ANDERSON'S
Law School Publications

Administrative Law Anthology
Thomas O. Sargentich

Administrative Law: Cases and Materials
Daniel J. Gifford

Alternative Dispute Resolution: Strategies for Law and Business
E. Wendy Trachte-Huber and Stephen K. Huber

American Legal Systems: A Resource and Reference Guide
Toni M. Fine

An Admiralty Law Anthology
Robert M. Jarvis

Analytic Jurisprudence Anthology
Anthony D'Amato

An Antitrust Anthology
Andrew I. Gavil

Appellate Advocacy: Principles and Practice: Cases and Materials, Second Edition
Ursula Bentele and Eve Cary

Basic Accounting Principles for Lawyers: With Present Value and Expected Value
C. Steven Bradford and Gary A. Ames

A Capital Punishment Anthology (and Electronic Caselaw Appendix)
Victor L. Streib

Cases and Problems in Criminal Law, Third Edition
Myron Moskovitz

The Citation Workbook: How to Beat the Citation Blues, Second Edition
Maria L. Ciampi, Rivka Widerman, and Vicki Lutz

Civil Procedure: Cases, Materials, and Questions
Richard D. Freer and Wendy C. Perdue

Clinical Anthology: Readings for Live-Client Clinics
Alex J. Hurder, Frank S. Bloch, Susan L. Brooks, and Susan L. Kay

Commercial Transactions: Problems and Materials
Louis F. Del Duca, Egon Guttman, Alphonse M. Squillante, Fred H. Miller, and Peter Winship
    Vol. 1: Secured Transactions Under the UCC
    Vol. 2: Sales Under the UCC and the CISG
    Vol. 3: Negotiable Instruments Under the UCC and the CIBN

Communications Law: Media, Entertainment, and Regulation
Donald E. Lively, Allen S. Hammond, IV, Blake D. Morant, and Russell L. Weaver

A Conflict-of-Laws Anthology
Gene R. Shreve

A Constitutional Law Anthology, Second Edition
Michael J. Glennon, Donald E. Lively, Phoebe A. Haddon, Dorothy E. Roberts, and Russell L. Weaver

Constitutional Conflicts, Parts I & II
Derrick A. Bell, Jr.

Constitutional Law: Cases, History, and Dialogues
Donald E. Lively, Phoebe A. Haddon, Dorothy E. Roberts, and Russell L. Weaver

The Constitutional Law of the European Union
James D. Dinnage and John F. Murphy

The Constitutional Law of the European Union: Documentary Supplement
James D. Dinnage and John F. Murphy

Constitutional Torts
Sheldon H. Nahmod, Michael L. Wells, and Thomas A. Eaton

Contracts
Contemporary Cases, Comments, and Problems
Michael L. Closen, Richard M. Perlmutter, and Jeffrey D. Wittenberg

A Contracts Anthology, Second Edition
Peter Linzer

A Corporate Law Anthology
Franklin A. Gevurtz

Corporate and White Collar Crime: An Anthology
Leonard Orland

A Criminal Law Anthology
Arnold H. Loewy

Criminal Law: Cases and Materials
Arnold H. Loewy

A Criminal Procedure Anthology
Silas J. Wasserstrom and Christie L. Snyder

Criminal Procedure: Arrest and Investigation
Arnold H. Loewy and Arthur B. LaFrance

Criminal Procedure: Trial and Sentencing
Arthur B. LaFrance and Arnold H. Loewy

Economic Regulation: Cases and Materials
Richard J. Pierce, Jr.

Elements of Law
Eva H. Hanks, Michael E. Herz, and Steven S. Nemerson

Ending It: Dispute Resolution in America
Descriptions, Examples, Cases and Questions
Susan M. Leeson and Bryan M. Johnston

Environmental Law, Second Edition
Jackson B. Battle, Robert L. Fischman, Maxine I. Lipeles, and Mark S. Squillace
    Vol. 1: Environmental Decisionmaking: NEPA and the Endangered Species Act
    Vol. 2: Water Pollution
    Vol. 3: Air Pollution
    Vol. 4: Hazardous Waste

An Environmental Law Anthology
Robert L. Fischman, Maxine I. Lipeles, and Mark S. Squillace

Environmental Protection and Justice
Readings and Commentary on Environmental Law and Practice
Kenneth A. Manaster

An Evidence Anthology
Edward J. Imwinkelried and Glen Weissenberger

Federal Evidence Courtroom Manual
Glen Weissenberger

Federal Income Tax Anthology
Paul L. Caron, Karen C. Burke, and Grayson M.P. McCouch

Federal Rules of Evidence, 1996-97 Edition
Rules, Legislative History, Commentary and Authority
Glen Weissenberger

Federal Rules of Evidence Handbook, 1996-97 Edition
Publisher's Staff

First Amendment Anthology
Donald E. Lively, Dorothy E. Roberts, and Russell L. Weaver

International Environmental Law Anthology
Anthony D'Amato and Kirsten Engel

International Human Rights: Law, Policy and Process, Second Edition
Frank C. Newman and David Weissbrodt

**Selected International Human Rights Instruments and
Bibliography For Research on International Human Rights Law, Second Edition**
Frank C. Newman and David Weissbrodt

International Intellectual Property Anthology
Anthony D'Amato and Doris Estelle Long

International Law Anthology
Anthony D'Amato

International Law Coursebook
Anthony D'Amato

Introduction to The Study of Law: Cases and Materials
John Makdisi

Judicial Externships: The Clinic Inside The Courthouse
Rebecca A. Cochran

Justice and the Legal System
A Coursebook
Anthony D'Amato and Arthur J. Jacobson

The Law of Disability Discrimination
Ruth Colker

ADA Handbook
Statutes, Regulations and Related Materials
Publisher's Staff

The Law of Modern Payment Systems and Notes
Fred H. Miller and Alvin C. Harrell

Lawyers and Fundamental Moral Responsibility
Daniel R. Coquillette

Microeconomic Predicates to Law and Economics
Mark Seidenfeld

Patients, Psychiatrists and Lawyers Law and the Mental Health System, Second Edition
Raymond L. Spring, Roy B. Lacoursiere, M.D., and Glen Weissenberger

Preventive Law: Materials on a Non Adversarial Legal Process
Robert M. Hardaway

Principles of Evidence, Third Edition
Irving Younger, Michael Goldsmith, and David A. Sonenshein

Problems and Simulations in Evidence, Second Edition
Thomas F. Guernsey

A Products Liability Anthology
Anita Bernstein

Professional Responsibility Anthology
Thomas B. Metzloff

A Property Anthology, Second Edition
Richard H. Chused

Public Choice and Public Law: Readings and Commentary
Maxwell L. Stearns

The Regulation of Banking
Cases and Materials on Depository Institutions and Their Regulators
Michael P. Malloy

Science in Evidence
D. H. Kaye

A Section 1983 Civil Rights Anthology
Sheldon H. Nahmod

Sports Law: Cases and Materials, Third Edition
Ray L. Yasser, James R. McCurdy, and C. Peter Goplerud

A Torts Anthology
Lawrence C. Levine, Julie A. Davies, and Edward J. Kionka

Trial Practice
Lawrence A. Dubin and Thomas F. Guernsey

Trial Practice Problems and Case Files
Edward R. Stein and Lawrence A. Dubin

Trial Practice and Case Files *with Video* Presentation
Edward R. Stein and Lawrence A. Dubin

Unincorporated Business Entities
Larry E. Ribstein

FORTHCOMING PUBLICATIONS

A Civil Procedure Anthology
David I. Levine, Donald L. Doernberg, and Melissa L. Nelken

Civil Procedure: Cases, Materials, and Questions, 2nd Edition
Richard D. Freer and Wendy C. Perdue

Contract Law and Practice: Cases and Materials
Michael L. Closen, Gerald E. Berendt, Doris Estelle Long, Marie A. Monahan, Robert J. Nye, and John H. Scheid

Environmental Law: Air Pollution (Vol. 3) 3rd Edition
Mark S. Squillace and David R. Wooley

Environmental Law: Hazardous Waste (Vol. 4) 3rd Edition
Jackson B. Battle and Maxine I. Lipeles

European Union Law Anthology
Anthony D'Amato and Karen V. Kole

Federal Antitrust Law: Cases and Materials
Daniel J. Gifford and Leo J. Raskind

Juvenile Law Anthology
Victor L. Streib and Lynn Sametz

Law and Economics: An Anthology
Kenneth G. Dau-Schmidt and Thomas S. Ulen

Readings in Criminal Law: An Anthology
Russell L. Weaver, Geoffrey J. G. Bennett, John M. Burkoff, Catherine Hancock, Matt O'Brien, James O'Reilly, Alan Reed, Peter Seago, and Sarah N. Welling

A Constitutional Law Anthology

Second Edition

A CONSTITUTIONAL LAW ANTHOLOGY

SECOND EDITION

Professor of Law
University of California at Davis

DONALD E. LIVELY
Dean
Florida Coastal School of Law

PHOEBE A. HADDON
Charles Klein Professor of Law and Government
Temple University

DOROTHY E. ROBERTS
Professor of Law
Rutgers State University of New Jersey

RUSSELL L. WEAVER
Professor of Law & Brown, Todd & Heyburn Fellow
Louis D. Brandeis School of Law
at the University of Louisville

ANDERSON PUBLISHING CO.
CINCINNATI, OHIO

A Constitutional Law Anthology, *Second Edition*
Michael J. Glennon, Donald E. Lively, Phoebe A. Haddon,
Dorothy E. Roberts, Russell L. Weaver

Anderson Publishing Co.
2035 Reading Road / Cincinnati, Ohio 45202
800-582-7295 / e-mail andpubco@aol.com / Fax 513-562-5430

ISBN: 0-87084-198-X

To my parents, William J. Glennon and Catherine A. Glennon   **M.J.G.**

To the memory of Professor Barbara McCalla   **D.E.L.**

This anthology is dedicated to my mother, Ida B. Haddon, who set the standard for hard work and for love of Family, and who continues to teach me about the indomitable human spirit.   **P.A.H.**

To my parents, Iris and Robert Roberts   **D.E.R.**

To Mary Kay and Loretta   **R.L.W.**

Table of Contents

Preface

Constitutional law, in addition to its primary function of amplifying the meaning of the nation's charter, has begotten an especially rich and varied body of commentary. Such output has served not only as a checkpoint but an inspiration point for the law's development. Because the "stakes are high"[1] when constitutional questions arise, a massive outpouring of literature in the field is not surprising. The volume of quality writing in the field, however, presents a challenge for even the most voracious reader.

This anthology has been constructed in the context of a veritable information glut that is daunting even to the editors. The book nonetheless reflects a selection process connected to what they regard as important pedagogical aims. As constitutional law has expanded at an explosive rate over the past few decades, and editorial manageability has become a compounding imperative, casebooks and instruction have tended to become increasingly detached from context. Attention to history has been a particularly unfortunate casualty.

Editorial decisions for this book have been driven primarily by an interest in identifying literature that engages the reader and enriches his or her understanding. Consistent with the editors' concern with significant missing links in many core course materials, the anthology devotes attention not only to contemporary understandings but to historical perspectives. Some early writings on issues that no longer may be debated extensively, for instance, have been included because they afford insight into the law's evolution and even may inspire inquiry into settled principle.

Judgments about what to include in this anthology have been a function of the editors' sense of content that is absorbing, inspires critical thinking and provokes discussion. Recognizing that the primary audience consists of law students, accessibility of thought and message has been a significant factor. As with other anthologies in the series, the editors believe that the book also will be useful to those with serious research interests in the field. Bibliographies at the end of each major section are provided to direct readers to other works which would merit inclusion if space permitted.

The anthology's organization parallels the structure of Donald E. Lively, Phoebe A. Haddon, Dorothy E. Roberts and Russell L. Weaver, *Constitutional Law: Cases, History and Dialogues* (Anderson 1996). It is adaptable, however, to other casebooks and may be used independently in appropriate courses. Consistent with the dominant model of basic constitutional law instruction, the anthology excludes the First Amendment. A separate book—Donald E. Lively, Dorothy E. Roberts and Russell Weaver, *A First Amendment Anthology* (Anderson 1994)—covers that territory.

The editors welcome feedback, including input relevant to development of future editions.

---

[1]   United States v. O'Brien, 391 U.S. 367, 383-84 (1968).

Part I
The Power and Role
of the Judiciary

The Power "To Say What the Law Is"

The power of judicial review gives the Supreme Court final authority to define the Constitution's meaning. Authority of the judiciary to bind the other branches of government with its interpretation is not provided by specific terms of the Constitution. The historical record on the subject has been debated to the point that one prominent critic has concluded that "[t]he people who say the framers intended [judicial primacy] are talking nonsense, and the people who say they did not intend it are talking nonsense."[2] Whatever the attention to the role of the judiciary (or lack thereof) at the republic's founding, it is evident that the function it historically has performed was established as a post-ratification phenomenon. In *Marbury v. Madison,* the Court effectively arrogated for itself "the power to say what the law is."[3] Nearly two centuries later, the *Marbury* decision and its implications persist as a departure point for the study of American constitutional law and a rich body of commentary. William W. Van Alstyne provides a critical perspective upon Chief Justice Marshall's resolution of the *Marbury* case. Felix Frankfurter praises Marshall's work but warns against an expanded judicial function that some regard as the logical extension of the *Marbury* decision. Edwin Meese III suggests that a distinction must be drawn between the binding properties of the law of the Constitution and constitutional law. From a literary and legal perspective, J. M. Balkin assesses the significance of Footnote Four of *United States v. Carolene Products Co.*[4] Bruce A. Ackerman urges a new model of review to supersede the *Carolene Products* model that he characterizes as obsolete.

---

2   Leonard W. Levy, Judicial Review and the Supreme Court 4 (1967) (quoting Edward Corwin before the Senate Committee on the Judiciary, 75th Cong., 1st Sess. (1976)).

3   Marbury v. Madison, 5 U.S. 137, 177 (1803).

4   304 U.S. 144 (1938).

William W. Van Alstyne, *A Critical Guide to* Marbury v. Madison, 1969 DUKE L.J. 1 (1969)*

I. JUDICIAL REVIEW

Assuming that section 13 of the Judiciary Act of 1789 . . . confer[red] original jurisdiction in *Marbury v. Madison*, is its constitutionality subject to judicial review? Marshall initially responds to this question, which, of course, is the issue which has made the case of historic importance, by posing his own rhetorical question: "whether an Act repugnant to the Constitution can become the law of the land." That it cannot is clear, he says, from the following consideration.

The people in an exercise of their "original right," established the government pursuant to a written constitution which defines and limits the powers of the legislature. A "legislative act contrary to the constitution is not law," therefore, as it is contrary to the original and supreme will which organized the legislature itself.

That the constitution is a "written" one yields little or nothing as to whether acts of Congress may be given the force of positive law notwithstanding the opinion of judges, the executive, a minority or majority of the population, or even of Congress itself (assuming that Congress might sometimes be pressed by political forces to adopt a law against its belief that it lacked power to do so) that such acts are repugnant to the Constitution. That this is so is clear enough simply from the fact that even in Marshall's time (and to a great extent today), a number of nations maintained written constitutions and yet gave national legislative acts the full force of positive law without providing any constitutional check to guarantee the compatibility of those acts with their constitutions.

This observation, moreover, leads to the conclusion that Marshall presents a false dilemma in insisting that "[t]he constitution is either a superior paramount law, unchangeable by ordinary means, or it is on a level with ordinary legislative acts, and, like other acts, is alterable when the legislature shall please to alter it." Remember, the question he has posed is "whether an Act repugnant to the Constitution can become the law of the land." The question is not whether Congress can alter the Constitution by means other than those provided by Article V, and the case raises no issue concerning an alteration of any provision in the Constitution. We may assume that Congress cannot, by simple act, alter the Constitution and still we may maintain that an act which the court or someone else *believes* to be repugnant to the Constitution shall be given the full force of positive law until repealed. Again, this is the situation which prevails in many other countries, and no absurdity is felt to exist where such a condition obtains.

To be sure, situations can be imagined (and may arise in fact) where an act of Congress seems so clearly repugnant to the Constitution that one may wonder what function the Constitution can usefully serve if such a law is nevertheless given the full force of positive law until repealed. Marshall's illustrations of such situations are quite compelling in this regard, *e.g.*, an act of Congress providing that one may be convicted of treason upon testimony of a single witness, or confession out of Court, in the "very teeth" of the provision in Article III, section 3, that "no person shall be convicted of treason unless on the testimony of two witnesses to the same overt Act, or on Confession in open Court."

---

*   Reprinted with permission.

This leads, then, directly to the third point Marshall makes with a rhetorical flourish: "To what purpose are powers limited, . . . if these limits may, at any time, be passed by those intended to be restrained?" Thus he argues by implication that no other purpose can be imagined and so it follows that the purpose of preventing acts of Congress repugnant to the Constitution from being given the effect of positive law is the necessary purpose of prescribing written limitations on its power. Again, however, a variety of excellent purposes are felt to be served in other countries with similar constitutional provisions but without detracting from the positive law effect of all legislative acts. Thus the written limitations serve as a conscientious check on the legislators, admonishing each and advising each concerning the responsibility he has to respect the limitations thus laid down. The very fact, for instance, that the minimum proof for treason is prescribed in Article III makes it far less likely than otherwise that Congress would attempt to enact a lesser standard, and this is so wholly aside from whether such an attempt would still be given the effect of positive law. Again, the written limitations may be useful politically; they may figure in congressional debates, furnishing argumentative force as well as a personal conscientious restraint, against the enactment of repressive bills. Finally, there is the purpose the Constitution would serve in providing a political check upon Congress by the people, even assuming that all acts of Congress were given the full effects of positive law by the Courts as well as by the executive. Indeed consistent with Marshall's own observation that *the people* themselves established these written limitations, the democratic approach is to leave the judgment and remedy for alleged legislative usurpation with the people. If *they* conclude the Constitution has been violated, they can exert political pressure to effect the repeal of the offending act or to replace their congressmen at times of election with representatives who will effectuate that repeal. The document thus provides the people with a firm, written normative standard to which to repair in making political decisions.

Unwillingness of the courts to give effect to acts of Congress which the Supreme Court might conclude were repugnant to the Constitution is thus quite unnecessary to the accomplishment of several significant purposes which might still be served. In certain respects, moreover, it may even be said to work at cross purposes with these other salutary aims. For instance, it tends to encourage congressional indifference to considerations of constitutionality by implying that questions of this sort are none of its concern and are entrusted, rather, only to the Court. Such a tendency was utilized by President Roosevelt when he urged a House subcommittee chairman to resolve all constitutional doubts about a given bill in favor of the bill, "leaving to the courts, in an orderly fashion, the ultimate question of constitutionality." In addition it may frustrate acts of Congress even when the people, whose "original and supreme will organizes the government," find no repugnance to their own Constitution.

Finally, however, there is the reference to the supremacy clause in Article VI which Marshall uses partly to show, again, "that a law repugnant to the constitution is void" (as well as to show that it does not bind the judiciary). To be sure, the clause does provide that "[t]his Constitution, and the Laws of the United States which shall be made in *Pursuance* thereof . . . shall be the supreme Law of the Land," and thus the text appears to require that acts of Congress be made "pursuant" to the authority (and limitations) of the Constitution to be effective as supreme law. But this does not necessarily support Marshall's conclusion that no act of Congress believed by the Court to be repugnant to the Constitution shall be given full positive-law effect.

The phrase "in pursuance thereof" might as easily mean *"in the manner prescribed by this Constitution,"* in which case acts of Congress might be judicially reviewable as to their procedural integrity, but not as to their substance. . . . Thus, the only constitutional issue to be raised in a judicial forum to determine whether an act of Congress should be given effect is whether the bill has been enacted according to the forms prescribed in the Constitution. Its substantive constitutionality, *e.g.* whether it exceeds the enumerated powers of Congress or violates a stated limitation on those powers, is reserved for the people to determine and for them to resolve through the political process. It is, therefore, significant that the clause does *not* provide as follows: "This Constitution, and the Laws of the United States *authorized and not limited thereby* . . . shall be the supreme Law of the Land."

The phrase might also mean merely that only those statutes adopted by Congress *after* the re-establishment and reconstitution of Congress pursuant to the Constitution itself shall be the supreme law of the land, whereas acts of the earlier Continental Congress, constituted merely under the Articles of Confederation, would not necessarily be supreme and binding upon the several states. Under this view, acts of Congress, like acts of Parliament, *are* the supreme law and not to be second-guessed by any court, state or federal, so long as they postdate ratification of the Constitution.

Finally, however, there is another point which also necessarily shades into Marshall's related discussion of whether an act repugnant to the Constitution is nonetheless binding upon the courts. The point is that Marshall arguably may have begged a critical question, *i.e.*, he failed to acknowledge and thus to answer a question critical to the position he takes. *Assuming that an act repugnant to the Constitution is not a law "in pursuance thereof" and thus must not be given effect as the supreme law of the land, who, according to the Constitution, is to make the determination as to whether any given law is in fact repugnant to the Constitution itself?* Such alleged repugnance is ordinarily not self-demonstrating in most cases, as we well know. Marshall never confronts this question. His substitute question, whether a law repugnant to the Constitution still binds the courts, *assumes* that such "repugnance" has appropriately been determined by those granted such power under the Constitution. It is clear, however, that the supremacy clause itself cannot be the clear textual basis for a claim by the judiciary that this prerogative to determine repugnancy belongs to it.

On its face, the clause does not say by whom or how or at what time it shall be determined whether certain laws of the United States were adopted pursuant to the Constitution. Again, the phrase that only such laws shall be part of the supreme law could mean merely that the people should regard the Constitution with deep concern and that *they* should act to prevent Congress from overstepping the Constitution. It might even imply, moreover, a right of civil disobedience or serve as a written reminder to government of the natural right of revolution against tyrannical government which oversteps the terms of the social compact. Such a construction would be consistent with philosophical writings of the period, consistent with the Declaration of Independence, and consistent also with the view of some antifederalists of the period. As a hortatory reminder to the Government of the ultimate right of the people, however, it clearly does not authorize the Court to make the critical judgment as to which laws, if any, were not made in pursuance of the Constitution.

* * *

But does the Chief Justice Finally strike paydirt when he observes that Article III provides that "the judicial Power . . . shall be vested in one supreme court," etc., and that this judicial power "shall extend to all Cases . . . arising under this Constitution," etc.? To paraphrase Marshall, what sense does it make to say that all cases arising under the Constitution are within the judicial power if, at the same time, the

Court is never free in such a case to consider the constitutionality of an act of Congress which has been drawn into question in that very case?

Is it sufficient to reply that the Court may consider the question of constitutionality, but that it must resolve that question according to Congress' interpretation of the Constitution rather than according to its own interpretation? Some have so suggested, noting again that the Constitution itself is silent as to whose constitutional interpretation shall be controlling even in the disposition of a case, and contending that the interpretation made by Congress and subject only to popular, but not judicial, review would be more compatible with the theory of democratic government. There are, however, several shortcomings to this criticism. One is that the business of deciding a *case* does seem emphatically to be a part of judicial business. In the absence of a provision expressly withdrawing from the courts the power to decide for themselves any significant issue which must be resolved in order to dispose of the whole case, including of course the challenged constitutionality of an act of Congress, or instructing the Court to resolve any such issue according to the decision of Congress or someone else, it would appear to be the more natural inference that the judicial prerogative is the same as to this issue as to any other unavoidably presented by the case. It is not a sufficient answer to this point merely to say that the issue of substantive constitutionality is so different in kind from all other issues and that its reservation to Congress and to the people is so fundamental to democratic theory that this difference alone is sufficient to withdraw it from the courts. If it *was* felt to be so different, we should expect the difference to be expressed and provided for in the Constitution itself.

If the Court is always to resolve a question of substantive constitutionality of an act of Congress only according to Congress' own constitutional interpretation of its authority, necessarily it will always uphold the act and the "judicial review" thus being exercised seems to amount to nothing at all. Under these circumstances, it seems trivial and strange that Article III would extend the judicial power to *all cases arising under the Constitution*. It seems that it would have been more logical not to bother with this category on the understanding that acts of Congress are simply not to be questioned, either by federal or by state courts, on grounds of constitutionality.

This necessarily leads to the question: Unless these phrases in Article III contemplate independent judicial review of the substantive constitutionality of acts of Congress drawn into question in cases arising under the Constitution, what purposes or functions can this category of judicial power possibly or usefully serve? Arguably, it would still serve a variety of very important functions.

A case may arise under the Constitution in a clear and straightforward sense *and not in the least involve an act of Congress*. Thus a person might file suit for damages from police officers who he claims broke into his house without a warrant, allegedly violating the fourth amendment via the fourteenth amendment. His "claim" arises under the Constitution in that he asserts that the due process clause of the fourteenth amendment *itself* furnishes him with a remedial right to damages under these circumstances. The case thus "arises" under the Constitution, it would be reviewable in due course under the Court's appellate jurisdiction (unless Congress excepted such jurisdiction), and the Court would be competent to decide for itself whether or not the claim was well made. In the course of doing so, the Court might well interpret the Constitution to determine whether the fourth and fourteenth amendments implicitly provide for recovery in money damages or whether they do not. Here, in such a situation the case itself does arise under the Constitution, Congress has adopted no act which provides an interpretation of the constitutional issue in question, and quite naturally and necessarily the Court could review the matter. Thus, the clause has a function and an importance independent of extending it to mean that the substantive constitutionality of acts of Congress are judicially reviewable. In fact this reading of the clause seems more natural and straightforward than the one proposed by Marshall. Here the claim itself is asserted as arising under the Constitution. Marshall would read the clause as though it said "all cases in which an issue of constitutionality is presented." But, of course, it does not say this.

Again, the clause might permit judicial review of cases involving the federal constitutionality of state laws or state constitutional provisions where Congress has adopted no act dispositive of the question. Or the clause may even contemplate a limited review of acts of Congress drawn into question in a case thus alleged to arise under the Constitution, but the review would be strictly limited to *procedural* constitutionality of the congressional act, as discussed earlier.

It appears to follow, then, that cases may arise under the Constitution having nothing to do with acts of Congress, and that even in cases involving acts of Congress there is no inherent necessity for the Court to exercise a power of independent substantive constitutional review. To be sure, our analysis concedes the propriety of such review in certain cases, not involving acts of Congress, while denying it in others where acts of Congress are involved. To establish a final point in Marshall's favor, does not a simple principle of consistency require that judicial review should either be granted in *all* cases, whether or not an act of Congress is challenged on constitutional grounds, or in none of the cases which arise under the Constitution? An argument can be made that the answer is "no." Indeed we have already canvassed the argument and need only summarize it here. In cases raising constitutional issues *which Congress has not attempted to resolve*, the Court must of necessity render its own interpretation of the part of the Constitution in question if only to decide the case. Moreover, it should do so "to support the Constitution." Where Congress has considered the issue and has interpreted the Constitution in the course of adopting relevant legislation, however, the matter is properly foreclosed to the courts which are not to oppose themselves to Congress which is itself fully answerable to the people. The Court is not similarly answerable, of course, and thus certainly ought not supererogate a power of judicial review for which it is politically unaccountable in what we believe to be a democratic republic.

* * *

III. A SPECIFICATION OF THE HOLDING ON CONSTITUTIONAL REVIEW

In litigation before the Supreme Court, the Court may refuse to give effect to an act of Congress where the act pertains to the judicial power itself. In deciding whether to give effect to such an act, the Court may determine its decision according to its own interpretation of constitutional provisions which describe the judicial power.

Thus described, the holding in *Marbury v. Madison* is less remarkable than generally supposed. It is also, however, far more defensible because it draws upon one's sympathy to maintain the Court as a co-ordinate branch of government, and not as a superior branch. It represents a defensive use of constitutional review alone, acquiring considerable support from the concept of *separated* powers. It merely minds the Court's *own* business (*i.e.* what cases shall originate in the Court, what cases shall be treated on appeal or otherwise). Were the Court to lack *this* capacity, it could scarcely be able to maintain even the ordinary function of *non*custodial judicial review.

* * *

We have thus far described the holding respecting constitutional review in *Marbury* as a very limited thing by concentrating on the character of the act of Congress actually involved in the case. As thus limited, it is fair to conclude that the case does not establish constitutional review of acts of Congress regarding any subject other than the judicial power itself, *e.g.*, it does not establish such review for acts concerning "separation-of-powers conflicts between legislative and executive branches, which are of no such concern to the courts' own powers: to federalistic questions; and to direct limitations on the powers of government."

It must be conceded, however, that his view of "the holding" is one we bring to the case rather than one which clearly characterizes Marshall's opinion. Even a unhurried rereading of the case is not likely to suggest that Marshall was emphasizing, or limiting himself to, the legitimacy of constitutional review used only defensively in the protection of the balance of judicial power. For instance, he does not emphasize the concept of separation of powers in *this* limited sense, but considers it in the more grandiose sense that the whole business of interpreting "law," including the "law" of the Constitution is emphatically judicial business. Remember also his statement, which seems to look well beyond the character of the case at hand: "in some cases, then, the Constitution must be looked into by the judges. And if they can open it all, what part of it are they forbidden to read or to obey?"

It is unsurprising, therefore, that the "holding" has been generally regarded as a broader one which carries at least this far: *In litigation before the Supreme Court, the Court may refuse to give effect to an act of Congress where, in the Court's own view, that act is repugnant to the Constitution.*

This is, of course, a significantly broader holding than the first one suggested. It means that the Court will withhold its power even when the efficacy of an act of Congress depends on the co-operation of that power against private citizens, corporate interests, state interests, or executive interests, whenever the Court concludes that the act is repugnant to the Court's own interpretation of some constitutional provision. It may be characterized by the phrase "national, substantive constitutional review."

Even this breadth of holding, however, falls far short of cementing the notion of "judicial supremacy." It does not mean, for instance, that either Congress or the President need defer to Supreme Court interpretations of the Constitution so far as the efficacy of their power does not depend upon judicial co-operation.

When a bill is under consideration, for example, Congress might conscientiously reject the bill believing that bill to be unconstitutional even assuming that the Court has provided no precedent for that belief and even assuming that the Court has itself upheld similar legislation adopted by an earlier Congress. Similarly, the President may veto the bill on the grounds of his own interpretation of the Constitution— whether or not it is the same as the Court's. So, too, might he decline to enforce an act of Congress on such a basis.

The concept of national, substantive judicial *review*, moreover, does not preclude independent prerogatives of Congress and the President to prefer their own constitutional interpretations even when the Court, for its part, has interpreted the Constitution in such a manner as to sustain the bill. A clear instance might involve the use of the executive clemency power, used by Jefferson to pardon those convicted under the Alien and Sedition Acts which had been upheld in the lower federal courts, on the grounds that in the President's own view those acts were repugnant to the Constitution. A harder instance might involve the decision of the President not to enforce an act of Congress because of his own belief that it was unconstitutional, even after the act had been tested and upheld in the Supreme Court.

There is, then, no doctrine of national, substantive judicial *supremacy* which inexorably flows from *Marbury v. Madison* itself, *i.e.*, no doctrine that the only interpretation of the Constitution which all branches of the national government must employ is the interpretation which the Court may provide in the course of litigation.

Beyond this lies the observation that *Marbury* does not pass upon the separate question of *federal* substantive constitutional review or *federal* substantive judicial supremacy. The case provides no occasion to determine the role of the states in the interpretation of the Constitution; no issue of federalism is present in the case. By itself, it does not settle any of these questions: (1) Are state courts bound by Supreme Court interpretations of the Constitution respecting the constitutionality of the *federal* laws, and (2) are state courts bound by Supreme Court interpretations of the Constitution respecting the constitutionality of *state* laws? To put the matter more orthodoxly, are state court judgments involving interpretations of the United States Constitution subject to revision by the Supreme Court? This question presents new considerations of federalism not treated in *Marbury*. They might have been answered in favor of state determinism, without disturbing *Marbury's* "holding" as to national, substantive judicial review. The issue was, of course, resolved in favor of federal constitutional review.

If, at this juncture, it should be thought surprising that *Marbury v. Madison* could sensibly be considered by anyone as authoritatively establishing the doctrine of federal substantive judicial supremacy, however, one need look no further than the Supreme Court itself to find an example of such a view! In *Cooper v. Aaron*, the Court said the following with respect to the exclusiveness of its own constitutional interpretations as applied to state laws and the obligations of state officials:

> This decision [*Marbury v. Madison*] declared the basic principle that the federal judiciary is supreme in the exposition of the law of the Constitution, and that principle has ever since been respected by this Court and the Country as a permanent and indispensable feature of our constitutional system.

* * *

Felix Frankfurter, *John Marshall and the Judicial Function*, 69 HARV. L. REV. 217 (1955)*

* * *

When Marshall came to the Supreme Court, the Constitution was still essentially a virgin document. By a few opinions—a mere handful—he gave institutional direction to the inert ideas of a paper scheme of government. Such an achievement demanded an undimmed vision of the union of states as a nation and the determination of an uncompromising devotion to such insight. Equally indispensable was the power to formulate views expressing this outlook with the persuasiveness of compelling simplicity.

It is shallow to deny that general ideas have influence or to minimize their importance. Marshall's ideas, diffused in all sorts of ways, especially through the influence of the legal profession, have become the presuppositions of our political institutions. He released an enduring spirit, a mode of approach for generations of judges charged with the awesome duty of subjecting the conduct of government and the claims of individual rights to the touchstone of a written document, binding the Government and safe-guarding such rights. He has afforded this guidance not only for his own country. In the federalisms that have evolved out of the British Empire, Marshall's outlook in constitutional adjudications has been the lodestar. Unashamedly I recall the familiar phrase in which he expressed the core of his constitutional philosophy:

"it is a *constitution* we are expounding."

M'Culloch v. Maryland. It bears repeating because it is, I believe, the single most important utterance in the literature of constitutional law—most important because most comprehensive and comprehending.

I should like to follow James Bradley Thayer in believing that the conception of the nation which Marshall derived from the Constitution and set forth in *M'Culloch v. Maryland* is his greatest single judicial performance. It is that, both in its persuasiveness and in its effect. As good a test as I know of the significance of an opinion is to contemplate the consequences of its opposite. The courage of *Marbury v. Madison* is not minimized by suggesting that its reasoning is not impeccable and its conclusion, however wise, not inevitable. I venture to say this though fully aware that, since Marshall's time and largely, I suspect, through the momentum of the experience which he initiated, his conclusion in *Marbury v. Madison* has been deemed by great English-speaking courts an indispensable, implied characteristic of a written constitution. Holmes could say, as late as 1913, "I do not think the United States would come to an end if we lost our power to declare an Act of Congress void." But he went on to say, "I do think the Union would be imperiled if we could not make that declaration as to the laws of the several States. For one in my place sees how often a local policy prevails with those who are not trained to national views and how often action is taken that embodies what the Commerce Clause was meant to end." One can, I believe, say with assurance that a failure to conceive the Constitution as Marshall conceived it in *M'Culloch v. Maryland*, to draw from it the national powers which have since been exercised and to exact deference to such powers from the states, would have been reflected by a very different United States than history knows. Marshall surely was right when he wrote, a month after he rejected the argument for Maryland: "If the principles which have been advanced on this occasion were to prevail, the Constitution would be converted into the old Confederation."

Marshall's intrinsic achievements are too solid and his personal qualities too homespun to tolerate mythical treatment. It is important not to make untouchable dogmas of the fallible reasoning of even our greatest judge, and not to attribute god-like qualities to the builders of our nation. . . .

* * *

Marshall's significance could not be more fittingly celebrated than by scrutinizing . . . the state of "government under law," more particularly under the legal system to which Marshall so heavily contributed, a hundred and twenty years after he wrote his last opinion. . . . [N]othing would be bound to strike him more than the enlarged scope of law since his day. He would, of course, think of law as legally enforceable rights. For, while he occasionally referred to "natural law," it was not much more than literary garniture, even as in our own day, and not a guiding means for adjudication. He would have sympathized, as other judges have, with Sir Frederick Pollock's remark, "In the Middle Ages natural law was regarded as the senior branch of divine law and therefore had to be treated as infallible (but there was no infallible way of knowing what it was)." Marshall would be amazed by the interpretation of law in government, because during his whole era he was concerned with the Constitution as an instrument predominantly regulating the machinery of government, and more particularly, distributing powers between the central government and the states. The Constitution was not thought of as the repository of the supreme law limiting all government, with a court wielding the deepest-cutting power of deciding whether there is any authority in government at all to do what is sought to be done.

* * *

The vast change in the scope of law between Marshall's time and ours is at bottom a reflection of the vast change in the circumstances of society. The range of business covered by Marshall's Court, though operating under a written Constitution, was in the main not very different from the concerns of the English courts, except that the latter dealt much more with property settlements. The vast enveloping present-day role of law is not the design of a statesman nor attributable to the influence of some great thinker. It is a reflection of the great technological revolution which brought in its train what a quiet writer in The Economist could call "the tornado of economic and social change of the last century." Law has been an essential accompaniment of the shift from "watchdog government"—the phrase is George Kennan's—to the service state. For government has become a service state, whatever the tint of the party in power and whatever time-honored slogans it may use and promote measures that hardly vindicate the slogans. Profound social changes continue to be in the making, due to movements of industrialization, urbanization, and permeating egalitarian ideas.

With crude accuracy I have just summarized the situation in the countries of the English-speaking world, about which alone I may speak. But when these transforming economic and social forces got under full swing in the United States, lawyers and courts found available in the Fourteenth Amendment resources for curbing legislative responses to new pressures. That Amendment was gradually invoked against the substance of legislation and not merely to support claims based on traditionally fair procedure.

* * *

In his first inaugural Jefferson spoke of the "sacred principle" that "the will of the majority is in all cases to prevail." Jefferson himself hardly meant all by "all." In any event, one need not give full adherence to his view to be deeply mindful of the fact that judicial review is a deliberate check upon democracy through an organ of government not subject to popular control. In relation to the judiciary's task in the type of cases I am now discussing, I am raising difficulties which I think must in all good conscience be faced, unless perchance the Court is expected to register a particular view and unless the profession that the judiciary is the disinterested guardian of our Constitution be pretense.

It may be that responsibility for decision dulls the capacity of discernment. The fact is that one sometimes envies the certitude of outsiders regarding the compulsions to be drawn from vague and admonitory constitutional provisions. Only for those who have not the responsibility of decision can it be easy to decide the grave and complex problems they raise, especially in controversies that excite public interest. This is so because they too often present legal issues inextricably and deeply bound up in emotional reactions to sharply conflicting economic, social, and political views. It is not the duty of judges to express their personal attitudes on such issues, deep as their individual convictions may be. The opposite is the truth; it is their duty not to act on merely personal views. But "due process," once we go beyond its strictly procedural aspect, and the "equal protection of the laws" enshrined in the Constitution, are precisely defined neither by history nor in terms. . . .

It is, of course, no longer to be questioned that claims under the Fourteenth Amendment are subject to judicial judgment. This makes it all the more important to realize what is involved in the discharge of this function of the Court, particularly since this is probably the largest source of the Court's business. It is important, that is, fully to appreciate the intrinsic nature of the issues when the Court is called upon to determine whether the legislature or the executive has regulated "liberty" or "property" "without due process of law" or has denied "equal protection of the laws"; to appreciate the difficulties in making a judgment upon such issues, difficulties of a different order from those normally imposed upon jural tribunals; and, not least, to appreciate the qualifications requisite for those who exercise this extraordinary authority, demanding as it does a breadth of outlook and an invincible disinterestedness rooted in temperament and confirmed by discipline. Of course, individual judgment and feeling cannot be wholly shut out of the judicial process. But if they dominate, the judicial process becomes a dangerous sham. The conception by a judge of the scope and limits of his function may exert an intellectual and moral force as much as responsiveness to a particular audience or congenial environment.

We are dealing with constitutional provisions the nature of which can be best conveyed compendiously by Judge Learned Hand's phrase that they "represent a mood rather than a command, that sense of moderation, of fair play, of mutual forbearance, without which states become the prey of faction." Alert search for enduring standards by which the judiciary is to exercise its duty in enforcing those provisions of the Constitution that are expressed in what Ruskin called "chameleon words," needs the indispensable counterpoise of sturdy doubt that one has found those standards. Yesterday the active area in this field was concerned with "property." Today it is "civil liberties." Tomorrow it may again be "property." Who can say that in a society with a mixed economy, like ours, these two areas are sharply separated, and that certain freedoms in relation to property may not again be deemed, as they were in the past, aspects of individual freedom? Concerned as I am with the evolution of social policy by way of judicial application of Delphic provisions of the Constitution, recession of judicial doctrine is as pertinent as its expansion.

* * *

No matter how often the Court insists that it is not passing on policy when determining constitutionality, the emphasis on constitutionality, and its fascination for the American public seriously confound problems of constitutionality with the merits of a policy. Industrial relations are not alone in presenting problems that suffer in their solution from having public opinion too readily assume that because some measure is found to be constitutional it is wise and right, and contrariwise, because it is found unconstitutional it is intrinsically wrong. That such miseducation of public opinion, with its effect upon action, has been an important consequence of committing to the Court the enforcement of "the mood" represented by these vague constitutional provisions, can hardly be gainsaid by any student of their history.

* * *

Is it the tenor of these remarks that courts should have no concern with other than material interests, that they must be unmindful of the imponderable rights and dignities of the individual which are, I am sure I shall have your agreement in saying, the ideals which the Western world holds most high? Of course not. Recognition of them should permeate the law, and it does so effectively even in courts that do not have veto power over legislation. They constitute presuppositions where parliaments have not spoken unequivocally and courts are left with the jural task of construction in its fair sense.

* * *

If government under law were confined to what is judicially enforced, law in government would be very restricted, no matter how latitudinarian one's conception of what is fitting for judicial examination of governmental action. For one thing, courts have a strong tendency to abstain from constitutional controversies. Thereby, they may avoid conflict, at least prematurely if not permanently, with the other branches of the government and they may avoid also the determination of conflict between the nation and the states. Moreover, settlement of complicated public issues, particularly on the basis of constitutional provisions conveying indeterminate standards, is subject to the inherent limitations and contingencies of the judicial process. For constitutional adjudications involve adjustment of vast and incommensurable public interests through episodic instances, upon evidence and information limited by the narrow rules of litigation, shaped and intellectually influenced by the fortuitous choice of particular counsel.

Mr. Justice Brandeis made a fair estimate in saying that by applying its restrictive canons for adjudication, the Court has in the course of its history "avoided passing upon a large part of all the constitutional questions pressed upon it for decision." This is true not only of our Supreme Court, which cannot render advisory opinions however compelling the appeal for legal guidance, even at times of national emergency. Insistence on an immediate, substantial, and threatened interest in raising such constitutional issues is a characteristic of all high courts with power to pass upon them. But even where advisory opinions are constitutionally authorized, tribunals are reluctant to pronounce in situations that are hypothetical or abstract or otherwise not conducive to judicial disposition. It is, I believe, not inaccurate to say that most of the occasions when the Supreme Court has come into virulent conflict with public opinion were those in which the Court disregarded its settled tradition against needlessly pronouncing on constitutional issues.

The confining limits within which courts thus move in expounding law is not the most important reason for a conception of government under law far transcending merely law that is enforced in the courts. The day has long gone by when Austin's notions exhaust the content of law. Law is not set above the government. It defines its orbit. But government is not law except insofar as law infuses government. This is not wordplaying. Also indispensable to government is ample scope for individual insight and imaginative origination by those entrusted with the public interest. If society is not to remain stagnant, there is need of action beyond uniformities found recurring in instances which sustain a generalization and demand its application. But law is not a code of fettering restraints, a litany of prohibitions and permissions. It is an enveloping and permeating habituation of behavior, reflecting the counsels of reason on the part of those entrusted with power in reconciling the pressures of conflicting interests. Once we conceive of "the rule of law" as embracing the whole range of presuppositions on which government is conducted and not as a technical doctrine of judicial authority, the relevant question is not, has it been achieved, but, is it conscientiously and systematically pursued.

What matters most is whether the standards of reason and fair dealing are bred in the bones of people. Hyde Park represents a devotion to free speech far more dependable in its assurances, though unprotected by formal constitutional requirement, than reliance upon the litigious process for its enjoyment. . . .

You will note that the instances I have given of manifestations of law responsive to the deep feelings of a people are drawn from a nation that does not rely on a written constitution. I need not add that the distinctive historical development in Great Britain, in the context of its progressive cultural and economic homogeneity, has made possible accommodation between stability and change, defining the powers of government and the limits within which due regard for individual rights require it to be kept, without embodying it in a single legal document enforceable in courts of law.

* * *

If what I have brought you, in my endeavor to give you as frankly as I may the distillation of sixteen years of reflection from within the tribunal peculiarly concerned with government under law, is charged with being an old-fashioned liberal's view of government and law, I plead guilty. For the charge implies allegiance to the humane and gradualist tradition in dealing with refractory social and political problems, recognizing them to be fractious because of their complexity and not amenable to quick and propitious solutions without resort to methods which deny law as the instrument and offspring of reason.

I have not been able to submit to you large generalizations that illumine or harmoniously assimilate discrete instances. Still less have I been able to fashion criteria for easier adjudication of the specific cases that will trouble future judges. They are bound to be troubled whether they will be faced with variant aspects of old problems—old conflicts between liberty and authority, between the central government and its constituent members—or new problems inevitably thrown up by the everlasting flux of life.

Believing it still important to do so, I have tried to dispel the age-old illusion that the conflicts to which the energy and ambition and imagination of the restless human spirit give rise can be subdued, even if not settled, by giving the endeavors of reason we call law a mechanical or automatic or enduring configuration. Law cannot be confined within any such mould because life cannot be so confined. Man's most piercing discernment of the future cannot see very far beyond his day, even when guided by the prophet's insight and the compassionate humility of a Lincoln. And I am the last to claim that judges are apt to be endowed with these gifts. But a fair appraisal of Anglo-American judicial history ought to leave us not without encouragement that modest goals, uncompromisingly pursued, may promote what I hope you will let me call civilized ends without the need of defining them.

In what I have been saying you have no doubt heard undertones of a judge's perplexities—particularly of a judge who has to construe, as it is called, vague and admonitory constitutional provisions. But I am very far from meaning to imply a shriveled conception of government under law. Quite the contrary. The intention of my emphasis has been not on the limited scope of judicial enforcement of laws. My concern is an affirmation—my plea is for the pervasiveness throughout the whole range of government of the spirit of law, at least in the sense of excluding arbitrary official action. But however limited the area of adjudication may be, the standards of what is fair and just set by courts in controversies appropriate for their adjudication are perhaps the single most powerful influence in promoting the spirit of law throughout government. These standards also help shape the dominant civic habits and attitudes which ultimately determine the ethos of a society.

In exercising their technical jurisdiction, courts thus release contagious consequences. Nothing is farther from my mind than to suggest that judges should exceed the professional demands of a particular decision. If judges want to be preachers, they should dedicate themselves to the pulpit; if judges want to be primary shapers of policy, the legislature is their place. Self-willed judges are the least defensible offenders against government under law. But since the grounds of decisions and their general direction suffuse the public mind and the operations of government, judges cannot free themselves from the responsibility of the inevitable effect of their opinions in constricting or promoting the force of law throughout government. Upon no functionaries is there a greater duty to promote law.

Edwin Meese III, *The Law of the Constitution,* 61 TUL. L. REV. 979 (1987)*

* * *

During its nearly two hundred years, the Constitution, which Gladstone pronounced "the most wonderful work ever struck off at a given time by the brain and purpose of man," has been reflected upon and argued about from many perspectives by great men and lesser ones. The scrutiny has not always been friendly. The debates over ratification, for example, were often rancorous, and scorn was poured on many of the constitutional provisions devised by the Federal Convention in 1787. The Federalists and the Anti-Federalists were, to say the very least, in notable disagreement. Richard Henry Lee of Virginia, a leading Anti-Federalist, was convinced, for example, that the new Constitution was "in its first principles, [most] highly and dangerously oligarchic." He feared, as did a good many others, for the fate of democratic government under so powerful an instrument. Still others thought it unlikely that so large a nation could survive without explicit provision for cultivating civic virtue among the citizens. The critics of the proposed Constitution had serious reservations about this new enterprise in popular government, an effort even the friends of the Constitution conceded was a novel experiment.

No sooner was the Constitution adopted than it became an object of astonishing reverence. The losers in the great ratification debates pitched in to make the new government work. Indeed, so vast was the public enthusiasm that one Senator complained that, in praising the new government, "declamatory gentlemen" were painting "the state of the country under the old congress"—that is, under the Articles of Confederation—"as if neither wood grew nor water ran in America before the happy adoption of the new Constitution."

It has not all been easy going, of course. There has been some pretty rough sailing during the nearly 200 years under the Constitution. In fact, the greatest political tragedy in American history was played out in terms of the principles of the Constitution. You see, the debate over nationalism versus confederalism, that had

----

*   Reprinted with permission.

first so divided the Federal Convention and later had inflamed the animosities of Federalists and Anti-Federalists, lingered on. Its final resolution was a terrible and bloody one—the War Between the States. And in the war's wake, the once giddy, almost unqualified adoration of the Constitution subsided into realism.

* * *

The Constitution is—to put it simply but one hopes not simplistically—the Constitution. It is a document of our most fundamental law. It begins "We the People of the United States, in Order to form a more perfect Union . . ." and ends up, some 6,000 words later, with the twenty-sixth amendment. It creates the institutions of our government, it enumerates the powers those institutions may wield, and it cordons off certain areas into which government may not enter. It prohibits the national authority, for example, from passing ex post facto laws while it prohibits the states from violating the obligations of contracts.

The Constitution is, in brief, the instrument by which the consent of the governed—the fundamental requirement of any legitimate government—is transformed into a government complete with the powers to act and a structure designed to make it act wisely or responsibly. Among its various internal contrivances (as James Madison called them) we find federalism, separation of powers, bicameralism, representation, an extended commercial republic, an energetic executive, and an independent judiciary. Together, these devices form the machinery of our popular form of government and secure the rights of the people. The Constitution, then, is the Constitution, and as such it is, in its own words, "the supreme Law of the Land."

Constitutional law, on the other hand, is that body of law that has resulted from the Supreme Court's adjudications involving disputes over constitutional provisions or doctrines. To put it a bit more simply, constitutional law is what the Supreme Court says about the Constitution in its decisions resolving the cases and controversies that come before it.

In its limited role of offering judgment, the Court has had a great deal to say. In almost two hundred years, it has produced nearly 500 volumes of reports of cases. While not all these opinions deal with constitutional questions, of course, a good many do. This stands in marked contrast to the few, slim paragraphs that have been added to the original Constitution as amendments. So, in terms of sheer bulk, constitutional law greatly overwhelms the Constitution. But in substance, it is meant to support and not overwhelm the Constitution from which it is derived.

This body of law, this judicial handiwork, is in a fundamental way unique in our scheme. For the Court is the only branch of our government that routinely, day in and day out, is charged with the awesome task of addressing the most basic, the most enduring, political questions: What is due process of law? How does the idea of separation of powers affect the Congress in certain circumstances? And so forth. The answers the Court gives are very important to the stability of the law so necessary for good government. Yet as constitutional historian Charles Warren once noted, what's most important to remember is that "[h]owever the Court may interpret the provisions of the Constitution, it is still the Constitution which is the law and not the decision of the Court."

By this, of course, Charles Warren did not mean that a constitutional decision by the Supreme Court lacks the character of law. Obviously it does have binding quality: it binds the parties in a case and also the executive branch for whatever enforcement is necessary. But such a decision does not establish a supreme law of the land that is binding on all persons and parts of government henceforth and forevermore.

This point should seem so obvious as not to need elaboration. Consider its necessity in particular reference to the Court's own work. The Supreme Court would face quite a dilemma if its own constitutional decisions really were the supreme law of the land, binding on all persons and governmental entities, including the Court itself, for then the Court would not be able to change its mind. It could not overrule itself in a constitutional case. Yet we know that the Court has done so on numerous occasions. . . .

These and other examples teach effectively the point that constitutional law and the Constitution are not the same. Even so, although the point may seem obvious, there have been those throughout our history—and especially, it seems, in our own time—who have denied the distinction between the Constitution and constitutional law. Such denial usually has gone hand in hand with an affirmation that constitutional decisions are on a par with the Constitution in the sense that they too are the supreme law of the land, from which there is no appeal.

Perhaps the most well-known instance of this denial occurred during the most important crisis in our political history. In 1857, in the *Dred Scott* case, the Supreme Court struck down the Missouri Compromise by declaring that Congress could not prevent the extension of slavery into the territories and that blacks could not be citizens and thus eligible to enjoy the constitutional privileges of citizenship. This was a constitutional decision, for the Court said that the right of whites to possess slaves was a property right affirmed in the Constitution.

This decision sparked the greatest political debate in our history. In the 1858 Senate campaign in Illinois, Stephen Douglas went so far in his defense of *Dred Scott* as to equate the decision with the Constitution. In his third debate with his opponent, Abraham Lincoln, he said:

> It is the fundamental principle of the judiciary that its decisions are final.
> It is created for that purpose so that when you cannot agree among your-
> selves on a disputed point you appeal to the judicial tribunal which steps
> in and decides for you, and that decision is binding on every good citizen.

Furthermore, he later said, "The Constitution has created that Court to decide all Constitutional questions in the last resort, and when such decisions have been made, they become the law of the land." It plainly was Douglas's view that constitutional decisions by the Court were authoritative, controlling, and final, binding on all persons and parts of government the instant they are made—from then on.

Lincoln, of course, disagreed. In his response to Douglas we can see the nuances and subtleties and the correctness of the position that makes most sense in a constitutional democracy like ours—a position that seeks to maintain the important function of judicial review while at the same time upholding the right of the people to govern themselves through the democratic branches of government.

Lincoln said that insofar as the Court "decided in favor of Dred Scott's master and against Dred Scott and his family"—the actual parties in the case—he did not propose to resist the decision. But Lincoln went on to say:

> We nevertheless do oppose [*Dred Scott*] . . . as a political rule which shall
> be binding on the voter, to vote for nobody who thinks it wrong, which shall
> be binding on the members of Congress or the President to favor no mea-
> sure that does not actually concur with the principles of that decision.

I have provided this example, not only because it comes from a well-known episode in our history, but also because it helps us understand the implications of this important distinction. If a constitutional decision is not the same as the Constitution itself, if it is not binding in the same way that the Constitution is, we as citizens may respond to a decision with which we disagree. As Lincoln in effect pointed out, we can make our responses through the presidents, the senators, and the representatives we elect at the national level. We can also make them through those we elect at the state and local levels. Thus, not only can the Supreme Court respond to its previous constitutional decisions and change them, as it did in *Brown* and has done on many other occasions, but so can the other branches of government, and through them, the American people. As we know, Lincoln himself worked to overturn *Dred Scott* through the executive branch. The Congress joined him in this effort. Fortunately, *Dred Scott*—the case—lived a very short life.

Once we understand the distinction between constitutional law and the Constitution, once we see that constitutional decisions need not be seen as the last words in constitutional construction, once we comprehend that these decisions do not necessarily determine future public policy, once we see all of this, we can grasp a correlative point: constitutional interpretation is not the business of the Court only, but also properly the business of all branches of government.

The Supreme Court, then, is not the only interpreter of the Constitution. Each of the three coordinate branches of government created and empowered by the Constitution—the executive and legislative no less than the judicial—has a duty to interpret the Constitution in the performance of its official functions. In fact, every official takes an oath precisely to that effect.

For the same reason that the Constitution cannot be reduced to constitutional law, the Constitution cannot simply be reduced to what Congress or the President say it is either. Quite the contrary. The Constitution, the original document of 1787 plus its amendments, is and must be understood to be the standard against which all laws, policies, and interpretations must be measured. It is the consent of the governed with which the actions of the governors must be squared. And this also applies to the power of judicial review. For as Felix Frankfurter once said, "[t]he ultimate touchstone of constitutionality is the Constitution itself and not what we have said about it."

Judicial review of congressional and executive actions for their constitutionality has played a major role throughout our political history. The exercise of this power produces constitutional law. In this task even the courts themselves have on occasion been tempted to think that the law of their decisions is on a par with the Constitution.

Some thirty years ago, in the midst of great racial turmoil, our highest Court seemed to succumb to this very temptation. By a flawed reading of our Constitution and *Marbury v. Madison*, and an even more faulty syllogism of legal reasoning, the Court in a 1958 case called *Cooper v. Aaron* appeared to arrive at conclusions about its own power that would have shocked men like John Marshall and Joseph Story.

In this case, in dictum, the Court characterized one of its constitutional decisions as nothing less than "the supreme law of the land." Obviously constitutional decisions are binding on the parties to a case; but the implication of the dictum that everyone should accept constitutional decisions uncritically, that they are judgments from which there is no appeal, was astonishing; the language recalled what Stephen Douglas said about *Dred Scott*. In one fell swoop, the Court seemed to reduce the Constitution to the status of ordinary constitutional law, and to equate the judge with the lawgiver. Such logic assumes, as Charles Evans Hughes once quipped, that the Constitution is "what the judges say it is." The logic of the dictum in *Cooper v. Aaron* was, and is, at war with the Constitution, at war with the basic principles of democratic government, and at war with the very meaning of the rule of law.

* * *

My message today is that such interpretations are not and must not be placed in such a position. To understand the distinction between the Constitution and constitutional law is to grasp, as John Marshall observed in *Marbury*, "that the framers of the constitution contemplated that instrument as a *rule* for the government of courts, as well as of the legislature." This was the reason, in Marshall's view, that a written Constitution is "the greatest improvement on political institutions."

Likewise, James Madison, expressing his mature view of the subject, wrote that as the three branches of government are coordinate and equally bound to support the Constitution, "each must in the exercise of its functions be guided by the text of the Constitution according to its own interpretation of it." And, as his lifelong friend and collaborator, Jefferson, once said, the written Constitution is "our peculiar security."

Perhaps no one has ever put it better than did Abraham Lincoln, seeking to keep the lamp of freedom burning bright in the dark moral shadows cast by the Court in the *Dred Scott* case. Recognizing that Justice Taney, in his opinion in that case, had done great violence not only to the text of the Constitution but to the intentions of those who had written, proposed, and ratified it, Lincoln argued that if the policy of government upon vital questions affecting the whole people is to be irrevocably fixed by decisions of the Supreme Court the instant they are made, in ordinary litigation between parties, in personal actions, the people will have ceased to be their own rulers, having to that extent, practically resigned their government into the hands of that imminent tribunal.

Once again, we must understand that the Constitution is and must be understood to be superior to ordinary constitutional law. This distinction must be respected. To confuse the Constitution with judicial pronouncements allows no standard by which to criticize and to seek the overruling of what University of Chicago Law Professor Philip Kurland once called the "derelicts of constitutional law"—cases such as *Dred Scott* and *Plessy v. Ferguson*. To do otherwise, as Lincoln said, is to submit to government by judiciary. But such a state could never be consistent with the principles of our Constitution. Indeed, it would be utterly inconsistent with the very idea of the rule of law to which we, as a people, have always subscribed.

* * *

J.M. Balkin, *The Footnote*, 83 Nw. U. L. Rev. 275 (1989)*

I. THE PROBLEM OF THE FOOTNOTE

* * *

When constitutional scholars talk about the "problem of the footnote," they are referring to a specific footnote, *the* Footnote, footnote four of *United States v. Carolene Products*, an opinion written by Justice Harlan Fiske Stone. Here indeed is a footnote that has become more important than the text; that is often read separated from its text; that can stand alone. Nor is this footnote a trifle, or an insignificant bauble. It has inspired countless books and law review articles.

---

*   Reprinted with permission.

* * *

II. THE OPINION AS FOOTNOTE

Carolene Products concerned the constitutionality of the Filled Milk Act of 1923, "which prohibit[ed] the shipment in interstate commerce of skimmed milk compounded with any fat or oil other than milk fat, so as to resemble milk or cream." Section 62 of the Act declared that "filled milk . . . is an adulterated article of food, injurious to the public health, and its sale constitutes a fraud upon the public." The appellee, Carolene Products Co., was indicted for shipping in interstate commerce packages of "Milnut," a product which combined skim milk with coconut oil to produce a substance resembling whole milk or cream. Such artificial substitutes were also marketed under the trade name "Carolene," from which the company derived its name. Carolene Products Co. argued that the statute was beyond the power of the federal government both under the commerce clause and the due process clause of the fifth amendment. (It is often forgotten that *Carolene Products* is not only a due process case but also a commerce clause case, a fact which is usually excluded from edited versions appearing in contemporary Constitutional Law casebooks).

* * *

[In the part of the opinion that the author depicts as "second,"] for a brief moment (a second perhaps), it appears as if Stone has provided us with a new approach to judicial scrutiny, of which footnote *two* is the centerpiece. Here, in "Second," he suggests that the test of legislative reasonableness is whether Congress has held hearings, gathered evidence, made detailed findings of fact—in short, whether there are indicia of a sound and considered judgment by the elected representatives of the people based upon reliable scientific information. If the Congress has made an effort to learn the facts, if it has sought dispassionately and conscientiously to ascertain the public interest through a process of deliberation and self-education, it is not for the courts to second-guess its judgment. The theory of "Second," had it been allowed to flourish, might have developed into something reminiscent of what later writers would call "Due Process of Lawmaking"—a concern for the procedural purity of the process by which Congress makes decisions in the public interest, posed as an alternative to the Lochnerian concern with the end results of the political process. Or, the theory of "Second" might have developed into a republican conception of politics, with a judicial role that sought to promote sincere deliberation over cynical logrolling, and public interest over private advantage.

Yet as soon as these alternatives are suggested, they are hurriedly whisked off the stage, and another, superficially similar, line of reasoning takes their place. This seemingly harmless and uninteresting rationale appears in the section labelled "Third," which at first glance appears to be no more than the warm up act for the real celebrity, its neighbor, the famous footnote four.

. . . [In Part III of the opinion], the Court makes it clear that even if the Congress had held no hearings, had called no witnesses, had engaged in no factfinding or deliberations whatsoever, the constitutionality of the statute would remain unaffected. The Court will simply make up facts and reasons to justify the distinctions made by the legislation it is presented with, and it will not strike down the legislation unless the Court cannot invent a scenario in which a rational legislature might have produced the bill before it.

Here we are brought to the difficulty and the interest in this easy and uninteresting case. Stone reveals himself supremely unconcerned with the actual method by which Congress reached its conclusion, or with the actual purpose that motivated the legislators in banning filled milk. Indeed, in his fidelity to judicial deference, Stone commits the Court to an enterprise of disguise and misrepresentation. The goal of a Court faced with a due process or equal protection challenge henceforth is to paint the rosiest possible picture of the process of deliberation and of the legislature's purpose. We now see why the results of the Congressional hearings were relegated to footnote two—they were mere window dressing, a surplusage ultimately unnecessary to the decision of the case. Indeed, the whole section of the opinion marked "Second" has itself been a sham, a diversionary tactic.

* * *

By refusing to inquire into less restrictive alternatives, and by rejecting attacks based upon over- and underinclusiveness, Stone wholeheartedly embraces agnosticism as to purpose. The rationale of every governmental action almost always has a nice version and a naughty version; inquiry using such proxies as means-ends fit is important, for the real legislative purpose is not always easily determined otherwise. A poor fitting of means to ends is the surest sign that the legislature's stated goals are not its real goals, and that the bill disguises some unseemly machination or invidious prejudice.

The "nice" version of the Filled Milk Act, for example, is that the bill was designed as a paternalistic measure to prevent uneducated and even illiterate consumers from purchasing a less expensive but less nutritious substitute for milk and cream. The legislature was concerned that consumers would purchase Milnut under the influence of unscrupulous merchants motivated more by private profit than by public concern. Conceivably, lack of consumer education might have undermined the efficacy of labelling Milnut as a milk substitute as required by the Food and Drug Act.

On the other hand, the rationale of the Filled Milk Act also has a naughty version, as Professor Komesar tells us:

> It does not take much scrutiny to see the dairy lobby at work behind the passage and enforcement of the "filled milk" act. Indeed, the dairy industry's efforts to employ legislation to keep "adulterated" products from grocery shelves and vending booths have a long history, extending from before *Lochner v. New York* to the present. It is not too uncharitable, perhaps, to suggest that concern for the dairies' pocketbooks rather than for the consumer's health best explains the diary lobby's efforts. In fact, though the filled milk legislation seemed to be aimed at helping consumers, it may have harmed them. They were "saved" from "adulterated" products, but only at the cost of higher prices, while the diary industry benefited from reduced competition.

Komesar's explanation leaves us wondering who was really sacrificing public interest for personal profit. And the doctrine of "Third" gives us only this reply: Who Cares? This is a very *uninteresting* opinion, indeed. But, the deficiency of interest is not ours, but the opinion's, in its lack of concern with the integrity of the legislative process.

Moreover, if we dig deeper, forgetting for the moment that we are lawyers attempting to divine the *legal meaning* of this text—a text which, as we have just seen, suffers from an acute case of ennui—we will again witness how the opinion comments upon and even mocks itself. The portion we have nicknamed "Third" is a remarkable exercise in judicial deference to the legislature. Yet this judicial deference is a deferral both to and of the legislature. By fabricating a rational basis for this legislation, the Court not only marginalizes its own role (scrutiny of legislative action), but, ironically, also defers and puts off the legislature itself. The rational basis test requires the Court to disregard the actual legislative process, and substitute in place of the real legislature (with its adulterated motivations and flaws of reasoning) an ideal legislature, armed with precisely those facts and considerations that would make a statute reasonable and thus worthy of judicial deference. The Court adopts the stance of the infatuated lover in the first stages of a crush, who substitutes an ideal picture of the beloved for a less flattering reality.

This legislative deference is legislative *deferral* substitution—a substitution uncannily mocked by the subject of the opinion. Even as the Court recites Congress' concerns about adulterated products that substitute nondairy fat for milk fat, it engages in its own substitution. It delivers its own adulterated product (a theory of judicial scrutiny) by substituting the constitutional theory of "Third" for that of "Second"—a bait and switch game whose contours have already been noted. The Court replaces one conception of the judicial role—the inquiry into the actual deliberative process in democratic institutions—with another: the creation of excuses for pluralist hardball. In like fashion, the cream of actual legislative deliberation is skimmed away, and replaced with the artificial substitute of an imagined and ideal purpose. The Court then passes off its product to the ultimate consumer, claiming that this new judicial role is better (and less costly to society) than a more active judicial role (read here substantive due process). Finally, not only is the Court's new product adulterated, but it is even *mislabeled* as judicial scrutiny.

Here too, the issue of purity reappears in a highly problematical fashion. It is hard to know what is pure and what is impure in the portions of the opinion marked "Second" and "Third." Consider: the Court, suspecting that the legislative motivation behind the Filled Milk Act is not pure—that the Act is rather an attempt by the dairy lobby to subdue its economic competitors—hides this impurity by constructing a "purer" purpose for public consumption. Yet the purity of this purpose is artificial (and hence also impure). Consider: usurpation of the legislature's role introduces an impurity into our democratic system; requiring actual purity of motive on the legislature would encroach upon the purity of democracy. Yet abdication of the judicial role leaves no protection of the process from self-adulteration; it may reduce the courts to apologists for a process that is really impure.

The issues of substitution, purity, and deferral do not escape us. They return with each investigation into this seemingly unremarkable opinion. The Carolene product of *Carolene Products* is already, also, and always adulterated, a substitution of an unhealthy and artificial filler (institutional considerations, appeal to a nonexistent legislative consideration) for a more searching inquiry. Might we not inquire, as Congress did, whether this substitution will not ultimately injure the public's health? When, as here, the Court offers us a less costly product, will we not be tempted to choose it instead of a healthier, albeit more difficult inquiry into the processes of democratic deliberation? Will this purchase of shoddy goods not leave us worse off in the long run?

III. THE NEW CIVIL RELIGION AND ITS PROPHETS

In developing the problematics of this uninteresting opinion—an opinion which professes no interest in the interests of special interests—we seem to have garnered for ourselves a tidy sum (of interest). How could our interpretations of so marginal a product have borne so much fruit? Perhaps *Carolene Products* is not so unimportant an opinion after all. Perhaps Stone was right to place his famous footnote in the margin of the opinion, for the problems that give rise to this footnote are already implicated in the text.

Carolene Products is the post-1937 Court's first extended discussion and elaboration of a theory of judicial review proclaimed in a very famous opinion: *West Coast Hotel Co. v. Parrish*. *West Coast Hotel*, and its companion in the Commerce Clause area, *NLRB v. Jones & Laughlin Steel Corporation*, announce the end of the *Lochner* period in Supreme Court jurisprudence; together they constitute the boundary that separates modern from premodern constitutional law. Yet if *West Coast Hotel* forms the boundary, *Carolene Products* is the first way station in this hitherto uncharted territory.

West Coast Hotel is never mentioned in *Carolene Products*; the former dealt with a line of cases involving labor regulations while the latter concerned itself mainly with cases involving regulation of adulterated foodstuffs. Yet the revolution of *West Coast Hotel* was *very* much on the minds of the justices as they decided *Carolene Products*. The former decision had left many important and unanswered questions. What was the promise of *West Coast Hotel v. Parrish*? . . .

. . . Similarly, *West Coast Hotel* could have been understood as questioning the political neutrality of the status quo through its deconstructive claim that "[t]he community is not bound to provide what is in effect a subsidy for unconscionable employers." This delightfully perverse statement responds to an unstated premise in *Lochner* era jurisprudence. Alterations of common law rules of contract—for example, those designed to ameliorate the inequality of bargaining power between the parties—were viewed by the *Lochner* Court as subsidizing one of the parties (or the public at large) at the expense of the other. Such alterations were impermissible redistributions of wealth unless they fell within the Court's limited conception of the police power or were otherwise in aid of common law rights.

Yet, as Professor Sunstein points out, "[t]he notion of subsidy is . . . incoherent without a baseline from which to make a measurement." If the employer suffered from the public's decision to enact a minimum wage law, the employee suffered from the public's decision not to enact a minimum wage law. One might object that in the latter case the state did nothing by failing to enact such a law, but the logic of *West Coast Hotel* implies that having a common law of contracts that protects some expectations but not others is a type of action for which the state is ultimately responsible. Hence, *West Coast Hotel* might have led to a rejection of the common law or the status quo as the benchmark for determining whether economic, political, or civil rights had been violated. This too, would have substituted a new kind of substantive protection for the older, common law inspired jurisprudence of the *Lochner* Court.

Thus, *West Coast Hotel* represented a revolution, but a revolution of imprecise contours. It could have been a revolution, as Tribe suggests, in which economic liberty was still protected, but through a different system of values. Or, as Sunstein suggests, it could have been a decision to reject the belief in a neutral market ordering created by a common law for which the state was not responsible. In either case the Court would not have foresworn the legitimacy of substantive review of legislative enactments, or the requirement that legislation demonstrate a "fair and substantial relation" to its stated objectives. In either case, the Court could have claimed that it was a true servant of the revolution. Yet *Carolene Products* took a third approach. It saw the vice of *Lochner*, and the virtue of *West Coast Hotel*, in purely institutional terms. Under this interpretation, the revolution of 1937 was fought not over the content of values but over who was to choose those values—after the revolution, such choices were excluded from the purview of courts and placed solely in the hands of legislatures. Thus, the portion of *Carolene Products* marked "Third" is by no means insignificant or unimportant. It represents the reinterpretation of the revolution in terms of a seemingly value neutral deference to legislative will.

And here the significance of *Carolene Products'* seeming insignificance is revealed. *Carolene Products* is the humble servant of the messianic *West Coast Hotel*, playing St. Paul to the latter's Jesus. If Jesus came to offer a message of salvation for the world, St. Paul told us what that message was. And in interpreting that message for the Gentiles, St. Paul did more than act as a messenger. He invented an entirely new religion—Christianity.

One must pardon the temptation to see the religious analogy here, in this New Testament of our Civil Religion (the Constitution), in this most ecclesiastical of cases, which even bears the name *Parrish*. Here is the long hoped for Messiah, come to sweep away the old law and replace it with the new (yet at the same time insisting that He came not to abolish the law but to fulfill it). Here is the faithful servant, St. Paul, who in an effort to attract the heathen, downplays the role of good works (read here substantive review) in his Master's sayings, and informs us that faith alone (in the democratic process) is both necessary and sufficient for salvation. The antiestablishment and revolutionary elements of the Master's message, the identification with the disadvantaged and the poor, are all marginalized, deemphasized. Good works will not save us, for no one is without sin, and hence no one can gain salvation merely by pursuing the right values; all will ultimately fall short of the mark. The way to heaven is not by good works, the enforcement of the proper choice of values, but through faith in the new civil religion—democracy.

And who writes the epistles that champion this interpretation? Who creates this new civil religion of salvation through faith alone? It is Justice Stone, the apostle whose faith in democracy disguises his agnosticism towards legislative purpose. Stone's opinion is both St. Paul and St. Peter—Stone's opinion is the *petros* (or rock) upon which this new church is founded.

What was the advantage of the interpretation Stone created in *Carolene Products*, the promise of this new civil religion? Quite simply, *Carolene Products* seemed to offer an alternative to, and a retreat from, value-laden decisionmaking by the judiciary. To Stone and his brethren, the erratically high level of judicial scrutiny adopted by the old Court had only resulted in a superimposition of its economic and political views onto those of legislatures. In the new constitutional regime, a strong presumption of constitutionality of majoritarian acts and a low level of judicial scrutiny would prevent the judiciary's intervention into controversial value choices that were properly the concern of the democratic process. Stone's interpretation of the 1937 revolution counseled that preemptive impositions of value by the judiciary should be eliminated, or at the very least, seriously curtailed.

Ideally, the judiciary would have avoided imposing substantive value choices entirely. Yet this ideal was impossible to achieve in practice, for taken seriously, one would have to overrule *Marbury v. Madison* and the doctrine of judicial review itself. Moreover, it presented a potential embarrassment. Stone and his allies on the Court were quite concerned that majorities might seek to abridge civil liberties of speech, press, and peaceable assembly, and had joined in several opinions dispensing with the presumption of constitutionality and applying a relatively high level of judicial scrutiny where freedom of speech as opposed to contract was involved. Under the judicial nonscrutiny envisioned in "Third," an unscrupulous majority could soon make short work of political opponents, and America might easily degenerate into the very sort of fascism that Stone and his brethren saw percolating on the other side of the Atlantic. The problem for Stone and his like-minded colleagues was how to reconcile their instinct for the preservation of civil liberties with their commitment to legislative deference and judicial self-restraint. The revolution they had fought for was in serious danger of unravelling intellectually at the very moment of its success.

According to the institutional interpretation of the 1937 revolution, preemptive value choices had to be excluded from the judicial role. They represented the evil of the old religion, an impurity and a danger to the democratic faith. Yet the need for such preemptive choices reasserted itself as soon as they were excluded. A high level of judicial scrutiny—a serious commitment to judicial review—was both necessary and dangerous to the new civil religion; necessary because of the desire to preserve civil liberties, dangerous because it threatened the intellectual coherence of the new Court's teachings.

If a serious commitment to judicial scrutiny could not be eliminated in all cases, perhaps it could be confined to its appropriate sphere. The dirty and disgusting job of judicial review might be banished to areas demarcated in advance, much as one places lepers, criminals, or the insane in a colony, prison, or asylum. The messy and questionable task of judicial scrutiny might be *confined* to particular types of legislation, to a particular group of factual situations, without infecting the purity of the general commitment to democracy. This confinement, this quarantine, might allow the disease or abnormality to be treated on its own terms without risking an infection of the general populace. Here is the solution of *Carolene Products*—a partial exclusion, which divides the constitutional world into a rule (deference, the kingdom of "Third") and an exception (scrutiny, the *hospital* of the footnote, where diseases are treated, or otherwise prevented from injuring the outside world).

And with this exclusion comes a new myth to justify the exile, the marginalization, the neat division of the world into rule and exception, normal case and abnormal, healthy and sick. It is well stated by Justice Powell:

> The fundamental character of our government is democratic. Our constitution assumes that majorities should rule and that the government should be able to govern. Therefore, for the most part, Congress and the state legislatures should be allowed to do as they choose. But there are certain groups that cannot participate effectively in the political process. And the political process therefore cannot be trusted to protect these groups in the way it protects most of us.

The key words in this passage—the words that establish and justify the logic of exclusion and marginalization—are "for the most part." Note their implications: The political process works effectively most of the time; representative democracy can generally be trusted to act in the public interest. Nevertheless, in a small, selected group of cases, which can be readily identified, the process malfunctions. In that marginal set of cases the judiciary properly may subject legislation to a higher level of scrutiny, not because it is authorized to impose its value choices upon the majority, but because the process itself is defective, undemocratic, impure. And in the very act of excluding these marginal situations from the norm, the judiciary demonstrates a double fidelity to democracy: First, because it avoids interfering in the normal processes of democratic institutions, and second, because it intervenes in those and only those abnormal cases in which the democratic ideals that justify judicial deference have been disserved.

Here the Court takes for itself a new role—the physician who tends to the diseased, or the pastor who brings succor and comfort to the criminal or to the leper. And it is well that the Court should confine its work to this very small class of cases—the derelicts of the democratic process. For as Jesus tells us, "[t]hose who are well have no need of a physician, [only] those who are sick." The Court's proper role is as master of the marginal, like the doctor who preserves health by treating the sick, the prison warden who preserves safety by sequestering the dangerous, the minister who preserves morality by preaching to the sinful.

The metaphors of purity and impurity, sickness and health, inclusion and exclusion, are busily at work in the language of the third paragraph of the footnote. Stone speaks of prejudice against discrete and insular minorities as a "special condition, which tends seriously to curtail the operation of those political processes ordinarily to be relied upon to protect minorities." Thus, prejudice is a special condition, an impurity or illness that is limited in scope, unusual, a defect that one is not likely to find everywhere. It is precisely because of its limited nature that it can be excluded, cut off, placed outside the political process through judicial supervision. The task of the judiciary, then, is to exclude or set aside those legislative enactments that are the result of this special condition. The rhetoric of inclusion and exclusion closes in upon itself, for exclusion will be remedied by a form of exclusion. The judiciary outlaws those decisions and actions that result from an imperfect political process, leaving the purer, democratic products of the process untouched and uncontaminated.

Yet at the very moment in which Stone makes this division, impurities have already infiltrated into the political system. For we have no reason to believe that prejudice, lack of deliberation, stereotypical thinking, and invidious motivation appear magically only during consideration of legislation that tramples upon civil liberties. If the political process is impure where noneconomic rights are at stake, it is equally impure when economic rights are concerned. Yet this is the governing myth of the new Civil Religion—the process will never fail us when the legislature considers particular subject matters (economic rights) while it often fails us when considering others (political rights).

Merely to state this myth is to reveal its fictional character. Yet the task Stone set for the judiciary in "Third" was to perpetuate that myth, and where economic rights were involved, to disguise every prejudice as a principle, every adulterated action as the servant of the public interest. Once again we see that the substitution of "Third" for "Second" was more than accidental, that it was essential to the logic of Stone's work. Stone could not have taken what he said in "Second" seriously: to do so would have admitted the possibility that the impurity in the political process could not be cabined in, that it might infect even purely economic legislation. He would have had to admit that legislation that does not directly address civil liberties or the rights of suspect categories, even legislation neutral on its face, might be contaminated by the same disease and deformity that abides in the exile of the footnote. Yet how could he concede that the epidemic had spread beyond the confines of the hospital, that the criminal population had escaped their prison, without destroying the essential *myth*, the faith of the new Civil Religion? Such an alternative was too horrible to be contemplated. And so, *Carolene Products* perpetuates a deception through the artful substitution of "Third" for "Second," clinging all the while to its pluralist faith in a discernible public interest—a public interest that is more than just the vector sum of political forces and yet is achieved only through their summation.

IV. THE FOOTNOTE AS OPINION

* * *

Stone's institutional interpretation of *West Coast Hotel* (the third section of *Carolene Products*) raised the embarrassing question why judicial deference was not appropriate in every case. The reasoning of "Third" seemed to offer no way of picking and choosing among subjects for more searching judicial review. Yet the Court did, in actual practice, strike down some statutes but not others. If so, the Court's decision to defer in a particular case might be seen as just as much a value choice as the decision to scrutinize strictly in another case, and one was back to the vices of *Lochner*.

Thus, whenever the Court decided an economic regulation case, the logic of the footnote hovered at the periphery, supporting the Court's decision by answering the unspoken objection: "Why did you defer here and not elsewhere?" Only by characterizing the Court's role as properly concerned with marginal failures of process (the subject of the footnote) that called for more searching judicial scrutiny could the Court justify its new role (or nonrole) in the general area of social and economic regulation (the subject of the text). Only by explaining that higher levels of scrutiny were justified by the ideals of democracy themselves and not by a particular substantive conception of values could the new Roosevelt Court distinguish its work from the substantive due process review of the hated *Lochner* Court. And only by linking the Court's abandonment of the presumption of constitutionality to the ideals that justified the presumption could the Court explain why it deferred to the legislature in some cases but not others.

Thus in every economic due process case the logic of the footnote is deferred yet present, silent yet secretly evoked. In the doctrinal picture painted by the Court, it is kept outside the canvas, yet through this very act of exclusion it becomes the frame that keeps the canvas taut. Here, then, is yet another sense in which the footnote dominates the text. For not only has footnote four become more famous than the opinion in *Carolene Products*, it also supports and justifies the pluralist conception of politics in post-1937 constitutional jurisprudence. It is aptly called a footnote—for just as the body cannot stand or move without feet, the edifice of modernist constitutional law cannot support itself without complementary theories of judicial review and nonreview.

Yet, at the same time, if the logic of the footnote supported the logic of the opinion (and hence by extension the logic of post-1937 economic regulation cases in general), the converse was also true: The logic of the famous footnote four was predicated upon the very interpretation of *West Coast Hotel* that necessitated the footnote's existence. Footnote four owes as much to "Third" as "Third" owes to it. This footnote is the remedy to a disease, yet like a vaccine it bears the characteristics of the sickness it seeks to cure. The articulation of a justification of judicial review based upon failures of process is the natural result of the institutional interpretation of the 1937 revolution which saw the rough and tumble of legislative bargaining as the appropriate method for ascertaining and enforcing values. Because the text of *Carolene Products* defends judicial deference in pluralist terms, the footnote also defends judicial nondeference in pluralist terms—that (putting enforcement of the Bill of Rights to one side) judicial review is only justified to the extent that it can be tied to the correction of the limited flaws of democratic pluralism.

The faith of *Carolene Products* was that one could exclude values from the judicial role, and by casting them out substitute the task of purifying the democratic process. Yet, as so many commentators have noted, the purported exclusion of value that justified *Carolene Products* is a false exclusion, for controversial value choices arise anew the moment that others are avoided. The Supreme Court still had to identify those minorities and those fundamental liberties that were to be protected by more searching judicial scrutiny. Thus, the problem of the footnote reappeared insistently, for the more value choices were marginalized and excluded, the more the Court depended upon them in its appointed task of purifying the democratic process. Justice Powell aptly notes that

> [f]ar from initiating a jurisprudence of judicial deference to political judgments by the legislature, Footnote 4—in this view—undertook to substitute one activist judicial mission for another. . . . Where the Court before had used the substantive due process clause to protect property rights, now it should use the equal protection clause—a generally forgotten provision that Holmes once dismissed as 'the usual last resort of constitutional arguments'—as a sword with which to promote the liberty interests of groups disadvantaged by political decisions.

The problem of the footnote is especially powerful in this passage. Here the excluded, the marginalized, and the cast out—judicial activism, the equal protection clause, and disadvantaged minorities—combine to subvert the new constitutional regime. The previously discredited equal protection clause becomes the new champion of substantive values. Arguments about liberty are easily disguised as claims about equality and vice-versa—an interchangeability familiar to every student who has taken an introductory course in constitutional law.

Moreover, as soon as the Court tried to exclude substantive due process from consideration, it simply reappeared in a new guise. As many scholars have noted, one needs a substantive vision—of what kinds of discrimination are invidious, of what kinds of groups are deserving of judicial protection, of the substantive content of fairness, of the rights of due process—in order to determine whether the democratic process has in fact misfired. And here, says Justice Powell,

> [one] must pause to wonder. If I am correct about the implicit link between a substantive judgment and a malfunction of process, then one may inquire whether we have not returned in some cases to a kind of substantive due process. And one may also wonder what Stone—who had fought so vigorously against substantive due process—would have had to say about that.

V. THE PARTIALITY OF *CAROLENE PRODUCTS*

* * *

We have already seen how *Carolene Products* excluded the impurities of *Lochner* only to introduce new impurities in its own conception of judicial review, how it demarcated areas in which the political process was defective only by refusing to see deficiencies in the process as a whole, how it banished value choices from the judicial role only to see them reemerge in other contexts. The history of *Carolene Products* is the history of our discovery of its partiality, of its intellectual marginalizations. For history deconstructs—revealing that the dominant conceptions we use to understand the world at a particular point in time are increasingly inappropriate for solving the problems of later years. As events progress, altering our awareness of social reality, we discover the importance of what our theories marginalized or neglected, and how our conception has sown the seeds of its own destruction, adulteration, and purification in what it has overlooked, in what it has excluded. Ironically, the impurity of a dominant conception—the source of its eventual decomposition and decay—is due less to what it lets in than to what it leaves out. Thus, as we enter the next decade, the next century, we will find that, for all the good *Carolene Products* has done us, its shortcomings will become more and more apparent.

For example, in the innocent division of the world into text and footnote cases, between the heightened scrutiny of footnote four and the non-scrutiny of "Third," we can see the beginnings of the bankruptcy of equal protection jurisprudence in the 1970s. We cannot place the blame for these difficulties entirely on Justice Stone, who offered footnote four as the beginning of a search for a modern constitutional jurisprudence. Rather, the fault lies in the shortsightedness of his successors, who allowed his suggestions to ossify into an unthinking paradigm of judicial practice. Thus, by the 1970s, Stone's revolutionary approach had hardened into an equal protection doctrine featuring two tiers of scrutiny, where government action either received no review at all or a virtually irrebuttable presumption of unconstitutionality. The only issue in most cases was which level of scrutiny applied, which in turn reduced to the question whether a suspect class or a fundamental right was affected.

At first, this ossification did not appear to create any significant disadvantages. During the last years of the Warren Era and the first years of the Burger Era, the Supreme Court continued to add new fundamental rights, such as the right to travel in *Shapiro v. Thompson*, the right to marry in *Loving v. Virginia*, and the right of access to courts in *Boddie v. Connecticut*. Yet because the two-tier theory seemed to offer no alternative between total deference and total unconstitutionality, the recognition of new fundamental rights and suspect classes was made increasingly difficult. This difficulty suited conservatives like Justice Rehnquist perfectly well, for it guaranteed that the Court would be loath to introduce new theories requiring strict scrutiny. In such situations, the federal courts were left with only the alternative of rational basis review, which in most cases would do little to disturb the economic status quo.

* * *

This is not to say that the Supreme Court would not revise the list of suspect classes later on, as it did in the case of gender, or that it would not devise alternative theories of scrutiny, as it did in cases like *Plyler v. Doe* or *City of Cleburne v. Cleburne Living Center*. Nevertheless, the two tier system of equal protection of the 1970s created an orthodoxy, a doctrinal hurdle, that any new theories of discrimination or essential rights had to overcome. The gender and illegitimacy cases, for example were regarded as exceptional situations that did not fit easily into the "normal" mode of constitutional analysis. And in those cases where the Court was unable or unwilling to abandon theoretical normalcy—*Dandridge v. Williams, Rodriguez, Harris v. McCrae* and *Beazer*—it relegated many of the most important types of flaws of the democratic process to the nonprotections of the rational basis test. In this sense, later cases like *Plyler* and *Cleburne* must be understood as sports that reflect a profound dissatisfaction with the gradual stagnation of equal protection doctrine. Moreover, as cases like these become less and less exceptional, they announce the incipient rejection and transformation of the two-tier system, a transformation that we are living through even now.

The process of doctrinal ossification culminated in the 1973 decision in *San Antonio Independent School District v. Rodriguez,* in which the Court not only held that education was not a fundamental right but reiterated that poverty was not a suspect classification. With that decision the Court seemingly closed off, for a time, the list of rights and classes that would be counted as "footnote cases"—and would thus receive the benefits of heightened judicial scrutiny. In *Rodriguez,* Justice Powell surveyed the list of fundamental rights and decided arbitrarily that the Court would accept no more of them. In support of this decision, he announced that henceforth no right would be considered fundamental unless it had been explicitly or implicitly recognized in the Constitution. This statement was itself an ossification of doctrine, a decision to consolidate constitutional principles at a particular point in history. For the right to procreate in *Skinner v. Oklahoma* and the right to travel in *Shapiro v. Thompson* were no more and no less implicated in the Constitution than the right to education in *Rodriguez.* The only difference was that the former rights had been mentioned in cases decided before 1973. All Powell could offer in justification of his ipse dixit was that these rights had already been let in the door—and that the Court would not compound that error by adding new rights. Thus, *Rodriguez* symbolized not only a form of doctrinal stagnation, but, ironically, a new form of exclusion—an attempt to place a hermetic seal on the logic of footnote four, to prevent the accelerating conversion of text cases into footnote cases.

* * *

How did this state of affairs come about? How was the progressive vision of Justice Stone twisted into a heartless orthodoxy? How was revolutionary politics stultified into conservative dogma, the religious fervor of 1937 made pharisaic? The beginnings of the problem of the 1970s may be found in the articulation and division in footnote four itself, an articulation originally designed to remove obstacles in the path of progressive economic and social policies. Yet within this strategy lay the possibility of its own emasculation and deradicalization.

* * *

The source of the problem is in the ideology of democratic pluralism reflected in the intellectual framework of *Carolene Products*—in footnote four and the text, "Third," that surrounds it. Within Justice Stone's list of the causes of failures of democratic process, no mention is made of what seems today to be the most obvious cause of all—disparities in political power caused by differences in economic power. In 1938, Stone saw unreasoning prejudice, censorship, and limited access to the ballot box as the chief factors adulterating the purity of self-rule, and given the experiences of his day, these assumptions cannot be too much faulted. Yet fifty years of history would prove this viewpoint seriously inadequate. Today, in a country where traditional civil liberties are relatively well protected, we can see that disparities in wealth and economic power may poison the democratic process every bit as much as the imperfections Stone identified in his famous footnote.

Footnote four's blindness to these impurities is not accidental—it is inherent in its logical structure. The importance of this logic consists less in what footnote four says than in what it does *not* say. In the second paragraph of footnote four, when Stone decries "legislation which restricts those political processes which can ordinarily be expected to bring about repeal of undesirable legislation," he does not consider the possibility that relative economic strength also affects the possibility of subsequent repeal. Nor does he imagine that governmental action that *creates or rein-*

forces disparities in economic wealth and power might have exactly the same self-sustaining effect as governmental action that more directly affects political rights of speech and suffrage. To use the famous example of *Williamson v. Lee Optical*, if opthamologists and optometrists use draconian regulations to drive opticians out of business, it is hardly likely that the latter group's weakened economic condition will enhance their political effectiveness in a subsequent battle for repeal. Moreover, as proponents of campaign finance laws have argued for years, freedom of speech means little if no one can hear you, either because you lack the money to make yourself heard effectively or because your opponents have drowned out your message by means of their superior resources.

Similarly, in paragraph three of footnote four, Stone speaks of "prejudice against discrete and insular minorities [as] a special condition, which tends seriously to curtail the operation of those political processes ordinarily to be relied upon to protect minorities." This implies that minorities are closed out of the process because others will not deal with them in the political arena. Yet paragraph three does not consider that the true cause of political powerlessness of minorities might be disparities in economic status which are the effects of previous prejudice or previous exclusions from the political process. By focusing on pluralist bargaining strategies, paragraph three captures the important insight that majorities can adopt *self-reproducing* strategies for retaining power. Yet at the same time, paragraph three declines to push the analysis of self-reproduction of status and power back one step further—it does not contemplate that dominant economic and social forces might combine to perpetuate an economic underclass, or create minority subcultures that feature poverty, lack of education, learned helplessness, and self-destructive behavior.

If the footnote is blind to these possibilities, it is because it defines itself in terms of a text (the body of the opinion) which thrives upon that blindness. For the argument of "Third" depends upon the assumption that differences in wealth or economic power cannot by themselves be possible causes of failures of the political process, cannot result in self-reproducing stratifications of political power. This assumption was in turn necessitated by *Carolene Products'* peculiar interpretation of *West Coast Hotel* and the particular blindness of the *Lochner* era.

From the failures of the *Lochner* era, *Carolene Products* gleaned two important and interrelated lessons. The first lesson was that regulation with redistributive consequences could be in the public interest in spite of, and indeed because of, its redistributive effects. The second, which appeared to follow from the first, was that the judiciary should no longer concern itself with struggles over economic rights. If the faith of the revolution of 1937 consisted precisely in the belief that the distribution of wealth in society was none of its business (except in the case of a simple taking), how could the Court concern itself with the effect of wealth in other contexts—that is, with its effects on the democratic process? Thus, once again we see how much the logic of footnote four depends upon the logic of the opinion that surrounds it. The agnosticism of Stone, the faith of "Third," was that a properly functioning political process would regulate the economy and redistribute wealth in the public interest— the Court would only remain concerned with the formal structures of the political process (the subject of the footnote).

In divorcing the structure of procedure from the structure of the economy, *Carolene Products* proclaimed the essential independence of political from economic liberty, and political from economic equality. That this, too, was the lesson of the *Lochner* era seemed the most obvious reading of the revolution wrought by *West Coast Hotel*. Yet here again everything depended upon the partiality of a particular reading and upon its accompanying blindnesses. We have seen that an institutional reading of *West Coast Hotel* misses its more radical, humanitarian aspects. For by daring to label the common law regime of property and contract a "subsidy for unconscionable employers," *West Coast Hotel* affirmed the connection between economic equality and substantive liberty, between economic power and political right. If the legislature was *right* to alter the economic status quo because that regime violated human liberty, then the distribution of economic power in society had everything to do with the liberty guaranteed by the due process clause. The lesson of *Lochner* was that courts should not hinder legislatures from pursing human rights through alteration of property rights; and that the state was responsible for the reproduction of disparities in economic power achieved through maintenance of the status quo.

By neglecting this possible interpretation of *West Coast Hotel*, by understanding it as the strict separation of political and economic liberty (conceived in non-common-law terms), the pluralist faith of *Carolene Products* reintroduced, at a new level, the very evil that *West Coast Hotel* found in *Lochner*. If the *Lochner* court had seen differences in economic status as natural and not seriously affecting human rights, so now *Carolene Products* saw differences in political power stemming from differences in economic power as prepolitical and not seriously threatening the purity of the democratic process. Just as *Lochner* saw the right of economic participation as unaffected by differences in wealth, so now *Carolene Products* assumed that the rights of political participation were unaffected by these differences. Indeed, the pluralist credo of *Carolene Products* is hardly different than the famous Lochnerian credo of *Coppage v. Kansas*, with the notion of political liberty substituted for that of liberty of contract.

* * *

Why was the abandonment of *West Coast Hotel*'s more progressive tendencies so easy for a Court that viewed itself as liberal and progressive? Why was it content to exchange the wheat for the chaff? We must remember that in *West Coast Hotel*, the Court believed that the Washington legislature had acted to protect the rights of the poor. The Court was optimistic that the democratic process usually would recognize the need to move towards egalitarian measures, if only the heavy hand of the federal judiciary were removed. In this sense, the paradigm of *West Coast Hotel* gave the Court a false optimism; it led the Court to believe that there was something about the institution of democratic legislatures that made them more likely to regulate the economy and redistribute wealth in the public interest. Conversely, the Court assumed that the *Lochner* Court's reactionary tendencies were inherent in the structure of an unelected judiciary, even though the result in *West Coast Hotel* itself belied this very assumption. Thus, from the perspective of a particular moment in history, the new liberal Roosevelt majority believed that institutional and substantive concerns were tied together in a much more permanent way than later historical experience would confirm. If the assumption of a connection between institutions and values seems particularly naive today, we should remember that it is a mistake frequently made. The Warren Court led many liberal thinkers to precisely the opposite institutional conclusions, and it was not until the rise of the Burger Court that liberal commentators once again began to recognize the ambivalent relationship between substantive and institutional considerations.

The historical situation in which the Roosevelt Court acted led to its institutional delusions, its value-free rhetoric of deference to democracy. Yet by disregarding the effects of differences in economic power on the proper functioning of the political process, the *Carolene Products* Court betrayed the revolutionary ideas of *West Coast Hotel*. In the very act of casting out *Lochner* it depended upon *Lochner*-like premises. In its exclusion of impurities from the democratic process, it left untouched the strongest source of adulteration. The Carolene product of *Carolene Products* is, and always has been, adulterated

* * *

Bruce A. Ackerman, *Beyond* Carolene Products, 98 HARV. L. REV. 713 (1985)*

I. THE PROMISE OF CAROLENE PRODUCTS

"[P]rejudice against discrete and insular minorities may be a special condition . . . curtail[ing] the operation of those political processes ordinarily to be relied upon to protect minorities, and [so] may call for a correspondingly more searching judicial inquiry."

THESE famous words, appearing in the otherwise unimportant *Carolene Products* case, came at a moment of extraordinary vulnerability for the Supreme Court. They were written in 1938. The Court was just beginning to dig itself out of the constitutional debris left by its wholesale capitulation to the New Deal a year before. With the decisive triumph of the activist welfare state over the Old Court, an entire world of constitutional meanings, laboriously built up over two generations, had come crashing down upon the Justices' heads. Indeed, the Court had been so politically discredited by its constitutional defense of laissez-faire capitalism that it was hardly obvious whether any firm ground remained upon which to rebuild the institution of judicial review. How, then, to begin the work of reconstruction?

Only once before had the Court confronted a similar challenge. Just as the triumphant New Deal Democrats had destroyed the laissez-faire Constitutionalism of *Lochner v. New York*, so too a triumphant Republican Congress had destroyed the slavocratic constitutionalism of *Dred Scott v. Sanford* after the Civil War. Just as many contemporary observers doubted the institutional independence—let alone the constitutional importance—of the Supreme Court during Reconstruction, nobody could be confident about the future of judicial review in the aftermath of the Court-packing crisis.

Only one thing was clear. If the Court were to reassert itself after the Great Depression, it could not do so through the same constitutional rhetoric with which it had rehabilitated itself after the Civil War. During the long period between Reconstruction and New Deal, the Court had risen to the heights of power by insisting upon the fundamental right of free men to pursue their private aims in a free market system. Yet it was precisely this ideological elixir, which had given the judiciary new life after the Civil War, that proved nearly fatal during the constitutional birth agony of the activist welfare state. *If* the Court were to build a new foundation for judicial review, it would need an entirely new constitutional rhetoric—one that self-consciously recognized that the era of laissez-faire capitalism had ended.

Against this historical background, we may glimpse the promise of *Carolene Products*. Rather than look back longingly to a repudiated constitutional order, *Carolene* brilliantly endeavored to turn the Old Court's recent defeat into a judicial victory. As far as *Carolene* was concerned, lawyers could dispense with their traditional effort to organize their concern for individual rights through a constitutional rhetoric glorifying private property and free contract. Instead, *Carolene* proposed to make the ideals of the victorious activist Democracy serve as a primary foundation for constitutional rights in the United States.

Fifty years onward, the basic idea is familiar, but it requires restatement if we are to examine it carefully. *Carolene* promises relief from the problem of legitimacy raised whenever nine elderly lawyers invalidate the legislative decisions of a majority of our elected representatives. The *Carolene* solution is to seize the high ground of democratic theory and establish that the challenged legislation was produced by a profoundly defective process. By demonstrating that the legislative decision itself resulted from an undemocratic procedure, a *Carolene* court hopes to reverse the spin of the countermajoritarian difficulty. For it now may seem that the original legislative decision, not the judicial invalidation, suffers the greater legitimacy deficit.

Assume, for example, that the people of a state, after excluding blacks from the polls, elect an all-white legislature that proceeds to enact some classic Jim Crow legislation. Under the *Carolene* approach, the court does not purport to challenge the substantive value judgments underlying the legislative decision; instead, it simply denies that the Jim Crow statute would have emerged from a fair and open political process in which blacks were allowed to participate. In essence, the court is trumping the statutory conclusions of the deeply flawed real-world legislature by appealing to the hypothetical judgment of an ideally democratic legislature.

No wonder, then, that *Carolene Products* seemed so promising in 1938. Not only did it point the Supreme Court toward the path of racial justice and minority rights, but it also explained why the new road to minority rights was fundamentally different from the old road to property rights that had so recently led the Court to the brink of self-destruction. Whereas the Old Court had protected property owners who enjoyed ample opportunity to safeguard their own interests through the political process, the New Court would accord special protection to those who had been deprived of their fair share of political influence.

No less significantly, the *Carolene* Court sketched its new mission in exceptionally broad strokes. It did not limit its prospective intervention to the straightforward cases in which blacks or other unpopular groups were excluded from the polls or denied other fundamental rights of political expression. *Carolene* suggested an enduring role for the judiciary, one that would continue even after every adult American had secured his right to participate in politics. To take the case that will serve as a paradigm in this essay: the *Carolene* footnote suggests that, even in a world in which blacks voted no less frequently than whites, and in which election districts strictly conformed to the Court's reapportionment decisions, blacks would still possess, by virtue of their discreteness and insularity, a disproportionately small share of influence on legislative policy—a disproportion of such magnitude as to warrant the judicial conclusion that a fair democratic process would have generated outcomes systematically more favorable to minority interests. This suggestion, moreover, animates countless modern discussions—judicial as well as academic—in which the political weakness of "discrete and insular minorities" is a crucial, if unexamined, premise in the elaboration of intricate constitutional doctrines. I shall argue, however, that the *Carolene* formula cannot withstand close scrutiny.

* * *

My concern here, however, is with the future, not the past. Although America has by no means worked itself clear of past practices of political exclusion, it is not visionary to hope that we will indeed put this grim aspect of history behind us and that, during the next generation, we will inhabit a world that increasingly resembles my paradigm case: a world in which, despite the existence of pervasive social prejudice, minorities can and do participate in large numbers within the normal political process. In light of this prospect, a reappraisal of *Carolene* is a pressing necessity: its approach to minority rights is profoundly shaped by the old politics of exclusion and yields systematically misleading cues within the new participatory paradigm.

Indeed, if we fail to rethink *Carolene*'s dictum about discrete and insular minorities, we will succeed only in doing two different kinds of damage. On the one hand, we will fail to do justice to the very racial and religious groups that *Carolene* has done so much to protect in the past half-century. By tying their rights to an increasingly unrealistic model of politics, we will place them on the weakest possible foundation. On the other hand, we will fail to do justice to *Carolene*'s basic insight into the problem posed by prejudice in a pluralist democracy. The end of the politics of exclusion hardly implies that pluralist democracy now functions fairly; it does mean, however, that the groups most disadvantaged by pluralism in the future will be different from those excluded under the old regime. The victims of sexual discrimination or poverty, rather than racial or religious minorities, will increasingly constitute the groups with the greatest claim upon *Carolene*'s concern with the fairness of pluralist process.

* * *

II. DISCRETE AND INSULAR MINORITIES?

The *Carolene* formula limits its attention to the asserted political weakness of minorities and fails to consider the analogous case of a politically ineffective majority. In view of *Carolene*'s larger ambition to deflect the countermajoritarian difficulty, this is an especially odd omission. Consider again the paradigm case: blacks are participating no less frequently than whites in a political system that satisfies the standards for electoral fairness elaborated in the Court's modern decisions. Despite these formal safeguards, imagine that an all-white legislature manages to get elected, and then enacts a series of laws prohibiting interracial marriage and forbidding interracial adoptions. Would we be less concerned about this outcome if we completed the scenario by assuming that blacks amounted to 75 percent, rather than 12 percent, of the relevant electorate?

Of course not. Indeed, the existence of a commanding black majority would encourage us to intensify our search for a set of structural factors that somehow allowed whites to dominate the ostensibly democratic political process. *Carolene* casually disregards the easiest case for finding a substantive defect in a formally fair electoral process: the case in which organizational difficulties have prevented a commanding majority of the population from influencing the ongoing flow of legislative decisions. After all, if democracy means anything, it means a regime designed to further the majority's basic interests; that is certainly not what is going on in the case we have hypothesized.

* * *

. . . Other things being equal, "discreteness and insularity" will normally be a source of enormous bargaining advantage, not disadvantage, for a group engaged in pluralist American politics. Except for special cases, the concerns that underlie *Carolene* should lead judges to protect groups that possess the opposite characteristics from the ones *Carolene* emphasizes—groups that are "anonymous and diffuse" rather than "discrete and insular." It is these groups that both political science and American history indicate are systematically disadvantaged in a pluralist democracy.

A. The Free-Rider Problem

To see my point, start with insularity and consider a thought-experiment suggested by the previous argument. Imagine two groups, I and D, of equal size (say each accounts for 12 percent of the population). The members of one group, the I's, are distributed in an insular way, concentrated in a single massive island within the sea of American life; the D's, on the other hand, are diffused evenly throughout the sea. Is it really so clear that, by virtue of their diffusion throughout American life, the D's will gain systematic advantages over the I's in the normal course of pluralist politics?

Hardly. To begin with the basics, a political interest gains a great advantage if its proponents can form a well-organized lobby to press their cause in the corridors of power. Yet the construction of a pressure group is no easy task. The main obstacle is the familiar free-rider problem. Simply because a person would find his interests advanced by the formation of a pressure group, it does not follow that he will spend his own scarce time and energy on political organization. On the contrary, from each individual's selfish viewpoint, abstaining from interest-group activity is a "heads-I-win-tails-you-lose" proposition. If only a few people adopt the do-nothing strategy, the do-nothings will free-ride on the successful lobbying effort of others. If free-riding becomes pervasive, things will not improve much if a single member of the group adds his money and time to the floundering political effort. Either way, it pays for a selfish person to remain a free rider even if he has a lot to gain from concerted lobbying. For this reason, many interests remain ineffectively organized even in pressure-group America. How, then, does a minority's insularity affect the probability that it will break through the free-rider barrier and achieve organizational effectiveness?

Far from being a patent disadvantage, insularity can help I-groups in at least four different ways, all of which depend upon a single sociological assumption that we should identify at the outset: however oppressed the I's may be in other respects, they have not been prevented from building up a dense communal life for themselves on their tight little island. Thus, wherever an I looks, he will find himself in businesses and churches, schools and labor unions, composed largely of people speaking in distinctively I-accents about the daily problems of social life. This fundamental fact will generate a whole series of advantages for I-members who seek to organize for political purposes.

* * *

But insularity does more than engender the sentiment of group solidarity that encourages symbolic contributions—contributions that, when multiplied thousands of times, add up to very substantial resources for the interest group receiving them. It also aids the I-group in a second way by providing it with a new range of social sanctions to impose upon would-be free riders . . ..

B. Organizational Costs

It follows, then, that the average I is more likely to contribute his time and money to the group cause than is an otherwise comparable D. Yet this conclusion tells only half the story: not only will an I-group receive more resources from its constituency, but I's will also find it cheaper to organize themselves for effective political action. . . .

. . . If the term is conceived in this sociological way, people who live far apart from one another may still be members of a single I-group, especially under modern conditions. Conversely, it is easy for people living cheek by jowl to fail to qualify as an insular minority from a sociological point of view.

We have reached a point, however, where it is necessary to introduce an explicitly geographic concept of insularity into the discussion—for the simple reason that geography is of the first importance in assessing a group's influence within the American political system. For present purposes, it will suffice to restrict our speculations to two simple geographic alternatives. On the one hand, our sociologically insular minority might also be geographically insular: concentrated in a relatively small number of places in the United States. On the other hand, geographic insularity might not accompany sociological insularity. Indeed, at the limit, the *I*-group might be evenly spread over the fifty states and 435 congressional districts. For heuristic purposes, let us begin with the alternative that is empirically less common, but analytically more tractable. Suppose that an *I*-group is distributed in a geographically diffuse way: if it contains 12 percent of the national population, it accounts for 12 percent of each congressional district. Now compare this geographically diffuse *I*-group with a *D*-group that is both sociologically and geographically diffuse. Other things being equal, which group is more likely to succeed in influencing Congressmen?

The previous analysis suggests that the *I*-group will probably have greater influence. Such a group is more likely to form a political lobby peopled by credible leaders who remain in close touch with the insular constituency they represent. When such lobbyists threaten a Congressman with electoral retribution, they can expect a respectful hearing. Even if the interest-group leaders can influence only 10 to 20 percent of their 12 percent of the population, no sensible politician would lightly forfeit 1 to 2 percent of the vote. Of course, if it happens that the *I*-group's interests are diametrically opposed to those of other groups within a Congressman's electoral coalition, a reelection-maximizing politician might decide to ignore the *I*-group's demands. Yet his reluctance to forsake the group will be greater than it would be if he were dealing with a comparable *D*-group. The *D*-group is less likely to have a well-organized lobby to press its cause. It is also less likely to have the communications network necessary for the lobby's leaders credibly to threaten Congressmen with the prospect of electoral retribution. In short, even if the *I*-group is distributed evenly throughout the nation, it has a greater ability to exert political influence through the ultimate currency of democratic politics: votes on election day.

This conclusion is reinforced when we turn to the more realistic case in which the middling *I*-group is distributed very unevenly throughout the country. In this scenario, a middling minority could reasonably expect to be a local majority—or at least a decisive voting bloc—in 20 to 30 congressional districts. For the representatives of these districts, the support of the *I*- group amounts to nothing less than the stuff of political survival. In fact, for all our *Carolene* talk about the powerlessness of insular groups, we are perfectly aware of the enormous power such voting blocs have in American politics. The story of the protective tariff is, I suppose, the classic illustration of insularity's power in American history. Over the past half-century, we have been treated to an enormous number of welfare-state variations on the theme of insularity by the farm bloc, the steel lobby, the auto lobby, and others too numerous to mention. In this standard scenario of pluralistic politics, it is precisely the diffuse character of the majority forced to pay the bill for tariffs, agricultural subsidies, and the like, that allows strategically located Congressmen to deliver the goods to their well-organized local constituents. Given these familiar stories, it is really quite remarkable to hear lawyers profess concern that insular interests have too little influence in Congress. Instead, the American system typically deprives *diffuse* groups of their rightful say over the course of legislative policy. If there is anything to *Carolene Products,* then, it cannot be a minority's insularity, taken by itself—something more must be involved.

IV. DISCRETE AND INSULAR MINORITIES?

Could that something be the "discreteness" of a *Carolene* minority?

I begin with a question because it is not obvious whether most constitutional lawyers endow the word "discrete" with independent significance in their understanding of the *Carolene* doctrine. Nonetheless, we can conceive the term in a way that adds something important to the overall formula. I propose to define a minority as "discrete" when its members are marked out in ways that make it relatively easy for others to identify them. For instance, there is nothing a black woman may plausibly do to hide the fact that she is black or female. Like it or not, she will have to deal with the social expectations and stereotypes generated by her evident group characteristics. In contrast, other minorities are socially defined in ways that give individual members the chance to avoid easy identification. A homosexual, for example, can keep her sexual preference a very private affair and thereby avoid much of the public opprobrium attached to her minority status. It is for this reason that I shall call homosexuals, and groups like them, "anonymous" minorities and contrast them with "discrete" minorities of the kind paradigmatically exemplified by blacks.

This way of defining terms allows us to complement our analysis of insularity in a natural way. While the insularity-diffuseness continuum measures the intensity and breadth of intragroup interaction, the discreteness-anonymity continuum measures the ease with which people *outside* a group can identify group members. It should be plain that these two continua are not invariably associated with one another. Blacks, for example, are both discrete and insular, whereas women are discrete yet diffuse; homosexuals are anonymous but may be somewhat insular, whereas the poor are both relatively anonymous and diffuse. Because there is no necessary correlation between discreteness and insularity, I shall treat discreteness as a distinct subject for analysis and consider how a group's place on the discreteness-anonymity continuum can be expected to add to, or detract from, its probable political influence.

Carolene takes a straightforward position on this question. In its view, discreteness is a political liability. Once again, however, the only thing that is obvious is that this is not obvious. The main reason why has been elegantly developed in Albert Hirschman's modern classic, *Exit, Voice and Loyalty.* The book's title refers to three nonviolent ways of responding to an unsatisfactory situation: if you dislike something, you may try to avoid it (exit), you may complain about it (voice), or you may grin-and-hope-for-improvement (loyalty). Although these three responses may be related to one another in a number of ways, the relationship between two of them— exit and voice—is of special relevance here. People do not respond to a bad situation by engaging in a random pattern of avoidance and protest. Instead, according to Hirschman, an inverse relationship obtains: the more exit, the less voice, and vice versa. The reason for this is straightforward: the easier it is to avoid a bad situation, the less it will seem worthwhile to complain, and vice versa.

This inverse relationship holds significant implications for the relative political strength of minorities at different points on the discreteness-anonymity scale. If you are a black in America today, you know there is no way you can avoid the impact of the larger public's views about the significance of blackness. Because exit is not possible, there is only one way to do something about disadvantageous racial stereotypes:

complain about them. Among efficacious forms of complaint, the possibility of organized political action will surely rank high.

This is not to say, of course, that individual blacks, or members of other discrete minorities, will necessarily lend their support to interest-group activity. They may, instead, succumb to the temptations of free-riding and thus deprive the group of vital political resources. But even if discreteness is no cure-all for selfishness, it does free a minority from the organizational problem confronting an anonymous group of comparable size. To see my point, compare the problem faced by black political organizers with the one confronting organizers of the homosexual community. As a member of an anonymous group, each homosexual can seek to minimize the personal harm due to prejudice by keeping his or her sexual preference a tightly held secret. Although this is hardly a fully satisfactory response, secrecy does enable homosexuals to "exit" from prejudice in a way that blacks cannot. This means that a homosexual group must confront an organizational problem that does not arise for its black counterpart: somehow the group must induce each anonymous homosexual to reveal his or her sexual preference to the larger public and to bear the private costs this public declaration may involve.

Although some, perhaps many, homosexuals may be willing to pay this price, the fact that each must individually choose to pay it means that this anonymous group is less likely to be politically efficacious than is an otherwise comparable but discrete minority. For, by definition, discrete groups do not have to convince their constituents to "come out of the closet" before they can engage in effective political activity. So it would seem that *Carolene Products* is wrong again: a court concerned with pluralist bargaining power should be more, not less, attentive to the claims of anonymous minorities than to those of discrete ones.

* * *

A. Questions of Fact

Carolene's empirical inadequacy stems from its underinclusive conception of the impact of prejudice upon American society. It is easy to identify groups in the population that are not discrete and insular but that are nonetheless the victims of prejudice, as that term is commonly understood. Thus, the fact that homosexuals are a relatively anonymous minority has not saved the group from severe prejudice. Nor is sexism a nonproblem merely because women are a diffuse, if discrete, majority. Prejudice is generated by a bewildering variety of social conditions. Although some *Carolene* minorities are seriously victimized, they are not the only ones stigmatized; nor is it obvious that all *Carolene* minorities are stigmatized more grievously than any other non-*Carolene* group. Why should the concern with "prejudice" justify *Carolene*'s narrow fixation upon "discrete and insular" minorities?

The answer seemed easy in a world in which members of the paradigmatic *Carolene* minority group—blacks—were effectively barred from voting and political participation. Something is better than nothing: whatever the organizational problems engendered by anonymity and diffuseness, surely they are not nearly so devastating as total disenfranchisement. As we turn toward the future, however, it is far less clear that such selective perception makes constitutional sense. . . .

B. Questions of Value

. . . *Carolene*'s failure to recognize the political predicament of anonymous or diffuse groups that are victims of prejudice is only half the problem; the other half is more conceptual, but no less troubling. The idea of "prejudice" is simply unequal to the task assigned it within the overall *Carolene* analysis. Recall that *Carolene*'s promise is a form of argument that allows a court to say that it is purifying the democratic process rather than imposing its own substantive values upon the political branches. And yet it is just this process orientation that is at risk when a *Carolene* court undertakes to identify the prejudices that entitle a group to special protection from the vagaries of pluralist politics. One person's "prejudice" is, notoriously, another's "principle." How, then, do we identify a group for *Carolene* protection without performing the substantive analysis of constitutional values that *Carolene* hopes to avoid?

The kind of answer required is clear enough. To redeem *Carolene*'s promise, the judicial identification of a prejudice cannot depend upon the substance of the suspect view, but must turn on the way in which legislators come to hold their belief. The process-oriented argument goes something like this: although each of us cannot always expect to convince our legislators, we can at least insist that they treat our claims with respect. At the very least, they should thoughtfully consider our moral and empirical arguments, rejecting them only after conscientiously deciding that they are inconsistent with the public interest. If a group fails to receive this treatment, it suffers a special wrong, one quite distinct from its substantive treatment on the merits. And it is this purely processual kind of prejudice that constitutes the grievance *Carolene* courts may endeavor to remedy without engaging in the suspect task of prescribing substantive values.

Of course, no one imagines that it will be easy for the courts to act effectively on behalf of the victims of purely processual prejudice. To the contrary, a rich and provocative literature describes the difficulties involved in legislative mind reading. For present purposes, I shall assume that the partisans of the process approach can solve these problems in one way or another. My own objections to the enterprise arise only after these threshold difficulties have been overcome. Thus, I shall assume that judges can accurately gauge the quality of legislative deliberation behind a statute, and I shall ask you to speculate about what they would find if they deployed their highpowered techniques on a representative range of legislation.

The critical question, instead, is whether purely processual prejudice is more characteristic in this context than in the political treatment of other interests and opinions. What of the prejudice middle-class legislators may have toward the poor? Heterosexuals toward homosexuals? More fundamentally, are we right to assume that only those *opposed* to "progressive" causes can be processually prejudiced?

Let me propose a test case. Imagine that, after reading Herbert Wechsler's famous essay, a group of conservative legalists becomes sincerely convinced that *Brown v. Board of Education* could not in fact be based on neutral principles and so does not deserve its place as a cornerstone of our constitutional law. Acting on this conviction, the group begins a campaign advocating a constitutional amendment to repeal *Brown* and generates some modest interest among conservatives across the country. Arriving in Washington, D.C., with their legal process arguments elaborately developed, the group proceeds to the lobbies of Congress. How do you think the group would be received? Would most Representatives be willing and able to confront the Wechslerian arguments with a thoughtful defense of our constitutional commitment to equality? Or would they respond in a *processually* prejudiced fashion—

peremptorily brushing aside the Wechslerians' arguments with a catch-phrase or two that fails to join issue?

This is, in principle, an empirical question—though, like many others, it will never get a good empirical answer. Nonetheless, if my study of politics has taught me anything, I would not expect the agitating Wechslerians to receive a processually unprejudiced response on Capitol Hill. As far as I can tell, any large representative assembly will contain a bewildering variety of human types—from the elaborately thoughtful to the superficially unquestioning. It is simply self-congratulatory to suppose that the members of our own persuasion have reached their convictions in a deeply reflective way, whereas those espousing opinions we hate are superficial. Instead, a thoughtful judge can expect to find an abundance of stereotype-mongers and knee-jerks on *all* sides of *every* important issue—as well as many who have struggled their way to more considered judgments. Given the complexity of the human comedy, a judge is bound on a fool's errand if he imagines that the good guys and bad guys of American politics can be neatly classified according to the seriousness with which they have considered opposing points of view. Processual prejudice is a pervasive problem in the American political system.

But if this is right, *Carolene* cannot justify its concern with discrete and insular minorities without calling on judges to engage in a very different kind of judgment, one dealing with the *substance* of racial and religious prejudice. In doing so, the judge need not try to play the elaborate psychological and political guessing game required to assess the extent to which a statute is the product of a prejudiced refusal to give a respectful hearing to disfavored interests and opinions. Instead, she proceeds to a more familiar judicial inquiry into the nature of the substantive reasons that might plausibly justify the legislature's assertion of authority. If the only plausible reasons for the statute's enactment offend substantive constitutional principles, the groups aggrieved by the statute are declared victims of "prejudice"; if not, not. Although this judicial inquiry into the rational foundations of a statute may sometimes require a focused inquiry into the data available to, or even the subjective opinions of, particular public officials, the critical legal question is of a very different kind: why are the political principles endorsed by some groups judicially recognized as vindicating the constitutionality of a statute, while others are viewed as inadmissible "prejudices" delegitimating a statute's claim to constitutionality?

If *Carolene* somehow hoped to find a shortcut around this substantive inquiry into constitutional values, its journey was fated to fail from the outset. The difference between the things we call "prejudice" and the things we call "principle" is in the end a substantive moral difference. And if the courts are authorized to protect the victims of certain "prejudices," it can only be because the Constitution has placed certain normative judgments beyond the pale of legitimacy.

VI. FROM CRITIQUE TO RECONSTRUCTION

Paradoxically, it is by reflecting upon this last mistake that we may begin to reorganize *Carolene* in a way that will renew its promise for the next generation. Our discussion suggests that, in responding to "prejudice against discrete and insular minorities," *Carolene* courts have in fact been trying to force a single formula to express two very different insights. *Carolene*'s first insight is that some groups suffer from systematic disadvantages in pursuing their interests in the pluralist bargaining process normally central to American politics. In this view, the Court appears as a perfecter of pluralist democracy. It corrects political results generated by unfair bargaining advantages but does not question the substantive values pursued by the participants.

Carolene's emphasis on "prejudice," however, announces a second, quite different, conception of judicial review. Here the courts do not enter as the perfecters of pluralist democracy, but as pluralism's ultimate critics. In exercising this critical function, courts insist that there are certain substantive principles—*Carolene* calls them "prejudices"—that pluralist politicians are simply not allowed to bargain over in normal American politics. It is only when statutes emerging from the pluralist process do not offend these constraining constitutional values that they have the force of law in our political system.

By collapsing the perfecting and critical functions of judicial review into a single formula, *Carolene* poses a formidable intellectual problem for lawyers in the years ahead. Indeed, I believe the future vitality of both functions will significantly depend upon the success with which constitutional lawyers manage to disentangle the two themes from one another—and so permit each to receive the sustained doctrinal elaboration it deserves.

Consider first the Supreme Court's function as a perfecter of pluralist democracy. Here *Carolene's* fundamental concern seems more salient today than when first announced a half-century ago. In 1938, Americans were only just beginning to move beyond a political system that limited interest-group struggle over federal policy to a few classic pork-barrel issues: the tariff, internal improvements, land distribution, and the like. Yet *Carolene* was remarkably prescient in recognizing that the downfall of the Old Court's laissez-faire jurisprudence had transformed the structure of pluralist bargaining into an issue of prime constitutional importance. In the system of activist government inaugurated by the New Deal, the course of pluralist bargaining would have a profound and pervasive impact upon the shape of every American's life. Within this setting, the existence of systematic bargaining disadvantage erodes the perceived legitimacy of our constitutional regime in the eyes of broad segments of the American population. If *Carolene* had not already impressed a concern with the integrity of the pluralist process onto our constitutional consciousness, another case would inevitably have made the same point.

The problem comes only in the way in which *Carolene* elaborates its fundamental insight in terms of judicial doctrine. Even in this regard it would be wrong to judge *Carolene's* focus upon "discrete and insular minorities" too harshly. The case was handed down in the shadow of the infamous Nuremberg laws, which had stripped German Jews of all their previously established civil rights. This served to recall, in the starkest way, the grim process by which black Americans had been stripped of their civil rights in the aftermath of Reconstruction. In both cases, the dreadful consequences of political exclusion were plain to all who cared to look. Moreover, it was—and remains—obvious that the political decision to disenfranchise these groups was made vastly easier by virtue of their discreteness and insularity. It was precisely these characteristics that permitted German Nazis and American white supremacists to portray Jews and blacks as aliens within the body politic, to be used and abused in any way the master race desired.

Against this historical background, the *Carolene* Court was absolutely right to emphasize the special vulnerability of discrete and insular minorities, as well as the fundamental importance of ensuring their effective participation in the democratic process. After a generation of renewed struggle for civil rights, however, it no longer follows that the discreteness or insularity of a group will continue to serve as a decisive disadvantage in the ongoing process of pluralist bargaining. Rather than find this fact embarrassing, constitutional lawyers ought to be proud of it. It suggests that, despite the racial and religious prejudices that still haunt our society, Americans *have* made some progress toward a more just polity.

It will be a tragedy, however, if the progress we have made serves to justify a refusal to develop and extend *Carolene*'s concern with the integrity of pluralist process to contemporary conditions. Long after discrete and insular minorities have gained strong representation at the pluralist bargaining table, there will remain many other groups who fail to achieve influence remotely proportionate to their numbers: groups that are discrete and diffuse (like women), or anonymous and somewhat insular (like homosexuals), or *both* diffuse and anonymous (like the victims of poverty). If we are to treat *Carolene* as something more than a tired formula, constitutional lawyers must develop paradigms that detail the systematic disadvantages that undermine our system's legitimacy in dealing with the grievances of these diffuse or anonymous groups.

At the same time that we enrich the capacity of constitutional law to perfect pluralist democracy, we must also reaffirm a second fundamental mission for judicial review: to expound the ultimate limits imposed on pluralist bargaining by the American constitutional system. In the exercise of this critical function, the courts insist that, for all our plural differences, We the People of the United States *do* have a set of fundamental commitments that bind us together in ways that our interest-group representatives are not normally elected to modify. It is this idea of higher law that must be taken with renewed seriousness if we are to sustain judicial protection for racial and religious minorities in the coming generation. Although, as we have seen, the *Carolene* effort to protect minorities ultimately required the elaboration of substantive constitutional principles, the *Carolene* tradition's reliance on bad political science has made it seem possible to avoid the sustained inquiry into democratic theory that substantive judicial review entails. More particularly, *Carolene*'s focus on pluralist bargaining has subtly encouraged the belief that pluralism is the alpha and the omega of the American constitutional system, and that any effort by the courts to challenge the substantive values generated by legislative compromise is necessarily antidemocratic.

We must repudiate this reduction of the American Constitution to a simple system of pluralist bargaining if we are to reassert the legitimacy of the courts' critical function. Although the bargaining model captures an important aspect of American politics, it does not do justice to the most fundamental episodes of our constitutional history. We make a mistake, for example, to view the enactment of the Bill of Rights and the Civil War Amendments as if they were outcomes of ordinary pluralist bargaining. Instead, these constitutional achievements represent the highest legal expression of a different kind of politics—one characterized by mass mobilization and struggle that, after experiences like the Revolution and the Civil War, yielded fundamental principles transcending the normal processes of interest-group accommodation. It is only by reasserting the relevance of this tradition of constitutional politics, as I have called it, that we shall gain the necessary perspective to put pluralist bargaining in its place as one—but only one—form of American democracy, and the lesser form at that.

Not that the *Carolene* tradition—or *Carolene* itself—is entirely oblivious to the limits of pluralist bargaining. Indeed, it was just this issue that initially provoked Chief Justice Hughes to press for a revision of *Carolene* in the opinion-writing process. While Justice Stone's early draft had focused exclusively on the pluralist perfection rationale, the Chief Justice believed that something essential was missing in the case for judicial review. In response to this expression of concern, Justice Stone added a first paragraph to footnote four that takes our higher-law tradition more explicitly into account. Thus, before addressing the pluralist themes we have considered here, *Carolene* noted that "the presumption of constitutionality" may also be overcome "when legislation appears on its face to be within a specific prohibition of the Constitution, such as those of the first ten amendments."

In calling the Bill of Rights "specific," Justice Stone doubtless wished to emphasize that the Court had learned its lesson in 1937 and would not use the Constitution's grand abstractions to revive the laissez-faire capitalism of the *Lochner* era. Nonetheless, by framing its pledge of judicial restraint in this way, *Carolene* added a distortion of its own. For it intimated that the judicial process of articulating the nature of our higher law values can be reduced to a mechanical effort to apply "specific" constitutional rules to predetermined facts. Such a position requires judges to repudiate the main line of modern American legal thought, which—from Pound to Dworkin— is one long elaboration of the inadequacies of mechanical jurisprudence. Even more fundamentally, it trivializes the nature of the American people's higher-law achievement. Our Constitution does not even attempt to provide a detailed set of rules that might suggest the possibility of pseudomechanical application. Instead, our higher law tradition gains its distinctive character precisely by speaking in abstract and general terms about the nature of our basic rights. Hence, in endowing the Bill of Rights with a false "specificity," *Carolene* not only proffered a misleading and unattainable picture of responsible judicial decisionmaking. It also diverted us from the main question: having cleared away the laissez-faire debris of the *Lochner* era, can we still reconstruct, out of authoritative sources, a legally cogent set of higher-law principles that can continue to govern the pluralist process in the name of We the People?

The point of this essay is not to answer this question, but to convince you that it needs asking if we are to preserve the constitutional rights of discrete and insular minorities during the coming decades. I do not believe that the weaknesses in *Carolene*'s defense of minority rights will long remain a professional secret locked in the pages of the *Harvard Law Review*. Instead, *Carolene*'s errors will become increasingly apparent on the surface of American political life. Thanks largely to the achievements of the generation that looked to *Carolene* for inspiration, black Americans today are generally free to participate in democratic politics—and do so by the millions in every national election. Moreover, the predicted consequences of the discreteness and insularity of black voters are beginning to be obvious at every level of American government. From City Hall to Capitol Hill, black politicians now aggressively represent their constituencies in the citadels of power. Similarly, religious organizations are increasingly involved in pressure-group politics.

I am not suggesting that America is on the way to becoming a religious and racial utopia. Despite their political gains, blacks still suffer under the weight of grossly disproportionate economic, educational, and social disadvantage, as well as sheer racial prejudice. In light of these facts, it is far too early to say that we have redeemed the promise of the thirteenth and fourteenth amendments. In contrast to black political mobilization, the heightened involvement of organized religion can readily undermine our substantive constitutional legacy—threatening the very values of religious toleration and free exercise to which our higher law is committed.

Yet as long as we use *Carolene* rhetoric to express our constitutional concerns with racial equality and religious freedom, we will find ourselves saying things that are increasingly belied by political reality. While constitutional lawyers decry the political powerlessness of discrete and insular groups, representatives of these interests will be wheeling and dealing in the ongoing pluralist exchange—winning some battles, losing others, but plainly numbering among the organized interests whose electoral power must be treated with respect by their bargaining partners and competitors. Gradually, this clash between constitutional rhetoric and political reality can have only one result. As time goes by, the constitutional center will not hold: the longer *Carolene* remains at the core of the constitutional case for judicial review, the harder lawyers will find it to convince themselves, let alone others, that judicial protection for the rights of "discrete and insular minorities" makes constitutional sense.

For those who are constitutional conservatives in the deepest sense, and who look upon our tradition of civil liberties as one of the greatest achievements of American law, the challenges are clear. On the one hand, if we are to remain faithful to *Carolene*'s concern with the fairness of pluralist politics, we must repudiate the bad political science that allows us to ignore those citizens who have the most serious complaints: the anonymous and diffuse victims of poverty and sexual discrimination who find it most difficult to protect their fundamental interests through effective political organization. On the other hand, we must explain to our fellow Americans that there are constitutional values in our scheme of government even more fundamental than perfected pluralism—most notably, those that bar prejudice against racial and religious minorities. If we persist in holding these rights hostage to pluralist theory, we shall only end up mocking the proud role that *Carolene* has played in the pursuit of constitutional values over the past half-century. By failing to adapt *Carolene*'s constitutional theory to a changing political reality, we shall have passively allowed the Constitution's profound concern for racial equality and religious freedom to be trivialized into a transparent apologia for the status quo.

Bibliography

The Power "To Say What the Law Is"

Abraham, Henry, JUSTICES AND PRESIDENTS (1978)

Ackerman, Bruce A., *The Storrs Lectures: Discovering the Constitution,* 93 YALE L.J. 1013 (1984)

Beard, Charles, THE SUPREME COURT AND THE CONSTITUTION (1912)

Berger, Raoul, CONGRESS V. THE SUPREME COURT (1969)

Corwin, Edward, *The Establishment of Judicial Review,* 9 MICH. L. REV. 102 (1910)

Crosskey, William W., POLITICS AND THE CONSTITUTION IN THE HISTORY OF THE UNITED STATES (1953)

Farber, Daniel A., *The Supreme Court and the Rule of Law:* Cooper v. Aaron *Revisited,* 1982 U. ILL. L. REV. 387

McCloskey, Robert, THE AMERICAN SUPREME COURT (1960)

Nelson, William E., *Changing Conceptions of Judicial Review: The Evolution of Constitutional Theory in the States, 1790-1860,* 120 U. PA. L. REV. 1166 (1972)

Thayer, James Bradley, *The Origin and Scope of the American Doctrine of Constitutional Law,* 7 HARV. L. REV. 1 (1893)

Warren, Charles, THE SUPREME COURT IN UNITED STATES HISTORY (1922)

Constitutional Interpretation

Even if the power of judicial review is conceded, debate is certain to exist over the permissible reference points for decision-making. Disagreement over whether the judiciary may factor only the terms of the Constitution and discernible intent of the framers and ratifiers, or gloss the document with rights or liberties that are not textually enumerated, predates and survives the *Marbury* decision. Contours of the controversy were etched by Justices Iredell and Chase in *Calder v. Bull.* Iredell expounded the premise that the judicial invocation of natural law to void a legislative act was an anti-democratic exercise.[5] Chase countered that "certain vital principles in our free republican government" apart from those enshrined in the Constitution itself could override the exercise of legislative power.[6] The debate between Iredell and Chase has been forwarded largely intact to successive generations of constitutional commentators who have embellished it with reference to the evolution of fundamental law over the past two centuries. Henry P. Monaghan asserts that "perfectionist" commentators improperly view the Constitution as a body of common law subject to flexible contemporary interpretation. H. Jefferson Powell suggests that the framers did not intend their subjective purposes to bind constitutional interpretation by future generations. Herbert Wechsler proposes that neutrality of principle is essential to the legitimacy of judicial review in a democratic society. Robert H. Bork amplifies and extends interpretive methodologies of originalism and neutrality. Mark V. Tushnet critiques originalist and neutralist premises. Thomas H. Grey suggests that judicial reliance upon values that are not textually identified may represent a legitimate means of resolving constitutional controversies. Gerald E. Lynch criticizes theories of heightened constitutional review premised upon process defect.

Henry P. Monaghan, *Our Perfect Constitution*, 56 N.Y.U. L. REV. 353, 353-60, 391-95 (1981)*

Some lawyers, many judges, and perhaps most academic commentators view the constitution as authorizing courts to nullify the results of the political process on the basis of general principles of political morality not derived from the constitutional text or the structure it creates. The supreme court is plainly committed to such an endeavor in the sex-marriage-children area, where some fifty written opinions order these relationships ostensibly in the name of securing due process and equal protection. Indeed, the court seems well on its way to "constitutionalizing" the entire subject of family law, which two short decades ago was bereft of constitutional restraints.

The court's efforts at developing a constitutional *lex non scripta* are modest when compared with those of its admiring academic commentators. For well over twenty years these commentators have been industriously formulating substantive

---

5   Calder v. Bull, 3 U.S. 386, 398-400 (1798).

6   *Id.* at 396-98.

*   Reprinted with permission.

limits on the political process in the name of equal protection of the laws. More recently, these commentators have been "taking rights seriously"—so seriously in fact that they outdo one another in urging the imposition of constitutional constraints on the basis of "rights" whose origins cannot be traced to either the constitutional text or the structure it creates. The current academic emphasis on rights, rather than equality, has two sources: the general perception that concerns over political morality are not exhausted by, and cannot be reduced to, concepts of equality; and a more focused concern for according protection to those specified areas of individual autonomy that are most highly esteemed by the commentators. Thus, the commentators eagerly defend limitations on government based upon the rights of "personhood," "intimate association," and "personal lifestyles." Quite plainly, the old fear of substantive due process is dead; it has been succeeded by a confidence that "good" and "bad" varieties of substantive due process can be distinguished.

Some commentators would go still further. Mixing concepts of rights and equality, they would hold government to an affirmative constitutional duty to satisfy the "just wants" of its citizens. In their view, government is constitutionally obliged to provide "adequate" levels of food, housing, education, and whatever other "goods" the commentators deem necessary to a decent existence.

Academic commentary of this character is more than simply intriguing. It vividly highlights a core issue in modem constitutional theory—the legitimacy of judicial review under (in the characterization of a former student) the "due substance clauses": substantive due process and substantive equal protection. Most commentators welcome "due substance" review in some form, proclaim that it is "here to stay," and admonish that further resistance is "unwise" and "hopeless." The fun, for them, begins in seeking to domesticate their creations. Since the meaning of the constitution is not to be found in its history or in judicial precedent, but in current social consensus—or, as now seems the fashion, in Kant, Rawls, or Nozick—the commentator's initial task is the selection of a preferred source from which to extract concepts of equality and justice. Next, the substance of political activity is expressed and weighed in scales, or even calibrated on charts. Finally, the commentator concludes, usually after the most meticulous and detailed comparison of the "interests at stake," that certain political outcomes are simply prohibited. No matter how "fair" or "open" the underlying political process, these outcomes must be set aside because they conflict with some ideal normative pattern "out there" that circumscribes the permissible distribution of governmental benefits or burdens.

"Due substance" methodology is profoundly different from one premised on a view that (in general) the constitution legitimately sanctions inquiry only into the openness and fairness of the political process. Professor Ely's process-oriented *Democracy and Distrust* is, I think, the classic affirmation in our time for those recalcitrants who, like me, oppose any further extension of an approach that tests political outcomes for their consistency with some external, ideal pattern of distributive justice. And since we recalcitrants are, as yet, unwilling to yield the battlefield, one can expect that this controversy will occupy the center of constitutional debate for some time to come.

My concern here is with an aspect of the controversy that in this context has escaped notice. Virtually every adherent to the "due substance" school of judicial review shares in whole or in large part a critical culture theme, to borrow a phrase from cultural anthropology: that of "Our perfect Constitution."

The practice of "constitution worship" has been quite solidly ingrained in our political culture from the beginning of our constitutional history. Initially, the constitution symbolized the unity of the new nation. With the advent of national prosperity, "the exultation over the new America was converted into the tradition of a perfect constitution." Not surprisingly, the Civil War placed considerable strain on the perfection theme; but with the resurgence of nationalism at the war's conclusion, perfectionism took firm hold again.

A counterculture has always existed, of course. Before the Civil War, for example, many abolitionists denounced the constitution for its recognition of slavery. The most salient modem challenge to the perfect constitution came from progressive historians who attacked the constitution (and the court) as an impediment to social change. In essence, they saw the constitution as the American Thermidor to the democracy of the Declaration of Independence. J. Allen Smith's influential text, *Spirit of American Government*, epitomized this view. Smith described his purpose as "call[ing] attention to the spirit of the Constitution, its inherent opposition to democracy, the obstacles which it has placed in the way of majority rule . . .," and he entitled a chapter "The Constitution As A Reactionary Document." But when the court began to sustain New Deal legislation, one consequence was to eliminate as a working theme of political and social theory any concept of the constitution as a fundamentally undemocratic, let alone a thoroughly reactionary, document. This, in turn, tended to deflect attention from any inadequacies in the document, thereby indirectly reinforcing the culturally dominant symbolism of the constitution as the embodiment of political justice as well as national unity.

"Due substance" theorists would, of course, insist that they are aware of this history, and that they neither worship the constitution nor view it as perfect. Perhaps indignantly, they would observe that they recognize that issues such as international peace, poverty, inflation, and crime control are not amenable to resolution simply by invoking the premises contained in our "perfect constitution." All this is certainly true, but I think at one important level their disclaimers would be misleading. One cannot read the works of Professors Tribe, Karst, Michelman, and a whole host of other due substance theorists without a profound feeling that, however much they might otherwise disagree, for them the constitution is essentially perfect in one central respect: *properly construed, the constitution guarantees against the political order most equality and autonomy values which the commentators think a twentieth century Western liberal democratic government ought to guarantee to its citizens.* For these commentators, the constitution is not Perfect with a capital "P"; it, however, perfect in the more limited sense that a necessary link is asserted between the constitution and currently "valid" notions of rights, equality and distributive justice. The constitution is, in sum, "perfect" with a small "p."

Of course, I overstate my point. Few due substance commentators hold a "perfection" premise fully. Nevertheless, each commentator can be fairly described as "perfectionist." Each asserts that there is a clear and substantial connection between the constitution and *current* conceptions of political morality, a linkage not *exhausted* by any assumed constitutional guarantee of a fair political process. To be sure, the commentators display important differences among themselves in terms of the relative weight each places upon historical tradition, current sociological formulations, and political philosophy in defining the content of political morality. But the important fact is that they share a distinctive and controversial underlying premise: the "outputs" of even a fairly structured political process must satisfy some core substantive notions of political morality.

For example, in "an avowed effort to construct a more just constitutional order," Professor Tribe elaborates a wide range of equality and autonomy claims. His colleague Professor Michelman has devoted much of his academic career to cementing a union between the distributional patterns of the modern welfare state and the federal constitution. Professor Karst would guarantee a whole range of nontextually based rights against government to ensure "the dignity of full membership in society," which, he asserts, inheres in the "right of equal citizenship." Professor Fiss argues that the courts should give "concrete meaning and application" to those values that "give our society an identity and inner coherence [and] its distinctive public morality." Professor Dworkin charges the courts with enforcing our "constitutional morality," namely, the moral principles "presupposed by the law and institutions of the community." Professor Perry sees the court as having a "prophetic" role in developing moral standards in a "dialectical relationship" with congress, from which he sees emerging a "more mature" political morality. Professor Richards urges that the court apply the contractarian moral theory of Professor Rawls' *A Theory of Justice* to constitution questions. Professor Alfange tells us that the court should "translate . . . the national will into constitutional terms." Professor White's urging that the courts invoke "reasons that appeal to deeply embedded cultural values" is echoed in Professor Lupu's invitation that the court protect those "fundamental values" that have a solid underpinning in our historical traditions. Dean Sandalow describes constitutional law as "the means by which we express the values that we hold to be fundamental in the operations of government." Professor Brest summarizes the view of many when he states that "constitutional adjudication should enforce those . . . values which are fundamental to our society." So doing, Professor Brest states, will "contribute to the well being of our society—or more narrowly, to the ends of constitutional government." So it goes. For all these commentators, the constitution "has to some extent been assigned the function of defining the American way of life, both descriptively and prescriptively."

All of these formulations view the constitution as positively forbidding "wrongs"—distribution of burdens and benefits by the political process that offend some *current* conception of political morality. Emphasis must be placed on "current," because no pretense is made that these conceptions were viewed as constitutional limitations on the political branches in either the eighteenth or nineteenth centuries.

* * *

The perfectionists' discomfort with interpretative modes grounded in original intent and precedent is offset by their enthusiasm for viewing constitutional law as similar in method and substance to the common law of torts. Thus, Professor Brest proposes to derive and elaborate constitutional principles from "custom, social practices, conventional morality, and precedents." Other commentators rely more explicitly on insights derived from currently fashionable philosophical or economic concepts to generate both common law and constitutional principles. Application of common law approaches to the constitutional law area has important consequences for interpretation. First, it invites the extraction of quite general political principles from the specific constitutional guarantees. Second, and more important, the common law method encourages the elaboration of supplemental, nontextually grounded principles of political morality to fill in any gaps. So supplemented, the constitution manifests a unified, coherent conception of political justice, and not simply a series of separate and incompletely related provisions which, taken together, are insufficiently expressive of the substantive values of a twentieth-century liberal democracy.

The common law approach is particularly congenial to professors of law, whose training and experience heavily emphasize this technique. The advantages of transplanting the common law method to the constitutional arena are obvious. The tedious labor associated with the historical search for original intent is eliminated. With the concerns of the past out of the way, attention may be focused exclusively on present realities. Armed with the insights of current social, political, and economic thinking, these commentators can "reason" about contemporary needs and the public good in much the same way that they would reason about tort problems—with interest balancing providing the solution to every constitutional problem, just as it purports to do for the creative common law judge. The constitutional values themselves become one set of interests—important ones to be sure, but in the end only interests—to be weighed against competing social values.

Our constitutional origins suggest a different perspective: the constitution as a superstatute. Like important statutes, the constitution emerged as a result of compromises struck after hard bargaining. In addition, its intellectual underpinnings invite a statutory perspective. The dominant conceptions of popular sovereignty and limited government realized by the device of a social compact suggest that the constitution be construed as a compact whose contents could not be altered by any organ of government. That is a great deal more like the way statutes are construed than the way common law is made. These origins make plausible, even if they do not compel, a conclusion that constitutional interpretation should be assimilated to the process of statutory interpretation. While I do not wish to overstate the differences between common law development and statutory interpretation, important interpretational consequences do flow from viewing the constitution as a statute (a super one, to be sure) rather than as declaration of common law. Statutory interpretation involves a blend of emphases upon original intention and historical context, and a full recognition of the unprincipled, and imperfect, nature of an enactment produced by compromise. By contrast, the common law method, if applied to either a statute or a constitution, tends to obscure the compromise character of the enactment, and thus renders opaque its "imperfect" quality when measured against ideal norms.

Candor requires that one recognize that the common law approach, and not the statutory approach, best describes the development of constitutional law under the bill of rights. Substantive elaboration of the bill of rights has increasingly followed the incremental, case-by-case method employed by common law judges. Viewed retrospectively, this was perhaps inevitable. Courts have had to cope with the relative paucity and indeterminacy of the underlying historical materials, as well as the difficulty of relating ancient norms to a world radically different from that of the Framers. Not surprisingly, as the text got older and interpretative materials accumulated, "the focus of professional and judicial attention . . . [shifted] from the . . . text and history to the . . . norm[s] to be derived by analysis and synthesis of the judicial precedents." More importantly, adoption of the method of the common law, with its emphasis on precedent (albeit without the constraining influence of stare decisis) and analogical reasoning, brought with it a belief that the *substance* of the judicial task in each sphere is similar: balancing the interests at stake, with the constitutional guarantees assessed in functional, rather than historical, terms. At least in bill of rights cases, therefore, there is considerable force in Professor Brest's observation that reliance upon original intent "has played a very small role compared to the elaboration of the Court's own precedents. It is rather like having a remote ancestor who came over on the Mayflower."

Thus, the perfectionist has much on which to rely in drawing upon a common law approach to the development of civil liberties—but not nearly enough to justify the perfectionists' central need to legitimate the existence of a supplemental, nontextually based list of autonomy, privacy, and equality claims that are assertable against the political organs of government. One could, after all, argue that elaboration of the specific guarantees of the bill of rights exhibits characteristics of both common law and statutory interpretation: common law because their content is worked out in the manner of the analogical and precedential reasoning characteristic of the common law courts; statutory because, so far as is practicable, emphasis has been and still should be placed on historical setting and original intent. A supplemental list of nontextual rights lacks the latter characteristics by definition.

More importantly, the bill of rights should constitute the paradigmatic illustration of the American reluctance to reason from the equity of the statute. That the constitution specifically guarantees the enumerated freedoms of the bill of rights does not, stated alone, imply that it guarantees a list of unstated freedoms such as the rights of "intimate association" and "personhood." The validity of any such approach is entirely dependent upon a showing that constitutional text authorizes it. Only the ninth amendment and the privileges or immunities clause of the fourteenth amendment could provide a basis for such guarantees, a contention that I have already indicated is arguable but unpersuasive. Perfectionist autonomy, privacy, and equality rights are different in kind from the process rights explicitly guaranteed by the constitutional text, as Professor Ely shows. Moreover, the substantive rights now asserted by the perfectionists, were wholly foreign to both eighteenth and nineteenth century constitutional jurisprudence. Perfectionists cannot point to a textual authorization for their views without demonstrating that the ninth amendment and the privileges or immunities clause were intended to possess a strong, dynamic component, one that would authorize courts to enlarge *materially* over time the sphere insulated from the reach of the ordinary political process. Thus, even if both the form and the substance of common law method are properly utilized by the court in the development of "specific" constitutional guarantees, a *general* judicial prerogative to constrain the outcomes of an open and fair political process cannot be supported.

* * *

H. Jefferson Powell, *The Original Understanding of Original Intent*, 98 HARV. L. REV. 885, 902-13 (1985)*

* * *

III. EARLY VIEWS ON INTERPRETING THE CONSTITUTION

Friend: 'You have given us a good Constitution.'
Gouverneur Morris: 'That depends on how it is construed.'

A. The Framers and the Battle for Ratification

Constitutional debate was not the invention of Revolutionary America, and the invocation of written documents was a wholly traditional move in English high political controversy. America's innovation was to identify 'the Constitution' with a single normative document instead of a historical tradition, and thus to create the possibility of treating constitutional interpretation as an exercise in the traditional legal activity of construing a written instrument. The proceedings of the Philadelphia convention reflect the delegates' awareness of this innovation and their desire to craft a document that would be understood, at least in part, through the traditional processes of legal interpretation.

The Philadelphia framers' primary expectation regarding constitutional interpretation was that the Constitution, like any other legal document, would be interpreted in accord with its express language. This expectation is evident in the framers' numerous attempts to refine the wording of the text, either to eliminate vagueness or to allay fears that overprecise language would be taken literally and that the aim of a given provision would thus be defeated. Debates over the language of the document were abundant, yet in none of them did any delegate suggest that future interpreters could avoid misconstruing the text by consulting evidence of the intentions articulated at the convention. Although the Philadelphia framers certainly wished to embody in the text the most 'distinctive form of collecting the mind' of the convention, there is no indication that they expected or intended future interpreters to refer to any extratextual intentions revealed in the convention's secretly conducted debates. The framers shared the traditional common law view—so foreign to much hermeneutical thought in more recent years—that the import of the document they were framing would be determined by reference to the intrinsic meaning of its words or through the usual judicial process of case-by-case interpretation.

In accepting the common law's objective approach to discerning the meaning of a document, the framers did not endorse strict literalism as the proper stance of future interpreters. The framers were aware that unforeseen situations would arise, and they accepted the inevitability and propriety of construction. When a motion was made to extend the jurisdiction of the Supreme Court to cases arising under 'this Constitution' as well as under 'the laws of the United States,' James Madison expressed concern that this would extend the Court's power to matters not properly within judicial cognizance:

> Mr. MADISON doubted whether it was not going too far, to extend the jurisdiction of the Court generally to cases arising under the Constitution, and whether it ought not to be limited to cases of a judiciary nature. The right of expounding the Constitution, in cases not of this nature, ought not to be given to that department.

> The motion of Docr. JOHNSON [to extend the Court's jurisdiction] was agreed to, *nem. con.* [without dissent], it being generally supposed, that the jurisdiction given was constructively limited to cases of a judiciary nature.

Although the Philadelphia framers did not discuss in detail how they intended their end product to be interpreted, they clearly assumed that future interpreters would adhere to then-prevalent methods of statutory construction.

The political struggle over the ratification of the Constitution elicited, both in print and on state convention floors, a considerable body of commentary on the Constitution's 'intent,' and on the means that future interpreters would use to determine that 'intent.' Americans generally agreed that the Articles of Confederation were a compact among the several states. The Federalist proponents of the Constitution identified the contractual basis of the Articles as one of their chief weaknesses. One of the Constitution's virtues, in the Federalists' view, lay in its rejection of a contractual model for the polity of the United States. The Federalists analogized the ratification process to the passage by a legislature (the people) of a statute (the Constitution) drafted by a committee (the Philadelphia convention). Without the people's approval, the convention's work would remain a mere proposal lacking any intrinsic authority. This analogy led many Federalists to assume or assert that the Constitution would be construed in accord with the same basic principles that the common law had developed for statutory interpretation. Perhaps for their own polemical purposes, the

Anti-Federalists usually agreed with the statutory analogy for the proposed Constitution, and with the corollary analogy between constitutional and statutory interpretation. Their complaint was that this methodology, applied to the sweeping
language of the Constitution, would lead inexorably to the effective consolidation of
the states into a single body politic with a single, omnipotent government.

Once the Constitution was proposed to the states, a central element of the
campaign to prevent ratification was the charge that the Constitution would be the
object of interpretation and that judges and legislators would read into it doctrines
present only 'constructively' and not textually. All of the anti-hermeneutic resources
of Protestant biblicism and Enlightenment rationalism were enlisted in an effort to
show that the Constitution was an open invitation to political corruption and oligarchic usurpation. The Constitution was ambiguous by design, the Anti-Federalists
claimed, and thereby invited construction. Through such construction the new federal
rulers would gradually extend their power and so finally subvert American liberties.
The Supreme Court's power to interpret the Constitution would make the Court, not
the people or their representatives, the true lawgiver. Disputes over the scope of the
Constitution's grants of power, the Anti-Federalists argued, showed that no one
could predict how the instrument would be interpreted once adopted. The good intentions of the Philadelphia delegates, or of the proponents of the Constitution in the
state conventions, were irrelevant, because the Constitution's intention was expressed
'[s]o loosely . . . [and] inaccurately' that misconstructions were certain to occur. The
Protestant tradition taught that God's Word is its own interpreter, and the philosophers had warned against the dangers of any law not plainly comprehensible on its
face; the proposed Constitution, however, contained no acceptable internal criteria to
guide its interpreters. Some Anti-Federalists viewed the document in an even darker
light: to them it revealed a conscious desire on the part of the Philadelphia delegates,
who had clothed their proceedings in a veil of secrecy, to overthrow the free and republican constitutions of the states and substitute for them a centralized despotism.

The Federalist supporters of ratification offered a variety of responses to the
barrage of criticism leveled against the Constitution and its alleged susceptibility to
corrupting interpretation. First, to those who questioned the good faith of the
Philadelphia delegates, the Federalists responded by invoking not only the great
names of Washington and Franklin, but also the common law's understanding of
'intent.' The Anti-Federalists' fears were misguided, they asserted, because whatever
the private sentiments of the Philadelphia delegates had been, those sentiments
would not be the legally significant 'intent' of the Constitution. The members of the
federal convention had been mere scriveners or attorneys appointed to draw up an
instrument; the instrument's true makers were the people of the United States
assembled in state conventions. It was thus the people's unquestionably republican
intention, evinced in the plain, obvious meaning of the text, that would control
future interpretations. The Federalists additionally denied allegations that they
were already corrupting the meaning of the Constitution. It was not they but their
opponents, the Federalists claimed, who were engaged in lawyers' quibbles over the
language of an instrument that the common sense of the people found perfectly
clear. As John Jay explained, Federalist statements of the document's meaning were
not products of a suspect hermeneutical process; they involved 'no sophistry; no construction; no false glosses, but simple inferences from the obvious operation of
things.' Finally, Federalists argued that the Anti-Federalist attack on the Constitution's indeterminacy ignored the limits of human communicative powers: 'no compo-
sitions which men can pen, could be formed, but wh[ich] would be liable to the same

charge [of ambiguity].' When interpretation was necessary, it would take place in accord with the rules of 'universal jurisprudence,' subject to correction by the amendment process provided for in article V.

A series of essays published in the *New York Journal* from October 1787 through April 1788 under the byline 'Brutus' constituted by far the most powerful and sustained attack on the Constitution from an anti-hermeneutical perspective. 'Brutus' read the first sentence of the second section of article III ('The judicial power shall extend to all cases, in law and equity, arising under this Constitution . . . .') to authorize the federal courts to give the Constitution both 'a legal construction' and an interpretation 'according to the reasoning spirit of it, without being confined to the words or letter.' Courts frequently would employ the latter 'mode of construction' out of necessity, because the Constitution's grants of authority were 'conceived in general and indefinite terms, which are either equivocal, ambiguous, or which require long definitions to unfold the extent of their meaning.' The courts' exercises in construction 'according to the reasoning spirit,' therefore, would necessarily amount to the creation of constitutional norms by judges themselves.

'Brutus' felt that the courts' interpretations 'according to the rules laid down for construing a law' would be just as unfortunate. The common law tradition of statutory interpretation, he pointed out, permitted and even required the court to take the end or purpose of the statute into account. Like many statutes, the Constitution declared its purpose in a Preamble, the wording of which made it 'obvious,' to 'Brutus,' that the Constitution 'has in view every object which is embraced by any government,' leaving no separate sphere of responsibility for the state authorities and reducing the present confederation to a single, consolidated nation. Most horrifying of all to 'Brutus' was the realization, gathered from the Preamble, from the grants of power to Congress, and from the interpretive authority entrusted to the federal judiciary, that the Constitution identified the separate existence and autonomy of the states as the mischief and defect it was to cure. 'Brutus' insisted that the most disinterested judge, interpreting the Constitution with strict regard for the proprieties of common law statutory construction, would agree that the document 'was calculated to abolish entirely the state governments, and to melt down the states into one entire government.' And of course, he argued, judges would not in fact be disinterested. Electorally irresponsible, endowed with that absolute authority to interpret against which English religious and political tradition warned, the federal judges would be from the beginning the final lawgivers of the system, and in the end its absolute rulers.

'Brutus' therefore saw the Constitution as flawed at a deeper level than that reached by criticisms of its ambiguities or of its broad grants of power to the federal legislature. Its basic evil was its framers' misconception, deliberate or not, of the nature of fundamental law in a free society. The Philadelphia convention had devised a constitution patterned after a statute, a command issued by a legal superior and subject to technical interpretation in accord with the traditional rules of construction. But for 'Brutus,' a constitution should be a contract, 'a compact of a people with their rulers,' framed in simple and nontechnical language and enforced by the people's right to remove those rulers 'at the period when the rulers are to be elected.' A constitution, for 'Brutus,' should articulate in plain terms the agreement of the community on the rightful powers of government, not establish a superior authority to determine what those powers are. Under such a political compact there could be no danger of effective usurpation by the rulers, save by force, for the compact's meaning would be clear to all and would be interpreted by the equal parties to the compact, not by a legal superior. The Philadelphia framers, unfortunately, had followed a different model. Their proposed constitution did not express consensus; it issued commands—mandates at once so complicated and so obscure that it would be impossible to give them meaning without resort by the federal political bodies to the artificial techniques of traditional legal hermeneutics. By drafting an instrument requiring such interpretation, the Philadelphia framers had ensured that future authority over the parameters of American political society would ultimately be transferred from the ordinary people to a small coterie of legal quibblers.

Commentators have suggested that Alexander Hamilton's discussion of article III in *The Federalist* Nos. 78 through 83, which appeared in late May 1788, was written as a direct response to the Essays of 'Brutus.' Whether or not intended as such, those papers in fact offered the most coherent Federalist rebuttal of the arguments of 'Brutus.' Hamilton had already observed in *The Federalist* No. 22 that one of the defects of the Articles of Confederation was their failure to establish an effective federal judiciary. In addition, in *The Federalist* No. 37 James Madison had launched a devastating counterattack on the standard Anti-Federalist charge of ambiguity. Madison stressed the inescapable fallibility and tentativeness of all human acts of discrimination—sensory, mental, or experiential—and responded to the religious overtones in the Anti-Federalist critique with the observation that the meaning even of God's Word 'is rendered dim and doubtful, by the cloudy medium through which it is communicated' when He 'condescends to address mankind in their own language.' Mortals' efforts at the framing of law obviously could not be hoped to better those of Omnipotence; Madison thus concluded that '[a]ll new laws, though penned with the greatest technical skill, and passed on the fullest and most mature deliberation, are considered as more or less obscure and equivocal, until their meaning be liquidated and ascertained by a series of particular discussions and adjudications.' Madison's argument, which Hamilton had anticipated in *The Federalist* No. 22, was of course a restatement in somewhat abstract terms of the old common law assumption, shared by the Philadelphia framers, that the 'intent' of any legal document is the product of the interpretive process and not some fixed meaning that the author locks into the document's text at the outset. In his Essays 'Brutus' underscored this confession that the Constitution would be subject to judicial construction whose results were not completely foreseeable at present, and he labored with considerable success to demonstrate that the necessary consequence was judicial tyranny.

In *The Federalist* Nos. 78 through 83, Hamilton returned his attention to the legal character of the Constitution and its provisions for a federal judiciary. He steadfastly reiterated *The Federalist*'s earlier claims that it was appropriate and necessary for the courts to 'liquidate and fix [the] meaning and operation' of laws, including the Constitution. Hamilton rejected the inference that the future federal courts would find in the Constitution anything shocking or surprising to the ordinary reader: 'The rules of legal interpretation are rules of *common sense*, adopted by the courts in the construction of the laws. . . . In relation to such a subject [a constitution of government], the natural and obvious sense of its provisions, apart from any technical rules, is the true criterion of construction.'

Faced with the argument of 'Brutus' that the court's powers of constitutional interpretation and judicial review of legislative acts would inexorably result in uncontrollable and ultimately despotic oligarchy, Hamilton countered by suggesting that 'Brutus' had not taken the statutory analogy seriously enough. Both agreed, Hamilton approvingly and 'Brutus' disapprovingly, that the Constitution was to be viewed as a quasi-statute, a command from a legal superior to those under its authority. According to this view, Hamilton argued, the legal superior issuing the command must be considered the ultimate repository of sovereignty in a republic: the people. But 'the nature and reason of the thing,' Hamilton wrote,

> teach us that the prior act of a superior ought to be preferred to the subsequent act of an inferior and subordinate authority; and that, accordingly, whenever a particular statute contravenes the constitution, it will be the duty of the judicial tribunals to adhere to the latter, and disregard the former.

Far from exalting the judiciary over all, the doctrine of judicial review based on the courts' construction of the Constitution simply safeguarded the authority of the people who had 'ordained and established' the Constitution in the first place.

Hamilton and 'Brutus' therefore disagreed primarily over the nature of legal interpretation. 'Brutus' feared that interpretation would inevitably convert the Constitution's open-textured language into a license for omnipotent federal government. Hamilton countered that legal interpretation was simply the application of common sense to text. Because the people can exercise common sense, they could tell for themselves what the Constitution meant—and no sensible reader would take it to be a charter for tyranny. Hamilton scornfully dismissed the notion that judges could exploit their interpretive authority to make themselves despots: lacking influence 'over either the sword or the purse,' he remarked, courts would possess 'neither Force nor Will, but merely judgment.' The insulation of judges from electoral accountability was not a threat to liberty, but rather an essential condition to the judiciary's role as independent guardian of the Constitution's limitations on power. In reality, as Hamilton had argued earlier, the seeds of tyranny lurked not within the statutory analogy proposed by the Federalists, but within the contract analogy favored by 'Brutus.' A government with no justification other than a contractual meeting of the minds could not long endure without resorting to force to resolve the disagreements that would inevitably splinter society. The debate between Hamilton and 'Brutus' was ultimately irresolvable, for they started from different premises that paralleled the conflicting hermeneutical perspectives discussed above in Part II. 'Brutus' assumed the validity of the anti-interpretive tradition's equation of construction and corruption. In sharp contrast, Hamilton accepted the validity of the common law's hermeneutical techniques as means to discovering a document's 'intent.'

The public debate over the adoption of the Constitution thus revealed that Americans of all political opinions accepted the applicability to constitutional interpretation of hermeneutical views developed in relation to quite different documents—the Bible, parliamentary statutes, and private contracts. But there were sharp disagreements over which interpretive approach was acceptable. An important element in the Anti-Federalists' critique was their implicit appeal to the distrust of interpretation cultivated by the British Protestant tradition and Enlightenment thought. The Federalists, on the other hand, treated the availability of common law hermeneutics as a positive good: precisely because there was a developed tradition of legal interpretation, they argued, the people could predict with confidence the results of future constitutional construction.

* * *

Herbert Wechsler, *Toward Neutral Principles of Constitutional Law,* 73 HARV. L. REV. 1 (1959)*

* * *

II. THE STANDARDS OF REVIEW

If courts cannot escape the duty of deciding whether actions of the other branches of the govemment are consistent with the Constitution, when a case is properly before them in the sense I have attempted to describe, you will not doubt the relevancy and importance of demanding what, if any, are the standards to be followed in interpretation. Are there, indeed, any criteria that both the Supreme Court and those who undertake to praise or to condemn its judgments are morally and intellectually obligated to support?

Whatever you may think to be the answer, surely you agree with me that I am right to state the question as the same one for the Court and for critics. An attack upon a judgment involves assertion that a court should have decided otherwise than as it did. Is it not clear that the validity of assertion of this kind depends upon assigning reasons that should have prevailed with the tribunal and that any other reasons are irrelevant? That is, course, not only true of a critique of a decision of the courts; it applies whenever a determination is questioned, a determination that it is essential to make either way. Is it the irritation of advancing years that leads me to lament that our culture is not rich with critics who respect these limitations of the enterprise in which they are engaged?

You may remind me that, as someone in the ancient world observed—perhaps it was Josephus—history has little tolerance for any of those reasonable judgments that have turned out to be wrong. But history, in this sense, is inscrutable, concealing all its verdicts in the bosom of the future; it is never a contemporary critic.

I revert then to the problem of criteria as it arises for both courts and critics—by which I mean criteria that can be framed and tested as an exercise of reason and not merely as an act of willfulness or will. Even to put the problem is, of course, to raise an issue no less old than our culture. Those who perceive in law only the element of fiat, in whose conception of the legal cosmos reason has no meaning or no place, will not join gladly in the search for standards of the kind I have in mind. I must, in short, expect dissent in limine from anyone whose view of the judicial process leaves no room for the antinomy Professor Fuller has so gracefully explored. So too must I anticipate dissent from those more numerous among us who, vouching no philosophy to warranty, frankly or covertly make the test of virtue in interpretation whether its result in the immediate decision seems to hinder or advance the interests or the values they support.

I shall not try to overcome the philosophic doubt that I have mentioned, although to use a phrase that Holmes so often used—"it hits me where I live." That battle must be fought on wider fronts than that of constitutional interpretation; and I do not delude myself that I can qualify for a command, great as is my wish to render service. The man who simply lets his judgment turn on the immediate result may not, however, realize that his position implies that the courts are free to function as a naked power organ, that it is an empty affirmation to regard them, as ambivalently he so often does, as courts of law. If he may know he disapproves of a decision when all he knows is that it has sustained a claim put forward by a labor union or a taxpayer, a Negro or a segregationist, a corporation or a Communist—he acquiesces

---

in the proposition that a man of different sympathy but equal information may no less properly conclude that he approves.

You will not charge me with exaggeration if I say that this type of ad hoc evaluation is, as it has always been, the deepest problem of our constitutionalism, not only with respect to judgments of the courts but also in the wider realm in which conflicting constitutional positions have played a part in our politics.

Did not New England challenge the embargo that the South supported on the very ground on which the South was to resist New England's demand for a protective tariff? Was not Jefferson in the Louisiana Purchase forced to rest on an expansive reading of the clauses granting national authority of the very kind that he had steadfastly opposed in his attacks upon the Bank? Can you square his disappointment about Burr's acquittal on the treason charge and his subsequent request for legislation with the attitude towards freedom and repression most enduringly associated with his name? Were the abolitionists who rescued fugitives and were acquitted in defiance of the evidence able to distinguish their view of the compulsion of a law of the United States from that advanced by South Carolina in the ordinance that they despised?

To bring the matter even more directly home, what shall we think of the Harvard records of the Class of 1829, the class of Mr. Justice Curtis, which, we are told, praised at length the Justice's dissent in the *Dred Scott* case but then added, "Again, and *seemingly adverse to the above,* in October, 1862, he prepared a legal opinion and argument, which was published in Boston in pamphlet form, to the effect that President Lincoln's Proclamation prospective emancipation of the slaves in the rebellious States is unconstitutional."

Of course, a man who thought and, as a Justice, voted and maintained that a free Negro could be a citizen of the United States and therefore of a state, within the meaning of the constitutional and statutory clauses defining the diversity jurisdiction; that Congress had authority to forbid slavery within a territory, even one acquired after the formation of the Union; and that such a prohibition worked emancipation of a slave whose owner brought him to reside in such a territory—a man who thought all these things detracted obviously from the force of his positions if he also thought the President without authority to abrogate a form of property established and protected by state law within the states where it was located, states which the President and his critic alike maintained had not effectively seceded from the Union and were not a foreign enemy at war.

How simple the class historian could make it all by treating as the only thing that mattered when Mr. Justice Curtis had, on the occasions noted, helped or hindered the attainment of the freedom of the slaves.

I have cited these examples from the early years of our history since time has bred aloofness that may give them added force. What a wealth of illustration is at hand today! How many of the constitutional attacks upon congressional investigations of suspected Communists have their authors felt obliged to launch against the inquiries respecting the activities of Goldfine or of Hoffa or of others I might name? How often have those who think the Smith Act, as construed, inconsistent with the first amendment made clear that they also stand for constitutional immunity for racial agitators fanning flames of prejudice and discontent? Turning the case around, are those who in relation to the Smith Act see no virtue in distinguishing between advocacy of merely abstract doctrine and advocacy which is planned to instigate unlawful action, equally unable to see virtue in the same distinction in relation, let us say, to advocacy of resistance to the judgments of the courts, especially perhaps to judgments vindicating claims that equal protection of the laws has been denied? I may live a uniquely sheltered life but am I wrong in thinking I discerned in some extremely warm enthusiasts for jury trial a certain diminution of enthusiasm as the issue was presented in the course of the debate in 1957 on the bill to extend federal protection of our civil rights?

All I have said, you may reply, is something no one will deny, that principles are largely instrumental as they are employed in politics, instrumental in relation to results that a controlling sentiment demands at any given time. Politicians recognize this fact of life and are obliged to trim and shape their speech and votes accordingly, unless perchance they are prepared to step aside; and the example that John Quincy Adams set somehow is rarely followed.

That is, indeed, all I have said but I now add that whether you are tolerant, perhaps more tolerant than I, of the ad hoc in politics, with principle reduced to a manipulative tool, are you not also ready to agree that something else is called for from the courts? I put it to you that the main constituent of the judicial process is precisely that it must be genuinely principled, resting with respect to every step that is involved in reaching judgment on analysis and reasons quite transcending the immediate result that is achieved. To be sure, the courts decide, or should decide, only the case they have before them. But must they not decide on grounds of adequate neutrality and generality, tested not only by the instant application but by others that the principles imply? Is it not the very essence of judicial method to insist upon attending to such other cases, preferably those involving an opposing interest, in evaluating any principle avowed?

Here too I do not think that I am stating any novel or momentous insight. But now, as Holmes said long ago in speaking of "the unrest which seems to wonder vaguely whether law and order pay," we "need education in the obvious." We need it more particulary now respecting constitutional interpretation, since it has become a commonplace to grant what many for so long denied: that courts in constitutional determinations face issues that are inescapably "political"—political in the third sense that I have used that word—in that they involve a choice among competing values or desires, a choice reflected in the legislative or executive action in question, which the court must either condemn or condone.

I should be the last to argue otherwise or to protest the emphasis upon the point in Mr. Justice Jackson's book, throughout the Marshall conference, and in the lectures by Judge Hand. I have, indeed, insisted on the point myself. But what is crucial, I submit, is not the nature of the question but the nature of the answer that may validly be given by the courts. No legislature or executive is obligated by the nature of its function to support its choice of values by the type of reasoned explanation that I have suggested is intrinsic to judicial action—however much we may admire such a reasoned exposition when we find it in those other realms.

Does not the special duty of the courts to judge by neutral principles addressed to all the issues make it inapposite to contend, as Judge Hand does, that no court can review the legislative choice—by any standard other than a fixed "historical meaning" of constitutional provisions—without becoming "a third legislative chamber"? Is there not, in short, a vital difference between legislative freedom to appraise the gains and losses in projected measures and the kind of principled appraisal, in respect of values that can reasonably be asserted to have constitutional dimension, that alone is in the province of the courts? Does not the difference yield a middle ground between a judicial House of Lords and the abandonment of any limitation on the other branches—a middle ground consisting of judicial action that embodies what are surely the main qualities of law, its generality and its neutrality? This must, it seems to me, have been in Mr. Justice Jackson's mind when in his chapter on the Supreme Court "as a political institution" he wrote in words that I find stirring, "Liberty is not the mere absence of restraint, it is not a spontaneous product of majority rule, it is not achieved merely by lifting underprivileged classes to power, nor is it the inevitable by-product of technological expansion. It is achieved only by a rule of law." Is it not also what Mr. Justice Frankfurter must mean in calling upon judges for "allegiance to nothing except the effort, amid tangled words and limited insights, to find the path through precedent, through policy, through history, to the best judgment that fallible creatures can reach in that most difficult of all tasks: the achievement of justice between man and man, between man and state, through reason called law"?

You will not understand my emphasis upon the role of reason and of principle in the judicial, as distinguished from the legislative or executive, appraisal of conflicting values to imply that I depreciate the duty of fidelity to the text of the Constitution, when its words may be decisive—though I would certainly remind you of the caution stated by Chief Justice Hughes: "Behind the words of the constitutional provisions are postulates which limit and control." Nor will you take me to deny that history has weight in the elucidation of the text, though it is surely subtle business to appraise it as a guide. Nor will you even think that I deem precedent without importance, for we surely must agree with Holmes that "imitation of the past, until we have a clear reason for change, no more needs justification than appetite." But after all, it was Chief Justice Taney who declared his willingness "that it be regarded hereafter as the law of this court, that its opinion upon the construction of the Constitution is always open to discussion when it is supposed to have been founded in error, and that its judicial authority should hereafter depend altogether on the force of the reasoning by which it is supported." Would any of us have it otherwise, given the nature of the problems that confront the courts?

At all events, is not the relative compulsion of the language of the Constitution, of history and precedent—where they do not combine to make an answer clear—itself a matter to be judged, so far as possible, by neutral principles—by standards that transcend the case at hand? I know, of course, that it is common to distinguish, as Judge Hand did, clauses like "due process," cast "in such sweeping terms that their history does not elucidate their contents," from other provisions of the Bill of Rights addressed to more specific problems. But the contrast, as it seems to me, often implies an overstatement of the specificity or the immutability these other clauses really have, at least when problems under them arise.

No one would argue, for example, that there need not be indictment and a jury trial in prosecutions for a felony in district courts. What made a question of some difficulty was the issue whether service wives charged with the murders of their husbands overseas could be tried there before a military court. Does the language of the double-jeopardy clause or its preconstitutional history actually help to decide whether a defendant tried for murder in the first degree and convicted of murder in the second, who wins a reversal of the judgment on appeal, may be tried again for murder in the first or only murder in the second? Is there significance in the fact that it is "jeopardy of life or limb" that is forbidden, now that no one is in jeopardy of limb but only of imprisonment or fine? The right to "have the assistance of counsel" was considered, I am sure, when the sixth amendment was proposed, a right to defend by counsel if you have one; contrary to what was then the English law. That does not seem to me sufficient to avert extension of its meaning to imply a right to court-appointed counsel when the defendant is too poor to find such aid—though I admit that I once urged the point sincerely as a lawyer for the Government. It is difficult for me to think the fourth amendment freezes for all time the common law of search and of arrest as it prevailed when the amendment was adopted, whatever the exigencies of police problems may now be or may become. Nor should we, in my view, lament the fact that "the" freedom of speech or press that Congress is forbidden by the first amendment to impair is not determined only by the scope such freedom had in the late eighteenth century, though the word "the" might have been taken to impose a limitation to the concept of that time—a time when, President Wright has recently reminded us, there was remarkable consensus about matters of this kind.

Even "due process," on the other hand, might have been confined, as Mr. Justice Brandeis urged originally, to a guarantee of fair procedure, coupled perhaps with prohibition of executive displacement of established law—the analogue for us of what the barons meant in Magna Carta. Equal protection could be taken as no more than an assurance that no one may be placed beyond the safeguards of the law, outlawing, as it were, the possibility of outlawry, but nothing else. Here too I cannot find it in my heart to regret that interpretation did not ground itself in ancient history but rather has perceived in these provisions a compendious affirmation of the basic values of a free society, values that must be given weight in legislation and administration at the risk of courting trouble in the courts.

So far as possible, to finish with my point, I argue that we should prefer to see the other clauses of the Bill of Rights read as an affirmation of the special values they embody rather than as statements of a finite rule of law, its limits fixed by the consensus of a century long past, with problems very different from our own. To read them in the former way is to leave room for adaptation and adjustment if and when competing values, also having constitutional dimension, enter on the scene.

Let me repeat what I have thus far tried to say. The courts have both the title and the duty when a case is properly before them to review the actions of the other branches in the light of constitutional provisions, even though the action involves value choices, as invariably action does. In doing so, however, they are bound to function otherwise than as a naked power organ; they participate as courts of law. This calls for facing how determinations of this kind can be asserted to have any legal quality. The answer, I suggest, inheres primarily in that they are—or are obliged to be—entirely principled. A principled decision, in the sense I have in mind, is one that rests on reasons with respect to all the issues in the case, reasons that in their generality and their neutrality transcend any immediate result that is involved. When no sufficient reasons of this kind can be assigned for overturning value choices of the other branches of the Government or of a state, those choices must, of course, survive. Otherwise, as Holmes said in his first opinion for the Court, "a constitution, instead of embodying only relatively fundamental rules of rights, as generally understood by all English-speaking communities, would become the partisan of a particular set of ethical or economical opinions. . . ."

The virtue or demerit of a judgment turns, therefore, entirely on the reasons that support it and their adequacy to maintain any choice of values it decrees, or, it is vital that we add, to maintain the rejection of a claim that any given choice should be decreed. The critic's role, as T. R. Powell showed throughout so many fruitful years, is the sustained, disinterested, merciless examination of the reasons that the courts advance, measured by standards of the kind I have attempted to describe. I wish that more of us today could imitate his dedication to that task.

* * *

Robert H. Bork, *Neutral Principles and Some First Amendment Problems,* 47 IND. L.J. 1 (1971)*

A persistently disturbing aspect of constitutional law is its lack of theory, a lack which is manifest not merely in the work of the courts but in the public, professional and even scholarly discussion of the topic. The result, of course, is that courts are without effective criteria and, therefore, we have come to expect that the nature of the Constitution will change, often quite dramatically, as the personnel of the Supreme Court changes. In the present state of affairs that expectation is inevitable, but it is nevertheless deplorable.

The remarks that follow do not, of course, offer a general theory of constitutional law. They are more properly viewed as ranging shots, an attempt to establish the necessity for theory and to take the argument of how constitutional doctrine should be evolved by courts a step or two farther. The first section centers upon the implications of Professor Wechsler's concept of "neutral principles," and the second attempts to apply those implications to some important and much-debated problems in the interpretation of the first amendment. The style is informal since these remarks were originally lectures and I have not thought it worthwhile to convert these speculations and arguments into a heavily researched, balanced and thorough presentation, for that would result in a book.

THE SUPREME COURT AND THE DEMAND FOR PRINCIPLE

The subject of the lengthy and often acrimonious debate about the proper role of the Supreme Court under the Constitution is one that preoccupies many people these days: when is authority legitimate? I find it convenient to discuss that question in the context of the Warren Court and its works simply because the Warren Court posed the issue in acute form. The issue did not disappear along with the era of the Warren Court majorities, however. It arises when any court either exercises or declines to exercise the power to invalidate any act of another branch of government. The Supreme Court is a major power center, and we must ask when its power should be used and when it should be withheld.

Our starting place, inevitably, is Professor Herbert Wechsler's argument that the Court must not be merely a "naked power organ," which means that its decisions must be controlled by principle. "A principled decision," according to Wechsler, "is one that rests on reasons with respect to all the issues in a case, reasons that in their generality and their neutrality transcend any immediate result that is involved."

Wechsler chose the term "neutral principles" to capsulate his argument, though he recognizes that the legal principle to be applied is itself never neutral because it embodies a choice of one value rather than another. Wechsler asked for the neutral application of principles, which is a requirement, as Professor Louis L. Jaffe puts it, that the judge "sincerely believe in the principle upon which he purports to rest his decision." "The judge," says Jaffe, "must believe in the validity of the reasons given for the decision at least in the sense that he is prepared to apply them to a later case which he cannot honestly distinguish." He must not, that is, decide lawlessly. But is the demand for neutrality in judges merely another value choice, one that is no more principled than any other? I think not, but to prove it we must rehearse fundamentals. This is familiar terrain but important and still debated.

The requirement that the Court be principled arises from the resolution of the seeming anomaly of judicial supremacy in a democratic society. If the judiciary really is supreme, able to rule when and as it sees fit, the society is not democratic. The anomaly is dissipated, however, by the model of government embodied in the structure of the Constitution, a model upon which popular consent to limited government by the Supreme Court also rests. This model we may for convenience, though perhaps not with total accuracy, call "Madisonian."

A Madisonian system is not completely democratic, if by "democratic" we mean completely majoritarian. It assumes that in wide areas of life majorities are entitled to rule for no better reason that they are majorities. We need not pause here to examine the philosophical underpinnings of that assumption since it is a "given" in our society; nor need we worry that "majority" is a term of art meaning often no more than the shifting combinations of minorities that add up to temporary majorities in the legislature. That majorities are so constituted is inevitable. In any case, one essential premise of the Madisonian model is majoritarianism. The model has also a counter-majoritarian premise, however, for it assumes there are some areas of life a majority should not control. There are some things a majority should not do to us no matter how democratically it decides to do them. These are areas properly left to individual freedom, and coercion by the majority in these aspects of life is tyranny.

Some see the model as containing an inherent, perhaps an insoluble, dilemma. Majority tyranny occurs if legislation invades the areas properly left to individual freedom. Minority tyranny occurs if the majority is prevented from ruling where its power is legitimate. Yet, quite obviously, neither the majority nor the minority can be trusted to define the freedom of the other. This dilemma is resolved in constitutional theory, and in popular understanding, by the Supreme Court's power to define both majority and minority freedom through the interpretation of the Constitution. Society consents to be ruled undemocratically within defined areas by certain enduring principles believed to be stated in, and placed beyond the reach of majorities by the Constitution.

But this resolution of the dilemma imposes severe requirements upon the Court. For it follows that the Court's power is legitimate only if it has, and can demonstrate in reasoned opinions that it has, a valid theory, derived form the Constitution, of the respective spheres of majority and minority freedom. If it does not have such a theory but merely imposes its own value choices, or worse if it pretends to have a theory but actually follows its own predilections, the Court violates the postulates of the Madisonian model that alone justifies its power. It then necessarily abets the tyranny either of the majority or of the minority.

This argument is central to the issue of legitimate authority because the Supreme Court's power to govern rests upon popular acceptance of this model. Evidence that this is, in fact, the basis of the Court's power is to be gleaned everywhere in our culture. We need not canvass here such things as high school civics texts and newspaper commentary, for the most telling evidence may be found in the U.S. Reports. The Supreme Court regularly insists that its results, and most particularly its controversial results, do not spring from the mere will of the Justices in the majority but are supported, indeed compelled, by a proper understanding of the Constitution of the United States. Value choices are attributed to the Founding Fathers, not to the Court. The way an institution advertises tells you what it thinks its customers demand.

This is, I think, the ultimate reason the Court must be principled. If it does not have and rigorously adhere to a valid and consistent theory of majority and minority freedoms based upon the Constitution, judicial supremacy, given the axioms of our system, is, precisely to that extent, illegitimate. The root of its illegitimacy is that it opens a chasm between the reality of the Court's performance and the constitutional popular assumptions that give it power.

I do not mean to rest the argument entirely upon the popular understanding of the Court's function. Even if society generally should ultimately perceive what the Court is in fact doing and, having seen, prove content to have major policies determined by the unguided discretion of judges rather than by elected representatives, a principled judge would, I believe, continue to consider himself bound by an obligation to the document and to the structure of government that it prescribes. At least he would be bound so long as any litigant existed who demanded such adherence of him. I do not understand how, on any other theory of judicial obligation, the Court could, as it does now, protect voting rights if a large majority of the relevant constituency were willing to see some groups or individuals deprived of such rights. But even if I am wrong in that, at the very least an honest judge would owe it to the body politic to cease invoking the authority of the Constitution and to make explicit the imposition of his own will, for only then would we know whether the society understood enough of what is taking place to be said to have consented.

Judge J. Skelly Wright, in an argument resting on different premises, has severely criticized the advocates of principle. He defends the value-choosing role of the Warren Court, setting that Court in opposition to something he refers to as the "scholarly tradition," which criticizes that Court for its lack of principle. A perceptive reader, sensitive to nuance, may suspect that the Judge is rather out of sympathy with that tradition from such hints as his reference to "self-appointed scholastic mandarins."

The "mandarins" of the academy anger the Judge because they engage in "haughty derision of the Court's powers of analysis and reasoning." Yet, curiously enough, Judge Wright makes no attempt to refute the charge but rather seems to adopt the technique of confession and avoidance. He seems to be arguing that a Court engaged in choosing fundamental values for society cannot be expected to produce principled decisions at the same time. Decisions first, principles later. One wonders, however, how the Court or the rest of us are to know that the decisions are correct or what they portend for the future if they are not accompanied by the principles that explain and justify them. And it would not be amiss to point out that quite often the principles required of the Warren Court's decisions never did put in an appearance. But Judge Wright's main point appears to be that value choice is the most important function of the Supreme Court, so that if we must take one or the other, and apparently we must, we should prefer a process of selecting values to one of constructing and articulating principles. His argument, I believe, boils down to a syllogism. 1. The Supreme Court should "protect our constitutional rights and liberties." II. The Supreme Court must "make fundamental value choices" in order to "protect our constitutional rights and liberties." III. Therefore, the Supreme Court should "make fundamental value choices."

The argument displays an all too common confusion. If we have constitutional rights and liberties already, rights and liberties specified by the Constitution, the Court need make no fundamental value choices in order to protect them, and it certainly need not have difficulty enunciating principles. If, on the other hand, "constitutional rights and liberties" are not in some real sense specified by the Constitution but are the rights and liberties the Court chooses, on the basis of its own values, to give to us, then the conclusion was contained entirely in the major premise, and the Judge's syllogism is no more than an assertion of what it purported to prove.

If I am correct so far, no argument that is both coherent and respectable can be made supporting a Supreme Court that "chooses fundamental values" because a Court that makes rather than implements value choices cannot be squared with the presuppositions of a democratic society. The man who understands the issues and nevertheless insists upon the rightness of the Warren Court's performance ought also, if he is candid, to admit that he is prepared to sacrifice democratic process to his own moral views. He claims for the Supreme Court an institutionalized role as perpetrator of limited coups d'etat.

Such a man occupies an impossible philosophic position. What can he say, for instance, of a Court that does not share his politics or his morality? I can think of nothing except the assertion that he will ignore the Court whenever he can get away with it and overthrow it if he can. In his view the Court has no legitimacy, and there is no reason any of us should obey it. And, this being the case, the advocate of a value-choosing Court must answer another difficult question. Why should the Court, a committee of nine lawyers, be the sole agent of change? The man who prefers results to processes has no reason to say that the Court is more legitimate than any other institution. If the Court will not listen, why not argue the case to some other group, say the Joint Chiefs of Staff, a body with rather better means for implementing its decisions?

We are driven to the conclusion that a legitimate Court must be controlled by principles exterior to the will of the Justices. As my colleague, Professor Alexander Bickel, puts it, "The process of the coherent, analytically warranted, principled declaration of general norms alone justifies the Court's function. . . . Recognition of the need for principle is only the first step, but once that step is taken much more follows. Logic has a life of its own, and devotion to principle requires that we follow where logic leads."

Professor Bickel identifies Justice Frankfurter as the leading judicial proponent of principle but concedes that even Frankfurter never found a "rigorous general accord between judicial supremacy and democratic theory." Judge Wright responds, "The leading commentators of the scholarly tradition have tried ever since to succeed where the Justice failed." As Judge Wright quite accurately suggests, the commentators have so far had no better luck than the Justice.

One reason, I think, is clear. We have not carried the idea of neutrality far enough. We have been talking about neutrality in the *application* of principles. If judges are to avoid imposing their own values upon the rest of us, however, they must be neutral as well in the definition and the *derivation* of principles.

It is easy enough to meet the requirement of neutral application by stating a principle so narrowly that no embarrassment need arise in applying it to all cases it subsumes, a tactic often urged by proponents of "judicial restraint." But that solves very little. It certainly does not protect the judge from the intrusion of his own values. The problem may be illustrated by *Griswold v. Connecticut,* in many ways a typical decision of the Warren Court. *Griswold* struck down Connecticut's statute making it a crime, even for married couples, to use contraceptive devices. If we take the principle of the decision to be a statement that government may not interfere with any acts done in private, we need not even ask about the principle's dubious origin for we know at once that the Court will not apply it neutrally. The Court, we may confidently predict, is not going to throw constitutional protection around heroin use or sexual acts with a consenting minor. We can gain the possibility of neutral application by refraining the principle as a statement that government may not prohibit the use of contraceptives by married couples, but that is not enough. The question of neutral definition arises: Why does the principle extend only to married couples? Why, out of all forms of sexual behavior, only to the use of contraceptives? Why, out of all forms of behavior, only to sex? The question of neutral derivation also arises: What justifies any limitation upon legislatures in this area? What is the origin of any principle one may state?

To put the matter another way, if a neutral judge must demonstrate why principle X applies to cases A and B but not to case C (which is, I believe, the requirement laid down by Professors Wechsler and Jaffe), he must, by the same token, also explain why the principle is defined as X rather than as X minus, which would cover A but not cases B and C, or as X plus, which would cover all cases, A, B and C. Similarly, he must explain why X is a proper principle of limitation on majority power at all. Why should he not choose non-X? If he may not choose lawlessly between cases in applying principle X, he may certainly not choose lawlessly in defining X or in choosing X, for principles are after all only organizations of cases into groups. To choose the principle and define it is to decide the cases.

It follows that the choice of "fundamental values" by the Court cannot be justified. Where constitutional materials do not clearly specify the value to be preferred, there is no principled way to prefer any claimed human value to any other. The judge must stick close to the text and the history, and their fair implications, and not construct new rights. The case just mentioned illustrates the point. The *Griswold* decision has been acclaimed by legal scholars as a major advance in constitutional law, a salutary demonstration of the Court's ability to protect fundamental human values. I regret to have to disagree, and my regret is all the more sincere because I once took the same position and did so in print. In extenuation I can only say that at the time I thought, quite erroneously, that new basic rights could be derived logically by finding and extrapolating a more general principle of individual autonomy underlying the particular guarantees of the Bill of Rights.

The Court's *Griswold* opinion, by Justice Douglas, and the array of concurring opinions, by Justices Goldberg, White and Harlan, all failed to justify the derivation of any principle used to strike down the Connecticut anti-contraceptive statute or to define the scope of the principle. Justice Douglas, to whose opinion I must confine myself, began by pointing out that "specific guarantees in the Bill of Rights have penumbras, formed by emanations from those guarantees that help give them life and substance." Nothing is exceptional there. In the case Justice Douglas cited, *NAACP v. Alabama,* the State was held unable to force disclosure of membership lists because of the chilling effect upon the rights of assembly and political action of the NAACP's members. The penumbra was created solely to preserve a value central to the first amendment, applied in this case through the fourteenth amendment. It had no life of its own as a right independent of the value specified by the first amendment.

But Justice Douglas then performed a miracle of transubstantiation. He called the first amendment's penumbra a protection of "privacy" and then asserted that other amendments create "zones of privacy." He had no better reason to use the word "privacy" than that the individual is free within these zones, free to act in public as well as in private. None of these penumbral zones—from the first, third, fourth or fifth amendments, all of which he cited, along with the ninth—covered the case before him. One more leap was required. Justice Douglas asserted that these various "zones of privacy" created an independent right of privacy, a right not lying within the penumbra of any specific amendment. He did not disclose, however, how a series of specified rights combined to create a new and unspecified right.

The *Griswold* opinion fails every test of neutrality. The derivation of the principle was utterly specious, and so was its definition. In fact, we are left with no idea of what the principle really forbids. Derivation and definition are interrelated here. Justice Douglas called the amendments and their penumbras "zones of privacy," though of course they are not that at all. They protect both private and public behavior and so would more properly be labelled "zones of freedom." If we follow Justice Douglas in his next step, these zones would then add up to an independent right of freedom, which is to say, a general constitutional right to be free of legal coercion, a manifest impossibility in any imaginable society.

Griswold, then, is an unprincipled decision, both in the way in which it derives a new constitutional right and in the way it defines that right, or rather fails to define it. We are left with no idea of the sweep of the right of privacy and hence no notion of the cases to which it may or may not be applied in the future. The truth is that the Court could not reach its result in *Griswold* through principle. The reason is obvious. Every clash between a minority claiming freedom and a majority claiming power to regulate involves a choice between the gratifications of the two groups. When the Constitution has not spoken, the Court will be able to find no scale, other than its own value preferences, upon which to weigh the respective claims to pleasure. Compare the facts in *Griswold* with a hypothetical suit by an electric utility company and one of its customers to void a smoke pollution ordinance as unconstitutional. The cases are identical.

In Griswold a husband and wife assert that they wish to have sexual relations without fear of unwanted children. The law impairs their sexual gratifications. The State can assert, and at one stage in that litigation did assert, that the majority finds the use of contraceptives immoral. Knowledge that it takes place and that the State makes no effort to inhibit it causes the majority anguish, impairs their gratifications.

The electrical company asserts that it wishes to produce electricity at low cost in order to reach a wide market and make profits. Its customer asserts that he wants a lower cost so that prices can be held low. The smoke pollution regulation impairs his and the company's stockholders' economic gratifications. The State can assert not only that the majority prefer clean air to lower prices, but also that the absence of the regulation impairs the majority's physical and aesthetic gratifications.

Neither case is covered specifically or by obvious implication in the Constitution. Unless we can distinguish forms of gratification, the only course for a principled Court is to let the majority have its way in both cases. It is clear that the Court cannot make the necessary distinction. There is no principled way to decide that one man's gratifications are more deserving of respect than another's or that one form of gratification is more worthy than another. Why is sexual gratification more worthy than moral gratification? Why is sexual gratification nobler than economic gratification? There is no way of deciding these matters other than by reference to some system of moral or ethical values that has no objective or intrinsic validity of its own and about which men can and do differ. Where the Constitution does not embody the moral or ethical choice, the judge has no basis other than his own values upon which to set aside the community judgment embodied in the statute. That, by definition, is an inadequate basis for judicial supremacy. The issue of the community's moral and ethical values, the issue of the degree of pain an activity causes, are matters concluded by the passage and enforcement of the laws in question. The judiciary has no role to play other than that of applying the statutes in a fair and impartial manner.

One of my colleagues refers to this conclusion, not without sarcasm, as the "Equal Gratification Clause." The phrase is apt, and I accept it, though not the sarcasm. Equality of human gratifications, where the document does not impose a hierarchy, is an essential part of constitutional doctrine because of the necessity that judges be principled. To be perfectly clear on the subject, I repeat that the principle is not applicable to legislatures. Legislation requires value choice and cannot be principled in the sense under discussion. Courts must accept any value choice the legislature makes unless it clearly runs contrary to a choice made in the framing of the Constitution.

It follows, of course, that broad areas of constitutional law ought to be reformulated. Most obviously, it follows that substantive due process, revived by the *Griswold* case, is and always has been an improper doctrine. Substantive due process requires the Court to say, without guidance from the Constitution, which liberties or gratifications may be infringed by majorities and which may not. This means that *Griswold*'s antecedents were also wrongly decided, *e.g., Meyer v. Nebraska,* which struck down a statute forbidding the teaching of subjects in any language other than English; *Pierce v. Society of Sisters,* which set aside a statute compelling all Oregon school children to attend public schools; *Adkins v. Children's Hospital,* which invalidated a statute of Congress authorizing a board to fix minimum wages for women and children in the District of Columbia; and *Lochner v. New York,* which voided a statute fixing maximum hours of work for bakers. With some of these cases I am in political agreement, and perhaps *Pierce*'s result could be reached on acceptable grounds, but there is no justification for the Court's methods. In *Lochner,* Justice Peckham, defending liberty from what he conceived as a mere meddlesome interference, asked, "[A]re we all . . . at the mercy of legislative majorities?" The correct answer, where the Constitution does not speak, must be yes.

Mark V. Tushnet, *Following the Rules Laid Down: A Critique of Interpretivism and Neutral Principles,* 96 HARV. L. REV. 781 (1983)*

* * *

II. INTERPRETIVISM AND HISTORICAL KNOWLEDGE

* * *

The dilemma of interpretivism is that, if it is to rely on a real grasp of the framers' intentions—and only this premise gives interpretivism its intuitive appeal—its method must be hermeneutic, but if it adopts a hermeneutic approach, it is foreclosed from achieving the determinacy about the framers' meanings necessary to serve its underlying goals. The interpretivists' premise of determinate intentions is essential to their project of developing constraints on judges. But the hermeneutic approach to historical understanding requires that we abandon this premise. In imaginatively entering the world of the past, we not only reconstruct it, but—more importantly for present purposes—we also creatively construct it. For such creativity is the only way to bridge the gaps between that world and ours. The past, particularly the aspects that the interpretivists care about, is in its essence indeterminate; the interpretivist project cannot be carried to its conclusion.

Consider an example. We have already seen that interpretivism's most plausible version leads one to conclude that school segregation is not unconstitutional. In *Brown v. Board of Education*, however, the Supreme Court said, "In approaching this problem, we cannot turn the clock back to 1868 when the [Fourteenth] Amendment was adopted. . . . We must consider public education in the light of its full development and its present place in American life throughout the Nation." Chief Justice Warren was not rejecting the use of historical inquiries in constitutional law; he was instead approaching the task of discovering the past in a hermeneutic way.

Suppose that we did turn back the clock so that we could talk to the framers of the fourteenth amendment. If we asked them whether the amendment outlawed segregation in public schools, they would answer "No." But we could pursue our conversation by asking them what they had in mind when they thought about public education. We would find out that they had in mind a relatively new and peripheral social institution designed (say) to civilize the lower classes. In contrast, they thought that freedom of contract was extremely important because it was the foundation of individual achievement, and they certainly wanted to outlaw racial discrimination with respect to this freedom. Returning to 1954 and the question for the Court in *Brown*, we might, in an antic moment, challenge the interpretivists with their own weapons. Our hermeneutic enterprise has shown us that public education as it exists today—a central institution for the achievement of individual goals—is in fact the functional equivalent not of public education in 1868, but of freedom of contract in 1868. Thus, *Brown* was correctly decided in light of a hermeneutic interpretivism.

The problem raised by this interpretation of *Brown* is that the need to identify functional equivalents over time necessarily imports significant indeterminacy—and therefore discretion—into the interpretivist account; alternative hermeneutic accounts of *Brown* are also possible. Consider, for example, the implications of Herbert Wechsler's argument that *Brown* was problematic because it failed to consider the effect of desegregation on the interest of white parents and students in associating only with those of whom they approved. A hermeneutic defense of that criticism might argue that education today is an important part of American civil religion and that it is therefore the secular functional equivalent of true religion in 1868. The framers would certainly have considered forced association in churches to be improper; thus, Wechsler's point is established. Interpretivists claim that their approach is at least able to limit judges, but, by allowing judges to look hermeneutically for functional equivalents, interpretivism reintroduces the discretion that it was intended to eliminate.

But the difficulty runs deeper than the indeterminacy of identifications of functional equivalents. The hermeneutic tradition tells us that we cannot understand the acts of those in the past without entering into their mental world. Because we live in our own world, the only way to begin the hermeneutic enterprise is by thinking about what in our world initially seems like what people in the past talked and thought about. Usually we begin with a few areas in which we and they use the same rather abstract words to talk about apparently similar things. Thus, we and the framers share a concern for democracy, human rights, and limited government. But as we read what the framers said about democracy and limited government, we notice discontinuities: they described their polity as a democratic one, for example, when we would think it obviously nondemocratic. As we examine this evidence, we adjust our understanding and attempt to take account of the "peculiarities." With a great deal of imaginative effort, we can indeed at the end of the process understand their world, because we have become immersed in it. But the understanding we achieve is not the unique, correct image of the framers' world. On the contrary, our imaginative immersion is only one of a great many possible reconstructions of that segment of the past, a reconstruction shaped not only by the character of the past, but also by our own interests, concerns, and preconceptions. The imagination that we have used to adjust and readjust our understandings makes it impossible to claim that any one reconstruction is uniquely correct. The past shapes the materials on which we use our imaginations; our interests, concerns, and preconceptions shape our imaginations themselves.

* * *

Nonetheless, the hermeneutic tradition does identify something that constitutional theory should take seriously. The point is not, as some fanatic adherents of hermeneutic method might have it, that, because the world of the past is not the world in which we have developed our ways of understanding how others act, we can never understand that past world. That view would go too far. We can gain an interpretive understanding of the past by working from commonalities in the use of large abstractions to reach the unfamiliar particulars of what those abstractions really meant in the past. The commonalities are what make the past *our* past; they are the links between two segments of a single community that extends over time. The commonalities are both immanent in our history and constructed by us as we reflect on what our history is. Interpretivism goes wrong in thinking that the commonalities are greater than they really are, but we would go equally wrong if we denied that they exist. The task is to think through the implications of our continued dedication to the large abstractions when the particulars of the world have changed so drastically. That project will lead us to face questions about the kind of community we have and want.

III. NEUTRAL PRINCIPLES AND THE RECOGNITION OF RULES

The hermeneutic tradition suggests that historical discontinuities are so substantial that interpretivism must make incoherent claims because it can achieve the necessary determinacy of past intentions only at the cost of an implausible claim about consistency of meaning across time. The theory of neutral principles fails for similar reasons. It requires that we develop an account of consistency of meaning— particularly of the meaning of rules or principles—within liberal society. Yet the atomistic premises of liberalism treat each of us as autonomous individuals whose choices and values are independent of those made and held by others. These premises make it exceedingly difficult to develop such an account of consistent meaning. The autonomous producer of choice and value is also an autonomous producer of meaning.

The rule of law, according to the liberal conception, is meant to protect us against the exercise of arbitrary power. The theory of neutral principles asserts that a requirement of consistency, the core of the ideal of the rule of law, places sufficient bounds on judges to reduce the risk of arbitrariness to an acceptable level. The question is whether the concepts of neutrality and consistency can be developed in ways that are adequate for the task. My discussion examines various candidates for a definition of neutrality, beginning with a crude definition and moving toward more sophisticated ones. Yet each candidate suffers from similar defects: each fails to provide the kinds of constraints on judges that liberalism requires. Some candidates seek to limit the results judges might reach, others the methods they may use. The supposed substantive bounds that consistency imposes on judges, however, are either empty or parasitic on other substantive theories of constitutional law, and the methodological bounds are either empty or dependent on a sociology of law that undermines liberalism's assumptions about society.

A. Neutral Content

Robert Bork's version of neutral principles theory would require that decisions rest on principles that are neutral in content and in application. Bork's formulation may be an attempt to generalize Wechsler's definition, which characterizes neutrality as judicial indifference to who the winner is. For Wechsler, such indifference was a matter of judicial willingness to apply the present case's rule in the next case as well, regardless whether the beneficiary in the later case was less attractive than the earlier winner in ways not made relevant by the rule itself. Neutral content for Bork might mean a similar indifference, but now within the case: the principle governing the case should be developed in a form that employs only general terms and that avoids any express preference for any named groups. This outcome, however, is impossible. We might coherently require that rules not use proper names, but there is no principled way to distinguish between the general terms that in effect pick out specific groups or individuals and those that are "truly" general. Any general term serves to identify some specific group; hence if the notion of content neutrality is to make any sense, it must depend on a prior understanding of which kinds of distinctions are legitimately "neutral" and which are not. The demand for neutrality in content thus cannot provide an independent criterion for acceptable decisions.

Standing alone, the theory that principles must be neutral in content cannot constrain judicial discretion. But it could be coupled with some other theory—such as interpretivism, Ely's reinforcement of representation, or a moral philosophy. When coordinated with some such substantive theory, the demand for neutral principles stipulates that a decision is justified only if the principles derived from the other theory are neutrally applied. Yet to require neutral application of the principles of the other theory is merely to apply those principles in given cases; the requirement of content neutrality adds nothing.

B. Neutral Method

If neutrality is to serve as a meaningful guide, it must be understood not as a standard for the content of principles, but rather as a constraint on the process by which principles are selected, justified, and applied. Thus, the remaining candidate explications of neutrality all focus on the judicial process and the need for "neutral *application*." This focus transfers our attention from the principles themselves to the judges who purport to use them.

* * *

1. Prospective Application.—What then are methodologically neutral principles? To Wechsler, such principles are identified primarily by a forward-looking aspect: a judge who invokes a principle in a specific instance commits himself or herself to invoking it in future cases that are relevantly identical. For example, a judge who justifies the holding in *Brown v. Board of Education* that segregated schools are unconstitutional by invoking the principle that the state may not take race into account in any significant policy decision is thereby also committed to holding state-developed affirmative action programs unconstitutional. The judge's interior monologue involves specifying the principle about to be invoked, imagining future cases and their proper resolution, determining whether those cases are different from the present one in any ways that the proposed principle itself says are relevant, and asking whether the principle yields the proper results.

There are two levels of problems with the idea that commitment to prospective neutral application constrains judicial choices. First, there are two features of our judicial institutions that dissipate any constraining force that the demand for prospective neutrality may impose. Second, there is a conceptual problem that robs the very idea of prospective neutrality of any normative force.

(a) Institutional Problems.—The first institutional problem is that Supreme Court decisions are made by a collective body, which is constrained by a norm of compromise and cooperation. Suppose that in case 1 Justices M, N, and O have taken neutral principles theory to heart and believe that the correct result is justified by principle A. Justices P, Q, R, and S have done likewise but believe that the same result is justified by principle B. Justices T and V, who also accept principle A but believe it inapplicable to case 1, dissent. The four-person group gains control of the writing of the opinion, and the three others who agree with the result accede to the institutional pressure for majority decisions and join an opinion that invokes principle B. Now case 2 arises. Justices T and V are convinced that, because case 2 is relevantly different from case 1, principle A should be used. They join with Justices M, N, and O and produce a majority opinion invoking principle A. If principle B were used, the result would be different; thus, there are four dissenters.

Kent Greenawalt has argued that neutral principles theory is required to acknowledge that neutrality sometimes must yield to other considerations, such as the institutional pressure for majority decisions. If the norm of compromise is thought to authorize submersion of individual views in the selection of principles, we could not charge anyone with prospective nonneutrality in the handling of case 1. When case 2 subsequently arises, however, it would be odd—and ultimately destructive of the willingness to compromise—to demand that Justices M, N, and O follow principle B to a result that they, on principled grounds, believe wrong. But at the same time, to allow a judge criticized for nonneutrality to reply that in the particular situation neutrality had to yield to more pressing circumstances is to give the game of theory away. If we allow neutrality to yield to the institutional need here (a need that is quite weak—we all can live with fragmented Courts and decisions), a sufficiently pressing need will likely be available to justify virtually any deviation from neutrality.

A second institutional problem is that prospective neutrality involves unreasonable expectations concerning the capacities of judges. Every present case is connected to every conceivable future case, in the sense that a skilled lawyer can demonstrate how the earlier case's principles ought to affect (although perhaps not determine) the outcome in any later case. In these circumstances, neutral application means that each decision constrains a judge in every future decision; the import of the prospective approach is that, the first time a judge decides a case, he or she is to some extent committed to particular decisions for the rest of his or her career.

There are two difficulties here. First, even if we confine our attention to cases in the same general area as the present one, this formulation of the neutrality requirement is obviously too stringent. We cannot and should not expect judges to have fully elaborated theories of race discrimination in their first cases, much less theories of gender, illegitimacy, and other modes of discrimination as well. Second, to the extent that perceptions of connections vary with skill, the theory has the curious effect of constraining only the better judges. The less skilled judge will not think to test a principle developed in a race-discrimination case against gender-discrimination or abortion cases; a more skilled judge will.

Wechsler responded to these difficulties by relaxing the requirement: the judge must test the principle against "applications that are now foreseeable," and must either agree with the result in such applications or be able to specify a relevant difference between the cases. But now the judge charged with nonneutrality will often be able to defend by saying that he or she simply had not foreseen the case at hand when the prior one was decided. That defense may lead us to conclude that the judge is not terribly competent, but it defeats the charge of nonneutrality.

(b) Conceptual Difficulty.—The third, largely conceptual difficulty with the theory of neutral principles was foreshadowed by the example of a case whose result could be justified by either of two principles. Neutral application requires that we be able to identify *the* principle that justified the result in case 1 in order to be sure that it is neutrally applied in case 2. This requirement, however, cannot be fulfilled, because there are always a number of justificatory principles available to make sense of case 1 and a number of techniques to select the "true" basis of case 1. Of course, the opinion in case 1 will articulate a principle that purports to support the result. But the thrust of introductory law courses is to show that the principles offered in opinions are never good enough. And this indefiniteness bedevils—and liberates—not only the commentators and the lawyers and judges subsequently dealing with the decision; it equally affects the author of the opinion.

* * *

. . . At the moment a decision is announced, we cannot identify the principle that it embodies. Even when we take account of the language of the opinion, each decision can be traced to many different possible principles, and we often learn the justifying principle of case 1 only when a court in case 2 states it. Behind the court's statement of what case I meant lies all the creativity to which the hermeneutic theory of historical understanding directed our attention. . . . The theory of neutral principles thus loses almost all of its constraining force when neutrality has a prospective meaning. What is left is something like a counsel to judges that they be sincere within the limits of their ability. But this formulation hardly provides a reassuring constraint on judicial willfulness.

2. *Retrospective Application.*—Although Wechsler framed the neutral principles theory in prospective terms, it might be saved by recasting it in retrospective terms. The theory would then impose as a necessary condition for justification the requirement that a decision be consistent with the relevant precedents. This tack links the theory to general approaches to precedent-based judicial decisionmaking in nonconstitutional areas. It also captures the natural way in which we raise questions about neutrality. The prospective theory requires that we pose hypothetical future cases, apply the principle, and ask whether the judges really meant to resolve the hypothetical cases as the principle seems to require. Because the hypothetical cases have not arisen, we cannot know the answer; we can do little more than raise our eyebrows, as Wechsler surely did, and emphasize the "really" as we ask the question in a skeptical tone.

. . . We need only compare case 2, which is now decided, with case 1 to see if a principle from case 1 has been neutrally applied in case 2. But if the retrospective demand is merely that the opinion in case 2 deploy some reading of the earlier case from which the holding in case 2 follows, the openness of the precedents means that the demand can always be satisfied. And if the demand is rather that the holding be derived from the principles actually articulated in the relevant precedents, differences between case 2 and the precedents will inevitably demand a degree of reinterpretation of the old principles. New cases always present issues different from those settled by prior cases. Thus, to decide a new case, a judge must take some liberties with the old principles, if they are to be applied at all. There is, however, no principled way to determine how many liberties can be taken; hence this second reading of the retrospective approach likewise provides no meaningful constraints.

The central problem here is that, given the difficulty of isolating a single principle for which a given precedent stands, we lack any criteria for distinguishing between cases that depart from and those that conform to the principles of their precedents. In fact, any case can compellingly be placed in either category. Although such a universal claim cannot be validated by example, examples can at least make the claim plausible. Therefore, the following paragraphs present several instances of cases that simultaneously depart from and conform to their precedents.

The first is *Griswold v. Connecticut*, in which the Supreme Court held that a state could not constitutionally prohibit the dissemination of contraceptive information or devices to married people. *Griswold* relied in part on *Pierce v. Society of Sisters*, which held unconstitutional a requirement that children attend public rather than private schools, and *Meyer v. Nebraska*, which held that a state could not prohibit the teaching of foreign languages to young children. In *Griswold*, the Court said that these cases relied on a constitutionally protected interest, conveniently labeled "privacy," that was identical to the interest implicated in the contraceptive case.

On one view, *Griswold* tortures these precedents. Both were old-fashioned due process cases, which emphasized interference "with the calling of modern language teachers . . . and with the power of parents to control the education of their own." On this view, the most one can fairly find in *Meyer* and *Pierce* is a principle about freedom of inquiry that is rather narrower than a principle of privacy. Yet of course one can say with equal force that *Griswold* identifies for us the true privacy principle of *Meyer* and *Pierce*, in the same way that the abortion funding cases identify the true principle of *Roe v. Wade*. Just as hermeneutic interpretivism emphasizes the creativity that is involved when judges impute to the framers a set of intentions, so the retrospective approach to neutral principles must recognize the extensive creativity exercised by a judge when he or she imputes to a precedent "the" principle that justifies both the precedent and the judge's present holding.

A second example is *Brandenburg v. Ohio*. The state of Ohio had prosecuted a leader of the Ku Klux Klan for violating its criminal syndicalism statute, which prohibited advocating the propriety of violence as a means of political reform. The Court held that the conviction violated the first amendment, which, according to the decision, permits punishment of advocacy of illegal conduct only when "such advocacy is directed to inciting or producing imminent lawless action and is likely to incite or produce such action." Remarkably, the Court derived this test from *Dennis v. United States*, in which the Court had upheld convictions of leaders of the Communist Party for violating a federal sedition law. This reading was, to say the least, an innovative interpretation of *Dennis*, which explicitly stated a different test—"the gravity of the 'evil,' discounted by its improbability"—that left the decision largely to the jury. Putting aside the obvious effects of cold war hysteria on the 1951 decision in *Dennis*, a dispassionate observer would find it hard to reconcile the results in *Dennis* and *Brandenburg*. But again the requirement of retrospective neutrality may be satisfied if we interpret *Brandenburg*'s use of *Dennis* as the creative reworking of precedents within fair bounds.

* * *

The difficulties with this variety of neutral principles theory are on a par with the problems in understanding interpretivism that were noted earlier. Understanding the intentions of the framers required a special kind of creative re-creation of the past; the creativity involved in such a re-creation dashed any hopes that interpretivism could effectively constrain judicial decisions, because many alternative re-creations of the framers' intentions on any given issue are always possible. In the same way, the result of the inquiry into retrospective neutral principles theory indicates that, though it is possible to discuss a given decision's consistency with previous precedents, requiring consistency of this kind similarly fails to constrain judges sufficiently and thereby fails to advance the underlying liberal project.

3. The Craft Interpretation.—This critique of the retrospective-application interpretation points the way to a more refined version—what I will term the craft interpretation—of the calls of the neutral principles theorists for retrospective consistency. The failings of this final alternative bring out the underlying reasons that the demand for consistency cannot do the job expected of it.

The preceding discussion has reminded us that each decision reworks its precedents. A decision picks up some threads that received little emphasis before, and places great stress on them. It deprecates what seemed important before by emphasizing the factual setting of the precedents. The techniques are well known; indeed, learning them is at the core of a good legal education. But they are techniques. This recognition suggests that we attempt to define consistency as a matter of craft. When push comes to shove, in fact, adherents of neutral principles simply offer us lyrical descriptions of the sense of professionalism in lieu of sharper characterizations of the constraints on judges. Charles Black, for example, attempts to resolve the question whether law can rely on neutral principles by depicting "the art of law" living between the two poles of subjective preference and objective validation in much the same way that "the art of music has its life somewhere between traffic noise and a tuning fork—more disciplined by far than the one, with an unfathomably complex inner discipline of its own, far richer than the other, with inexhaustible variety of resource." The difficulty then is to specify the limits to permissible craftiness. One limit may be that a judge cannot lie about the precedents—for example, by grossly mischaracterizing the facts. And Black adds that "decision [must] be taken in knowledge of and with consideration of certainly known facts of public life," such as the fact that segregation necessarily degrades blacks. But these limits are clearly not terribly restrictive, and no one has suggested helpful others.

If the craft interpretation cannot specify limits to craftiness, another alternative is to identify some decisions that are within and some that are outside the limits in order to provide the basis for an inductive and intuitive generalization. As the following discussion indicates, however, it turns out that the limits of craft are so broad that in any interesting case any reasonably skilled lawyer can reach whatever result he or she wants. The craft interpretation thus fails to constrain the results that a reasonably skilled judge can reach, and leaves the judge free to enforce his or her personal values, as long as the opinions enforcing those values are well written. Such an outcome is inconsistent with the requirements of liberalism in that, once again, the demand for neutral principles fails in any appreciable way to limit the possibility of judicial tyranny.

The debate over the propriety of the result in *Roe v. Wade* illustrates this problem. It seems to be generally agreed that, as a matter of simple craft, Justice Blackmun's opinion for the Court was dreadful. The central issue before the Court was whether a pregnant woman had a constitutionally protected interest in terminating her pregnancy. When his opinion reached that issue, Justice Blackmun simply listed a number of cases in which "a right of personal privacy, or a guarantee of certain areas or zones of privacy," had been recognized. Then he said, "This right of privacy, whether it be founded in the Fourteenth Amendment's concept of personal liberty . . . or . . . in the Ninth Amendment's reservation of rights to the people, is broad enough to encompass a woman's decision whether or not to terminate her pregnancy." And that was it. I will provisionally concede that this "argument" does not satisfy the requirements of the craft.

But the conclusion that we are to draw faces two challenges: it is either uninteresting or irrelevant to constitutional theory. Insofar as *Roe* gives us evidence, we can conclude that Justice Blackmun is a terrible judge. The point of constitutional theory, though, would seem to be to keep judges in line. If the result in *Roe* can be defended by judges more skilled than Justice Blackmun, the requirements of the craft would mean only that good judges can do things that bad judges cannot without subjecting themselves to professional criticism.

There is in fact a cottage industry of constitutional law scholars who concoct revised opinions for controversial decisions. Thus, the craft interpretation of neutrality in application is ultimately uninteresting for reasons that we have already seen. At most it provides a standard to measure the competence of judges, a standard that by itself is insufficient to constrain adequately the risk of tyranny.

The other difficulty with the craft interpretation runs deeper. Craft limitations make sense only if we can agree what the craft is. But consider the craft of "writing novels." Its practice includes Trollope writing *The Eustace Diamonds*, Joyce writing *Finnegan's Wake*, and Mailer writing *The Executioner's Song*. We might think of Justice Blackmun's opinion in *Roe* as an innovation akin to Joyce's or Mailer's. It is the totally unreasoned judicial opinion. To say that it does not look like Justice Powell's decision in some other case is like saying that a Cubist "portrait" does not look like its subject as a member of the Academy would paint it. The observation is true, but irrelevant both to the enterprise in which the artist or judge was engaged and to our ultimate assessment of his product.

C. Rules and Institutions

We can now survey our progress in the attempt to define "neutral principles." Each proposed definition left us with judges who could enforce their personal values unconstrained by the suggested version of the neutrality requirement. Some of the more sophisticated candidates, such as the craft interpretation, seemed plausible because they appealed to an intuitive sense that the institution of judging involves people who are guided by and committed to general rules applied consistently. But the very notions of generality and consistency can be specified only by reference to an established institutional setting. We can know what we mean by "acting consistently" only if we understand the institution of judging in our society. Thus, neutral principles theory proves unable to satisfy its demand for rule-guided judicial decisionmaking in a way that can constrain or define the judicial institution; in the final analysis, it is the institution—or our conception of it—that constrains the concept of rule-guidedness.

Consider the following multiple choice question: "Which pair of numbers comes next in the series 1, 3, 5, 7? (a) 9, 11; (b) 11, 13; (c) 25, 18." It is easy to show that any of the answers is correct. The first is correct if the rule generating the series is "list the odd numbers"; the second is correct if the rule is "list the odd prime numbers"; and the third is correct if a more complex rule generates the series. Thus, if asked to follow the underlying rule—the "principle" of the series—we can justify a tremendous range of divergent answers by constructing the rule so that it generates the answer that we want. As the legal realists showed, this result obtains for legal as well as mathematical rules. The situation in law might be thought to differ, because judges try to articulate the rules they use. But even when an earlier case identifies the rule that it invokes, only a vision of the contours of the judicial role constrains judges' understanding of what counts as applying the rule. Without such a vision, there will always be a diversity of subsequent uses of the rule that could fairly be called consistent applications of it.

There is, however, something askew in this anarchic conclusion. After all, we know that no test maker would accept (c) as an answer to the mathematical problem; and indeed we can be fairly confident that test makers would not include both (a) and (b) as possible answers, because the underlying rules that generate them are so obvious that they make the question fatally ambiguous. Another example may sharpen the point. The examination for those seeking driver's licenses in the District of Columbia includes this question: "What is responsible for most automobile accidents? (a) The car; (b) the driver; (c) road conditions." Anyone who does not know immediately that the answer is (b) does not understand what the testing enterprise is all about.

In these examples, we know something about the rule to follow only because we are familiar with the social practices of intelligence testing and drivers' education. That is, the answer does not follow from a rule that can be uniquely identified without specifying something about the substantive practices. Similarly, although we can, as I have argued elsewhere, use standard techniques of legal argument to draw from the decided cases the conclusion that the Constitution requires socialism, we know that no judge will in the near future draw that conclusion. But the failure to reach that result is not ensured because the practice of "following rules" or neutral application of the principles inherent in the decided cases precludes a judge from doing so. Rather, it is ensured because judges in contemporary America are selected in a way that keeps them from thinking that such arguments make sense. This branch of the argument thus makes a sociological point about neutral principles. Neither the principles nor any reconstructed version of a theory that takes following rules as its focus can be neutral in the sense that liberalism requires, because taken by itself, an injunction to follow the rules tells us nothing of substance. If such a theory constrains judges, it does so only because judges, before they turn to the task of finding neutral principles for the case at hand, have implicitly accepted some image of what their role in shaping and applying rules in controverted cases ought to be.

There is something both odd and important here. The theory of neutral principles is initially attractive because it affirms the openness of the courts to all reasonable arguments drawn from decided cases. But if the courts are indeed open to such arguments, the theory allows judges to do whatever they want. If it is only in consequence of the pressures exerted by a highly developed, deeply entrenched, homeostatic social structure that judges seem to eschew conclusions grossly at odds with the values of liberal capitalism, sociological analysis ought to destroy the attraction of neutral principles theory. Principles are "neutral" only in the sense that they are, as a matter of contingent fact, unchallenged, and the contingencies have obvious historical limits.

At the same time, however, the theory shows us an institution at the heart of liberalism that contains the potential for destroying liberalism by revealing the institution's inconsistencies and its dialectical instability. The neutral rule of law was Locke's solution to the Hobbesian problem of order. But the rule of law requires that preexisting rules be followed. If we accept substantive limitations on the rules that courts can adopt, we abandon the notion of rule-following as a neutral enterprise with no social content; yet if we truly allow all reasonable arguments to be made and possibly accepted, we abandon the notion of rule-following entirely, and with it we abandon the ideal of the rule of law. What is odd is that liberalism has generated an institution that reveals these irresolvable tensions.

IV. CONCLUSION

The critiques of interpretivism and neutral principles have each led to the same point. To be coherent, each theory requires that our understandings of social institutions be stable. Interpretivism requires that judges today be able to trace historical continuities between the institutions the framers knew and those that contemporary judges know. The theory of neutral principles requires that judges be able to rely on a shared conception of the proper role of judicial reasoning. The critiques have established that there are no determinate continuities derivable from history or legal principle. Rather, judges must choose which conceptions to rely on . . ..

Thomas C. Grey, *Do We Have an Unwritten Constitution,* 27 STAN. L. REV. 703 (1975)*

It seems to me that the courts do appropriately apply values not articulated in the constitutional text, and appropriately apply them in determining the constitutionality of legislation.

This view, it seems to me, tacitly underlies much of the affirmative constitutional doctrine developed by the courts over the last generation. The trouble is that the view has been too tacit. It has not been clearly stated and articulately defended, as basic constitutional doctrine should be. Nor, for that matter, has the opposing general view received adequate theoretical statement and defense—except by Mr. Justice Black. Unfortunately, the professional world concerned with constitutional law has not taken Mr. Justice Black's theoretical position sufficiently seriously. Perhaps there was too much of a tendency to accept at face value the great Justice's pose as a rather old-fashioned and simple-minded country lawyer, with sound intuition and a good nose for the concrete issues, but lacking any claim to jurisprudential sophistication.

If the articles by Messrs. Bork, Linde, and Ely mark the emergence of an important trend—as I suspect they do—this basic theoretical issue will no longer be swept under the rug. These critics simply cannot be dismissed as unsophisticates or out-of-date legal primitives.

The truth is that the view of constitutional adjudication that they share with Mr. Justice Black is one of great power and compelling simplicity. That view is deeply rooted in our history and in our shared principles of political legitimacy. It has equally deep roots in our formal constitutional law; it is, after all, the theory upon which judicial review was founded in *Marbury v. Madison.*

The chief virtue of this view is that it supports judicial review while answering the charge that the practice is undemocratic. Under the pure interpretive model (as I shall henceforth call the view in question), when a court strikes down a popular statute or practice as unconstitutional, it may always reply to the resulting public outcry: "We didn't do it—you did." The people have chosen the principle that the statute or practice violated, have designated it as fundamental, and have written it down in

---

the text of the Constitution for the judges to interpret and apply. The task of interpretation of the people's commands may not always be simple or mechanical; there is no warrant to condemn Mr. Justice Black or his allies with the epithet "mechanical jurisprudence." But the task remains basically one of interpretation, the application of fixed and binding norms to new facts.

The contrary view of judicial review, the one that I espouse and that seems to me implicit in much of the constitutional law developed by the courts, does not deny that the Constitution is a written document, expressing some clear and positive restraints upon governmental power. Nor does it deny that part of the business of judicial review consists of giving effect to these explicit commands.

Where the broader view of judicial review diverges from the pure interpretive model is in its acceptance of the courts' additional role as the expounder of basic national ideals of individual liberty and fair treatment, even when the content of these ideals is not expressed as a matter of positive law in the written Constitution. It must at once be conceded that such a role for our courts is more difficult to justify than is the role assigned by the pure interpretive model. Why, one asks, are the courts better able to discern and articulate basic national ideals than are the people's politically responsible representatives? And one recalls Learned Hand's remark that he would find it "most irksome to be ruled by a bevy of Platonic Guardians, even if I knew how to choose them, which I assuredly do not."

These grave difficulties no doubt explain, although they do not excuse, the tendency of our courts—today as throughout our history—to resort to bad legislative history and strained reading of constitutional language to support results that would be better justified by explication of contemporary moral and political ideals not drawn from the constitutional text. Of course, this tendency of the courts in no way helps to establish the legitimacy of noninterpretive judicial review. Indeed, standing alone it tends to establish the opposite; for if judges resort to bad interpretation in preference to honest exposition of deeply held but unwritten ideals, it must be because they perceive the latter mode of decisionmaking to be of suspect legitimacy.

However, the tendency to slipshod history and text-parsing does not stand alone. The courts do not only effectuate unwritten ideals and values covertly. Rather, in a very large proportion of their important constitutional decisions, they proceed in a mode that is openly noninterpretive. If this assertion seems at first glance surprising, it may be so partly because of the way in which constitutional law is taught in our law schools.

In the academic teaching of constitutional law, the general question of the legitimacy of judicial review is addressed largely through the vehicle of *Marbury v. Madison*. Students examine the arguments made for judicial review by Chief Justice Marshall, and perhaps contrast them with some of the counterarguments of later judges or commentators. The discussion concludes with the point that, whatever the validity of those arguments as an original matter, history has firmly decided in favor of judicial review. Thereafter, debates about judicial review focus on the question of how "activist" or how "deferential" it should be. It is always assumed to be the single unitary practice established and justified in *Marbury*.

This seems to me a seriously misleading way of proceeding. *Marbury* defends (and its detractors attack) what I have here called the pure interpretive model of judicial review. The case itself involves the close interpretation of a technical and explicit constitutional provision, which is found, upon conventional linguistic analysis, to conflict with a statute. The argument for judicial review as a general matter is made in terms appropriate to that sort of case. Chief Justice Marshall's stress is on the *writ-*

tenness of the Constitution, and on its supremacy in cases of clear conflict with ordinary law. His heuristic examples all involve obvious conflicts between hypothetical (and unlikely) statutes on the one hand, and particularly explicit constitutional commands on the other.

All this makes *Marbury* a most atypical constitutional case, and an inappropriate paradigm for the sort of judicial review that has been important and controversial throughout our history, from *Dred Scott* to the *Legal Tender Cases* to *Lochner* to *Carter Coal* and on to *Brown v. Board of Education, Baker v.* Carr, and the Death Penalty and Abortion cases in our own day. In the important cases, reference to and analysis of the constitutional text plays a minor role. The dominant norms of decision are those large conceptions of governmental structure and individual rights that are at best referred to, and whose content is scarcely at all specified, in the written Constitution—dual federalism, vested rights, fair procedure, equality before the law.

The question of the legitimacy of this very different sort of judicial review is scarcely addressed, much less concluded, by the arguments of *Marbury v. Madison*. To approach that question, we might better examine the debate between Justices Chase and Iredell in *Calder v. Bull*. And if exposure to the matchless rhetoric of John Marshall is desired, *Fletcher v. Peck* provides an excellent example. In that case, the Georgia statute is struck down on two alternative grounds. The first is a strained interpretation of the contract clause, comparable in flimsiness to some of the poorer interpretive efforts of the Warren Court. The second ground is expressed in the Court's conclusion that the statute violates "general principles which are common to our free institutions"—in particular, the principle of the inviolability of vested rights. Conspicuously absent is a dissent arguing that this principle is nowhere stated in the constitutional text. Indeed, the other opinion in the case—that of Justice Johnson—expresses agreement with the result on the ground of "general principles," but disavows the strained reading of the contract clause.

The parallel between *Fletcher* and most contemporary judicial review is striking. Today, the Court will formally invoke one of the majestic generalities of the Constitution, typically the due process or equal protection clause, as the textual basis for its decision. Even this much specificity is not always vouchsafed us. Thus we are told of the constitutional "right to travel" that the Court has "no occasion to ascribe the source of this right to . . . a particular constitutional provision." And in the Abortion Cases, the Court's reference to the textual cover for the "right of privacy" is strikingly casual:

> This right of privacy, whether it be founded in the Fourteenth Amendment's concept of personal liberty and restrictions upon state action, as we feel it is, or, as the District Court determined, in the Ninth Amendment's reservation of rights to the people, is broad enough to encompass a woman's decision whether or not to terminate her pregnancy.

It should be clear that in these cases the Court is quite openly not relying on constitutional text for the content of the substantive principles it is invoking to invalidate legislation. The parallel reliance on the ninth amendment and the due process clause in the Abortion Cases is instructive on the point. The ninth amendment on its face has no substantive content. It is rather a license to constitutional decisionmakers to look beyond the substantive commands of the constitutional text to protect fundamental rights not expressed therein. In this case at least, the due process clause is being used in the same way.

Much of our substantive constitutional doctrine is of this kind. Where it arises "under" some piece of constitutional text, the text is not invoked as the source of the values or principles that rule the cases. Rather the broad textual provisions are seen as sources of legitimacy for judicial development and explication of basic shared national values. These values may be seen as permanent and universal features of human social arrangements—natural law principles—as they typically were in the 18th and 19th centuries. Or they may be seen as relative to our particular civilization, and subject to growth and change, as they typically are today. Our characteristic contemporary metaphor is "the living Constitution"—a constitution with provisions suggesting restraints on government in the name of basic rights, yet sufficiently unspecific to permit the judiciary to elucidate the development and change in the content of those rights over time.

This view of constitutional adjudication is at war with the pure interpretive model. As Mr. Justice Black said often and forcefully enough, he had no truck with the notion of changing, flexible, "living" constitutional guarantees. The amendment process was the framers' chosen and exclusive method of adopting constitutional values to changing times; the judiciary was to enforce the Constitution's substantive commands as the framers meant them.

This is not to say that the interpretive model is incompatible with one limited sense of the concept of a "living" constitution. The model can contemplate the application of the framers' value judgments and institutional arrangements to new or changed factual circumstances. In that sense, its proponents can endorse Chief Justice Marshall's view of the Constitution as "intended to endure for ages to come, and consequently, to be adapted to the various crises of human affairs."

But the interpretive model cannot be reconciled with constitutional doctrines protecting unspecified "essential" or "fundamental" liberties, or "fair procedure," or "decency"—leaving it to the judiciary to give moral content to those conceptions either once and for all or from age to age. That sort of "interpretation" would drain from the interpretive model its animating strength. Once it was adopted, the courts could no longer honestly defend an unpopular decision to a protesting public with the transfer of responsibility: "We didn't do it—you did." No longer would the Court's constitutional role be the technical and professional one of applying given norms to changing facts; instead the Court would assume the large and problematic role of discerning a society's most basic contemporary values.

* * *

Gerard E. Lynch, *Review of John Hart Ely's*, Democracy and Distrust, 80 COLUM. L. REV. 857, 857-64 (1980)*

* * *

Professor Ely wants to reject both sides of what most writers have seen as the fundamental division between theories of judicial review that are interpretivist and ones that are noninterpretivist—"the former indicating that judges deciding constitutional issues should confine themselves to enforcing norms that are stated or clearly implicit in the written Constitution, the latter the contrary view that courts should go beyond that set of references and enforce norms that cannot be discovered within the four corners of the document." As Professor Ely rightly recognizes, each theory "racks up rhetorical points by exposing the unacceptability of the only alternative." In this war of destruction, Professor Ely suggests that both sides are correct, for both theories are indeed unacceptable.

The interpretivists are Professor Ely's first target. However unfashionable in the academy, interpretivism remains a kind of conventional wisdom; the courts, for example, inevitably purport, except in the very last resort, to fit their interventions into an interpretivist mold. Professor Ely suggests two reasons for "the allure of interpretivism": first, that doctrine "better fits our usual conceptions of what law is and the way it works," and second, its opposite faces "obvious difficulties . . . in trying to reconcile itself with the underlying democratic theory of our government."

But if interpretivism has its allure, it also has serious problems. Academic critics frequently argue the case against a narrow concentration on the intentions of the framers of constitutional provisions by pointing to the (to them) unacceptable consequences of such a position: the framers do not always seem to have intended results that most of us find of vital importance. Professor Ely's attack on interpretivism is especially devastating because it proceeds largely on the interpretivists' own premises. If "incompatibility with democratic theory" is a problem for the noninterpretivist, it is not much less a problem for the most faithful strict constructionist, for the most frequently litigated constitutional provisions, "to the extent that they ever represented the 'voice of the people[,]' represent the voice of people who have been dead for a century or two." If democracy requires that a majority of any group be empowered to set policy, it is constitutionalism itself, not any particular variant of it, that is the problem.

But Professor Ely's longer and even more compelling argument against interpretivism is his demonstration that several constitutional provisions plainly direct the importation into the Constitution of values not found in the text or its legislative history. The fourteenth amendment—most particularly, the privileges or immunities clause—and the ninth amendment constitute straightforward "delegation[s] to future constitutional decisionmakers to protect certain rights that the document neither lists, at least not exhaustively, nor even in any specific way gives directions for finding." One can ignore these provisions—indeed, the dominant constitutional tradition has ignored them—but, as Ely persuasively demonstrates, to do so one must be faithless to the idea of interpretivism.

But if the Constitution itself directs its interpreters to go beyond mere interpretation, where are they to look for the "privileges or immunities" of citizens, or the unenumerated rights "retained by the people"? Professor Ely rejects "[t]he prevailing academic line . . . that the Supreme Court should give content to the Constitution's open-ended provisions by identifying and enforcing upon the political branches those values that are, by one formula or another, truly important or fundamental." His argument here is rich and complex in presentation, but its essence is simple: few would find acceptable a theory of adjudication which held that "judges should use their own values to give content to the Constitution's open texture," since such a theory would be profoundly undemocratic. But, as Ely wittily though thoughtfully proceeds to demonstrate, all other potential sources of fundamental values—Professor Ely considers in turn natural law, neutral principles, reason, tradition, consensus, and predictions of the original direction of evolving values—when used by courts as bases for overturning legislative judgments, lack sufficient agreed-upon content to amount to much more than masks for precisely such imposition of the judges' policy preferences.

Having thus demolished both interpretivism and noninterpretivism, Ely proceeds to erect his own theory of judicial review. Heavily influenced by Justice Stone's *Carolene Products* footnote, Professor Ely suggests that in interpreting the open-ended provisions of the Constitution courts should not look for substantive values to elevate to a constitutional stature, but rather should restrict themselves to pursuing "procedural" or "participational" goals that open up and make effective the process of representative government, and ensure the fair representation of minority interests. In this way, constitutional interpretation can be freed from the narrowness and self-contradictions of "clause-bound" interpretivism, without opening the door to the imposition of substantive outcomes by unelected officials. Judicial review becomes an adjunct, rather than an adversary, of the democratic process.

II

It is worth asking, I think, where these limitations on judicial review come from. Professor Ely states three arguments in support of "a participation-oriented, representation-reinforcing approach to judicial review." Close analysis of these arguments suggests to me, however, that Professor Ely has not really escaped the potholes he has found the interpretivists and noninterpretivists driving into.

The first argument, presented at greatest length, is that the Constitution "is overwhelmingly concerned, on the one hand, with procedural fairness in the resolution of individual disputes (process writ small) and, on the other, with what might capaciously be designated process writ large—with ensuring broad participation in the processes and distributions of government." As Professor Ely recognizes, this is essentially an interpretivist argument, proceeding by the maxim *ejusdem generis*: the framers must have meant the content of an open-ended catchall provision like the ninth amendment to refer to additional rights somehow analogous to those enumerated.

Surely Professor Ely is correct that the Constitution as a whole is principally concerned with process and structure. That, of course, is to be expected; it is, after all, a Constitution we are expounding, and constitutions are primarily concerned with creating institutions—a business of structure and process. But the ninth amendment, the principal open-ended provision that Professor Ely wants to tame, is not a part of the original body of the Constitution. Instead, it is part of a Bill of Rights that at least some of the framers thought was not appropriately included in a constitutional document precisely because it *does* attempt to insulate substantive values from majoritarian decision in exactly the way Professor Ely finds objectionable. If we are playing by interpretivist rules, the other "rights . . . retained by the people" protected by the ninth amendment must be of the same genus as those enumerated in the first eight amendments.

Recognizing this, Professor Ely proceeds to examine the Bill of Rights, with a view to establishing that there, too, "participational" and procedural concerns predominate. This portion of the book contains some of the most brilliant law-professing I have seen in a while. Professor Ely is remarkably adept at finding procedural values lurking behind apparently substantive values, and for that matter at identifying substantive strands in what might have seemed primarily procedural protections. The result of these intellectual fireworks is a sense that even in the Bill of Rights, the enshrinement of substantive value choices is rarer than we might have thought.

But this effect is created, I fear, as much by the smoke as by the light generated by Ely's flares. A more pedestrian account suggests that the framers of the Bill of Rights made no sharp distinction between the designation of protected substantive entitlements and the protection of the democratic political process, and at the very least had no aversion to including the former in their document. The first amendment, for example, mingles in the same sentence the protection of religious freedom (which Professor Ely concedes was for the framers "an important substantive value they wanted to put significantly beyond the reach of at least the federal legislature") and the rights of assembly and petition (in Ely's terms, procedural values)—with the freedoms of speech and press, which can be seen in either light, poised neatly between. Is the second amendment a protection of a substantive right "to keep and bear arms" or a structural provision preserving state militias? I'd like to agree with Professor Ely that it's the latter, but if the object of the game is to figure out what sort of document the framers thought the Bill of Rights was, I would agree more with his concession that "the point is debatable." The third and fourth amendments seem primarily concerned with substantive rights of privacy, personal security, and property. Professor Ely concedes the third (after hinting at a partial separation of powers rationale), but incredibly finds the fourth "another harbinger of the Equal Protection Clause, concerned with avoiding indefensible inequities in treatment." Well, in a way, perhaps; let's just say, with Professor Ely, that this perspective "obviously is only one of several." To finish the catalogue more briefly, I remain unconvinced by Professor Ely's ingenious arguments that the fifth amendment's prohibition of the taking of property without just compensation is anything other than a (limited) protection of the substantive value of private property, or that the eighth is not in essence a prohibition of substantive abuses. The rest of the fifth, sixth and seventh amendments, as Professor Ely agrees, are primarily concerned with fair procedure, with some substantive components.

On my scorecard, then, we have three amendments, the third, fourth and eighth, that are primarily concerned with protecting substantive rights; one, the seventh, that is purely procedural, plus two, the fifth and sixth, that contain a mixture of mostly procedural requirements with a few protections of substantive values; and two draws—the first, because its substantive and participational values are so exactly balanced, and the second, because of the difficulty of deciding what it was intended to do. But the point, of course, is not to be decided by counting heads. What does emerge is that if we are to determine the content of the ninth amendment by the rule of *ejusdem generis*, we can only conclude that the framers of the Bill of Rights saw values of both a substantive and a participational nature (as Professor Ely uses the terms) as of the same kind, and that we therefore cannot limit ourselves, in giving content to that amendment, to rights of the latter sort. Professor Ely's analysis of the content of the Constitution contains not only skillful worrying of particular provisions, but also a useful reminder of the extent to which our constitutional scheme does rely on procedural strategies to safeguard liberty. It does not, however, in the end provide a convincing interpretivist demonstration that the protection of substantive values from the majoritarian process is not also a significant aspect of that scheme and a legitimate basis for judicial elucidation of open-ended constitutional provisions.

Professor Ely's second argument in favor of his proposed limitations on judicial review is the most important, and constitutes the major message of the book. The "representation-reinforcing orientation" he urges on the courts, "unlike an approach geared to the judicial imposition of 'fundamental values,' . . . is not inconsistent with, but on the contrary is entirely supportive of, the American system of representative democracy." Of course, Professor Ely is correct that the kind of review he suggests is less intrusive into the representative political process than a theory that permits the courts to constitutionalize substantive value choices, and that the dominant constitutional tradition in the United States is democratic and majoritarian. I do have two problems with this argument, however.

The first is that Professor Ely seems to think that the question of an institution's consistency with democratic principles can be answered yes or no, rather than more or less. No one can question that the elected branches of government are more responsible to popular majorities than unelected judges. But both our formal political institutions and our actual structure of power abound in significant checks on majoritarian power. These checks are hardly as trivial as they seem to Professor Ely. The representational nature of our democracy is not just a concession to the impracticality of large-scale town-meetings, but a significant moderation of majoritarian control that fosters the influence of political elites and activist minorities. The separation of powers between executive and legislature makes our system considerably less responsive to popular majorities than a parliamentary system. Major powers are assigned to a Senate not elected according to population, increasing the influence of certain regions. Constitutionalism, even with review far more narrowly constrained than Professor Ely would permit, puts certain questions beyond the wishes of a simple majority. Permitting judges to reject political choices they find inconsistent with their views of the nation's basic values may be just another part of a system that on the whole does not require instant effectuation of the will of today's majority, but that rather commonly requires major decisions to be based on broader, more lasting consensus, occasionally with formal or de facto veto powers lodged in particular social or regional groups.

There isn't space here to debate the significance of these or other limits on majoritarianism that are built into our political system, or the related question of just how unresponsive to popular sentiments the courts really are. I wouldn't for a moment argue that Professor Ely is wrong in concluding that majoritarian democracy is at the core of our political institutions, and that the courts are further from that core than the elected branches of government. What I would say is that the thesis that judges should have a role in substantive policy choices is not so alien to the spirit of American institutions as to be illegitimate.

My second problem with Professor Ely's argument concerns the type of argument it is. Professor Ely is in effect arguing that substantive judicial review is illegitimate because it is inconsistent with what he sees as the dominant theme in the American political tradition. But that argument is vulnerable to the same criticisms Professor Ely has made of attempts to find substantive values in that tradition. The American political tradition is a rich one, and contains many contradictory elements. As I have argued above, without questioning that majoritarianism is a dominant element in that tradition, other elements are present as well, many of which directly limit the majoritarian tendency.

My point, in short, is this: Professor Ely complains that the noninterpretivist who would have judges give content to open-ended constitutional provisions by deciding what political decisions are contrary to our traditions is essentially deceiving herself—the judge will in the end be applying her own values to thwart the popular will. But that is just what Mr. Justice Ely himself is doing. Reading such provisions in light of his view of our traditions, he would override majoritarian decisions that conflict with his preferred portion of that tradition, that which favors broad political participation and relatively few substantive constraints on majority choices.

Professor Ely's third argument in favor of "representation-reinforcing" judicial review only makes this point clearer. I would agree with him that judges, as outsiders to the political system, are better able than legislators to decide when legislators have perverted the process of popular representation. But this argument implies that a judge applying an open-textured constitutional provision should give it content by asking what role the courts can most effectively play in a representative democracy. In that case, what ultimately divides Professor Ely from the judge who would embark on the admittedly personal and fallible search for basic values that the legislature should not be allowed to tamper with is not a question of legitimacy but of practical political philosophy. Professor Ely's reminder to judges that they are not necessarily in closer harmony than elected officials with popular values, or with what popular values would be if people would only stop to think, is extremely important. But I am not convinced that the presence of an institution composed of politically selected but tenured members that is officially commissioned, in a way the political branches of government are not, to compare political decisions with a rationalized account of the longer-range value commitments our political tradition has made is not on balance a valuable addition to a system of representative democracy.

III

I have concentrated on Professor Ely's arguments for his "participation-oriented, representation-reinforcing approach to judicial review" because I think they reveal his failure to get beyond the dichotomy between interpretivist and noninterpretivist approaches. His essentially interpretivist argument that "the sort of document our forbears thought they were writing" dictates that open-ended provisions of the Constitution should be read in accordance with his scheme fails because if the intention of the authors is to be our guide, at least one such provision, the ninth amendment, is embedded in that part of the Constitution that more than any other embodies substantive value choices. On the other hand, his attempt to read those provisions in light of what he sees as the genius of American democracy suffers from precisely the weaknesses he identifies in other non-interpretivist efforts to find other sorts of values in our political traditions: the tradition is too rich and contradictory to support a confident assertion that one or another of any complex set of values, including Professor Ely's participational values as well as various substantive ones, is mandated or forbidden sufficiently plainly to justify overriding political decisions. In the end, Professor Ely is reduced to arguing, just as he predicts the noninterpretivist would be, that judges should adopt his approach because it's a good one—that is, because it represents his own values and ought to represent theirs.

Bibliography

Constitutional Interpretation

Bickel, Alexander, THE LEAST DANGEROUS BRANCH (1962)

Bickel, Alexander, THE SUPREME COURT AND THE IDEA OF PROGRESS (1969)

Black, Charles, THE PEOPLE AND THE COURT (1960)

Choper, Jesse, *The Supreme Court and the Political Branches: Democratic Theory and Practice,* 122 U. PA. L. REV. 810 (1974)

Dworkin, Ronald, *Hard Cases,* 88 HARV. L. REV. 1057 (1957)

Greenwalt, Kent, *The Enduring Significance of Neutral Principles,* 78 COLUM. L. REV. 982 (1978)

Hand, Learned, THE BILL OF RIGHTS (1958)

Kurland, Philip B., *Toward a Political Supreme Court,* 37 U. CHI. L. REV. 19 (1969)

Monaghan, Henry P., *The Supreme Court, 1974 Term—Foreword: Constitutional Common Law,* 89 HARV. L. REV. 1 (1975)

Perry, Michael J., *The Authority of Text, Tradition and Reason: A Theory of Constitutional "Interpretation,"* 58 S. CAL. L. REV. 551 (1985)

Sandalow, Terrance, *Constitutional Interpretation,* 79 MICH. L. REV. 1033 (1981)

Wright, J. Skelly, *Professor Bickel, The Scholarly Tradition and the Supreme Court,* 84 HARV. L. REV. 769 (1971)

Fundamental Rights Analysis

Generally

Controversy over interpretive and noninterpretive methods has been especially intense in the context of fundamental rights. The most pitched debate comprehends the Court's usage of the due process clause as a check upon legislative power. Common focal points of commentary are the development of economic rights doctrine during the late nineteenth and early twentieth century and the evolution of privacy as a fundamental right over the past few decades. Cass R. Sunstein contends that a prohibition against "naked preferences" underlies much constitutional doctrine.

Cass R. Sunstein, *Naked Preferences and the Constitution*, 84 COLUM. L. REV. 1689 (1984)*

One of the most striking facts of modern constitutional law is the overlap—almost the identity—of current tests under many of the most important clauses of the Constitution: the dormant commerce, privileges and immunities, equal protection, due process, contract, and eminent domain clauses. Although these clauses have different historical roots and were originally directed at different problems, they are united by a common theme and focused on a single underlying evil: the distribution of resources or opportunities to one group rather than another solely on the ground that those favored have exercised the raw political power to obtain what they want. I will call this underlying evil a naked preference.

The prohibition of naked preferences captures large areas of doctrine under all six clauses. The privileges and immunities clause, for example, prohibits a state from preferring its citizens over outsiders unless "there are perfectly valid independent reasons for" the preference. The dormant commerce clause allows discrimination against interstate commerce, with its attendant costs to out-of-staters, only if the discrimination is a means of promoting some goal unrelated to protectionism. The equal protection clause allows a state to distinguish between one person and another only if there is a plausible connection between the distinction and a legitimate public purpose. The contract clause does not forbid an impairment of contractual obligations if the impairment is the "incidental" consequence of "a generally applicable rule of conduct" designed to promote legitimate government goals. The eminent domain clause embodies similar principles, both in the requirement that a "public use" must be shown to justify a taking of private property and in the distinction that has been developed between permissible exercises of the police power and prohibited takings.

Because of their common concern with naked preferences, these clauses share a number of features. They are all directed in large part at discrimination based on an impermissible purpose. Effects are relevant, if at all, only to show such a purpose. A number of devices—most prominently, the required showing of some degree of

---

*   This article originally appeared at 84 Colum. L. Rev. 1689 (1984). Reprinted by permission.

means-ends connection and the identification of a category of impermissible government ends—are applied under all of these clauses to filter out naked preferences.

The prohibition of naked preferences captures a significant theme in the original intent. It is closely related to the central constitutional concern of ensuring against capture of government power by faction. The framers' hostility toward naked preferences was rooted in the fear that government power would be usurped solely to distribute wealth or opportunities to one group or person at the expense of another. The constitutional requirement that something other than a naked preference be shown to justify differential treatment provides a means, admittedly imperfect, of ensuring that government action results from a legitimate effort to promote the public good rather than from a factional takeover. The Court's adherence to this requirement under the various clauses and over long historical periods showing otherwise considerable doctrinal change reflects a striking continuity in general approach.

The prohibition of naked preferences also reflects the Constitution's roots in civil republicanism and accompanying conceptions of civic virtue. The notion that government actions must be responsive to something other than private pressure is associated with the idea that politics is "not the reconciling but the transcending of the different interests of the society in the search for the single common good." Civil republicanism embodies a conception of politics in which preferences are not viewed as private and exogenous. Their selection is the object of the governmental process. The model for this conception of government is the town meeting, where decisions are made during a process of collective self-determination.

In accordance with the original Madisonian understanding, the prohibition is focused on the motivations of legislators, not of their constituents. The prohibition therefore embodies a particular conception of representation. Under that conception, the task of legislators is not to respond to private pressure but instead to select values through deliberation and debate.

Finally, the prohibition of naked preferences is reflected in the structural provisions of the Constitution. Indeed, the framers believed that those provisions would provide the most important means of implementing the prohibition. The separation of powers, both in general and in its concrete constitutional manifestations, was designed to limit the power of self-interested groups or factions by ensuring that government power would be exercised in accordance with certain predetermined constraints. It is no coincidence that the most celebrated case employing the nondelegation doctrine involved a delegation of legislative authority to private groups. Similarly, the general welfare provision of the spending clause was designed to ensure that public resources would be devoted to broad social interests. Nor is it surprising that the Court's legislative veto decision—perhaps the most important separation of powers decision in recent years—focused on the factional dangers produced by evasion of the presentment and bicameralism requirements of article I.

Quite apart from its roots in original intent, the prohibition of naked preferences captures the judicial understanding that the Constitution requires all government action to be justified by reference to some public value. The "reasonableness" constraint of the due process clause is perhaps the most obvious example. The minimum requirement that government decisions be something other than a raw exercise of political power has been embodied in constitutional doctrine under the due process clause before, during, and after the Lochner era. The equal protection clause, in its core requirement that classifications be justified by reference to some public value, reflects an identical understanding. The same principle has been embodied in constitutional doctrine under many other clauses as well. The contract and eminent domain clauses, for example, are efforts to apply the general prohibition of naked preferences to several specific instances of government action about which the framers were most concerned.

The notion that government action must be grounded in something other than an exercise of raw political power is in considerable tension with many of the most prominent theories of how government does and should operate. It is especially at odds with pluralism. Naked preferences are common fare in the pluralist conception; interest-group politics invites them. The prohibition of naked preferences, enforced as it is by the courts, stands as a repudiation of theories positing that the judicial role is only to police the processes of representation to ensure that all affected interest-groups may participate. It presupposes that courts will serve as critics of the pluralist vision, not as adherents striving only to "clear the channels" in preparation for the ensuing political struggle. In this respect, the prohibition of naked preferences reflects a distinctly substantive value and cannot easily be captured in procedural terms. Moreover, it reflects an attractive conception of politics, one that does not understand the political process as simply another sort of market. It is hardly surprising that the prohibition is reflected in many areas of constitutional law.

This Article will argue that the prohibition of naked preferences captures large areas of current constitutional doctrine and is therefore the best candidate for a unitary conception of the sorts of government action that the Constitution prohibits. But courts have interpreted the prohibition in different ways over time and among clauses, and these differences are of independent interest. In tracing the evolution of the prohibition, the focus of this Article will be primarily descriptive. In addition, however, it will suggest that the prohibition embodies an understanding of governance that has considerable appeal, and that, if taken seriously, could form the basis for a distinctive conception of politics and a distinctive judicial role.

I. NAKED PREFERENCES AND PUBLIC VALUES: THE FRAMEWORK

It will be useful to begin by distinguishing between two bases for treating one person or group differently from another. The first is a naked preference. When a naked preference is at work, one group or person is treated differently from another solely because of a raw exercise of political power; no broader or more general justification exists. For example, state A may treat its own citizens better than those of state B—say, by requiring people from state B to pay for the use of the local parks—simply because its own citizens have the political power and want better treatment. Or a city may treat blacks worse than whites—say, by denying them welfare benefits—because whites have the power to restrict state largesse to themselves. Or a state may relieve a group of citizens from a contractual obligation, thus benefiting them at the expense of another group of contracting parties, simply because the first group and its allies seized the political power to dispossess the second group of the rights that it previously had.

These examples illustrate a conception of the political process as a mechanism by which self-interested individuals or groups seek to obtain wealth or opportunities at the expense of others. Political ordering is assimilated to market ordering. The public interest is understood as the aggregation of private interests. The task of the legislator is to respond to the pressures imposed by those interests. This conception of the political process reflects a set of values within which any other conception appears mystical, potentially totalitarian, or both.

Contrast with this a conception of a political process in which differential treatment is justified not by reference to raw political power, but to some public value that the differential treatment can be said to serve. A public value can be defined as any justification for government action that goes beyond the exercise of raw political power. For example, a state may impose regulatory requirements on opticians, but not on optometrists, because the methods used by the former group create special risks of deception or overreaching. Or a state may relieve a group of people from a contractual obligation because the contract called for an act—say, the passing on of increased costs to consumers—that violated a public policy demanding that consumers be insulated from some of the dislocations caused by an unregulated marketplace. Or state A may treat its own citizens better than those of state B—say, by limiting welfare payments to its own citizens—because it wants to restrict social spending to those who in the past have made, or in the future might make, a contribution to state revenues. These examples reflect a conception of the political process as an effort to select and implement public values. The process is primarily one of collective self-determination, rather than of compromises or trade-offs among preexisting private interests. The role of the representative is to deliberate rather than to respond mechanically to constituent pressures. Politics cannot, in this view, be reduced to the aggregation of private interests. Such interests are not preexisting. They are themselves a product of the political process, whose function is not to choose among preselected values but instead to select values through public deliberation and debate.

These competing portraits of the political process are of course caricatures of a far more complex reality. It is rare that government action is based purely or exclusively on raw political power. Losers in the political process may have lost for a very good reason that has little or nothing to do with the power of their adversaries. Belief that an action will promote at least some conception of the public good almost always plays at least some role in government decisions. Moreover, it is rare for government action to be based on a disembodied effort to discern and implement public values, entirely apart from considerations of private pressure. What emerges is therefore a continuum of government decisions, ranging from those that are motivated primarily by interest-group pressures to those in which such pressures play a very minor role. The rest of Part I examines the devices used by the courts to determine which of these poles a particular measure approaches.

A. The Minimal Requirement

If naked preferences are a legitimate basis for government action, a significant judicial constraint on the exercise of government power is lifted. It is sufficient that a particular group has been able to assemble the raw political power to obtain what it seeks; might makes right.

* * *

B. Beyond the Minimal Requirement

* * *

Everything, in short, is at least potentially lawful. To develop a more vigorous set of constraints on government, it is necessary to go beyond the weak version described thus far.

The Constitution expressly provides a few—but only a few—of the elements of a more robust set of constraints. Under the privileges and immunities and dormant commerce clauses, a preference for in-staters at the expense of out-of-staters is impermissible. Under the equal protection clause, the same is true for discrimination against blacks. As a constitutional matter, both out-of-staters and blacks are entitled to special protection from discrimination; discrimination against either group for its own sake cannot be understood as a public value.

Even these apparently express constraints, however, can be ambiguous. What if a state justifies discrimination against out-of-staters on the ground that they have been the main factor contributing to in-state unemployment, or discrimination against blacks on the ground that, when blacks are jailed with whites, the likelihood of violence is dramatically increased? Outside of the narrow areas of discrimination against out-of-staters and blacks, the judicial inquiry is even more open-ended. To be sure, certain constitutional provisions give some guidance. For example, it may be possible to derive from the equal protection clause a general principle by which to judge all classifications. But in giving content to that principle, there is enormous room for judgment. In such cases, how do the courts enforce the prohibition of naked preferences?

In answering this question, we begin by examining several devices that have been of special importance under all six clauses. These devices, which are logically independent, have been the key elements in strengthening and supplementing the constraint imposed by the weak version of the prohibition.

1. Heightened Scrutiny.—The first device involves the scope of review of government claims that a public value is being served. "Heightened scrutiny" consists of a careful examination of the government's claim that a public value is in fact the motivating force behind its actions. Here courts find it insufficient, as a basis for a conclusion that a public value is at work, that the measure under review has satisfied all formal requirements and a connection can be hypothesized between it and some public value. Under this approach, a public value is what emerges from a well-functioning political process in which legislators do not respond only to raw political power, and courts will scrutinize the process to ensure that it is in fact well functioning.

Heightened scrutiny involves two principal elements. The first is a requirement that the government show a close connection between the asserted public value and the means that the legislature has chosen to promote it. If a sufficiently close connection cannot be shown, there is reason for skepticism that the asserted value in fact accounted for the legislation. The second element is a search for less restrictive alternatives—ways in which the government could have promoted the public value without harming the group in question. The availability of such alternatives also suggests that the public value justification is a facade.

Heightened scrutiny also requires that the government show that it actually considered the public value in enacting the measure in question. Such a requirement represents a similar effort to ensure that the values on which a statute rests are genuinely public, in the sense that they resulted not from private pressure but from broad deliberation about what the relevant rule should be. In this respect, the requirements of heightened scrutiny serve as a means, though very tentative and undeveloped, of implementing the republican ideal.

Heightened scrutiny is triggered by a concern that in the circumstances it is especially likely that the measure under review reflects a naked preference. The most familiar example is review of racial classifications under the equal protection clause. Review of statutes that discriminate on their face against noncitizens under the privileges and immunities clause falls into the same category. In both cases, heightened scrutiny is justified by a perception that the groups in question lack the political power to protect themselves against factional tyranny.

By contrast, more relaxed scrutiny—typified by rationality review—reflects a strong presumption that a public value is at work. That presumption is conventionally supported by reference to considerations of judicial competence and legitimacy. The underlying idea is, first, that courts lack the capacity to review the factual determinations of other branches of government and, second, that vigorous judicial scrutiny of whether a naked preference is at work would be inconsistent with what is taken to be the central constitutional commitment to representative democracy.

2. Theory of Impermissible Ends.—A second device in a more rigorous version of the prohibition, typified by doctrines developed under the due process and equal protection clauses, consists of judicial formulation of a normative theory designed to distinguish between legitimate and illegitimate bases for government action. The courts attempt to root this normative theory in the text or history of the Constitution. Under this approach, the weak version of the prohibition of naked preferences is buttressed by a conclusion that a number of ends are illegitimate even if they are not exercises of raw political power in the ordinary sense. This element thus supplements the procedural requirements of heightened scrutiny with a substantive constraint.

During the Lochner era, for example, the redistribution of resources from employer to employee was not thought to respond to a public value and was therefore placed in the category of naked preferences. Numerous goals now considered to fall within the realm of public values were not recognized as such, largely because common law conceptions of rights and obligations dominated early public law. If a measure enacted by the government was not a proper exercise of the police power under common law standards, it was impermissible under the due process clause as a naked preference for one group at the expense of another. Identical results occurred under the contract clause. In short, a particular normative theory sharply limited the category of public values.

Under current law, by contrast, all sorts of redistributive measures are permissible. The weak version of the prohibition of naked preferences still applies to such measures, but the normative theory supplementing the weak version has been dramatically altered in a way that has expanded the category of public values to include redistribution. When a normative theory outlaws certain kinds of government action even though such action is not solely an exercise of raw political power, the prohibition of naked preferences has gone well beyond the weak version. To develop a complete theory of the resulting "strong version," it is necessary to identify the expanded category of public values with precision.

Economic Rights and Liberty

Fundamental rights analysis for better or for worse is influenced heavily by the Court's performance earlier this century in accounting for marketplace freedom. What Justice Holmes characterized as the Court's prioritization of "Mr. Herbert Spencer's Social Statics theories," in *Lochner v. New York,*[7] defined a jurisprudential method from which the judiciary vigorously attempts to distance itself more than half a century after economic rights doctrine was abandoned. Primary incidents of the evolution of a fundamental right of privacy thus have been accusations of neo-Lochnerism[8] and disclamation of any such function.[9] Geoffrey P. Miller assesses the modern Court's abandonment of economic rights review against the political backdrop that begot the *Carolene Products* case. Frank H. Easterbrook argues that calculated judicial inattention to economic regulation is misconceived. Robert G. McCloskey suggests that, even if wholesale deference to the legislative wisdom of economic regulation was initially unwise, the judiciary's expanded interest in substantive due process warrants diminished attention to such political output.

The demise of economic rights as an imperative of substantive due process has rekindled interest in constitutional provisions that speak specifically to economic concerns. A student note contends that the constitutionality of legislation reviewed under the Contract Clause should depend upon the relative weight of the substantive principles governing expectations and public power. Joseph L. Sax analyzes the extent to which the "spillover" effect should be taken into account in takings cases. Frank Michelman examines doctrinal turmoil that has defined taking jurisprudence especially over the past decade.

Geoffrey P. Miller, *The True Story of* Carolene Products, 1987 SUP. CT. REV. 397 (1987)*

United States v. Carolene Products Corporation, as any second year law student knows, contains perhaps the most renowned footnote in constitutional history. In famous footnote four justice Stone, writing for himself and three others, suggested that the Court apply relatively, strict scrutiny to legislation interfering with the political processes or affecting the rights of "discrete and insular minorities." Because the Court had but recently abandoned strict scrutiny of economic regulation, the footnote is seen as paving the way for a two-tiered system of constitutional review in which individual rights are afforded greater protection than so-called economic liberties.

Today a half-century later, the footnote is widely honored as a cornerstone of constitutional law, a "great and modern charter for ordering the relations between judges and other agencies of government." . . .

---

7   198 U.S. 45, 75 (1905) (Holmes, J., dissenting).

8   *E.g.*, Roe v. Wade, 410 U.S. 113, 174 (1973) (Rehnquist, J., dissenting).

9   *E.g.*, Griswold v. Connecticut, 381 U.S. 479, 481-82 (1965).

*   Copyright © 1987 by the University of Chicago. Reprinted from 1987 Supreme Court Review 397 by permission.

The plaudits accorded the footnote are matched by the disregard of the case itself. The facts were not the stuff of great decisions. At issue was the constitutionality of the 1923 federal "Filled Milk Act," a statute that prohibited the shipment in interstate commerce of skimmed milk laced with vegetable oil. The case appeared to be a routine challenge to an unimportant economic regulation, with the outcome foreordained by recent opinions sustaining other forms of economic regulation. Commentators have denigrated its significance, finding it "unremarkable," "straightforward," even "easy."

The lack of attention to the case itself is unfortunate, because it is interesting in its own right, and because its facts shed light on the meaning of the footnote. The statute upheld in the case was an utterly unprincipled example of special interest legislation. The purported "public interest" justifications so credulously reported by justice Stone were patently bogus. If the preference embodied by this statute was not "naked," it was clothed only in gossamer rationalizations. The consequence of the decision was to expropriate the property of a lawful and beneficial industry; to deprive working and poor people of a healthful, nutritious, and low-cost food; and to impair the health of the nation's children by encouraging the use as baby food of a sweetened condensed milk product that was 42 percent sugar.

It is difficult to believe that members of the Court were unaware of the true motivation behind this legislation. That they should nonetheless vote to uphold the statute strongly suggested that all bets were off as far as economic regulation was concerned. Footnote four, in this light, can be seen as indicating that the Court intended to keep its hands off economic regulation, no matter how egregious the discrimination or patent the special interest motivation. Rational basis scrutiny, of the sort suggested in *West Cost Hotel* could not be taken seriously, if it precluded judicial protection of individual liberties. By separating economic and personal liberties, justice Stone suggested that the Court might really mean what it said about deference to the legislative will in economic cases. Two-tiered scrutiny did much more than facilitate the creation of preferred constitutional categories entitled to exacting judicial review. It also freed the forces of interest group politics from the stumbling block of the federal courts. *Carolene*'s legacy is not only *Brown v. Board of Education*, it is also the unrivaled primacy of interest groups in American politics of the last half-century.

Fortunately for the nation's consumers, the *Carolene Products* case itself is no longer the law. Go to any supermarket and you will find filled milk for sale under trade names such as "Melnot" or "Melloream." Some firms, including the aptly named Defiance Milk Products Company of Defiance, Ohio, are boldly marketing the product under its original colors. The Supreme Court's decision in *Carolene Products* has been overruled, and the statute declared to violate substantive due process. Yet while the injustice of the case itself has been remedied, the footnote remains.

* * *

I. POLITICS, TECHNOLOGY, MARKETS, AND LAW:
THE FILLED MILK ACT OF 1923

* * *

Filled milk appeared on the scene in the early teens. It was produced by a few of the bigger milk dealers incident to their manufacture of condensed and evaporated milk. By 1923 there were seven or eight brands on the market, going under trade names such as "Enzo," "Nutro," "Nyko," "Silver Key," and "Carolene." The industry leader was "Hebe," produced by a subsidiary of the Carnation Company, one of the industry's top ten firms.

The great selling point of filled milk was price. Skimmed milk was virtually worthless at the time. Produced in the billions of pounds a year, its principal cash market was in the manufacture of paint. Mostly it was fed to hogs or calves on the farm. The only element of real value in milk was butterfat. Because the coconut oil in filled milk was much cheaper than butterfat, filled milk could be sold for considerably less than canned whole milk. The wholesale cost of a case of filled milk was about $3.50 for forty-eight cans, while the cost of a case of canned whole milk was $5.00. At retail, filled milk typically sold for about 7½¢ a can, as compared with 10¢ for canned whole milk.

* * *

C. POLITICS

The politics of filled milk was a predictable expression of the self-interest of the various affected parties. The opponents of the product can appropriately be referred to as the "dairy industry," although the term is not completely accurate because limited segments of the industry were aligned on the other side. Pressing for prohibition were various farmer associations: breed groups; county, state, and national political organizations; dairy newspapers, agricultural colleges and universities; granges; and dairy promotional organizations. Farmers understood, correctly, that the imported coconut oil in filled milk undercut the domestic butterfat market. Although filled milk was mostly skimmed milk, a dairy product, the net impact on dairy farmers was negative. The demand for skimmed milk created by Hebe and similar products was largely a replacement for skimmed milk that would otherwise have been used in whole evaporated milk. Worse, filled milk displaced millions of pounds of butter into the market, driving down the price of that commodity. The loss in profits from the reduction in butter price outweighed any gain from an enhanced skimmed milk market. In this respect the impact of filled milk was similar to that of margarine, dairying's longtime bugaboo.

In addition to farmers, the other important member of this coalition was the Borden Company. Borden enjoyed substantial brandname capital in its various kinds of canned milk, especially its "Eagle" condensed milk. Perhaps because of its dominant position, Borden failed to introduce its own brand of filled milk. By 1920 the various other proprietary brand names had gained consumer acceptance; if Borden were to enter the market at this point it would have to struggle to do as well in filled milk as it was doing in other segments of the canned milk industry. Thus by 1920 Borden apparently calculated that it had more to gain by suppressing the trade in filled milk than by entering into competition with its rivals. Much of the opposition to filled milk appears to have been instigated and actively supported by Borden throughout. . . .

* * *

D. THE 1923 STATUTE

Despite the threat posed by filled milk, the dairy industry made few efforts to combat the product prior to the onset of the farm depression in 1920. In part this was because there was no basis for challenging the product under existing law. The federal pure food and drug act required that the product not be adulterated or misbranded, but a proviso stated that an article would not be considered adulterated or misbranded if it was a compound of ingredients offered for sale under its own name and not an imitation of another article. There was no question that filled milk, taken by itself, was a healthful product, since it was simply a compound of skimmed milk and vegetable oil, two substances universally recognized as healthful. Nor was there any basis to challenge the labeling of the various filled milks, under either state or federal law, since they correctly disclosed their ingredients and did not include "milk" in their names. Thus the executive branches of the state and federal governments, which might have been the first resort for the dairy industry, were not initially available in its campaign.

In Ohio, however, an existing statute prohibited the manufacture or sale of condensed skimmed milk. Ohio authorities threatened prosecution against the manufacturer of Hebe for violation of the statute. The case reached the Supreme Court of the United States in 1919, where, despite an argument for Hebe by Charles Evans Hughes, Justice Holmes upheld the statute. Holmes deferred to the legislature to a degree rarely matched even in the Court's pro-New Deal decisions after 1937. Even assuming that Hebe was wholesome, said Holmes, the legislative power "is not to be denied simply because some innocent articles or transactions may be found within the proscribed class. The inquiry must be whether, considering the end in the view, the statute passes the bounds of reason and assumes the character of a merely arbitrary fiat." Holmes had no difficulty concluding that the statute represented a valid exercise of the police power.

The result in *Hebe Co.*, coupled with the weakening in dairy prices that began in 1919, galvanized the industry into action. Prominent dairy journals sounded the alarm. *Hoard's Dairyman* accused Hebe of being oleo wearing "a tin jacket . . . instead of annatto paint and oil paper." The *Jersey Bulletin and Dairy World*, a national journal for the Jersey breed, disparaged the product as "milk business a la sausage grinder" and noted pointedly that the skimmed milk in Hebe was supplied by a Holstein herd. The equation of filled milk with margarine was well-calculated to capture the attention of farmers long conditioned to consider oleo the worst of all possible evils (except when served at their own dinner tables).

Industry leaders charged that filled milk was unhealthy because it lacked vitamins, and that it induced fraud because it could so easily be confused with evaporated milk. These arguments formed the basis for a sustained campaign by the industry, against filled milk at both the state and federal levels.

Around 1920 bills to outlaw or severely restrict filled milk were introduced in various state legislatures. California and Washington passed the first such laws in 1919, followed by seventeen more states within the next four years. The campaign for state legislation received a boost in 1922 when the Wisconsin Supreme Court upheld that state's filled milk statute against a challenge brought by the Hebe Company.

Beneficial as these statutes were for the opponents of filled milk, they did not provide complete protection. The product could still be manufactured where it was not prohibited, and could, under the original package doctrine, be freely transported into states that had enacted prohibitory legislation. As long as filled milk undersold canned whole milk by a significant amount, merchants, grocers, and peddlers could be found willing to risk prosecution for selling the product. To enforce the statute effectively prosecutors would have to go after these small-time operators, a strategy certain to prove both time-consuming and ineffective. Even if retailers could be apprehended, their defense costs would be paid by the filled milk manufacturers; and sympathy for defendants would often result in jury nullification or unfavorable judicial interpretations. Prosecutors were unlikely to enforce these statutes enthusiastically, given the many other demands on their resources. The dairy industry had experienced all this and more in its frustrating campaign against margarine, and it was well aware of the difficulties it would face in a similar attack on filled milk.

* * *

By 1921 the dairy industry as a whole had determined to support a direct federal prohibition of filled milk rather than a punitive tax, although segments of the industry worried about the constitutional difficulties. The leading congressional supporters of the bill were congressmen from dairy states such as Wisconsin, Minnesota, New York, and Iowa. The opponents were largely from the South, especially cotton states such as Arkansas, Mississippi, and Louisiana. The bill passed the House 250 to 40, passed the Senate by a voice vote, and was signed into law on March 4, 1923.

The federal statute removed some of the pressure for prohibitory legislation in states that had not yet acted, but state legislation was still needed to prevent intrastate manufacture and sale of the product. . . . By 1937 thirty-one states had enacted laws prohibiting the manufacture or sale of filled milk; three had prescribed standards for condensed milk that effectively outlawed filled milk, and three had imposed conditions and regulations on the manufacture and sale of filled milk.

The effect of the federal statute, coupled with prohibitory, state legislation, was to drive most producers out of business. A small trade in the product did continue, however, where permitted by law or where a producer was willing to risk prosecution in order to test a statute in court. The leading (perhaps the only) manufacturer of filled milk after 1923 was the Carolene Products Corporation. This firm continued to manufacture and sell the substance in a number of states, including several that had enacted prohibitory legislation.

Despite what appeared to be the unfavorable precedent in *Hebe Co.*, Carolene Products had some remarkable successes in its lonely legal odyssey. In 1931 the Supreme Court of Illinois—Carolene's home state—invalidated its filled milk statute on due process grounds. When an organization of evaporated milk producers caused the legislature to enact a new statute complete with suitable recitations of "fact," the Illinois Supreme Court again struck it down, holding that the purported fact finding intruded on the judicial function and denied due process and equal protection of the laws. These decisions established a safe harbor in which the company could operate its manufacturing plant and serve the large intrastate market, including the Chicago metropolitan area.

In 1934 the company won an even bigger victory when a judge in the Southern District of Illinois, in a sweeping if confused opinion, invalidated the federal statute. The act, said the court, "strikes down a well-known lawful industry, one which theretofore was entitled to and had the protection of the Constitution and laws of the United States. It amounts to a taking of private property ostensibly for the public good without compensation, and deprives the defendant and others similarly situated of liberty and property, without due process of law."

Carolene Products' situation improved still more in 1936 with decisions by the Supreme Courts of Michigan and Nebraska striking down their respective filled milk statutes. Although prohibitory legislation was still being enacted in a number of states, it began to appear as if the dairy industry's campaign of 1920-23 would founder completely upon the rocks of the Due Process Clause.

In fact, however, it was Carolene Products that was on a headlong course for disaster. In 1937 it attempted to eliminate interference from its archenemy, the Evaporated Milk Association, by bringing a bill of complaint alleging that the Association's activities violated the antitrust law. The strategy backfired when the Seventh Circuit upheld the federal statute, overruling the prior decision by the Southern District of Illinois.

The following year catastrophe struck. The Supreme Courts of Missouri and Pennsylvania upheld their states' prohibitory statutes. Worse, the United States Supreme Court Upheld the federal statute in *United States v. Carolene Products Co.* Justice Stone's opinion for the Court deferred totally to congressional committee "findings" that filled milk threatened the public health (because it lacked vitamins) and encouraged consumer fraud (because it could be confused with evaporated milk).

Despite the Court's apparent renunciation of any meaningful role in economic cases, Carolene Products refused to abandon the fight. It added a little cod liver oil and marketed the product as "New Vitamin A Carolene." The scheme failed. State supreme courts in Kentucky and Kansas sustained filled milk statutes as applied to the new formula. A renewed federal prosecution came to the United States Supreme Court in 1944. The Court rejected the company's arguments out of hand, holding that congressional concerns about consumer fraud were sufficient to sustain the statute even if the product were assumed to be completely wholesome and nutritionally equivalent to milk. In a companion case, *Sage Stores v. Kansas*, the Court sustained the Kansas filled milk statute as applied to the new product.

By the end of 1944 Carolene Products appeared to have run out of options. The Supreme Court had made it abundantly clear that it was not about to overturn filled milk statutes no matter what proof the company might offer. Filled milk had been banned in more than thirty states and heavily regulated in others. Carolene was relegated to marginal legal existence, able to survive by serving a few intrastate markets but without serious prospects for expansion. At this point the record falls almost silent on the fate of an organization known as the Carolene Products Corporation.

* * *

The federal statute remained. By the 1950s, however, it was evident that the federal government had lost all enthusiasm for prosecuting violations. The Agriculture Department determined that many new filled dairy products were not made "in imitation or semblance of milk," hence not within the statutes. Interpretation had its limits, however. No amount of bureaucratic legerdemain could twist the statute so as not to apply to its original intended victim, evaporated skimmed milk with vegetable oil. At some point the issue that had apparently been conclusively settled in the *Carolene Products* cases was bound to arise again.

It did so in 1972 in a suit brought by the Milnot Company, a manufacturer of filled milk. A federal district court struck the statute down as a violation of substantive due process, thus overruling the Supreme Court's decisions in *Carolene Products*. The statute was arbitrary and capricious, according to the court, because products virtually identical to Milnot were circulating in interstate commerce free of statutory infirmity. Moreover, the market conditions and dangers of confusion that led to the passage and judicial upholding of the statute "have long since ceased." Accordingly, Milnot had the right to market its product in interstate and foreign commerce free from federal interference under the Filled Milk Act.

The *Milnot* decision has once again reopened the channels of national commerce to trade in filled milk. Today, as noted, filled milk can be found on the canned milk shelves of any supermarket. Borden's "Eagle," meanwhile, is often ignominiously relegated to the baker department, it having been recognized that a product comprised 42 percent of sugar is not a particularly appropriate beverage, especially for infants. And in one sense filled milk has gained the sweetest revenge of all: concerns about dietary cholesterol have made filled milk appear the more healthful product, since the vegetable oils (principally soybean oil) now contained in filled milk are cholesterol free, a virtue notoriously lacking in butterfat.

A final footnote is in order. The Milnot Company, which managed to overturn the Supreme Court's opinions in *Carolene Products*, was not always known by that title. Years ago it had a different, more familiar name—the Carolene Products Corporation.

II. CONSTITUTIONALITY OF THE FEDERAL STATUTE

The campaign against filled milk was grounded on three arguments: (1) filled milk is a threat to the public health because it does not contain the vitamins that exist in butterfat; (2) filled milk is a threat to the public welfare because it can be confused with evaporated milk; (3) filled milk is a threat to the public interest because it undermines the dairy industry, an essential national institution. The first two arguments were designed to bring the proposed statute within the police power. They were credulously accepted by the Supreme Court in *Carolene Products*. Yet even on the legislative record compiled in 1923 they were a tissue of insubstantial rationalizations covering the real motivation of the statute, namely, the desire to suppress trade in one article of commerce in order to eliminate competition with another.

A. VITAMINS

The dairy industry's campaign against filled milk was based on one indisputable proposition: butterfat was a rich source of vitamin A while coconut oil was almost devoid of the vitamin. This proposition did not, however, justify legislative prohibition of filled milk.

. . . At the Wisconsin Agricultural Experiment Station a young research scientist, E. V. McCollum, began giving simplified diets to animals. By 1913 McCollum and a colleague had demonstrated that young rats on restricted diets would grow when butterfat was added but did not grow when olive oil or lard was added. They interpreted these results to mean that butterfat contained a previously unrecognized dietary essential. This mysterious substance . . . was quickly identified as one of the "vitamins" postulated by an earlier researcher, C. Funk, as necessary to prevent certain dietary deficiency diseases.

The case against filled milk had the appearance of scientific rigor. McCollum, a researcher of undoubted stature, was ready at a moment's notice to testify to the many virtues of milk and to inadequacies of vegetable oils. He came equipped with gruesome photographs of young animals fed on vegetable oil, showing them to be scraggly, undernourished, and afflicted by eye disorders. Young animals fed on butterfat, on the other hand, were shown with glossy coats, bright eyes, and healthy constitutions.

In spite of appearances, the case for prohibiting filled milk was utterly unproved. Filled milk was undoubtedly a wholesome food. No one would be harmed by drinking it. The entire argument against the product was based on the proposition that it would somehow crowd out consumption of other foods necessary to a well-balanced diet.

* * *

[T]he proposition that filled milk in an adult diet would crowd out other sources of vitamin A was absurd. The American diet was rich in many foods containing vitamin A, including butterfat products (whole milk, cheese, and butter), fish, eggs, greens, and yellow vegetables. There was no evidence that any adult would ever drink so much filled milk as to cause vitamin A deficiency. The argument for banning filled milk, in the case of adults, was no more substantial than that for banning the use of rice or flour because these substances were deficient in vitamin A.

* * *

The fact was that filled milk undoubtedly improved the national health. Its lower price increased consumption of skimmed milk and vegetable fats, both wholesome and nutritious foods. And to the extent that it displaced other dairy products, the result was far from undesirable. The sugar content of condensed milk (including Borden's "Eagle") was high enough to raise questions about its desirability as a baby food. Fresh whole milk was often positively dangerous. Milk was known to transmit typhoid fever, diphtheria, diarrhea, septic sore throat, and scarlet fever. It was suspected in the transmission of poliomyelitis. Most tragically, it was a leading cause of tuberculosis, a disease that carried away thousands of adults and tens of thousands of children annually. These dangers were largely absent in the case of filled milk, which was manufactured in modern plants under hygienic conditions and sterilized at high temperature.

* * *

The scientific case against filled milk, in short, was entirely bogus from the start.

B. FRAUD

Whatever the merits of the vitamin argument, it is clear that these contentions had no force as against filled milks to which vitamins had been added. The second *Carolene Products* case presented that fact situation. The filled milk in that case had been fortified with cod liver oil, a rich source of vitamins A and D. Although the new ingredient could not have enhanced the taste of the product, it did supply at least as many vitamins as were in evaporated whole milk. Accordingly, the second *Carolene Products* case isolated the fraud argument for separate analysis and consideration.

This argument was even more whimsical than the health contentions. To begin with, there was a certain irony in the idea that consumers would object to a product indistinguishable from evaporated whole milk in every practical way including vitamin content. Ironies aside, it was evident that filled milk simply did not present any dangers of fraud, or even serious dangers of confusion. It was sold in cans clearly marked with proprietary brand names and unequivocally stating that the products were not milk. The ingredients were listed for anyone to read. The product was in full compliance with the labeling requirements of the federal food and drug act and with virtually all state legislation. Filled milk producers were willing to accept any further labeling requirements that Congress might impose.

* * *

As with the health argument, the argument from consumer welfare cut in exactly the wrong direction. The interests of consumers would have been much better served by permitting and encouraging trade in filled milk than by outlawing a healthful, nutritious, and low-cost item of food.

C. THE "NATIONAL INTEREST"

The final argument for the statute was the contention that filled milk posed a threat to the dairy industry, a vital institution essential to the national welfare. At bottom the argument was a thinly disguised expression of self-interest. So interpreted, it was no doubt valid: filled milk did threaten the dairy industry. Yet the argument at least purported to consider the broader public interest as well.

One oft-repeated assertion was that dairying preserved the "fertility of American soil." The connection between dairying and the fertility of the soil was never spelled out, but it was obvious to anyone who had ever walked across a cow pasture.

So understood, the argument is easily seen to be made of the same substance that gave such fertility to the soil. While the by-product of the dairy cow was undoubtedly good fertilizer, it was no better, and considerably less convenient, than other commercially available fertilizers. There was no evidence that the fertility of the soil would suffer a whit by a marginal decrease in the number of dairy cows due to competition from the "coconut cow" of the South Seas.

The "national interest" argument also incorporated disquieting ideas about the alleged superiority of milk-consuming cultures. McCollum, who was an odd blend of hard scientist, dairy huckster, and muddleheaded racist, epitomized these attitudes. His grand scheme divided humanity into milk-drinking and vegetable-eating peoples. With breathtaking disregard of history he asserted that milk drinkers had always enjoyed cultural and physical superiority over their leaf-chewing cousins. Not a single plant-eating culture, he claimed, "has ever come to the front in a matter of human achievement in any field of activity." Take the Japanese. "These people . . . are the subjects or vassals; they are the peoples who multiply in considerable numbers, but whose life is short, who are inefficient, of low mentality, warped by peculiar religious prejudices which ruined them. . . . They are a failure from the standpoint of living a normal human life." Milk-drinking peoples, on the other hand, "become large, strong, vigorous people, who . . . have the best trades in the world, who have an appreciation for art and literature and music, who are progressive in science and in every activity of the human intellect." Unpleasant as it may now seem, this racial stereotype had considerable currency the dairy districts of the country and in the Congress. Farmers of the "coconut cow" were portrayed as lazy, ignorant, dark-skinned natives who had nothing to do all day, but run up a tree and shake down a few nuts. A milk industry cartoon showed Congress, as a large white American, booting filled milk, personified as a small dark-skinned savage, back to the South Sea islands from which he came, while an American dairy cow watched with evident satisfaction.

Aside from its crass appeal to self-interest, the various appeals to the "national interest" had even less to recommend them than the vitamin or fraud contentions. The arguments in support of the statute, in short, were entirely implausible under any reasonable view of the evidence.

III. THE STATUTE AS AN INTEREST GROUP MEASURE

The history recounted above suggests several thoughts about the dynamics of American politics as expressed in the filled milk controversy. The analysis is based on the interest group theory of regulation developed by (among others) Stigler, Peltzman, Posner, and Becker. The familiar claim of this theory is that regulations are principally determined by the influence of political pressure groups rather than by ideology or rational debate. As currently constructed, the theory posits the existence of a political equilibrium in which interest groups "maximize their incomes by spending their optimal amount on political pressure, given the productivity of their expenditures and the behavior of other groups." The theory recognizes that the outcome of the political struggle is rarely an absolute victory or defeat for any group, but rather reflects a balancing of interests in which each of the affected groups exerts equal pressure at the margin.

The battle over filled milk seems well-described by interest group theory. The most plausible inference is that the statute was enacted at the behest of a coalition of groups intent on advancing their own economic welfare at the expense of less powerful groups. An impressionistic view of the events surrounding the statute's enactment supports this inference: the sponsors were from big dairy states, while the chief opponents were from cotton states.

* * *

The filled milk controversy suggests some possible extensions of interest group analysis. First, the basic structural elements of the American constitutional system— federalism and separation of powers—mediated the process of interest group rivalry in quite different ways. A repeated phenomenon of dairy industry politics is that the interest groups would go first to the states before attempting federal legislation. This pattern held true in the case of filled milk, where the interest groups obtained discriminatory legislation in a number of states before presenting their case to Congress. The states acted as "laboratories," not in Brandeis's sense of experimental arenas for socially beneficial legislation, but in the sense that they provided an ideal testing ground for special interest measures. State legislation gave the dairy industry an opportunity to develop its case against filled milk, to assess the feasibility, enforceability, and constitutionality of different legislative approaches, and to organize coalitions at the state level before attempting to develop a national campaign.

Although the existence of overlapping state and federal sovereigns provided opportunities for the dairy industry, it also posed problems. Under the limited interpretation of the Commerce Clause then in effect, Congress was powerless to prohibit the manufacture or intrastate sale of the substance. And the dairy industry was never able to obtain prohibitory legislation in all states. Thus federalism prevented the industry from achieving its goal of an absolute ban on filled milk. Filled milk continued to be produced and sold in states that had not banned the product. In a unitary system the dairy industry might have administered the coup de grace.

Separation of powers also played a powerful mediating role in the politics of filled milk. It was not enough for the dairy industry to obtain legislation; the legislation had to be enforced by the executive branches of the state or federal governments and upheld by the judicial branches. Although the campaign against filled milk was more successful in this regard than the industry's battles against margarine, it nevertheless ran into difficulties outside the legislative arenas. After a period of relatively vigorous enforcement the executive branches of the state and federal governments grew lax about prosecuting violations of the filled milk statutes. The Department of Agriculture eviscerated the federal statute through interpretation, and it is likely that state attorneys general were similarly disinclined to enforce their statutes. The judicial branches also proved nettlesome, at least at the state level where a substantial number of filled milk statutes were struck down. At the federal level, the *Carolene Products* cases suggested that the judiciary would no longer block economic regulation. That prophecy has apparently been disproved in the case of filled milk, but it remains generally true for economic legislation. There is, however, the possibility that the Court may someday tighten up its scrutiny in economic matters.

On the other hand, separation of powers was not necessarily an unambiguous evil for the dairy industry. The system of divided powers allowed it to go first to the branch of government where it had the most influence—the legislature, where the votes of 5 million dairy farmers spoke loudly indeed. The industry was able to obtain some relief, even if the legislation was progressively weakened as it passed through the executive and judicial levels of the enforcement process. Moreover, it is not always the case that special interests will receive their most favorable reception in the legislature. Many groups find executive agencies to be the preferred forum from which to obtain protection. Others go first to the courts. In a unitary system, interest groups might have less, not more ability to obtain favorable action because they would have to present their petitions to the government as a whole.

* * *

IV. CONCLUSION

In the *Carolene Products* footnote, justice Stone suggested that special protections were needed for "discrete and insular minorities" because such groups would not be adequately served by the political process. The statement, if meant as a general observation about American politics, is obviously misplaced. Public choice theory demonstrates that, in general, "discrete and insular minorities" are exactly the groups that are likely to obtain disproportionately large benefits from the political process.

The insights of public choice theory are amply demonstrated by the battle over filled milk, where one discrete minority—the nation's dairy farmers—and their allies obtained legislation harmful to consumers and the public at large. To be sure, the legislation discriminated against another discrete minority—the filled milk industry—but this fact simply reflects the complexity of the dairy industry. Filled milk producers, if they had not been trumped by a politically more powerful group, might themselves have been able to obtain special legislative favors to the detriment of the public interest.

The political theory underlaying the *Carolene Products* footnote, now a half-century old, needs to be updated. The results of that process may call in question the Supreme Court's policy of blind deference to legislation favoring special industrial interests. Is it time to re-examine the wisdom of "see-no-evil, hear-no-evil" as the prevailing philosophy in economic regulation cases?

Frank H. Easterbrook, *Substance and Due Process*, 1982 SUP. CT. REV. 85 (1982)*

* * *

CONSTITUTIONAL HISTORY

* * *

An increasing number of scholars maintain that history is no sure guide—indeed no guide at all—to constitutional interpretation. Three overlapping arguments are available to this end. One is that the meaning of the words in 1791 is not controlling and that each generation must invent its own constitution. Another is that history is vague and manipulable and, worse, that there is no historical guide to the appropriate level of generality at which to read history. Finally, it is argued that the Framers put open-ended clauses into the Constitution so that the judiciary could revise the rules to meet the needs of each new age. The third, the "living constitution" approach, is the only one judges will confess to taking seriously.

One branch of the living constitution approach rests on the language and history of particular constitutional provisions. One could prove or disprove it clause by clause. Another branch, perhaps the dominant one today, simply asserts that the Constitution as an entity should be construed with great flexibility, perhaps because of

---

a meta-intent of the Framers, perhaps because there are a few clauses so elastic that the strictures of others are unimportant perhaps just because the absence of such flexibility produces undesirable consequences. To the extent this second branch prevails, the history of each clause is less important, and the three positions are barely distinguishable in practice. Any of them allows courts to proceed in accordance with the judges' own notions of justice.

It is easy to become mired in a discussion of these approaches to constitutional construction. Scholars who spend too much time debating how to conduct a discourse may never be able to say anything. I therefore reject all three approaches without extended discussion here. It is enough for now to say that I agree with justice Holmes, judges Bork and Hand, Professors Black and Monaghan, and many others, that language and structure, informed by constitutional history, are the proper basis of interpretation and that, perhaps, they are all that count.

To the extent we wish to make propositions about the Constitution we have, rather than about the one we wish we had, we must start with language, structure, and history, even if we do not end there. That these tools of interpretation do not answer all questions does not mean they are useless. History lays down the baseline against which other arguments are measured; it also lays down the principles by which we can elaborate further from the historical experience.

The three methods of evading history that I sketched above are—at least if the second meaning is given to the living constitution argument—a method of constituting the courts a council of revision. Yet the Framers considered and rejected a council of revision. They provided an amending clause to permit accommodation of changed circumstances but to make that accommodation difficult. Nothing else would assure the initial support by extraordinary majorities that characterizes constitutional structure. An easy process of alteration produces instability in the nation's fundamental institutions, an instability that becomes more pronounced as time passes, if only because the chance of error increases as the years separate us from 1789. The whole idea of having a written constitution is inconsistent with constant revisions in interpretation, and there is no good evidence that the Framers designed such flexibility into the document. Words are designed to control. We have a text and must make sense of it even at some cost to today's notions of moral philosophy.

It is hard, moreover, to take the position that judges have great flexibility without saying that the rest of the actors in the government have similar flexibility, unbounded by either language or the commands of courts. Consider, for example, why we adhere to the notion of judicial review, to the principle that the legislative and executive branches are bound by the judiciary's pronouncements. Judicial review, at least as Marshall proclaimed it, rests on the belief that the Constitution has an ascertainable meaning and, as the document granting power to Congress and the Court alike, limits what each may do.

When the Court states a judgment of unconstitutionality, it cannot just say why it finds its disposition a just result. It must also state a good reason why the other branches are required to pay attention. If the Court does not accept Congress's treatment of Congress's powers, why should Congress accept the Court's? When the Court claims a power of constitutional review, it must give a compelling reason why Congress and the President should follow the Court's view of Congress's power and of the Court's power too. The reason the Court states will usually take the form of an appeal to jointly held principles. It will assert, at a level of generality capable of generating belief: "Someone else decided this question, at an earlier time, in a way that you will agree binds all institutions of government." Such a claim to prior decision forecloses a claim to substantial powers of judicial revision. A Court that finds in the Constitution limits on the power of Congress and the states has found the limits on its own power.

Surely, it cannot avoid these limits by saying that it may update constitutional rules because the enunciation and application of principles is a function at which courts have become skilled, or because courts administer general principles better than any other institution. An argument based on experience begs the question whether the Court legitimately obtained (or maintains) this relative expertise. Moreover, the argument that power flows from aptitude is identical to the President's argument that he could seize and run the steel mills without Congress's authorization because Executives are good at such things, and to Congress's argument that Congress may appoint members to the Federal Election Commission because Members of Congress have special skills in election matters. The reasons the Court gave for rejecting the President's and Congress's arguments apply to it too.

* * *

A provision so limited would do little service unless, contrary to the expectations of the Federalists, the Executive began to behave in a monarchical fashion. (Congress was not worried in 1791 about judicial tyranny.) But monarchy and tyranny did not appear in the United States under the Constitution. Laws were passed and (usually) obeyed in the ordinary course. The Due Process Clause accordingly was largely irrelevant. The Clause that entered the Constitution without debate, indeed almost without notice, fell into desuetude. The Supreme Court was not even to mention it for sixty-five years, although in the interim it handed down hundreds of cases interpreting other provisions of the Constitution. The Due Process Clause escaped the Court's notice for the same reason it escaped the Framers': it stated an uncontroversial principle that was expected to be trivial.

Early commentators took what was, if possible, an even narrower reading of the clause than the one I have offered. They saw it as limited to criminal cases. Chancellor Kent remarked that due process meant only "law in its regular course of administration through courts of Justice" in criminal cases. Justice Story agreed, treating the due process language as limited to criminal trials and indictment and proceedings in conformity with the prevailing modes. Kent and Story thought that mere conformity to prevailing procedures, plus adherence to Coke's fundamental rights of indictment and jury, always would satisfy the constitutional demand. The Clause had no application at all to civil cases, and both Kent and Story would have found incoherent an assertion that the Clause had something to say about the procedures Congress could specify for poor relief, public employment, or the disposition of other new substantive entitlements.

Robert G. McCloskey, *Economic Due Process and the Supreme Court: An Exhumation and Reburial,* 1962 SUP. CT. REV. 34 (1962)*

* * *

II. THE DEMISE OF A DOCTRINE: THE METHOD

The judicial reaction against economic due process after 1937 is unique in the history of the Supreme Court. There have been gradual shifts from negativism to permissiveness, as in the antitrust field during the decades after *E. C. Knight*; there have been abrupt departures from salient negative doctrines as in *Nebbia* or in *Graves v. New York*. But it is hard to think of another instance when the Court so thoroughly and quickly demolished a constitutional doctrine of such far-reaching significance. The concomitant destruction of "dual federalism" in the commerce field is doubtless the closest analogue. But there the negative standard had rested in fact on a comparatively scanty handful of precedents, and the Court in *United States v. Darby* could draw on a line of contrary pronouncements beginning with Marshall. On the other hand, the judicial power to strike down an economic statute on the ground that it was "arbitrary, capricious, or unreasonable" had been frequently exercised and seemed to stand on a solid base. Most of the Court's critics and some of its friends might have hoped in the early 1930's that the "rational basis" standard would be applied more leniently. But only a singularly prescient observer could have dreamed that the Court would soon abandon the concept altogether.

* * *

III. ACTION AND REACTION

* * *

The harder question is: Why did the Court move all the way from the inflexible negativism of the old majority to the all-out tolerance of the new? Why did it not establish a halfway house between the extremes, retaining a measure of control over economic legislation but exercising that control with discrimination and self-restraint?

A[n] . . . explanation . . . .. It is that extremism had bred extremism in thinking about the role of the Supreme Court. Between 1923 and 1937, a conservative majority had, from time to time, embraced a policy of adamant resistance to economic experiment, and this obstructionist spirit had reached its zenith in the judicial reaction against the New Deal. . . .

This intransigence had tended to discredit the whole concept of judicial supervision in the minds of those who felt that government must have reasonable leeway to experiment with the economic order. The result was that the two winds of the Court (and of the country) had almost ceased to communicate with each other. The dissenting opinions of Stone in *United States v. Butler* and Sutherland in *West Coast Hotel* are not a dialogue between men who share a common ground but disagree about its implications. The opinions represent wholly different realms of discourse. If the position of the conservatives had been less extreme, there might have been in 1937

---

the basis for a viable, moderate doctrine of economic supervision. It is almost touching to observe Sutherland, in *Carmichael v. Southern Coal & Coke Co.*, after the "revolution" of 1937, urging that the State law could be cured of its constitutional infirmities and that, if it were, the objective of relieving unemployment could be attained despite the Due Process Clause. This language of sweet reason had not been conspicuous in the negative decisions of previous years. Now it came too late. The extreme of the past had generated the extreme of the present. The Court which had claimed the full loaf was winding up without even the half. Such a result is not surprising when dogmatism has been substituted for discussion.

Factors like these may help to explain the impulse to discard the old due process doctrine, bag and baggage. Yet one would like to think that a more thoughtful process was going on somewhere below the surface, that the policy of virtual abdication was not merely a reflex against the excesses of the past but a considered and justified decision about the proper scope of judicial review. The written record to support such a supposition is not, alas, very convincing. Scattered remarks in decisions cited above, and in others, assailed the dead horse of "the Allgeyer-Lochner-Adair-Coppage" doctrine, i.e., the justices argued against "social dogma" and for "increased deference to the legislative judgment" in the economic field. But they did not explain why the abuses of power in those earlier decisions justified abandonment of the power itself, nor why the deference to the legislature should be carried to the point of complete submission. The nearest thing to an explanation is perhaps to be found in Mr. Justice Frankfurter's concurrence in *American Federation of Labor v. American Sash & Door Co.*, where he argued that "the judiciary is prone to misconceive the public good" and that matters of policy, depending as they do on imponderable value issues, are best left to the people and their representatives. This is a coherent and not unconvincing viewpoint, but the trouble with it has always been that it implied similar judicial withdrawal, not only from the economic field, but from other areas that pose questions of policy, such as freedom of expression. Well aware of this difficulty, Frankfurter tried to meet it in this opinion by declaring that matters like press censorship and separation of church and state are different, because "history, through the Constitution, speaks so decisively as to forbid legislative experimentation" with them. Scholarship has since provided reason to doubt that history speaks so plainly after all, even on these subjects, and without a strong, historical rationale the argument falters badly, for the arguments against judicial intervention in economic affairs become arguments against intervention in the policy sphere generally. . . .

But it is certainly not the dominant doctrine of the modern Court, which has fairly consistently held to the "dual standard" enunciated by Stone in the *Carolene Products* case. So we are left with a judicial policy which rejects supervision over economic matters and asserts supervision over personal rights; and with a rationale, so far as the written opinions go, that might support withdrawal from both fields but does not adequately justify the discrimination between them.

IV. THE DOUBTFUL DISTINCTION BETWEEN ECONOMIC
AND CIVIL RIGHTS

* * *

The arguments for demoting economic rights to their modern lowly constitutional status—lowly when compared with "personal rights"—fall into two categories. First, there is a group of arguments based on judgments about the nature and relative importance of the rights concerned. For example, it is sometimes argued that laws limiting freedom of expression impinge on the human personality more grievously than do laws curbing mere economic liberty, and that the Court is therefore justified in protecting the former more zealously than the latter. The individual has, *qua* individual, "the right to be let alone." The right to free choice in the intellectual and spiritual realm is particularly precious to him. A major difficulty with this formulation is that there is the smell of the lamp about it: it may reflect the tastes of the judges and dons who advance it, rather than the real preferences of the commonality of mortals. Judges and professors are talkers both by profession and avocation. It is not surprising that they would view freedom of expression as primary to the free play of their personalities. But most men would probably feel that an economic right, such as freedom of occupation, was at least as vital to them as the right to speak their minds. Mark Twain would surely have felt constrained in the most fundamental sense, if his youthful aspiration to be a river-boat pilot had been frustrated by a State-ordained system of nepotism. Needless to say, no disparagement of freedom of expression is here intended. But its inarguable importance to the human spirit, on the one hand, does not furnish an adequate ground for downgradiing all economic rights, on the other.

So much for a purely individual-centered justification for the disparity between economic rights and other civil liberties. Another suggested rationale looks toward the community rather than the separate individuals within it. Progress, it is said, "is to a considerable extent the displacement of error which once held sway as official truth by beliefs which in turn have yielded to other beliefs." To encourage societal progress, it is important then to protect "those liberties of the individual which history has attested as the indispensable conditions of an open as against a closed society," *e.g.*, freedom of expression.

. . . In short, the special importance of certain civil rights derives from their special relationship to the process of self-government. Other rights, including the economic, can be abridged when the legislature deems abridgment desirable.

* * *

The whole "open society" line of argument in its various forms is convincing enough as a justification for protecting the free trade in ideas. If one feels the need to explain why the free speech guarantees are important, these explanations will do pretty well for a start. But they are rather less satisfactory as the basis for a policy of *not* protecting economic freedom, of regarding it as unimportant in a democratic system. For one thing, it is not entirely clear why liberty of economic choice is less indispensable to the "openness" of a society than freedom of expression. Few historians would deny that the growth of entrepreneurial and occupational freedom helped to promote material progress in England in the eighteenth and nineteenth centuries and in America after the Civil War (although they might of course argue that the price paid for this progress was unconscionably high). It is one thing to argue that economic liberty must be subject to rational control in the "public interest"; it is quite another to say in effect that it is not liberty at all and that the proponent of the "open society" can therefore regard it as irrelevant to progress.

As for the "political process" subthemes of the open-society argument . . . they too must be queried insofar as they purport to justify a downgrading of economic rights. In fact, their basic difficulty is that, in exalting the freedoms bearing on the political process, they bypass the question of other freedoms altogether. . . . Arguments for protecting liberty of expression are cogent, but they do not on their face explain why other, "private," rights should be neglected. A decision to protect Peter does not necessarily involve the decision to abandon Paul. . . . We can refuse to swallow whole the dogmas of nineteenth century rugged individualism and can still believe that some freedom of occupation and economic choice is also instrumental to the development of this self-determining and sensitive citizen-governor.

If [the above] argument contains the unexamined assumption that the political is primary and almost exclusive, the "Stone-Frankfurter" point described above contains this and an assumption of its own as well: the majoritarian idea in a peculiarly unqualified form. The notion seems to be that the citizen can have nothing really fundamental to complain about in a law if a free majority has enacted it and if he is protected in his right to agitate for its repeal. But this view ascribes a preponderance to the majority will that has certainly not been acknowledged by the American political tradition. In that tradition, it is not assumed that an unjust law becomes just by virtue of majority approval, not even if the victim has the theoretical right to persuade the majority to change its mind. The denial of that right would aggravate the injustice, but the granting of the right does not dispel it. As Justice Jackson said in the flag-salute dialogue, the very purpose of a Bill of Rights was to place certain fundamental rights beyond the reach of majorities. Of course, it may be argued that economic freedom in its various forms can never be so fundamental a right, but that shifts the discussion to a quite different level.

Furthermore this argument overlooks a difficulty partly recognized by Stone himself in the *Carolene Products* footnote and invoked by him in the first flag-salute case, the problem of "discrete and insular minorities," *i.e.*, those who have no realistic chance of influencing the majority to rescind the law that does them harm. Stone was speaking specifically of religious, national, or racial minorities, and his suggestion was that prejudice against them might curtail the political processes that would ordinarily be expected to protect their rights. Prejudice against Jehovah's Witnesses for their "queerness" makes repressive governmental action more probable, and precisely because of their queerness they are not likely to be numerous enough or influential enough in any given community so that their weight will be felt in the city council. To speak of their power to defend themselves through political action is to sacrifice their civil rights in the name of an amiable fiction. Yet it is not clear why the thrust of this point should be restricted to ethnic and religious minorities. Perhaps it is true that a prosperous corporation can effectively plead its case at the bar of legislative judgment by resort to publicity and direct lobbying. Economic power may be an adequate surrogate for numerical power; no tears need be shed for helpless General Electric. But the scattered individuals who are denied access to an occupation by State-enforced barriers are about as impotent a minority as can be imagined. The would-be barmaids of Michigan or the would-be plumbers of Illinois have no more chance against the entrenched influence of the established bartenders and master plumbers than the Jehovah's Witnesses had against the prejudices of Minersville School District. In fact the Witnesses may enjoy an advantage, for they are at least cohesive; and other "discrete" minorities, such as racial groups, have occasionally displayed respectable capacities to exert political leverage by virtue of their very discreteness. Not so the isolated economic man who belongs to no identifiable group at all.

V. JUDICIAL CAPACITY IN THE REALM OF ECONOMIC REGULATION

For one reason or another then, none of these justifications of the Court's modern hands-off policy in the economic field quite stands up. The distinctions they rely on, between economic rights on the one hand and personal rights on the other, tend to blur when we examine them. And, even if it were thought that the distinctions were tenable, the case would remain incomplete. It might, squeezing it hard, justify a difference in the kind and degree of protection afforded economic rights; but it would not warrant a policy of no protection at all.

Although the policy of abdication cannot be justified in terms of an analysis of the nature and relative unimportance of the rights concerned, there is a second line of thought that merits consideration. Perhaps the decision to leave economic rights to the tender mercy of the legislative power is based on the idea that the Supreme Court is peculiarly ill-equipped to deal with this subject. No one would argue that the right enshrined in Article IV, the guarantee of a republican form of government, is unimportant. Yet the Court has refused to protect it, because of well-founded doubts about judicial competence to make effective judgments in this field. It may be that similar doubts underlie the policy of abdication in the area of economic affairs.

At first blush, this argument seems highly persuasive, at least in broad terms. . . .

Those who remember the Court's crusades against the rise of the welfare state may be dubious about judicial competence on somewhat different grounds. They may feel that economic policy is not only beyond the reach of the Court's expertise, but beyond the reach of its practical power. Whether the nation shall have a minimum-wage law; whether the government shall control prices; whether social security shall be publicly guaranteed—these are questions so "high" and so basic that no court could determine them even if it should. They involve in a word the momentous issue of the welfare state itself, and that issue will be determined by "dominant opinion" with or without judicial approval.

There are, of course, economic subjects so recondite that judicial surveillance of them would be anomalous. The choice between "historical cost" and "placement cost" as a basis for rate making must be made by the legislature, not because it will always choose well, but because the judiciary lacks the knowledge and expertise for distinguishing good from bad in this area. But this point will carry only as far as its logic will bring it, and there are fields of economic regulation less intricate than the problem of public utility rates. To be sure, even the problems raised in these fields may not be simple. A fair evaluation of Oklahoma's need for its anti-optician law would require the Court to make judgments about a complex matter. But this can be said about most questions that reach the Supreme Court in any field. Our problem is not to identify the issues that present difficulties and then to discard them as improper subjects for judicial review. That would be to abandon judicial review in most of the fields where it is now exercised. Our problem is to determine whether economic statutes always or usually involve such extraordinary difficulties that a modest judiciary must eschew them, even though that same judiciary does claim the competence to judge other, more difficult, issues.

Is it easier for example for the Court to appraise a law empowering a board of censors to ban an "immoral movie" than a law empowering a real estate licensing board to deny a license unless the applicant is of "good moral character"? The two standards would seem to be equally vague and the possibility of arbitrary administrative action would seem to be as menacing in one situation as in the other. Is it easier to see that the State corporate registration law in *N.A.A.C.P. v. Alabama* was being used to facilitate private reprisals against Association members than it is to see that State boards of plumbers, barbers, and morticians sometimes use their publicly granted powers to protect the private financial interests of present guild members to the disadvantage of non-members?

The point is not that the cited cases should necessarily have been decided differently, but rather that the issues they present stand on a common level of difficulty and that judicial scrutiny seems as feasible (or unfeasible) for one issue as for the other. And the further, related, point is that there are kinds and kinds of economic subjects and that it is difficult to fashion a generalization that applies to all. Some subjects may be so inscrutable that judicial review cannot fruitfully cope with them; but this is not a justification for avoiding other economic subjects which are no more opaque than the "personal rights" issues that are the standard coinage of judicial discourse these days.

This point likewise applies to the suggestion that the Court, as the relatively weak and non-political branch, simply lacks the power to dictate the economic order, however otherwise competent its members may be. No doubt the Court was presumptuous to imagine, before 1917, that it could hold back such waves as the wage-control movement or the demand for social security. The tide of the welfare state was flowing, and no court could have reversed it. But neither does the judiciary have the practical power to halt any major social developments backed by insistent popular demand. And this would be so whether the development involved economic questions or questions of "personal rights." It was the dimension of the issues in the anti-New Deal cases that made them incongruous for judicial decision, not the mere fact that they were economic in character. No such judicial delusions of grandeur would be implied by enforcement of the requirement that an occupational qualification must be rationally based, or by similar modest applications of substantive due process. . . . In short, while doubts about judicial expertise and power may warrant withdrawal from some economic questions, they cannot justify withdrawal from all such questions, unless the doubter is willing to go the full distance and give up most of the residue of modern judicial review.

* * *

VI. REQUIESCAT IN PACE

* * *

. . . [I]t is legitimate, and perhaps timely, for an observer of the Court's work to ask whether constitutional law should move down that road again, whether the Court should reassert its claim to examine the reasonableness of economic legislation. . . .

. . . The Supreme Court is an agency of Government and, like other agencies of government, must work within the limits of political possibility. It has been suggested above that a revival of economic due process in connection with a subject like occupational freedom would not by itself overstrain the Court's power. But when the prospect of such a development is considered against the background of other recent assumptions of authority, the calculus may be very different. Various personal-rights decisions during that period have taxed not only the "time-chart" and the reasoning power of the justices but their effective prestige as well. . . . Doubtless it is regrettable that factors like these must be brought into an assessment of judicial capacities. A world in which the ethical-legal mandates of the Court were accepted without question by those affected would be a comfortable world for the justices and perhaps not a bad one for the United States as a whole. But it is not, and never has been, the world the Court lives in; and in the real world a friend of the Court quails at the thought of seeing it assume still another politically delicate task.

All things considered, then, it seems best that the cause of economic rights be left by the Supreme Court to lie in its uneasy grave. This need not mean that the legislatures of the nation are warranted in ignoring them, nor that the State courts, applying their own constitutions, should be indifferent to plausible due process claims. These rights, or some of them, do have a bearing on the justness of a society and on the happiness and well-being of the people who live in it. If the Supreme Court of today had a free hand in choosing the subjects of judicial review, there might well be an argument for choosing the right to work over some of the other subjects that engage Court attention. But it does not have a free hand; its liberty of choice has been considerably foreclosed by the episodic course of constitutional law since 1937. The Supreme Court, like the American political system of which it is a part, proceeds by impulse rather than by design, pragmatically rather than foresightedly. Like the United States, the Court derives advantages from this approach; but like the United States, the Court, too, is bound by its limitations.

Note, *A Process-Oriented Approach to the Contract Clause,* 89 YALE L.J. 1623 (1980)*

* * *

A. Threshold Inquiry

The preliminary stage of a court's analysis should be to determine whether the case involves a contract rather than some other form of legal interest. If a contract is involved, the court must determine whether, in the ordinary contract-law sense—that is, ignoring constitutional considerations—it has been impaired. The court would inquire whether, but for the challenged state law, either the full obligation of all parties would have been met or a state remedy would have been available to compensate for nonperformance of a contractual obligation. A negative answer would signify that the state has not interfered with the contract in violation of its tacit or express assurances of security.

B. The Elements of Process Scrutiny

Process scrutiny differs from the existing approaches to contract clause jurisprudence in that it recognizes the constraints on institutional role that caution against independent judicial determination of the public interest. If the legislature is functioning properly, selection of a public purpose and determinations of necessity and appropriateness should be left to it. Even if the legislative process is inadequate, the proposed approach would invalidate legislation only on process grounds, leaving open the possibility that the legislature could reenact the legislation after remedying the defects in process.

Judicial determination of the adequacy of process would focus on two related questions: whether the legislature made the judgments necessary to support the validity of the impairment, and whether political processes functioned effectively to provide all interested parties with a fair opportunity to argue their cases or to challenge an adverse decision. The requisite legislative judgments would depend upon whether a public or private contract is at issue. The adequacy of process would depend upon the grounds for suspecting insufficient legislative consideration of the interests of a burdened group.

Requiring explicit judgments in order to justify an impairment could render political checks effective for several reasons. Explicitness would enhance legislative responsibility by opening the action and its supporting judgments to public criticism

---

    *   Reprinted by permission of The Yale Law Journal Company and Fred B. Rothman & Company from The Yale Law Journal, Vol. 89, pages 1623-1651.

and electoral response. Explicitness would also constrain legislators more directly by forcing them to predict their constituents' reaction and to analyze more fully the justification for their action. By articulating the policy and factual judgments implicit in their decisions, legislators would invite more immediate and effective criticism from fellow legislators and other persons who monitor and influence legislation.

A court applying process review in contract clause cases would have to decide when to doubt that the legislature had fully considered the interests of all concerned parties. The legislative process might fail in two ways. First, the legislature could rely upon public willingness to accept the particular legislation even though it has not made the judgments necessary to support the impairment. Second, the burdened group could be politically weak or an easy target for the imposition of costs and hence chosen to bear those costs without fair attention to its interests. Failure of the process in either respect would warrant suspicion that the legislative decision was not supported by public policies sufficient to justify an impairment.

C. Requisite Legislative Judgments

Integration of the principles underlying the contract clause requires separate consideration of public-contract cases and private-contract cases in defining which judgments should suffice to justify an impairment. In public-contract cases, the proposed approach requires states to overcome the presumptive primacy of contractual security; in private-contract cases no such presumption should be established.

1. Public Contracts

In a public-contract case, a court should presume that impairment of the contract upset legitimate expectations. In entering into the contract, the state negotiated its terms and committed itself expressly to honoring the contract. As a consequence of this express commitment, other parties are strongly justified in relying upon enforcement of the contract. The stricture against the state's breaking its word therefore applies with great force. Impairment defeats a justified reliance interest, and courts should therefore require a legislature to address explicitly its failure to keep its word.

To justify the impairment, the state must find that enforcement of the contract conflicts with pursuit of a public goal and that imposition of the costs on the complaining party is appropriate. Courts should presume that the state continues to adhere to the policy and factual judgments implicit in the initial contractual undertaking. To overcome that presumption, the legislature must specify policies or conditions that have changed, or new information that has come forth, since the making of the contract. In addition to identifying the conflict, the state should be required to justify the fairness of impairing particular contracts to pursue the public purpose. In situations in which the state cannot persuasively identify the burdened party as responsible for harm, it could attempt to justify the appropriateness of the impairment on some other theory.

The adequacy of a legislature's support for its judgments would depend on the ability of interested parties to use political processes effectively to present their interests. The complaining party would be able to rebut the legislative judgments by establishing that the process was inadequate. If a court found reason to doubt that political processes ensure the genuineness of any of these legislative judgments, the impairment should be blocked.

2. *Private Contracts*

In private-contract cases, courts should not presume the primacy of contractual expectations. Because the state cannot be expected to anticipate every private contract, tacit assurances that the contract will be enforced cannot be treated as firm commitments. Impairment of a private contract, therefore, does not violate strong strictures against the state's breaking its word. In addition, because private contracts are made about virtually every conceivable subject, almost no legislation can escape upsetting some private contractual expectations. Courts therefore should not require a legislature to specify intervening changes of condition, information, or policy that necessitate impairment.

The state should, however, articulate the purpose that it claims requires impairment and explain the selection of the particular means chosen to pursue that purpose. In finding that pursuit of the goal and enforcement of the contract are in conflict, and in determining the fairness of imposing the costs upon contracting parties, the state would make the same judgments in a private-contract case as in a public-contract case. Those judgments would be subject to the same constraints: adequate political process to ensure fair consideration for interested parties, and sufficient explicitness and factual support to allay suspicions of legislative disingenuity. The judgments would also vary with the type of fairness justification being offered.

D. *Rethinking* United States Trust Co. *and* Spannaus

Under the proposed process approach, *United States Trust Co.,* a public-contract case, was correctly decided. The threshold inquiry would find at most a technical impairment. Furthermore, the state's claim that energy, environmental, and transportation policies had become significantly more important since 1962 was credible. Nevertheless, the state's necessity and appropriateness justifications were weak. Because obvious alternative means would have been politically unpopular, and because bondholders were a target group with little political strength, the process approach would require explicit support in the legislative record for judgments of necessity and appropriateness. Although the state might have shown necessity by articulating relevant legal constraints and subsidiary policies, and might have advanced a cost-benefit justification for imposing the minimal burden on bondholders, its failure to demonstrate adequate consideration of alternatives would justify invalidation.

The *Spannaus* legislation, on the other hand, would be upheld under the process approach. Interference with the pension agreement would constitute an impairment, but because a private contract was involved, the state would not need to demonstrate changed circumstances or policies; it would merely have to show that the impairment was necessary and appropriate. Though some evidence suggested hurried passage, the legislation was of a sufficiently common variety and was carefully enough drafted that the political process could be found to be functioning properly. Finally, a court could easily find that the state was protecting employees' reliance interests from actions of their employers that would harm those interests. The law therefore would be validated.

Conclusion

The process approach proposed in this Note would return to legislatures primary authority to resolve conflicts between public power and private expectations—authority that the recent revival of the contract clause has eroded. Although the new activism would thus be halted, the restoration of legislative authority would be accompanied by stringent requirements as to the process by which legislatures exercised that authority. The approach would foster responsible political processes and would direct courts to focus on the legislature's responsibility in making the public policy judgments upon which contract clause cases depend.

Joseph L. Sax, *Takings, Private Property and Public Rights,* 81 YALE L.J. 149 (1971)*

* * *

Current takings law assumes that when the government restricts the use of private property, the public has acquired something to which it did not previously have a right. While scrupulously preventing total loss to the particular owner, it often imposes that loss upon diffusely-held interests, such as those affected by drainage and erosion from a mining operation or those dependent upon the marine resources impaired by a wetlands filling and development project. The constitutional takings provision, it is assumed, assures compensation when government thus restrains the profit-making capacity of private property owners in favor of a more general public claim. To the extent that the courts adopt this perspective, they deny recognition of extant public rights.

The prevailing view of compensation law has a considerable practical effect on resource allocation, since the prospect of having to pay compensation is a constraint on government regulation of private property. Though it may be desirable, in terms of maximizing the net product of the aggregate resource base, to undertake a particular restriction on the use of private property, compelled compensation may deter a legislature from enacting the restriction. Notice that under current law, a failure to undertake restrictions may generate costs for diffuse interest-holders for which no compensation must be paid. Requiring compensation when a conflict among competing users is resolved in favor of diffuse interest-holders, and not when it is resolved against them, inevitably skews the political resolution of conflicts over resource use and discriminates against public rights.

Furthermore, a system which compels compensation in the event of severe diminution in value ignores the possible incentive function of leaving costs on private resource users. The question of allocating costs of conflict among competing resource users will be discussed below; for now it is sufficient to note that an important criterion in resource allocation is minimizing the costs of future conflict, and this goal is best served by a policy free to allocate costs on the party best equipped to avoid such conflict. To bring under the takings clause governmental restrictions designed to mediate between conflicting interests is to introduce a doctrinal rigidity inconsistent with the kind of planning essential to optimal resource allocation.

An important observation to be made about the analysis set out thus far is that it does not obliterate the distinction between mine and thine that lies at the heart of a system of private property. Rather, it notes that the simplistic way in which that distinction has been made under existing property law, attending solely to the physical boundaries of property, is insufficient. It does not make less valid a demand for compensation when government restricts uses that do not have spillover effects.

*   Reprinted by permission of The Yale Law Journal Company and Fred B. Rothman & Company from The Yale Law Journal, Vol. 81, pages 149-186.

The purpose of the analysis stated above is not to permit a redistribution of land to achieve the most socially beneficial use, but only to put competing resource-users in a position of equality when each of them seeks to make a use that involves some imposition (spillover) on his neighbors, and those demands are in conflict. In such cases, and such cases only, there is a conflict in which neither is a priori entitled to prevail, because neither claimant has any more right to impose on his neighbor than his neighbor does on him. Only in such situations may one use be curtailed by the government without triggering the takings clause.

It thus becomes necessary to explain what is meant by a use of property that has a spillover or inextricable effect on other property. The first and most obvious example of this situation is that in which my use of my land results in a physical restriction of the uses that may be made of other land, such as the mining of coal which results in drainage on lower-lying land.

A second type of spillover effect is the use of a common to which another landowner has an equal right, such as the dumping of water from industrial use into a stream upon which a landowner downstream depends for water supply. While a stream is the most obvious example of a common, it is by no means the only one. The ambient air is also a common of sorts. Thus putting smoke or noise or light into the air is the use of a common, and no use of land that has the effect of burdening this common can be claimed as a constitutionally insulated property right. Conversely, to use land in a way that demands silence, darkness or the absence of smoke on one's land is similarly to burden the common in air that belongs equally to one's neighbor and cannot be a matter of constitutional right. The water overlying wetlands that serves as a breeding ground for the adjacent ocean should also be viewed as a common as to conflicting demands of ocean users and the owner of the wetlands.

In a somewhat less conventional sense, a visual prospect is also a common. Thus, if the landscape as a visual prospect is not confinable to any single tract of land, no single landowner is entitled to dominate it. The effects of a vast tower built on a single tract spill over visually onto other lands just as smoke or noise does. Conversely, a majestic mountain or a forest generates positive spillover effects on nearby lands, and no owner has an unqualified constitutional right to destroy the mountain.

There is yet a third, less physical, kind of spillover effect. It is a use of property that affects the health or well-being of others, such as the treatment of land with toxic substances that results in the death of wildlife, or a use of property that imposes an affirmative obligation on the community, such as residential development in a remote area that would require the furnishing of police protection.

Any demand of a right to use property that has spillover effects in any of the three senses described above may constitutionally be restrained, however severe the economic loss on the property owner, without any compensation being required; for each of the competing interests that would be adversely affected by such uses has, a priori, an equal right to be free of such burdens.

Having thus defined spillover uses, it is essential to observe that any uses of property that do not involve such spillover effects are constitutionally entitled to protection, and may not be restricted without the payment of compensation. Notably, this distinction prevents a use of property from being restricted without compensation simply because a neighboring demand would provide a greater net benefit to the society.

The distinction may be illustrated by referring again to the strip mining-lower residence example. A legislature could, without compensation, prohibit mining resulting in drainage to protect the lower residences or it could protect residential uses that required freedom from drainage, since each of these uses imposes a spillover demand on the neighboring land. Assuming that mining were prohibited, however, the legislature could not require the mine land to be used as a parking lot for the cars of the lower residents, without compensation, regardless of the need for additional parking space. For to require the miner to submit to parking on his land without compensation would require him to forego profit from a use—such as farming, forestry or, indeed, operation of a private parking lot—that could be carried out by him without imposing spillover demands on uses the lower owners could make on their land. Assuming that uses can be made of the upper land which do not physically restrict a neighbor, burden a common, impose on the community an affirmative burden of providing public services, or adversely affect some interest in health or well-being (though of course they may adversely affect the usefulness of the lower land which badly needs additional parking space), the landowner has a constitutional right to make those uses. If he is restricted from doing so, he is entitled to receive as compensation the value of the highest and best use that could be made *without producing spillover effects.* If the legislature has restricted mining to prevent erosion, the landowner is not entitled to any special value the land may have as a coal mining site.

While the land described above would be physically invaded by a parking lot, note that the right to compensation does not arise simply because of that invasion. One's land may be invaded, as by a governmentally tolerated influx of noise or smoke, without triggering the takings clause, because both of the competing uses in question (e.g., residential as against industrial) put inconsistent demands on the other, and both are a priori equal in status. Either use may be restricted by the government without compensation.

Nor is a landowner better situated to receive compensation simply because the *surface* of his land, rather than the common in air above it, is invaded, for one may be required to tolerate a physical invasion of the surface without being constitutionally entitled to compensation (as where strip mining is permitted and water drainage over the lower lying land occurs). Similarly, one could constitutionally be prohibited from fencing his land, if that restriction were required to permit the free passage of wildlife, which could be viewed as a common resource not unlike a flowing river.

These examples are suggested only to emphasize that the traditional indicia of property right violation do not determine the question of compensation under the theory proposed here. The only appropriate question in determining whether or not compensation is due is whether an owner is being prohibited from making a use of his land that has no conflictcreating spillover effects. If the answer is affirmative, compensation is due for the value of land for that use.

* * *

Frank Michelman, *Takings, 1987*, 88 COLUM. L. REV. 1600, 1605-14, 1621-22 (1988)*

* * *

III. THE *NOLLAN* CASE: HEIGHTENED SCRUTINY AND
      PERMANENT PHYSICAL OCCUPATION

The Nollans owned a beachfront lot on which stood a small bungalow dilapidated (apparently) beyond the point of habitability. Rather than repair, they chose to demolish and replace the bungalow with a new and larger house. Under state statutes

*   This article originally appeared at 88 Colum. L. Rev. 1600 (1988). Reprinted by permission.

of unquestioned constitutionality, such new construction would be unlawful without a development permit issued by the California Coastal Commission. This agency's assigned purposes included protecting the public's interests in access to the shore, both bodily and visual (or "psychological"), and controlling shoreline congestion. The Supreme Court seemed to take for granted, at least arguendo, that the Commission would have committed no constitutional violation by denying the Nollans their permit unconditionally and without compensation on the ground (assuming it to be reasonably supportable on the facts) that their proposed development would, in combination with other, similarly restricted, proposed development in the neighborhood, "substantially impede" one or more of these public interests.

The complication comes because the Commission, instead of denying outright the Nollans' application, took what might seem the more lenient course of issuing a permit to the Nollans conditioned on their formally dedicating a public easement of passage across their land. Here there is a curiosity. Instead of demanding, as one might have expected, dedication of a passage from front to rear or street to shore, the Commission required a passage running laterally to the shore, along a narrow strip to the rear of the Nollans' house and beyond their seawall, adjacent to the mean high tide line that bounded their holding to the seaward side. (Presumably, this would have facilitated movement by members of the public between two public beach areas flanking the Nollans' land to both the north and south of it.) It was this lateral-passage condition that the Court found to constitute a taking.

The Court so found by a course of reasoning that turned, if somewhat ambiguously, on subjecting the instrumental merit of the Commission's action to a distinctly more active and intensive judicial reexamination than the kind of desultory, "rational basis" review that the Court has for the last half-century been applying to police-power regulations affecting economic interests, most notably including land-use regulations. Having posited, as the Commission's legitimate regulatory goals vis-à-vis the Nollans' proposal, a finite list of public interests meriting protection, the Court proceeded to find that these concededly legitimate goals were not substantially advanced by the regulatory device of exacting from the Nollans an easement of lateral passage and therefore could not justify the resultant imposition on the Nollans' property rights.

Prior to *Nollan,* a judicial determination of a property regulation's validity under the fifth or fourteenth amendment, to the extent that it involved any means-ends appraisal, involved only scrutiny of the public purposes plausibly ascribed to the regulation. If a regulation failed to meet the minimal test of plausibly serving some legitimate governmental purpose, it was a deprivation of property without due process of law. If, on the other hand, the regulation's plausible purpose lay in its restricting harmful or nuisance-like activity, that aspect of the regulation's "nature" would tend to exempt it from any further takings scrutiny. If neither of these conditions obtained, then there remained only the inquiry (rarely issuing in an affirmative answer) about whether the regulation's impact on the complaining owner was so grievous (invasive, discriminatory, or confiscatory) as to be a taking and, as such, unconstitutional unless attended by compensation. Thus, insofar as a takings inquiry might ever invalidate a regulation that could pass the desultory means-ends scrutiny involved in ordinary due process inspection, that additional inquiry was distinctively directed to the question of the severity of the regulation's impact on the complaining owner's interests. Takings (as distinguished from due process) inquiry was not about regulatory instrumental efficacy or urgency.

That is how matters stood, prior to *Nollan.* In *Nollan,* however, the Court did rely outright and crucially on its own censorious appraisal of instrumental efficacy in condemning as an uncompensated taking a regulation that in its degree of onerousness did not remotely approach the level of a total denial of economic value or "viability." What is even more striking is that the Court expressly endorsed a form of semi-strict or heightened judicial scrutiny of regulatory means-ends relationships in the course of invalidating, as a taking, the Commission's conditional regulatory imposition on the Nollans.

If this innovation is indeed now "the law" generally applicable to regulatory-takings claims across the board, its import is both clear and startling: Who knows how many land-use regulations, hitherto thought virtually immune from federal judicial censorship, might be destined for doom at the hands of lower federal courts now supremely licensed to apply to them an intensified means-ends scrutiny?

There may, however, be less to *Nollan*'s heightened-scrutiny lesson than first appears. The decision seems most satisfactorily understood as a further manifestation, albeit in somewhat surprising form, of the talismanic force of "permanent physical occupation" in takings adjudication. *Loretto v. Teleprompter Manhattan CATV Corp.* held that a regulation which directly and unconditionally imposes a permanent physical occupation on an unwilling owner is a taking per se. *Nollan* holds that when state regulatory action imposes permanent physical occupation conditionally rather than unconditionally, the aggrieved owner can challenge state regulatory action "as" a "taking," and thereby obtain a certain form of intensified judicial scrutiny of the condition's instrumental merit or urgency. There is no clear basis to be found in the opinion for concluding that the Court in *Nollan* decided or meant to decide anything beyond just that. Moreover, it is understandable, given *Loretto*, why the Court felt compelled to resort to heightened scrutiny (as opposed to either loose scrutiny or, at the other extreme, per se invalidation) in cases of conditional imposition of permanent physical occupation. Finally, this "narrow" reading of the decision has the virtue of fully explaining the opinion and its result without, implausibly, turning *Nollan* into *Lochner redivivus*. Indeed, when the case is thus understood, it is hardly a novelty at all.

Pointing strongly towards the narrow reading is the stark fact that Justice Scalia began his analysis of *Nollan* by taking pains to assert, as his argument's first premise, an analogy between the *Nollan* and *Loretto* cases. Scalia's point was to establish that the lateral-passage easement required of the Nollans by the Commission fell within the legal-doctrinal category of "permanent physical occupation," so that if the requirement had been imposed by direct regulation, rather than indirectly as a building-permit condition, the regulation imposing it would have been a per se taking under the *Loretto* doctrine.

Arguing against the narrow reading, it might be argued, are two other, equally stark features of the Court's opinion. First, the Court's reasoning did not rest where it started, that is, with the *Loretto* analogy and permanent physical occupation. Rather, it proceeded to what appears to be a more generally applicable, intensified scrutiny of the "nexus," or lack of it, between the Commission's specific imposition upon the Nollans—requiring that they not build without dedicating the lateral easement—and the Commission's public regulatory pursuits—protecting beach access. Second, the Court went out of its way to suggest that it might be prepared to uphold a demand from the Commission "that the Nollans provide a viewing spot on their property for passersby with whose sighting of the ocean their new house would interfere," thus indicating that it would uphold a regulatory imposition even of permanent physical occupation if satisfied that such an imposition would avoid or requite some interference with the regulator's public objectives threatened or caused by the regulated owner's activity. Do not those two features of the opinion taken together immediately refute any suggestion that it pivots on permanent physical occupation or that the Court is treating permanent physical occupation as the *sine qua non* of heightened scrutiny?

To understand why they do not, it is necessary to begin by noticing the obvious disanalogy, as well as analogy, between the *Nollan* and *Loretto* cases. In the *Nollan* case, the Court invalidated, as an uncompensated taking, a restrictive exercise of regulatory power in the indirect form of conditional denial of a building permit. In and of itself, denial of a permit is not physically invasive. Physical occupation enters the case only as the condition upon which the aggrieved landowners would be allowed to build. This indirectness is sufficient to explain why the Court would feel that its hypothetical case of the "viewing spot" condition would not be governed (in the Nollans' favor) by *Loretto.* In *Loretto,* the aggrieved owner's only alternative to suffering permanent physical occupation was destruction of her building's value as rental property—a taking, it would seem, in another form. But in the Court's hypothetical case—like *Nollan* itself a case not of direct regulation but of conditional issuance of a building permit—the alternative to permanent physical occupation is not so dire. In both the hypothetical and actual cases, the Nollans could have avoided any physical occupation by the alternative, readily available and economically viable so far as appears, of forgoing the new construction in return for which regulators were demanding an easement. There is, therefore, no logical ground for treating these cases as falling into the special *Loretto* category of a regulatory taking per se, rather than into the residual category of cases that simply fail the *Agins* test of denial of economic viability. But if we thus conclude that the availability to the Nollans of an economically viable alternative renders their case unfit for the *Loretto* taking-per-se treatment, the question then arises as to why that same fact should not entirely defeat their takings claim without the further ado of heightened means-ends scrutiny. The Court, after all, was apparently prepared to take it as a given that unconditional denial of the permit would not have been a compensable taking because it both would have been a suitable way of advancing the Commission's access-protection objectives and would not have left the Nollans with a valueless holding. How, then, can a *conditional* grant of the permit (which leaves the Nollans with more options than would a total denial) amount to an unconstitutional taking? The Court's answer to this question requires a little unpacking.

Let us imagine that California enacts a law simply declaring that no owner of privately held beachfront shall forbid or impede lateral public passage along a five-foot wide path bounded on the seaward side by mean high tide. The *Nollan* Court's first premise was that under the per se doctrine of *Loretto,* this, in effect, direct regulatory impressment of public easements on all privately held California littoral has to be a taking. Now imagine that the legislature, anticipating this response, enacts instead a law barring all private owners of California beachfront land from access to any public water supply or other utility service, except on condition of the owner's having dedicated a public easement of lateral passage across privately held dry sand. The Court understandably would perceive such a case as one of taking by subterfuge (or "extortion"), because the regulation's purpose is, too obviously to ignore, the constitutionally illicit one of evading the *Loretto* doctrine by "obtaining . . . an easement to serve some valid governmental purpose, but without payment of compensation."

The Court took the position that the only way to distinguish the actual *Nollan* case from hypothetical cases of this kind would be to show that something special about *the Nollans'* proposed activity makes it particularly appropriate to exact an easement from them as a condition of permitting *that activity,* or, in other words, to find a "nexus" between the Commission's dedication condition and some proper regulatory objective of the Commission's that the Nollans' development particularly threatened. What heightened judicial scrutiny of regulatory efficacy amounted to in *Nollan,* then, was the Court's insistence on being satisfied that the claimed nexus was sufficiently apparent and credible to counteract suspicion of taking by subterfuge. But nothing about the case or the opinion suggests that "taking" here means anything other than imposing a permanent physical occupation on an owner who prefers otherwise and whose specific actions cannot justly be deemed to have waived or forfeited that preference.

Such a qualified reading of *Nollan's* heightened-scrutiny message is not only fully consonant with everything found in the opinion, it is also the only way to contain that message within plausible bounds.

Justice Scalia defended his resort to heightened scrutiny in *Nollan* with the suggestion that takings claims (as distinguished from ordinary due process and equal protection claims arising in commercial or economic context) fall into a specially sensitive constitutional category much as do freedom of speech claims. What follows if we take at face value the proposition that takings claims, like free-speech claims, beget heightened scrutiny as compared with ordinary economic due process and equal protection claims? What most obviously follows is that, in order to be able to tell in any given case whether cursory or intensified scrutiny of the regulation's instrumental merit is in order, we need a trenchant legal criterion for selecting out of the mine run of land-use cases presenting due process or equal protection claims those that fall exceptionally into the aggravated category of takings claims. With freedom of speech, that is not usually a problem. If someone challenges an ordinary zoning restriction as an abridgement of the freedom of speech, it is usually, although not always, easy just to say that this regulation really is not, in purpose or effect, what constitutional law means by an abridgement of the freedom of speech, so no strict scrutiny is due. But whenever someone challenges a land-use regulation as a taking, rather than challenging it as a simple deprivation of property without due process, there will be an obvious problem of how to tell whether the case really and truly involves a takings challenge meriting intensified means-ends scrutiny.

One possible answer is that it is just a matter of pleading. For reasons that must be obvious, this cannot be what the *Nollan* Court means. Any aggrieved owner prefers intensified scrutiny and thus would plead "taking," not "deprivation without due process" or "denial of equal protection." The obvious alternative is that a litigant can challenge state regulatory action "as" a taking, and thereby obtain intensified judicial scrutiny of the regulation's instrumental merit or urgency, if and only if the challenged regulation has the effect of imposing a permanent physical occupation on an unwilling owner.

* * *

In hindsight, the Supreme Court's takings jurisprudence seems to have moved steadily from 1922 toward a highly nonformal, open-ended, multi-factor balancing method. In all the years between 1922 and 1987, however, the Court never once clearly applied the open-ended balancing test in favor of a takings claim and against a regulating government. Towards the end of this period, the Court could perhaps be heard confessing a sense of unease about the lack of definition and rigor in its regulatory-takings doctrine.

There are further signs in recent developments that the Court is finding its open-ended balancing posture hard to maintain and so is moving noticeably towards a reformalization of regulatory-takings doctrine. Doctrine appears to be moving in the direction of resolution into a series of categorical "either-ors": *either* (a) the regulation is categorically a taking of property because (i) it works a permanent physical occupation (however practically trivial) of private property by the government, or, perhaps, specifically undermines a "distinct investment-backed expectation," or (ii) it totally eliminates the property's economic value or "viability" to its nominal owner, *or* (b) the regulation is categorically not a taking.

* * *

Incorporation

At least as controversial as the judiciary's development of fundamental rights and liberties not enumerated by constitutional text has been the Court's application of most provisions of the Bill of Rights to the states. The incorporation debate over the middle of this century was reducible largely to whether all, none or some of the provisions of the Bill of Rights were accounted for by the Fourteenth Amendment. The case for total incorporation was advanced most notably by Justice Black who, in *Adamson v. California,* included in his dissenting opinion an appendix delineating the case for total incorporation. Charles A. Fairman rejects the notion of incorporation. Louis Henkin maintains that, although neither total nor partial incorporation theories were historically defensible, the same result could be achieved pursuant to an elastic reading of the Fourteenth Amendment's due process clause.

Charles Fairman, *Does the Fourteenth Amendment Incorporate the Bill of Rights?*, 2 STAN. L. REV. 5 (1949)*

The question to be explored is, was [incorporation of the Bill of Rights] the understanding of the import of the privileges and immunities, due process, and equal protection clauses of Section I of the Fourteenth Amendment, or of any one of those clauses, at the time the Amendment was adopted? This involves an attempt to apprehend the views of the members of the Congress that proposed the Amendment, and to appreciate the significance of the action of the state legislatures when they considered ratification.

We shall be sifting the historical evidence on a fine point of great present interest. But we must not suppose that the men who fashioned the Fourteenth Amendment were concentered upon our nice constitutional question. Whether the freedman should be given the suffrage, what should be the new basis of representation in Congress and what would be the consequences for the two parties, how could the Confederate leaders best be excluded from the councils of the nation—political questions such as these dominated the hour. No one could foresee that Section 2 would prove abortive—that the most interesting feature of Section 1, the privileges and immunities clause, would be virtually read out of the Constitution in 1873—that the due process clause would become, from the point of view of litigation, one of the two most

---

*   Copyright © 1949 by the Board of Trustees of the Leland Stanford Junior University. Reprinted by permission.

important clauses in the entire Constitution—or that it would be the judiciary, not the Congress, that most concerned itself with the protection of liberty, and property. We know so much more about the constitutional law of the Fourteenth Amendment than the men who adopted it that we should remind ourselves not to be surprised to find them vague where we want them to prove sharp. Eighty years of adjudication has taught us distinctions and subtleties where the men of 1866 did not even perceive the need for analysis.

We need to remind ourselves, too, that that was the Age of Hate in American politics—that a tremendous struggle was going on within the party that had saved the Union and between the Congressional leaders and the President. In inducing Congress to set up a Joint Committee to establish the basis for reconstruction, the Radical leaders had stolen a march, and in working out the Amendment and marshaling the Republican Party behind it these Radicals were exploiting their initial success. We shall isolate and magnify one line of constitutional development: a participant, could he have been presented with this perspective, would doubtless have thought it yielded a highly selective and artificial view of the entire episode. We should constantly make allowance for the distortion we inevitably produce by concentrating upon Section I of the Amendment.

. . . The current of thought in 1866 . . . ran strongly in the direction of *congressional* action. Congress was going to shove the President out of the driver's seat; Congress was going to preside over reconstruction. When one realizes how little the men of 1866 foresaw the part the Supreme Court was going to play in working out the Fourteenth Amendment's guaranties of civil rights, it is no wonder that they did not fix their minds squarely on the question the Court had to face in 1873, and which is raised again today: What is the *standard* by which to test state action alleged to violate the Fourteenth Amendment?

* * *

The constitutional amendment proposed by the Committee of Fifteen was introduced in each House on February 13, 1866. In the Senate it was ordered to lie on the table—and there it remained. Bingham presented his measure to the House. On February 26, 27, and 28 there was a lively debate, culminating in a postponement from which the proposal never emerged. Although this draft came to naught, the debate upon it is a chapter in the evolution of congressional thought and thus merits careful attention.

The proposal was a grant of *legislative* power—to secure

(1)   to all citizens in each State all privileges and immunities of citizens in the several States; and
(2)   to all persons in the several States equal protection in the rights to life, liberty, and property.

Bingham's opening speech outlined his conception of the problem. Every word of the proposed amendment, he said, was already in the Constitution, save only the grant of enforcing power to Congress. (This was not literally true, of course. The opening words of the second branch of the proposal were new.)

> Sir, it has been the want of the Republic that there was not an express grant of power in the Constitution to enable the whole people of every State, by congressional enactment, to enforce obedience to these requirements of the Constitution.

Nothing could be plainer, Bingham continued, than that, had Congress had and exercised this power, there would have been no rebellion.

> I ask the attention of the House to the further consideration that the proposed amendment does not impose upon any State of the Union, or any citizen of any State of the Union, any obligation which is not now enjoined upon them by the very letter of the Constitution.

For, recall, "this Constitution" has always been "the supreme law of the land."

> And, sir, it is equally clear by every construction of the Constitution, its contemporaneous construction, its continued construction legislative, executive, and judicial, that these great provisions of the Constitution, this immortal bill of rights embodied in the Constitution, rested for its execution and enforcement hitherto upon the fidelity of the States.

But, as the world knew, during the last five years, the officers of eleven states,

> in utter disregard of these injunctions of your Constitution, in utter disregard of that official oath which the Constitution required they should severally take and faithfully keep when they entered upon the discharge of their respective duties, have violated in every sense of the word these provisions of the Constitution of the United States, the enforcement of which are absolutely essential to American nationality.

By order of the joint Committee on Reconstruction, and "for the purpose of giving to the whole people the care in future of the unity of the Government which constitutes us one people," he proposed this amendment for adoption by the Congress and the loyal people of the whole country.

Because Bingham is a key figure in our inquiry, his point of view is of great significance. A careful reader will have remarked that he held a singular opinion on the constitutional problem. The states had all along been bound to accord the "privileges and immunities" of Article IV, Section 2, but Congress had no power to compel obedience. The states had all along been bound to protect the rights of life, liberty, and property; the Fifth Amendment recognized them and forbade the United States Government to infringe them; but again, Congress had not been given power to compel the states to observe these rights. If a state officer or legislator participated in making or enforcing a state law which, had such action been in the federal system would have amounted to a denial of the rights of life, liberty, or property, that state officer or legislator thereby violated his oath to observe the Constitution of the United States! But he did it with impunity, because the Fathers had given Congress no power to interfere. This is a novel, and one may think a befuddled construction of the Constitution. So be it. We are trying to catch Bingham's point of view.

Consider Bingham's expression, "these great provisions of the Constitution, this immortal bill of rights embodied in the Constitution." What is the antecedent? Evidently, the "privileges and immunities" (Art. IV, § 2), and the rights of "life, liberty, and property" of the Fifth Amendment—these comprise "the immortal bill of rights." In this spacious gesture Bingham certainly does not seem to be making any particular reference to Amendments I to VIII. Let us take note that, on this occasion at any rate, "the immortal bill of rights" is to Bingham a fine literary phrase not referring precisely to the first eight Amendments.

* * *

Presently Bingham moved to insert a new Section 5—and here at last emerges the formula that was to become a part of the Constitution:

> No State shall make or enforce any law which shall abridge the privileges or immunities of citizens of the United States; nor shall any State deprive any person of life, liberty or property without due process of law, nor deny to any person within its jurisdiction the equal protection of the laws.

* * *

The necessity for the first Section, Bingham tells us, is a lesson taught by the past four years of conflict. Surely this is an inapt way to express the idea that the provisions of Amendments I to VIII should be made applicable to the states! What is the great want this Section will fill? Once more we are told, the absence of power in Congress to protect the privileges and immunities of citizens of the Republic and the inborn rights of man. The rightful authority of the state will not be diminished; it is simply that Congress thereafter will be able to repress state action inconsistent with the Constitution. "Contrary to the express letter" of the Constitution, states have inflicted "cruel and unusual punishments." Admit, very frankly, that this necessarily implies that the first eight Amendments were already limitations—though not enforceable by congressional action—upon the states. Marshall's Court had said they were not limitations on the states, Bingham somehow believes that they are—but we need not go over that again. Supposing that the cruel punishments clause was such a limitation, though not directly enforceable by Congress, why did not the victims raise the federal question and if need be carry it to the Supreme Court? Bingham did not explain. If the answer is that the Southern States were in rebellion, then of course it was the whole Constitution that was denied enforcement. Bingham asserts that these "cruel and unusual punishments" were inflicted not only for crimes, but also for lawful acts of "sacred duty," presumably of fidelity to the Union. This is a new point, unsupported by anything previously brought out in debate. Perhaps we are puzzling over a wild sentence that comes to no more than this:

> (1) that in the South loyal men had been made to suffer for the their devotion to the Union, plus (2) that the cruel and unusual punishments clause denounced ancient wrongs which no state should perpetrate.

* * *

On May 23 the Senate turned to the joint resolution proposing the Amendment. Consideration had had to be postponed because of the illness of Senator Fessenden, chairman, on the part of the Senate, of the Joint Committee. But the matter was urgent, and now Senator Jacob M. Howard of Michigan substituted for him in presenting the measure:

> . . . . I can only promise to present to the Senate, in a very succinct way, the views and the motives which influenced that committee, so far as I understand those views and motives, in presenting the report which is now before us for consideration, and the ends it aims to accomplish.

Taking up Section I of the proposed Amendment, Howard observed that its privileges and immunities clause ran to "citizens of the United States." It was not, perhaps, very easy to define this expression. (Later, on Howard's motion, the Senate amended Section I by inserting the definition that now forms the opening sentence.) Leaving that point, he continued:

It would be a curious question to solve what are the privileges and immunities of citizens of each of the States in the several States. I do not propose to go at any length into that question at this time. It would be a somewhat barren discussion. But it is certain the clause was inserted in the Constitution [Art. IV, § 2] for some good purpose. It has in view some results beneficial to the citizens of the several States, or it would not be found there; yet I am not aware that the Supreme Court have ever undertaken to define either the nature or extent of the privileges and immunities thus guarantied. Indeed, if my recollection serves me, that court, on a certain occasion not many years since, when this question seemed to present itself to them, very modestly declined to go into a definition of them, leaving questions arising under the clause to be discussed and adjudicated when they should happen practically to arise. But we may gather some intimation of what probably will be the opinion of the judiciary by referring to a case adjudged many years ago in one of the circuit courts of the United States by Judge Washington; and I will trouble the Senate but for a moment by reading what that very learned and excellent judge says about these privileges and immunities of the citizens of each State in the several States. [He quotes in full the passage in *Corfield v. Coryell* where this clause was construed.]

Let us reread this language carefully. Howard starts with the "privileges and immunities" of Article IV, Section 2. (When we resume direct quotation we shall find him saying that these privileges and immunities are included within the privileges and immunities to be guaranteed by Section I of the proposed Amendment. That explains why he started on Article IV, Section 2.) "It would be a curious question" to say what the clause means but we will not go very deeply into that—it would be a "barren discussion." (Surely, this is completely wrong. A discussion that really established the meaning of words already in the Constitution and about to be repeated, would have been exceedingly useful.) Article IV, Section 2 must have been inserted for "some good purpose"; since we always assume that the Founders purposed nothing useless, we must go on saying that the clause doubtless produces some beneficial results. But the Supreme Court has never told us what they are, ...

It would be naive, of course, to expect Howard to provide a mechanical formula for determining the content of "privilege and immunities." But hard analysis could have produced a far clearer basic conception. Was the standard to be found in the law, of nature—or in national law (and if so, was it what was implicit in *federal* citizenship, or was it such civil rights as Congress might declare) or in the law of the state, impartially applied? If the new expression, "the privileges and immunities of citizens of the United States," was to include "the privileges and immunities of citizens in the several States" (Art. IV, § 2), what did it signify that the modifying phrase was varied? (In the *Slaughter-House Cases* as we know, Justice Miller was to give decisive importance to the qualification "of the United States.") In so far as the new clause would cover the same ground as the old, it would seem superfluous. If it were answered that the new clause was to be sanctioned by Section 5, giving Congress power to enforce, then why not reach that result directly by adding in Section 5 that Congress should also have power to enforce Article IV, Section 2? This is not mere minutiae of drafting, to be dismissed impatiently. As was inevitable, these points arose in the course of litigation. They might have been perceived by hard reflective thinking while the Amendment was being fashioned. But the air was charged with partisan feeling, the political sections were the center of interest, the clauses of Section I sounded excellent, and the need for rigorous analysis was not recognized.

Now back to Senator Howard's opening statement. . . .

Here at last is a clear statement that the new privileges and immunities clause is intended to incorporate the federal Bill Rights. For the first time, "the first eight amendments" are specified. On this point Howard's statement seems full and equivocal. It must be given very serious consideration, coming from the Senator who had the measure in charge. The question then becomes: did the Senate agree, did the House agree, did the State Legislatures that ratified the Amendment agree, that this was what the clause meant? (Presently we shall have reason to inquire, too, how should we construe Howard's statement, having regard to his subsequent conduct?)

Howard went on briefly to speak of the due process and equal protection clauses. These, he pointed out, ran not merely to the citizen but to any person, and abolished class legislation and the injustice of subjecting one caste of persons to a code not applicable to all. It was time, he said, that the black man was guaranteed the equal protection of the law.

If the new privileges and immunities clause incorporated the provisions of Amendments I to VIII, it must include the due process clause of Amendment V. But how can this be maintained in view of the fact that a separate due process clause was found necessary? Howard did not meet this obvious question. He did, however, note that the due process clause extended to *any person*, whereas the privileges and immunities were enjoyed by *citizens of the United States*. One who accepts Howard's view must admit the consequence, that the only essential function of the due process clause was to protect such "persons" as were not "citizens.". . .

Such a view would, however, be quite unrealistic. Although it was noted in debate that "person" was wider than citizen, no particular interest in either the alien or the corporation was expressed. They simply did not enter into the actual discussion, one way or the other. And if it was no special concern for their protection that produced the striking departure from the principles of drafting, how is Howard's statement to be squared with the presence of a due process clause in the Amendment?

* * *

The joint resolution was returned to the House for its concurrence in the amendments. Debate was completed on a single day, June 13. Nothing was said about the federal Bill of Rights: Howard's statement on that point was not mentioned. The only comment at all pertinent to our inquiry came from Representative Aaron Harding, a Kentucky Democrat opposing the Amendment. The effect of Sections 1 and 5, taken together, was, he said, to transfer all power over the citizens of a state from the state to the Federal Government. "Will not Congress then virtually hold all power of legislation over your own citizens and in defiance of you?" He thus professed to believe that the significance of the measure was to give Congress a general authority over the field of civil rights.

The House concurred in the Senate's amendments, 120 to 32, with 32 not voting.

Looking back, what evidence has there been to sustain the view that Section I was intended to incorporate Amendments I to VIII? Bingham, as we know, did a good deal of talking about "the immortal bill of rights," and once spoke of "cruel and unusual punishments." Senator Howard, explaining the new privileges and immunities clause, said that it included the privileges and immunities of Article VI, Section 2—whatever they may be—and also "the personal rights guarantied and secured by the first eight amendments. . . ." That is all. The rest of the evidence bore in the opposite direction, or was indifferent. Yet one reads in one of Justice Black's footnotes that:

A comprehensive analysis of the historical origin of the Fourteenth Amendment, Flack, The Adoption of the Fourteenth Amendment (1908), 94, concludes that "Congress, the House and the Senate, had the following objects and motives in view for submitting the first section of the Fourteenth Amendment to the States for ratification:

1. To make the Bill of Rights (the first eight Amendments) binding or applicable to, the States.
2. To give validity to the Civil Rights Bill.
3. To declare who were citizens of the United States.

We have been examining the same materials as did Flack, and have quoted far more extensively than he. How could he on that record reach the conclusion that Congress purposed by Section 1 to incorporate Amendments I to VIII? The explanation is supplied by a few sentences from his book:

The vote then [on the Amendment, in the House] was taken immediately after Mr. Bingham had spoken, and his position must have been understood by all the members present. His statement of the need and purpose of the section must, therefore, have been acquiesced in by those who supported it, especially since Mr. Bingham was the author of it as well as a member of the Committee which ordered it to be reported, and thus could speak with authority. . . . [Page 81.]

* * *

His [Senator Howard's] interpretation of the Amendment was not questioned by any one, and in view of his statement made at the beginning of his speech, this interpretation must be accepted as that of the Committee, since no member of the Committee gave a different interpretation or questioned his statements in any particular.

This is treated as being governed by a sort of legal presumption. The author of the measure said so and so in the House, the sponsor said it more clearly in the Senate; no one specifically contradicted. That concludes the matter: what they said must be deemed to be the purpose of the Congress.

Of course the search for historical truth is not governed by any such arbitrary presumption. What was said by the author of a measure, or by the member reporting for a committee, is ordinarily entitled to very special consideration. But others may, without challenging these views, have supported the measure for quite inconsistent reasons. We need not enter here into the large subject of extrinsic aids in constitutional interpretation. That would only complicate a fairly simple problem. Bingham said inconsistent things, and was very unsatisfactory when pressed for clarification. When other members were unable to find out what he meant, they can hardly be charged with consenting to his words. Senator Howard, however, spoke with more precision, and his interpretation carries much greater weight. While no Senator specifically contradicted him, [statements by other senators contradicted him or asserted uncertainty about] the effect of the privileges and immunities clause.

* * *

Flack, as a witness testifying to what he has observed, says that he has examined a good many newspapers and has not found *any statement at all*, one way or the other, about the incorporation of the Bill of Rights. Of course, in so far as people had not heard of the idea they would not comment on it. And such as may have heard of it—Senators in particular—appear to have ignored it. Certainly that evidence, fairly presented, counts heavily against the theory of incorporation.

Mr. Flack adds that where we find a man who believed that Section I carried with it freedom of speech and of the press, we may infer that he recognized it to be a logical result that Section I would impose all of the Bill of Rights. Maybe so—or maybe such a man would have believed in a selective incorporation. In any event, the man's recognizing that this result would be logical falls far short of making it the meaning understood by the American people. In the latter part of the paragraph quoted, Mr. Flack was no longer giving testimony as to facts he had observed.

This unsatisfactory passage from the United States Reports calls to mind the tendentious use of a headline by the *Detroit Free Press,* shortly after the destruction of the Maine in Havana harbor. A banner announced

MINES IN THE HARBOR

Then in cramped typography came this accurate report:

AGENTS OF THE UNITED STATES HAVE BEEN UNABLE TO FIND THE SLIGHTEST EVIDENCE OF THEIR EXISTENCE

* * *

If it was understood, in the legislatures that considered the proposed Amendment, that its adoption would impose upon the state governments the provisions of the federal Bill of Rights, then almost certainly each legislature would take note of what the effect would be upon the constitutional law and practice of its own state. If, for instance, the state permitted one charged with "a capital or otherwise infamous crime" to be tried upon information rather than "on a presentment or indictment of a Grand Jury" (Amend. V), if it did not provide a common-law jury of twelve, "in all criminal prosecutions" (Amend. VI), or if it failed to preserve "the right of trial by jury" "in suits at common law, where the value in controversy shall exceed twenty dollars" (Amend. VII)—if there was any state in this situation, presumably its legislature would not knowingly ratify such an Amendment without giving some thought to the implications. . . .

[Professor Fairman reviews the debates in the various states, and identifies no meaningful attention to issues that would support an incorporation understanding].

* * *

If the theory that the new privileges and immunities clause incorporated Amendments I to VIII found no recognition in the practice of Congress, or in the action of state legislatures, constitutional conventions, or courts, it is not surprising that the contemporary Supreme Court knew nothing of it either. *Mitchell v. Pennsylvania,* decided on April 5, 1869, is evidence that such was the case. The petitioner had been condemned to death for murder, in the courts of Pennsylvania. According to the statute, it was not necessary in an indictment for murder "to set forth the manner in which, or the means by which," the death was caused. In seeking a writ of error it was contended that this procedure violated the Fifth Amendment (indictment by grand jury) and the Sixth ("to be informed of the nature and cause of the accusation"). The Court granted leave to file a motion for the writ, and directed that notice be served on the Attorney General of Pennsylvania. No counsel appeared for the respondent.

* * *

Note that it did not occur to counsel for the petitioner to suggest that the Fourteenth Amendment, adopted less than a year before, had worked any change in the law applicable to the case. Note, too, that the Attorney General of Pennsylvania saw no reason to be on hand, evidently regarding the law as being perfectly cold. Even though counsel for the petitioner had failed to invoke the *Fourteenth* Amendment, one supposes that the Court, had it been stirred by the least uncertainty, would have suggested the question and heard argument before disposing of the petition of one sentenced to death.

* * *

This mountain of evidence has become so high, one may have lost sight of the few stones and pebbles that made up the theory that the Fourteenth Amendment incorporated Amendments I to VIII. Let them be recounted.

First, Representative Bingham, author of Section I, had much to say about "the immortal bill of rights," and referred once to "cruel and unusual punishments." Never in the reported debate on the passage of the Amendment did he refer specifically to Amendments I to VIII. On the hustings he included the right to teach of the eternal life.

Next, Senator Howard, who introduced the measure in the Senate, said that the new privileges and immunities clause included "the personal rights guaranteed and secured by the first eight amendments." That seems clear enough—and yet one can hardly believe that the Senator from Michigan ever thought that the Amendment expressing the congressional policy on reconstruction would require his own state to abandon its practice of prosecuting upon information.

Even if these statements be taken at face value, Bingham and Howard promptly repudiated them by their support of the admission of Nebraska and of the restoration of the Southern States.

Mr. Flack's conclusion, it has been pointed out, rested largely on a supposed presumption that what was said by the author and by the sponsor of a measure must, unless directly contradicted, be deemed to establish its meaning.

* * *

As one looks up from this protracted inquiry, certain broad reflections seem controlling. If Senator Howard's statement about Amendments I to VIII had really been accepted at the time, surely one would find it caught up and repeated in contemporary discussion. "Section I incorporates the Bill of Rights"—an intricate subject would have been compressed into a capsule. So pat a phrase would have been passed about. The Democratic opposition, if they had understood that any such object was in view, would have sought to turn it to their advantage in states whose practice would be disturbed. And yet one does not find the thought expressed—neither in newspaper editorials or campaign speeches so far as they have been examined, nor in the messages of governors. Lawyers would have urged the contention in the courts, and if need be carried their appeals to the Supreme Court. But this simply did not occur.

The freedom that the states traditionally have exercised to develop their own systems for administering justice, repels any thought that the federal provisions on grand jury, criminal jury, and civil jury were fastened upon them in 1868. Congress would not have attempted such a thing, the country would not have stood for it, the legislatures would not have ratified. The electoral campaign of 1866 was fought over the proposed Amendment: but the debates never took the turn of suggesting that ratification would involve major change in the administration of justice in the Northern States. Recall how the legislatures in many Northern States, obedient to the autumn mandate, had trooped to ratify the Amendment—even suspending rules, refusing to refer to committee, cutting off debate: surely all this haste was not to make Amendments V, VI, and VII the Constitution's rule for every state. As one ponders the matter, this consideration seems far more substantial than a few words uttered by Bingham and Howard in the debates of 1866—specially since we have found that their conduct denied their words.

If the founders of the Fourteenth Amendment did not intend the privileges and immunities clause to impose Amendments I to VIII, then what, it may be asked, did they mean? One cannot with grace plead that this invites a "barren discussion" or that to answer would be "more tedious than difficult." If one seeks some inclusive and exclusive definition, such that one could say, this is precisely what they had in mind—pretty clearly there never was any such clear conception. We may put to one side the utterances of the more zealous Democrats—they were magnifying the proposal to render it odious. Once it was adopted they would, of course, reverse their stand. The advocates of the measure offered illustrations of particular evils that would be repressed; they stayed away from any explanation of a fundamental principle. Some referred grandly to the spirit of the Declaration of Independence—the fundamental rights of citizens in a free government—law in its highest sense that is the perfection of reason even the spirit of Christianity. Some, down to earth, said the privileges and immunities clause would write into the Constitution what the Civil Rights Act had put upon the statute book. Evidently they had no clear idea as to the confines of the clause, and in the main no awareness either of their own want of understanding. A few sharp minds perceived the questions to be asked, and asked them—and went unanswered. The debates never established what was to be the basis or measure of the privileges and immunities of citizens of the United States.

Congress, we know, was moved by various purposes. It meant to insure that the Negro would be accorded the same civil rights as the white man: that was the object of the equal protection clause. It also meant to forbid state action that would deny to any citizen the faculties inherent in being a citizen *of the United States*. But it undoubtedly purposed to do still more, to establish a federal standard below which state action must not fall. At this point thinking became hazy. Brooding over the matter in the writing of this article has, however, slowly brought the conclusion that Justice Cardozo's gloss on the due process clause—what is "implicit in the concept of ordered liberty"—comes as close as one can to catching the vague aspirations that were hung upon the privileges and immunities clause. This accommodates the fact that freedom of speech was mentioned in the discussion of 1866, and the conclusion that, according to the contemporary understanding, surely the federal requirements as to juries were not included. When the *Slaughter-House Cases* put the privileges and immunities clause to a rigorous scrutiny, its looseness became apparent. Since then it has merely lingered on, performing virtually no duty as an operative part of the Constitution. The due process clause was increasingly invoked by litigants claiming protection against state action, and in passing upon those contentions the Court has gradually established that that provision embraces certain of the rights specifically mentioned in the first eight Amendments, yet not all of them. This is the selective process against which Justice Black has rebelled. In his contention that Section I was intended and understood to impose Amendments I to VIII upon the states, the record of history is overwhelmingly against him.

Justice Hugo Black, *Adamson v. California,* 322 U.S. 46, 92 (1947) (Black J., dissenting)

APPENDIX

I.

The legislative origin of the first section of the Fourteenth Amendment seems to have been in the Joint Committee on Reconstruction. That Committee had been appointed by a concurrent resolution of the House and Senate with authority to report "by bill or otherwise" whether the former Confederate States "are entitled to be represented in either House of Congress." The broad mission of that Committee was revealed by its very first action of sending a delegation to President Johnson requesting him to "defer all further executive action in regard to reconstruction until this committee shall have taken action on that subject." It immediately set about the business of drafting constitutional amendments which would outline the plan of reconstruction which it would recommend to Congress . . . .. On January 12, 1866, a subcommittee, consisting of Senators Fessenden (Chairman of the Reconstruction Committee) and Howard, and Congressmen Stevens, Bingham and Conkling, was appointed to consider those suffrage proposals. There was at the same time referred to this Committee a "proposed amendment to the Constitution" submitted by Mr. Bingham that: "The Congress shall have power to make all laws necessary and proper to secure to all persons in every State within this Union equal protection in their rights of life, liberty, and property." Another proposed amendment that "All laws, State or national, shall operate impartially and equally on all persons without regard to race or color," was also referred to the Committee. On January 24, 1866, the subcommittee reported back a combination of these two proposals which was not accepted by the full Committee. Thereupon the proposals were referred to a "select committee of three," Bingham, Boutwell and Rogers. On January 27, 1866, Mr. Bingham on behalf of the select committee, presented this recommended amendment to the full committee: "Congress shall have power to make all laws which shall be necessary and proper to secure all persons in every State full protection in the enjoyment of life, liberty and property; and to all citizens of the United States, in any State, the same immunities and also equal political rights and privileges." This was not accepted. But on February 3, 1866, Mr. Bingham submitted an amended version: "The Congress shall have power to make all laws which shall be necessary and proper to secure to the citizens of each State all privileges and immunities of citizens in the several States (art. 4, sec. 2); and to all persons in the several States equal protection in the rights of life, liberty, and property (5th amendment)." This won committee approval, Journal, 17, and was presented by Mr. Bingham to the House on behalf of the Committee on February 13, 1866.

II.

When, on February 26, the proposed amendment came up for debate, Mr. Bingham stated that "by order . . . of the committee . . . I propose adoption of this amendment." In support of it he said:

> ". . . The amendment proposed stands in the very words of the Constitution of the United States as it came to us from the hands of its illustrious framers. Every word of the proposed amendment is to-day in the Constitution of our country, save the words conferring the express grant of

power upon the Congress of the United States. The residue of the resolution, as the House will see by a reference to the Constitution, is the language of the second section of the fourth article, and of a portion of the fifth amendment adopted by the First Congress in 1789, and made part of the Constitution of the country. . . .

"Sir, it has been the want of the Republic that there was not an express grant of power in the Constitution to enable the whole people of every State, by congressional enactment, to enforce obedience to these requirements of the Constitution. Nothing can be plainer to thoughtful men than that if the grant of power had been originally conferred upon the Congress of the nation and legislation had been upon your statute-books to enforce these requirements of the Constitution in every State, that rebellion, which has scarred and blasted the land, would have been an impossibility. . . .

"And, sir, it is equally clear by every construction of the Constitution, its contemporaneous construction, its continued construction, legislative, executive, and judicial, that these great provisions of the Constitution, this immortal bill of rights embodied in the Constitution, rested for its execution and enforcement hitherto upon the fidelity of the States. . . ."

Opposition speakers emphasized that the Amendment would destroy states' rights and empower Congress to legislate on matters of purely local concern. Some took the position that the Amendment was unnecessary because the Bill of Rights were already secured against state violation. Mr. Bingham joined issue on this contention:

"The gentleman seemed to think that all persons could have remedies for all violations of their rights of 'life, liberty, and property' in the Federal courts.

"I ventured to ask him yesterday when any action of that sort was ever maintained in any of the Federal courts of the United States to redress the great wrong which has been practiced, and which is being practiced now in more States than one of the Union under the authority of State laws, denying to citizens therein equal protection or any protection in the rights of life, liberty, and property.

". . . A gentleman on the other side interrupted me and wanted to know if I could cite a decision showing that the power of the Federal Government to enforce in the United States courts the bill of rights under the articles of amendment to the Constitution had been denied. I answered that I was prepared to introduce such decisions; and that is exactly what makes plain the necessity of adopting this amendment.

"Mr. Speaker, on this subject I refer the House and the country to a decision of the Supreme Court, . . . in the case of *Barron v. The Mayor and City Council of Baltimore*, involving the question whether the provisions of the fifth article of the amendments to the Constitution are binding upon the State of Maryland and to be enforced in the Federal courts. The Chief Justice says:

"'The people of the United States framed such a Government for the United States as they supposed best adapted to their situation and best calculated to promote their interests. The powers they conferred on this Government were to be exercised by itself; and the limitations of power, if expressed in general terms, are naturally, and we think necessarily, applicable to the Government created by the instrument. They are limitations of power granted in the instrument itself, not of distinct governments, framed by different persons and for different purposes.

"'If these propositions be correct, the fifth amendment must be understood as restraining the power of the General Government, not as applicable to the States.'

"I read one further decision on this subject—the case of the *Lessee of Livingston v. Moore*. The court, in delivering its opinion, says:

"'As to the Amendments of the Constitution of the United States, they must be put out of the case, since it is now settled that those amendments do not extend to the States; and this observation disposes of the next exception, which relies on the seventh article of those amendments.'

"The question is, simply, whether you will give by this amendment to the people of the United States the power, by legislative enactment, to punish officials of States for violation of oaths enjoined upon them by their Constitution? . . . Is the Bill of Rights to stand in our Constitution hereafter, as in the past five years within eleven States, a mere dead letter? It is absolutely essential to the safety of the people that it should be enforced.

"Mr. Speaker, it appears to me that this very provision of the bill of rights brought in question this day, upon this trial before the House, more than any other provision of the Constitution, makes that unity of government which constitutes us one people, by which and through which American nationality came to be, and only by the enforcement of which can American nationality continue to be.

"What more could have been added to that instrument to secure the enforcement of these provisions of the bill of rights in every State, other than the additional grant of power which we ask this day? . . .

"As slaves were not protected by the Constitution, there might be some color of excuse for the slave States in their disregard for the requirement of the bill of rights as to slaves in refusing them protection in life or property. . . .

"But, sir, there never was even colorable excuse, much less apology, for any man North or South claiming that any State Legislature or State court, or State Executive, has any right to deny protection to any free citizen of the United States within their limits in the rights of life, liberty, and property. Gentlemen who oppose this amendment oppose the grant of power to enforce the bill of rights. Gentlemen who oppose this amendment simply declare to these rebel States, Go on with your confiscation statutes, your statutes of banishment, your statutes of unjust imprisonment, your statutes of murder and death against men because of their loyalty to the Constitution and Government of the United States.

". . . Where is the power in Congress, unless this or some similar amendment be adopted, to prevent the reenactment of those infernal statutes . . .? Let some man answer. Why, sir, the gentleman from New York [Mr. Hale] . . . yesterday gave up the argument on this point. He said that the citizens must rely upon the State for their protection. I admit that such is the rule under the Constitution as it now stands."

As one important writer on the adoption of the Fourteenth Amendment has observed, "Mr. Bingham's speech in defense and advocacy of his amendment comprehends practically everything that was said in the press or on the floor of the House in favor of the resolution. . . ." A reading of the debates indicates that no member except Mr. Hale had contradicted Mr. Bingham's argument that without this Amendment the states had power to deprive persons of the rights guaranteed by the first eight amendments. Mr. Hale had conceded that he did not "know of a case where it has ever been decided that the United States Constitution is sufficient for the protection of the liberties of the citizen." But he was apparently unaware of the decision of this Court in *Barron v. Baltimore, supra.* For he thought that the protections of the Bill of Rights had already been "thrown over us in some way, whether with or without the sanction of a judicial decision . . .." And in any event, he insisted, ". . . the American people have not yet found that their State governments are insufficient to protect the rights and liberties of the citizen." He further objected, as had most of the other opponents to the proposal, that the Amendment authorized the Congress to "arrogate" to itself vast powers over all kinds of affairs which should properly be left to the States.

When Mr. Hotchkiss suggested that the amendment should be couched in terms of a prohibition against the States in addition to authorizing Congress to legislate against state deprivations of privileges and immunities, debate on the amendment was postponed until April 2, 1866.

III.

Important events which apparently affected the evolution of the Fourteenth Amendment transpired during the period during which discussion of it was postponed. The Freedman's Bureau Bill which made deprivation of certain civil rights of negroes an offense punishable by military tribunals had been passed. It applied, not to the entire country, but only to the South. On February 19, 1866, President Johnson had vetoed the bill principally on the ground that it was unconstitutional. Forthwith, a companion proposal known as the Civil Rights Bill empowering federal courts to punish those who deprived any person anywhere in the country of certain defined civil rights was pressed to passage. Senator Trumbull, Chairman of the Senate Judiciary Committee, who offered the bill in the Senate on behalf of that Committee, had stated that "the late slaveholding States" had enacted laws ". . . depriving persons of African descent of privileges which are essential to freemen. . . . (S)tatutes of Mississippi . . . provide that if any person of African descent residing in that State travels from one county to another without having a pass or a certificate of his freedom, he is liable to be committed to jail and to be dealt with as a person who is in the State without authority. Other provisions of the statute prohibit any negro or mulatto from having fire-arms; and one provision of the statute declares that for 'exercising the functions of a minister of the Gospel free negroes . . . on conviction, may be punished by . . . lashes. . . .' Other provisions . . . prohibit a free negro . . . from keeping a house of entertainment, and subject him to trial before two justices of the peace and five slaveholders for violating . . . this law. The statutes of South Carolina make it a highly penal offense for any person, white or colored, to teach slaves; and similar provisions are to be found running through all the statutes of the late slaveholding States. . . . The purpose of the bill . . . is to destroy all these discriminations. . . ."

Mr. Bingham himself vigorously opposed and voted against the Bill. His objection was twofold: First, insofar as it extended the protections of the Bill of Rights as against state invasion, he believed the measure to be unconstitutional because of the Supreme Court's holding in *Barron v. Baltimore, supra*. While favoring the extension of the Bill of Rights guarantees as against state invasion, he thought this could be done only by passage of his amendment. His second objection to the Bill was that in his view it would go beyond his objective of making the states observe the Bill of Rights and would actually strip the states of power to govern, centralizing all power in the Federal Government. To this he was opposed. In vetoing the Civil Rights Bill, President Johnson said among other things that the Bill was unconstitutional for many of the same reasons advanced by Mr. Bingham:

> "Hitherto every subject embraced in the enumeration of rights contained in this bill has been considered as exclusively belonging to the States. . . . As respects the Territories, they come within the power of Congress, for as to them, the lawmaking power is the federal power; but as to the States no similar provisions exist, vesting in Congress the power 'to make rules and regulations' for them."

The bill, however, was passed over President Johnson's veto and in spite of the constitutional objections of Bingham and others.

IV.

Thereafter the scene changed back to the Committee on Reconstruction. There Mr. Stevens had proposed an amendment, § 1 of which provided "No discrimination shall be made by any State, nor by the United States, as to the civil rights of persons because of race, color, or previous condition of servitude." Mr. Bingham proposed an additional section providing that "No State shall make or enforce any law which shall abridge the privileges or immunities of citizens of the United States; nor shall any State deprive any person of life, liberty, or property without due process of law, nor deny to any person within its jurisdiction the equal protection of the laws." After the Committee had twice declined to recommend Mr. Bingham's proposal, on April 28 it was accepted by the Committee, substantially in the form he had proposed it, as § 1 of the recommended Amendment.

V.

In introducing the proposed Amendment to the House on May 8, 1866, Mr. Stevens speaking for the Committee said:

> "The first section [of the proposed amendment] prohibits the States from abridging the privileges and immunities of citizens of the United States, or unlawfully depriving them of life, liberty, or property, or of denying to any person within their jurisdiction the 'equal' protection of the laws.
>
> "I can hardly believe that any person can be found who will not admit that every one of these provisions is just. They are all asserted, in some form or other, in our DECLARATION or organic law. But the Constitution limits only the action of Congress, and is not a limitation on the States. This amendment supplies that defect, and allows Congress to cor-

rect the unjust legislation of the States, so far that the law which operates upon one man shall operate *equally* upon all."

On May 23, 1866, Senator Howard introduced the proposed amendment to the Senate in the absence of Senator Fessenden who was sick. Senator Howard prefaced his remarks by stating:

> "I . . . present to the Senate . . . the views and the motives [of the Reconstruction Committee]. . . . One result of their investigation has been the joint resolution for the amendment of the Constitution of the United States now under consideration. . . .

> "The first section of the amendment . . . submitted for the consideration of the two Houses, relates to the privileges and immunities of citizens of the several States, and to the rights and privileges of all persons, whether citizens or others, under the laws of the United States. . . .

> "It will be observed that this is a general prohibition upon all the States, as such, from abridging the privileges and immunities of the citizens of the United States. . . .

> "Such is the character of the privileges and immunities spoken of in the second section of the fourth article of the Constitution. To these privileges and immunities, whatever they may be—for they are not and cannot be fully defined in their entire extent and precise nature—to these should be added the personal rights guarantied and secured by the first eight amendments of the Constitution; such as the freedom of speech and of the press; the right of the people peaceably to assemble and petition the Government for a redress of grievances, a right appertaining to each and all the people; the right to keep and to bear arms; the right to be exempted from the quartering of soldiers in a house without the consent of the owner; the right to be exempt from unreasonable searches and seizures, and from any search or seizure except by virtue of a warrant issued upon a formal oath or affidavit; the right of an accused person to be informed of the nature of the accusation against him, and his right to be tried by an impartial jury of the vicinage; and also the right to be secure against excessive bail and against cruel and unusual punishments.

* * *

> "Now, sir, there is no power given in the Constitution to enforce and to carry out any of these guarantees. They are not powers granted by the Constitution to Congress, and of course do not come within the sweeping clause of the Constitution authorizing Congress to pass all laws necessary and proper for carrying out the foregoing or granted powers, but they stand simply as a bill of rights in the Constitution, without power on the part of Congress to give them full effect; while at the same time the States are not restrained from violating the principles embraced in them except by their own local constitutions, which may be altered from year to year. The great object of the first section of this amendment is, therefore, to restrain the power of the States and compel them at all times to respect these great fundamental guarantees."

Mr. Bingham had closed the debate in the House on the proposal prior to its consideration by the Senate. He said in part:

"... [M]any instances of State injustice and oppression have already occurred in the State legislation of this Union, of flagrant violations of the guarantied privileges of citizens of the United States, for which the national Government furnished and could furnish by law no remedy whatever. Contrary to the express letter of your Constitution, 'cruel and unusual punishments' have been inflicted under State laws within this Union upon citizens, not only for crimes committed, but for sacred duty done, for which and against which the Government of the United States had provided no remedy and could provide none.

"It was an opprobrium to the Republic that for fidelity to the United States they could not by national law be protected against the degrading punishment inflicted on slaves and felons by State law. That great want of the citizen and stranger, protection by national law from unconstitutional State enactments, is supplied by the first section of this amendment. . . ."

Except for the addition of the first sentence of § 1 which defined citizenship, the amendment weathered the Senate debate without substantial change. It is significant that several references were made in the Senate debate to Mr. Bingham's great responsibility for § 1 of the amendment as passed by the House.

VI.

Also just prior to the final votes in both Houses passing the resolution of adoption, the Report of the Joint Committee on Reconstruction, was submitted. This report was apparently not distributed in time to influence the debates in Congress. But a student of the period reports that 150,000 copies of the Report and the testimony which it contained were printed in order that senators and representatives might distribute them among their constituents. Apparently the Report was widely reprinted in the press and used as a campaign document in the election of 1866. According to Kendrick the Report was "eagerly . . . perused" for information concerning "conditions in the South."

The Report of the Committee had said with reference to the necessity of amending the Constitution:

"... (T)he so-called Confederate States are not, at present, entitled to representation in the Congress of the United States; that, before allowing such representation, adequate security for future peace and safety should be required; that this can only be found in such changes of the organic law as shall determine the civil rights and privileges of all citizens in all parts of the republic. . . ."

Among the examples recited by the testimony were discrimination against negro churches and preachers by local officials and criminal punishment of those who attended objectionable church services. Testimony also cited recently enacted Louisiana laws which made it "a highly penal offense for anyone to do anything that might be construed into encouraging the blacks to leave the persons with whom they had made contracts for labor . . .."

Flack, *supra* at 142, who canvassed newspaper coverage and speeches concerning the popular discussion of the adoption of the Fourteenth Amendment, indicates that Senator Howard's speech stating that one of the purposes of the first section was to give Congress power to enforce the Bill of Rights as well as extracts and digests of other speeches were published widely in the press. Flack summarizes his observation that:

> "The declarations and statements of newspapers, writers and speakers, . . . show very clearly, . . . the general opinion held in the North. That opinion, briefly stated, was that the Amendment embodied the Civil Rights Bill and gave Congress the power to define and secure the privileges of citizens of the United States. There does not seem to have been any statement at all as to whether the first eight Amendments were to be made applicable to the States or not, whether the privileges guaranteed by those Amendments were to be considered as privileges secured by the Amendment, but it may be inferred that this was recognized to be the logical result by those who thought that the freedom of speech and of the press as well as due process of law, including a jury trial, were secured by it."

Louis Henkin, "*Selective Incorporation*" *in the Fourteenth Amendment,* 73 YALE L.J. 74 (1963)*

"Selective incorporation" may represent a compromise with Mr. justice Black's view of incorporation of the whole Bill of Rights. Perhaps, indeed, it is an effort to achieve, more acceptably, substantially what Mr. Justice Black's position in *Adamson* sought to achieve and failed to achieve. It might be more acceptable in that it does not depend on justice Black's views of the history of the amendment and the intention of its draftsmen, views which historians have challenged. Selective incorporation does not so clearly require overruling the consistent, often reaffirmed, and almost unanimous jurisprudence of the Court for nearly a hundred years. And since it does not involve automatic absorption of the whole of the Bill of Rights, selective incorporation permits the abandonment, as regards the states, of one or more provisions of the Bill of Rights that seem less important and would be too onerous—say, that dated provision in the seventh amendment requiring a jury trial in civil cases where the value in controversy exceeds twenty dollars. For the rest, selective incorporation could apply to the states all the "important" provisions of the Bill of Rights in their full and growing vigor. Moreover, unlike Mr. Justice Black's position, this view, presumably, does not preclude the Court from finding in the due process clause additional protections not found in any of the specifics of the Bill of Rights.

Selective incorporation finds no support in the language of the amendment, or in the history of its adoption. Indeed it is more difficult to justify than justice Black's position that the Bill of Rights was wholly incorporated. There is some evidence that some persons associated with the adoption of the amendment contemplated that it might apply the Bill of Rights to the states. There is no evidence, and it is difficult to conceive, that anyone thought or intended that the amendment should impose on the states a selective incorporation. In the absence of any special intention revealed in the history of the amendment, we have only the language to look to. It is conceivable, again, that the phrase "privileges and immunities of citizens of the United States" might include a reference to the whole Bill of Rights. Surely there is no basis for find-

*   Reprinted by permission of The Yale Law Journal Company and Fred B. Rothman & Company from The Yale Law Journal, Vol. 73, page 74.

ing that some "specifics" of the Bill of Rights are, while others are not, privileges and immunities of national citizenship. Even the phrase "due process of law" might conceivably be a short-hand expression for the whole Bill of Rights. It is hardly possible to see in that phrase some purpose to select some specifics of the Bill of Rights and an insistence that they be selected whole.

* * *

In order to determine whether a particular procedural safeguard, in a particular case or in all cases, is "due" process, i.e., is required by the conscience of mankind, it does not appear apt or relevant to ask whether a particular provision of the Bill of Rights is "incorporated" in due process. In any event, in regard to standards of criminal procedure at least, no case has said that a specific provision in the Bill of Rights, or a federal standard, is being "incorporated." A right of counsel, one might say, was incorporated in the fourteenth amendment, but not necessarily the same right of counsel given in the fifth amendment. What is clear, too, is that the Court could—and did—justify any such "incorporation" only by finding it in the concept of ordered liberty that is due process. Incorporation then does not, and cannot, avoid reference to the uncertain, debatable, changeable touchstone of ordered liberty. And incorporation, by reference to ordered liberty, cannot claim that specific procedural provisions in the Bill of Rights are incorporated "whole." Ordered liberty, indeed, may for some safeguards require exactly what is required by the Bill of Rights. But it can as well require less, or more. Nothing in that concept suggests that if it includes some procedure akin to one in the Bill of Rights, it must be of exactly the same size, shape, scope as the federal protection.

Most important, perhaps, accepting the need or the desirability of increasing constitutional protections against the states, one may yet ask whether this doctrine is really necessary. If the federal standard is indeed the goal in some instances, the Court can, without any difficult new doctrine, find the federal standard to be required by ordered liberty or by other elements in the Court's jurisprudence. That is now the case with the right to counsel. The Court has also found it possible to justify identical standards in regard to exclusion of the fruits of unreasonable search and seizure, not from any notion of total incorporation, but because of convenience in administration and in federal-state cooperation in the enforcement of criminal law. Federalism and stare decisis apart, without any new doctrine the flexibility and vitality of the concept of ordered liberty would permit the extension today to the states of the heart of concepts against double jeopardy, perhaps even against self-incrimination—the only safeguards now apparently in issue—without necessarily saddling all the states with what may be peripheral survivals or accretions in the Bill of Rights. Of course, if the justices are not to be imposing their own notions of what is desirable procedure, they can only find these new protections in the fourteenth amendment if they are satisfied that they are indeed required by some impersonal, objective, determinable (if difficult to determine) standard of community conscience. But a similar reference to some similar standard, we have said, could not be avoided if the Court asked anew, for example, "whether the privilege against self-incrimination is incorporated." There is no constitutional language, no established doctrine, no old case, that can be invoked to avoid the inevitable question of ordered liberty.

There is indeed a kind of inversion about attempting today to increase the content of procedural due process vis-à-vis the states through wholesale incorporation of complete provisions of the Bill of Rights. For in regard to the federal government the Court has also been extending constitutional liberties and protections. It has done so in part by recognizing distinct content in the due process clause of the fifth amendment and applying notions of fairness and ordered liberty there. It has done so even more by developing the flexible standards of some of the provisions—"unreasonable" search and seizure, "cruel and unusual" punishment, even "double jeopardy." The Court, surely, is aware that though it is ostensibly applying a "specific," the specific is not very specific; and in seeking a standard for developing these and other ambiguities the Court has inevitably applied contemporary notions of fairness—not very different from "ordered liberty." Sometimes, it seems, the Court has stretched quite far the language of one of the specifics to achieve in effect what it thought required by new communal enlightenment. One may wonder, then, whether in regard to both state and federal governments, the Court might not better look less to the procedural specifics of the Bill of Rights and exploit rather the more flexible notion of due process in both the fifth and fourteenth amendments to achieve identical and contemporary standards of liberty under ordered government. To Mr. Justice Black this approach may still be abhorrent because it leaves the courts at large with too much discretion. Most of the justices, one might guess, would not find this discretion distressingly larger than is in play when the Court develops the mentioned ambiguities of the Bill of Rights, or applies the due process clause of the fifth amendment, or decrees notions of propriety under the Court's supervisory powers, where there is no applicable specifics.

Palko v. Connecticut, it seems clear, is not authority for any general doctrine that specifics of the Bill of Rights are incorporated into the fourteenth amendment. It is surely not authority—indeed it negates—a doctrine that insists that any federal specific which is at all reflected in "due process" must be incorporated whole. Neither *Palko* nor any other case, nor independent inquiry, has suggested any acceptable basis for incorporating whole federal specifics in the procedural amendments.

I venture to suggest that as to these provisions—the origin and perhaps a principal motivation for "selective incorporation"—one might arrive where that doctrine would take us, though by another path.

Substantive due process in concept and in its development is, of course, quite different from "procedural due process," although the Court has found them both in the same clause. Due process of law in the original Bill of Rights, while its total impact is less than clear, surely had procedural connotations. The same phrase was probably designed to impose some procedural limitations on the states when it was written into the fourteenth amendment. To determine the scope of these safeguards the Court interpreted the words "due process," holding that the process that is due is that which conforms to accepted notions of "dueness," to the demands of civilized conscience.

"Substantive due process," on the other hand, may be wholly a judicial creation. It was first found in the fifth amendment in the *Dred Scott* case. However, when "due process of law" appeared in the fourteenth amendment, it is far from agreed that it intended substantive limitations on what state legislatures might do. Substantive due process, as is well known, found its origin and its wild and questionable growth in regard to economic regulation; only comparatively recently has it begun to protect political and civil liberties. In regard to the latter, when the Court decided, say, that freedom of speech enjoyed protection from state encroachment, it was asserting that the "liberty" of which a person may not be deprived includes the freedom of speech. Liberty, it later held, included other freedoms, indeed "the full range of conduct which the individual is free to pursue." Surely, the Court has found, it included those liberties whose significance was expressly honored in the first and fourth amendments.

One may say, then, that the liberties mentioned in the Bill of Rights were, in this sense, "incorporated" or "absorbed" in the "liberty" protected by the fourteenth amendment. It remained to be determined what is the standard of protection accorded to these liberties. The scope of the protection has indeed been found in the phrase "due process," but here it means something different from what it means as procedural due process. The standard of substantive due process is not "conscience" or "fairness" as in the procedural cases. Substantive due process, we know, has suggested to the modern Court standards for permissible limitations on property different from those on liberty, and perhaps, too, different standards for limitations on different liberties. In regard to property, or even "economic liberties," the standard has been reduced to mere "reasonableness" of end and means. For "civil liberties" it has meant much greater protection. For property or liberty the standard has reflected developing values, developing attitudes on the relation of government and individual, of order and liberty, applied to the issues of a new day. Except to those who think that the first amendment speaks clearly and absolutely, however, these same developed values in fact determine the protection accorded by the substantive amendments too—the scope of "respecting an establishment" or "prohibiting the free exercise" of religion, of "abridging" the freedom of speech or of the press, and other ambiguities in the first amendment, as of "the right to be secure" against "unreasonable searches and seizures" in the fourth amendment. To those who see in these amendments flexible standards reflecting respective needs of order and of liberty, it is easy to suggest that there is no reason to assume different values in this regard as concerns the action of the states. In terms of incorporation, then, one may say that the liberties mentioned in the first and fourth amendments are incorporated in "liberty" in the fourteenth, and that the values of order and liberty which determine the protection accorded against the federal government by the substantive amendments are the same as—are congruent with if not "incorporated" in—substantive "due process of law" applicable to the states.

This suggestion, I emphasize, does not depend merely on linguistic parsing of the different phrases of the due process clause. The point is that if the fourteenth amendment is deemed to afford substantive protection for "liberty," it should surely protect the fundamental and established liberties. And if the Court is creating a standard of protection for these liberties, it may well look to the standards of protection which it has developed for these liberties in regard to the federal government. Surely it may look to those same standards if, as most of the justices accept, the substantive provisions are "specific" only in identifying the right protected, but not as to elaborating the standard of protection, and the latter must derive from contemporary enlightenment. The fact is that without having explicitly accepted incorporation, the Court never seems to have found in the explicit provisions of the early amendments some standard higher than that to be applied to the states. And even the individual justices who have insisted that the standard is different have not been able to articulate and justify two different standards. Whether one calls it incorporation or not, identical standards for state and federal governments apparently are established. Incorporating the procedural provisions of the Bill of Rights, on the other hand, would automatically apply to the states provisions of considerable specificity, including the accretions those amendments have acquired in the history of their application to the federal government. Some of these may not fall within the notion of fairness and ordered liberty that is the core of procedural due process. True, in some situations, as in the right to counsel, there may indeed be congruity with federal protection. In others, congruity may not be required by "due process." There seems no occasion to seek it by an artificial process of incorporation.

. . . What must be remembered is that for the states we start with the fourteenth amendment, not with the Bill of Rights. Unless, with justice Black, one relies on some special intention of the draftsmen of the amendment, that amendment has no relation to the Bill of Rights as a whole. . . .

. . . The suggestion that protections of the Bill of Rights must in all cases be applied exactly to the states, if they be applied at all, is difficult to support as a matter of constitutional language or of the jurisprudence of the Court, or to justify on any other relevant considerations. It creates its own rigidities and runs counter to the direction of growth of the Constitution to embody flexible standards permitting the increase of individual safeguards with the growing enlightenment of contemporary civilization. Even the strongest libertarian instincts do not need such a doctrine to increase protection for the rights of the criminally accused when greater communal enlightenment suggests higher standards to be required of the states as of the federal government.

Bibliography

Fundamental Rights Analysis

Generally

Bork, Robert H., THE TEMPTING OF AMERICA (1991)

Cooley, Thomas L., CONSTITUTIONAL LIMITATIONS (1868)

Corwin, Edward, *The Doctrine of Due Process of Law before the Civil War,* 24 HARV. L. REV. 366 (1911)

Craven, Jr., J. Braxton, *Personhood: The Right To Be Let Alone,* 1976 DUKE L.J. 699 (1976)

Royalty, Kenneth M., *Motorcycle Helmets and the Constitutionality of Self-Protective Legislation,* 38 OHIO ST. L.J. 355 (1969)

Economic Rights and Liberty

Blume, Lawrence & Rubinfeld, Daniel, *Compensation for Taking: An Economic Analysis,* 72 CAL. L. REV. 569 (1984)

Costonis, John J., *Presumptive and Per Se Takings: A Decisional Model for the Taking Issue,* 58 N.Y.U. L. REV. 465 (1983)

Currie, David P., *The Constitution in the Supreme Court: Contracts and Commerce, 1834-1864,* 1983 DUKE L.J. 471

Currie, David P., *The Constitution in the Supreme Court: The Protection of Economic Interests, 1889-1910,* 52 U. CHI. L. REV. 324 (1985)

Dunham, Allison, Griggs v. Allegheny County *in Perspective: Thirty Years of Supreme Court Expropriation Law,* 1962 SUP. CT. REV. 63

Epstein, Richard A., TAKINGS: PRIVATE PROPERTY AND THE POWER OF EMINENT DOMAIN (1985)

Hale, Robert L., *The Supreme Court and the Contract Clause,* 57 HARV. L. REV. 512 (1994)

Hetherington, John A.C., *State Economic Regulation and Substantive Due Process of Law,* 53 NW. U. L. REV. 13 (1958)

Karst, Kenneth L., *Legislative Facts in Constitutional Litigation,* 1960 SUP. CT. REV. 15

Nelson, William E., THE FOURTEENTH AMENDMENT: FROM POLITICAL PRINCIPLE TO JUDICIAL DOCTRINE (1988)

Siegel, Stephen A., Lochner *Era Jurisprudence and the American Constitutional Tradition,* 70 N.C. L. REV. 1 (1991)

Siegel, Stephen A., *Understanding the* Lochner *Era: Lessons from the Controversy over Railroad and Utility Rate Regulation,* 70 Va. L. Rev. 187 (1984)

Stoebuck, William B., *A General Theory of Eminent Domain,* 47 Wash. L. Rev. 553 (1972)

Incorporation

Amar, Akhil Reed, *The Bill of Rights and the Fourteenth Amendment,* 101 Yale L.J. 1193 (1992)

Friendly, Henry J., *The Bill of Rights as a Code of Criminal Procedure,* 53 Cal. L. Rev. 929 (1965)

Israel, Jerold H., *Selective Incorporation Revisited,* 71 Geo. L.J. 253 (1982)

Kelly, Alfred J., Clio *and the Court: An Illicit Love Affair,* 1965 Sup. Ct. Rev. 119

Morrison, Stanley, *Does the Fourteenth Amendment Incorporate the Bill of Rights?,* 2 Stan. L. Rev. 140 (1949)

Nowak, John E., *Due Process Methodology in the Postincorporation World,* 70 J. Crim. L. & Criminology 397 (1980)

ten Broek, Jacobus, Equal under Law (1965)

Modern Substantive Due Process

Although the Court abandoned its zealous protection of economic due process, it pursued another version of substantive due process in more recent decisions involving personal and family liberty. The modern concept of constitutional privacy can trace its origins to the expansive liberty notions developed in pre-*Carolene Products* decisions. But the Court first announced a constitutional "right of privacy" in its 1965 decision in *Griswold v. Connecticut,* which invalidated a state ban on the use of contraceptives by married couples. Justice Douglas' opinion for the Court, disclaiming a doctrinal connection to the repudiated *Lochner,* notably avoided any reliance on liberty, due process, or the Fourteenth Amendment. Instead, it elaborately pieced together a realm of constitutional protection not explicitly mentioned in the Constitution—the right of privacy. In the years since *Griswold,* justices and commentators have debated the scope of this modern version of substantive due process in such controversial contexts as abortion, nontraditional families, sexual orientation and expression, and "the right to die."

The Right of Privacy and Reproductive Freedom

The Court's next application of the right of privacy following *Griswold* embroiled the Court in one of the most divisive political and jurisprudential battles of our time. *Roe v. Wade* upheld a woman's constitutional right to terminate her pregnancy, explicitly acknowledging that the right of privacy articulated in *Griswold* was grounded in the due process clause of the Fourteenth Amendment. Moreover, because this right was "fundamental," the Court required the abortion law to pass strict scrutiny review. In so doing, the Court's opinion in *Roe* revived not only substantive due process but also the heated contest over "noninterpretivist" judicial review. Subsequent cases concerning state restrictions on the abortion right have significantly diminished *Roe*'s scheme of constitutional protection.

John Hart Ely questions *Roe*'s reliance on substantive due process principles and asserts that the Court lacked any constitutional justification for finding an abortion right. Jed Rubenfeld criticizes the most common interpretations of the right of privacy and proposes an alternative approach that centers on the totalitarian intervention of government into a person's life. Catharine MacKinnon rejects privacy law altogether for upholding male power and undermining state intervention needed to end women's subordination. She suggests instead a sex equality approach to the law of reproductive control that focuses on the status of the sexes. Dorothy Roberts addresses the reproductive rights of Black women, advocating a progressive concept of privacy that places an affirmative duty on government to guarantee liberty and recognizes the connection between the right of privacy and racial equality.

John Hart Ely, *The Wages of Crying Wolf: A Comment on Roe v. Wade*, 82 YALE L.J. 920, 923-937 (1973)*

* * *

II

Let us not underestimate what is at stake: Having an unwanted child can go a long way toward ruining a woman's life. And at bottom *Roe* signals the Court's judgment that this result cannot be justified by any good that anti-abortion legislation accomplishes. This surely is an understandable conclusion—indeed it is one with which I agree—but ordinarily the Court claims no mandate to second-guess legislative balances, at least not when the Constitution has designated neither of the values in conflict as entitled to special protection. But even assuming it would be a good idea for the Court to assume this function, *Roe* seems a curious place to have begun. Laws prohibiting the use of "soft" drugs or, even more obviously, homosexual acts between consenting adults can stunt "the preferred life styles" of those against whom enforcement is threatened in very serious ways. It is clear such acts harm no one besides the participants, and indeed the case that the participants are harmed is a rather shaky one. Yet such laws survive, on the theory that there exists a societal consensus that the behavior involved is revolting or at any rate immoral. Of course the consensus is not universal but it is sufficient, and this is what is counted crucial, to get the laws passed and keep them on the books. Whether anti-abortion legislation cramps the life style of an unwilling mother more significantly than anti-homosexuality legislation cramps the life style of a homosexual is a close question. But even granting that it does, the *other* side of the balance looks very different. For there is more than simple societal revulsion to support legislation restricting abortion: Abortion ends (or if it makes a difference, prevents) the life of a human being other than the one making the choice.

The Court's response here is simply not adequate. It agrees, indeed it holds, that after the point of viability (a concept it fails to note will become even less clear than it is now as the technology of birth continues to develop) the interest in protecting the fetus is compelling. Exactly why that is the magic moment is not made clear: Viability, as the Court defines it, is achieved some six to twelve weeks after quickening. (Quickening is the point at which the fetus begins discernibly to move independently of the mother and the point that has historically been deemed crucial—to the extent any point between conception and birth has been focused on.) But no, it is viability that is constitutionally critical: the Court's defense seems to mistake a definition for a syllogism.

> With respect to the State's important and legitimate interest in potential life, the "compelling" point is at viability. This is so because the fetus then presumably has the capacity of meaningful life outside the mother's womb.

With regard to why the state cannot consider this "important and legitimate interest" prior to viability, the opinion is even less satisfactory. The discussion begins sensibly enough: The interest asserted is not necessarily tied to the question whether the fetus is "alive," for whether or not one calls it a living being, it is an entity with the potential for (and indeed the likelihood of) life. But all of arguable relevance that follows are argu-

---

    *   Reprinted by permission of the Yale Law Journal Company and Fred B. Rothman & Company from The Yale Law Journal, Vol. 82, page 920.

ments that fetuses (a) are not recognized as "persons in the whole sense" by legal doctrine generally and (b) are not "persons" protected by the Fourteenth Amendment.

To the extent they are not entirely inconclusive, the bodies of doctrine to which the Court adverts respecting the protection of fetuses under general legal doctrine tend to undercut rather than support its conclusion. And the argument that fetuses (unlike, say, corporations) are not "persons" under the Fourteenth Amendment fares little better. The Court notes that most constitutional clauses using the word "persons"—such as the one outlining the qualifications for the Presidency—appear to have been drafted with postnatal beings in mind. (It might have added that most of them were plainly drafted with adults in mind, but I suppose that wouldn't have helped.) In addition, "the appellee conceded on reargument that no case can be cited that holds that a fetus is a person within the meaning of the Fourteenth Amendment." (The other legal contexts in which the question could have arisen are not enumerated.)

The canons of construction employed here are perhaps most intriguing when they are contrasted with those invoked to derive the constitutional right to an abortion. But in any event, the argument that fetuses lack constitutional rights is simply irrelevant. For it has never been held or even asserted that the state interest needed to justify forcing a person to refrain from an activity, whether or not that activity is constitutionally protected, must implicate either the life or the constitutional rights of another person. Dogs are not "persons in the whole sense" nor have they constitutional rights, but that does not mean the state cannot prohibit killing them: It does not even mean the state cannot prohibit killing them in the exercise of the First Amendment right of political protest. Come to think of it, draft cards aren't persons either.

Thus even assuming the Court ought generally to get into the business of second-guessing legislative balances, it has picked a strange case with which to begin. Its purported evaluation of the balance that produced anti-abortion legislation simply does not meet the issue: That the life plans of the mother must, not simply may, prevail over the state's desire to protect the fetus simply does not follow from the judgment that the fetus is not a person. Beyond all that, however, the Court has no business getting into that business.

III

Were I a legislator I would vote for a statute very much like the one the Court ends up drafting. I hope this reaction reflects more than the psychological phenomenon that keeps bombardiers sane—the fact that it is somehow easier to "terminate" those you cannot see—and am inclined to think it does: that the mother, unlike the unborn child, has begun to imagine a future for herself strikes me as morally quite significant. But God knows I'm not happy with that resolution. Abortion is too much like infanticide on the one hand, and too much like contraception on the other, to leave one comfortable with any answer; and the moral issue it poses is as fiendish as any philosopher's hypothetical.

Of course, the Court often resolves difficult moral questions, and difficult questions yield controversial answers. I doubt, for example, that most people would agree that letting a drug peddler go unapprehended is morally preferable to letting the police kick down his door without probable cause. The difference, of course, is that the Constitution, which legitimates and theoretically controls judicial intervention, has some rather pointed things to say about this choice. There will of course be difficult questions about the applicability of its language to specific facts, but at least the document's special concern with one of the values in conflict is manifest. It simply says nothing, clear or fuzzy, about abortion.

The matter cannot end there, however. The Burger Court, like the Warren Court before it, has been especially solicitous of the right to travel from state to state, demanding a compelling state interest if it is to be inhibited. Yet nowhere in the Constitution is such a right mentioned. It is, however, as clear as such things can be that this right was one the framers intended to protect, most specifically by the Privileges and Immunities Clause of Article IV. The right is, moreover, plausibly inferable from the system of government, and the citizen's role therein, contemplated by the Constitution. The Court in *Roe* suggests an inference of neither sort—from the intent of the framers, or from the governmental system contemplated by the Constitution—in support of the constitutional right to an abortion.

What the Court does assert is that there is a general right of privacy granted special protection—that is, protection above and beyond the baseline requirement of "rationality"—by the Fourteenth Amendment, and that that right "is broad enough to encompass" the right to an abortion. The general right of privacy is inferred, as it was in *Griswold v. Connecticut,* from various provisions of the Bill of Rights manifesting a concern with privacy, notably the Fourth Amendment's guarantee against unreasonable searches, the Fifth Amendment's privilege against self-incrimination, and the right, inferred from the First Amendment, to keep one's political associations secret.

One possible response is that all this proves is that the things explicitly mentioned are forbidden, if indeed it does not actually demonstrate a disposition not to enshrine anything that might be called a general right of privacy. In fact the Court takes this view when it suits its purposes. (On the same day it decided *Roe*, the Court held that a showing of reasonableness was not needed to force someone to provide a grand jury with a voice exemplar, reasoning that the Fifth Amendment was not implicated because the evidence was not "testimonial" and that the Fourth Amendment did not apply because there was no "seizure.") But this approach is unduly crabbed. Surely the Court is entitled, indeed I think it is obligated, to seek out the sorts of evils the framers meant to combat and to move against their twentieth century counterparts.

Thus it seems to me entirely proper to infer a general right of privacy, so long as some care is taken in defining the sort of right the inference will support. Those aspects of the First, Fourth and Fifth Amendments to which the Court refers all limit the ways in which, and the circumstances under which, the government can go about gathering information about a person he would rather it did not have. *Katz v. United States,* limiting governmental tapping of telephones, may not involve what the framers would have called a "search," but it plainly involves this general concern with privacy. *Griswold* is a long step, even a leap, beyond this, but at least the connection is discernible. Had it been a case that purported to discover in the Constitution a "right to contraception," it would have been *Roe's* strongest precedent. But the Court in *Roe* gives no evidence of so regarding it, and rightly not. Commentators tend to forget, though the Court plainly has not, that the Court in *Griswold* stressed that it was invalidating only that portion of the Connecticut law that proscribed the use, as opposed to the manufacture, sale, or other distribution of contraceptives. That distinction (which would be silly were the right to contraception being constitutionally enshrined) makes sense if the case is rationalized on the ground that the section of the law whose constitutionality was in issue was such that its enforcement would have been virtually impossible without the most outrageous sort of governmental prying into the privacy of the home. And this, indeed, is the theory on which the Court appeared rather explicitly to settle:

The present case, then, concerns a relationship lying within the zone of privacy created by several fundamental constitutional guarantees. And it concerns a law which, in forbidding the use of contraceptives rather than regulating their manufacture or sale, seeks to achieve its goals by means having a maximum destructive impact upon that relationship. Such a law cannot stand in light of the familiar principle, so often applied by this Court, that "a governmental purpose to control or prevent activities constitutionally subject to state regulation may not be achieved by means which sweep unnecessarily broadly and thereby invade the area of protected freedoms." NAACP v. Alabama, 377 U.S. 288, 307. Would we allow the police to search the sacred precincts of marital bedrooms for telltale signs of the use of contraceptives? The very idea is repulsive to the notions of privacy surrounding the marriage relationship.

Thus even assuming (as the Court surely seemed to) that a state can constitutionally seek to minimize or eliminate the circulation and use of contraceptives, Connecticut had acted unconstitutionally by selecting a means, that is a direct ban on use, that would generate intolerably intrusive modes of data-gathering. No such rationalization is attempted by the Court in *Roe*—and understandably not, for whatever else may be involved, it is not a case about governmental snooping.

The Court reports that some amici curiae argued for an unlimited right to do as one wishes with one's body. This theory holds, for me at any rate, much appeal. However, there would have been serious problems with its invocation in this case. In the first place, more than the mother's own body is involved in a decision to have an abortion; a fetus may not be a "person in the whole sense," but it is certainly not nothing. Second, it is difficult to find a basis for thinking that the theory was meant to be given constitutional sanction: Surely it is no part of the "privacy" interest the Bill of Rights suggests.

[I]t is not clear to us that the claim . . . that one has an unlimited right to do with one's body as one pleases bears a close relationship to the right of privacy . . ..

Unfortunately, having thus rejected the amici's attempt to define the bounds of the general constitutional right of which the right to an abortion is a part, on the theory that the general right described has little to do with privacy, the Court provides neither an alternative definition nor an account of why it thinks privacy is involved. It simply announces that the right to privacy "is broad enough to encompass a woman's decision whether or not to terminate her pregnancy." Apparently this conclusion is thought to derive from the passage that immediately follows it:

The detriment that the State would impose upon the pregnant woman by denying this choice altogether is apparent. Specific and direct harm medically diagnosable even in early pregnancy may be involved. Maternity, or additional offspring, may force upon the woman a distressful life and future. Psychological harm may be imminent. Mental and physical health may be taxed by child care. There is also the distress, for all concerned, associated with the unwanted child, and there is the problem of bringing a child into a family already unable, psychologically and otherwise, to care for it. In other cases, as in this one, the additional difficulties and continuing stigma of unwed motherhood may be involved.

All of this is true and ought to be taken very seriously. But it has nothing to do with privacy in the Bill of Rights sense or any other the Constitution suggests. I suppose there is nothing to prevent one from using the word "privacy" to mean the freedom to live one's life without governmental interference. But the Court obviously does not so use the term. Nor could it, for such a right is at stake in every case. Our life styles are constantly limited, often seriously, by governmental regulation; and while many of us would prefer less direction, granting that desire the status of a preferred constitutional right would yield a system of "government" virtually unrecognizable to us and only slightly more recognizable to our forefathers. The Court's observations concerning the serious, life-shaping costs of having a child prove what might to the thoughtless have seemed unprovable: That even though a human life, or a potential human life, hangs in the balance, the moral dilemma abortion poses is so difficult as to be heartbreaking. What they fail to do is even begin to resolve that dilemma so far as our governmental system is concerned by associating either side of the balance with a value inferable from the Constitution.

But perhaps the inquiry should not end even there. In his famous *Carolene Products* footnote, Justice Stone suggested that the interests to which the Court can responsibly give extraordinary constitutional protection include not only those expressed in the Constitution but also those that are unlikely to receive adequate consideration in the political process, specifically the interests of "discrete and insular minorities" unable to form effective political alliances. There can be little doubt that such considerations have influenced the direction, if only occasionally the rhetoric, of the recent Courts. My repeated efforts to convince my students that sex should be treated as a "suspect classification" have convinced me it is no easy matter to state such considerations in a "principled" way. But passing that problem, *Roe* is not an appropriate case for their invocation.

Compared with men, very few women sit in our legislatures, a fact I believe should bear some relevance—even without an Equal Rights Amendment—to the appropriate standard of review for legislation that favors men over women. But no fetuses sit in our legislatures. Of course they have their champions, but so have women. The two interests have clashed repeatedly in the political arena, and had continued to do so up to the date of the opinion, generating quite a wide variety of accommodations. By the Court's lights virtually all of the legislative accommodations had unduly favored fetuses: by its definition of victory, women had lost. Yet in every legislative balance one of the competing interests loses to some extent; indeed usually, as here, they both do. On some occasions the Constitution throws its weight on the side of one of them, indicating the balance must be restruck. And on others—and this is Justice Stone's suggestion—it is at least arguable that, constitutional directive or not, the Court should throw its weight on the side of a minority demanding in court more than it was able to achieve politically. But even assuming this suggestion can be given principled content, it was clearly intended and should be reserved for those interests which, as compared with the interests to which they have been subordinated, constitute minorities unusually incapable of protecting themselves. Compared with men, women may constitute such a "minority"; compared with the unborn, they do not. I'm not sure I'd know a discrete and insular minority if I saw one, but confronted with a multiple choice question requiring me to designate (a) women or (b) fetuses as one, I'd expect no credit for the former answer.

Of course a woman's freedom to choose an abortion is part of the "liberty" the Fourteenth Amendment says shall not be denied without due process of law, as indeed is anyone's freedom to do what he wants. But "due process" generally guarantees only that the inhibition be procedurally fair and that it have some "rational" connection—though plausible is probably a better word—with a permissible governmental goal. What is unusual about *Roe* is that the liberty involved is accorded a far more stringent protection, so stringent that a desire to preserve the fetus' existence is unable to overcome it—a protection more stringent, I think it fair to say, than that the present Court accords the freedom of the press explicitly guaranteed by the First Amendment. What is frightening about *Roe* is that this super-protected right is not inferable from the language of the Constitution, the framers' thinking respecting the specific problem in issue, any general value derivable from the provisions they included, or the nation's governmental structure. Nor is it explainable in terms of the unusual political impotence of the group judicially protected vis-à-vis the interest that legislatively prevailed over it. And that, I believe—the predictable early reaction to *Roe* notwithstanding ("more of the same Warren-type activism")—is a charge that can responsibly be leveled at no other decision of the past twenty years. At times the inferences the Court has drawn from the values the Constitution marks for special protection have been controversial, even shaky, but never before has its sense of an obligation to draw one been so obviously lacking.

* * *

Jed Rubenfeld, *The Right of Privacy*, 102 HARV. L. REV. 737, 737-40, 750-76, 782-805 (1989)*

* * *

. . . The changing membership of the High Court raises the possibility of a wholesale reconsideration of the privacy doctrine's propriety. Yet even when the doctrine was first ascendant, the Court never hazarded a definitive statement of what it was supposed to protect. At the heart of the right to privacy, there has always been a conceptual vacuum.

The reason for this, I will try to show, is that the operative analysis in privacy cases has invariably missed the real point. Past privacy analysis has taken the act proscribed by the law at issue—for example, abortion, interracial marriage, or homosexual sex—and asked whether there is a "fundamental right" to perform it. But the fundament of the right to privacy is not to be found in the supposed fundamentality of what the law proscribes. It is to be found in what the law imposes. The question, for example, of whether the state should be permitted to compel an individual to have a child—with all the pervasive, far-reaching, lifelong consequences that child-bearing ordinarily entails—need not be the same as the question of whether abortion or even child-bearing itself is a "fundamental" act within some normative framework. The distinguishing feature of the laws struck down by the privacy cases has been their profound capacity to direct and to occupy individuals' lives through their affirmative consequences. This affirmative power in the law, lying just below its interdictive surface, must be privacy's focal point.

I. A GENEOLOGY OF PRIVACY

* * *

What, then, is the right to privacy? What does it protect? A number of commentators seem to think that they have it when they add the word "autonomy" to the privacy vocabulary. But to call an individual "autonomous" is simply another way of saying that he is morally free, and to say that the right to privacy protects freedom adds little to our understanding of the doctrine. To be sure, the privacy doctrine involves the "right to make choices and decisions," which, it is said, forms the "kernel" of autonomy. The question, however, is *which* choices and decisions are protected.

On this point the Court has offered little guidance. We are told that privacy encompasses only those "personal rights that can be deemed 'fundamental' or 'implicit in the concept of ordered liberty,'" that it insulates decisions "important" to a person's destiny, and that it applies to "matters . . . fundamentally affecting a person." Perhaps the best interpretation of these formulations is that privacy is like obscenity: the Justices might not be able to say what privacy is, but they know it when they see it. How else can one explain the Court's astonishing introduction of its pivotal holding in *Eisenstadt v. Baird* with the phrase, "*If the right to privacy means anything,* it means . . ."?

That a doctrine might have to wait for a principle to "catch up" with it is nothing new to common-lawmaking in general or to constitutional lawmaking in particular. Yet a complete absence of conceptualization cannot be maintained. To define "fundamental" rights as those that cover matters "fundamentally affecting persons" is less than entirely satisfactory. Can no more be said?

II. PERSONHOOD

Into this conceptual breach steps "personhood." The late Judge Craven attributed the term's usage in privacy jurisprudence to Professor Freund, who in 1975 made the following observation:

> The theme of personhood is . . . emerging. It has been groping, I think, for a rubric. Sometimes it is called privacy, inaptly it would seem to me; autonomy perhaps, though that seems too dangerously broad. But the idea is that of personhood in the sense of those attributes of an individual which are irreducible in his selfhood.

It is worth recalling, however, that Brandeis and Warren traced their tort law right of privacy to an analogous but now archaic term: the individual's "inviolate personality." Whatever its genesis, "personhood" has so invaded privacy doctrine that it now regularly is seen either as the value underlying the right or as a synonym for the right itself.

Despite its ubiquity, "personhood" remains rather ill-defined. The word is meant, it seems, to capture some essence of our being—"those attributes . . . irreducible in [one's] selfhood"—with which the state must not be allowed to tamper. Yet the concept has a certain opacity, greater perhaps than that of analogous but no less abstract terms such as "dignity" or "liberty." We imagine that we know what it means for someone to be without dignity or liberty; what is it to be deprived of one's personhood?

This much of the idea is easily stated: some acts, faculties, or qualities are so important to our identity as persons—as human beings—that they must remain inviolable, at least as against the state. Yet even this basic formulation is ambiguous. Our "identity as persons" might mean either our identity qua persons or our personal identity. Personhood in the former sense would focus on whatever it is that makes you a person—a human being. Personhood in the latter sense would focus on whatever it is that makes you the person you are. Although these two strands of personhood theory are not always distinguished in the literature, and although they may intertwine at a certain point, the notion of personhood advanced in support of privacy is plainly the second one.

Proponents of personhood forge a link between the privacy case law and individuals' personal identity: the personhood thesis, as we shall pursue it here, is that a person must be free to "define himself." Certain decisions in life are so "central to the personal identities of those singled out" that the state must not be allowed to interfere with them. The right to privacy is, then, to use Justice Blackmun's word, a right to "self-definition."

This conception of a fundamental freedom to define oneself emerges from the second strand of personhood theory: the concern for personal identity. The conception draws its vitality, however, from the first: the concern for our identity as persons. Indeed, to give personhood its strongest formulation, it is at just this point—self-definition—that our "identity qua persons" and our "personal identity" intersect. For, it could be said, the definitive characteristic of human beings is precisely our capacity for self-conscious individuation: the ability to relate to one's past and future as a single being and to construct out of the multiplicity of one's experience and expectations an individual personality. Thus, the freedom of self-definition would be the fundamental human right, of which, for example, the freedoms of thought and belief embodied in the first amendment would count as necessary but insufficient components. Thus might personhood simultaneously account for privacy's constitutional status, its "derivation" from other, enumerated constitutional guarantees, and its moral and political exigency. Surely the state may not deprive us of that liberty on which our humanity fundamentally rests.

* * *

A. Analytic Critique

In demanding that personhood theory satisfy analytic criteria, we are going to subject it to traditional jurisprudential logic: fitting principles to cases, posing hypothetical counterexamples, and so forth. Such logic carries its own substantive premises about the structure, the function, and even the aesthetics of judicial reasoning. I confess at the outset that I do not see how to avoid these premises. At any rate, they seem to me necessary in order to engage in legal discourse and not merely speak of it.

The personhood thesis is this: where our identity or self-definition is at stake, there the state may not interfere. The paramount analytical difficulty is one of limitation. Where is our self-definition *not* at stake? Virtually every action a person takes could arguably be said to be an element of his self-definition. Decisions seemingly insignificant for constitutional purposes may well be felt by some to be central to their self-definition. Should our tonsorial preferences, for example, be constitutionally protected?

Clearly personhood must give us a conception of personal identity to show what acts are fundamental and hence constitutionally protected. The proponents of personhood, however, have not yet elaborated a conception of identity; and, for the moment, they have not yet had to do so. The reason for this lies in the emphasis on sexuality in the privacy case law. There has been a peculiar willingness simply to state or to assume—as if it required no explanation—that matters of sexuality go straight to the heart of personal identity. I shall have much more to say about this assumption below. For "analytic" purposes, however, let us accept the idea that matters of reproduction, contraception, marriage partners, and so on are somehow fundamental to self-definition. A whole range of activity, long the subject of state prohibitions, must still be confronted. Are laws against prostitution, adultery, incest, and rape unconstitutional?

We must do personhood justice, if we can. There is no reason for personhood to assert that every sexual act is fundamental to an individual's identity. Rather the *intimacy* of a sexual relationship—the bond between two people—might be what is central. Prostitution is sexual industry, not intimacy, it might be said; the parties are no more defining themselves through such transactions than are people who are having lunch at McDonald's.

Now it may well be that people *are* defining themselves when they have lunch at McDonald's. Yet even accepting the distinction between sexual activity traded for money and sexual activity more deeply tied to one's psychological and emotional life, we are still left with adultery, incest, and rape to consider. Adultery and incest may involve relations as "intimate" as marriage. And although there is no such intimacy in rape, rape still differs from prostitution in a way that personhood must confront. The rapist, from a psychological viewpoint, may be expressing and establishing his identity in the deepest sense through his acts. Surely personhood theorists do not envision a rapist defending himself with the claim that he needs to violate women in order to "define himself."

An advocate of personhood has two responses to this rather obvious but important hypothetical. She might say that being a rapist—or an adulterer, a practicer of incest, or for that matter a prostitute—is simply not the kind of identity to which the right she has in mind would offer any protection. It is a "bad" or "unhealthy" identity. Alternatively, she might say that harm is the answer: the right to self-definition is not absolute, it could be said, and acts that cause harm to others are not constitutionally protected even if central to a person's identity.

The difficulty with the former approach is that, once the personhood theorist enters the realm of "good" and "bad" identities, she is in danger of losing the battle entirely. . . . Thus the openly normative response appears to surrender what the personhood theorist must most strongly defend: the right to define oneself even in opposition to widespread, traditional, "normal" values.

In contrast, the harm response seems to offer a more solid, analytical distinction. It appears to avoid the abyss of subjectivity opened up by the yawning categories of "good" and "bad." We need not pass judgment on identities: as long as an individual does not harm others, he has a right to be whatever he chooses.

In this formulation, personhood is aligned with, and can draw support from, John Stuart Mill's well-known thesis concerning self-regarding acts. Mill conceived of an absolute privilege to perform those acts that have no effect on others or only such effects as have been consented to in advance. Mill's principle was "jurisdictional" in nature: society has authority to regulate only activity that affects it, and self-regarding acts by definition do not affect society. American jurisprudence has had a long flirtation with this simple but revolutionary idea. Several commentators have explicitly invoked the harm principle as the basis for a right to privacy.

Let us see whether Mill's logic can successfully limit the personhood thesis. Clearly a harm limitation would provide personhood with a coherent answer to the problem of rape. It is not so clear, however, that Mill's principle can achieve the desired results in the other contexts already mentioned. As to adultery, personhood's position could be that the potential emotional harm to one's spouse and children is sufficiently intense, confined, and foreseeable that it allows adultery laws to pass Mill's test, which ordinarily would be extremely skeptical about claims of "emotional harm." Or it could be said that, by marrying, the adulterer ceded to his spouse a right that ordinarily would not be legally cognizable. These arguments, although by no means air-tight, are serviceable enough; let us grant this point.

As to incest, the case is still more attenuated, provided we are speaking of incest not with a minor child but between adults. The former could be prohibited under Mill's logic even where both parties had "consented" on the ground that a minor's consent is not dispositive. The trick for personhood here is to categorize incest even between adults in the same fashion: the argument would be that consent to incestuous sex is always suspect because of the peculiar, mysterious pressures at work within the nuclear family. . . .

Say, then, that personhood has staked its claim on Mill's principle and that the conduct it seeks to exclude from its protective ambit is that which affects or harms others in the necessary ways. There remains a much harder problem: that the conduct personhood seeks to include may affect others in the same way.

The difficulty with the notion of "self-regarding" acts has always been that there are none—or, at least, that the only really self-regarding acts are completely uncontroversial. The minute someone starts defending her actions against a storm of protest with the claim that she is only affecting herself, we may be certain that the opposite is true. First there is the offense caused to others; then there are the indirect, unintended effects that may usually be found if the causal sequence is carried far enough along; and finally there may be direct but overlooked consequences as well. Such arguments against Mill's principle have been rehearsed many times. They are especially easy to apply to the particular conduct protected by the privacy doctrine. . . . These arguments, however, all retain the liberal vocabulary of "harm"; they do not depart from Mill's framework, but instead attempt to work within it. Their logic is unassailable, but they fail to capture what opponents of the right to privacy really challenge.

There is another way in which acts may not be "self-regarding" that is more difficult to articulate from a perspective that looks to the particular consequences of individual acts, but that offers a more profound challenge to Mill's principle. In personhood's own view, the right to privacy protects iconoclasm; it allows people to define themselves in defiance of certain widely held, deeply entrenched values. Iconoclasm throws into question such values, which make society cohere and which so often survive chiefly by their stamp of unchallengeability. Some opponents of the behavior that personhood seeks to protect firmly believe that their childrens' wellbeing and their society's disintegration may be at stake if their traditional values decline. What could more clearly constitute a potential harm to society, one might answer Mill, than that which portends society's disintegration?

* * *

It should be clear, I think, that personhood cannot escape its analytic difficulties by excluding conduct that affects others. The principle that society may not interfere with self-regarding acts cannot serve privacy's purpose. Yet this conclusion is hardly fatal; it is barely even unexpected.

Personhood's answer must be to relax the jurisdictional logic attempted above, to admit that the conduct it would protect has effects on others, and to acknowledge that society may have a considerable interest in such conduct. Personhood must abandon Mill—or rather, it must abandon the superficial construction of Mill encapsulated in the principle of immunity for self-regarding acts, in favor of a construction truer to Mill himself.

* * *

B. The Republican Critique

We have seen that personhood seeks to protect the freedom of individuals to define themselves in contradistinction to the values of the society in which they happen to live. The premise of such freedom is an individualist understanding of human self-definition: a conception of self-definition as something that persons are, and should be, able to do apart from society. Opposed to this individualist idea of self-definition stands the idea of political or communal self-definition. The latter idea is the nucleus of republicanism, a branch of political thought usually advanced as the chief opponent of, and alternative to, traditional liberalism. This "republican vision," which appears in the literature today with some frequency, presents a radical challenge to the personhood principle.

Liberalism and republicanism may be contrasted in a number of ways. One way is to see them as offering two competing understandings of self-government. Liberalism is grounded in a conception of *individual* self-government. Its institutions are designed primarily to secure individual autonomy: the freedom of each to choose and pursue his own ends, limited only by the principle that others must be free to do likewise. By contrast, the "self" that is to govern itself in the republican understanding is a political or communal entity. Republican political institutions are designed with a view to substantive popular participation; republicanism sees liberty as an active and supra-individual condition, a distinctly human potential realizable only through participation in political self-government.

When liberalism and republicanism are contrasted in this way, it becomes possible to see personhood not only as a liberal principle but as *the* liberal principle. Grounded in personhood's right to self-definition, privacy serves the classically liberal goals of preventing government from legislating morality and ensuring that individuals are free to make critical value-choices for themselves. Viewed thus, personhood is subject to an immediate republican rejoinder. We recognized earlier that, if individuals define themselves in opposition to established values, this could have a diffuse but profound effect on social relations. We spoke, rather vaguely, of a threat to the "social fabric." Personhood capitalized on our vagueness by saying that individuals' identities should not be sacrificed to abstract concerns about society's warp and woof.

We can now put the argument more incisively. It is *society's identity* that is at stake. Iconoclasm throws into question what a society stands for; it threatens to disrupt or even to remake the particular identity that a society has chosen and defined for itself. Self-definition is therefore a double-edged sword.

* * *

Hence, personhood remains trapped in the self-contradiction produced by its own premises concerning the nature of human identity. Personhood cannot exclude "intolerant" identities without abandoning its value-neutrality as between identities, and abandoning such value-neutrality undermines personhood's normative foundations. There is, however, one other avenue of escape available, if personhood dares to take it. From the first, we observed that personhood would eventually be obliged to deliver a conception of personal identity that could explain which decisions, being central to identity, deserve constitutional protection and which decisions, being peripheral or less significant, do not. Personhood must now take advantage of this necessity and attempt to refine the premises that have led it into self-contradiction.

No matter how exercised people get over their neighbors' skin color or sexual preferences, personhood may say, this intolerance is not genuinely constitutive of identity. The right to privacy really does ultimately come down to our private lives, and the neighbor's private life is precisely not one's own.

But what is that "private life" to which personhood now adverts? It is, of course, the field of sexuality: marriage, contraception, child-bearing, and so on. Personhood finally comes to rest its case on the fundamental importance of sexuality: a person's sexual life (in the broad sense of the term) is simply more definitive of and more deeply rooted in who that person is than his neighbors' conduct can ever be. That is personhood's final defense.

C. The Critique from Foucault

Thus the forefather of privacy, from personhood's view, is not Brandeis, but Freud. Personhood can resolve the contradiction it confronted in the last section by adopting a Freudian conception of identity. In this view, sexuality occupies a psychologically (or even biologically) privileged stratum in the formation of our identity and, at the same time, delineates an inner boundary of the strictly personal that the state ought not to be able to cross. In sexuality lies the hidden truth of our identity, and for the sake of our identity, society must not be allowed to repress that truth or to prevent us from discovering it.

By taking this Freudian turn, personhood scores a number of points. It suddenly possesses an elaborate theory of human identity on which to draw, replete with "experts" to back it up. In addition, this theory of identity miraculously happens to match up with the main thrust of the extant privacy cases; that is, personhood now has an explanation of privacy's preoccupation with sexuality. Finally, personhood even gains an emancipatory vision with which to supplement its own: the Freudian vision of the individual freeing himself from socio-sexual repression.

Although it would not be profitable here to analyze Freudian theory in any depth, it is necessary at a minimum for us to challenge the widely accepted connection that it draws between sexuality and identity. To see this task through, we will enlist the aid of the late Michel Foucault. What follows does not demand a complete acceptance of Foucault's views any more than it demands a rejection of Freud's. We will try to draw out just enough of the argument to make the point that concerns us. Here, however, our concerns have become more complicated. We are now looking to answer the most important questions posed earlier: what accounts for the strange attraction toward sexuality of the right-to-privacy decisions? And is the force behind this attraction a liberating one?

1. *Foucault's* History of Sexuality.—Foucault's last work, *The History of Sexuality,* begins with a description of and a challenge to what he calls the "repressive hypothesis": the view that "define[s] the relationship between sex and power in terms of repression." In this view, our sexuality has been systematically repressed for some time by society, which has enjoined us not to speak of our true sexual desires, not to act upon them, and indeed not to know them. From this repression a great host of maladies follows, but also a great hope: that by liberating our sexuality, we will rediscover the truth about ourselves and simultaneously remake our society. "[T]he essential thing," as Foucault describes this uniquely modern way of formulating the "problem" of sexuality, is "the existence in our era of a discourse in which sex, the rev-

elation of truth, the overturning of global laws, the proclamation of a new day to come, and the promise of a certain felicity are linked together."

Personhood, at the moment it adopts a Freudian perspective on personal identity, partakes of the repressive hypothesis. First, it perceives in sexuality "the deeply buried truth . . . about ourselves," so that sexual relations must be accorded central self-definitive status within the category of protected conduct. Second, it perceives itself as part of a process of liberating individuals from the constraints of a powerful state by permitting each individual to express his own sexuality freely.

Foucault challenges both aspects of this view. The critical point for Foucault is to see in all the discourse about liberating sexuality nothing other than the creation of a society captivated by sexuality. According to Foucault, Freud did not stand, as the repressive hypothesis would have it, at the turning point between a Victorian age of sexual repression and a modern era of dawning sexual enlightenment. To the contrary, the chief characteristic of psychoanalysis in particular and the repressive hypothesis in general is that they have continued—rather than broken with—the ongoing history of sexuality, which to Foucault has been a "centuries-long rise of a complex deployment for compelling sex to speak, for fastening our attention and concern upon sex."

* * *

Foucault's revolutionary "history of sexuality" indicates two points of vulnerability for the personhood theory. First, it challenges the connection between sex and identity on which personhood now crucially relies. In Foucault's view, sexuality occupies no biologically or psychologically privileged status in our identities. To the contrary, the belief that sexuality does play this privileged role is explained as a societal artifact or even a mystification. "The whole idea," as Charles Taylor has said, "turns out to be a stratagem of power." Second, Foucault's view implicates—in a manner we have yet to explore fully—the emancipatory vision to which personhood lays claim.

* * *

2. *Personhood's Liberating Potential.*—Foucault's critique of the Freudian (and by now almost universal) understanding of sexual repression is intimately connected with another theme central to Foucault's remarkable later works and indispensable here: a reformulation of the way that *power* operates in modern societies. Foucault's treatment of sexuality rejects the view that society's relation to sexuality is that of an external, essentially prohibitory force. Rather, as we have seen, Foucault's contention is that sexuality has been affirmatively and systematically insinuated into our lives in a variety of ways. For Foucault, this transition from a negative to an affirmative conception of societal power applies not only to the "deployment" of sexuality, but to power's operation in general.

We have too long adhered, Foucault tells us, to a conception of power tied to the image of a monarchical sovereign: a "purely juridical conception" that sees power as essentially prohibiting certain conduct. This conception may once have been useful, centuries ago, when the exercise of monarchical power was confined largely to public punishments, sanctions, and forcible seizures. Now, however, through expanded technologies and far more systematic methods of acculturation, the state's power works *positively* to watch over and shape our lives, to dispose and predispose us, and to inscribe into our lives and consciousnesses its particular designs. . . .

Thus, the primary characteristic of power in the modern era, as Foucault describes it, is what he calls its "productive" capacity: not production in the sense of goods or services, but the production of individuals' lives. This new productivity is achieved in two ways. First, Foucault stresses the increasing state control over the material, quotidian conditions of everyday life. He describes a "proliferation of political technologies . . . investing the body, health, modes of subsistence and habitation, living conditions, the whole of existence." Second, Foucault identifies a *normalizing* function exercised throughout the political and social apparatus, working to mold our identities into patterns designated as healthy, sane, law-abiding, or otherwise normal.

* * *

We must reject the personhood thesis, then, not because the concept of "self-definition" is analytically incoherent, nor because it is too "individualistic," but ultimately because it betrays privacy's—if not personhood's own—political aspirations. By conceiving of the conduct that it purports to protect as "essential to the individual's identity," personhood inadvertently reintroduces into privacy analysis the very premise of the invidious uses of state power it seeks to overcome.

Perhaps the example of abortion can best serve to drive this point home. Personhood must defend the right to abortion on the ground that abortion is essential to the woman's self-definition. But underlying the idea that a woman is *defining her identity* by determining not to have a child is the very premise of those institutionalized sexual roles through which the subordination of women has for so long been maintained. Only if it were "natural" for a woman to want to bear children—and unnatural if she did not—would it make sense to insist that the decision not to have a child at one given moment was centrally definitive of a woman's identity. Those of us who believe that a woman has a right to abort her pregnancy must defend the position on other grounds. The claim that an abortion is a fundamental act of self-definition is nothing other than a corollary to the insistence that motherhood, or at least the desire to be a mother, is the fundamental, inescapable, natural backdrop of womanhood against which every woman is defined.

Women should be able to abort their pregnancies so that they may *avoid being forced into an identity,* not because they are defining their identities through the decision itself. Resisting an enforced identity is not the same as defining oneself. Therein lies the real flaw of the personhood account of privacy—and therein the core of the alternative view of privacy advanced in what follows.

III. AN ALTERNATIVE FOR PRIVACY

Despite the maxim, it is always easier, as everyone knows, to dispose than to propose. But negation must come to an end, and criticism, however sharp its edge, must also have a point. What follows, then, is the point.

A. *Method*

The methodology heretofore universal in privacy analysis has begun with the question, "What is the state trying to forbid?" The proscribed conduct is then delineated and its significance tested through a pre-established conceptual apparatus: for its role in "the concept of ordered liberty," its status as a "fundamental" right, its importance to one's identity, or for any other criterion of fundamentality upon which a court can settle. Suppose instead we began by asking not what is being *prohibited,* but what is being *produced.* Suppose we looked not to the negative aspect of the law— the interdiction by which it formally expresses itself—but at its positive aspect: the real effects that conformity with the law produces at the level of everyday lives and social practices.

The derivation of this turn lies in the ideas discussed in the foregoing section. In Foucault's conception, the significance of a law does not reside in the interdiction itself, but in the extent to which the law interjects us in a network of norms and practices that affirmatively shape our lives. The critical methodological step is to look away from what the law would keep us from doing and instead look to what the law would have us do.

B. Substance

Consider the three principal areas in which the right to privacy has been applied: child-bearing (abortion and contraception), marriage (miscegenation laws, divorce restrictions, and so on), and education of children (*Meyer* and *Pierce*). According to the prevailing method of privacy analysis, certain decisions concerning these matters cannot be proscribed because they are "fundamental." But what is fundamental about these decisions? Are they fundamental in themselves? If, for example, the right to decide whom to marry is inherently fundamental, how is it, for example, that the proscriptions against incestuous and bigamous marriage do not offend it? In fact, a "liberty of fundamental decisions" cannot serve as a constitutional principle any more than could that quite similar quantity—the "liberty of contract"—that animated the *Lochner* jurisprudence. There is something fundamental at stake in the privacy decisions, but it is not the proscribed conduct, nor even the freedom of decision—it is not what is being taken away.

The distinctive and singular characteristic of the laws against which the right to privacy has been applied lies in their *productive* or *affirmative* consequences. There are perhaps no legal proscriptions with more profound, more extensive, or more persistent affirmative effects on individual lives than the laws struck down as violations of the right to privacy. Anti-abortion laws, anti-miscegenation laws, and compulsory education laws all involve the forcing of lives into well-defined and highly confined institutional layers. At the simplest, most quotidian level, such laws tend to *take over* the lives of the persons involved: they occupy and preoccupy. They affirmatively and very substantially shape a person's life; they direct a life's development along a particular avenue. These laws do not simply proscribe one act or remove one liberty; they inform the totality of a person's life.

The principle of the right to privacy is not the freedom to do certain, particular acts determined to be fundamental through some ever-progressing normative lens. It is the fundamental freedom not to have one's life too totally determined by a progressively more normalizing state.

Someone might say, I suppose, that anti-abortion or anti-contraception laws do not force women to bear children because women can simply refrain from having sex. Similarly one might say that whites and blacks, confronted by laws forbidding interracial marriage, can simply decline to marry if they do not wish to live with members of their own race.

This is no answer at all. To begin with, it is no answer to the pregnant woman seeking an abortion. More fundamentally, it is no answer because it is merely another attempt to hide behind a factitious focus on the prohibitory aspect of the law. The practical consequence of obeying laws against contraception or interracial marriage is that people become pregnant or marry intraracially. Indeed these laws derive the depth of their affirmative force from the fact that they operate on drives and desires too strong or too subtle for most to resist.

The danger, then, is a particular kind of creeping totalitarianism, an unarmed *occupation* of individuals' lives. That is the danger of which Foucault as well as the right to privacy is warning us: a society standardized and normalized, in which lives are too substantially or too rigidly directed. That is the threat posed by state power in our century.

* * *

Consider now the cases of *Meyer* and *Pierce,* which, as noted earlier, may be considered the true progenitors of the privacy decisions.

* * *

. . . The threat of the state using the public schools to inculcate one acceptable way of thinking—"our" way, as opposed to "foreign" ways—was genuinely present in *Meyer.* It was a threat not of coercing uniformity from without, but of producing uniformity from within.

Pierce presented this threat even more starkly because there the state had prohibited all organized elementary education outside the public schools. That the Court was reacting to this threat—and not merely to a deprivation of the "liberty of contract"—cannot be doubted. In language that implicitly derived its force from the same sources on which the Court drew in *Meyer,* the Court struck down the law and held that the "fundamental theory of liberty upon which all governments in this Union repose excludes any general power of the State to *standardize its children.*"

This concept of standardization as applied in *Pierce* is critical for our purposes. It includes both quantitative and qualitative components. The law struck down in *Pierce*—like the Platonic or Spartan regimes described by the *Meyer* Court, but unlike *Barnette*'s flag-salute law—had the effect of affirmatively occupying a substantial portion of the material, day-to-day lives of those individuals subject to it. At the same time, this occupation potentially subjected these individuals to a narrowly directed existence: a regimen, a discipline, a curriculum in which the totality of their personhood or identity could be forcefully compressed into a particular mold.

These two elements—the affirmative occupation of one's time and the directedness of this occupation—are crucial in understanding why the mandatory public schooling law in *Pierce* implicated a constitutional concern, now called the right to privacy, even though no explicit constitutional guarantee could be said to forbid it. Privacy takes its stand at the outer boundaries of the legitimate exercise of state power. It is to be invoked only where the government threatens to take over or ocucpy our lives—to exert its power in some way over the totality of our lives.

In a few, rare instances this "totalitarian" intervention into a person's life may occur as a result of a single legal prohibition. The burden of elaborating a conception of privacy based on an anti-totalitarian principle is to perceive how a single law may operate positively to take over and direct the totality of our lives.

C. Application

Let us briefly revisit the past privacy cases. The purpose of this revisiting is twofold. We must first test the general principles suggested above against the actual decisions in order to assess their fit. In addition, we need to mix these general principles with concrete cases to give them more color and definition. If in the process we settle into some sort of "reflective equilibrium"—we will have only ourselves to blame.

1. *Abortion and Contraception.*—*Roe v. Wade* is probably the most important privacy case decided. Let us see whether our analysis can provide an adequate foundation for its result.

In what way, if any, do laws against abortion effect a standardization? Do they operate in any way to confine, normalize, and functionalize identities? Even if this is so, do anti-abortion laws operate in this way any more than do other laws?

The answer to these questions is a most emphatic yes. Considered solely in terms of their prohibition, anti-abortion laws are no more "standardizing" than laws against murder. There can be nothing totalitarian, it might be said, in an injunction against the taking of life or of potential life. Considered, however, in productive rather than proscriptive terms, the picture looks quite different.

Anti-abortion laws produce motherhood: they take diverse women with every variety of career, life-plan, and so on, and make mothers of them all. To be sure, motherhood is no unitary phenomenon that is experienced alike by all women. Nonetheless, it is difficult to imagine a state-enforced rule whose ramifications within the actual, everyday life of the actor are more far-reaching. For a period of months and quite possibly years, forced motherhood shapes women's occupations and preoccupations in the minutest detail; it creates a perceived identity for women and confines them to it; and it gathers up a multiplicity of approaches to the problem of being a woman and reduces them all to the single norm of motherhood.

The point at which the state is exerting its power in this context is important too, just as it was in *Pierce*. Education involves the shaping of minds. If state-controlled education necessarily involves certain dangers, in *Pierce* these dangers were exacerbated precisely because the education at issue there involved minds as yet unshaped. The particular danger of state-controlled elementary education lies in the exertion of power in the *formation* of identity, thereby preceding and preempting resistance.

Yet power need not be directed at the undeveloped mind to have this effect; it may also do so if directed at the fully-developed body. A person's life and identity may be shaped as forcefully through taking control over her body—as is done, for example, in some military or religious disciplines—as through the attempted control of her mind. Indeed, bodily control may be the more effective medium to the extent that thought cannot, as it were, meet such control head on, as it might when confronted by an idea that it is told to accept. The exertion of power over the body is in this respect comparable to the exertion of power over a child's mind: its effect can be *formative,* shaping identity at a point where intellectual resistance cannot meet it.

Now, it is quite clear that *Roe v. Wade* had something to do with control over the body; indeed, it has become conventional to interpret *Roe* as resting at least in part on women's right to "bodily integrity" or to "control their own bodies." This supposed right of bodily control, however, has been either poorly articulated or simply misunderstood. The right to control one's body cannot possibly be a right to do as one pleases with it even where the state can rationally identify harms being caused thereby; otherwise common law crimes or torts would be constitutionally immunized. Nor, however, should the bodily control theme in *Roe* be reduced to the woman's interest in deciding whether a certain surgical operation is to be performed upon her. In fact, anti-abortion laws produce a far more affirmative and pronounced bodily intervention: the compulsion to carry a fetus to term, to deliver the baby, and to care for the child in the first years of its life. All of these processes, in their real daily effects, involve without question the most intimate and strenuous exercises of the female body. The woman's body will be subjected to a continuous regimen of diet, exercise, medical examination, and possibly surgical procedures. Her most elemental biological and psychological impulses will be enlisted in the process. In these ways, anti-abortion laws exert power productively over a woman's body and, through the uses to which her body is put, forcefully reshape and redirect her life.

A further point of similarity between *Pierce* and *Roe* should be noted. The danger of standardization that the Court noted in *Pierce* can in part be understood as the danger of treating individuals as mere instrumentalities of the state, rather than as citizens with independent minds who themselves constitute the state. Instrumentalization and the undermining of independence are also critically implicated in the abortion context. Women forced to bear children are compelled to devote both body and mind to their children. Many will, moreover, be thrown into positions of economic dependency from which it may be difficult ever to escape. Finally, all will be, by the act of reproduction itself, involuntarily drafted into the service of the state, the first requirement of which is the reproduction of its populace.

Thus it is difficult to imagine a single proscription with a greater capacity to shape lives into singular, normalized, functional molds than the prohibition of abortions. Even if the propensity of anti-abortion laws to exert power over the body and to instrumentalize women is discounted, it remains the case that such laws radically and affirmatively redirect women's lives. Indeed it is difficult to conceive of a particular legal prohibition with a more total effect on the life and future of the one enjoined. It is no exaggeration to say that mandatory childbearing is a totalitarian intervention into a woman's life. With regard to the occupation and direction of lives, the positive ramifications of anti-abortion laws are unparalleled. *Roe v. Wade* was, in this view, correctly decided.

Griswold is explicable along the same lines. At least at the time it was decided, when abortion was still generally prohibited, the ban on contraception was equivalent in its positive aspect to enforced child-bearing. The ban ensured, moreover, that sex would not only be a matter of individuals' pleasure; or rather it put individuals' sexual desire and sexual pleasure to use. At the same time, it operated within a normative regimen of sexual relations leading from chastity straight to marriage, which, no matter how beneficent its effects, stands as one of the clearest forms of social standardization possible. *Griswold* too is readily understandable in the terms we are developing here.

* * *

D. *Distinctions*

* * *

Every law could be called "standardizing" to the extent that it directs all of us to follow a particular command; every law could be said to operate "on the body" to the extent that it impinges upon some physical acts; and every law could be said to make us serve some social end. But this is not the sort of standardization that we have been discussing. When a person obeys the law against murder, or almost any other law, his life is constrained but not usually informed or taken over to any substantial degree with a set of new activities and concerns. He is not thrust into a set of new institutions or relations. The category of "non-murderer" is essentially a formal one; it is not a defined role or identity with substantial, affirmative, institutionalized functions. And although a person can refrain from murder only by refraining from certain physical actions, his body is in no affirmative way taken over or put to use.

* * *

. . . The anti-totalitarian right to privacy, it might be said, prevents the state from imposing on individuals a defined identity, whereas the personhood right to privacy ensures that individuals are free to define their own identities. Is the anti-totalitarian theory of privacy nothing more in reality than a restatement of the personhood idea from another angle?

On the contrary: first, when personhood speaks of the "freedom to define oneself," it speaks for the most part of a chimera. We are all so powerfully influenced by the institutions within which we are raised that it is probably impossible, both psychologically and epistemologically, to speak of defining one's own identity. The point is not to save for the individual an abstract and chimerical right of defining himself; the point is to prevent the state from taking over, or taking undue advantage of, those processes by which individuals are defined in order to produce overly standardized, functional citizens.

Second, because personhood concentrates on the fundamentality of the act or decision at stake in a given case—whether to have a child, whom to marry, and so on—it will produce a different analysis and different results from the anti-totalitarian principle.

* * *

For another, more difficult illustration of the doctrinal differences between a personhood account of privacy and the anti-totalitarian principle advanced here, imagine a law passed in the next century limiting families to two or three children each. If, as personhood would have it, the decision whether to bear a child is fundamental and must be protected, then this case is doctrinally straightforward. The hypothesized law restricts this "fundamental right" in precisely the same way that a law forbidding abortions does, and therefore, from personhood's perspective, it equally impinges on the right to privacy. Personhood—and any other mode of privacy analysis that concentrates on the fundamentality of the proscribed decision—must look on such a law as doctrinally *identical* to a law forbidding abortion: both laws deprive the individual of the "fundamental right" to make her child-bearing decisions for herself.

Yet the two laws are in fact enormously different in their real, material effect on individuals' lives, and we should not be misled by their formal similarities. Recall our grounds for supporting *Roe*. Compelled child-bearing occupies a woman's life in the largest and subtlest respects, puts her body to use in the most extreme and intrusive ways, and forces upon her a well-defined and, to some degree, dependent role or identity. These factors are not present in a law prohibiting one from having a third or fourth child. The person's life is constrained in a way that might be deeply important to her, but not affirmatively taken over and directed as a result of the law.

To be sure, there is a disturbing standardization potentially effected by a law limiting families to two children. In the absence of a compelling state need, we might well feel that such a law was an outrageous governmental intrusion into our lives. Indeed, even on the anti-totalitarian principles developed here, there is an argument that the law should be struck down. There is, however, clearly a chasm between a law (let us vary the comparison somewhat) *requiring* persons to have at least two children and a law *forbidding* them to have more than two children. The former enlists, directs, and takes over individuals' lives far more than does the latter. Yet because both laws equally impinge on the child-bearing decision, both would receive doctrinally identical treatment from a personhood account of privacy. According to our principles, however, whereas the former law would plainly violate the right to privacy, the latter law would at least present a very different question.

There remains a third and final differentiation to be made between personhood and the right to privacy as understood here. To speak of resisting state-imposed identities—as we have done—does not commit privacy to personhood's central premise: that each individual's defining his identity is an act of such value that it is of constitutional importance. Indeed the right to privacy as developed here may suggest a repudiation of personal identity altogether.

The concept of personal identity—that sense of a unitary, atomic self that we all tend to consider ourselves to "have"—is complex and difficult. It has an almost theological or metaphysical aspect, as if one's "identity" were a kind of hypostatic quantity underlying the multiplicity of his vastly different relations in the world and the mutability of his nature over time. The concept borders on hypostatization in the other sense as well, as if it were attempting to concretize under the name of "personhood" or "selfhood" something that had no existence without such reification. This conception of a unitary personal identity has been radically challenged again and again this century in various fields, including psychoanalysis, literature, and—most recently and surprisingly—analytic philosophy. Personhood, reflecting an essentially liberal philosophy, is obliged to embrace and valorize the idea of a unitary personal identity; the right to privacy is not.

Nor, however, does privacy on our terms embrace a republican or communitarian conception of a supra-individual identity. To the contrary, it suggests a critique of republicanism as much as of liberalism, for both of these rest on the concept of a unitary identity. The republicans aspire to a well-defined and self-constructed identity as much as do the liberals; the difference is between a somewhat inchoate political identity on the one hand and an equally inchoate individual identity on the other.

* * *

It is no coincidence that liberals and republicans each see the others' vision of freedom as a form of self-subjugation. At the root of this self-subjugation in both conceptions is the exaltation of self-definition: the impulse to locate those institutions or qualities "central to our identity" in which our truth is revealed and to which we must therefore be true. From this impulse arises both the reification of the self and the suppression of the self that each theory correctly attributes to the other. The right to privacy as described here embraces neither alternative.

* * *

IV. CONCLUSION: THE CONSTITUTIONAL GROUNDING OF THE RIGHT TO PRIVACY

A. *Privacy and* Lochner

The right to privacy, in its constitutional incarnation, was discovered in the "penumbras" and "emanations" of other constitutional guarantees. The liberty of contract, in its day, was invoked as a matter of "substantive due process." A devious irony is at work in these phrases, as if a consciousness of the charade had inadvertently crept into the judicial language itself, announcing the one doctrine as mystification and the other as oxymoron. Yet what drove privacy into the penumbras, it should be recalled, was a perceived need to differentiate the privacy doctrine from the language of substantive due process. Unfortunately, this insecurity on privacy's part—an identity complex no doubt—resulted in the very thing feared; by resorting to shadows, the right to privacy has simply invited critics to expose it—and to brand it, of course, with the scarlet letter of Lochnerism.

* * *

One way to distinguish privacy from *Lochner* is to say that the overruled *Lochner* era cases involved economic regulations. The *Lochner* error, it might be said, was the failure to recognize that the Constitution does not enact any particular economic theory; thus the repudiation of *Lochner* means only that courts cannot sit as superlegislatures overseeing state or federal economic regulation. In the privacy cases, the courts do no such thing.

This distinction betrays a superficial understanding of both *Lochner* and privacy. The *Lochner* Court almost certainly did not understand itself to be sitting as a super-legislature for economic regulation, protecting American commerce or prosperity. In its own eyes, the *Lochner* Court was not regulating economics; it was protecting liberty—the liberty of contract. That a man was free to do as he pleased with his own property—that is, property in which he had a "vested right"—was axiomatic in the thinking of many at that time. From this point of view, *Lochner* did not involve mere "economics" but rather the most fundamental liberties of man against the state.

* * *

Instead consider the following: the rights protected by the *Lochner* doctrine were pre-political. Vested property rights and the liberty of contract did not have to be explicitly protected by the Constitution because, in the Lochnerian view, they existed outside the Constitution. They *pre-existed* the Constitution. Indeed, these rights antedated the formation of society itself. Property was the reason why men instituted government, and contract was the means by which they did so.

There is nothing pre-political in the right to privacy. If the kind of creeping totalitarianism that I have described is a danger to us, it is so solely because of our commitment to democracy—to a set of political values. The right to privacy, as I have sought to elucidate it, became a right only at the moment when we constituted ourselves as a democratic polity. For this reason the right to privacy is not, like the rights protected under *Lochner*, extraneous to the Constitution. It does not purport to antedate the Constitution or to arise from a source, such as the "social contract," superior in authority to the Constitution. The right to privacy is a constitutional right because the Constitution is the document that establishes democracy in this country.

The right to privacy is a political doctrine. It does not exist because individuals have a sphere of "private" life with which the state has nothing to do. The state has everything to do with our private life; and the freedom that privacy protects equally extends, as we have seen, into "public" as well as "private" matters. The right to privacy exists because democracy must impose limits on the extent of control and direction that the state exercises over the day-to-day conduct of individual lives.

* * *

Catharine A. MacKinnon, *Reflections on Sex Equality Under Law,* 100 YALE L.J. 1281, 1308-24 (1991)*

* * *

The inequality of women to men deserves a theory of its own. The status of women resembles other bases for inequality, but, like every inequality, is also particular and unique. Women's situation combines unequal pay with allocation to dis-

*   Reprinted by permission of the author, The Yale Law Journal Company and Fred B. Rothman & Company from The Yale Law Journal, vol. 100, pages 1281-1328.

respected work; sexual targeting for rape, domestic battering, sexual abuse as children, and systematic sexual harassment; depersonalization, demeaned physical characteristics, and use in denigrating entertainment; deprivation of reproductive control and forced prostitution. These abuses have occurred, in one form or another, for a very long time in a context characterized by disenfranchisement, preclusion from property ownership, ownership and use as object, exclusion from public life, sex-based poverty, degraded sexuality, and a devaluation of women's human worth and contributions throughout society. Like other inequalities, but in its own way, the subordination of women is socially institutionalized, cumulatively and systematically shaping access to human dignity, respect, resources, physical security, credibility, membership in community, speech, and power. Composed of all its variations, the group women has a collective social history of disempowerment, exploitation, and subordination extending to the present. To be treated like a woman is to be disadvantaged in these ways as an incident of being assigned to the female sex. To speak of social treatment "as a woman" is thus not to invoke any universal essence or homogeneous generic or ideal type, but to refer to this diverse material reality of social meanings and practices such that to be a woman "is not yet the name of a way of being human."

In this context, the failure of the law of sex equality to address sexual abuse and reproductive exploitation stands out. The law typically considers these abuses, cardinal experiences of sex inequality, to be crimes or privacy violations, not acts of sex discrimination. Equality doctrine does not seem to fit them. Equality law privileges recognition of facial classifications, in which the group descriptor is the legal inequality, because such devices have enforced much racial inequality. For the most part, the laws of sexual assault and reproductive control do not mention women or men, not any more. Yet these laws are not exactly neutral with an adverse impact either, at least not in the usual sense. They are too gendered to be neutral, and any law on rape or pregnancy affects the sexes differentially, without necessarily being discriminatory.

Existing legal equality templates utterly fail to capture the particular way in which the legal system organizes its participation in the subordination of women. Consider whether the law of sex classifications has the same relation to the realities of women's subordination as the law of racial classifications has to the realities of racial subordination. Does a law preferring men as administrators of estates have the same relation to women's subjection as a law prescribing "white only" railway cars has to racial subordination? Does a law prohibiting eighteen- to twenty-year-old boys in Oklahoma from drinking 3.2% beer while permitting it to girls have the same relation to sex inequality as a law requiring Black children in Kansas to attend racially segregated schools has to racial inequality? I mention the two seminal sex discrimination cases to suggest that facial sex classifications may be relatively peripheral to women's inequality, including by law. For claims based on sex, what the constitutional inequality net is made to catch has always been relatively rare and is now virtually extinct, while sex inequality, including through law, remains predatory and flourishing.

Much sex inequality is successfully accomplished in society without express legal enforcement and legitimation. Yet the law is deeply implicated in it. Law actively engages in sex inequality by apparently prohibiting abuses it largely permits, like rape, and by hiding the deprivations it imposes beneath ostensibly gender-neutral terms, like abortion. In the areas of sexual assault and reproductive control specifically, these legal concepts have been designed and applied from the point of view of the accused rapist and the outsider/impregnator respectively, and in the absence of the point of view of the sexually assaulted or pregnant woman. Most of the sexual assaults women experience do not fit the legal model of the ideal violation.

Most rapes are by familiars not strangers, by members of one's own ethnic group not others, at home not on the street. The notion of consent here, the law's line between intercourse and rape, is so passive that a dead body could satisfy it. The law of rape is designed so that rape is what somebody else does and what almost never happens: so that what is done all the time, presumably including by those who design and interpret and enforce the laws, can be done.

Similarly, when convenient to do away with the consequences of sexual intercourse (meaning children), women get abortion rights. Women can have abortions so men can have sex. When not convenient, and for those men who seek to control women through controlling their children instead of through controlling their ability to have them, and for those women (such as women of color) for whom more drastic means are deemed more convenient, women are deprived of procreative choice through sterilization abuse the law either actively promotes or fails to recognize or redress, forced obstetrical interventions the law permits, fetal rights the law defines against women's rights, and criminalized and unfunded and bureaucratically burdened abortions the law deems adequate. In this light, the theme of the laws of sexual assault and reproduction is male control of, access to, and use of women.

* * *

Usually, sex precedes reproduction. In part through its connections with forced sex, procreation has also provided a crucial occasion, pretext, and focus for the subordination of women to men in society. Many of the social disadvantages to which women have been subjected have been predicated upon their capacity for and role in childbearing. Although reproduction has a major impact on both sexes, men are not generally fired from their jobs, excluded from public life, beaten, patronized, confined, or made into pornography for making babies. This point is not the biological one that only women experience pregnancy and childbirth in their bodies, but the social one: women, because of their sex, are subjected to social inequality at each step in the process of procreation. Encompassed are women's experiences of "fertility and infertility, conception and contraception, pregnancy and the end of pregnancy, whether through miscarriage, abortion, or birth and child-rearing." As with most sex inequality, it is unclear whether an attribute distinctive to women is targeted for abuse and hatred because it is women's, or women are targeted for abuse and hatred because of a distinctive attribute. I suspect the former is closer to the truth. Either way, under male dominance, pregnancy, analyzed by Andrea Dworkin as "the primary physical emblem of female negativity," and the potential to become pregnant, are socially fundamental in women's inequality to men.

Grounding a sex equality approach to reproductive control requires situating pregnancy in the legal and social context of sex inequality and capturing the unique relationship between the pregnant woman and her fetus. The legal system has not adequately conceptualized pregnancy, hence the relationship between the fetus and the pregnant woman. This may be because the interests, perceptions, and experiences that have shaped the law have not included those of women. The social conception of pregnancy that has formed the basis for its legal treatment has not been from the point of view of the pregnant woman, but rather from the point of view of the observing outsider, gendered male. Traditionally, fetuses have not fared much better under this vantage point than have women. This may be changing at women's expense as increasingly, despite the explicit Supreme Court ruling to the contrary, the fetus becomes endowed with attributes of personhood. Men may more readily identify with the fetus than with the pregnant woman if only because all have been fetuses and none will ever be a pregnant woman.

Accordingly, the law of reproductive issues has implicitly centered on observing and controlling the pregnant woman and the fetus using evidence that is available from the outside. The point of these interventions is to control the woman through controlling the fetus. Technology, also largely controlled by men, has made it possible to view the fetus through ultrasound, fueling much of the present crisis in the legal status of the fetus by framing it as a free-floating independent entity rather than as connected with the pregnant woman. Much of the authority and persuasiveness of the ultrasound image derives from its presentation of the fetus from the standpoint of the outside observer, the so-called objective standpoint, so that it becomes socially experienced in these terms rather than in terms of its direct connection to the woman. Presenting the fetus from this point of view, rather than from that which is uniquely accessible to the pregnant woman, stigmatizes her unique viewpoint as subjective and internal. This has the epistemic effect of making the fetus more real than the woman, who becomes reduced to the "grainy blur" at the edge of the image.

The law of reproductive control has developed largely as a branch of the law of privacy, the law that keeps out observing outsiders. Sometimes it has. The problem is that while the private has been a refuge for some, it has been a hellhole for others, often at the same time. In gendered light, the law's privacy is a sphere of sanctified isolation, impunity, and unaccountability. It surrounds the individual in his habitat. It belongs to the individual with power. Women have been accorded neither individuality nor power. Privacy follows those with power wherever they go, like and as consent follows women. When the person with privacy is having his privacy, the person without power is tacitly imagined to be consenting. At whatever time and place man has privacy, woman wants to have happen, or lets happen, whatever he does to her. Everyone is implicitly equal in there. If the woman needs something—say, equality—to make these assumptions real, privacy law does nothing for her, and even ideologically undermines the state intervention that might provide the preconditions for its meaningful exercise. The private is a distinctive sphere of women's inequality to men. Because this has not been recognized, the doctrine of privacy has become the triumph of the state's abdication of women in the name of freedom and self-determination.

Theorized instead as a problem of sex inequality, the law of reproductive control would begin with the place of reproduction in the status of the sexes. A narrow view of women's "biological destiny" has confined many women to childbearing and childrearing and defined all women in terms of it, limiting their participation in other pursuits, especially remunerative positions with social stature. Women who bear children are constrained by a society that does not allocate resources to assist combining family needs with work outside the home. In the case of men, the two are traditionally tailored to a complementary fit, provided that a woman is available to perform the traditional role that makes that fit possible. Law has permitted women to be punished at work for their reproductive role. The option of pregnancy leave mandated by law was not even regarded as legal until recently; in the United States, it still is not required. When women begin to "show," they are often treated as walking obscenities unfit for public presentation. Inside the home, battering of women may increase during pregnancy. Pornography makes pregnancy into a sexual fetish, conditioning male sexual arousal to it, meaning targeting sexualized hatred against it. Whether or not women have children, they are disadvantaged by social norms that limit their options because of women's enforced role in childbearing and childrearing. For a woman who does become pregnant, these consequences occur even when a pregnancy is wanted.

Women often do not control the conditions under which they become pregnant; systematically denied meaningful control over the reproductive uses of their bodies through sex, it is exceptional when they do. Women are socially disadvantaged in controlling sexual access to their bodies through socialization to customs that define a woman's body as for sexual use by men. Sexual access is regularly forced or pressured or routinized beyond denial. Laws against sexual assault provide little to no real protection. Contraception is inadequate or unsafe or inaccessible or sadistic or stigmatized. Sex education is often misleading or unavailable or pushes heterosexual motherhood as an exclusive life possibility and as the point of sex. Poverty and enforced economic dependence undermine women's physical integrity and sexual self-determination. Social supports or blandishments for women's self-respect are simply not enough to withstand all of this.

After childbirth, women tend to be the ones who are primarily responsible for the intimate care of offspring—their own and those of others. Social custom, pressure, exclusion from well-paying jobs, the structure of the marketplace, and lack of adequate daycare have exploited women's commitment to and caring for children and relegated women to this pursuit which is not even considered an occupation but an expression of the X chromosome. Women do not control the circumstances under which they rear children, hence the impact of those conditions on their own life chances. Men, as a group, are not comparably disempowered by their reproductive capacities. Nobody forces them to impregnate women. They are not generally required by society to spend their lives caring for children to the comparative preclusion of other life pursuits.

It is women who are caught, to varying degrees, between the reproductive consequences of sexual use and aggression on the one side and the economic and other consequences of the sex role allocations of labor in the market and family on the other. As a result of these conditions, women are prevented from having children they do want and forced to have children they do not want and cannot want because they are not in a position responsibly to care for them because they are women. This is what an inequality looks like.

Reproduction is socially gendered. Women are raped and coerced into sex. When conception results from rape or incest, it is a girl or a woman who was violated, shamed, and defiled in a way distinctively regarded as female. When a teenager gets pregnant because of ignorance or the negative social connotations of contraception, it is a young woman who is pregnant. When miscarriage results from physical assault, it is a woman who was beaten. When there is not enough money for another child or for an abortion, it is a woman who is forced to have a child she cannot responsibly care for. When a single parent is impoverished as a result of childbearing, usually that parent is female. When someone must care for the children, it is almost always a woman who does it, without her work being valued in terms of money or social status. Men, regardless of race, have not generally been sterilized without their knowledge and against their will, as have women of color. It has been held illegal to sterilize a male prisoner but legal to sterilize a mentally disabled woman. Those who have been defined and valued and devalued as breeders and body servants of the next generation are not usually men, except under circumstances recognized as slavery. The essential social function of nurturing new life has been degraded by being filled by women, as the women who fill it have been degraded by filling it. And it is women who, for reasons not always purely biological, may pay for giving birth with their lives.

In this context, the relationship between the woman, gendered female, and her fetus needs to be reconsidered. Although it hardly presents new facts, this relation has never been accorded a legal concept of its own. Because legal method traditionally proceeds by analogy and distinction, attempts at analogy between the relationship between the fetus and the pregnant woman and relations already mapped by law are ubiquitous. Had women participated equally in designing laws, we might now be trying to compare other relationships—employer and employee, partners in a business, oil in the ground, termites in a building, tumors in a body, ailing famous violinists and abducted hostages forced to sustain them—to the maternal/fetal relationship rather than the reverse. Sometimes there are no adequate analogies. As it is, the fetus has no concept of its own, but must be like something men have or are: a body part to the Left, a person to the Right. Nowhere in law is the fetus a fetus.

Considering the fetus a body part has been the closest the law has come to recognizing fetal reality and protecting women at the same time. Since men have body parts over which they have sovereignty, deeming the fetus to be "like that" has seemed the way to give women sovereignty over what is done to their bodies, in which the fetus inevitably resides. Because persons are sovereign, deeming the fetus to be a person, "like me," has seemed the way to take away women's control over it, hence over themselves. The body part analogy derives its credibility from the intricate and intimate connection between the fetus and woman. It derives nourishment from her and is accessible only through her. From before viability until fully completed live birth, the fetus is within the person of the woman and at one with her bodily systems. What happens to it happens to her and what happens to her happens to it—if not always in the same way. By telescoping the fetus into the woman, the body part analogy at once recognizes the unity of interest between fetus and pregnant woman that the personhood model is predicated on severing, and consolidates the woman as the decisionmaker for the unit.

Yet the fetus is not a body part. The fetus is ordinarily created through intercourse, a social relation through which impregnation occurs. Although some body parts are donated (as are some fertilized ova), no body part is created from a social relation—one between the sexes at that. Physically, no body part takes as much and contributes as little. The fetus does not exist to serve the woman as her body parts do. The relation is more the other way around; on the biological level, the fetus is more like a parasite than a part. The woman's physical relation to her fetus is expected to end and does; when it does, her body still has all of its parts. She is whole with it or without it; a miscarriage leaves her body as such intact, although the loss may diminish her. On the level of feeling, she has lost a part of her, but this is also true of loss of children who are fully born alive. Fetal dependence upon the pregnant woman does not make the fetus a part of her any more than fully dependent adults are parts of those on whom they are dependent. The fetus is a unique kind of whole that, after a certain point, can live or die without the mother. Whatever credibility the body part analogy has evaporates at the moment of viability, placing tremendous pressure on the viability line and its determination as a consequence. No other body part gets up and walks away on its own eventually.

The fetus is not even like gendered body parts. A fetus is lived by the pregnant woman through her pregnancy. A pregnancy is not, in fact or in social meaning, a body part, even a female body part. The cultural meanings of pregnancy are distinct. Pregnancy can be an emblem of female inferiority or adulation, of denigration or elevation; it can bring closeness or estrangement, can give a new sense of the meaning of life and new depth or desperation to the experience of family. It attracts violence against women, sentimentality, attempts at control, gives rise to financial costs and the need for difficult decisions. Women have lost jobs and been stigmatized and excluded from public life because they are pregnant—jobs and access they had in spite of having breasts and uteruses. It seems that it is one thing to have them, another to use them. No body part has the specific consequences pregnancy has on women's social destiny.

Now place the legal status of the fetus against the backdrop of women's tenuous to nonexistent equality. Women have not been considered "persons" by law very long; the law of persons arguably does not recognize the requisites of female personhood yet. Separate fetal status of any sort, in a male-dominated legal system in which women have been controlled through the control of their procreative capacity, risks further entrenchment of women's inequality. If the fetus were deemed a person, it may well have more rights than women do, especially since fetal rights would be asserted most often by men in traditionally male institutions of authority: progenitors, husbands, doctors, legislators, and courts. Fetal rights as such are thus in direct tension with sex equality rights.

Indeed, the only point of recognizing fetal personhood, or a separate fetal entity, is to assert the interests of the fetus *against* the pregnant woman. There would be two persons in one skin—hers—the rationale being that its life depends upon her, but the reverse is not usually true. The fetus could be given the right to the use of the pregnant woman's body from conception to birth. In arguments for fetal personhood, the fetus is "born in the imagination." But it is not born in the world. Gestation and birth involve the mother and often entail considerable medical uncertainty. Even well toward the end of pregnancy, the view that the fetus is a person vaults over this process in a way that is unrealistic and dangerous for the birthing woman, who can be made invisible and chattel in a situation in which she is deeply implicated.

Personhood is a legal and social status, not a biological fact. As gestation progresses, the fetus grows from something that is more like a lump of cells to something that is more like a baby. As the body part analogy draws on the earlier reality to define the later one, the personhood analogy draws on the later reality to define the earlier one. In my opinion and in the experience of many pregnant women, the fetus is a human form of life. It is alive. But the existence of sex inequality in society requires that completed live birth mark the personhood line. If sex equality existed socially—if women were recognized as persons, sexual aggression were truly deviant, and childrearing were shared and consistent with a full life rather than at odds with it—the fetus still might not be considered a person but the question of its political status would be a very different one.

So long as it gestates in utero, the fetus is defined by its relation to the pregnant woman. This is why its status turns on her status. More than a body part but less than a person, where it is, is largely what it is. From the standpoint of the pregnant woman, it is both me and not me. It "is" the pregnant woman in the sense that it is in her and of her and is hers more than anyone's. It "is not" her in the sense that she is not all that is there. In a legal system that views the individual as a unitary self, and that self as a bundle of rights, it is no wonder that the pregnant woman has eluded legal grasp, and her fetus with her.

The legal status of the fetus cannot be considered separately from the legal and social status of the woman in whose body it is. The pregnant woman is more than a location for gestation. She is a woman, in the socially gendered and unequal sense of the word. In an analysis of women's status as socially disadvantaged, the woman is not a mere vehicle for an event which happens to occur within her physical boundaries for biological reasons. Women's relation to the fetus is not that of a powerful, fully capacitated being in relation to a powerless, incapacitated, and incomplete one. Indeed, it shows how powerless women are that it takes a fetus to make a woman look powerful by comparison. The relation of the woman to the fetus must be seen in the social context of sex inequality in which women have been kept relatively powerless compared with men. The fetus may have been conceived in powerlessness and, as a child, may be reared in powerlessness—the woman's. The effects of women's inequality in procreation can range from situations in which the woman does not choose to conceive but is forced to deliver to those in which the woman chooses to conceive and deeply desires to deliver but the baby dies.

The range of procreative events along which inequality is experienced contextualizes the fact that when women are forced into maternity, they are reproductively exploited. Short of achieving sexual and social equality—short of changing the context—abortion has offered the only way out. However difficult an abortion decision may be for an individual woman, it provides a moment of power in a life otherwise led under unequal conditions which preclude choice in ways she cannot control. In this context, abortion provides a window of relief in an unequal situation from which there is no exit. Until this context changes, only the pregnant woman can choose life for the unborn.

Because the discussion of the political status of the fetus has been framed by the abortion controversy, it has proceeded from the premise that there is a conflict between what is good for the woman and what is good for the fetus. Sometimes there is. Usually there is not, in large part because when there is, women tend to resolve it in favor of the fetus. Women may identify with the fetus because, like them, it is invisible, powerless, derivative, and silent. Grasping this unity in oppression, it has most often been women who have put the welfare of the fetus first, before their own. While most women who abort did not choose to conceive, many women who keep their pregnancies did not choose to conceive either. The priority women make of their offspring may be more true in the abortion context than it seems. Many women have abortions as a desperate act of love for their unborn children. Many women conceive in battering relationships; subjecting a child to a violent father is more than they can bear. When women in a quarter to a third of all American households face domestic violence, this motivation cannot be dismissed as marginal. Some women conceive in part to cement a relationship which dissolves or becomes violent when the man discovers the conception. Even where direct abuse is not present, sex inequality is. Many abortions occur because the woman needs to try to give herself a life. But many also occur because the woman faces the fact that she cannot give this child a life. Women's impotence to make this not so may make the decision tragic, but it is nonetheless one of absolute realism and deep responsibility as a mother.

Reproduction in the lives of women is a far larger and more diverse experience than the focus on abortion has permitted. The right to reproductive control I have in mind would include the abortion right but would not center on it. Women would have more rights when they carry a fetus: sex equality rights. Women who are assaulted and miscarry, women who are forced to have abortions and women who are denied abortions, women who are sterilized, and women who are negligently attended at birth all suffer deprivation of reproductive control. Under such circumstances, existing laws that regulate these areas should be interpreted consistent with constitutional sex equality mandates. If affirmative legislative pursuit of this principle were desired, this concept of reproductive control would encourage programs to support the fetus through supporting the woman, including guaranteed prenatal care, pregnancy leaves, and nutritional, alcohol, and drug counseling. If pursued in a context in which sexual coercion was effectively addressed, such programs would promote women's equality, not constitute inducements and pressures to succumb to women's subordinate roles. In this light, purported concern for the well-being of pregnant women and subsequently born children expressed by policing women's activities during pregnancy and forcing women to carry pregnancies to term is not only vicious and counterproductive, but unconstitutional.

Because the social organization of reproduction is a major bulwark of women's social inequality, any constitutional interpretation of a sex equality principle must prohibit laws, state policies, or official practices and acts that deprive women of reproductive control or punish women for their reproductive role or capacity. Existing examples include nonconsensual sterilization, forced obstetrical intervention, supervision of women's activities during pregnancy under the criminal law, and denials of abortion through criminalization or lack of public funding where needed. Women's right to reproductive control is a sex equality right because it is inconsistent with an equality mandate for the state, by law, to collaborate with or mandate social inequality on the basis of sex, as such legal incursions do. This is not so much an argument for an extension of the meaning of constitutional sex equality as a recognition that if it does not mean this, it does not mean anything at all.

Under this sex equality analysis, criminal abortion statutes of the sort invalidated in *Roe v. Wade* violate equal protection of the laws. They make women criminals for a medical procedure only women need, or make others criminals for performing a procedure on women that only women need, when much of the need for this procedure as well as barriers to access to it have been created by social conditions of sex inequality. Forced motherhood is sex inequality. Because pregnancy can be experienced only by women, and because of the unequal social predicates and consequences pregnancy has for women, any forced pregnancy will always deprive and hurt one sex only as a member of her gender. Just as no man will ever become pregnant, no man will ever need an abortion, hence be in a position to be denied one by law. On this level, only women can be disadvantaged, for a reason specific to sex, through state-mandated restrictions on abortion. The denial of funding for Medicaid abortions obviously violates this right. The Medicaid issue connects the maternity historically forced on African American women integral to their exploitation under slavery with the motherhood effectively forced on poor women, many of whom are Black, by deprivation of government funding for abortions. For those who have not noticed, the abortion right has already been lost: this was when.

Although the sex equality argument for equal funding is doctrinally simpler than that for the abortion right itself, statutes that recriminalize abortion would be invalidated under this argument. To recast the argument in a more doctrinal guise, statutes that draw gender lines are unconstitutional under the equal protection clause if they do not bear a valid or substantial relation to an important or legitimate and compelling state purpose. Initially, a state's purposes in passing criminal abortion statutes could be challenged as invalid. If states wanted to protect the fetus, rather than discriminate against women, they would help the woman, not make her a criminal. The most effective route to protecting the fetus—given illegal abortion, perhaps the only effective route—is supporting the woman. Further, the seeming appropriateness of forcing women to bear children when no such bodily impositions are made upon men by any state law—even after fetuses men have participated in creating become children (persons) and even when no alternatives are available—is transparently based on the view that the purpose of women is breeding. If using women as a sex as a means to an end is discriminatory, if naturalizing as destiny a role that is rooted in the history of sex inequality is discriminatory, the state purpose in restricting abortions is discriminatory and not valid.

But even assuming the state purpose were found valid—the purpose was not to harm women but to help fetuses, and this need not be pursued in the best way but only nonpretextually—the issue would remain whether such a statute were based on sex. Criminal abortion laws hurt women through a biological correlate of femaleness and a socially defining characteristic of gender long used to disadvantage women and keep them in a subject status. For this reason, criminal abortion statutes should be treated as closer to facially discriminatory than to neutral distinctions disparate in effect. By analogy, sexual harassment is legally treated more like facial than disparate impact discrimination, even though it is not done by express law or policy. Certainly, more men are sexually harassed than are denied abortions. Criminal abortion laws hurt no men the way they hurt only women. They single out women exclusively. Criminalizing providers, which does affect men, is merely a pretextually gender-neutral means of accomplishing the same goal: depriving women and only women, by law, of relief from a situation of sex inequality which begins in unequal sex and ends in unequal childrearing. If such statutes are treated as facial, not neutral, it is unnecessary to prove that they discriminate intentionally.

If intent had to be proven, states would doubtless argue that criminal abortion statutes aim to help fetuses, not hurt women. But intent can be inferred from impact. No men are denied abortions, even if some doctors, regardless of sex, are made criminals for providing them. Such a statutory impact would be far more one-sided than, for example, the impact of veterans' preference statutes, which have been found to lack the requisite discriminatory intent because, although most of those benefited by them are men, many men—nonveterans—are also harmed. No men are damaged in the way women are harmed by an abortion prohibition. Even those who can be prosecuted are harmed for performing what is, in essence, a female procedure, a procedure only women need, with the clear aim of keeping women and only women from access to it. Male providers can avoid liability by refusing to perform the procedure and be, as men, no worse off, while pregnant women who seek to abide by the law must continue the pregnancy, damaging them in a way that only women are or could be damaged.

* * *

Because forced maternity is a sex equality deprivation, legal abortion is a sex equality right. "Women's access to legal abortion is an attempt to ensure that women and men have more equal control of their reproductive capacities, more equal opportunity to plan their lives and more equal ability to participate fully in society than if legal abortion did not exist." Sex equality would be advanced if women were permitted to control sexual access to their bodies long before an unwanted pregnancy. Sex equality would be advanced if society were organized so that both sexes participated equally in daily child care. Sex equality would be advanced by economic parity between women and men. Equality for women would gain from racial equality. All these changes would overwhelmingly reduce the numbers of abortions sought. The abortion controversy would not be entirely eliminated, but its ground would shift dramatically.

Those who support the abortion right in the name of "a woman's right to control her own body" might start earlier, before women are pregnant, with the issue of sexual access. If women are not socially accorded control over sexual access to their bodies, they cannot control much else about them. Those who think that fetuses should not have to pay with their lives for their mothers' inequality might direct themselves to changing the conditions of sex inequality that make abortions necessary. They might find the problem largely withered away if they, too, opposed sex on demand.

* * *

Dorothy E. Roberts, *Punishing Drug Addicts Who Have Babies: Women of Color, Equality, and the Right of Privacy,* 104 HARV. L. REV. 1419, 1420-36, 1445-50, 1456-81 (1991)*

Prologue

A former slave named Lizzie Williams recounted the beating of pregnant slave women on a Mississippi cotton plantation: "I['] s seen nigger women dat was fixin' to be confined do somethin' de white folks didn't like. Dey [the white folks] would dig a hole in de ground just big 'nuff fo' her stomach, make her lie face down an whip her on de back to keep from hurtin' de child."

In July 1989, Jennifer Clarise Johnson, a twenty-three-year-old crack addict, became the first woman in the United States to be criminally convicted for exposing her baby to drugs while pregnant. Florida law enforcement officials charged Johnson with two counts of delivering a controlled substance to a minor after her two children tested positive for cocaine at birth. Because the relevant Florida drug law did not apply to fetuses, the prosecution invented a novel interpretation of the statute. The prosecution obtained Johnson's conviction for passing a cocaine metabolite from her body to her newborn infants during the sixty-second period after birth and before the umbilical cord was cut.

I. INTRODUCTION

A growing number of women across the country have been charged with criminal offenses after giving birth to babies who test positive for drugs. The majority of these women, like Jennifer Johnson, are poor and Black. Most are addicted to crack cocaine. The prosecution of drug-addicted mothers is part of an alarming trend towards greater state intervention into the lives of pregnant women under the rationale of protecting the fetus from harm. This intervention has included compelled medical treatment, greater restrictions on abortion, and increased supervision of pregnant women's conduct.

Such government intrusion is particularly harsh for poor women of color. They are the least likely to obtain adequate prenatal care, the most vulnerable to government monitoring, and the least able to conform to the white, middle-class standard of motherhood. They are therefore the primary targets of government control.

The prosecution of drug-addicted mothers implicates two fundamental tensions. First, punishing a woman for using drugs during pregnancy pits the state's interest in protecting the future health of a child against the mother's interest in autonomy over her reproductive life—interests that until recently had not been thought to be in conflict. Second, such prosecutions represent one of two possible responses to the problem of drug-exposed babies. The government may choose either to help women have healthy pregnancies or to punish women for their prenatal conduct. Although it might seem that the state could pursue both of these avenues at once, the two responses are ultimately irreconcilable. Far from deterring injurious drug use, prosecution of drug-addicted mothers in fact deters pregnant women from using available health and counseling services because it causes women to fear that,

---

if they seek help, they could be reported to government authorities and charged with a crime. Moreover, prosecution blinds the public to the possibility of nonpunitive solutions and to the inadequacy of the nonpunitive solutions that are currently available.

The debate between those who favor protecting the rights of the fetus and those who favor protecting the rights of the mother has been extensively waged in the literature. This Article does not repeat the theoretical arguments for and against state intervention. Rather, this Article suggests that both sides of the debate have largely overlooked a critical aspect of government prosecution of drug-addicted mothers. Can we determine the legality of the prosecutions simply by weighing the state's abstract interest in the fetus against the mother's abstract interest in autonomy? Can we determine whether the prosecutions are fair simply by deciding the duties a pregnant woman owes to her fetus and then assessing whether the defendant has met them? Can we determine the constitutionality of the government's actions without considering the race of the women being singled out for prosecution?

Before deciding whether the state's interest in preventing harm to the fetus justifies criminal sanctions against the mother, we must first understand the mother's competing perspective and the reasons for the state's choice of a punitive response. This Article seeks to illuminate the current debate by examining the experiences of the class of women who are primarily affected—poor Black women.

Providing the perspective of poor Black women offers two advantages. First, examining legal issues from the viewpoint of those whom they affect most helps to uncover the real reasons for state action and to explain the real harms that it causes. It exposes the way in which the prosecutions deny poor Black women a facet of their humanity by punishing their reproductive choices. The government's choice of a punitive response perpetuates the historical devaluation of Black women as mothers. Viewing the legal issues from the experiential standpoint of the defendants enhances our understanding of the constitutional dimensions of the state's conduct.

Second, examining the constraints on poor Black women's reproductive choices expands our understanding of reproductive freedom in particular and of the right of privacy in general. Much of the literature discussing reproductive freedom has adopted a white middle-class perspective, which focuses narrowly on abortion rights. The feminist critique of privacy doctrine has also neglected many of the concerns of poor women of color.

My analysis presumes that Black women experience various forms of oppression simultaneously, as a complex interaction of race, gender, and class that is more than the sum of its parts. It is impossible to isolate any one of the components of this oppression or to separate the experiences that are attributable to one component from experiences attributable to the others. The prosecution of drug-addicted mothers cannot be explained as simply an issue of gender inequality. Poor Black women have been selected for punishment as a result of an inseparable combination of their gender, race, and economic status. Their devaluation as mothers, which underlies the prosecutions, has its roots in the unique experience of slavery and has been perpetuated by complex social forces.

Thus, for example, the focus of mainstream feminist legal thought on gender as the primary locus of oppression often forces women of color to fragment their experience in a way that does not reflect the reality of their lives. Angela Harris and others have presented a racial critique of this gender essentialism in feminist legal theory. By introducing the voices of Black women, these critics have begun to reconstruct a feminist jurisprudence based on the historical, economic, and social diversity of women's experiences. This new jurisprudence must be used to reconsider the more particular discourse of reproductive rights.

This Article advances an account of the constitutionality of prosecutions of drug-addicted mothers that explicitly considers the experiences of poor Black women. The constitutional arguments are based on theories of both racial equality and the right of privacy. I argue that punishing drug addicts who choose to carry their pregnancies to term unconstitutionally burdens the right to autonomy over reproductive decisions. Violation of poor Black women's reproductive rights helps to perpetuate a racist hierarchy in our society. The prosecutions thus impose a standard of motherhood that is offensive to principles of both equality and privacy. This Article provides insight into the particular and urgent struggle of women of color for reproductive freedom. Further, I intend my constitutional critique of the prosecutions to demonstrate the advantages of a discourse that combines elements of racial equality and privacy theories in advocating the reproductive rights of women of color.

* * *

II. BACKGROUND: THE STATE'S PUNITIVE RESPONSE TO DRUG-ADDICTED MOTHERS

A. The Crack Epidemic and the State's Response

Crack cocaine appeared in America in the early 1980s, and its abuse has grown to epidemic proportions. Crack is especially popular among inner-city women. Indeed, evidence shows that, in several urban areas in the United States, more women than men now smoke crack. Most crack-addicted women are of childbearing age, and many are pregnant. This phenomenon has contributed to an explosion in the number of newborns affected by maternal drug use. Some experts estimate that as many as 375,000 drug-exposed infants are born every year. In many urban hospitals, the number of these newborns has quadrupled in the last five years. A widely cited 1988 study conducted by the National Association for Perinatal Addiction Research and Education (NAPARE) found that eleven percent of newborns in thirty-six hospitals surveyed were affected by their mothers' illegal-drug use during pregnancy. In several hospitals, the proportion of drug-exposed infants was as high as fifteen and twenty-five percent.

Babies born to drug-addicted mothers may suffer a variety of medical, developmental, and behavioral problems, depending on the nature of their mother's substance abuse. Immediate effects of cocaine exposure can include premature birth, low birth weight, and withdrawal symptoms. Cocaine-exposed children have also exhibited neurobehavioral problems such as mood dysfunction, organizational deficits, poor attention, and impaired human interaction, although it has not been determined whether these conditions are permanent. Congenital disorders and deformities have also been associated with cocaine use during pregnancy. According to NAPARE, babies exposed to cocaine have a tenfold greater risk of suffering sudden infant death syndrome (SIDS).

Data on the extent and potential severity of the adverse effects of maternal cocaine use are controversial. The interpretation of studies of cocaine-exposed infants is often clouded by the presence of other fetal risk factors, such as the mother's use of additional drugs, cigarettes, and alcohol and her socioeconomic status. For example, the health prospects of an infant are significantly threatened because pregnant addicts often receive little or no prenatal care and may be malnourished. Moreover, because the medical community has given more attention to studies showing adverse effects of cocaine exposure than to those that deny these effects, the public has a distorted perception of the risks of maternal cocaine use. Researchers have not yet authoritatively determined the percentage of infants exposed to cocaine who actually experience adverse consequences.

The response of state prosecutors, legislators, and judges to the problem of drug-exposed babies has been punitive. They have punished women who use drugs during pregnancy by depriving these mothers of custody of their children, by jailing them during their pregnancy, and by prosecuting them after their babies are born.

The most common penalty for a mother's prenatal drug use is the permanent or temporary removal of her baby. Hospitals in a number of states now screen newborns for evidence of drugs in their urine and report positive results to child welfare authorities. Some child protection agencies institute neglect proceedings to obtain custody of babies with positive toxicologies based solely on these tests. More and more government authorities are also removing drug-exposed newborns from their mothers immediately after birth pending an investigation of parental fitness. In these investigations, positive neonatal toxicologies often raise a strong presumption of parental unfitness, which circumvents the inquiry into the mother's ability to care for her child that is customarily necessary to deprive a parent of custody.

A second form of punishment is the "protective" incarceration of pregnant drug addicts charged with unrelated crimes. In 1988, a Washington, D.C. judge sentenced a thirty-year-old woman named Brenda Vaughn, who pleaded guilty to forging $700 worth of checks, to jail for the duration of her pregnancy. The judge stated at sentencing that he wanted to ensure that the baby would be born in jail to protect it from its mother's drug abuse. Although the *Vaughn* case has received the most attention, anecdotal evidence suggests that defendants' drug use during pregnancy often affects judges' sentencing decisions.

Finally, women have been prosecuted after the birth of their children for having exposed the fetuses to drugs or alcohol. Creative statutory interpretations that once seemed little more than the outlandish concoctions of conservative scholars are now used to punish women. Mothers of children affected by prenatal substance abuse have been charged with crimes such as distributing drugs to a minor, child abuse and neglect, manslaughter, and assault with a deadly weapon.

This Article considers the constitutional implications of criminal prosecution of drug-addicted mothers because, as Part IV explains, this penalty most directly punishes poor Black women for having babies. When the government prosecutes, its intervention is not designed to protect babies from the irresponsible actions of their mothers (as is arguably the case when the state takes custody of a pregnant addict or her child). Rather, the government criminalizes the mother as a consequence of her decision to bear a child.

B. The Disproportionate Impact on Poor Black Women

Poor Black women bear the brunt of prosecutors' punitive approach. These women are the primary targets of prosecutors, not because they are more likely to be guilty of fetal abuse, but because they are Black and poor. Poor women, who are disproportionately Black, are in closer contact with government agencies, and their drug use is therefore more likely to be detected. Black women are also more likely to be reported to government authorities, in part because of the racist attitudes of health care professionals. Finally, their failure to meet society's image of the ideal mother makes their prosecution more acceptable.

To charge drug-addicted mothers with crimes, the state must be able to identify those who use drugs during pregnancy. Because poor women are generally under greater government supervision—through their associations with public hospitals, welfare agencies, and probation officers—their drug use is more likely to be detected and reported. Hospital screening practices result in disproportionate reporting of poor Black women. The government's main source of information about prenatal drug use is hospitals' reporting of positive infant toxicologies to child welfare authorities. Hospitals serving poor minority communities implement this testing almost exclusively. Private physicians who serve more affluent women perform less of this screening both because they have a financial stake both in retaining their patients' business and securing referrals from them and because they are socially more like their patients.

Hospitals administer drug tests in a manner that further discriminates against poor Black women. One common criterion triggering an infant toxicology screen is the mother's failure to obtain prenatal care, a factor that correlates strongly with race and income. Worse still, many hospitals have no formal screening procedures, relying solely on the suspicions of health care professionals. This discretion allows doctors and hospital staff to perform tests based on their stereotyped assumptions about drug addicts.

Health care professionals are much more likely to report Black women's drug use to government authorities than they are similar drug use by their wealthy white patients. A study recently reported in *The New England Journal of Medicine* demonstrated this racial bias in the reporting of maternal drug use. Researchers studied the results of toxicologic tests of pregnant women who received prenatal care in public health clinics and in private obstetrical offices in Pinellas County, Florida. Little difference existed in the prevalence of substance abuse by pregnant women along either racial or economic lines, nor was there any significant difference between public clinics and private offices. Despite similar rates of substance abuse, however, Black women were *ten times* more likely than whites to be reported to public health authorities for substance abuse during pregnancy. Although several possible explanations can account for this disparate reporting, both public health facilities and private doctors are more inclined to turn in pregnant Black women who use drugs than pregnant white women who use drugs.

It is also significant that, out of the universe of maternal conduct that can injure a fetus, prosecutors have focused on crack use. The selection of crack addiction for punishment can be justified neither by the number of addicts nor the extent of the harm to the fetus. Excessive alcohol consumption during pregnancy, for example, can cause severe fetal injury, and marijuana use may also adversely affect the unborn. The incidence of both these types of substance abuse is high as well. In addition, prosecutors do not always base their claims on actual harm to the child, but on the mere delivery of crack by the mother. Although different forms of substance abuse prevail among pregnant women of various socioeconomic levels and racial and ethnic backgrounds, inner-city Black communities have the highest concentrations of crack addicts. Therefore, selecting crack abuse as the primary fetal harm to be punished has a discriminatory impact that cannot be medically justified.

Focusing on Black crack addicts rather than on other perpetrators of fetal harms serves two broader social purposes. First, prosecution of these pregnant women serves to degrade women whom society views as undeserving to be mothers and to discourage them from having children. If prosecutors had instead chosen to prosecute affluent women addicted to alcohol or prescription medication, the policy of criminalizing prenatal conduct very likely would have suffered a hasty demise. Society is much more willing to condone the punishment of poor women of color who fail to meet the middle-class ideal of motherhood.

In addition to legitimizing fetal rights enforcement, the prosecution of crack-addicted mothers diverts public attention from social ills such as poverty, racism, and a misguided national health policy and implies instead that shamefully high Black infant death rates are caused by the bad acts of individual mothers. Poor Black mothers thus become the scapegoats for the causes of the Black community's ill health. Punishing them assuages any guilt the nation might feel at the plight of an underclass with infant mortality at rates higher than those in some less developed countries. Making criminals of Black mothers apparently helps to relieve the nation of the burden of creating a health care system that ensures healthy babies for all its citizens.

For a variety of reasons, then, an informed appraisal of the competing interests involved in the prosecutions must take account of the race of the women affected. . . .

* * *

VI. A CRITICAL ASSESSMENT OF ARGUMENTS AGAINST INTERVENTION

There is now a substantial body of scholarship challenging state intervention in pregnant women's conduct. Yet much of the literature has not sufficiently taken into account the experience of poor Black women, the very women who are most affected. In addition, the literature has failed to address adequately the arguments on behalf of fetal protection. In this Part, I will critique various reproductive rights theories that have been used to challenge the control of pregnant women and show why they are not helpful in addressing the prosecution of drug-addicted mothers. In Part VII, I will present a privacy argument that more effectively confronts the government's policy. That analysis better explains the constitutional injury caused by the prosecutions because it recognizes race as a critical factor.

A. Bodily Autonomy and Integrity

Much of the discourse challenging state intervention in the decisions of pregnant women has occurred in the context of forced medical treatment. Many commentators have argued that judicial decisions that allow doctors to perform surgery and other procedures on a pregnant woman without her consent violate women's right to bodily autonomy and integrity. It is difficult, however, to transfer the scholarship addressing compelled medical procedures to the issue of drug-addicted mothers.

The interests of the drug-addicted mother appear to be weaker for three reasons. First, unlike forced medical treatment, punishing the pregnant drug addict does not require her to take affirmative steps to benefit the fetus. She is not asked to be a good samaritan; rather, she is punished for affirmatively doing harm to the fetus. Second, the prosecution of drug-addicted mothers involves no direct physical intrusion. Nor do prosecutions deprive women of control over their bodies by directly compelling them to undergo an unwanted biological process, as is the case with the prohibition of abortion. On this level, punishing drug-addicted mothers does not seem to implicate a mother's right to bodily integrity at all.

Third, the mother's drug use has potentially devastating effects on the fetus and lacks any social justification. Indeed, forcing a woman to refrain from using harmful drugs through incarceration or court order may be seen as a benefit *to the women herself*, whereas forced medical procedures often aid the fetus only at the expense of the mother's health or her deeply held religious beliefs. It is therefore harder to identify how the government's action infringes a constitutionally protected interest. Consequently, some commentators who oppose the regulation of some potentially harmful conduct during pregnancy at the same time justify punishment of pregnant drug users. We must therefore draw on another principle of autonomy to describe the infringement caused by these prosecutions: the right to make decisions about reproduction (here, the choice of carrying a pregnancy to term).

In addition, many of the issues raised by forced medical treatment seem disconnected from the experiences of poor women of color. For example, much of the literature focuses on ethical issues arising from treating the fetus as a patient and its impact on the relationship between the pregnant woman and her physician. This debate is largely irrelevant to poor Black women, the majority of whom receive inadequate prenatal care. Their major concern is not having an ethical conflict with their doctor, but affording or finding a doctor in the first place. The issue of whether intricate fetal surgery may be performed against a mother's will is far removed from the urgent needs of poor women who may not have available to them the most rudimentary means to ensure the health of the fetus.

Forced treatment decisions equate women with inert vessels, disregard their own choices, and value them solely for their capacity to nurture the fetus. Although this view of women is reflected as well in the prosecution of drug-addicted mothers, it does not grasp the full indignity of the state's treatment of poor Black women. Government control of pregnancy perpetuates stereotypes that value women solely for their procreative capacity. But the prosecutions of crack addicts deny poor Black women even this modicum of value. By punishing them for having babies, they are deemed not even worthy of the dignity of childbearing. Thus, the prosecutions debase Black women even more than forced medical treatment's general devaluation of women.

B.   The Right to Make Medical and Lifestyle Decisions

A second approach challenges restrictions on maternal conduct during pregnancy by advocating a woman's right to make medical and lifestyle decisions. Rather than focus on a woman's right to protect her body from physical intrusion, this approach focuses on a woman's right to engage in activities of her choice free from government interference. This argument also loses its force in the context of maternal drug addiction. While the danger of government restrictions on a pregnant woman's *normal* conduct may be apparent, drug use during pregnancy arguably belongs in a separate category. The pregnant drug addict is not asked to refrain from generally acceptable behavior, such as sexual intercourse, work, or exercise. Rather, society demands only that she cease conduct that it already deems illegal and reprehensible.

Arguments based on a woman's right to make decisions about her pregnancy and her fetus also appear weak in the context of maternal drug addiction. Unlike healthy mothers, pregnant drug addicts are not better able to make lifestyle and medical decisions that affect the fetus than the state or physicians. Nor can we say that a decision to carry a fetus to term automatically demonstrates that a drug-addicted mother cares deeply for it and is in a better position to monitor her own conduct during pregnancy than the state. Most would agree that the pregnant drug addict has exercised poor judgment in caring for herself and her fetus. The state should not substitute its judgment for that of the "normal" mother, but intervention in the case of the drug addict seems more justified.

Although the government is arguably better able to make decisions about the care of the fetus than the drug-addicted mother, it is quite a different matter to allow the government to determine who is entitled to be a mother. State interference in the decision to bear a child is constitutionally more significant than state control of lifestyle decisions.

The interference-in-women's-lifestyles approach also neglects the concerns of poor women of color. A common criticism of the prosecution of drug-addicted mothers is that the imposition of maternal duties will lead to punishment for less egregious conduct. Commentators have predicted government penalties for cigarette smoking, consumption of alcohol, strenuous physical activity, and failure to follow a doctor's orders. Although valid, this argument ignores the reality of poor Black women whom are currently being arrested. The reference to a parade of future horribles to criticize the fetal rights doctrine belittles the significance of current government action. It seems to imply that the prosecution of Black crack addicts is not enough to generate concern and that we must postulate the prosecution of white middle-class women in order for the challenge to be meaningful.

C. The Focus on Abortion

Another aspect of the reproductive rights literature that limits our understanding of reproductive choice is its focus on abortion rights. One problem is that this focus provides an inadequate response to a central argument in support of the regulation of pregnancy. John Robertson, for example, has contended that if a woman forgoes her right to an abortion, she forfeits her right to autonomy and choice. If abortion is the heart of women's reproductive rights, then state policies that do not interfere with that right are acceptable. Similarly, if the full extent of reproductive freedom is the right to have an abortion, then a policy that encourages abortion—such as the prosecution of crack-addicted mothers—does not interfere with that freedom.

As in the previous approaches, the emphasis on abortion fails to incorporate the needs of poor women of color. The primary concern of white, middle-class women are laws that restrict choices otherwise available to them, such as statutes that make it more difficult to obtain an abortion. The main concern of poor women of color, however, are the material conditions of poverty and oppression that restrict their choices. The reproductive freedom of poor women of color, for example, is limited significantly not only by the denial of access to safe abortions, but also by the lack of resources necessary for a healthy pregnancy and parenting relationship. Their choices are limited not only by direct government interference with their decisions, but also by government's failure to facilitate them. The focus of reproductive rights discourse on abortion neglects this broader range of reproductive health issues that affect poor women of color. Addressing the concerns of women of color will expand our vision of reproductive freedom to include the full scope of what it means to have control over one's reproductive life.

VII. CLAIMING THE RIGHT OF PRIVACY FOR WOMEN OF COLOR

A. Identifying the Constitutional Issue

In deciding which of the competing interests involved in the prosecution of drug-addicted mothers prevails—the state's interest in protecting the health of the fetus or the woman's interest in preventing state intervention—it is essential as a matter of constitutional law to identify the precise nature of the woman's right at stake. In the *Johnson* case, the prosecutor framed the constitutional issue as follows: "What constitutionally protected freedom did Jennifer engage in when she smoked cocaine?" That was the wrong question. Johnson was not convicted of using drugs. Her "constitutional right" to smoke cocaine was never at issue. Johnson was prosecuted because she chose to carry her pregnancy to term while she was addicted to crack. Had she smoked cocaine during her pregnancy and then had an abortion, she would not have been charged with such a serious crime. The proper question, then, is "What constitutionally protected freedom did Jennifer engage in when she decided to have a baby, even though she was a drug addict?"

Understanding the prosecution of drug-addicted mothers as punishment for having babies clarifies the constitutional right at stake. The woman's right at issue is not the right to abuse drugs or to cause the fetus to be born with defects. It is the right to choose to be a mother that is burdened by the criminalization of conduct during pregnancy. This view of the constitutional issue reveals the relevance of race to the resolution of the competing interests. Race has historically determined the value society places on an individual's right to choose motherhood. Because of the devaluation of Black motherhood, protecting the right of Black women to choose to bear a child has unique significance. In the following section, I argue that the prosecutions of addicted mothers violate traditional liberal notions of privacy. I also demonstrate how the issue of race informs the traditional analysis and calls for a reassessment of the use of privacy doctrine in the struggle to eliminate gender and racial subordination.

B. Overview of Privacy Arguments

Prosecutions of drug-addicted mothers infringe on two aspects of the right to individual choice in reproductive decisionmaking. First, they infringe on the freedom to continue a pregnancy that is essential to an individual's personhood and autonomy. This freedom implies that state control of the decision to carry a pregnancy to term can be as pernicious as state control of the decision to terminate a pregnancy. Second, the prosecutions infringe on choice by imposing an invidious government standard for the entitlement to procreate. Such imposition of a government standard for childbearing is one way that society denies the humanity of those who are different. The first approach emphasizes a woman's right to autonomy over her reproductive life; the second highlights a woman's right to be valued equally as a human being. In other words, the prosecution of crack-addicted mothers infringes upon both a mother's right to make decisions that determine her individual identity and her right to be respected equally as a human being by recognizing the value of her motherhood.

Inherent in the thesis of this Article is a tension between the reliance on the liberal rhetoric of choice and an acknowledgement of the fallacy of choice for poor women of color. This Article also seeks to incorporate liberal notions of individual autonomy while acknowledging the collective injury perpetrated by racism. . . . Working through the privacy analysis from the perspective of poor Black women uncovers unexplored benefits to be gained from liberal doctrine while revealing liberalism's inadequacies. . . .

C. The Right to Choose Procreation

Punishing drug-addicted mothers unconstitutionally burdens the right to choose to bear a child. . . . Considerable support exists for the conclusion that the decision to procreate is part of the right of privacy. The decision to bear children is universally acknowledged in the privacy cases as being "at the very heart" of these constitutionally protected choices. In *Eisenstadt v. Baird*, for example, the Court struck down a Massachusetts statute that prohibited the distribution of contraceptives to unmarried persons. Although the case was decided on equal protection grounds, the Court recognized the vital nature of the freedom to choose whether to give birth to a child: "If the right of privacy means anything, it is the right of the individual, married or single, to be free from unwarranted governmental intrusion into matters so fundamentally affecting a person as the decision whether to bear or beget a child."

The right of privacy protects equally the choice to bear children and the choice to refrain from bearing them. The historical experiences of Black women illustrate the evil of government control over procreative decisions. Their experiences demonstrate that the dual nature of the decisional right recognized in the privacy cases goes beyond the logical implications of making a choice. The exploitation of Black women's foremothers during slavery to breed more slaves and the sterilization abuse that they have suffered reveal society's pervasive devaluation of Black women as mothers.

Burdening both the right to terminate a pregnancy and the right to give birth to a child violates a woman's personhood by denying her autonomy over the self-defining decision of whether she will bring another being into the world. Furthermore, criminalizing the choice to give birth imposes tangible burdens on women, as well as the intangible infringement on personhood. Punishing women for having babies is in this sense at least as pernicious as forced maternity at the behest of the state.

* * *

These privacy concepts have two benefits for advocating the reproductive rights of women of color in particular: the right of privacy stresses the value of personhood, and it protects against the totalitarian abuse of government power. First, affirming Black women's constitutional claim to personhood is particularly important because these women historically have been denied the dignity of their full humanity and identity. The principle of self-definition has special significance for Black women. Angela Harris recognizes in the writings of Zora Neale Hurston an insistence on a "conception of identity as a construction, not an essence . . . . [B]lack women have had to learn to construct themselves in a society that denied them full selves." Black women's willful self-definition is an adaptation to a history of social denigration. Rejected from the dominant society's norm of womanhood, Black women have been forced to resort to their own internal resources. Harris contrasts this process of affirmative self-definition with the feminist paradigm of women as passive victims. Black women willfully create their own identities out of "fragments of experience, not discovered in one's body or unveiled after male domination is eliminated."

The concept of personhood embodied in the right of privacy can be used to affirm the role of will and creativity in Black women's construction of their own identities. Relying on the concept of self-definition celebrates the legacy of Black women who have survived and transcended conditions of oppression. The process of defining one's self and declaring one's personhood defies the denial of self-ownership inherent in slavery. Thus, the right of privacy, with its affirmation of personhood, is especially suited for challenging the devaluation of Black motherhood underlying the prosecutions of drug-addicted women.

Another important element of the right of privacy is its delineation of the limits of governmental power. The protection from government abuse also makes the right of privacy a useful legal tool for protecting the reproductive rights of women of color. Poor women of color are especially vulnerable to government control over their decisions. The government's pervasive involvement in Black women's lives illustrates the inadequacy of the privacy critique presented by some white feminist scholars. Catharine MacKinnon, for example, argues that privacy doctrine is based on the false liberal assumption that government nonintervention into the private sphere promotes women's autonomy. The individual woman's legal right of privacy, according to MacKinnon, functions instead as "a means of subordinating women's collective needs to the imperatives of male supremacy."

This rejection of privacy doctrine does not take into account the contradictory meaning of the private sphere for women of color. Feminist legal theory focuses on the private realm of the family as an institution of violence and subordination. Women of color, however, often experience the family as the site of solace and resistance against racial oppression. For many women of color, the immediate concern in the area of reproductive rights is not abuse in the private sphere, but abuse of government power. The prosecution of crack-addicted mothers and coerced sterilization are examples of state intervention that pose a much greater threat for women of color than for white women.

Another telling example is the issue of child custody. The primary concern for white middle-class women with regard to child custody is private custody battles with their husbands following the termination of a marriage. But for women of color, the dominant threat is termination of parental rights by the state. Again, the imminent danger faced by poor women of color comes from the public sphere, not the private. Thus, the protection from government interference that privacy doctrine affords may have a different significance for women of color.

D. Unconstitutional Government Standards for Procreation: The Intersection of Privacy and Equality

The equal protection clause and the right of privacy provide the basis for two separate constitutional challenges to the prosecution of drug-addicted mothers. The singling out of Black mothers for punishment combines in a single government action several wrongs prohibited by both constitutional doctrines. Black mothers are denied autonomy over procreative decisions because of their race. The government's denial of Black women's fundamental right to choose to bear children serves to perpetuate the legacy of racial discrimination embodied in the devaluation of Black motherhood. The full scope of the government's violation can better be understood, then, by a constitutional theory that acknowledges the complementary and overlapping qualities of the Constitution's guarantees of equality and privacy. Viewing the prosecutions as imposing a racist government standard for procreation uses this approach.

Poor crack addicts are punished for having babies because they fail to measure up to the state's ideal of motherhood. Prosecutors have brought charges against women who use drugs during pregnancy without demonstrating any harm to the fetus. Moreover, a government policy that has the effect of punishing primarily poor Black women for having babies evokes the specter of racial eugenics, especially in light of the history of sterilization abuse of women of color. These factors make clear that these women are not punished simply because they may harm their unborn children. They are punished because the combination of their poverty, race, and drug addiction is seen to make them unworthy of procreating.

This aspect of the prosecutions implicates both equality and privacy interests. The right to bear children goes to the heart of what it means to be human. The value we place on individuals determines whether we see them as entitled to perpetuate themselves in their children. Denying someone the right to bear children—or punishing her for exercising that right—deprives her of a basic part of her humanity. When this denial is based on race, it also functions to preserve a racial hierarchy that essentially disregards Black humanity.

* * *

Skinner [*v. Oklahoma*] rested on grounds that linked equal protection doctrine and the right to procreate. Justice Douglas framed the legal question as "a sensitive and important area of human rights." The reason for the Court's elevation of the right to procreate was the Court's recognition of the significant risk of discriminatory selection inherent in state intervention in reproduction. The Court also understood the genocidal implications of a government standard for procreation: "In evil or reckless hands [the government's power to sterilize] can cause races or types which are inimical to the dominant group to wither and disappear." The critical role of procreation to human survival and the invidious potential for government discrimination against disfavored groups makes heightened protection crucial. The Court understood the use of the power to sterilize in the government's discrimination against certain types of criminals to be as invidious "as if it had selected a particular race or nationality for oppressive treatment."

Although the reasons advanced for the sterilization of chicken thieves and the prosecution of drug-addicted mothers are different, both practices are dangerous for similar reasons. Both effectuate ethnocentric judgments by the government that certain members of society do not deserve to have children. As the Court recognized in *Skinner*, the enforcement of a government standard for childbearing denies the disfavored group a critical aspect of human dignity.

The history of compulsory sterilization demonstrates that society deems women who deviate from its norms of motherhood—in 1941, teenaged delinquent girls like Carrie Buck who bore illegitimate children, today, poor Black crack addicts who use drugs during pregnancy—"unworthy of the high privilege" of procreation. The government therefore refuses to affirm their human dignity by helping them overcome obstacles to good mothering. Rather, it punishes them by sterilization or criminal prosecution and thereby denies them a basic part of their humanity. When this denial is based on race, the violation is especially serious. Governmental policies that perpetuate racial subordination through the denial of procreative rights, which threaten both racial equality and privacy at once, should be subject to the highest scrutiny.

E. Toward a New Privacy Jurisprudence

Imagine that courts and legislatures have accepted the argument that the prosecution of crack-addicted mothers violates their right of privacy. All pending indictments for drug use during pregnancy are dismissed and bills proposing fetal abuse laws are discarded. Would there be any perceptible change in the inferior status of Black women? Pregnant crack addicts would still be denied treatment, and most poor Black women would continue to receive inadequate prenatal care. The infant mortality rate for Blacks would remain deplorably high. In spite of the benefits of privacy doctrine for women of color, liberal notions of privacy are inadequate to eliminate the subordination of Black women. In this section, I will suggest two approaches that I believe are necessary in order for privacy theory to contribute to the eradication of racial hierarchy. First, we need to develop a positive view of the right of privacy. Second, the law must recognize the connection between the right of privacy and racial equality.

The most compelling argument against privacy rhetoric, from the perspective of women of color, is the connection that feminist scholars have drawn between privacy and the abortion funding decisions. Critics of the concept of privacy note that framing the abortion right as a right merely to be shielded from state intrusion into private choices provides no basis for a constitutional claim to public support for abortions. As the Court explained in *Harris v. McRae*, "although government may not place obstacles in the path of a woman's exercise of her freedom of choice, it need not remove those not of its own creation." MacKinnon concludes that abortion as a private privilege rather than a public right only serves to perpetuate inequality:

> Privacy conceived as a right from public intervention and disclosure is the opposite of the relief that *Harris* sought for welfare women. State intervention would have provided a choice women did *not* have in [the] private [realm]. The women in *Harris*, women whose sexual refusal has counted for particularly little, needed something to make their privacy effective.

The logic of the Court's response resembles the logic by which women are supposed to consent to sex. Preclude the alternatives, then call the sole remaining option "her choice." The point is that the alternatives are precluded *prior* to the reach of the chosen legal doctrine. They are precluded by conditions of sex, race, and class—the very conditions the privacy frame not only leaves tacit but exists to *guarantee.*

This critique is correct in its observation that the power of privacy doctrine in poor women's lives is constrained by liberal notions of freedom. First, the abstract freedom to choose is of meager value without meaningful options from which to choose and the ability to effectuate one's choice. The traditional concept of privacy makes the false presumption that the right to choose is contained entirely within the individual and not circumscribed by the material conditions of the individual's life. Second, the abstract freedom of self-definition is of little help to someone who lacks the resources to realize the personality she envisions or whose emergent self is continually beaten down by social forces. Defining the guarantee of personhood as no more than shielding a sphere of personal decisions from the reach of government—merely ensuring the individual's "right to be let alone"—may be inadequate to protect the dignity and autonomy of the poor and oppressed.

The definition of privacy as a purely negative right serves to exempt the state from any obligation to ensure the social conditions and resources necessary for self-determination and autonomous decisionmaking. Based on this narrow view of liberty, the Supreme Court has denied a variety of claims to government aid. MacKinnon notes that "[i]t is apparently a very short step from that which the government has a duty *not* to intervene in to that which it has *no* duty to intervene in." An evolving privacy doctrine need not make the step between these two propositions. Laurence Tribe, for example, has suggested an alternative view of the relationship between the government's negative and affirmative responsibilities in guaranteeing the rights of personhood: "Ultimately, the affirmative duties of government cannot be severed from its obligations to refrain from certain forms of control; both must respond to a substantive vision of the needs of human personality."

This concept of privacy includes not only the negative proscription against government coercion, but also the affirmative duty of government to protect the individual's personhood from degradation and to facilitate the processes of choice and self-determination. This approach shifts the focus of privacy theory from state nonintervention to an affirmative guarantee of personhood and autonomy. Under this post-liberal doctrine, the government is not only prohibited from punishing crack-addicted women for choosing to bear children; it is also required to provide drug treatment and prenatal care. Robin West has eloquently captured this progressive understanding of the due process clause in which privacy doctrine is grounded: "The ideal of due process, then, is an individual life free of illegitimate social coercion facilitated by hierarchies of class, gender, or race. The goal is an affirmatively autonomous existence: a meaningfully flourishing, independent, enriched individual life."

This affirmative view of privacy is enhanced by recognizing the connection between privacy and racial equality. The government's duty to guarantee personhood and autonomy stems not only from the needs of the individual, but also from the needs of the entire community. The harm caused by the prosecution of crack-addicted mothers is not simply the incursion on each individual crack addict's decisionmaking; it is the perpetuation of a degraded image that affects the status of an entire race. The devaluation of a poor Black addict's decision to bear a child is tied to the dominant society's disregard for the motherhood of all Black women. The diminished value placed on Black motherhood, in turn, is a badge of racial inferiority worn by all Black people. The affirmative view of privacy recognizes the connection between the dehumanization of the individual and the subordination of the group.

Thus, the reason that legislatures should reject laws that punish Black women's reproductive choices is not an absolute and isolated notion of individual autonomy. Rather, legislatures should reject these laws as a critical step towards eradicating a racial hierarchy that has historically demeaned Black motherhood. Respecting Black women's decision to bear children is a necessary ingredient of a community that affirms the personhood of all of its members. The right to reproductive autonomy is in this way linked to the goal of racial equality and the broader pursuit of a just society. This broader dimension of privacy's guarantees provides a stronger claim to government's affirmative responsibilities.

Feminist legal theory, with its emphasis on the law's concrete effect on the condition of women, calls for a reassessment of traditional privacy law. It may be possible, however, to reconstruct a privacy jurisprudence that retains the focus on autonomy and personhood while making privacy doctrine effective. Before dismissing the right of privacy altogether, we should explore ways to give the concepts of choice and personhood more substance. In this way, the continuing process of challenge and subversion—the feminist critique of liberal privacy doctrine, followed by the racial critique of the feminist analysis—will forge a finer legal tool for dismantling institutions of domination.

* * *

Homosexuality and Sexual Privacy

Are sexual orientation and sexual expression aspects of personhood that are protected from state interference under substantive due process? In *Bowers v. Hardwick,* the Supreme Court held that homosexuals' sexual conduct was not protected by the right of privacy against criminal prohibition by state sodomy laws. Anne Goldstein recalls the Hart-Devlin debate in Britain in analyzing *Bowers v. Hardwick*. Janet Halley criticizes the Court's reading of the unstable relationship between act and identity in sodomy statutes and advocates a strategy that emphasizes acts. Michael Sandel rejects liberal theory's tendency to bracket moral arguments about homosexuality, arguing that the justice of laws against homosexual sodomy depend on the morality or immorality of this practice. Kendall Thomas also rejects the liberal right of privacy for ignoring the corporeality at issue in sodomy laws and their legitimation of private homophobic violence. He proposes a less abstract, embodied model that views sodomy statutes as an unconstitutional invasion of political rights.

Anne B. Goldstein, *History, Homosexuality, and Political Values: Searching for the Hidden Determinants of* Bowers v. Hardwick, 97 YALE L.J. 1073, 1091-1098 (1988)*

* * *

III. SUBTEXT AND TEXT: THE POLITICAL PHILOSOPHIES UNDERLYING *BOWERS V. HARDWICK*

The Justices' debate over the scope of constitutional "privacy" masked not only disagreement about the nature of Hardwick's activity, but also a dispute over fundamental values. Two competing political philosophies, classical conservatism and classical liberalism, respectively, underlie the Supreme Court majority and dissenting opinions. The *Hardwick* majority accepted Georgia's argument that even irrational popular prejudices should be enforced in order to preserve the very existence of society, because these prejudices may embody ancient wisdom. This argument resembles the classical conservatism of Edmund Burke and FitzJames Stephen. Justice Blackmun's dissent implied that an individual's right to behave as he chooses may be limited only in order to prevent him from causing harm to others, a view reminiscent of the classical liberalism of Jeremy Bentham and John Stuart Mill. Disputes over similar issues in other contexts have been framed in these terms, most notably the extended written debate between Professor H.L.A. Hart and Lord Patrick Devlin when the Wolfenden Committee recommended in 1957 that criminal penalties for private and consensual sexual acts between men be repealed in Great Britain. Thus, the Supreme Court's discussion and resolution of *Bowers v. Hardwick* was shaped by thirty years of lively public, forensic, and scholarly debate about whether consensual lovemaking between two persons of the same sex ought to be a crime.

A. *The Hart-Devlin Debate*

The writings of H.L.A. Hart and Patrick Devlin provide a particularly instructive comparison with *Bowers v. Hardwick* because they consider the underlying philosophical questions raised by *Hardwick* with depth and rigor. Hart and Devlin debated the political philosophy which undergirded the Wolfenden Report's jurisprudential support for its substantive recommendations: the theory that protection of an individual from external harm was the only valid justification for criminal prohibitions; no other goal, and certainly no other moral theory, could be sufficient.

Lord Devlin attacked one of the Wolfenden Report's key premises: that there is a realm of private morality that may not properly be enforced by the criminal law. Devlin argued that judgments about private morality must be made every day by sentencing judges, and are implicit in the mere proscription of some, although perhaps not all, crimes. Claiming that the Wolfenden Committee had conceded homosexuality to be morally wrong, Lord Devlin argued against a "freedom to be immoral," because "[s]ociety is entitled by means of its laws to protect itself from dangers, whether from within or without." He thought the "viewpoint of the man in the street"—especially when reflecting a visceral response—should be the only measure of both morality and danger to society. Although Lord Devlin conceded that the state might protect individual privacy from the criminal law by restricting methods of police investigation or by lenient sentences for private behavior, he argued that the community needed to be able to enforce the majority's moral views in order to preserve its own existence.

Lord Devlin's arguments were explicitly and self-consciously conservative. Indeed, he argued that basing the law upon rational considerations would be undemocratic and elitist. He acknowledged that his argument that the law should enforce majoritarian morality was conservative, naming James FitzJames Stephen as his intellectual ancestor.

Like Lord Devlin, Professor Hart was at least as interested in the Wolfenden Committee's jurisprudential theory as in its practical recommendations. His arguments therefore defended both John Stuart Mill and the Wolfenden Report, and attacked the theories of Edmund Burke and FitzJames Stephen along with those propounded by Lord Devlin himself. In defending the Wolfenden Committee's jurisprudence, Hart argued that although "we should attempt to adjust the severity of punishment to the moral gravity of offences," it does not follow "that punishment merely for immorality is justified." Hart explained that although "the only justification for having a *system* of punishment is to prevent harm and only harmful conduct should be punished," nevertheless using moral judgments to decide on the quantum of punishment for harmful conduct may support social morality and prevent the law from falling into disrepute. Pointing out that criminal laws affect both those persons actually punished under them and those persons "coerced into obedience by the threat of legal punishment," Hart argued that proscribing harmless sexual activities was particularly pernicious because of the "recurrent and insistent part" sexual impulses play in daily life: "[T]he suppression of sexual impulses generally is[ ] something which affects the development or balance of the individual's emotional life, happiness, and personality." Professor Hart characterized Lord Devlin's argument that society must enforce majoritarian morality to protect itself as "a highly ambitious empirical generalization" for which Devlin had offered neither evidence nor even any "indication . . . of the kind of evidence that would support it." Professor Hart acknowledged that it might be possible to discriminate empirically between those portions of society's moral code necessary for social existence and those that were superfluous, but noted that it would be difficult to do so. Until empirical evidence demonstrating the necessity for any particular moral rule was available, Hart concluded, Lord Devlin's arguments rested entirely upon the "conservative thesis" that "the majority have the right to enforce its . . . convictions that their moral environment is a thing of value to be defended from change."

One of Lord Devlin's most enduring contributions to the debate about the role of morality in the criminal law was his development of a list of existing crimes which he used to challenge the liberal argument that "private immorality should altogether and always be immune from interference by the law." This list included: treason, euthanasia or the killing of another at his own request, suicide, attempted suicide and suicide pacts, dueling, abortion, incest between brother and sister, gambling, drunkenness, living on the earnings of a prostitute, bestiality, conspiracy to corrupt morals, bigamy, and polygamy. Some version of Lord Devlin's list has become a staple in arguments over whether private lovemaking between consenting adults should be legal, and a version of it appears in *Bowers v. Hardwick.*

Professor Hart responded to Devlin's list in two ways. First, he argued that "the actual existence of laws of any given kind is wholly irrelevant to [the] contention . . . that it would be better if laws of such a kind did not exist." Second, he attempted to show that many of the crimes on Lord Devlin's list were not solely attempts to enforce morality.

B.   Bowers v. Hardwick *Recasts the Hart-Devlin Debate*

In many respects, *Bowers v. Hardwick* recast the Hart-Devlin debate in constitutional terms. Understanding White's majoritarian justifications for seeing "homosexual sodomy" as immoral, and Blackmun's responses to it, is key to understanding the philosophical similarities between *Bowers v. Hardwick* and the Hart-Devlin debate. Like Lord Devlin, Justice White and Chief Justice Burger defended the criminal proscription of homosexual lovemaking by appealing to tradition and morality. Like Professor Hart, Justices Blackmun and Stevens would have required proof that private homosexual lovemaking was harmful before permitting the state to proscribe it. These differences reflect, respectively, the conservative position, for which the desirability of protecting society's existing form is unquestioned, and the liberal position, for which individual liberty is the primary value. Liberal values and conservative values are incommensurable. Although one can make an intelligible choice between them, this cannot be done from an Archimedean perspective.

In addition to his misleading historical claims, White relied on "the presumed belief of a majority of the Georgia electorate that homosexual sodomy is immoral and unacceptable." Although careful analysis suggests that White was working within the conservative perspective, his majoritarian justification can be interpreted in both conservative and liberal ways. The conservative interpretation assumes that White agreed with FitzJames Stephen and Lord Patrick Devlin that strongly held popular prejudices are by themselves sufficient justification for criminal proscriptions. The liberal interpretation assumes that White accepted Jeremy Bentham's principle that criminal proscriptions must be limited to curbing behavior causing harm to others. Many of the dissenters' arguments, and almost all of the scholarly commentary, have been written from within the liberal perspective, and assume White to have been asserting that homosexuality is harmful. Yet White's argument fails in liberal terms, since he never attempts to identify any harm caused by consensual adult sodomy.

In conservative terms, however, White's argument is coherent. When he relied on "the presumed belief of a majority of the Georgia electorate," White meant that

Georgia might proscribe homosexuality solely because it was abhorred by the majority. When he compiled a list strikingly similar to Lord Devlin's by comparing "homosexual sodomy" to '[v]ictimless crimes, such as the possession and use of illegal drugs[,] . . . possession in the home of drugs, firearms, or stolen goods[,] . . . adultery, incest, and other sexual crimes," White, like Devlin, was arguing that society often legislates on the basis of morality alone, and that this is entirely proper.

Blackmun explicitly repudiated White's conservative premises at some points, but at others merely implicitly assumed the primacy of liberal values. Although, as just argued, Justice White's opinion is more coherent when understood in conservative terms, Justice Blackmun sometimes interpreted it as a liberal argument. Treating White's use of his Devlin-like list as shorthand for the liberal argument that all these crimes cause harm, Blackmun retorted that private, consensual, violations of Georgia's law were obviously neither the cause nor the effect of harm to any individual. Blackmun's implicit assertion that the crimes on White's list are proscribed because they harm identifiable individuals may be correct for most of the crimes. Adultery and sexual crimes involving the use of actual or constructive force may be distinguished from "homosexual sodomy" on this basis. Yet incest between adults is not clearly harmful.

Blackmun's own liberal assumptions prevented him from recognizing that White's use of the list was shorthand for the conservative argument that the criminal law may properly be used 'to preserve order and decency.' Professor Hart responded to this argument by requesting empirical evidence of the necessity for any criminal prohibition based upon morality; had Blackmun done so, his rhetorical position would have been stronger. Instead, Justice Blackmun attempted to refute the majority's argument on liberal terms by seeking to distinguish homosexual love from incest between adults. He may have tried to do so in order to contain the anarchic risks implied by a rule favoring individual sexual freedom. Yet he set himself a formidable task, because incest between adults seems not to cause any discernable harm to an identifiable individual.

The dissenters' most creative responses to the majority pushed beyond the Hart-Devlin debate, turning the conservative argument against itself. Instead of accepting the assertion that homosexuality is universally considered immoral, as Hart implicitly did, Stevens denied that homosexuality is abhorred even in Georgia. Blackmun did not challenge this factual premise. Recalling that the values of pluralistic diversity and individual liberty form a traditional part of our society's morality, he paradoxically asserted that these liberal values should be considered paramount in constitutional interpretation, even by those who consider conserving our society in its present form a primary value.

* * *

Janet E. Halley, *Reasoning About Sodomy: Act and Identity in and After* Bowers v. Hardwick, 79 VA. L. REV. 1721, 1721-26, 1731-72 (1993)*

> *Heterosexuals don't practice sodomy. . . .*
> — Senator Strom Thurmond

> *THIS IS NOT A CASE ABOUT ONLY HOMOSEXUALS. . . .*
> *ALL SORTS OF PEOPLE DO THIS KIND OF THING.*
> — Daniel C. Richman

INTRODUCTION

The criminalization of sodomy is crucial to the generation and ordering of sexual-orientation identities. Sodomy statutes generate at least part of the personhood of anyone who wishes to engage in debates about whether such measures should be adopted, modified or repealed. By contributing to the terms on which sexual-orientation identities may be adopted and maintained, sodomy statutes interfere indirectly in the conventions and practices of reasoning about their own propriety. They function to maintain themselves.

Sodomy statutes place certain people at risk of surveillance, arrest, indictment, conviction and incarceration, while they simultaneously provide for certain other people spaces of relative immunity. What is interesting and complicated about sodomy statutes is that the first group is not exclusively the group of "homosexuals," and the second group is not exclusively the group of "heterosexuals." This is because sodomy, as it has been criminalized in the United States, is not only about identities: it is also about acts. To think of this is to resist the obvious: we all tend to imagine that sodomy is about homosexuals, but if we think for a moment we recall that many resolute homosexuals never do any acts that could be called sodomy, while many resolute heterosexuals are, where sodomy is concerned, avid recidivists. The recollection is a gestalt switch: we have stopped thinking about sodomy as an indicator and regulator of identities, and have recalled its reference to acts.

Sodomy statutes maintain themselves in part by their equivocal reference to identities *and/or* acts. The duality of the sodomy statutes—sometimes an index of identity, sometimes an index of acts—is a rhetorical mechanism in the subordination of homosexual identity and the superordination of heterosexual identity. Designating homosexual identity as the personal manifestation of sodomy confirms its subordination. At the same time, the ways in which homosexual identity is not sodomy are subject to an organized forgetting. And heterosexual identity becomes superordinate not because it is absolutely immune, but because it is *intermittently and provisionally* immune from regulation under the sodomy statutes. This instability can be a source of rhetorical and political power. For the designation "heterosexual," the instability of sodomy along the parallel registers of act and identity generates a form of self-interestedness that is also a fragile and fearfully-to-be-maintained identity.

Resisting power in this form provides gay men, lesbians, bisexuals, and their allies with a political opportunity. We can form new alliances along the register of acts. From that vantage point the instability of heterosexual identity can be exploited, and indeed, undermined from within. To be sure, adopting this approach requires that

---

lesbians, gay men, and bisexuals place their identities as such in abeyance at least from time to time. This is dangerous, but it may be the only way that lesbians, gay men, and bisexuals can gain some kind of rhetorical leverage in a rhetorical system whose instability normally places us in a double bind.

Before launching on this argument, I offer two methodological points. . . . First, to argue that sodomy prohibitions shape heterosexual and homosexual identities, as I do, is to imply that those identities do not emerge unproblematically from nature or stably describe the persons who bear them. I want to embrace that implication explicitly. In this Article I use the terms "homosexuality" and "homosexual"—and more tendentiously, the terms "heterosexuality" and "heterosexual"— without any implication that they accurately describe any persons living or dead. As I try to use them here, these terms describe rhetorical categories that have real, material importance notwithstanding their failure to provide adequate descriptions of any one of us. Sexual-orientation identities are, then, *facilities* that we use when we attempt to explain ourselves to ourselves, when we seek to situate ourselves in relation to others or others in relation to ourselves, and thus when we seek to gain and wield power, including the power of persuasion.

Second, this Article does not pursue the well-established inquiry into the relationship between gender and sexual orientation, and focuses instead on the dynamics peculiar to sexual-orientation identities. The former line of investigation has produced powerful social and political as well as legal analyses arguing that the social and legal interdiction of homosexuality produces gender hierarchy by enforcing a rigid distinction between the genders, and by requiring women to associate intimately with men and thus to be dependent on them. . . .

I do not disagree with this approach, but I think it is only part of the picture. Heterosexuality exceeds and thus differs from masculinity, just as homosexuality exceeds and differs from the so-called passive role in anal sex. Though they intersect, gender and sexuality exceed and differ from one another. As Andrew Parker notes in a deft summary of the recent articulation of sexuality or queer studies as a body of work distinct from that developed in women's, gender, and feminist studies, "a growing number of critics, 'male' and 'female' alike, no longer find gender *the* inevitable or even appropriate optic through which to explore 'issues of sexuality in general.'" In an inaugurating essay for the study of sexuality, Gayle Rubin invoked Michel Foucault's conception of sexuality as a system of social practices and knowledge "concerned with the sensations of the body, the quality of pleasures, and the nature of impressions," and argued that the study of sexuality so described should not be equated with the study of gender:

> I want to challenge the assumption that feminism is or should be the privileged site of a theory of sexuality. Feminism is the theory of gender oppression. To automatically assume that this makes it the theory of sexual oppression is to fail to distinguish between gender, on the one hand, and erotic desire, on the other. . . .
>
> . . . .
>
> . . . Gender affects the operation of the sexual system, and the sexual system has had gender-specific manifestations. But although sex and gender are related, they are not the same thing, and they form the basis of two distinct arenas of social practice.

Indeed, any assumption that hetero/homosexual dynamics must originate in, or ultimately produce, gender hierarchy or gender identity gives analytic priority to heterosexuality, with its definitional dependence on the concept of male and female, of masculine and feminine, as matching opposites. . . .

The sheer plausibility of gender as the source of and explanation for erotic differences makes it especially necessary to look at sexuality independently (though not instead). Sidestepping the pervasive explanatory power of that norm requires an analysis of sexuality that is distinctively queer, in the sense that it seeks to describe the peculiar operations of sexual-orientation taxonomies insofar as they are not articulated through gender. The present Article is such an effort.

* * *

I. REASONS AND REASONERS

* * *

The criminalization of sodomy is crucial to the ordering of sexual-orientation identities, particularly to the subordination of homosexual identity and the superordination of heterosexual identity. Sodomy statutes are materially important for concrete, material reasons: under their authority, people are in jail. They are materially important for symbolic reasons as well. Sodomy statutes acquire symbolic importance in part because they are, most often, facially neutral. Twenty-eight states and Washington D.C. have repealed their provisions governing sodomy, either by statute or through adjudication. Of the twenty-three statutes (including the Military Code of Justice) that retain prohibitions on consensual sodomy, only five prohibit same-sex sodomy alone and leave cross-sex sodomy unregulated. Eighteen statutes (including the Military Code of Justice) prohibit sodomy no matter whether it is engaged in by people of the same or of different sexes. It is not clear how many prosecutions for consensual, noncommercial sodomy between adults are threatened or brought every year in the U.S., but it is clear that these statutes are at least sporadically enforced, more often against same-sex conduct, though with surprising frequency against cross-sex conduct as well.

Though discriminatory enforcement of sodomy statutes against parties in same-sex erotic contacts may be difficult to prove, selective prosecution is widely recognized, and has even been held, in the military context, to "bear[] a substantial relationship to an important governmental interest." Commentators have argued that an invidious legislative intent to target same-sex conduct often underlies facially neutral statutes, rendering them indistinguishable under the Equal Protection Clause from the very few statutes that target same-sex conduct. I agree that it is most often entirely appropriate to consider the main run of sodomy statutes "homosexual sodomy law." But most sodomy statutes are in fact facially neutral. This Article focuses on the cultural dynamics set in motion by the *possibility*—a possibility that is more than merely theoretical—that cross-sex conduct will be prosecuted.

The facially neutral sodomy statutes make complex and unstable reference to erotic acts *and* to the public identities of persons. Conversely, act and identity are incommensurable articulations of sodomy. The next Part argues that prying act and identity apart in this context exposes the political character of that equivocation.

II. RHETORICS OF ACT AND IDENTITY

* * *

Two apparently disparate trends encourage us to imagine that sodomy and homosexual identity are identical, or that, in the relation of metonymy, sodomy is to homosexual identity as burglary is to burglars. The first of these trends is explicitly unfriendly to gay men, lesbians, bisexuals, and queers; the second has been crucial to the development of anti-homophobic thinking and litigation strategy.

In the post-*Hardwick* environment, what Justice White described as "homosexual sodomy" has become homosexuals *as* sodomy. Several federal courts have held that *Hardwick* forecloses heightened equal protection scrutiny of discrimination disadvantageous to gay men, lesbians, and bisexuals on the ground that sodomy is the *"behavior that defines the class"* of homosexuals. Other courts have refused to acknowledge that a gay public employee who comes out of the closet has engaged in First Amendment protected speech, or indeed any speech at all, on the ground that an acknowledgement of gay identity is an admission of membership in a criminal— or at least criminalizable—class. The Alabama legislature has banned public funding of any student group "that fosters or promotes a lifestyle or actions prohibited by the [state's] sodomy and sexual misconduct laws," relying on the state Attorney General's opinion that, under *Hardwick,* Alabama's sodomy statute—a prohibition of oral/genital and genital/anal contacts between any unmarried persons—constitutionally prohibits "homosexuality." In these applications of *Hardwick,* the case is construed to authorize state decisionmakers to demote gay men, lesbians, and bisexuals socially, and to exclude them from certain public debates, on the grounds that their identity alone gives rise to an irrebuttable presumption that they have committed criminalizable sodomy, and that this inferred conduct is, in turn, the essential defining feature of their identity.

* * *

Sodomy in these formulations is such an intrinsic characteristic of homosexuals, and so exclusive to us, that it constitutes a rhetorical proxy for us. It is our metonym. In the contexts identified so far this equation seems so unfriendly that it is hard to recognize that pro-gay advocates frequently make a formally identical argument. A familiar example is the practice of outing, when justified on the grounds that the true sexual-orientation identity of a person living as straight is conclusively demonstrated by his or her same-sex erotic contacts. Such outings characterize the heterosexuality of people who engage in same-sex contacts as a hypocritical veneer; underlying that veneer is the outed person's "true" homosexuality. This practice reinforces the homo/hetero dichotomy by insisting that the objects of outing, once evicted from the class of heterosexuals, are necessarily and unproblematically homosexuals. It thus denies any value to bisexuality as a social position or project. In addition, it seriously depletes the remarkable range of meanings layered under the identity "heterosexual." These are serious political mistakes because they deny the political possibility of alliances along a register of acts. And they rest on a categorical error: outing of this type merges acts discourse into identities discourse, and makes invisible the relative autonomy of each. It oversimplifies the meanings of sodomy.

Michel Foucault's famous periodization of sodomitical acts and homosexual persons has been widely misconstrued to confirm this powerful equation, but, read carefully, it provides a useful means of decoupling it. In the first volume of his *History of Sexuality,* Foucault claimed that the late nineteenth century saw "a new specification of individuals":

> As defined by the ancient civil or canonical codes, sodomy was a category of forbidden acts; their perpetrator was nothing more than the juridical subject of them. The nineteenth-century homosexual became a personage, a past, a case history, and a childhood, in addition to being a type of life, a life form, and a morphology, with an indiscreet anatomy and possibly a mysterious physiology. Nothing that went into his total composition was

unaffected by his sexuality. It was everywhere present in him. . . . It was consubstantial with him, less as a habitual sin than as a singular nature[,] . . . [and was] constituted . . . less by a type of sexual relations than by a certain quality of sexual sensibility. . . . The sodomite had been a temporary aberration; the homosexual was now a species.

These celebrated lines do not explain what Foucault thought happened to sodomy after the great nineteenth-century shift from acts to sexualities. One reading, depending on the equation of sodomy with homosexual identity, assumes that sodomy (a regime of acts) was *transformed into* homosexuality (a regime of identities). Wherever this assumption operates, sodomy-the-act is thought to have been subsumed into homosexuality-the-identity; if sodomy nevertheless stubbornly reasserts its importance as a category of acts, the move is to save appearances by absorbing it into the newly invented personage of the homosexual.

An alternative reading of Foucault's paragraph assumes less, and leaves in place a more complex and more adequate set of analytic categories for understanding the reasoning of sodomy. On this reading, the rhetoric of acts has not been evaporated or transformed; it has merely been displaced, set to one side and made slightly more difficult to discern by the rhetoric of identity. Thus sodomy—even sodomy between two people of the same sex or gender—is not necessarily the equivalent of acts or of identities; it is now unstably available for characterization as a species of act *and/or* as an indicator of sexual-orientation personality. As Sedgwick has argued, the application of gender-neutral sodomy statutes in a culture that simultaneously punishes disfavored identities creates a "threat of . . . juxtaposition [that] . . . can only be exacerbated by the insistence of gay theory that the discourse of acts can represent nothing but an anachronistic vestige." And as Jonathan Goldberg argues, this "juxtaposition" is threatening because sodomy, "that utterly confused category," as Foucault memorably put it, identifies neither persons nor acts with any coherence or specificity. This is one reason why the term can be mobilized—precisely because it is incapable of exact definition; but this is also how the bankruptcy of the term, and what has been done in its name, can be uncovered.

The volatility of sodomy appears when legislatures, courts, prosecutors, juries, voters, and public opinion attempt to determine which bodily acts come within its scope; and again when these players attempt to determine which sexual-orientation identities it governs. But a more complex range of flexibility is offered by the possibility that volatility of the first type is interlinked with volatility of the second. The Supreme Court's decision in the *Hardwick* case itself provides a laboratory for exploring these complex links.

III. "HOMOSEXUAL CONDUCT" IN *BOWERS V. HARDWICK*

Like gender, sexuality is political.
— Gayle Rubin

Justice White's majority opinion in *Hardwick* and the concurring opinion filed by Chief Justice Burger purport to be transparent frames through which we may behold not the Justices' contributions to the rhetoric of sexual acts and orientations, but those prepared before-hand by the people of Georgia and by Western civilization itself. Such transparency is a rhetorical posture; to resist it, to understand it as rhetorical, one must see the text of *Hardwick* as opaque. In this Part, I read *Hardwick* as a cultural gesture, a "social text," of a particularly authoritative kind. Rather than attribute to the majority Justices an analysis better than the one they have produced, this Part will examine *what they have in fact done* with the complex of act and identity described above—even at the cost of describing their work product as systematically incoherent. The fact that similar incoherencies have emerged elsewhere, before or since, does not relieve the severity and the cultural salience of an assertion from the apex of the federal judiciary.

The *Hardwick* decision set the stage for its peculiar contribution to act/identity incoherence, and for the posture the Justices would assume in the end, when it framed the question it would answer. As all the dissenters and virtually every academic commentator on the case have noted, Michael Hardwick challenged a gender neutral sodomy statute on its face. Georgia defined sodomy to be *"any sexual act involving the sex organs of one person and the mouth or anus of another,"* thus imposing a facially neutral prohibition of the specified bodily contacts notwithstanding the gender of the actors. Not only is it not limited to "homosexuals," it does not even mention them. And yet the Court limited its review to the question

> whether the Federal Constitution confers a fundamental right *upon homosexuals* to engage in sodomy and hence invalidates the laws of the many States that still make such conduct illegal and have done so for a very long time.

The by-now classic response to this move is to exclaim at the transparent fictionality of the Court's determination that the case involved homosexual sodomy. I have done this a number of times myself. But to stop there is to oversimplify what is going on in the case. The majority Justices' deft manipulation of act and identity responded to Hardwick's own efforts to manage these elements by trapping Hardwick under the rubric "homosexual sodomy" and permitting heterosexual sodomy—and identity—to escape from view.

[The author turns to examine the plaintiff's case and the majority Justices' opinions as examples of the resulting double bind.]

A. Plaintiff's Case

Only politics could save you now.
                                —William E. Connolly

Justice White's designation of Hardwick's case as a claim for a right to engage in "homosexual sodomy" captures a tension that permeated Hardwick's litigation papers, which sought throughout to present a facial challenge to a facially neutral statute, and to acknowledge that Hardwick, as a homosexual, claimed protection due to all persons. The discourse of identities thus permeated Hardwick's own litigation of his claim; Justice White was not the first person to put it there. Instead, plaintiff's case was structured by a tension between the rhetoric of acts and the rhetoric of identity as they sought to capture the meaning of sodomy.

Hardwick was charged with sodomy after a Georgia police officer entered his bedroom and observed him engaged in mutual fellatio with another man. This act of male-male sodomy was the only one in the record after the district court dismissed for lack of standing a married couple, John and Mary Doe, who alleged that they wished to engage in sodomy in the privacy of their home but were deterred from doing so by fear of prosecution. When the Does appealed their dismissal, the Eleventh Circuit affirmed it. The Does' claim to standing relied on an unsupported assertion that they were faced with a credible threat of prosecution, and in any event, their presence was not a prerequisite to Hardwick's facial challenge to the sodomy statute. In light of these circumstances, and unaware of the surprising rearrangement of act and identity that would be made by the majority Justices, the Does did not further challenge their dismissal when Georgia took Hardwick's claim to the Supreme Court on certiorari. Like any other person, Hardwick was entitled to challenge the statute facially, and to insist on adjudication directed to criminalization of certain bodily acts.

Framing that facial challenge in light of the act/identity dynamic produced two noticeably different strategies. A team of lawyers with the ACLU of Georgia, headed by Kathleen L. Wilde, litigated Hardwick's case before the district court and the Eleventh Circuit and filed the plaintiff's briefs before the Supreme Court arguing that Georgia's petition for certiorari should be denied. After the Supreme Court granted certiorari, Laurence Tribe and Kathleen Sullivan convened a new group of attorneys to handle the case. Though both teams insisted on Hardwick's facial challenge, their approaches diverged.

Up to and including the briefs on the petition for certiorari, Hardwick's attorneys consistently framed his case as raising a question of homosexual rights, emphasizing his sexual-orientation identity and deemphasizing the acts for which he was arrested. In his complaint, Hardwick characterized himself as a "practicing homosexual," and his brief opposing Georgia's petition for a writ of certiorari stated that "as Hardwick regularly engages in private homosexual acts, and will do so in the future, he, like all other homosexuals in Georgia, is in imminent danger of arrest, prosecution, and potential imprisonment." This formulation implicitly equates all "homosexual acts" with sodomy and subsumes them both under the rubric of homosexual identity. It subtly distinguishes sodomitical conduct from homosexual personhood and presents the latter to the court as its real concern. Hardwick's first strategy was therefore to call on the court to protect a group of persons from intimate invasion by making their acts a merely adventitious (in Aristotelian terms, an accidental) characteristic that renders them vulnerable to arrest. Though the early briefs emphasized Hardwick's continuing commitment to "homosexual acts," they were written to *hold at bay* the conclusion that a "practicing homosexual" is a sodomite.

Hardwick's second team of attorneys, pursuing a different strategy, worked to *exclude* that conclusion altogether. After certiorari was granted, Hardwick's attorneys consistently emphasized that his challenge was a facial one. Accordingly they recast Hardwick's claim with painstaking care as a bid for protection along the register not of identities but of acts—"the associational intimacies of private life in the sanctuary of the home." Hardwick's Supreme Court brief acknowledged "homosexual sodomy" only once, and then it argued that Georgia's decision to prosecute selectively, targeting only homosexual sodomy, required "particularized explanation" above and beyond the mere recitation of moral condemnation of homosexuality. The brief attempted to distance the plaintiff from his identity as "homosexual" by designating it as part of the *state's* analysis rather than plaintiff's. Identity appears here in the defensive posture of a justification for discriminatory enforcement of a facially neutral statute challenged on its face.

The decision to alienate identity in this way reflects anxiety—amply justified in retrospect—about the relationship between Hardwick's entry into reasoning *as a homosexual* and his act of sodomy. Hardwick's Supreme Court briefs were drafted in the shadow of the possibility that sodomy can remain a "category of forbidden acts" and can form the object of a facial attack only if all mention of gay identity is excluded. If that possibility were to materialize, the briefs seem to suggest, Hardwick would emerge as "a homosexual" and simultaneously would claim sodomy as the peculiar province of "a personage, a past, a case history, and a childhood, in addition to being a type of life, a life form, and a morphology. . . ." And as Justice White's decision was soon to reveal, when identity captures Michael Hardwick's act of sodomy, it captures him too.

The almost Sisyphean struggles reflected in these briefs indicate a particular form of vulnerability borne by the "reasoning homosexual." Anyone occupying this position risks becoming the human sign that acts rhetoric and identities rhetoric are one and the same. Keeping these rhetorics apart may be the only way to resist the peculiar form that power takes when it appears, as it did in Justice White's majority opinion, as heterosexual reasoning.

B.   The Majority and Concurring Opinions

I holde a mouses herte nat worth a leek
That hath but oon hole for to sterte to.
—The Wife of Bath

While Michael Hardwick was subject to a terrible fixity at the crux of the act/identity intersection, Justice White and Chief Justice Burger disaggregated these discourses. By this means the majority Justices framed an unstable relationship between the rhetoric of acts, the rhetoric of identity, and Michael Hardwick's act of sodomy. Repointing the passage in which the Court presented its question indicates how the volatility of act and identity operate in this context. As Justice White informed us,

> The issue presented is whether the Federal Constitution confers a fundamental right upon *homosexuals* to engage in *sodomy* and hence invalidates the laws of the many States that still make *such conduct* illegal and have done so for a very long time.

What does the "such" of "such conduct" refer to? To sodomy generally? Or does it refer to sodomy as inflected by the homosexuals who do it? When Justice White invoked a historical argument to justify rejecting the fundamental rights claim framed in this way, he found that "[p]roscriptions against *that conduct* have ancient roots"—a conclusion that maintains a binocular vision of its object, hanging in delicate equipoise between act and identity.

Are "homosexuals" definitive of "such conduct" or not? These formulations (and others appearing throughout Justice White's opinion for the majority and Chief Justice Burger's concurring opinion) keep the Court in suspense: it remains ready to answer yes or no. Sodomy can receive its definitive characteristic from the "homosexuals" who do it, or can stand free of persons and be merely a "bad act." The majority Justices have enabled themselves to treat sodomy as a metonym for homosexual personhood—or not, as they wish. The question Justice White sets out to answer is thus apparently single but actually multiple: "such conduct" represents not a purely act-based categorical system but an unstable hybrid one, in which identity and conduct simultaneously diverge and implicate one another.

A classic deconstructive claim at this point is to say that detecting the instability of the decision's figural structure undermines it and threatens to dissolve its claims to authority. Such a claim is implicit in the virtually ubiquitous conclusion that the *Hardwick* majority vitiated its credibility when it framed the question of the case. But such instability is not per se a source of weakness; in the majority and concurring opinions it can be seen instead as positively constituting the peculiar powers and securities belonging to the style of reasoning adopted by the majority Justices. That reasoning style produces not only certain ideas about sodomy, but also, through them, certain positions from which to reason about it, and especially a *heterosexual* position from which to reason about it. We can say the Justices occupied this heterosexual posture even though we know nothing about their personal erotic preferences. It is a public posture, a public identity, and a point of vantage in public discourse. Unlike Hardwick's position—fixed, exposed, visible in the klieg lights trained on the homosexual sodomite—the Justices' heterosexual position is fluid, hidden, ever retaining a rhetorical place to hide.

A comparison of the Court's fundamental rights holding with its application of rational basis review reveals the advantages of the majority Justices' labile strategy by exposing the systematic ways in which acts and identities generate incoherence and instability. In his fundamental rights analysis, Justice White (cheered on by Chief Justice Burger) exploited the rhetoric of acts to make plausible his claim that sodomy has been, transhistorically and without surcease, the object of intense social disapprobation. In the rational basis holding, on the other hand, Justice White moved into a rhetoric of identities, holding that Georgia's sodomy statute rationally implements popular condemnation of *homosexuality*. Even within these distinct and opposed arguments, however, the two rhetorics are interlocked: that of acts implies and depends upon, even as it excludes, that of identities—and vice versa. The fundamental rights holding cannot actually constitute a coherent history of sodomy based on acts alone, for the acts that constitute sodomy are too various: Justice White achieves the appearance of coherence here only through persistent, implicit invocations of homosexual identity as the unifying theme of sodomy's prohibition. Conversely, his rational basis claim—that a facially neutral sodomy statute is reasonable because it makes a legitimate popular statement condemning homosexuality—is frontally incoherent. If the rational basis holding and its invocation of identity make sense at all, it is because they confer invisibility and immunity on a certain type of act. Indeed, heterosexual acts of sodomy are so thoroughly detached from the rhetoric of identity that those who do them are not even acknowledged as a class of persons.

The result of these arrangements is a chiastic relationship shaped like this:

	Primary Rhetoric	Secondary Rhetoric
Fundamental Rights Holding	Acts	Identities
Rational Basis Holding	Identities	Acts

This diagram schematizes a double bind. In everyday language, you are in a double bind when you cannot win because your victorious opponent is willing to be a hypocrite and to "damn you if you do and damn you if you don't." More strictly examined, a double bind involves a systematic arrangement of symbolic systems with at least three characteristics. First, two conceptual systems (or "discourses") are matched in their opposition to one another; one is consistently understood to be not only different from but the logical alternative of the other. Second, the preferred discourse actually requires the submerged one to make it work. It is at this point that a naive deconstructive claim is often made, that the secret inclusion of the nonpreferred discourse as a prerequisite for the smooth operation of the express one reveals the whole system to be fatally unstable. But third, that very instability can be the source of suppleness and resilience, because the two stacked discourses can be flipped: the one that was submerged and denied can become express, and it in turn can be covertly supported by the one that was preferred. The master of a double bind always has somewhere to go.

But who is to be the master? As Sedgwick concludes in her examination of a much wider range of paired opposites, or "binarisms," than I am studying here,

> rather than embrace an idealist faith in the necessarily, immanently self-corrosive efficacy of the contradictions inherent to these definitional binarisms, I will suggest instead that contests for discursive power can be specified as competitions for the material or rhetorical leverage required to set the terms of, and to profit in some way from, the operations of such an incoherence of definition.

The majority Justices in *Hardwick*, having at their disposal quite a bit of "material [and] rhetorical leverage," were able to exploit the systematic instability of the act/identity system by treating it as a double bind. Hardwick, although his attorneys strove with steady insight to tame the act/identity problem, was cinched by the double bind in the end.

It does not always have to be that way. The denied and submerged element in a double bind provides a point for resistance. Several authors in this volume recommend that pro-gay analysis directly address the problem of acts—a focus that suggests a sense that acts must be evaluated as a potential place from which to articulate the claims of gay men, lesbians, and bisexuals as oppositional. To be sure, the dominant group can at any moment make such resistance futile by flipping the system. And where the dominant group is willing, as were the majority Justices in *Hardwick*, to keep the paired dynamics of the double bind in action simultaneously, the danger of such destabilization is perpetually present, and imposes on the less powerful player a range of strategic options in which fluidity will always be at least potentially valuable.

1. Fundamental Rights

> *"When I started this, I didn't even know there was a sodomy law!"*
> —Michael Hardwick

> *"I had no idea that I was incriminating myself."*
> —James Moseley

The linchpin of the Supreme Court's fundamental rights holding in *Hardwick* is a history of anti-sodomy regulation that, both Justice White and Chief Justice Burger claim, is univocal and continuous over time. Justice White wrote for the Court that Hardwick could assert no "fundamental right to engage in homosexual sodomy" unless he could show that the liberty he aspired to is *"deeply rooted in this Nation's history and tradition."*

Though the Court could have held for the state of Georgia on a finding that Hardwick had failed to make a positive showing that the liberty he claimed was so "deeply rooted," Justice White's decision set out to prove more: that the liberty Hardwick claimed has been transhistorically rejected. It represents "such conduct" as a stable, univocal signifier for act(s) that have a monolithic history: the states "still make such conduct illegal and have done so for a very long time." And he went on to hold:

> It is obvious to us that [the requirement that fundamental rights be "deeply rooted in this Nation's history and tradition"] would [not] extend a fundamental right to homosexuals to engage in acts of consensual sodomy. Proscriptions against that conduct have ancient roots. Sodomy was a criminal offense at common law and was forbidden by the laws of the original 13 States when they ratified the Bill of Rights. In 1868, when the

Fourteenth Amendment was ratified, all but 5 of the 37 States in the Union had criminal sodomy laws. In fact, until 1961, all 50 States outlawed sodomy, and today, 24 States and the District of Columbia continue to provide criminal penalties for sodomy performed in private and between consenting adults. Against this background, to claim that a right to engage in such conduct is 'deeply rooted in this Nation's history and tradition' . . . is, at best, facetious.

Chief Justice Burger reached a similar conclusion: "there is no such thing as a fundamental right to commit homosexual sodomy" because to recognize such a right "would be to cast aside millennia of moral teaching."

It is now commonplace to disparage the *Hardwick* Justices' performance as historians, though it is less common to specify what was wrong with it. At first blush the problem with the Court's sweeping claim about the Georgia sodomy statute's "ancient roots" is simply that it rests on a single, unexamined secondary source, the University of Miami Survey. Justice White's clerk gave only the lightest copy-editing to the Survey's conclusion that "[c]urrent state laws prohibiting homosexual intercourse are ancient in origin," and the Court adopts this posture of slavish dependency unwisely, as even a passing acquaintance with the relevant literature indicates.

What gives structure to the Court's historiographical embarrassment is not the sheer bad scholarship represented by its uncritical reliance on the Survey, however, but its handling of the act/identity problem in history. To claim that present sodomy statutes prohibit the same thing as ancient sodomy prohibitions and as the colonial proscriptions which Justice White so lovingly cited, is to promote formal sameness over radical historical discontinuity. As the following discussion of sodomy's various definitions in Georgia will indicate, the history of sodomy shows a startling variation in the kinds of physical acts deemed to be sodomitical. Moreover, even when the condemned act and the degree of condemnation are the same in two instances, the *identities* which the act is supposed to demonstrate, and which bring the act under disapprobation, have differed sharply: sodomy has been objected to not because of the sexual but the *political* personality of its supposed performers; not for the erotic but the *religious* identity of those said to have done it. And sodomy may not be inflected by identities at all: it may be a species of bad act *simpliciter,* or be deemed bad because of other contextual factors that do not involve the articulation of contested identities. The Court submerges all these discontinuities, proposing, as the basis for its fundamental rights holding, a uniform history of sodomy throughout Western history.

That history, by default, is necessarily a history of sodomy not as various acts, but as *an act*. But because of the way Justice White framed the question before him, identities are always implicitly available as a rhetorical resource: "such conduct" can always escape its provisional meaning as a set of physical acts and recapture its reference to the "homosexuals" who are said to be its characteristic performers. Indeed, if it does not—if sodomy remains an act attributable to any and all persons—the Court's reliance on a discourse of acts endorses the condemnation of the very heterosexual conduct which the Justices worked so hard to exclude from the question on review.

In a pioneering article on *Hardwick,* Anne B. Goldstein exposed the way in which the majority Justices thus trapped themselves in their own logic. My reading of *Hardwick* depends pervasively on Goldstein's, but diverges from it by critiquing not only the content, but the method of the Court's history. Though Goldstein very deftly catches the Justices in their own double bind by forcing recognition that the Court's rationale cannot differentiate heterosexual sodomy, she does so by invoking a positivistic, objectively ascertained history of sodomy. To insist on such an account of sodomy's history excludes from consideration the crime's most salient characteristics: its mutability, its shiftingness, its plasticity, its volatility. A meta-historical approach to sodomy better reveals the ways in which its past is always a reflection of, and a rhetorical resource for, its present, and the ways in which precisely that rhetorical mirroring can expose the hidden artificer located in, and protecting, heterosexual identity. Concealment of heterosexual identity, even more than exposure of homosexual identity, is the product of *Hardwick*'s historiography: only by examining the judicial historian's method can we detect the flickering relationship between sodomy and heterosexual identity.

As Chief Justice Burger reminds us in celebratory cadences, sodomy is "a heinous act 'the very mention of which is a disgrace to human nature,' and 'a crime not fit to be named.'" And as Samuel Pepys, a busy-bodied know-it-all ensconced in the governing elite of seventeenth-century London, wrote to his diary, "blessed be God, I do not to this day know what is the meaning of this sin, nor which is the agent nor which the patient." *Not knowing* what sodomy is, *not naming* it at all, *not describing* it accurately, *not acknowledging* its presence, are all important parts of its historical profile. Obscurity is part of what sodomy is, a means by which it attains its social effects.

Pepys' is not a quaint and outdated posture. After *Hardwick* more acutely than before, ignorance of one's own vulnerability to a sodomy prosecution is a social privilege, a "privilege of unknowing." *Hardwick* renders inhabitants of homosexual identity markedly less capable of retaining this privilege, and confers it more peculiarly on inhabitants of heterosexual identity. But as long as acts discourse has legitimacy, and sodomy between persons of the different sexes is sodomy, inhabitants of heterosexual identity can find their blithe immunity stripped away. The instability of act and identity that the majority Justices deployed in *Hardwick* thus both protects and exposes heterosexual identity. Heterosexual reasoning about sodomy is, ultimately, about managing that instability.

The Supreme Court's decision to base its fundamental rights holding in *Hardwick* on a history of sodomy made sodomy's historiography a crucial means of instability management, a point that is exemplified by the Court's misrepresentation of the history of sodomy in Georgia itself. Justice White's and Chief Justice Burger's opinions concluded with composure that sodomy was a crime at common law when, in 1784, Georgia adopted the common law of England. Yet Georgian sodomy persistently resists arguments seeking to fix exactly what it was, and when.

* * *

Goldstein describes this record as "unclear" and tentatively concludes that "it appears that no proscription against buggery was 'in force' [in Georgia] at the time the Bill of Rights was adopted." Even such a provisional conclusion should probably await further investigation, however. Deciding whether the 1784 statute incorporated a ban on sodomy through its adoption of English common law requires some definition of English common law. Lawrence Friedman argues that colonial common law, where it existed, emerged in inchoate ways from "remembered folk-law" and "norms and practices that the colonists adopted because of who they were—the ideological element." Such sources could well have introduced incipient legal norms about sexual conduct that came to be understood and applied as common law. And what are the standards for determining that a statute is "usually in force?" Must there be prosecutions? Must there even be violations? To be sure, when in 1826 William Schley compiled the English statutes then in force in Georgia pursuant to the 1784 Act, he made no mention of sodomy. Goldstein cites Schley's compilation as evidence suggesting that sodomy was not implicitly included in the 1784 Act, but it is conceivable that Schley omitted sodomy because he thought the positive legislation promulgated in the years 1816 to 1817 was sufficient to displace any adoption of the English sodomy statute by the 1784 Act.

When an act is not fit to be named among Christians, a court seeking to find its first prohibition might be expected to have difficulty. But the real heavy lifting in the Supreme Court's management of sodomy's instability involves the scope of sodomy's prohibition. In *Hardwick,* the Court refused to specify what it steadfastly termed "sodomy." Although it set out to determine whether a right to commit sodomy was denied at constitutionally significant moments in the past, it failed to ask itself what an act of sodomy *is.* Throughout Justice White's footnote history of sodomy, and even more sweepingly in Chief Justice Burger's concurring opinion, sodomy is always and only "sodomy"; "homosexual sodomy" is treated as its equivalent, and no specification of bodily contacts is offered.

By this means the Court can hide—but just barely!—the problem exposed with great care by Goldstein: that *fellatio,* the act for which Hardwick was in fact arrested, cannot be shown to have been sodomy in 1791 or 1868. Instead the Court informs us that "Hardwick . . . was charged with violating the Georgia statute criminalizing *sodomy* by committing *that act* with another adult male. . . ." As the Court proposes to use it, the term "sodomy" is not a general analytic category that includes more specific bodily acts; it is not a legal fiction devised to describe a set of physical practices; rather, it *is* the act: "*sodomy*" is what Michael Hardwick *did.* But Goldstein argues that, in many of the states Justice White cited for his claim of historical continuity, fellatio was not sodomy at the time the Bill of Rights and the Fourteenth Amendment were adopted. Considering a series of cases, the earliest dated 1897, holding that oral-genital contact was not sodomy *then,* Goldstein infers that fellatio had not been sodomy *before* the cases were decided either. The force of her argument is to break the continuity of sodomy upon which the Supreme Court's reasoning depends for its constitutional justification of the Georgia statute "as applied" to Hardwick's act of fellatio.

I think the legal historical record is too equivocal to support Goldstein's claim at full strength, as a positive statement of what happened. It is not just that I hesitate to conclude from cases decided after a certain date that the meaning they attribute to a statute constitutes a retroactive construction of its meaning before that date. More to the point, it appears that the volatility of sodomy wheels with particular rapidity around the question whether sodomy includes oral sex. Once confronted with the question in the late nineteenth and early twentieth centuries, state courts diverged sharply, though without generating any striking patterns, in their willingness to define felatio as sodomy. In some states, courts refused to interpret sodomy statutes to include cunnilingus or fellatio. In many other states, courts were willing to take this step—even though their statutes were not discernably different in scope. Georgia courts, with admirable inconsistency, did both.

Uncertainty pervaded Georgian sodomy even when the legislature did define it, in 1833, as "the carnal knowledge and connection against the order of nature by man with man, or in the same unnatural manner with woman." It is only in the modern era that states have decided to put relentlessly asserted, but most often futile, void-for-vagueness challenges to sodomy statutes to rest by adopting, as Georgia did in 1968, statutory language specifying the exact body parts that must not touch one another. Where such amendments have not been adopted, obscure and highly general language describing sodomy keeps the tradition of sodomy's unnameability alive. The gradient between the general language of a definition, and the specific referential acts deemed to fall within it, establishes a semantic of *multivocality*: like a roadsign that spins on its post, the general term has a range of possible meanings, leaving open the possibility of nonce selections among them.

* * *

The volatility of sodomy is a problem. Goldstein tames it by giving sodomy a clearer historical transformation than the record will support. The Supreme Court goes to the other extreme. It exploits sodomy's volatility by eliding the acts into which sodomy dis- and reaggregates. The centrifugal forces of sodomy's internal differences are there within the field of the Court's decision, even though the Court does not explicitly mention them. Ultimately, the only coherence the Court can offer depends not on its express acts discourse, but on intermittent, and often only implicit, invocation of persons as bearers of sexual identity.

What gives definitional coherence to the *Hardwick* Court's sodomy, and makes possible its legally crucial equation of past with present prohibitions, is not conduct (for the classes of conduct defined as sodomy are mutable) but the *person of the homosexual*. The Court's apparent focus on acts, that is, depends on a less obvious focus on persons. Its strict act-based traditionalism covertly supplies a transhistorical homosexual person who has always (Justice White implies) been the real target of legal condemnation and who alone can unite within the tentative grasp of logical coherence the vast array of different sodomy statutes and of different sorts of conduct which the Court treats as the same.

The fundamental-rights holding's express discourse of acts displays *heterosexual* identity in equally crucial but diametrically opposed ways. First, and most noticeably, the Justices only fleetingly acknowledge heterosexual identity. But second, heterosexual identity is the location from which the Justices decide the case without appearing to. The very dynamic that Goldstein criticizes as a failure of logical consistency that traps the Justices in their own positivist history can also be described as a peculiarly resilient and supple form of rhetorical activity, in which heterosexual identity makes possible the Justices' self-fashioning as the exemplars of judicial restraint. By insisting that sodomy is nothing but a species of act and that as such it is identical to itself over time, Justice White pretends that his decision plays no intervening role in the history of sodomy, that he merely defers to past decisions about it. Framed as a case about mere bodily acts and not messy, contested, relentlessly political identities, *Hardwick* purports to take the Justices out of politics. Inasmuch as it is about acts and not identities, their ruling is a gesture of deference to majority sentiment. They carry their posture of neutrality so far that they even claim to refrain from deciding whether criminal prohibitions of "sodomy . . . between homosexuals in particular, are wise or desirable." Far from acting on anti-gay animus, they are, they say, evenhandedly indifferent to *all* sexual-orientation identities; they claim to be equally without a view "on whether laws against sodomy between consenting adults in general . . . are wise or desirable." While the fundamental rights holding, with its express reliance on a discourse of acts, ultimately confers on homosexuals and homosexuality glaring and definitive identities, heterosexuals and heterosexuality disappear from view, and take the Justices with them.

* * *

IV. CONCLUSION

As a conceptual matter, criticism of *Hardwick* isolates itself by posing the questions whether the Court's analysis is more fundamentally act-based or identity-based, and whether it can be better refuted from an act- or identity-based position. It is the unstable relationship between act and identity—not the preference of one to the other—that allows the Justices to exploit confusion about what sodomy is in ways that create opportunities for the exercise of homophobic power, and that create in particular the heterosexual subject position from which the opinion's reasoning issues.

Heterosexual identity as it is implied by the *Hardwick* Court's rational basis holding is (1) immune from the stigma and vulnerability of sodomy understood as a species of identities regulation; and (2) subject to the stigma and vulnerability of sodomy understood as a species of acts regulation. It is therefore (3) unstable, provisional, internally volatile—both sodomitical and not-sodomitical; and (4) able to maintain its appearance of coherence and its status of immunity by remaining *invisible*. The conceptual complexity of heterosexual superordination thus produced should be reflected in pro-gay strategic analysis.

Any attempt to exploit the rhetorical possibilities created as *Hardwick* becomes part of our legal and extra-legal culture . . . should embrace the multiplicity of strategies adopted by the Court. Anti-homophobic strategy should look *both* to identities *and* to acts as conceptual locations for opposition. More specifically, it is time to recognize that further destabilizing the identity "heterosexual" is an important goal that can be partly accomplished by an emphasis on acts. The subordinating dynamics that generate social privilege for its members will require that we deal directly with acts rhetoric.

To do so, however, those of us who inhabit gay and lesbian identity must loosen our grip on these identities, and admit into the field of our self-identification a cross-cutting set of identities founded on acts. This is a grave and dangerous move for a hated minority rhetorically involved in a double bind. Gay men, lesbians, and bisexuals must organize insistently around their stigmatized identities in order to remain players in the social process of giving those identities meaning, and in order to consolidate a recognizably "minority" movement in pluralistic politics. . . .

* * *

Two benefits emerge from an emphasis on acts, one material and one symbolic. First, it can engage anti-homophobic heterosexuals, providing a place for them in gay, lesbian, bisexual, and queer movements and making possible a range of alliances capable of diversifying *heterosexual* identity by displaying its multiple relationships to sodomy—both cross-sex and same-sex. Second, it forces heterosexual identity to share some of the glaring light that shines, thanks to *Hardwick*'s privacy holding, on the profane homosexual bed, and exposing the immunity which invisibly gives heterosexuality its rationale. These goals are important enough that pro-gay advocates should pursue them even at the expense of a rigid—and, as it happens, also unsafe—loyalty to identities.

Michael J. Sandel, *Moral Argument and Liberal Toleration: Abortion and Homosexuality*, 77 CAL. L. REV. 521, 521-31, 533-38 (1989)*

People defend laws against abortion and homosexual sodomy in two different ways: Some argue that abortion and homosexuality are morally reprehensible and therefore worthy of prohibition; others try to avoid passing judgment on the morality of these practices, and argue instead that, in a democracy, political majorities have the right to embody in law their moral convictions.

In a similar way, arguments against antiabortion and antisodomy laws take two different forms: Some say the laws are unjust because the practices they prohibit are morally permissible, indeed sometimes desirable; others oppose these laws without reference to the moral status of the practices at issue, and argue instead that individuals have a right to choose for themselves whether to engage in them.

These two styles of argument might be called, respectively, the "naive" and the "sophisticated." The naive view holds that the justice of laws depends on the moral worth of the conduct they prohibit or protect. The sophisticated view holds that the justice of such laws depends not on a substantive moral judgment about the conduct at stake, but instead on a more general theory about the respective claims of majority rule and individual rights, of democracy on the one hand, and liberty on the other.

I shall try in this paper to bring out the truth in the naive view, which I take to be this: The justice (or injustice) of laws against abortion and homosexual sodomy depends, at least in part, on the morality (or immorality) of those practices. This is the claim the sophisticated view rejects. In both its majoritarian and its liberal versions, the sophisticated view tries to set aside or "bracket" controversial moral and religious conceptions for purposes of justice. It insists that the justification of laws be neutral among competing visions of the good life.

In practice, of course, these two kinds of argument can be difficult to distinguish. In the debate over cases like *Roe v. Wade* and *Bowers v. Hardwick,* both camps tend to advance the naive view under cover of the sophisticated. (Such is the prestige of the sophisticated way of arguing.) For example, those who would ban abortion and sodomy out of abhorrence often argue in the name of deference to democracy and judicial restraint. Similarly, those who want permissive laws because they approve of abortion and homosexuality often argue in the name of liberal toleration.

This is not to suggest that all instances of the sophisticated argument are disingenuous attempts to promote a substantive moral conviction. Those who argue that law should be neutral among competing conceptions of the good life offer various grounds for their claim, including most prominently the following:

> (1) the *relativist* view says law should not affirm a particular moral conception because all morality is relative, and so there are no moral truths to affirm; (2) the *utilitarian* view argues that government neutrality will, for various reasons, promote the general welfare in the long run; (3) the *voluntarist* view holds that government should be neutral among conceptions of the good life in order to respect the capacity of persons as free citizens or autonomous agents to choose their conceptions for themselves; and (4) the *minimalist,* or pragmatic view says that, because people inevitably disagree about morality and religion, government should bracket these controversies for the sake of political agreement and social cooperation.

---

* Copyright 1989 by Michael J. Sandel. Reprinted by permission.

In order to bring out the truth in the naive way of arguing, I look to the actual arguments judges and commentators have made in recent cases dealing with abortion and homosexuality. Their arguments, unfailingly sophisticated, illustrate the difficulty of bracketing moral judgments for purposes of law. Because their reasons for trying to be neutral among conceptions of the good life are drawn primarily from voluntarist and minimalist assumptions, I focus on these arguments. Finally, although much of my argument criticizes leading theories of liberal toleration, I do not think it offers any comfort to majoritarianism. The cure for liberalism is not majoritarianism, but a keener appreciation of the role of substantive moral discourse in political and constitutional argument.

I

PRIVACY RIGHTS: INTIMACY AND AUTONOMY

In the constitutional right of privacy, the neutral state and the voluntarist conception of the person are often joined. In the case of abortion, for example, no state may, "by adopting one theory of life," override a woman's right to decide "whether or not to terminate her pregnancy." Government may not enforce a particular moral view, however widely held, for "no individual should be compelled to surrender the freedom to make that decision for herself simply because her 'value preferences' are not shared by the majority."

As with religious liberty and freedom of speech, so with privacy, the ideal of neutrality often reflects a voluntarist conception of human agency. Government must be neutral among conceptions of the good life in order to respect the capacity of persons to choose their values and relationships for themselves. So close is the connection between privacy rights and the voluntarist conception of the self that commentators frequently assimilate the values of privacy and autonomy: Privacy rights are said to be "grounded in notions of individual autnomy," because "[t]he human dignity protected by the constitutional guarantees would be seriously diminished if people were not free to choose and adopt a lifestyle which allows expression of their uniqueness and individuality." In "recognizing a constitutional right to privacy," the Court has given effect to the view "that persons have the capacity to live autonomously and the right to exercise that capacity." Supreme Court decisions voiding laws against contraceptives "not only protect the individual who chooses not to procreate, but also the autonomy of a couple's association." They protect men and women "against an unchosen commitment" to unwanted children, and "against a compelled identification with the social role of parent."

In Supreme Court decisions and dissents alike, the justices have often tied privacy rights to voluntarist assumptions. The Court has thus characterized laws banning the use of contraceptives as violating "the constitutional protection of individual autonomy in matters of childbearing." It has defended the right to an abortion on the grounds that few decisions are "more properly private, or more basic to individual dignity and autonomy, than a woman's decision . . . whether to end her pregnancy." Justice Douglas, concurring in an abortion case, emphasized that the right of privacy protects such liberties as "the autonomous control over the development and expression of one's intellect, interests, tastes, and personality," as well as "freedom of choice in the basic decisions of one's life respecting marriage, divorce, procreation, contraception, and the education and upbringing of children." Writing in dissent, Justice Marshall found a regulation limiting the hair length of policemen "inconsistent with the values of privacy, self-identity, autonomy, and personal integrity" he believed the Constitution was designed to protect. And four justices would have extended privacy protection to consensual homosexual activity on the grounds that "much of the richness of a relationship will come from the freedom an individual has to *choose* the form and nature of these intensely personal bonds."

Although the link between privacy and autonomy is now so familiar as to seem natural, even necessary, the right of privacy need not presuppose a voluntarist conception of the person. In fact, through most of its history in American law, the right of privacy has implied neither the ideal of the neutral state nor the ideal of a self freely choosing its aims and attachments.

Where the contemporary right of privacy is the right to engage in certain conduct without government restraint, the traditional version is the right to keep certain personal facts from public view. The new privacy protects a person's "independence in making certain kinds of important decisions," whereas the old privacy protects a person's interest "in avoiding disclosure of personal matters."

The tendency to identify privacy with autonomy not only obscures these shifting understandings of privacy; it also restricts the range of reasons for protecting it. Although the new privacy typically relies on voluntarist justifications, it can also be justified in other ways. A right to be free of governmental interference in matters of marriage, for example, can be defended not only in the name of individual choice, but also in the name of the intrinsic value or social importance of the practice it protects. As the Court has acknowledged, "certain kinds of personal bonds have played a critical role in the culture and traditions of the Nation by cultivating and transmitting shared ideals and beliefs; they thereby foster diversity and act as critical buffers between the individual and the power of the State." The Court's greater tendency, however, has been to view privacy in voluntarist terms, as protecting "the ability independently to define one's identity."

II
FROM THE OLD PRIVACY TO THE NEW

The right to privacy first gained legal recognition in the United States as a doctrine of tort law, not constitutional law. In an influential article in 1890, Louis Brandeis, then a Boston lawyer, and his one-time law partner Samuel Warren argued that the civil law should protect "the right to privacy." Far from later-day concerns with sexual freedoms, Brandeis and Warren's privacy was quaint by comparison, concerned with the publication of high society gossip by the sensationalist press, or the unauthorized use of people's portraits in advertising. Gradually at first, then more frequently in the 1930s, this right to privacy gained recognition in the civil law of most states. Prior to the 1960s, however, privacy received scant attention in constitutional law.

Two members of the Supreme Court first addressed the right of privacy as such in 1961 when a Connecticut pharmacist challenged the state's ban on contraceptives in *Poe v. Ullman*. Although the majority dismissed the case on technical grounds, Justices Douglas and Harlan dissented, arguing that the law violated the right of privacy. The privacy they defended was privacy in the traditional sense. The right at stake was not the right to use contraceptives but the right to be free of the surveillance that enforcement would require. "If we imagine a regime of full enforcement of the law," wrote Douglas, "we would reach the point where search warrants issued and officers appeared in bedrooms to find out what went on. . . . If [the State] can make this law, it can enforce it. And proof of its violation necessarily involves an inquiry into the relations between man and wife." Banning the sale of contraceptives would be different from banning their use, Douglas observed. Banning the sale would restrict access to contraceptives but would not expose intimate relations to public inspection. Enforcement would take police to the drugstore, not the bedroom, and so would not offend privacy in the traditional sense.

Justice Harlan also objected to the law on grounds that distinguish the old privacy from the new. He did not object that the law against contraceptives failed to be neutral among competing moral conceptions. Although Harlan acknowledged that the law was based on the belief that contraception is immoral in itself, and encourages such "dissolute action" as fornication and adultery by minimizing their "disastrous consequence," he did not find this failure of neutrality contrary to the Constitution. In a statement clearly opposed to the strictures of neutrality, Harlan argued that morality is a legitimate concern of government.

> The very inclusion of the category of morality among state concerns indicates that society is not limited in its objects only to the physical well-being of the community, but has traditionally concerned itself with the moral soundness of its people as well. Indeed to attempt a line between public behavior and that which is purely consensual or solitary would be to withdraw from community concern a range of subjects with which every society in civilized times has found it necessary to deal.

Though he rejected the ideal of the neutral state, Harlan did not conclude that Connecticut could prohibit married couples from using contraceptives. Like Douglas, he reasoned that enforcing the law would intrude on the privacy essential to the prized institution of marriage. He objected to the violation of privacy in the traditional sense, to "the intrusion of the whole machinery of the criminal law into the very heart of marital privacy, requiring husband and wife to render account before a criminal tribunal of their uses of that intimacy." According to Harlan, the state was entitled to embody in law the belief that contraception is immoral, but not to implement "the obnoxiously intrusive means it ha[d] chosen to effectuate that policy."

Four years later, in *Griswold v. Connecticut,* the dissenters prevailed. The Supreme Court invalidated Connecticut's law against contraceptives and for the first time explicitly recognized a constitutional right of privacy. Although the right was located in the Constitution rather than tort law, it remained tied to the traditional notion of privacy as the interest in keeping intimate affairs from public view. The violation of privacy consisted in the intrusion required to enforce the law, not the restriction on the freedom to use contraceptives. "Would we allow the police to search the sacred precincts of marital bedrooms for telltale signs of the use of contraceptives?," wrote Justice Douglas for the Court. "The very idea is repulsive to the notions of privacy surrounding the marriage relationship."

The justification for the right was not voluntarist but unabashedly teleological; the privacy the Court vindicated was not for the sake of letting people lead their sexual lives as they choose, but rather for the sake of affirming and protecting the social institution of marriage.

> Marriage is a coming together for better or for worse, hopefully enduring, and intimate to the degree of being sacred. It is an association that promotes a way of life, . . . a harmony in living, . . . a bilateral loyalty. . . . [I]t is an association for as noble a purpose as any involved in our prior decisions.

Although commentators and judges often view *Griswold* as a dramatic constitutional departure, the privacy right it proclaimed was consistent with traditional notions of privacy going back to the turn of the century. From the standpoint of shifting privacy conceptions, the more decisive turn came seven years later in *Eisenstadt v. Baird,* a seemingly similar case. Like *Griswold,* it involved a state law restricting contraceptives. In *Eisenstadt,* however, the challenged law restricted the distribution of contraceptives, not their use. While it therefore limited access to contraceptives, its enforcement could not be said to require governmental surveillance of intimate activities. It did not violate privacy in the traditional sense. Furthermore, the law prohibited distributing contraceptives only to unmarried persons, and so did not burden the institution of marriage as the Connecticut law did.

Despite these differences, the Supreme Court struck down the law with only a single dissent. Its decision involved two innovations, one explicit, the other unacknowledged. The explicit innovation redescribed the bearers of privacy rights from persons *qua* participants in the social institution of marriage to persons *qua* individuals, independent of their roles or attachments. As the Court explained, "It is true that in *Griswold* the right of privacy in question inhered in the marital relationship. Yet the marital couple is not an independent entity with a mind and heart of its own, but an association of two individuals each with a separate intellectual and emotional makeup."

The subtler, though no less fateful change in *Eisenstadt* was in the shift from the old privacy to the new. Rather than conceiving privacy as freedom from surveillance or disclosure of intimate affairs, the Court found that the right to privacy now protected the freedom to engage in certain activities without governmental restriction. Although privacy in *Griswold* prevented intrusion into "the sacred precincts of marital bedrooms," privacy in *Eisenstadt* prevented intrusion into *decisions* of certain kinds. Moreover, as the meaning of privacy changed, so did its justification. The Court protected privacy in *Eisenstadt* not for the social practices it promoted but for the individual choice it secured. "If the right of privacy means anything, it is the right of the *individual,* married or single, to be free from unwarranted governmental intrusion into matters so fundamentally affecting a person as the decision whether to bear or beget a child."

One year later, in *Roe v. Wade,* the Supreme Court gave the new privacy its most controversial application by striking down a Texas law against abortion and extending privacy to "encompass a woman's decision whether or not to terminate her pregnancy." First with contraception, then with abortion, the right of privacy had become the right to make certain sorts of choices, free of interference by the state. The choice had also to be free of interference by husbands or parents. In *Planned Parenthood of Missouri v. Danforth,* the Court struck down a law requiring a husband's consent, or parental consent in the case of unmarried minors, as a condition for an abortion. Since the state may not prevent even minors from having abortions in the first trimester, it cannot delegate to "a third party" such as a husband or parent the authority to do so.

The voluntarist grounds of the new privacy found explicit statement in a 1977 case invalidating a New York law prohibiting the sale of contraceptives to minors under age sixteen. For the first time, the Court used the language of autonomy to describe the interest privacy protects, and argued openly for the shift from the old privacy to the new. Writing for the Court in *Carey v. Population Services International,* Justice Brennan admitted that *Griswold* focused on the fact that a law forbidding the use of contraceptives can bring the police into marital bedrooms. "But subsequent decisions have made clear that the constitutional protection of individual autonomy in matters of childbearing is not dependent on that element." Surveying the previous cases, he emphasized that *Eisenstadt* protected the "*decision* whether to bear or beget a child," and *Roe* protected "a woman's *decision* whether or not to terminate her pregnancy." He concluded that "the teaching of *Griswold* is that the Constitution protects individual decisions in matters of childbearing from unjustified intrusion by the State."

Given the voluntarist interpretation of privacy, restricting the *sale* of contraceptives violates privacy as harshly as banning their *use*; the one limits choice as surely as the other. "Indeed, in practice," Brennan observed, "a prohibition against all sales, since more easily and less offensively enforced, might have an even more devastating effect upon the freedom to choose contraception." Ironically, the very fact that a ban on sales does *not* threaten the old privacy makes it a greater threat to the new.

Later decisions upholding abortion rights also used the language of autonomy to describe the privacy interest at stake. The Court held in a recent opinion that "[f]ew decisions are ... more properly private, or more basic to individual dignity and autonomy than a woman's decision ... whether to end her pregnancy. A woman's right to make that choice freely is fundamental."

Despite its increasing tendency to identify privacy with autonomy, the Court refused, in a 5-4 decision, to extend privacy protection to consensual homosexual activity. Writing for the majority, Justice White emphasized that the Court's previous privacy cases protected choice only with respect to child rearing and education, family relationships, procreation, marriage, contraception, and abortion. "[W]e think it evident," he held, "that none of the rights announced in those cases bears any resemblance to the claimed constitutional right of homosexuals to engage in acts of sodomy. . . ." He also rejected the claim that Georgia's citizens could not embody in law their belief "that homosexual sodomy is immoral and unacceptable." Neutrality to the contrary, "[t]he law . . . is constantly based on notions of morality, and if all laws representing essentially moral choices are to be invalidated under the Due Process Clause, the courts will be very busy indeed."

Writing for the four dissenters, Justice Blackmun argued that the Court's previous privacy decisions did not depend on the virtue of the practices they protected but on the principle of free individual choice in intimate matters. "We protect those rights not because they contribute . . . to the general public welfare, but because they form so central a part of an individual's life. '[T]he concept of privacy embodies the "moral fact that a person belongs to himself and not others nor to society as a whole.'"

Blackmun argued for the application of earlier privacy rulings in the consideration of homosexual practices by casting the Court's concern for conventional family ties in individualist terms: "We protect the decision whether to have a child because parenthood alters so dramatically an individual's self-definition . . . . And we protect the family because it contributes so powerfully to the happiness of individuals, not because of a preference for stereotypical households." Because the right of privacy in sexual relationships protects "the freedom an individual has to *choose* the form and nature of these intensely personal bonds," it protects homosexual activity no less than other intimate choices.

Defending the ideal of the neutral state, Blackmun added that traditional religious condemnations of homosexuality "give[ ] the State no license to impose their judgments on the entire citizenry." To the contrary, the State's appeal to religious teachings against homosexuality undermines its claim that the law "represents a legitimate use of secular coercive power."

Despite the Court's reluctance to extend privacy rights to homosexuals, the privacy cases of the last twenty-five years offer ample evidence of assumptions drawn from the liberal conception of the person. They also raise two questions about the liberalism they reflect: First whether bracketing controversial moral issues is even possible; and second whether the voluntarist conception of privacy limits the range of reasons for protecting privacy.

* * *

IV

THE VOLUNTARIST CASE FOR TOLERATION:
HOMOSEXUALITY

The dissenters' argument for toleration in *Bowers v. Hardwick* illustrates the difficulties with the version of liberalism that ties toleration to autonomy rights alone. In refusing to extend the right of privacy to homosexuals, the majority in *Bowers* declared that none of the rights announced in earlier privacy cases resembled the rights homosexuals were seeking: "No connection between family, marriage, or procreation on the one hand and homosexual activity on the other has been demonstrated . . .." Any reply to the Court's position would have to show some connection between the practices already subject to privacy protection and the homosexual practices not yet protected. What then is the resemblance between heterosexual intimacies on the one hand, and homosexual intimacies on the other, such that both are entitled to a constitutional right of privacy?

This question might be answered in at least two different ways—one voluntarist, the other substantive. The first argues from the autonomy the practices reflect, whereas the second appeals to the human goods the practices realize. The voluntarist answer holds that people should be free to choose their intimate associations for themselves, regardless of the virtue or popularity of the practices they choose so long as they do not harm others. In this view, homosexual relationships resemble the heterosexual relationships the Court has already protected in that all reflect the choices of autonomous selves.

By contrast, the substantive answer claims that much that is valuable in conventional marriage is also present in homosexual unions. In this view, the connection between heterosexual and homosexual relations is not that both result from individual choice but that both realize important human goods. Rather than rely on autonomy alone, this second line of reply articulates the virtues homosexual intimacy may share with heterosexual intimacy, along with any distinctive virtues of its own. It defends homosexual privacy the way *Griswold* defended marital privacy, by arguing that, like marriage, homosexual union may also be "intimate to the degree of being sacred . . . a harmony in living . . . a bilateral loyalty," an association for a "noble . . . purpose."

Of these two possible replies, the dissenters in *Bowers* relied wholly on the first. Rather than protect homosexual intimacies for the human goods they share with intimacies the Court already protects, Justice Blackmun cast the Court's earlier cases in individualist terms, and found their reading applied equally to homosexuality because "much of the richness of a relationship will come from the freedom an individual has to choose the form and nature of these intensely personal bonds." At issue was not homosexuality as such but respect for the fact that "different individuals will make different choices" in deciding how to conduct their lives.

Justice Stevens, in a separate dissent, also avoided referring to the values homosexual intimacy may share with heterosexual love. Instead, he wrote broadly of "'the individual's right to make certain unusually important decisions'" and "'respect for the dignity of individual choice,'" rejecting the notion that such liberty belongs to heterosexuals alone. "From the standpoint of the individual, the homosexual and the heterosexual have the same interest in deciding how he will live his own life, and, more narrowly, how he will conduct himself in his personal and voluntary associations with his companions."

The voluntarist argument so dominates the *Bowers* dissents that it seems difficult to imagine a judicial rendering of the substantive view. But a glimmer of this view can be found in the appeals court opinion in the same case. The United States Court of Appeals had ruled in Hardwick's favor and had struck down the law under which he was convicted. Like Blackmun and Stevens, the appeals court constructed an analogy between privacy in marriage and privacy in homosexual relations. But unlike the Supreme Court dissenters, it did not rest the analogy on voluntarist grounds alone. It argued instead that both practices may realize important human goods.

The marital relationship is significant, wrote the court of appeals, not only because of its procreative purpose but also "because of the unsurpassed opportunity for mutual support and self-expression that it provides." It recalled the Supreme Court's observation in *Griswold* that "[m]arriage is a coming together for better or for worse, hopefully enduring, and intimate to the degree of being sacred." And it went on to suggest that the qualities the Court so prized in *Griswold* could be present in homosexual unions as well: "For some, the sexual activity in question here serves the same purpose as the intimacy of marriage."

Ironically, this way of extending privacy rights to homosexuals depends on an "old-fashioned" reading of *Griswold* as protecting the human goods realized in marriage, a reading the Court has long since renounced in favor of an individualist reading. By drawing on the teleological dimension of *Griswold,* the substantive case for homosexual privacy offends the liberalism that insists on neutrality. It grounds the right of privacy on the good of the practice it would protect, and so fails to be neutral among conceptions of the good.

The more frequently employed precedent for homosexual rights is not *Griswold* but *Stanley v. Georgia,* which upheld the right to possess obscene materials in the privacy of one's home. *Stanley* did not hold that the obscene films found in the defendant's bedroom served a "noble purpose," only that he had a right to view them in private. The toleration *Stanley* defended was wholly independent of the value or importance of the thing being tolerated.

In the 1980 case of *People v. Onofre,* the New York Court of Appeals vindicated privacy rights for homosexuals on precisely these grounds. The court reasoned that if, following *Stanley,* there is a right to the "satisfaction of sexual desires by resort to material condemned as obscene," there should also be a right "to seek sexual gratification from what at least once was commonly regarded as 'deviant' conduct," so long as it is private and consensual. The court emphasized its neutrality toward the conduct it protected: "We express no view as to any theological, moral or psychological evaluation of consensual sodomy. These are aspects of the issue on which informed, competent authorities and individuals may and do differ." The court's role was simply to ensure that the State bracketed these competing moral views, rather than embodying any one of them in law.

The case for toleration that brackets the morality of homosexuality has a powerful appeal. In the face of deep disagreement about values, it seems to ask the least of the contending parties. It offers social peace and respect for rights without the need for moral conversion. Those who view sodomy as sin need not be persuaded to change their minds, only to tolerate those who practice it in private. By insisting only that each respect the freedom of others to live the lives they choose, this toleration promises a basis for political agreement that does not await shared conceptions of morality.

Despite its promise, however, the neutral case for toleration is subject to two related difficulties. First, as a practical matter, it is by no means clear that social cooperation can be secured on the strength of autonomy rights alone, absent some measure of agreement on the moral permissibility of the practices at issue. It may not be accidental that the first practices subject to the right of privacy were accorded constitutional protection in cases that spoke of the sancity of marriage and procreation. Only later did the Court abstract privacy rights from these practices and protect them without reference to the human goods they were once thought to make possible. This suggests that the voluntarist justification of privacy rights is dependent—politically as well as philosphically—on some measure of agreement that the practices protected are morally permissible.

A second difficulty with the voluntarist case for toleration concerns the quality of respect it secures. As the New York case suggests, the analogy with *Stanley* tolerates homosexuality at the price of demeaning it; it puts homosexual intimacy on a par with obscenity—a base thing that should nonetheless be tolerated so long as it takes place in private. If *Stanley* rather than *Griswold* is the relevant analogy, the interest at stake is bound to be reduced, as the New York court reduced it, to "sexual gratification." (The only intimate relationship at stake in *Stanley* was between a man and his pornography.)

The majority in *Bowers* exploited this assumption by ridiculing the notion of a "fundamental right to engage in homosexual sodomy." The obvious reply is that *Bowers* is no more about a right to homosexual sodomy that *Griswold* was about a right to heterosexual intercourse. But by refusing to articulate the human goods that homosexual intimacy may share with heterosexual unions, the voluntarist case for toleration forfeits the analogy with *Griswold* and makes the ridicule difficult to refute.

The problem with the neutral case for toleration is the opposite side of its appeal; it leaves wholly unchallenged the adverse views of homosexuality itself. Unless those views can be plausibly addressed, even a Court ruling in their favor is unlikely to win for homosexuals more than a thin and fragile toleration. A fuller respect would require, if not admiration, at least some appreciation of the lives homosexuals live. Such appreciation, however, is unlikely to be cultivated by a legal and political discourse conducted in terms of autonomy rights alone.

The liberal may reply that autonomy arguments in court need not foreclose more substantive, affirmative arguments elsewhere; bracketing moral argument for constitutional purposes does not mean bracketing moral argument altogether. Once their freedom of choice in sexual practice is secured, homosexuals can seek, by argument and example, to win from their fellow citizens a deeper respect than autonomy can supply.

The liberal reply, however, underestimates the extent to which constitutional discourse has come to constitute the terms of political discourse in American public life. While most at home in constitutional law, the main motifs of contemporary liberalism—rights as trumps, the neutral state, and the unencumbered self—figure with increasing prominence in our moral and political culture. Assumptions drawn from constitutional discourse increasingly set the terms of political debate in general.

CONCLUSION

Admittedly, the tendency to bracket substantive moral questions makes it difficult to argue for toleration in the language of the good. Defining privacy rights by defending the practices privacy protects seems either reckless or quaint; reckless because it rests so much on moral argument, quaint because it recalls the traditional view that ties the case for privacy to the merits of the conduct privacy protects. But as the abortion and sodomy cases illustrate, the attempt to bracket moral questions faces difficulties of its own. They suggest the truth in the "naive" view, that the justice or injustice of laws against abortion and homosexual sodomy may have something to do with the morality or immorality of these practices after all.

Kendall Thomas, *Beyond the Privacy Principle*, 92 COLUM. L. REV. 1431, 1431-43, 1459-69, 1476-90, 1509-13 (1992)*

The law may not be able to make a man love me,
but at least it can keep him from lynching me.
                                                    —Martin Luther King, Jr.

INTRODUCTION

* * *

In the past five years, the Court's decision in [*Bowers v.*] *Hardwick* has been the object of considerable scholarly commentary. Much of the critical literature has revolved around the question whether the Court's refusal to invalidate the Georgia "sodomy" statute challenged in *Hardwick* comports with, or contradicts, its earlier decisions regarding the so-called constitutional "right to privacy." Given the historically close relationship between the terms of judicial discourse and legal academic discourse, it is not surprising that scholarly analysis of *Hardwick* has been dominated by the same conceptual framework in which the Court articulated and adjudicated Hardwick's claim. However, if one believes, as I do, that the intellectual concerns and commitments of students of constitutional jurisprudence overlap but are not congruent with those of the Supreme Court itself, one might well ask whether this strategy of assessing the Court's work exclusively or primarily on its own terms helps or hinders the distinctively *critical* project of constitutional scholarship.

Two separate but related questions may be posed in this connection. In theoretical discourse, does the language of privacy provide an adequate vocabulary for critically assessing the Court's reasoning and result in *Hardwick*? In political discourse, does it permit a sufficiently precise articulation of the concrete social interests for which *Hardwick* served as a constitutional flashpoint? A careful reading of the text and surrounding context of the *Hardwick* decision suggests that the rhetoric of privacy is indeed incapable of discharging either of these tasks. The limitations of privacy rhetoric as a conceptual resource for discussing the constitutional issues at stake in *Hardwick* lead me to follow a somewhat different itinerary than has been pursued in most scholarly discussion of the decision.

* * *

I. THE PRISONHOUSE OF PRIVACY

A. *Trail of Blood: The Untold Story of* Bowers v. Hardwick

By 1986, when the Supreme Court rendered its judgment in *Bowers v. Hardwick,* the concept of the right to privacy had become a central term in the lexicon of twentieth century constitutional argument. From our present perspective, it may be difficult to imagine another root concept that would have served as well as this one to articulate and advance the concerns at stake in *Griswold v. Connecticut* and its progeny. With *Hardwick,* however, privacy's term of service seems to have run its course. This, at least, is the lesson I draw from the case and from the terms in which the Supreme Court discussed the constitutional issues it presented.

Let me acknowledge at the outset that the view of *Hardwick* urged here may seem something of a paradox. *Hardwick* seems to be the most private of all privacy

---

cases. After all, one might note, Michael Hardwick was arrested in the privacy of his own bedroom, for conduct that took place there. On this view, *Hardwick* lends itself perfectly to analysis through the lens of privacy, since it appears to present a textbook example of the kind of state practices against which the doctrine was designed to protect. In this perspective, the most likely explanation for the *Hardwick* Court's refusal to apply the doctrine to the private consensual sexual conduct of Michael Hardwick and his partner has more to do with the disposition of the Supreme Court than with any purported defects in the doctrine of constitutional privacy itself.

The first step in response to this claim is to note two crucial and contestable factual predicates on which it may be said to rest. The first assumption is that the relevant focal point for constitutional analysis of the statute challenged in *Hardwick* is, indeed, the time and place of his arrest. The second assumption is that *Hardwick* was in fact arrested for engaging in the act of homosexual sodomy with which he was formally charged. I want to suggest that both of these assumptions are belied by other, and to my mind, more significant facts of the case. Thus, to the extent that the argument for viewing *Hardwick* in particular through the prism of privacy depends on these empirical premises, it is deeply flawed.

In order to establish this contention, we need to recall certain "public" facts about *Bowers v. Hardwick* that never found their way into the record before the Supreme Court. Taken together, they tell an all too typical story of the gay and lesbian experience under the American legal system. Although we shall have occasion to review that larger history, my immediate theoretical interest is in the local history of the *Hardwick* case itself. When *Hardwick* is viewed in the light of this history, it becomes possible to argue—indeed impossible to deny—that the case presents a number of issues that require a more realistic analysis than the privacy principle can provide.

Michael Hardwick's first encounter with the police power of the state of Georgia took place one morning a block away from the gay bar in Atlanta where he worked. An Atlanta police officer named K.R. Torick stopped Hardwick after seeing him throw a beer bottle into a trashcan outside the bar. As Hardwick recounts the story, the officer "made me get in the car and asked me what I was doing. I told him that I worked there, which immediately identified me as a homosexual, because he knew it was a homosexual bar." Torick then issued Hardwick a ticket for drinking in public. Because of a discrepancy on the ticket between the day and the date he was to appear in court, Hardwick failed to appear. Within two hours of Hardwick's scheduled appearance, Torick went to Hardwick's house with a warrant for his arrest, only to find that he was not at home. When Hardwick returned to his apartment, his roommate told him of the police officer's visit. Hardwick then went to the Fulton County courthouse, where he paid a $50 fine. In Hardwick's words:

> I told the county clerk the cop had already been at my house with a warrant and he said that was impossible. He said it takes forty-eight hours to process a warrant. He wrote me a receipt just in case I had any problems with it further down the road. That was that, and I thought I had taken care of it and everything was finished, and I didn't give it much thought.

Three weeks later, Hardwick arrived home from work to find three men whom he did not know outside his house. In his account of the incident, Hardwick admits that he has no proof that these men were police officers, "but they were very straight, middle thirties, civilian clothes."

> I got out of the car, turned around, and they said 'Michael' and I said yes, and they proceeded to beat the hell out of me. Tore all the cartilage out of my nose, kicked me in the face, cracked about six of my ribs. I passed out. I don't know how long I was unconscious. . . . I managed to crawl up the stairs into the house, into the back bedroom. What I didn't realize was that I'd left a trail of blood all the way back.

A few days after this incident, and nearly a month after his first visit, Officer Torick again appeared at Hardwick's home. Torick found Hardwick in his bedroom having sex with another man.

> He said, My name is Officer Torick. Michael Hardwick, you are under arrest. I said, For what? What are you doing in my bedroom? He said, I have a warrant for your arrest. I told him the warrant isn't any good. He said, It doesn't matter, because I was acting under good faith.

Torick handcuffed Hardwick and his partner and took them to jail, where they were booked, fingerprinted, and photographed. As the two men were taken to a holding tank, Hardwick recalls that the arresting officer "made sure everyone in the holding cells and guards and people who were processing us knew I was in there for 'cock-sucking' and that I should be able to get what I was looking for. The guards were having a real good time with that." Some hours later, Hardwick and his partner were transferred to another part of the building in which he was being held, in the course of which the jail officers made it clear to the other inmates that the men were gay, remarking "Wait until we put [him] into the bullpen. Well, fags shouldn't mind—after all, that's why they are here." Hardwick and his partner remained in jail for the greater part of the day, when friends were permitted to post bail for their release.

Shortly after his release, Hardwick accepted an offer from the Georgia affiliate of the American Civil Liberties Union to undertake his defense in the state courts. Hardwick and his attorneys planned to challenge the constitutionality of the state sodomy law's criminalization of the sexual conduct for which he had been arrested. Before the case came to trial, however, the Fulton County District Attorney declined to seek a grand jury indictment against Hardwick on the sodomy charges. In legal terms, this did not mean that the matter was at an end; the governing statute of limitations rendered Hardwick subject to indictment on the sodomy charges at any time within the next four years. In political terms, it meant that Hardwick (and gays and lesbians throughout the state) continued to be vulnerable to harassment and violence that would likely go unchecked and unchallenged so long as the sodomy statute remained in the Georgia criminal code. Faced with this prospect, Hardwick agreed to take his constitutional claim to the federal courts.

For those who are familiar with the history of sodomy statutes, the story recounted here contains few surprises. *Hardwick* is merely the most visible recent chapter of a larger, unfinished plot. What bears remarking is the degree to which so much of the background biography of *Hardwick* resists translation into the language and logic of sexual privacy. Obviously, I do not want to deny the significance of Hardwick's arrest or discount the importance of the fact that the arrest took place in his bedroom. Nor do I wish to suggest that Officer Torick did not in fact find and arrest Hardwick for engaging in sexual acts prohibited by Georgia criminal law. I mean to make two rather different observations.

The first is that Hardwick's arrest in the privacy of his bedroom was the culmination of a series of events that was set in motion long before, beginning with his public, on-the-street encounter with Officer Torick outside that Atlanta gay bar. A second, related observation is that while Hardwick had certainly engaged in sexual acts punishable by eight to twenty years imprisonment under Georgia law, it is not implausible to think that Hardwick would never have been charged for violating that law had Officer Torick not gone to Hardwick's home to serve the expired warrant. Recall that the first piece of information Hardwick gave Officer Torick outside the bar was about the kind of work he did, not about the kind of sex he practiced. In my view, this aspect of the case provides some basis for a belief that the officer's visit on the day of the arrest had less to do with what Hardwick had done, than with his discovery some weeks before of who and what Hardwick was. Had Michael Hardwick not first been ascribed a homosexual *identity,* it is unlikely that he would ever have been observed or arrested for engaging in prohibited homosexual acts.

Two related points of theoretical import are suggested by this sequence of events. I shall have more to say below about their precise doctrinal ramifications. Here it suffices to note the respects in which *Hardwick* requires a broader conception of the constitutional interests at stake in the case than the privacy paradigm allows.

First, as a temporal matter, Hardwick's arrest at his home must be situated in a *chronological sequence* whose inaugural moment was the earlier, involuntary revelation of his sexuality during his initial encounter with Officer Torick. Furthermore, an adequate analytical "time chart" of *Hardwick* must also include the bloody beating Hardwick sustained outside his home, as well as the threat of sexualized violence to which he and his partner were deliberately exposed while in police custody. These incidents are not isolable events; they inhabit the same temporal field, whose horizons exceed privacy's chronometry.

Second, as a conceptual matter, when situated in its broader factual context, the formal claim raised and rejected in *Hardwick* must be viewed as a semantic conductor for a complex current of substantive concerns. The criminalization of homosexual sodomy challenged in *Hardwick* belongs to, and must be analyzed as, a *constellation* of diverse practices. My image of homosexual sodomy statutes as the site of a "constellation" of practices is intended to capture the essential inseparability of these laws from the actual methods—public or private, official or unofficial, sanctioned or unsanctioned, act-based or identity-based, instrumental or symbolic—by which the social control of those to whom they are directed is undertaken and achieved. Thus, I am going to take it as a basic premise that the factual background of *Hardwick* undermines the traditional distinction between the formal prohibition of homosexual sodomy and the substantive means by which that prohibition is enforced (or not enforced, as the case may be): form and substance are inextricably linked.

This constellation of prohibitive practices interdicts (homo)social identity *and* (homo)sexual intimacy; enlists the unauthorized, unofficial disciplinary power of private actors and the authorized, official police power of state institutions; subjects those designated as "homosexual" to lawless and random aggression and violence and lawful and regularized constraint and control; targets the bodies and the behavior of those to whom its edicts are directed; enjoins homosexual existence *and* homoerotic acts. Given this complexity, the question becomes whether the factual predicates of the issues presented in *Hardwick* can be cleanly or comprehensively contained within the constitutional category of privacy.

At least three possible answers to this question suggest themselves. One might flatly deny that anything of theoretical consequence flows from what I have said about the public biography of *Hardwick*. This position holds that there is still a close enough conceptual connection between the privacy paradigm and the more public dimensions of *Hardwick* to warrant rejection of an alternative perspective, even if that perspective illuminates aspects of the case that escape the view of privacy. In my view, this position is indefensible. The unmodified privacy framework fails to satisfy a basal requirement that any interpretive model must meet: namely, that the model fit the data it aims to explain. While the resolute refusal to come to grips with *Hardwick's* public biography may preserve the purity of privacy analysis, the perceived benefits of its preservation entail too great a conceptual cost. We may ignore the mentioned public determinants and dimensions of *Hardwick,* but we cannot erase them altogether: they remain substantive and significant facts of the case.

A second possible response to the claim that *Hardwick* raises issues that cannot be forced into the conceptual grid of the privacy paradigm does not deny the claim's force, but tries instead to deflect it. This response concedes that an adequate constitutional analysis of *Hardwick* cannot justifiably overlook the apparently public features of the case, but rejects the implication that attention to these concerns necessarily entails the abandonment of privacy analysis *tout court*. It begins by noting that the reservations mentioned regarding the value of the privacy model as a framework for analysis of *Hardwick* fail to distinguish between the larger concepts associated with the privacy principle, on the one hand, and the local factual premises that inform its analysis, on the other. With this distinction in mind, one can accept the claim that the factual premises that typically inform privacy thinking overlook the public features of *Hardwick*. At the same time, one can insist that nothing I have said about the contingent factual assumptions of the privacy paradigm warrants repudiation of its core ideas. To put the point another way, one might argue that the basic conceptual framework of privacy analysis is sufficiently elastic to cover these dimensions of *Hardwick*. Our task, then, is simply to reformulate or redescribe the particular public facts of the case in terms that reveal their family resemblance to already acknowledged privacy interests. I criticize this position in greater detail below. I would simply note here that it is far from clear why this semantic sleight-of-hand is preferable to an open admission that *Hardwick* might be better understood by use of a richer conceptual vocabulary than that which the privacy paradigm is able to offer.

A third response is to contend, as I do, that privacy's narrow temporal and categorical frameworks render it too blunt a tool for the critical task before us. *Hardwick* is not just a story about private homoerotic acts and their interdiction; it is also an account of the harassment, the humiliation, and the violence that await the mere assertion or imputation of homosexual identities and existences in the public sphere. A more extended and unified account of the events that preceded and followed the encounter in Hardwick's bedroom militates toward a broader conception of our analytic object than the privacy principle permits. These events do not simply straddle the boundaries between the public and private; they overrun them altogether. Thus, against the sheer taken-for-grantedness of the view that *Hardwick* is most productively understood within the language and logic of privacy, I would urge that close attention to the public dimensions of *Hardwick* demands analysis in other, more comprehensive terms. We must, in short, force privacy to go public.

* * *

In my view, in order to develop a sufficiently precise conception of the human beings whose "personhood" is the target of homosexual sodomy statutes, we need a "concrete" rather than an "abstract" understanding of the body. I have already suggested why it would be a mistake to view *Hardwick* as raising only the question whether the State of Georgia could prohibit and punish Michael Hardwick for engaging in sexual acts with another consenting adult male in the privacy of his own home. Close attention to its factual background indicates that an even more fundamental issue presented in *Hardwick* was whether the State of Georgia could constitutionally permit its police power, specifically, its criminalization of homosexual sodomy, to serve as a justification for threatened and actual violence toward one of its citizens. We would do well here to remember that the road that led Michael Hardwick to the bar of the Supreme Court was, in his words, "a trail of blood"—his own. Hence, I believe that it would be a mistake to view *Hardwick* as a case about the state's power to regulate sexual intimacy or personal morality. Rather, *Hardwick* ought to be understood as a case about Michael Hardwick's right to be protected from state-sanctioned invasion of his corporal integrity, that is, of his very bodily existence.

From this perspective, *Hardwick* casts the limitations of the theory of the subject in which privacy principle is grounded into stark, unflattering relief. The "personhood" privileged in privacy analysis relies too heavily on an abstract image of the human subject as a moral self. The "personhood" at stake in *Hardwick*, however, calls for a more materialist view of the human subject as an *embodied* self. *Hardwick* powerfully underscores the fact that the interests privacy analysis seeks to defend are initially, and indispensably, *body-generated*. In the instant context, this means simply that the bodies of the actual, empirical individuals to whom homosexual sodomy statutes are addressed are not merely a derivative supplement, but the generative substrate of the constitutional rights the privacy principle attempts to secure. The rights claimed under privacy doctrine live and move and have their being in the material body of the human subject. Without the prior and primary recognition of a basal right of corporal integrity, the right of privacy is not only incomplete, but quite literally impossible.

* * *

II. ONE BODY, MANY MEMBERS: CORPOREALITY AND AMERICAN CONSTITUTIONALISM

The preceding section argued that the regnant emphasis on abstract, private personhood can never provide more than a partial account of the actual individual against whom homosexual sodomy statutes operate. The constitutional theory we need now must move beyond the axiological premises and perspectives that inform privacy analysis. If the core issue presented by these statutes concerns limitations on the power of the body politic to intervene in the sexual lives of its actual or potential members, it is only fitting that we begin by thinking about the embodied experience of the people who are touched by sodomy laws. It is, after all, the bodies of the individuals that homosexual sodomy laws address that provide the "raw material" on which the police power acts. Reaching a clear understanding of the concrete corporal implications of homosexual sodomy statutes is a crucial task. In order to discharge it, we must be prepared to abandon the assumption that since the laws at issue have to do with sexuality, the language of sexuality ought accordingly to provide the governing terms of analysis. I begin instead from a rather different assumption that the conceptual framework that will best enable us to understand the concrete operations of homosexual sodomy law focuses on political power rather than on personal pleasure.

This is a political analysis because it poses and aims to answer one of the most basic questions of our constitutional law: What is the substance of the relationship between the government of the individual and the government of the body politic? Building on an empirical account of the concrete "body politics" of homosexual sodomy law, I want to suggest that the beginnings of an answer to this question may be found in the Cruel and Unusual Punishments Clause of the Eighth Amendment, whose terms allow us to flesh out the rights of "personhood" that privacy analysis so abstractly purports to comprehend. As I read it, the Eighth Amendment is the constitutional marker of a basic political right to be free from state-sanctioned torture and terror. However, the lived experience of gay men and lesbians under the legal regime challenged and upheld in *Bowers v. Hardwick* is one in which government not only passively permits, but actively protects, acts of violence directed toward individuals who are, or are taken to be, homosexual. In my view, this state-legitimized violence represents an unconstitutional abdication of one of the most basic duties of government.

A. *"Choked to Death, Burnt to Ashes": A Political Anatomy of Homophobic Violence*

In October 1987, hundreds of people were arrested during the course of a demonstration against the decision in *Bowers v. Hardwick*. Those arrested had participated in a massive act of civil disobedience in which they had literally laid their bodies on the steps outside the Supreme Court building. The protest dramatically underscored the concrete corporal interests that the *Hardwick* Court ignored and evoked the tangible historical experience of gay and lesbian Americans in which the case must be situated.

Stated bluntly, that history is a story of homophobic aggression and ideology. Its central theme is the fear, hatred, stigmatization, and persecution of homosexuals and homosexuality. Over the course of American history, gay men and lesbian women have been discursively marked as "faggots" (after the pieces of kindling used to burn their bodies), "monsters," "fairies," "bull dykes," "perverts," "freaks," and "queers." Their intimate associations have been denominated "abominations," "crimes against nature," and "sins not fit to be named among Christians." This symbolic violence has produced and been produced by congeries of physical violence. Gay men and lesbians in America have been "condemned to death by choking, burning and drowning; . . . executed, [castrated], jailed, pilloried, fined, court-martialed, prostituted, fired, framed, blackmailed, disinherited, [lobotomized, shock-treated, psychoanalyzed and] declared insane, driven to insanity, to suicide, murder, and self-hate, witch-hunted, entrapped, stereotyped, mocked, insulted, isolated . . . castigated . . . despised [and degraded]."

The historical roots of this violence are older than the nation itself. The 1646 Calendar of Dutch Historical Manuscripts reports the trial, conviction, and sentence on Manhattan Island, New Netherland Colony of one Jan Creoli, "a negro, [for] sodomy; second offense; this crime being condemned of God (Gen., c. 19; Levit., c. 18:22, 29) as an abomination, the prisoner is sentenced to be conveyed to the place of public execution, and there choked to death, and then burnt to ashes." On the same date the Calendar records the sentence of "Manuel Congo . . . on whom the above abominable crime was committed," whom the Court ordered "to be carried to the place where Creoli is to be executed, tied to a stake, and faggots piled around him, for justice sake, and to be flogged; sentence executed."

The continuity between the seventeenth-century experience and homophobic violence in our own time is startling. A report issued by Community United Against Violence, an organization that monitors incidents of homophobic violence, offers a picture of the violent face of homophobia in contemporary America:

> One man's body was discovered with his face literally beaten off. Another had his jaw smashed into eight pieces by a gang of youths taunting "you'll never suck another cock, faggot!" Another had most of his lower intestine removed after suffering severe stab wounds in the abdomen. Another was stabbed 27 times in the face and upper chest with a screwdriver, which leaves a very jagged scar. Another had both lungs punctured by stab wounds, and yet another had his aorta severed.

Some months before the Supreme Court rendered its judgment in *Hardwick*, the *New York Daily News* printed the story of a homeless gay man in that city who "had his skull crushed by three men who beat him unconscious with two-by-fours while screaming anti-gay epithets"; the same article recounted an incident in which a motorist "who saw a lesbian standing on a sidewalk in [Manhattan] stopped his car, got out and beat her so badly (while shouting anti-lesbian epithets) that she suffered broken facial bones and permanent nerve damage." Two years after the *Hardwick* decision, the coordinator of a victim assistance program at a New York City hospital reported that "attacks against gay men were the most heinous and brutal I encountered." The hospital routinely treated gay male victims of homophobic violence, whose injuries "frequently involved torture, cutting, mutilation, and beating, and showed the absolute intent to rub out the human being because of his [sexual] orientation."

One would be mistaken to view these stories as aberrant, isolated instances of violence perpetrated by the psychologically imbalanced against individual gay men and women. They are not. All the evidence suggests that there are hundreds, if not thousands of such stories, most of them untold. Violence against gay men and lesbians—on the streets, in the workplace, at home—is a structural feature of life in American society. A study commissioned by the National Institute of Justice (the research arm of the U.S. Department of Justice) concluded that gay men and women "are probably the most frequent victims [of hate violence today]." We may never know the full story of the violence to which gay men and gay women are subjected. In spite of their frequency, it is estimated that a full 80% of bias violence against gay men and women is never reported to the police. This under-reporting is not surprising, since victims of anti-gay violence have reason to be fearful that the response of state and local officials may be unsympathetic or openly hostile, or that the disclosure of their sexual orientation may lead to further discrimination.

Indeed, government officials and agencies are themselves often complicit in the phenomenon of homophobic violence. Governmental involvement ranges from active instigation to acquiescent indifference. A recent survey of violence against gay men and lesbians cites a 1951 case study of police practices in which a patrolman describes his typical treatment of homosexuals:

> Now in my own cases when I catch a guy like that I just pick him up and take him into the woods and beat him until he can't crawl. I have had seventeen cases like that in the last couple of years. I tell the guy if I catch him doing that again I will take him out to the woods and I will shoot him. I tell him that I carry a second gun on me just in case I find guys like him and that I will plant it in his hand and say that he tried to kill me and that no jury will convict me.

At October 1986 hearings on homophobic violence convened by the House of Representatives Committee on the Judiciary, Subcommittee on Criminal Justice, the district attorney of New York County noted that "at times, [lesbians and gay men] have been, and in many areas of the country continue to be, taunted, harassed, and even physically assaulted by the very people whose job it is to protect them."

Even if we were able to document every instance of homophobic violence in America, our understanding of its effects would still be incomplete. To be sure, many men and women in the gay and lesbian communities have escaped direct physical attack by perpetrators of homophobic violence. However, the horror and sinister efficacy of homophobic violence are in many ways like those of racist violence. Like people of color, gay men and lesbians always and everywhere have to live their lives on guard, knowing that they are vulnerable to attack at any time. As one observer has noted, "being gay means living with the reality that although you may not personally be the victim of outright homophobic attacks every day, at any moment you could be attacked—walking down the street, going to work, on the job, shopping, or in a restaurant." Indeed, much of the efficacy of homophobic violence lies in the message it conveys to those who are not its immediate victims.

In this respect, homophobic violence bears many of the characteristics associated with terrorism. As in the case of terrorism, much of the force of violence against gay men and lesbians lies in its randomness: individuals may know that the assertion or ascription of gay or lesbian identity marks them as potential targets of homophobic violence, but they cannot know until too late whether or when they will actually be hit. Like the terrorist, the perpetrator of homophobic violence strikes without giving warning. A second characteristic common to terrorism and homophobic violence is its utter impersonality. Like perpetrators of terrorist acts, those who attack gays and lesbians do not know, and are most often unknown to, their victims.

Another feature that homophobic violence shares with terrorism is its "communicative" thrust. Although attacks on gays and lesbians might be random and impersonal, such attacks are far from meaningless. The communicative dimensions of homophobic violence may be seen on a number of levels. Survivors of homophobic violence have reported that their attackers verbally expressed hatred of homosexuality, boasted of heterosexuality, or otherwise taunted them. However, in most instances, perpetrators of violence against gays and lesbians have no need to resort to language to communicate: the expressive force of the violence itself makes verbal communication unnecessary. One of the most salient features of homophobic violence is its excessive brutality. . . .

The terroristic dimensions of homophobic violence compel us to understand it as a mode of power. To put the point in slightly different terms, homophobic violence is a form of "institution," in the sense that John Rawls elaborates that concept. Homophobic violence is a social activity "structured by rules that define roles and positions, powers and opportunities, thereby distributing responsibility for consequences." Viewed systemically, the objective and outcome of violence against lesbians and gays is the social control of human sexuality. Homophobic violence aims to regulate the erotic economy of contemporary American society, or more specifically, to enforce the institutional and ideological imperatives of what Adrienne Rich has termed "compulsory heterosexuality." Insofar as homophobic violence functions to prevent and punish actual or imagined deviations from heterosexual acts and identities, it carries a determinate political valence and value.

* * *

I have argued that homophobic violence is an exercise of political power. I have suggested that the purpose of this violence is to terrorize the population to whom its victims belong. I have also referred to the record of state instigation of, and acquiescence in, the phenomenon of homophobic violence. I want now to explore more fully the constitutional implications of the connection between governmental instigation of and acquiescence in criminal attacks on gay men and lesbians on the one hand, and criminal statutes against homosexual sodomy on the other. It might be said that the coincidence of the law of homosexual sodomy and the lawlessness of homophobic violence by itself presents a question with which a constitutional analysis of these statutes must reckon.

However, I hope by now to have said enough to clear the ground for a somewhat stronger claim. I contend that the involvement of the state in the phenomenon of homophobic violence is in fact no coincidence at all. A close examination of the political terror directed against gay men and lesbians suggests that the relationship between homosexual sodomy law and homophobic violence is not merely coincident, but coordinate: the criminalization of homosexual sodomy and criminal attacks on gay men and lesbians work in tandem. My task, of course, is to specify the terms of their coordinal interaction. How should we think about the role the state plays in permitting, promoting or participating in homophobic violence?

* * *

C. *"Keep Your Laws Off My Body": Homophobic Violence, Homosexual Sodomy Laws and the Right of Corporal Integrity*

To appreciate the ways in which the relationship between homosexual sodomy law and homophobic violence presents constitutional analysis with a "political question," we might recall Seneca's claim that the body politic "can be kept unharmed only by the mutual protection" of its parts. I take this principle to mean that one of the first duties of the state is to protect the citizens from whom its powers derive against random, unchecked violence by other citizens, or by government officials.

For gay men and lesbians, the state has honored this fundamental obligation more in the breach than in the observance. As I have shown, few members of our body politic are more vulnerable to violent terrorist attack than the gay or lesbian citizen. This violence takes two forms. One form is violence at the hand of state officials such as the police. This official violence is an important part of the political history of the criminalization of homosexual sex. The second form of homophobic violence is that perpetrated by private individuals. Although this type of violence is of lower visibility than that committed by public officials, the available evidence suggests that it is even more extensive. Both involve the unlawful use of state power as a tool of law enforcement. With respect to homophobic violence perpetrated by state officials, no one would deny that a court can and should forbid a state from using terror and random violence as a standard tactic for enforcing homosexual sodomy law. Accordingly, I shall focus my discussion on the hidden constitutional dimensions of the brutal violence inflicted on gay men and lesbians at the hands of other citizens.

* * *

Recent scholarship on the theory of power . . . represents a powerful challenge to traditional understandings. The central proposition established in contemporary work on power is that the effective exercise of state power in the modern period does not require a formal apparatus or agency. This is not to say that the forms in which the political is clothed are utterly illusory and without ideological consequence. It is to suggest that the substantive operation and effects of state power cannot always be determined solely (or even primarily) by reference to its formal agency; the state power in contemporary American society can be seen not only in the force relations involving public officials and private citizens, but in those among citizens as well. As Nicos Poulantzas writes: "[A] number of sites of power which [appear] to lie wholly outside the State . . . are all the more sites of power in that they are included in the strategic field of the state." "[R]elations of power *go far beyond the State*." In consequence, any adequate analysis of the political technologies of the modern state must attend not only to the form power takes, but to its function as well. Power relations do not have to be localized within the formal institutions of the state in order to serve the substantive interests of the state.

Taking these theoretical lessons about state power as a point of reference, one may now specify precisely why the relationship between homosexual sodomy statutes and homophobic violence is constitutionally suspect. In assessing the constitutionality of these laws, I would argue that violence against gays and lesbians perpetrated by other citizens represents the states' *constructive delegation* of governmental power to these citizens. As a constitutional matter, the covert, unofficial character of this violence does not render it any less problematic than open, official attacks against gay men and lesbians. To state the point in slightly different terms, the fact that homophobic violence occurs within the context of "private" relations by no means implies that such violence is without "public" origins or consequence. The apparently private character of homophobic violence should not blind us to the reality of the state power that enables and underwrites it. The functional privatization of state power that structures the triangular relationship among victim, perpetrator, and state does not render the phenomenon of homophobic violence any less a matter of constitutional concern.

In order to see why the private lawlessness of homophobic violence is very much a problem for constitutional law, we must turn from considering *who* perpetrates this violence to considering *how* the state responds to the fact of its occurrence. The sheer difficulty of writing about the role of government in private homophobic violence may be traced in part to the insidious hidden forms state involvement takes. The political sociology of homophobic violence reveals that more often than not, the complicity of the state in private attacks on gay men and lesbians may be characterized as complicity through a consistent and calculated pattern of inaction. To paraphrase Justice Brandeis, the most important thing state governments do with respect to homophobic violence is to do nothing.

State officials seem unwilling or unable to use the criminal justice system to reach crimes of homophobic violence. In this respect, the response to private violence against gays and lesbians apparently mirrors the reaction of state governments to private violations of homosexual sodomy law. However, in the case of homophobic violence, the practical and ideological effects of government indifference are not at all the same. This difference lies in the very nature of the crime.

When political pressures or the persistence of victims have forced state officials to prosecute perpetrators of homophobic violence, those accused have very often been acquitted. The relatively few individuals who have been convicted of criminal violence against gay men or lesbians have often received reduced sentences or been granted a mitigation in the degree of criminal offense. These outcomes result from the emergence of two curious defenses, which are termed "homosexual panic" and "homosexual advance." The "homosexual panic" defense permits individuals accused of attacking or murdering a gay man or lesbian to assert that their acts stemmed from a violent reaction to their own "latent" homosexual tendencies, triggered after the accused was homosexually propositioned. The "homosexual advance" defense allows the accused to claim that he was the subject of a homosexual overture. The "homosexual advance" defense differs from the "homosexual panic" defense insofar as it does not require the defendant to introduce evidence about his "latent homosexual tendencies." The critical point is that the effect of both of these defenses is to create a doctrinal space within the criminal justice system that permits the perpetrators of violent crimes against gay men and lesbians to lay the blame for their brutality at the feet of their victims.

Thus, the problem faced by those who have sought to place private violence against gay men and lesbians on the public agenda is not simply that state officials seem all too capable of either shutting their eyes to homophobic violence or looking the other way. The problem runs much deeper. Because gay men and lesbians are seen as members of a criminal class, it is almost as though state governments view prosecution of those who commit crimes of homophobic violence as an invasion of the perpetrator's rights.

The constitutional implications of this deliberate policy and practice of government indifference will likely elude us so long as we cling to the impoverished understanding of state power reflected in the regnant doctrine of state action. It bears remarking, however, that this doctrine does not represent the only plausible understanding of state power:

> [The state action doctrine] does not *have* to be construed as ruling out affirmative governmental duties to protect citizen against citizen. While insisting that the fourteenth amendment does not apply to private conduct *per se*, and that such conduct does not become state action merely because the state has chosen not to prohibit it, the doctrine can be understood as leaving open the substantive constitutional question whether the state's own failure to control certain types of private conduct (whether that failure be called "action" or "inaction") violates the amendment. The constitutional enforcement of a citizen's natural right to affirmative governmental protection against victimization by fellow citizens can thus be squared with the state action doctrine through a holding that nonprovision of such protection is unconstitutional state action.

The point here is that government may effectively exercise its powers in a variety of forms, of which positive, affirmative state action is only one, and not always the most efficient means.

In the instant context, this more nuanced understanding of the combined force of the private action and state inaction that are so violently brought to bear on the bodies of gay men and lesbians clears the ground for clearer specification of the coordinal relationship between criminal laws against homosexual sodomy on one side, and criminal acts of homophobic violence perpetrated by private citizens on the other. It will be recalled that the question I posed and proposed to address was this: How ought we to think about the role state governments play in the phenomenon of homophobic violence? I believe my preceding discussion of the political sociology of power permits two inferences regarding this question, one general and one more specific. Broadly speaking, homosexual sodomy statutes express the official "theory" of homophobia; private acts of violence against gay men and lesbians "translate" that theory into brutal "practice." In other words, private homophobic violence punishes what homosexual sodomy statutes prohibit. When situated within this framework, the terms and target of my Eighth Amendment-based account of the criminal laws against homosexual sodomy become clear: one might call it an "anti-terrorist" case for judicial invalidation of homosexual sodomy laws, whose textual grounding is a functional, rather than formal interpretation of the prohibition against the infliction of cruel and unusual punishments.

I read the Eighth Amendment as a constitutional reflection of an important political principle. This principle presupposes a constitutive conceptual connection between the legitimacy of a government and the methods that government employs to enforce its commands. In other words, the reason our Constitution prohibits the infliction of cruel and unusual punishments is because we cannot countenance the practices the Eighth Amendment forbids without doing violence to the very concept of governmentality, or at least to the liberal conception of legitimate government that underlies our constitutional tradition. If we accept the view that under our political system, a state may not resort to terror or random violence as a standard tool of governmental control, a functional interpretation of the Eighth Amendment permits us to make two claims about the constitutionality of laws against homosexual sodomy. The Eighth Amendment prohibition against cruel and unusual punishments may be construed not only to forbid open and official government use of violence to enforce the criminal laws against homosexual sodomy, but also to bar a state from effecting the enforcement of these laws by instigating, encouraging, or permitting private attacks on gay men and lesbians.

Turning to the question of the judicial role, we see that the Eighth Amendment may thus be interpreted as empowering constitutional courts to invalidate homosexual sodomy statutes on the grounds that the actual, concrete effect of these laws is to *legitimize* the lawless infliction of homophobic violence. After *Hardwick*, the starting point of the constitutional case against homosexual sodomy statutes is a recognition that the Court's reasoning and result in *Hardwick* necessarily presupposed certain "constitutional facts" about the actual operation of the Georgia law. It is plausible to think that among the assumptions on which the *Hardwick* Court based its decision was a belief that the methods employed by the State of Georgia to enforce its criminal sodomy laws did not entail violation of other, independent constitutional rights. That is, whatever the *Hardwick* Court may have thought about the existence of "a fundamental right to engage in homosexual sodomy," it could not have upheld the Georgia law in the face of evidence that the *actual administration* of the criminal sodomy statute violated other constitutional rights, such as those protected by the Eighth Amendment.

Because of the procedural posture of the case, the *Hardwick* Court possessed relatively little information regarding the actual application of the challenged law. Moreover, nothing in the *Hardwick* decision warrants a reading of the Court's judgment regarding the right of privacy as foreclosing invalidation of the Georgia sodomy law on alternative constitutional grounds. Thus, if it can be shown that the "real effect" of the Georgia statute is to inflict cruel and unusual punishment on individuals who engaged in the conduct prohibited by the statute, a court could properly declare the statute constitutionally invalid.

I hope by now to have justified the claim that there is a firm factual basis on which a post-*Hardwick* court could so hold. The factual premises regarding the enforcement of sodomy laws on which *Hardwick* appears to have been based do not comport with past or present realities. As I have shown, it is not only possible to argue, but difficult to deny, that the criminalization of homosexual sodomy and crimes of homophobic violence mutually reinforce one another.

* * *

IV. FROM PRIVACY TO POLITICS

Although it has taken a different path than arguments couched in the language of privacy, the account proffered here of homosexual sodomy statutes has ultimately arrived at the same destination. Like the proponents of the right of privacy, I firmly believe that homosexual sodomy laws like the statute upheld in *Bowers v. Hardwick* are illegitimate as a matter of constitutional law. My discussion has broken most markedly with the privacy model by placing greater accent and emphasis on a problem that is anterior to the issue of individual rights, a problem that has traditionally provided an important, but characteristically undertheorized, frame of reference for proponents of privacy. That is, I have chosen a theoretical framework in which the first and focal question for constitutional analysis is not the problem of individual or personal rights, but the question of political power.

I have adopted this approach for four reasons. First, in general, I believe a "political power" model best comports with my own understanding that the chief object of constitutional law in America is to define the scope and limits of legitimate political power. On this view, the primary function of constitutional adjudication is to identify and check unconstitutional uses of political power.

A second reason I have emphasized the question of power rather than that of privacy is because current realities demand such emphasis. Contemporary political developments in the United States have produced nothing short of a "paradigm" shift in the very meaning of the political. The recent history of constitutional politics in America (the women's movement most readily comes to mind) represents a powerful challenge to the strict division between "public" and "private" spheres on which the privacy principle depends. The implications of this challenge are both ideological and institutional. By insisting that the "personal" and "private" are the "public" and "political," feminist theory and practice have forced us to question long-held assumptions about the relations among gender, sexuality, power, and politics. As Iris Marion Young observes, feminism "expresses the principle that no social practices or activities should be excluded as improper subjects for public discussion, expression, or collective choice."

The rethinking of these assumptions has produced a distinctive "sexual politics" whose influence on the national political consciousness cannot be denied. Discussions of issues regarding sexuality that were conducted in the rhetoric of privacy have increasingly come to be posed as public issues about relations of power and domination. Struggles over sexuality and its social meaning are now firmly fixed on our national political agenda. The state, of course, is a key arena of contest over the terms and understandings that inform and determine decisions of public law and policy with respect to sexuality.

It has become increasingly clear that to frame the public issues presented by homosexual sodomy statutes in the language of "privacy" rights is to grasp only one side of the constitutional problem. The stakes, however, are not merely conceptual. As I have argued, reliance on the language of privacy as a framework for constitutional analysis of the intersection of homosexual sodomy statutes and homophobic violence carries other and deeper dangers. I suggested earlier that the history of the concept of sexual privacy is not the history of a neutral principle. Much as feminist theorists have demonstrated that the concept of privacy is "gendered," I have called attention to the degree to which the concept of privacy is "sexuated": for gay men and lesbians, privacy has always represented privation. In short, the rhetoric of privacy has historically functioned to perpetuate the oppressive politics of the "closet": privacy is the ideological substrate of the very secrecy that has forced gay men and lesbians to remain hidden and underground, and thus rendered them vulnerable to private homophobic violence. There is no reason to think that we can rid privacy of its sedimented history.

In my view, these considerations force the recognition that we lose something by continuing to treat the questions of public law and politics posed by the existence of homosexual sodomy statutes exclusively, or even primarily, as a matter of private rights. The issue here is not simply that the categories "[p]ublic and private [have developed] *together.*" It is rather a question of exposing the ways in which the violent subjugation of gay men and lesbians in America has been made possible by an exercise of public power cloaked as private prejudice. I have tried to set forth a conceptual vocabulary in which that political interaction, and its constitutional dimensions, can be described.

This brings me to a third reason for my choice of a decidedly political framework for analysis of homosexual sodomy law. Premature emphasis on rights discourse tends to give unnecessary ground to a claim often made in debates about the privacy rights (if any) to be accorded the consensual intimate conduct of gay and lesbian Americans.

This argument warns that challenges against the constitutionality of "sodomy" statutes are disguised but aggressive demands for "endorsement" of "their lifestyle." I have framed the issue as involving the use and limits of political power to preempt such a reading of my project in these pages. As I see it, recourse to the *courts* by gay and lesbian Americans is driven not so much by a desire to seek new privileges, as by a desire to end the complicity of the state in old persecutions.

My approach thus partially converges with the view of those legal scholars who have insisted on the importance in constitutional analysis and adjudication of the distinction between a "state power" and an "individual rights" framework. Clearly, attention to this distinction carries important implications, not only for the interpretation of particular instances of judicial review, but for the assessment of its institutional legitimacy under our form of government. At the same time, however, I am rather more skeptical than these scholars about the possibility or desirability of any absolute separation of questions of individual rights and state power. In the final instance, assertion of a limit on the use of state power necessarily implies some position regarding the rights of the individuals on whom that power is brought to bear. On this understanding, positive rights of the individual and negative limitations on state power are the *recto* and *verso* of the same constitutional charter. Thus, while my discussion has stressed the degree to which constitutional analysis of homosexual sodomy statutes can be cast as a question of the use and abuse of "state power," I am by no means indifferent to the relation between this body of law and the rights of the individuals whose bodies it aims to contain, coerce or control. To the contrary, my argument has been aimed throughout at building the constitutional case for an individual right of corporal integrity generally, and a right to be free from homophobic violence in particular. Ultimately, however, I remain convinced that neither the "state power" nor the "individual rights" framework, standing alone, can begin to address the tangled cluster of descriptive and normative issues that the existence, operation, and effects of homosexual sodomy statutes present for constitutional law. In order to grasp the complex intersection of homosexual sodomy law and homophobic violence, we must closely attend to the constitutional consequences these practices entail for political power as well as personal rights.

* * *

As I have shown, the argument from privacy is predominantly an axiological case against the legal regulation of private, consensual sexual conduct. It draws on concepts of moral and ethical theory to make claims about sexuality and personhood. The corporal paradigm developed here differs from the privacy framework in that its case against homosexual sodomy laws relies first and primarily on concepts about power and the state taken from political theory. This is so in at least two senses. First, the corporal model elaborated here proceeds from the recognition that like the criminal law generally, sodomy statutes necessarily presuppose a political conception regarding the relationship between the arm of the state and the body of the individual. Second, the corporal model permits us to apprehend the unique way in which homosexual sodomy law has historically promoted and reflected illegitimate power relationships among the citizens who make up the body politic. In my view, close attention to the politics of sodomy statutes illuminates aspects of these laws that will be indispensable to future debate and discussion about their constitutionality after *Hardwick*.

* * *

The "Right to Die"

As medical science has improved the technological means for prolonging life, states have had to grapple with patients' requests to "die with dignity" by refusing life-sustaining medical treatment and even by taking affirmative steps to end their own lives. State courts have taken diverse approaches in finding a right to refuse treatment, relying primarily on state constitutions, statutes, and common law. More recently, courts have considered the more controversial issue of whether the Constitution protects assisted suicide or voluntary euthanasia. In *Cruzan v. Director, Missouri Department of Health,* the Supreme Court considered for the first time whether the United States Constitution conferred a right to terminate life-sustaining medical treatment. Some commentators have compared the right to terminate a pregnancy with the right to end one's life. But Yale Kamisar powerfully repudiates arguments in favor of "mercy killing" by pointing out the potential for error and social injustice. Thomas Mayo argues that the Supreme Court should not recognize a fundamental right to die because there is no societal consensus on the issue. Sanford Kadish rejects the reliance on individual autonomy in deciding a range of issues involving dying patients, favoring an approach that centers on the current compassionate interests of the patient.

Yale Kamisar, *Some Non-Religious Views Against Proposed "Mercy-Killing" Legislation,* 42 MINN. L. REV. 969, 969-70, 976-98, 1005-30 (1958)*

A recent book, Glanville Williams' *The Sanctity of Life and the Criminal Law,* once again brings to the fore the controversial topic of euthanasia, more popularly known as "mercy killing." In keeping with the trend of the euthanasia movement over the past generation, Williams concentrates his efforts for reform on the *voluntary* type of euthanasia, for example, the cancer victim begging for death; as opposed to the *involuntary variety,* that is, the case of the congenital idiot, the permanently insane or the senile.

When a legal scholar of Williams' stature joins the ranks of such formidable criminal law thinkers as America's Herbert Wechsler and the late Jerome Michael, and England's Hermann Mannheim in approving voluntary euthanasia, at least under certain circumstances, a major exploration of the bases for the euthanasia prohibition seems in order. This need is underscored by the fact that Williams' book arrives on the scene so soon after the stir caused by a brilliant Anglican clergyman's plea for voluntary euthanasia.

* * *

The "freedom to choose a merciful death by euthanasia" may well be regarded, as does Professor Harry Kalven in a carefully measured review of another recent book

---

*   Reprinted with permission.

urging a similar proposal, as "a special area of civil liberties far removed from the familiar concerns with criminal procedures, race discrimination and freedom of speech and religion." The civil liberties angle is definitely a part of Professor Williams' approach:

> If the law were to remove its ban on euthanasia, the effect would merely be to leave this subject to the individual conscience. This proposal would . . . be easy to defend, as restoring personal liberty in a field in which men differ on the question of conscience. . . .

> On a question like this there is surely everything to be said for the liberty of the individual.

I am perfectly willing to accept civil liberties as the battlefield, but issues of "liberty" and "freedom" mean little until we begin to pin down *whose* "liberty" and "freedom" and for *what* need and at *what* price. This paper is concerned largely with such questions.

It is true also of journeys in the law that the place you reach depends on the direction you are taking. And so, where one comes out on a case depends on where one goes in.

So it is with the question at hand. Williams champions the "personal liberty" of the dying to die painlessly. I am more concerned about the life and liberty of those who would needlessly be killed in the process or who would irrationally choose to partake of the process. Williams' price on behalf of those who are *in fact* "hopeless incurables" and *in fact* of a fixed and rational desire to die is the sacrifice of (1) some few, who, though they know it not, because their physicians know it not, need not and should not die; (2) others, probably not so few, who, though they go through the motion of "volunteering," are casualties of strain, pain or narcotics to such an extent that they really know not what they do. My price on behalf of those who, despite appearances to the contrary, have some relatively normal and reasonably useful life left in them or who are incapable of making the choice, is the lingering on for awhile of those who, if you will, *in fact* have no desire and no reason to linger on.

I. A CLOSE-UP VIEW OF VOLUNTARY EUTHANASIA

A. *The Euthanasiast's Dilemma and Williams' Proposed Solution.*

As if the general principle they advocate did not raise enough difficulties in itself, euthanasiasts have learned only too bitterly that specific plans of enforcement are often much less palatable than the abstract notions they are designed to effectuate. In the case of voluntary euthanasia, the means of implementation vary from (1) the simple proposal that mercy-killings by anyone, typically relatives, be immunized from the criminal law; to (2) the elaborate legal machinery contained in the bills of the Voluntary Euthanasia Legalisation Society (England) and the Euthanasia Society of America for carrying out euthanasia.

The English Society would require the eligible patient, *i.e.,* one over twenty-one and "suffering from a disease involving severe pain and of an incurable and fatal character," to forward a specially prescribed application—along with two medical certificates, one signed by the attending physician, and the other by a specially qualified physician—to a specially appointed Euthanasia Referee "who shall satisfy himself by means of a personal interview with the patient and otherwise that the said conditions shall have been fulfilled and that the patient fully understands the nature and purpose of the application"; and, if so satisfied, shall then send a euthanasia permit to the patient; which permit shall, seven days after receipt, become "operative" in the presence of an official witness; unless the nearest relative manages to cancel the permit by persuading a court of appropriate jurisdiction that the requisite conditions have not been met.

The American Society would have the eligible patient, *i.e.,* one over twenty-one "suffering from severe physical pain caused by a disease for which no remedy affording lasting relief or recovery is at the time known to medical science," petition for euthanasia in the presence of two witnesses and file same, along with the certificate of an attending physician, in a court of appropriate jurisdiction; said court to then appoint a committee of three, of whom at least two must be physicians, "who shall forthwith examine the patient and such other persons as they deem advisable or as the court may direct and within five days after their appointment, shall report to the court whether or not the patient understands the nature and purpose of the petition and comes within the [act's] provisions"; whereupon, if the report is in the affirmative, the court shall—"unless there is some reason to believe that the report is erroneous or untrue"—grant the petition; in which event euthanasia is to be administered in the presence of the committee, or any two members thereof.

As will be seen, and as might be expected, the simple negative proposal to remove "mercy-killings" from the ban of the criminal law is strenuously resisted on the ground that it offers the patient far too little protection from not-so-necessary or not-so-merciful killings. On the other hand, the elaborate affirmative proposals of the euthanasia societies meet much pronounced eye-blinking, not a few guffaws, and sharp criticism that the legal machinery is so drawn-out, so complex, so formal and so tedious as to offer the patient far too little solace.

* * *

Nothing rouses Professor Williams' ire more than the fact that opponents of the euthanasia movement argue that euthanasia proposals offer either inadequate protection or overelaborate safeguards. Williams appears to meet this dilemma with the insinuation that because arguments are made in the antithesis *they must each be invalid, each be obstructionist, and each be made in bad faith.*

It just may be, however, that each alternative argument is quite valid, that the trouble lies with the euthanasiasts themselves in seeking a goal which is *inherently inconsistent:* a procedure for death which *both* (1) provides ample safeguards against abuse and mistake; and (2) is "quick" and "easy" in operation. Professor Williams meets the problem with more than bitter comments about the tactics of the opposition. He makes a brave try to break through the dilemma:

> [T]he reformers might be well advised, in their next proposal, to abandon all their cumbrous safeguards and to do as their opponents wish, giving the medical practitioner a wide discretion and trusting to his good sense.

> [T]he essence of the bill would then be simple. It would provide that no medical practitioner should be guilty of an offense in respect of an act done intentionally to accelerate the death of a patient who is seriously ill, unless it is proved that the act was not done in good faith with the consent of the patient and for the purpose of saving him from severe pain in an illness believed to be of an incurable and fatal character. Under this formula it would be for the physician, if charged, to show that the patient was seri-

ously ill, but for the prosecution to prove that the physician acted from some motive other than the humanitarian one allowed to him by law.

Evidently, the presumption is that the general practitioner is a sufficient buffer between the patient and the restless spouse or over-wrought or overreaching relative, as well as a depository of enough general scientific know-how and enough information about current research developments and trends, to assure a minimum of error in diagnosis and anticipation of new measures of relief. Whether or not the general practitioner will accept the responsibility Williams would confer on him is itself a problem of major proportions. Putting that question aside, the soundness of the underlying premises of Williams' "legislative suggestion" will be examined in the course of the discussion of various aspects of the euthanasia problem.

B. The "Choice."

Under current proposals to establish legal machinery, elaborate or otherwise, for the administration of a quick and easy death, it is not enough that those authorized to pass on the question decide that the patient, in effect, is "better off dead." The patient must concur in this opinion. Much of the appeal in the current proposal lies in this so-called "voluntary" attribute.

But is the adult patient really in a position to concur? Is he truly able to make euthanasia a "voluntary" act? There is a good deal to be said, is there not, for Dr. Frohman's pithy comment that the "voluntary" plan is supposed to be carried out "only if the victim is both sane and crazed by pain."

By hypothesis, voluntary euthanasia is not to be resorted to until narcotics have long since been administered and the patient has developed a tolerance to them. *When,* then, does the patient make the choice? While heavily drugged? Or is narcotic relief to be withdrawn for the time of decision? But if heavy dosage no longer deadens pain, indeed, no longer makes it bearable, how overwhelming is it when whatever relief narcotics offer is taken away, too?

"Hypersensitivity to pain after analgesia has worn off is nearly always noted." Moreover, "the mental side-effects of narcotics, unfortunately for anyone wishing to suspend them temporarily without unduly tormenting the patient, appear to outlast the analgesic effect" and "by many hours." The situation is further complicated by the fact that "a person in terminal stages of cancer who had been given morphine steadily for a matter of weeks would certainly be dependent upon it physically and would probably be addicted to it and react with the addict's response."

The narcotics problem aside, Dr. Benjamin Miller, who probably has personally experienced more pain than any other commentator on the euthanasia scene, observes:

> Anyone who has been severely ill knows how distorted his judgment became during the worst moments of the illness. Pain and the toxic effect of disease, or the violent reaction to certain surgical procedures may change our capacity for rational and courageous thought.

If, say, a man in this plight were a criminal defendant and he were to decline the assistance of counsel would the courts hold that he had "intelligently and understandingly waived the benefit of counsel?"

Undoubtedly, some euthanasia candidates will have their lucid moments. How they are to be distinguished from fellow-sufferers who do not, or how these instances are to be distinguished from others when the patient is exercising an irrational judgment is not an easy matter. Particularly is this so under Williams' proposal, where no specially qualified persons, psychiatrically trained or otherwise, are to assist in the process.

Assuming, for purposes of argument, that the occasion when a euthanasia candidate possesses a sufficiently clear mind can be ascertained and that a request for euthanasia is then made, there remain other problems. The mind of the pain-racked may occasionally be clear, but is it not also likely to be uncertain and variable? This point was pressed hard by the great physician, Lord Horder, in the House of Lords debates:

> During the morning depression he [the patient] will be found to favour the application under this Bill, later in the day he will think quite differently, or will have forgotten all about it. The mental clarity with which noble Lords who present this Bill are able to think and to speak must not be thought to have any counterpart in the alternating moods and confused judgments of the sick man.

The concept of "voluntary" in voluntary euthanasia would have a great deal more substance to it if, as is the case with voluntary admission statutes for the mentally ill, the patient retained the right to reverse the process within a specified number of days after he gives written notice of his desire to do so—but unfortunately this cannot be. The choice here, of course, is an irrevocable one.

The likelihood of confusion, distortion or vacillation would appear to be serious draw-backs to any voluntary plan. Moreover, Williams' proposal is particularly vulnerable in this regard, since, as he admits, by eliminating the fairly elaborate procedure of the American and English Societies' plans, he also eliminates a time period which would furnish substantial evidence of the patient's settled intention to avail himself of euthanasia. . . .

If consent is given at a time when the patient's condition has so degenerated that he has become a fit candidate for euthanasia, when, if ever, will it be "clear and incontrovertible?" Is the suggested alternative of consent in advance a satisfactory solution? Can such a consent be deemed an informed one? Is this much different from holding a man to a prior statement of intent that if such and such an employment opportunity would present itself he would accept it, or if such and such a young woman were to come along he would marry her? Need one marshal authority for the proposition that many an "iffy" inclination is disregarded when the actual facts are at hand?

Professor Williams states that where a pre-pain desire for "ultimate euthanasia" is "reaffirmed" under pain, "there is the best possible proof of full consent." Perhaps. But what if it is alternately renounced and reaffirmed under pain? What if it is neither affirmed or renounced? What if it is only renounced? Will a physician be free to go ahead on the ground that the prior desire was "rational," but the present desire "irrational"? Under Williams' plan, will not the physician frequently "be walking in the margin of the law"—just as he is now? Do we really accomplish much more under this proposal than to put the euthanasia principle on the books?

Even if the patient's choice could be said to be "clear and incontrovertible," do not other difficulties remain? Is this the kind of choice, assuming that it can be made in a fixed and rational manner, that we want to offer a gravely ill person? Will we not sweep up, in the process, some who are not really tired of life, but think others are tired of them; some who do not really want to die, but who feel they should not live on, because to do so when there looms the legal alternative of euthanasia is to do a selfish or cowardly act? Will not some feel an obligation to have themselves "eliminated" in order that funds allocated for their terminal care might be better used by their families or, financial worries aside, in order to relieve their families of the emotional strain involved?

It would not be surprising for the gravely ill person to seek to inquire of those close to him whether he should avail himself of the legal alternative of euthanasia. Certainly, he is likely to wonder about their attitude in the matter. It is quite possible, is it not, that he will not exactly be gratified by an inclination on their part—however noble their motives may be in fact—that he resort to the new procedure? At this state, the patient-family relationship may well be a good deal less than it ought to be. . . .

* * *

. . . Are these the kind of pressures we want to inflict on any person, let alone a very sick person? Are these the kind of pressures we want to impose on any family, let alone an emotionally-shattered family? And if so, why are they not also proper considerations for the crippled, the paralyzed, the quadruple amputee, the iron lung occupant and their families?

* * *

C. The "Hopelessly Incurable" Patient and the Fallible Doctor.

Professor Williams notes as "standard argument" the plea that "no sufferer from an apparently fatal illness should be deprived of his life because there is always the possibility that the diagnosis is wrong, or else that some remarkable cure will be discovered in time." But he does not reach the issue until he has already dismissed it with this prefatory remark:

> It has been noticed in this work that writers who object to a practice for theological reasons frequently try to support their condemnation on medical grounds. With euthanasia this is difficult, but the effort is made.

Does not Williams, while he pleads that euthanasia not be theologically prejudged, at the same time invite the inference that non-theological objections to euthanasia are simple camouflage?

It is no doubt true that many theological opponents employ medical arguments as well, but it is also true that the doctor who has probably most forcefully advanced medical objections to euthanasia of the so-call incurables, Cornell University's world-renowned Foster Kennedy, a former president of the Euthanasia Society of America, *advocates* euthanasia in other areas where error in diagnosis and prospect of new relief or cures are much reduced, *i.e.*, the "congenitally unfit". In large part for the same reasons, Great Britain's Dr. A. Leslie Banks, then Principle Medical Officer of the Ministry of Health, maintained that a better case could be made for the destruction of congenital idiots and those in the final stages of dementia, particularly senile dementia, than could be made for the doing away of the pain-stricken incurable. Surely, such opponents of voluntary euthanasia cannot be accused of wrapping theological objections in medical dressing!

Until the euthanasia societies of England and America had been organized and a party decision reached, shall we say, to advocate euthanasia only for incurables on their request, Dr. Abraham L. Wolbarst, one of the most ardent supporters of the movement, was less troubled about putting away "insane or defective people [who] have suffered mental incapacity and tortures of the mind for many years" than he was about the "incurables." He recognized the "difficulty involved in the decision as to incurability" as one of the "doubtful aspect of euthanasia."

Doctors are only human beings, with few if any supermen among them. They make honest mistakes, like other men, because of the limitations of the human mind.

He noted further that "it goes without saying that, in recently developed cases with a possibility of cure, euthanasia should not even be considered," that "the law might establish a limit of, say, ten years in which there is a chance of the patient's recovery."

Dr. Benjamin Miller is another who is unlikely to harbor an ulterior theological motive. His interest is more personal. He himself was left to die the death of a "hopeless" tuberculosis victim only to discover that he was suffering from a rare malady which affects the lungs in much the same manner but seldom kills. Five years and sixteen hospitalizations later, Dr. Miller dramatized his point by recalling the last diagnostic clinic of the brilliant Richard Cabot, on the occasion of his official retirement:

He was given the case records [complete medical histories and results of careful examinations] of two patients and asked to diagnose their illnesses. . . . The patients had died and only the hospital pathologist knew the exact diagnosis beyond doubt, for he had seen the descriptions of the postmortem findings. Dr. Cabot, usually very accurate in his diagnosis, that day missed both.

The chief pathologist who had selected the cases was a wise person. He had purposely chosen two of the most deceptive to remind the medical students and young physicians that even at the end of a long and rich experience one of the greatest diagnosticians of our time was still not infallible.

* * *

Faulty diagnosis is only one ground for error. Even if the diagnosis is correct, a second ground for error lies in the possibility that some measure of relief, if not a full cure, may come to the fore within the life expectancy of the patient. . . .

* * *

D. "Mistakes Are Always Possible."

Under Professor Williams' "legislative suggestion" a doctor could "refrain from taking steps to prolong the patient's life by medical means" solely on his own authority. Only when disposition by affirmative "mercy-killing" is a considered alternative need he do so much as, and only so much as, consult another general practitioner. There are not other safeguards. No "euthanasia referee," no requirement that death be administered in the presence of an official witness, as in the English society's bill. No court to petition, no committee to investigate and report back to the court, as in the American society's bill. Professor Williams' view is:

It may be allowed that mistakes are always possible, but this is so in any of the affairs of life. And it is just as possible to make a mistake by doing nothing as by acting. All that can be expected of any moral agent is that he should do his best on the facts as they appear to him.

* * *

A relevant question, then, is what is the need for euthanasia which leads us to tolerate the mistakes, the very fatal mistakes, which will inevitably occur? What is the compelling force which requires us to tinker with deeply entrenched and almost universal precepts of criminal law?

Let us first examine the qualitative need for euthanasia:

Proponents of euthanasia like to present for consideration the case of the surgical operation, particularly a highly dangerous one: risk of death is substantial, perhaps even more probable than not; in addition, there is always the risk that the doctors have misjudged the situation and that no operation was needed at all. Yet it is not unlawful to perform the operation.

The short answer is the witticism that whatever the incidence of death in connection with different types of operations "no doubt, it is in all cases below 100 per cent, which is the incidence rate for euthanasia." But this may not be the full answer. There are occasions where the law permits action involving about a 100 per cent incidence of death, for example, self-defense. . . .

* * *

Reasonable mistakes, then, may be tolerated if as in the above circumstances and as in the case of the surgical operation, these mistakes are the inevitable by-products of efforts to save one or more human lives.

The need the euthanasiast advances, however, is a good deal less compelling. It is only to ease pain.

Let us next examine the quantitative need for euthanasia:

No figures are available, so far as I can determine, as to the number of say, cancer victims, who undergo intolerable or overwhelming pain. That an appreciable number do suffer such pain, I have no doubt. But that anything approaching this number whatever it is, need suffer such pain, I have—viewing the many sundry palliative measures now available—considerable doubt. The whole field of severe pain and its management in the terminal stage of cancer is, according to an eminent physician, "a subject neglected far too much by the medical profession." Other well-qualified commentators have recently noted the "obvious lack of interest in the literature about the problem of cancer pain" and have scored "the deplorable attitude of defeatism and therapeutic inactivity found in some quarters."

* * *

That of those who do suffer and must necessarily suffer the requisite pain, many *really* desire death, I have considerable doubt. Further, that of those who may desire death at a given moment, many have a fixed and rational desire for death, I likewise have considerable doubt. Finally, taking those who may have such a desire, again I must register a strong note of skepticism that many cannot do the job themselves. It is not that I condone suicide. It is simply that for reasons discussed in subsequent sections of this paper I find it easier to prefer a *laissez-faire* approach in such matters over an approach aided and sanctioned by the state.

* * *

Even if the need for voluntary euthanasia could be said to outweigh the risk of mistake, this is not the end of the matter. That "all that can be expected of any moral agent is that he should do his best on the facts as they appear to him" may be true as far as it goes, but it would seem that where the consequence of error is so irreparable it is not too much to expect of society that there be *a good deal more than one moral agent* "to do his best on the facts as they appear to him." It is not too much to expect for example, that something approaching the protection thrown around one who appears to have perpetrated a serious crime be extended to one who appears to have an incurable disease. Williams' proposal falls far short of this mark.

II. A LONG-RANGE VIEW OF EUTHANASIA

A. *Voluntary v. Involuntary Euthanasia.*

Ever since the 1870's, when what was probably the first euthanasia debate of the modern era took place, most proponents of the movement—at least when they are pressed—have taken considerable pains to restrict the question to the plight of the unbearably suffering incurable who *voluntarily seeks* death while most of their opponents have striven equally hard to frame the issue in terms which would encompass certain involuntary situations as well, *e.g.,* the "congenital idiots," the "permanently insane," and the senile.

* * *

No sooner had the English Society been organized and a drive to attain "easy death" legislation launched than Dr. Harry Roberts, one of the most distinguished sympathizers of the movement, disclosed some basis for alarm as to how far the momentum would carry:

> So far as its defined objects go, most informed people outside the Catholic Church will be in general sympathy with the new Society; but lovers of personal liberty may feel some of that suspicion which proved so well justified when the Eugenics movement was at its most enthusiastic height.

> In the course of the discussion at the [1935] Royal Sanitary Institute Congress, two distinguished doctors urged the desirability of legalizing the painless destruction of 'human mental monstrosities' in whom improvement is unattainable; and at the inaugural meeting of the Euthanasia Legislation Society, the Chairman of the Executive Committee said that 'they were concerned today only with voluntary euthanasia; but, as public opinion developed, and it became possible to form a truer estimate of the value of human life, further progress along preventive lines would be possible. . . . The population was an aging one, with a larger relative proportion of elderly persons—individuals who had reached a degenerative stage of life. Thus the total amount of suffering and the number of useless lives must increase.'

> We need to discriminate very carefully between facilitating the death of an individual at his own request and for his own relief, and the killing of an individual on the ground that, for the rest of us a course would be more economical or more agreeable than keeping him alive.

In the 1936 debate in the House of Lords, Lord Ponsonby of Shulbrede, who moved the second reading of the voluntary euthanasia bill, described two appealing actual cases, one where a man drowned his four-year-old daughter "who had contracted tuberculosis and had developed gangrene in the face," another where a woman killed her mother who was suffering from "general paralysis of the insane." Both cases of course were of the compulsory variety of euthanasia. True, Lord Ponsonby readily admitted that these cases were not covered by the proposed bill, but the fact remains that they were the *only* specific cases he chose to describe.

In 1950, Lord Chorley once again called the voluntary euthanasia bill to the attention of the House of Lords. He was most articulate, if not too discreet, on excluding compulsory euthanasia cases from coverage:

Another objection is that the Bill does not go far enough, because it applies only to adults and does not apply to children who come into the world deaf, dumb and crippled, and who have a much better cause than those for whom the Bill provides. That may be so, but we must go step by step.

In 1938, two years after the English Society was organized and its bill had been introduced into the House of Lords, the Euthanasia Society of America was formed. At its first annual meeting the following year, it offered proposed euthanasia legislation:

Infant imbeciles, hopelessly insane persons . . . and any person not requesting his own death would not come within the scope of the proposed act.

Charles E. Nixdorff, New York lawyer and treasurer of the society, who offered the bill for consideration, explained to some of the members who desired to broaden the scope of the proposed law, that it was *limited purposely to voluntary euthanasia because public opinions is not ready to accept the broader principle.* He said, however, that *the society hoped eventually to legalize the putting to death of nonvolunteers* beyond the help of the medical science.

About this time, apparently, the Society began to circulate literature in explanation and support of voluntary euthanasia, as follows:

The American and English Euthanasia Societies, after careful consideration, have both decided that more will be accomplished by devoting their efforts at present to the measure which will probably encounter the least opposition, namely *voluntary euthanasia.* The public is readier to recognize the right to *die* than the right to *kill,* even though the latter be in mercy. To take someone's life without his consent is a very different thing from granting him release from unnecessary suffering at his own express desire. The freedom of the individual is highly prized in democracies.

The American Society's own "Outline of the Euthanasia Movement in the United States and England" states in part:

1941. A questionnaire was sent to all physicians of New York State asking (1) Are you in favor of legalizing voluntary euthanasia for incurable adult sufferers? (2) Are you in favor of legalizing euthanasia for congenital monstrosities, idiots and imbeciles? Because only 1/3 as many physicians answered 'yes' to question 2 as to question 1, we decided that we would limit our program to voluntary euthanasia.

At a meeting of the Society of Medical Jurisprudence held several weeks after the American Society voluntary euthanasia bill had been drafted, Dr. Foster Kennedy, newly elected president of the Society, "urged the legalizing of euthanasia primarily in cases of born defectives who are doomed to remain defective, rather than for normal persons who have become miserable through incurable illness" and scored the "absurd and misplaced sentimental kindness" that seeks to preserve the life of a "person who is not a person." "If the law sought to restrict euthanasia to those who could speak out for it, and thus overlooked these creatures who cannot speak, then, I say as Dickens did, 'The law's an ass.'" As pointed out elsewhere, *while president* of the Society, Dr. Kennedy not only eloquently advocated involuntary euthanasia but strenuously *opposed* the voluntary variety. Is it any wonder that opponents of the movement do not always respect the voluntary-involuntary dichotomy?

At the same time that Dr. Kennedy was disseminating his "personal" views, Dr. A.L. Wolbarst, long a stalwart in the movement, was adhering much more closely to the party line. In a persuasive address to medical students published in a leading medical journal he pointed out that "a bill is now in preparation for introduction in the New York State Legislature authorizing the administration of euthanasia to incurable sufferers on their own request" and stressed that "the advocates of voluntary euthanasia do not seek to impose it on any one who does not ask for it. It is intended as an act of mercy for those who need it and demand it." What were Dr. Wolbarst's views before the English and American societies had been organized and substantial agreement reached as to the party platform? Four years earlier, in a debate on euthanasia, he stated:

> The question as usually submitted limits the discussion of legal euthanasia to those 'incurables whose physical suffering is unbearable to themselves.' That limitation is rather unfortunate, because the number of incurables within this category is actually and relatively extremely small. Very few incurables have or express the wish to die. However great their physical suffering may be . . . they prefer to live.
>
> If legal euthanasia has a humane and merciful motivation, it seems to me the entire question should be considered from a broad angle. There are times when euthanasia is strongly indicated as an act of mercy even though the subject's suffering is not 'unbearable to himself,' as in the case of an imbecile.
>
> It goes without saying that, in recently developed cases with a possibility of cure, euthanasia should not even be considered; but when insane or defective people have suffered mental incapacity and tortures of the mind for many years—forty-three years in a case of my personal knowledge— euthanasia certainly has a proper field.

In his 1939 address, Dr. Wolbarst also quoted in full the stirring suicide of Charlotte Perkins Gilman, "described as one of the twelve greatest American women [who] had been in failing health for several years and chose self-euthanasia rather than endure the pains of cancer." He would have presented Mrs. Gilman's views more fully if he had quoted as well from her last article, left with her agent to be published after her death, where she advocates euthanasia for "incurable invalids," "hopeless idiots," "helpless paretics," and "certain grades of criminals." Citing with approval the experience of "practical Germany," Miss Gilman's article asserted that "the dragging weight of the grossly unfit and dangerous could be lightened" by legalized euthanasia, "with great advantage to the normal and progressive. The millions spent in restraining and maintaining social detritus should be available for the safe-guarding and improving of better lives."

In 1950, the "mercy killings" perpetrated by Dr. Herman N. Sander on his cancer-stricken patient and by Miss Carol Ann Paight on her cancer-stricken father put the euthanasia question on page one. In the midst of the fervor over these cases, Dr. Clarence Cook Little, one of the leaders in the movement and a former president of the American Society, suggested specific safeguards for a law legalizing "mercy killings" for the "incurably ill but mentally fit" *and* for "mental defectives." The Reverend Charles Francis Potter, the founder and first president of the American Society hailed Dr. Sander's action as "morally right" and hence that which "should be legally right." Shortly thereafter, at its annual meeting, the American Society "voted to continue support" of both Dr. Sander and Miss Paight.

Now, one of the interesting, albeit underplayed, features of these cases—and this was evident all along—was that both were *involuntary* "mercy killings." There was considerable conflict in the testimony at the Sander Trial as to whether or not the victim's *husband* had pleaded with the doctor to end her suffering, but nobody claimed that the victim herself had done such pleading. There was considerable evidence in the *Paight* case to the effect that the victim's *daughter* had a "cancer phobia," the cancer deaths of two aunts having left a deep mark on her, but nobody suggested that the victim had a "cancer phobia."

It is true that Mother Paight said approvingly of her mercy-killing daughter that "she had the old Paight guts," but it is no less true that Father Paight had no opportunity to pass judgment on the question. He was asleep, still under the anesthetic of the exploratory operation which revealed the cancer in his stomach when his daughter, after having taken one practice shot in the woods, fired into his left temple. Is it not just possible that Father Paight would have preferred to have the vaunted Paight intestinal fortitude channelled in other directions, *e.g.,* by his daughter bearing to see him suffer?

The *Sander* and *Paight* case amply demonstrate that to the press, the public, and many euthanasiasts, the killing of one who does not or cannot speak is no less a "mercy killing" than the killing of one who asks for death. Indeed, the overwhelming majority of known or alleged "mercy killings" have occurred without the consent of the victim. . . .

* * *

The boldness and daring which characterizes most of Glanville Williams' book dims perceptibly when he comes to involuntary euthanasia proposals. As to the senile, he states:

> At present the problem has certainly not reached the degree of seriousness that would warrant an effort being made to change traditional attitudes toward the sanctity of life of the aged. Only the grimmest necessity could bring about a change that, however cautious in its approach, would probably cause apprehension and deep distress to many people, and inflict a traumatic injury upon the accepted code of behaviour built up by two thousand years of the Christian religion. It may be however, that as the problem becomes more acute it will itself cause a reversal of generally accepted values.

* * *

How "serious" does a problem have to be to warrant a change in these "traditional attitudes"? If, as the statement seems to indicate, "seriousness" of a problem is to be determined numerically, the problem of the cancer victim does not appear to be as substantial as the problem of the senile. For example, taking just the 95,837 first admissions to "public prolonged-care hospitals" for mental diseases in the United States in 1955, 23,561—or one fourth—were cerebral arteriosclerosis or senile brain disease cases. I am not at all sure that there are 20,000 cancer victims per year who die *unbearably painful* deaths. Even if there were, I cannot believe that among their ranks are some 20,000 per year who, when still in a rational state, so long for a quick and easy death that they would avail themselves of legal machinery for euthanasia.

If the problem of the incurable cancer victim "has reached the degree of seriousness that would warrant an effort being made to change traditional attitudes toward the sanctity of life," as Williams obviously thinks it has, then so has the problem of senility. In any event, the senility problem will undoubtedly soon reach even Williams' degree of seriousness. . . .

When Williams turns to the plight of the "hopelessly defective infants," his characteristic vim and vigor are, as in the senility discussion, conspicuously absent:

> While the Euthanasia Society of England has never advocated this, the Euthanasia Society of America did include it in its original program. The proposal certainly escapes the chief objection to the similar proposal for senile dementia: it does not create a sense of insecurity in society, because infants cannot, like adults, feel anticipatory dread of being done to death if their condition should worsen. Moreover, the proposal receives some support on eugenic grounds, and more importantly on humanitarian grounds—both on account of the parents, to whom the child will be a burden all their lives, and on account of the handicapped child itself. (It is not, however, proposed that any child should be destroyed against the wishes of its parents.) Finally, the legalization of euthanasia for handicapped children would bring the law into closer relation to its practical administration, because juries do not regard parental mercy-killing as murder. For these various reasons the proposal to legalize humanitarian infanticide is put forward from time to time by individuals. They remain in a very small minority, and the proposal may at present be dismissed as politically insignificant.

It is understandable for a reformer to limit his present proposals for change to those with a real prospect of success. But it is hardly reassuring for Williams to cite the fact that only "a very small minority" has urged euthanasia for "hopelessly defective infants" as the *only* reason for not pressing for such legislation now. If, as Williams sees it, the only advantage voluntary euthanasia has over the involuntary variety lies in the organized movements on its behalf, that advantage can readily be wiped out.

In any event, I do not think that such "a very small minority" has advocated "humanitarian infanticide." Until the organization of the English and American societies led to a concentration on the voluntary type, and until the by-products of the Nazi euthanasia program somewhat embarrassed, if only temporarily, most proponents of involuntary euthanasia, about as many writers urged one type as another. Indeed, some euthanasiasts have taken considerable pain to demonstrate the superiority of defective infant euthanasia over incurably ill euthanasia.

* * *

Nor do I think it irrelevant that while public resistance caused Hitler to yield on the adult euthanasia front, the killing of malformed and idiot children continued unhindered to the end of the war, the definition of "children" expanding all the while. Is it the embarrassing experience of the Nazi euthanasia program which has rendered destruction of defective infants presently "politically insignificant"? If so, is it any more of a jump from the incurably and painfully ill to the unorthodox political thinker than it is from the hopelessly defective infant to the same "unsavory character"? Or is it not so much that the euthanasiasts are troubled by the Nazi experience as it is that they are troubled that the public is troubled by the Nazi experience?

I read Williams' comment on defective infants for the proposition that there are some very good reasons for euthanatizing defective infants, but the time is not yet ripe. When will it be? When will the proposal become politically significant? After a voluntary euthanasia law is on the books and public opinion is sufficiently "educated"?

Williams' reasons for not extending euthanasia—once we legalize it in the narrow "voluntary" area—to the senile and the defective are much less forceful and much less persuasive than his arguments for legalizing voluntary euthanasia in the first place. I regard this as another reason for not legalizing voluntary euthanasia in the first place.

* * *

Thomas W. Mayo, *Constitutionalizing the "Right to Die,"* 49 MD. L. REV. 103, 125-46 (1990)*

* * *

II. FUNDAMENTAL RIGHTS

Judicial self-restraint will not, I suggest, be brought about in the 'due process' area by the historically unfounded incorporation formula . . .. It will be achieved in this area, as in other constitutional areas, only by continual insistence upon respect for the teachings of history, solid recognition of the basic values that underlie our society, and wise appreciation of the great roles that the doctrines of federalism and separation of powers have played in establishing and preserving American freedoms.[1]

A. Overview

Is the right of a PVS [persistent vegetative state] patient to refuse life-sustaining treatment a fundamental right that should enjoy the protection of the fourteenth amendment? This simple question simply begets more questions. How can we tell if the fourteenth amendment recognizes such a fundamental right? To what kinds of sources will we look to find an answer? How are institutional and political concerns to be balanced against individual ones?

This part of the article proposes an answer to these questions. In brief, my answer is this:

> 1. By most traditional measures—reason, tradition, natural law, consensus—the right of an incompetent patient to refuse life-sustaining treatment does not enjoy enough support to be accurately labeled a "fundamental" right, at least not when the patient is, like Nancy Beth Cruzan, in a persistent vegetative state and has not executed an advance directive. More significantly, even if broad agreement could be found for the general proposition that under some circumstances incompetent patients should be able to refuse life-sustaining treatment, there is not widespread agreement as to many of the important procedural and substantive issues implicit in that statement.

---

*   Reprinted by permission of Thomas William Mayo and the Maryland Law Review.

1   Griswold v. Connecticut, 381 U.S. 479, 501 (1965) (Harlan, J., concurring).

2. The Court should not extend federal constitutional protection to the right, because constitutionalization will cause more damage to evolving standards of medical practice and consensus-building on this important subject than it cures.

B. The "Rights" Stuff

The Supreme Court's forays into fundamental-rights analysis fall roughly into two groups. First are those cases involving democratic rights of political participation—having to do, for example, with voter qualifications, the weighing of votes, apportionment and districting, and access to the ballot. These decisions fall into that category of cases, in Professor Ely's words, "fueled . . . by a desire to ensure that the political process . . . was open to those of all viewpoints on something approaching an equal basis."

The second grouping of cases involves all other rights, not limited to rights of democratic participation, that the Court has identified as so important that state restrictions on them shall be given "heightened judicial scrutiny." These rights include the right to travel, the right to marry, and the broadly defined right of privacy. The Court also has held that some rights properly are not included on this list of fundamental rights, including the right to receive welfare; the right to basic levels of education, health care, or housing; and the right to government employment. Most, if not all, of these exclusions from the list of fundamental rights are explained, at least in part, by the Court's continued refusal to regard governmental classifications based upon wealth as "suspect" classifications that can be justified only by reference to a suitably "compelling" state interest.

How does the Court decide, with respect to this second group of cases, which rights are "fundamental" in some important enough way to warrant heightened judicial protection under the fourteenth amendment? Members of the Court can seldom agree among themselves as to the precise source of these rights or the justification for regarding them as "fundamental." The absence from the text of the Constitution of any mention of these rights makes the job of justifying these decisions doctrinally difficult. The Court's tendency to identify these rights and then, as in the case of privacy, to expand on them, has thrown constitutional scholars into one of the most divisive and enduring battles of the past thirty years.

Professor Ely has surveyed the various rationales put forward to explain and to justify the occasions when the Court has settled upon one right or another as "fundamental." Ely is a skeptic, but his guide is useful. Concluding that all of these external sources of value are wanting in one way or another, Ely discusses the personal values of the deciding judge, natural law, neutral principles, reason, tradition, consensus, and the judge's "best estimate of what tomorrow's observers would be prepared to credit as progress." In the course of his survey of constitutional law scholarship on the subject of "fundamental rights," Dean Choper produced a similar list of approaches.

Considered together, these sources might be expressed by Dean Choper's necessarily loose phrase, "some evolving societal consensus." Indeed, of all of the approaches on Ely's list, the Supreme Court has appeared, especially in its recent cases, to rely most explicitly upon consensus—focusing especially upon ostensibly objective indicia of society's "widely shared values," of conventional morality—which Ely says "turns out to be at the core of most 'fundamental values' positions." This article will apply this sense of "consensus"—broad, inclusionary, historical, and progressive—to the constitutional issue raised by Cruzan.

First, however, some words of caution are in order. In Ely's view, the use of consensus as a guide to discovering fundamental values has three major flaws. The first is the assumption that consensus may exist at all, when in fact the United States may have devolved into a system of special interest domination through temporary coalitions and legislative logrolling. Developments in public choice theory tend to support this conclusion.

The second and more serious flaw focuses on our inability to define the content and scope of a consensus, even if we assume the possibility that a consensus may exist. As Ely puts it, "when one gets down to cases, one finds much the same mix we found when the reference was to 'natural law'—a mix of the uselessly general and the controversially specific."

The most serious flaw of all for Ely is the illogic of appealing to majoritarian consensus on questions of fundamental rights. One reason for the appeal to fundamental rights might be to assure that the majority's interest in a fundamental right is protected adequately, a job the legislature clearly is better suited to perform. On the other hand, if the reason for appealing to fundamental rights is to protect the rights of an individual or minority from the tyranny of the majority, it seems somewhat self-defeating to appeal to the sense of the majority to determine whether such fundamental individual or minority rights exist.

Most of Ely's objections are illustrated by a recent privacy case in which the Supreme Court justified its limitation upon the fundamental right to privacy by noting the absence of consensus. In *Bowers v. Hardwick,* the Court concluded that prior cases "would [not] extend a fundamental right to homosexuals to engage in acts of consensual sodomy." The Court reached this conclusion by noting that "[s]odomy was a criminal offense at common law and was forbidden by the laws of the original 13 States when they ratified the Bill of Rights" and "[i]n 1868, when the Fourteenth Amendment was ratified, all but 5 of the 37 states in the Union had criminal sodomy laws." The Court's reliance upon historical consensus presumably is justified by one of the Court's alternative definitions of "fundamental rights": "those liberties that are 'deeply rooted in this Nation's history and tradition.'"

Yet, the *Bowers* Court could not conclude with any real justification that consensual sodomy—along with other decisions that profoundly touch individual notions of sexuality and identity such as contraception and abortion—is not included within our core understanding of "privacy rights." The Court's notion of consensus on this subject lacks credibility when twenty-four states and the District of Columbia have criminalized sodomy but twenty-six states have not. Whatever the level of consensus in the past, the Justices' figures illustrate a clear historical shift away from criminalizing sodomy. Yet that trend was not factored into the majority's discussion of consensus. For that matter, it is difficult to say how a historical shift in attitudes should be factored into the Court's analysis.

Finally, "consensus" requires an issue, a proposition, that a majority can agree on, and that issue or proposition should be relevant to the case at hand. Imagine that a representative sampling of citizens or legislators was asked, "Should the constitution protect consensual homosexual sodomy?" and another sampling was asked, "Should the constitution protect the right to be left alone or the right to conduct intimate relationships in the intimacy of your own home?" How would the answers to either set of questions provide an answer to whether the fundamental right to privacy permitted Georgia's punishment of Michael Hardwick?

The foregoing discussion illustrates how tenuous—as a matter of logic, history, and constitutional doctrine—the Court's reliance upon consensus can be as a guide to identifying and defining fundamental rights. Having charted a course in this area that relies upon consensus, however, the Court appears unwilling or unable to turn back, and it could not do so without undoing settled law. For example, *Roe v. Wade* and its progeny depend upon a non-statutory consensus for their conclusion that the constitution protects a woman's right to choose to have an abortion. With all of these difficulties in mind, we turn next to the question whether any such consensus exists on the question of an incompetent patient's right to refuse life-sustaining treatment.

C. Terminating Treatment

"No answer is what the wrong question begets. . . ."

The question of the legal status of an incompetent patient's right to refuse life-sustaining medical treatment produces different answers depending upon how the question is framed. Consider, for example, the states' "living will" legislation. As of 1988, thirty-eight states and the District of Columbia had enacted some type of statute that empowered a competent patient to execute an advance medical directive that would allow life-sustaining treatment to be withheld or withdrawn in the event the patient becomes incompetent and is terminally ill. At one level of generality, these thirty-nine statutes reflect a national consensus (based upon the agreement of nearly eighty percent of the states) that life-sustaining treatment can be withheld or withdrawn from incompetent patients, at least under some limited circumstances, when the patient has executed an advance written directive.

Only two of these state statutes, however—Arkansas and, very recently, Texas—would appear to permit patients who are not in a terminal condition to execute advance written directives. Thus, with respect to PVS patients with no other illness or injury (and whose life expectancy may be measured in years or decades), the vast majority of these statutes do not confer a right to have life-sustaining treatment withdrawn on the basis of a living will.

"Terminal condition" is, of course, a nontechnical term that is capable of being infused with different meanings. For example, it does not specify a period of time within which death is expected to occur. Even if this limitation can be finessed by physicians acting within their reasonable clinical, professional judgment, however, it is difficult to find in these statutes a national consensus in support of the termination of life-sustaining treatment for patients, like Nancy Beth Cruzan, in a persistent vegetative state. This is because the medical needs of such patients, absent infections and the like, are limited to nutrition and hydration (as well as basic nursing care), and nineteen of these thirty-nine statutes do not permit nourishment to be withheld pursuant to a living will. Commentators are dramatically and heatedly in disagreement over the issue, as well.

The search for a national consensus on the treatment issues for PVS patients, however, need not be limited to the legislative enactments of the various states. There are at least two reasons why this should be so. First, most patients, like Nancy Beth Cruzan, do not execute living wills before they become incompetent to make their own medical care decisions. Thus, "living will" legislation is only an indirect source of guidance in cases similar to hers. Second, the Natural Death Acts and "living will" statutes generally are regarded as having added rights to those that existed at common law, not as being in derogation of those pre-existing rights. Consequently, a complete picture of the national consensus, if any, on this issue must look to other statutes, the case law, and the commentary that has come out of this area. Although there is no logical reason why the Supreme Court could not look to state and lower federal court decisions to determine whether there exists a common-law right to have life-sustaining treatment withdrawn or withheld, it would not be helpful in this case.

The doctrine of informed consent to medical treatment, for example, does not help in the search for a consensus concerning medical decision making for incompetent patients such as Nancy Beth Cruzan. There undoubtedly is widespread support in the courts for the doctrine, with its twin duties to inform and to obtain consent and its correlative right to refuse consent. Its acceptance within the medical profession, however, has been somewhat grudging, and fidelity to the dictates of informed consent in the clinical setting remains a matter not wholly free from doubt. Finally, there is a lack of realism in looking to informed consent, which posits the right of competent patients to make their own medical treatment decisions, as a basis for finding consensus concerning the rights of incompetent patients to choose a certain course of medical treatment.

The "right to die" cases are also an unsatisfactory source of consensus. Professor Alan Meisel's recent summary of these cases deserves to be quoted in full:

> Although the case law since *Quinlan* has added some clarity, it has also added a great deal of confusion to the issue of the right to die. A large majority of jurisdictions still have no case law on the issue. Looking to the law of other jurisdictions is complicated by the fact that it may be unsettled, incomplete, or conflicting. Furthermore, judicial decisions frequently raise more questions than they answer. The New Jersey courts, for example, despite repeated attempts to put the matter to rest with far-reaching if not seemingly definitive opinions, have appeared to be seriously frustrated in their efforts. Indeed, the experience in those jurisdictions (California, Florida, Massachusetts, New Jersey, and New York) that have experienced relatively frequent litigation over these matters has been that litigation raises more questions and breeds more litigation rather than definitive resolution.

Professor George Annas, who has been a rather consistent defender of the right to refuse life-sustaining treatment, would agree. He describes the decision as to "[w]ho has the right to refuse lifesaving treatment for an incompetent patient as one of the most controversial areas of medical jurisprudence." As anyone who has attempted to wade through the opinions knows, this is a field in which distinctions and contradictions abound.

Nor, for that matter, has the medical profession itself developed a consensus as to the proper method of dealing with PVS patients. As the Supreme Judicial Court of Massachusetts noted in *Brophy v. New England Mount Sinai Hospital, Inc.,* "There is substantial disagreement in the medical community over the appropriate medical action." The steady stream of books and articles about the "right to die" is a further illustration of the lack of general agreement on even first principles, let alone the details of the implementation of such principles.

As evidence of the deep, fundamental disagreements that so mark this area, consider the status of the debate over active and passive euthanasia. If there is a dominant position with respect to these terms, it is that passive euthanasia may be ethically and legally permissible under certain circumstances, while active euthanasia is not ethically permissible and constitutes homicide, at least under some circumstances. The distinction between active and passive euthanasia typically is seen as a difficult one to defend logically but important to retain for legal and policy reasons. As the controversy over the following article in the Journal of the American Medical Association (JAMA) illustrates, however, a strong riptide of dissent runs just below the seemingly placid surface of this general agreement.

In 1988, JAMA published *It's Over, Debbie,* an anonymous account of a gynecology resident's decision to inject a young cancer patient with a lethal dose of morphine. The circumstances surrounding the resident's decision to administer the lethal injection were so unusual, some readers were tempted to conclude that the story was apocryphal. In a subsequent editorial defending JAMA's decision to print the article, the journal's editor, Dr. George Lundberg, stated that there are "at least six identifiable major types of euthanasia," beginning with "passive," ending with "active," and with at least four presumably intermediate types in between. Lundberg regarded only "active euthanasia," such as that performed by the resident in *It's Over, Debbie,* to be both illegal and "outside the bounds of thousands of years of medical tradition." William Gaylin and three other well-known medical ethicists agreed, condemning the resident for committing premeditated murder and "behav[ing] altogether in a scandalously unprofessional and unethical manner." Kenneth Vaux, however, chose to recharacterize the resident's act as "morally acceptable double-effect euthanasia." This disagreement might be written off merely as evidence of the difficult moral distinction between passive euthanasia (and its moral equivalents) and active euthanasia, since Vaux avoided the label of "active euthanasia" in his analysis of the resident's conduct. But Vaux's disagreement with the other writers is more fundamental. He stated: "[W]hile positive euthanasia must be proscribed in principle, in exceptional cases it may be abided in deed."

Other authors, perhaps less cagey than Vaux, have supported the proposition that active euthanasia should not even be proscribed in principle. Thus, in a famous essay, James Rachels wrote: "[T]here is really no moral difference between the two, considered in themselves (there may be important moral differences in some cases in their consequences, but, as I pointed out, these differences may make active euthanasia, and not passive euthanasia, the morally preferable option)." For its time, Rachels' argument was a notably minority position. Four years later, Joseph Fletcher argued forcefully in favor of "active or direct euthanasia, which helps the patient to die, not merely the passive or indirect form of euthanasia which 'lets the patient go' by simply withholding life-preserving treatments." His argument ended with the prediction, not quite fully realized in 1990, that "other forms [of euthanasia than indirect and involuntary euthanasia] will one day be socially accepted and enacted into law." Others have since embraced the Rachels-Fletcher position that no principled basis exists between active and passive euthanasia and that active euthanasia is, therefore, morally defensible.

After the infamous "Debbie" piece appeared, physicians and laypeople wrote to JAMA and expressed opinions that cover the entire spectrum from Gaylin to Rachels. As the Vaux article intimates, it may well be that there exists a significant chasm between medical ethical theory and medical practice in fact. The differences of opinion in this area have led to recent scholarly efforts to redefine the terms of the debate in an attempt to clarify the moral terms over which there is so much disagreement. In the spring of 1989, an influential group of physicians added their voices to the debate by concluding that physician-assisted suicide is not unethical. Stopping short of a similar endorsement of active euthanasia, the group wrote that physicians "should not feel morally coerced to participate in [euthanasia]. . . . [T]he medical profession and the public will continue to debate the role that euthanasia may have in the treatment of the terminally or hopelessly ill patient." Answers may not be obvious, but the lack of consensus is.

The shifting attitudes toward passive and active euthanasia should be of great concern to the Court as it considers whether and to what extent it should approve the withholding or withdrawal of nutrition and hydration from Nancy Beth Cruzan. We in the United States already have seen a quite dramatic change in attitudes toward nutrition and hydration, from 1976, when Karen Ann Quinlan's father (who already had petitioned to have his daughter's respirator turned off) reacted with horror at the suggestion to remove her nasogastric tube ("Oh no, that is her nourishment") to the present, when "courts . . . typically do not give th[e] fact [that nutrition and hydration are being removed] particular note." How long will it take for our acceptance of passive euthanasia to lead to a grudging and limited acceptance of active euthanasia, followed by a greater willingness to tolerate active euthanasia?

Although it is fashionable in some circles to sneer at slippery slope arguments such as this, one should not do so unthinkingly in this area. Those who support passive euthanasia but oppose active euthanasia, for example, believe the two forms of euthanasia to be different and that the differences are morally significant. But, as Professor Frederick Schauer has pointed out, most slippery slope arguments are based upon the potentially valid assumption of the inability of future decision makers to understand or defend distinctions we deem important today. The ability or willingness of future decision-makers to maintain the active-passive distinction still thought by most observers to be significant depends upon at least two factors: the logical strength of the distinction and the effect that experience has upon our willingness to maintain the distinction. As to the former, one only need read some of the arguments currently being put forth by proponents of the active-passive distinction to wonder how long the arguments will satisfy the proponents themselves, let alone those who follow some years later.

As for the effect that our experience with legalized passive euthanasia might have on our ability to maintain moral distinctions we currently believe are significant, a few comments may be made. First, the history of our activities and beliefs concerning the ethics of death and dying is a history of lost distinctions of former significance. Slippery slopes simply may go with this psychological and emotional territory. Moreover, the courts (and the Supreme Court in particular) cannot be unmindful of their influence not only as definers of conventional morality but as shapers of it as well. The role of Dutch courts in moving the Netherlands toward legalized active euthanasia provides an example. As Professor Tribe recently has noted, the courts and the legal system affect reality by changing the conditions of our relations with one another and the state, yet the courts (or at least the Supreme Court) repeatedly fail to take this into account when they address subsequent legal issues without recognizing the extent to which their own past decisions fundamentally altered the experiences, expectations, and conduct of the parties.

Again, the Netherlands may provide an example. One of the essential preconditions for the use of active euthanasia by a Dutch physician is that the patient freely request the termination of his or her life, a precondition that proponents of active euthanasia in the United States probably would accept. The notion of free choice, however, becomes troubling as soon as the euthanasia option becomes legalized. As Professor Yale Kamisar noted thirty years ago:

> Even if the patient's choice could be said to be "clear and incontrovertible," do not other difficulties remain? Is this the kind of choice, assuming that it can be made in a fixed and rational manner, that we want to offer a gravely ill person? Will we not sweep up, in the process, some who are not really tired of life, but think others are tired of them; some who do

not really want to die, but who feel they should not live on, because to do so when there looms the legal alternative of euthanasia is to do a selfish or cowardly act? Will not some feel an obligation to have themselves "eliminated" in order that funds allocated for their terminal care might be better used by their families or, financial worries aside, in order to relieve their families of the emotional strain involved?

In short, just as technology often has seemed to have its own moral imperative ("If it is available, it should be used"), options given the blessings of the law may well become not only thinkable but presumptively so. For the reasons explained in the remainder of this article, the Supreme Court should let these issues continue to develop at the grassroots, with the vigorous debate and the cross-fertilization from one state to another that can happen best, if at all, with the least control from the Court. This seems so at least until the dynamic and fluid "consensus" on these issues coalesces around both conclusions and rationales acceptable to at least the proponents of passive or active euthanasia themselves. Two recent commentaries on the *Cruzan* case by authors who criticize and approve the Missouri Supreme Court's decision support this cautious approach. Both suggest that recognizing a constitutional right to die in a case such as *Cruzan* will seriously threaten the rights of incapacitated patients. One or the other of these positions is likely to be correct, and the resolution of this most difficult of problems will not be furthered by Supreme Court activism in this case.

* * *

Sanford H. Kadish, *Letting Patients Die: Legal and Moral Reflections,* 80 CAL. L. REV. 857 (1992)*

Since World War II dramatic advances in the power of medicine to sustain life have led to profound changes in the types of illness from which people die. At one time pneumonia, influenza, and other communicable diseases were the most common causes of death. Today chronic, degenerative diseases such as cancer, heart disease, and cerebrovascular disease have become predominant, accounting for approximately seventy percent of all deaths in the United States. This in turn has shifted the locus of dying. Whereas at the turn of the century most patients died at home, today nearly eighty percent of deaths occur in hospitals. Patients with degenerative diseases can be kept biologically alive for long periods of time through the use of drugs and machines, though sensate and functional life has gone forever. As a consequence, in the language of one court, "[q]uestions of fate have . . . become matters of choice raising profound 'moral, social, technological, philosophical, and legal questions. . . .'" For example, does keeping people biologically alive in these circumstances make sense? Whose interests are served by sustaining a life so limited in scope? In what does the value of a life lie? What is the role of the patient's preferences in cases where he has made a competent current choice, where he has made an earlier choice, where he has made no choice? These questions, thrust upon us by advances in medical technology, raise doubts about the continued validity of some of our most deeply held moral beliefs about life and death.

Despite some paradoxes and inconsistencies (for example, in our attitudes toward war, capital punishment, and risk), preservation of human life is generally seen as a supreme good in our culture. Intentionally taking a life, at least an innocent life, is among the worst wrongs a person can commit. It is everywhere a crime, punishable by the severest penalties known to the law. Every innocent person, no matter what the quality of his life, has a legal right that his life not be taken. Moreover, so great a value is put on life that a person may not waive his right to life; killing does not become non-culpable because the victim consented. For similar reasons, suicide and attempted suicide were crimes at common law, and helping another kill himself is still a crime in many American states. Finally, although the law does not generally criminalize failure to save another, a physician who intentionally fails to save a patient's life when able to do so may be guilty of some form of culpable homicide. These norms constitute the moral tradition threatened by the remarkable power of medicine to prolong life. How can this moral tradition ever accommodate a deliberate decision not to use all available medical power to save a life?

Departures from the official pieties usually occur first in our practices and only later in our professions. So it has been with the issue of life-sustaining treatment. Doctors and hospitals have long engaged in or tolerated practices that contravene the moral tradition I have just described. For decades doctors and hospitals have accepted what is called negative euthanasia. "Every day . . . respirators are turned off, life-perpetuating intravenous infusions stopped, proposed surgery canceled, and drugs countermanded. So-called Code 90 stickers are put on many record-jackets, indicating 'Give no intensive care or resuscitation.'" And though medical killing on request (active euthanasia) is apparently not common, neither is it unknown in American hospitals.

The public has come largely to accept these practices, principally through the impact of such dramatic and highly publicized cases as *In re Quinlan.* In 1976, the New Jersey Supreme Court held that a parent of Karen Quinlan, a young woman in a permanent vegetative state, could authorize removal of a respirator that was keeping Karen biologically alive. Since then, public opinion polls have revealed an impressive shift of opinion in just one generation from a majority opposed to "pulling the plug" on permanently comatose patients to a large majority—sometimes nearing 90%—in favor of such measures. Opinion as to whether doctors should be permitted to actively kill incurable and comatose patients has also changed. In 1947, a majority disapproved. Since then, majorities of up to 64% have favored such proposals.

There appears to be even less dissent when the patient is not comatose and competently chooses to die. A recent national survey showed that 79% of adults support laws allowing terminally ill patients to refuse life-sustaining treatment or to order that it be stopped. A recent California poll indicates that about 70% of Californians feel that the assisted suicide of seriously ill patients who wish to die should be legalized. In Washington state, voters defeated a referendum proposing that doctors be permitted to kill terminally ill patients at their request by a vote of 56% to 44%. But a month earlier a poll showed that, of those likely to vote, 61% were in favor, 27% were opposed, and 12% were undecided. The defeat of the referendum might have been a manifestation of the "cold feet" phenomenon that sometimes occurs when the voter enters the voting booth. Despite this apparent setback, the marked increase in public acceptance of killing terminally ill patients, both in Washington and nationally, has been striking.

Equally striking are the changes in enacted laws. When Karen Quinlan became comatose in 1975, no state recognized a patient's right to set limits on life-prolonging medical efforts. Now, over forty states have passed "living will" statutes giving effect to a person's choice of medical treatment in the event of incompetency. Although these laws tend to be highly restrictive, they nonetheless represent a radical departure from what could have been expected of a legislature a decade earlier. More significantly, many states have enacted statutes allowing a person to authorize an agent, in the event of the patient's incompetence, to make those health care decisions that the patient could have made if competent.

* * *

I

AUTONOMY AND THE COMPETENT PATIENT

The fulcrum on which the courts moved the law away from its traditional hostility to forgoing treatment was the concept of consent. The requirement of consent goes back to the common law, which made it a battery to subject a person to any force to which he had not consented, including such force as might be involved in providing medical treatment. In dealing with such issues as the constitutionality of laws prohibiting contraception and abortion, the United States Supreme Court gave new and powerful support to the common law concept of consent. The Court developed a jurisprudence of autonomy (sometimes under the misleading label of privacy), finding in the Constitution a fundamental right of individuals to make choices with regard to their own bodies. The lesson of the new autonomy jurisprudence for refusals of medical treatment was plain, and the *Quinlan* case was one of the first to draw it explicitly. In that case the New Jersey court found that just as the constitutional right of autonomy over one's body encompasses a woman's decision to have an abortion, so does it "encompass a patient's decision to decline medical treatment," at least under some circumstances. Other courts soon followed the *Quinlan* lead.

In *Cruzan v. Director, Missouri Department of Health,* the United States Supreme Court, in an opinion by Chief Justice Rehnquist, went a good distance toward lending its authority to a constitutional right to refuse medical treatment. The case involved a Missouri statute requiring that before artificial nutrition and hydration could be withdrawn from a patient in a permanent vegetative state, it must be established by "clear and convincing" evidence that she had decided when competent not to be kept alive in these circumstances. Although upholding the constitutionality of the Missouri standard, the opinion stated that the logic of the Court's prior opinions supported the existence of a patient's constitutionally protected interest in refusing life-sustaining medical treatment, including artificial nutrition and hydration.

As the Court further noted in *Cruzan,* however, the existence of a constitutionally protected interest does not necessarily preclude state regulation, for a state might have sufficiently weighty interests to override that of the individual. Indeed, state and lower federal courts have recognized four distinct state interests that weigh against the choice of a competent patient to decline treatment: 1) its interest in preserving life as such; 2) its interest in preventing suicide; 3) its interest in protecting the interests of innocent third parties; and 4) its interest in maintaining the ethical integrity of the medical profession. Only the first two figure at all seriously in the decisions, however. Though some courts have treated the interest in preserving life and the interest in preventing suicide separately, they are obviously interrelated considerations. It is noteworthy, however, that lower courts in virtually all cases have upheld the right of a patient to reject life-sustaining treatment as required by a constitutional right of autonomy, and as such outweighing these state interests.

The problem that naturally arises concerning this right of autonomy is its extent. Does it come into play only in these medical contexts, or does it extend to all cases in which the person chooses to achieve his own death, including perhaps those in which he obtains the help of another to further his choice? Courts have declined to extend the right of autonomy to nonmedical contexts and have sought to avoid doing so by distinguishing medical letting-die situations from conventional suicide and consensual euthanasia. Since such an extension would profoundly unsettle existing mores and might raise formidable problems for the law in preventing exploitation and abuse, it is not hard to understand the courts' motivation. Still, putting prudential considerations aside for the moment, can these distinctions withstand principled analysis?

One ground on which courts have sought to distinguish letting-die situations from conventional suicide is that the latter requires affirmative life-taking actions. On this view a patient refusing to be attached to an apparatus necessary for his survival is not taking his life, but is simply letting nature take its course. Hence death is caused by the disease, not by the person himself, nor by the physician who respects his wishes. How persuasive is this distinction? Perhaps there is some support for this approach in the legal principle that imposes no duty to act to prevent a prohibited harm except in specified circumstances. After all, the traditional formulation of the ban on suicide is cast in terms of action, so it is arguable that one who seeks death through inaction would not fall within the ban. Yet it would be odd if that were so. The traditional disinclination of Anglo-American courts to interpret prohibitions on causing certain results as requiring action to prevent those results is based on the value of the freedom of the individual not to be constrained by the interests of others. That value is not at stake in the prohibition of suicide for two reasons: first, because the interests of others are not necessarily involved, and second, because the ban on suicidal actions already constitutes a major inroad upon the person's freedom, so that excluding cases of passive choice to die out of concern for that very freedom would be eccentric at best.

In any event, if we view the issue in terms of moral principle rather than legal doctrine and take the traditional anti-suicide position as a serious starting point, the distinction between intentionally killing oneself and intentionally submitting to an avoidable death is suspect. There is disagreement over the general moral significance of the distinction between doing and letting happen, but the intuitive appeal of the distinction is less in some cases than in others, and its appeal seems particularly weak in cases of treatment refusal.

Consider a patient who finds himself attached against his will to some life-sustaining apparatus he had earlier explicitly rejected. He removes it for the same reason he earlier rejected it—he prefers death to living attached to a machine—and dies moments later. Presumably this would constitute suicide, since he achieved his death by positive actions. But could we justifiably say that if the doctors had followed his instructions and he had died, this would not be suicide because his death would then not have been caused by the patient's actions? Or consider an analogous case: a paralyzed man, sitting on a beach threatened by an incoming tide, deliberately, in order to end his life, declines to allow a lifeguard to move him out of harm's way, and drowns in consequence. (To make the analogy closer, assume he took no action to place himself in danger from the tide—say, for example, he was initially placed there against his will.) Would it not be correct to see this as a suicide? Yet the person dying of a disease who chooses not to permit some medical intervention that would save him is in no different a situation.

We might have good reasons to think that in certain circumstances intentionally achieving one's death is justifiable, or that it is less blameworthy in some circumstances than in others. Moreover, we may for these reasons, or indeed for other reasons of a more practical and prudential character, want to call it something else. But as a matter of principle, that a person achieves his goal by refusing necessary medical intervention hardly seems a better reason to treat his action differently than that a person achieves his goal by letting the tide come to him rather than going to it.

Another approach some courts have taken is to define suicide to require a purpose to take one's own life, sometimes called a specific intent. Those who reject treatment, it is reasoned, do not want to die; indeed, as one court put it, "they may fervently wish to live, but to do so free of unwanted medical technology, surgery, or drugs, and without protracted suffering." When they reject treatment, therefore, they are not committing suicide. Recently Ronald Dworkin has lent his considerable authority to this position.* In the course of criticizing Justice Scalia's argument in *Cruzan* that the venerability of the tradition of state condemnation of suicide establishes the state's equal entitlement to regulate treatment refusal, Dworkin asserts that it is "bizarre to classify as suicide someone's decision to reject treatment that would keep him alive but at a cost he and many other people think too great." He appears to be making two points: the first, that death is achieved by failing to act, I have already discussed; the second, that the person's decision is not suicide because his intention is not to achieve his death as such, but to avoid a life whose burdens are not worth the living, is an argument I take to be equivalent to the specific intent argument.

A case may be made for the specific intent argument in this context along the following lines. The purpose of the classic suicide in inflicting a mortal injury on himself, in the sense of purpose as the "conscious object" of an action, is to cause his own death. The same cannot be said of all cases where the person refuses treatment he knows is necessary to keep him alive. In some of these cases his mental state with respect to his death is more properly characterized as knowledge rather than purpose; that is, although he knows that his conduct will result in his death, his conscious object is not to die, but to be free of the medical treatment. That his object is not to die may be seen by noticing that if, contrary to the prediction of his doctors, he recovered without the treatment, his purpose would not be frustrated. The same could not be said of the classic attempted suicide.

The trouble with this line of argument is that the distinction between purpose and knowledge in this context is without moral relevance. The cases where the refusal of treatment can be said not to reflect a specific intent to die are those in which the irremediable condition which makes living not worthwhile to the person is prospective rather than already existing. If it is in prospect, we are able to see his purpose as avoiding his affliction. But when the afflicted condition already exists, the ending of the person's afflicted life would presumably be seen as his purpose in refusing treatment. So, for example, if a patient refuses amputation of his gangrenous legs (because he doesn't want to live without them), his purpose is to avoid the amputation, not to die, so that his subsequent death would not be considered a suicide. He would have been pleased to live if his legs could have been saved. But if a person whose legs have already been amputated refuses medical treatment neces-

---

*   *See* Ronald Dworkin, *The Right to Death*, N.Y. REV. BOOKS, Jan. 31, 1991, at 14.

sary for his recovery (again because he doesn't want to live without his legs), his purpose is to die, so that his subsequent death *would* be deemed a suicide. But except in the case where death is itself sought as an end (the insured who wants his beneficiary to recover on his life insurance, for example), all suicides are motivated by the desire to end experiencing something unbearable in that person's life. It is hard to see any point in treating choices to end one's life differently depending on whether the motivating condition is present or anticipated.

I suggest, therefore, that the efforts by courts maintain to traditional authority of the state over suicide by distinguishing it from refusal of treatment do not withstand scrutiny. I do not mean to suggest that the law cannot justifiably make distinctions on pragmatic grounds; it frequently does so for all kinds of prudential considerations. I mean only to suggest that the distinctions under discussion cannot be defended *except* on pragmatic grounds.

* * *

II

AUTONOMY AND THE INCOMPETENT PATIENT

The right of autonomy, then, is what ensures that a patient may refuse treatment. But autonomous choice requires a competent chooser. What of the many cases where the patient is not competent? The response of the courts has been to rest on the intriguing argument that since incompetency cannot diminish a person's rights, denial of an incompetent's choice would constitute unconstitutional discrimination on grounds of personal handicap. At the outset, therefore, the cases of incompetents raise a formidable conceptual problem. How can the right of autonomy over one's own body have any application where the patient is incompetent to make a choice? Whatever rights an incompetent person may be said to possess, how can autonomous choice be one of them when incompetency means precisely the inability to exercise choice?

The current state of law in the area can be briefly summarized. If the incompetent patient, at some time when he was competent, exercised his right to refuse medical treatment under circumstances like those now presented (possibly, but not necessarily, by a formal "advance directive" in a living will), the courts have been willing in most situations to give effect to that choice. Courts have also given effect to choices by patients who, while competent, authorized another to make the choice in the event of his incompetence (by a so-called "durable power of attorney"). If, during competency, the patient did not execute an advance directive, appoint an agent, or indicate a choice in some other way (which is the usual case), the courts have invoked the concept of "substituted judgment" (sometimes called "surrogate decision-making"). Under this approach, the decider (the court, the family, or others—courts have disagreed on whether judicial intervention is necessary) makes the choice on behalf of the incompetent.

A. *Where the Patient Made a Competent Choice in the Past: Advance Directives*

I will start with situations that seem to me to present the least difficulty, those where the patient has made an actual choice in the past. One set of such cases occurs when the patient is in a vegetative state that is known to be permanent. Lacking capacity now and forever for having experiences of any kind or for making a different choice, there is no basis for not respecting his earlier competent choice to die.

Cases at the other extreme, those in which the person remains competent, are also easy. If a competent patient decides to change his mind for some reason—perhaps because of new medical treatments, or because facing dying as a present reality is different from facing it as a future possibility, or perhaps because he has simply mellowed with age—the principle of autonomy requires, not just permits, that he may do so. Assuming there is no question of the patient's competence (a problem I will return to shortly), the principle of autonomy requires the person's latest choice to govern.

The hard case is presented when a patient, plainly incompetent on traditional criteria, is still sentient. Consider this hypothetical. Composer Then is a famous musician whose whole life centers around music. She executes a durable power of attorney in favor of her son, instructing him that if she becomes permanently unable to experience music in any way, needs medical treatment to save her life, and is not competent to exercise choice, then no medical treatment should be administered to keep her alive. Assume that years later she is in precisely this condition, a victim of senile dementia, as well as of a life-threatening but readily curable disease. Call her Composer Now. Though disabled in the ways I have described and lacking competence as traditionally conceived, she still has some awareness and has the capacity for sensations. For example, suppose Composer Now smiles at the sight of her grandchildren, she is apparently comforted by sitting in a garden or by being attended and talked to, and she shows preferences in foods and television programs. Moreover, she gives no sign of being uncomfortable, in pain, or unhappy. Finally, when asked if she prefers to be left to die, she becomes agitated and says no, though how much she understands is unclear. (Shortly I will also consider the hypothetical without this last circumstance.)

Should doctors be authorized or required not to treat the curable disease Composer Now has contracted because Composer Then would not have wanted her life to continue in these circumstances? Does vindication of Composer Then's autonomy require it? Or must Composer Then's earlier choice yield to Composer Now's present interest in continuing to experience the limited life available to her, as she now seems to want?

Ronald Dworkin would apparently hold that Composer's right of autonomy requires that her earlier competent wish be respected:

> A competent person's right to autonomy requires that his past decisions, about how he is to be treated if he becomes demented, be respected even if they do not represent, and even if they contradict, the desires he has when we respect them, provided he did not change his mind while he was still in charge of his own life.

As Dworkin emphasizes elsewhere, he reaches this conclusion even in the harder case where the demented person "insists on and pleads for" medical treatment. He argues that autonomy is the right to govern one's life as a whole and not only part of it, so the right must extend throughout the life of the person—including the period of his incompetency, whether permanent or temporary (Dworkin calls this the "integrity" view of the person). To fail to recognize the right of the person when competent to control his fate when incompetent violates what Dworkin calls the right of "precedent autonomy," whose point is to enable us "to lead our own lives rather than being led along them, so that each of us can be . . . what he has made himself."

I do not dispute that the right of autonomy extends to having one's earlier choices govern during periods of later incompetence—Ulysses' sailors would have been on solid moral ground in refusing to untie him as they passed the sirens, even if they could have heard his orders to do so. Nor do I hold that a person's right of autonomy may not be violated if he can never experience its violation, as is true of a person who will never regain his competence. Rather I will argue two propositions: first, that in our Composer case (in contrast to Ulysses' case) precedent autonomy is not as compelling as an exercise of contemporary autonomy (a current choice) would be; second, that such moral force as precedent autonomy has is morally overridden by considerations of human compassion.

Dworkin tells us that he asked a number of people what they would prefer if they were suffering from senile dementia. He reports that they expressed a preference to be left to die. I think he would have gotten a much more mixed response if he had asked a different question—not what they would prefer for themselves if they were someone like Composer Now, but what they would do if they were responsible for deciding whether to treat Composer Now. A number of people to whom I have put both questions answer Dworkin's question the way he reports, but answer my question the opposite way. They themselves would prefer to be left to die rather than to hang on to a life so limited. They are not so ready, however, to inflict the same fate on another person on the basis of their own preference. But why not, if the patient indicated in her advance directive that that was her preference also? The reason, I suggest, is a well-founded lack of confidence in the force of the earlier directive not to treat.

Some discounting of the advance directive in the Composer case is warranted on two grounds. First, the fact that advance directives are executed as future hypotheticals deprives them of the full moral force of contemporary choices. Unforeseen changes, such as new medical treatments, may substantially alter the person's interests. Moreover, the effect of severe, life-imperilling illness may well produce a marked revision in the attitudes and values of the person. Indeed, even absent such traumas, it is common for a person to reach very different conclusions depending on whether he is imagining a future hypothetical situation or confronting an immediate, real predicament. What people thought they would want often turns out to be very different from what they do want. Finally, as Buchanan and Brock have pointed out, an advance decision to forgo life-preserving treatment is less likely than a contemporaneous choice to elicit protective and supportive responses from persons close to the patient; hence, this informal safeguard against hasty and ill-considered action is not usually present in the case of advance directives. In view of these considerations, disregard of the advance directive would not constitute as deep an inroad into the autonomy principle as would disregard of a contemporaneous choice.

This conclusion, of course, rests on the premise that at least one major element in the rationale for respecting autonomy is that people are normally the best judges of their own interests—for the reasons just given, this rationale is less well-grounded in cases of decisions to die in future circumstances radically different from those experienced by the person at the time of decision. Dworkin rejects this rationale of autonomy, however, (the "evidentiary" view, he calls it) in favor of the integrity view, which makes the decisive point of autonomy the right to govern the course of one's life, including one's incompetency, according to a "recognized and coherent scheme of value." Certainly this is one of the virtues of autonomy, but as I argue below, it is unduly limiting to give it the paramount place that Dworkin gives it.

The second ground for discounting the advance directive is simply that Composer Now has subsequently indicated that she prefers to live. Of course, this would be determinative if she were competent. The question is whether to disregard it because she is not. I do not think that we should. Competence is a matter of degree and depends upon the kinds of action at issue. Impaired people have varying capacities to think, reason, and evaluate, and some actions will call for less of these capacities than will others. A person may lack competence to make a will, for example, but be perfectly competent to choose whether to watch television or go to the beach. It seems to me that an expression of a wish to live, even by a person incompetent for most other purposes, is entitled to carry weight, even if less than the full weight which a fully competent expression would command.

Why should we defer to a decision to continue living made by someone with the barest minimum of capacity for understanding and judgment? At bottom, I think the reason has to do with a general presumption favoring respect for a wish to live. At least two factors seem to be involved. First, there is the universality of the struggle to survive that we perceive in all living things, which makes it odd to justify disqualifying an expressed wish to live simply because of the person's cognitive limitations. Second, there is the seriousness and finality of what is at stake—the ending of a person's life. Buchanan and Brock have developed the case for taking into account the seriousness of the harmful consequences for the person in deciding whether he is competent. I follow them here. Their approach is usually employed to justify overriding a person's choice to take a course that would greatly injure him or his interests (for example, a decision to refuse medical treatment necessary to sustain life). But I see no reason why it should not also justify complying with his choice to take a course that would avoid those serious and permanent consequences. Indeed, I am inclined to think that no person should be regarded as so incompetent that his expressed wish to live should be given no weight. I do not take issue with Professor Feinberg that greater harm may possibly be done to a person by sustaining his life than by allowing it to expire. But I do not believe that this is the case where the patient, even though generally incompetent, is asking to be kept alive.

Dworkin, to the contrary, believes that "autonomy, on the integrity view of that right, must be a *general* judgment about [the person's] overall capacity to seek integrity and authenticity, not a specific, task-sensitive judgment." In his view, an autonomous person must have "the capacity to see and evaluate particular decisions in the structured context of an overall life organized around a coherent conception of character and conviction." This seems to me too restrictive a limitation on the right of autonomy, for it would jeopardize the right to autonomy of many ordinary people who, by virtue of qualities of temperament or character, appear to lack an ability to make choices on the basis of consistent life-organizing conceptions. I think, rather, that a major point of autonomy is to enhance the freedom to decide for oneself, whether one decides with authenticity and a sense of coherence or just on the basis of immediate preferences and transient urges. An unwise, uninformed, and eccentric choice is still a choice. It may be that ideally, autonomy functions to permit people, to the extent they can, to make choices that create a coherent whole of their lives. But to deny a person his choices because he cannot choose in terms of a "structured context of an overall life organized around a coherent conception of character and conviction" would deny choice to an unacceptably large segment of the population.

But while precedent autonomy (as Dworkin calls it) in our Composer's case falls short of the full moral force of contemporary autonomy, I have not argued that it has no force. What is there about the circumstances of Composer Now which warrants overriding the force it has? For me, and I expect for many, it is compassion for the human being before us, living her limited life in apparent contentment and evidencing no wish to end it. Letting her die when a cure is readily at hand requires a certain distancing of ourselves from our human impulses, the suppression of a fundamental human empathy for another.

The choice to allow Composer Now to die is supported because earlier, when in full possession of her faculties, she stated that such a life for her would not be worth living. I do not mean to suggest that this is of slight moment. As I said, it has moral significance. But it does not have determinative significance. Without going so far as to regard Composer Now as a different person from Composer Then, I believe it is plain that there has occurred a great transformation in her capacities and perspectives. If we deny her the treatment that would save her, the harm we do is immediate and palpable—we end a life of sharply limited but still contented experiences, in stark violation of our humane sensibilities. If we grant her the treatment we also do harm, but the harm we do is remote and intangible—we violate an exercise of precedent autonomy which is so far separated and distant from her present circumstances that its entitlement to govern is severely compromised.

In the last analysis judgment turns on how much weight to give to the compassionate appeal of the person before us, as compared to the value of autonomy as a right to govern one's life according to a coherent normative structure. . . .

. . . [C]ompassion is not another word for personal squeamishness of the person making the decision. If it were, it would have the status of just one more competing interest of another person, comparable to the interest of a relative in being relieved of the financial and psychological burdens attendant to the patient's continued life. But it is not just another's competing interest; it rises to the level of a moral concern. This is because morality has a dimension that has to do with the person doing the action as well as with the person being acted upon. The patient's right of autonomy is a moral concern of the latter kind; the actor's motivation stemming from the impulse of human compassion is a moral concern of the former kind. The well-known phenomenon of agent-centered restrictions on actions—moral restraints that make it wrong for an agent to do an action that would produce the best available outcome overall (including the fewest actions of that same kind by others)—would not raise the profound problems for moral theory that it does were it not that morality has these separate dimensions.

One final comment on the Composer hypothetical is in order. I have been addressing it on the assumption that Composer expressed a desire to be kept alive—an assumption that makes it harder to justify letting her die. I have done so to allow me to consider Dworkin's argument, which accepts the challenge of this harder case. It is apparent, however, that the argument from compassion I have made applies as well to a modified Composer hypothetical in which it is not possible for her to express a wish one way or the other. That she expresses a wish to live adds the appeal of autonomy to the appeal of compassion (as well as contributing to it), but I believe the appeal of compassion is enough without it.

B. Where the Patient Never Chose: Substituted Judgment

I turn now to what are called "substituted judgment" cases, those in which a person now incompetent never exercised a choice when competent. As I have indicated, the courts try to deal with incompetents the same way they deal with competents, namely by seeking to determine the person's choice. But how do you find a choice when none has been made? Courts have responded by looking for what the patient *would* have chosen: What would this patient choose if he were competent to appraise his situation, including his medical condition and prognosis, as well as his present and future incompetency?

This standard is puzzling because it implies that we are to ask what the permanently incompetent person would now choose if he were competent to choose and aware of his incompetency, as if this would tell us what an incompetent would choose. But it cannot be known what an incompetent person would choose precisely because he cannot choose. We can try to imagine that he is temporarily competent and making a choice that takes into account his anticipated incompetency. But this is a very different thing. Like an advance directive, it would be the choice of a competent patient anticipating, but not actually experiencing, his life as an incompetent; the choice, in short, of the person as he was, not as he now is, because he is now incapable of choosing. This is, I think, all that courts can mean by the usual statement of the substituted-judgment standard.

* * *

Another question raised by the substituted-judgment standard, even interpreted as I have argued it should be interpreted, is this: To what extent is it required by the patient's right of self-determination? In the Composer hypothetical, I considered that question in connection with advance choices generally, and concluded that while the right of autonomy was indeed involved (because the patient exercised choice at some time in the past), the advance choice might in some circumstances lack the full moral force of a contemporaneous choice. The substituted-judgment standard entails the same difficulty since the evidence of what the patient would have chosen is in the patient's past. But this standard has an additional difficulty; namely, that it is invoked where there has been no choice by the patient at all, either in the past or now. Courts applying this standard search for evidence of the patient's past life in order to determine how he would have chosen. But whatever the justification for this standard may be (I shall argue it is best understood as part of a best-interests assessment), it cannot be based on the autonomy principle. In these cases we cannot say that the patient has the right that his choice be respected, because he has made none.

The reason for this lies in the distinction between evidence of what a patient would choose and an actual choice. The right of autonomy is the right to have your own choices respected, not to have someone else make the choice he believes you would (or should) have made. The right protects your act of choosing. When someone else makes the choice, even if he chooses as he thinks you would, he is making the choice, not you. Since you made no actual choice, if he chose to disregard evidence of what you would have chosen, he would not be violating your autonomous right to choose.

Why should an actual choice be that crucial? Aren't there many cases in which the past life of the patient allows us to conclude with reasonable assurance that, if competent, he would have chosen a certain way? Surely this is so. The reason this is nonetheless not equivalent to an actual choice turns on a view of what an exercise of will entails. The view I am taking is that the will of a person stands apart from his character and dispositions; it is not one among other characteristics that, summed up, go to make the person what he is. Everything the person is and was may point to him doing X in some particular circumstance. But he is free to do not-X, and may do so, no matter how out of character it seems. The phenomenon of weakness of the will illustrates this point. Even when a person acknowledges that, from the standpoint of every relevant criterion he accepts he should do X, he may still choose not to do X. Just as a baseball game, in a notable aphorism, is "not over till it's over," so a choice is not made till it's made.

* * *

It does not follow from this distinction that evidence of the patient's preferences has no relevance. It plays a role in assessing his best interests, as I will argue. I only want to claim that cases of presumed preference are not morally equivalent to cases of actual choice, express or implied. This point is important because it allows us to see that, while in cases of contemporaneous choices (and, though to a lesser degree, in cases of advance choices as well) respect for autonomy requires doing as the patient directed, this is not so in substituted-judgment cases. Here, the deciding agent is obliged to make its own choice, the values and preferences of the patient in his competent state serving as guide to a best-interests judgment. Recall Composer Now and Composer Then. In order to make the case for treatment I had to justify compromising Composer Then's right of autonomy. Absent her directive not to treat, however, I would not have had to face that issue, because her autonomy would not have been involved.

The point has further import. So long as the ultimate issue is narrowly thought of as one of substituted judgment—that is, what the patient would choose if he could—there is some logic to courts insisting on a demonstration of that fact with a high degree of evidentiary certitude. This was the narrow issue in the *Cruzan* case, in which the Supreme Court upheld the Missouri law requiring "clear and convincing proof" that the patient would choose to terminate treatment. Viewing the task more broadly, however, as involving a construction from all the circumstances of what treatment decision comports best with the life and character of the patient and therefore furthers his best interests, changes the focus of inquiry. It puts the issue of proof in a more appropriate and realistic framework: not "Unless it is demonstrated with a high level of certainty what the patient would have chosen, treatment must continue," but rather, "From the evidence that is available, including the character and attitudes of the patient, what decision—to continue or terminate treatment—will serve his best interests?"

III

BEST INTERESTS

* * *

A fundamental objection arises from what is implicit in the standard, at least when understood apart from the setting of the patient's inferred preferences: that in certain circumstances the quality of a person's life may be so low that it is not worth living. This stands in stark opposition to the tradition that human life is always valuable. It is one thing for courts to defer to the patient's choice to die. This has proved difficult enough for some courts, as we saw, but at least the decision requires no judgment by the court or some other agent that the patient's life is no longer worth living—only that this is the choice of the patient whose life it is. It is quite different when the best-interests standard is applied independently of the patient's inferred preferences, because this requires the deciding authority itself—the court or some other agent—to make the substantive judgment of whether what is left of the patient's life is worth the candle.

One concern animating this objection is that assessing the quality of the patient's life requires a judgment of its social worth. As one court put it, it is improper "to authorize decision-making based on assessments of the personal worth or social utility of another's life, or the value of that life to others" because to do so creates "an intolerable risk for socially isolated and defenseless people suffering from physical or mental handicaps." Yet this concern seems misplaced, for there is nothing in the nature or history of the standard that requires judgments of the patient's worth to society generally or to particular others. Applied to the decision whether to treat, the accepted understanding of the best-interests standard is that it seeks to assess what would be best for the patient, not for his family, others, or the community as a whole.

Even so, courts have found that judging whether a patient's future life is not worth living is a troubling decision for anyone to make. First, what makes a life not worth living anyway? Loss of the patient's cognitive powers, his ability to function independently, his ability to interact with others, his dependence on constant medical intervention? How much ability to sense and take comfort from experiences is required before we can say his life is not worth living? At bottom, the difficulty is that we have no way to make confident judgments about how far cognitive and physical deterioration must go before life ceases to be worth living, because the value judgments implicit in such a conclusion are in sharp contention in our society. Second, there is the challenge of "don[ning] the mental mantle of the incompetent," understanding and judging his experiences as he lives and feels them, rather than from the biased perspective of a normally healthy person with unimpaired faculties. Finally, courts are often troubled by the specter of the slippery slope—the fear that once the precedent is established that a person may be left to die because someone judges his life not satisfying enough to be worth living, there will be nothing, or at least less, to stand in the way of that judgment being made of socially, mentally, and physically handicapped people on the margins of society.

* * *

Certainly evidence of the values that guided the patient's competent life (what Ronald Dworkin calls his "evaluative interests")—his character, how he led his life, his attitude toward medical treatment, what it was about life that he thought made it worthwhile, how much it mattered to him that he was burdening others, how sensitive he was to considerations of privacy and personal dignity—bears directly on a best-interests judgment. But there is another kind of consideration that needs consulting as well; namely, the patient's present experiences or lack of them (what Dworkin calls his "experiential interests"). These include the patient's medical prognosis, the extent of his suffering, the degree of his mental and physical impairment, and the kind of experiences he would be capable of if he survived. The question then becomes whether, on the basis of both kinds of evidence, we can conclude that a decision to forgo treatment would be consonant with the kind of life he led and the kind of person he was, as well as with the kind of person he is now. If so, we can conclude that it is in his best interests to deny treatment.

Some regard evidence of the first kind—evaluative interests—as irrelevant, on the ground that one can have no interest in what is not and can never be experienced; under this view, only experiential interests count in cases of serious and permanent mental disability. This argument has an attractively down-to-earth appeal, but as Joel Feinberg and others have shown, denying that a person's interests may be harmed when he does not and can never experience the harm takes too narrow a view of an interest. Consider posthumous harms. There is a natural sense in which the interests of a person who is no longer alive may be harmed. Such harm occurs when that which he deeply cherished and to which he devoted his life suffers destruction, when his valued reputation as a person of honor and distinction is destroyed by malicious lies, or when significant promises he exacted to be performed after his death are foresworn. For like reasons, the evaluative interests of a living person (his sensibilities, his concerns for his own dignity and for not burdening others, his prized self-determination) may be harmed by how we deal with him after he has permanently lost capacity to be aware that these harms are being done to him. The Composer hypothetical would not have been so difficult were it not that Composer's interest in having her right of autonomy respected continued even though she could not (and could never) experience it. It is important to stress that this approach to ascertaining best interests offers some protection against the feared precedent of permitting someone else's judgment of the quality of a patient's life to determine whether the patient should be permitted to die. It does so because it makes the patient's own value structure controlling of whether it is consistent with the patient's best interests to forego treatment.

Ronald Dworkin, to the contrary, has proposed that except in cases where the patient has made a competent choice for treatment sufficient to invoke his right of autonomy (Dworkin agrees that evidence of preferences short of such choice are insufficient to invoke this right), the standard of evaluation of the worth of the patient's continued life (his evaluative interests) should be objective rather than subjective. In other words, the standard should not be necessarily what the patient himself would regard as in his best interests, but what is in his best interests, period. Referring to patients with permanent and severe dementia, he concludes that:

> a fiduciary should take over a person's responsibility to make his life as good a life as it can be when that person is no longer capable of this himself. . . . [I]t follows that the right to beneficence includes the right not to be given life-prolonging treatment when seriously and permanently demented.

This follows for Dworkin because a permanently and seriously demented person's life can contain nothing that would make his life better. Lacking a "sense of personality and agency," his experiences could not be rewarding. And lacking "continuity of project and fulfillment," they could not be regarded as achievements. On the other hand, a demented life can contain experiences that make the life of which it is a part worse—experiences of anxiety and pain, for example.

What I have given of Dworkin's argument for an objective best-interests judgment is the barest outline, which fails to convey its subtlety and complexity, but it is enough to allow me to say why I find it troubling. First, a basic premise of Dworkin's argument is that it is in the best interests of a patient that a decision makes of the patient's life as a whole as good a thing as it can be, one marked by a sensitivity to values of privacy and dignity, by respect for and deference to the interests of others, and so on. This evokes his theory of adjudication as interpretation, requiring the judge to make of the law as good a thing as it can be. But there is an important difference, for I doubt that a person's life is made better by decisions that are not rooted in him as a person. If a person during the course of his competent life has been indifferent to matters of respect for his person and for the interests of others, it does not seem to me that it serves to make his whole life a better one that in the end someone has made decisions for him which manifest these virtues. They are, after all, imposed on him and hardly do him credit.

Moral luck plays some role in the living of a good life, and on that basis an argument can be made that the patient's good fortune in being permitted to die after suffering serious and permanent dementia makes his whole life, on balance, a better one than it would be if he were kept alive. But this seems unconvincing. Luck may be a factor in permitting a person to lead a good life, but to say that his life is made a better one because a good thing luckily happened to him after he had finished leading his life yields too much to the authority of fortune. It is a bit like flowers on a grave: they make lots of things better, but scarcely the life of the person beneath them. Consider the example of being a burden to others, often given as one among a set of reasons for declining treatment: it is a virtue for a person to permit himself to die to save burdening others, and he makes his whole life a better one for doing so. But it hardly makes his life a better one that a third party decides to sacrifice it for the benefit of others.

My second reason for demurring to Dworkin's conclusion is practical: it invites the danger that many courts and commentators have seen in best-interests standards—the danger that those making the decision cannot be relied on to keep separate what is objectively best and what is best for them. It is often in the interest of those around the demented patient that he be permitted to die—he is a psychological burden to them, the ministrations required for his bodily functions often offend their sensibilities, he requires the use of valuable resources, and the positive qualities of his limited life seem slight compared to the negative influence on the lives of others. We may insist that it is in his best interest that he be allowed to die, but when that decision is one that serves the interests of others (who often are the ones making the decision) there is the ever-present danger that it is their interests, not his, that are motivating the decision.

Another problem with Dworkin's position is that it is, most uncharacteristically for him, paternalistic, at least in the sense that it makes the final act in a person's life turn on the normative standards of others rather than on those of the person himself. Dworkin accepts that a demented person's earlier competent choice for treatment must prevail even if it is against what Dworkin would regard as his best evaluative interests, considered from an objective perspective. But there are plainly going to be cases where the person's life has left evidence consistent with a preference for continued treatment, although he made no actual or implied choice to which his right of autonomy would require deferring. It seems to me that we should want to say that such a person has an interest, that it is in *his* best interests, that the decision accord with his own values and preferences as best we can discern them. I agree that it would not violate his right to autonomy to disregard his inferred preferences (since he made no choice). Nonetheless, it would be inconsistent with his interest in having the end of his life governed by the kind of choices he made to govern his competent earlier life, and therefore, in this sense, paternalistic.

Nonetheless, there are situations where Dworkin's analysis has a strong appeal. These are the cases where we can make no reliable judgment based on the person's past values and commitments, either because the evidence is totally indeterminate or because he never was competent. Here it is not possible to tailor the choice to the character of the person. In this situation a decision that can be supported as better on impersonal, objective grounds is obviously preferable to a decision that cannot be so supported.

My final concern, which I suggested earlier in a related context, is that Dworkin's position unduly discounts the experiential interests of a demented person— the satisfactions that can come from sensory experiences and comforting feelings that do not require higher-order mentation. To paraphrase Bentham, the question is not whether demented people can reason, nor whether they can talk, but whether they can feel.

* * *

Bibliography

Modern Substantive Due Process

Burt, Robert A., *The Constitution of the Family,* 1979 SUP. CT. REV. 329

Chemerinsky, Erwin, *Rationalizing the Abortion Debate: Legal Rhetoric and the Abortion Controversy*, 31 BUFF. L. REV. 107 (1982)

Davis, Peggy Cooper, *Neglected Stories and the Lawfulness of* Roe v. Wade, 28 HARV. C.R.–C.L. L. REV. 299 (1933)

Dolgin, Janet, *The Family in Transition: From* Griswold *to* Eisenstadt *and Beyond*, 82 GEO. L.J. 1519 (1994)

Eskridge, William, *A Social Constructionist Critique of Posner's* Sex and Reason*: Steps Toward a Gaylegal Agenda*, 102 YALE L.J. 333 (1992)

Estrich, Susan, & Sullivan, Kathleen, *Abortion Politics: Writing for an Audience of One*, 138 U. PA. L. REV. 119 (1989)

Henkin, Louis, *Privacy and Autonomy*, 74 COLUM. L. REV. 1410 (1974)

Kreimer, Seth, *Does Pro-Choice Mean Pro-Kervorkian? An Essay on Roe, Casey, and the Right to Die*, 44 AM. U. L. REV. 803 (1995)

Law, Sylvia, *Homosexuality and the Social Meaning of Gender*, 1988 WISC. L. REV. 1

McConnell, Michael, *How Not to Promote Serious Deliberation about Abortion*, 58 U. CHI. L. REV. 1181 (1991)

Minow, Martha, *The Free Exercise of Families*, 1991 U. ILL. L. REV. 925

Olsen, Frances, *Unravelling Compromise*, 103 HARV. L. REV. 105 (1989)

Posner, Richard, *The Uncertain Protection of Privacy by the Supreme Court*, 1979 SUP. CT. REV. 173

Rhoden, Nancy K., *Litigating Life and Death*, 102 HARV. L. REV. 375 (1988)

Siegel, Reva, *Reasoning From the Body: A Historical Perspective on Abortion Regulation and Questions of Equal Protection*, 44 STAN. L. REV. 261 (1992)

Thompson, Judith Jarvis, THE REALM OF RIGHTS (1990)

Part II
Separation of Powers

The articles appearing in this section attempt to define the doctrine of separation of powers and critically analyze its applications. In Gerhard Casper's article entitled *An Essay in Separation of Powers: Some Early Versions and Practices*, the author explores the late eighteenth century political thinking about separation of powers, concluding that no one principle reflective of the concerns emerged. Moreover, he posits that in the constitutional framing no consensus existed as to the institutional arrangements that would satisfy the requirements of separation of powers. William Gwyn, in *The Indeterminacy of the Separation of Powers in the Age of the Framers*, connects the absence of a clear articulation of the separation of powers doctrine and its goals at the time of constituional framing to the confusion in the modern doctrine, arguing that a formalistic approach which is often promoted is not justified by history. In *The Rise and Fall of the "Doctrine" of Separation of Powers*, Philp B. Kurland argues that the Framers' expectation that separation of powers would prevent one governmental branch from becoming dominant has failed and pertinently the growth in the stature of the judicial branch flows from the failure of the principle of separation of powers. E. Donald Elliott, in *Why Our Separation of Powers Jurisprudence Is So Abysmal,* argues that literalism in judicial interpretation has stifled the development of separation of powers jurisprudence because it limits the creative potential of discussion about the modern meaning of the principle of separation of powers.

Peter L. Strauss writes in *Was There a Baby in the Bathwater? A Comment on the Supreme Court's Legislative Veto Decision* that the *Chadha* decision called into question the dispersal of governmental authority, particularly our understanding of what is within the "legislative" sphere of action. Examining the range of circumstances in which legislative vetoes have been used, the author argues that the Court majority's formal approach eliminates a device which is useful and appropriate in limited contexts. In his article, *The Independent Counsel Mess*, Stephen L. Carter examines the Court's disposition of the statute providing for the independent counsel which he believes abandoned its "de-evolutionary, history-focused" approach to separation of powers issues, permitting congressional judgment to overcome the Framers' vision of the proper distribution of governmental powers. For Carter, the essential problem confronting the Court is the longstanding and unchallenged legitimacy of independent agencies. Abner S. Greene, in *Checks and Balances in an Era of Presidential Lawmaking*, seeks to clarify the circumstances where congressional oversight and delegation of power insulated from executive control are appropriate and consistent with the Constitution's framing. He asserts as an organizing

271

principle of caselaw that independent agencies restore the balance of power between executive and legislative power but that Congress may not draw executive power to itself nor exercise its legislative power outside the Articel I, Section 7 framework. In *"If Angels Were to Govern": The Need for Pragmatic Formalism in Separation of Powers Theory,* Martin H. Redish and Elizabeth J. Cisar propose "pragmatic formalism" as a mode of interpretation in separation of powers cases, limiting the Court's role in the cases to determining whether the challenged branch action falls within that branch's constitutionally derived powers. In fashioning its defininiton of branch power, however, the authors invite the Court to look to a combination of factors, including policy, tradition, precedent and linguisitic analysis. In conclusion, Rebecca L. Brown, in *Separated Powers and Ordered Liberty*, rejects the functional and formalistic approaches to separation of powers issues, arguing that the doctrine which both have produced is incoherent and devoid of a theoretical framework. The author urges the Court to apply the principle of ordered liberty or evenhanded government as an explicit factor in the analysis of structural issues related to separation of powers.

Gerhard Casper, *An Essay in Separation of Powers: Some Early Versions and Practices,* 30 WM. & MARY L. REV. 211 (1989)*

* * *

[T]he very centrality of the separation of powers doctrine in the last quarter of the eighteenth century quickly produced a sharpened sense of its uncertainty as the "first constitutional generation" encountered specific tasks of governmental organization and statecraft. Indeed, the doctrine itself mirrored the complexities of life and its symbolisms. It was "tentative, reflective, suggestive, contradictory, and incomplete." It did not provide a major premise for easy syllogisms concerning the organization of government.

* * *

"A society in which the guarantee of rights is not assured, nor the separation of powers provided for, has no constitution." This stringent formulation is that of article 16 of the French Declaration of the Rights of Man of 1789. With respect to the separation of powers, it expressed what had become an almost sacred article of faith in the deliberations of the constitutional assemblies of the United States and France.

When these words were written, the separation of executive and judicial, legislative and executive powers had been the subject of ever increasing attention on both sides of the Atlantic for about 150 years. Nedham, Locke, Bolingbroke, Montesquieu, Blackstone, Rousseau, Siyes, Adams, Jefferson, and Madison are only some of the names associated with this debate. Their respective contributions reflected rather diverse political, constitutional, and theoretical concerns. It is therefore

---

*   Reprinted with permission.

hardly surprising that, by the last quarter of the eighteenth century, no single doctrine using the label of separation of powers had emerged that could command general assent.

* * *

Unfortunately, many political writers, Montesquieu included, tended to amal-
gamate (and thus obscure) separation of powers notions with another possible condition of liberty, or at least of good government: the institution of "mixed" government,
which was aimed primarily at balancing different classes or interests. . . .

* * *

Although great differences in the institutional arrangements of government in
the various colonies existed, to say that, by and large, the colonies had "mixed" government based on the British model with monarchic, aristocratic, and democratic elements manifested in their governors, councils, and legislatures is not an exaggeration.
. . .

[S]eparation of powers notions were intertwined with older notions reflecting the
allocation of powers in the mixed colonial regimes. In these mixed regimes, only the
popular house of the legislature represented the people, the often predominating
gubernatorial powers possessed legislative, executive, and judicial elements, and the
functionally differentiated judiciary was kept less than completely separate. . . .

The challenge faced after the Declaration of Independence was how to adapt the
institutions of mixed government to the doctrine of popular sovereignty. The issue was
no longer the separation of differently based powers, but the separation of power (in
the singular) flowing from one source: the people. If the separation of powers was a
necessary condition of liberty, the task was to reconcile it to the notion of popular sovereignty, which was invoked explicitly and dramatically in the majority of the new
state constitutions and was the foremost expression of that liberty.

A further problem was that the people in the former colonies were stratified:
there were old inhabitants and newcomers, revolutionaries and loyalists, free men
and indentured servants and slaves. Often, there was a "gentry" as distrustful of the
"people" as the "people" were distrustful of the "gentry." The tensions resulting from
these stratifications were bound up with the organizational tasks of the new states.

* * *

Although the absence of separation of powers was not generally viewed as the
main weakness of the Confederation, Hamilton criticized the Articles as early as July
1783 for "confounding legislative and executive powers in a single body" and for lacking a federal judicature "having cognizance of all matters of general concern.". . .

When Randolph opened the substantive deliberations of the 1787 Convention
with his enumeration of the defects of the Confederation, he apparently made no reference to separation of powers. The Virginia Plan, submitted the same day, however,
implied separation of powers and called for a quadripartite governmental structure:
a bicameral legislature, a national executive, a national judiciary (to serve during
good behavior), and a council of revision to be composed of the executive and members
of the judiciary. . . .

Other plans for a constitution all presupposed a three-branch structure of government. . . . [I]n the subsequent discussions of the structure and powers of the legislative, executive, and judicial branches as well as in the repeated debates concerning
a council of revision, the delegates raised many points about the independence of the

respective branches, the dangers of encroachments, and the need for checks and balances. What was strikingly absent, however, was anything that might be viewed as a coherent and generally shared view of separation of powers.

The constitutional text itself, although implying the notion of distinct branches, did not invoke the separation of powers as a principle. Some of the state ratifying conventions attempted to remedy this omission in their original proposals for bills of rights to be added to the Constitution. Madison also sought a remedy. In 1788, in the Federalist Papers, Madison had considered it necessary to defend the Constitution against the charge that it paid no regard to the separation of powers. His core argument in The Federalist No. 47 was the "impossibility and inexpediency of avoiding any mixture" as demonstrated by the state constitutions and as supported by the "oracle who is always consulted and cited on this subject . . . the celebrated Montesquieu." Montesquieu, according to Madison, did not mean to suggest that the three departments "ought to have no partial agency in, or no control over, the acts of each other."

Madison's 1789 proposal for a new article VII to precede the existing one (which was to be renumbered) was ingenious in the manner in which it formulated a separation of powers doctrine that took account of the constitutional scheme of checks and balances:

> The powers delegated by this constitution, are appropriated to the departments to which they are respectively distributed: so that the legislative department shall never exercise the powers vested in the executive or judicial; nor the executive exercise the powers vested in the legislative or judicial; nor the judicial exercise the powers vested in the legislative or executive departments.

The separation of powers provision of Roger Sherman's draft bill of rights, also dating from the summer of 1789, captured even more clearly the point made by Madison's proposed article VII:

> The legislative, executive and judiciary powers vested by the Constitution in the respective branches of the Government of the United States shall be exercised according to the distribution therein made, so that neither of said branches shall assume or exercise any of the powers peculiar to either of the other branches.

The House adopted Madison's amendment (with a minor change) despite objections that it was unnecessary and "subversive of the Constitution.". . . Alas, the Senate rejected the amendment for reasons we shall never know. One can only surmise that the Senate was not eager to adopt separation of powers as an independent doctrine or even as a mere principle of construction for the many and subtle "mixing" decisions of the framers, some of which benefitted the Senate.

* * *

The Convention debates, taken as a whole, hardly suggest a strong consensus that the "[s]tate experience . . . contributed, nothing more strongly, to discredit the whole idea of the sovereign legislature, [than] to bring home the real meaning of limited government and coordinate powers." Forrest McDonald, in his recent book on the origins of the Constitution, has concluded from the decisions of the Convention that the "doctrine of the separation of powers had clearly been abandoned in the framing of the Constitution." This judgment presupposes that a doctrine existed that could be abandoned. Given the state of the discussion of the framers in the last quarter of the eighteenth century and the constitutions enacted after 1776, a "pure" doctrine of separation of powers can be no more than a political science or legal construct.

No consensus existed as to the precise institutional arrangements that would satisfy the requirements of the doctrine. The only matter on which agreement existed was what it meant not to have separation of powers: it meant tyranny. This insight is not to be belittled. Madison and Sherman were right when, in their 1789 proposals, they claimed that the particular distribution of powers found in the Constitution could be legitimately seen as a version of an uncertain doctrine.

* * *

William B. Gwyn, *The Indeterminacy of the Separation of Powers in the Age of the Framers,* 30 WM. & MARY L. REV. 263 (1989)*

* * *

From the time when the idea of separation of powers first became popular in North America, much disagreement prevailed as to what institutional arrangements would satisfy the doctrine. . . . This absence of agreement about the institutional arrangements required by the doctrine probably encouraged its use as a rhetorical weapon with which to belabor political opponents or legitimize one's own constitutional preferences, rather than as a clear guide for the construction of a safe and effective system of government. Such absence of agreement was not confined to the United States, for it occurred also in seventeenth-century England when the doctrine was first articulated and continues in our own century with respect to forms of government different from our own. Disagreement about the doctrine is probably inherent because, as stated in The Federalist No. 47, a large variety of institutional arrangements can satisfy the separation of powers norm. The most extreme embodiment is not necessarily the best, for it might reduce the achievement of other values.

Most late eighteenth-century American accounts of the separation of powers doctrine were very superficial. Rarely does one find an explanation for why such a separation is desirable beyond vague references to its necessity in achieving "liberty" and avoiding "tyranny," two highly emotive words dear to eighteenth-century Anglo-American rhetoric. . . .

* * *

First, the absence of a clear articulation of the separation of powers doctrine leads modern courts to apply the doctrine without understanding its purposes. As in the days of the framers and possibly in part as a result of the superficiality of thinking about the separation of powers at that time, lawyers and judges today continue to invoke the doctrine without indicating either the intended goals of the separation or the range of institutional arrangements that might satisfy the doctrine. Without an idea of the values to be maximized by separating the exercise of legislative, executive, and judicial powers, intelligent discussion about the institutional means for achieving the values is impossible. . . .

---

*   Reprinted with permission.

Second, from the time of the framers, the distinction between legislative, executive, and judicial powers has been inexact and highly misleading. Professor Casper reminds us that the doctrine of the separation of powers is not stated explicitly in the Constitution, and that the Senate defeated later efforts to include it in the Bill of Rights. Nevertheless, commentators frequently maintain that the doctrine is implied in the first three articles, in which Congress is given "[a]ll legislative powers" granted in the Constitution, the "executive power" is vested in the President, and the "judicial power of the United States" is vested in the Supreme Court and inferior courts created by Congress. What the Constitution does not tell us is the meaning of the terms "legislative," "executive," and "judicial power."

The framers clearly were not functioning as political theorists, carefully distinguishing each type of power. Nor were they relying solely on the traditional British understanding of governmental activities considered legislative or executive. Yet the framers and their English forbearers did share the view that legislative power involved much more than simply enacting general legal rules and that executive power involved immensely more than executing those rules. Indeed, during the seventeenth century, the term "executive power" usually included what has been labeled "judicial power" since the eighteenth century. Furthermore, the terms "legislative power" and "executive power," which date in English only from the seventeenth century, were coined to refer, not to single governmental functions, but to the variety of functions exercised by the two houses of Parliament on the one hand and those exercised by the monarch, his officials, and his advisers, on the other hand. Executive power was then, as it remains today, particularly multifunctional. . . . The concept of legislative powers that we inherited from England, however, was itself multifunctional, and, in addition to making laws, included taxation, appropriation of public funds, and impeachment and trial of officials accused of abusing their authority. Additionally, as we have seen, the framers further expanded the scope of legislative powers and at times, as in the case of the appointing power, were extremely uncertain as to which branch to assign a particular governmental function.

. . . In some cases, whether a function is given either to the legislative or to the executive branch probably has no bearing on the quality of government. In other cases, however, the allocation of an activity to one branch of government rather than to another could be critical to maintaining the rule of law, the accountability of officials, and the efficiency of government.

Philip B. Kurland, *The Rise and Fall of the "Doctrine" of Separation of Powers*, 85 MICH. L. REV. 592 (1986)*

* * *

The original constitutional notions of division of powers and functions were based not only on "separation of powers," but on a concept of "balanced government" and of "checks and balances" as well. If the three ideas rested on a single base of mistrust—a mistrust of governmental authority concentrated in the same hands—they were far from the same in their forms. Checks and balances suggested the joinder, not

---

    *   Originally published in 85 Mich. L. Rev. 592 (1986). Reprinted with permission of the Michigan Law Review Association.

separation, of two or more governmental agencies before action could be validated—or the oversight of one by another. Balanced or mixed government involved separation, but by way of providing different voices for the different elements in a society. . ... In fact, Madison's rationalization for the division of powers suggests a more substantial notion of balancing forces, but for him the forces to be balanced were multitudinous and not few.

Separation of powers certainly encompasses the notion that there are fundamental differences in governmental functions—frequently but not universally denoted as legislative, executive, and judicial—which must be maintained as separate and distinct, each sovereign in its own area, none to operate in the realm assigned to another. The tendency even today is to think of the constitutional separation of powers in these terms. What Madison wrote in 1788, however, remains true today and has proved true in the interim. He said in the 37th Federalist:

> Experience has instructed us that no skill in the science of Government has yet been able to discriminate and define, with sufficient certainty, its three great provinces, the Legislative, Executive, and Judiciary; or even the privileges and powers of the different Legislative branches. Questions daily occur in the course of practice, which prove the obscurity which reigns in these subjects, and which puzzle the greatest adepts in political science.

The consequence has been that problems of separation of powers have more often been sought to be resolved by invoking one or the other of the classifications as a shibboleth, what Holmes and Cardozo referred to as judgment by labels.

The life of the Constitution, however, from its birth to its bicentennial has not been theory but experience. . . .

The American concept of separation of powers—if I may now use that term as shorthand—is the prime example of the proposition that experience rather than theory grounds the Constitution. In no small part, this consequence is attributable to necessity rather than choice. In part, the necessity derives from the fact that, . . . separation of powers as adopted by the American Constitution had no true precedents either in fact or in theory. [B]ecause the new American government was sui generis, it was not possible to trace all its provisions to any of the almost unlimited antecedents invoked at the Convention or to the only slightly smaller number of political savants to whom appeal was equally readily made.

* * *

The American constitution of 1787 made the notion of separation of powers both more simple and more complex than it had been under previous regimes or in earlier texts. As Professor Gordon Wood has told us:

> . . . Separation of powers, whether describing executive, legislative, and judicial separation or the bicameral division of the legislature (the once distinct concepts now thoroughly blended), was simply a partitioning of political power, the creation of a plurality of discrete governmental elements, all detached from yet responsible to and controlled by the people, checking and balancing each other, preventing any one power from asserting itself too far. The libertarian doctrine of separation of powers was expanded and exalted by the Americans to the foremost position in their constitutionalism, premised on the belief, in John Dickinson's words, that "government must never be lodged in a single body." Enlightenment and

experience had pointed out "the propriety of government being committed to such a number of great departments"—three or four, suggested Dickinson—"as can be introduced without confusion, distinct in office, and yet connected in operation." Such a "repartition" of power was designed to provide for the safety and ease of the people, since "there will be more obstructions interposed" against errors and frauds in the government. "The departments so constituted," concluded Dickinson, "may therefore be said to be balanced." But it was not a balance of "any intrinsic or constitutional properties," of any social elements, but rather only a balance of governmental functionaries without social connections, all monitored by the people who remained outside, a balanced government that worked, "although," said Wilson, "the materials, of which it is constructed, be not an assemblage of different and dissimilar kinds."

The new form of separation of powers was not wholly appreciated when the ratification processes were in place. As Madison said in Federalist No. 47: "One of the principal objections inculcated by the more respectable adversaries to the constitution, is its supposed violation of the political maxim, that the legislative, executive, and judiciary departments ought to be separate and distinct." Federalist Nos. 47 through 51 were devoted to refuting that charge, largely by revising the classic notions of separation of powers.

It was evident from Montesquieu's resort to the British model, said Madison, that he did not mean that there could be no partial overlap of governmental functions in different departments. Montesquieu meant only "that where the whole power of one department is exercised by the same hands which possess the whole power of another department, the fundamental principles of a free constitution, are subverted." So, too, Madison pointed out: "If we look into the constitutions of the several states we find that notwithstanding the emphatical, and in some instances, the unqualified terms in which this axiom has been laid down, there is not a single instance in which the several departments of power have been kept absolutely separate and distinct." Having disposed of Montesquieuan theory and American experience in No. 47, he proceeded in No. 48 to demonstrate that it is not sufficient merely "to mark with precision the boundaries of these departments in the constitution of the government, and to trust to these parchment barriers against the encroaching spirit of power." It is to be recalled that he had conceded in No. 37 that it was impossible sharply to delineate the different powers labeled legislative, executive, and judicial. In No. 51, he justified the melange as "so contriving the interior structure of the government, that its several constituent parts may, by their mutual relations, be the means of keeping each other in their proper places." The result was a new conception of a balancing of powers so well described in the quotation from Professor Wood. And here Madison recited one of his most frequently quoted arguments:

> Ambition must be made to counteract ambition. The interest of the man must be connected with the constitutional rights of the place. It may be a reflection on human nature, that such devices should be necessary to controul the abuses of government. But what is government itself but the greatest of all reflections on human nature? If men were angels, no government would be necessary. If angels were to govern men, neither external nor internal controuls on government would be necessary. In framing a government which is to be administered by men over men, the great difficulty lies in this: You must first enable the government to controul the

governed; and in the next place, oblige it to controul itself. A dependence on the people is no doubt the primary controul on the government; but experience has taught mankind the necessity of auxiliary precautions.

It must be remembered that some fundamental differences dividing the Framers were never mediated at the Convention. One concerned the identity of that part of government which posed the greatest threat to individual liberty. One group of some of its most powerful thinkers—Madison and Hamilton, for example—believed that the great danger was that a democratic legislature threatened to absorb all government power. The other group saw the danger of tyranny in a singular executive, an attitude that had been expressed in the Declaration of Independence's indictment of the King and in the omnipresent fear that, unless he were George Washington, the man who controlled the army could use it to subjugate the people. The objective of separation of powers was to preclude the concentration of legitimate government authority in either Congress or the President. . . .

. . . [T]he debates and arguments over separation of powers expressed little fear of judicial hegemony. Their worries focused on legislative or executive usurpation of power. Whether the judiciary as used in the tripartite systems of separation was regarded in the image of juries, which seemed to be Montesquieu's idea, or to be like the Courts at Westminster, the Framers were generally of a mind that the executive and the legislature ought to keep their hands off the courts. No concern was displayed that the courts themselves represented a threat to the other two national branches or to the people. . . .

The national judiciary was recognized, as Hamilton put it in Federalist No. 78, as the "least dangerous branch.". . . Nevertheless, the judiciary was at the cornerstone of the concept of a "limited constitution" for which separation of powers was to be a guarantee, especially where the concern was to limit the authority of the legislature.

"By a limited constitution," Hamilton said, again in No. 78,

> I understand one which contains certain specified exceptions to the legislative authority; such for instance as that it shall pass no bills of attainder, no ex post facto laws, and the like. Limitations of this kind can be preserved in practice in no other way than through the medium of the courts of justice; whose duty it must be to declare all acts contrary to the manifest tenor of the constitution void. Without this, all the reservations of particular rights or privileges would amount to nothing.

Thus, the American invention of judicial review became an essential ingredient in the American version of separation of powers. Indeed, it was to become a most important practical element. In doing so, the judiciary may long since have exceeded the limits of its own authority as contemplated by the authors of the Constitution. Such a grand role for judges as presently exercised was certainly not in keeping with their status on either side of the Atlantic at the turn of the eighteenth century. Passing on the validity of legislative acts certainly could not be said to be intrinsically or exclusively a judicial function in 1787; it was equally exercisable by an executive council, as in Pennsylvania and New York, or by one part of the legislature itself. Madison would have provided for congressional—rather than judicial—review of state legislation. But, as experience of the last two hundred years has shown, the American judiciary need not be given power in order to exercise it.

* * *

I should reiterate that the underlying, if unstated, premise of all theories of separation seems to have been a minimalist government. The doctrine has afforded less and less adequate protection for the individual as government has grown into the Leviathan it has become. Constitutional law seems to have remained truer to the goal of separation of powers—the liberty of the people—than to the specific means it adopted toward that end.

* * *

At the beginning then, I would repeat that it was clear that the doctrine of separation of powers was not a rule of decision. The inefficacy of resorting to a general notion of separation of powers to resolve contests between two branches of government has long since been demonstrated by our history. There are probably many reasons for this. Two of them are patent. First, to resort to the idea that there is a tripartite division of powers, legislative, executive, and judicial, each term self-defining, is to deal with phantasms. If we take the basic arguments usually asserted that it is for the legislature to make the rules governing conduct, for the executive to enforce those rules, and for the judiciary to apply those rules in the resolution of justiciable contests, it soon becomes apparent that it is necessary to government that sometimes the executive and sometimes the judiciary has to create rules, that sometimes the legislature and sometimes the judiciary has to enforce rules, and sometimes the legislature and sometimes the executive has to resolve controversies over the rules. And these variations became more imperative as government became more invasive and complex. Moreover, some parts of government have nothing to do with rules of conduct. There is nothing implicit or self-evident in any of the three labels that permits resort to the generalization about separation as a device, especially for the resolution of hard cases.

When we shift our focus from the general proposition to an interpretation of the particular allocations of power specified in the Constitution, we face different difficulties. Most of these difficulties derive from the movement away from the idea that the national government was a government of limited powers to the current recognition that somewhere in the grants of power to the national government is to be found authority to act. The limits on government are not substantive, they are now essentially procedural; they no longer depend on what the Constitution says that any branch can do but what it says that it cannot do. In sum, one would have to say that if the separation of powers doctrine rested on a desire to protect the liberty of the individuals subject to government actions, the protection is no longer to be found in the separation of powers but rather in the Bill of Rights, in the provisions of article I, sections 9 and 10, and in the fourteenth amendment's due process and equal protection clauses. Incidentally, if this be true, it explains in part why the realm of the judiciary has become more and more expansive in the totality of our governance. Limited government, or minimalist government, in Lockean or Harringtonian terms, is a matter of ancient history; its demise is probably coincident with the growth of the idea of implied powers.

* * *

[O]ver our history, the most important contests for power between the legislative and executive branches of the national government have been resolved by confrontation. Each side has weapons at its command to wound and maul the other. The most devastating at Congress' disposition, the power of impeachment, has had to be used with caution. . . . But ordinarily the threat of its use is sufficient, if the only goal is to remove a man from office rather than to change policy. Usually, impeachment and its threat do not cure the excessive aggrandizement of the office, as President Nixon's case clearly demonstrates. The judicial power of injunction, the legislative power over appropriations and of contempt, the executive power to ignore challenges by other branches to its power by appeals to the electorate and its control of disbursements and appointments have been the usual weapons employed. Compromise has more often prevailed than total victory by either contestant. But it is in this way that the separation of powers has tended to work, not in terms of pure doctrine, nor yet in terms of what assures the liberties of the people.

Where the alleged overreaching of one branch or another impinges on the rights of a person, association, or corporation, the judicial branch has more and more often been called on to determine whether the challenged authority is legitimate. With the extension of national power to a general hegemony over the lives of the people living within its domain, however, the question thus raised ordinarily is not whether the governmental power exists, but by which office can it be exercised. For this reason, the claims resolved by judicial action have tended to be of not much moment because, at least as between the legislature and the executive, whichever choice the judiciary makes is subject to direct renegotiation by the principals. Thus, for example, when the Supreme Court declares the legislative veto unconstitutional, as it did in *INS v. Chadha*, the legislative choice is to submit or to withdraw the delegation that was conditioned on the legislative veto. Were it not so weak-willed, Congress would reclaim its legislative power, most of which it has delegated without any grumbling about separation of powers. When the Court declares that the President has an executive privilege to withhold documents from legislative scrutiny, as it did in dicta in *United States v. Nixon*, without a phrase or scintilla of legislative history in the Constitution or its origins to support it, the legislature can still resort to its other powers to compel delivery. For the most part, however, what Learned Hand said in 1942 remains true today:

> To this point, I have concentrated on the origins and development of the constitutional concept of separation of powers. If the Founding Fathers had been right, that concept should have limited the growth of each branch lest any of them become dominant. If I turn to the question of the growth of each of the three divisions, I think I have to say that the notion of separation has had little or nothing to do with it. Contrary to the expectations of such as Madison and Jefferson, far from bringing all government power within its ambit, the legislative branch has become the least of the three both as threat to and protector of the people's liberty. The executive branch has become imperial and imperious. And the judiciary has developed from that "98-lb. weakling" into the muscular giant, just as the ads of Charles Atlas said he could in the pulp magazines of yesteryear.

It is true that the legislative power and the executive power have been like occupants of opposite ends of a seesaw: as one rises, the other declines. It is equally true that the balance has not remained constant, so that for much of our earlier history legislative power was the more dominant. But for the last half century, the executive has been up and the legislature down.

Explanations are not hard to come by. The first remains the growth of national government power so that almost nothing is beyond its scope. Early Congresses were in session for very short periods of time. Even the first Congress, which had to establish the government, produced a volume of statutes that may best be described as miniscule. Today the Congress is almost never out of session, and its output fills volumes that can barely be lifted. But the result has been that the legislation that passes tends to be merely an outline of the problem plus a delegation of power to make the necessary rules to effectuate solutions. Congress has thus given away most of its authority to make the rules for the governance of society. Second, there is an absence of discipline among the 535 members of Congress. It is a huge body without a head. Most of its legislation does not originate within Congress but is a response to demands or instructions from executive authorities. Too much congressional time is spent as agents of constituents seeking relief in the myriad of government agencies that Congress has created but does not control. The rest of its time seems to be spent in trying to oversee the execution of the laws by way of investigatory hearings which, in theory, are held to help frame legislation but which, in fact, are more devoted to exposure than to cure. The image of Gulliver among the Lilliputians readily comes to mind.

The executive branch, on the other hand, has burgeoned. It constantly grows stronger. Part of the cause for the disparity was well stated by Mr. Justice Jackson in the *Steel Seizure Case*:

> Executive power has the advantage of concentration in a single head in whose choice the whole Nation has a part, making him the focus of public hopes and expectations. In drama, magnitude and finality his decisions so far overshadow any others that almost alone he fills the public eye and ear. No other personality in public life can begin to compete with him in access to the public mind through modern methods of communications. By his prestige as head of state and his influence upon public opinion he exerts a leverage upon those who are supposed to check and balance his power which often cancels their effectiveness.

* * *

In part, the rise of the presidency can be attributed to the emergence of the United States as the prime actor on the stage of world affairs. Whether this should be dated from the Spanish-American War, or from World War I, it must certainly be acknowledged as a fait accompli since World War II. Wars create conditions in which even so reticent a president as Abraham Lincoln will place necessities over the niceties of political or constitutional theories. By the time of the second Roosevelt, the necessity for marshaling the forces of the nation toward the single goal of victory consolidated powers in the executive. We have been in a continuing crisis of foreign affairs ever since. . . .

* * *

In the middle of the nineteenth century, the Supreme Court described itself as "equal in origin and equal in title to the legislative and executive branches of the government." That might have been a bit of braggadocio at the time. It is a claim easily defended today.

Whence comes the explanation? I suppose we can start with Jefferson's early insight that it would be the Supreme Court that would channel state power into federal hands, from which it might follow that the Court implicitly lays claim to part of the national power that is largely of its own creation. That is perhaps too subtle an argument. The fact is, however, that the Court, over the years, has been able to make a greater claim to public support than either of the two political branches. It has consistently wielded a wider and wider power of judicial review. After a hesitant start in

Marbury v. Madison, and a disastrous effort in *Dred Scott v. Sandford*, the Court has been more and more willing to fashion new constitutional rules limiting both national and state action, with less and less reliance on the terms of the Constitution, its origins, or even the Court's own precedents. . . .

Nor is the accretion of power solely in the constitutional field: it is at least as much to be found in the remedial powers exercised. And it would seem that the people are turning to the courts more and more rather than to the political branches for relief of their individual problems. One of our most eminent federal judges expressed the thought that resort to the judiciary by the citizenry is as much due to lack of faith in the other branches as to faith in the courts. . . .

* * *

In addition to the fact that the courts seem to be the place to go because they tend to give the customer what he wants, making for popularity and power if not sensibility and good judgment, the growth of the courts' authority derives from the same source as that of the executive. An extraordinarily large part of the judiciary's power has been delegated to it by Congress. Legislation that, in effect, leaves its meaning and effect to be determined by the courts is almost as prolific as that delegating authority to the administrative agencies.

Finally, I would suggest, the growth in the stature of the judicial branch derives directly from the failure of the principle of separation of powers to effectuate the objective behind its invocation. The powers of government were to be separated in order to protect the liberty of the people. With the growth of government, the safeguard thought to be inherent in separation of powers has largely failed. The country has fallen back on the specific negatives in the Constitution which, as I have already suggested, are to be found in the Bill of Rights, the provisions of article I, sections 9 and 10, and the clauses of the fourteenth amendment. The enforcement of these restraints has fallen largely to the judiciary; neither the legislature nor the executive seems capable of abiding by these negative commandments without help from the judiciary. . . .

We are left now not with substantive limitations against government tyranny, but with procedural ones. We have become dependent for what freedoms are left to us on another underlying principle of the Constitution—like federalism and separation of powers not mentioned in haec verba in the document—one that is also an inheritance from the English, "the rule of law." The rule of law requires that government not act except according to preestablished rule, that it apply the rule according to preestablished procedure, and that the same rule be applied equally to all. Obviously, like federalism and the separation of powers, the concept of the rule of law is an ideal. It is the last best hope for avoiding the arbitrary tyranny of government.

* * *

E. Donald Elliott, *Why Our Separation of Powers Jurisprudence Is So Abysmal,* 57 GEO. WASH. L. REV. 506 (1989)*

Separation of powers jurisprudence in the United States is in an abysmal state. Our separation of powers jurisprudence is abysmal because the Supreme Court has failed for over two hundred years of our history to develop a law of separation of powers. The Court has reached a collection of results in separation of powers cases—some sensible and pragmatic, others utterly asinine. But what the Court has undeniably failed to do through all of these cases is to develop a body of principle and theory that is coherent and useful in enabling the system "to be wiser than the individuals who constitute it." In interpreting most of the familiar texts in constitutional law, for example, the Free Press Clause of the First Amendment or the Due Process Clause of the Fourteenth Amendment, the Supreme Court is construing a discrete, "uni-directional" passage that creates a linguistic representation for a specific constitutional value. That is simply not true in separation of powers law. There is no discrete "Separation of Powers Clause" in the Constitution. Rather, the term "separation of powers" is used to encapsulate the general principles of constitutional structure and design that are imminent throughout the Framers' Constitution. In a sense, the "text" in separation of powers law is everything that the Framers did and said in making the original Constitution plus the history of our government since the founding.

The essential flaw in prevailing separation of powers jurisprudence is that it (mis)understands the task of constitutional interpretation in too literal a way. In a sense, separation of powers cases are being decided as if there were a "Separation of Powers Clause" in the Constitution that the Court could read and apply like the wording of a statute or a contract.

Literalism as a theory of constitutional interpretation is responsible for generating both the "formalistic" and the "functional" strands that have been observed in our current separation of powers jurisprudence. By enforcing the words of the Constitution too mechanically and uncreatively in its "formalistic" decisions, the Court loses sight of, and frequently violates, the true meaning of the Constitution. On the other hand, when the Court eschews a formalist result, its "functionalist" decisions seem to lose their moorings in the Constitution. They come across as ipse dixits because literalism was the only mode of constitutional interpretation that seemed available to the Court for grounding a result in the Constitution.

My contention is that literalism is stifling separation of powers jurisprudence and preventing if from becoming a positive, creative force in our constitutional law. The source of the prevailing literalism is a fundamental misconception of the judicial role in separation of powers cases. This misconception can be traced to the undue emphasis that lawyers, judges, and law professors have placed on *Marbury v. Madison* and the problems of legitimating judicial review as the central issue in constitutional law. . . .

I. Separation of Powers Jurisprudence Evaluated

Unlike some other areas of constitutional law, such as civil liberties, where the work of the federal courts has been dynamic and creative and has arguably even made contributions to improving the well-being of citizens in our society, in separation of powers cases the work of our courts has been characterized by literalism and negativity. . . .

An additional consequence of the literalistic, negative tone of our separation of powers jurisprudence is that the role of the courts in this area must be measured primarily by how much net harm they have done. Hardly anyone thinks that the federal courts have played an affirmative role in moving the evolution of the structure of our government forward; discussion of their contribution (if "contribution" it be on balance) is almost entirely in terms of how much harm they have (allegedly) prevented, and at what cost in terms of efficiency or other values.

Again a comparison to other areas of constitutional law may be instructive. American lawyers are justly proud of the affirmative role that the federal courts have played during the past generation in goading our society to deal with issues of racial justice. Contrast their consistent refusal to become involved in the decades-long struggle between Congress and the executive branch over control of the power to make war, and it should be clear that the courts cannot claim much credit for what they have brought to fruition in separation of powers law, but rather only for what they have prevented.

The negative, literalistic tone of this area of our constitutional law is even evident from the term that we conventionally apply to it, separation of powers. The term itself conjures up simplistic notions about our tripartite structure of government and how the roles of the three branches of government should be kept "separate." In fact, however, "separation of powers" jurisprudence is nothing less than our constitutional law about questions of governmental structure.

In their obeisance to the Framers' intentions on the specifics of governmental organization and structure, the courts violate the deeper, more fundamental spirit of the Framers' vision that power should be divided and balanced creatively to prevent misuse. . . . Ironically, this structural "separation of powers" approach to the problems of governing—creatively designing and balancing complex institutional systems to deal with governmental problems—has become increasingly unavailable because the courts' understanding of this constitutional principle has been literal and unimaginative. In their zeal to enforce the letter of the Constitution, they deny its essence.

* * *

. . . Were it not so sad, it would be laughable for the Supreme Court to make pronouncements about the constitutionality of innovations in governmental structure that are reminiscent of the old farmer's edict that if God had intended us to fly, He would have given us wings.

The Constitution was intended to create a structure of government for the ages, not to provide an exhaustive laundry list of all the things that the government may do to deal with changing problems. By looking at the language of the Constitution for hints as to "what the Framers thought about" the legislative veto, or Gramm-Rudman, when they never really thought at all about the problems that these devices were created to solve, the courts trivialize the process of turning to our history and traditions for wisdom and guidance. The proper question is whether a new measure or device is consistent with the Framers' vision of government as reflected and made manifest to us by the constitutional structure that they created, and elaborated by our subsequent history and traditions. This the courts almost never ask.

* * *

II. Beyond *Marbury* and the Jurisprudence of Inputs

From the beginning, American judges and legal scholars have been obsessed with questions concerning the legitimacy of judicial review and corollary problems of what sources of law judges may properly consider in deciding constitutional cases. For convenience, let us call this "the jurisprudence of inputs," because it focuses almost exclusively on what judges may take into account in deciding constitutional cases.

. . . I want to suggest, that the prevailing definition of constitutional law in terms of *Marbury* and the jurisprudence of inputs has been a crucial factor in impoverishing constitutional thought in the field of separation of powers, and perhaps more broadly as well.

The essential justification for judicial review that Chief Justice Marshall posits in *Marbury* turns on an analogy between the Constitution and other legal documents, such as contracts or statutes. . . . Textuality, however, is not the only plausible justification that might be given for judicial review. For example, Alexander Hamilton's justification for judicial review in The Federalist No. 78 is really quite different from Marshall's in *Marbury*, and relies far less, if at all, on the written nature of the Constitution. In a similar vein, Professor Barbara Black has suggested that judicial review by courts on issues of constitutional law is "obvious enough to go without saying" from the nature of courts and their role in the structure of government created by the Constitution.

. . . Under the justification for judicial review given in *Marbury*—but not under the others that might have been given—the strongest, most legitimate constitutional argument is one based on the text of the Constitution itself. A close second is an argument based on other closely related texts from the founding period, such as the debates of the Constitutional Convention and The Federalist Papers.

Unlike most other areas of constitutional law, separation of powers law was "blessed" with a comparative wealth of these early texts. These early texts applying separation of powers concepts to various problems encountered during the founding period have made it easy to decide separation of powers cases literally. For example, in *Bowsher*, Chief Justice Burger can point to the Founders' fears that the Congress might aggrandize its power at the expense of the other branches. . . . But does the fact that the Framers feared legislative (rather than presidential) aggrandizement in 1787 really imply that it should be our primary concern in 1987?

Just as wealth that comes too easily in other spheres of life may stifle and impoverish the spirit, so too a wealth of relevant textual material in separation of powers law has made it easy to decide, but may make it harder to learn to decide well. By this line of reasoning, separation of powers law has failed to develop a rich theoretical foundation precisely because these concepts were so prominent during the Founders' era.

* * *

Rather than applying separation of powers texts literally, the courts should be striving to reach a deeper, more fundamental, and therefore more relevant understanding of our separation of powers traditions, as they sometimes have in other areas of constitutional law.

III.   Toward Interpretation in Separation of Powers Jurisprudence

The central fallacy that ails our separation of powers jurisprudence grows out of a failure to distinguish between interpretation and literalism in applying the Constitution.

No text applies itself. A text, like any other set of symbols, must be related to its environment through a process by which meaning is created. But the environment is always changing, and consequently, relating a text to its environment and thereby giving it meaning is problematic. Literalism does not escape this problem; it merely obscures the problem by abandoning the choice of meanings to the general cultural evolution of language.

* * *

The problem I have just described is a general one for constitutional law, where we must always try to give meaning to symbols across two hundred years of historical distance. It is exacerbated for separation of powers by the absence of a single, general text that states a broad, constitutional principle.

In lieu of such a "Separation of Powers Clause," we are given a number of specific clauses that constitute the three branches of government and define relationships among them. It is a mistake to imagine, however, that the constitutional doctrine of separation of powers is coterminous with the specific provisions of the Constitution creating the government. These words, in historical context, created the doctrine of separation of powers, but they do not exhaust it.

* * *

The saddest casualty of the literalism that now pervades our separation of powers jurisprudence is that literalism cuts short discussion and thought. Lawyers and judges rarely think or talk today about how government works, or what history teaches are the characteristic flaws in particular governmental designs, and how these weaknesses may be overcome through creatively designing and combining institutions. It was just these types of questions that the Framers asked themselves when they met together in the summer of 1787 in Philadelphia.

We need to think of our separation of powers jurisprudence as a continuation of the creative discussions about governmental structure that began at Philadelphia. This we cannot do, however, so long as we insist on applying the Framers' words but neglecting their meaning.

Peter L. Strauss, *Was There a Baby in the Bathwater? A Comment on the Supreme Court's Legislative Veto Decision,* 1983 Duke L.J. 789 (1983)*

* * *

. . . Written following what was evidently a difficult internal process, the Chief Justice's majority opinion in *Immigration and Naturalization Service v. Chadha,* seems intended to sweep all of the 200-plus legislative veto provisions from the statute books, in addition to the one provision necessarily before the Court in the case. That impression is confirmed by subsequent summary actions affirming unanimous opinions of the District of Columbia Circuit striking down legislative vetoes affecting regulatory agency rulemaking, as well as by the disapproval evident in three separate opinions in *Chadha.* The immediate and pained response of Congress suggested as well the understanding that it had been deprived, in all contexts, of a valued legislative tool.

---

*   Reprinted with permission.

* * *

Faced with uses of the legislative veto that allowed the President and Congress to resolve directly constitutional and policy differences on issues of high political and small legal moment, uses that accommodate a necessarily continuing dialogue between Congress and the President on matters internal to government (its budget and structure), uses for deciding questions of individual status such as deportability, and uses for oversight of agency conduct such as public rulemaking directly affecting obligations of the public, the Court might have been expected to distinguish among these uses or, at least, to decide in a way that reserved consideration of those uses not presented in *Chadha*. The Court did not do so; the argument of this essay is that the Court's actions would have been far more acceptable, had it attended to the multiplicity of settings in which the veto has been used.

. . . [T]he use of legislative veto provisions may empower the President as much as Congress. Use of the veto as an instrument of the continuing political dialogue between President and Congress, on matters having high and legitimate political interest to both, and calling for flexibility for government generally, does not present the same problems as its use to control, in random and arbitrary fashion, those matters customarily regarded as the domain of administrative law. That none of the disputants before the Court may have found it in their interest to argue for such distinctions and that the Court itself did not suggest them, only illustrates once more the problems presented by the Court's limited capacity to entertain and decide issues of national importance, and the resulting temptation to make doctrine governing the future, rather than decision of the pending case, the centerpiece of the Court's effort.

* * *

The *Chadha* decision would be less important—as the result in the case is the right one—if it did not call into question so much that had been thought established about the dispersal of governmental authority. The opinion repudiates the now deeply engrained proposition that Congress' legislative authority may be exercised conditionally; yet that proposition was the initial engine by which delegation of "legislative powers" was effected, with the conditions, in this instance, supervised by the courts. The Court recognizes the possible inconsistency when it worries in a lengthy footnote that its reasoning might be seen as casting some doubt on rulemaking or other forms of agency action. [T]he Court concludes that no such inconsistency is presented. . . . "The President's power to see that the laws are faithfully executed refutes the idea that he is to be a lawmaker." Of course, the President and the agencies are lawmakers, in any conventional sense of the term, when they engage in rulemaking pursuant to constitutional or statutory authorization. However one might label what the Department of Justice and the House did in considering the cancellation of Mr. Chadha's deportation for compassionate reasons, the action of each seems to have been of the same nature and to have had precisely the same kind of legal effect on Mr. Chadha's rights. . . . The Court does not adequately explain why one actor is regarded as behaving "legislatively," and the other is not. The Court seems to make the *Youngstown* passage mean that the "President does not act legislatively because he is the chief executive; the House does, because it is part of Congress. What the President does is ipso facto executive; what Congress does, legislative."

Whether an action is "legislative in character and effect" might have been thought a function of its characteristics, rather than the identity of the actor. This approach would have led the Court to consider the arguable differences between "legislative" and "adjudicative" action. . . .

* * *

Perhaps one should take seriously the notion that whatever is done by the House or Senate is definitionally legislative, not because of the characteristics of what is done but because of the identity of the body acting. The same propositions would then apply to the President and the Supreme Court; their actions would, of necessity, be "executive" or "judicial," respectively. Some suggestion that the Court intends that approach is found in a repeated "presumption" that a governmental body is acting within its intended sphere. What follows, however, is that there is then no magic in the word "legislative" to aid in determining whether the House and/or Senate are acting constitutionally. Because the House and Senate often act outside the structure of presentment and bicameralism, and in fact use it only when enacting laws, one must have reasons not supplied by the label "legislative" for insisting upon that structure, or for otherwise finding constitutional fault with the legislative scheme. . . .

* * *

IV. JUSTICE WHITE'S DISSENT

Justice White's intellectual approach to the legislative veto question, although flawed, seems more consistent with the Court's recent analyses of separation of powers/checks and balances issues than the majority's approach. . . .

For Justice White, the legislative veto "has become a central means by which Congress secures the accountability of executive and independent agencies"—"an important if not indispensable political intervention that allows the President and Congress to resolve major constitutional and policy differences, assures the accountability of independent regulatory agencies, and preserves Congress' control over lawmaking." In light of the relatively limited use of the device to date, one wonders if he does not overstate the case. His judgment is particularly questionable respecting use of the veto for regulatory oversight; at least until recently, enhancing the accountability of independent regulatory agencies and preserving congressional control over public rulemaking were not significant uses for the legislative veto, in either actual or political terms.

The Political Uses of Legislative Vetoes.

. . . Justice White's detailed account of the history of the legislative veto reflects its initial use in reorganization acts, and subsequent expansion to problems of national security and foreign affairs. In these contexts it seems proper to characterize the veto, as he does, as a means by which Congress could "transfer greater authority to the President . . . while preserving its own constitutional role." Withdrawals of federal lands, international agreements and tariffs, . . . national emergency legislation, and the impoundment issue each concern chiefly public measures, primarily related to the internal organization of government and affecting the interests of private persons only indirectly; they reflect areas of direct presidential initiative and responsibility. In these contexts, too, the veto represents an accommodation between the branches, often mutually desired as Justice White demonstrated, on matters of legitimate interest to each. Reorganization acts, measures concerned with budgetary adjustment (impoundment), foreign relations, and war . . . rarely appear in a form likely to attract or, more importantly, to justify judicial review. They may all be described fairly as a setting for horse-trading between the President and Congress . . .. To the extent Justice White speaks of the legislative veto in terms of congressional accommodation directly with a powerful President requiring more power—as a means of preserving balance while accomplishing needed delegation to that other potential tyrant—his dissent is persuasive.

The Regulatory Uses of Legislative Vetoes.

At other points Justice White's dissent is far less persuasive, notably those bearing on the regulatory context, where it speaks only in terms of Congress' accomplishment of its own "designated role under Article I as the nation's lawmaker," independent of any relational concerns. The legislative veto did not begin to appear with any frequency in that context until the 1970's. In that setting, Justice White's assertion that the legislative veto should be understood as a check on the President corresponding to the bicameral legislature/presidential veto regime, one of the principal engines of his analysis, is at best questionably relevant. The difficulties arise for two reasons: first, ordinarily the President is not the delegate under these statutes and his authority to direct the proceedings over which the veto is reserved is, at best, controversial; second, even if he were the delegate, reservation of an unconditional congressional negative would not protect Congress' "designated role . . . as the nation's lawmaker." . . .

[O]ne premise of Justice White's argument is that, as the President is the source of the action subject to the veto, the effect of the mechanism is merely to invert the ordinary processes of legislative action; the agreement of all three actors is in any event required, and in that way the essentials of the constitutional scheme are preserved. That premise will not always be true; some proposals subject to legislative vetoes come from the President, but others come from rulemakers not subject to direct presidential control or, as here, administrative judges acting "on the record," and thus also not subject to presidential direction. In particular, congressional delegations of regulatory authority are most often made not to the President, but to some agency or official—whether executive branch or independent regulatory commission. The legal authority to act is then that of the delegate, and even for indisputably executive agencies the President's power of direction appears limited in ways that make it difficult to characterize him as the delegate. . . . The more difficult Congress makes it, in its original delegation, for the President to participate and instruct, the greater the reason to suspect that the legislative veto does in fact operate as a device for evasion of the President's participation in governance rather than the simple redressing of an imbalance created by the practical need to delegate.

The second difficulty with the "functional equivalency" argument in the regulatory context is that presidential (or agency) shaping of rules followed by an up-or-down congressional "veto" is not the equivalent of the Article I legislative process. The possibility that any one of the three political arms of government can prevent the enactment of legislation is only part of the constitutional scheme. Of at least equal significance is that, where legislation is to be created, the opportunities for shaping and constructive change are to be focused in two of them, the House and the Senate. Congress does not act as a lawmaker when it leaves to other entities all possibility of shaping and accommodating that go into the drafting of a rule, reserving for itself only the possibility of an unconditional negative; it then serves the same function as the President does respecting the legislation Congress does enact. The drafters of the Constitution meant the shaping of legislation to be done by Congress; and that adjustment seems important to the overall acheme (sic). . . .

To be sure, the constitutional design has suffered considerable erosion. Even absent the legislative veto, Congress' work has frequently been wanting. We permit Congress to delegate notably open-ended rulemaking authority to agencies, subject only to the now limited constraints of the delegation doctrine: that the authority has been clearly delegated; and that the authority be described with clarity sufficient to permit a court to assess whether it has been exceeded. Even so, and putting aside the question whether the courts are not now, and properly, reinvigorating these controls, use of the legislative veto to control agency rulemaking—the generation of statute-like prescriptions binding upon the citizenry—aggravates the delegation problem rather than ameliorates it. Congress may have been encouraged by the availability of the veto both to employ vague standards of delegation to proxy statute-shapers, and to respond to its proxies' "excesses" with unexplained, ad hoc negatives rather than with the construction of revised statutory prescriptions. . . . Room thus exists at least for suspicion that legislative vetoes will produce less careful initial drafting by providing a mechanism whereby difficult issues can be cheaply revisited. The threat of their exercise may also enhance the aggressiveness of political oversight by congressmen or congressional committees. In sum, the existence of a legislative veto in a regulatory statute may look much more like political self-aggrandizement than "a means of defense" against the Imperial Presidency. . . .

* * *

V. PRESERVING THE POLITICAL VETO

This consideration of the "functional equivalency" argument suggests a broad distinction between use of the legislative veto as a check on the chief executive, and use of the legislative veto as a check on any agency to which power has been delegated. . . .

* * *

One wishes the Court had limited itself to the particular measures before it, or that it or Justice White had shown some sensitivity in addressing the variety of settings in which legislative vetoes might be employed. In the three cases it had to decide, the Court reached a sound result: Congress has no business determining that the individual circumstances of a particular alien warrant his deportation; and in the regulatory rulemaking context, especially as it concerns the independent regulatory commissions, the legislative veto does seem to exclude the President rather than mediate a continuing dialogue between the President and the Congress. Yet for the cases it did not have to decide, Justice White's premises seem stronger than the majority's.

The argument that a legislative veto can be the functional equivalent of "normal" constitutional processes—or, perhaps more properly, works no threatening rearrangement of initiative and authority—is persuasive for the settings in which the device was earliest and most commonly used:

- where the President himself takes or directs the action subject to the legislative veto;
- where the subject matter principally concerns the internal arrangements of government rather than rules of conduct applicable to the public, and judicial consideration at any stage is unlikely;
- where both the President and Congress have an important interest in the subject matter of the action to be taken, and congressional participation through the veto may prompt less grudging recognition of the President's participation and/or a sense of moral commitment to provide fiscal or other support for the resulting arrangements.

The argument is far less persuasive, however, in the regulatory setting, where, on the other hand:

- the President ordinarily is not a direct participant, and may even be excluded from direct participation;
- judgments affecting individual interests or obligations are to be made, and judicial review of agency action is readily available;
- permitting use of the legislative veto may tempt Congress to believe that it can easily correct the excesses of a careless formula governing the obligations of the public, and correct them without the need to articulate a fresh or limiting principle; and
- the justification offered for use of the veto is framed not in terms of political accommodation between a Congress and President, both interested in the premises, but only in terms of Congress' performance of its own legislative function.

Neither the majority opinion nor Justice White's dissent seem to leave much room for accommodations of this character.

* * *

Stephen L. Carter, *The Supreme Court, 1987 Term, Comment: The Independent Counsel Mess*, 102 HARV. L. REV. 105 (1988)*

To many contemporary commentators, the doctrine of separation of powers is a hoary non sequitur used to justify reactionary results. To the evident frustration of the critics, however, the Supreme Court has recently been quite solicitous of the original understanding on the way in which federal power is to be distributed. In the face of a chorus of calls for innovative legislative action to undo a supposed government paralysis or to reverse a perceived concentration of authority in the executive branch, the Supreme Court has generally stuck to its guns, consistently reminding the Congress and the nation that policy inconsistent with the structure of government mandated by the Constitution is impermissible. . . .

Against this background, many observers were surprised by the Court's 7-1 vote last Term in *Morrison v. Olson*, which sustained the constitutionality of a key provision of the Ethics in Government Act. That statute, passed in the heady days after Richard Nixon was toppled from office, permits judicial appointment of independent counsels, popularly known as special prosecutors, to investigate allegations of criminal wrongdoing in the executive branch, and, if necessary, to prosecute the wrongdoers.

* * *

[I]f *Morrison* marks a move away from originalism and toward deference to the Congress in the resolution of separation of powers disputes, something important and in many ways troubling is plainly in the wind. The other tantalizing possibility is that in *Morrison* the originalist approach to separation of powers cases finally and inevitably came into conflict with the Court's other structural project, a project of longer standing: the legitimation and preservation of the independent agencies.

---

*   Copyright © 1988 by the Harvard Law Review Association. Reprinted by permission.

Thus, far from signalling a change in direction, the decision to sustain the independent counsel provision of the Ethics in Government Act might herald the Supreme Court's resolution to stay the course as Court and Congress work together to build an administrative, managerial government independent of effective executive control. If so, the decision arguably does no more than maintain the status quo on the constitutionality of the independent agencies. . . .

I.

* * *

In 1978, evidently convinced that the abuses of Watergate would have been reined in and punished far sooner had they been independently investigated—not a bad hypothesis—the Congress adopted the Ethics in Government Act. Title VI of the Act requires the Attorney General of the United States, in certain clearly defined circumstances, to apply to a judicial panel known as the Special Division for the appointment of an independent counsel. The Act provides that the independent counsel, not the Attorney General, will be charged with investigating and prosecuting violations of federal law by executive branch employees. Because the statute tries to remove from the Attorney General any discretion in the matter once the statutory conditions are met, it is plainly designed to make the decision whether to apply for appointment of an independent counsel an essentially ministerial act. The Congress that passed the Act plainly contemplated, moreover, that the independent counsel would undertake her duties in the manner that the name implies—independently. Hence, the counsel was to be independent of the President's control and, a fortiori, independent of the Attorney General's control as well.

The premise of the Act is that the executive branch cannot be trusted to investigate allegations of criminality by its own high officials. And it is certainly true, as supporters of the independent counsel provision insist, that there always has been, and always will be, malfeasance by employees of the executive branch. It is also true that those with the power to do so always have been, and always will be, tempted to limit the political damage that any investigation might cause.

Under the approach to separation of powers questions that the Court has followed in recent years, however, such policy concerns as these are essentially irrelevant. The Supreme Court's jurisprudence on separation of powers represents an admixture of two traditions. The first might be called the evolutionary tradition, for it holds that as the needs of the nation change over time, the Congress may guide the evolution of fresh institutional forms to meet these changing needs. The second might be called the de-evolutionary tradition, for it holds that the constitutional scheme of balanced and separated powers should be used as a brake on efforts to alter the form of government that the Framers envisioned.

Over the past decade or so, a rather strict originalist form of the de-evolutionary tradition has come to dominate the Court's separation of powers jurisprudence. Relying heavily on James Madison's notes of the Philadelphia Convention of 1787 (a less than ideal source, because they played no significant role in the debate over ratification of the Constitution, the process that transformed the document into fundamental law), the Court has tried to measure the federal government's deployment of its powers against what it has determined the views of the Founders to have been. . . .

The common theme running through these and other de-evolutionary decisions is that, whatever disagreements might exist over the appropriate interpretive method in other constitutional cases, there is only one correct method when the structure of the federal government is at issue: enforcing the Founders' shared vision of the way in which the federal government was to work. Claims of necessity, claims of good policy, and claims of efficiency are not sufficient, under this approach, to justify a new institutional form that runs afoul of the system of balanced and separated powers that the Founders devised. . . .

. . . [T]he majority opinion in *Morrison*, quite unlike the Court's recent de-evolutionary analyses, treated the history as virtually irrelevant, and in the end subordinated it to the very policy concerns that earlier decisions had chosen to ignore. The independent counsel provision, the majority announced, is constitutional, evidently because it does not transgress too far onto any specific presidential power, and also because the Congress has determined that independence is necessary to the prosecutor's function.

The independent counsel provisions of title VI were challenged on several grounds. First, the appointment of the independent counsel by the Special Division was said to violate the appointment clause of article II, either because the counsel was a "principal" executive officer whose appointment could not be delegated, or because executive officers could not in any case be appointed by the courts. Second, the continuing supervision of the counsel by the Special Division was said to violate the "case or controversy" requirement for judicial action under article III. Third, the cornerstone of the Act, the very independence of the counsel from presidential control, was said to intrude in a variety of ways on presidential prerogative, and, as a consequence, to violate the separation of powers.

. . . In assessing the appointment power claim, Chief Justice Rehnquist's majority opinion did discuss some of the history of the appointments clause (not of article III), but considered only the third-best evidence of the original understanding, Madison's secret notes of the Convention. In the end, the Justices dismissed the assault on the appointment process in a passage as predictable as it was lengthy.

. . . The Court construed the statute to deny the Special Division any supervisory role over the counsel "in the exercise of her investigative or prosecutorial authority." The majority reached this construction notwithstanding its admission that the Special Division may select the counsel, define the counsel's jurisdiction, alter that jurisdiction, refer additional matters to the counsel, decide what to do with the counsel's reports, and decide when the counsel's task is "so substantially completed" that the counsel should be discharged.

The challenges to title VI on the ground that it interferes with executive authority could not be so easily dismissed, and the arguments that the majority selected suggest a considerable struggle to find a way of evading them. Even as it sustained title VI, the Court seemed to acknowledge by the very awkwardness of its arguments that the constitutional difficulties raised by the independent counsel provision are substantial. Chief among the problems is this: article II vests the executive power in the President, and it was assumed on all sides that the investigative and prosecutorial powers exercised by the independent counsel are entirely executive in nature. If one who indulges the de-evolutionary approach accepts that assumption, then no matter who appoints the prosecutors there is at least a colorable case to be made that the President is constitutionally entitled to control them.

* * *

In *Morrison*, however, the Justices seemed unwilling to concede that the Attorney General—and therefore the President—lacks all effective ability to control the independent counsel. The Act, the majority explained, merely "reduces the amount of control or supervision" that the President and the Attorney General may exercise. As evidence of the President's continuing supervisory authority, the Court pointed out that the independent counsel may be removed for good cause and that no judicial review is available of the Attorney General's decision to decline to ask the Special Division for appointment in the first place.

. . . [T]he *Morrison* majority faced the need to explain how a prosecutor—assumed on all sides to be within the executive branch—could nevertheless be exempt from removal by the President. . . . [T]he Justices proceeded to analyze the functions of the independent counsel and concluded that "because the independent counsel may be terminated for 'good cause,' the Executive, through the Attorney General, retains ample authority to assure that the counsel is competently performing her statutory responsibilities in a manner that comports with the provisions of the Act." Consequently, the opinion concluded, the removal restriction does not "sufficiently deprive[ ] the President of control over the independent counsel to interfere impermissibly with his constitutional obligation to ensure the faithful execution of the laws."

* * *

What, then, can one make of the analysis in *Morrison*? One possibility is that the Justices have simply abandoned the de-evolutionary tradition in separation of powers jurisprudence, and have decided to allow congressional judgment about necessity to dominate the Founders' vision. Yet so extraordinary a development would surely find hints and precursors in other recent opinions, and there simply are none to be found.

* * *

The Court may have supposed that it was preserving a strong executive in the general case, but that the President's prerogative had to yield in this specific matter, because the Congress had determined that independence of the counsel was vital to the operation of the Ethics in Government Act. If this was what the Justices had in mind, then although the opinion might have been poorly drafted, it stands in an established constitutional tradition. The trouble is that it is a tradition that may rest on sand. This tradition holds that when the Congress decides that independence is necessary for an agency to do its job, even a job partly executive, it may insulate the agency from presidential control. This is the tradition that undergirds the modern administrative state, but it has never been adequately justified by the Court as a matter of constitutional law. In a constitutional world in which the Justices understand the link between legitimacy and originalism in separation of powers disputes, a constitutional reexamination of the tradition of independent administrative government is long overdue.

* * *

Consider, first, the possibility that we have a multitude of Constitutions, for the Constitution of the United States is many documents, and not all of these documents serve the same purpose. One of the many lines along which the Constitution might be sliced is this one: some clauses relate to rights of individuals within the system of government, and others relate to the structure of the system itself. The individual rights clauses are usually written in the glowing and evocative terms of moral appeal, and, taken together, might be called our Natural Law Constitution. The structural clauses, which constitute what might be called our Political Constitution, are relatively dry and relatively concrete. The individual rights clauses, when considered as ordinary language, seem to deny by their very words the possibility that they have very specific referents. The structural clauses, on the other hand, carry with them the suggestion that the authors had in mind a very specific vision of the system under construction.

It is a mistake to assume that the Political Constitution and the Natural Rights Constitution, with their different emphases and different forms of language, ought necessarily to be subjected to the same rules for interpretation. Every act of interpretation is an act undertaken for a specific purpose, and the purpose of the interpretation generates the question that the interpreter ought to ask. The error of conflating interpretation under the Political and Natural Law Constitutions arises from the assumption that the interpretations share a common purpose, usually captured in the word "adjudication." But although it is true that the happenstance of adjudication occasions judicial interpretation, it is not correct to call adjudication the purpose. To do so takes too narrow a view of the role that the Founding Generation and the Constitution itself play in American political iconography.

Constitutional interpretation is (or ought to be) a narrative activity. . . . For the Constitution, at its heart, is not a document but a continuing saga—the saga of We, the People of the United States, in whose name the document speaks. The story provides us with continuity, by linking our world to the world that has gone before; and it provides us with immortality, by linking our world to the world that is yet to come. It is not a story told by the judges alone, or by the historians, or by the politicians; it is also a constitutional story that we—We, the People—tell about ourselves.

* * *

What the Supreme Court apparently recognizes in its separation of powers jurisprudence, however, is that adjudication under the Political Constitution requires more concrete rules for interpretation to match the Political Constitution's quite different status. . . .

* * *

A judge who is concerned about the legitimacy of the government, and about the legitimacy of the judicial function, which is prescribed in the same Political Constitution that establishes the other branches, will obviously be cautious in permitting the evolution of new institutional forms not contemplated in the system of checks and balances that the Founders set forth. If the judge accepts the notion that much of the public respect for government and for law rests on the supposition that the government operates in accordance with the rules handed down by the Founding Generation, it would be logical for her to decide that the government must play by the rules under which the public supposes that the game is played. . . . If the rules of the game are not the ones devised by the Founders, then there really may be no practical sense in which the federal government, in all its institutional complexity, enjoys the consent of the governed. Thus the judge could sensibly conclude that the ideal theory of interpretation is one that encourages the search for the vision shared by the Founders on the fundamental rules that would control the structure of the government.

This reasoning might explain how the Justices could end up where they were before *Morrison*: insisting on a form of originalism in cases arising under the Political Constitution, and applying other interpretive rules, sometimes radically inconsistent ones, in cases arising under the Natural Rights Constitution. The Justices might well believe that originalism in structural cases is the key to legitimacy—including the legitimacy of the judicial freedom to exercise greater discretion in interpretation of the Natural Law Constitution. The originalist project of rendering the Political Constitution relatively concrete might then be viewed as a pragmatic choice as well as one dictated by theory. . . .

The choice to pursue and enforce the original understanding privileges one set of values over another; there is nothing "objective" about the selection. Nor can originalism do all that some of its most ardent advocates may pretend. . . .

* * *

[A] Supreme Court interested in discerning the original understanding on separation of powers issues would make a grave error (and perhaps has occasionally made one) by insisting in an intentionalist way on evidence of what the Founders thought the answer was. There is more to originalism than intentionalism. . . . The task is to ensure that the fundamental value choices made by the Founders in devising the system of balanced and separated power continue to guide the structure of the federal government. Thus the de-evolutionary project requires an answer not to the question "Did the Founders intend that the President control all executive officers or not?" but to the quite different question "Is independence of this kind consistent with the values underlying the scheme of balanced and separated powers or not?" If the second question accurately captures what the Justices have been doing, then they may have discovered something important.

Although this de-evolutionary project, like all efforts at reading history, possesses certain obvious limitations, it avoids many of the pitfalls that have snared other originalist efforts. The judge is searching only for those aspects of constitutional history that provide the continuity linking the nation in which we live with the one that the Founders envisioned, and that is a task that requires only that the judge identify those aspects of the system that were originally understood as fundamental to the transformation of political science into political practice. Implementing this project means avoiding the mistakes of the many "law office" originalists who confine themselves to the records of deliberations on concise constitutional clauses rather than immersing themselves in the intellectual currents of the Founding Generation, a far richer path toward identifying the fundamental postulates standing behind particular provisions of the Constitution.

This might or might not be what the Justices are actually up to, but, if it is, it is no easy theory for them to sell. In the post-liberal legal world, law is policy, not structure. Advocates of particular devices and institutions for the efficient deployment of government authority to attain particular ends have little patience with de-evolutionary review. They would prefer a world in which, as long as individual rights are protected, the government may reconstitute itself in a fresh image, one in which all that matters in selecting the proper legal rule to govern the society's transformation is an appreciation of the learning of the policy scientists. . . .

. . . The de-evolutionary project tries to give people the government that they already think they have, by preserving the basic structure that the Founders designed. The project, in short, tries to treat the Founders as the larger-than-life figures that the popular imagination insists that they are. Their fundamental structural choices must be respected and there can be no tampering with their handiwork. If this be ancestor worship, then the Justices are apparently prepared to make the most of it.

And this is where the Justices could have, and perhaps should have, made their stand in *Morrison*. The majority could have gone to the history of ratification and the political science of the Founding Era, could have delved and burrowed and studied and filled the opinion with whatever it discovered. Quite conceivably, the Court would have reached the same result. The Justices might have noted, for example, that in England, as late as the eighteenth century, criminal prosecution was still something instigated by private individuals, and although the Attorney General brought some cases and could defeat a private prosecution by filing a writ of nolle prosequi, the system was essentially private. A dual system of public and private prosecution, together with some appointments of prosecutors by the courts, was the practice in most of the colonies at the time of the Founding. In the first decades of the Republic, federal prosecutors—then known as district attorneys—bore a somewhat ambiguous relationship to the executive branch. They were appointed by the President, but had no direct superior in the federal government, and they acted with considerable independence, often as aides to the federal courts and the judicially controlled grand juries. Such historical evidence as this might have led the majority to conclude that title VI of the Ethics in Government Act simply harks back to an earlier constitutional status quo.

Or the Justices might have reached the opposite conclusion, reading the Constitution, with its carefully crafted system of checks and balances, as so radical a departure from previous models of government that continuity with past practice should not be assumed. These tiny bites of history, the Court might have said, are not enough to overcome the plain historical tradition that the President has always retained effective, ultimate control over criminal prosecution for the violation of federal law. First principles of separation of powers, the Justices could have argued, hold that if one branch makes the laws and a second determines guilt or innocence, a third must be vested with the discretion whether to prosecute or not.

The point is that whichever route the Justices chose to follow, they would at least have placed us in history once more, adding to the constitutional saga with the message: "The political science of the Founding Generation created a system flexible enough to accommodate this necessary device." Or, had the result been different, the Justices would have been saying: "The establishment of an investigator and prosecutor outside of the executive branch is inconsistent with the political science underlying our system of government." . . .

Yet despite the years that the Supreme Court has spent building its de-evolutionary project into fundamental structural law, the project was suddenly abandoned in *Morrison* in favor of a balancing test and a deference to a congressional judgment about necessity. . . . If the reason for the Court's sudden retreat from de-evolution is its fear of jeopardizing the status of the independent administrative agencies, then perhaps the time has come to subject those agencies to a bit of the de-evolutionary discipline that the Justices have recently used to analyze other institutions of government. . . .

III.

[In *Humphrey's Executor v. United States,*] the Justices ruled that the Congress possesses the authority to constitute agencies beyond the direction of the President and to imbue these independent agencies with authority that is partly executive in nature. This the Congress can do by directing that specified presidential appointees serve for a term of years rather than at the pleasure of the President. The Court has subsequently made clear that it will police the manner of appointment of the heads of these agencies to guarantee that the Congress' role is no more substantial than the senatorial confirmation power specified in article II, and that it will also guard the manner of removal of the heads of these agencies to ensure that the manner of removal can strip them of their commissions only through the device of impeachment. Nevertheless, the policy judgment on whether the agencies should be constituted independent of presidential control is left entirely to the Congress.

Humphrey's Executor was never an easy case to understand. Did Mr. Humphrey, the Federal Trade Commissioner whom President Roosevelt sought to fire, exercise executive authority or not? The Justices waffled on the point, explaining only that the FTC was not in the executive branch, and that the agency acted "in part quasi-legislatively and in part quasi-judicially." The constitutional basis for the delegation (or indeed, the existence) of these "quasi" powers was not specified, which led Justice Jackson to complain two decades later: "The mere retreat to the qualifying "quasi" is implicit with confession that all recognized classifications have broken down, and "quasi" is a smooth cover which we draw over our confusion as we might use a counterpane to conceal a disordered bed." *Humphrey's Executor*, moreover, seemed to fly in the face of *Myers v. United States*, which was decided just a decade earlier. In *Myers*, a divided Court had apparently settled the question of removal in the President's favor. According to Chief Justice Taft's majority opinion, the President's discretion to remove executive officials was designed to be plenary, and the Congress lacks constitutional authority to interfere with it. . . .

Like the Court in *Humphrey's Executor*, the *Morrison* majority evidently saw no need to discuss constitutional history in reaching a conclusion about constitutional structure. In explaining why the Congress possesses constitutional authority to clothe a prosecutor with some degree of independence—the Justices never said how much—the majority relied heavily on *Humphrey's Executor*, treating *Myers* as an interesting but no longer useful historical relic. . . . *Myers*, according to the *Morrison* opinion, turns out not really to have been about the removal power at all, but about ensuring that the "Congress does not interfere with the President's exercise of the "executive power" and his constitutionally appointed duly to "take care that the laws be faithfully executed." "As a matter of preserving the constitutional system of balanced and separated powers, it is obviously vital to have some limits on congressional interference with presidential prerogative, so the Court's revision of *Myers* states a sensible rule. It would surely come as some surprise to the authors of the four opinions in *Myers*, however, to learn that they were writing about the theoretical standard to be applied in separation of powers cases rather than arguing, as they evidently thought, over the precise historical origins and limits of the removal power.

Having thus disposed of *Myers*, the Justices rested on *Humphrey's Executor* to ground the independent counsel firmly in the tradition of establishing officers protected from presidential removal. . . .

> In *Humphrey's Executor*, we found it "plain" that the Constitution did not give the President "illimitable power of removal" over the officers of independent agencies. Were the President to have the power to remove FTC commissioners at will, the "coercive influence" of the removal power would "threate[n] the independence of [the] commission."

If this is what *Humphrey's Executor* stands for, then there is a substantial cart-and-horse problem. In the first place, to say that the Constitution does not grant the President "illimitable power of removal" over the heads of the independent agencies implies that the Constitution says something about independent agencies. But of course, it doesn't. The Constitution describes three forms of federal authority—legislative, executive, and judicial—and sets out in some detail who shall exercise each. There is no suggestion in the document, or in its ratification history, that the Congress ought to be free to create new forms of federal authority and new officials independent of the control of any branch.

And then there is the last part of the quote from *Humphrey's Executor*: should the President be able to remove the heads of the agencies at will, then the agencies will no longer be independent of executive control. This much is undeniable. What is left undiscussed in the majority opinion in *Morrison* is why this makes a difference. After all, one might reasonably reply that if presidential power to fire those who exercise executive authority renders it impossible to make them independent of presidential control, then perhaps the answer is that all those who exercise executive authority are, as a matter of constitutional law, subject to presidential control. The independent agencies, to the extent that they exercise executive authority, would then be unconstitutional.

This is heady stuff, but asking whether the Congress possesses authority under the Constitution to assign executive functions to nonexecutive officials is perfectly logical. The casual reader of *Morrison*, aware that this point is never broached, might imagine that the answer is found in *Humphrey's Executor*, because that is the case that the majority discusses at greatest length. . . . *Humphrey's Executor*, like *Morrison*, simply takes the permissibility of independence for granted. . . . The embarrassing truth is that in the long line of cases since the 1930's discussing the various facts of administrative government, not one makes a serious effort to justify the independent agencies in constitutional terms. There is talk of necessity, talk of chilling, and talk of coercion—in short, talk of policy—but there is nothing about constitutional structure, or the vision of the Founders. In short, the Justices have never undertaken a de-evolutionary analysis of independent administrative government.

* * *

. . . It would be nice, however, if at some point the Court itself would apply its recent de-evolutionary discipline to this fundamental constitutional question about modern American government. The answer that the Justices would find might well be the same as the one offered by *Humphrey's Executor* and expanded in *Morrison*. If judicial review is to retain its constitutional legitimacy, however, the process of reasoning is more important than the end result.

Even should a de-evolutionary analysis find no significant constitutional difficulties attaching to the independent agencies, there would remain the problem of deciding whether, as the *Morrison* opinion suggests, the independent counsel is analogous to the independent agency. The agencies, according to *Humphrey's Executor*, "cannot in any proper sense be characterized as an arm or an eye of the executive." In *Morrison*, by contrast, the parties characterized the independent counsel in just that way. To make the counsel fit the independent agency model, the Justices were forced to lump together all executive authority as one malleable whole, and to test restrictions on that authority only for the degree of their intrusiveness. In so doing, the Court presented the Congress with what Justice Scalia called "an open invitation . . . to experiment.". . .

Already wending its way through the Congress is a proposal for a special environmental prosecutor to handle those cases too explosive to leave to politically accountable officials. What might be next? Well, perhaps the Congress, angered by the direction and policies of the Justice Department under the recently resigned Edwin Meese, could decree (over the President's likely veto) that the entire Justice Department is to become an independent agency, like the FTC, thereby placing all criminal prosecution beyond direct presidential control. Nor is there any reason to think that the *Morrison* invitation is limited to situations involving prosecution. The principal cases cited by the majority on this point have nothing to do with prosecution as such, and besides, the Court itself said that the nature of the power is not the issue. Thus, if the Congress determines that foreign policy is too important a matter to be left to the politically expedient judgments of the White House, it might command the independence of the Department of State, to be called perhaps the Foreign Policy Agency, placing it under the command of a commission of experts nominated by the President and confirmed by the Senate. . . .

* * *

. . . The problem with the *Morrison* opinion is that it provides no reliable guide . . .. The reader is left with the uneasy sense that there may, in fact, be no rule at all, and that the principal practical restraint on the Congress is its own discretion.

The struggling, haunted quality of the majority opinion suggests that the Justices understood this and worried about it, but saw no way to escape the slippery slope. And perhaps there is, at this late date, no escape, for title VI of the Ethics in Government Act really does grow quite logically from the line of cases permitting the Congress to vest executive authority in agencies beyond presidential control. Perhaps the constitutional assault on the independent counsel was too late and directed at the wrong target; perhaps, given what has gone before, there was no way that the Court could have avoided reaching the decision that it did. In that case, it may be that legislative government, with a profoundly weaker executive, is indeed what the future holds, or, at least, that nothing more than the wisdom and discretion of one-third-plus-one of the members of either House of the Congress will be available to prevent the legislature from taking us there. It is a shame that a Court that has lately devoted so much effort to ensuring a de-evolutionary approach to the distribution of power refuses to undertake such an approach when the issue is the independence of executive officers from executive control. It is a shame because, if government by independent agency is indeed our future, it would be nice to get there by constitutional amendment rather than legislative fiat.

* * *

Abner S. Greene, *Checks and Balances in an Era of Presidential Lawmaking*, 61 U. CHI. L. REV. 123 (1994)*

* * *

Madison's admonition against mingling executive and legislative powers was central to the federal government as devised in 1787. Today, though, this precept is often ignored. We accept, perhaps uneasily, the delegation of substantial lawmaking power to the President, who executes the laws he makes. Of course we don't call the President's power "lawmaking." We have euphemisms—we call this power "regulatory," or "interpretive," or "gap-filling." . . .

Presidential lawmaking presents an unusual problem for constitutional theory. After all, the Constitution's text gives lawmaking power to Congress, reserving to the President only a qualified veto. So on a straightforward textualist view, presidential lawmaking would be unconstitutional. But we live with an enormous amount of

---

*   Reprinted with permission.

such lawmaking, and few appear ready to condemn the system as invalid. If, therefore, we have accepted presidential lawmaking as constitutional, must we accept without reservation this concentration of executive and legislative power, or should we deem appropriate other structural responses that seek to reduce the agglomeration of presidential power?

. . . I suggest that if we accept sweeping delegations of lawmaking power to the President, then to capture accurately the framers' principles—principles that deserve our continuing adherence—we must also accept some (though not all) congressional efforts at regulating presidential lawmaking. Just as the framers saw their structural choices as parts of a package separating legislative from executive power to protect liberty and avoid governmental tyranny, so should we view checks and balances doctrine as a package, its specific elements subject to revision to ensure fidelity to the constitutional premise of divided governmental powers. . . . [B]y paying close attention to the principles that led the framers to make specific structural choices, we can better understand the sometimes confusing array of twentieth century cases addressing "framework" legislation, that is, legislation that structures the relationship between Congress and the President. . . .

* * *

. . . The principle that synthesizes the case law is this: Congress may give away legislative power and insulate such delegated power from total presidential control, but Congress may neither draw executive power to itself nor seek to legislate outside the Article I, Section 7 framework. Insulation from presidential control, often accomplished through the establishment of independent agencies, restores a balance of powers by preventing the agglomeration of executive and legislative power in the President, without creating an unjustifiable "accountability gap" for undisciplined agencies. Other methods of congressional control risk replacing presidential with congressional tyranny.

I. ASSUMPTIONS OF THE PROJECT

* * *

[I]n this Article, I argue that to preserve in the late twentieth century what the framers meant by dividing legislative from executive power, we must reconceptualize the congressional-presidential power structure. In so doing, we will not be altering the Constitution, but rather maintaining its identity over time.

But what, precisely, were the framers' principles regarding the division of congressional and presidential power? And which of these principles should we deem so fundamental as to merit preservation through a sea of other structural changes? In Section II, I argue that the best reading of the Convention Debates and The Federalist Papers reveals a heavy emphasis on creating not simply a strong executive, but rather a strong enough executive to check what the framers expected to be an overreaching legislature.

* * *

II. THE DECISION OF 1787: DIVIDING AND BALANCING LEGISLATIVE AND EXECUTIVE POWERS

. . . Some have argued that the framers of the Constitution established a strong executive to combat a mischievous legislature, and thus that twentieth century congressional attempts at regulating the executive run afoul of the original structure.

Some evidence from the framing materials does reveal a focus on limiting congressional power. But when one examines the entire picture, one discovers a concern not with establishing a strong executive alone, but rather with establishing a strong enough executive to keep a strong legislature in check. The bottom line was not strength in the executive, but rather balance between the branches, secured through a division of power.

A. Pre-1787: Balance in Theory, Concern with Executive Tyranny in Practice

* * *

For the colonists, the potential for abuse of delegated, governmental power was of central importance. As Bernard Bailyn has written, "[m]ost commonly the discussion of power centered on its essential characteristic of aggressiveness: its endlessly propulsive tendency to expand itself beyond legitimate boundaries." Delegated public power was not in itself evil; "[w]hat made it so, what turned power into a malignant force, was not its own nature so much as the nature of man—his susceptibility to corruption and his lust for self-aggrandizement."

The Americans sought to thwart the self-aggrandizing tendencies of governmental agents by turning to British principles of constitutionalism. In England, the various elements of society had "entered [into government] simultaneously, so to speak, in a balanced sharing of power. The functions, the powers, of government were so distributed among these components of society that no one of them dominated the others." But the colonists transmuted the British system of mixed government based on social classes to a government in which three branches, the legislative, executive, and judicial, would check each other, regardless of the social class from which the officials were drawn.

* * *

B. The Constitution of 1787: Reclaiming Balance through Creating a Strong Enough Executive

But all was not well with the governmental structures in place during the 1780s. Many state legislatures succumbed to pure majoritarian tendencies; rather than reflecting upon greater notions of the public good, state legislatures confiscated property, issued paper money, and eliminated debts. To be sure, these laws were "enacted by legislatures which were probably as equally and fairly representative of the people as any legislatures in history," but the problem was that government was acting too easily, interfering with property rights without sufficient structural encumbrances. . . .

Thus, although providing greater power to the national government was the framers' central concern when they met in Philadelphia in the spring and summer of 1787, the framers of our Constitution also sought to ensure against future legislative abuse. One method was to establish a strong executive power, vested not in a commission or group of people, but in one person, the "President.". . .

All agree that the framers deliberately chose a unitary rather than plural executive at least in a limited sense, that is, they consciously decided that one person, rather than a team of people, should be atop the executive branch. The hard questions are: What precisely was the nature of the "executive" that the framers established? What relevance do the framers' decisions about the executive branch have for us today? . . .

* * *

. . . The framers started from Montesquieu's basic maxims regarding the need to separate executive power from legislative power. To limit legislative overreaching, they created a unitary executive not elected by Congress and prohibited simultaneous executive and legislative service. But to ensure that the executive itself would not become too powerful, thereby creating the same problem in a different guise, the framers were careful to limit executive power. Importantly, they assumed that although Congress could delegate executive powers to the executive, it could not delegate legislative powers.

* * *

The Federalist Papers reinforce and add to the arguments made during the debates. . . .

* * *

. . . All of the framers' discussions of executive power must be understood from the predicate of a strong legislature and a limited executive that did not exercise any legislative powers. This was true when the delegates agreed that although Congress could delegate powers to the executive, such powers had to be "not legislative nor judiciary in their nature." And it was true during the ratification period which was influenced by The Federalist Papers. . . .

III. AFTER THE DEMISE OF THE NONDELEGATION DOCTRINE: IMPLEMENTING THE DECISION OF 1787 FROM A NEW PREMISE

A. Updating the Original Understanding

Proper regard to originalism requires that we not simply jettison the 1787 understanding in light of twentieth-century developments. But requiring a literal replication of the framers' strong, unitary executive in the new, post-nondelegation doctrine world distracts from the more significant task of ensuring that in such a world, power is not overly concentrated in one branch of government.

. . . [T]he framers' conception was not of executive power plain and simple, but rather of the proper amount of executive power to counterbalance what they perceived would be a strong, overreaching, self-aggrandizing Congress. A properly originalist approach would recognize that to be true to the framers, that is, to our constitutional tradition, we must carry over their basic structural understandings to a time when some of the structural elements have shifted. . . .

[M]y argument is that we must evaluate twentieth-century congressional framework legislation in light of the great twentieth-century giveaway of legislative power. If the feared Congress starts giving away its broad-reaching legislative power to the very actor who was thought to provide a check on such power, then for the essential balance of powers to be maintained, the President himself must now be checked.

* * *

. . . Congress not only passed more laws, requiring more execution; it also passed more laws requiring broad-scale policy making before execution. A law requiring the enforcement of particular rules governing communications, for example, delegates typical executive enforcement discretion, but a law authorizing administrative action in the "public convenience, interest, or necessity" delegates something much closer to pure lawmaking power. To be sure, the administrator of the latter law would technically be acting as "agent" to the legislative "principal." But when the principal's command merely sets forth a jurisdiction (communications, say) and then provides virtually no further guidance, so long as the agent acts within this jurisdiction, almost any action it takes will not be inconsistent with the principal's "intent." Thus, an executive branch "interpretation" of a law that provides virtually no guidance is best dubbed "lawmaking," or at a minimum "interpretive lawmaking."

The Court tried only twice to halt such broad delegations before realizing that it was too difficult to draw a line between delegations that are unconstitutionally broad, because they give the executive something that looks like lawmaking power, and those that are sufficiently narrow, because they grant something that looks like enforcement discretion. The Court's refusal to enforce the nondelegation doctrine seriously—to strike down broad delegations of lawmaking power to the executive—must be seen as the premise for all other checks and balances cases in the post-New Deal era. From the prior premise, executive power was cabined narrowly enough (at least in the domestic sphere) to prevent concern about the balance of power shifting toward the executive. But now that the nondelegation doctrine no longer provides an enforceable rule against excessive delegation, the balance of power tips toward the executive every time Congress delegates lawmaking power.

Much of checks and balances law since the demise of the nondelegation doctrine can be seen as a response to congressional efforts to assure the framers' balance between Congress and the President. Reacting to presidential power made extraordinary by broad delegations of lawmaking power, Congress has enacted legislation that checks presidential tyranny in three ways. First, Congress has given itself a role in the appointment of officers or in the execution of the laws. Second, it has attempted to legislate outside the Article I, Section 7 process. Third, Congress has sought to check executive-branch tyranny by removing various agencies that exercise executive, legislative, and judicial power from the direct control of the President, and by providing for investigations of intra-executive branch corruption by an officer outside the presidential chain of command.

The first and second efforts properly have been invalidated. For controlling executive power through the threat of congressional aggrandizement exacerbates rather than solves the concentration of powers problem. Although only the first category concentrates legislative and executive power (in the hands of Congress), the second category also involves Congress's efforts to skew the division of governmental power in its favor. For when Congress tries to make law outside the constitutionally mandated process, the comparative reduction of presidential power reduces the multiple repositories of power that are so central to the structure of national government. The third category of legislation, on the other hand, avoids the vice of concentrating power in either named branch of government. Here, Congress's efforts properly have been validated, for they check presidential aggrandizement without the concomitant risk of congressional aggrandizement.

Let me address one obvious problem at the outset. How can independent agencies—which often combine legislative and executive (not to mention adjudicative) functions—not contravene the core tenet against execution by the lawmaker? I have three responses. First, and most importantly, independent agencies still represent an important curtailment of presidential power. The concentration of lawmaking and executing powers in the President reduces the multiple repositories of power established by the framers; selecting certain jurisdictional areas for independent lawmaking and executing helps ensure that the repositories of power are truly multiple.

Second, judicial review of the action of any agency that combines legislative and executive power might be a constitutionally required check. Such judicial review should pay special attention to the use of these combined powers to help certain narrowly defined groups at the expense of other groups or the public at large. . . .

Third, even with power diffused rather than concentrated in the President, and even with hands-on judicial review, many independent agencies are still deviations from the norm of divided legislative and executive powers. But what else should we expect in a post-nondelegation doctrine world? By enforcing the nondelegation doctrine along with rules against congressional execution, we could ensure against combined legislative/executive powers. . . .

The following is a description of how the Court's twentieth-century checks and balances doctrine fits together. In many instances, the Court's explanation of its holding does not match the structural constitutional explanation I have just given. In particular, independent agencies have often been defended as enabling politically insulated experts to make "good government" decisions. . . . I am not defending the Court's exegesis of its checks and balances doctrine; I defend only its holdings as both consistent and correct.

1. Congress may not play a role in appointing officers or in executing the laws.

Allowing Congress to play a role in appointing officers or in executing the laws would be an easy way to ensure against excessive presidential power. But when Congress tries to give power to itself in a way that the Constitution does not clearly authorize—particularly when Congress vests itself with functions best deemed executive—the danger of excessive, concentrated congressional power looms. Without always recognizing this as the central problem, the Court has invalidated a number of laws that, we can now see, improperly aggrandized Congress.

* * *

2. Congress may not make law outside the finely wrought Article I, Section 7 bicameralism and presentment process.

Congressional attempts to evade the requirements of Article I, Section 7 bicameralism and presentment also represent a grab for power outside clear constitutional lines. The problem here is somewhat different from the problem in the previous category of cases. Here, rather than trying to do someone else's job (execute the law), Congress tries to do its own job (legislate), but without the strictures of bicameralism and presentment. By excluding the President from the lawmaking process, Congress threatened, in these cases, to concentrate power in its own hands in a potentially dangerous manner.

* * *

3. Congress may try to hem in executive action not by reaching for power itself, but by regulating the executive's power.

It is undisputed that Congress may curtail executive action by limiting agency funding, personnel, or jurisdiction. Rather, the principal dispute has been over whether Congress can regulate the removal of agency personnel, to ensure that the President does not control all the power delegated away from Congress. In this third category of cases, the Court has consistently answered yes.

* * *

. . . Much of post-New Deal checks and balances doctrine makes sense if we (a) recall that the framers' core checks and balances value was to ensure a balance of power among the branches—to prevent the tyranny of any one branch (and thus help preserve individual liberty), to avoid placing legislative and executive power in the same branch of government—and (b) start from a premise in which broad delegations of lawmaking power from Congress to the President are accepted as constitutional. Thus, we can (c) approve congressional attempts to regulate presidential action where such action would otherwise enlarge presidential power beyond execution or would involve executive branch self-dealing, but (d) invalidate congressional attempts to control execution itself or to make law outside the Article I, Section 7 process, because such aggrandizement concentrates power back in the hands of Congress. In this way, the Court's checks and balances jurisprudence can be rendered both internally consistent and consistent with the framers' understanding of the balance of power in the federal government. In a new world in which Congress gives away legislative power, additional congressional efforts to control the now-enlarged executive are faithful to, rather than in tension with, the Constitution of 1787.

The twentieth-century checks and balances doctrine, which is often unjustly criticized as shifting inconsistently between formalism and functionalism, is thus rendered coherent. To be sure, the Court's explanations for its holdings have changed and often have evidenced an ad hoc quality when clearer principles would have been welcome. But the holdings in these cases are quite consistent; the resulting doctrine, although no doubt in need of elaboration, makes a great deal of sense, both in terms of internal coherence and as measured by constitutional values. The Court permits Congress to regulate executive branch lawmaking or self-dealing so long as Congress does not expand its own powers in so doing and thus threaten the return of congressional aggrandizement. The Court's doctrine thus comports with the legitimate translation of the framers' Constitution outlined above.

* * *

B. The Comparative Irrelevance of Accountability

One result of these developments—an underenforced nondelegation doctrine, independent agencies, and a rule against Congress giving itself control over execution or lawmaking outside Article I, Section 7—is that national policy is sometimes made by neither of the elected actors (Congress or the President), but rather by unelected "independent" agencies. This seems to violate a basic constitutional value. But as I have shown . . ., the framers' discussions of a "unitary" executive, though sometimes mentioning "responsibility," were focused primarily on the need for balance, for nonagglomeration. In fact, the principle behind our checks and balances structure is in tension with the norm of accountability. The framers knew they could have ensured an energetic, efficient government by vesting lawmaking and executing powers in one person, or by creating a unicameral legislature with no presidential veto. Accountability would be quite clear in such a structure—the citizens would know precisely whom to blame. But the framers were more concerned with making the machinery of government somewhat cumbersome, thus ensuring against the hegemony of one branch or person. By dividing powers and insisting upon a complex system of checks—bicameralism, presentment, and judicial review (not to mention federalism)—the framers ensured against such hegemony, but simultaneously sacrificed accountability. It is pretty hard for citizens to know precisely whom to blame when something goes wrong in such a system.

* * *

Furthermore, independent agencies are not totally unaccountable. Although the President may not remove the heads of such agencies for policy disagreements, he does control (with the Senate) appointment and reappointment; he may often select the chairperson of the agency; the agency might depend on the President for information and for support during budgetary negotiations with Congress; the agency's budget probably goes through the Office of Management and Budget for review; and most agencies must work through the Department of Justice with regard to litigation. Furthermore, citizens can still hold both Congress and the President accountable for appointments to the independent agencies, and for the legislative delegations to those agencies. Therefore, there is enough accountability to prevent the independent agencies from being truly free-floating. . . .

* * *

CONCLUSION

We cannot properly examine the constitutional balance of power between the President and Congress if we assume that Congress legislates and the President executes. Rather, we should begin from a new premise, that of presidential lawmaking. For since the New Deal, Congress has delegated much lawmaking power to the President, without judicial invalidation. The framers of the Constitution were centrally concerned with avoiding the concentration of executive and legislative powers in the same hands. This concern should be ours as well, both because of the harm that concentrated power can bring and the good that can result from diffused power. Much, but not all, of post-New Deal checks and balances jurisprudence can be justified from these premises—that the delegation of legislative power is permissible, but that the concentration of power in one branch is still troublesome. Thus, the Court has properly upheld laws that fracture the executive by establishing independent agencies, which help to diffuse the power that would otherwise be concentrated in the President. At the same time, the Court has properly invalidated laws that, while seeking the end of balance between the branches, operate through the means of concentrating power back in Congress.

* * *

Martin H. Redish & Elizabeth J. Cisar , *"If Angels Were to Govern": The Need for Pragmatic Formalism in Separation of Powers Theory*, 41 DUKE L.J. 449 (1991)*

INTRODUCTION

It has become fashionable in certain academic circles to urge a dramatically reduced role for the courts in enforcement of the Constitution's structural provisions. In the separation of powers area, however, the modern Court has evinced something of a split personality, seemingly wavering from resort to judicial enforcement with a formalistic vengeance to use of a so-called "functional" approach that appears to be designed to do little more than rationalize incursions by one branch of the federal government into the domain of another.

---

*   Reprinted with permission.

Those constitutional theorists who have urged this stance of judicial indifference toward issues of constitutional structure have chosen instead to focus their attention on issues surrounding the scope of individual rights. The sad irony in this is that the body of the Constitution—the document to which the Framers devoted so much time and energy at the Convention in Philadelphia—contained precious few direct references to the protection of individual rights. Rather, the document was primarily devoted to the implementation of an intricate and innovative political theory: a constitutionally limited, federally structured, representative democracy. Although one may of course debate the scope or meaning of particular constitutional provisions, it would be difficult to deny that in establishing their complex structure, the Framers were virtually obsessed with a fear—bordering on what some might uncharitably describe as paranoia—of the concentration of political power. [T]he Framers chose to rely on a number of different structural devices to check what they assumed to be the natural and inherent tendency of government to proceed toward tyranny.

In structuring their unique governmental form, the Framers sought to avoid undue concentrations of power by resort to institutional devices designed to foster three political values: checking, diversity, and accountability. By simultaneously dividing power among the three branches and institutionalizing methods that allow each branch to check the others, the Constitution reduces the likelihood that one faction or interest group that has managed to obtain control of one branch will be able to implement its political agenda in contravention of the wishes of the people. By dividing power on a vertical as well as lateral plane (i.e., between the state and federal governments), they sought to assure that not all policy decisions would be made at one political level. And by implementing a diluted form of popular sovereignty, they assured that those in power would be generally responsive to those they represent while reducing the danger of a tyrannical majority.

It is our position that the centrality of the separation of powers concept to American political theory should be recognized, and that as a result the Court's enforcement of that concept needs to become considerably more vigorous than it has been in the recent past. Several political theorists have challenged the viability of the Constitution's system of separation of powers for modern society. However, we believe that the separation of powers provisions of the Constitution are tremendously important, not merely because the Framers imposed them, but because the fears of creeping tyranny that underlie them are at least as justified today as they were at the time the Framers established them. What is called for, then, is an interpretational model that will avoid the diluting impact that recent Supreme Court doctrine has sometimes had on the beneficial protective force of separation of powers. The model we recommend is a type of "formalistic" approach to the interpretation and enforcement of separation of powers—one grounded on the deceptively simple principle that no branch may be permitted to exercise any authority definitionally found to fall outside its constitutionally delineated powers.

"Pragmatic formalism," is a "street-smart" mode of interpretation, growing out of a recognition of the dangers to which a more "functional" or "balancing" analysis in the separation of powers context may create.

The pragmatic nature of the formalistic approach we advocate is manifested in two ways. Initially, pragmatic factors lead to the choice of formalism in the first place: No conceivable alternative adequately guards against the dangers that the system of separation of powers was adopted to avoid. Secondly, pragmatism influences how the differing concepts of branch power are ultimately to be defined. It is important to emphasize that formalism, as we employ the term, is not intended to imply imposition of rigid, abstract interpretational formulas derived from an originalistic perspective. All the term is intended to suggest is that the constitutional validity of a particular branch action, from the perspective of separation of powers, is to be determined not by resort to functional balancing, but solely by the use of a definitional analysis. In other words, the Court's role in separation of powers cases should be limited to determining whether the challenged branch action falls within the definition of that branch's constitutionally derived powers—executive, legislative, or judicial. If the answer is yes, the branch's action is constitutional; if the answer is no, the action is unconstitutional. No other questions are to be asked; no other countervailing factors are to be considered.

In fashioning its definitions of branch power, the Court should look to a combination of policy, tradition, precedent, and linguistic analysis. To be sure, a Court not acting in good faith could manipulate our suggested standard into meaninglessness. But that is just as true of any conceivable doctrinal standard, or the interpretation of any constitutional provision. In any event, to do so would impose costs on the Court's institutional capital that open and admitted use of functionalism would not.

Mixed government was designed to prevent absolutism—the arbitrary use of power—by avoiding the concentration of all state power in one body. Separation of powers has the same function, but operates on different assumptions. Two major changes are required to transform mixed government into a government based on separation of powers. First, particular departments must be restricted to certain functions. Second, an independent judiciary must be established.

Two methodological insights may be drawn from the Framers' virtual obsession with the concentration of power. First, to be meaningful, the separation of powers must be institutionalized in a manner that provides each branch with the formal tools necessary to limit the excesses of its rivals. Second, and of greater importance for modern doctrinal purposes, the separation of powers must operate in a prophylactic manner—in other words, as a means of preventing a situation in which one branch has acquired a level of power sufficient to allow it to subvert popular sovereignty and individual liberty.

This was by no means the only conceivable method one might have chosen to deal with the undue accumulation of power, even under a separation of powers structure. Presumably, the Framers could have established a system in which each branch could exercise any form of governmental power, unless its exercise of that power was found to reach a level that enabled that branch to impose tyranny—what might be labeled the "undue accretion" model of separation of powers theory. Alternatively, they could have chosen a slightly more protective format, in which each branch would be allowed to exercise any form of governmental power until it was determined (by whom, we suppose, could be subject to debate) that that branch's power had reached a level at which the potential for undue accretion was evident—what might be labeled the "clear-and-present danger" model. A third alternative would have been to reject separation of powers completely—to impose no prophylactic barriers to the undue accretion of power—but instead simply to prohibit the tyrannical misuse of that power in its particular exercise.

Given their recent experience with the usurpations of power under state constitutions, not to mention the generally poor survival rate of republican governments throughout history, it should not be surprising that the Framers chose none of these alternatives. Each branch is limited to the exercise of the power given to it, which, in turn, is exclusive of the power exercised by the other branches (with the limited exceptions explicitly provided in the text that allow one branch to check another).

Under this structure, no case-by-case inquiry is made into the likelihood that tyranny will be threatened by a breach of branch separation, for the simple reason that there is no effective method of making that inquiry—at least until it is too late to avoid the danger.

Separation of Powers as a Zero Sum Game: The Modern Theoretical Assault

A comparison of separation of powers to the alternative models that have been suggested to replace it reveals that, whatever its faults, separation of powers provides the optimum methodology for attaining the goal of assuring the maintenance of popular sovereignty and individual liberty.

1. The Radical Attack. Some of the most strident criticisms of separation of powers have come from those who argue that it deadlocks government. These arguments rest on the proposition that modern governments need to be able to act more quickly than a separation of powers system permits.

The solutions that these critics offer vary. Cutler proposes that we adopt a parliamentary system similar to the one employed in England. Professor Wilson suggests that the crumbling two-party system be reforged and strengthened to "overcome the separation of powers by bringing together under informal arrangements what the founders were at pains to divide by formal ones." Professor Robinson suggests that bicameralism be abolished, power to call new elections be given to the majority of Congress and the President, terms of office be limited to five years, and that a national council of about 100 persons be established to manage the new election system and to advise the President.

One difficulty with these solutions is the underlying assumption that more federal governmental action is necessarily better than less. Making innovation difficult ensures that "foolish or sinister schemes [are] . . . exposed and defeated" and that there is "deep and broad consensus" about proposed changes.

The disruption caused by the threat of dissolution would create a more serious problem than the deadlock it seeks to avoid. The new check would weld Congress to the President in all but the most egregious situations. Further, the valuable deliberative powers of Congress might well be lost, because the executive has no need to consult it. Thus, such a system could seriously undermine limited government, by reducing the legislature's influence on executive decisionmaking.

2. The Moderate Attack. Other, less radical solutions to the problems of separation of powers do not require constitutional amendment, as Cutler's obviously would. One commentator, for example, suggests that we reforge the party system and rely on it to overcome legislative-executive deadlock. This solution, however, shares the weaknesses of the parliamentary proposal. Strong parties require both a single set of policies and strict adherence to party lines in voting. But the same diverse population that prevents accommodation of many interests in a parliamentary system would also prevent them in a strong party system.

A less drastic method proposed to alleviate the fragmenting of federal power is to make changes in our "unwritten constitution." "The first step in the right direction," according to one commentator, "would be to quit talking about the constitutional separation of powers." Initially, ensuring executive efficiency by imposing informal (i.e., non-statutory, non-constitutional) restraints on Congress seems naive at best. If the restraints are not enforceable, what will keep self-interested members of Congress from encroaching on the executive sphere? If the "unwritten constitution" can modify the tenets of the written one, this proposal effectively advocates a circumvention of the amendment process.

The Costs of Abandoning Separation of Powers.

The most significant problem with the modern attacks on separation of powers is that they completely ignore the very real fears that led to the adoption of the system in the first place. No critic has adequately demonstrated either that the fears of undue concentrations of political power that caused the Framers to impose separation of powers are unjustified, or that separation of powers is not an important means of deterring those concentrations.

The decision regarding whether to employ a particular prophylactic device, then, must come down to a comparison of the costs incurred as a result of the device's use with an estimate of both the likelihood and severity of the feared harm. Although some undoubtedly believe that separation of powers imposes severe costs on the achievement of substantive governmental goals, it would be inaccurate to suggest that government has been paralyzed as a result of separation of powers.

[N]o defender of separation of powers can prove with certitude that, but for the existence of separation of powers, tyranny would be the inevitable outcome. But the question is whether we wish to take that risk, given the obvious severity of the harm that might result. Given both the relatively limited cost imposed by use of separation of powers and the great severity of the harm sought to be avoided, one should not demand a great showing of the likelihood that the feared harm would result.

PRAGMATIC FORMALISM AS AN ANALYTICAL MODEL IN SEPARATION OF POWERS CASES

The Case for Pragmatic Formalism

Once one accepts (as we do) that separation of powers is an essential means of preserving both individual liberty and representative government, the next task is to find the most effective doctrinal model to preserve those protections. Our answer to that inquiry is "pragmatic formalism"—an approach that requires a "formal" separation of branch power, to be determined by means of a pragmatically-based definitional analysis of the concepts of "executive," "legislative," and "judicial" power. In the sense in which we employ the term, "formalism" implies merely the formal separation of "executive," "legislative," and "judicial" power, without either an attempt to discern whether a breach of those barriers presents a danger of "undue" accretion of power in a particular instance or any discounting for countervailing political or social interests. This approach is chosen because of the pragmatic assessment that it is far and away the best means of ensuring the viability of separation of powers, which is itself designed to foster broader social and political values. Thus, far from representing a formal separation of law on the one hand and politics and morality on the other, the brand of formalism we advocate is adopted for the very purpose of implementing carefully reasoned political values.

The justification for the use of pragmatic formalism flows from a recognition of the purposes served by separation of powers in the first place. Central to that concept are three simultaneous insights: (1) the very fact of the concentration of political power in the hands of one governmental organ is unacceptable, even absent a showing of misuse of that power; (2) it will, as a practical matter, be all but impossible to determine when the level of the concentration of political power has reached the danger point; and (3) the point at which such an unacceptable concentration is actually reached is too late for the situation to be remedied. Separation of powers guarantees are, then, prophylactic in nature. They are designed to avoid a situation in which one might even debate whether an undue accretion of power has taken place.

No doctrinal model other than a formalistic approach can assure that a system of separation of powers will perform its prophylactic function. The key advantage of a formalistic analysis is that it frees a reviewing court from the impossible task of determining whether a particular usurpation of branch power presents a serious step toward tyranny.

Resort to formalism in the shaping of separation of powers doctrine has been severely criticized. The use of formalism in separation of powers doctrine, one commentator has alleged, "tends to produce excessively mechanical results," and also "tends to straitjacket the government's ability to respond to new needs in creative ways, even if those ways pose no threat to whatever might be posited as the basic purposes of the constitutional structure." But such criticisms fail to recognize the manner in which formalism uniquely fosters one of the central structural elements of separation of powers theory: its inherently prophylactic nature. Criticism of formalism for imposing an unrealistic "straitjacket" on governmental innovation likewise misses the point. Quite obviously, separation of powers protections, like many other structural elements of the Constitution, were inserted for the very purpose of preventing precipitant governmental action. If one believes that the use of such "speed bumps" to action are unwise, presumably one would concur with one or more of the proposals for radically reshaping our governmental structure—proposals that we believe to be extremely dangerous to the values of liberty and representationalism central to our nation's political theory.

The Problem of Definition

1. The Issue of Linguistic Skepticism. One who is skeptical about the meaning of text might well respond to our defense of pragmatic formalism that this doctrinal model provides no more protection against undue accretions of power than would a case-by-case standard because of the inherently vague and manipulable nature of the constitutional terms to be defined. If the terms "executive," "legislative," and "judicial" are incapable of any meaningful distinction, then reliance on the definitional analysis inherent in the pragmatic formalist model would actually prove to be counter-productive, in that it would force a reviewing court to engage in a meaningless, abstract linguistic analysis, instead of attempting to deal with cold, hard political realities.

Concededly, one who believes that words are inherently capable of infinite, equally acceptable meanings will not likely be impressed with our interpretational model. However, we proceed on the assumption—previously both articulated and defended—that the constitutional text is not so easily manipulable.

2. Defining Branch Power. Construction of the terms "legislative," "executive," and "judicial," as employed in Articles I, II, and III respectively, provides a classic illustration of this mode of textual interpretation. With relatively narrow, historically-based exceptions, "legislative" power includes only the authority to promulgate generalized standards and requirements of citizen behavior or to dispense benefits—to achieve, maintain, or avoid particular social policy results. So broadly phrased, of course, such a standard could conceivably be employed also to describe the functions performed by the judicial and executive branches. However, the difference is the structural "baggage" that the exercise of the judicial and executive powers are required to carry, baggage that does not affix itself to the exercise of the legislative power.

The executive branch, on the other hand (with certain exceptions specified by the Constitution), is confined to the function of "executing" the law. Such a function inherently presupposes a pre-existing "law" to be executed. Thus, the executive branch is, in the exercise of its "executive" power, confined to the development of means to enforce legislation already in existence. Hence, every exercise of executive power not grounded in another of the executive's enumerated powers must accurately purport to enforce existing legislation.

It should be emphasized that this requirement in no way implies that the executive branch's power should somehow be confined to the performance of "ministerial" functions, bereft of any room for the exercise of creativity, judgment, or discretion. All it means is that, unless some other specifically delegated executive branch power applies, the executive branch must be exercising that creativity, judgment, or discretion in an "implementational" context. In other words, the executive branch must be interpreting or enforcing a legislative choice or judgment; its actions cannot amount to the exercise of free-standing legislative power.

3. The "Inherent Executive Power" Theory. Some scholars have suggested that the President's authority is not limited to those powers specifically enumerated in Article II, but rather includes an ill-defined group of "inherent" powers not explicitly embodied in the Constitution's text. If this theory were accepted, the preceding effort to define the meaning of "executive" power would be pointless: Any exercise of power by the President not found to fall within the terms of Article II could simply be justified as falling within his "inherent" authority. But although such a theory actually does find support on some levels in Supreme Court doctrine, it represents a highly dubious, and arguably very dangerous, construction of constitutional power.

Most damning to the inherent executive power theory, however, is its inescapable inconsistency with the fundamental "horizontal" and "vertical" tenets of American political theory. In the "horizontal" sense (i.e., relations among the coordinate branches of the federal government) it would make little sense, given the deeply ingrained mistrust of the concentration of political power in general and the mistrust of executive power in particular that prevailed at the time, to tie two of the branches to specifically enumerated authority, yet simultaneously vest in the executive branch what amounts to unlimited political authority. Such a construction of Article II would effectively circumvent the separation of powers structure that the Framers had so carefully crafted.

So broad a reading of executive power would also seriously disrupt the intended "vertical" relationship between the state and federal governments. It was clearly understood by all involved that, under the Constitution, the federal government was one of enumerated (and therefore limited) powers. To assuage any lingering doubts, the Tenth Amendment was enacted expressly declaring the limited nature of federal power. Yet the "inherent authority" model of executive power automatically extends the power of one branch of the federal government beyond any constitutionally described limits. Such a model therefore undermines the carefully crafted structure of constitutional federalism.

4. The "Cumulative Effects" Approach. Another important issue to be examined from the perspective of the definitional analysis of the pragmatic formalist model is what might be labeled the "cumulative effects" approach to separation of powers. This approach is most often associated with Justice Jackson's famed concurrence in *Youngstown Sheet & Tube Co. v. Sawyer*, the so-called "steel seizure" case. In key respects, such an approach is fundamentally inconsistent with the definitional analysis associated with the pragmatic formalist model. Although Justice Jackson's analysis appears consistent with some form of a definitional approach to separation of powers, by positing a principle of transferability of branch power (at least for the executive and legislative branches) he has largely rejected the premise that underlies the pragmatic formalist model.

It might be argued, however, that as long as Congress has voluntarily chosen to convey its power to the executive branch (an assumption of Justice Jackson's first category), no separation of powers violation has occurred. Congress has effectively waived that protection, deciding that separation of powers concerns are outweighed by the competing need for an increase in executive authority. Separation of powers values are preserved, the argument proceeds, as long as Congress retains the option of curbing executive usurpation. But both theoretically and practically, this waiver analysis is unacceptable. From the perspective of American political theory, the concept of congressional waiver ignores the fact that separation of powers protections were not inserted to protect the other branches, but rather to protect the populace. From a practical perspective, the waiver theory ignores the obvious possibility that Congress may be controlled by the same party as the executive branch, effectively reducing Congress's check on the President. In such a situation, the only means of assuring the prevention of branch usurpation is by judicial enforcement of separation of powers.

IV. CONCLUSION

The Constitution's drafters knew all too well—from a study of history as well as from their own experience—that those who govern are anything but angels. The danger of tyranny is always present, yet it may develop in forms so insidiously subtle that its recognition will come at a point too late to avoid the ultimate danger. For this reason, power must be divided, and not only in those instances in which a threat to liberty is discerned; additional constitutional enclaves of liberty have been inserted to deal with such individualized threats. Rather, it must be divided always and for all time. To be sure, the limited definitional flexibility traditionally associated with constitutional terminology may provide a reviewing court some degree of pragmatically-based maneuverability. But, for pragmatic reasons of the most compelling sort, the judicial inquiry must still be limited to defining the scope of each branch's delegated authority. Such an inquiry must be untied to any investigation of whether the ultimate political goal of separation of powers is threatened by inter-branch usurpation in the particular case, or whether harm to competing social or political interests would result from enforcement of separation of powers. Analytical models that fail to engage in such an inquiry give rise to all of the dangers that those who established our system correctly sought to avoid.

Rebecca L. Brown, *Separated Powers and Ordered Liberty*, 139 U. PA. L. REV. 1513 (1991)*

Our Constitution originated as seven articles dealing almost exclusively with the structure of the federal government. Those seven articles are all that the states ratified when the people voted to adopt the Constitution of the United States. The Framers, most of them ardent supporters of civil liberty, were willing to establish a nation under the real possibility that an enumeration of rights might not follow.

What if there had been no bill of rights? One might think the consequences for individual liberty would have been disastrous. But perhaps the authors of the Con-

---

stitution had already made provision for the requirements of ordered liberty through the structure of the government they had crafted in the original Constitution.

The principle of separated powers is a prominent feature of the body of the Constitution, dictating the form, function, and structure of a government of limited powers. "Ordered liberty," a phrase coined by Justice Cardozo, has come to represent a counter-majoritarian protection of the rights of the individual against arbitrary or unfair treatment at the hands of the government, rights now embodied in the due process clauses of the fifth and fourteenth amendments. It is curious, however, that the relationship between these two core concepts has yet to be explored.

The Supreme Court has treated separation of powers as an isolated area of the law, governed by its own glacial dynamic and insulated from the social changes that stimulate development of other constitutional doctrines. I reject that approach and, repairing to the norms that inspired the embrace of the mechanism of separated powers at its inception, seek to demonstrate that the structure of the government is a vital part of a constitutional organism whose final cause is the protection of individual rights. From this perspective, it is unsurprising that the revolution in individual rights of the fifties and sixties was followed in the seventies and eighties by renewed interest and profound changes in the doctrine of separated powers.

A link between constitutional structure and liberty has been acknowledged by political philosophers for centuries. The importance of the relationship between governmental structure and individual freedom is borne out by a comparison with authoritarian nations in which the people actually enjoy comparatively little freedom, despite very generous verbal constitutional commitments to individual liberties. Such constitutions contain liberal bills of rights, but they do not provide for separated powers, so that those who execute the laws also interpret and enforce them. The Framers of our own Constitution preferred to err in the opposite direction; some opposed the addition of a bill of rights on the ground that the structure of the government, with its own self-limiting principles, would make any express protection of individual liberties superfluous or even counterproductive.

As if to confirm its central importance in protecting individual rights, the judges and academics who take up the subject of separated powers almost invariably invoke James Madison: "The accumulation of all powers, legislative, executive, and judiciary, in the same hands, whether of one, a few, or many, and whether hereditary, self-appointed, or elective, may justly be pronounced the very definition of tyranny." I argue that the Madisonian goal of avoiding tyranny through the preservation of separated powers should inform the Supreme Court's analysis in cases raising constitutional issues involving the structure of government. Moreover, that goal should be understood as a concern for protecting individual rights against encroachment by a tyrannical majority. The protection of individual rights—specifically, evenhanded treatment by the government, or "ordered liberty"—should be an explicit factor in the analysis of structural issues and should provide an animating principle for the jurisprudence of separated powers. Thus when government action is challenged on separation-of-powers grounds, the Court should consider the potential effect of the arrangement on individual due-process interests.

* * *

THE JURISPRUDENCE OF SEPARATED POWERS

Unanimity among constitutional scholars is all but unheard of. But one point on which the literature has spoken virtually in unison is no cause for celebration: the Supreme Court's treatment of the constitutional separation of powers is an incoherent muddle. The criticism here is not the familiar lament that the Court has gotten it wrong. In the field of separated powers the Court has not really "gotten it" at all. It has adopted no theory, embraced no doctrine, endorsed no philosophy, that would provide even a starting-point for debate. The Court has appeared to decide each case as if it were the first of its kind, with each individual justice apparently weighing costs and benefits according to some idiosyncratic scale of values, often unarticulated, and which may vary from case to case. The decisions reached in this ad hoc manner have not necessarily been wrong, but neither have they required the Court to take a stand on what values the structural provisions of the Constitution should promote.

The judicial opinions addressing the separation of powers over the past decade tend to place primary emphasis on the advancement of the institutional interests of the branches themselves, as if that goal were itself a good—a proposition with no historical support. When possible excesses by one branch present issues that cannot be resolved easily by resort to the text of the Constitution, the Court simply asks whether the territorial boundaries of the "victim" branch have been violated. Hence, the Court has viewed the separation of powers as "a self-executing safeguard against the encroachment or aggrandizement of one branch at the expense of another."

* * *

Critical Approaches: Formalism and Functionalism

The lack of analytic consistency has exasperated the critics. Most writers in the field have proceeded by selecting the interpretative theory they consider superior, then evaluating each of the Court's separation-of-powers decisions against the template of that theory. Because the Court has failed to adopt its own theory, invariably some of its opinions pass muster and others do not, depending upon the perspective of the scholar. Even those decisions that do correspond in result to the author's recommendations generally do so for the wrong reasons—again because of the absence of theoretical foundation.

The most prominent theories of constitutional interpretation to be superimposed upon the separation-of-powers cases by and large track the traditional "formalist" and "functionalist" approaches to constitutional interpretation. Other terminology has been offered by various scholars, who have staked claims for a "de-evolutionary" versus an "evolutionary" approach; a "neoclassical" versus a "pragmatic" approach; an "originalist" versus a "non-originalist" interpretation, or judicial "literalism" versus judicial "interpretation." On closer inspection these theories appear to present pretty much the same dichotomy, and fit reasonably well within the general descriptions of the formalist and functionalist schools.

Those who espouse the formalist view of separated powers seek judicial legitimacy by insisting upon a firm textual basis in the Constitution for any governmental act. They posit that the structural provisions of the Constitution should be understood solely by their literal language and the drafters' original intent regarding their application. The formalist approach finds support in the traditional expositions of the theme of "pure" separated powers, such as the maxim that "the legislature makes, the executive executes, and the judiciary construes the law." Under formalist thinking, the creation of independent administrative agencies, for example, is considered a violation of the Constitution because such agencies require the exercise of governmental power in ways that involve an overlap of expressly assigned functions, subject to the control of none of the three branches.

The implications and consequences of formalism are significant. First, it depends upon a belief that legislative, executive, and judicial powers are inherently distinguishable as well as separable from one another—a highly questionable premise. . . . However, "to insist upon the maintenance of an absolute separation merely for the sake of doctrinal purity could severely hinder the quest for 'a workable government' with no appreciable gain for the cause of liberty or efficiency." Moreover, formalism appears to be concerned primarily with forcing the Court to adhere to bright-line rules to foster predictability and restraint in judging. Thus, the the liberty that separation of powers theoretically protects may be sacrificed in a given case to the principal objective of determinacy in judicial decisionmaking.

An additional consequence of formalism is that it tends to straitjacket the government's ability to respond to new needs in creative ways, even if those ways pose no threat to whatever might be posited as the basic purposes of the constitutional structure. And ironically, in light of the usual textualist support for judicial restraint, the Court is forced to engage in a relatively high degree of judicial activism. Formalism, although conceiving a narrow role for the Court, forces it to strike down any action for which it cannot find express textual justification in the Constitution, even when two branches of the federal government may have agreed or acquiesced in the use of certain powers.

Finally, formalism supports majoritarianism. It is no accident that many of those who advocate the formalist view of constitutional interpretation for separation-of-powers issues also strongly favor greater strength for the Executive Branch—a majoritarian institution—through a "unitary" theory of executive power. Formalism restricts innovation in sharing power and encourages independence of the branches; in the modern era it has most often been Congress, as the instigator of political change through legislation, that has initiated new modes of allocating or sharing power, at least in the domestic sphere. . . .

In contrast, advocates of the "functionalist" approach urge the Court to ask a different question: whether an action of one branch interferes with one of the core functions of another. The sharing of powers, in itself, is not repugnant to the functionalists, nor is the formation of alliances. The functionalist view stresses the interdependence of the branches. "While the Constitution diffuses power the better to secure liberty, it also contemplates that practice will integrate the dispersed powers into a workable government. It enjoins upon its branches separateness but interdependence, autonomy but reciprocity."

Functionalism appears to bestow on judges a much greater discretion than does formalism to determine what values or functions are central to the constitutional structure, and define the extent to which changed circumstances should be permitted to influence that determination. Functionalist analysis is criticized, therefore, for its indeterminacy and the inevitability of ad hoc decisionmaking under its influence. In reality, however, the deference contemplated by functionalism has resulted in a less activist role for the Judiciary than has formalism—or at least it fosters activism of a different kind. While formalism nearly always results in striking down the challenged measure, functionalism nearly always upholds it.

The functionalist approach, like the formalist, is majoritarian in outcome. Because it encourages cooperation among branches, it would likely permit schemes to which Congress and the Executive, the two majoritarian branches, give their assent. Thus it is a theory that employs the principle of judicial restraint, and relies largely upon the departments of government themselves to work out what is best for them politically. This approach pays little attention to the effects of such inter-institutional alliances on those outside the government, namely private individuals.

An alternative to these two mechanisms for resolving separation-of-powers issues would leave all disputes between the Executive and Congress to the political process and rule them non-justiciable political questions. The justification for this approach is that the branches are capable of protecting themselves, through the weapons provided them in the Constitution in the form of "checks and balances," against encroachments by the others. It is not at all clear, however, that such protection is possible. Moreover, even if true balance could be achieved through judicial deference to the political branches, this would be insufficient to protect individuals. . . .

Thus the scholarly debate about separated powers goes wrong because it hangs in midair, moored to no grander objective than the abstract merits of the two relatively mechanical theories themselves—in the end no more than a question of where the proper point lies on the flexibility/determinacy matrix. Missing from the analysis of both camps is an external value consistent with the reasons for separating powers in the first place. . . .

Unlike both the formalist and functionalist schools, an "ordered-liberty" analysis would have the Court examine governmental acts in light of the degree to which they may tend to detract from fairness and accountability in the process of government. If process is impaired in this way, then the action poses a threat to individual liberty. . . .

THE HISTORICAL RELATIONSHIP BETWEEN ORDERED LIBERTY AND SEPARATED POWERS

The best evidence that the Framers intended to reject a strict separation of powers is that they created a system of checks and balances requiring participation by each branch in some functions that may be considered part of the power of the others. "Checks and balances do not arise from separation theory, but are at odds with it. Checks and balances have to do with corrective invasion of the separated powers.". . .

* * *

"The doctrine of the separation of powers was adopted by the Convention of 1787, not to promote efficiency but to preclude the exercise of arbitrary power." In general, then, separation of powers aimed at the interconnected goals of preventing tyranny and protecting liberty. Of course, different writers have defended different notions of what those terms meant, but it is not inaccurate to define tyranny as fear of "arbitrary government.". . .

From a modern perspective, twentieth-century due process prevents a court from retroactively expanding the reach of certain laws, which ensures separation of legislative and judicial functions—a concern Montesquieu identifies. Due process also guarantees trial by independent tribunal, which ensures the separation of executive and judicial functions—another of Montesquieu's stated goals. Thus, it is fair to say that, for Montesquieu, the unification or combination of the institutional powers would mean the loss of the values that now underlie the protections of due process.

John Locke is credited with the same insight, criticizing "absolute monarchies, which, by violating the separation of powers, frustrate the possibility of achieving an impartial administration of the laws"—another danger coextensive with the breakdown of due process of law.

Montesquieu articulated other potential hazards that separation of powers was thought to forestall. He saw the exercise of judicial power as posing the greatest threat to the liberty of the people. He recognized that the legislature and executive are concerned with general rules, which might be good or bad for the masses. A genuine loss of liberty, however, could come only from a judicial decision, which determines how the laws affect individuals under specific circumstances. Consequently, Montesquieu emphasized the importance of judicial procedures, even when costly or cumbersome, as a protection for the individual from this type of harm—as a guarantor of "liberty." Montesquieu, for whom separated powers were essential to liberty, contended that fair process was similarly essential, suggesting a syllogistic link between the structure of government and the protection of individual rights—specifically, the right to fair treatment by the government, or ordered liberty.

* * *

THE THEORY APPLIED

The theory of ordered liberty as a component of separated powers can supply strong guidance to the courts in their efforts to resolve specific cases. Applying the ordered-liberty analysis to a separation-of-powers attack, a court first would inquire whether the challenged action tends to foster unaccountable, biased, or otherwise arbitrary government decisionmaking and, if so, whether that impairment of government process will affect individuals.

The objective of this approach is not to substitute a due-process claim for a separation-of-powers claim. Clearly, situations often arise in which an individual suffers an actual violation of due process because of a deviation from structural norms, but those cases can be disposed of under the due process clause; no separation-of-powers analysis is required. Rather, the goal of the ordered-liberty approach is to interpret the structural provisions of the Constitution consistently with their purpose and spirit.

There are three general types of cases in which a party challenges some action as structurally flawed, but does not claim to have suffered an actual violation of due-process rights: (1) those in which an individual claims direct injury as a result of government action; (2) those in which no individual has clearly been injured directly, but the government action has had some effect on persons; and (3) those in which the challenged action has no discernible effect on any identifiable person. . . .

* * *

CONCLUSION

Judicial efforts to protect the institutional interests of the various branches of government are misguided. The Court's role in cases involving separated powers, no less than in those involving the Bill of Rights, ought to be as vigilant arbiter of process for the purpose of protecting individuals from the dangers of arbitrary government. When exercises of power by one branch of government, or by coalitions of two or more acting together, threaten the integrity of government process, then the Court should consider interfering to restore a balance of power, a balance of process. In the absence of such a threat, however, there is no need for the Court to step in, and the political branches should be allowed to use their powers of mutual checks and balances to work out the conflict.

In short, courts should not be in the business of protecting government. They should be protecting people. That is true, even—or perhaps especially—in cases involving governmental structure. Only with that proper mission in mind will the Court be able to bring a new rationality to its jurisprudence in the area of law devoted to the separated powers of government. Only then will that jurisprudence offer any fidelity to the original genius of the tripartite division of power, and only then will it do justice to the Constitution "proper," which, after all, was all that we had from the start.

Bibliography

Separation of Powers

Alfange, Dean, Jr. *The Supreme Court and the Separation of Powers: A Welcome Return to Normalcy?* 58 GEO. WASH. L. REV. 668 (1990)

Breyer, Stephen, *The Legislative Veto After* Chadha, 72 GEO. L.J. 785 (1984)

Calabresi, Stephen G. & Rhodes, Kevin H., *The Structural Constitution: Unitary Executive, Plural Judiciary*, 105 HARV. L. REV. 1153 (1992)

Carter, Stephen L., *From Sick Chicken to* Synar: *The Evolution and Subsequent De-Evolution of the Separation of Powers*, 1987 B.Y.U. L. REV. 719

Dorsen, Norman & Shattuck, John H.F., *Executive Privilege, The Congress and the Courts*, 35 OHIO ST. L.J. 1 (1974)

Froomkin, A. Michael, *The Imperial Presidency's New Vestments*, 88 NW. U. L. REV. 1346 (1994)

Henkin, Louis, *The Treaty Makers and the Law Makers: The Law of the Land and Foreign Relations*, 107 U. PA. L. REV. 903 (1959)

Karst, Kenneth L. & Horowitz, Harold W., *Presidential Prerogatives and Judicial Review*, 22 UCLA L. REV. 47 (1974)

Kauper, Paul G., *The* Steel Seizure Case: *Congress, the President and the Supreme Court*, 51 MICH. L. REV. 141 (1952)

Lofgren, Charles A., *War-Making Under the Constitution: The Original Understanding*, 81 YALE L.J. 672 (1972)

Strauss, Peter L., *The Place of Agencies in Government: Separation of Powers and the Fourth Branch*, 84 COLUM. L. REV. 573 (1984)

Werhan, Keith, *Toward an Eclectic Approach to Separation of Powers:* Morrison v. Olsen *Examined*, 16 HASTINGS CONST. L.Q. 393 (1989)

Part III
Legislative Power Over the National Economy

Federal Commerce Power

This section examines the federal commerce power. The first article, Robert L. Stern's, *The Commerce Clause and the National Economy, 1933-1946*, traces the Supreme Court's Commerce Clause decisions from the earliest days through the constitutional crisis of the 1930s. The remaining articles give perspectives on the Court's post-1930s Commerce Clause decisions.

Two articles seek to justify an expansive view of the Commerce Clause. Robert L. Stern's article *That Commerce Which Concerns More States Than One* argues that the Constitution's structure and history give the federal government the power to deal with desperate social and economic situations like the Great Depression. Robert Eugene Cushman's article *The National Police Power under the Commerce Clause of the Constitution* also argues for broad federal power, but does so based on a "national police power."

The next two articles question the scope of federal power. Professor Richard Epstein responds to Stern and Cushman's more expansive interpretations of the Commerce Clause in his article *The Proper Scope of the Commerce Power*. Professor Epstein argues that the "expansive construction of the [commerce] clause accepted by the New Deal Supreme Court is wrong, and clearly so, and [a] host of other interpretations are more consistent with both the text and the structure of our constitutional government." Justice Vincent Cirillo and Jay Eisenhofer's article *Reflections on the Congressional Commerce Power* argues that the Court's interpretation of the Commerce Clause has caused huge "federal budget deficits resulting, in part, from the public's desire to maintain public services without a parallel commitment to fund these services." They suggest that "the most effective check on spending" might be found in "a more restrictive reading" of the Commerce Clause that would limit "governmental growth and federal deficits."

The final article, Russell L. Weaver's article, Lopez *and the Federalization of Criminal Law*, analyzes the Supreme Court's recent decision in *United States v. Lopez*. In *Lopez*, for the first time in more than half a century, the Court struck down a statute enacted under the Commerce Clause. Professor Weaver argues that, despite *Lopez's* surprising holding, that decision was not as revolutionary as it seemed.

Robert L. Stern, *The Commerce Clause and the National Economy, 1933-1946,* 59 HARV. L. REV. 645 (1946)*

[Although] not for a century was the Court required to determine the scope of the regulatory power of Congress under the Commerce Clause, its opinions had not been silent as to the meaning of the constitutional provision. The early cases and a great number of later ones had held that the Commerce Clause barred the states from enacting laws which intruded too far into the interstate domain. In the very first of these cases—and indeed the first case under the Commerce Clause—Chief Justice Marshall had "described the federal commerce power with a breadth never yet exceeded." . . .

[*Gibbons'*] interpretation of the [commerce] clause as reaching all commercial matters affecting the states generally, by a judge who had lived through the period when the Constitution was adopted and even taken some part in that process, finds support both in the usage of language during that period and in the proceedings in the Constitutional Convention. . . .

Many of the subsequent decisions as to the validity of state legislation took a different course, however. In many of the cases, though by no means all, the technique by which the Court proceeded was to decide whether a subject was or was not interstate commerce; if it was, Congress alone could regulate it, and if not, only the states could. Pronouncements that "manufacturing," "production," and "mining" were subject to state taxation and regulation were frequently accompanied by statements indicating that these matters were not subject to the regulatory power of Congress. [Directly] concerned with the limits of the federal power was *Hammer v. Dagenhart*, which invalidated the Federal Child Labor Act of 1916 on the ground that Congress could not prohibit the interstate transportation of child-made goods if the purpose or effect was to control conditions in productive industry. . . .

But in the great majority of cases decided during the same general period, 1900-1930, the Court was upholding the application of the commerce power even to intrastate transactions. The principle that the power over interstate commerce extended to intrastate acts relating to interstate commerce was most explicitly embodied in the *Minnesota Rate Cases*, the *Shreveport Case* and other decisions sustaining regulations of railroads. Intrastate rates could be controlled by the Federal Government because of their competitive relation to interstate rates and their general effect upon railroad revenues. Intrastate trains were subject to federal safety appliance legislation because of the danger to interstate traffic on the same rails if they were not. Maximum hours could be prescribed for employees engaged in intrastate work connected with the movement of interstate trains. . . .

The cases sustaining the constitutionality of such statutes as the Lottery Act, the Pure Food and Drug Act, the White Slave Act, the Motor Vehicle Theft Act and the Animal Industries Act dealt with laws which were in substance police measures enacted in the interests of the public health and morality. But these laws were concerned with interstate transportation of the prohibited commodities or persons, and were not very close authority for the application of the commerce power to intrastate affairs. This was true even to a greater degree of the cases upholding statutes such as the Webb-Kenyon Act, which prohibits interstate transportation, as a means of

---

assisting the states in enforcing their own liquor and prison-made goods laws. The Court has uniformly favored such efforts at federal-state cooperation.

* * *

II. THE NATIONAL INDUSTRIAL RECOVERY ACT—1933-1935

The depression which began in the Fall of 1929 had, by 1933, produced an economic crisis probably unequalled in the history of the United States. At least thirteen million persons were unemployed; the average wages of those still employed in twenty-five selected industries had dropped to $16.13 per week in February 1933; wages received in mining, manufacturing, construction and transportation had declined from 17 to 6.8 billion dollars. Prices had fallen 37 per cent and industrial production had been cut almost in half. Insolvencies were mounting, and the banks were closed. The amount of revenue freight carried by Class I railroads, a fair measure of the quantity of interstate commerce, had declined 51 per cent.

Title I of the National Industrial Recovery Act, which became law June 16, 1933, was one of a series of statutes enacted by the Roosevelt Administration in an effort to halt the downward spiral of the depression and reinvigorate the national economy. While other measures dealt with different aspects of the problem, the Recovery Act grappled with the depression as it directly affected labor and industry. The deflated purchasing power of the masses was to be increased through the establishment of minimum wages and free collective bargaining; employment was to be increased through maximum-hour regulations. Business men, in combinations subject to Government approval, were to be allowed to eliminate wasteful competitive practices and cut-throat competition so as to enable them to halt the decline in prices, to pay the higher wage bills and to restore business to a healthy condition. This, all too briefly, was the background and the purpose of the Recovery Act.

The Act was passed in June, 1933. The first "Code of Fair Competition"—a code of regulations proposed by the members of an industry—was approved by the President in August of that year. At the beginning the Act functioned with the benefit of a great wave of public enthusiasm. The Administration sought to insure the necessary compliance through resort to voluntary cooperation and the pressure of public opinion. At first this was successful. But obviously violations were bound to occur, and unless violators were penalized, competitors of those who broke the law would be forced to follow their example to insure their own survival.

The first litigation arose in the Texas oil fields. The petroleum industry had been subjected not merely to the ordinary effects of the depression but to the ruinous consequences of uncontrolled overproduction from newly discovered fields. The opening of the vast East Texas field brought prices in 1931 down to as low as five and two and one-half cents a barrel. For reasons discussed at length elsewhere, attempts by Texas authorities to limit production under State proration laws proved futile. Again in 1933 the posted price of crude oil fell to ten cents per barrel in Texas, a price which broke the market both in crude oil and in petroleum products throughout the entire nation. The prices affected obviously included those of all petroleum and petroleum products sold in interstate commerce.

In order to meet the petroleum problem the Recovery Act contained a special provision—Section 9(c)—which authorized the President to prohibit the transportation in interstate commerce of petroleum and petroleum products produced in violation of state law. In addition, the Code for the petroleum industry made it a federal offense for any person to produce oil in excess of the amount fixed by a state, or by the Federal Government if a state failed to prescribe proper quotas.

In [the] *Panama [Refining]*, or "Hot Oil" case, [the Court focused on] Section 9(c), an almost overlooked portion of the Recovery Act, [where] it found an unlawful delegation of legislative power by Congress—the first time in American history that a federal law had ever been nullified on that ground. Only Mr. Justice Cardozo dissented. Section 9(c) had authorized the President to prohibit the interstate transportation of illegally produced, or "hot," oil without indicating when or under what circumstances he should do so. . . .

The direct impact of the decision was thus not very serious; the defect in draftsmanship was easily cured. But by January 1935, when the decision came down, violations of the Recovery Act Codes were getting out of control. Prosecutions were being lost in the district courts, and competitors of the violators were rightly objecting to having the Codes bind only those who voluntarily complied. Nothing short of a Supreme Court decision sustaining the statute and giving the enforcing officials power could have turned the tide. . . .

[The] Monday after the *Schechter* case was argued and three weeks before it was decided, the Court held, five to four, that the Railroad Retirement Act of 1934 contravened the Commerce Clause. After holding the entire statute in violation of due process and inseverable, the opinion of Mr. Justice Roberts went further and concluded that Congress could not reasonably have found that a plan for the retirement on pensions of superannuated employees would promote the efficiency and safety of interstate transportation, and that there was no other basis for federal control of the retirement of employees of the interstate railroads. Mr. Chief Justice Hughes, dissenting for himself and for Justices Brandeis, Stone, and Cardozo, thought the very fact that many of the carriers themselves had established such systems, not out of "largesse unrelated to legitimate transportation ends," proved that Congress was not unreasonable in assuming that the termination of excessive superannuation would be helpful to railroad service. The opinion of the majority demonstrated the hostility with which five justices viewed the federal commerce power. Clearly, it would not have been feasible or practicable for the separate states to have established pension plans for railroad employees. If the Federal Government lacked the power to impose such requirements, no government could do so. And the railroads, of course, were engaged primarily in interstate commerce, so that there could be no question that any regulation of them was substantially related to their interstate activities. This decision was a bad omen for the much more difficult *Schechter* case.

On May 27, 1935, the Court unanimously, speaking through Chief Justice Hughes, struck down the Recovery Act. To no one's great surprise, it held that power had been unlawfully delegated to the Administrator without standards sufficiently definite to limit his discretion in any way at all. . . .

After holding the entire Act invalid for want of standards, the Court somewhat unnecessarily—and perhaps non-judicially—went further and also held that its particular application in the Poultry Code did not come within the power of Congress under the Commerce Clause. Only intrastate practices "directly" affecting interstate commerce were subject to the federal power. Which effects were "direct" and which "indirect" apparently was to be largely determined by the fact that ours was a federated system in which many things were to be left to state control. Instead of determining the extent of the effect on commerce, the Court seemed to be guided by its view as to where the dividing line between the state and the federal jurisdiction should be drawn. Applying this test, it was easy for the Court to find that the practices in the New York poultry market could not be said directly to affect interstate commerce without finding such effects everywhere and thus leaving all industry subject to federal control. As Mr. Justice Cardozo said in his concurring opinion, "To find immediacy or directness here is to find it almost everywhere." The theory that the very existence of the states furnishes an independent limitation upon the national power permitted an abrupt rejection of the argument that because depressions which undoubtedly greatly affect commerce can be treated only on a nationwide basis, Congress may undertake any reasonable means of combatting them, without being restricted to acts which individually "directly" affect commerce.

The very weakness of the *Schechter* case, from the Government's viewpoint, was its saving grace. For in dealing with processors of poultry in the New York local market, the Court had not passed upon the power of Congress to control trade practices or labor relations in any interstate industry, and particularly not in any major industry, such as petroleum, lumber, coal or steel. Although the language in the opinion suggested that even the regulation of such industries might be invalid, the case—and perhaps its language—could clearly be distinguished when and if such regulation was attempted.

The code structure of the National Recovery Act—which had only three weeks to go unless renewed—collapsed with the *Schechter* decision. It had proved too cumbersome and unworkable, in part because in seeking to regulate all industry it had attempted to cover too much ground, in part because of the absence of any effective sanction after the original enthusiasm and public support began to fade. It had to some extent achieved its objectives of improving wages and hours and encouraging collective bargaining. Whether the program was economically beneficial to the nation is a matter far beyond the scope of this discussion.

The destruction of the National Recovery Act codes terminated the federal regulation of industry as a whole. But the pressures from employers and employees in particularly weak industries and from employees unwilling to lose the right to collective bargaining and the wages and hours protected by the Recovery Act could not be downed by a Supreme Court decision. The petroleum industry had been brought under control by the prohibition of interstate hot oil shipments and the resulting federal enforcement of state quotas in the Connally Hot Oil Act of February 22, 1935. The most immediate demands for some substitute for the Recovery Act came from the coal industry and from labor, which did not intend to lose their hard-won gains. Although the National Labor Relations Act was passed shortly before the Bituminous Coal Conservation Act of 1935, the latter comes first in our story.

III. THE GUFFEY COAL CASE—1936

The bituminous coal industry had suffered from low prices and too much competition long before the economic crisis responsible for the National Industrial Recovery Act. Its physical nature is such that once a mine is opened it becomes advantageous to the owner to produce as much coal as possible as long as the price exceeds his out-of-pocket costs. The industry's capacity to produce—except in war time—had long exceeded the national demand. The inroads of fuel oil and other competing fuels into coal's markets and increased efficiency in the use of fuel aggravated the maladjustment of demand and supply. The depression, which greatly diminished purchasing power and consumer demand, brought the industry to a state of collapse.

Coal mining is peculiar in that labor costs constitute approximately 60 per cent of the total cost of production and are the only substantial cost item which is susceptible of reduction by an operator in order to meet competition. The struggle between the operators to get as much coal out of their mines as possible was inevitably taken out on labor. A mine owner could, in entire good faith, tell his employees, who often lived in company towns around the mine and could not secure jobs elsewhere, that he could not sell his coal unless he reduced his prices, that he could only do so by cutting wages, and that it was better for them to accept lower wages than none at all. Although large portions of the industry had been organized by the United Mine Workers and covered by collective bargaining agreements, the operators in the large fields of Southern West Virginia and Kentucky had persistently refused to recognize the principle of collective bargaining. They had fought unionization with all possible weapons, and even before the depression were able through their control of wages to fix prices below those of their northern rivals who complied with a higher union wage scale. As a consequence, in order to stay in business, the latter felt themselves forced to drive union wage rates down, and, when the union resisted this move, to abandon collective bargaining. The United Mine Workers struggled to maintain decent rates of pay; in recognition of the Achilles heel in the structure of the industry—the absence of universal collective bargaining—the union had over the years fought fiercely to organize the entire industry, but with the help of the courts the operators had usually won the battles. During the depression the cutthroat competition in the industry resulted in average mine prices falling to $1.31 per ton and the average annual income of the ordinary miner falling to approximately $500. Chaotic competitive conditions—which have only briefly been sketched here— and their close relationship to working conditions had in the past brought on numerous strikes, some nationwide in extent. The strike in 1922 had closed down 73 per cent of the industry. These strikes threatened to stifle substantially all commerce and industry, since transportation and manufacture were both largely dependent on coal for fuel.

The NRA Bituminous Coal Code fixed minimum prices for coal and minimum wages for the miners and also guaranteed the latter the right to bargain collectively. Its effect in eliminating competition below the cost of production was beneficial to both the miners and operators. Its protection to collective bargaining spurred on the organization of the miners, so that the membership of the United Mine Workers expanded tremendously between 1932 and 1935.

Both the United Mine Workers and most of the operators were, with justification, afraid that the abrogation of the Code by the *Schechter* decision might restore the pre-existing disastrous competitive situation. Accordingly, they joined in seeking legislation which would preserve for them the benefits of the Code. Inasmuch as the downward spiral of prices and wages depended upon the operators' freedom to cut both, stability in the industry could have been achieved by putting a floor under either the one or the other. The operators and miners drafted a bill which provided for both of these things, and it was introduced by Senator Guffey and Representative Snyder of Pennsylvania. It also contained provisions for conservation which were subsequently eliminated by Congress, but which left the bill with the misleading title "Bituminous Coal Conservation Act."

The bill as introduced and as passed imposed a heavy tax on the sale of coal by producers who had not joined the "Bituminous Coal Code." The substantive provisions of the Act were found in the "Code." This contained an elaborate machinery for the establishment of minimum prices by district boards and the National Bituminous Coal Commission, all prices being subject to the latter's approval. Numerous "unfair methods of competition" were proscribed in order to aid in the stabilization of the price structure. These provisions were modeled on those of the National Industrial Recovery Act Coal Code. A separately numbered part of the Code created a Coal Labor Board, contained provisions guaranteeing the right to bargain collectively without employer interference, and provided for the establishment of binding minimum wages and maximum hours at whatever was agreed upon by producers of two-thirds of the tonnage and representatives of the majority of the coal miners in specified areas. The Code was preceded by the statement that its provisions "all tend to regulate interstate commerce in bituminous coal and transactions directly affecting" such commerce.

The tax device was undoubtedly employed in the hope, not subsequently shared by Government counsel, that the plan might stand as a tax if it was not supportable under the commerce power. The Code system was taken from the Recovery Act—perhaps originally in the expectation that those who joined the Code would be found to have voluntarily assented to it.

[President] Roosevelt requested Congress to pass the bill, despite admitted doubts as to whether the Supreme Court would uphold its constitutionality, and the bill became law on August 30, 1935.

[Undoubtedly] in an effort to demonstrate the futility of leaving the coal industry to state regulation, the attorneys general of seven coal-producing states filed briefs in support of the validity of the Guffey Coal Act. They pointed out that no producing state could regulate prices or wages without subjecting its own producers to a competitive disadvantage as against those elsewhere, and that the Commerce Clause itself precluded a state from protecting its citizens against the entrance of outside competition. In view of the legal and practical incapacities of the states, they disavowed the "states' rights" argument as one which would result in no regulation but only in continued chaos in a national industry, to the particularly great disadvantage of all of the producing states. Other briefs were filed by groups of operators on both sides, and by the United Mine Workers. The briefs for the Government and for Carter were over 300 pages in length. In all, the Court was deluged with 1344 pages of briefs.

The case was argued in March by Mr. Wood and Assistant Attorney General Dickinson. In order to defeat the portion of the Act authorizing the fixing of prices for coal most of which was sold in commerce Mr. Wood was forced to the novel contention that Congress lacked power under the Commerce Clause to impose restrictive regulations on commerce (except transportation)—that the purpose of the clause was to free commerce from state control, not to permit affirmative federal regulation.

Mr. Justice Sutherland, speaking for five members of the Court, did not go quite that far. He managed to sidestep the entire issue of the constitutionality of the price-fixing provisions—on which he might have had difficulty carrying Mr. Justice Roberts—by holding them inseparable from the labor provisions and holding the latter unconstitutional. The opinion re-emphasized the need for preserving the powers of the states, irrespective of whether the subject might be one on which the states would be incompetent separately to legislate. Mr. Dickinson's argument that the Commerce Clause should be construed to avoid any such practical hiatus in governmental power, and that the Constitutional Convention's repeated approval of the Sixth Randolph Resolution demonstrated that the granted powers should be so construed, was transformed by the majority opinion into the easily refutable contention that regardless of the enumerated powers Congress could act whenever a subject was beyond the capacity of the several states.

The opinion also, for the first time (and the last), sought to give definite content to the direct-indirect test. The Court could not deny the tremendous effects of labor disputes in the coal industry upon interstate commerce, and it did not attempt to do so. Instead, it declared that "The word 'direct' implies that the activity or condition invoked or blamed shall operate proximately—not mediately, remotely, or collaterally—to produce the effect. It connotes the absence of an efficient intervening agency or condition. And the extent of the effect bears no logical relation to its character. The distinction between a direct and an indirect effect turns, not upon the magnitude of either the cause or the effect, but entirely upon the manner in which the effect has been brought about." Since a strike halts production, and the cessation of production interferes with commerce, the strike only "indirectly" affects commerce—even though it might block it completely.

The Court held that the use of a tax as a sanction did not give the Act any constitutional basis other than the commerce power. As had been predicted, it found the wage and hour provisions of the Act unlawful on the additional ground that the delegation of the right to fix wages and hours to a majority of the operators and representatives of the miners constituted both an invalid delegation of legislative power, because lacking in any standards, and a violation of the Due Process Clause because the power to legislate was vested in private interest groups. Mr. Chief Justice Hughes, and Justices Cardozo, Brandeis and Stone, dissenting, did not take direct issue with these pronouncements; indeed, the Chief Justice concurred in the view that the labor provisions of the Act were invalid. The opinions of the Chief Justice and of Mr. Justice Cardozo asserted that the price provisions of the Act were separable and constitutional, and that the entire statute should not be held invalid. Mr. Justice Cardozo's opinion manifested obvious dissatisfaction with the majority's dialectic as to the meaning of "direct" and "indirect." Those words, and others of similar import, must, he said, be "interpreted with suppleness of adaptation and flexibility of meaning. The power is as broad as the need that evokes it." The facts of the particular situation must determine whether a relationship to interstate commerce is too tenuous in a practical sense to warrant federal control, not theories of proximate causation. "[A] great principle of constitutional law is not susceptible of comprehensive statement in an adjective."

* * *

IV. LABOR RELATIONS—1937

[The] National Labor Relations Act[,] most carefully drafted, prohibited only unfair labor practices—interference by an employer with his employees' freedom to choose their own representatives and to bargain collectively—which threatened to obstruct interstate commerce. . . .

As a result, an overwhelming majority of the lower courts denied the numerous applications to enjoin the enforcement of the National Labor Relations Act. All but one circuit court of appeals held that the Act was not invalid on its face, that it could legitimately apply to some employers, and that, since no employer would be harmed until after the Board's order had been affirmed by a circuit court of appeals, employers must proceed through the orderly and adequate protective machinery contained in the statute.

[A]fter the *Carter* decision, the cause of the NLRB, insofar as it attempted to apply the Act to anyone but employers engaged in interstate commerce, seemed hopeless. The Coal Act had contained collective bargaining provisions substantially the same as those in the Labor Relations Act, and the evidence in the *Carter* case had shown beyond doubt that labor disputes in the coal industry had interfered not only with interstate commerce in coal itself but with interstate rail transportation and a great proportion of all industry as well. That strong a case could be presented for no other productive industry. The argument that the collective bargaining provisions of the Coal Act failed because the purpose of the statute was to stabilize an industry, not to eliminate obstructions to commerce, was the best distinction that Government counsel could contrive.

[While the labor cases] were on their way to the Court two events took place which undoubtedly played a vital role in their determination. In November, 1936, the nation re-elected President Roosevelt by a tremendous electoral and popular majority. The President construed this popular mandate as an indorsement of his program to improve the conditions of the under-privileged in industry and in agriculture through federal regulation despite the recent Supreme Court decisions which seemingly blocked his path. Since those decisions had been rendered by majorities of only five or six justices, the President determined not to permit the Court to flout the popular will by what he, as well as Justices Brandeis, Stone and Cardozo, felt to be a reactionary interpretation of the Constitution. On Friday, February 5, 1937, the President proposed the plan for appointing as many as six new justices to the Supreme Court of the United States, one to sit in addition to each justice over seventy years of age.

Three days later, the *Virginian* case and the NLRB cases came on for argument. [T]he Government presented the cases in a manner which would have enabled the Court, if it were so disposed, to hold the Act applicable to such vertically integrated enterprises as the Jones & Laughlin Steel Corp.—which even owned its own shipping lines—without necessarily reaching ordinary manufacturing concerns. [The] arguments of the attorneys in the three manufacturing cases were the same as those which had been accepted by the Court in the *Carter* case.

While the cases were awaiting decision, the efforts of the newly formed CIO to organize the automobile, steel and other mass production industries came to a head. The employers had refused to obey the new law, and the unions, unwilling to rely exclusively on the Act, which might or might not be held applicable and which would in any event operate very tardily, sought to force recognition by strikes many of which involved the "sit-down" technique and resulted in considerable violence. Whether deliberately or not, these strikes vividly illustrated how the refusal of employers to bargain with freely chosen representatives of their employees could result in the closing down of plants and the halting of all interstate commerce in major segments of industry.

On March 29, 1937 the Court unanimously affirmed the decisions below in the *Virginian* case. It held that the Railway Labor Act could lawfully be applied to back shop employees, inasmuch as a strike by such employees "would seriously cripple petitioner's interstate transportation." Mr. Justice Stone's opinion distinguished *The Employers' Liability Cases* in a manner which left little doubt that they would not be followed in the future. The opinion also upheld the majority rule provisions of the Railway Labor Act, which were substantially the same as those contained in the National Labor Relations Act. On the same day, in an amazing reversal of a decision less than a year old, the Court in *West Coast Hotel Co. v. Parrish* held that statutes prescribing minimum wages for women did not so interfere with liberty of contract as to violate the Due Process Clause. This decision removed a judicial barrier to minimum-wage legislation which had existed since the oft-criticized ruling in *Adkins v. Children's Hospital* in 1923, and which had been reaffirmed by five judges only ten months before in *Morehead v. New York ex rel. Tipaldo*. Justice Roberts abandoned the four justices with whom he had agreed during the previous Term to join Chief Justice Hughes and Justices Brandeis, Stone and Cardozo in overruling both the *Morehead* and *Adkins* cases.

The courtroom was jammed on Monday, April 12, 1937. Mr. Justice Roberts announced opinions sustaining the Board in the *Associated Press* and bus line cases, both of which involved companies engaged in interstate commerce. The latter decision was unanimous; the four conservative justices dissented in the former on the ground that the application of the Act to the Associated Press violated the freedom of the press. But no one disputed the validity of the Act as it related to employees in interstate commerce. This result had been anticipated—at least by Government counsel.

The suspense was great as Chief Justice Hughes began to read his opinion in the *Jones & Laughlin* case. The Act as a whole was declared valid, since it reached only activities which obstructed commerce, a phrase which the Court found was obviously intended to be conterminous with the federal commerce power and not extending beyond it. There remained the inquiry "whether in the instant case the constitutional boundary has been passed."

The Chief Justice then reviewed the cases upholding the exercise of the federal power over intrastate activities. Citing the same authorities that the Government had relied upon to no avail in the *Carter* and NRA arguments, he declared that:

> The close and intimate effect which brings the subject within the reach of federal power may be due to activities in relation to productive industry although the industry when separately viewed is local. . . .
>
> It is thus apparent that the fact that the employees here concerned were engaged in production is not determinative.

Shades of *Butler* and *Carter*, in which a majority had indicated that to brand a statute as reaching production was sufficient to condemn it without more! The opinion then went on to "distinguish" the *Carter* case, on the ground that the production provisions of the Coal Act were invalid because "the requirements not only went beyond any sustainable measure of protection of interstate commerce" but because there was improper delegation of legislative power and a violation of due process. But the last two objections had run only to the wage and hour provisions of the Coal Act; its labor relations sections were substantially the same as those of the National Labor Relations Act.

Finally the opinion reached the crucial point. Did labor relations in the vast Jones & Laughlin steel-manufacturing organization sufficiently affect interstate commerce? Gone was the verbalism of the *Carter* case, the reliance upon such metaphysical concepts as proximate or intermediate causation. Instead the opinion spoke in terms which anyone, be he layman, economist or even lawyer, could understand:

> [the] fact remains that the stoppage of those operations by industrial strife would have a most serious effect upon interstate commerce. In view of respondent's far-flung activities, it is idle to say that the effect would be indirect or remote. It is obvious that it would be immediate and might be catastrophic. We are asked to shut our eyes to the plainest facts of our national life and to deal with the question of direct and indirect effects in an intellectual [vacuum]. When industries organize themselves on a national scale, making their relation to interstate commerce the dominant factor in their activities, how can it be maintained that their industrial labor relations constitute a forbidden field into which Congress may not enter when it is necessary to protect interstate commerce from the paralyzing consequences of industrial war? We have often said that interstate commerce itself is a practical conception. It is equally true that interferences with that commerce must be appraised by a judgment that does not ignore actual experience.

"Actual experience," actual relation to commerce, was henceforth to be the criterion. The same test was applied to sustain the Board's position in the trailer and clothing company cases. Mr. Justice McReynolds, in a bitter dissent on behalf of himself and Justices Van Devanter, Sutherland, and Butler, accused the majority of abandoning the precepts of the *Schechter* and *Carter* decisions.

No other opinions were rendered that day, and the courtroom rapidly cleared. The corridors and the cafeteria buzzed with excited conversation. For the second time in two weeks the Court had in substance overruled cases decided less than one year before on major constitutional issues. No serious effort had been made to distinguish the *Carter* case; the connection between interstate commerce and labor relations in the coal mines shown in the *Carter* record far exceeded in quantity and effect anything appearing in the Labor Board cases. There had been no change in the membership of the Court. What had induced Mr. Justice Roberts to switch his vote, after his opinion in the *Butler* case emphasizing the limitations imposed by the Tenth Amendment upon control of production and his full concurrence in *Carter*? What of the Chief Justice, who had joined in the *Butler* decision and approved of *Carter* insofar as it nullified the labor relations provisions of the Coal Act?

No one who did not participate in the conferences of the Court will know the answers to those questions. But few attributed the difference in results between the decisions in 1936 and those in 1937 to anything inherent in the cases themselves—their facts, the arguments presented, or the authorities cited. Perhaps the series of violent strikes had educated Mr. Justice Roberts as to the close relationship between labor relations and interstate commerce. But the consensus among the lawyers speculating on the Court's sudden reversal was that the Chief Justice and Mr. Justice Roberts believed that the continued nullification of the legislative program demanded by the people and their representatives—as manifested in the 1936 election—would lead to acceptance of the President's Court plan, and that this would seriously undermine the independence and prestige of the federal judiciary, and particularly of the Supreme Court, without preventing the President from attaining his objective. Chief Justice Hughes was subsequently cited for his "statesmanship" in using the cases as potent weapons in a successful campaign, in which he was somewhat inhibited by his judicial position, to combat the plan. Whether or not there was any basis for these conjectures, Government counsel, or most of them, accredited their victory more to the President than to anything they had said or done.

It may be noted in passing that the Chief Justice's strategy, if such it was, succeeded. A few weeks later the Court sustained the constitutionality of the Social Security Act, in two of the three cases by the same votes of five to four. At the end of the Term, Mr. Justice Van Devanter announced his retirement from the bench. Since the new appointee would undoubtedly not share his constitutional philosophy, the balance of power on the Court would shift from Mr. Justice Roberts, whose vacillating course from his outstanding opinion in the *Nebbia* case through the *Railroad Retirement*, *Butler*, *Morehead* and *Carter* cases to the Labor Board and Social Security cases was an unsafe foundation upon which to predicate the entire economic policy of the United States. There was thus no longer need for the Court plan, and although the President continued, many thought unnecessarily, to press it, it was eventually defeated. But the campaign had been won even though not in the manner anticipated.

Senator Black succeeded Mr. Justice Van Devanter at the beginning of the October Term, 1937. Mr. Justice Sutherland retired in January, 1938, and Solicitor General Stanley Reed took his place.

In the 1937 and 1938 Terms the Court further defined the scope of the Commerce Clause in cases under the National Labor Relations Act. The original Labor Act cases had been concerned with manufacturers in the center of the interstate movement, who both received materials and shipped finished products in interstate commerce. *Santa Cruz Fruit Packing Co. v. NLRB* made it clear that industries at the beginning of the flow, producing raw materials within a state for shipment outside, were subject to the Act, since labor disputes in such concerns would undoubtedly obstruct the interstate movement. The case involved a fruit packing plant, but Chief Justice Hughes emphasized that it was covered by the same principles as "coal mined." The *Carter* case, somewhat inexplicably, was said not to "establish a different principle." The Court also held it immaterial that only 37 per cent of the product of the plant was shipped out of the state. This amounted to approximately one half a million cases of fruits and vegetables annually, and a strike provoked by the employer's anti-union tactics had previously closed down the plant and directly interfered with his substantial flow of commerce. The opinion was also significant for its effort to redefine "direct" and "indirect"; this terminology was said merely to embody the distinction between "remote" and "close and substantial," a "criterion [necessarily] one of degree" and not susceptible of expression in "mathematical or rigid formulas" such as had been prescribed by Mr. Justice Sutherland in the *Carter* case. Justices Butler and McReynolds dissented on the ground that the *Carter* case, still not definitely overruled, was controlling.

Robert L. Stern, *That Commerce Which Concerns More States Than One*, 47 HARV. L. REV. 1335 (1934)*

Let us assume—in the proper law school classroom manner—a situation in which 25 percent of the people in the United States are unemployed and in which business is prostrate. Let us likewise assume that this state of affairs has been in part caused by national maladjustment of production and consumption—production in excess of purchasing power—and that business will grow steadily worse unless measures are taken to remedy these conditions. And, finally, let it be assumed that to be effective such measures must be nation-wide in scope, that because of the integrated character of the national economic structure action by the states separately would be impracticable and ineffectual, and that unless steps to alleviate the situation can be taken on a national scale, the people of the United States will be entirely unable to help themselves through any existing social or governmental agency. This classroom method of assuming a situation has been invoked in order to avoid, in the analysis which follows, any dispute as to the need for the particular measures which have been recently utilized to relieve the depression.

Under such circumstances, any one but a constitutional lawyer would immediately agree that if the Federal Government alone is able to revive business throughout the country, that government should take the necessary action. But the constitutional lawyer rightly enough perceives that no matter how serious the nation's plight may be, the Federal Government cannot act unless it has been granted the power to do so by the Constitution. And a number of constitutional lawyers will

---

explain that the only section of the Constitution which gives to the Federal Government any power over business is the commerce [clause]. If asked to define "interstate" commerce, they would quickly reply, "the movement of commodities or persons or information across state lines." . . .

Under this conception of the commerce power a hiatus would exist between those commercial matters subject to federal regulation and those which the state could effectively control. For even though each state might pass laws regulating those subjects within its own boundaries, it could not cure itself of its portion of a national economic disease. As well might a person whose entire body was seriously afflicted hope to cure his right hand by applying bandages and ointments to that hand alone. The analogy is even more complete. The doctored hand of the afflicted individual would be receiving tainted blood from the rest of the body. Similarly, the state which attempted to doctor itself in this wise would receive commodities from other states which by competition with domestic products would render its efforts to protect its own commercial establishment unavailing. And the commerce clause itself is the constitutional factor in the body politic which prevents the state from closing the artery carrying the tainted stream of goods into its territory.

[An] interpretation of the commerce clause which would permit any such weakness to exist in the power of the nation to protect itself against commercial disaster would do violence both to the fundamental concepts which guided those men who prepared the Constitution and to the principles which the Supreme Court has professed since the days of John Marshall. For the commerce clause, above all others, was, and has been universally regarded as, the great unifying clause of the Constitution, as the section of that document in which the authors indicated their desire to give the national government as much control over commercial transactions as was then or would in the future be essential to the protection of the commercial interests of the union.

[The] Constitutional Convention was called because the Articles of Confederation had not given the Federal Government any power to regulate [commerce]. Representatives [who] met at Annapolis [determined] that [the] adequate protection of commerce required a complete revision of the structure of government. Accordingly, they recommended that a convention be called for the purpose of revising the Articles of Confederation. . . .

[The] commerce clause was the only one of the enumerated powers in which Congress was given any broad power to regulate trade or business. [In] view of the fact that the need for centralized commercial regulation was universally recognized as the primary reason for preparing a new constitution, the Convention would not have been likely to have meant the commerce clause to have a narrow or restrictive meaning.

[It] was the clear understanding of the state conventions called to consider the ratification of the Constitution that the division of power gave to the national government control of all matters of national, as contrasted with local, concern. On this point both the proponents and opponents of ratification [agreed].

There can be no question, of course, that in 1787 the framers and ratifiers of the Constitution did not contemplate either the close-knit economic structure which exists today, or the need for a far-reaching system of national control to preserve that structure from disintegration. When they considered the need for regulating "commerce with foreign nations and among the several states," they were thinking only in terms of the national control of trade with the European countries and the removal of barriers obstructing the physical movements of goods across state lines. For in 1787 there was no need for further national regulation of trade or business; the states were not then separately incompetent to cope with those commercial problems which did not involve the movement of goods from one state to another.

But the framers of the Constitution did not use language which would restrict the federal power to regulation of the movement of physical goods, even though that was the only kind of regulation which they immediately contemplated. The history and proceedings of the Convention and of the ratifying conventions in the states indicate that the purpose of the commerce clause was to give the Federal Government as much control over commercial transactions as was and would in the future be essential to the general welfare of the union, and there is no suggestion that this power was to be limited to control over movement. The framers of the Constitution would have been exceedingly surprised if they had thought that by the language employed to accomplish that purpose—"the commerce among the several states"—they had so restricted the national power as to create a union incapable of dealing with a commercial condition even more serious than the one that had brought them together. They were acutely conscious that they were preparing an instrument for the ages, not a document adapted only for the exigencies of the time.

[Moreover,] an analysis of the meaning during that early period of the words in the expression "commerce among the several states" shows that when the Constitution was adopted the phrase was understood to include much more than the movement of goods between the states. Commerce, according to the dictionaries of that time, primarily denoted trade, traffic, buying and selling, or the exchange of goods, and the movement of goods was only one of its connotations. The definition in the early decisions of the Supreme Court contains the same emphasis. In fact, the inclusion of transportation in "commerce" in *Gibbons v. Ogden* was regarded as a radical innovation. "Commerce" in those days, then, was the practical equivalent of the word "trade." Although it would not have covered manufacturing, mining, or agriculture as such, it would have included the marketing of the products after the processing had been completed. . . .

[The] use of the convenient phrase "interstate commerce" instead of the words of the Constitution has unfortunately tended to cause the connotation of "intermingling" in the phrase "commerce among the states" to be neglected, and the element of interstate movement to be over-emphasized. Thus, the impression is often given that the commerce power of Congress is dependent upon the existence of movement *between* the states. But the Constitution says "among," rather than "between," and the difference between the two words is ignored if the commerce power is limited to the control of acts affecting movement across state lines.

[A]n analysis of the commerce decisions will demonstrate that since the first case in which the commerce clause came before it, the Supreme Court has consistently recognized that the clause should be interpreted to meet the needs of a rapidly, expanding nation. [In] *Gibbons v. Ogden*, Chief Justice Marshall, who himself had been a member of the Virginia Ratifying Convention, laid down the basic doctrine that the phrase "commerce among the states" comprehended "that commerce which concerns more states than one"—not merely commerce moving across state lines. . . .

[As] Congress found it necessary to regulate additional specific abuses—in each instance because the states were unable satisfactorily to deal with the problems raised—the Court kept pace with it in recognizing the need for extending the application of the commerce power. Each new type of statute, when passed, seemed novel and dangerous, though often the control of interstate movements alone sufficed to meet the situation. But the Lottery Act, the Pure Food and Drug Act, the White Slave Act, the Adamson Act, the Bill of Lading Act, the Motor Vehicle Theft Act, and the Animal Industry Act were all upheld. And in the most recent of the leading commerce decisions—*Stafford v. Wallace, Board of Trade v. Olsen*, and *Tagg Bros. & Moorehead v. United States*—the Court has upheld detailed federal regulation of stockyards and grain exchanges located in only a few cities but affecting business transactions throughout the country.

These cases and the Anti-Trust decisions illustrate most vividly the willingness of the Supreme Court to uphold the application of federal power to ordinary business practices which concern and affect acts in other states although the Court always found or was able to assume that interstate movement was present or affected, in many of the decisions this element was very slight and incidental. An examination of the cases indicates very clearly that it was not the effect upon movement which was important, but the effect of the practices upon business in other states—upon price, upon supply, or upon competitors. . . .

[A]lthough the Court has continued to talk of interstate commerce in terms of movement, it has repeatedly sanctioned the application of federal power to situations in which the effect upon movement was only a subordinate factor where it was apparent that the subject of regulation demanded national control. . . .

[Before] the nation had become the economic unit that it is today, commercial activities in one state concerned other states only through actual movements of goods across state lines. There was no need for applying the federal power to anything but actual shipments. Then, as intra- and interstate business grew more and more unified, congressional control of those intrastate acts which *affected* movement between the states became essential. The emphasis could still be on physical movement, however, and since movement alone had previously been considered within the federal power, the language of movement was employed as a matter of course. . . .

Movement, it is true—or the potentiality of movement—was, in these cases, and will continue to be the connecting link which makes business transactions in the various states affect each other. If things could not be rapidly transported from state to state, if the United States did not for that reason constitute a national market, most intrastate commercial transactions would not concern other states at all. The two approaches to the problem are entirely consistent, and it may often be true, as it has been in the past, that the same decision can be reached regardless of whether the effect upon movement or the effect upon trade in other states is emphasized. For whenever business in one state does affect business in others, it is also likely to affect—by diminishing, increasing, or diverting from its normal channels—movements between the states. The difference between the approaches is largely a question of which element should be stressed.

The adoption of the proper approach is tremendously important, however, as Congress has been obliged, in an effort to relieve the nation from the business depression, to exert its power over practices the effect of which upon the movement or potential movement of goods may be slight, although the detrimental effect of a practice in one state upon business in other states may be considerable. No one has pretended that the National Industrial Recovery Act, the Agricultural Adjustment Act, the Securities Act, or the Stock Exchange bill were designed to enable the Federal Government to control acts affecting movements across state lines. The known basis of these measures is the unity of the national business structure which makes it impossible for the states separately to meet the problems of the business cycle. All of the statutes have been so drafted, however, that their application can be restricted to transactions coming within the movement test. Moreover, if a realistic attitude be applied even to that test, all the recovery legislation may be supported on the theory that the termination of the depression will substantially increase interstate shipments of goods, and that therefore any measures which will assist in the improvement of business generally are valid. Thus, it is possible for the Court to uphold the recovery legislation to the fullest extent without shifting its verbal approach to the subject. But this tack is dangerous, in view of the necessary restrictive doctrine that the federal power does not extend to acts which affect "commerce among the states" remotely or indirectly. If commerce among the states be regarded as limited to movement across state lines, the application of the new statutes may be greatly narrowed, and their effectiveness as an aid to national business recovery greatly diminished.

[The] answer to the constitutional lawyer's objection, then, is that although the Court has generally talked of interstate commerce as if it meant interstate movement, there has heretofore been no need for a broader definition. The time has now arrived for the Court to cut loose from the "old" approach and to select the "new" one marked out by the fathers of the Constitution, by the first great expounder of that document, by the Court's own holdings, and by its present chief.

[The] states do not, as a practical matter, lose any power they now possess, for the application of federal power to intrastate transactions is posited on the assumption that the states separately are unable to take effective action. The states, furthermore, will not be deprived of the power to regulate business within their borders except to the extent that Congress chooses to enter the field. As has been pointed out, the same transaction may be within the sphere both of state and federal regulation.

[If] business in the United States has become a single integrated whole, if the state can no longer effectively regulate those acts formerly regarded as purely local, if the welfare of the nation depends upon the treatment of national problems on a national scale, if almost all business substantially affects business in other states, why should not Congress possess whatever power is necessary to assume some social control of the national economy? The Constitution does not provide that Congress may regulate commerce among the several states only when such commerce is ten per cent of the whole, but not when it becomes ninety per cent. The entire purpose of the fathers was to give the national government the powers which must be vested in a central authority "to promote the general welfare" of the union.

The history of the commerce clause, both in the Constitutional Convention and in the decisions of the Supreme Court, makes it clear that no hiatus between the powers of the state and federal governments to control commerce effectively was intended to exist—that it was not intended to leave the people of the United States powerless to combat the play of destructive economic forces. The Court has a number of times regarded the possibility of creating such a situation as strong reason for avoiding a decision which would hold a particular course of conduct exempt from federal control. The Court can avoid the possibility of placing the nation in a defenseless position by returning to the original conception of the commerce clause—by allowing federal control of those business transactions which occur in and concern more states than one and which the individual states are separately incompetent to control.

Robert Eugene Cushman, *The National Police Power Under the Commerce Clause of the Constitution*, 3 MINN. L. REV. 289 (1919)*

[Congress] has come gradually to legislate in affairs over which it has been supposed to have no jurisdiction—to assume responsibility for the safety, health, morals, good order, and general welfare of the nation, and thus to exercise what may be called a national police power.

It seems clear that it is entirely proper to use the term "national police power." To borrow a definition of the police power from the authority perhaps most competent to lend, it is that power of government which "aims directly to secure and promote the public welfare" by subjecting to restraint or compulsion the members of the community. It is the power by which the government abridges the freedom of action or the free use of property of the individual in order that the welfare of the state or nation may not be jeopardized. It is obvious, then, that when Congress places a prohibitive tax upon poisonous matches, excludes obscene literature from the mails, or enacts an employers' liability law, it is exercising police power. What is the source and nature of this police power which Congress enjoys and what are the limitations upon it?

THEORY OF THE NATIONAL POLICE POWER

Principle of Enumerated Powers of Congress

To understand clearly the nature of the national police power it is necessary to bear in mind one of the abc's of our constitutional law, namely, that Congress enjoys those powers of legislation, and only those, which are positively given to it by the constitution. Unlike the states, which enjoy all powers which have not been taken away from them, it has only the powers which are delegated to it. The subjects over which it may exercise control are carefully enumerated. [Nothing] is clearer than that the purpose of the Convention of 1787 was to confer upon the new Congress a certain group of powers definitely delimited and to leave the other powers of government in the hands of the states.

The effect of this doctrine of enumerated powers upon the right of Congress to exercise a national police power is perfectly plain. The enumeration of congressional powers in the constitution does not include any general grant of authority to pass laws for the protection of the health, morals, or general welfare of the nation. It follows, then, that if Congress is to exercise a police power at all it must do so by a process something akin to indirection; that is, by using the powers which are definitely confided to it, for the purposes of the police power. If it would enter upon an ambitious program to protect public morals or safety or health or to promote good order, it must cloak its good works under its authority to tax, or to regulate commerce, or to control the mails, or the like, and say, "By this authority we pass this law in the interest of the public welfare." In short, Congress exercises a generous police power not because that power is placed directly in its hands but because it has the power to regulate commerce, to lay taxes and to control the mails, and uses that authority for the broad purposes of the general welfare.

That Congress can exercise police power only in so far as it is possible to utilize one of its enumerated powers for that purpose is not due to accident or inadvertence. The limited nature of that police power has been emphasized and re-emphasized by the unsuccessful efforts of those who from 1787 to the present time have sought to

---

*   Copyright © 1919 by the Minnesota Law Review. Reprinted by permission.

secure its enlargement and invest Congress with a power adequate to deal with any truly national problem. The earliest of these efforts was made in the Convention of 1787. Four resolutions were introduced during the sessions of that body, varying somewhat in phraseology but similar in purpose. That purpose, to quote the language of the one introduced by Mr. Bedford, was to confer upon Congress the power "to legislate in all cases for the general interests of the Union, and also in those to which the States are severally incompetent, or in which the harmony of the United States may be interrupted by the exercise of individual legislation." In defeating these resolutions the Convention passed squarely upon the question whether or not Congress should enjoy a general police power for the protection of the national welfare apart from its specifically enumerated powers and decided that it should not.

[It] remained for President [Theodore] Roosevelt to discover or at least to label the neutral or "twilight" zone in our constitutional system—a zone lying between the jurisdictions of the state and the nation, to which lawbreakers of great wealth might repair and be free from punishment or restraint. Large corporations had come to be beyond the reach of the state because they had grown to national dimensions; they were outside the effective control of Congress because the constitution does not confer upon Congress a positive grant of authority to deal with them directly. It was to meet this situation that President Roosevelt urged his doctrine of "New Nationalism," first as a principle of constitutional interpretation, and, failing in that, as a constitutional amendment. That doctrine may be best stated in his own words: "It should be made clear that there are neither vacancies nor interferences between the limits of state and national jurisdictions, and that both jurisdictions together compose only one uniform and comprehensive system of government and laws; that is, whenever the states cannot act, because the need to be met is not one merely of a single locality, then the national government, representing all the people, should have complete power to act." In public addresses delivered after 1906 President Roosevelt reverted again and again to this subject, urging always that the federal government should be competent to deal with every truly national problem and expressing his impatience at "the impotence which springs from overdivision of government powers, the impotence which makes it possible for local selfishness or for legal cunning, hired by wealthy special interests, to bring national activities to a deadlock."

[W]hile the doctrine of enumerated powers imposes upon Congress the necessity of finding among its delegated powers what has been aptly termed "a definite constitutional peg" upon which to hang every exercise of the national police power, the doctrine of implied powers, or the liberal construction of congressional authority, has made it possible to hang upon those "pegs" an enormous amount of salutary legislation in the interest of the national health, safety, and well being. The "pegs" themselves are few in number, the only important ones being the power to regulate commerce, the power to tax, and the power to establish and run the postal system; but the police legislation which they have been made to support deals with anything from the white slave traffic to speculation in cotton.

[While] the police regulations which Congress has passed under its authority to regulate interstate commerce have been exceedingly numerous and have dealt with a wide range of topics, from locomotive ashpans to obscene literature, they may all be placed for convenience in four groups, according to the general purpose of their enactment and the constitutional principles upon which they are based. (I) In the first group may be placed those regulations in which Congress has exercised police power for the protection and promotion of interstate commerce itself by the enactment of such laws as the safety appliance acts, the anti-trust acts, and other regulations designed to keep that commerce safe, efficient, and unobstructed. (II) The second group comprises the cases in which the law forbids the use of interstate commerce as a medium or channel for transactions which menace the national health, morals, or welfare. In this class would be placed the Pure Food Act, the White Slave Act, and other statutes by which Congress, instead of protecting commerce itself from danger, protects the nation from the misuse of that commerce. (III) The third group consists of the enactments by which Congress co-operates with the states by forbidding the use of the facilities of interstate commerce for the purpose of evading or violating state police regulations. Here would be found such laws as the Webb-Kenyon Act, excluding from interstate commerce shipments of liquor consigned to dry territory. (IV) In the last group should be placed the Keating-Owen Child-Labor Act of 1916, by which Congress attempted to deny the privileges of interstate commerce to articles produced under conditions which Congress disapproved but which it had no direct power to control. Careful consideration may profitably be given to each of these groups.

Richard A. Epstein, *The Proper Scope of the Commerce Power*, 73 VA. L. REV. 1387 (1987)*

[T]he expansive construction of the [commerce] clause accepted by the New Deal Supreme Court is wrong, and clearly so, and [a] host of other interpretations are more consistent with both the text and the structure of our constitutional government.

I. THE PROBLEM: STRUCTURE AND INDIVIDUAL RIGHTS

The commerce power is not a comprehensive grant of federal power. It does not convert the Constitution from a system of government with enumerated federal powers into one in which the only subject matter limitations placed on Congress are those which it chooses to impose upon itself. Nor does the "necessary and proper" clause work to change this basic design; although it seeks to insure that the federal power may be exercised upon its appropriate targets, it is not designed to run roughshod over the entire scheme of enumerated powers that precedes it in the Constitution. If forced to summarize what the commerce clause means, I would say that it refers more to "commerce" as that term has been developed in connection with the "negative" or "dormant" commerce clause cases, which concern the instrumentalities of interstate commerce and the goods that are shipped into it. [More] generally, the idea of commerce seems closer to the idea of "trade" than to other economic activities. It is in just this sense that the term was used in ordinary discourse at the time of the founding. Hume's essay Of Commerce, for example, explicitly places the idea of commerce in opposition to that of manufacturing. The same usage, restrictive by modern standards, was adopted by Hamilton, who for example in the Federalist No. 11 uses commerce as a synonym for trade and navigation, and links his discussion of the commerce power with the need to have an American navy to police and protect the seas. But whatever the uncertainties, commerce does not comprise the sum of all productive activities in which individuals may engage. There is at least a slight irony here, for the Uniform Commercial Code is enacted under state law, whereas everything from manufacturing to welfare is regulated comprehensively at the federal level.

---

*   Reprinted with permission.

* * *

II. THE TEXT

The first place to look to find the meaning of the commerce clause is the text of the clause itself. Here one notices that the word "commerce" governs three separate sets of relations—those with foreign nations, among the states, and with Indian tribes. One should assume that the word commerce applies with equal force to all three cases, and bears the same meaning with respect to each of its objects. . . .

[O]ne does not want a meaning of the term commerce which renders any one of these three heads of the commerce power redundant or unnecessary. The modern view which says that commerce among the several states includes all manufacture and other productive activity within each and every state, because of the effect that such manufacture has upon commerce, violates this constraint. If commerce includes all that precedes trade with foreign nations, among the states, and with Indian tribes, then the three heads of jurisdiction cover the same ground; that is, each by itself covers manufacturing or agriculture within each of the states. The scope of the clause would thus be plenary even if it said only that Congress shall have power to regulate commerce with foreign nations, or even with the Indian tribes, and remained silent about commerce among the several [states].

Taking the alternative position, that commerce means trade, or as Chief Justice Marshall said, "intercourse," with or among the parties named, changes the situation dramatically. By Chief Justice Marshall's account, "intercourse" covered both shipping and navigation, and the contracts regulating buying and selling. Using that two-part definition it becomes clear that trade with foreign nations is not trade among the several states or with the Indian tribes. Each part of the clause attributes the same meaning to the term commerce, and each of the objects of the clause—foreign nations, the states, and Indian tribes—becomes an indispensable part of the constitutional structure. The power to regulate commerce with foreign nations, for example, is needed to ensure that trade negotiations with foreign nations are not conducted by each of the several states in its own individual capacity.

[T]his view of commerce as trade is consistent with the other prominent mention of the word commerce in the Constitution. Article I also states that "[n]o preference shall be given by any Regulation of Commerce or Revenue to the Parts of one State over those of [another]." The term "commerce" is used in opposition to the term "revenue," and seems clearly to refer to shipping and its incidental activities; this much seems evident from the use of the term "port." The clause itself would sound odd if it referred, for example, to preferences "given by any Regulation of Commerce, Manufacture or Revenue to the ports of one State." The term commerce in this commerce provision does not carry with it the extensive baggage placed upon it by the better-known New Deal cases concerning the commerce clause.

III. THE STRUCTURE

One obtains the same interpretation of the commerce clause when considering the clause in light of the overall constitutional structure. Article I, section 8, contains an extensive list of separate, discrete, and enumerated powers granted to Congress, whereas article I, section 9, contains a comparable list of powers specifically denied to it. The lists of inclusion and exclusion suggest that the provisions contained in any one section should be read to recognize the existence and necessity of other specific powers and limitations contained elsewhere in article I, as well as the certainty that some matters are wholly beyond the power of Congress.

This view certainly appears to agree with the original theory of the Constitution. The federal government received delegated powers from the states and the individuals within the states. The exact source of the granting power might be somewhat unclear; after all, the preamble begins with "We the People," yet ratification was by nine of the thirteen sovereign states. Yet whatever the pedigree of the Constitution, there was clearly no sense that either grantor conferred upon the Congress the plenary power to act as a roving commission, in order to do whatever it thought best for the common good. The looseness of vague grants of power would have given rise to the possibility of massive abuse, a possibility the framers seemed determined to control. The federal government was to have supremacy in the areas under its control, but the quid pro quo was that these areas were to be limited by specific jurisdictional grants. A system which says that the commerce clause essentially allows the government to regulate anything that even indirectly burdens or affects commerce does away with the key understanding that the federal government has received only enumerated powers. The doctrine of "internal relations" is not only a philosophical creed that says every event is related to every other separate event; it is also something of an economic truth in a world in which the price of any given commodity depends upon the costs of its inputs and upon the alternatives available to potential buyers. To say that Congress may regulate X because of its price effects upon any goods in interstate commerce, or because of its effects upon the quantity of goods so shipped, is to say that Congress can regulate whatever it pleases, a theory that cases such as *Wickard v. Filburn* have so eagerly inferred.

On this score, moreover, there is no reason to distinguish the commerce of the eighteenth and nineteenth centuries from that of the twentieth. Business in one state has always had profound economic effects upon the fortunes of other states. The pre-Civil War battles between North and South over the tariff show just how much the fate of each state has always depended upon national economic policies. There was no economic revolution during the Progressive Era or the New Deal that justifies the convenient escape of saying that it is only the nature of business and trade that has changed, not the appropriate construction of the commerce clause. . . .

Nor is any of this understanding upset by the "necessary and proper" clause of the Constitution, which may expand the power of Congress, but does not provide for an unlimited grant of federal power. . . .

IV. THE CASE LAW BEFORE THE NEW DEAL: 1824-1936

The elaborate case law under the commerce clause can be profitably interpreted in light of the above understandings. Thus it is often said today that the New Deal does not represent violent revolution but prudent reformation (one thinks of Martin Luther and that other reformation). More precisely, the newer cases are said only to have returned to the wisdom of Chief Justice Marshall, who understood the importance of an expansive interpretation of the commerce clause to the maintenance of the Union. In between, in such cases as *United States v. E.C. Knight Co.*, the courts are said to have strayed from the original understanding to a view that effectively hampered the power of Congress to impose much-needed social and economic regulation. This set of insights has even been dressed up in plausible philosophical garb. Professor Tribe's treatise, AMERICAN CONSTITUTIONAL LAW, tells us that the Supreme Court between 1887 and 1937 substituted a "formal classification" of economic activities for the "empiricism" that characterized Chief Justice Marshall's great judgment in the pivotal case of *Gibbons v. Ogden*.

The New Deal was not a reformation, but a sharp departure from previous case law, and one that moved federal power far beyond anything Chief Justice Marshall had in mind. *Gibbons* is often regarded as an expansive interpretation, and for its time so it was. Yet when the critical passages of the opinion are read as a whole, it seems quite clear that the case strongly adumbrated the subsequent holding in *E.C. Knight*, with which it is said to contrast so clearly. . . .

A. *Gibbons v. Ogden*

[Professor] Tribe has summarized his view of the broad scope of *Gibbons* as follows:

> [I]n an elaborate preliminary discussion, [Chief Justice] Marshall indicated that, in his view, congressional power to regulate "commercial intercourse" extended to all activity having any interstate impact—however indirect. Acting under the commerce clause, Congress could legislate with respect to all "commerce which concerns more states than one." This power would be plenary: absolute within its sphere, subject only to the Constitution's affirmative prohibitions on the exercise of federal authority.

This passage suggests that Chief Justice Marshall in *Gibbons* gave a very extensive reading to the reach of the commerce clause. But that is only because of the redactor's power of selection. Consider the fuller context of the quotation from *Gibbons*:

> Commerce among the States, cannot stop at the external boundary line of each State, but may be introduced into the interior.
> It is not intended to say that these words comprehend that commerce, which is completely internal, which is carried on between man and man in a State, or between different parts of the same State, and which does not extend to or affect other States. Such a power would be inconvenient, and is certainly unnecessary.

Comprehensive as the word "among" is, it may very properly be restricted to that commerce which concerns more States than one. The phrase is not one which would probably have been selected to indicate the completely interior traffic of a State, because it is not an apt phrase for that purpose; and the enumeration of the particular classes of commerce to which the power was to be extended, would not have been made, had the intention been to extend the power to every description. The enumeration presupposes something not enumerated; and that something, if we regard the language or the subject of the sentence, must be the exclusively internal commerce of a State.

The passage gives a quite different sense of the commerce clause's scope than the one that Tribe suggests. It is hard to find in the phrase "commerce which concerns more States than one" a total jurisdiction over all commercial activity, especially when the phrase is preceded by the word "restricted." Quite the opposite; it looks as though Chief Justice Marshall wanted only to refute the argument (see his first sentence quoted) that interstate commerce can only take place on the narrow boundary between the two states. Such a position, if carried into law, would have rendered the commerce clause a dead letter. Commerce between two states, or among many, must take place physically within the confines of one or both of them. It is therefore the nature of a transaction, rather than its location, that stamps it as part of interstate commerce. Navigation between states takes place at one instant in one state, and at another instant in another. Both portions of the journey are covered by the commerce clause, even if purely intrastate navigation is excluded. The power may be plenary, but it is surely limited as to its objects. Matters outside its scope are fully reserved to the states. Chief Justice Marshall did write, as Tribe suggests, of the "plenary" nature of the commerce power. But again his words must be set in context. Chief Justice Marshall thus wrote: "This power, like all others vested in Congress, is complete in itself, may be exercised to its utmost extent, and acknowledges no limitations other than are prescribed in the constitution." But he continued:

> If, as has always been understood, the sovereignty of Congress, though limited to specified objects, is plenary as to those objects, the power over commerce with foreign nations, and among the several states, is vested in Congress as absolutely as it would be in a single government, having in its constitution the same restrictions on the exercise of the power as are found in the constitution of the United States.

It follows therefore that "plenary" powers were understood by Chief Justice Marshall to be wholly consistent with powers "limited to specified objects."

This view is, moreover, reinforced when we take into account Chief Justice Marshall's own principles of construction, which should give caution to advocates of both judicial restraint and judicial activism. His attitude was essentially that the Constitution should be construed in its "natural sense." He was rightly suspicious of any effort to impose principles of "strict construction," but by the same token did not wish to give words an extravagant meaning given their function and purpose within the framework of the Constitution. He followed a middle course on the issue of construction, that of ordinary meaning, no different from that which a good contracts judge follows when he attaches ordinary meaning to contractual provisions. Even with an explicit reference to the necessary and proper clause, Chief Justice Marshall acknowledged that the commerce clause was itself directed toward specific ends, as was captured by the distinction between "internal" and "external" commerce, where internal commerce was that trade "between man and man in a State, or between different parts of the same State." By that definition internal commerce is as commonplace in our own time as it was in Marshall's: every purchase at a supermarket is internal commerce, even if the market itself acquired its own goods from a supplier out of state.

Nor is this balance between internal and external commerce undone because Chief Justice Marshall used the word "affects" to round out the scope of Congress' power. Those references to activities that "affect" interstate commerce cannot be read in isolation from the rest of the text, as an effort to nullify the basic doctrine of enumerated powers. Instead, his purpose was to counter prior contentions about the scope of internal commerce. . . .

Further elaboration of Chief Justice Marshall's meaning appeared elsewhere in his opinion. At one point he addressed whether the states could pass inspection laws, or whether these laws fell solely within the domain of the congressional commerce power. He finessed that question by giving a very narrow definition of what interstate commerce included:

> That inspection laws may have a remote and considerable influence on commerce, will not be denied; but that a power to regulate commerce is the source from which the right to pass them is derived, cannot be admitted. The object of inspection laws, is to improve the quality of articles produced by the labour of a country; to fit them for exportation; or, it may be,

for domestic use. They act upon the subject before it becomes an article of foreign commerce, or of commerce among the States, and prepare it for that purpose.

It is instructive to compare this passage with the most famous sentence of *E.C. Knight*, which has been cited as a sign of its narrow and indefensible rigidity: "Commerce succeeds to manufacture, and is not a part of it." Chief Justice Marshall himself could have written that sentence, citing *Gibbons* as authority. His style was anything but "empirical," if that term is used to identify the necessary economic connection between intrastate and interstate commerce. Indeed the passage just quoted is wholly inconsistent with the indirect burden on interstate commerce approach taken in the modern law. Chief Justice Marshall's greatness rests upon his appreciation of the boundaries which should dominate the constitutional playing field. Individual cases may fall close to the boundary lines, and must be placed on one side or the other. Yet the position of the boundary lines must remain fixed if the power to adjudicate is to remain. Things cannot be partly in and partly out of interstate commerce. As long as one government or the other must regulate, the boundaries must be sharp—such as the foul lines in baseball—and not fuzzy. It has been said that modern constitutional law represents the triumph of "formalism" over "realism." If this is true, then Chief Justice Marshall was the great formalist, not the precursor of the modern realists.

* * *

B. The Expansion of Commerce Clause Jurisdiction

[The] expansion of the affirmative power [took] place along three separate lines. The first line took its cue from the narrow holding of *Gibbons* that navigation counted as commerce under the clause, and concerned the "instrumentalities of commerce." This Article follows the expansion of the clause, briefly in connection with navigable waterways, and more extensively with the systematic and inexorable expansion of the federal power to regulate the railroads under the Interstate Commerce Act of 1887, as amended.

The second line of cases involved the regulation of goods admittedly in interstate commerce (that is, goods in transit across state lines) in order to control the primary conduct of persons in either the sending or receiving state. This line of cases might be called the "indirect regulation" cases. The third line of cases, emanating from *E.C. Knight* itself, explored the distinction between manufacture and commerce among the several states.

Between 1870 and 1937 the scope of federal power under these three lines of case law continued to expand, but in ways that still left an extensive area of economic life outside the power of Congress. In particular, the distinction between manufacture and commerce laid down in *E.C. Knight* in 1895 retained its validity until it was at last overturned in 1937 by *NLRB v. Jones & Laughlin Steel Corp.* In general the expansion of the first and second heads of the commerce power fall within the general scheme set out by Chief Justice Marshall in *Gibbons* in that they address both the power of Congress to regulate the means by which goods are shipped in interstate commerce, as well as the types of goods that can be shipped. In my judgment, the scope of the federal power under these two heads moved, prior to 1937, a step or two beyond where proper argument would take them. But although these difficult cases can be argued at the margin, nothing in the case law under these two heads undermined the essential validity of the line between commerce, on the one hand, and manufacture and agriculture on the other, clearly adumbrated in *Gibbons* and accepted in *E.C. Knight*. It is only when that last distinction is rejected that a system of enumerated powers is dismantled. Yet there is no conceptual necessity for saying that power to regulate commerce among the several states must reach everything if it is to reach anything. The modern generation of negative commerce clause cases is instructive because it proves that it is possible, and sensible, to articulate an enduring conception of interstate commerce—just as Chief Justice Marshall had insisted.

* * *

V. THE NEW DEAL TRANSFORMATION OF THE COMMERCE CLAUSE

The New Deal [expansion] of federal power [is] better understood, but hardly justified, as a response to two separate but related forces. First, the 1936 Roosevelt mandate and the prospect of court packing could hardly have been lost on the Court. Second, a narrow majority of the Court was in sympathy with the dominant intellectual belief of the time that national problems required national responses. The New Deal cases worked a revolution in constitutional theory as well as in textual interpretation. The original theory of the Constitution was based on the belief that government was not an unrequited good, but was at best a necessary evil. The system of enumerated powers allowed state governments to compete among themselves, thus limiting the risks of governmental abuse even absent explicit, substantive limitations on the laws that states could pass. The various limitations upon the federal power helped achieve this end. The New Deal conception, on the other hand, saw no virtue in competition, whether between states or between firms. The old barriers were stripped away; in their place has emerged the vast and unwarranted concentration of power in Congress that remains the hallmark of the modern regulatory state.

The first major case to test the traditional analysis of the commerce clause was *NLRB v. Jones & Laughlin Steel Corp.*, which involved a challenge to the National Labor Relations Act (Wagner Act). The Wagner Act in essence removed employers' power to hire and fire at will, instead requiring extensive collective bargaining in good faith between employers and unions if the union is approved by a majority of employees. The unions were selected by a majority of workers, but had the power to bind workers who dissented. Individual contracts inconsistent with the master agreement were unenforceable, lest the union's power be undermined by dissatisfied workers.

The Wagner Act was based squarely upon the commerce clause. The draftsmen sought to meet the fundamental challenge of jurisdiction by providing that federal jurisdiction extended not only to cases of "commerce" but also to cases "affecting commerce": "The term 'affecting commerce' means in commerce, or burdening or obstructing commerce or the free flow of commerce, or having led or tending to lead to a labor dispute burdening or obstructing commerce or the free flow of commerce."

This extended definition proves that Congress used a legal fiction to expand federal jurisdiction beyond its original grant. The commerce clause does not say "Congress shall have the power to regulate commerce, and all matters affecting commerce with foreign nations, among the several states, and with the Indian tribes." The statutory text, moreover, invited a favorable outcome on the jurisdictional question by smuggling into its expanded definition of commerce the desirable effects that the labor statute was intended to achieve. Yet there was no real evidence that local regulation of employment markets was incapable of achieving desired economic goals. It was only the distinct New Deal bias for worker monopolies protected by explicit barriers to entry (here, against rival workers who would work for less) that could have led to the conclusion that the Wagner Act would improve the free flow of commerce.

How cartelization of labor markets would remove barriers or obstructions to interstate commerce has never been explained. Labor cartelization generally raises the level of wages and reduces the quantity of goods produced. When a cartel is legally protected against new entrants into its market, the new entrants are no longer able to take advantage of the price "umbrella" that an unregulated cartel necessarily creates for enterprising rivals. The Wagner Act surely had an effect on commerce, and that effect was negative.

A system of limited government keeps local governments in competition with each other. This sensible institutional arrangement was wholly undermined by Congress' decision, in the teeth of the commerce clause, to subject all employment markets to nationally uniform regulation. As in the case of child labor laws, the power of states to impose collective bargaining requirements on firms is effectively limited by the ability of old firms to leave the state and of new ones not to enter it. Also, since domestic firms can escape whatever misguided tariff barriers may be thrown up against international suppliers of goods and services, the level of state regulation is effectively curtailed, and the volume of goods and services in commerce increases.

The transformation in legislative and judicial thinking about the commerce clause is revealed by the reversal in substantive outcomes. *Gibbons v. Ogden* ensured free trade by overturning a state-granted legal monopoly. The Sherman Act cases were also directed against private monopolies—a lesser peril—which were seen improperly as "regulating" interstate commerce. Both *Gibbons* and the Sherman Act cases were attempts to facilitate free trade in open markets—one at the constitutional, the other at the statutory, level. With the later expansion of congressional jurisdiction by such laws as the Transportation Act of 1920, however, the commerce clause became an instrument to suppress competition, rather than one to further it. It is only if one thinks that government can neutrally determine when there is too much competition as well as when there is too little that the broader interpretation of the commerce power becomes plausible. And it is clear that the New Deal thinkers thought they understood the vices of competition.

It is always, however, a precarious venture for judges to make independent normative judgments about the desirability of certain social arrangements when passing on the constitutionality of certain acts. In a sense, the task of interpretation should depend, as Chief Justice Marshall did in *Gibbons v. Ogden*, on the natural and ordinary sense of the word. The approach also leads, however, to the conclusion that the Wagner Act goes beyond the scope of the commerce clause under the authority of *E.C. Knight* and, most notably, *Carter*. The three decisions of the United States Courts of Appeals that passed upon the Wagner Act declared it unconstitutional by applying the precedents mechanically. Recall that the hard question in *E.C. Knight* was whether prospective restraints of trade in interstate markets could justify an intrusion into manufacture, an area normally regulated by the states. *Jones & Laughlin*, of course, involved no effort to monopolize an interstate market. Quite the opposite; the contracts at issue concerned only matters of local employment which, as the Court's opinion in *Carter* had confirmed, had never been thought a federal matter under any prior conception of the commerce clause.

To respond to this difficulty, the Court in *Jones & Laughlin* resurrected the losing argument of *Carter*—that anything which had a substantial effect upon interstate commerce could be regulated regardless of its source. In so doing, the Court in effect borrowed the language of those cases concerned with the instrumentalities of interstate commerce and applied it generally, as if the original subject-matter restriction had not been integral to the earlier decisions. Manufacture was no longer distinguishable from commerce, because the manufacturing process involved "a great movement of iron ore, coal and limestone along well-defined paths to the steel mills, thence through them, and thence in the form of steel products into the consuming centers of the country—a definite and well-understood course of business."

To be sure, Chief Justice Hughes acknowledged in *Jones & Laughlin* that some "internal concerns" of the state remained outside the power of Congress to regulate. But it was all lip service; the companion cases to *Jones & Laughlin* showed that the "internal concerns of a state" had become an empty vessel. *NLRB v. Fruehauf Co.* applied the Wagner Act to a manufacturer of commercial trailers that obtained more than fifty percent of its material out of state and sold eighty percent of its output to out-of-state customers. *NLRB v. Friedman-Harry Marks Clothing Co.* used the same logic, applying the statute to a clothing manufacturer that purchased most of its raw cloth out of state, and sold a majority of its finished garments there as well. The commerce clause was thus hardly limited to the integrated multistate firms like *Jones & Laughlin*. And beneath the legal analysis lay the ultimate policy reason for the decisions: Congress and the NLRB believed that industry-wide unionizations could not succeed without federal assistance, and the Court accepted this belief, and the desirability of the substantive conclusion, at face value.

The cases that followed *Jones & Laughlin* continued to sustain the power of the federal government to regulate interstate commerce expansively, on the ground that any competition among states necessarily restricted the scope of government action. The government's argument in *United States v. Darby* in defense of the Fair Labor Standards Act (FLSA), for example, was essentially identical to that made unsuccessfully a generation before in *Hammer v. Dagenhart*:

> No State, acting alone, could require labor standards substantially higher than those obtaining in other States whose producers and manufacturers competed in the interstate market. Employers with lower labor standards possess an unfair advantage in interstate competition, and only the national government can deal with the problem.

The Court's unanimous decision upholding the FLSA accepted the substantive case for the statute at face value, and regarded the FLSA as essentially public interest rather than interest-group legislation. Arguments in favor of *Hammer's* limits on federal power were curtly dismissed: "The motive and purpose of a regulation of interstate commerce are matters for the legislative judgment upon the exercise of which the Constitution places no restriction and over which the courts are given no control."

There remained only the question whether federal power extended to those goods of local manufacture which were not shipped in interstate commerce. In this regard Justice Stone cited the Shreveport Rate Case to support the proposition that a "familiar like exercise of power is the regulation of intrastate transactions which are so commingled with or related to interstate commerce that all must be regulated if the interstate commerce is to be effectively controlled." Justice Stone omitted any reference to the desire to fight local discrimination against interstate commerce that was so critical to the earlier decision, or to any recognition that the Shreveport Rate Case did not apply to all "intrastate transactions" but only to the "instrumentalities" of interstate commerce—in particular to interstate railroad operations. Nor did Justice Stone acknowledge that the Shreveport Rate Case never challenged the distinction between commerce and manufacture defended in *E.C. Knight*. Justice Holmes in his *Hammer* dissent defending federal authority still recognized that some manufacture was part of the purely internal commerce of the state. Yet such was the strength of the federal tide that Justice Stone abandoned that vestige of state autonomy in *Darby*. The question of state autonomy, so critical to *E.C. Knight*, also received back-of-the-hand treatment in *Darby*; the Court brushed aside the tenth amendment, and the principle of enumerated powers that it articulated, as "but a truism that all is retained which has not been surrendered."

Justice Stone's cavalier treatment of jurisdictional objections to the FLSA resulted from his powerful belief in the soundness of the basic social legislation involved. To him, the suppression of "unfair" competition from exploited labor was the dominant "evil" the FLSA attacked. The possibility that the minimum wage law could be a barrier to the entry of unskilled labor into the labor market, and hence the very evil to be avoided, was never assessed. What failed in *Darby* was not the language of the Constitution, but the willingness of the Justices to accept the theory of limited government upon which it rested.

The same failure was repeated in cases that sustained the powerful system of agricultural price supports and acreage restrictions that was introduced by the New Deal. The question in *United States v. Wrightwood Dairy* was whether Congress could authorize the Secretary of Agriculture to set minimum prices for milk that was produced and consumed within a single state. The usual language which spoke of a transaction "which directly burdens, obstructs, or affects, interstate or foreign commerce in such commodity or product thereof," was duly set out in the statutory language. Ironically, the anticompetitive effect of federal interstate milk regulation became the justification for a further expansion of federal power:

> As the court below recognized, and as seems not to be disputed, the marketing of intrastate milk which competes with that shipped interstate would tend seriously to break down price regulation of the latter. Under the conditions prevailing in the milk industry, as the record shows, the unregulated sale of the intrastate milk tends to reduce the sales price received by handlers and the amount which they in turn pay to producers.

Even after *Wrightwood* plugged the loophole of intrastate sales, another obstacle remained to comprehensive federal agricultural regulation. Farmers could still influence the price of agricultural products in interstate commerce simply by keeping and using them on their own farms. The scope of agricultural regulation expanded to meet this challenge. *Wickard v. Filburn* upheld the statutory authority of the Secretary of Agriculture to limit the consumption of wheat on the very farms that grew it. Here there was no sale transaction at all, but this did not matter to the Court. The government's ability to maintain artificially high regulated prices for goods shipped across interstate lines would surely have been compromised if local consumption had been allowed to expand supply to meet demand. The economic interdependence of the various activities was held to preclude any watertight division between production and commerce. The Court regarded the distinction between direct and indirect effects on interstate commerce as quite beside the point (as indeed it was), and the entire issue of enumerated powers and state autonomy disappeared from view. Once the Court decided to ignore the limitations of the *Shreveport Rate Case*, it saw *Wickard* as a natural extension of the *Shreveport Rate Case* doctrine. This is just the approach that Justice Jackson took:

> The opinion of Mr. Justice Hughes found federal intervention constitutionally authorized because of matters having such a close and substantial relation to interstate traffic that the control is essential or appropriate to the security of that traffic, to the efficiency of the interstate service, and to the maintenance of conditions under which interstate

commerce may be conducted upon fair terms and without molestation or hindrance.

Carefully excised from the quotation was the beginning of Justice Hughes's sentence: "[Congress'] authority, extending to these interstate carriers as instruments of interstate commerce, necessarily embraces the right to control their operations in all [matters]." This excision, doubtless deliberate, completed the transformation of the commerce clause.

The question then arises as to how is it possible to stand a clause of the Constitution upon its head. I do not think that the explanation comes from any vagueness in the language of the commerce clause. If a Court innocent of political theory or of any predeliction on the merits of the underlying legislation approached a commerce case, it could not possibly parse the words of the clause so as to reach the extravagant interpretations of federal power accepted in *Jones & Laughlin, Darby, Wrightwood*, and *Wickard*. Could anyone say with a straight face that the consumption of homegrown wheat is "commerce among the several states"? A powerful principle must have led to so fanciful a conclusion. That principle has to go to the idea of what kind of government and social organization is thought to be just and proper for society at large.

I have no doubt that the Justices of the Supreme Court who forged so powerful a doctrine had such a conception in mind. At one level they rejected the idea of limited federal government and decentralized power. That idea only made sense if there was a risk that governments could misbehave. If it was thought that they always acted in the public interest, then any effort to deny them substantive power would have hobbled the forces of virtue and enhanced those of wickedness. It is noticeable that all the key New Deal commerce clause opinions took the substantive findings of Congress at face value. None was prepared to identify the powerful interest group politics that were so evident in both the labor and agricultural cases—the very policy areas in which the commerce clause reached its present scope. Once government is thought to be the source of risk, however, then competition between governments makes sense, and there is good reason to uphold the ideas of limited government and enumerated federal powers that were part of the original design. The New Deal's change in attitude toward the commerce clause thus depended upon a radical reorientation of judicial views toward the role of government that in the end overwhelmed the relatively clean lines of the commerce clause.

In addition, the key federal laws of the New Deal cartelized either labor or product markets that would otherwise have been highly competitive absent government regulation. Indeed, there were substantive challenges to each of these laws, usually under the due process clause. These developments were not unrelated, for jurisdictional limitations upon the power of Congress only made sense if there was reason to think that use of the power would have been harmful. Yet once the idea that markets performed useful functions was cast aside, the jurisdictional limitations ceased to make any sense. The war cry became a call for Congress to act because, in an age of economic interdependence, national problems demanded national solutions.

Yet the point about economic interdependence mistakes the disease for the cure. It is precisely because markets are interdependent that there is reason to fear comprehensive federal regulation. Competitive markets are the best way to allocate scarce goods and services. They promise to bring price into line with the marginal cost of production, and they hold out some hope that all the possible gains from trade will be achieved by voluntary transactions. Markets are not just a good in themselves. They are powerful instruments for human happiness and well-being.

Legal monopolies have precisely the opposite effect. They raise price above marginal cost and they prevent many voluntary transactions from taking place, so that the total social output is reduced by the deadweight loss that they cause. Worse still, the ability to obtain legal protection against competition invites individuals and groups to spend valuable resources in order to obtain (or resist obtaining) economic rents. Even though no market is an ideal competitive market, there is absolutely no reason to impose economic regulations, such as minimum price laws or cartelization of labor markets, whose only effect is to drive quantity and price further from the competitive equilibrium. When viewed from this perspective, the Wagner Act, the Fair Labor Standards Act, and the Agricultural Marketing Acts appear to be long-standing social disasters that could not long have survived with their present vigor solely at the state level.

There is a dangerous tendency to assume that competitive injury and physical injury form part of a seamless web, so that the power to regulate the one necessarily confers the authority to regulate the other. It is as though the power to protect interstate commerce against robbers and thieves is sufficient warrant for the far more extensive social controls that treat competitive activities undertaken within different states, when the social consequences of violence and competition are so radically different. The ability to conceive of competitive injury as a justification for the exercise of federal power lies at the root of all the modern commerce clause decisions. The ability to perceive the essential difference between violence and competition is all that is needed to respect the limitation on federal power that is implicit in the commerce clause.

VI. CONCLUSION

[Hamilton] may not have had it all correct when he said that sound limitations on government jurisdiction obviated the need for a bill of rights. But he was surely correct when he said that the maintenance of those jurisdictional limitations is one essential bulwark to sound constitutional government.

The problem of sovereignty remains: How do the people compel the holders of governmental monopoly power to act as though they could only obtain a competitive return for their services? Federalism facilitates a solution by allowing easy exit, as well as by allowing voice. National regulation prevents unhealthy types of competition among jurisdictions, such as were present in *Gibbons*. Under this view, the old construction of the commerce clause makes sense; it facilitates national markets by preventing state balkanization. This was the achievement of *Gibbons*. The great peril of national regulation is that it may be taken too far, to impose national uniformity which frustrates, rather than facilitates markets. This was the New Deal. I cannot help thinking that a sound view of the commerce clause is one that returns to *Gibbons*. The affirmative scope of the commerce power should be limited to those matters that today are governed by the dormant commerce clause: interstate transportation, navigation and sales, and the activities closely incident to them. All else should be left to the states.

I realize that this conclusion seems radical because of the way the clock has turned. One is hesitant to require dismantling of large portions of the modern federal government, given the enormous reliance interests that have been created. And I do not have, nor do I know of anyone who has, a good theory that explains when it is appropriate to correct past errors that have become embedded in the legal system. It is far easier to keep power from the hands of government officials than it is to wrest it back from them once it has been conferred. We had our chance with the commerce clause, and we have lost it.

Still, the argument from principle seems clear enough, even if one is left at a loss as to what should be done about it. And in a sense that is just the point. Congress and the courts can proceed merrily on their way if they are convinced that the basis for an extensive federal commerce power is rooted firmly in the original constitutional text or structure. But uneasiness necessarily creeps into the legislative picture if, as I have argued, the commerce clause is far narrower in scope than modern courts have held. There is a powerful tension between the legacy of the past fifty years and the original constitutional understanding. It is a tension that we must face, even if we cannot resolve it.

Honorable Vincent A. Cirillo & Jay W. Eisenhofer, *Reflections on the Congressional Commerce Power*, 60 TEMPLE L. REV. 901 (1987)*

[O]ur national political scene has witnessed a ferocious debate over growing federal government. Huge budget deficits have resulted, in part, from the public's desire to maintain public services without a parallel commitment to fund these services. Recently, congressional opponents of the mounting deficits have imposed an automatic limit on spending. Nevertheless, the most effective check on spending may exist in the text of the Constitution itself. Indeed, because much of the growth of the federal government has been pursuant to the commerce clause, a more restrictive reading of that clause may aid in limiting governmental growth and federal deficits.

[A] more appropriate commerce clause doctrine would impose a two-part test based on Chief Justice Marshall's view of limited federal power. First, Congress could continue to exercise its plenary power over interstate movements and shipments by directly regulating the terms and conditions of those movements. Second, Congress may regulate activity that is not itself interstate commerce provided its objective is to correct a problem in the interstate commercial marketplace. However, because the regulation of intrastate activity to effectuate regulation of interstate commerce is an implied use of power under the necessary and proper clause, Congress may exercise such power only to further a permissible end.

This is the test proposed by Chief Justice Marshall in *McCulloch*: an implied use of an enumerated power for a purpose not associated with that power is unconstitutional. Chief Justice Marshall reasoned that because the necessary and proper clause gave Congress implied authority to implement the enumerated powers, only protection against pretextual use can prevent those powers from expanding beyond their proper scope.

This theory is consistent with the text, structure, and history of the Constitution. It would allow Congress sufficient flexibility to solve national economic problems, and the constitutional concern for local interests would be well protected because the return of enumerated power to Congress would also mean the revival of nonenumerated and reserved power to the states.

The most difficult issue raised by a test focusing on congressional purpose involves the determination whether the purpose is commercial in nature. In most cases, however, economic matters are distinguishable from social, health, and safety concerns. Moreover, the Supreme Court has endorsed an analysis of legislative motives in other contexts.

Critics also argue that the legislature may simply reenact the law based on a "sham" legislative record reflecting the judicially approved goals. Courts will only invalidate legislation, however, if it is clear that its dominant goal is noncommercial. Reenactment would not camouflage the legislature's noncommercial purpose.

The most alarming aspect of this proposed commerce clause doctrine would be its impact on our current national government. There are legions of agencies, laws, and activities that might immediately become grounded on unconstitutional legislation. Could the federal government, under the commerce clause, regulate workplace safety or plant emissions? Would it be able to prosecute local Mafia chieftains whose crimes do not contain an interstate element? Could the federal government continue its vast array of social programs, from Social Security to welfare to food stamps?

Viewed from another perspective, these inquiries reflect just how far the Supreme Court has allowed Congress to stray from the constitutional scheme of limited, enumerated power. The drastic dislocation necessary to restore this scheme is a testament to the Court's overbroad reading of the commerce clause. Moreover, the suggested approach is feasible. Because it is the only way to realistically reconcile the various policies underlying the commerce clause, the supremacy of federal power, federalism and enumerated powers, the difficulties should be addressed and challenged, not avoided.

Russell L. Weaver, Lopez *and the Federalization of Criminal Law*, 98 W. VA. L. REV. 815 (1996)*

[In] *United States v. Lopez*, for the first time in nearly six decades, the judiciary reasserted itself. In that case, the Court struck down the Gun Free School Zones Act (Gun Free Schools Act) as applied to a student who brought a gun to school. The Court held that Congress had exceeded its power under the Commerce Clause. *Lopez* set off a storm of controversy. One commentator described *Lopez* as "one of the opening cannonades in the coming constitutional revolution." Another stated that "[t]he *Lopez* holding, even as cautiously explained by Chief Justice Rehnquist [is], as Justice John P. Stevens says in dissent, 'radical.' There is no other way to reverse nearly 60 years of total deference to Congress on the meaning of the commerce clause."

Was *Lopez* "one of the opening cannonades in the coming constitutional revolution?" Undoubtedly, *Lopez* marks the end of an era of extreme deference to legislative determinations, but will it lead to an avalanche of decisions striking down federal statutes, and does it signal a return to pre-1937 Commerce Clause jurisprudence? In fact, *Lopez* ends a period of extreme deference to legislative judgments, but the decision's ramifications may be less profound than many initially thought.

II. THE HOLDING

Justice Rehnquist delivered the Court's decision, and sought to portray the Court's holding as decidedly unrevolutionary. The opinion did not explicitly overrule or overtly question the Court's post-'37 Commerce Clause precedent. On the contrary,

---

*   Reprinted with permission.

the opinion embraced that precedent and strived to characterize its holding as consistent with that precedent:

> *Jones & Laughlin Steel*, *Darby*, and *Wickard* ushered in an era of Commerce Clause jurisprudence that greatly expanded the previously defined authority of Congress under that Clause. In part, this was a recognition of the great changes that had occurred in the way business was carried on in this country. Enterprises that had once been local or at most regional in nature had become national in scope. But the doctrinal change also reflected a view that earlier Commerce Clause cases artificially had constrained the authority of Congress to regulate interstate commerce.
>
> But even these modern-era precedents which have expanded congressional power under the Commerce Clause confirm that this power is subject to outer limits. In *Jones & Laughlin Steel*, the Court warned that the scope of the interstate commerce power "must be considered in the light of our dual system of government and may not be extended so as to embrace effects upon interstate commerce so indirect and remote that to embrace them, in view of our complex society, would effectually obliterate the distinction between what is national and what is local and create a completely centralized government." [Since] that time, the Court has heeded that warning and undertaken to decide whether a rational basis existed for concluding that a regulated activity sufficiently affected interstate commerce.

Of course, in terms of result, the opinion was decidedly revolutionary. For nearly six decades, the Court had virtually rubberstamped congressionally-passed commercial legislation, including criminal legislation, enacted under the Commerce Clause. In *Lopez*, the Court articulated Madisonian themes regarding the scope of federal power. The opinion characterized the Constitution as creating a government of limited, enumerated, powers. And, specifically quoting James Madison, the Court flatly stated that "[t]he powers delegated by the proposed Constitution to the federal government are few and defined. Those which are to remain in the state governments are numerous and indefinite." Then for the first time in over half a century, the Court seriously reviewed a federal statute to see whether Congress had exceeded its commerce power. The Court articulated three situations in which congressional regulation of commerce is permissible:

> [W]e have identified three broad categories of activity that Congress may regulate under its commerce [power]. First, Congress may regulate the use of the channels of interstate [commerce]. Second, Congress is empowered to regulate and protect the instrumentalities of interstate commerce, or persons or things in interstate commerce, even though the threat may come only from intrastate [activities]. Finally, Congress' commerce authority includes the power to regulate those activities having a substantial relation to interstate commerce, *i.e.*, those activities that substantially affect interstate [commerce].

The Court concluded that Section 922(q) did not fit within any of the three situations:

> We now turn to consider the power of Congress, in the light of this framework, to enact § 922(q). The first two categories of authority may be quickly disposed of: § 922(q) is not a regulation of the use of the channels

of interstate commerce, nor is it an attempt to prohibit the interstate transportation of a commodity through the channels of commerce; nor can § 922(q) be justified as a regulation by which Congress has sought to protect an instrumentality of interstate commerce or a thing in interstate commerce. Thus, if § 922(q) is to be sustained, it must be under the third category as a regulation of an activity that substantially affects interstate commerce.

[W]e have upheld a wide variety of congressional Acts regulating intrastate economic activity where we have concluded that the activity substantially affected interstate [commerce].

[Section] 922(q) is a criminal statute that by its terms has nothing to do with "commerce" or any sort of economic enterprise, however broadly one might define those terms. Section 922(q) is not an essential part of a larger regulation of economic activity, in which the regulatory scheme could be undercut unless the intrastate activity were regulated. It cannot, therefore, be sustained under our cases upholding regulations of activities that arise out of or are connected with a commercial transaction, which viewed in the aggregate, substantially affects interstate commerce.

The Court might have upheld the law had the statute contained a jurisdictional provision requiring that the firearm possession in question affected interstate commerce. But the law contained no such provision. The Court might also have upheld the law had Congress made explicit findings regarding the effect of gun possession in a school zone on interstate commerce. But, as the Court noted, "to the extent that congressional findings would enable us to evaluate the legislative judgment that the activity in question substantially affected interstate commerce, even though no such substantial effect was visible to the naked eye, they are lacking here."

The opinion then expressed specific concerns about the scope of federal power. The Court rejected the notion that guns in schools have a definite impact on "national productivity." The Court noted that, if Congress were free to regulate in this case, it would be free to regulate virtually all aspects of the educational process and society:

[U]nder the Government's "national productivity" reasoning, Congress could regulate any activity that it found was related to the economic productivity of individual citizens: family law (including marriage, divorce, and child custody), for example. Under the theories that the Government presents in support of § 922(q), it is difficult to perceive any limitation on federal power, even in areas such as criminal law enforcement or education where States historically have been sovereign. Thus, if we were to accept the Government's arguments, we are hard-pressed to posit any activity by an individual that Congress is without power to regulate.

To uphold the Government's contentions here, we would have to pile inference upon inference in a manner that would bid fair to convert congressional authority under the Commerce Clause to a general police power of the sort retained by the [States].

If that were to happen, then the distinction between "national" and "local" activities would disappear.

Although Justice Rehnquist tried to portray his opinion as consistent with the Court's modern Commerce Clause decisions, his result and approach were strikingly inconsistent with those decisions. In its modern precedent, the Court had reviewed commercial legislation under a rational basis analysis. As the Court stated in *Katzenbach v. McClung*, "where we find that the legislators, in light of the facts and testimony before them, have a rational basis for finding a chosen regulatory scheme necessary to the protection of commerce, our investigation is at an end." If the Court had applied the rational basis test to the Gun Free Schools Act, it would have been forced to sustain that Act. Justice Breyer made this point in his dissent: Congress had the power to pass the Act "as this Court has understood [Congress' Commerce Clause power] over the last half-century."

Justice Breyer construed that precedent as giving Congress the right to "regulate local activities insofar as they significantly affect interstate commerce," and as requiring the Court to "give Congress a degree of leeway in determining the existence of a significant factual connection between the regulated activity and interstate commerce." Justice Breyer characterized this deferential approach as requiring affirmance if Congress' determinations had a "rational basis." Justice Breyer then sought to demonstrate that Congress had a rational basis for concluding that the presence of guns in a school zone affects commerce:

> [N]umerous reports and studies—generated both inside and outside government—make clear that Congress could reasonably have found the empirical connection that its law, implicitly or explicitly, [asserts].
>
> Having found that guns in schools significantly undermine the quality of education in our Nation's classrooms, Congress could also have found, given the effect of education upon interstate and foreign commerce, that gun-related violence in and around schools is a commercial, as well as a human, problem. Education, although far more than a matter of economics, has long been inextricably intertwined with the Nation's [economy].
>
> The economic links I have just sketched seem fairly obvious. Why then is it not equally obvious, in light of those links, that a widespread, serious, and substantial physical threat to teaching and learning also substantially threatens the commerce to which that teaching and learning is inextricably tied? That is to say, guns in the hands of six percent of inner-city high school students and gun-related violence throughout a city's schools must threaten the trade and commerce that those schools support. The only question, then, is whether the latter threat is (to use the majority's terminology) "substantial." And, the evidence of (1) the extent of the gun-related violence problem, (2) the extent of the resulting negative effect on classroom learning and (3) the extent of the consequent negative commercial effects, when taken together, indicate a threat to trade and commerce that is "substantial." At the very least, Congress could rationally have concluded that the links are "substantial."

Justice Breyer argued that the Gun Free Schools Act did not transgress the boundaries between state and federal authority, and concluded by arguing that "[u]pholding this legislation would do no more than simply recognize that Congress had a rational basis for finding a significant connection between guns in or near schools and (through their effect on education) the interstate and foreign commerce they [threaten]."

Mr. Justice Stevens, who also dissented, agreed that the Court's recent precedent required affirmance of Congress' determinations. In his view, "Congress has ample power to prohibit the possession of firearms in or near schools—just as it may protect the school environment from harms posed by controlled substances such as asbestos or alcohol."

III. LOPEZ'S IMPLICATIONS FOR THE FUTURE

What are *Lopez's* implications for the future? Does that decision signal a radical restructuring of the Court's Commerce Clause jurisprudence?

A. *Lopez* in the Supreme Court

In the short term, *Lopez* is unlikely to have cataclysmic effect, and certainly does not signal a return to pre-1937 Commerce Clause jurisprudence. The decision was rendered by a fragmented court which produced two concurring opinions (Justices Kennedy and Thomas with O'Connor concurring in Kennedy's opinion), and three dissenting opinions joined by four justices (Justices Stevens, Souter and Breyer with Stevens, Souter and Ginsberg joining Breyer's opinion). Several members of the Court expressed concern about the potential consequences of a radical shift in the Court's Commerce Clause jurisprudence. Justice Kennedy supported the Court's result but felt compelled to issue a concurring opinion urging the Court "not to call in question the essential principles now in place respecting the congressional power to regulate transactions of a commercial nature." Justice Kennedy noted:

> [The] fundamental restraint [of stare decisis forecloses] us from reverting to an understanding of commerce that would serve only an 18th-century economy, dependent then upon production and trading practices that had changed but little over the preceding centuries; it also mandates against returning to the time when congressional authority to regulate undoubted commercial activities was limited by a judicial determination that those matters had an insufficient connection to an interstate system. Congress can regulate in the commercial sphere on the assumption that we have a single market and a unified purpose to build a stable national economy.

He joined the Court's opinion only because he felt that Congress had gone too far, and had intruded on state power.

Other justices also counseled restraint including dissenting Justices Breyer and Souter. Although not a swing vote, Justice Souter's dissent expressly invoked the specter of the 1930s' constitutional crisis. He reminded the Court of the "chastening experiences" which led the Court to repudiate "an earlier and untenably expansive conception of judicial review in derogation of congressional commerce power." And he expressed concern that the majority's decision "tugs the Court off course, leading it to suggest opportunities for further developments that would be at odds with the rule of restraint to which the Court still wisely states adherence." Justice Souter then traced the history of the Commerce Clause noting that "the period from the turn of the century to 1937 is better noted for a series of cases applying highly formalistic notions of 'commerce' to invalidate federal social and economic [legislation]." In Justice Souter's view, the Gun Free Schools Act passed muster under the Court's more recent precedent and did not improperly infringe the scope of state authority. Justice Souter also argued that the Court's tendency to apply rational basis review in Commerce Clause cases constitutes "a paradigm of judicial restraint" and "reflects our respect for the institutional competence of the Congress on a subject expressly assigned to it by the Constitution and our appreciation of the legitimacy that comes from Congress's political accountability in dealing with matters open to a wide range of possible choices."

Thus, six justices expressed concern for stare decisis. And, although Justices Kennedy and O'Connor joined in the Court's judgment, they argued for a more moderate application of *Lopez*'s holding. Only one justice, Justice Thomas, pushed for more sweeping changes in the Court's Commerce Clause jurisprudence, and his opinion was not joined by any other justice. Justice Thomas argued that the Court should undertake a review of the Court's precedent under the Commerce Clause:

> [O]ur case law has drifted far from the original understanding of the Commerce Clause. In a future case, we ought to temper our Commerce Clause jurisprudence in a manner that both makes sense of our more recent case law and is more faithful to the original understanding of that Clause.

He then urged the Court to return to a more historically justified approach to the Commerce Clause and the Tenth Amendment:

> [Our] cases all establish a simple point: from the time of the ratification of the Constitution to the mid-1930's, it was widely understood that the Constitution granted Congress only limited powers, notwithstanding the Commerce Clause. Moreover, there was no question that activities wholly separated from business, such as gun possession, were beyond the reach of the commerce power. If anything, the "wrong turn" was the Court's dramatic departure in the 1930's from a century and a half of precedent.

Justice Thomas took particular issue with the "substantial effects" test which he viewed as historically unjustified and as having permitted Congress to exercise sweeping power with few limits. He concluded by noting that "[a]t an appropriate juncture, I think we must modify our Commerce Clause jurisprudence. Today, it is easy enough to say that the Clause certainly does not empower Congress to ban gun possession within 1,000 feet of a school." In his view, this modification need not be "radical."

Thus far, at least, the Court has not been inclined to follow Justice Thomas' concurrence. In two post-*Lopez* actions, the Court had the chance to extend *Lopez* to other contexts and refused to do so. . . .

Even though *Lopez* did not overturn the Court's Commerce Clause jurisprudence, *Lopez* did produce a significant difference in the Court's approach to Commerce Clause issues. The deferential approach used in cases like *Katzenbach*, in which the Court applied rational basis review, was rejected by a substantial number of justices. Justice Rehnquist's first reference to the rational basis test was an historical reference. His second reference came when he responded to the government's argument "that Congress could rationally have concluded that § 922(q) substantially affects interstate commerce." When Rehnquist finally addressed the test head-on, he rejected it:

> Justice BREYER rejects our reading of precedent and argues that "Congress [could] rationally conclude that schools fall on the commercial side of the line." Again, Justice BREYER's rationale lacks any real limits because, depending on the level of generality, any activity can be looked upon as [commercial].

Thus, if Justice Rehnquist has his way, the era of blind deference to legislative determinations would be over.

What test replaces the rational basis test? Justice Rehnquist's opinion focuses on whether the regulated activity has a "substantial" relationship to interstate commerce. To the extent that Congress is not regulating the channels of interstate commerce themselves, or attempting to "regulate and protect the instrumentalities of interstate commerce, or persons or things in interstate commerce," Congress can only regulate when the activity being regulated has a "substantial relation" to interstate commerce. In *Lopez*, the Court struck down the Gun Free Schools Act because it found that

> the possession of a gun in a local school zone is in no sense an economic activity that might, through repetition elsewhere, substantially affect any sort of interstate commerce. Respondent was a local student at a local school; there is no indication that he had recently moved in interstate commerce, and there is no requirement that his possession of the firearm have any concrete tie to interstate commerce.

Although the *Lopez* decision may not result in a complete reversal of the Court's post-'37 precedent, or the invalidation of numerous federal statutes, that decision will likely force Congress to be more careful in exercising its Commerce Clause power. If Congress wishes to spare future legislation the same fate as the Gun Free Schools Act, it will need to provide more support in the form of a jurisdictional provision, requiring that an activity being criminalized affect interstate commerce, or in the form of specific findings regarding the effect of the activity on interstate commerce. If *Lopez* forces Congress to more carefully delineate its findings, the decision may have a healthy effect on the legislative process.

B. *Lopez* in the Lower Federal Courts

In the lower federal courts, *Lopez* generated a predictable avalanche of litigation challenging other federal statutes. Defendants eagerly embraced *Lopez* in the hope of avoiding prosecution or overturning a conviction. But these so-called "*Lopez* challenges" have not been well-received. The lower courts have upheld numerous federal criminal statutes prohibiting many different types of conduct: the non-payment of child support, the use or possession of weapons, possession of a firearm by a convicted felon, possession of firearms with obliterated serial numbers, possession of an unregistered destructive device, conspiracy to possess an unregistered firearm, possession or transfer of a machine gun, malicious destruction of property, the use of a residence located within 1000 feet of a secondary school for the distribution of cocaine and crack cocaine, possession of cocaine with intent to distribute, the obstruction of commerce, and aiding and abetting the manufacture of marijuana. In addition, the courts have upheld the Hobbs Act, the Drug Act, the federal carjacking statute, and the Freedom of Access to Clinic Entrances Act. In one case, a sheriff unsuccessfully tried to use *Lopez* to challenge the Brady Handgun Violence Prevention Act which required him to run background checks on those wishing to purchase handguns.

This response by the lower courts could have been predicted. Under the "modern view" of the Commerce Clause, which has been taught in law schools for decades, the idea of striking down a federal statute on the ground that Congress exceeded its authority under the Commerce Clause is a "radical" concept. When Congress passes legislation under the Commerce Clause, the courts are supposed to "defer" to rational legislative judgments. The *Lopez* decision, surprising as it was, did not break lower-court judges out of this mindset.

In a significant number of *Lopez* challenges, the lower courts summarily reject the challenge. Most of these decisions distinguish or limit *Lopez*. . . .

Even those courts that engage in more extended review of federal statutes tend to tread very carefully. . . .

IV. CONCLUSION

Whether *Lopez* will lead to an outright reversal of the Court's Commerce Clause precedent, and with it an end to the federalization of the criminal law, is far from clear. In any event, it seems unlikely that the Court will reverse that precedent in the short term. Only one justice (Justice Thomas) argued for a sweeping review of the Court's Commerce Clause precedent. Four justices dissented (Souter, Stevens, Ginsberg & Breyer), and two of the concurring justices (Kennedy & O'Connor) counseled restraint. As a result, absent a change in position or a shift in the Court's composition, a reversal seems unlikely.

In the short term, practical considerations virtually preclude the Court from radically altering its position on the Commerce Clause. Since the 1930s, Congress has used its commerce power to pass hundreds of commercial and criminal statutes. If the Court began overturning those statutes in quantity, the Court would cause an earthquake in the business and legal communities. Even Justice Thomas recognized this fact in his concurrence:

> Although I might be willing to return to the original understanding, I recognize that many believe that it is too late in the day to undertake a fundamental reexamination of the past 60 years. Considerations of stare decisis and reliance interests may convince us that we cannot wipe the slate clean.

As a result, it is not surprising that the lower federal courts have restrictively construed *Lopez*, and have not used that decision to strike down other federal statutes.

Nevertheless, *Lopez* does signal the end of an era. For the first time in more than half a century, the Court struck down a federal criminal statute enacted under Congress' Commerce Clause authority. In so doing, the Court ended an era of almost complete deference to legislative decisions as manifested by the rational basis test. In order to pass muster now, a statute must have a "substantial effect" on interstate commerce. And Congress, in light of *Lopez*, will be more forced to include jurisdictional statements and findings designed to demonstrate that effect. Otherwise, the Court may strike down other statutes.

Bibliography

Federal Commerce Power

Corwin, Edward S., *The Passing of Dual Federalism*, 36 VA. L. REV. 1 (1950)

Corwin, Edward S., *The Power of Congress to Prohibit Commerce*, 18 CORNELL L. REV. 477 (1933)

Frankfurter, Felix, *Mr. Justice Roberts*, 104 U. PA. L. REV. 311 (1955)

Jackson, Robert H., THE STRUGGLE FOR JUDICIAL SUPREMACY (1941)

Leuchtenberg, *The Origins of Franklin D. Roosevelt's Court-Packing Plan*, 1966 SUP. CT. REV. 347

Morison, Samuel Elliott & Commager, Henry Steele, THE GROWTH OF THE AMERICAN REPUBLIC (1950)

Ribble, Frederick Deane, STATE AND NATIONAL POWER OVER COMMERCE (1937)

Schlesinger, Arthur M., THE COMING OF THE NEW DEAL (1951)

The Dormant Commerce Clause

This section examines the power of the states to regulate interstate commerce. During the first third of the twentieth century, the Supreme Court construed the Tenth Amendment as giving the states a reserved power over "purely local" commerce. Although Congress controlled commerce "among" the states, it was precluded from violating the states' reserved power. Following the Switch of 1937, the distinction between "local" commerce and commerce "among" the states began to disappear. Under decisions like *Wickard* and *Perez,* the federal government assumed much broader authority over both interstate and local commerce. Moreover, the Court began to treat the Tenth Amendment as a truism thereby depriving states of their reserved power over commerce.

In the post-Switch era, the federal courts have faced quite different questions regarding the scope of state power. Most post-Switch cases involve "dormant" power situations—situations in which the federal government has the power to regulate a subject, but has not done so (or has done so incompletely). In these dormant power situations, courts are forced to determine whether, and to what extent, the states have the power to regulate commerce.

The articles in this section examine how the courts have addressed that problem. Professor Noel Dowling's influential article *Interstate Commerce and State Power* provides historical analysis and articulates Professor's Dowling's balancing approach to dormant Commerce Clause cases. Donald H. Regan's article *The Supreme Court and State Protectionism: Making Sense of the Dormant Commerce Clause* analyzes how the Supreme Court has applied its antiprotectionism and balancing theories in *Pike v. Bruce Church* and subsequent cases. Mark V. Tushnet's article *Rethinking the Dormant Commerce Clause* argues that the Court's Commerce Clause cases reveal "enhanced due process scrutiny parading in the guise of a balancing process" and develops a "positive argument for a return to substantive due process analysis in economic cases." Finally, Julian N. Eule's article *Laying the Dormant Commerce Clause to Rest* "[i]t no longer makes sense for the Court to invalidate evenhanded state legislation merely because it burdens interstate commerce. Under the Court's present standard, the likelihood of judicial invalidation increases with the degree of burden imposed by state law, and the weight of the national interest. But this is precisely the situation in which action by Congress or administrative agencies is likely."

Noel J. Dowling, *Interstate Commerce and State Power*, 27 VA. L. REV. 1 (1940)*

[Mr.] Justice Holmes once said that while he did "not think the United States would come to an end if we lost our power to declare an Act of Congress void," he did "think the Union would be imperiled if we could not make that declaration as to the laws of the several States." The reason he gave was that "one in my place sees how often a local policy prevails with those who are not trained to national views and how often action is taken that embodies what the commerce clause was meant to end."

* * *

I. Prior Theories

The views which have been entertained as to the effect of the commerce clause on state power may be summarized under four heads. Each of them has been held by the Court, or a number of Justices, at one time or another, and one of them contains in substance, as I will try to show, the desirable doctrine for the future. They are:

1. That the clause impliedly prohibits all state regulation or taxation of interstate commerce;
2. That the clause itself prohibits nothing, the states being free to regulate and tax as they see fit unless and until they are stopped by Congressional action;
3. That the clause prohibits some, but not all, state regulation and taxation—that is, sometimes it prohibits and sometimes it does not;
4. That though the clause itself prohibits nothing, an impediment may arise from the express or implied will of Congress.

The first is of historical interest as that to which the Court inclined at the beginning. In *Gibbons v. Ogden*, counsel contended that "as the word 'to regulate' implies in its nature full power over the thing to be regulated, it excludes, necessarily, the action of all others that would perform the same operation on the same thing," and further that "regulation is designed for the entire result, applying to those parts which remain as they were, as well as to those which are altered." "Great force" was conceded to this argument by Chief Justice Marshall, and the Court was "not satisfied that it has been refuted." But it was unnecessary in that case to decide whether the power of the states was surrendered by the mere grant to Congress, or is retained until Congress shall exercise the power, for the reason that the power had been exercised, and the regulations which Congress deemed it proper to make were in full operation. And the narrow holding was that the Act of Congress prevailed over the inconsistent regulation of the New York statute. As to taxation, *Brown v. Maryland* all but committed the Court to the first view. There the doctrine, developed in *McCulloch v. Maryland*, that there is a "total failure" of power in the states to tax the operations of a federal instrumentality was brought over and declared to be "entirely applicable" to state taxation of foreign and interstate commerce. And as late as 1887 *Robbins v. Shelby County* was saying that a state cannot tax interstate commerce at all.

The second view is, in substance, the one expounded by Chief Justice Taney, particularly in the *License* cases. Though his opinion did not win the support of a full majority of the Court, there was agreement in the conclusion to which it led. In gen-

---

*   Reprinted with permission.

eral, this view would remove the commerce clause from judicial consideration. There would be nothing for the Court to do on the subject of the validity of a state law, assuming of course that it violated no other provision in the Constitution and collided with no national action. There is no indication that he would have looked differently upon the matter if the state law had been discriminatory in nature. The presence of an Act of Congress might give rise, as it did in *Gibbons v. Ogden*, to questions concerning its interpretation and the reconciliation of state laws with it, but that would be a statutory inquiry.

The third view, a compromise between the two earlier views, represents the first definite position taken by the Court on the commerce clause; and this occurred in *Cooley v. The Board of Wardens*, in 1851. In the course of the opinion the Court undertook to explain the cause of its prior diversities of opinion, saying that they arose "from the different views taken of the nature of the power." But when, the Court added, the nature of a power like this is spoken of, when it is said that the nature of the power requires that it should be exercised exclusively by Congress, "it must be intended to refer to the subjects of that power, and to say they are of such a nature as to require exclusive legislation by Congress." For the power to regulate commerce, the Court observed, embraces a vast field, containing not only many, but exceedingly various subjects, quite unlike in their nature; some imperatively demanding a single uniform rule, and some as imperatively demanding that diversity which alone can meet local necessities.

> "Whatever subjects of this power are in their nature national, or admit only of one uniform system, or plan of regulation, may justly be said to be of such a nature as to require exclusive legislation by Congress."

So, at the half-century mark the Court had progressed to a point where it could say that a state may or may not regulate interstate commerce depending upon whether the "subjects of this power" are "local" or "national." If the former, the states were free until Congress acted contrariwise; if the latter, only Congress could regulate. On the face of the opinion the principal inquiry centered on the need for uniformity of regulation, the determination of which involved (the Court did not enlarge upon the point) at least some weighing of the advancement of local interests as against interference with national interests. And at this stage there was distinctly a job for the courts to do.

The fourth view may be described as a composite of the second and third, and a limited version of it was announced by the Court in 1890. It originally covered only interstate commerce in intoxicating liquors, though it was later enlarged. This view squares with the second in the sense that no prohibition inheres in the commerce clause itself, and it preserves the results of the third in that some state action would be upheld—*e.g.*, where "matters of local concern" are involved—and some overturned. Also it calls for the same kind of inquiry as under *Cooley v. The Board*, but with this difference in result: if the subject were held "national," a congressional negative would be presumed rather than a constitutional prohibition applied. This view admitted the power of Congress to exercise complete control in both fields: to supersede state action in local matters, to permit it in national. The significant and salutary effect was to take constitutional rigidity out of the commerce clause problem and substitute the flexible and adaptable will of Congress. At the same time it recognized a definite function for the courts in the ascertainment of that will. To them fell the initial task of drawing the line between what the states could and could not do. Congress could then effect a readjustment if it thought necessary in the interests of the country as a whole.

In the intervening period up to 1938 no distinctive theory appears to have been formulated or urged. New terminology crept into the opinions, and the Court talked increasingly of "direct" and "indirect" effects or burdens on interstate commerce, the former being held invalid and the latter valid. The "direct-indirect" test had this much at least in common with *Cooley v. The Board*, that it upheld some and overturned other state action; but it was far from satisfying since it offered so little of a criterion for determining on which side a case would fall. Quarantine laws, for example, which hit interstate commerce head-on and stopped it dead in its tracks at the border, surely would have to be classed as "direct," yet they were sustained. The oleomargarine laws of Massachusetts had a no less direct impact on traffic than did Iowa's liquor laws, but Massachusetts won and Iowa lost. And in 1927 came a broadside attack upon this test in the Court. Mr. Justice Stone led off with a dissenting opinion in *Di Santo v. Pennsylvania*. He thought it "too mechanical, too uncertain in its application, and too remote from actualities to be of value." To employ it was "little more than using labels to describe a result rather than any trustworthy formula by which it is reached." He sought to discover the factors that had influenced the Court in its decisions on this subject in the past, and this is the way he summed the matter up: "those interferences not deemed to be forbidden are to be sustained * * * because a consideration of all the facts and circumstances, such as the nature of the regulation, its function, the character of the business involved, and the actual effect on the flow of commerce, lead to the conclusion that the regulation concerns interests peculiarly local and does not infringe the national interest in maintaining the freedom of commerce across state lines." Justices Holmes and Brandeis concurred in his dissent.

* * *

III. What of the Future?

From what has gone before, a doctrine can be drawn which offers, I believe, desirable and helpful guidance for the Court in the future. It is, that in the absence of affirmative consent a Congressional negative will be presumed in the courts against state action which in its effect upon interstate commerce constitutes an unreasonable interference with national interests, the presumption being rebuttable at the pleasure of Congress. Such a doctrine would free the states from any constitutional disability but at the same time would not give them license to take such action as they see fit irrespective of its effect upon interstate commerce. With respect to such commerce, the question whether the states may act upon it would depend upon the will of Congress expressed in such form as it may choose. State action falling short of such interference would prevail unless and until superseded or otherwise nullified by Congressional action.

Five principal reasons support the foregoing:

1. The congressional consent aspect of the doctrine would entail no sharp break with the past, and its adoption would constitute the acceptance of some of the best efforts of the Court. Indeed, except for explicitness and generalization, it is the position to which the Court itself had come by a process of trial and error over nearly a hundred years. It is true that on the surface the first indication of the doctrine had a semblance of the casual, though I have always thought that it was implicit in *Cooley v. The Board*, which came at an earlier date and whose opposing opinions belie any casual imputation. It is also true that the doctrine was slow in taking form and did not acquire definite proportions until *Leisy v. Hardin* in 1890. The fact that the Court's arrival at this position culminated a long consideration accentuates the burden upon those who would depart from it. Not that the past stays the

hand of the present, but that the cumulative judgment of the Court is entitled to great respect and that particularly in the field of constitutional law much may be said for the continuity and stability of a doctrine until its error or undesirability is plainly shown.

2.   The substantive standard embodied in the doctrine, "unreasonable interference with national interests," would commit the Court to no new or untried principle. It would, to be sure, involve an avowal that the Court is deliberately balancing national and local interests and making a choice as to which of the two *should* prevail. That, as I see the matter, is a policy judgment. But the test of reasonableness in interstate commerce cases is not the same as, for example, in due process cases. Additional factors are involved. In a sense, a state law must take the hurdle of due process before it comes to the interstate barrier. The blow post law case from Georgia affords a striking illustration. The requirement that trains slow down at crossings was deemed, as well as it can be gleaned from the report and with regard to the situation in Georgia, an appropriate and permissible means for securing safety of life and property notwithstanding the inconvenience to local traffic and to the companies. At that stage the judicial scales tipped in favor of the statute. But other factors thrown into the other side of the scales—*e.g.*, convenience and economy of time in through traffic, more efficient and less expensive operation of railway systems— tipped them back against the statute.

As already indicated, *Cooley v. The Board* comprehended a certain balancing of state and national interests, though the Court did not go into the subject in detail. And it was just there, in an effort to discover the relevant considerations for answering the question whether the "national interest in maintaining freedom of commerce across state lines" has been infringed, that Mr. Justice Stone tackled the problem in his *Di Santo* dissent. His approach in that opinion appears to be well calculated to produce a "realistic" judgment whether any given state action constitutes an unreasonable interference with national interests. The several considerations to which he referred have been noted and discussed above. He essayed no exhaustive list, nor would he exclude such factors as the desirability of uniform regulation (the principal point of *Cooley v. The Board*); or the consequences to the state if its action were disallowed—how serious and widespread the evil and what the prospect for national action; or the intangible but nevertheless real benefits to be had from giving the people of the states the satisfaction of, and stimulus to responsibility from, home government as against distant government. And in order to bring all such considerations into the judicial forum, could not the rules of evidence be made more generous and elastic? It is true that the litigation is between private parties, but the issue touches the relative jurisdictions of nation and state. After all, this is statecraft in which the courts are engaged.

3.   This doctrine would provide flexibility in the adjustment and accommodation of national and state interests, at the same time preserving the judicial and amplifying the legislative function. From the judicial point of view it would preserve a role which the Court, beginning with the leadership of Marshall, has worked out for itself and which has conspicuously contributed to the functioning of the federal system. That role brings to constitutional cases the best of the common law methods in the building up of principles from specific decisions. The trial courts would operate out on the front line, where the impact of state action on interstate commerce is first felt, and they could appraise at close range the conflicting state and national interests. Furthermore, the judicial sifting of the facts would have the manifest merit of sharpening the issues and facilitating legislative efforts in the event that Congress, dissatisfied with the judicial results, should desire to take corrective action of its own.

From the legislative standpoint, the fullest power of Congress would be guaranteed. In no event could the courts forestall or impede Congressional action. If the state law complained of were sustained in the courts, Congress could step in and occupy the field if in its judgment the state action went too far. On the other hand, if the state law were disallowed in the courts, Congress could obviate the results by giving its consent for the operation of the law. In this respect the doctrine would amplify the power of Congress, for no longer would congressional consent be thought of as somehow dependent upon the nature of the subject matter involved. And such consent would be given (the point is worth repeating) in the light of the issues developed in the litigation. It can hardly be doubted, for instance, that the liquor cases gave Congress a clear lead for its own part in establishing the disputed power of the states.

There is no assurance that the commerce problem would be as well handled by Congress alone as where both Congress and the courts participate in its solution. I say "would," drawing a distinction between what seems likely and what is theoretically possible. Congress is a big and heavy machine to set in motion, and its progress is sometimes impeded even when national interests of the highest order are at stake. Meanwhile much damage to interstate commerce, to say nothing of the otherwise amicable relationships among the states, might be caused by unrestrained state action. Nor is this merely conjecture: the last few years have seen a wide upsurge of economic nationalism on state lines. Whether or not there is cause and effect between the letdown of the judicial bars and this nationalistic upsurge, it can be said that they are more or less contemporaneous. And it seems somehow as if the times are out of joint when, in a world seething with animosities some of which feed upon nothing more substantial than geographical lines separating peoples and countries, the Supreme Court should give so much encouragement to trade wars among the states of this union as it appears to do by stepping aside from the interstate commerce problem and leaving it to Congress.

Even if Congress should accept the task it would not find it an easy one. It would have to labor with much of the same evidence that would be offered in the courts, as well as other matters bearing upon various phases of policy (including sheer political pressures); and perhaps more often than not the solution would have to be stated in general terms. And then, after all that were done, it is not at all unlikely that the whole thing would be thrown into the courts for final settlement, but with this difference, that whereas formerly the courts could turn to the judicially developed principles and feel their way along, henceforth they would have to interpret and apply new and general formulas from Congress.

The most that can be said for shifting from courts to Congress is that it is a debatable question whether quicker or better results can be had through initial action by Congress followed by interpretative proceedings in the courts than by initial determination in the courts followed, if necessary, by corrective action in Congress. Admittedly that is a basic question, involving a study of the relations of the courts to Congress in the functioning of the federal system. Until that study is pursued further there can hardly be a satisfying conclusion to the debate. But as well as I can see it, and particularly in the absence of a persuasive showing for the abandonment of an unbroken line of procedure since *Brown v. Maryland*, over a century ago, the choice lies on the side of a progression of specific judicial determinations rather than out-of-hand legislative pronouncements.

4. It is fairly certain that the adoption of this doctrine by the Court would be agreeable to Congress. This is an important feature in view of the fact that the doctrine is built on the notion that the will of Congress controls. Its agreeability to Con-

gress is shown by negative as well as affirmative evidence. Negatively, Congress has never, so far as I am aware, repudiated or seriously questioned its underlying idea. Affirmatively, Congress has acted upon the basis of the doctrine's soundness. To be sure, Congress did find difficulty in grasping and understanding the consent theory in its first experiment, the Wilson Act of 1890. That difficulty resulted, I think, from the assumption that *Leisy v. Hardin*, the case whose effect was to be overcome, had held the state constitutionally disabled from regulating the traffic. But the Court did not so hold. Its language was unequivocally to the contrary: "Up to that point of time [sale within the state], we hold that, in the absence of congressional permission to do so, the State had no power to interfere by seizure, or by any other action, in prohibition of importation and sale." Beyond question the impediment to state action was ascribed not to the Constitution but to the will of Congress; and the Court went a step further to offer the suggestion that Congress could remove the impediment and thus enable state power to apply. Congress answered the suggestion with the passage of the Wilson Act, and it in turn was forthwith sustained by the Court. Since then Congress has become accustomed to the doctrine and has repeatedly indicated its will that, in respect of certain subject matters, the states shall be free in the interstate field.

5. The doctrine would afford a common ground on which the divergent views in the Court could be brought together. No bothersome concession should be required of any one, and the ultimate aims of each might be secured. All members of the Court are agreed, it may of course be assumed, in desiring that the states have the fullest governmental freedom consistent with national interest. In a sense the differences in the Court are largely of a procedural nature—as to the methods for determining whether any challenged state action interferes too much with those interests—and to some extent they are verbal—as to the theories of the effect of the commerce clause and the bases for determining that effect.

[One] further and final point needs to be added, not by way of support for the doctrine, but as an indication of the new, or at all events more emphatic, responsibility which its adoption by the Court would impose upon the Bar. To a very considerable extent the success of the doctrine will depend upon the thoroughness with which the lawyers perform their task in the conduct of constitutional litigation. Here, as in many other fields, constitutionality is conditioned upon the facts, and to the lawyers the courts are entitled to look for garnering and presenting the facts. There are other media by which relevant matters may be brought into consideration—for example, judicial notice, not to say judicial ingenuity, industry and knowledge—but by and large the lawyers ought to furnish the most helpful assistance; and the breadth of the questions in such cases would justify lenient rules on admissibility of evidence. A competent handling of the case under fairly flexible judicial rules would take most of the sting out of Mr. Justice Black's point that "from inherent limitations of the judicial process" the courts could only "treat the subject by the hit and miss method of deciding single local controversies upon evidence and information limited by the narrow rules of litigation." So it is, that in the interstate commerce cases it may depend upon how worthily and well the lawyers do their jobs whether a traditional function of the courts, which I believe to be appropriate and essential for the working of our federal system, shall be preserved.

> "Great as is the practical wisdom exhibited in all the provisions, of the Constitution, and important as were the character and influence of those who secured its adoption, it will, I believe, be the judgment of history that the Commerce Clause and the wise interpretation of it, perhaps more than any other contributing element, have united to bind the several states into a nation."

Donald H. Regan, *The Supreme Court and State Protectionism: Making Sense of the Dormant Commerce Clause*, 84 MICH. L. REV. 1091, 1209-20, 1269-71 (1986)*

. . . *Pike v. Bruce Church, Inc.* illustrates the neglected adage, "Odd cases make bad law." *Pike* is not a particularly hard case, but it is decidedly odd, and Stewart, who writes for the Court, is bemused by the oddity. Let us therefore begin not with the opinion, but with the facts of the case and the application to the facts of the anti-protectionism theory.

In issue is the constitutionality of an order by an Arizona agricultural supervisor forbidding Bruce Church to transport cantaloupes grown by it in Arizona into California for packing. The effect of the order is to require that Arizona-grown cantaloupes be processed and packed in Arizona.

As a consequence of being packed in Arizona, these cantaloupes will end up *labeled* as coming from Arizona. The Court is not clear whether it is an independent requirement of Arizona law that cantaloupes packed in Arizona be so labeled, or whether it is merely standard practice of the industry. But the entire discussion proceeds on the assumption that cantaloupes packed in Arizona will be labeled as Arizona cantaloupes and cantaloupes packed in California will be labeled as California cantaloupes. In fact, that asserted purpose of the Supervisor's order is precisely to guarantee that these Arizona-grown cantaloupes end up labeled as the product of Arizona. Stewart quotes from the brief for that Supervisor: "It is within Arizona's legitimate interest to require that interstate cantaloupe purchasers be informed that this high quality Parker fruit was grown in Arizona."

Now, applying the anti-protectionism theory, the first question is whether Arizona's purpose is protectionist. The answer is clearly, Yes. This is not a matter of disbelieving the Supervisor's claim. The *asserted* purpose is protectionist. Why does the Supervisor want interstate cantaloupe purchasers to be informed about the origin of this fruit? Neither the Supervisor nor the purchasers regard that bit of knowledge as valuable in itself. The Supervisor wants purchasers to know where these cantaloupes came from because they are unusually good cantaloupes, and knowledge that they came from Arizona will dispose purchasers of them to buy other cantaloupes from Arizona. If the cantaloupes are labeled as coming from California, California will reap the reputational benefit. In short, the Supervisor wants these cantaloupes labeled as Arizona cantaloupes because that will improve the competitive position of the Arizona cantaloupe industry, in general and as compared to its California competition. Arizona's avowed purpose is protectionist.

On the other hand, this purpose of promoting the reputation of local products is a protectionist purpose that the states are often allowed to pursue, because it is often pursued by permissible techniques such as media advertising paid for by a state agency. What about the technique in this case?

The technique in this case turns out to be a forbidden one—an explicit embargo on the export of unprocessed goods. There is no doubt about that technique's being sufficiently like the traditional weapons of protectionism to be forbidden. It *is* one of the traditional weapons of protectionism. Some people, including even Stewart in the early portions of his opinion, seem to miss the fact that the Supervisor's order is an

---

*   Reprinted with permission.

explicit embargo. Perhaps they miss this because the order does not distinguish in terms between packers who operate in Arizona and packers who operate in California. The order may therefore seem to confer no advantage on local actors. But the order does confer advantage on locals. The order is stated explicitly in terms of state lines. Its immediate effect is to require packing in Arizona and its inevitable tendency is to advantage Arizona packing workers. In addition, the usual effect of a statute like this, expectable just from its language and with no further empirical knowledge, would be to advantage packing companies that operate in Arizona. If this order will not, it is only because Bruce Church has said that if it is required to conform in the order it will itself become a packing company that operates in Arizona (by building a new packing shed there). This order is an entirely different kettle of fish from the facially neutral statutes with protectionist effect involved in, say, *Hunt* or *Exxon*.

So, the Supervisor's order promotes a protectionist purpose by a standard protectionist technique. Under the anti-protectionism theory, the order is unconstitutional.

The conclusion that the order is unconstitutional may, however, be a little harder to swallow than our analysis suggests. Let us see why the case may seem less straightforward than our analysis so far makes it appear. There is a protectionist purpose in *Pike*, and there is a standard protectionist technique. But the relationship between purpose and technique is non-standard. The embargo technique usually aims at promoting local business or employment directly; in *Pike* the embargo (supposedly) promotes local business or employment indirectly through the medium of product reputation. This peculiar indirect relation of technique to ultimate purpose is the main thing that makes *Pike* odd. And there are subsidiary aspects of the situation that contribute to the oddity. If we rule against Arizona here, it seems that we are ruling against the dissemination of true information, which is normally a great constitutional good. (Ironically, the information in this case, about the origin of these particular cantaloupes, will tend to be misleading if it persuades consumers that all Arizona cantaloupes are exceptionally good. It seems to be agreed these cantaloupes are special. Still, the pure factual information is indisputably true.) Furthermore, Arizona would be perfectly free to disseminate information about the quality of its cantaloupes by normal advertising. Also, the local packing requirement is imposed by the Supervisor under a long-existing statutory scheme whose *general* purpose is to maintain the reputation of Arizona cantaloupes by preventing deceptive packing. Such a scheme, we have seen, is another standard instance of permissible protectionism.

None of the above considerations should incline us to alter our conclusion that the Supervisor's order is unconstitutional. In striking down the order, we would not be disfavoring information, but only the embargo as a technique of disseminating information. State advertising and schemes to promote honesty in packing are permissible, despite protectionist purpose, just because they do not involve any technique like an embargo that is coercive and hostile and that produces substantial market effect at slight expense to the state. The fact that Arizona claims to be interested only in the remote (informational and reputational) effects of its embargo does not alter the coerciveness of the embargo with regard to packers, nor does it raise the cost of the embargo to the state.

And to tell the truth, it is hard to believe that Arizona is motivated only by the remote effects of its embargo, when the immediate effects are similarly pro-local and much more certain. If we had no direct evidence at all concerning Arizona's purpose, the Supervisor's order would fall under the *per se* rule against explicit embargoes that we discussed in section II.A. It would be supremely silly to say Arizona can avoid the effect of that *per se* rule by proving a nonstandard, but still protectionist, purpose aiming only at remote protectionist effects.

We are ready now to consider Stewart's opinion, which is as odd in its way as the case itself. Despite his talk of balancing, Stewart actually decides the case by virtually the same analysis we have generated in applying the anti-protectionism principle.

After stating the facts and disposing of the Supervisor's contention that his order has nothing to do with interstate commerce because it affects only what is done in Arizona, Stewart states the famous *Pike* test. I reproduce it here, complete with all citations:

> Although the criteria for determining the validity of state statutes affecting interstate commerce have been variously stated, the general rule that emerges can be phrased as follows: Where the statute regulates evenhandedly to effectuate a legitimate local public interest, and its effects on interstate commerce are only incidental, it will be upheld unless the burden imposed on such commerce is clearly excessive in relation to the putative local benefits. *Huron Cement Co. v. Detroit*, 362 U.S. 440, 443. If a legitimate local purpose is found, then the question becomes one of degree. And the extent of the burden that will be tolerated will of course depend on the nature of the local interest involved, and on whether it could be promoted as well with a lesser impact on interstate activities. Occasionally the court has candidly undertaken a balancing approach in resolving these issues, *Southern Pacific Co. v. Arizona*, 325 U.S. 761, but more frequently it has spoken in terms of "direct" and "indirect" effects and burdens. *See, e.g., Shafer v. Farmers Grain Co.*, [268 U.S. 189].

Note in passing that none of the cases Stewart cites gives any support to balancing in movement-of-goods cases. *Huron Cement* and *Southern Pacific* are both transportation cases. The third case, *Shafer*, Stewart cites mainly as an example of misleading language. Stewart does not explicitly disapprove the argument or result of *Shafer*; and he may think *Shafer* is a balancing case beneath its obsolete rhetoric. But if Stewart thinks that, he is almost certainly mistaken. The Court in *Shafer* does not discuss at all the local benefits claimed for the statute under review. Indeed, the Court explicitly refuses to consider these benefits: "If the [local] evils suggested [by North Dakota] are real, the power of correction does not rest with North Dakota but with Congress. . . ." *Shafer* was written before the modern era by a Justice (Van Devanter) who believed in the direct/indirect test; it was decided by a Court that believed in the test; and by modern standards, mine or Stewart's, it was probably decided wrongly. To repeat, Stewart's precedents give no support to balancing in movement-of-goods cases.

Having stated his famous test, Stewart proceeds virtually to ignore it. (In fairness, he may not have known it was destined to become famous.) The first question raised by Stewart's test as he states it is whether the order regulates "evenhandedly"; but Stewart skips over that question without comment. This would be understandable if it were obvious that the order was evenhanded. But in fact it is obvious that it is not. The order is an explicit embargo; it requires that certain cantaloupes, which could be well packed in California, be packed in Arizona instead. What is more, Stewart's eventual resolution of the case is going to turn on the fact that the order is thus unevenhanded. Already we wonder what is going on.

Instead of considering at this point whether the order is evenhanded, Stewart embarks on a meandering discussion of the purpose of the Supervisor's order and the purpose of the statute on which the order is based. This discussion of purpose takes up more than half of the remainder of the opinion. Stewart's attention to purpose does not prove he is following the anti-protectionist approach; purpose is central under the anti-protectionist approach, but it is relevant also to Stewart's test, both because the state is required by Stewart's test to have a legitimate purpose and because the purpose is a good guide to what is actually accomplished. Even so, Stewart's perplexity about the legitimacy of the purpose parallels very closely our own discussion from the anti-protectionist point of view. Stewart regards the specific purpose here as a manifestation of a general purpose, to enhance product reputation, which he can neither reject nor endorse without qualification. The reason, we know, is that such a purpose is acceptable if pursued by certain means, but objectionable if pursued by other means such as the order in the case at hand.

In the end Stewart writes: "Although it is not easy to see why the other growers of Arizona are entitled to benefit at [Bruce Church's] expense from the fact that [Bruce Church] produces superior crops, we may assume that the asserted state interest is a legitimate one." Notice that Stewart is plainly viewing even the reputation enhancement purpose as protectionist; he speaks of the growers of Arizona benefiting at Bruce Church's expense. (The unfairness is magnified by the fact that they are capitalizing on the quality of Bruce Church's fruit.) Notice also that Stewart cannot bring himself to say the reputation enhancement purpose in the present context is legitimate; he only "assumes" so. And he reveals some doubt about the Supervisor's *bona fides*, referring for the first time to the reputation enhancement purpose as "asserted."

Stewart has now brought us to the crux of his opinion. After the quoted sentence in which he assumes that the asserted state interest is legitimate, he continues:

> But the State's tenuous interest in having the company's cantaloupes identified as originating in Arizona cannot constitutionally justify the requirement that the company build and operate an unneeded $200,000 packing plant in the State. The nature of that burden is, constitutionally, more significant than its extent. For the Court has viewed with particular suspicion state statutes requiring business operations to be performed in the home State that could more efficiently be performed elsewhere. Even where the State is pursuing a clearly legitimate local interest, this particular burden on commerce has been declared to be virtually *per se* illegal.

In these four sentences, the case is effectively decided. And if we look closely, we will see a balancing opinion turn into an anti-protectionist opinion before our very eyes.

The first sentence, which concludes with a reference to the $200,000 cost to Bruce Church, could be the start of open-ended private interest balancing. But we are told in the next sentence that the nature of the burden is more significant than its extent. Already, then, the balancing is not simply a matter of totting up costs and benefits. Some costs are special. Incidentally, the famous *Pike* test from earlier in Stewart's opinion says nothing about the nature of the burden being significant. It says the nature of the local interest is significant, but not the nature of the burden. This is one more example of the general lack of connection between the stated test and Stewart's actual process of decision.

Very well, what burdens are specially problematic? The third sentence tells us. The specially suspect statutes are those "requiring business operations to be performed in the home State. . . ." (Let me ignore for the moment Stewart's reference to efficiency. I shall return to it.) So, the burden that is specially problematic, at least in the context of this case, is protectionist effect. Or rather, under the broadest possible interpretation of Stewart's language, it is protectionist effect. There is a splendid triple ambiguity in Stewart's word "requiring." "Requiring" could mean "having the purpose of bringing it about that [business operations are performed in-state]"; or it could mean "formulated in terms which explicitly direct that [business operations be performed in-state]"; or it could mean "producing the effect that [business operations are performed in-state]." In other words, statutes that "require" business operations to be performed locally might be (1) statutes with protectionist purpose, or (2) statutes that (purpose aside) make explicit reference to state lines, or (3) statutes that (purpose and explicit language aside) have protectionist effect.

Perhaps the fourth and final sentence will clarify the meaning of "requiring." The fourth sentence claims to find in *Foster-Fountain Packing Co. v. Haydel, Johnson v. Haydel*, and *Toomer v. Witsel* the rule that "this particular burden on commerce" (that is, whatever burden it is that we are talking about) is "virtually *per se* illegal." So the question becomes, what rule could those cases be thought to establish? Keeping in mind that if we are going to infer a *per se* rule from only three cases that do not explicitly announce any rule we should be conservative in our inference, the answer is: at most a *per se* rule against statutes that explicitly require that business operations be performed locally.

In all three cases, the statutes under review were explicit. There was no question of mere protectionist effect from a facially neutral ("evenhanded") statute. As it happens, the Court probably also thought there was protectionist purpose in all three cases. The Court is completely explicit about finding protectionist purpose in the two *Haydel* cases. In *Toomer* the Court is nowhere explicit about its view of the purpose of the local processing requirement; but the Court clearly believes the general scheme under review, which includes discriminatory licensing provisions, has a protectionist purpose. The *Toomer* Court never focuses on whether bad purpose is necessary to the result. The reason the Court can ignore this issue about the role of purpose, so interesting to us, is not that the case is decided by pure balancing. It is rather that South Carolina practically conceded the existence of protectionist purpose by relying primarily on the argument that even purposeful protectionism is permitted in a state's dealings with local fish and wildlife.

In sum, we might well say that Stewart's cases establish a *per se* rule only against statutes with protectionist purpose. But that would be no *per se* rule at all, since it is apparently agreed on all hands that protectionist purpose is objectionable in itself. Let us concede one more step. Let us allow that the cases establish a *per se* rule against explicit embargoes. (We have seen that such a *per se* rule is justified whether these cases establish it or not.) But Stewart's cases most certainly do not justify a *per se* rule covering facially neutral statutes with an incidental "embargo effect." Granting Stewart the benefit of the doubt about his precedents, what he has established, and what he relies on to decide *Pike*, is a *per se* rule against explicit embargoes.

To complete our analysis of Stewart's crucial four sentences, we must tie up one loose end. In the third sentence of the four, Stewart describes as specially suspect statutes requiring local performance of business operations "that could more efficiently be performed elsewhere." I have so far ignored this qualification, which may seem to sound a balancing note. I wanted to get on and see that Stewart is moving toward a *per se* rule. Once we know Stewart is moving toward a *per se* rule, it becomes clear that an inquiry into efficiency can be no part of the actual rule of decision Stewart is suggesting. The question where some business operation can most efficiently be performed is the sort of question that requires a complex investigation. Efficiency is simply not the right sort of thing to use as a trigger for a *per se* rule.

(Explicitness, in contrast, is the right sort of thing, precisely because explicitness is easy to identify.) The reader might suggest that Stewart is not really talking about efficiency in any sophisticated sense; Stewart is merely pointing to the fact that the Supervisor's order will increase Bruce Church's short-term packing costs. Such a cost increase may be easy enough to identify, but there are other reasons for not regarding it as part of the *per se* rule Stewart is aiming at. A *per se* rule triggered simply by a cost increase standing alone would be much too restrictive. And if we make the rule less restrictive by adding explicitness (the obvious candidate) as a further necessary trigger, then we find we can dispense with reference to the cost increase. We have a *per se* rule (in terms of explicitness alone) that is already satisfactory without bothering about the cost increase.

So, efficiency plays no role in Stewart's actual rule of decision. But Stewart does refer to efficiency. What do we make of that? The reference may well be mere window dressing. References to efficiency often are. But there is one other possibility we should at least consider, namely, that efficiency is part of the underlying justification for the *per se* rule against explicit embargoes that Stewart ends up with.

Now, we know that if the underlying justification that moves Stewart is the anti-protectionism theory, then efficiency indeed is a part of that justification. I have argued that the role of efficiency in anti-protectionism theory is minor and that the relevant sense of efficiency is weak. But there is enough connection between concern for efficiency and the anti-protectionism principle so that a reference to efficiency in this context is perfectly consistent with the notion that Stewart's underlying theory is anti-protectionism.

One might argue, of course, that the reference to efficiency suggests that the underlying justification for the *per se* rule against explicit embargoes, in Stewart's mind, is a balancing justification. Notice, however, that the balancing justification for a *per se* rule against explicit embargoes must itself depend on the anti-protectionist's assumption that explicit embargoes will normally reflect protectionist purpose. After all, if states never had bad purpose, then the only explicit embargoes would be laws like the Wyoming embargo on the export of unprocessed wuzzie meat or the Wisconsin law excluding eighteen-year-old residents of Illinois from Wisconsin bars. It is far from clear that such laws would be bad on balance more often than not; so it is far from clear that a *per se* prohibition on explicit embargoes would be justified by a balancing analysis if bad purpose is not assumed. But if the balancing argument against explicit embargoes depends on the likelihood of bad purpose, while the anti-protectionist argument, which makes purpose central, depends not at all on claims about the balance of effects (remember the minor role played in the anti-protectionist analysis by a special notion of efficiency), then is not the anti-protectionist analysis to be preferred? And is not the anti-protectionist analysis what we should attribute to Stewart as his underlying analysis, given that his opinion makes no serious attempt to ground the *per se* rule against explicit embargoes (except in precedent)?

To summarize our discussion of Stewart's crucial paragraph: In the space of four sentences, Stewart goes from a beginning that looks like open-ended private interest balancing to a conclusion based on a *per se* rule against explicit embargoes that is best justified by an anti-protectionism analysis. At this point, the case is effectively decided. *Pike* is meet for decision by a *per se* rule against explicit embargoes because, as we have noted, the Supervisor's order is an explicit embargo. What Stewart ignored before (the un-evenhandedness of the order) he relies on now.

There are two further paragraphs in Stewart's opinion. In the paragraph that follows immediately the passage we have been dissecting, Stewart addresses the Supervisor's claim that the *Haydel* cases and *Toomer* are distinguishable from *Pike* because they involved statutes with express or concealed purpose to promote local employment while the Supervisor's order does not. ("Employment" must be taken to cover not only the existence of jobs but also general business activity if the Supervisor's claim is to be evidently true about the three precedents.) Stewart does not respond, as he might, that the Supervisor's order has the same ultimate purpose, only pursued indirectly. Instead, Stewart says that the *Toomer* Court "indicated" that bad purpose was unnecessary. Presumably Stewart says "indicated" out of awareness that the *Toomer* Court does not say this explicitly. Indeed, I think the Toomer Court does not say this even implicitly. As I have mentioned, the role of purpose was not the issue in *Toomer*. The passage Stewart quotes from *Toomer* has some language that suggests a balancing approach; but taken as a whole, and especially in the context of the whole *Toomer* opinion, the passage suggests only our per se rule against explicit embargoes.

(Of course, if we have a *per se* rule against explicit embargoes, then when the *per se* rule is triggered it is not necessary for the party challenging the state law to adduce further positive proof of bad purpose. In that sense, bad purpose is unnecessary when the *per se* rule is triggered. But nonnecessity of bad purpose in that sense is consistent with, indeed flows from the general purpose-based anti-protectionism approach, and it does nothing to suggest that balancing is ever appropriate.)

In his next and final paragraph, Stewart does a remarkable aboutface. The paragraph continues the discussion of *Toomer* and of *Pike*'s relation to *Toomer*, and it concludes with an argument *a fortiori*:

> If the Commerce Clause forbids a State to require work to be done within its jurisdiction to promote local employment, then surely it cannot permit a State to require a person to go into a local packing business solely for the sake of enhancing the reputation of other producers within its borders.

In the first clause, Stewart implicitly describes *Toomer* as involving the purpose "to promote local employment." There is no evidence this is an assumption Stewart has made only for purposes of argument. This is the last sentence of Stewart's opinion; we may assume it reflects what Stewart really thinks about *Toomer*. So, Stewart thinks of *Toomer* as involving protectionist purpose, and he here makes use of just the fact about *Toomer* that he said in his previous paragraph was irrelevant.

This last sentence of the opinion includes what looks like a limited reappearance of the balancing motif, when the state's interest in product reputation is compared unfavorably to the state's interest in employment. But the force of the comparison in context is just to say that an explicit embargo with the purpose of promoting reputation fares no better than an explicit embargo with the purpose of promoting jobs directly. That, of course, is just what we decided at the end of our analysis of the facts of *Pike* under the anti-protectionist approach.

Considering now the whole opinion: What is Stewart doing in *Pike*? At some level, Stewart may think he is balancing; but read as a whole, the opinion strongly suggests that Stewart is moved by more specific considerations. (I am willing to claim that even Stewart would have seen this, if he had *read* the opinion dispassionately.) Certainly there is no trace of the open-ended private interest balancing or the wide-ranging national interest balancing that the much-quoted *Pike* test might lead us to expect. The only thing that appears in the balance against the Supervisor's order (supposing for the moment that there is balancing at all) is protectionist effect; and it is important to Stewart that this is "the nature of the burden." The weight of what goes into the other side of the balance is also determined by anti-protectionist considerations. After a longish discussion of the Supervisor's purpose, revealing the same perplexity we would expect from an anti-protectionist, Stewart grudgingly decides to assume that the reputation enhancement purpose is legitimate (as it is, considered in itself). But he is troubled by the fact that it is protectionist (recall his observation that the other growers of Arizona benefit at Bruce Church's expense); and in his final sentence he sums up his opinion by telling us with a rhetorical flourish that this protectionist purpose cannot be pursued by the protectionist technique of an embargo. (He does not use the word "protectionist," but he says everything necessary to make it clear that the word applies to both purpose and technique.) In between, after revealing that he suspects the Supervisor of even more flagrant protectionist purpose (remember "asserted"), Stewart decides the case by reference to a *per se* rule against a standard protectionist technique. This *per se* rule is better justified by anti-protectionist considerations than by balancing; and Stewart infers it from cases that he later reveals he understands as involving protectionist purpose.

This I submit is not a balancing opinion. . . .

The most interesting and important of the post-*Pike* cases that we have not already discussed at length is *City of Philadelphia v. New Jersey*. Speaking through Justice Stewart, the Court struck down a New Jersey statute that effectively closed New Jersey landfills to solid or liquid waste from outside the state.

Of greater general significance is the Court's clear recognition that protectionist motivation of *any feature* of a statute makes the statute unconstitutional. Stewart says it is unnecessary to decide whether the purpose of the statute as a whole is primarily to preserve New Jersey's environment or primarily to make landfill space cheaper for residents of New Jersey. Even assuming the general purpose is environmental, New Jersey cannot place the burden of achieving its environmental goal solely on the shoulders of foreigners while exempting their local competitors.

The Court also correctly decides that the New Jersey statute cannot be upheld on the authority of the old quarantine cases. There are two reasons. First, although the quarantine cases indicate that a law can be valid despite being an explicit import embargo, there is always an implicit assumption in those cases either that the problem the quarantine is aimed at (say, a disease of cattle) simply does not exist locally, or else that local measures for control and suppression of the problem are in force that are generally comparable in their impact to the embargo on imports. There was no suggestion in *Philadelphia v. New Jersey* that New Jersey had done anything to discourage the internal creation of waste or to minimize the internal transportation of waste.

Second, and even more important, the easy assumption that quarantines are permissible depends on an implicit belief that *disposal* of unwanted goods is not a problem. Until recently the popular consciousness, the economic and technological consciousness, and the judicial consciousness took it for granted that when an object lost its value, it evaporated. We toss it in the garbage, we toss it in the ocean—but when we no longer want it, getting rid of it is easy. We have recently learned, of course, that getting rid of it may *not* be easy. Disposal has become a problem. As a result, resources that play a role in the disposal process (such as landfill space) have suddenly become scarce.

Landfill space is now a valuable commodity, and it is a commodity used in a special way. Instead of buying it and taking it off to one's home for one's factory for consumption or further transformation, one uses landfill space by bringing something else, one's waste, to it. So, a quarantine on the import of waste becomes in effect an embargo on the export of landfill space. Explicit export embargoes, we know, are virtually *per se* illegal; and it does not matter to that illegality whether the (privately owned) landfill space is regarded as a natural resource or as the product of economic development.

We should notice that there are many things New Jersey can still do to slow the use of its landfills and to protect itself from the dangers of solid and liquid waste. It can tax the consumption of landfill space. It can tax and regulate (evenhandedly) the internal transportation of waste. (This might technically produce a transportation case, under my classification of dormant commerce clause cases, but even-handed taxation or regulation designed to reflect the nonmarket costs and to minimize the dangers of waste transporting would surely be upheld.) In my opinion, New Jersey could set out measures for discouraging the generation of waste and could deny access to landfills to entities, local or foreign, that did not comply with these measures. If New Jersey then legally required compliance with these waste reduction measures throughout New Jersey, all New Jersey residents would have access to the landfills, along with foreigners who took similar measures to stop generating waste. (My suggestion that New Jersey might condition access to landfills on adoption of waste reduction measures will raise eyebrows and will attract the complaint that as applied to foreigners such legislation would be impermissibly extraterritorial. I think not. In any event, it is not the only thing I have suggested New Jersey could do. It is only, in some respects, the best thing they could do.)

Two quick final points; In deciding *Philadelphia v. New Jersey*, the Court implicitly reaffirmed the protection of local consumers counts as protectionism. The Court also implicitly recognized that municipal governments, who are important purchasers of landfill space, are in economic competition with each other as consumers of landfill space even though from the point of view of their residents they are performing a governmental function.

Mark V. Tushnet, *Rethinking the Dormant Commerce Clause*, 125 WIS. L. REV. 125, 141-50 (1979)*

* * *

Once standards for evaluating discriminatory legislation have been established, the free trade policies underlying the dormant commerce clause have been satisfied. The Supreme Court has nonetheless invalidated nondiscriminatory statutes on the ground that they unduly burden interstate commerce. Judicial intervention in undue burden cases can also be justified by the political theory because a state's political process may not take account of the price increases that its regulations spread throughout the nation. However, once efficiency considerations are held to have constitutional status, it makes little sense to confine them to the dormant commerce clause area. Rather, because the courts properly force states to consider efficiency in the dormant commerce clause area, they should also do so with respect to economic regulation generally, even in the absence of a commerce clause challenge. Thus, substantive due process, a doctrine that should be responsive to efficiency concerns, should become the articulated basis for constitutional analysis.

A. A Justification for Undue Burdens Analysis

In *Southern Pacific Co. v. Arizona*, the Court invalidated a statute limiting the length of trains passing through the state as an undue burden on interstate commerce. Undoubtedly the statute increased the cost of running trains in Arizona, but the relation between that cost increase and interstate commerce was more complicated than the Court thought. When rail costs increase, there need be no direct impact on interstate commerce at all. If the increased costs cannot be absorbed, shippers will shift from rail to other modes of transportation. The state law simply has the effect of transferring business from one interstate carrier to another, and no free trade concerns should be aroused.

The law does, however, increase the cost to consumers of goods shipped in interstate commerce, because producers will have been switched from the lowest-cost shipping method to the next higher cost one. Either these cost increases will be paid by consumers, or consumers will switch to less expensive substitutes, which themselves probably will have moved in interstate commerce and necessarily will be more expensive than the initial goods. Thus there will be a reduction in interstate commerce to the extent that consumer buying power is reduced or some consumers drop out of the market entirely. The Court has never attempted to measure the size of this reduction, however. Its sole focus has been on the increased cost of shipping or production, which has an indeterminate relation to reduced consumption of interstate goods.

"Burden," therefore, cannot mean "reduction." The only burden the Court has been concerned with has been increased cost to producers. The national free trade unit remains, although the pattern of trade within it may change. But the change is not advantageous to the state adopting the regulation. If it were, burden cases would be transformed into discrimination ones, for the state would have adopted a law that increased prices of foreign goods as compared to local ones.

Burden cases involve across-the-board price increases. To invalidate statutes with such effects, a general efficiency criterion must be read into the commerce clause. In light of the Court's national responsibilities, burden analysis is justified. State regulation increases the price of goods sold outside the state, when, for example, the increased costs of shipping goods through Arizona are passed on to California consumers. But Californians are not represented in the Arizona Legislature. Thus, the local legislatures may be unconcerned with the real costs of regulation even as it acknowledges the willingness of its own citizens to bear a portion of the increased costs. A national viewpoint must be inserted in the process if the real costs are to be fully considered. In a sense, national supervision is designed to guarantee that the external costs of regulation are considered by local legislatures.

B. The Ambiguity of "Burdens" Balancing and Substantive Due Process

If a safety device were cost-justified, businesses would adopt it without compulsion. For example, if running long trains caused accidents and railroads had to bear the costs of those accidents, then railroads would voluntarily run shorter trains, provided that the accident costs exceeded the cost of running shorter trains. Regulation by statute occurs either when the legislature rejects efficiency as a criterion or when it seeks to remedy problems arising in the process of internalizing the external costs of a business, such as difficulty in determining the costs of accidents caused by long trains. Judicial balancing is difficult when the legislature rejects efficiency, but it is possible when regulation is an internalizing device.

1. THE PROBLEM OF BALANCING INCOMMENSURABLES

Not surprisingly, Justice Black, a vigorous opponent of judicial inquiry into the reasonableness of economic legislation under the due process clause, took an equally vigorous position regarding the dormant commerce clause. His views were most clearly stated in an opinion upholding a state law requiring that trains carry full crews. The state had claimed that full crew laws promoted safety, but the district court concluded that any increase in safety was small "and not worth the cost." Justice Black responded:

> Nor was it open to the District Court to place a value on the additional safety in terms of dollars and cents, in order to see whether this value, as calculated by the court, exceeded the financial cost to the railroads. . . . It is difficult at best to say that financial losses should be balanced against the loss of lives and limbs of workers and people using the highways.

For Justice Black, therefore, inefficiency is not sufficient to invalidate a statute, for a state is entitled to treat life and limb in nonmarket-oriented ways.

This approach, however, would entirely eliminate dormant commerce clause review. If that review involved balancing, economic interests would be on one side and noneconomic ones on the other, and it is impossible to balance incommensurable items. Even if the metaphor of balancing were maintained, Justice Black would allow the state to place whatever weight it chose on the side of safety, so that the state interests would always prevail. While Justice Black would have accepted such a result, the Court has not embraced it. The Court has assumed that it makes sense to balance, but it has not yet confronted the implications of its contemporaneous approval of state laws that reject the efficiency criteria which make all interests commensurable.

Perhaps the Court's reluctance to bring this contradiction into the open is an indication that it has not fully adopted the efficiency criteria either. It has responded to Justice Black by saying, in effect, that a state may place any weight *within reason* on noneconomic interests. Due process review has thus reentered through the back door. This should not be surprising, for the efficiency concerns that alone justify burden analysis under the dormant commence clause are precisely the same as the concerns that had once been expressed through due process analysis. The linkage between the two types of review can be seen again if burden problems are examined in a somewhat different light.

2. INTERNALIZING COSTS THROUGH TORT LAW, USER FEES, AND REGULATIONS

Justice Black's reluctance to require that life and limb be monetized was almost certainly derived from his sense that monetary awards were in reality inadequate. One is troubled by an award of $50,000 for loss of both legs, when one is reasonably confident that the victim would have rejected an offer of $50,000 for the loss before the accident. To some extent, this uneasiness is based on the implicit judgment that existing damage criteria are inadequate. A liability system aimed at fully internalizing the external costs of enterprise should measure damages by the difference between the victim's post-accident position and what his position would have been but for the accident. If a $50,000 post-accident award is troubling, it is because the award is inconsistent with the standards needed to make the liability system work.

The state could remedy this flaw by adjusting its damage rules. It could, for example, make awards for intangibles such as pain and suffering easier to receive. If needed, excess compensation for intangibles could be used to compensate for a perceived undercompensation for tangible injuries. The Supreme Court has indicated that a state could force the industry involved to absorb the new administrative costs by charging fees for using some service or for invoking new damage rules so long as the fees charged were "not wholly unreasonable." Indeed, the fees, if reasonable, could exceed the administrative costs of the service or the new damage rules, although here the meaning of "reasonable" is not immediately apparent. Analytically, changes in state damage rules, whether or not accompanied by user charges, should be subject to commerce clause review, for they do raise prices. But no significant challenges to such charges have bene made in the modern era. The reason must be that standards of reasonableness are easily met, and litigation is accordingly fruitless.

There is no substantive difference between new damage rules plus user charges and regulation. Damage rules and user charges force each enterprise to bear the external costs it imposes, while regulation places the burden on the industry as a whole. If the cost of regulation is reasonable in light of the external costs of an industry, regulation should be allowed on the same principle that allows user charges. Thus, the inquiry in burden cases also ought to focus on a test of reasonableness.

3. BALANCING AS A SURROGATE FOR DUE PROCESS INQUIRY

So far, it has been established that challenges to regulations on undue burden grounds are indistinguishable from challenges to changes in tort law on economic due process grounds. In both cases, the challenges rest on claims that the state's law unreasonably raises prices, in the sense that it raises prices to an extent that is not justified by the benefits flowing from the law. But the Supreme Court has explicitly rejected efficiency criteria in due process cases, while it remains attached to such criteria in undue burden cases. By examining some recent decisions, it can be seen that undue burden analysis incorporates what should be called "enhanced due process" analysis. The stage is then set for an open return to the application of substantive due process doctrines in economic cases.

Although the Court has purported to use balancing tests in burden cases, in practice its review has not involved a difficult balancing of interests of similar weight. Typically, the Court will acknowledge the importance, or at least the legitimacy, of the state interest asserted, but will conclude that the regulation at issue does virtually nothing to advance that interest. Since very little is left on the state's side of the balance, the national interest prevails. Every significant modern case invalidating a state regulation follows this pattern.

For example, the Court in *Southern Pacific Co. v. Arizona*, concluded that the limitation on train length "afford[ed] at most slight and dubious advantage, if any, over unregulated train lengths." The state interest in *Pike v. Bruce Church, Inc.* was to guarantee that Arizona retained its reputation as a state in which high quality cantaloupes were grown. The Court "assume[d]" that this was a legitimate interest, but it characterized the interest as "tenuous," a semantically odd term, and "minimal at best." The argument advanced by Mississippi in *Great Atlantic & Pacific Tea Co. v. Cottrell* that its requirement of reciprocity in the sale of milk, which permitted foreign milk to be sold in the state only if the state of origin allowed Mississippi milk to be sold without inspection, promoted health was deemed by the Court to "border [on] the frivolous."

Standing alone, these quotations might suggest that the Court was simply invoking a due process test by invalidating statutes that raise prices but provide no offsetting advantages. The last two cases, though, were decided in 1970 and 1976, years when economic due process arguments were not given a warm reception by the Court. The *Cottrell* case demonstrates that the Court is using a more vigorous standard than the current due process one. In addition to the health purpose, the state asserted that requiring reciprocity reduced the cost of administering an inspection system. The Court responded that a reasonable alternative existed, since foreign producers could be charged with the cost of the inspection. Modern due process cases eschew analysis of equally effective alternatives. In addition, when the Court has upheld regulations against commerce clause challenges, it has sometimes done so only after a relatively detailed examination of the effectiveness of the state's regulation as a means of achieving its purpose.

4. SUBSTANTIVE DUE PROCESS AS A BASIS FOR DECISION

When the Court's decisions are viewed as a group, they show enhanced due process scrutiny parading in the guise of a balancing process. Due process scrutiny is enhanced by adding to the deference accorded most state economic regulations, a concern for efficiency that is absent from most cases labelled "due process." The Court has been attracted to balancing tests under the "burden" label for two reasons related to its discomfort over the abandonment of overt due process scrutiny. When those reasons are aired, they can be augmented to provide a positive argument for a return to substantive due process analysis in economic cases.

First, in the substantive due process area, standards of reasonableness are so loose that the test of reasonableness is satisfied by almost any law. Transferring those standards to the dormant commerce clause area would entirely eliminate any judicial supervision of state economic regulation. When Justice Stone first suggested that the test under the dormant commerce clause was "whether the means of regulation chosen are reasonably adapted to the end sought," tests of reasonableness in the due process area had not yet been emptied of content. In contrast, by the time Justice Stone proposed that balancing was appropriate in commerce clause inquiry, the ultimate fate of the due process clause as applied to economic regulation was clear. Reasonableness was already well on its way to meaning anything goes. Thus, balancing tests are used to preserve some role for the Court in view of the emptiness of existing due process standards.

Second, the Court must have felt some discomfort over its abdication in the due process field, as it should have. Efficiency criteria, while they certainly need not be the only ones invoked by legislature, are relevant to the legislative task. Due process review ought to be used to guarantee that efficiency is not wholly disregarded by the legislature.

This defense of burden analysis, when expanded, is also a defense of due process scrutiny. National intervention has been justified on the ground that one state's regulation imposes costs on consumers both within and without the state, and that local political processes were likely to underestimate the external costs of regulation. But this argument holds with respect to regulation generally. In an interdependent economy, it is unrealistic to bifurcate laws into those that have effect outside the state and those that do not. Just as doctrine regarding Congress' power under the commerce clause long ago came to recognize that everything is interstate commerce, so too should dormant commerce clause doctrine reflect the economic facts of American life. In addition, due process review would embody concerns for efficiency shared most directly by the consuming public. General difficulties in organizing the consumer interest support judicial intervention within the general political theory sketched by Justice Stone in order to guarantee that efficiency concerns are taken into account at some point in the process of enforcing a statute.

An appropriately restrained stance would allow judicial intervention in those cases, perhaps few in number, where no organized interest group appears to oppose inefficient regulations and incidentally enlists general efficiency arguments on behalf of parochial concerns. Several facets of due process review should be brought out. First, authorizing such review would give the court the opportunity to overturn statutes even where the political process was entirely adequate to protect the consumer interest. Indeed, due process review has been discredited in precisely those circumstances. What is striking to the student of the dormant commerce clause, though, is how well the Court has already done in subjecting statutes to a scrutiny indistinguishable from that which due process review would impose. A Court conscious of the political theory is unlikely to be misled by the label "due process." Overreaching is likely to be rare and the Court's occasional errors may well be a cost worth bearing in light of other instances of appropriate intervention.

Second, Congress' power to suspend judicial determinations in this area would formally be absent were the Court to use due process review as the articulated basis for its actions. Here too the risk of judicial overreaching is likely to be small. Where national legislation is involved, the Court's deliberations are not likely to be colored by a perception of local parochialism. Thus, due process scrutiny can be expected to proceed in a relatively straight-forward manner. Further, the investigative resources of Congress and representation before the Court by federal authorities are likely to lead Congress to develop evidence that the costs of regulation are outweighed by its benefits. State investigations and representation may not make the case so persuasively.

It cannot be said, of course, that open adherence to substantive due process review in economic cases is free of risk, or that its risks will surely be outweighed in practice by its benefits. But enhanced due process scrutiny has an additional attraction: it would rationalize the impact of national law on federalism. Present doctrine allows invalidation of statutes under the dormant commerce clause that would survive due process review. In effect, the Court tells the states in one breath that they are free to experiment and to disregard efficiency criteria, only to say, in apparently unrelated contexts, that their disregard of efficiency will be limited. A unified doctrine of enhanced due process would make it clear that the states can experiment, but not too much. And clarity is a virtue that cannot be valued too much in constitutional law.

* * *

Julian N. Eule, *Laying the Dormant Commerce Clause to Rest*, 91 YALE L.J. 425, 435-44 (1982)*

* * *

The time-honored rationales for traditional dormant commerce clause jurisprudence have become historical vestiges. Because the Constitution does not protect free trade or a national market, the Court's current role as the trumpeter of these values can only be viewed as that of congressional spokesman. In 1789 Congress needed this crutch. Congress can now fend for itself. A number of commentators have suggested,

* Reprinted by permission of The Yale Law Journal Company and Fred B. Rothman & Company from The Yale Law Journal, Vol. 91, pp. 425-485.

however, that Congress cannot provide adequate or satisfactory guidance to the states. This defense of an active judicial role under the dormant commerce clause ignores the obvious role played by the regulatory agencies in translating the general into the particular and thus fleshing out the commands of Congress. More important, Congress' inability to anticipate the diverse situations to which its guidelines may have to be applied is not a compelling argument for judicial usurpation of the law-making responsibility. It is one thing to say that courts often have to construe the scope and intent of federal legislative efforts under the preemption doctrine. It is quite another to say that where Congress has refused or failed to enact guidelines at all, the courts may substitute their own formulations. The argument that Congress is too busy, that attention to state commercial legislation would divert it from its "usual" and "more pressing" business is similarly unconvincing. The national commercial interest ought to be the "usual" business of Congress and its regulatory agencies. After all, nothing could be "more pressing" than combatting the threat to "the solidarity and prosperity of this Nation" posed by excessively burdensome or protectionist legislation. If the internal machinery of Congress and its agencies is inadequate to deal with the "myriad of state and local rules" intruding on the national domain, then Congress can modify that machinery.

It no longer makes sense for the Court to invalidate evenhanded state legislation merely because it burdens interstate commerce too heavily. Under the Court's present standard, the likelihood of judicial invalidation increases with the degree of burden imposed by state law, and the weight of the national interest. But this is precisely the situation in which action by Congress or administrative agencies is most likely. There is something fundamentally wrong with a judicial framework that prompts judicial intervention by the same trigger that induces political response. One might have thought that the revolutionary expansion of congressional power and the proliferation of federal regulatory agencies would prompt a re-examination of the role of the Court under the dormant commerce clause. The Court, in fact, appears not merely to have continued its campaign to impart content to congressional silences, but to have significantly stepped up its effort. It has invalidated seven state commercial regulations over the past six terms (a rate of more than one per term) as compared to four times over the preceding twenty-four terms (a rate of one every six terms).

A. An Alternative Role

Much attention has been paid in recent legal literature to the dichotomy between process-based interpretations of the United States Constitution and value-laden searches for fundamental rights protected by that document. The seemingly cyclical revival of this jurisprudential schism was no doubt precipitated by the Supreme Court's pronouncements in *Roe v. Wade*. To one school of thought, that decision is no more defensible than the now discredited protection of liberty of contract in *Lochner v. New York*. Both decisions make the same mistake. They purport to authorize judicial imposition of fundamental values that are not derived from the text, history or structure of the Constitution. The process-based theorists reject the proposition that the Framers regarded jurists as "better reflectors of conventional values than elected representatives," and instead view the constitutionally envisioned judicial role as "policing the mechanisms by which the system seeks to ensure that our elected representatives will actually represent." Accordingly, where the political system proves responsive, deference to the democratic structure is warranted. The opposing school of thought finds no inherent obstacle to judicial selection and application of contemporary norms that are neither demonstrably expressed nor implied by the Framers and expresses puzzlement at the persistence of process-based constitutional theories.

Surprisingly, the dormant commerce clause is seldom viewed as a productive battleground for academic warfare between the value-protectors and the process-preservers. Perhaps this can best be explained by the Court's unearthing of something for everyone in this invisible clause. For the process-oriented among us, the Court has found a prohibition against discriminatory or disproportional state legislative treatment of interstate commerce. In an approach akin to that of his famous footnote in *Carolene Products*, Justice Harlan Stone pointed out the defects inherent in a legislative scheme whose purpose or effect is to gain an advantage for those within the state at the expense of those without. "[W]hen the regulation, is of such a character that its burden falls principally upon those without the state, legislative action is not likely to be subjected to those political restraints which are normally exerted on legislation where it affects adversely some interests within the state." This approach is hereinafter referred to as the "process" standard because of its focal concern for the integrity of the mechanics that produce the legislation rather than the desirability of the impact thus produced.

The needs of the value-oriented have not been neglected either. In a distinct strand of the fabric of the commerce clause's negative implications, the Court has mystically found a restriction against unduly burdening the free flow of interstate trade, even where an identical burden has been imposed on intrastate commerce. Unlike the process-oriented approach, whose inquiry is directed at the *proportional division* of the burden, the focus of the value-oriented theme (hereinafter referred to as the "free trade" standard) is the *weight* of the burden imposed. Four permutations may be invoked to illustrate the interrelationships between those two strands of dormant commerce clause jurisprudence.

In the first, the burden of the state legislative effort is minimal in effect and evenhanded in distribution. This scheme encounters no commerce clause difficulties under either branch of review. The second permutation, reflecting the opposite end of the scale, imposes a burden which is both "excessive" and disproportionally distributed. In other words, the heavy burden imposed falls either exclusively or predominantly on foreign interests not represented in the law-making body. This legislative effort will be invalidated under either approach, although it is by no means clear which the Court finds preferable or why. In the third permutation, the impact is disproportional, but not excessive. This variation must overcome the considerable obstacles of a process-based inquiry, but if it does so, it will encounter no problem under the value-based free trade standard.

In the last of these simplistic categorizations, the burden, while "excessive," falls evenhandedly on both represented local and unrepresented foreign interests. This final legislative permutation proves the most troublesome. While the legislation will survive the representation-reinforcing scrutiny of the process standard, it faces judicial veto under the free trade standard if the Court disagrees with the state's accommodation of the competing demands of the state and national interest involved. It is judicial commitment to such balancing that has so offended the adherents of the process strand. The process standard and the free trade standard cannot be regarded as complementary, therefore, because they inevitably clash when an "excessive" state regulatory burden falls equally on represented and on unrepresented interests.

It is necessary to bifurcate the objection to such a "super-legislature" approach in order better to understand the nature of this conflict. The challenge to judicial interest-weighing may be one of competence—that courts lack the tools to make such judgments, or one of separation of powers—that making such determinations would transcend the judiciary's proper constitutional role. Both objections, of course, share the crucial assumption that judicial intervention is unnecessary in this fourth legislative permutation. Regardless of the correctness of such an assumption in the 1930's and 1940's when the "super-legislature" approach was first opposed, its validity today seems far more certain. Determining that judicial response is superfluous in view of congressional omnipotence, however, is one step away from concluding that it is unwise. The competency objection to the balancing approach seems to fall considerably short of bridging the gap between lack of need and danger of usage. To begin with, accepting the proposition that courts lack the needed skills ignores the reality of modern constitutional decisionmaking. It is unavoidable that courts, faced with the application of nonabsolutist constitutional provisions, frequently must balance interests. If skills are the product of experience, judges must, at the very least, be regarded as accomplished apprentices. The competency objection labors, however, under a more serious defect. If it is, as that objection implies, the *accuracy* rather than the *propriety* of judicial action that troubles us, the dormant commerce clause seems a strange target toward which to direct our concerns. Regardless of the rate of error here, Congress retains the right to correct any erroneous weighing because of the nonconstitutional nature of the court's ruling.

It is, therefore, the alternative objection—that judicial invalidation of evenhanded state commercial legislation through the current weighing process is inconsistent with our constitutional system of representative democracy—that highlights the incompatibility of the process and value-based themes.

The representation-enforcing approach commands judicial intervention where the mechanisms of participatory government have failed to operate, but it also requires deference where no such defect appears. The failure to defer to the legislative product undercuts the democratic process in a multitude of ways. It permits substitution of judicially imposed policies for evenhanded and rationally based state legislation efforts. It encourages politically influential interest groups to seek remedies in judicial rather than legislative tribunals. It induces congressional and agency abrogation of responsibility. Finally, it subverts the silently expressed will of the majority by imposition of national uniformity despite Congress' considered refusal or inability to achieve legislatively the same result.

In the commerce clause context, selecting between competing approaches, the process-based and value-oriented, ought to pose no serious dilemma. The Framers unquestionably rejected free trade as a constitutionally protected value. Invalidation of state commercial legislation can only, therefore, be done on some basis other than its interference with the "right" of an individual or corporation to engage in interstate trade unhindered by government restrictions. Two alternatives immediately suggest themselves. The legislation may be invalidated because its burdensome nature "invades or nullifies federal prerogatives" or because its discriminatory or protectionist nature represents a breakdown of the mechanism of democratic government. The continued need for judicial intervention on the former ground, the reader will recall, was challenged earlier. In the end, therefore, we are left with only a single justification for judicial displacement of state legislative judgments in the commercial area—the process-oriented protection of representational government. This theme, heralded in *McCulloch v. Maryland* has had, and continues to have its champions. What is not at all clear, however, is why this inquiry should take place under the umbrella of the dormant commerce clause.

B. *The Inappropriate Commercial Focus*

Identifying process protection as the preferred goal in scrutinizing state commercial regulation admittedly raises as many problems as it purports to resolve. That judicial efforts ought properly to be directed toward ensuring a legislative process consistent with the concept of representional government sounds admirable in principle, but in practice it is often difficult to identify actual instances of the breakdown of represential democracy. In commerce clause jurisprudence, the traditional watchword has been "discrimination." Those unsympathetic with the process theme have criticized the term "discrimination" as mere "shibboleth," offering "not a great deal in either understanding or guidance." To be sure the term is not "self-defining" but a large part of the problem is the Court's failure to identify unambiguously who or what it is that state legislatures may not discriminate against. The Court's standard response—that it is "interstate commerce" which may not be discriminated against— is of little help. It leaves unsettled whether the entities protected against discrimination are the articles of commerce themselves, or those out-of-state individuals and corporations engaged in their production, shipment and sale. . . .

Bibliography

The Dormant Commerce Clause

Barrett, Jr., Edward L., *State Taxation of Interstate Commerce—"Direct Burdens," "Multiple Burdens," or What Have You?* 4 VAND. L. REV. 496 (1951)

Collins, Richard B., *Economic Union as a Constitutional Value*, 63 N.Y.U. L. REV. 43 (1988)

Dunham, Allison, *Gross Receipts Taxes on Interstate Transactions,* 47 COLUM. L. REV. 211 (1947)

Farber, Daniel A., *State Regulation and the Dormant Commerce Clause*, 3 CONST. COMM. 395 (1986)

Hartman, Paul J., STATE TAXATION OF INTERSTATE COMMERCE (1953)

Lockhart, William B., *State Tax Barriers to Interstate Commerce*, 53 HARV. L. REV. 1253 (1940)

Sedler, Robert A., *The Negative Commerce Clause as a Restriction on State Regulation and Taxation: An Analysis in Terms of Constitutional Structure*, 31 WAYNE L. REV. 885 (1985)

Part IV
Equality Concepts

Equal protection jurisprudence, regardless of any criticism that it elicits, has substantially exceeded early expectations. Earlier this century Justice Holmes dismissed the equal protection guarantee as "the usual last resort of constitutional arguments."[1] In its first interpretation of the Fourteenth Amendment, the Supreme Court doubted "whether any action of a State not directed by way of discrimination against the negroes as a class, or on account of their race, will ever be held to come within the purview of this provision."[2] Contrary to such expectations, the Equal Protection Clause has emerged as an especially prolific source of constitutional litigation and judicially driven societal change that transcends concern with race. Even so, equal protection remains a function of relatively discrete concern insofar as heightened scrutiny is triggered only by certain classifications or by discriminations in the distribution of fundamental rights.

Race

Slavery

Founding of the union two centuries ago was a function of brokering and negotiation among the initial thirteen states. No issue was more divisive at the Constitutional Convention than slavery. As James Madison observed, friction among the delegates owed less to differences between large and small states than "the effects of their having or not having slaves."[3] Despite some sentiment against slavery, the interests in establishing a viable union were prioritized over such concern. The result was a document that, without ever specifically using the term "slavery," included several provisions that accommodated the institution. A. Leon Higginbotham, Jr. examines the Declaration of Independence, notes the hypocrisy of its terms when viewed in relationship to the practices of its authors and traces how its basic equality principle over the long run has proved difficult to contain. Thurgood Marshall notes the same phenomenon of exclusion and subordination as a defining aspect of the Constitution's framing and ratification.

---

1   Buck v. Bell, 274 U.S. 200, 208 (1927).

2   Slaughter-House Cases, 83 U.S. 36, 81 (1873).

3   2 Max Farrand, The Records of the Federal Convention of 1787, 486 (1937).

A. Leon Higginbotham, Jr., IN THE MATTER OF COLOR (1978)*

THE DECLARATION OF INDEPENDENCE
A SELF-EVIDENT TRUTH OR A SELF-EVIDENT LIE?

When we were the political slaves of King George, and wanted to be free, we called the maxim that "all men are created equal" a self-evident truth; but now when we have grown fat, and lost all dread of being slaves ourselves, we have become so greedy to be masters that we call the same maxim "a self-evident lie." The Fourth of July has not quite dwindled away; it is still a great day for burning fire-crackers!

—Abraham Lincoln, 1855

Roots of the Revolution

Did the Declaration of Independence announce a self-evident truth or a self-evident lie? The answer depends on whose equality one considers. As Abraham Lincoln later noted, the success of the first Revolution in no way altered the degraded status of most black Americans. Nor did it free the more than one-half million slaves in the colonies. As we have noted in the introduction of this book, Frederick Douglass spoke out three years before Lincoln, much to the same point when he noted: "This Fourth [of] July is yours, not mine . . . the sunlight that brought light and healing to you, has brought stripes and death to me." From the perspective of the black masses, the Revolution merely assured the plantation owners of their right to continue the legal tyranny of slavery.

It is sad to note that the first emancipation proclamation applying to American slaves was issued during the Revolutionary era by the representatives of George III. On November 7, 1775, John Murray, Earl of Dunmore and Governor-General of the Colony and Dominion of Virginia, issued a proclamation that freed "all indented Servants, Negroes or others . . . able and willing to bear Arms . . ." with His Majesty's troops. In contrast, some of the colonists equivocated as to whether they would free blacks who fought for the colonists' cause. Tragically the colonists wanted both their freedom from the King and simultaneously the right to deny that freedom to blacks.

Some blacks were active on the battle fronts and behind the lines. In his illuminative work, Professor Benjamin Quarles noted:

> The Negro's role in the Revolution can best be understood by realizing that his major loyalty was not to a place nor to a people, but to a principle. Insofar as he had freedom of choice, he was likely to join the side that made him the quickest and best offer in terms of those "unalienable rights" of which Mr. Jefferson had spoken.

As to blacks who fought for the independence of the new nation, Harriet Beecher Stowe observed:

> We are to reflect upon them as far more magnanimous [because they served] a nation which did not acknowledge them as citizens and equals, and in whose interests and prosperity they had less at stake. It was not for their own land they fought, not even for a land which had adopted them,

---

*   Excerpted from IN THE MATTER OF COLOR, RACE AND THE AMERICAN LEGAL PROCESS: THE COLONIAL PERIOD by A. Leon Higginbotham, Jr. Copyright © by Oxford University Press, Inc. Reprinted by permission.

but for a land which had enslaved them, and whose laws, even in freedom, oftener oppressed than protected. Bravery, under such circumstances, has a peculiar beauty and merit.

Relatively few blacks were freed by the colonists, by either Lord Dunmore's proclamation or the fact that several thousand blacks had fought on behalf of the American forces. The war had no immediate impact on the struggle to deny slavery its legitimacy as an institution. Yet half a century later, the documents and rhetoric of this successful "white" revolution did indeed become catalysts, if not rallying points, for blacks and their white allies in the abolitionist struggles. In the decades preceding the Civil War, abolitionists would point to the forefathers' Revolutionary assertion of inalienable rights and the obligation of those who govern to obtain the consent of the governed. Affirming the essential dignity of all mankind, they stressed the inherent hypocrisy in this nation's exclusion of blacks from those rights of mankind that at its very birth this nation proclaimed inalienable.

Paradoxically, then, the first Declaration, impotent though it was to change black servitude, did ultimately play a part in the evolutionary process that was to free blacks from slavery. Accordingly, the history of the first Declaration of Independence is relevant to an understanding of the process through which blacks came to be freed from slavery and through which post-emancipation gains were made.

Though the temptation exists to equate the opening of hostilities with the start of revolutions, revolutions do not begin in the hour when the first shots are fired. Revolutions, like most historic moments, are born and acted out in men's minds well before they become history. As Chateaubriand noted with regard to the revolution in France, it was "accomplished before it occurred." Similarly, among its more radical leaders, the American Revolution started long before 1776. As John Adams wrote:

> What do we mean by the revolution? The war with Britain? That was no part of the revolution; it was only the effect and consequence of it. The revolution was in the minds and hearts of the people, and this was effected from 1760 to 1775, in the course of fifteen years, before a drop of blood was shed at Lexington.

Though Adams and a few revolutionary thinkers were manifestly discontent even before 1760, until 1764 the colonists "were in the main well satisfied" despite some occasional tensions with Great Britain. The vast majority seemed "proud to be counted British subjects and citizens within the empire, the burdens of which, such as they were, had never rested heavily upon them." They had been displeased with those Imperial regulations that hindered the manufacture of iron products, hats, or woolen cloth, but the vast majority "had inspired no thoughts of outright resistance." However, upon the passage of the 1764 Sugar Act, this "gentle current of tranquility" was shaken.

The 1764 Sugar Act put the American colonists in a significantly disadvantageous position in their competition in the triangular trade. This trade involved the shipping of products, basically molasses, from the West Indies to the New England colonies for distillation into rum, generally at Boston or Newport. The rum and other New England products were shipped to Africa in exchange for slaves; the slaves were then transported to the American colonies. The 1764 Act precluded American colonies from obtaining molasses at the French Islands, such as Santo Domingo, where the products were superior and cheaper. This one act of Parliament had, as James Otis declared, "set people a-thinking in six months, more than they had done in their whole lives before." Starting with the protest to the 1764 Act, more colonists began to agree with Patrick Henry's later prediction that England would:

> drive us to extremities; no accommodation *will* take place; hostilities *will* *soon* commence; and a desperate and bloody touch it will be.

In their new thinking the soon to be revolutionary leaders were greatly influenced by the concepts of natural rights that John Locke and others had articulated. Locke's categorization of the natural rights of "property, liberty and estate" were broadened to "life, liberty and the pursuit of happiness" by Jefferson. Armed with the natural rights arguments asserted by Locke and the earlier declared "liberties of Englishmen" it was but an "easy step" for these men to move "to the universalist assertion that all men had a right to be free."

Though influenced by these Lockean concepts, when the representatives to the First Continental Congress met in Philadelphia in 1774 they still did not plan "to set in train a movement for independence from Great Britain." The delegates had been charged by their constituencies "to reestablish the harmony that before 1763 had characterized colonial relations with the mother country." Their primary task was "to persuade the British government to abandon its efforts to tax the colonies without their consent" and to free the colonies from the Coercive Acts. Yet while they were meeting, King George III declared: "The dye is now cast, the Colonies must either submit or triumph." As the colonists became more and more reluctant to submit, the argument that the British denial to them of the natural rights of man constituted an enslavement gained wider appeal.

The White Colonists' Perception of Their Enslavement

Although the enslavement of whites was never legally permissible at any time in any of the colonies, nevertheless revolutionary leaders persistently described the political plight of the colonists as one of enslavement. In noting his opposition to the Sugar Act of 1764, Governor Stephen Hopkins of Rhode Island started his diatribe by asserting that "Liberty is the greatest blessing that men enjoy, and slavery the heaviest curse that human nature is capable of." Of course, Governor Hopkins was not speaking of the enslavement of blacks. Ironically, he argued that white colonists were being enslaved by England because the Sugar Act of 1764 decreased the profits from Rhode Island's involvement in the international slave trade.

Pennsylvania's John Dickinson in 1768 likewise argued:

> *Those* who are *taxed* without their own consent expressed by themselves or their representatives . . . are *slaves*. *We are taxed* without our consent expressed by ourselves or our representatives. *We* are therefore—SLAVES.

Five years later Boston's Josiah Quincy proclaimed:

> I speak it with grief—I speak it with anguish—Britons are our oppressors: I speak it with shame—I speak it with indignation—*we are slaves.*

John Adams concurred that we are "the most abject sort of the worst sort of masters!" Almost every statement of political principles linked the status of white colonists to a concept of slavery.

As a political term then, slavery had two meanings. For whites it described any enactment that limited their economic freedom of action or reduced the value of their property when they had not previously elected representatives to vote on that impediment. Concurrently, however, those arbitrary acts of physically enslaving blacks, were not embraced within the slavery definition whites used in condemning the king's abuses.

Nowhere is this racially bifurcated construction of slavery more manifest than in the July 6, 1775 Declaration of the Causes and Necessities of Taking Up Arms. Franklin, John Rutledge, Johnson, Livingston, John Jay, Jefferson, and Dickinson constituted the committee that drew up this declaration, though the final draft appeared to be primarily the work of Dickinson and Jefferson. They started the Declaration by asking whether it was possible for men "who exercise their reason to believe that the Divine author of our existence intended a part of the human race to hold an absolute power in, and an unbounded power over others . . . as the objects of a legal domination never rightfully resistible, however severe and oppressive." Then they responded:

> the great Creator['s] principles of humanity, and the dictates of common sense, must convince all those who reflect upon the subject, that government was instituted to promote the welfare of mankind, and ought to be administered for the attainment of that end.

They condemned the legislature of Great Britain for "enslaving these colonies by violence," which acts "have thereby rendered it necessary for us to close with [our] last appeal from reasons to arms." They emphasized that when "reduced to the alternative of choosing an unconditional submission to the tyranny of irritated ministers, or resistance by force" that they must respond by force:

> We have counted the cost of this contest, . . . *and find nothing so dreadful as voluntary slavery.*—Honour, justice, and humanity, forbid us tamely to surrender that freedom which we received from our gallant ancestors, and which our innocent posterity have a right to receive from us. We cannot endure the infamy and guilt of resigning succeeding generations to that wretchedness which inevitably awaits them, if we basely entail hereditary bondage upon them.

Several times in their Declaration they referred to their slavery or enslavement. "With hearts fortified" they pledged "before God and the world" that they would use arms "in defiance of every hazard with unabating firmness and perseverance," and they resolved that "we are of one mind" determined *"to die freemen rather than to live slaves."*

Yet while the revolutionary leaders had resolved to die freemen rather than to live slaves, they did not perceive blacks as having the same human right to be free. By their statutes the colonists had made it an act of treason, often punishable by death, for blacks to dare to flee from slavery and seek to live as free men.

The colonists were ridiculed often in England because the protest against their alleged enslavement was inconsistent with their insistence that blacks should be slaves. In 1775 in response to the resolution and address of the American Congress, Dr. Samuel Johnson said:

> If slavery be thus fatally contagious, how is it that we hear the loudest yelps for liberty among the drivers of negroes.

Finally, Johnson summed up the colonists' arguments as "too foolish for buffoonery [and] too wild for madness."

The Moral Antecedents for Challenging, in 1776, the Continuance of Slavery

Although the 1776 statesmen were insistent on their right to revolt for their freedom, they did not mean to even inferentially condemn their enslavement of a half-million blacks. Long before July 4, 1776, many forceful arguments had been asserted as to the immorality of slavery, had our forefathers sought precedent for a commitment to universal freedom. The first organizational resolution as a protest against slavery had occurred, as we have noted in our chapter on the Pennsylvania colony, eighty-eight years previously in the same city where the Declaration of Independence was ultimately written. On February 18, 1688, the Germantown Mennonites at Philadelphia had asserted that maintenance of slavery was inconsistent with Christian principles. They concluded by recognizing the moral right of slaves to revolt and the contradictions of principle if Christians opposed the slaves' fight for freedom:

> If once these slaves (which they say are so wicked and stubborn men,) should join themselves—fight for their freedom, and handel their masters and mistresses, as they did handel them before; will these masters and mistresses take the sword at hand and war against these poor slaves, like, as we were able to believe, some will not refuse to do? Or, have these poor negers not as much right to fight for their freedom, as you have to keep them slaves?

After this 1688 resolution there were many further protestations against slavery. Some challenged slavery on moral grounds. Others opposed slavery because of fears of revolt. Some argued that the existence of slavery precluded white settlers from coming to the new country and still others asserted that slavery deterred the general economic growth of the country.

During this pre-Revolutionary era, none wrote more eloquently in condemnation of slavery than James Otis and Anthony Benezet. In 1764, James Otis wrote "The Rights of the British Colonies Asserted and Proved." First he asserted that all men, black and white, were born equal. Then he asked:

> Does it follow that 'tis right to enslave a man because he is black? Will short curled hair like wool instead of Christian hair . . . help the argument? Can any logical inference in favor of slavery be drawn from a flat nose, a long or short face?

He condemned the slave trade as a "most shocking violation of the law of nature" for it "makes every dealer in it [slavery] a tyrant." Otis also argued that "those who every day barter away other men's liberty will soon care little for their own." Benezet, as the leading Quaker spokesman, argued unrelentingly against slavery.

After reading Benezet's 1772 book, which attacked the slave trade, Patrick Henry noted the incompatibility of Christian precepts and enlightenment values, on the one had, and the practice of slavery on the other. Then, moving from the serene level of abstract analysis to the more difficult task of facing these same contradictions within himself, he noted:

> Would any one believe that I am Master of Slaves of my own purchase! I am drawn along by ye general Inconvenience of living without them; I will not, I cannot justify it.

Yet Patrick Henry was able, as were most "enlightened" slave holders, to soothe his conscience by proclaiming that "a time will come when an opportunity will be offered to abolish this lamentable evil." He urged that if he and his fellow man failed to abolish this evil within "our day" then "let us transmit to our descendants together with our Slaves a pity for their unhappy Lot, and an abhorrence for Slavery."

Even the Harvard University Commencement of July 21, 1773 included "A Forensic Dispute On The Legality of Enslaving Africans." The opponent to slavery argued:

> To me, I confess, it is matter of painful astonishment, that in this enlightened age and land, where the principles of natural and civil Liberty, and consequently the natural rights of mankind are so generally understood, the case of these unhappy *Africans* should gain no more attention;—that those, who are so readily disposed to urge the principles of natural equality in defense of their own Liberties, should, with so little reluctance, continue to exert a power, by the operation of which they are so flagrantly contradicted. For what less can be said of that exercise of power, whereby such multitudes of our fellow-men, descendants, my friend from the same common parent with you and me, and between whom and us nature has made no distinction, save what arises from the stronger influence of the sun in the climate whence they originated, are held to groan under the insupportable burden of the most abject slavery, without one chearing beam to refresh their desponding souls; and upon whose dreary path not even the feeblest ray of hope is permitted to dawn, and whose only prospect of deliverance is—in death. If indeed the law protects their lives, (which is all that can be said even here, and more—shame to mankind!—more than can be said in some of our sister colonies) the only favor these unhappy people receive, from such protection, is a continuation of their misery; the preservation of a life, every moment of which is worse than non-existence.

From Benezet to Patrick Henry, from the Germantown Mennonites to the Harvard commencement, the moral issue had been pleaded with escalating vigor. Shortly before the Declaration of Independence was drafted, theologian Samuel Hopkins petitioned the Continental Congress for the abolishment of slavery. Like others, he linked slavery with immorality and on his cover page he quoted, "Open thy mouth, judge righteously, and plead the cause of the poor and needy" [Pr. XXXI:9] and "as ye would that men should do to you, do ye also to them likewise" [Luke VI:31]. Through these biblical precepts, he argued that slavery was a "shocking, intolerable . . . bare faced inconsistence."

During this era the revolutionaries at Carpenter's Hall were all men—thus, in a political participatory context we had no fore-mothers. But Abigail Adams also had made clear her concerns on the slavery issue. Writing to her husband, John, who was then in Philadelphia, she commented on some petitions slaves in Massachusetts had filed with the governor seeking their freedom, "telling him they would fight for him provided he would arm them, and engage to liberate them if he conquered."

> I wish most sincerely there was not a slave in the province; it always appeared a most iniquitous scheme to me to fight ourselves for what we are daily robbing and plundering from those who have as good a right to freedom as we have.

Obviously, Thomas Jefferson, the man to whom would fall the ominous task of drafting the Declaration of Independence, was aware of these compelling indictments on the immorality of slavery. It is intriguing to observe how he ignored them and instead attempted to single out the international slave trade for condemnation, perhaps thereby partially soothing his conscience as to the injustices which he, a purported spokesman for liberty, perpetuated by his ownership of slaves.

The Discarded July 2 Draft:
A Futile Diatribe on the International Slave Trade

THE DELETED CLAUSE

As finally adopted, the Declaration of Independence contained no references at all to the plight of blacks or slaves, or to the international slave trade. It is particularly ironic that the revolutionary forefathers struck out the one and only provision in an earlier draft that even condemned by inference the international slave trade. Between June 11, 1776 and June 28, 1776, Jefferson had written a passage condemning the international slave trade. Basically, this provision was not altered in the final draft presented by the Committee of Five to the Continental Congress for their debate and deliberations on July 2. The full significance of the deletion at this July 2 debate stage is apparent only to those familiar with the different stages in the writing of the Declaration of Independence.

There were at least three stages in the writing of the Declaration of Independence. On June 11, 1776 the Committee of Five—Jefferson, Franklin, Sherman, Adams, and Robert R. Livingston—was appointed to prepare the Declaration of Independence. The committee gave Jefferson the responsibility to prepare the first draft.

In Jefferson's original rough draft and in the draft approved by the Committee of Five as submitted on June 28 to the Congress, the climax of charges against the king was a significant diatribe against the international slave trade:

> He has waged cruel war against human nature itself, violating it's most sacred rights of life and liberty in the persons of a distant people who never offended him, captivating and carry them into slavery in another hemisphere or to incur miserable death in their transportation thither. This piratical warfare, the opprobrium of *infidel* powers, is the warfare of the Christian king of Great Britain. Determined to keep open a market where MEN should be bought and sold, he has prostituted his negative for suppressing every legislative attempt to prohibit or to restrain this execrable commerce. And that this assemblage of horrors might want no fact of distinguished die, he is now exciting these very people to rise in arms among us, and to purchase that liberty of which *he* has deprived them, by murdering the people on whom *he* also obtruded them; thus paying off former crimes committed against the *Liberties* of one people, with crimes which he urges them to commit against the *lives* of another.

As a matter of logic, in many respects the diatribe was substantively deficient. For George III did not initiate the slave trade; it had been started centuries before. Further, there is an inherent hypocrisy wherein Jefferson is so vehement against the international slave trade and yet is totally silent about the continuance of slavery in the colonies. If, in Jefferson's phrase, the international slave trade was initiated by "cruel war against human nature itself," why was it not just as depraved for him to keep in lifetime servitude in the colonies those who had been so cruelly captured abroad or their children?

Furthermore, even in 1776 many of the colonies had never taken steps to prevent the further importation of slaves, and most had profited from it. Even Virginia's sporadic opposition to the international slave trade may have been based more on a fear of slave revolts or on economic considerations than on any concern about the immorality of either the international slave trade or slavery itself.

Unfortunately, there is just as much reason to believe that Jefferson was not truly troubled about the international slave trade. Perhaps his insertion of this provision had more pragmatic ends, one being to mitigate the impact of Lord Dunmore's emancipation proclamation. Jefferson had responded to Dunmore's proclamation by arguing that the king was:

> now exciting those very people to rise in arms among us, and to purchase that liberty of which *he* was deprived them, by murdering the people upon whom *he* also obtruded them: thus paying off former crimes committed against the *liberties* of one people, with crimes which he urges them to commit against the *lives* of another.

Was Jefferson's greatest fear that the slaves might believe that they too were entitled to the natural rights of man Jefferson had proclaimed for the white colonists? Was Jefferson most fearful that the slaves believing in the natural rights of man might take arms against their slave master oppressors, just as the colonists felt they had the obligation to take arms against the king? Was he merely fearful of the economic loss that Dunmore's proclamation might cause because Jefferson's "livelihood depended" on the continuance of slavery?

Nevertheless, when Jefferson's draft was debated by the Congress on July 2 to 4, the members eliminated even this one reference to slavery. Jefferson's notes of July 2 state:

> The clause too, reprobating the enslaving the inhabitants of Africa, was struck out in complaisance to South Carolina and Georgia, ... Our Northern brethren felt a little tender for they had been pretty considerable carriers of [slaves].

Rather than risk any negative votes from South Carolina and Georgia, the Congress opted for unanimity because of an attitude that Franklin reportedly expressed: "We must, indeed all hang together, or most assuredly we shall all hang separately." Despite Thomas Jefferson's purported chagrin over the deletion, as John Hope Franklin pointedly observed, "The record does not indicate that Jefferson made any effort to save the section" against the international slave trade. For a mulatto slave Sandy, the following excerpted advertisement of Thomas Jefferson's was far more significant than his flourish of words condemning the international slave trade:

> Run away a Mulatto slave Sandy, 35 years, complexion light, shoemaker by trade, can do coarse carpenters work, a horse jockey, when drunk insolent and disorderly, swears much, and his behavior is artful and knavish. Took a horse. Whoever conveys the said slave to me shall have reward . . . .
> THOMAS JEFFERSON

The July 2nd draft probably reflected the tensions within Jefferson—his simultaneous desire to protect his estate and his moral inability to justify slavery. Five years later, Jefferson, once again commenting on slavery, further noted:

> Indeed I tremble for my country when I reflect that God is just; that his justice cannot sleep forever.

The Impact of the Declaration of Independence:
"The Tendency of a Principle to Expand Itself
to the Limit of its Logic"

After reading the sordid history of a nation that spoke nobly that all men are created equal and then, nevertheless, excluded blacks from the equality promised all, the unsophisticated might argue that the Declaration of Independence had no ultimate impact or significant in eradicating slavery or diminishing racial discrimination. Yet in the corridors of history, there is a direct nexus between the egalitarian words uttered, even if not yet meant, and many of the changes that later took place.

No one has written more precisely than has Dean Louis Pollak of the University of Pennsylvania law school on the ultimate impact of the embryonic idea of equality expressed in the Declaration of Independence.

> The ever-widening impact of the nation's early commitment to the equality of "all men" compellingly illustrates what Benjamin N. Cardozo, one of the handful of great American judges, termed "the tendency of a principle to expand itself to the limit of its logic." In this sense, the Declaration of Independence is the apt progenitor of the Emancipation Proclamation, the Gettysburg Address, the Fourteenth Amendment's guarantee of "the equal protection of the laws," and the Supreme Court's recent decisions invalidating governmentally ordained racial segregation in public schools and elsewhere.

If the authors of the Declaration of Independence had said—"all *white* men are created equal" or even "all white men who own property . . ." they would have more honestly conveyed the general consensus. But when they declared, as they did, that "all men are created equal" without introducing any qualifications, they created a document that put moral demands on all Americans who would ever quote it. Thus, on the authority of the Declaration of Independence blacks and their white sympathizers urged that they were obligated to abolish the present government that denied blacks "Life, liberty and the pursuit of happiness."

The irony of the unfulfilled American dream of equality is that of all those in the long line of dreamers who have sought the ultimately just society, none had to seek out alien sources for moral authority. They had only to say to the American people fulfill the largest promise in your first statement as a nation.

By its very language, the Declaration of Independence introduced to the nation, from its inception, the problem of a "moral overstrain," a burden from which it has ever since suffered in varying degrees—that ". . . tension caused between high ideals and low achievement, between the American creed including equalitarian individualism and the historical American reality of unjust, unequal and class treatment for blacks."

From 1776 to 1863 abolitionists repeatedly used the language and logic of the Declaration of Independence to stoke the American conscience. Abolitionist William Lloyd Garrison, in commencing his newspaper, "The Liberator," stressed that because he:

> Assent[ed] to the "self-evident truths" maintained in the American Declaration of Independence, "that all men are created equal, and endowed by their Creator with certain inalienable rights—. . ." I shall strenuously contend for the immediate enfranchisement of our slave population. . . .

After quoting from the Declaration, the Quaker David Cooper asserted:

If these solemn truths, uttered at such an awful crisis, are *self-evident*: unless we can shew that the African race are not *men*, words can hardly express the amazement which naturally arises on reflecting, that the very people who make these pompous declarations are slave-holders, and by their legislative conduct, tell us, that these blessing were only meant to be the rights of *white-men* not of all *men*.

At the end of the Revolutionary War, Cooper wrote:

We need not now turn over the libraries of Europe for authorities to prove that blacks are born equally free with whites: it is declared and recorded as the sense of America.

Further, reflect on the following cry of outrage by Frederick Douglass regarding Independence Day celebrations and consider how much less moral force his arguments would have had if the framers of the Declaration of Independence had not declared all men created equal.

your denunciation of tyrants, [are] brass fronted impudence; your shouts of liberty and equality, hollow mockery; your prayers and hymns, your sermons and thanksgivings, with all your religious parade and solemnity, are, to Him mere bombast, fraud, deception, impiety, and *hypocrisy*—a thin veil to cover up crimes which would disgrace a nation of savages. There is not a nation on the earth guilty of practices more shocking and bloody than are the people of the United States, at this very hour.

But the impact of the Declaration of Independence goes beyond its implied criticism of the hypocrisy of slavery; for the document not only asserts that all men were endowed with these inalienable rights but "That whenever any Form of Government becomes destructive of those ends, it is the Right of the People to alter or to abolish it, and to institute new Government. . . ."

In 1831 black abolitionist David Walker wrote:

that if any people were ever justified in throwing off the yoke of their tyrants, the slaves are that people. It is not we, but our guilty countrymen, who put arguments into the mouths, and swords into the hands of the slaves. Every sentence that they write—every word that they speak— every resistance that they make, against foreign oppression, is a call upon their slaves to destroy them. Every Fourth of July celebration must embitter and inflame the minds of the slaves.

Born to a free black woman, David Walker wrote a series of tracts that placed fear in the hearts of every slaveholder, partially because he cited their Declaration of Independence as his justification for inciting blacks to rise with force and militancy to destroy their white oppressors. In "Walker's Appeal in Four Articles Together with a Preamble to the Colored Citizens of the World, But in Particular and very Expressly to those of the United States of America," he asserted:

Are we men!!—I ask you . . . are we MEN? Did our creator make us to be slaves to dust and ashes like ourselves? Are they not dying worms as well as we? . . . How we could be so *submissive* to a gang of men, whom we cannot tell whether they are as good as ourselves or not, I never could conceive. . . . America is more our country than it is the whites—we have enriched it with our *blood and tears.* The greatest riches in all America have arisen from our blood and tears:—and will they drive us from our property and homes, which we earned with our *blood*?

In one letter to "The Liberator," a free Negro wrote:

Nothing was ever more true, sir, than the sentiment put forth by Mr. Jefferson in the Declaration of Independence, that all men are born free and equal:—and there is no stronger proof of this truth, than to see, whenever an opportunity presents itself, the oppressed grasping the banner of liberty and breathing forth this sentiment in peals of thunder. That the spirit of liberty is born in the breast of every man is an undeniable truth: it is also true that the sensation accompanies him from his cradle to the grave; and through sometimes suppressed by the sword and bayonet, it often bursts forth, like the smoking volcano, striking terror into the heart of the oppressor. May its mighty power shake the pillars of oppression until they crumble like "the baseless fabric of a vision."

The Declaration of Independence's relevance to blacks was not debated solely in the political and religious forums. Finally the courts were asked to adjudicate its applicability to blacks. In the *Amistad* case, when arguing before the United States Supreme Court for the freedom of Africans who had mutinied against a slave trader, former President of the United States, John Quincy Adams, arguing in behalf of the slaves said:

The moment you come, to the Declaration of Independence, that every man has a right to life and liberty, an inalienable right, this case is decided. I ask nothing more in behalf of these unfortunate men, than this Declaration.

Shortly before the Civil War Abraham Lincoln construed the Declaration of Independence as having a broader scope and impact than that suggested by Taney. President Lincoln said the framers:

meant to set up a standard maxim for free society, which should be . . . constantly looked to, constantly labored for, and even though never perfectly attained, constantly approximated, and thereby constantly spreading and deepening its influence, and augmenting the happiness and value of life to all people of all colors everywhere.

Even after slavery was abolished, Charles Sumner, the major author of the 14th and 15th Amendments, emphasized the continuing relevance of the Declaration. In his moving letter to the American Antislavery Society for their final meeting on April 8, 1870, he said:

The Antislavery Society may now die in peace. Slavery is ended. But I do not doubt that the same courage and fidelity which through long years warred against this prodigious Barbarism will continue determined to the end in protecting and advancing the work begun.

I do not think the work finished, so long as the word "white" is allowed to play any part in legislation,—so long as it constrains the courts in naturalization,—so long as it bars the doors of houses bound by law to receive people for food and lodging, or licensed as places of amusement,— so long as it is inscribed on our common schools;—nor do I think the work finished until the power of the Nation is recognized, supreme and beyond question, to fix the definition of a "republican government," and to enforce the same by the perfect maintenance of rights everywhere throughout the land, *according to the promise of the Declaration of Independence*, without any check or hindrance from the old proslavery pretension of State Rights.

Even after legal emancipation, the Declaration of Independence continued to be part of the moral authority for the dream of true equality. Martin Luther King in his dramatic speech on August 28, 1963 in the celebrated March on Washington referred to it:

> I shall have a dream. It is a dream deeply rooted in the American dream that one day this nation will rise up and live out the true meaning of its creed—we hold these truths to be self-evident, that all men are created equal.

U.S. Supreme Court Chief Justice Earl Warren emphasized its relevance when stating:

> There are many causes [in American justice], but none I believe as basic as our neglect in reaching the ideal we fashioned for ourselves in the Declaration of Independence that "All men are created equal. . . ."

The impact of the Declaration of Independence can be seen in the Civil Rights acts of the 1960s; fortunately the scope has been expanded beyond the Declaration's chauvinistic categorization of "men" to the Civil Rights acts' guarantees for all persons. Title II provides:

> *All persons* shall be entitled to the full and equal enjoyment of the goods, services, facilities, privileges, advantages, and accommodations of any place of accommodation, . . . without discrimination or segregation on the ground of race, color, religion, or national origin.

In Title VII, these rights are expanded to preclude discrimination against any *individual* "with respect to his compensation, terms, conditions, or privileges of employment, because of such individual's race, color, religion, sex, or national origin."

Thus the recent Civil Rights act exemplifies the formation of an idea expanded far beyond what the forefathers intended when they said "all men are created equal." Perhaps if the framers of 1776 had not declared the concept of equality in such universal terms it may have been more difficult to challenge and partially eradicate the pervasive barriers of discrimination on race and sex. But once the drafters and signers of the Declaration of Independence made the decision not to weaken their moral argument for nationhood by attempting to rationalize the lie many of them were living, they made inevitable the irony that the truth they espoused, and not their example, would eventually guide their progeny to a society more just than their own.

Thurgood Marshall, *Commentary: Reflections on the Bicentennial of the United States Constitution*, 101 HARV. L. REV. 1 (1987)*

The year 1987 marks the 200th anniversary of the United States Constitution. A Commission has been established to coordinate the celebration. The official meetings, essay contests, and festivities have begun.

The planned commemoration will span three years, and I am told 1987 is 'dedicated to the memory of the Founders and the document they drafted in Philadelphia.' We are to 'recall the achievements of our Founders and the knowledge and experience that inspired them, the nature of the government they established, its origins, its character, and its ends, and the rights and privileges of citizenship, as well as its attendant responsibilities.'

Like many anniversary celebrations, the plan for 1987 takes particular events and holds them up as the source of all the very best that has followed. Patriotic feelings will surely swell, prompting proud proclamations of the wisdom, foresight, and sense of justice shared by the framers and reflected in a written document now yellowed with age. This is unfortunate—not the patriotism itself, but the tendency for the celebration to oversimplify, and overlook the many other events that have been instrumental to our achievements as a nation. The focus of this celebration invites a complacent belief that the vision of those who debated and compromised in Philadelphia yielded the 'more perfect Union' it is said we now enjoy.

I cannot accept this invitation, for I do not believe that the meaning of the Constitution was forever 'fixed' at the Philadelphia Convention. Nor do I find the wisdom, foresight, and sense of justice exhibited by the framers particularly profound. To the contrary, the government they devised was defective from the start, requiring several amendments, a civil war, and momentous social transformation to attain the system of constitutional government, and its respect for the individual freedoms and human rights, that we hold as fundamental today. When contemporary Americans cite 'The Constitution,' they invoke a concept that is vastly different from what the framers barely began to construct two centuries ago.

For a sense of the evolving nature of the Constitution we need look no further than the first three words of the document's preamble: 'We the People.' When the Founding Fathers used this phrase in 1787, they did not have in mind the majority of America's citizens. 'We the People' included, in the words of the framers, 'the whole Number of free Persons.' On a matter so basic as the right to vote, for example, Negro slaves were excluded, although they were counted for representational purposes—at three-fifths each. Women did not gain the right to vote for over a hundred and thirty years.

These omissions were intentional. The record of the framers' debates on the slave question is especially clear: the Southern states acceded to the demands of the New England states for giving Congress broad power to regulate commerce, in exchange for the right to continue the slave trade. The economic interests of the regions coalesced: New Englanders engaged in the 'carrying trade' would profit from transporting slaves from Africa as well as goods produced in America by slave labor. The perpetuation of slavery ensured the primary source of wealth in the Southern states.

Despite this clear understanding of the role slavery would play in the new republic, use of the words 'slaves' and 'slavery' was carefully avoided in the original document. Political representation in the lower House of Congress was to be based on the population of 'free Persons' in each state, plus three-fifths of all 'other Persons.' Moral principles against slavery, for those who had them, were compromised, with no explanation of the conflicting principles for which the American Revolutionary War had ostensibly been fought: the self-evident truths 'that all men are created equal, that they are endowed by their Creator with certain unalienable Rights, that among these are Life, Liberty and the pursuit of Happiness.'

It was not the first such compromise. Even these ringing phrases from the Declaration of Independence are filled with irony, for an early draft of what became that declaration assailed the King of England for suppressing legislative attempts to end the slave trade and for encouraging slave rebellions. The final draft adopted in 1776 did not contain this criticism. And so again at the Constitutional Convention eloquent objections to the institution of slavery went unheeded, and its opponents eventually consented to a document which laid a foundation for the tragic events that were to follow.

Pennsylvania's Gouverneur Morris provides an example. He opposed slavery and the counting of slaves in determining the basis for representation in Congress. At the Convention he objected that

> the inhabitant of Georgia [or] South Carolina who goes to the coast of Africa, and in defiance of the most sacred laws of humanity tears away his fellow creatures from their dearest connections and damns them to the most cruel bondages, shall have more votes in a Government instituted for protection of the rights of mankind, than the Citizen of Pennsylvania or New Jersey who views with a laudable horror, so nefarious a practice.

And yet Gouverneur Morris eventually accepted the three-fifths accommodation. In fact, he wrote the final draft of the Constitution, the very document the bicentennial will commemorate.

As a result of compromise, the right of the Southern states to continue importing slaves was extended, officially, at least until 1808. We know that it actually lasted a good deal longer, as the framers possessed no monopoly on the ability to trade moral principles for self-interest. But they nevertheless set an unfortunate example. Slaves could be imported, if the commercial interests of the North were protected. To make the compromise even more palatable, customs duties would be imposed at up to ten dollars per slave as a means of raising public revenues.

No doubt it will be said, when the unpleasant truth of the history of slavery in America is mentioned during this bicentennial year, that the Constitution was a product of its times, and embodied a compromise which, under other circumstances, would not have been made. But the effects of the framers' compromise have remained for generations. They arose from the contradiction between guaranteeing liberty and justice to all, and denying both to Negroes.

The original intent of the phrase, 'We the People,' was far too clear for any ameliorating construction. Writing for the Supreme Court in 1857, Chief Justice Taney penned the following passage in the Dred Scott case, on the issue of whether, in the eyes of the framers, slaves were 'constituent members of the sovereignty,' and were to be included among 'We the People':

> We think they are not, and that they are not included, and were not intended to be included. . . .

They had for more than a century before been regarded as beings of an inferior order, and altogether unfit to associate with the white race . . .; and so far inferior, that they had no rights which the white man was bound to respect; and that the negro might justly and lawfully be reduced to slavery for his benefit. . . .

. . . [A]ccordingly, a negro of the African race was regarded . . . as an article of property, and held, and bought and sold as such. . . . [N]o one seems to have doubted the correctness of the prevailing opinion of the time. And so, nearly seven decades after the Constitutional Convention, the Supreme Court reaffirmed the prevailing opinion of the framers regarding the rights of Negroes in America. It took a bloody civil war before the thirteenth amendment could be adopted to abolish slavery, though not the consequences slavery would have for future Americans.

While the Union survived the civil war, the Constitution did not. In its place arose a new, more promising basis for justice and equality, the fourteenth amendment, ensuring protection of the life, liberty, and property of all persons against deprivations without due process, and guaranteeing equal protection of the laws. And yet almost another century would pass before any significant recognition was obtained of the rights of black Americans to share equally even in such basic opportunities as education, housing, and employment, and to have their votes counted, and counted equally. In the meantime, blacks joined America's military to fight its wars and invested untold hours working in its factories and on its farms, contributing to the development of this country's magnificent wealth and waiting to share in its prosperity.

What is striking is the role legal principles have played throughout America's history in determining the condition of Negroes. They were enslaved by law, emancipated by law, disenfranchised and segregated by law; and, finally, they have begun to win equality by law. Along the way, new constitutional principles have emerged to meet the challenges of a changing society. The progress has been dramatic, and it will continue. The men who gathered in Philadelphia in 1787 could not have envisioned these changes. They could not have imagined, nor would they have accepted, that the document they were drafting would one day be construed by a Supreme Court to which had been appointed a woman and the descendent of an African slave. 'We the People' no longer enslave, but the credit does not belong to the framers. It belongs to those who refused to acquiesce in outdated notions of 'liberty,' 'justice,' and 'equality,' and who strived to better them. And so we must be careful, when focusing on the events which took place in Philadelphia two centuries ago, that we not overlook the momentous events which followed, and thereby lose our proper sense of perspective. Otherwise, the odds are that for many Americans the bicentennial celebration will be little more than a blind pilgrimage to the shrine of the original document now stored in a vault in the National Archives. If we seek, instead, a sensitive understanding of the Constitution's inherent defects, and its promising evolution through 200 years of history, the celebration of the 'Miracle at Philadelphia' will, in my view, be a far more meaningful and humbling experience. We will see that the true miracle was not the birth of the Constitution, but its life, a life nurtured through two turbulent centuries of our own making, and a life embodying much good fortune that was not. Thus, in this bicentennial year, we may not all participate in the festivities with flag-waving fervor. Some may more quietly commemorate the suffering, struggle, and sacrifice that has triumphed over much of what was wrong with the original document, and observe the anniversary with hopes not realized and promises not fulfilled. I plan to celebrate the bicentennial of the Constitution as a living document, including the Bill of Rights and the other amendments protecting individual freedoms and human rights.

History and Understanding of the Fourteenth Amendment

The unfinished business of the Constitutional Convention eventually became the focal point of Reconstruction. After slavery was abolished pursuant to the Thirteenth Amendment, the union effectively was reinvented as a function of the Fourteenth Amendment. The nature and extent of the framers' vision have been a primary subject of debate of case law and commentary ever since. Raoul Berger contends that the Fourteenth Amendment reflects a relatively limited accounting for equality. Robert H. Bork expresses similar sentiment in arguing that the Court's decision in *Brown v. Board of Education* reflects a faulty understanding of history. Paul R. Dimond argues that Berger's understanding of the Fourteenth Amendment is misplaced even from a strict interpretivist perspective. John P. Frank and Robert Munro suggest that the farmers possessed a broader equal protection vision.

Raoul Berger, GOVERNMENT BY JUDICIARY (1971)*

The key to an understanding of the Fourteenth Amendment is that the North was shot through with Negrophobia, that the Republicans, except for a minority of extremists, were swayed by the racism that gripped their constituents rather than by abolitionist ideology. At the inception of their crusade the abolitionists peered up at an almost unscalable cliff. Charles Sumner, destined to become a leading spokesman for extreme abolitionist views, wrote in 1834, upon his first sight of slaves, "My worst preconception of their appearance and their ignorance did not fall as low as their actual stupidity . . . They appear to be nothing more than moving masses of flesh unendowed with anything of intelligence above the brutes." Tocqueville's impression in 1831-32 was equally abysmal. He noticed that in the North, "the prejudice which repels the negroes seems to increase in proportion as they are emancipated," that prejudice appears to be stronger in the States which have abolished slavery, than in those where it still exists."

Little wonder that the abolitionist campaign was greeted with loathing! In 1837 Elijah Lovejoy, an abolitionist editor, was murdered by an Illinois mob. How shallow was the impress of the abolitionist campaign on such feelings is graphically revealed in a Lincoln incident. A delegation of Negro leaders had called on him at the White House, and he told them,

> There is an unwillingness on the part of our people, harsh as it may be, for you free colored people to remain with us . . . [E]ven when you cease to be slaves, you are far removed from being placed on an equality with the white man . . . I cannot alter it if I would. It is a fact.

---

* Raoul Berger, GOVERNMENT BY JUDICIARY (Indianapolis: Liberty Fund, Inc., 1997). Reprinted by permission.

Fear of Negro invasion—that the emancipated slaves would flock north in droves—alarmed the North. The letters and diaries of Union soldiers, Woodward notes, reveal an "enormous amount of antipathy towards Negroes"; popular convictions "were not prepared to sustain" a commitment to equality. Racism, David Donald remarks, "ran deep in the North," and the suggestion that "Negroes should be treated as equals to white men woke some of the deepest and ugliest fears in the American mind."

One need not look beyond the confines of the debates in the 39th Congress to find abundant confirmation. Time and again Republicans took account of race prejudice as an inescapable fact. George W. Julian of Indiana referred to the "proverbial hatred" of Negroes, Senator Henry S. Lane of Indiana to the "almost ineradicable prejudice," Shelby M. Cullom of Illinois to the "morbid prejudice," Senator William M. Stewart of Nevada to the "nearly insurmountable" prejudice, James F. Wilson of Iowa to the "iron-cased prejudice" against blacks. These were Republicans, sympathetic to emancipation and the protection of civil rights. Then there were the Democratic racists who unashamedly proclaimed that the Union should remain a "white man's" government. In the words of Senator Garrett Davis of Kentucky, "The white race . . . will be proprietors of the land, and the blacks its cultivators; such is their destiny." Let it be regarded as political propaganda, and, as the noted British historiographer Sir Herbert Butterfield states, it "does at least presume an audience—perhaps a 'public opinion'—which is judged to be susceptible to the kinds of arguments and considerations set before it." Consider, too, that the Indiana Constitution of 1851 excluded Negroes from the State, as did Oregon, that a substantial number of Northern States recently had rejected Negro suffrage, that others maintained segregated schools. It is against this backdrop that we must measure claims that the framers of the Fourteenth Amendment swallowed abolitionist ideology hook, line, and sinker.

The framers represented a constituency that had just emerged from a protracted, bitterly fought war, a war that had left them physically and emotionally drained. It had begun with a commitment to save the Union and had gone on to emancipate the slaves. Now the war-weary North was far from anxious to embark on fresh crusades for the realization of still other abolitionist goals. While emancipation largely hit slavery in the South, eradication of inequality, as Vann Woodward reminded, required "a revolution for the North as well," a revolution for which most Republicans were utterly unprepared. Then too, the fact that Republicans and Democrats had been pretty evenly matched over the years, that some districts definitely were swing areas, led Republicans in those areas to be cautious of affronting their constituents. Many moderate and conservative Republicans, as we shall see, were acutely aware of the impact on elections of sweeping radical claims for political, let alone, social, equality for the blacks. While most men were united in a desire to protect the freedmen from outrage and oppression in the South by prohibiting discrimination with respect to "fundamental rights," without which freedom was illusory, to go beyond this with a campaign for political and social equality was, as Senator James R. Doolittle of Wisconsin confessed, "frightening" to the Republicans who "represented States containing the despised and feared free negroes."

* * *

. . . [M]ost Republicans were politicians first and ideologues afterward. Not civil rights for blacks but the dreaded take-over of the federal government by the South was their obsessive preoccupation. Emancipation brought the startling realization that Southern representation would no longer be limited in the House of Representatives to three-fifths of the blacks, as Article 1, § 3, provided. Now each voteless freedman counted as a whole person; and in the result Southern States would be entitled to increased representation and, with the help of Northern Democrats, would have, Thaddeus Stevens pointed out at the very outset of the 39th Congress, "a majority in Congress and in the Electoral College." With equal candor he said that the Southern States "ought never to be recognized as valid States, until the Constitution shall be amended . . . as to secure perpetual ascendancy" to the Republican party. The North had not fought and quelled rebellion in order to surrender the fruits of victory to the unrepentant rebels. How to circumvent this possibility was the central concern of the Republicans, and it found expression in § 2 of the Fourteenth Amendment, which reduced representation in proportion as the right to vote was denied or abridged. Unless we seize hold of the fact that, to borrow from Russell R. Nye, "what lies beneath the politics of the Reconstruction period, so far as it touched the Negro, is the prevailing racist policy tacitly accepted by both parties and by the general public," we shall fail to appreciate the limited objectives of the Fourteenth Amendment. That is the reality underlying the limited purposes of the framers of the Fourteenth Amendment, and which circumscribes the so-called "generality" of "equal protection" and "due process."

* * *

The "privileges or immunities" clause was the central provision of the Amendment's § 1, and the key to its meaning is furnished by the immediately preceding Civil Rights Act of 1866, which, all are agreed, it was the purpose of the Amendment to embody and protect. The objects of the Act were quite limited. The framers intended to confer on the freedmen the auxiliary rights that would protect their "life, liberty, and property,"—no more. For the framers those words did not have the sprawling connotations later given them by the Court but, instead, restricted aims that were expressed in the Act. . . .

* * *

THE CIVIL RIGHTS ACT OF 1866

The meaning and scope of the Fourteenth Amendment are greatly illuminated by the debates in the 39th Congress on the antecedent Civil Rights Act of 1866. As Charles Fairman stated, "over and over in this debate [on the Amendment] the correspondence between Section One of the Amendment and the Civil Rights Act is noted. The provisions of the one are treated as though they were essentially identical with those of the other." George R. Latham of West Virginia, for example, stated that "the 'civil rights bill' which is now a law . . . covers exactly the same ground as this amendment." In fact, the Amendment was designed to "constitutionalize" the Act, that is, to "embody" it in the Constitution so as to remove doubt as to its constitutionality and to place it beyond the power of a later Congress to repeal. An ardent advocate of an abolitionist reading of the Amendment, Howard Jay Graham, stated that "virtually every speaker on the Fourteenth Amendment—Republican and Democrat alike—said or agreed that the Amendment was designed to embody or incorporate the Civil Rights Act."

Section 1 of the Civil Rights Bill provided in pertinent part,

> That there shall be *no discrimination in civil rights or immunities* . . . on account of race . . . but the inhabitants of every race . . . shall have the *same* right to make and enforce contracts, to sue, be parties, and give evidence, to inherit, purchase, lease, sell, hold and convey real and personal property,

and to full and *equal* benefit of all laws and proceedings for the security of person and property, and shall be subject to *like* punishment . . . and no other.

* * *

. . . Shortly stated, freedmen were to have the same *enumerated* rights (as white men), be subject to like punishment, suffer no discrimination with respect to civil rights, and have the equal benefit of all laws for the security of person and property. Patently these were limited objectives; the rights enumerated, said William Lawrence of Ohio, "were the *necessary incidents* of these absolute rights," that is, of "life, liberty, and property," lacking which those "fundamental rights" could not be enjoyed. It was these "enumerated rights," "stated in the bill," said Martin Thayer of Pennsylvania, that were "the fundamental rights of citizenship."

Section 1 of the Bill was a studied response to a perceived evil, the Black Codes, which the Republicans averred were designed to set emancipation at naught, to restore the shackles of the prior Slave Codes, and to return the blacks to serfdom. The Bill was necessary, Senator Henry Wilson of Massachusetts said, because the new Black Codes were "nearly as iniquitous as the old slave codes." Citing the prewar Slave Code of Mississippi, which prohibited the entry of a free Negro into the State, travel from one county to another, serving as a preacher, teaching slaves, and so on, Senator Trumbull stated that "the purpose of the bill . . . is to destroy all these discriminations." References to the Black Codes studded the debates: they were described as "atrocious" and "malignant."

The explanations of the Civil Rights Bill by the respective committee chairmen made its limited objectives entirely clear. Speaking to "civil rights and immunities," House Chairman Wilson asked,

> What do these terms mean? Do they mean that in all things, civil, social, political, all citizens, without distinction of race or color, shall be equal? By no means can they be so construed . . . Nor do they mean that all citizens shall sit on juries, or that their children shall attend the same schools. These are not civil rights and immunities. Well, what is the meaning? What are civil rights? I understand civil rights to be simply the absolute rights of individuals, such as "The right of personal security, the right of personal liberty, and the right to acquire and enjoy property."

* * *

Such views had been expressed in the Senate by Trumbull, who drafted the Bill: "The bill is applicable exclusively to civil rights. It does not propose to regulate political rights of individuals; it has nothing to do with the right of suffrage, or any other political right." Commenting on *Corfield v. Coryell*, Trumbull stated that such cases had held that under the "privileges and immunities" of Article IV, § 2, a citizen had "certain great fundamental rights, such as the right to life, to liberty, and to avail oneself of all the laws passed for the benefit of the citizen to enable him to enforce his rights." These were the rights with which the Civil Rights Bill would clothe the Negro.

* * *

Since *Corfield v. Coryell* is cited on all hands, it will profit us to consider its bearing on the scope of "privileges or immunities." The actual holding was that the phrase did not confer on an out-of-state citizen the right to dredge for oysters in New Jersey waters. In passing, Justice Washington stated:

We feel no hesitation in confining these expressions to those privileges and immunities which are, in their nature, *fundamental* . . . They may, however, be all comprehended under the following general heads: Protection by the government, the enjoyment of life and liberty, with the right to acquire and possess property of every kind and to pursue and obtain happiness and safety . . . The right of a citizen of one state to pass through, or reside in any other state, for purposes of trade, agriculture, professional pursuits, or otherwise; to claim the benefit of the writ of habeas corpus; to institute and maintain actions of any kind in the courts of the state; to take, hold and dispose of property, either real or personal; and an exemption from higher taxes or impositions than are paid by the citizens of the other state; may be mentioned as some of the particular privileges and immunities of citizens, which are clearly embraced by the general description of privileges deemed to be fundamental; to which may be added, the elective franchise, as regulated and established by the laws or constitution of the state in which it is to be exercised . . . But we cannot accede to the proposition . . . that the citizens of the several states are permitted to participate in *all* the rights which belong exclusively to the citizens of any other particular state.

Shortly stated, [the historical] facts are that the "fundamental" rights which the framers were anxious to secure were those described by Blackstone—personal security, freedom to move about and to own property; they had been picked up in the "privileges and immunities" of Article IV, § 1; the incidental rights necessary for their protection were "enumerated" in the Civil Rights Act of 1866; that enumeration, according to the framers, marked the bounds of the grant; and at length those rights were embodied in the "privileges or immunities" of the Fourteenth Amendment. An argument to the contrary, it may be stated categorically, will find no solid ground in the debates of the 39th Congress.

Robert H. Bork, THE TEMPTING OF AMERICA (1990)*

Brown was a great and correct decision, but it must be said in all candor that the decision was supported by a very weak opinion. Those two facts, taken together, have caused an enormous amount of trouble in the law.

The *Brown* Court found the history of the fourteenth amendment inconclusive because public education in 1868 was embryonic in the South and the effect of the amendment on public schools in the North was ignored in the congressional debates. The opinion did not choose to face the uncomfortable fact that the effect on public education was ignored because no one then imagined the equal protection clause might affect school segregation. The Chief Justice concluded for the Court that to "separate [children in grade and high schools] from others of similar age and qualifications solely because of their race generates a feeling of inferiority as to their status in the community that may affect their hearts and minds in a way unlikely ever to be undone. . . . Whatever may have been the extent of psychological knowledge at the time of *Plessy v. Ferguson*, this finding is amply supported by modern authority." There followed a footnote citing psychological studies.

There are obvious difficulties with the opinion. In the first place, it failed to deal with the fact that a number of Northern states had ratified the fourteenth amendment and had continued to segregate their public schools without even supposing there was any conflict between the two actions. It was no answer to say, as Warren did, that public education had not then advanced to the condition it has achieved today. The inescapable fact is that those who ratified the amendment did not think it outlawed segregated education or segregation in any aspect of life. If the ratifiers had intended segregation as the central meaning of the equal protection clause, it is impossible to see how later studies on the baleful psychological effects of segregation could change that meaning. Indeed, *Plessy* had recognized that segregation could have a psychological impact and found it essentially irrelevant. It is difficult to believe that those who ratified the fourteenth amendment and also passed or continued in force segregation laws did not similarly understand the psychological effects of what they did. They didn't care.

The second difficulty is that nobody who read *Brown* believed for a moment that the decision turned on social science studies about such matters as the preference of black children for white or black dolls, which supposedly showed something about their self-esteem, which in turn supposedly was related to the presence or absence of legal segregation. This was disingenuous. The real rationale for *Brown* was deeper, and the pretense that it was not cheapened a great moment in constitutional law. Finally, in focusing on the effects of segregation on young children's capacity to learn—a question by no means as simple as the Court made it sound—the decision's rationale limited its principle to primary and secondary public education.

That the Court had not been straightforward in *Brown* quickly became apparent. Cases soon came up in which the professed rationale of *Brown*, the psychological effects of segregation on children of tender years, could not conceivably apply. Plaintiffs challenged legally segregated beaches, golf courses, parks, and courtrooms. The Supreme Court simply issued orders that such segregation was unconstitutional with nothing more than the citation of *Brown v. Board of Education*. That necessarily meant that the rationale of *Brown* was not the rationale offered in the opinion. Racial segregation by order of the state was unconstitutional under all circumstances and had nothing to do with the context of education or the psychological vulnerability of a particular age group. The real meaning of *Brown*, therefore, was far better than its professed meaning.

But the combined disingenuousness of the *Brown* opinion and the obvious moral rightness of its result had, I believe, a calamitous effect upon the law. This was massively ironic, because the result in *Brown* is consistent with, indeed is compelled by, the original understanding of the fourteenth amendment's equal protection clause. The disastrous fact was that the Supreme Court did not think so. The Court, judging by its opinion, thought that it had departed from the original understanding in order to do the socially desirable thing. What is more, the Court triumphed over intense political opposition despite that fact. Those of us of a certain age remember the intense, indeed hysterical opposition that *Brown* aroused in parts of the South. Most Southern politicians felt obliged to denounce it, to insist that the South would continue segregation in defiance of any number of Supreme Court rulings. We remember the television pictures of adult whites screaming obscenities at properly dressed black children arriving to attend school. We remember that at one point President Eisenhower had to send in airborne troops to guarantee compliance with the Court's rulings.

Imagine, then, what the Justices of the Supreme Court thought. They had issued, so they apparently believed, a ruling based on nothing in the historic Constitution, and that decision had prevailed despite the fact that it had ordered a change in an entrenched social order in much of the nation. Scholars used to worry that the Court would damage its authority if it acted politically. I have written a few such naive lines myself. The fact is quite the contrary. The Court is virtually invulnerable, and *Brown* proved it. The Court can do what it wishes, and there is almost no way to stop it, provided its result has a significant political constituency. (These days the significance of a political constituency is greatly magnified if the constituency includes a large part of the intellectual or knowledge class, which means that the Court has greater freedom to the left than it has to the right.) Much of the rest of the Warren Court's history may be explained by the lesson it learned from its success in *Brown*.

But *Brown* taught lessons to others as well. It was accepted by law professors as inconsistent with the original understanding of the equal protection clause. That fact was crucial. The end of state-mandated segregation was the greatest moral triumph constitutional law had ever produced. It is not surprising that academic lawyers were unwilling to give it up; it *had* to be right. Thus, *Brown* has become the high ground of constitutional theory. Theorists of all persuasions seek to capture it, because any theory that seeks acceptance must, as a matter of psychological fact, if not of logical necessity, account for the result in *Brown*. In fact, those who wish to be free of the restraints of original understanding in the hope that courts will further a particular policy agenda regularly seek to discredit that philosophy by claiming that it could not have produced the outcome in *Brown*. Since *Brown* is the test, the argument runs, and since original understanding cannot meet that test, then the philosophy is discredited, and courts may do as they wish, or as the intellectual class wishes, in all future policy issues. The charge is false, but if it were correct, that would not affect the legitimacy of the philosophy. Constitutional philosophy is a theory of what renders a judge's power to override democratic choice legitimate. It is no answer to say that we like the results, no matter how divorced from the intentions of the lawgivers, for that is to say that we prefer an authoritarian regime with which we agree to a democracy with which we do not.

But so great is the allegiance to *Brown* that when a respected law professor, Herbert Wechsler of Columbia, questioned the case in a Holmes Lecture at Harvard, he created a sensation in academic circles, and many professors rushed into print to rebut him. Wechsler did not actually say the case was wrong, but he had confessed to being unable to discern the "neutral principle" upon which it rested.

* * *

. . . [I]f we accept Wechsler's requirement that a court must apply neutral principles, and I think we must, *Brown* must rest, if it is a correct decision, on the original understanding of the equal protection clause of the fourteenth amendment. It is clear that it can be rested there. . . .

Let us suppose that *Plessy v. Ferguson* correctly represented the original understanding of the fourteenth amendment, that those who ratified it intended black equality, which they demonstrated by adopting the equal protection clause. But they also assumed that equality and state-compelled separation of the races were consistent, an assumption which they demonstrated by leaving in place various state laws segregating the races. Let us also suppose, along with the Court in *Plessy*, as I think we must, that the ratifiers had no objection to the psychological harm segregation inflicted. If those things are true, then it is impossible to square the *opinion* in *Brown* with the original understanding. It is, however, entirely possible to square the *result* in *Brown* with that understanding.

Perhaps because of their anxiety to deny that *Brown v. Board of Education* could have been arrived at consistently with the original understanding of the fourteenth amendment, those who oppose that philosophy always talk as though segregation was the primary thrust of the equal protection clause. But, of course, it was not. Segregation is not mentioned in the clause, nor do the debates suggest that the clause was enacting segregation. The ratifiers probably assumed that segregation was consistent with equality but they were not addressing segregation. The text itself demonstrates that the equality under law was the primary goal.

By 1954, when *Brown* came up for decision, it had been apparent for some time that segregation rarely if ever produced equality. Quite aside from any question of psychology, the physical facilities provided for blacks were not as good as those provided for whites. That had been demonstrated in a long series of cases. The Supreme Court was faced with a situation in which the courts would have to go on forever entertaining litigation about primary schools, secondary schools, colleges, washrooms, golf courses, swimming pools, drinking fountains, and the endless variety of facilities that were segregated, or else the separate-but-equal doctrine would have to be abandoned. Endless litigation, aside from the burden on the courts, also would never produce the equality the Constitution promised. The Court's realistic choice, therefore, was either to abandon the quest for equality by allowing segregation or to forbid segregation in order to achieve equality. There was no third choice. Either choice would violate one aspect of the original understanding, but there was no possibility of avoiding that. Since equality and segregation were mutually inconsistent, though the ratifiers did not understand that, both could not be honored. When that is seen, it is obvious the Court must choose equality and prohibit state-imposed segregation. The purpose that brought the fourteenth amendment into being was equality before the law, and equality, not separation, was written into the text.

Had the *Brown* opinion been written that way, its result would have clearly been rooted in the original understanding, and its legitimacy would have been enhanced for those troubled by the way in which the Court arrived at a moral result without demonstrating its mooring in the historic Constitution. There might have been an even more important benefit. The Court might not have been encouraged to embark on more adventures in policymaking, which is what it thought it had done in *Brown*, and academic constitutional lawyers might not have gone on to construct the apparently endless set of theories that not only attempt to justify *Brown* on grounds other than the original understanding but, in order to do so, advance arguments that necessarily justify departure from the historic Constitution in general. Perhaps constitutional theory would be in a far happier state today if *Brown* had been written, as it could have been, in terms of the original understanding.

* * *

Paul R. Dimond, *Strict Construction and Judicial Review of Racial Discrimination Under the Equal Protection Clause: Meeting Raoul Berger on Interpretivist Grounds,* 80 MICH. L. REV. 462 (1982)*

In *Government by the Judiciary*, Raoul Berger argues that the legislative debates on the Reconstruction amendments and their enforcement acts reveal that the equal protection clause was intended to prohibit only racially partial state legislation that affects specific civil rights concerning the security of person and property. Berger urges that this narrow reading of the framers' intent should limit review under the fourteenth amendment of all claims of racial discrimination and that any broader judicial interpretation of the equal protection clause, as in the 1954 school desegregation ruling, usurps the policy-making functions vested in Congress or reserved to the states and to the people. Berger's theses are not new, but their application would immunize much official racial discrimination from judicial scrutiny and challenge the legitimacy of many court decisions that protect racial minorities from majoritarian abuse or neglect.

Berger's construction has been challenged elsewhere on a number of grounds. Some argue that its interpretivist theory of judicial review falls to comprehend the Supreme Court's institutional mission, such as its role in articulating the contemporary meaning of sweeping phrases like equal protection and in policing our democratic system to ensure that the majority will neither exclude the minority from the political process nor systematically ignore its interests. Others argue that Berger's preoccupation with the legislative debates leads to a disabling myopia concerning the nature of the regional struggles and political battles joined during Reconstruction. These conflicts both complicate and enrich any analysis of the Reconstruction era's response to the problems of federalism, the economy, politics, and racism. In this Article, however, I will meet Berger's argument on his own interpretivist turf.

* * *

II. THE OBJECTS OF RECONSTRUCTION REDRESS

The sorts of evils that the framers sought to redress after the Civil War provide another clue to the original understanding of the scope of Reconstruction law. A brief examination of the context in which the fourteenth amendment arose indicates that it was not directed solely at state legislation that was expressly partial concerning certain limited rights; rather, it was also intended to strike at discriminatory implementation of facially neutral laws, and at the states' failure to protect blacks from pervasive private discrimination.

The passage of the thirteenth amendment, which outlawed the institution of slavery, and the end of the Civil War set the stage for the developments leading to the fourteenth amendment. It is undisputed that slavery was more than a formal legal status; it involved a complex system of state laws and local ordinances (or "Slave Codes"), executive and judicial enforcement, community custom, and private action. The slave states also enforced a reciprocal system of discrimination to subjugate the "free blacks" in their midst, lest they serve as a festering symbol of freedom constantly

---

*   Reprinted with permission.

threatening the slave regime. Whether the legislative history shows that the framers intended "full freedom" as a necessary corollary of the abolition of slavery, for both historically "free blacks" and emancipated slaves alike, is still debated. Many proponents of the thirteenth amendment argued (and many of its opponents feared) that it should be construed broadly. Others declared that it outlawed only the status of slavery and left the rest, including the framework of customary caste subjugation of blacks, to the states for decision. Under either view, there remained the problem of defining what acts of racial discrimination—whether public, customary, or private—amounted to such "badges and incidents of slavery" that they perpetuated conditions of servitude under section 1 or supported legislation by Congress under section 2 to enforce the prohibition against slavery. Unless the thirteenth amendment was intended by its framers to be a vain act, its object of redress must have included something more than the formal legal status of slavery and the Slave Codes.

Contemporary understanding of the thirteenth amendment thus may shed some light on the background leading to consideration of the fourteenth. Yet Berger barely addresses the relevance of the thirteenth amendment. In contrast, Berger argues that the fourteenth amendment merely "constitutionalized" the 1866 Civil Rights Act. Therefore, the following discussion turns to the sorts of evils which that Act was intended to remedy.

At the end of the Civil War, the rebel states sought to preserve their racial caste systems. When restructuring their civil governments, these states formed legislatures dominated by conservatives. In the winter of 1865-1866, all but Texas enacted Black Codes to keep the "free" blacks in a second-class position, beneath both their former masters and poor whites. Many of the Codes expressly excluded blacks from voting, owning land, making contracts, securing access to the courts, working without a license, traveling without a pass, or engaging in certain trades.

Other provisions, however, made no reference to race; instead, their oppressive racial impact depended on selective enforcement, customary caste relations, and private discrimination against blacks. The invidious quality of these laws lay in their failure to protect blacks from the white majority's efforts to maintain blacks as a servile class. Many of the vagrancy and apprenticeship laws, for example, applied on their face to blacks and whites alike, but nonetheless threatened to relegate blacks to virtual peonage. Whites refused to convey land to blacks or to employ "free" blacks at a living wage, and the laws imposed harsh penalties on those hapless victims, predominantly black, who could find neither land to till nor paying jobs at which to work. Federal military commanders in Virginia, South Carolina, Alabama, and Mississippi quashed such facially race-neutral acts. In the face of "combinations by [white] employers" leading to inadequate wages for blacks throughout the states, these Reconstruction generals found that the laws would "reduce the freedmen to a condition of servitude worse than that from which they have been emancipated—a condition which will be slavery in all but its name."

Raoul Berger agrees that section I of the 1866 Civil Rights Act was a studied response to a perceived evil, the Black Codes. Yet, by ignoring the significance of the Codes' facially neutral provisions, he fails to "recognize the *sweep* of the evil" that the 1866 Act addressed. . . .

If eliminating race-neutral but oppressive acts was one object of the 1866 Act, its goals were not as "limited" as Berger claims. Based on the sorts of evil addressed, the Act can be understood as limited to "discriminatory legislation with respect to specified rights" only if (a) these rights included the terms and conditions of employment, the opportunity to lead a productive life in a chosen profession, and freedom from racially disparate punishments for conditions of racial inequality caused by the legacy of slavery and continuing prejudice, and (b) the discrimination included facially neutral laws that failed to redress private combinations and other customary discriminations. This sort of evil included a state's denial of protection to blacks by the passage of penal or regulatory laws that ignored customary discrimination and thus relegated blacks to second-class citizenship.

The 1866 Civil Rights Act dealt with the specific wrongs that Congress thought should be outlawed at that time. The underlying evil that Congress attacked was the legacy of slavery—invidious racial discrimination. The legislation was directed at the ways in which this evil was manifested most harshly in 1866. Decades or centuries later, however, the manifestations of such discrimination might be quite different. Unless the framers believed that time would stand still, they might have foreseen that the future would bring such changes. Thus, even an amendment incorporating "only" the thrust of the 1866 Act could authorize different applications than those enumerated in the Act.

This brings us to the sorts of evils sought to be remedied by the fourteenth amendment. For Raoul Berger, the answer is the *same* object as the 1866 Act, which he argues was aimed only at expressly racially discriminatory legislation affecting certain rights. Yet the 1866 Act responded to evils extending beyond such express discrimination. The language of the fourteenth amendment, moreover, is markedly different from that of the Act: it is more general and open-ended. There can be no question that at least one object of the amendment was to constitutionalize the 1866 Act, both to prevent its repeal by a hostile future Congress and to resolve any doubts concerning Congress's power to pass the 1866 Act under the thirteenth amendment. In so doing, however, the framers consciously used broad language that is not a mere substitute for the 1866 Act.

. . . The Joint Committee of Fifteen on Reconstruction that drafted the fourteenth amendment and presented it to Congress reported extensively on the evils of these Black Codes. The Report did not ignore facially neutral laws that operated in practice to oppress blacks. In addition, the Report stressed the *failure* of the states to *protect* against continuing community bias and provide intimidation:

> The feeling in many portions of the country towards emancipated slaves, especially among the uneducated and ignorant, is one of vindictive and malicious hatred. This deep-seated prejudice against color is assiduously cultivated by the public journals, and leads to acts of cruelty, oppression and murder, which the local authorities are at no pains to prevent or punish.

Section 1 was designed to redress this denial by the states of the equal protection of their laws. How the duty to protect against this evil would be measured, policed, and enforced in the future could not be known in 1866.

Following the passage of the fourteenth amendment in Congress, a flood of remedial legislation was enacted to bring the rebel states up short and to protect blacks and their white (*i.e.*, Republican) sympathizers. . . .

Thus, in the years immediately after the adoption of the fourteenth amendment, the Congressmen who framed its language acted with the understanding that it covered a broad range of state behavior. The evils addressed by the constitutional amendments of the Reconstruction Congress extended beyond racially discriminatory state statutes that affected limited rights concerning the security of person and property. Congress regulated state executive, judicial, and local governmental action to protect the freedmen and other citizens against a new from of white supremacy rooted in private conspiracy and intimidation, fueled by Democratic opposition to Republican Reconstruction and by community hostility to blacks, and condoned by state default, official blindness, and public disregard of minority interests. The Reconstruction Congress did not, of course, address every form of caste discrimination authorized, condoned, or neglected by the states in all of their branches and subdivisions. But it did serve notice, consistent with the text of the fourteenth amendment, that the states' affirmative duty to provide "equal protection of the laws" to the freedmen could be interpreted broadly, applied to a variety of state action and inaction, subjected to judicial review, and supplemented with remedial regulation by Congress. But this open-ended quality also left open both the ultimate status of the free blacks and the final fate of caste discrimination and race relations throughout the country.

* * *

IV. THE DEBATES ON THE FOURTEENTH AMENDMENT: CODE WORDS OR GENERALITY?

. . . [T]he Joint Committee introduced the fourteenth amendment in both Houses on April 30, 1866. Because of the political power struggle between Republicans and Democrats, the debates focused primarily on the terms for Reconstruction—including disqualifying rebel leaders from office and reducing the representation of any state that denied freedmen the vote. In the limited debate concerning sections 1 and 5, "declamation abounded where hard analysis was wanting." The amount of evidence that supports an open-ended reading of the amendment makes it difficult to see how such general debate could prove Berger's claims that the fourteenth amendment dealt solely with the rights enumerated in the 1866 Act, and that "equal protection of the laws" was limited to statutes concerning "privileges or immunities." The discussion of the amendment's language also casts doubt on Berger's assertion that it was constructed of narrow code words with generally accepted meanings.

* * *

Comments about "constitutionalizing" the 1866 Civil Rights Act are not free from ambiguity, but they do not prove that was the *only* purpose of section 1. The general, broad-brush descriptions of section 1's reach, the different roads to framing section 1 and the 1866 Civil Rights Act, and their contrasting texts and structures all suggest otherwise. In addition, conservative opponents, who had previously argued that the 1866 Civil Rights Act broadly intruded on the power reserved to the states, claimed that the clauses of section 1 possessed no precise or agreed meaning but embraced "all the rights we have under the laws of the country." Joint Committee member Rogers, for example, opposed the fourteenth amendment by charging that such conditions as marriage, jury service, and office-holding were covered by the broad and undefined phrases. Although exaggerating the scope of pending legislation to make it appear more unattractive is a classic opposition technique, the proponents did not dispute these broad interpretations of section 1 of the fourteenth amendment, as they had so vigorously in the prior debate on the Civil Rights Bill. Rather than delete broad phrases or enumerate specific rights, the House passed the general text of the fourteenth amendment intact. In conjunction with Bingham's reading of section 1, the House debates on the fourteenth amendment provide additional evidence of the broad sweep of its language.

* * *

Although debate on section 1 was relatively meager and is subject to conflicting interpretations, the evidence that is there does not show that the privileges or immunities clause was intended to have a precisely limited scope or that it incorporates only the rights enumerated in the 1866 Civil Rights Act. There is even less evidence that the framers intended to restrict the equal protection clause to the terms of the Civil Rights Act, to the Black Codes, or to "privileges or immunities," however they might be defined. In fact, the only consistently mentioned limit on the amendment was that it did not give black citizens the right to vote. Consistent with the text, the evils addressed, and John Bingham's drafting, the congressional debates suggest that section 1—particularly the equal protection clause—was framed in general terms and did not have a generally accepted and narrowly limited meaning.

V. THE RECONSTRUCTION CONGRESS AND SCHOOL SEGREGATION: CONDONED, CONDEMNED, OR LEFT OPEN FOR DECISION UNDER THE EQUAL PROTECTION CLAUSE?

This interpretation of the fourteenth amendment is supported by an examination of the Reconstruction Congress's handling of a particular form of racial discrimination that even then attracted attention: segregation in the schools. Berger notes that Congress repeatedly rejected legislation providing for integrated schools, and he concludes that the framers did not intend the fourteenth amendment to authorize desegregation. Berger's conclusion, however, does not necessarily follow: It proves nothing to say that the framers had no present intent to outlaw school segregation by specific statute; the question is whether they could have intended that future Congresses or the Court be free to do so under the authority of the more general fourteenth amendment.

Berger's conclusion apparently rests on two grounds: first, that school segregation does not implicate any of the fundamental rights to which he limits the amendment; and second, that the pervasiveness of segregation at that time indicates that equal protection was not intended to prohibit racially dual schooling and, at most, guaranteed only "separate but equal" facilities. The materials discussed in the preceding sections of this Article do not support Berger's assertion that the fourteenth amendment protects only a narrow range of rights affecting the security of person and property; the subsequent legislative proposals regarding schools do not suggest a different conclusion. Proponents of contemporary legislation to prohibit segregation asserted that schools were covered by the fourteenth amendment. These proposals necessarily suggest that some Congressmen believed that school segregation was unconstitutional. The proposals were not rejected because Congress considered segregation in general or in public schools in particular to be beyond the scope of the fourteenth amendment, but because passage was politically impossible at that time.

Before we examine the debates on legislation regarding the schools, one point regarding segregation in general should be noted. Segregation was not uncommon when the fourteenth amendment was ratified. Schools were segregated in many areas, including by local action in the District of Columbia, and some states prohibited publicly supported education for blacks. Some other public facilities, including the galleries of the House and Senate, were segregated. Similar racial restrictions were imposed in some areas with respect to the rights that Berger argues were specifically intended by the framers for protection under the 1866 Civil Rights Act and section 1 of the fourteenth amendment. But even congressional refusal to pass statutes specifically outlawing all segregation in the enjoyment of these protected rights would not imply that the framers intended the fourteenth amendment to condone segregation for all time. It would only suggest that the Reconstruction Congress was then unable to perceive segregation as imposing caste or unwilling to legislate against such discriminatory practices in every instance.

Concerning public schools, the record of Congress indicates just such a reluctance to legislate. Senator Charles Sumner led the frontal assault on separate schools in Congress, as he had earlier in Massachusetts. He opened his campaign on March 16, 1867, after Congress had passed both the fourteenth amendment and the Military Reconstruction Act, by introducing a rider requiring the rebel states to establish "public schools open to all, without distinction of race or color." The lack of popular support for mixed schools generally frustrated Sumner's eight-year campaign in Congress to legislate specifically against separate schools. But Congress also repeatedly refused to declare that it would be unconstitutional to pass such legislation.

VI. IS *PLESSY* OR *BROWN* THE STRICT CONSTRUCTION?

According to Berger, *Brown v. Board of Education* is wrong for two reasons: schools are not within the limited scope of the fourteenth amendment, and the requirements of equal protection are satisfied by separate but equal facilities. Thus, the major surprise of Berger's book is not that it criticizes *Brown*, but that it never addresses the propriety of the Supreme Court's 1896 decision in *Plessy v. Ferguson*. Unlike public schooling, freedom of movement on a common carrier is arguably within the fundamental rights recognized by Berger, and is thus protected by the equal protection clause. Although Berger's materials on the separate but equal question imply that *Plessy* was nevertheless correctly decided, he does not forthrightly state that conclusion.

This Article undercuts Berger's assertion that the scope of the amendment is limited, and suggests that the framers left open the question whether state-mandated and state-condoned segregation denies equal protection. *Plessy* was the Court's response. It assumed that the fourteenth amendment applied to the case before it, treated the question whether separate is equal as one of fact to be decided by the Court, and found that state-mandated segregation in railroad cars was constitutionally permissible because it did not discriminate against blacks. On these terms, *Plessy* was wrongly decided.

Homer Plessy, an octoroon who could not be distinguished by his color from whites, argued that the evils of Louisiana's statute requiring separate coaches for blacks and whites lay in the compulsory nature of the segregation and its stigmatization of blacks as a servile class. But the majority rejected this charge of racial discrimination on *factual* grounds:

> We consider the underlying fallacy of the plaintiff's argument to consist in the assumption that the enforced separation of the two races stamps the colored with a badge of inferiority. If this be so, it is not by reason of anything found in the act, but solely because the colored race chooses to put that construction upon it. The plaintiff's argument necessarily assumes that if, as has been more than once the case, and is not unlikely to be so again, the colored race should become the dominant power in the state legislature, and should enact a law in precisely similar terms, it would thereby relegate the white race to an inferior position. We imagine that the white race, at least, would not acquiesce in this assumption.

As Charles Black aptly characterized this view, "the curves of callousness and stupidity intersect at their respective maxima."

* * *

... The "separate-but-equal" rationale had always been an excuse for state-sanctioned racism. As Edmund Cahn so aptly put the point:

> The moral factors involved in racial segregation are not new ... but exceedingly ancient. What, after all, is the most elementary and conspicuous fact about a primitive community if not the physical proximity of human beings mingling together? ... Hardly anyone has been hypocritical enough to contend that no stigma or loss of status attaches to ... physical separation. Segregation does involve stigma; the community knows it does.

On balance, then, the decision in *Brown* has a stronger claim than *Plessy* to being a "strict" construction of the meaning of the discrimination prohibited by the equal protection clause. The evidence indicates that the fourteenth amendment was not intended to protect only Berger's enumerated civil rights relating to the security of person and property. It also suggests that the issue of segregation, particularly in schools, was left open for decision under the equal protection clause. Chief Justice Warren's finding that the amendment's history is "inconclusive ... with respect to segregated schools" is not far off the mark. The conclusion in *Brown* that governmentally fostered or officially condoned segregation in fact imposes caste discrimination and thereby denies the equal protection of the laws represents a fair interpretivist construction of section 1 of the fourteenth amendment.

CONCLUSION

The weight of the interpretivist materials demonstrates that section 1 of the fourteenth amendment does not precisely define the general antidiscrimination obligations that it imposes on the states. Under settled principles of judicial review, repeatedly confirmed by the framers of the amendment, the Supreme Court is empowered to define those duties and to determine whether states are adequately discharging their responsibilities to all of their citizens. Whatever label is applied to this judicial review—interpretivist, structural, or fundamental value—the substance of the Court's work is to interpret the amendment's core prohibition against caste and to apply it, as the Court did in *Brown*, to contemporary circumstances. Under our federal system, such judicial vigilance will help the people, the Congress and the states meet their own constitutional responsibilities to grapple with the monumental task that the amendment's framers only began.

John P. Frank and Robert F. Munro, *The Original Understanding of "Equal Protection of the Laws,"* 1972 WASH. U. L.Q. 421 (1972)*

I. INTRODUCTION

* * *

To describe the Civil War as the Second American Revolution is apt enough, and yet the label obscures reality. This was a two-way revolution. Specifically it was the revolt by the southern region against the established government; but it quickly became as well a revolt of northern forces against southern hegemony in government. Jefferson Davis revolted against Thaddeus Stevens, but in the course of a hard war, Thad Stevens was also revolting against Davis and all he stood for.

This revolution was, in the most awful and real sense, a revolution of guns and death, a true military convulsion. As is customary with revolutions, it discarded much of the legal system which it found, and substituted a legal order of its own. The three Civil War amendments, adopted both to take and to perpetuate the fruits of the revolution for the victors, were the charter of the new order. Reconstruction was the device of the victors to govern the conquered territory, a device not radically different from the immediate post-World War II occupations.

The termination of the reconstruction was the great counterrevolution. While revolutions are normally of violence, violence, while likely, is not essential. Revolution by force unseated and beheaded Charles I and ruled the country; the Glorious Revolution of 1688 put an end to the Stuarts a second time and forever without any war at all. So in America, the Second American Revolution unseated southern power and utterly changed the complexion of the country. Reconstruction enforced the new mandate. The counterrevolution, ending without significant military action, set the country on a new path as surely as did the accession of William and Mary in England 200 years before.

These changing seasons of government, in very rapid order, dominated the development of the fourteenth amendment. Nowhere is this rapidity more dramatic than the course of events relating to the Negroes. In 1860, slavery was solidly entrenched in the United States. In a short five years had come the progression: the freeing of slaves used for military purposes by the army; the prohibition against returning slaves who crossed Union lines; the termination of slavery in the District of Columbia; the abandonment of fugitive slave laws; the Emancipation Proclamation; the first equal rights laws for the District of Columbia; the establishment of schools for all in the District; the admission of Negroes into the military forces; the elimination of restrictions against Negroes carrying the mails; the prohibitions of exclusion of Negroes from transportation in the District; and the thirteenth amendment itself.

Two more amendments, the fourteenth and fifteenth, quickly followed. They were accompanied by a series of civil rights acts and by active reconstruction aimed at establishing Negro freedom in the South. This program met incredibly large obstacles to effectiveness, including the southern resistance, the discovery by many of the northern bloc that their interests were best served by collaboration and numerous other factors. These led to the abandonment of the whole effort to dominate the South by troops or by law after 1877, when the counterrevolution had prevailed.

---

*   Reprinted with permission.

This means that the entirety of the active life of the Second American Revolution was, realistically, from about 1861 to 1877 at the outside. Insofar as the period of turbulent reform was directed at slavery, the active years may be measured as January 1, 1863 (Emancipation Proclamation) to the Civil Rights Act of 1875. In terms of sheer time span, comparison with other revolutions shows a highly comparable active life, a period of overwhelming dominance followed in these instances by exhaustion of early dynamism and a replacement by another form of government.

	BEGIN	END	YEAR SPAN
Puritan Revolution in England	1641	1660	19
American Revolution, Lexington to Constitutional Government	1775	1789	14
French Revolution to Napoleon's Empire	1789	1804	15
Civil War to End of Reconstruction	1861	1877	16

It is a quality of revolution that events reshape the law rather than that the law controls the revolution.

This reshaping of the law by the Second American Revolution gave birth to the thirteenth, fourteenth and fifteenth amendments as the new American Constitution. They were the legal structure for consolidating, perpetuating, and controlling the results of that revolution. They were as radical in their conception as the 1791 revolutionary constitution of France.

The counterrevolution derailed the amendments as an instrument for perpetuating the revolution. Any effort to comprehend the history of the fourteenth amendment in the last third of the nineteenth century and the first half of the twentieth by purporting to relate it to original purposes is simply hopeless. It altogether fails to take into account that the counterrevolution changed the legal system fundamentally, just as the amendments themselves changed the system which they replaced.

Emancipation did not necessarily move the Negroes from the one class to the other. In ancient civilizations, "the world was not a place inhabited solely by free persons and slaves. Between men of these extremes of status stood special classes which lived outside the boundary of slavery but not yet within the circle of those who might rightly be called free." In this respect, antiquity might be reproduced, and a new class might be created by which the ex-slave would be placed in a social limbo, equivalent perhaps to that of the less happy castes of India. If the range of status from slavery to complete freedom may be thought of as a scale, the reconstruction generation had to decide where within that scale the freedman should be placed.

The driving force of the thirteenth amendment was something more than to strike off the manacles and end the slave trade. Its key sponsors would have been appalled to discover that they were substituting a caste system for a slave system. As Speaker of the House Schuyler Colfax said in a speech at the opening of the 39th Congress, "I call them free men, not freedmen," but the rest of the century never witnessed the creation of truly free men.

The counterrevolution took full-fledged freedom out of the thirteenth amendment. It was thereafter applied to allow a caste system holding Negroes as a separate group with permanent disabilities. Not until the most recent times has any legal significance been given to the removal of the "badge of slavery," as distinguished from slavery itself.

The fifteenth amendment is the last of the three, and this is no accident. As other devices failed, this amendment was intended to give the Negro the possibility of looking after himself as well as the opportunity of holding the Republican Party, as the Negro's instrument of freedom, in office. After 1877, by one device or another, this policy was robbed of all meaning until it was revived again in recent decisions, new civil rights acts, and militant voter registration.

We come then to the late nineteenth and pre-Warren twentieth century interpretation of the fourteenth amendment. We do so realizing that the thirteenth amendment for very nearly a hundred years had been shrunk to its most minimal meaning, extinguishing slavery but substituting a kind of serfdom, and that the fifteenth amendment had been even more drastically reduced to a dead letter.

It is no surprise, therefore, to know that the fourteenth amendment, after the counterrevolution, was so totally reshaped as to have only a minimal resemblance, and at times not even that, to its original purposes. The forces of counterrevolution here, too, were too strong for the exhausted forces of the revolution. Like the thirteenth and fifteenth amendments, the fourteenth was not repealed. There was no need. Rather, the successor social order demanded an entirely new interpretation and this amendment, like the others, was rewritten by interpretation to accommodate. Twenty-five years after each of the three other revolutions tabulated above, there was little still alive of the Articles of Confederation, or the French Constitution of 1791, or Cromwell's Instrument of Government. In the same way, by 1900 there was not much left of the Second American Constitution.

* * *

II. EQUAL PROTECTION

* * *

We conclude that the fundamental working legal theory of equality before the law, or equal rights, or equal protection, based on well-established tradition, was formulated for American law by Sumner, and popularized under his leadership. The actual language of equal protection found its way into the Constitution from the Sumner draft of the thirteenth amendment, to the Wilson draft of the Civil Rights Act of 1866, through Trumbull as public sponsor of the Civil Rights Act and certainly through Bingham.

To this group of the four "insiders" must be added the eleven majority members other than Bingham of the Joint Committee on Reconstruction, from which the amendment actually emerged. The total number of "insiders" is thus fifteen, and a central inquiry is the determination of the meaning of equal protection to them.

This group had a unified meaning as to the nature of the equal right to testify, to sue and to hold property. Their stand on other specific questions is outlined in sections following. On the broader question of whether equal protection would, under any circumstances, permit laws making distinctions based on race or color, there is less uniformity and less precise evidence. We conclude that of the fifteen, eight, Sumner, Wilson, Bingham, Howard, Stevens, Conkling, Boutwell and Morrill, probably accepted an interpretation of equal protection which precluded any use whatsoever of color as a basis of legal distinctions. Trumbull, Fessenden and Grimes on some occasions countenanced some types of segregation, at least as to miscegenation. The positions of Harris, Williams, Blow and Washburne are unascertained.

III. INTERPRETATION OF EQUAL PROTECTION
DURING RECONSTRUCTION

The *Slaughter-House Cases* in 1873 gave this interpretation to the equal protection clause: "We doubt very much whether any action of a State not directed by way of discrimination against the Negroes as a class, or on account of their race, will ever be held to come within the purview of this provision. It is so clearly a provision for that race and that emergency [the black codes], that a strong case would be necessary for its application to any other." This was narrow construction with a vengeance, and Justice Miller, its author, quickly recanted. It was obvious from the discussion of the amendment, its background, and its contemporary interpretation, that the clause reached all racial classifications, including groups other than Negroes.

Miller's observation, however, certainly did not conflict with contemporary understanding as to economic regulatory action unrelated to racial distinctions. Although there is little doubt that Republicans would have approved of restraints upon regulation of business had they thought of it, we have not found anywhere even a single intimation that this possibility did in fact occur to them. In other words, there was no contemporary understanding of the relation of equal protection to business regulation.

A. Equality in the Courts and Commerce

Under the pre-rebellion black codes, the free Negro's position differed little from that of the slave, except that a freedman had the right to the fruits of his own labor, usually the right to hold personal property, and in a few states the right to hold real property. Also, he ranked a step above the slave in the law courts. The slave, of course, could not sue in the courts, since any rights of action arising out of transactions in which he was involved were the property of his master. The free Negro could own rights of action, but like a minor, could frequently enforce them only by a suit through a guardian or next friend, a white man; and he could be a witness only in actions where only Negroes were involved.

In criminal law, the status of the free Negro was about on a par with that of the slave. Frequently statutes imposing liability on one imposed it on the other as well. Arson, burglary, mayhem (against a white person), rape or attempted rape (against a white person) were typical capital crimes both for slave and for free Negro. Preaching the gospel, using insulting language to white persons, assembling together to learn to read and write: these were typical misdemeanors for the Negro, slave or free. Except in capital cases, the Negro, slave or free, was tried by a jury of slaveholders, who could convict by a majority vote.

The black codes after the war perpetuated or created many discriminations in the criminal law by applying unequal penalties to Negroes for recognized offenses and by specifying offenses for Negroes only. Laws which prohibited Negroes from keeping weapons or from selling liquor were typical of the latter. Examples of discriminatory penalties were the laws which made it a capital offense for a Negro to rape a white woman, or to assault a white woman with intent to rape, or the ingenious bit of foresight by which the South Carolina Legislature made it a felony without benefit of clergy "for a person of color to have sexual intercourse with a white woman by impersonating her husband."

In addition to the discriminations of the criminal laws, post-war black codes hedged in the Negroes with a series of restraints on their business dealings of even the simplest from. Though in many states the Negro could acquire property, Mississippi put sharp limitations on that right. But most restrictive were the provisions concerning contracts for personal service. Many statutes called for specific enforcement of labor contracts against freedmen, with provisions to facilitate capture should a freedman try to escape. Vagrancy laws made it a misdemeanor for a Negro to be without a long-term contract of employment; conviction was followed by a fine, payable by a white man who could then set the criminal to work for him until the benefactor had been completely reimbursed for his generosity. Minors were remembered in compulsory apprenticeship laws which arranged for long term instruction in the arts of hoeing and cotton-picking. Not infrequently there were provisions that the former owner should have first call upon the labor of an ex-slave.

Congress began the uprooting of these codes outside the District of Columbia with the Civil Rights Act of 1866. It provided:

> [C]itizens, of every race and color . . . shall have the same right, in every State and Territory in the United States, to make and enforce contracts, to sue, be parties, and give evidence, to inherit, purchase, lease, sell, hold, and convey real and personal property, and to full and equal benefit of all laws and proceedings for the security of person and property, as is enjoyed by white citizens, and shall be subject to like punishment, pains, and penalties, and to none other, any law, statute, ordinance, regulation, or custom, to the contrary notwithstanding.

As can be seen, that Act dealt explicitly with the inequalities of the black codes in criminal and commercial law, and its principles passed into the equal protection clause. . . . The Act and the amendment obliterated the commercial discriminations by giving Negroes equal rights to contract and to be subject to no vagrancy laws which did not apply to whites.

Considerable doubt exists as to whether the equal protection clause was meant to confer equality in jury service. The Civil Rights Act of 1866, which was quite explicit in its language, said nothing of jury service; "equal benefit of all laws and proceedings for the security of person and property" was the only language under which jury service could conceivably come. Representative Wilson, floor leader for the Bill, stated in debate that the Act would not affect jury service. During the passage of the fourteenth amendment itself, no discussion of this point was had.

. . . It seems fair to conclude that, while Congress did not have jury service in mind in 1866 as a civil right, the language of the amendment was broad enough to cover jury service in the apparent absence of any intent to the contrary.

* * *

In its criminal law aspect, the clause was the broadest possible generalization. To some it was the American equivalent of the pledge of Magna Carta: "We will sell to no man, we will deny to no man, we will delay to no man right or justice."

* * *

B. Segregation

* * *

Segregation, with its legal corollary of "separate but equal," is a term which our generation has applied loosely as a unitary concept to cover the entire area in which separation of the races is feasible. This concept has been applied to such disparate situations as separation in transportation, schools, drinking fountains, housing, churches, hotels, restaurants, theaters, health services, employment opportunities, and cemeteries.

Difficulty exists in discovering the original meaning of equal protection as it relates to this problem because it never occurred to a substantial number of persons in the decade under study to approach this question in any such unitary way. Three distinct views can be identified. The abolitionist view of equality, represented by Sumner, permitted absolutely no distinctions of any kind based on color. Directly opposite was the view of the opponents of the Civil Rights Act and the fourteenth amendment with their rough slogan of "no nigger equality." Both of these groups may fairly be described as having a unitary concept of segregation. The abolitionists were against it in every context, though on this point no direct discussion among them has been found for the critical year of 1866. Some conservatives approved of segregation in all respects, professing to believe that equal protection obliterated every restraint on intermingling. This interpretation of equal protection probably was taken by them only as conventional opposition party Cassandras, for after the amendment was adopted the conservatives frequently gave a very narrow construction of the terms they had once thought so broad.

Between these two extreme positions was a middle group which, in the years 1865-68 in particular, never had to take a stand on the problems as a whole because its outlines were not clearly perceived. Segregation, as compared, for instance, with twenty days' hard labor for preaching the gospel, is a fairly refined development in the history of discrimination. In the South, with slavery just abolished, discrimination against the Negro which angered Congress was of a much cruder kind.

It is not surprising that Congress, concerned with securing to the freedman the most fundamental rights of life, liberty, and property, should not have devoted much time in its first post-war sessions to considering where he should sit in theaters and trains. Because the problem of segregation was never squarely faced during the incubation period of the amendment, the task of interpreting mass opinion on equal protection with absolute assurance becomes impossible. This difficulty is heightened by acceptance in the middle group of a formula which evades precise analysis. Under that middle approach, there were three types of equality with corresponding rights: political equality, civil equality, and social equality. The equal protection clause was clearly not intended to include the right to vote. Putting the question of political equality aside, this group made a hazy division between the other two terms, believing that equal protection granted "civil equality" but not "social equality." A typical example of a use of this conception by a supporter of the amendment is Greeley's observation: "You can't make all men equal socially. One is stronger, better, braver than the other. Now what I want is that all men should be equal before the law. I want the black man to have his rights all over the South. The law should know nothing about a man's color."

One central theme emerges from the talk of "social equality": there are two kinds of relations of men, those that are controlled by the law and those that are controlled by purely personal choice. The former involves civil rights, the latter social rights. There are statements by proponents of the amendment from which a different definition could be taken, but this seems to be the usual one. Frequently, of course, the terms were used with no content at all, as when a Pennsylvania Republican simply told his audience that the amendment granted civil rights but not social rights; but when analysis began, the explanation given above usually appeared.

Thus, in one debate Senator Harlan of Iowa explained that the right of Negroes to use the streetcars did not involve social equality since the right was legal in origin. Normally the hotelkeeper's responsibility not to discriminate was explained in terms of a distinction between taking a Negro into the hotel or dining room, as distinguished from putting him into a particular room or at a particular table: the hotelkeeper's obligation to take customers rested on law, but the right to choose one's own tablemate was social. Stevens himself stressed the vital distinction between matters of law and matters of taste: "This doctrine does not mean that a Negro shall sit on the same seat or eat at the same table with a white man. That is a matter of taste which every man must decide for himself. The law has nothing to do with it."

Thus the original distinction appears to have been that the law should know no distinctions of color, but that personal taste should be left to govern itself. In this, the practical difference between the abolitionist and the middle position was that the abolitionists as a moral matter encouraged complete intermingling even though this entered the zone of taste, while the middle group lacked any such fervor.

Because the civil-social distinction was misty, it is easiest to diagnose original opinion by studying its application to concrete cases.

1. *Geographical segregation.* Restrictions of Negroes to particular regions of the country or to particular areas in a city by limiting their right to buy and live on particular pieces of property is the most obvious kind of segregation to have been forbidden by equal protection. As has already been noted, Illinois and Indiana excluded all Negro immigration into the state prior to the Civil War; and the southern states by old and new codes for freedmen excluded them from particular areas and from buying real estate.

Section 1 of the Civil Rights Act of 1866 provided that "citizens, of every race and color . . . shall have the *same* right, in every State . . . to inherit, purchase, lease, sell, hold, and convey real and personal property. . . ." President Johnson, in his veto message, specifically challenged the right of Congress to "abrogate all State laws of discrimination between the two races in the matter of real estate. The veto was overridden, and it was proclaimed by every advocate of the fourteenth amendment that it carried the principles of the Act into the Constitution.

There are many points of doubt in the determination of the original understanding of the fourteenth amendment, but on this one we think, there is no room for serious difference of opinion. In view of the specific grant in the Civil Rights Act of "*the same right*" to hold and use property, no distinctions whatsoever based on race or color could be made in respect to this right. Geographic segregation was completely forbidden.

2. *Segregation in transportation.* The type of segregation most frequently considered between 1865 and 1875 was segregation in transportation. Before the Civil Rights Act of 1866, attention focused largely on transportation in Washington. Thereafter, the issue was widespread as Negroes sought to utilize the privileges they thought the Act had given them. The central legal theory of the attack on segregated transportation was that transportation companies had a common law duty to take all comers and that making any distinctions in the operation of this duty because of color denied an equal right to contract for transportation. The vital distinctions are highlighted by Senator Reverdy Johnson of Maryland, perhaps the ablest constitutionalist of the conservative faction:

> It may be convenient, because it meets with the public wish or with the public taste of both classes, the white and the black, that there should be cars in which the white men and ladies are to travel, designated for that purpose, and cars in which the black men and black women are to travel, designated for that purpose. But that is a matter to be decided as between these two classes. There is no more right to exclude a black man from a car designated for the transportation of white persons than there is a right to refuse to transport in a car designated for black persons white men.

The matter was repeatedly before Congress. The Senate voted against segregated transportation in one from or another at least six times from 1863 to 1875. In 1863, Congress amended the charter of the Alexandria and Washington Railroad and provided that "No person shall be excluded from the cars on account of color." A year later the Washington and Georgetown Railroad, a street railway in the District of Columbia, excluded a Negro army officer from a car. The District Committee, after an investigation in response to a request by Sumner, reported that no legislation was necessary; the officer could sue because "colored persons are entitled to all the privileges of said road which any other persons have." The company attempted to propitiate this sentiment by putting on more cars for the exclusive use of Negroes, a concession which gave Sumner no comfort because "whenever they exclude a colored person from any one of their cars they do it in violation of law."

Sumner thereupon embarked upon a crusade to eliminate streetcar segregation in the District. He successfully carried an amendment to the charter of the Depot and Ferry Co. Railway by a vote of 24 to 6, that "no person shall be excluded from any car on account of color." He lost, 14 to 16, an effort to put a similar provision into the Washington and Georgetown Railway charter because some Radicals thought it unnecessary in view of the clarity of the law; but finally he achieved complete victory in 1864 and 1865 when he carried an amendment to the Metropolitan Railway Company's charter by which the prohibition against exclusions from any car because of color was "extended to every other railroad in the District of Columbia."

All this debate upon the whole issue of segregation in transportation took place before the enactment of the fourteenth amendment. Those who opposed the measures contended that segregation was perfectly valid. Senator Saulsbury of Delaware, for example, said such legislation would be "a war against nature and nature's God." More restrained Senators, such as Grimes and Doolittle, argued merely that there was no harm in separation. Those who supported the legislation did so on grounds of equality. Senator Wilson denounced the "Jim Crow car"—to make Negroes stand on a front platform, he said, was "in defiance of decency." Sumner observed of Massachusetts that there "the rights of every colored person are placed on an equality with those of white persons. They have the same right with white persons to ride in every public conveyance in the commonwealth." He asked the same rule of equality for the District.

The first of the Sumner amendments came before the Supreme Court in *Railroad Co. v. Brown*, a case which is an important part of this history. On February 8, 1868, Catharine Brown, colored, bought a ticket on the Alexandria and Washington Railway. That company, its charter containing the amendment providing that "no person shall be excluded from the cars on account of color," maintained two identical and connected cars, using one for colored and the other for white passengers. When Mrs. Brown attempted to sit in the "white" car, she was ejected with great violence.

The episode attracted immediate attention because Mrs. Brown was in charge of the ladies' rest room at the Senate. An immediate Senate investigation was undertaken to explore whether the company's charter should be repealed. One hearing was held in the shanty in which Mrs. Brown lived and was recuperating. The Committee concluded that the company had violated its charter. It recommended against repeal of the charter because it thought compensation by judicial proceedings would be adequate, but it concluded: "If the result of the legal proceedings which Mrs. Brown has instituted should not be satisfactory, or if the conduct of the said Company in the future shall not be satisfactory, the resolution can be taken from the table, and the charter of the Company repealed."

The company, contending that segregation was "reasonable and legal," asked for a charge to the jury that it was under no obligation to plaintiff to do more than offer separate but equal cars. The trial court rejected the charge, and the Supreme Court unanimously affirmed, rejecting the "separate but equal" argument as "an ingenious attempt to evade a compliance with the obvious meaning of the requirement." The Court declared that the object of Congress was not merely to afford transportation for Negroes, which anyone selling transportation would of course want to give them if they had the money to buy it. Rather:

> It was the discrimination in the use of the cars on account of color, where slavery obtained, which was the subject of discussion at the time, and not the fact that the colored race could not ride in the cars at all. Congress, in the belief that this discrimination was unjust, acted. It told this company, in substance, that it could extend its road into the District as desired, but that this discrimination must cease, *and the colored and white race, in the use of the cars, be placed on an equality.* This condition it had the right to impose, and in the temper of Congress at the time, it is manifest the grant could not have been made without it.

Clearly "in the temper of the Congress at the time," segregation in transportation was "discrimination," not "equality." We believe that the equal protection clause, in the eyes of its contemporaries, froze into constitutional law the existing common law obligation of transportation companies to take all comers and to eliminate any possibility of their segregation. Congress decided so often in this period that color classifications were not permissible for purposes of transportation that it is difficult to understand how equal protection could possibly be given another meaning. In 1872, under the leadership of Carpenter, the Senate passed a bill forbidding the making of any distinctions because of color by railroads, inns, and theaters; the conservative opposition confined its attack—unsuccessfully—to the inns and theaters sections, apparently conceding the point as to transportation. By the Civil Rights Act of 1875, Congress made a final attempt to obliterate completely segregation in transportation.

3. *Segregation in hotels and theaters.* The hotel and theater problem was considered much the same as the transportation problem. As to all of these facilities, the Radicals believed that there was a common law right to admittance which had obtained constitutional status. There was this difference in some minds: the common law right of transportation was wholly "civil" while the right to a hotel was partially "social." It was felt that the innkeeper must accept a Negro applicant, give him a room and access to the dining room, and in no way treat him as an inferior guest. On the other hand, the white person renting a room or taking a table had his own right to decide whom he would have as his guest in what had become, for the moment, his own room and his own table; and the Radicals conceded that such a guest could exercise dominion as he chose in the selection of his own guests and companions.

There was an even more substantial difference as to theaters. Though highly regulated, theaters were not subject to a common law right of general use, as were trains or hotels. We find no thinking directed squarely at the consequences of this fact, but the inclusion of theaters in the Civil Rights Act of 1875 seems to have been based on a theory that since theaters were extensively regulated they were creatures of the law, and therefore subject to the requirements of equality.

4. *Segregation in education.* To understand the relation of equal protection to education, it is necessary to recall two crusades, abolitionism and the public school movement, both of which began major aggressive development in the 1830's. The

rapid spread of abolitionism from a few print shops and meeting places occurred because the whole society was ripe for a wave of good works, such as land reforms, suffrage, temperance agitation, women's rights, and many other ameliorative movements. As abolition was a crusade, so was the movement for public schools, which was spread throughout the North in the years between 1830 and the Civil War. Frequently the abolitionists and the public school men were the same people. There was no limit to the social good which was expected of the schools by their sponsors. Said Thaddeus Stevens, as Pennsylvania leader of the free school movement: "What earthly glory is there equal in luster and duration to that conferred by education?"

The public school system made much less headway in the South. The children of the well-to-do went to private academies, while others usually had little or no schooling at all. By the census of 1850, illiteracy among native whites was twenty percent in the South, three percent in the Midwest, and less than one percent in New England. In New England particularly, education was the vehicle for the indoctrination of Puritan morality, and nowhere was its use as an auxiliary to other crusades more fully appreciated. Hence in the wake of the northern troops came the schoolteachers of the Freedmen's Aid Societies, ready to make abolition a success by educating the South. A substantial part of post-war education in 1865 and 1866 was in the hands of these societies; the task of teachers included a mingling of education and propaganda for children and adults.

To these societies with a blind confidence in the capacity of education to solve all of the nation's social ills, nothing was impossible; and this is an important element in the social psychology from which the fourteenth amendment emerged. In this philosophy, of course, schools should be mixed rather than segregated. The constitution of the American Freedmen's and Union Commission, a central agency for these educational societies, specifically provided that "No schools or supply depots shall be maintained from the benefits of which any person shall be excluded because of color."

Like the objects of many of the rest of the pre-Civil War crusades, commingled education was easier to dream than to achieve. At the close of the war Negroes were excluded from education altogether in states both north and south. The first task was to achieve any kind of Negro education, and in the South efforts to do even this were sometimes met by violence or ostracism.

As will be shown, there is room for substantial difference of opinion concerning the dominant intent of the Reconstruction as to mixed schools; but it does seem clear that if the schools were to be separate, genuine equality was required. Governor Morton of Indiana, at the same time that he recommended ratification by his state of the amendment, recommended that the state terminate its policy of barring Negroes from public education and that tax funds proportionate with their number be allocated for their benefit. On the specific ground that the South was not offering opportunities for Negro education, Representative Donnelly sponsored an amendment to the Freedmen's Bureau Bill to permit the Bureau to aid education: "[W]e must make all the citizens of the country equal before the law . . . [and] we must offer equal opportunities to all men." Senator Howe, in one of the leading Senate addresses in support of section 1 of the fourteenth amendment, explained in detail that the equal protection clause would illegalize a Florida system whereby Negroes paid taxes for educational purposes without getting full benefits in return.

The confused picture in respect to mixed schools from 1865 to 1875 is a product of several factors. In the first place, there was genuine difference of opinion in the North on the merits. To the abolitionists, to New England, and to the Freedmen's Aid Societies, it was clear that equality banned compulsory segregation. Yet to Governor

Morton, also a good Republican, the schools in his state should remain separate "in the present state of public opinion." In the second place, so long as the South made going to school optional, collisions were avoided by voluntary choices. Although the Freedmen's Aid Society threw its schools open to anyone who chose to come, it was only occasionally that white students attended. In the third place, the issue was a difficult one and its resolution could usually be postponed without the necessity of decision.

One measure of the contemporary radical attitude of the requirement of equality can be seen in the acts of the reconstruction governments in the South. In each reconstruction convention, mixed schools were debated, and in South Carolina, Florida, Mississippi and Louisiana they were authorized. The South Carolina constitution, for example, provided that all public schools "shall be free and open to all . . . without regard to race or color." In the debate on this clause, opposition was expressed on the ground that the whites would not attend under such circumstances; the answer was made that this was a necessary part of securing to everyone his full political and civil equality.

The attitude of Congress toward mixed schools in the reconstructed states prior to the consideration of the Civil Rights Bill of 1875 was inconclusive.

Final consideration of mixed schools during Reconstruction came in connection with the Civil Rights Act of 1875. More than any other major measure of reconstruction, this bill was Sumner's. It was a bill to forbid segregation in conveyances, theaters, inns, and schools.

* * *

The debate over the measure which eventually became the Civil Rights Act of 1875 resulted in the most thorough analysis of the segregation problem during the Reconstruction. Sumner himself rested the claim for the legality of such legislation on both the thirteenth and the fourteenth amendments, claiming that the right not to be segregated was both a privilege of a citizen and an aspect of equality. . . .

The passage of the Civil Rights Act by the Senate represents a contemporary constitutional judgment that segregation in conveyances, theaters, inns, and schools violated either the privileges and immunities clause or the equal protection clause. While reference was frequently made to both provisions, the total impression of the debate is that the violation was thought by most to be of equal protection. . . .

The result in the House was a different story. Almost a year elapsed between the time of consideration in the Senate and in the House. In that interim there was sufficient change of sentiment to cause the House to delete the school clause, and the measure passed onto the statute books without it. The provisions forbidding separate conveyances, inns and theaters and requiring equality in jury service remained.

* * *

We conclude that it was accepted virtually unanimously by all who supported the fourteenth amendment that it required equal schools and that a very large number of its supporters thought that the amendment forbade segregated schools.

5. *Miscegenation.* We find it impossible to reach an assured conclusion as to the original understanding concerning segregation in matrimony, or the prohibition of miscegenation. Senator Reverdy Johnson made a typical attack on the Civil Rights Bill by suggesting that equality of the right to contract extended to the marriage contract and thus permitted miscegenation; but certainly the moderately radical Senators Trumbull and Fessenden thought otherwise. The abolitionists affirmatively and

enthusiastically advocated miscegenation on other occasions, but not in 1866; and such an extreme Radical as Wilson of Massachusetts, who twenty-two years before had led the fight on the Massachusetts anti-miscegenation law, confined his remarks, perhaps discreetly, to the broadest possible generalities.

Charges that the amendment permitted miscegenation were typically countered by the Republicans with a joke to the effect that possible elimination of anti-miscegenation statutes was not disturbing to them because Republicans had no intention of marrying Negroes. Aside from the campaign oratory, it appears probable that miscegenation was so remote a possibility to the majority of persons who supported the amendment that they never seriously thought out the relationship of the two.

* * *

THE PLACE OF HISTORY

The thirteenth, fourteenth, and fifteenth amendments were the new constitution which emerged from the Second American Revolution. Drafted and carried to ratification by a group of stern and willful men, they were intended to make complete changes in the American political system and to facilitate an economic revolution. One may easily challenge the wisdom of this Second American Constitution by asserting that it permitted the federal government to reach unprecedentedly far into the internal affairs of the states, giving enormous discretion to Congress; but the challenge to wisdom is no challenge to the fact that this was exactly what was intended. The Second American Constitution gave no greater power to the federal government than, for example, the commerce clause gave in the first American Constitution.

The differentiating factors in the fates of these two American constitutions were these: the economic and political elements that made up a major part of the original force behind the war amendments eventually found that the policies they once espoused were no longer useful to them, while the original Constitution had the consistent support of the wealthy class. Moreover, the original Constitution was interpreted by a Court determined to maximize its underlying purposes, while the war amendments came to a Court inclined to construe them narrowly. But vastly the most important difference was that the war amendments, unlike the original Constitution, were thrust by force upon a community whose deepest mores they outraged. The net result was that the industrialist element in the original movement for the fourteenth amendment eventually found it considerably more to their liking than they had ever anticipated, but the element in the movement which had desired to use all three of the war amendments to create an America in which all citizens were truly equal was seriously disappointed.

When Chief Justice Warren came to the Supreme Court he found himself confronted with the great issue of segregation in the public schools. In the spring preceding his appointment, the Court had asked for reargument of the school cases in highly historical terms.

The effect of the course of decision has been to put historical analysis of original intention of the fourteenth amendment into a secondary role, helpful or illuminating on occasion, but short of controlling.

This course by the Supreme Court seems inescapable wisdom. There is no escaping the fact, developed earlier, that the counterrevolution ending Reconstruction did wipe out the anticipated scope of all three of the Civil War amendments. The course of social and political life and of interpretation twisted the fourteenth amendment in particular beyond even a likely possibility of recognition by its sponsors.

A judge who picked up the problems of the 1950's was thus confronted with two absolutely conflicting histories. He had the history of 1866 to 1875. He also had the reversing history of 1875 to, say, 1954. The judge in 1954 was not a historical puzzle-solver, fascinated with the long-terminated truth of Who Was Shakespeare?, or Who Killed the Prince in the Tower? He needed instead to relate living problems to living law. If one did have a sure answer to intent in the 1860's, which on marginal problems is hard to find, he might still wisely be reluctant to vault over seventy-nine years of conflicting subsequent history to embrace the purpose of the first ten.

Some clauses of the Constitution permit a concept of truly historical growth, no matter how different the present is from the past. But the fourteenth amendment had no historical growth; it was absolutely cut off and replaced by a fresh start after the mid-1870's. Chief Justice Warren used great good judgment when he dropped the historical inquiry as profitless and turned to other sources of law.

CONCLUSION

For whatever utility it may have, and for the sake of intellectual inquiry on a great theme, it is possible to know, at least generally, what equal protection meant in its original conception in the reconstruction decade. Closer than this we cannot come; the extreme volatility of this revolutionary era means that understandings may have altered between passage of the amendment in 1866, its ratification in 1868, and the Civil Rights Act of 1875. Our interpretations are those of the reconstruction decade, wherever that evidence may be, and not the interpretation of any particular year.

The equal protection clause was, with the foregoing qualification, originally understood to mean the following: All men, without regard to race or color, should have the same rights to acquire real and personal property and to enter into business enterprises; criminal and civil law, in procedures or penalties, should make no distinctions whatsoever because of race or color; there should be no segregation of individuals on the basis of race or color as to the right to own or use land; there should be no segregation of individuals on the basis of race or color in the use of utilities, such as transportation or hotels; with reservations, for here there is substantial divergence, there should be no segregation in the schools. It was generally understood that Congress could legislate to secure these ends, without regard to whether the particular objective was frustrated by state action or by state inaction. On the other hand, the clause was meant to have no bearing on the right to vote; the evidence of its contemplated effect on state anti-miscegenation laws is unclear; and it was generally understood to have no bearing on segregation of a purely private sort in situations fairly independent of the law, as in churches, cemeteries, or private clubs.

What has been said goes to the measure of equal protection as a rule of law. But equal protection deserves measure as more than a rule of law, for it represents a part of a symbol, the symbol of equality. The enormous potentiality which made that symbol the banner of the abolitionists manifested itself not only in the equal protection clause but also in the remainder of the war amendments. The strongest advocates of "equality before the law" in Congress during the Reconstruction hoped to place the recent slaves, not halfway on the scale between slavery and freedom, but at a level substantially equivalent and undistinguished from that of the white population. That ultimate goal was to be achieved through equal freedom, equal privileges and immunities, equal due process, equal rights to vote, and equal protection of the laws.

Separate but Equal

For most of the time since Reconstruction, the Fourteenth Amendment has been interpreted to accommodate public and private discrimination. Such reality is consistent with the Supreme Court's observation, in the *Civil Rights Cases,* that the Fourteenth Amendment was never intended to eradicate "[m]ere discriminations."[14] From the end of the late nineteenth century until the middle of the twentieth century, official segregation was the defining racially significant social reality. Although upheld as a reasonable exercise of a state's police power, "reference[d] to the established usages, customs, and traditions of the people, and with a view to the promotion of their comfort, and the preservation of the public peace and good order,"[15] prescriptive segregation was conceived and executed as a methodology of group subordination.[16] In operation, it was defined by a commitment to separation with little if any attention to equality. Paul Oberst examines the origins and nature of prescriptive segregation. Thurgood Marshall recounts the NAACP strategy that ultimately succeeded in defeating official segregation in education. W.E.B. DuBois raises questions about a desegregation strategy in the context of a society that indulges racism.

Paul Oberst, *The Strange Career of* Plessy v. Ferguson, 15 ARIZ. L. REV. 389 (1973)*

In 1955 Vann Woodward, in his book *The Strange Career of Jim Crow*, challenged the conventional history of the times with his demonstration that racial segregation, far from being a long standing and inevitable American folkway, came gradually on the scene in the late nineteenth century and attained its most absurd developments only in the twentieth century. Indeed, it was only after the decision of the United States Supreme Court in *Plessy v. Ferguson*, upholding an 1890 railroad segregation statute and validating state-imposed segregation as equality, that rigid segregation-in-fact began to run rampant. Then, with increasing frequency, it began to be transmitted by legislation into an elaborate, but unsystematic and often conflicting, body of Jim Crow laws. Segregation statutes "lent the sanction of law to a racial ostracism that extended to churches and schools, to housing and jobs, to eating and drinking . . . to virtually all forms of public transportation, to sports and recreations, to hospitals, orphanages, prisons, and asylums, and ultimately to funeral homes, morgues, and cemeteries." It seems today that *Plessy* was indeed one of the pivotal decisions of the Supreme Court.

* * *

---

14   Civil Rights Cases, 109 U.S. 3, 25 (1883).

15   Plessy v. Ferguson, 163 U.S. 544, 550 (1896).

16   See, e.g., Leonard W. Levy, Plessy v. Ferguson, in Civil Rights and Equality 174 (Kenneth Karst ed. 1989).

PLESSY V. FERGUSON IN HISTORICAL PERSPECTIVE

Segregation Before Plessy

It is commonly and erroneously believed that racial segregation has always been the southern way of life, except for a decade of Reconstruction following the Civil War, when the South was under the aegis of federal troops and Northern carpetbaggers. This misconception arises because slavery is confused with segregation, and the franchise with integration. Four eras might be identified: The era of slavery was ended in 1865 with emancipation. After a brief postwar period of Restoration under Lincoln and Johnson, the Radical Reconstruction was established. Reconstruction was in turn terminated a decade later with the Compromise of 1877, and the "Redemption" instituted a long period of discrimination, suppression and disenfranchisement at the hands of dominant whites. It was only during the last of these four eras that segregation became the rule and was converted into statutory law.

In the midst of these shifting times in the last quarter of the nineteenth century, segregation had its own separate development. As W.E.B. Du Bois pointed out, a rigid segregation code could not exist under slavery. Black domestics lived in daily intimacy with whites, lived in the same houses, shared the same food, went to the same church and conversed constantly with each other.

* * *

The era of Redemption was a strange period when the interests of the conservatives, the radical populists and the liberals led many of them—each for a different reason—to oppose extension of racial segregation. The conservatives believed in white supremacy, but did not believe that blacks should be disenfranchised, degraded or segregated. "An excessive squeamishness or fussiness about contact with Negroes was commonly identified as a lower-class white attitude, while the opposite attitude was as popularly associated with 'the quality.' The blacks and conservatives sought a mutual alliance against the 'crackers.'" The Populists, on the other hand, sought to approach the Negro on the ground of mutual economic interests in opposition to the conservative establishment. In the 1890's Tom Watson of Georgia was promising that the Populists would "wipe out the color line and put every man on his citizenship irrespective of color."

With both the conservatives and radicals seeking to enlist the support of the black, not to segregate him, how did the Jim Crow regime begin? Vann Woodward attributes it to the coincidence of the abandonment of the Negro by Northern liberals after 1877, a series of Supreme Court cases narrowly construing the fourteenth amendment, turn-of-the-century American imperialism and, finally, a sudden crumbling of internal Southern resistance to the racial extremists. The radicals and conservatives, locked in a struggle for supremacy, both turned against the black as a scapegoat and abandoned their policy of racial moderation. Segregation laws were enacted, not because of "any spontaneous public demand, but because of the clamor of demagogues who endeavored to outdo each other in running for office against the Negro as a fictitious opponent." The first priority was to disenfranchise the Negro and then to "keep him in his place" with newly designed discrimination laws. The first of these laws were directed at segregation on railroads, and one of the first states to adopt such legislation was Louisiana.

The Origins of Plessy

By all accounts Louisiana, and especially New Orleans with its Spanish and French background, had a society which permitted the freest intermingling of the races anywhere in the South and in which many Negroes had acquired wealth and dignity. It is not surprising that when a bill to require segregation on railroad cars was introduced in the Louisiana legislature in 1890 there was vigorous opposition to its passage.

A Memorial addressed to the Louisiana House of Representatives by "The American Citizens Equal Rights Association of Louisiana Against Class Legislation," and signed by 17 prominent New Orleans Negroes, attacked the bill as unjust, discriminatory and a denial of equality. It was characterized as a gratuitous indignity and legal degradation. The bill's opponents argued that "under such circumstances the promotion of good will among inhabitants of the same State would be almost impossible." The bill was originally defeated in the Senate on July 8, 1890, but due to political treachery it was passed later that same month.

Subsequently, New Orleans Negroes formed the "Citizens Committee to Test the Constitutionality of the Separate Car Law" and collected funds to make a test case. They had the encouragement of Albion W. Tourgee, an upstate New York lawyer, who was one of the founders of the biracial Citizens Equal Rights League in 1890. Judge Tourgee offered to direct the attack without fee and was named "leading counsel . . . [with] control from beginning to end." James C. Walker, a white New Orleans criminal lawyer, was retained as local counsel.

Tourgee from the outset insisted that the plaintiff in the test suit be a "nearly white" Negro, perhaps in order that the issue of denial of "property rights" might be introduced. The chosen plaintiff was Homer Adolph Plessy, who was "seven-eighths" white and, as the petition states, "the mixture of colored blood was not discernible in him." On June 7, 1892, Homer Plessy boarded a passenger tram in New Orleans with a first class ticket to an intrastate destination. He seated himself in a coach reserved for whites and refused to move to the car reserved for Negroes, as the conductor commanded, apparently pursuant to previous arrangement with the railroad. He was arrested, imprisoned in the county jail and released on $500 bond. Plessy was tried before Judge John H. Ferguson in the Criminal District Court of the New Orleans Parish in November 1892 and convicted, over objections of his attorney that the Louisiana statute of 1890 violated the Federal Constitution.

On appeal to the Supreme Court of Louisiana, it was contended that the statute violated both the thirteenth and fourteenth amendments. The court denied the thirteenth amendment claim that the statute "perpetuates involuntary servitude" with a brief reference to the decision of the United States Supreme Court in the *Civil Rights Cases*. In denying any violation of the fourteenth amendment, the opinion of the Louisiana court by Justice Charles E. Fenner relied principally on the opinion of Massachusetts Chief Justice Shaw in *Roberts v. City of Boston*, and the decision of the Supreme Court of Pennsylvania in *Westchester and Philadelphia R.R. v. Miles* for the principle that "separate but equal" treatment of the races was constitutionally permissible. . . .

ANALYSIS OF *PLESSY*

* * *

The Fourteenth Amendment Contentions

* * *

2. Segregation as a Denial of Due Process

Turning from precedent to principle, the opinion of Justice Brown then addressed an issue of procedural due process. It is on this point that the effort of Tourgee to have a "nearly white" plaintiff for his test case was more relevant. Tourgee's brief began with his peculiar argument that "in any mixed community, the reputation of belonging to the dominant race . . . is property." He stressed that the reputation of being white was a property of great pecuniary value, "the master-key that unlocks the golden door of opportunity." From this premise, Tourgee argued that the provision of the act authorizing the railroad officials "to assign a person to a car set aside for a particular race" deprives the passenger of his property without due process of law. This argument has been characterized as an "unconscious paradox," and one writer erroneously suggested that Plessy might have been more interested in proving himself white than in defeating the discrimination against blacks. Olsen suggests that Tourgee's purpose was twofold: to appeal to a property-conscious Court, and to establish Plessy's rights as a "nearly white" man, in the expectation that this would not only complicate enforcement of segregation, but would convince the Court that "since the holder of the smallest bit of property was entitled to the same right as the largest, one drop of white blood would suffice."

The brief dealt at length with the arbitrary nature of the right of the railroad official to assign a person to a specific car. The statute bestowed on the "officers" of passenger trains the power and duty to assign each passenger to the coach used for the race to which such passenger belonged, with power to refuse to carry any noncompliant passenger. Moreover, it immunized the officers and the railway from any damage suits arising out of refusal to carry the passenger. The procedural due process shortcomings of such a proposal are perhaps made clearer when the interest of Plessy is alternatively characterized as a "property" interest and dramatized by consideration of the possible financial impact on the individual incorrectly classified. The Court solved its procedural due process dilemma by deciding that a suit for damages would provide an ample opportunity for review of the railroad's decision and vindication of the property rights injured by the error, if any, and that whether a person was to be stamped as colored or white was a matter of state law. The Court indicated that the conductor who assigned passengers according to race acted at his peril. Consequently, the provisions of the Louisiana statute which purported to exempt the official and the railroad from damages for an erroneous assignment were declared in dictum to be unconstitutional, as the state's attorney had conceded. Summarizing, the Court observed:

> If he be a white man and assigned to a colored coach, he may have his action for damages against the company for being deprived of his so-called property. Upon the other hand, if he be a colored man and be so assigned, he has been deprived of no property, since he is not lawfully entitled to the reputation of being a white man.

Although this neat hypothetical case may have logically solved the Court's procedural due process problem, it raises some question of the Court's sensitivity to the equal protection problem, since it inadvertently suggests a great deal about the inequality of the "separate but equal" formula and about the realities of equality before the law, as opposed to logical symmetries.

3. The "Nature of Things": Segregation and Psychology

Precedents and procedure disposed of, Mr. Justice Brown turned back to the "nature of things." He had announced at the outset that laws requiring separation of the two races "in places where they are liable to be brought into contact do not necessarily imply the inferiority of either race to the other . . . ." Expanding on this position, he found that "the underlying fallacy" of plaintiff's argument consisted "in the assumption that the enforced separation of the two races stamps the colored race with a badge of inferiority. If this be so, it is not by reason of anything found in the act, but solely because the colored race chooses to put that construction upon it." His "proof" of the proposition was simple: if the colored race had passed a racial segregation law when it had a legislative majority, whites would not have assumed they were inferior.

* * *

The proposition that any implication of inferiority arising from segregation by law was not any part of the intent of the segregator but was merely a psychological quirk in the minds of the segregated does seem to raise questions of candor, rather than capacity. Certainly many of those who enacted segregation laws were imbued with strong feelings of white superiority. They were determined to maintain the supremacy of the whites politically, economically and socially; segregation by law and ordinance was only one of the last resorts of the dominant whites in securing and maintaining a status of semi-servitude for the black population.

As Friedman puts it, the "Negro problem" in the South following Reconstruction was more properly a white problem: "If a servile pattern of Negro behavior was to be restored—if anarchy was to be resisted—new techniques of racial control were required." Various theories were espoused to maintain white control—total exclusion, integrated subservience and differential segregation—but the impossibility of the first and the practical difficulties of the latter in urban society ultimately drove the racists to indiscriminate segregation by law.

The black citizens of New Orleans who protested the enactment of the Louisiana statute had no doubts as to its intent and consequence. Neither did the Negro representatives in the Louisiana legislature, who protested bitterly as they voted against the Jim Crow bill. And neither did Tourgee, as he argued that the Louisiana statute was intended to assert the inferiority of the Negro:

> The title of an Act does not make it a 'police provision' and a discrimination intended to humiliate or degrade one race in order to promote the pride of ascendancy in another, is not made a 'police regulation' by insisting that the one will not be entirely happy unless the other is shut out of their presence. . . .

The Court rejected Tourgee's psychological insight, however. American justice was not yet prepared to confront the full reality of racism.

4. The "Nature of Things": Segregation and Sociology

The majority opinion found additional support for state-imposed segregation in several dubious ventures into social theory. First, the Court said that a legislature in its discretion might reasonably require segregation by law "with a view to the . . . preservation of the public peace and good order." Mr. Justice Brown did not elaborate upon this thought, but Harlan, in dissent, attacked the argument with considerable force. Not only would the decision upholding such statutes stimulate aggressions against the admitted rights of Negroes, but it would create reciprocal feelings of distrust. . . .

At this point Mr. Justice Brown turned to a discussion of the first caveat which he had mentioned earlier in the opinion: that the fourteenth amendment granted civil and political equality, but not "social equality." While a public railroad car is hardly a private social club, Mr. Justice Brown apparently concluded that any "commingling" necessarily amounted to social equality, and any constitutional prohibition of segregation by law in railway transportation was "enforced commingling." He observed that "in the nature of things" the amendment could not have intended that. Just what is the "nature of things" was not discussed. Apparently the Court was postulating that social prejudices cannot be overcome by legislation; that legislation is powerless to eradicate racial instincts or to abolish distinctions based upon physical differences; indeed, that "if one race be inferior to the other socially, the Constitution of the United States cannot put them on the same plane." Therefore, despite any intent of Congress or the Constitution, efforts to do away with segregation—and force "social equality by law"—apparently were considered by Mr. Justice Brown to be so fruitless as to be beyond judicial consideration.

Mr. Justice Harlan considered the suggestion that "social equality" did not exist between the white and black races in this country to be wholly beside the point. To him travel in a passenger coach no more involved social equality than using the streets or approaching the ballot box.

Even more dubious was the proposition in the majority opinion that "social prejudices" cannot be overcome by legislation. Indeed, there is mounting evidence to the contrary. "The fact is," says Harris, "that laws do change customs and traditions even to the extent of up-rooting them. Law and its penal sanctions have indeed changed the most stubborn of customs with respect to the legal status of Negroes. Unfortunately, of course, it took the Congress of the United States some 75 years after *Plessy* to rediscover this fact and act upon it.

Mr. Justice Brown was merely espousing a jurisprudence and social theory of his day. It is part of the strange career of *Plessy* that the case was decided at a moment when southern political factions were all turning against the Negro in the struggle for power, and at the same time discrimination and segregation were becoming tolerable elsewhere in a United States which was beguiled by the theories of Social Darwinism. Mr. Justice Brown's observation that "legislation is powerless to eradicate racial instincts" sounds very much like William Graham Sumner's "stateways cannot change folkways."

* * *

PLESSY: THE AFTERMATH

Social Impact

For a decision of the Court purporting to respond to the folkways, *Plessy* was greeted with a surprising lack of popular enthusiasm . . . Woodward says:

> [T]he country as a whole received the news of [the Court's] momentous decision upholding the 'separate but equal' doctrine in relative silence and apparent indifference. Thirteen years earlier the Civil Rights Cases had precipitated pages of news reports, hundreds of editorials, indignant raffles, congressional bills, a Senate report, and much general debate. In striking contrast, the *Plessy* decision was accorded only short, inconspicuous news reports and virtually no editorial comment outside the Negro press.

Olsen reported a more negative reaction:

> Although this decision did not arouse the furor provoked thirteen years earlier by the Civil Rights Cases, neither was it endorsed with marked enthusiasm outside of the white South, and not even always there. The Negro press was unanimous in its denunciation, and a random survey of the northern white press reveals that the *Plessy* decision almost invariably attracted some attention, that it aroused significant opposition, and that it seldom won strong support. Only three out of forty-three newspapers surveyed ignored the decision altogether, while twelve displayed some hostility toward the decision and four, two of which were south of the Mason Dixon line, approved it. Due notice was frequently given to Harlan's telling dissent, and out of nine New York City publications, only one, the *Journal,* positively endorsed the majority opinion while four (*Tribune, Recorder, Independent*, and *Mail & Express*) favored the views of Harlan.

On the other hand, although the platforms of the Populist and Democratic parties in the presidential campaign of 1896 each contained an anti-Supreme Court plank criticizing the decisions of the Court in three 1895 cases—involving income tax, the sugar monopoly and the Pullman strike—they made no mention of the recently decided *Plessy* case.

Whatever the immediate popular response, the long range results of *Plessy* were certainly devastating to the freedom of a sizeable number of Americans. As Vann Woodward wrote:

> The racial aggressions [Harlan] foresaw came in a flood after the decision of 1896. Even Harlan indicated by his opinion of 1899 in *Cummings v. Board of Education* that he saw nothing unconstitutional in segregated public schools. Virginia was the last state in the South to adopt the separate-car law, and she resisted it only until 1900. Up to that year this was the only law of the type adopted by a majority of the southern states. But on January 12, 1900, the editor of the Richmond *Times* was in full accord with the new spirit when he asserted: 'It is necessary that this principle be applied in every relation of Southern life. God Almighty drew the color line and it cannot be obliterated. The negro must stay on his side of the line and the white man must stay on his side, and the sooner both races recognize this fact and accept it the better it will be for both.'

With a thoroughness approaching the incredible, the color line *was* drawn and the Jim Crow principle was applied even in those areas that Tourgee and Harlan had suggested a few years before as absurd extremes. In sustaining all these new laws, courts universally and confidently cited *Plessy v. Ferguson* as their authority.

It was this dynamic character of the new movement toward de jure segregation that was most remarkable. Like a snowball rolling downhill it gathered mass and momentum. Says Vann Woodward: "The Jim Crow laws, unlike feudal laws, did not assign the subordinate group a fixed status in society. *They were constantly pushing the Negro farther down.*"

It is all too easy to forget the excesses of segregation in the first half of the twentieth century. Laws, ordinances and regulations were passed in incredible volume and detail. And where law did not supply the rule, custom took over. It is difficult for old men to recall or young men to believe. Those who lived in the North did not experience its greatest rigors; for many of those who lived in the South, black and white, it was part of life, unnoticed and unremarked as the air one breathed. Trains, waiting rooms, ticket windows, street cars, entrances and exits in theatres, hotels, toilets and water fountains, industrial employment, hospitals, sports, telephone booths, barber shops and beauty shops, taxis, airport facilities, elevators, beaches, parks, soda fountains, bars, circuses, and even courtroom Bibles for swearing witnesses, all were segregated at some time in some places.

* * *

Plessy *Overruled?*

There is no time here to dwell on the social forces which assisted the end of legal segregation. Our principal concern is with the end of legal segregation by the Supreme Court. . . .

However sound the holding in *Brown*, and however content one is with the opinion, Mr. Justice Warren said only that the separate but equal doctrine "has no place in the field of public education." *Plessy* was not expressly overruled. Acknowledging this, many writers have speculated whether *Plessy* has been overruled. Blaustein and Zangrando say it was overruled in *Gayle v. Browder*. Loren Miller insists that it was not overruled until 1962 in *Bailey v. Patterson* when it was "choked to death on buttermilk." Indeed, no less an authority than Shepard's Citator apparently believes that *Plessy v. Ferguson* has never been directly overruled.

Mr. Justice Douglas, furthermore, in several In Chambers opinions, has found some life in the old case. He has noted that it "has not yet been overruled on its mandate that separate facilities be equal," and in a dissenting opinion he said:

> There is, moreover, an ancient American doctrine that as, if, and when public facilities are separate for the races, they must be equal. *Plessy v. Ferguson* held that a State could maintain separate facilities for different races providing the facilities were equal. . . . But there *can* be *de facto* segregation without the State's being implicated in the creation of the dual system and it is in such situations that *Plessy*'s mandate that separate facilities be equal has continuing force.

He contends, therefore, that where the state is not implicated in the actual creation of a de jure dual system, but is maintaining a school system which is segregated de facto, the *Plessy v. Ferguson* equality principle mandates an order that the inferior facilities be shared by the whites and the superior facilities be shared by the minority groups. This road to integration in a school system segregated de facto might lead to a program of school building and upgrading in the black areas which would match the efforts in some southern states on the eve of *Brown* in the early fifties!

* * *

CONCLUSION

Plessy was a catastrophe. Ill-conceived, ill-supported and rife with gratuitous psychological and social theory, the decision did great damage to the concept of freedom in America. The concern today is whether we are again about to settle for separate but equal facilities. There was a time a hundred years ago when many Americans were not, but then came the 1890's. There are some interesting parallels today. In 1895 Booker T. Washington was willing to settle for a distinctive role for blacks; today, to some, black identity and black separatism have become the most important values. Theories of racial differences being advanced by William Graham Sumner in his theories of folkways seem to find an echo in Jensenism. Some of the northern white ethnic groups have taken a position which parallels the abandonment of the Negro by the northern Republican politicians after 1877 and by southern Populists in the 1890's. Similarities might be suggested between the Hayes Compromise of 1877 and Nixon's 1972 "Southern Strategy." Above all there is a great yearning for peace.

At times one wonders if the nation is ready to settle for "separate but equal" facilities all over again, at least in housing and in neighborhood schools. Young voters can scarcely remember the climate of the 1960's that produced the Freedom Rides and the March, the federal and state public accommodations Acts, open housing and equal employment opportunity laws, all intended to put the nation on the road to equality, not to segregation. So was the Civil Rights Act of 1875, intended to end segregation, however, and it was succeeded in Congress by the long night of 1875 to 1957—with the early help of the Supreme Court.

Plessy v. Ferguson is dead, but the acquiescence in the inevitability of segregated society which was at the roots of that case seems to be with us again. Let us hope that the Court, the Congress, and President and the Nation will do better this time around. People, said Santayana, who do not know their history are doomed to repeat it. We cannot afford another round of "separate but equal."

Thurgood Marshall, *An Evaluation of Recent Efforts to Achieve Racial Integration in Education Through Resort to the Courts*, 21 J. NEGRO EDUC. 316 (1952)*

In order to evaluate recent efforts to achieve racial integration in education through legal action, it is necessary first to consider the legal background of these cases. There are three distinct periods to be considered. The period between 1896 and 1930; between 1930 and 1945; and from 1945 to date.

---

* Reprinted with permission.

1896-1930 PERIOD

The Supreme Court in 1896 in the case of *Plessy v. Ferguson* involving the validity of a statute of Louisiana requiring segregation in intrastate transportation used certain state cases upholding segregation in public education as the basis for its decision upholding the statute. This decision started the "separate but equal" doctrine. During the period between 1896 and 1930, this separate-but-equal doctrine became ingrained in our case law through a lack of carefully planned legal action. Many cases were decided in state and Federal courts during that period; and almost without exception these courts cited with approval the separate-but-equal doctrine. The important point to be considered during this period is that no effort was made in any of these cases to present to the court testimony and other evidence aimed at challenging the validity of the segregation statues in these states. A good example of this is the case of *Lum v. Rice* in which the Court followed the separate-but-equal doctrine. An examination of the record and briefs in this case demonstrates that the Chinese complainant did not object to the segregation statutes of the State of Mississippi but objected to being assigned to the Negro school. This period can be summed up for our purposes by recognizing that the separate-but-equal doctrine of *Plessy v. Ferguson* was set forth without critical analysis on the part of the Supreme Court and with a record which did not give them an opportunity to consider the question adequately. This doctrine established in a case involving intrastate transportation was seized upon and used by state and Federal courts in school cases again and again without any effort being made to analyze the legality of the segregation statutes involved. This separate-but-equal doctrine thus became a rule of law sacred and apparently beyond legal attack.

1930-1945 PERIOD

The N.A.A.C.P. in 1930 started the attack on the inequalities in public education. A special fund was set up to begin the campaign. A careful study was made by the late Nathan Margold. This study formed the groundwork for the first attack which was aimed at the professional school level. The late Charles H. Houston, armed with the Margold report, amplified this report and began the blueprint for the extended legal attack against the inequalities in public education. Many of Houston's associates and students at Howard University Law School worked closely with him on this new project.

* * *

This campaign moved along slowly for three reasons: (1) There was a lack of full support from the Negro community in general; (2) few Negroes were interested enough to ask to be plaintiffs and; (3) there was a lack of sufficient money to finance the cases.

An evaluation of this period would be that it marked the beginning period of planned legal strategy [against] racial segregation. It was the beginning of the period of closing of doors used by the courts in disregarding the fundamental equality of law. The greatest [object] from this period was the public education of school officials, the courts and the general public in the lawlessness of school officials, in depriving Negroes of their constitutional rights. It is the period whereby all of us found by experience that the tangential approach to this legal problem did not produce results in keeping with time, efforts and money expended.

This period is also noted for the cases to equalize the salaries of White and Negro public school teachers. The theory behind these cases was twofold—one, it was hoped that cases would add to the cost of the segregated school system and be an additional burden making segregation too costly to survive. At the same time, these cases were establishing the basic principle of equal pay for work without regard to race and color in the hope that these principles established in public school education would filter down into other of life and employment.

1945-1952 PERIOD

During the period between 1910 and 1945, this legal program was being checked and rechecked and was constantly being evaluated. It shortly became obvious that the only solution to the problem was an all out attack against segregation in public education so that by 1945 plans were ready for a direct attack on the validity of segregation statutes insofar as they applied to public education on the graduate and professional school level.

It appeared that the university level was the best place to begin a campaign that had as its ultimate objective the total elimination of segregation in public educational institutions in the United States. In the first place, at the university level no provision for Negro education was a rule rather than the exception. Then, too, the difficulties incident to providing equal educational opportunities even within the concept of the "separate-but-equal" doctrine were insurmountable. To provide separate medical schools, law schools, engineering schools and graduate schools with all the variety of offerings available at most state universities would be an almost financial impossibility. Even if feasible, it would be impractical to undertake such expenditures for the few Negroes who desired such training. It was felt, therefore, that if effort at this level was pressed with sufficient vigor many states would capitulate without extended litigation. Here also it was easy to demonstrate to the courts that separate facilities for Negroes could not provide equal training to that available in the state universities which for many years had been expanding and improving their facilities in an effort to compete with the great educational centers of the North and West.

The first case filed in this program was the *Sweatt* case against the law school of the University of Texas in 1946. When the case was first filed, the State of Texas assumed that it was a case seeking a separate-but-equal law school. Consequently, the Legislature met and merely changed the name of the Negro state college from Prairie View to "Prairie View University" without doing anything in the line of increased appropriations or building funds. After preliminary hearings on the case and after an amendment to the pleadings, it became evident that this case was actually making a direct attack on the segregation laws as they applied to the University of Texas. Upon discovering this, the same Texas Legislature reconvened and appropriated $2,600,000 plus $500,000 per annum to establish a brand new university for Negroes.

These two moves in and of themselves demonstrated that a direct attack on segregation would produce more in dollars and cents than the other method of seeking equal facilities. It was, therefore, clear, at least in Texas, that the new approach not only produced more education for Negroes than the other approach but also presented the opportunity to break down segregation itself at the same time.

As all of you know, the University of Texas set up a Jim Crow law school and made every effort to show that if it was not equal to the University of Texas law school insofar as physical facilities were concerned, it would be made equal in short order. During the trial of the *Sweatt* case, the first efforts were made to give to the court the necessary expert testimony to make a competent judgment of the validity of segregation statutes as applied to law schools. To do this, it was necessary to demonstrate that segregation of students on the basis of race was an unreasonable classification within the accepted rules for measuring classification statutes by the states. Experts in anthropology were produced and testified that given a similar learning situation a Negro student tended to react the same as any other student, and that there were no racial characteristics which had any bearing whatsoever to the subject of public education. Experts in the field of legal education testified that it was impossible for a Negro student to get an equal education in a Jim Crow law school because of the lack of opportunity to meet with and discuss their problems with other students of varying strata of society. These witnesses also testified that even if two law schools could be made absolutely equal insofar as physical facilities, equipment, curricula and faculties, the Jim Crow law school would nevertheless not offer an education equal to that offered at the other school for the reasons set forth above. Although the Texas courts refused to follow this testimony, the United States Supreme Court reversed these decisions and ordered Sweatt admitted to the law school of the University of Texas.

You also remember the *McLaurin* decision which was in many respects an even more clear-cut decision on the question of segregation. For in the *McLaurin* case, the plaintiff has the same teacher, the same curricula, was in the same building, and, as a matter of fact, was in the same classroom, although set apart from the other students.

It is significant that the decisions in both the *McLaurin* and *Sweatt* cases were unanimous. In the *Sweatt* case the court held: " . . . petitioner may claim his full constitutional right: legal education equivalent to that offered by the State to students to other races. Such education is not available to him in a separate law school as offered by the State . . . We hold that the Equal Protection Clause of the Fourteenth Amendment required that petitioner be admitted to the University Of Texas Law School." . . .

What effect have these university cases had upon the general public? In the first place, it is significant that in each university case the local white student bodies have openly shown their willingness to accept Negro students. Despite the predictions of horrible catastrophes by die-hard state officials, the admission of qualified Negroes has been smooth and without incident. . . .

When the *Sweatt* and *McLaurin* cases were pending in the Supreme Court the attorneys-general for the Southern States filed a joint brief alleging that "The Southern States trust this Court will not strike down power to keep peace, order and support of their public schools by maintaining equal separate facilities. If, the states are shorn of this police power and physical conflict takes place the states are left with no alternative but to close their schools to prevent violence." What happened to this dire prediction? No schools have been closed. More than a thousand Negroes are now attending graduate and professional schools in the South. . . .

* * *

While the right of Negroes to attend state graduate and professional schools has now been established, most Negroes who have received their early education in segregated schools are handicapped because their early training was inadequate and inferior. It became increasingly apparent that the supreme test would have to be made—an attack on segregation at the elementary and high school levels. Acceptance of segregation under the separate-but-equal doctrine had become so ingrained that overwhelming proof was sorely needed to demonstrate that equal educational opportunities for Negroes could not be provided in a segregated system.

It is relatively easy to show that a Negro graduate student offered training in a separate school, thrown up overnight, could not get an education equal to that available at the state universities. Public elementary and high schools, however, present a more difficult basis for comparison. They are normally not specialized institutions with national or even statewide reputations. Public school teachers at these levels are not likely to gain eminence in the profession comparable to that of teachers in colleges and universities. For years, however, exposure of the evils of segregation and discrimination has come from social scientists, and their help was elicited for this phase of the campaign. Social scientists are almost in universal agreement that segregated education produces inequality. Studies have been made of the personality problems caused by discrimination and segregation and most social scientists have reached the conclusion that artificial and arbitrary barriers, such as race and color bars, are likely to have an adverse effect on the personality development of the individual. The energy and strength which the individual might otherwise use in the development of his mental resources is dissipated in adjustment to the problem of segregation.

Unfortunately, the effects of segregation in education have not been related for study by social scientists. They have dealt with the whole problem of segregation, prejudice, and although no social scientist can say that segregated schools alone give the Negroes feelings of insecurity, self-hate, undermines his ego, makes him feel inferior and warps his outlook on life, yet school provides the most important contact with organized society. What he learns, feels, and how he is affected there is apt to determine the type of adult he will become. Social scientists have found that children at an early age are affected by and react to discrimination and prejudices. They have agreed that it is sound to conclude that segregated schools, perhaps more than any other single factor, are of major concern to the individual of public school age and contributes greatly to the unwholesomeness and unhappy development of the personality of Negroes which the caste system in the United States has produced.

The elimination of segregation in public schools may not remove all of the causes of insecurity, self-hate, etc., among Negroes, but since this is a state-sponsored program, certainly the state, consistent with the requirements of the Fourteenth Amendment, should not be a party to a system which does help produce these results. This is the thesis which is now being used to demonstrate the unconstitutionality of segregation at the public elementary and high school levels.

* * *

The primary objective of this recent litigation has been to obtain full and complete integration of all students on all levels of public education without regard to race or color. The stumbling block in the path toward this objective is the separate-but-equal doctrine. In the beginning the Courts prevented litigants from either attacking the doctrine head on or circumventing the doctrine. In the next phase of this program the courts eventually permitted the tangential approach by ordering equality of physical facilities while upholding segregation.

Finally in the *Sweatt* and *McLaurin* decisions the tangential approach was discarded and segregation on the graduate and professional school levels was removed. Even there the Supreme Court refused to strike down the separate-but-equal doctrine as such. The elementary and high school cases are the next steps in this campaign toward the objective and complete integration of all students.

The earlier legal approach to this problem failed to bring about either integration or equality of physical facilities. The direct attack on segregation even if successful in its all-out attack on segregation nevertheless produces immediate serious efforts toward physical equality.

* * *

W. E. Burghardt Du Bois, *Does the Negro Need Separate Schools?*, 4 J. NEGRO EDUC. 328 (1935)*

There are in the United States some four million Negroes of school age, of whom two million are in school, and of these, four-fifths are taught by forty-eight thousand Negro teachers in separate schools. Less than a half million are in mixed schools in the North, where they are taught almost exclusively by white teachers. Beside this, there are seventy-nine Negro universities and colleges with one thousand colored teachers, beside a number of private secondary schools.

The question which I am discussing is: Are these separate schools and institutions needed? And the answer, to my mind, is perfectly clear. They are needed just so far as they are necessary for the proper education of the Negro race. The proper education of any people includes sympathetic touch between teacher and pupil; knowledge on the part of the teacher, not simply of the individual taught, but of his surroundings and background, and the history of his class and group; such contact between pupils, and between teacher and pupil, on the basis of perfect social equality, as will increase this sympathy and knowledge; facilities for education in equipment and housing, and the promotion of such extra-curricular activities as will tend to induct the child into life.

If this is true, and if we recognize the present attitude of white America toward black America, then the Negro not only needs the vast majority of these schools, but it is a grave question if, in the near future, he will not need more such schools, both to take care of his natural increase, and to defend him against the growing animosity of the whites. It is of course fashionable and popular to deny this; to try to deceive ourselves into thinking that race prejudice in the United States across the Color Line is gradually softening and that slowly but surely we are coming to the time when racial animosities and lines will be so obliterated that race schools will be anachronisms.

Certainly, I shall welcome such a time. Just as long as Negroes are taught in Negro schools and whites in white schools; the poor in the slums, and the rich in private schools; just as long as it is impracticable to welcome Negro students to Harvard, Yale and Princeton; just as long as colleges like Williams, Amherst and Wellesley tend to become the property of certain wealthy families, where Jews are not solicited: just so long we shall lack in America that sort of public education which will create the intelligent basis of a real democracy.

Much as I would like this, and hard as I have striven and shall strive to help realize it, I am no fool; and I know that race prejudice in the United States today is such that most Negroes cannot receive proper education in white institutions. If the public schools of Atlanta, Nashville, New Orleans and Jacksonville were thrown open to all races tomorrow, the education that colored children would get in them would be worse than pitiable. It would not be education. And in the same way, there are many public school systems in the North where Negroes are admitted and tolerated, but they are not educated, they are crucified. There are Northern universities where Negro students, no matter what their ability, desert, or accomplishment, cannot get fair recognition, either in classroom or on the campus, in dining halls and student activities, or in human courtesy. It is well known that in certain faculties of the University of Chicago, no Negro has yet received the doctorate and seldom can

---

* Reprinted with permission.

achieve the mastership in arts; at Harvard, Yale and Columbia, Negroes are admitted but not welcomed; while in other institutions, like Princeton, they cannot even enroll.

Under such circumstances, there is no room for argument as to whether the Negro needs separate schools or not. The plain fact faces us, that either he will have separate schools or he will not be educated. There may be, and there is, considerable difference of opinion as to how far this separation in schools is today necessary. There can be argument as to what our attitude toward further separation should be. Suppose, for instance, that in Montclair, New Jersey, a city of wealth and culture, the Board of Education is determined to establish separate schools for Negroes; suppose that, despite the law, separate Negro schools are already established in Philadelphia, and pressure is being steadily brought to extend this separation at least to the junior high school; what must be our attitude toward this?

Manifestly, no general and inflexible rule can be laid down. If public opinion is such in Montclair that Negro children cannot receive decent and sympathetic education in the white schools, and no Negro teachers can be employed, there is for us no choice. We have got to accept Negro schools. Any agitation and action aimed at compelling a rich and powerful majority of the citizens to do what they will not do, is useless. On the other hand, we have a right and a duty to assure ourselves of the truth concerning this attitude; by careful conferences, by public meetings and by petitions, we should convince ourselves whether this demand for separate schools is merely the agition of a prejudiced minority, or the considered and final judgment of the town.

There are undoubtedly cases where a minority of leaders force their opinions upon a majority, and induce a community to establish separate schools, when as a matter of fact, there is no general demand for it; there has been no friction in the schools; and Negro children have been decently treated. In that case, a firm and intelligent appeal to public opinion would eventually settle the matter. But the futile attempt to compel even by law a group to do what it is determined not to do, is a silly waste of money, time, and temper.

On the other hand, there are also cases where there has been no separation in schools and no movement toward it. And yet the treatment of Negro children in the schools, the kind of teaching and the kind of advice they get, is such that they ought to demand either a thorough-going revolution in the official attitude toward Negro students, or absolute separation in educational facilities. To endure bad schools and wrong education because the schools are "mixed" is a costly if not fatal mistake. . . .

Recognizing the fact that for the vast majority of colored students in elementary, secondary, and collegiate education, there must be today separate educational institutions because of an attitude on the part of the white people which is not going materially to change in our time, our customary attitude toward these separate schools must be absolutely and definitely changed. As it is today, American Negroes almost universally disparage their own schools. They look down upon them; they often treat the Negro teachers in them with contempt; they refuse to work for their adequate support; and they refuse to join public movements to increase their efficiency.

The reason for this is quite clear, and may be divided into two parts: (1) the fear that any movement which implies segregation even as a temporary, much less as a relatively permanent institution, in the United States, is a fatal surrender of principle, which in the end will rebound and bring more evils on the Negro than he suffers today. (2) The other reason is at bottom an utter lack of faith on the part of Negroes that their race can do anything really well. If Negroes could conceive that Negroes could establish schools quite as good as or even superior to white schools; if Negro colleges were of equal accomplishment and in scientific work with white colleges; then separation would be a passing incident and not a permanent evil; but as long as American Negroes believe that their race is constitutionally and permanently inferior to white people, they necessarily disbelieve in every possible Negro Institution.

The first argument is more or less metaphysical and cannot be decided *a priori* for every case. There are times when one must stand up for principle at the cost of discomfort, harm, and death. But in the case of the education of the young, you must consider not simply yourself but children and the relation of children to life. It is difficult to think of anything more important for the development of a people than proper training for their children; and yet I have repeatedly seen wise and loving colored parents take infinite pains to force their little children into schools where the white children, white teachers, and white parents despised and resented the dark child, made mock of it, neglected or bullied it, and literally rendered its life a living hell. Such parents want their child to "fight" this thing out,—but, dear God, at what a cost!

Sometimes, to be sure, the child triumphs and teaches the school community a lesson; but even in such cases, the cost may be high, and the child's whole life turned into an effort to win cheap applause at the expense of healthy individuality. In other cases, the result of the experiment may be complete ruin of character, gift, and ability and ingrained hatred of schools and men. For the kind of battle thus indicated, most children are under no circumstances suited. It is the refinement of cruelty to require it of them. Therefore, in evaluating the advantage and disadvantage of accepting race hatred as a brutal but real fact, or of using a little child as a battering ram upon which its nastiness can be thrust, we must give greater value and greater emphasis to the rights of the child's own soul. We shall get a finer, better balance of spirit; an infinitely more capable and rounded personality by putting children in schools where they are wanted, and where they are happy and inspired, than in thrusting them into hells where they are ridiculed and hated.

Beyond this, lies the deeper, broader fact. If the American Negro really believed in himself; if he believed that Negro teachers can educate children according to the best standards of modern training; if he believed that Negro colleges transmit and add to science, as well as or better than other colleges, then he would bend his energies, not to escaping inescapable association with his own group, but to seeing that his group had every opportunity for its best and highest development. He would insist that his teachers be decently paid; that his schools were properly housed and equipped; that his colleges be supplied with scholarship and research funds; and he would be far more interested in the efficiency of these institutions of learning, than in forcing himself into other institutions where he is not wanted.

As long as the Negro student wishes to graduate from Columbia, not because Columbia is an institution of learning, but because it is attended by white students; as long as a Negro student is ashamed to attend Fisk or Howard because these institutions are largely run by black folk, just so long the main problem of Negro education will not be segregation but self-knowledge and self-respect.

There are not many teachers in Negro schools who would not esteem it an unparalleled honor and boast of it to their dying day, if instead of teaching black folk, they could get a chance to teach poor-whites, Irishmen, Italians or Chinese in a "white" institution. This is not unnatural. This is to them a sort of acid test of their worth. It is but the logical result of the "white" propaganda which has swept civilization for the last thousand years, and which is now bolstered and defended by brave words, high wages, and monopoly of opportunities. But this state of mind is suicidal and must be fought, and fought doggedly and bitterly: first, by giving Negro teachers decent wages, decent schoolhouses and equipment, and reasonable chances for advancement; and then by kicking out and leaving to the mercy of the white world those who do not and cannot believe in their own.

Lack of faith in Negro enterprise leads to singular results: Negroes will fight frenziedly to prevent segregated schools; but if segregation is forced upon them by dominant white public opinion, they will suddenly lose interest and scarcely raise a finger to see that the resultant Negro schools get a fair share of the public funds so as to have adequate equipment and housing; to see that real teachers are appointed, and that they are paid as much as white teachers doing the same work. Today, when the Negro public school system gets from half to one-tenth of the amount of money spent on white schools, and is often consequently poorly run and poorly taught, colored people tacitly if not openly join with white people in that Negroes cannot run Negro enterprises, and cannot educate themselves, and that the very establishment of a Negro school means starting an inferior school.

The N.A.A.C.P. and other Negro organizations have spent thousands of dollars to prevent the establishment of segregated Negro schools, but scarcely a single cent to see that the division of funds between white and Negro schools, North and South, is carried out with some faint approximation of justice. There can be no doubt that if the Supreme Court were overwhelmed with cases where the blatant and impudent discrimination against Negro education is openly acknowledged, it would be compelled to hand down decisions which would make this discrimination impossible. We Negroes do not dare to press this point and force these decisions because, forsooth, it would acknowledge the fact of separate schools, a fact that does not need to be acknowledged, and will not need to be for two centuries.

* * *

There was a time when the ability of Negro brains to do first-class work had to be proven by facts and figures, and I was a part of the movement that sought to set the accomplishments of Negro ability before the world. But the world before which I was setting this proof was a disbelieving white world. I did not need the proof for myself. I did not dream that my fellow Negroes needed it; but in the last few years, I have become curiously convinced that until American Negroes believe in their own power and ability, they are going to be helpless before the white world, and the white world, realizing this inner paralysis and lack of self-confidence, is going to persist in its insane determination to rule the universe for its own selfish advantage.

Does the Negro need separate schools? God knows he does. But what he needs more than separate schools is a firm and unshakable belief that twelve million American Negroes have the inborn capacity to accomplish just as much as any nation of twelve million anywhere in the world ever accomplished, and that this is not because they are Negroes but because they are human.

So far, I have noted chiefly negative arguments for separate Negro institutions of learning based on the fact that in the majority of cases Negroes are not welcomed in public schools nor treated as fellow human beings. But beyond this, there are certain positive reasons due to the fact that American Negroes have, because of their history, group experiences and memories, a distinct entity, whose spirit and reactions demand a certain type of education for its development.

I know that this article will forthwith be interpreted by certain illiterate "nitwits" as a plea for segregated Negro schools and colleges. It is not. It is simply calling a spade a spade. It is saying in plain English: that a separate Negro school, where children are treated like human beings, trained by teachers of their own race, who know what it means to be black in the year of salvation 1935, is infinitely better than making our boys and girls doormats to be spit and trampled upon and lied to by ignorant social climbers, whose sole claim to superiority is ability to kick "niggers" when they are down. I say, too, that certain studies and discipline necessary to Negroes can seldom be found in white schools.

It means this, and nothing more.

To sum up this: theoretically, the Negro needs neither segregated schools nor mixed schools. What he needs is Education. What he must remember is that there is no magic, either in mixed schools or in segregated schools. A mixed school with poor and unsympathetic teachers, with hostile public opinion, and no teaching of truth concerning black folk, is bad. A segregated school with ignorant placeholders, inadequate equipment, poor salaries, and wretched housing, is equally bad. Other things being equal, the mixed school is the broader, more natural basis for the education of all youth. It gives wider contacts; it inspires greater self-confidence; and suppresses the inferiority complex. But other things seldom are equal, and in that case, Sympathy, Knowledge, and the Truth, outweigh all that the mixed school can offer.

Brown and Beyond

Having determined in 1954 that "(s)eparate educational facilities are inherently unequal,"[17] the Supreme Court commenced what proved to be an immensely vexing task of desegregation. Responding to a decade of widespread evasion, resistance and delay, the Court eventually insisted upon "remedies that promise realistically to work now."[18] Two decades after *Brown,* the desegregation mandate increasingly was defined by limiting principles qualifying constitutional obligations pursuant to considerations of causation, geography and time. By the 1990s, the obligation to eliminate the vestiges of discrimination "root and branch"[19] had devolved into a duty of eradicating them "to the extent practicable."[20] Derrick A. Bell, Jr. suggests that the potential for racial progress, including the achievements of desegregation, is defined by the limited extent to which the interests of the dominant and subordinate races merge. Donald E. Lively suggests that the desegregation mandate was destined to be a source of underachievement. Kimberlé Williams Crenshaw stresses the significance of formal rights even as an incomplete and independently inadequate method of progress.

Derrick A. Bell, Jr., Brown v. Board of Education *and the Interest-Convergence Dilemma,* 93 HARV. L. REV. 518 (1980)*

In 1954, the Supreme Court handed down the landmark decision *Brown v. Board of Education,* in which the Court ordered the end of state-mandated racial segregation of public schools. Now, more than twenty-five years after that dramatic decision, it is clear that *Brown* will not be forgotten. It has triggered a revolution in civil rights law and in the political leverage available to blacks in and out of court. As judge Robert L. Carter put it, *Brown* transformed blacks from beggars pleading for decent treatment to citizens demanding equal treatment under the law as their constitutionally recognized right.

Yet today, most black children attend public schools that are both racially isolated and inferior. Demographic patterns, white flight, and the inability of the courts to effect the necessary degree of social reform render further progress in implementing *Brown* almost impossible. The late Professor Alexander Bickel warned that *Brown* would not be overturned but, for a whole array of reasons, "may be headed for—dread word—irrelevance." Bickel's prediction is premature in law where the *Brown* decision remains viable, but it may be an accurate assessment of its current practical value to millions of black children who have not experienced the decision's promise of equal educational opportunity.

---

17   Brown v. Board of Education, 347 U.S. 483, 495 (1954).

18   Green v. County School Board of New Kent County, Virginia, 391 U.S. 430, 439 (1968).

19   *Id.* at 438.

20   Board of Education of Oklahoma City Public Schools v. Dowell, 111 S. Ct. 630, 838 (1991).

*   Copyright © 1980 by the Harvard Law Review Association. Reprinted by permission.

Shortly after *Brown*, Professor Herbert Wechsler rendered a sharp and nagging criticism of the decision. Though he welcomed its result, he criticized its lack of a principled basis. Professor Wechsler's views have since been persuasively refuted, yet within them lie ideas which may help to explain the disappointment of *Brown* and what can be done to renew its promise.

* * *

Wechsler reviewed and rejected the possibility that *Brown* was based on a declaration that the fourteenth amendment barred all racial lines in legislation. He also doubted that the opinion relied upon a factual determination that segregation caused injury to black children, since evidence as to such harm was both inadequate and conflicting. Rather, Wechsler concluded, the Court in *Brown* must have rested its holding on the view that "racial segregation is, in *principle*, a denial of equality to the minority against whom it is directed; that is, the group that is not dominant politically and, therefore, does not make the choice involved." Yet, Wechsler found this argument untenable as well, because, among other difficulties, it seemed to require an inquiry into the motives of the legislature, a practice generally foreclosed to the courts.

After dismissing these arguments, Wechsler then asserted that the legal issue in state-imposed segregation cases was not one of discrimination at all, but rather of associational rights: "the denial by the state of freedom to associate, a denial that impinges in the same way on any groups or races that may be involved." Wechsler reasoned that "if the freedom of association is denied by segregation, integration forces an association upon those for whom it is unpleasant or repugnant." And concluding with a question that has challenged legal scholars, Wechsler asked:

> Given a situation where the state must practically choose between denying the association to those individuals who wish it or imposing it on those who would avoid it, is there a basis in neutral principles for holding that the Constitution demands that the claims for association should prevail?

In suggesting that there was a basis in neutral principles for holding that the Constitution supports a claim by blacks for an associational right, Professor Wechsler confessed that he had not yet written an opinion supporting such a holding. "To write it is for me the challenge of the school-segregation cases."

II. THE SEARCH FOR A NEUTRAL PRINCIPLE RACIAL EQUALITY AND INTEREST CONVERGENCE

Scholars who accepted Professor Wechsler's challenge had little difficulty finding a neutral principle on which the *Brown* decision could be based. Indeed, from the hindsight of a quarter century of the greatest racial consciousness-raising the country has ever known, much of Professor Wechsler's concern seems hard to imagine. To doubt that racial segregation is harmful to blacks, and to suggest that what blacks really sought was the right to associate with whites, is to believe in a world that does not exist now and could not possibly have existed then. Professor Charles Black, therefore, correctly viewed racial equality as the neutral principle which underlay the *Brown* opinion. In Black's view, Wechsler's question "is awkwardly simple," and he states his response in the from of a syllogism. Black's major premise is that "the equal protection clause of the fourteenth amendment should be read as saying that the Negro race, as such, is not to be significantly disadvantaged by the laws of the states." His minor premise is that "segregation is a massive intentional disadvantaging of the Negro race, as such, by state law." The conclusion, then, is that the equal protection clause clearly bars racial segregation because segregation harms blacks and benefits whites in ways too numerous and obvious to require citation.

Logically, the argument is persuasive, and Black has no trouble urging that "[w]hen the directive of equality cannot be followed without displeasing the white[s], then something that can be called a 'freedom' of the white[s] must be impaired." It is precisely here, though, that many whites part company with Professor Black. Whites may agree in the abstract that blacks are citizens and are entitled to constitutional protection against racial discrimination, but few are willing to recognize that racial segregation is much more than a series of quaint customs that can be remedied effectively without altering the status of whites. The extent of this unwillingness is illustrated by the controversy over affirmative action programs, particularly those where identifiable whites must step aside for blacks they deem less qualified or less deserving. Whites simply cannot envision the personal responsibility and the potential sacrifice inherent in Professor Black's conclusion that true equality for blacks will require the surrender of racism-granted privileges for whites.

This sober assessment of reality raises concern about the ultimate import of Black's theory. On a normative level, as a description of how the world ought to be, the notion of racial equality appears to be the proper basis on which *Brown* rests, and Wechsler's framing of the problem in terms of associational rights thus seem misplaced. Yet, on a positivistic level—how the world is—it is clear that racial equality is not deemed legitimate by large segments of the American people, at least to the extent it threatens to impair the societal status of whites. Hence, Wechsler's search for a guiding principle in the context of associational rights retains merit in the positivistic sphere, because it suggests a deeper truth about the subordination of law to interest-group politics with a racial configuration.

Although no such subordination is apparent in *Brown*, it is possible to discern in more recent school decisions the outline of a principle, applied without direct acknowledgment, that could serve as the positivistic expression of the neutral statement of general applicability sought by Professor Wechsler. Its elements rely as much on political history as legal precedent and emphasize the world as it is rather than how we might want it to be. Translated from judicial activity in racial cases both before and after *Brown*, this principle of "interest convergence" provides: The interest of blacks in achieving racial equality will be accommodated only when it converges with the interests of whites. However, the fourteenth amendment, standing alone, will not authorize a judicial remedy providing effective racial equality for blacks where the remedy sought threatens the superior societal status of middle and upper class whites.

It follows that the availability of fourteenth amendment protection in racial cases may not actually be determined by the character of harm suffered by blacks or the quantum of liability proved against whites. Racial remedies may instead be the outward manifestations of unspoken and perhaps subconscious judicial conclusions that the remedies, if granted, will secure, advance, or at least not harm societal interests deemed important by middle and upper class whites. Racial justice—or its appearance—may, from time to time, be counted among the interests deemed important by the courts and by society's policymakers.

In assessing how this principle can accommodate both the *Brown* decision and the subsequent development of school desegregation law, it is necessary to remember that the issue of school segregation and the harm it inflicted on black children did not first come to the Court's attention in the *Brown* litigation: blacks had been attacking the validity of these policies for 100 years. Yet, prior to *Brown*, black claims that segregated public schools were inferior had been met by orders requiring merely that facilities be made equal. What accounted, then, for the sudden shift in 1954 away from the separate but equal doctrine and towards a commitment to desegregation?

I contend that the decision in *Brown* to break with the Court's long-held position on these issues cannot be understood without some consideration of the decision's value to whites, not simply those concerned about the immorality of racial inequality, but also those whites in policymaking positions able to see the economic and political advances at home and abroad that would follow abandonment of segregation. First, the decision helped to provide immediate credibility to America's struggle with Communist countries to win the hearts and minds of emerging third world peoples. At least this argument was advanced by lawyers for both the NAACP and the federal governments. And the point was not lost on the news media. *Time* magazine, for example, predicted that the international impact of *Brown* would be scarcely less important than its effect on the education of black children: "In many countries, where U.S. prestige and leadership have been damaged by the fact of U.S. segregation, it will come as a timely reassertion of the basic American principle that 'all men are created equal.'"

Second, *Brown* offered much needed reassurance to American blacks that the precepts of equality and freedom so heralded during World War II might yet be given meaning at home. Returning black veterans faced not only continuing discrimination, but also violent attacks in the South which rivaled those that took place at the conclusion of World War I. . . .

Finally, there were whites who realized that the South could make the transition from a rural, plantation society to the sunbelt with all its potential and profit only when it ended its struggle to remain divided by state-sponsored segregation. Thus, segregation was viewed as a barrier to further industrialization in the South.

These points may seem insufficient proof of self-interest leverage to produce a decision as important as *Brown*. They are cited, however, to help assess and not to diminish the Supreme Court's most important statement on the principle of racial equality. Here, as in the abolition of slavery, there were whites for whom recognition of the racial equality principle was sufficient motivation. But, as with abolition, the number who would act on morality alone was insufficient to bring about the desired racial reform.

* * *

[R]ecent decisions, most notably by the Supreme Court, indicate that the convergency of black and white interests that led to *Brown* in 1954 and influenced the character of its enforcement has begun to fade. In *Swann v. Charlotte-Mecklenburg Board of Education*, Chief justice Burger spoke of the "reconciliation of competing values" in desegregation cases. If there was doubt that "competing values" referred to the conflicting interests of blacks seeking desegregation and whites who prefer to retain existing school policies, then the uncertainty was dispelled by *Milliken v. Bradley*, and by *Dayton Board of Education v. Brinkman (Dayton I)*. In both cases, the Court elevated the concept of "local autonomy" to a "vital national tradition." "No single tradition in public education is more deeply rooted than local control over the operation of schools; local autonomy has long been thought essential both to the maintenance of community concern and support for public schools and to the quality of the educational process." Local control, however, may result in the maintenance of a status quo that will preserve superior educational opportunities and facilities for whites at the expense of blacks. As one commentator has suggested, "It is implausible to assume that school boards guilty of substantial violations in the past will take the interests of black school children to heart."

As a result of its change in attitudes, the Court has increasingly erected barriers to achieving the forms of racial balance relief it earlier had approved. Plaintiffs must now prove that the complained-of segregation was the result of discriminatory actions intentionally and invidiously conducted or authorized by school officials. It is not enough that segregation was the "natural and foreseeable" consequence of their policies. And even when this difficult standard of proof is met, courts must carefully limit the relief granted to the harm actually proved. Judicial second thoughts about racial balance plans with broad-range busing components, the very plans which civil rights lawyers have come to rely on, is clearly evident in these new proof standards.

* * *

At the very least, these decisions reflect a substantial and growing divergence in the interests of whites and blacks. The result could prove to be the realization of Professor Wechsler's legitimate fear that, if there is not a change of course, the purported entitlement of whites not to associate with blacks in public schools may yet eclipse the hope and the promise of *Brown*.

INTEREST-CONVERGENCE REMEDIES UNDER *BROWN*

Further progress to fulfill the mandate of *Brown* is possible to the extent that the divergence of racial interests can be avoided or minimized. Whites in policy-making positions, including those who sit on federal courts, can take no comfort in the conditions of dozens of inner-city school systems where the great majority of nonwhite children attend classes as segregated and ineffective as those so roundly condemned by Chief Justice Warren in the *Brown* opinion. Nor do poorer whites gain from their opposition to the improvement of educational opportunities for blacks: as noted earlier, the needs of the two groups differ little. Hence, over time, all will reap the benefits from a concerted effort towards achieving racial equality.

The question still remains as to the surest way to reach the goal of educational effectiveness for both blacks and whites. I believe that the most widely used programs mandated by the courts—"antidefiance, racial balance" plans—may in some cases be inferior to plans focusing on "educational components," including the creation and development of "model" all-black schools. . . .

There was a problem with school desegregation decisions framed in this antidefiance form that was less discernible then than now. . . . [T]he remedies set forth in the major school cases following *Brown*—balancing the student and teacher populations by race in each school, eliminating one-race schools, redrawing school attendance lines, and transporting students to achieve racial balance—have not in themselves guaranteed black children better schooling than they received in the pre-*Brown* era. Such racial balance measures have often altered the racial appearance of dual school systems without eliminating racial discrimination. Plans relying on racial balance to foreclose evasion have not eliminated the need for further orders protecting black children against discriminatory policies, including resegregation within desegregated schools, the loss of black faculty and administrators, suspensions and expulsions at much higher rates than white students, and varying forms of racial harassment ranging from exclusion from extracurricular activities to physical violence. Antidefiance remedies, then, while effective in forcing alterations in school system structure, often encourage and seldom shield black children from discriminatory retaliation.

The educational benefits that have resulted from the mandatory assignment of black and white children to the same schools are also debatable. If benefits did exist, they have begun to dissipate as whites flee in alarming numbers from school districts ordered to implement mandatory reassignment plans. In response, civil rights lawyers sought to include entire metropolitan areas within mandatory reassignment plans where so many white parents sought sanctuary for their children.

Thus, the antidefiance strategy was brought full circle from a mechanism for preventing evasion by school officials of *Brown*'s antisegregation mandate to one aimed at creating a discrimination-free environment. This approach to the implementation of *Brown*, however, has become increasingly ineffective; indeed, it has in some cases been educationally destructive. A preferable method is to focus on obtaining real educational effectiveness which may entail the improvement of presently desegregated schools as well as the creation or preservation of model black schools.

* * *

Desegregation remedies that do not integrate may seem a step backward toward the *Plessy* "separate but equal" era. Some black educators, however, see major educational benefits in schools where black children, parents, and teachers can utilize the real cultural strengths of the black community to overcome the many barriers to educational achievement. As Professor Laurence Tribe argued, "[J]udicial rejection of the 'separate but equal' talisman seems to have been accompanied by a potentially troublesome lack of sympathy for racial separateness as a possible expression of group solidarity."

This is not to suggest that educationally oriented remedies can be developed and adopted without resistance. Policies necessary to obtain effective schools threaten the self-interest of teacher unions and others with vested interests in the status quo. But successful magnet schools may provide a lesson that effective schools for blacks must be a primary goal rather than a secondary result of integration. Many white parents recognize a value in integrated schooling for their children but they quite properly view integration as merely one component of an effective education. To the extent that civil rights advocates also accept this reasonable sense of priority, some greater racial interest conformity should be possible.

* * *

Is this what the *Brown* opinion meant by "equal educational opportunity"? Chief justice Warren said the Court could not "turn the clock back to 1868 when the [Fourteenth] Amendment was adopted, or even to 1896 when *Plessy v. Ferguson* was written." The change in racial circumstances since 1954 rivals or surpasses all that occurred during the period that preceded it. If the decision that was at least a catalyst for that change is to remain viable, those who rely on it must exhibit the dynamic awareness of all the legal and political considerations that influenced those who wrote it.

Professor Wechsler warned us early on that there was more to *Brown* than met the eye. At one point, he observed that the opinion is "often read with less fidelity by those who praise it than by those by whom it is condemned." Most of us ignored that observation openly and quietly raised a question about the sincerity of the observer. Criticism, as we in the movement for minority rights have every reason to learn, is a synonym for neither cowardice nor capitulation. It may instead bring awareness, always the first step toward overcoming still another barrier in the struggle for racial equality.

Donald E. Lively, *Desegregation and the Supreme Court: The Fatal Attraction of* Brown, 20 HASTINGS CONST. L.Q. 649 (1993)*

Introduction

The desegregation era has been notable for exceptional demands and disappointing results. The desegregation mandate, as introduced by *Brown v. Board of Education*, deviated from principles of constitutional review that had routinely accommodated or deferred to classifications and distinctions on the basis of race. Recent Supreme Court decisions have, however, trimmed constitutional requirements for a society that has left behind formal segregation, but not realities of racism and discrimination. As ultimately defined, the law of the land is that the achievements of *Brown* need not be preserved and the undoing of segregation itself is required only "to the extent practicable."

Investment in the desegregation mandate for less than four decades contrasts with the use of the separate but equal doctrine for half of the Fourteenth Amendment's existence. The result is consistent, however, with two centuries of constitutional jurisprudence that belatedly responded to issues of race, and has since consistently qualified and narrowed the principles that would reckon with discrimination and its legacy. The Thirteenth Amendment prohibited slavery, which northern states had accommodated as a cost of establishing a viable union. When southern states attempted to reintroduce slavery in function rather than form immediately after the Thirteenth Amendment's enactment, the Fourteenth Amendment was framed and ratified to secure the citizenship of all persons born or naturalized in the United States, including those of African descent. It also established privileges and immunities incidental to national citizenship and prohibited states from denying to any person due process or equal protection of the law. For nearly a century, judicial review of the Fourteenth Amendment was notable for its deference to official schemes and policies that favored whites and burdened other racial groups.

The recharting of equal protection principles in 1954 was thus performed against a backdrop of profound racial prejudice and discrimination. As central features in the nation's traditions, these were potent factors that could not be erased by a single judicial decree or series thereof. To the extent that racism survived the recasting of legal principle, it presented a persistent risk of diluting or defeating any constitutional commitment toward reckoning with the nation's legacy of racial injustice. The danger was compounded by the possibility that fatigue, indifference, or impatience with the intractable problem of race might set in and undermine grand objectives in much the same way that fading interest sapped motivation to achieve the goals of the Civil War amendments in the post-Reconstruction period.

The desegregation mandate's devitalization, despite the reality that racially identifiable and unequal schools endure as pervasive rather than exceptional phenomena, suggests the possibility that history has repeated itself. It invites attention not only to the wisdom of ending the era but to the decision to commence it. Desegregation essentially has been an affirmative action policy that in significant ways has

failed and, absent evidence that society was reasonably likely to adhere to its requirements in a comprehensive and enduring way, may have been a misplaced investment.

* * *

The *Brown* decision radically redirected equal protection doctrine and required
extensive cultural upheaval, but was premised upon assumptions that eventually limited its achievements. Given the backdrop against which *Brown* emerged, and the
manifestly racist tradition that it repudiated, the *Brown* decision has presented a
unique challenge to critics. To question the quality of its calculus runs a risk of being
typed as racist or reactionary. Not surprisingly, therefore, the *Brown* decision has
been treated with deference even by some of its most logical critics. Although not
grounded in interpretive norms ordinarily acceptable to exponents of judicial restraint
and political conservativism, *Brown* nonetheless is a decision they strive to rationalize
and accept. Robert Bork, an ardent advocate of originalism, has noted the deviation
between the desegregation principle and the Framers' acceptance of formal racial separation. Still, he has embraced the *Brown* ruling as the necessary function of a
choice between revising the meaning of equal protection or effectively reading it out
of the Constitution. Justice Scalia has identified desegregation as an exception to his
otherwise unbending view that race-conscious policies are constitutionally unacceptable. Such efforts at accommodation are mystifying in some ways, revealing in
others, and ultimately as unconvincing as they are disproportionate to the significance of *Brown* as it has devolved. The inclination to except *Brown* from interpretive
norms suggests theoretical maneuvers that are more patronizing than honest. The
abiding effort to square doctrine with incompatible theories of judicial restraint, especially as the desegregation principle itself has been gutted, indicates analytical confusion, selective distortion prompted by concern for appearance, and perhaps an
unconscious concession to the rightness of a result that if fully acknowledged would
undermine a favored judicial theory or political agenda.

Given the historical significance of race and impediments to the elimination of
racial distinctions, the desegregation formula, if not programmed for failure, was at
least a high risk proposition. It has been noted that, especially in the South, official
segregation was not merely a means of separation, but involved "one in-group enjoy-
ing full normal communal life and one out-group that is barred from this life and
forced into an inferior life of its own." Repudiation of such a system was appropriate,
and a compelling justification existed for policies that would repair a legacy of accumulated group disadvantage. The provision for relief "with all deliberate speed,"
rather than demanding immediate compliance, signaled judicial equivocation that
eventually would undermine the realization of *Brown*'s full potential. Inadequate or
incomplete enforcement also illuminated an unfortunate overemphasis upon assimilation as the sole path to destigmatization. Such an emphasis disregarded the more
profound reality that stigmatic harm ultimately is traceable to racial assumptions
that were capable of surviving the system of formal, legal segregation. Because
racial prejudice could not reasonably have been expected to dissipate by virtue of constitutional reformulation alone, a major risk to the fulfillment of *Brown*'s promise was
that doctrine would freeze as discriminatory methodologies changed from overt to subtle and resistance to change was compounded by indifference. The risk has materi-
alized into reality, as standards have not developed beyond the point of reckoning with
formal segregation or discrimination. The remedial methodology of desegregation
itself, moreover, may actually have enhanced stigmatic injury to the extent that it tied
perceptions of personal or group adequacy to full acceptance by a society resistant to

comprehensive integration. Compounding the negative fallout from *Brown* have been reduced desegregative demands and a failure to account effectively for educational opportunity.

* * *

I. The Rise and Fall of the Desegregation Principle

* * *

When conceived and as pursued, the aim of undoing segregation was not consensually subscribed to even among critics of the established order. W.E.B. DuBois noted, contemporaneously with the NAACP's initial success, that "[o]ther things being equal" desegregated schools were the ideal, but "things seldom are equal, and in that case, Sympathy, Knowledge, and the Truth, outweigh all the mixed school can offer." The pertinence of DuBois's observation was renewed in the post-*Brown* era as desegregation evolved in the direction of formal equality, without concern for equal educational opportunity, in a still largely segregated environment. The Court in *Brown* determined that racially segregated public schools never could be equal for purposes of the Fourteenth Amendment. Implicit in that conclusion and corresponding doctrinal revision was the sense that equal opportunity would be secured and connotations of racial inferiority would vanish through desegregation. Constitutional redirection was premised, however, upon dubious assumptions about the past and risky calculations of the future.

* * *

By encouraging affected states to participate in the framing of relief and vesting state and local officials and lower courts with implementation and oversight responsibilities, the Court anticipated cooperation in the transition from dual to unitary schools. Expectations of acquiescence were confounded initially by resistance to and evasion of the mandate. The efficacy of the *Brown* principle ultimately would depend upon the Court's ability to have it enforced. In one notable instance, desegregation was accomplished by armed intervention. It was boosted further by federal legislation authorizing the United States Attorney General to bring desegregation actions and denying federal funding to school districts not complying with *Brown*.

Efforts to avoid the process persisted throughout the desegregation era. After more than a decade of intransigence and evasion by many school districts, the Court insisted upon desegregation remedies that "promise[ ] realistically to work *now*." By then, however, the changes contemplated by the *Brown* Court had eluded nearly an entire generation of public school students. One school system subject to the original desegregation order in *Brown* itself remained unchanged a decade after the decision. At the same time, barely two percent of southern black students attended schools where they did not constitute the dominant racial group.

Unresponsiveness to *Brown* was reminiscent of early reaction to the Fourteenth Amendment itself. Although the Amendment reflected a new federal interest in civil rights and equality and provided a tool for attacking state devices for denying or limiting basic rights and equality, the Amendment's initial agenda was weakened by competing priorities and continued resistance to change. As reunification and economic development became more pressing, the nation's commitment to civil rights and societal change lapsed. Similarly, after several years of judicial and legislative activity on behalf of civil rights, the Court began to trim the scope of the *Brown* mandate.

The Supreme Court enunciated the first significant qualification in *Keyes v. School District No. 1*. Unlike the South, where segregation was maintained by legal prescription, the North and West achieved similar results through official decisions with respect to district lines, school siting, pupil placement, and other race-dependent variables. In *Keyes*, the Court determined that such policy-making "establishe[d] a prima facie case of intentional segregation." Of particular long-term significance was the Court's illusory distinction between de jure and de facto segregation, and its determination that only the former was constitutionally objectionable. Since *Keyes* required courts to discern de jure segregation before ordering desegregation, it became the plaintiff's responsibility to demonstrate that racial separation was attributable to intentional official action. The finding of a constitutional violation in *Keyes* itself may have suggested that its analytical framework could be used to support demands for desegregation. In fact, as motive-referenced standards have evolved in response to challenged policies by schools and other public institutions, the *Keyes* requirement of official action has proved effective primarily in curtailing the Fourteenth Amendment's demands.

Further qualifying the demands of the desegregation mandate was the Court's determination, one year after *Keyes*, that interdistrict relief was not a remedial option. In *Milliken v. Bradley*, it rejected the trial court's findings that state involvement in the segregation of Detroit schools justified a desegregation plan comprehending the city and its suburbs. The Court emphasized that suburban communities had not colluded directly with the city for segregative purposes and, notwithstanding their common status with the city as subdivisions of the state, were immune from responsibility for fixing any constitutional violation. As a consequence of the *Milliken* decision, the phenomenon of white flight received constitutional blessing. Justice Marshall objected that the Court was abandoning its responsibility for the consequences of the desegregation command which it had entered two decades earlier. He perceived in the decision a sense that the desegregation process "ha[d] gone far enough."

The *Milliken* decision established geographical restrictions upon the desegregation mandate. In *Pasadena City Board of Education v. Spangler*, the Court emphasized that desegregation responsibilities also were subject to time limitations. Specifically, the Court concluded that once a racially neutral attendance pattern was implemented, further constitutional duties would not be imposed in response to demographic change. Barring proof of official contribution to or manipulation of racial composition, therefore, resegregation was not a basis for further remediation. Justice Marshall argued unsuccessfully that when a state has "created a system where whites and Negroes were intentionally kept apart so that they could not become accustomed to learning together, [it] is responsible for the fact that many whites will react to the dismantling of that segregated system by attempting to flee to the suburbs." By the 1970s, the desegregation principle had been redefined to the point that it functioned only in rare instances where official wrong was manifest, afforded few meaningful remedies in major urban centers, and became only a passing obligation.

The principles enunciated in *Keyes, Milliken*, and *Spangler* profoundly limited the prospective operation of the desegregation mandate. They also generated obvious questions with respect to whether the accomplishments of the *Brown* mandate could be preserved and whether any constitutional obligation existed to maintain them. Integration maintenance efforts in some cities have led to sometimes incongruous and unsettling results. One city, for instance, reverted to racially identifiable schools at the primary level in hopes of preserving integration at the secondary level. Another restricted transfers from minority dominated schools to integrated settings out of concern that white flight would be exacerbated. Such policies have responded to abiding difficulties in actualizing the goals of *Brown* and desegregation itself. So elusive did the aims of *Brown* become that preservation of the process was prioritized above and to the detriment of the opportunity it was intended to secure. Recent case law has emphasized that such "heroic efforts" are not obligatory, and effectively has reduced desegregation to a ritual that must be performed to render segregation constitutionally permissible.

II. Reversion to Constitutional Norms

A persistent aspect of relevant constitutional review has been the misperception of racial reality, or manipulation of it, to avoid constitutional strictures. Such analytical failure is a phenomenon that precedes and postdates the *Brown* decision. The Supreme Court upheld slavery and denied citizenship status to all persons of African descent, for instance, in the belief that they were "beings of an inferior order and altogether unfit to associate with the white race . . . and lawfully . . . reduced to slavery." Even after the Fourteenth Amendment was framed and ratified, the Court regarded exclusion of blacks from public accommodations and reservation of social privileges for whites as "mere discriminations." The separate but equal doctrine advanced a premise that any harm from official segregation was attributable not to the law itself but to the construction that "the colored race chooses to put . . . on it." Such rationalization was a jurisprudentially polished veneer upon a policy that was the cornerstone of white supremacy, which assumed that "blacks were inherently inferior . . ., a conviction being stridently trumpeted by white supremacists from the press, the pulpit, and the platform, as well as the legislative halls of the South."

The *Brown* Court eventually recognized that prescriptive separation on the basis of race was a constitutionally significant source of stigmatizing injury and an impediment to opportunity. Consistent with, and perhaps a reason for, the desegregation mandate's demise, however, has been a reversion to traditional perceptual norms. Refusal to recalibrate the desegregation principle so that it would account for demographic change, for instance, reflects a perception of population redistribution as a "quite normal pattern of human migration." This dismissal of any constitutional significance with respect to population resettlement following court-ordered desegregation is reminiscent of the *Plessy* Court's deference to distinctions "in the nature of things." Similarly evidencing a sense of invariability, and thus acceptability, is the view that "[e]ven if the Constitution required it, and it were possible for the federal courts to do it, no equitable decree can fashion an 'Emerald City' where all the races, ethnic groups, and persons of various income levels live side by side. . . ." Such a perception is akin to the denial of relief for racially motivated deprivation of voting rights at the turn of this century because, given dominant attitudes of the time and place, judicial intervention would be "pointless."

The limiting principles which diminished the operation and significance of the desegregation mandate suggested that *Brown* itself was an exception to perceptual and analytical norms. Constrictive as they were, the decisions of the 1970s did not entirely enervate the desegregation principle. Even after those rulings, the Court found constitutional violations in the school systems of . . . northern cities and struck down an antibusing initiative in a northern state. Recent decisions have effectively relegated desegregation to a historical episode which now is largely past.

* * *

Decisions before and after *Brown* have acknowledged society's racial hierarchy, but have accommodated it for constitutional purposes. The *Brown* Court fashioned doctrine that largely ignored or underestimated the significance of the cultural factors it sought to contain. It may have assumed that it could overcome resistance or indifference. Subsequent jurisprudence and results have disclosed a fundamental miscalculation. The desegregation era commenced with a principle that responded to the existence and consequences of racial discrimination and has waned with results that are incomplete and fleeting. Addressing the reality and consequences of discrimination and disadvantage thus remains a challenge, rather than achievement, of the past four decades.

III. Desegregation and Assimilative Premises:
The Consequences of Miscalculation

As the nation courses into its third century and toward the centennial of the separate but equal doctrine, desegregation has been consigned to a unique but brief role in over 200 years of racially significant constitutional law. Justice Thurgood Marshall, in response to the limiting principles prefacing the era's foreclosure, observed that "[d]esegregation is not and was never expected to be an easy task." The *Brown* Court itself sensed some possibility that its transformation of the Fourteenth Amendment represented a perilous constitutional undertaking. Its invitation of state and local participation in the framing of relief represented an effort to defuse resistance that backfired. Later insistence upon relief that "works now" marked the desegregation mandate's peak assertiveness. Whether legal demands actually might have reshaped reality beyond what was achieved is at least dubious, given the prevalence of tracking, dual standards of discipline, and other race-dependent phenomena that have internalized duality in formally desegregated environments. The question, however, is largely academic. Given personnel turnover and ideological change on the Court, its demand for effective desegregation merely prefaced the circumscription and eventual demise of the *Brown* mandate.

* * *

Seldom acknowledged in the undoing of desegregation requirements, and criticism thereof, is *Brown*'s own contribution to racial stigmatization. Such results are not surprising given certain misperceptions and miscalculations by the *Brown* Court. Although recognizing that official segregation connoted inferiority, the Court's understanding of harm was somewhat misplaced. Implicit in its derogation of the separate but equal doctrine was the sense that black children were psychologically deprived by not having the opportunity to mix with white children. The real source of injury in a society that prioritizes personal liberty, autonomy, and determination, however, was a policy that denied choice concerning matters of self-development including where and with whom to attend school. By wrongly assuming the source and nature of harm, the *Brown* Court offered doctrine intimating that blacks needed whites to obtain a proper education and thereby reinforced traditional assumptions of racial superiority and inferiority. By concluding that racially separate education was inherently unequal, without attention to circumstance or alternative, it underestimated the abiding reality of racism that, until addressed, would undermine any constitutional principle or mandate. Demands for societal change, linking destigmatization and opportunity to compulsory mixing, compromised not only the remedy, but its objective as well.

Post-*Brown* case law has delimited the possibilities for desegregation and diminished the predicates for constitutional attention to discriminatory or segregative conditions. The Court in 1954 emphasized the Fourteenth Amendment significance of official action that was racially stigmatizing and that impaired equal educational opportunity. The attempt to remedy such action has been confounded by standards that require proof of discriminatory purpose rather than consideration of injury or persisting disadvantage. Despite well-established case law to the effect that the Fourteenth Amendment requires elimination of dual schools and attainment of unitary status, the Court now notes that "it is a mistake to treat words such as 'dual' and 'unitary' as if they were actually found in the Constitution." The observation is technically accurate, but it applies with equal force to discriminatory purpose standards that are selectively enshrined in modern equal protection analysis. In 1954, the Court intimated that education was a liberty interest protected by the Fourteenth Amendment. Twenty years later, at the same time the Court was limiting the reach of desegregation, it held that access to education was not a fundamental right. Except to the extent that overt discrimination is provable, and notwithstanding claims of stigmatic harm or linkage to a segregative past, the net result is prohibition of formal segregation and discrimination but tolerance of their legacy and even reversion to their functional likenesses.

The defensibility of *Brown* as a legitimate exercise of constitutional review does not afford it immunity from criticism with respect to its wisdom and foresight. Taken by itself, *Brown* expanded dramatically the national demands of constitutional equality. The ruling may have been a catalyst for enforcement action by the political branches that for decades had evinced limited interest in civil rights. In 1957, President Eisenhower dispatched federal troops to enforce the desegregation mandate despite his own reservations. A decade after *Brown*, Congress enacted comprehensive civil rights and voting rights legislation. The Civil Rights Act of 1964 prohibited discrimination in employment, housing, public accommodations and facilities, and in federally supported programs. The Voting Rights Act of 1965 barred schemes and devices that excluded minorities from the political system. Whether Congress would have acted sooner or later, or more or less effectively, absent *Brown*, is entirely speculative. What is certain is that, given widespread resistance to and evasion of the Court's edict, it was not until Congress intervened with appropriate legislation that substantial desegregative progress was realized. It is equally evident that, soon after the Supreme Court fortified the desegregation principle with demands for remedies that "work now," it began announcing limiting principles that curbed and eventually eviscerated the *Brown* mandate. The federal interest in civil rights waned, as it did a century ago, at the end of the Reconstruction era. The post-Reconstruction Court expressed fears of developing a federally inspired "code of municipal law." It consequently invalidated civil rights legislation and deferred to official segregation. Similarly, the modern Court emphasizes that education is a normatively local function and that the federal interest is essentially aberrational and transitory.

Given *Brown*'s achievement in dispatching formal segregation, but its subsequent limitations and failures, the ultimate question is whether *Brown* rates as a success or failure. Doctrinal wisdom is ultimately a function not only of the quality of the Court's analysis, but also of its durability and acceptance. In enunciating the desegregation mandate as the future wave of equal protection, the *Brown* Court was at an especially significant disadvantage since mid-twentieth century society was on the brink of extensive change that would complicate its implementation. The Court could not have anticipated how increased personal mobility, emerging transportation networks, and suburban development would facilitate the reconfiguration of community life and demographic patterns. By the 1970s, such changes presented a substantially reconstituted Court with the opportunity to distinguish current conditions from the relatively static social order which was considered in 1954.

Although the precise societal changes and the curtailment of doctrinal potential that ensued may have been unforeseeable, the *Brown* Court legitimately may be second-guessed for its sensitivity to a historical record characterized by sporadic and aborted attention to racial justice, vacillating concern with discrimination, competing priorities, and the risk that such factors would influence future doctrinal development. It also is subject to questions regarding its appreciation of deep seated racial antagonism and discomfort, how such realities would foil efforts to equalize educational opportunity, and how the dynamics of racial stigmatization operate. The *Brown* Court assumed that a redefined equal protection guarantee would account more effectively over the long run for interests which had been slighted by its analytical predecessor. It recognized the possibility of resistance to its mandate but took the chance that it could make the new constitutional formula work. What the Court in 1954 apparently did not anticipate was the relatively quick demise of the desegregation mandate in a way that ensured "the same separate and inherently unequal education in the future as . . . ha[s] been unconstitutionally afforded in the past." Had it possessed the vision to foresee that resistance, decreased interest, and diminished commitment would permit the substitution of functional for formal segregation, the Court may not have announced the desegregation decision as it did or when it did. What *Brown* thus may be primarily faulted for are too predictable consequences of underachievement and backlash when the judiciary fast-forwards the law beyond the society's moral development or capacity. The aftermath of *Brown* suggests that the nation was ready to disown formal segregation but not prepared to accept broad-spectrum integration or policies designed to rectify past injustice on a broad scale. Lost in doctrinal calculus now is any constitutional formula that might meaningfully account for persisting group separation and disadvantage.

Even if not directly responsible for the actual glosses that cramped development of its work, the *Brown* Court nonetheless assumed the risk that the desegregation principle, like any jurisprudential precept, would be distinguished, curtailed, or abandoned. Considering the desegregation mandate in historical context, the prospects for an unhappy ending should have seemed at least a distinct possibility. The history of the Fourteenth Amendment is dominated by resistance to its goals and perversion of its central meaning. Intransigence and evasion defined southern reaction to the desegregation mandate; hostility to its possible expansion characterized northern and western response to it. To some extent, the Court factored in the possibility of societal opposition to desegregation, as evidenced by its efforts to involve state and local communities in framing and effectuating relief. What it seems not to have anticipated was the long-term efficacy of resistance, as desegregation became a determinative issue in national politics, and the potential for interpretive translation of the *Brown* mandate into a relatively short-lived phenomenon.

Because such a response had been so historically typical, the *Brown* Court also might be criticized for failing to establish a constitutional safety net in the event the new doctrine failed. As it has devolved, the desegregation mandate seldom demands real desegregation and has established no lasting obligation. Its limited significance for modern circumstances warrants attention to whether other alternatives might have worked better under the conditions that largely foiled *Brown*'s potential.

One alternative to desegregation was enhanced attention to equalization, a proposition forcefully urged by states where official segregation was being challenged. To ward off the possibility of desegregation, states affected by the *Brown* decision promised a more meaningful accounting for the equality requirements of the separate but equal doctrine. The Court already had noted that such a policy was limited in its potential, because it could reckon only with tangible but not intangible inequalities. Nearly four decades later, the *Brown* mandate has succeeded in effectively addressing neither desegregation nor equality interests. Given the indisputably racist premises of official segregation, elimination of the separate but equal doctrine was unquestionably correct. As a singular remedy, however, desegregation afforded no effective relief in school systems that were resistant to change and provided no methodology to account for equalization in the event desegregation failed. To the extent it suggested that dignity and esteem were dependent upon mixing with whites, rather than a function of full opportunity and choice, the *Brown* decision also displaced one stigmatizing assumption in favor of another.

In different but nonetheless pertinent circumstances, Justice Harlan observed that animation of the Fourteenth Amendment requires close attention to the nation's history and values. Careful consideration of risks to the desegregation mandate's future, given the Fourteenth Amendment's jurisprudential record, favored at least some means of reckoning with societal traditions and tendencies that were certain not to vanish or abate merely because constitutional doctrine changed. In deciding upon remedial methodology, the Court invested in the dismantling of dual school systems "with all deliberate speed." An alternative, repudiated by the Court for two decades until allowing for a reversion to functional segregation, was that desegregation did not necessarily require integration. Such an option, advanced initially by southern courts in response to the *Brown* mandate, accepted elimination of prescriptive racial separation but would have minimized judicial restructuring of the established social order. Given the intransigence that confronted the desegregation mandate, investment in the less demanding alternative probably would not have accomplished less than what ultimately was achieved. Meaningful desegregative progress was not realized until after the Civil Rights Act of 1964 was passed and significant leverage became available for the federal government to compel compliance. Soon thereafter, the Court's relaxed Fourteenth Amendment standards limited desegregation's potential and permitted resegregation. Still unrealized is a durable constitutional means of reckoning with a persisting legacy of discrimination, stigmatization, and impaired educational opportunity.

* * *

The Brown decision presents a major challenge to critics who support its repudiation of official segregation, agree with its general aims, and recognize that it was inspired by a constitutional wrong more profound than any miscalculation in response. As the Court's mandate evolved, however, acceleration of the law beyond its moral base created a disincentive for society to directly confront and meaningfully examine a compounding legacy of racial discrimination. Achievement of formal equality and insistence on constitutional colorblindness for all purposes are the work of decisions that have elicited much public attention but not necessarily extensive public reflection. The resultant imagery of judicially defined standards implies that the business of the Fourteenth Amendment, at least with respect to accounting for discrimination against racial minorities, has been successfully completed. Such a consequence is reminiscent of the conclusion a century ago that, despite historical disadvantage and a brief remedial interlude, victims of discrimination must "cease[]" to be the special favorite of the laws." That sense is as misplaced now as it was then, insofar as the work of the Fourteenth Amendment remains unfinished. A dominant modern impression, evidenced by the waning of the desegregation mandate and resistance to affirmative action, seems to be that further efforts to account for accumulated racial disadvantage are unwarranted and excessive. Such a condition may owe to an appearance of achievement that surpasses actual progress but nonetheless defines popular understanding. The tragedy of *Brown* may be that in attempting to advance both the law and morality, it ended up retarding both.

IV. Conclusion

For its uniqueness and brevity, the desegregation interval is rich with instruction. The defusing of the *Brown* mandate, from insistence upon elimination of segregation "root and branch" to allowance of its regrowth or persistence, illustrates how radical constitutional redirection was translated eventually into limited achievements conserving much of the legacy it sought to change. *Brown* also demonstrates the risks of recontouring constitutional law in anticipation of significant cultural progress without doctrinal insurance for unexpected consequences. Critical response that excuses *Brown* from interpretive standards, vigorously pressed in other areas of constitutional doctrine, demonstrates how race continues to be a profoundly distorting factor in the law's development. Even more poignant is how the Court, in attempting to defeat racial stigma, contributed to it.

To expect more from the desegregation experience may disregard an especially pertinent lesson of *Brown* and its progeny. The central point, reinforced by two centuries of historical reality, is that the judiciary is more likely to accommodate than contest racial hierarchy in the established social order. Evidence of that tendency is gleaned not only from endorsement of slavery, allowance of "[m]ere discriminations," and support for official segregation, but also from the recent circumscription of remedial policies calculated to repudiate and remedy an acknowledged "sorry history."

In its early incarnation, the *Brown* decision heralded the possibility of constitutional litigation as a cost-efficient methodology for effecting social change. Standards that prohibit official segregation and formal discrimination have made a meaningful contribution to the pool of thoughts and ideas from which collective moral and legal principles emerge. Long-term jurisprudential performance evidences that law is an extension of moral development, however, and assumptions of a converse relationship may result in expectations that are unrealistic, in part because the process diverts attention from the necessary groundwork for real and lasting progress. The desegregation era's achievements are not insignificant. Their place in the broader stream of history, however, is notable also for relaxing anti-discrimination standards, confounding initiatives for reckoning with the nation's discriminatory legacy, and transforming constitutional obligations into a policy option.

Kimberlé Williams Crenshaw, *Race, Reform, and Retrenchment: Transformation and Legitimation in Antidiscrimination Law*, 101 HARV. L. REV. 1331 (1988)*

* * *

II. THE NEW RIGHT ATTACK: CIVIL RIGHTS AS "POLITICS"

A. *The Neoconservative Offensive*

The Reagan Administration arrived in Washington in 1981 with an agenda that was profoundly hostile to the civil rights policies of the previous two decades. The principal basis of its hostility was a formalistic, color-blind view of civil rights that had developed in the neoconservative "think tanks" during the 1970's. Neoconservative doctrine singles out race-specific civil rights policies as one of the most significant threats to the democratic political system. Emphasizing the need for strictly color-blind policies, this view calls for the repeal of affirmative action and other race-specific remedial policies, urges an end to class-based remedies, and calls for the Administration to limit remedies to what it calls "actual victims" of discrimination.

A number of early episodes sent a clear message that the Reagan Administration would be inhospitable to the civil rights policies adopted by earlier administrations. For example, the Civil Rights Division of the Justice Department, under Deputy Attorney General William Bradford Reynolds, abruptly changed sides in several cases. Other serious attacks on the civil rights constituency included Reagan's attempt to fire members of the United States Commission on Civil Rights, the Administration's opposition to the 1982 amendment of the Voting Rights Act, and Reagan's veto of the Civil Rights Restoration Act.

These fervent attempts to change the direction of civil rights law generated speculation that the Reagan Administration was anti-Black and ideologically opposed to civil rights. Yet the Administration denied that any racial animus motivated its campaign. Far from viewing themselves as opponents of civil rights, Reagan, Reynolds, and others in the Administration apparently saw themselves as "true" civil rights advocates seeking to restore the original meaning of civil rights.

Neoconservative scholar Thomas Sowell perhaps best articulates the philosophy underlying the New Right policies on race and law. Sowell presents the neoconservative struggle against prevailing civil rights policies as nothing less than an attempt to restore law to its rightful place and to prevent the descent of American society into fascism. Sowell suggests that the growing popularity of white hate groups is evidence of the instability wrought by improvident civil rights policies. To Sowell, the growth of anti-Black sentiment is an understandable reaction to a vision that has threatened to undermine democratic institutions, delegitimize the court system, and demoralize the American people.

The culprit in this epic struggle is a political view which Sowell has dubbed "the civil rights vision." According to Sowell, this view developed as the leaders of the civil rights movement shifted the movement's original focus on equal treatment under the law to a demand for equal results notwithstanding genuine differences in ability, delegitimizing the movement's claim in a democratic society. The civil rights vision has nothing to do with the achievement of civil rights today, according to Sowell, because in reality "the battle for civil rights was fought and won—at great cost—many years

---

ago." Sowell's central criticism is that the visionaries have attempted to infuse the law with their own political interpretation, which Sowell characterizes as separate from and alien to the true meaning of civil rights. He argues that, although these visionaries have struggled and sacrificed in the name of civil rights, they nonetheless merit censure for undermining the stability of American society through their politicization of the law.

Sowell singles out the judiciary for especially harsh criticism. Judges, according to Sowell, have ignored the original understanding of title VII and imposed their own political views instead. "The perversions of the law by federal judges . . . have been especially brazen," Sowell charges. According to Sowell, judges have participated in a process by which "law, plain honesty and democracy itself [have been] sacrificed on the altar of missionary self-righteousness." Sowell cautions that when judges allow law to be overridden by politics, the threat of fascism looms ever large:

> When judges reduce the law to a question of who has the power and whose ox is gored, they can hardly disclaim responsibility, or be morally superior, when others respond in kind. We can only hope that the response will not someday undermine our whole concept of law and freedom. Fascism has historically arisen from the utter disillusionment of the people with democratic institutions.

* * *

B. A Critique of the Critique:
The Indeterminacy of Civil Rights Discourse

Given the seriousness of his accusations, particularly those against the judiciary, one would expect Sowell's proof of subversion to be substantial. His repeated accusations that the true law has been subverted raise expectations that he will eventually identify some determinate, clearly discernible version of that law. Sowell's true law would presumably stand apart from the politics of race, yet control it, without being influenced by inappropriate political factors. Sowell's only "proof" that the law has been subverted, however, rests on his assumption that such subversion is self-evident. In the context of voting, for example, Sowell declares simply: "The right to vote is a civil right. The right to win is not. Equal treatment does not mean equal results."

Sowell fails to substantiate his accusations because he cannot tell us *what* the real law is, or whether it ever existed as he claims. He simply embraces language from antidiscrimination texts, imports his own meaning of its purpose, and ignores contradictory purposes and interpretations. Here Sowell, apparently without realizing it, merely embraces one aspect of a tension that runs throughout antidiscrimination law—the tension between equality as a process and equality as a result.

This basic conflict has given rise to two distinct rhetorical visions in the body of antidiscrimination law—one of which I have termed the expansive view, the other the restrictive view. The expansive view stresses equality as a result, and looks to real consequences for African-Americans. It interprets the objective of antidiscrimination law as the eradication of the substantive conditions of Black subordination and attempts to enlist the institutional power of the courts to further the national goal of eradicating the effects of racial oppression.

The restrictive vision, which exists side by side with this expansive view, treats equality as a process, downplaying the significance of actual outcomes. The primary objective of antidiscrimination law, according to this vision, is to prevent future wrongdoing rather than to redress present manifestations of past injustice. . . .

* * *

As the expansive and restrictive views of antidiscrimination law reveal, there simply is no self-evident interpretation of civil rights inherent in the terms themselves. Instead, specific interpretations proceed largely from the world view of the interpreter. For example, to believe, as Sowell does, that color-blind policies represent the only legitimate and effective means of ensuring a racially equitable society, one would have to assume not only that there is only one "proper role" for law, but also that such a racially equitable society already exists. In this world, once law had performed its "proper" function of assuring equality of process, differences in outcomes between groups would not reflect past discrimination but rather real differences between groups competing for societal rewards. Unimpeded be irrational prejudices against identifiable groups and unfettered by government-imposed preferences, competition would ensure that any group stratification would reflect only the cumulative effects of employers' rational decisions to hire the best workers for the least cost. The deprivations and oppression of the past would somehow be expunged from the present. Only in such a society, where all other societal functions operate in a nondiscriminatory way, would equality of process constitute equality of opportunity.

This belief in color-blindness and equal process, however, would make no sense at all in a society in which identifiable groups had actually been treated differently historically and in which the effects of this difference in treatment continued into the present. If employers were thought to have been influenced by factors other than the actual performance of each job applicant, it would be absurd to rely on their decisions as evidence of true market valuations. Arguments that differences in economic status cannot be redressed, or are legitimate because they reflect cultural rather than racial inferiority, would have to be rejected; cultural disadvantages themselves would be seen as the consequence of historical discrimination. One could not look at outcomes as a fair measure of merit since one would recognize that everyone had not been given an equal start. Because it would be apparent that institutions had embraced discriminatory policies in order to produce disparate results, it would be necessary to rely on results to indicate whether these discriminatory policies have been successfully dismantled.

These two visions of society correspond closely to those held by Sowell and the civil rights visionaries. In each vision, all arguments about what the law *is* are premised upon what the law *should be*, given a particular world view. The conflict is not, as Sowell has suggested, between the true meaning of the law and a bastardized version, but between two different interpretations of society. Thus, though they attempt to lay claim to an apolitical perch from which to accuse civil rights visionaries of subverting the law to politics, the neoconservatives as well rely on their own political interpretations to give meaning to their respective concepts of rights and oppression. The crucial point that Sowell overlooks is that law itself does not dictate which of various visions will be adopted as an interpretive base. The choice between various visions and the values that lie within them is not guided by any determinate organizing principle. Consequently, Sowell has no basis from which to argue that color-conscious, result-oriented remedies are political perversions of the law, but that his preference, color-blind, process-oriented remedies are not.

C. The Constituency's Dilemma

The passage of civil rights legislation nurtured the impression that the United States had moved decisively to end the oppression of Blacks. The fanfare surrounding the passage of these Acts, however, created an expectation that the legislation would not and could not fulfill. The law accommodated and obscured contradictions that led to conflict, countervision, and the current vacuousness of antidiscrimination law.

Because antidiscrimination law contains both the expansive and the restrictive view, equality of opportunity can refer to either. This uncertainty means that the societal adoption of racial equality rhetoric does not itself entail a commitment to end racial inequality. Indeed, to the extent that antidiscrimination law is believed to embrace colorblindness, equal opportunity rhetoric constitutes a formidable obstacle to efforts to alleviate conditions of white supremacy. . . .

Society's adoption of the ambivalent rhetoric of equal opportunity law has made it that much more difficult for Black people to name their reality. There is no longer a perpetrator, a clearly identifiable discriminator. Company X can be an equal opportunity employer even though Company X has no Blacks or any other minorities in its employ. Practically speaking, all companies can now be equal opportunity employers by proclamation alone. Society has embraced the rhetoric of equal opportunity without fulfilling its promise; creating a break with the past has formed the basis for the neoconservative claim that present inequities cannot be the result of discriminatory practices because this society no longer discriminates against Blacks.

Equal opportunity law may have also undermined the fragile consensus against white supremacy. To the extent that the objective of racial equality was seen as lifting formal barriers imposed against participation by Blacks, the reforms appear to have succeeded. Today, the claim that equal opportunity does not yet exist for Black America may fall upon deaf ears—ears deafened by repeated declarations that equal opportunity exists. . . .

The recognition on the part of civil rights advocates that deeper institutional changes are required has come just as the formal changes have begun to convince people that enough has been done. Indeed, recent cases illustrate that the judiciary's commitment to racial equality has waned considerably. These doctrinal and procedural developments, taken along with the overall political climate, indicate that the policy of redressing discrimination no longer has the high priority it once had. As Derrick Bell argues, "At heart, many of the cases seem to reflect an unwillingness that has been evident since *Washington v. Davis* to further expand remedies for discrimination." In discussing what he views as the waning of the commitment to achieve a non-racist society, Bell observes, "Discrimination claims, when they are dramatic enough, and do not greatly threaten majority concerns, are given a sympathetic hearing, but there is a pervasive sense that definite limits have been set on the weight that minority claims receive when balanced against majority interests."

The flagging commitment of the courts and of many whites to fighting discrimination may not be the only deleterious effect of the civil rights reforms. The lasting harm must be measured by the extent to which limited gains hamper efforts of African-Americans to name their reality and to remain capable of engaging in collective action in the future. The danger of adopting equal opportunity rhetoric on its face is that the constituency incorporates legal and philosophical concepts that have an uneven history and an unpredictable trajectory. If the civil rights constituency allows its own political consciousness to be completely replaced by the ambiguous discourse of antidiscrimination law, it will be difficult for it to defend its genuine interests against those whose interests are supported by opposing visions that also lie within the same discourse. The struggle, it seems, is to maintain a contextualized, specified world view that reflects the experience of Blacks. The question remains whether engaging in legal reform precludes this possibility.

III. THE NEW LEFT ATTACK: THE HEGEMONIC FUNCTION OF LEGAL RIGHTS DISCOURSE

Various scholars connected with the Critical Legal Studies movement have offered critical analyses of law and legal reform which provide a broad framework for explaining how legal reforms help mask and legitimate continuing racial inequality. The Critics present law as a series of ideological constructs that operate to support existing social arrangements by convincing people that things are both inevitable and basically fair. Legal reform, therefore, cannot serve as a means for fundamentally restructuring society. This theory, however, is a general one, the utility of which is limited in the context of civil rights by its insufficient attention to racial domination. Removed from the reality of oppression and its overwhelming constraints, the Critics cannot fairly understand the choices the civil rights movement confronted or, still less, recommend solutions to its current problems.

* * *

A. *The Critical Vision*

* * *

1. *The Role of Legal Ideology.*

Some Critics see the destructive role of rights rhetoric as [a] symptom of the law's legitimating function. Mark Tushnet has offered a four-tiered critique of rights:

> (1) Once one identifies what counts as a right in a specific setting, it invariably turns out that the right is unstable; significant but relatively small changes in the social setting can make it difficult to sustain the claim that a right remains implicated. (2) The claim that a right is implicated in some settings produces no determinate consequences. (3) The concept of rights falsely converts into an empty abstraction (reifies) real experiences that we ought to value for their own sake. (4) The use of rights in contemporary discourse impedes advances by progressive social forces . . . .

Tushnet's first and second arguments crystallize the doctrinal dilemmas faced by the civil rights community. Antidiscrimination doctrine does not itself provide determinate results. To give rights meaning, people must specify the world; they must create a picture of "what is" that grounds their normative interpretation.

Tushnet's third and fourth arguments spell out pragmatic reasons to approach rights with caution. According to Tushnet, the language of rights undermines efforts to change things by absorbing real demands, experiences, and concerns into a vacuous and indeterminate discourse. The discourse abstracts real experiences and clouds the ability of those who invoke rights rhetoric to think concretely about real confrontations and real circumstances.

According to Tushnet, the danger that arises from being swept into legal rights discourse is that people lose sight of their real objectives. Their visions and thoughts of the possible become trapped within the ideological limitations of the law. Tushnet suggests that, "[i]f we treated experiences of solidarity and individuality as directly relevant to our political discussions, instead of passing them through the filter of the language of rights, we would be in a better position to address the political issues on the appropriate level."

* * *

2. *Transformation in the Critical Vision.*

The vision of change that Critical scholars express flows directly from their focus on ideology as the major obstacle that separates the actual from the possible. Because it is ideology that prevents people from conceiving of—and hence from implementing—a freer social condition, the Critics propose the exposure of ideology as the logical first step toward social transformation.

* * *

Although the focus of their critiques may differ, the Critics all premise their views of transformative possibility on the necessity of critically engaging dominant ideology. Viewing the structures of legal thought as central to the perception of the world as necessary and the status quo as legitimate, they believe it is crucial to demonstrate the contingency of legal ideology. Once false necessity or contingency is revealed, the Critics suggest, people will be able to remake their world in a different way.

B. A Critique of the Critique: The Problem of Context

The Critics offer an analysis that is useful in understanding the limited transformative potential of antidiscrimination rhetoric. There are difficulties, however, in attempting to use Critical themes and ideas to understand the civil rights movement and to describe what alternatives the civil rights constituency could have pursued, or might now pursue. While Critical scholars claim that their project is concerned with domination, few have made more than a token effort to address racial domination specifically, and their work does not seem grounded in the reality of the racially oppressed.

This deficiency is especially apparent in critiques that relate to racial issues. Critical scholars have criticized mainstream legal ideology for its tendency to portray American society as basically fair, and thereby to legitimate the oppressive policies that have been directed toward racial minorities. Yet Critical scholars do not sufficiently account for the effects or the causes of the oppression that they routinely acknowledge. The result is that Critical literature exhibits the same proclivities of mainstream scholarship—it seldom speaks to or about Black people.

The failure of the Critics to incorporate racism into their analysis also renders their critique of rights and their overall analysis of law in America incomplete. Specifically, this failure leads to an inability to appreciate fully the transformative significance of the civil rights movement in mobilizing Black Americans and generating new demands. Further, the failure to consider the reality of those most oppressed by American institutions means that the Critical account of the hegemonic nature of legal thought overlooks a crucial dimension of American life—the ideological role of racism itself. . . .

The Critics' failure to analyze the hegemonic role of racism also renders their prescriptive analysis unrealistic. Critics often appear to view the trashing of legal ideology "as the only path that might lead to a liberated future." Yet if trashing is the only path that might lead to a liberated future, Black people are unlikely to make it to the Critics' promised land.

The Critics' commitment to trashing is premised on a notion that people are mystified by liberal legal ideology and consequently cannot remake their world until they see how contingent such ideology is. The Critics' principal error is that their version of domination by consent does not present a realistic picture of racial domination. Coercion explains much more about racial domination than does ideologically induced consent. Black people do not create their oppressive worlds moment to moment but rather are coerced into living in worlds created and maintained by others. Moreover, the ideological source of this coercion is not liberal legal consciousness, but racism. If racism is just as important as, if not more important than, liberal legal ideology in explaining the persistence of white supremacy, then the Critics' single-minded effort to deconstruct liberal legal ideology will be futile.

Finally, in addition to exaggerating the role of liberal legal consciousness and underestimating that of coercion, Critics also disregard the transformative potential that liberalism offers. Although liberal legal ideology may indeed function to mystify, it remains receptive to some aspirations that are central to Black demands, and may also perform an important function in combating the experience of being excluded and oppressed. This receptivity to Black aspirations is crucial given the hostile social world that racism creates. The most troubling aspect of the Critical program, therefore, is that "trashing" rights consciousness may have the unintended consequences of disempowering the racially oppressed while leaving white supremacy basically untouched.

C. Questioning the Transformative View: Some Doubts About Trashing

The Critics' product is of limited utility to Blacks in its present form. The implications for Blacks of trashing liberal legal ideology are troubling, even though it may be proper to assail belief structures that obscure liberating possibilities. Trashing legal ideology seems to tell us repeatedly what has already been established—that legal discourse is unstable and relatively indeterminate. Furthermore, trashing offers no idea of how to avoid the negative consequences of engaging in reformist discourse or how to work around such consequences. Even if we imagine the wrong world when we think in terms of legal discourse, we must nevertheless exist in a present world where legal protection has at times been a blessing—albeit a mixed one. The fundamental problem is that, although Critics criticize law because it functions to legitimate existing institutional arrangements, it is precisely this legitimating function that has made law receptive to certain demands in this area.

The Critical emphasis on deconstruction as the vehicle for liberation leads to the conclusion that engaging in legal discourse should be avoided because it reinforces not only the discourse itself but also the society and the world that it embodies. Yet Critics offer little beyond this observation. Their focus on delegitimating rights rhetoric seems to suggest that, once rights rhetoric has been discarded, there exists a more productive strategy for change, one which does not reinforce existing patterns of domination.

Unfortunately, no such strategy has yet been articulated, and it is difficult to imagine that racial minorities will ever be able to discover one. . . .

IV. THE CONTEXT DEFINED: RACIST IDEOLOGY AND HEGEMONY

* * *

B. The Role of Race Consciousness in a System of Formal Equality

* * *

Prior to the civil rights reforms, Blacks were formally subordinated by the state. Blacks experienced being the "other" in two aspects of oppression, which I shall designate as symbolic and material. Symbolic subordination refers to the formal denial of social and political equality to all Blacks, regardless of their accomplishments. Segregation and other forms of social exclusion—separate restrooms, drinking fountains, entrances, parks, cemeteries, and dining facilities—reinforced a racist ideology that Blacks were simply inferior to whites and were therefore not included in the vision of America as a community of equals.

Material subordination, on the other hand, refers to the ways that discrimination and exclusion economically subordinated Blacks to whites and subordinated the life chances of Blacks to those of whites on almost every level. This subordination occurs when Blacks are paid less for the same work, when segregation limits access to decent housing, and where poverty, anxiety, poor health care, and crime create a life expectancy for Blacks that is five to six years shorter than for whites.

Symbolic subordination often created material disadvantage by reinforcing race consciousness in everything from employment to education. In fact, the two are generally not thought of separately: separate facilities were usually inferior facilities, and limited job categorization virtually always brought lower pay and harder work. Despite the pervasiveness of racism, however, there existed even before the civil rights movement a class of Blacks who were educationally, economically, and professionally equal—if not superior—to many whites, and yet these Blacks suffered social and political exclusion as well.

It is also significant that not all separation resulted in inferior institutions. School segregation—although often presented as the epitome of symbolic and material subordination did not always result in inferior education. It is not separation *per se* that made segregation subordinating, but the fact that it was enforced and supported by state power, and accompanied by the explicit belief in African-American inferiority.

The response to the civil rights movement was the removal of most formal barriers and symbolic manifestations of subordination. Thus, "White Only" notices and other obvious indicators of the societal policy of racial subordination disappeared—at least in the public sphere. The disappearance of these symbols of subordination reflected the acceptance of the rhetoric of formal equality and signaled the demise of the rhetoric of white supremacy as expressing America's normative vision. In other words, it could no longer be said that Blacks were not included as equals in the American political vision.

Removal of these public manifestations of subordination was a significant gain for all Blacks, although some benefited more than others. The eradication of formal barriers meant more to those whose oppression was primarily symbolic than to those who suffered lasting material disadvantage. Yet despite these disparate results, it would be absurd to suggest that no benefits came from these formal reforms, especially in regard to racial policies, such as segregation, that were partly material but largely symbolic. Thus, to say that the reforms were "merely symbolic" is to say a great deal. These legal reforms and the formal extension of "citizenship" were large achievements precisely because much of what characterized Black oppression was symbolic and formal.

Yet the attainment of formal equality is not the end of the story. Racial hierarchy cannot be cured by the move to facial race-neutrality in the laws that structure the economic, political, and social lives of Black people. White race consciousness, in a new form but still virulent, plays an important, perhaps crucial, role in the new regime that has legitimated the deteriorating day-to-day material conditions of the majority of Blacks.

The end of Jim Crow has been accompanied by the demise of an explicit ideology of white supremacy. The white norm, however, has not disappeared; it has only been submerged in popular consciousness. It continues in an unspoken form as a statement of the positive social norm, legitimating the continuing domination of those who do not meet it. Nor have the negative stereotypes associated with Blacks been eradicated. The rationalizations once used to legitimate Black subordination based on a belief in racial inferiority have now been reemployed to legitimate the domination of Blacks through reference to an assumed cultural inferiority.

Thomas Sowell, for example, suggests that underclass Blacks are economically depressed because they have not adopted the values of hard work and discipline. He further implies that Blacks have not pursued the need to attain skills and marketable education, and have not learned to make the sacrifices necessary for success. Instead, Sowell charges that Blacks view demands for special treatment as a means for achieving what other groups have achieved through hard work and the abandonment of racial politics.

Sowell applies the same stereotypes to the mass of Blacks that white supremacists had applied in the past, but bases these modern stereotypes on notions of "culture" rather than genetics. Sowell characterizes underclass Blacks as victims of self-imposed ignorance, lack of direction, and poor work attitudes. Culture, not race, now accounts for this "otherness." Except for vestigial pockets of historical racism, any possible connection between past racial subordination and the present situation has been severed by the formal repudiation of the old race-conscious policies. The same dualities historically used to legitimate racial subordination in the name of genetic inferiority have now been adopted by Sowell as a means for explaining the subordinated status of Blacks today in terms of cultural inferiority.

Moreover, Sowell's explanation of the subordinate status of Blacks also illustrates the treatment of the now-unspoken white stereotypes as the positive social norm. His assertion that the *absence* of certain attributes accounts for the continued subordination of Blacks implies that it is the *presence* of these attributes that explains the continued advantage of whites. The only difference between this argument and the older oppositional dynamic is that, whereas the latter explained Black subordination through reference to the ideology of white supremacy, the former explains Black subordination through reference to an unspoken social norm. That norm—although no longer explicitly white supremacist—remains, nonetheless, a white norm. As Martha Minow has pointed out, "[t]he unstated point of comparison is not neutral, but particular, and not inevitable, but only seemingly so when left unstated."

White race consciousness, which includes the modern belief in cultural inferiority, acts to further Black subordination by justifying all the forms of unofficial racial discrimination, injury, and neglect that flourish in a society that is only formally dedicated to equality. In more subtle ways, moreover, white race consciousness reinforces and is reinforced by the myth of equal opportunity that explains and justifies broader class hierarchies.

Race consciousness also reinforces whites' sense that American society is really meritocratic and thus helps prevent them from questioning the basic legitimacy of the free market. Believing both that Blacks are inferior and that the economy impartially rewards the superior over the inferior, whites see that most Blacks are indeed worse off than whites are, which reinforces their sense that the market is operating "fairly and impartially"; those who should logically be on the bottom are on the bottom. This strengthening of whites' belief in the system in turn reinforces their beliefs that Blacks are *indeed* inferior. After all, equal opportunity is the rule, and the market is an impartial judge; if Blacks are on the bottom, it must reflect their relative inferiority. Racist ideology thus operates in conjunction with the class components of legal ideology to reinforce the status quo, both in terms of class and race.

To bring a fundamental challenge to the way things are, whites would have to question not just their own subordinate status, but also both the economic and the racial myths that justify the status quo. Racism, combined with equal opportunity mythology, provides a rationalization for racial oppression, making it difficult for whites to see the Black situation as illegitimate or unnecessary. If whites believe that Blacks, because they are unambitious or inferior, get what they deserve, it becomes that much harder to convince whites that something is wrong with the entire system. Similarly, a challenge to the legitimacy of continued racial inequality would force whites to confront myths about equality of opportunity that justify for them whatever measure of economic success they may have attained.

Thus, although Critics have suggested that legal consciousness plays a central role in legitimating hierarchy in America, the otherness dynamic enthroned within the maintenance and perpetuation of white race consciousness seems to be at least as important as legal consciousness in supporting the dominant order. Like legal consciousness, race consciousness makes it difficult—at least for whites—to imagine the world differently. It also creates the desire for identification with privileged elites. By focusing on a distinct, subordinate "other," whites include themselves in the dominant circle—an arena in which most hold no real power, but only their privileged racial identity. . . .

C. Rights Discourse as a Challenge to the Oppositional Dynamic

The oppositional dynamic, premised upon maintaining Blacks as an excluded and subordinated "other," initially created an ideological and political structure of formal inequality against which rights rhetoric proved to be the most effective weapon. Although rights rhetoric may ultimately have absorbed the civil rights challenge and legitimated continued subordination, the otherness dynamic provides a fuller understanding of how the very transformation afforded by legal reform itself has contributed to the ideological and political legitimation of continuing Black subordination.

Rights discourse provided the ideological mechanisms through which the conflicts of federalism, the power of the Presidency, and the legitimacy of the courts could be orchestrated against Jim Crow. Movement leaders used these tactics to force open a conflict between whites that eventually benefited Black people. Casting racial issues in the moral and legal rights rhetoric of the prevailing ideology helped create the political controversy without which the state's coercive function would not have been enlisted to aid Blacks.

Simply critiquing the ideology from without or making demands in language outside the rights discourse would have accomplished little. Rather, Blacks gained by using a powerful combination of direct action, mass protest, and individual acts of resistance, along with appeals to public opinion and the court couched in the language of the prevailing legal consciousness. The result was a series of ideological and political crises. In these crises, civil rights activists and lawyers induced the federal government to aid Blacks and triggered efforts to legitimate and reinforce the authority of the law in ways that benefited Blacks. Simply insisting that Blacks be integrated or speaking in the language of "needs" would have endangered the lives of those who were already taking risks—and with no reasonable chance of success. President Eisenhower, for example, would not have sent federal troops to Little Rock simply at the behest of protesters demanding that Black schoolchildren receive an equal education. Instead, the successful manipulation of legal rhetoric led to a crisis of federal power that ultimately benefited Blacks.

Some critics of legal reform movements seem to overlook the fact that state power has made a significant difference—sometimes between life and death—in the efforts of Black people to transform their world. Attempts to harness the power of the state through the appropriate rhetorical/legal incantations should be appreciated as intensely powerful and calculated political acts. In the context of white supremacy, engaging in rights discourse should be seen as an act of self-defense. This was particularly true because the state could not assume a position of neutrality regarding Black people once the movement had mobilized people to challenge the system of oppression: either the coercive mechanism of the state had to be used to support white supremacy, or it had to be used to dismantle it. We know now, with hindsight, that it did both.

Blacks did use rights rhetoric to mobilize state power to their benefit against symbolic oppression through formal inequality and, to some extent, against material deprivation in the from of private, informal exclusion of the middle class from jobs and housing. Yet today the same legal reforms play a role in providing an ideological framework that makes the present conditions facing underclass Blacks appear fair and reasonable. The eradication of barriers has created a new dilemma for those victims of racial oppression who are not in a position to benefit from the move to formal equality. The race neutrality of the legal system creates the illusion that racism is no longer the primary factor responsible for the condition of the Black underclass; instead, as we have seen, class disparities appear to be the consequence of individual and group merit within a supposed system of equal opportunity. Moreover, the fact that there are Blacks who are economically successful gives credence both to the assertion that opportunities exist, and to the backlash attitude that Blacks have "gotten too far." Psychologically, for Blacks who have not made it, the lack of an explanation for their underclass status may result in self-blame and other self-destructive attitudes.

Another consequence of the formal reforms may be the loss of collectivity among Blacks. The removal of formal barriers created new opportunities for some Blacks that were not shared by various other classes of African-Americans. As Blacks moved into different spheres, the experience of being Black in America became fragmented and multifaceted, and the different contexts presented opportunities to experience racism in different ways. The social, economic, and even residential distance between the various classes may complicate efforts to unite behind issues as a racial group. Although "White Only" signs may have been crude and debilitating, they at least presented a readily discernible target around which to organize. Now, the targets are obscure and diffuse, and this difference may create doubt among some Blacks whether there is enough similarity between their life experiences and those of other Blacks to warrant collective political action.

Formal equality significantly transformed the Black experience in America. With society's embrace of formal equality came the eradication of symbolic domination and the suppression of white supremacy as the norm of society. Future generations of Black Americans would no longer be explicitly regarded as America's second-class citizens. Yet the transformation of the oppositional dynamic—achieved through the suppression of racial norms and stereotypes, and the recasting of racial inferiority into assumptions of cultural inferiority—creates several difficulties for the civil rights constituency. The removal of formal barriers, although symbolically significant to all and materially significant to some, will do little to alter the hierarchical relationship between Blacks and whites until the way in which white race consciousness perpetuates norms that legitimate Black subordination is revealed. This is not to say that white norms alone account for the conditions of the Black underclass. It is instead an acknowledgment that, until the distinct racial nature of class ideology is itself revealed and debunked, nothing can be done about the underlying structural problems that account for the disparities. The narrow focus of racial exclusion—that is, the belief that racial exclusion is illegitimate only where the "White Only" signs are explicit—coupled with strong assumptions about equal opportunity, makes it difficult to move the discussion of racism beyond the societal self-satisfaction engendered by the appearance of neutral norms and formal inclusion.

D. Self-Conscious Ideological Struggle

Rights have been important. They may have legitimated racial inequality, but they have also been the means by which oppressed groups have secured both entry as formal equals into the dominant order and the survival of their movement in the face of private and state repression. The dual role of legal change creates a dilemma for Black reformers. As long as race consciousness thrives, Blacks will often have to rely on rights rhetoric when it is necessary to protect Black interests. The very reforms brought about by appeals to legal ideology, however, seem to undermine the ability to move forward toward a broader vision of racial equality. In the quest for racial justice, winning and losing have been part of the same experience.

* * *

Optimally, the deconstruction of white race consciousness might lead to a liberated future for both Blacks and whites. Yet, until whites recognize the hegemonic function of racism and turn their efforts toward neutralizing it, African-American people must develop pragmatic political strategies—self-conscious ideological struggle—to minimize the costs of liberal reform while maximizing its utility. A primary step in engaging in self-conscious ideological struggle must be to transcend the oppositional dynamic in which Blacks are cast simply and solely as whites' subordinate "other."

Motive-Based Inquiry

Meaningful equal protection review beginning in the 1970s was conditioned upon proof of discriminatory purpose. Motive-based standards were invested in for equal protection purposes, despite its rejection in other constitutional contexts where the Court expressed misgivings with such criteria.[21] The evidentiary requirement of intent has been a significant factor in blunting the utility of the equal protection guarantee in contexts where a classification is not overt. David A. Straus discusses how the discriminatory purpose requirement has effectively dulled the significance of *Brown*. Paul Brest makes a case for motive-based inquiry. Daniel R. Ortiz suggests that a search for intent is largely futile. Charles R. Lawrence, III argues that motive-referenced criteria are irrelevant to modern racial reality and should be adjusted to account for problems of subtle discrimination and unconscious racism. Barbara J. Flagg suggests that discriminatory purpose standards represent a false norm of neutrality that actually is a function of white values and perceptions.

David A. Strauss, *Discriminatory Intent and the Taming of* Brown, 56 U. CHI. L. REV. 935 (1989)*

I. INTRODUCTION

From the beginning, nearly everyone has agreed that the central purpose of the Equal Protection Clause is to outlaw certain kinds of discrimination. But what is "discrimination"? Only recently has the Supreme Court given a clear answer to that question: discrimination in violation of the Equal Protection Clause consists of acting with discriminatory intent. In this paper I will argue that although this conception of discrimination is sometimes useful, it is inadequate in a fundamental way; that its inadequacy explains the problematic character of several of the most controversial decisions of recent times; and that this inadequacy is the result of what I will call the taming of *Brown v Board of Education*—an excessively cautious and conservative approach to the implications of the Supreme Court's greatest anti-discrimination decision.

The discriminatory intent standard has both defenders and critics. But often neither side recognizes either the genuine strengths or the deep weaknesses of the discriminatory intent approach. Both its strengths and weaknesses lie in the fact that the discriminatory intent test reflects a requirement of impartiality: according to the discriminatory intent standard, invidious discrimination consists of a failure to be impartial. That is a strength because impartiality is not an empty notion; on the contrary, it is useful and important in many contexts.

Ultimately, however, impartiality—and discriminatory intent—fail as a comprehensive account of discrimination.

* * *

---

21   E.g., United States v. O'Brien, 391 U.S. 367, 383-84 (1969).

*   Reprinted with permission.

If the discriminatory intent standard were the only conception of discrimination with significant support in precedent, it would be difficult to criticize the Court for adopting it. But in fact when the Supreme Court adopted the discriminatory intent standard—in *Washington v Davis*, which was decided twenty-two years after *Brown*—several alternative conceptions of discrimination were possible. These alternatives—rooted in notions like stigma, subordination, and second-class citizenship—had substantial support in the first decisions interpreting the Equal Protection Clause, in *Brown* itself, and in the decisions that followed *Brown*. The Court's evident objection to these alternatives was twofold: they seemed far more vague than the discriminatory intent standard, and they seemed far more threatening to established institutions. To adopt any test other than the discriminatory intent test, the Court reasoned in *Washington v Davis*, would "raise serious questions about, and perhaps invalidate, a whole range of tax, welfare, public service, regulatory, and licensing statutes."

It is in this sense that *Washington v Davis* constituted a "taming" of *Brown* and a conservative approach to that decision: of the several possible conceptions of discrimination, the Court chose the one that appeared to be the most determinate and the least far reaching. But these supposed virtues of the discriminatory intent standard are illusory. The discriminatory intent standard is in fact at least as vague and indeterminate as the alternatives; and rigorously applied, it is no less threatening to established institutions.

II. THE TAMING OF *BROWN*

Until *Washington v Davis* was decided, there were several possible answers to the question: what constitutes impermissible discrimination under the Equal Protection Clause? *Washington v Davis*, in settling on the discriminatory intent standard, chose the most tame of those possible answers.

* * *

A. Five Conceptions of Discrimination

At the time *Washington v Davis* was decided, there were available to the Court roughly five possible approaches to the question: what constitutes impermissible discrimination in violation of the Equal Protection Clause?

* * *

1. Lack of impartiality.

According to this approach, discrimination is an impermissible failure to be impartial between the races. However the government treats whites, it must treat blacks the same way. No more should the government have different rules for people based on their race than a judge should have different rules for litigants based on their personal relationship to her. As the Court said in *Strauder v West Virginia*—the 1880 decision invalidating a law that explicitly excluded blacks from juries—"the law in the States shall be the same for the black as for the white." . . . This approach and the discriminatory intent standard are essentially equivalent.

2. Subordination.

This is a popular modern notion, and it has support in several opinions. In 1880, *Strauder* condemned "discriminations which are steps toward reducing [blacks] to the condition of a subject race"; in 1967, *Loving v Virginia* invalidated anti-miscegenation laws partly on the ground that they are "justifi[ed only] as measures designed to maintain White Supremacy."

There seem to be two ways of understanding subjugation or subordination. One focuses on the accumulation of disadvantages. A racial group that is worse off than all others in nearly every significant measure of human welfare might be said to be a "subject race." The second emphasizes the state of being personally subject to the will of another. Slavery was the clearest case of subordination. Under this view, the distinctive characteristic of a subordinated group is that its members are systematically subject to violence at the hands of members of another group, or must systematically yield to the commands of members of another group. This conception of subordination has obvious applications in the areas of both race and sex discrimination.

3. Stigma.

This approach focuses less on the concrete effects that a government action has on a group's position and more on the message that the action conveys to others. Stigma in this sense is related to defamation. It is also related to the notions of stigma used elsewhere in the law—for example, in defining the difference between criminal and civil penalties and in determining when a person has been deprived of liberty within the meaning of the Due Process Clause.

One of the most famous sentences in *Brown* emphasized that racial segregation of black children "generates a feeling of inferiority as to their status in the community that may affect their hearts and minds in a way unlikely ever to be undone." This suggests that the evil of racial segregation is the stigma it inflicts. (The emphasis on "status in the community" might also reflect a subordination approach.) Similarly, the *Strauder* Court suggested that the vice of excluding blacks from juries was that it was "practically a brand upon them . . . an assertion of their inferiority."

Because stigma has analogies in relatively well-developed areas of the law, it may seem somewhat less vague than subordination. But the class of stigmatizing measures may be larger than appears at first. In particular, this approach (like the subordination approach) might lead to the conclusion that certain measures conventionally viewed as affirmative action—constitutionally suspect, but possibly permissible—are actually constitutionally required. For example, an explicitly race-neutral policy that had the effect of excluding all blacks from admission to a state university might brand blacks as inferior by conveying the message that, as a group, they are not as capable as whites. If so, a race-conscious deviation from this policy would, under the "stigma" conception of discrimination, be required by the Equal Protection Clause.

4. Second-class citizenship.

This approach, too, has roots in *Strauder*, which interpreted the Equal Protection Clause as granting blacks an "exemption from legal discriminations, implying inferiority in civil society." This language seems to describe what we today would call second-class citizenship. The government may not create superior and inferior classes of people "in civil society." Whatever the attributes of membership in civil society are, the government may not grant them to whites while denying them to blacks.

If "civil society" were broadly understood to include all aspects of social life, the principle that the government may not relegate blacks to second-class citizenship would be essentially equivalent to the principle that blacks may not be subordinated. Alternatively, one might concede that "civil society" is narrowly defined to include only those activities closely connected to politics and political participation—there is some evidence that the framers of the Fourteenth Amendment held this view—but argue that the question is not whether a law explicitly disables blacks from engaging in those activities, but whether it has the effect of making blacks substantially less able to engage in them. Under this view, even if education is viewed as an aspect of "social life" rather than "civil society," the government might still violate the Equal Protection Clause if it allows blacks, as a group, to receive a level of education that is insufficient to enable them to participate in politics and government, or that enables them to participate only in a way grossly inferior to whites.

However far removed this approach might be from what the Court had in mind in *Strauder*, it gives realistic content to the notion of second-class citizenship, instead of emphasizing formalities. Moreover, this approach resonates both with the distinction between political and social rights that was an important aspect of post-Civil War thought, and with the emphasis on rights to political participation that is a central element of current justifications of judicial review. This approach would support those post-*Brown* decisions that have aggressively protected minority participation in the political process.

5. Encouragement of prejudice.

In *Strauder*, the Court also suggested that the West Virginia statute violated the Equal Protection Clause because it was "a stimulant to that race prejudice which is an impediment to securing . . . equal justice." Several modern cases, including cases decided after *Washington v Davis*, have suggested that the Equal Protection Clause forbids states from encouraging private prejudice.

This approach overlaps with the stigma and subordination approaches somewhat: measures that brand a group as inferior or place it in an inferior position certainly encourage prejudice. The most direct implication of this standard would be to preclude certain forms of government aid to private prejudice, including unusually elaborate guarantees of the right of private persons to engage in racially prejudiced private behavior.

* * *

The last four approaches I described differ from the first—impartiality—in several important respects. First, the impartiality approach focuses on the government; it requires that the government treat blacks and whites alike. Each of the other approaches focuses on the alleged victims of discrimination; they ask what effect the government's action has on blacks. It is conventional to distinguish between "intent tests" and "effects tests"—tests that consider the intent of the government actor and tests that consider the effects of the action on the alleged victims of discrimination. Impartiality is an intent standard. The other four approaches all consider effects. They differ from each other in that they are concerned with different kinds of effects.

The second apparent difference between the impartiality approach and the four effects-based conceptions is that the impartiality approach seems much more clearly defined. Each of the others seems vague and open-ended. One of my principal arguments in this paper is that this apparent contrast is an illusion. The impartiality approach, seriously and rigorously applied, mandates an inquiry no less open-ended than that required by other approaches.

The third difference is that the effects-based conceptions of discrimination seem potentially much more far-reaching than the impartiality approach. The impartiality approach appears to affect only a discrete category of government actions that are based on race. The effects-based conceptions can be interpreted to call into question many established practices and institutions, such as race-neutral measures that exclude blacks from positions of power and prestige and failures to provide disadvantaged groups with an education that permits adequate participation in the political process. . . . The impartiality approach is in fact not only as open-ended as the others but potentially as threatening to established institutions.

B. The Uncertain Meaning of *Brown*

The central development in modern equal protection law was the decision that Jim Crow—the system of state-enforced, explicit racial segregation—was unconstitutional. The pivotal event in that development was the decision in *Brown v Board of Education*. . . .

In *Brown*, the Court held that de jure segregation in public education violates the Equal Protection Clause. The Court soon extended the holding of *Brown* to all forms of state-enforced explicit segregation, effectively overruling *Plessy*. *Brown* has come to stand for the principle that the Equal Protection Clause almost never permits explicit racial classifications.

While the principle of *Brown* seems clear to this extent, it was not clear, until *Washington v Davis*, which conception of discrimination *Brown* embraced, or how far the principle of *Brown* extended. Did it reach only explicit segregation? Did it extend to all actions that in some sense helped perpetuate the vices of the Jim Crow system, by stigmatizing blacks or keeping them in a subordinate position, even if those actions made no explicit reference to race? Did it require states to ensure substantive equality for black and white citizens, at least in areas like education, even if state-sponsored discrimination had not caused inequality?

It quickly became clear that the principle of *Brown* had to extend beyond fully explicit racial classifications to measures that, although neutral on their face, were obviously based on surrogates for race. The perfect example was *Gomillion v Lightfoot*, where a state used a grotesque racial gerrymander to exclude all black citizens from a city. The statute did not explicitly mention race, but if the Court had not invalidated the gerrymander, states would been free effectively to nullify *Brown*. They could simply have replaced explicitly racial school assignments with racially motivated gerrymanders. If explicit racial classifications are unlawful, it makes little sense to allow a government that is subtle enough to use an ostensibly neutral surrogate for race to get away with maintaining the Jim Crow regime. In this sense, the principle of *Brown* had to extend beyond explicit racial classifications. *Brown* had to stand at least for the principle that government decisions, whatever their explicit language, must not in fact be based on race.

That was the minimum necessary content of the *Brown* principle. Anything less would have opened the door to massive evasion. A few cases decided between *Brown* and *Washington v Davis* suggested that the principle of *Brown* extended no further than this. But in the twenty years between *Brown* and *Washington v Davis*, the opinions of the Court, of individual Justices, and of the lower courts suggested other, more far-reaching interpretations of *Brown*.

1. As I have noted, the opinion in *Brown* itself emphasized the effects of racial segregation on the "hearts and minds" of black children and on "their status in the community"—language suggesting one of the more far-reaching conceptions of discrimination, such as stigma or subordination. Several post-*Brown* opinions contained comparable language, and in other decisions, the Court suggested that the government had an obligation to combat, or at least not to encourage, private discrimination.

2. Several post-*Brown* school desegregation decisions suggest (without unequivocally embracing) the far-reaching principle that governments are required to bring about actual integration. The Court repeatedly ruled that school districts that had

been segregated by law did not bring themselves into compliance with the Constitution merely by enacting race-neutral measures (for example, a so-called freedom of choice plan). The question, the Court implied, was whether those measures actually brought about racially integrated schools. In a concurring opinion, Justice Powell carried this approach even further by urging that the government had an obligation to ensure actual integration in whether or not segregation had ever been enforced by law.

The Court's approach in the desegregation cases can probably be best understood as reflecting an expanded notion of second-class citizenship: education is such an important benefit that it must not be distributed in a way that places blacks in a separate and inferior position, even if the criterion used in assigning students to schools is race-neutral and is in no sense a covert use of a racial classification. Alternatively, these opinions might reflect an anti-subordination principle: any measure, no matter why it was adopted, violates the Equal Protection Clause if it places blacks in a racially segregated and inferior position.

3. In *Griggs v Duke Power Co.*, the Supreme Court interpreted Title VII of the Civil Rights Act of 1964, which prohibits employment discrimination in general terms, to prohibit any hiring practice that disqualifies a disproportionate number of blacks unless it is justified by a "business necessity." The Court made it clear that this rule applied even to practices "neutral on their face, and even neutral in terms of intent." While *Griggs* was an interpretation of a statute, not the Equal Protection Clause, nothing obvious in the language or legislative history of Title VII suggested that its general ban on discrimination should be interpreted differently from the Equal Protection Clause.

Accordingly, several decisions by the courts of appeals that extended the *Griggs* approach to the Equal Protection Clause decisions suggested that the government may not adopt a measure that has a harsh impact on racial minorities unless it can provide a strong justification. The *Griggs* approach is probably best understood as an effort to develop a judicially administrable standard that loosely expresses the subordination, stigma, and second-class citizenship conceptions: because a measure that disproportionately burdens blacks has the power to stigmatize or subordinate them in an unacceptable way, such measures are acceptable only if the alternatives impose great costs on the employer or the government.

C. *Washington v Davis* and the Taming of *Brown*

In *Washington v Davis*, the Supreme Court set out to eliminate this uncertainty about the reach of *Brown*. The plaintiffs in *Washington v Davis* challenged a race-neutral testing program for the District of Columbia police force that failed many more blacks than whites. The Court rejected this challenge and ruled that "the basic equal protection principle" is "that the invidious quality of a law claimed to be racially discriminatory must ultimately be traced to a racially discriminatory purpose." Subsequent decisions reaffirmed this holding, and also established that "discriminatory purpose," "discriminatory intent," and "discriminatory motive" are interchangeable terms.

Washington v Davis was significant for two reasons. First, it established that courts could inquire into legislative intent or motive. A great deal of attention had been devoted to this issue. In *Gomillion* itself the Court had strained to avoid using the language of motive or intent. Although *Gomillion* and several other cases seemed explicable only as cases concerning legislative motive or intent, the Court continued, from time to time, to disclaim any authority to make such an inquiry. Just four years before *Washington v Davis*, in *Palmer v Thompson*, the Court had refused to entertain a claim that a city violated the Equal Protection Clause by closing its municipal swimming pools in order to avoid desegregation. In *Washington v Davis*, the Court explicitly retreated from its position in *Palmer* that intent was irrelevant.

The more important aspect of *Washington v Davis*, however, was the Court's ruling that the discriminatory intent standard is a *comprehensive* account of what constitutes impermissible discrimination under the Equal Protection Clause. Not only was a showing of discriminatory intent sufficient to establish a violation, it was also (in the absence of an explicit classification) necessary. Explicit classifications aside, *Washington v Davis* held that only actions taken with discriminatory intent violate the Equal Protection Clause. As the Court said in a subsequent case, "[p]roof of racially discriminatory intent or purpose is required to show a violation of the Equal Protection Clause."

The claim that the discriminatory intent standard is a comprehensive account of discrimination is, in my view, what makes *Washington v Davis* problematic. There is a category of cases in which the discriminatory intent standard works reasonably well. But in general, as I will argue below, the discriminatory intent standard leads to speculative or meaningless questions. Consequently, if the Court had held that a party can establish a violation of the Equal Protection Clause either by proving discriminatory intent or by showing, perhaps, stigma or subordination, the holding would not be subject to the criticisms I will make in this paper.

The opinion in *Washington v Davis* itself did not make it entirely clear that the discriminatory intent standard was to be a comprehensive approach; the opinion can be read as leaving open the possibility that other conceptions of discrimination might play a role, and as rejecting only the position that a measure is presumptively unconstitutional whenever it adversely affects a disproportionate number of blacks. Subsequent decisions, however, made it clear that the Court had rejected all of the more far-reaching, effects-based conceptions of discrimination—stigma, subordination, second-class citizenship, and the encouragement of prejudice. The sole test (leaving aside explicit classifications) is whether the government acted with discriminatory intent.

The most revealing aspect of the opinions in *Washington v Davis* and its sequelae is the cases the Court cited as examples of impermissible discrimination. Virtually every example the Court gave involved a situation like *Gomillion* or a more subtle version of *Gomillion*: cases in which voting or school district lines were ostensibly neutral but were in fact drawn along racial lines; cases in which the officials in charge of selecting jurors purported to act neutrally but in fact used race as a criterion; and cases in which supposedly neutral voting qualifications were in fact deliberate efforts to disqualify blacks. These are all, in essence, *Gomillion* situations—cases in which the government was using a racial classification but, in contrast to the classic Jim Crow laws of *Strauder* or *Plessy*, was trying to conceal the fact that it was doing so.

Moreover, in *Washington v Davis* and the cases that followed it, the Court did not mention (except to limit and distinguish) any of its previous opinions suggesting that the principle of *Brown* extended beyond explicit classifications and *Gomillion* situations. The Court said nothing, for example, about the suggestions in its opinions that race-neutral state action that encouraged private prejudice or excluded blacks from political power would violate the Equal Protection Clause. Nor did the Court refer to the "hearts and minds" language in *Brown*. In other words, the Court recognized that *Brown* cannot be confined to explicit racial classifications; it must extend to the equivalent of racial gerrymanders, subtle or unsubtle. But the Court was unwilling to extend the principle of *Brown* any further.

It is in this sense that *Washington v Davis* tamed *Brown*. The precedents—*Brown*, the cases decided in the two decades after *Brown*, and the antecedents in *Strauder*—all left open the possibility that *Brown* would stand for a principle that mandated relatively far-reaching changes in society. In *Washington v Davis*, the Court closed off that possibility. It returned to what I have called the minimum necessary content of *Brown*: that the Equal Protection Clause prohibits only explicit classifications and the equivalent of racial gerrymanders—facially neutral actions that are in fact based on race.

D. *Washington v Davis* and *Plessy*

Plessy v Ferguson is now universally condemned, and it would be unfair to equate *Washington v Davis* with *Plessy*. But there are several similarities, enough to suggest a more general pattern. Both *Strauder* and *Brown* were associated with eras of great change in American race relations. *Strauder* reflected the new understandings about race relations that developed after the Civil War. *Brown* both reflected and helped shape another set of new understandings, those of the civil rights movement. During Reconstruction and the civil rights era, it was unclear, in both the law and society, how far the changes would go.

Plessy and *Washington v Davis* were both decided after those eras had ended. *Plessy* did not overrule, or even explicitly question, the understandings that developed after the Civil War. *Washington v Davis*, of course, neither overruled nor questioned *Brown*. But *Plessy* adopted the narrowest possible interpretation of the Reconstruction understanding, and *Washington v Davis* adopted the narrowest plausible interpretation of *Brown*. Both decisions dismissed—*Plessy* explicitly, in the notorious passage about "the construction they choose to put on it," and *Washington v Davis* implicitly—the possibility that a notion like opposition to stigma or subordination might be the core of the prohibition against discrimination.

Finally, both decisions made it clear that the Equal Protection Clause would not be used to bring about large-scale changes in society. After *Plessy*, it was clear that the Supreme Court would not be a barrier to entrenching Jim Crow. *Washington v Davis*, to reiterate, did not do anything nearly so bad. But it seems fair to say that *Washington v Davis* also signaled a withdrawal from the front lines of social change. The Court in *Washington v Davis* explained that the alternatives to the discriminatory intent standard "would be far reaching and would raise serious questions about, and perhaps invalidate, a whole range of tax, welfare, public service, regulatory, and licensing statutes that may be more burdensome to the poor and to the average black than to the more affluent white."

Obviously these parallels do not establish that *Washington v Davis* is wrong, much less that it is another *Plessy*. I do not at all want to suggest that the discriminatory intent standard is either as obtuse or as evil as the doctrine of separate but equal. But the parallels may suggest the existence of some systematic process in the law, a process of taming. Great principles are announced in a form that is both vague and potentially far-reaching. Pressure then develops to tame them by reducing them to something that is both apparently more clear and objective, and apparently less threatening to established institutions. The post-Civil War revolution in race relations was tamed by being reduced to separate but equal; that standard emphasized "hard facts" like tangible equality instead of requiring courts to consider vague notions like stigma, and it did not threaten the basic way in which much of society was organized. *Brown* was tamed by being reduced to discriminatory intent, a standard that seems to have the same virtues—it appears to avoid the need to deal with "soft," open-ended notions like stigma, subordination, or second-class citizenship, and it appears not to call a wide range of established institutions into question.

But the consequence of the taming is a degree of infidelity to the great principle. The principle itself may be relatively vague, and it may threaten many institutions. Understanding what is wrong with discrimination may require some tolerance for relatively vague notions; there is no guarantee that the prohibition against discrimination can be expressed in a way that is not somewhat vague. And there is no guarantee that the principles that underlie that prohibition do not threaten many existing institutions.

Paul Brest, Palmer v. Thompson: *An Approach to the Problem of Unconstitutional Legislative Motive*, 1971 SUP. CT. REV. 95 (1971)*

* * *

V. THE CASE FOR JUDICIAL REVIEW OF MOTIVATION

* * *

A. ILLICIT MOTIVATION

The following four points set out what I believe to be the central argument for judicial invalidation of an illicitly motivated law.

1. Governments are constitutionally prohibited from pursuing certain objectives—for example, the disadvantage of a racial group, the suppression of a religion, or the deterring of interstate migration.

2. The fact that a decisionmaker gives weight to an illicit objective may determine the outcome of the decision. The decision-making process consists of weighing the foreseeable and desirable consequences of the proposed decision against its foreseeable costs. Considerations of distributive fairness play an important role. To the extent that the decisionmaker is illicitly motivated, he treats as a desirable consequence one to which the lawfully motivated decisionmaker would be indifferent or which he would view as undesirable.

3. Assuming that a person has no legitimate complaint against a particular decision merely because it affects him adversely, he does have a legitimate complaint if it would not have been adopted but for the decisionmaker's consideration of illicit objectives. If in fact the rule adopted is useful and fair, the adversely affected party might have no legitimate grievance, whatever considerations went into its adoption. In our governmental system, however, only the political decisionmaker—and not the judiciary—has general authority to assess the utility and fairness of a decision. And, since the decisionmaker has (by hypothesis) assigned an incorrect value to a relevant factor, the party has been deprived of his only opportunity for a full, proper assessment.

4. If the decisionmaker gave weight to an illicit objective, the court should presume that his consideration of the objective determined the outcome of the decision and should invalidate the decision in the absence of clear proof to the contrary. Evidence sufficient to establish that the decisionmaker gave any weight to an illicit objective will also often establish that the decision would not have been made but for the pursuit of that objective. A complainant may, however, prove clearly and convincingly that the decisionmaker gave weight to an illicit objective and yet fail to establish with equal certainty that this affected the outcome of the decision. It is conceivable—though seldom likely—that the same decision would have been made even in the absence of illicit motivation. In this case, proof that the decisionmaker took account of an illicit objective rebuts whatever presumption of regularity otherwise attaches. For this reason, and because of the constitutional interests at stake, the court should place on the decisionmaker a heavy burden of proving that his illicit objective was not determinative of the outcome.

B. SUSPECT MOTIVATION

A court may find that an operative rule innocent on its face was adopted with the objective of causing a result such that, had the operative rule in terms mandated that result, the rule would have been deemed constitutionally "suspect." For example, the court may find that an operative rule that does not classify by race has the purpose (and effect) of segregation by race.

It would be inappropriate to hold that the motivation as such invalidated the rule, for even if the rule explicitly classified by race it would not automatically fall, but would only trigger the demand for an extraordinary justification. It would be equally inappropriate to treat the motivation as innocent. For the same considerations that render an explicit racial classification suspect—the probability of an underlying prejudicial motivation, the antieducative effects, and the dangers of systematic injury to minorities—apply as well to the decisionmaker's objective of classifying on the basis of race.

The appropriate solution is to treat the objective itself as "suspect." If an operative rule mandating segregation under the circumstances could be justified by a compelling state interest, the decisionmaker's motivation is licit. If the operative rule could not be justified, the decisionmaker's motivation should invalidate the decision—for the same reasons that his consideration of an objective that is illicit per se should invalidate it.

VI. THE ARGUMENT AGAINST JUDICIAL REVIEW

. . . [O]bjections to Judicial review of motivation concern the difficulty of ascertaining motivation and the futility of invalidating an otherwise permissible law. Professors Tussman and ten Broek have suggested a third objection: the disutility of invalidating what may otherwise be a perfectly good law. And one also can find in some of the commentaries a fourth objection, based on the general impropriety of the inquiry.

A. ASCERTAINABILITY

Mr. Justice Black asserted in *Palmer* that it is generally "extremely difficult" to determine a decisionmaker's motivation and that it is especially difficult, or impossible, "to determine the 'sole' or 'dominant' motivation behind the choices of a group of legislators." I shall consider these propositions in reverse order.

1. *"'Sole' or 'dominant' motivation."* A complainant who can prove that, but for the decisionmaker's desire to promote an illicit objective, the decision would not have been made, should clearly have won his case. But such rigorous proof is not essential. It should suffice to demonstrate that illicit motivation played a nontrivial part in the decisionmaking process, so that it might have affected the outcome. Whichever of these ways one poses the inquiry, it is inappropriate to ask which of several possible objectives was "sole" or "dominant" in the decisionmaker's mind: an illicit motive may have been "subordinate" and yet have determined the outcome of the decision.

Nothing in the nature of a multimember decisionmaking body makes the search for sole or dominant motivation more appropriate than in the case of a single decisionmaker. Indeed, as the discussion below suggests, the main techniques for determining motivation treat the multimember body as a unit no different from the single decisionmaker.

2. *The general difficulty.* It is often impossible to establish that a decisionmaker entertained an illicit or suspect objective. But this does not justify a blanket refusal to undertake the inquiry if a decisionmaker's motivation can sometimes be determined with adequate certainty. And the Supreme Court and lower courts have rested judgments on findings of improper motivation—on records supporting those findings beyond serious dispute. In view of the doubts that have been expressed over the possibility of ascertaining motivation, I shall identify some general recurrent bases for such findings.

a) *Circumstantial evidence.* The chief method of ascertaining a decisionmaker's motivation involves the drawing of inferences from his conduct, viewed in the context of antecedent and concurrent events and situations. The process does not differ from that of inferring ultimate facts from basic facts in other areas of the law. It is grounded in an experiential, intuitive assessment of the likelihood that the decision was designed to further one or another objective.

* * *

. . . The courts possess no general authority to invalidate a decision because it is "undesirable," and an allegation of illicit motivation does not enlarge their authority. A conscientious decisionmaker, however, considers the costs of a proposal, its conduciveness to the ends sought to be attained, and the availability of alternatives less costly to the community as a whole or to a particular segment of the community. That a decision obviously falls to reflect these considerations with respect to any legitimate objective supports the inference that it was improperly motivated.

For example, a court would not question a city's decision to locate a park at site X rather, than site Y, merely because X seemed extremely costly, unattractive, and inaccessible, while Y seemed ideal. But this information, taken together with the fact that site X is the proposed location for a private interracial housing development strongly opposed by the white community, supports the inference that X was chosen to thwart construction of the project. Similarly, the fact that a regulation, though minimally related to the promotion of health or educational achievement, is poorly or dubiously suited to its supposed legitimate objectives, would lend support to other evidence of illicit motivation.

The juxtaposition of a decision with some prior event or sequence of events often bears on the inference of illicit motivation. The following chronological sequence, for example, is typical of a variety of cases: the decisionmaker enforces a discriminatory operative rule; a court enjoins this practice; the decisionmaker then adopts a constitutionally "innocent" rule that effectively maintains the *status quo ante*. For example, state voting officials are enjoined from refusing to register black applicants and the state then adopts difficult but apparently neutral registration requirements; or, school districts are ordered to cease assigning students by race and the state then enacts a tuition grant law, or abandons a public school system, or engages in other practices that tend to maintain segregation.

Each of these innovative practices serves conceivable permissible objectives. In considering the question, "Why did the decisionmaker adopt this practice?" the court, however, may properly consider the subquestion, "Why did the decisionmaker adopt this practice at this time?" The sequence of events may thus support the inference that the decisionmaker's objective was to do covertly that which he was forbidden to do overtly. The strength of the inference will also be affected by the tenacity of the decisionmaker's past commitment to the forbidden rule, the extent to which the innovation marks a departure from traditionally established practices, and the existence of other decisions that seem designed to serve the same illicit objective.

b) *Direct evidence of motivation.* In theory, the decisionmaker's statements can provide the most reliable evidence of his actual objectives: usually no one knows a person's reasons for acting better than the actor himself. On occasion, a decisionmaker will concede his actual objectives in a judicial proceeding. The utility of direct testimony, however, is seriously limited by the ease with which one can lie successfully about one's motives, by the costs of obtaining the testimony of the members of multimember decisionmaking bodies, and by legal doctrines that immunize legislators and high executive officials from having to account for their decisions.

Of greater practical utility are statements made by decisionmakers in the course of the decisionmaking, process statements of the sort often used in statutory interpretation. Where the decisionmaker consists of a single person, such statements may be conclusive. But only a few members of a multimember body usually will have stated their objectives. Attribution of the statements of some members of the decisionmaking body to the others cannot properly be justified on a theory of adoption by silence or the fiction of delegated authority to speak. Nonetheless, often the uncontested avowals of illicit motivation by the sponsors of a measure are in fact typical of the views of many others who vote for the measure. Such statements thus lend some support to an inference of illicit motivation, and have properly been used for this purpose, though alone they would not provide a sufficient basis for invalidation.

B. FUTILITY

[T]here is an element of futility in a judicial attempt to invalidate a law because of the bad motives of its supporters. If the law is struck down for this reason, rather than because of its facial content or effect, it would presumably be valid as soon as the legislature or other relevant governing board repassed it for different reasons.

If this means that the mere possibility of reenactment for proper purposes necessarily makes futile the invalidation of an illicitly motivated law, it misses the point of judicial review of motivation, which assumes that the law as such is constitutional and that only the process of its adoption—the decisionmaker's consideration of improper objectives—is constitutionally impermissible. Thus, in theory the decisionmaker remains free to readopt a motive-invalidated law at any time—provided that he does so solely for legitimate reasons. Judicial review of motivation is no more "futile" merely because reenactment is possible than appellate review is futile because an appellee may prevail again on remand after a trial court is reversed for giving weight to inadmissible evidence or misapplying the law.

The "futility" argument, however, has two other, more substantial components. First, if courts engage in review of motivation, decisionmakers may take greater care to conceal their illicit objectives. The judicial practice will thus be self-defeating: once it is engaged in, decisionmakers will cease providing the data on which it depends.

The empirical assumptions underlying this argument are not obviously correct. Determinations of motivation often do not depend on manipulable data such as legislative history. Moreover, decisionmakers may not take cognizance of the practice of judicial inquiry into motivation and, in any case, may not take measures to conceal their actual purposes in enacting a law.

The second argument is that a particular decisionmaker whose law is once struck down because it was illicitly motivated will readopt the law, retaining his illicit motivation but taking care to conceal it. This has more force, and it poses serious practical problems of formulating prospective relief. Since the law might be readopted for wholly licit reasons, a permanent injunction against its readoption could impose high costs on society without any countervailing justification in the policies supporting review of motivation. On the other hand, to treat readoption as an entirely new matter, ignoring the decisionmaker's past motivation, would be unrealistic and would subvert those policies.

In general, the most satisfactory response to this dilemma will be to presume that the decisionmaker continues to entertain the motives that led to the original decision (and to its invalidation). In operational terms, the court should enjoin an administrative decisionmaker from making the same decision again unless he comes forward with persuasive evidence that this time it will be made only for legitimate reasons. Sometimes a material change of circumstances, or the passage of time accompanied by a change of community attitudes, will be persuasive of the decisionmaker's good faith. In other circumstances the decisionmaker may be required to demonstrate that the proposed decision is in fact desirable on the merits and that no practicable alternative is less burdensome to the class at whom the original decision was adversely aimed; and the court might require additionally that the decisionmaker take steps to protect that class. If the court invalidates a legislative enactment, it should similarly scrutinize reenactment of the identical or a similar law if it is challenged in a properly maintained action.

This degree of judicial intrusion into the decisionmaking process is extraordinary. The decisionmaker's past behavior, however, usually justifies the court's strong suspicion of his motives and its concomitant scrutiny of the merits of a new decision and requirement of prophylactic measures. In some cases, the likelihood that a decision was readopted for legitimate reasons is so small that no inquiry into its merits is necessary. The evaluation of many other decisions calls for little or no substantive expertise, and when expertise is required the court can often gain sufficient information from documentary evidence and expert testimony.

C. DISUTILITY

The invalidation of an unconstitutional rule is desirable: as a matter of law the rule is bad. But "it is altogether possible for a law which is the expression of a bad motive to be a good law . . ., [to make] a positive contribution to the public good." As an argument against judicial review of motivation, this is misleading: it confuses the court's competence with that of the decisionmaker. It is beyond the court's normal authority to determine whether a law is "good." This is the central task delegated to the decisionmaker. But when the decisionmaker has treated an illicit objective as desirable—as a benefit rather than as a cost or a neutral factor—he has not properly evaluated the "goodness" of the decision. The argument for judicial review of motivation is that it is the court's task to assure, to the limited extent of forbidding the decisionmaker to weigh improper objectives, that the decisionmaker himself determines that his decision is good.

Suppose, for example, that a school board adopts an ability grouping system that has the effect of segregating black and white pupils. This system might have been adopted to promote educational achievement, but the court finds that the board's objective was in fact to preserve segregation. Conceding, *arguendo*, that a child has no constitutional right to be assigned to classes with children of other races, he does have a right not to be segregated on the basis of race. It is no response that "reasonable men" might adopt the tracking system to serve legitimate objectives. The court is not authorized to make this educational decision. And the authorized decisionmaker, the school board, did not make the decision on proper grounds. The board may not even have considered the utility of the scheme as a means of promoting educational achievement; and if the board did, it might not have found enough utility to justify the rule's adoption absent the added, impermissible, benefit of segregation. The proper allocation of decisionmaking competence requires that the board make this decision on proper grounds—or that it not be made at all.

D. IMPROPRIETY

The argument against judicial review of motivation on the ground of its impropriety has focused largely on inquiries into the motives of legislative bodies and high executive officials. By contrast, inquiry into the motivation of administrative officials is deemed permissible. The argument has two components: first, the process of proving legislative motivation requires an undesirable intrusion into the political process; second, inquiry into motivation entails a lack of proper respect for a government's chief policymaking agencies.

The first point assumes that the inquiry into legislative motivation requires the "cross-examination" of each individual legislator.

* * *

This argument is persuasive that legislators should not be subject to subpoena to explain their reasons for voting for a measure. To the extent that proof of illicit motivation depends on such testimony, the case must fail. But proof of illicit motivation need not depend on such testimony.

The second point involves "considerations of regard for 'the station,' so strong when the Court reviews the work of the legislature." "[A] finding of impure motive sufficient to void an act of a legislature impugns the essential integrity of a coordinate branch of government."

This argument has some force. To declare a law unconstitutional on its merits is to hold that the decisionmaker made an error. But a finding of illicit motivation often is tantamount to an accusation that the decisionmaker violated his constitutional oath of office. Especially where the decisionmaker claims to have pursued only legitimate objectives, a judicial determination of illicit motivation carries an element of insult; it is an attack on the decisionmaker's honesty. These concerns apply to lower-echelon officials as well as to legislators and high executive officials. Our constitutional traditions, however, accord greater respect to the integrity of the higher agencies.

Nevertheless, legislators sometimes do act out of illicit motivations. And against the argument for nonintervention one must set the interests favoring judicial invalidation of an illicitly motivated legislative act—the injury and insult felt by those at whom it is aimed; the harm to the integrity of a system of government that pretends officially not to know what everyone knows is true. The critical commentators themselves have conceded the propriety of invalidation when the case is clear, and the courts have so acted. Herein lies the proper reconciliation of these competing interests: the courts should not refuse to inquire into the motivation of any governmental body, but they should not invalidate a decision on the ground that it was designed to serve illicit objectives unless that fact has been established by clear and convincing evidence.

VII. SUMMARY OF AN APPROACH TO UNCONSTITUTIONAL MOTIVATION

I have arrived at the following position: A court should entertain an action challenging an otherwise constitutional decision—whether made by a legislature or an executive or administrative official—on the ground that it was designed in part to serve illicit or suspect objective. The complainant must establish by clear and convincing evidence that such an objective played an affirmative role in the decision-making process. He need not, however, establish that consideration of the objective was the sole, or dominant, or a "but-for" cause of the decision—only that its consideration may have affected the outcome of the process.

If the objective is illicit, the decision should simply be invalidated. If the objective is suspect, the court should treat it essentially as it treats a suspect operative rule, and invalidate the decision unless the defendant comes forward with an extraordinary justification.

The court should permit the decisionmaker to readopt the same decision only upon a showing that its readoption is designed to serve entirely legitimate objectives.

* * *

Daniel R. Ortiz, *The Myth of Intent in Equal Protection*, 41 STAN. L. REV. 1105 (1989)*

In 1976, the last major piece of traditional equal protection doctrine fell into place. That year the Supreme Court held in *Washington v. Davis* that in the absence of a racially discriminatory purpose a facially neutral governmental action having an adverse racial impact would not be subject to strict scrutiny. Some commentators have supported the intent requirement; some have quarreled with it; and many have argued with how the Court has applied it. All agree, however, that current doctrine makes intent the key to equal protection, and nearly all agree why.

The ascendancy of process theory in constitutional law has led the Court to avoid review of the substance of government decisionmaking. Instead, the Court tries to limit review to the processes of decisionmaking and invalidate only those laws resulting from process failure. Applied to equal protection, this approach implies that the Court should work only to keep the government's decisionmaking process pure. The Court should seek not to judge the substantive fairness of the outcomes of decisionmaking processes but only to screen out all impurifying motivations. In particular, it should strike down only those laws reflecting a discriminatory animus.

* * *

IV. THE OVERALL DESIGN

The Supreme Court has developed the intent requirement so unevenly that it now fails to fit either its name, the Court's description of it, or the theory its champions and opponents alike claim gave it birth. What are we to make of intent, then? Perhaps we can begin reconstructing the concept by noting certain similarities of function in the different areas in which the Court has applied it. Although the intent doctrine appears to operate quite differently in these different contexts, structurally it functions the same in each.

In each area discussed, the intent requirement serves to allocate burdens of proof between the individual and the state. In the housing and employment discrimination cases, for example, it allocates to individuals the burden of producing evidence of discriminatory motivation; if this is shown, it then shifts the burden of proof to the state to show legitimate reasons for the disparate treatment. Similarly, in the jury selection cases, the doctrine places on individuals the burden of showing adverse impact on an identifiable group and the susceptibility of the selection procedure to manipulation; if this is met, it then shifts the burden to the state to show that valid reasons underlie the selection of particular jurors.

In the voting cases, intent requires that the individual show adverse impact in voting plus discrimination in other areas of life, and then shifts the burden to the state to offer a compelling reason for the electoral discrimination. In the school desegregation cases, the rule is more complicated. At the initial liability stage, the individual must come forth with evidence of discriminatory motivation at some time from *Brown I* on and then, to rebut, the state must come forward with a compelling reason for segregation—which no state has ever done. Once liability is found, the district falls under an affirmative obligation to remedy segregation, a duty which effectively judges its actions under an effects test. After the declaration of unitariness, however, the test becomes much more strict. Since the district has cured the original violations, plaintiffs can no longer point to any discriminatory motivation from the time before the unitariness finding. Thus, after the school district has achieved unitariness, the intent doctrine requires the same showing on the plaintiff's side that it requires in the housing and employment cases: actual discriminatory motivation. The only difference lies in the state's burden. In the school cases, the state has never negated intent by arguing 'legitimate' interests.

The irony of intent is that over time it has come to embrace an approach it was originally adopted to avoid. In *Washington v. Davis*, the Court required intent largely to escape the implications of the analysis the lower courts were applying to facially neutral governmental actions having disparate effects. The lower courts at that time were for the most part treating this type of equal protection claim the same way they treated disparate impact claims under Title VII. If the plaintiff showed disparate impact in an employment case, for example, then the burden shifted to the state to show what, in *Griggs v. Duke Power Co.*, the Court variously described as 'business necessity,' 'relat[ionship] to job performance,' and 'manifest relationship to the employment in question.' Through this sometimes complex shifting of burdens of proof, Title VII doctrine aimed to evaluate 'the *consequences* of employment practices, not simply the motivation.' In other words, it tested the outcomes of decisionmaking, not the inputs. *Griggs*'s particular allocation of the burden of proof, moreover, served to balance the interests of minorities and employers. Title VII did not proscribe all employment practices having harmful disparate effects, but only those practices not justified by bona fide business interests. In the words of *Griggs*, the allocation roughly pit the cost of "built-in headwinds' for minority groups' against businesses' legitimate need to 'measur[e] job capability.' In origin at least, Title VII focused unabashedly on the substance of decisionmaking, not its motivation.

The intent doctrine has come to resemble Title VII in both focus and structure. In many contexts, it too centers on outcome, rather than input, and it too weighs the claims of both sides through its allocation of the burden of proof between the parties. More important, intent doctrine allocates the various burdens of proof in a systematic way. As the individual's interest becomes greater, the doctrine places a correspondingly lesser burden on the individual and a greater burden on the state. This observation contradicts one of the central doctrinal claims of process theorists, who believe that under the traditional suspect classification strand of equal protection the importance of the individual interest does not matter. As Ely puts it in arguing against the view that the Court considers the *'amount* of harm': '[Such an] account would make sense if the Court followed the practice of reviewing more strenuously those distinctions that hurt more, which it doesn't. A taxation distinction worth $1,000,000 receives about the same review as one worth $100—that is, virtually none.'

Ely's point is well taken, but only so far. The Court does not vary review according to the size of individual penalties, but it does distinguish between various categories of interests. In particular, it appears to follow the familiar hierarchy the Court employs in the fundamental rights strand of equal protection in deciding what level of scrutiny to accord various kinds of interests. In that area, voting and certain criminal process rights, along with the right to travel, receive heightened scrutiny; education receives somewhat elevated scrutiny, in practice, if not in theory; and traditional economic interests receive reduced scrutiny. Contrary to the claims of the Court and commentators, then, the fundamental rights and suspect classification strands of equal protection are not totally separate. Intent takes into account not only the invidiousness of the government's classification but also the importance of the individual interest at stake. At the heart of this most confusing stage of the equal protection inquiry, the seemingly disparate strands of larger equal protection doctrine meet.

This description of the intent requirement poses two major questions which are, in fact, related. First, why this particular hierarchy of value? Why should the law treat these particular kinds of cases more seriously than others? Second, why the great gap between the housing and employment cases and all the others? In the housing and employment cases, the plaintiff must show current, actual discriminatory motivation; in the others, current disparate effects plus some other showing—at most of motivation in the past or in decisions unrelated to the one under consideration—suffice. Not only is it much more difficult to prove intent in the housing and employment cases, but, more interestingly, they involve a completely different kind of inquiry. Why such a great difference in approach and result between these two groups of cases? Why require motivation in the one and pay only lip service to it in the other?

In *Washington v. Davis*, the Supreme Court gave three reasons for requiring discriminatory motivation: precedent, institutional role, and the slippery slope. Ironically, the precedents on which it relied consisted of jury selection, voting, and school desegregation cases—contexts where today, at least, the Court does not require a meaningful showing of discriminatory motivation on the part of the government decisionmaker. The Court's argument based on institutional role was more straight-forward. Absent invidious motivation, it thought, review as searching as that under Title VII was simply too disruptive of government decisionmaking. Congress could permit such intrusive judicial intervention, to be sure, but the courts could not undertake it themselves without statutory authorization.

The Court's final reason, the often throwaway slippery slope, reveals the most about its fears in this area. At the point of choosing between an effects and an intent test, the Court looked ahead to see where an effects test might lead:

> A rule that a statute designed to serve neutral ends is nevertheless invalid, absent compelling justification, if in practice it benefits or burdens one race more than another would be far reaching and would raise serious questions about, and perhaps invalidate, a whole range of tax, welfare, public service, regulatory, and licensing statutes that may be more burdensome to the poor and to the average black than to the more affluent white.

And in a footnote, the Court paraded even more horribles:

> [One commentator] suggests that disproportionate-impact analysis might invalidate 'tests and qualifications for voting, draft deferment, public employment, jury service, and other government-conferred benefits and opportunities . . .; [s]ales taxes, bail schedules, utility rates, bridge tolls, license fees, and other state-imposed charges.' It has also been argued that minimum wage and usury laws as well as professional licensing require-ments would require major modifications in light of the unequal-impact rule.

This parade of horribles, as the Court's comparison of 'the poor and . . . the average black' with 'the more affluent white' shows, arises out of the overlap of race with other classifications in our society, particularly wealth. As the Court's identification of 'poor' with 'average black' and of 'more affluent' with 'white' makes clear, any rule classi-fying on the basis of wealth has disproportionate racial effects because race and wealth are cohort classifications in our society. In other words, it is the case both that blacks are disproportionately poor and that the poor are disproportionately black. The two classifications correlate to some degree. According to the Bureau of the Census, for example, the median household net worth of blacks in 1984 was $3397, while that of whites was $39,135—a difference of over 1100 percent. One difficulty with allow-ing racial effects alone to cast suspicion on governmental action, then, is that such a rule would cast doubt on the validity of many laws reflecting differences in wealth. In a society like ours, however, wealth classifications can hardly be suspect. In an advanced market economy, wealth is in many ways a foundational classification, one on whose legitimacy large parts of the economic and social structure stand. If the Court were to hold that wealth was a suspect classification, the government could not simply accept the market as a background assumption for most of its programs. In many areas, it would have an affirmative obligation to work to revise market allo-cations. A simple effects test, then, might well have threatened many of our most tra-ditional and commonly accepted social and economic structures, and made more difficult any particular legislative efforts to reform them.

As originally developed in *Washington v. Davis*, the intent doctrine served a very critical and difficult function. It attempted to separate race from other classifica-tions—particularly wealth—to which it was very closely related. If these other clas-sifications served as mere pretexts for race, intent condemned them. If they did not, intent preserved them from searching scrutiny. Intent aimed, in other words, to separate racial proxies from mere racial cohorts. This task was critical because race had become as culturally odious as some of its cohorts had become foundational. Seen this way, the intent requirement serves as much a protective as a condemnatory function. It works not just to identify troubling classifications but also to insulate others—which largely constitute our society—from serious review. The market, if not exactly a constitutional value, is protected from constitutional concern.

Seeing intent in this way helps explain both the gap between the housing and employment cases and the others, and the rest of the hierarchy of value that the intent doctrine reflects. In those areas traditionally relegated primarily to market control, like housing and employment, the intent doctrine requires actual motivation. This not only makes judicial supervision of government participation in and regulation of these markets difficult, but it also places beyond constitutional question differences, like those in education or wealth, upon which market rewards at least in part depend. Intent thus protects not only the government's decision to participate, intervene, or not intervene in traditional markets, but also the criteria, like wealth endowments, through which we structure society in these areas.

In other contexts, such as voting, jury selection, and school desegregation, the Court does not protect these cohort classifications. In fact, in these areas, the Court has independently condemned discrimination on the basis of those classifications, like wealth, on which the market operates. In *Douglas v. California* and *Griffin v. Illinois*, for example, the Court held that the states had to extend certain rights to indigent criminal defendants that were available to those defendants who could pay. The state could not simply rely on the market to allocate these goods. Similarly, many of the voting rights cases under the fundamental rights strand of equal protection, particularly the poll tax cases, effectively outlaw use of wealth classifications in the electoral process. And finally, although the Court has held that education is not a fundamental right, it has also suggested certain limits to how much the state can discriminate in this area on the basis of wealth. In particular, it appears that the state may comparatively, but not absolutely, deprive the poor of education. As these fundamental rights strand cases show, in those contexts where the Court has significantly eased the intent requirement in the suspect classification strand it generally finds discrimination on the basis of wealth to be an independent problem. In these cases there is simply no need for a court to sort out race from wealth. Where we do not traditionally relegate an area of social activity largely to market control, equal protection can condemn both proxies and cohorts.

As this discussion suggests, the intent doctrine distinguishes between two types of goods. The first kind, which it fairly aggressively protects, consists primarily of political, criminal, and educational rights. The second kind, over which it allows the state much control, consists of 'ordinary' social and economic goods, like jobs and housing. In making this distinction, intent doctrine reflects our prevailing political ideology—liberalism—which is a system of values rooted in the belief that the state should allow every individual to pursue his own conception of the good. Since such an aim requires the state to remain neutral between competing conceptions of the good, the state can legitimately act only to allow individuals more fully to pursue their own private conceptions. Thus, in its most extreme from, libertarianism, this ideology permits the state only to create basic property law, to criminalize private behavior hindering others' ability to choose their own ends, to educate society's youngest citizens so that they too may learn to choose their own ends, and to enforce private bargains. In this extreme system, nearly all remaining social interaction is governed by free markets since that mechanism is thought best to allow persons to achieve their individually chosen objectives in free trade. Like libertarianism, liberalism also aggressively protects those basic rights, like voting, education, and freedom from unwarranted physical restraint, which are necessary for a person to be able to choose her own ends. And, like libertarianism, liberalism also relegates most remaining social behavior to the market. Liberalism does, however, differ from libertarianism in permitting the state to interfere somewhat in the market—certainly to overcome market failure and also to ensure a certain minimum level of dignity and welfare to all individuals.

In this description, liberalism has two central features. First, it grants the first type of goods priority over the second. In nearly all forms of liberalism, the state cannot seriously infringe these first-order goods and the individual cannot even voluntarily trade them away for others. Since they are foundational in the sense that they enable the individual to choose and pursue her own private conception of the good, they are necessarily primary. Second, while liberalism relies primarily on the market to allocate ordinary social and economic goods, it does allow the state to intervene to some degree in market allocation. Only strict libertarianism commands the state to leave the market inviolate. In prescribing the burdens borne by the parties, the intent doctrine thus reflects both of the core features of liberalism: the aggressive protection of those rights and liberties that enable the individual to pursue her own vision of the good and the permissive supervision of government intervention in traditional economic and social markets.

VI. CONCLUSION

Given the rigidification of the rest of equal protection law, and the increasing predictability of its results, it seems inevitable that the Court would invent a doctrine to balance competing interests. The puzzle is why the Court did so through intent, a concept seemingly unrelated to interest-balancing. In many areas of constitutional law, the Court freely employs balancing tests. Dormant commerce clause jurisprudence, for example, in many cases straightforwardly weighs the benefits to a state against the burdens to interstate commerce in determining the constitutionality of a state regulation. Equal protection, however, has always carefully avoided the appearance of balancing. The rigid tiers of scrutiny framework, together with the well-settled suspect classification analysis, appears to leave no room for the weighing of various interests. In fact, whenever a justice suggests departing from the tiers of scrutiny framework, if only in the name of judicial honesty, other members of the Court either ignore his noises or pounce for apostasy. The other justices are concerned at bottom that interest-balancing may move the Court beyond law into politics. Justices would appear to be legislating rather than judging as they make the many value choices balancing requires.

The intent doctrine, as developed by the Court, offers a way out of this difficulty. By allocating burdens of proof according to the balance of individual and public interests, intent overcomes the problem of doctrinal rigidity and offers a degree of flexibility in an otherwise inflexible area. It does so, however, without appearing overtly to weigh and compare interests. When the Court strikes down a governmental action, it can still avoid the charge of judicial legislation. Although it is actually weighing interests, it can claim to be just looking at motivation—a seemingly objective inquiry unrelated to the balance of interests at stake—to determine which particular tier of scrutiny to apply. In the end, the intent doctrine submerges judicial discretion to the level where it becomes invisible to those outside the system.

Anxious not to appear to weigh interests any more than absolutely necessary, the Court has retained its rigid overall doctrinal structure. It has at the same time, however, reconceptualized the key to the whole inquiry—intent—so that it can flexibly consider both the individual and public interests without appearing to do so. Not surprisingly, the balances it reaches in particular kinds of cases reflect our reigning cultural, political, and economic values. We should be surprised if it were otherwise. Intent insulates government participation in or regulation of traditional markets from judicial supervision while aggressively protecting the individual in certain other areas (notably voting, criminal procedure, and education) which we have traditionally excepted from market control.

In a sense, the intent doctrine fulfills two central purposes in equal protection. Through its allocation of burdens of proof in particular kinds of cases, the intent doctrine makes many of the ultimate value choices implicit in equal protection. Furthermore, through its name and widely-held descriptions based in process theory, it obscures these choices. Thus, it helps both to reinforce a particular vision and understanding of society, and to hide the fact that it is doing so. In short, the intent doctrine both perpetuates and mystifies, and, one could argue, perhaps it better perpetuates because it mystifies. By 'covering its own tracks,' so to speak, intent helps insulate its choices and the judicial process in general from certain kinds of criticism.

In this respect, the intent doctrine runs against the movement of much postmodern political theory, which advocates institutional arrangements that announce their commitments and proclaim their own contingency. Only in this way can our social and political structures open themselves up to our revision and thus continually reflect our changing desires, values, and aspirations. By obstructing proper understanding, the intent doctrine frustrates change because those who would revise the law's values must first be able to see what they are. Perhaps, then, intent is interesting more for what it says about us than for what it says about equal protection. In the end, it confronts us with a series of large and somewhat troubling questions: Why do we make central a doctrine that masks its own objectives and thereby resists revision? And if law is indeed one of our most important cultural activities, what does this need to mystify tell us about ourselves and our political institutions?

Charles R. Lawrence, III, *The Id, the Ego, and Equal Protection: Reckoning with Unconscious Racism*, 39 STAN. L. REV. 317 (1987)*

It is 1948. I am sitting in a kindergarten classroom at the Dalton School, a fashionable and progressive New York City private school. My parents, both products of a segregated Mississippi school system, have come to New York to attend graduate and professional school. They have enrolled me and my sisters here at Dalton to avoid sending us to the public school in our neighborhood where the vast majority of the students are black and poor. They want us to escape the ravages of segregation, New York style.

It is circle time in the five-year old group, and the teacher is reading us a book. As she reads, she passes the book around the circle so that each of us can see the illustrations. The book's title is *Little Black Sambo*. Looking back, I remember only one part of the story, one illustration: Little Black Sambo is running around a stack of pancakes with a tiger chasing him. He is very black and has a minstrel's white mouth. His hair is tied up in many pigtails, each pigtail tied with a different color ribbon. I have seen the picture before the book reaches my place in the circle. I have heard the teacher read the "comical" text describing Sambo's plight and have heard the laughter of my classmates. There is a knot in the pit of my stomach. I feel panic and shame. I do not have the words to articulate my feelings—words like "stereotype" and "stigma" that might help cathart the shame and place it outside of me where it began. But I am slowly realizing that, as the only black child in the circle, I have some kinship with the tragic and ugly hero of this story—that my classmates are laughing at me as well as at him. I wish I could laugh along with my friends. I wish I could disappear.

I am in a vacant lot next to my house with black friends from the neighborhood. We are listening to *Amos and Andy* on a small radio and laughing uproariously. My father comes out and turns off the radio. He reminds me that he disapproves of this show that pokes fun at Negroes. I feel bad—less from my father's reprimand than from a sense that I have betrayed him and myself, that I have joined my classmates in laughing at us.

I am certain that my kindergarten teacher was not intentionally racist in choosing *Little Black Sambo*. I knew even then, from a child's intuitive sense, that she was a good, well-meaning person. A less benign combination of racial mockery and profit motivated the white men who produced the radio show and played the roles of Amos and Andy. But we who had joined their conspiracy by our laughter had not intended to demean our race.

A dozen years later I am a student at Haverford College. Again, I am a token black presence in a white world. A companion whose face and name I can't remember seeks to compliment me by saying, "I don't think of you as a Negro." I understand his benign intention and accept the compliment. But the knot is in my stomach again. Once again, I have betrayed myself.

This happened to me more than a few times. Each time my interlocutor was a good, liberal, white person who intended to express feelings of shared humanity. I did not yet understand the racist implications of the way in which the feelings were conceptualized. I am certain that my white friends did not either. We had not yet grasped the compliment's underlying premise: To be thought of as a Negro is to be thought of as less than human. We were all victims of our culture's racism. We had all grown up on *Little Black Sambo* and *Amos and Andy*.

Another ten years pass. I am thirty-three. My daughter, Maia, is three. I greet a pink-faced, four-year old boy on the steps of her nursery school. He proudly presents me with a book he has brought for his teacher to read to the class. "It's my favorite," he says. The book is a new edition of *Little Black Sambo*.

INTRODUCTION

This article reconsiders the doctrine of discriminatory purpose that was established by the 1976 decision, *Washington v. Davis*. This now well-established doctrine requires plaintiffs challenging the constitutionality of a facially neutral law to prove a racially discriminatory purpose on the part of those responsible for the law's enactment or administration.

* * *

Much of one's inability to know racial discrimination when one sees it results from a failure to recognize that racism is both a crime and a disease. This failure is compounded by a reluctance to admit that the illness of racism infects almost everyone. Acknowledging and understanding the malignancy are prerequisites to the discovery of an appropriate cure. But the diagnosis is difficult, because our own contamination with the very illness for which a cure is sought impairs our comprehension of the disorder.

Americans share a common historical and cultural heritage in which racism has played and still plays a dominant role. Because of this shared experience, we also inevitably share many ideas, attitudes, and beliefs that attach significance to an individual's race and induce negative feelings and opinions about nonwhites. To the extent that this cultural belief system has influenced all of us, we are all racists. At the same time, most of us are unaware of our racism. We do not recognize the ways in which our cultural experience has influenced our beliefs about race or the occasions on which those beliefs affect our actions. In other words, a large part of the behavior that produces racial discrimination is influenced by unconscious racial motivation.

There are two explanations for the unconscious nature of our racially discriminatory beliefs and ideas. First, Freudian theory states that the human mind defends itself against the discomfort of guilt by denying or refusing to recognize those ideas, wishes, and beliefs that conflict with what the individual has learned is good or right. While our historical experience has made racism an integral part of our culture, our society has more recently embraced an ideal that rejects racism as immoral. When an individual experiences conflict between racist ideas and the societal ethic that condemns those ideas, the mind excludes his racism from consciousness.

Second, the theory of cognitive psychology states that the culture—including, for example, the media and an individual's parents, peers, and authority figures—transmits certain beliefs and preferences. Because these beliefs are so much a part of the culture, they are not experienced as explicit lessons. Instead, they seem part of the individual's rational ordering of her perceptions of the world. The individual is unaware, for example, that the ubiquitous presence of a cultural stereotype has influenced her perception that blacks are lazy or unintelligent. Because racism is so deeply ingrained in our culture, it is likely to be transmitted by tacit understandings: Even if a child is not told that blacks are inferior, he learns that lesson by observing the behavior of others. These tacit understandings, because they have never been articulated, are less likely to be experienced at a conscious level.

In short, requiring proof of conscious or intentional motivation as a prerequisite to constitutional recognition that a decision is race-dependent ignores much of what we understand about how the human mind works. It also disregards both the irrationality of racism and the profound effect that the history of American race relations has had on the individual and collective unconscious.

* * *

In pursuit of that goal, this article proposes a new test to trigger judicial recognition of race-based behavior. It posits a connection between unconscious racism and the existence of cultural symbols that have racial meaning. It suggests that the "cultural meaning" of an allegedly racially discriminatory act is the best available analogue for, and evidence of, a collective unconscious that we cannot observe directly. This test would thus evaluate governmental conduct to determine whether it conveys a symbolic message to which the culture attaches racial significance. A finding that the culture thinks of an allegedly discriminatory governmental action in racial terms would also constitute a finding regarding the beliefs and motivations of the governmental actors: The actors are themselves part of the culture and presumably could not have acted without being influenced by racial considerations, even if they are unaware of their racist beliefs. Therefore, the court would apply strict scrutiny.

I. "THY SPEECH MAKETH THEE MANIFEST": A PRIMER ON THE UNCONSCIOUS AND RACE

A. *Racism: A Public Health Problem*

Not every student of the human mind has agreed with Sigmund Freud's description of the unconscious, but few today would quarrel with the assertion that there is an unconscious—that there are mental processes of which we have no awareness that affect our actions and the ideas of which we are aware. There is a considerable, and by now well respected, body of knowledge and empirical research concerning the workings of the human psyche and the unconscious. Common sense tells us that we all act unwittingly on occasion. We have experienced slips of the tongue and said things we fully intended not to say, and we have had dreams in which we experienced such feeling as fear, desire, and anger that we did not know we had.

The law has, for the most part, refused to acknowledge what we have learned about the unconscious. . . .

But the body of law and legal theory that governs the application of the equal protection clause to cases of alleged racial discrimination should not blind itself to what we know about the unconscious. Racism is in large part a product of the unconscious. It is a set of beliefs whereby we irrationally attach significance to something called race. I do not mean to imply that racism does not have its origins in the rational and premeditated acts of those who sought and seek property and power. But racism in America is much more complex than either the conscious conspiracy of a power elite or the simple delusion of a few ignorant bigots. It is a part of our common historical experience and, therefore, a part of our culture. It arises from the assumptions we have learned to make about the world, ourselves, and others as well as from the patterns of our fundamental social activities.

* * *

B. *Psychoanalytic Theory: An Explanation of Racism's Irrationality*

The division of the mind into the conscious and the unconscious is the fundamental principle of psychoanalysis. Psychoanalytic theory explains the existence of pathological mental behavior as well as certain otherwise unexplained behavior in healthy people by postulating two powerful mental processes—the primary and the secondary—which govern how the mind works. The primary process, or Id, occurs outside of our awareness. It consists of desires, wishes, and instincts that strive for gratification. It follows its own laws, of which the supreme one is pleasure. The secondary process, or Ego, happens under conscious control and is bound by logic and reason. We use this process to adapt to reality: The Ego is required to respect the demands of reality and to conform to ethical and moral laws. On their way to gratification, the Id impulses must pass through the territory of the Ego where they are criticized, rejected, or modified, often by some defensive measure on the part of the secondary process. Defensive mechanisms such as repression, denial, introjection, projection, reaction formation, sublimation, and reversal resolve the conflicts between the primary and secondary processes by disguising forbidden wishes and making them palatable.

Several observations about the nature of racial prejudice give credence both to the theory of repression and to the suggestion that racial antagonism finds its source in the unconscious. For example, when we say that racism is irrational, we mean that when people are asked to explain the basis of their racial antagonism they either express an instinctive, unexplained distaste at the thought of associating with the out-group as equals or they cite reasons that are not based on established fact and are often contradicted by personal experience.

In psychoanalytic terms, this irrational behavior indicates poor "reality-testing." When people of normal intelligence behave in a way that rejects what they experience as real, it requires some explanation. Psychoanalytic theory assumes that inadequacy in reality-testing fulfills a psychological function, usually the preservation of an attitude basic to the individual's makeup. If adequate reality-testing threatens to undermine such functionally significant attitude, it is avoided. In such cases, the dislike of out-groups is based on rationalization—that is, on socially acceptable pseudoreasons that serve to disguise the function that the antagonism serves for the individual.

* * *

Of course, not all inadequate reality-testing is a rationalization of hidden motives. The occasion for reality-testing is not always available, and all of us make prejudgments based on insufficient evidence. But when these prejudgments become rigidly stereotyped thinking that eschews reality even when facts are available, there is reason to search for a psychological function that the rigidity of the prejudgment fulfills.

An examination of the beliefs that racially prejudiced people have about out-groups demonstrates their use of other mechanisms observed by both Freudian and non-Freudian behavioralists. For example, studies have found that racists hold two types of stereotyped beliefs: They believe the out-group is dirty, lazy, oversexed, and without control of their instincts (a typical accusation against blacks), or they believe the out-group is pushy, ambitious, conniving, and in control of business, money, and industry (a typical accusation against Jews). These two types of accusation correspond to two of the most common types of neurotic conflict: that which arises when an individual cannot master his instinctive drives in a way that fits into rational and socially approved patterns of behavior, and that which arises when an individual cannot live up to the aspirations and standards of his own conscience. Thus, the stereotypical view of blacks implies that their Id, the instinctive part of their psyche, dominates their Ego, the rationally oriented part. The stereotype of the Jew, on the other hand, accuses him of having an overdeveloped Ego. In this way, the racially prejudiced person projects his own conflict into the form of racial stereotypes.

The preoccupation among racially prejudiced people with sexual matters in race relations provides further evidence of this relationship between the unconscious and racism. Taboos against interracial sexual relations, myths concerning the sexual prowess of blacks, and obsessions with racial purity coexist irrationally with a tendency to break these taboos. Again, psychoanalytic theory provides insights: According to Freud, one's sexual identity plays a crucial role in the unending effort to come to terms with oneself. Thus, the prominence of racism's sexual component supports the theory that racial antagonism grows in large part out of an unstable sense of identity.

Another piece of evidence that supports the contention that racism originates in the unconscious is the fact that racially discriminatory behavior usually improves long before corresponding attitudes toward members of the out-group begin to change.

Again, this is to be expected in light of the underlying psychological processes. Behavior is more frequently under Ego control than is attitude. Attitude reflects, in large part, the less conscious part of the personality, a level at which change is more complex and difficult. It also seems reasonable for a change in behavior to stimulate a change in attitude, if for no other reason than that flagrant inconsistency between what one does and what one thinks is uncomfortable for most people.

Thus far we have considered the role the unconscious plays in creating overtly racist attitudes. But how is the unconscious involved when racial prejudice is less apparent—when racial bias is hidden from the prejudiced individual as well as from others? Increasingly, as our culture has rejected racism as immoral and unproductive, this hidden prejudice has become the more prevalent form of racism. The individual's Ego must adapt to a cultural order that views overtly racist attitudes and behavior as unsophisticated, uninformed, and immoral. It must repress or disguise racist ideas when they seek expression.

* * *

C. A Cognitive Approach to Unconscious Racism

Cognitive psychologists offer a contrasting model for understanding the origin and unconscious nature of racial prejudice. This is essentially a rational model. The cognitivists acknowledge the importance of emotional and motivational factors, but they do not embrace the Freudian belief that instinctive drives dominate individuals' concepts, attitudes, and beliefs. Instead, they view human behavior, including racial prejudice, as growing out of the individual's attempt to understand his relationship with the world (in this case, relations between groups) while at the same time preserving his personal integrity. But while the ultimate goal of the cognitive process is understanding or rationality, many of the critical elements of the process occur outside of the individual's awareness. This is especially true when there is tension between the individual's desire for simplification and the complexity of the real world or conflict between an understanding of a situation that preserves the individual's self-image and one that jeopardizes a positive view of himself.

Cognitivists see the process of "categorization" as one common source of racial and other stereotypes. All humans tend to categorize in order to make sense of experience. Too many events occur daily for us to deal successfully with each one on an individual basis; we must categorize in order to cope. When a category—for example, the category of black person or white person—correlates with a continuous dimension—for example, the range of human intelligence or the propensity to violence—there is a tendency to exaggerate the differences between categories on that dimension and to minimize the differences within each category.

The more important a particular classification of people into groups is to an individual, the more likely she is to distinguish sharply the characteristics of people who belong to the different groups. Here, cognitivists integrate the observations of personality theorists and social psychologists with their own. If an individual is hostile toward a group of people, she has an emotional investment in preserving the differentiations between her own group and the "others." Thus, the preservation of inaccurate judgments about the out-group is self-rewarding. This is particularly so when prejudiced judgments are made in a social context that accepts and encourages negative attitudes toward the outgroup. In these cases, the group judgment reinforces and helps maintain the individual judgment about the out-group's lack of worth.

The content of the social categories to which people are assigned is generated over a long period of time within a culture and transmitted to individual members of society by a process cognitivists call "assimilation." Assimilation entails learning and internalizing preferences and evaluations. Individuals learn cultural attitudes and beliefs about race very early in life, at a time when it is difficult to separate the perceptions of one's teacher (usually a parent) from one's own. In other words, one learns about race at a time when one is highly sensitive to the social contexts in which one lives.

Piaget, in his work on the development of moral judgment in children, described the transition from the stage when children judge pronouncements by their source rather than their content to the stage when children begin to cooperate with equals and to take the role of the other. This ability to see the same data from more than one point of view is the basis of intellectual and moral development. According to Piaget, this transition cannot take place when a child is exposed to only one source of information. These pretransition conditions, when the child remains in awe of the source of truth, tend to be precisely the conditions under which children learn socially sanctioned truths about race. Lessons learned at this early developmental stage are not questioned: They are learned as facts rather than as points of view.

Furthermore, because children learn lessons about race at this early stage, most of the lessons are tacit rather than explicit. Children learn not so much through an intellectual understanding of what their parents tell them about race as through an emotional identification with who their parents are and what they see and feel their parents do. Small children will adopt their parents' beliefs because they experience them as their own. If we do learn lessons about race in this way, we are not likely to be aware that the lessons have even taken place. If we are unaware that we have been taught to be afraid of blacks or to think of them as lazy or stupid, then we may not be conscious of our internalization of those feelings and beliefs.

All of these processes, most of which occur outside the actor's consciousness, are mutually reinforcing. Furthermore, there is little in our environment to counteract them; indeed, our culture often supports and rewards individuals for making hostile misjudgments that exaggerate the differences between themselves and members of a racial outgroup. Cultural prejudice also removes the possibility of checking judgments against outside reality, further inhibiting the chance that the holder of a prejudiced belief will perceive his mistake and correct it. Thus, through personal and cultural experience the individual comes to associate characteristics such as "intelligence," "laziness," "honesty," or "dirtiness" with classifications of people. In ambiguous social situations, it will always be easier to find evidence supporting an individual's assumed group characteristics than to find contradictory evidence. Furthermore, whenever one is confronted with the need to interpret the behavior of members of a particular group en masse, there will be little opportunity to observe behavior that conflicts with the group's assumed characteristics.

Case studies have demonstrated that an individual who holds stereotyped beliefs about a "target" will remember and interpret past events in the target's life history in ways that bolster and support his stereotyped beliefs and will perceive the target's actual behavior as reconfirming and validating the stereotyped beliefs. While the individual may be aware of the selectively perceived facts that support his categorization or simplified understanding, he will not be aware of the process that has caused him to deselect the facts that do not conform with his rationalization. Thus, racially prejudiced behavior that is actually the product of learned cultural preferences is experienced as a reflection of rational deduction from objective observation, which is nonprejudicial behavior. The decisionmaker who is unaware of the selective perception that has produced her stereotype will not view it as a stereotype. She will believe that her actions are motivated not by racial prejudice but by her attraction or aversion to the attributes she has "observed" in the groups she has favored or disfavored.

D. *Unconscious Racism in Everyday Life*

Whatever our preferred theoretical analysis, there is considerable commonsense evidence from our everyday experience to confirm that we all harbor prejudiced attitudes that are kept from our consciousness.

When, for example, a well-known sports broadcaster is carried away by the excitement of a brilliant play by an Afro-American professional football player and refers to the player as a "little monkey" during a nationally televised broadcast, we have witnessed the prototypical parapraxes, or unintentional slip of the tongue. This sportscaster views himself as progressive on issues of race. Many of his most important professional associates are black, and he would no doubt profess that more than a few are close friends. After the incident, he initially claimed no memory of it and then, when confronted with videotaped evidence, apologized and said that no racial slur was intended. There is no reason to doubt the sincerity of his assertion. Why would he intentionally risk antagonizing his audience and damaging his reputation and career? But his inadvertent slip of the tongue was not random. It is evidence of the continuing presence of a derogatory racial stereotype that he has repressed from consciousness and that has momentarily slipped past his Ego's censors. Likewise, when Nancy Reagan appeared before a public gathering of then-presidential-candidate Ronald Reagan's political supporters and said that she wished he could be there to "see all these beautiful white people," one can hardly imagine that it was her self-conscious intent to proclaim publicly her preference for the company of Caucasians.

Incidents of this kind are not uncommon, even if only the miscues of the powerful and famous are likely to come to the attention of the press. But because the unconscious also influences selective perceptions, whites are unlikely to hear many of the inadvertent racial slights that are made daily in their presence.

* * *

II. A TALE OF TWO THEORIES

The second likely challenge to my proposal acknowledges the existence of unconscious racism but questions whether it is important or even useful to take it into account in interpreting and applying the equal protection clause. This question can best be answered by posing a more general question: What is the wrong that the equal protection clause seeks to address? More specifically, what wrong do we seek to address in applying heightened scrutiny to racial classifications? If we can determine the nature of this wrong, we can determine whether identifying the existence of unconscious racial motivation is important to its prevention or remediation.

Two theories have attempted to specify the central function of suspect classification doctrine. The first, the "process defect" theory, sees the judicial intervention occasioned by strict scrutiny of suspect classifications as an appropriate response to distortions in the democratic process. The second theory cites racial stigma as the primary target of suspect classification doctrine. By examining whether and why the determination of self-conscious motive is important to each of these theories, we will be able to determine whether recognizing the presence of unconscious motive furthers the central rationale of each theory.

A. *The Process Defect Theory*

The chief proponent of the process defect theory has been John Ely. He identifies the systematic exclusion of a group from the normal workings of the political process as the harm that heightened judicial scrutiny for suspect classifications seeks to prevent or remedy. The theory begins with Justice Stone's *Carolene Products* footnote four, which states that "discrete and insular" minorities deserve special constitutional protection. . . .

Motive and intent are at the center of Ely's theory. The function of suspect classification doctrine is to expose unconstitutional motives that may have distorted the process. A statute that classifies by race is strictly scrutinized, because the requirement of "close fit" between end sought and means used will reveal those instances where the actual motive of the legislature was to disadvantage a group simply because of its race.

Under present doctrine, the courts look for Ely's process defect only when the racial classification appears on the face of the statute or when self-conscious racial intent has been proved under the *Davis* test. But the same process distortions will occur even when the racial prejudice is less apparent. Other groups in the body politic may avoid coalition with blacks without a conscious awareness of their aversion to blacks or of their association of certain characteristics with blacks. They may take stands on issues without realizing that their reasons are, in part, racially oriented. Likewise, the governmental decisionmaker may be unaware that she has devalued the cost of a chosen path, because a group with which she does not identify will bear that cost. Indeed, because of her lack of empathy with the group, she may have never even thought of the cost at all.

Process distortion exists where the unconstitutional motive of racial prejudice has influenced the decision. It matters not that the decisionmaker's motive may lie outside her awareness. For example, in *Village of Arlington Heights v. Metropolitan Housing Development Corp.*, a predominantly white, upper middle class Chicago suburb prevented the construction of a proposed housing development for low and moderate income families by refusing to rezone the projected site to allow multifamily units. The Supreme Court agreed that the decision not to rezone had racially discriminatory effects, but it rejected the black plaintiffs' equal protection claim on the ground that they had "simply failed to carry their burden of proving that discriminatory purpose was a motivating factor in the Village's decision." The Court focused on the lack of any evidence of conscious intent to discriminate on the part of either the city council in enacting the zoning ordinance that restricted use to single family homes or the planning commission in administering the ordinance.

We can envision several possible scenarios that demonstrate the possible process-distorting effects of unconscious racism on a governmental decision like that in *Arlington Heights*:

(1) The city council refused to rezone for the sole purpose of stigmatizing and denying housing to blacks. This case resembles *Plessy v. Ferguson* and *Gomillion v. Lightfoot*, in which the only motives were unconstitutional, and the ordinances were, therefore, per se unconstitutional.

(2) The city claims a legitimate economic or environmental purpose, but evidence shows that it sought to exclude blacks in order to achieve that purpose. This case is the same as a classification by race on the face of a statute for which a legitimate goal is claimed. It is the case Ely describes where blacks are consciously excluded from the political process and deval-

ued in the assessment of costs and benefits. When this self-conscious motive can be proved, the resulting classification is subject to strict scrutiny under existing doctrine.

(3) The purpose of the ordinance was economic—i.e., to keep property values up by keeping poor people out—but the decisionmakers associated poverty with blacks and would have weighed the costs and benefits differently if the poor people they envisioned excluding were elderly white people on social security. This "selective sympathy or indifference" could have occurred at a conscious or unconscious level. It is more than likely that the decision-makers knew that the poor people they were excluding were black, but they would not be likely to have known that they undervalued the cost to poor people because they thought of them as black rather than white.

(4) A constituency within Arlington Heights—for example, elderly whites—did not actively campaign for the rezoning because of aversion to blacks who might have benefitted from it. This occurred despite the fact that this constituency's interest in low income housing would otherwise have outweighed its interest in property values. This inability or unwillingness to apprehend and act upon an overlapping interest is precisely the kind of process distortion through group vilification that Ely describes. It is as likely as not that these elderly voters are largely unaware of the vilification and resulting aversion that preempted their potential coalition with blacks.

(5) No one in Arlington Heights thought about blacks one way or the other—i.e., it was a fight between environmentalists and developers—but an inadvertent devaluing of black interests caused inattention to the costs blacks would have to bear. If one asked the decisionmakers how they had valued the cost to blacks of the exclusionary zoning, they might have responded, "I never thought of that." This is an example of selective indifference or misapprehension of costs that occurs entirely outside of consciousness.

The process defect theory sees suspect classification doctrine as a roundabout way of uncovering unconstitutional motive by suspecting those classifications that disadvantage groups we know to be the object of widespread vilification. But by only suspecting laws that classify by race on their face or are the result of overtly self-conscious racial motivation, the theory stops an important step short of locating and eliminating the defect it has identified. Where a society has recently adopted a moral ethic that repudiates racial disadvantaging for its own sake, governmental decisionmakers are as likely to repress their racial motives as they are to lie to courts or to attempt after-the-fact rationalizations of classifications that are not racial on their face but that do have disproportionate racial impact. Unconscious aversion to a group that has historically been vilified distorts the political process no less than a conscious decision to place race hatred before politically legitimate goals.

Moreover, unconscious prejudice presents an additional problem in that it is not subject to self-correction within the political process. When racism operates at a conscious level, opposing forces can attempt to prevail upon the rationality and moral sensibility of racism's proponents; the self-professed racist may even find religion on the road to Damascus and correct his own ways. But when the discriminator is not aware of his prejudice and is convinced that he already walks in the path of righteousness, neither reason nor moral persuasion is likely to succeed. The process defect is all the more intractable, and judicial scrutiny becomes imperative.

B. *The Stigma Theory*

A second theory posits elimination of racially stigmatizing actions as the central concern of the equal protection clause. Under this theory, racial classifications should be strictly scrutinized when they operate to shame and degrade a class of persons by labeling it as inferior. Stigmatization is the process by which the dominant group in society differentiates itself from others by setting them apart, treating them as less than fully human, denying them acceptance by the organized community, and excluding them from participating in that community as equals. If the equal protection clause guarantees the right to be treated as an equal, "the constitutional claim in question can be reduced to a claim to be free from stigma." This theory acknowledges a historical experience in which the dominant group has systematically used stigmatizing labels against blacks and other nonwhites and has developed a social system of laws, practices, and cultural mores that looks down upon these groups, treating them as different from, and inferior to, the norm.

The prevention of stigma was at the core of the Supreme Court's unanimous declaration in *Brown v. Board of Education* that segregated public schools are inherently unequal. In observing that the segregation of black pupils "generates a feeling of inferiority as to their status in the community," Chief Justice Warren recognized what a majority of the Court had ignored almost sixty years earlier in *Plessy v. Ferguson*: The social meaning of racial segregation in the United States is the designation of a superior and an inferior caste, and segregation proceeds "on the ground that colored citizens are . . . inferior and degraded."

Stigmatizing actions harm the individual in two ways: They inflict psychological injury by assaulting a person's self-respect and human dignity, and they brand the individual with a sign that signals her inferior status to others and designates her as an outcast. The stigma theory recognizes the importance of both self-esteem and the respect of others for participating in society's benefits and responsibilities.

Proponents of this theory have also observed that racial stigma is self-perpetuating. Labeling blacks as inferior denies them access to societal opportunities; as a result, inadequate educational preparation, poverty of experience, and insufficient basic necessities limit their ability to contribute to society, and the prophecy of their inferiority is fulfilled. Furthermore, separate incidents of racial stigmatization do not inflict isolated injuries but are part of a mutually reinforcing and pervasive pattern of stigmatizing actions that cumulate to compose an injurious whole that is greater than the sum of its parts.

The injury of stigmatization consists of forcing the injured individual to wear a badge or symbol that degrades him in the eyes of society. But in most cases the symbol is not inherently pejorative. Rather, the message obtains its shameful meaning from the historical and cultural context in which it is used and, ultimately, from the way it is interpreted by those who witness it. Thus the woman who is asked to use a separate public bathroom from her husband is unlikely to be stigmatized by that action: Our society does not ordinarily interpret sex-segregated toilet facilities as designating the inferiority of women. By contrast, the black who is asked to use a different public bathroom from that of a white companion of the same gender is stigmatized. As Richard Wasserstrom has noted, racially segregated bathrooms were an important part of the system of segregation. That system's ideology held not only that blacks were less than fully human but also that they were dirty and impure. Racially segregated bathrooms ensured that blacks would not contaminate the facilities used by whites.

If stigmatizing actions injure by virtue of the meaning society gives them, then it should be apparent that the evil intent of their authors, while perhaps sufficient, is not necessary to the infliction of the injury. For example, a well-meaning if misguided white employer, having observed that her black employees usually sat together at lunch, might build a separate dining room for them with the intent of making them more comfortable. This action would stigmatize her black employees despite her best intentions. Similarly, when the city of Jackson, Mississippi closed its public pools after a federal court ordered it to integrate them, the action stigmatized blacks regardless of whether the government's purpose was racial or economic.

Given that stigma occurs whether there is racial animus or not, the answer to our initial question, "Is knowledge about the intent of the governmental actor significant to the achievement of the equal protection clause's purpose?" would seem an obvious "No." But many of the stigma theory's advocates find themselves in a quandary when faced with the question of how the Court should approach laws that are not apparently "race-dependent" but that result in disparate and stigmatizing effects. Kenneth Karst, for example, notes the Supreme Court's recent inhospitality to constitutional claims of disproportionate effect and argues that "[s]urely it is still a responsible from of advocacy to argue that some racially disproportionate effects of governmental action ought to be subjected to judicial scrutiny at a level higher than minimum rationality." He does not, however, elaborate on how the Court should determine which cases to include among that "some." Moreover, the origin of his reluctance to advocate increased scrutiny of all racially discriminatory impact lies in the disproportionate presence of blacks among the poor. He argues that, because the persistence of a racially identifiable economic underclass is probably beyond the capacity of courts to remedy, it is unrealistic to expect the Supreme Court to endorse this increased use of strict scrutiny in the near future.

Similarly, Paul Brest, having persuasively argued the need to eliminate racially disproportionate impact that stigmatizes, cautions that the impact doctrine "cannot reasonably be applied across the board" and urges that the doctrine be used "selectively." He warns that "remedies for disproportionate impact may impose heavy costs on institutions and individuals, and cannot be tailored narrowly to compensate all those and only those whose present situation is the result of past discrimination." Brest's reference to the overbreadth of remedies for disproportionate impact adds to the general concern about unduly limiting legislative discretion and the particular concern about the legitimacy of courts imposing costs on "blameless" individuals and conferring benefits on those who have not been directly harmed.

The consideration of unconscious intent responds to both of these concerns. Identifying stigmatizing actions that were affected by the actor's unconscious racial attitudes achieves two benefits. First, it significantly decreases the absolute number of impact cases subject to heightened scrutiny without eviscerating the substantive content of the equal protection clause. The bridge toll, the sales tax, and the filing fee can no longer be numbered among the parade of horribles that Justice White suggested in *Davis*. At the same time, cases where racially discriminatory impact results directly from past intentional discrimination or from current but unprovable racial animus will be well within judicial reach. A law does not stigmatize blacks simply because exclusion itself is stigmatizing, and, in this instance, they are disproportionately represented among the excluded group. Instead, the stigma stems at least in part from society's predisposition to exclude blacks. The fact that unconscious racial attitudes affected a governmental action is evidence that the racially stigmatizing symbolism preexisted the present impact.

Second, consideration of unconscious motivation provides a neutral principle for judicial intervention—i.e., the identification of a process defect. This counters the argument made against the impact test that the judiciary has no principled basis for imposing a priority for the removal of racial stigma over other social goods to which the political branch might choose to give preeminence. In short, stigma often occurs regardless of the intent of those who have engaged in the stigmatizing action. Thus, it is arguable that under the stigma theory neither conscious nor unconscious intent should be considered, and heightened judicial scrutiny should apply in all cases when governmental action produces a stigmatizing effect. Nonetheless, recognizing unconscious racism provides a mechanism for effectively responding to continuing race-based inequalities while minimizing the costs of judicial overreaching.

While the cultural meaning test identifies the same elements of the injury of racial discrimination as does the stigma theory, it differs from that theory in two regards. First, it identifies the injury at a different point in the constitutional analysis. The stigma theory explains why recognized racial classifications—i.e., laws whose racial classification is apparent on their face or laws whose racial motive has been proved—should be subject to heightened judicial scrutiny. In noting that the harm of stigma occurs irrespective of the presence of conscious motive, the cultural meaning test refocuses the stigma theory's inquiry to a different point in time. The presence of racial stigma is viewed as evidence of the existence of a racial classification, not simply as a justification for the heightened scrutiny of such classifications.

Second, the cultural meaning test adds content to the stigma theory's analysis. It locates the origin of racial stigma in the accumulation of the individual unconscious and finds the origin of unconscious racism in the presence of widely shared, tacitly transmitted cultural values. The recognition of these mutually reciprocal origins joins the theoretical description of human action as arising out of autonomous individual choice with the view that such action is socially determined. The cultural meaning theory thus describes a dialectic rather than a dichotomy. It demonstrates that ultimately the proponents of the process defect theory and the stigma theory have identified different manifestations of the same cultural phenomenon.

III. READING THE MIND'S SYMBOLS: HOW DO WE IDENTIFY UNCONSCIOUS RACISM IN SPECIFIC CASES?

A. *The "Cultural Meaning" Test*

This article's discussion of the stigma theory has anticipated the third likely challenge to my thesis that equal protection doctrine must address the unconscious racism that underlies much of the racially disproportionate impact of governmental policy. This challenge questions how a court would identify those cases where unconscious racism operated in order to determine whether to subject an allegedly discriminatory act to strict scrutiny.

I propose a test that would look to the "cultural meaning" of an allegedly racially discriminatory act as the best available analogue for and evidence of the collective unconscious that we cannot observe directly. This test would evaluate governmental conduct to see if it conveys a symbolic message to which the culture attaches racial significance. The court would analyze governmental behavior much like a cultural anthropologist might: by considering evidence regarding the historical and social context in which the decision was made and effectuated. If the court determined by a preponderance of the evidence that a significant portion of the population thinks of the governmental action in racial terms, then it would presume that socially shared, unconscious racial attitudes made evident by the action's meaning had influenced the decisionmakers. As a result, it would apply heightened scrutiny.

* * *

Thus, an action such as the construction of a wall between white and black communities in Memphis would have a cultural meaning growing out of a long history of whites' need to separate themselves from blacks as a symbol of their superiority. Individual members of the city council might well have been unaware that their continuing need to maintain their superiority over blacks, or their failure to empathize with how construction of the wall would make blacks feel, influenced their decision. But if one were to ask even the most self-deluded among them what the residents of Memphis would take the existence of the wall to mean, the obvious answer would be difficult to avoid. If one told the story leading to the wall's construction while omitting one vital fact—the race of those whose vehicular traffic the barrier excluded—and then asked Memphis citizens to describe the residents of the community claiming injury, few, if any, would not guess that they were black.

The current racial meanings of governmental actions are strong evidence that the process defects of group vilification and misapprehension of costs and benefits have occurred whether or not the decisionmakers were conscious that race played a part in their decisionmaking. Moreover, actions that have racial meaning within the culture are also those actions that carry a stigma for which we should have special concern. This is not the stigma that occurs only because of a coincidental congruence between race and poverty. The association of a symbol with race is a residuum of overtly racist practices in the past: The wall conjures up racial inferiority, not the inferiority of the poor or the undesirability of vehicular traffic. And stigma that has racial meaning burdens all blacks and adds to the pervasive, cumulative, and mutually reinforcing system of racial discrimination.

* * *

E. *Applying the Cultural Meaning Test*

* * *

1. *When "bad" means "good": conflicting cultural meanings.*

An initial difficulty with applying the cultural meaning test arises from the fact that we are not a monolithic culture. There may be instances in which governmental action is given different meanings by two subcultures within the larger culture. For example, the court might find that blacks see the decision to fund AFDC recipients at lower levels than other need-categories in racial terms while whites do not, or the court may find that people in northern urban areas give racial meaning to restrictions on federally funded abortions while people in southern rural areas do not.

The easiest solution to this problem is to acknowledge racial meaning for constitutional purposes only when the evidence indicates that the racial understanding will be widely shared within the predominant culture. This solution is better than the *Davis/Arlington Heights* intent test in that, at a minimum, it will correctly identify unconscious intent in cases like *Memphis v. Greene* or even *Arlington Heights.*

2. *The blind interpreting for the blind: the problem of judicial bias.*

A second difficulty with the cultural meaning test rests in the inevitable cultural biases of judges. Judges are not immune from our culture's racism, nor can they escape the psychological mechanisms that render us all, to some extent, unaware of our racist beliefs.

We must recognize, however, that this difficulty inheres in all judicial interpretation. The advantage of the cultural meaning test is that it makes the issue of culturally induced bias explicit. The judge who is hearing evidence regarding how our history and culture have influenced our racial beliefs is more likely to be made aware of his own heretofore unrecognized biases. Judges continue to come primarily from elite white backgrounds. They undoubtedly share the values and perceptions of that subculture, which may well be insensitive or even antagonistic toward the values, needs, and experiences of blacks and other minorities. The benefit of the cultural meaning test is that it confronts judges with this conflict and forces them to take responsibility for their own biases and preconceptions.

3. *"Media meaning": the problem of the self-fulfilling prophecy.*

A third difficulty in applying the cultural meaning test arises where the parties, particularly the plaintiffs, create a racial issue where there seemingly was none. How, for example, should a court treat a challenge to a state bar exam where the racial issues were not apparent until mass demonstrations or a media campaign attracted public attention to them? Again, the answer must be found in the sophistication of the interpretive process. Is the newfound awareness of the racial issue merely a result of media hype, or has the media campaign succeeded because it has touched a cultural nerve lying just below the surface of our consciousness?

Each of these potential problems indicates that the cultural meaning test will not create an easily recognizable bright line for judges to follow. The test's advantage lies not so much in its ease of application as in its ability to spotlight the source of injury in cases of racial discrimination: the unconscious racism that continues to pervade our culture and influence our decisionmaking.

* * *

CONCLUSION

Ultimately, the greatest stumbling block to any proposal to modify the intent requirement will not be its lack of jurisprudential efficacy but the perception among those who give substance to our jurisprudence that it will operate against their self-interest. Derrick Bell has noted that the interests of blacks in achieving racial equality have been accommodated only when they have converged with the interests of powerful whites: The legal establishment has not responded to civil rights claims that threaten the superior societal status of upper and middle class whites. Alan Freeman has argued persuasively for the more radical proposition that antidiscrimination law has affirmatively advanced racism by promoting an ideology that justifies the continued economic subjugation of blacks. The intent requirement is a centerpiece in an ideology of equal opportunity that legitimizes the continued existence of racially and economically discriminatory conditions and rationalizes the superordinate status of privileged whites.

* * *

I do not anticipate that either the Supreme Court or the academic establishment will rush to embrace and incorporate the approach this article proposes. It has not been my purpose to advance an analysis that is attractive for its ease of application or for its failure to challenge accepted and comfortable ways of thinking about equal protection and race. Rather, it is my hope that the preliminary thoughts expressed in the preceding pages will stimulate others to think about racism in a new way and will provoke a discussion of how equal protection doctrine can best incorporate this understanding of racism.

This article has argued that judicial exploration of the cultural meaning of governmental actions with racially discriminatory impact is the best way to discover the unconscious racism of governmental actors. This exploration will be beset by the complexities and inadequacies of social interpretation and buffeted by the head winds of political resistance. Perhaps I am overly optimistic in believing that in the process of this difficult exploration we may discover and understand a collective self-interest that overshadows the multitude of parochial self-interests the unconscious seeks to disguise and shield. But of one thing I am certain. A difficult and painful exploration beats death at the hands of the disease.

Barbara J. Flagg, "Was Blind, but Now I See": White Race Consciousness and the Requirement of Discriminatory Intent, 91 MICH. L. REV. 953 (1993)*

Advocating race consciousness is unthinkable for most white liberals. We define our position on the continuum of racism by the degree of our commitment to colorblindness; the more certain we are that race is never relevant to any assessment of an individual's abilities or achievements, the more certain we are that we have overcome racism as we conceive of it. This way of thinking about race is a matter of principle as well as a product of historical experience. It reflects the traditional liberal view that the autonomous individual, whose existence is analytically prior to that of society, ought never be credited with, nor blamed for, personal characteristics not under her own control, such as gender or race, or group membership or social status that is a consequence of birth rather than individual choice or accomplishment. The colorblindness principle also grows out of the historical development of race relations in the United States, in which, until quite recently, race-specific classifications have been the primary means of maintaining the supremacy of whites. In reaction to that experience, whites of good will tend to equate racial justice with the disavowal of race-conscious criteria of classification.

Nevertheless, the pursuit of colorblindness progressively reveals itself to be an inadequate social policy if the ultimate goal is substantive racial justice. Blacks continue to inhabit a very different America than do whites. They experience higher rates of poverty and unemployment and are more likely to live in environmentally undesirable locations than whites. They have more frequent and more severe medical problems, higher mortality rates, and receive less comprehensive health care than whites. Blacks continue disproportionately to attend inferior and inadequate primary and secondary schools. Proportionately fewer blacks than whites complete college, and those who do so still confront the "glass ceiling" after graduation. Blacks are no better off by many of these measures than they were twenty years ago, and in the recent past even the colorblindness principle itself, once seen as a promise of a brighter future for blacks, has been deployed instead to block further black economic progress.

Arguments that race consciousness has a positive face have begun to appear in the legal literature. Critical race theorists in particular have focused on the salience

---

*   Reprinted with permission.

of race to legal analysis, arguing compellingly that race does and should matter in all aspects of the law, from legal doctrine and theory to the conduct of legal education and the composition of the legal academy. Many of these authors have articulated critiques of colorblindness in the course of developing the critical perspective on race. . . .

The most striking characteristic of whites' consciousness of whiteness is that most of the time we don't have any. I call this the transparency phenomenon: the tendency of whites not to think about whiteness, or about norms, behaviors, experiences, or perspectives that are white-specific. Transparency often is the mechanism through which white decisionmakers who disavow white supremacy impose white norms on blacks. Transparency operates to require black assimilation even when pluralism is the articulated goal; it affords substantial advantages to whites over blacks even when decisionmakers intend to effect substantive racial justice.

Reconceptualizing white race consciousness means doing the hard work of developing a positive white racial identity, one neither founded on the implicit acceptance of white racial domination nor productive of distributive effects that systematically advantage whites. One step in that process is the deconstruction of transparency in the context of white decisionmaking. We can work to make explicit the unacknowledged whiteness of facially neutral criteria of decision, and we can adopt strategies that counteract the influence of unrecognized white norms. These approaches permit white decisionmakers to incorporate pluralist means of achieving our aims, and thus to contribute to the dismantling of white supremacy. Making nonobvious white norms explicit, and thus exposing their contingency, can begin to define for white people a coequal role in a racially diverse society.

In constitutional law, facially race-neutral criteria of decision that carry a racially disproportionate impact violate the Equal Protection Clause only if adopted with a racially discriminatory intent. This rule provides an excellent vehicle for reconsidering white race consciousness, because it perfectly reflects the prevailing white ideology of colorblindness and the concomitant failure of whites to scrutinize the whiteness of facially neutral norms. In addition, the discriminatory intent rule is the existing doctrinal means of regulating facially neutral government decisionmaking. When government imposes transparently white norms it participates actively in the maintenance of white supremacy, a stance I understand the Fourteenth Amendment to prohibit. We need, therefore, to reevaluate the existing discriminatory intent rule from the perspective of the transparency phenomenon, and to consider a revised approach to disparate impact cases that implements the insights gained from that reassessment.

* * *

I. THE REQUIREMENT OF DISCRIMINATORY INTENT

* * *

One relatively simple explanation for the stability of the requirement of discriminatory purpose is its intuitive appeal, or more precisely the appeal of the principles it embodies. Colorblindness is extremely attractive to white liberals, and process theory's promise to regulate only the inputs to legislative decisionmaking, but not the substance of the resulting decisions, is extremely attractive to jurists confronting the countermajoritarian difficulty. But there is, I think, another explanation: the *Davis* rule reflects a distinctively white way of thinking about race.

First, white people tend to view intent as an essential element of racial harm; nonwhites do not. The white perspective can be, and frequently is, expressed succinctly and without any apparent perceived need for justification: "[W]ithout concern about past and present intent, racially discriminatory effects of legislation would be quite innocent." For black people, however, the fact of racial oppression exists largely independent of the motives or intentions of its perpetrators. Second, both in principle and in application the *Davis* rule presupposes the existence of race-neutral decisionmaking. Whites' level of confidence in race neutrality is much greater than nonwhites'; a skeptic (nonwhite, more likely than not) would not adopt a rule that presumes the neutrality of criteria of decision absent the specific intent to do racial harm. Finally, retaining the intent requirement in the face of its demonstrated failure to effectuate substantive racial justice is indicative of a complacency concerning, or even a commitment to, the racial status quo that can only be enjoyed by those who are its beneficiaries - by white people.

A raised white consciousness of race would produce a very different rule in disparate impact cases. In particular, white people who take seriously the transparency phenomenon, and who want to foster racial justice, will look for ways to diffuse transparency's effects and to relativize previously unrecognized white norms. Existing doctrinal tools are adequate, in large measure, to accomplish these goals, if they are tailored to correct the evil of transparency. The process of reconstructing a disparate impact rule must begin, however, with a careful examination of the transparency phenomenon.

II. DECONSTRUCTING RACE NEUTRALITY

In this Part the white reader is invited to reexamine her customary ways of thinking about whiteness and, consequently, to reevaluate her attitude toward the concept of race-neutral decisionmaking. There is a profound cognitive dimension to the material and social privilege that attaches to whiteness in this society, in that the white person has an everyday option not to think of herself in racial terms at all. In fact, whites appear to pursue that option so habitually that it may be a defining characteristic of whiteness: to be white is not to think about it. I label the tendency for whiteness to vanish from whites' self-perception the transparency phenomenon.

A. *The Transparency Phenomenon*

* * *

White people externalize race. For most whites, most of the time, to think or speak about race is to think or speak about people of color, or perhaps, at times, to reflect on oneself (or other whites) in relation to people of color. But we tend not to think of ourselves or our racial cohort as racially distinctive. Whites' "consciousness" of whiteness is predominantly unconsciousness of whiteness. We perceive and interact with other whites as individuals who have no significant racial characteristics. In the same vein, the white person is unlikely to see or describe himself in racial terms, perhaps in part because his white peers do not regard him as racially distinctive. Whiteness is a transparent quality when whites interact with whites in the absence of people of color. Whiteness attains opacity, becomes apparent to the white mind, only in relation to, and contrast with, the "color" of nonwhites.

I do not mean to claim that white people are oblivious to the race of other whites. Race is undeniably a powerful determinant of social status and so is always noticed, in a way that eye color, for example, may not be. However, whites' social dominance allows us to relegate our own racial specificity to the realm of the subconscious. Whiteness is the racial norm. In this culture the black person, not the white, is the one who is different. The black, not the white, is racially distinctive. Once an individual is identified as white, his distinctively racial characteristics need no longer be conceptualized in racial terms; he becomes effectively raceless in the eyes of other whites. Whiteness is always a salient personal characteristic, but once identified, it fades almost instantaneously from white consciousness into transparency.

The best "evidence" for the pervasiveness of the transparency phenomenon will be the white reader's own experience: critically assessing our habitual ways of thinking about ourselves and about other white people should bring transparency into full view. The questions that follow may provide some direction for the reader's reflections.

In what situations do you describe yourself as white? Would you be likely to include white on a list of three adjectives that describe you? Do you think about your race as a factor in the way other whites treat you? For example, think about the last time some white clerk or salesperson treated you deferentially, or the last time the first taxi to come along stopped for you. Did you think, "That wouldn't have happened if I weren't white"? Are you conscious of yourself as white when you find yourself in a room occupied only by white people? What if there are people of color present? What if the room is mostly nonwhite?

Do you attribute your successes or failures in life to your whiteness? Do you reflect on the ways your educational and occupational opportunities have been enhanced by your whiteness? What about the life courses of others? In your experience, at the time of Justice Souter's nomination, how much attention did his race receive in conversations among whites about his abilities and prospects for confirmation? Did you or your white acquaintances speculate on the ways his whiteness might have contributed to his success, how his race may have affected his character and personality, or how his whiteness might pre-dispose him to a racially skewed perspective on legal issues?

If your lover or spouse is white, how frequently do you reflect on that fact? Do you think of your white friends as your white friends, other than in contrast with your friends who are not white? Do you try to understand the ways your shared whiteness affects the interactions between yourself and your white partner, friends, and acquaintances? For example, perhaps you have become aware of the absence of people of color on some occasion. Did you move beyond that moment of recognition to consider how the group's uniform whiteness affected its interactions, agenda, process, or decisions? Do you inquire about the ways white persons you know have dealt with the fact, and privilege, of their whiteness?

Imagine that I am describing to you a third individual who is not known to you. I say, for example, "She's good looking, but rather quiet," or "He's tall, dark, and handsome." If I do not specify the race of the person so described, is it not culturally appropriate, and expected, for you to assume she or he is white?

B. *Race-Neutral Decisionmaking*

* * *

Transparency casts doubt on the concept of race-neutral decisionmaking. Facially neutral criteria of decision formulated and applied by whites may be as vulnerable to the transparency phenomenon as is the race of white people itself. This Part suggests that whites should respond to the transparency phenomenon with a deliberate skepticism concerning race neutrality.

At a minimum, transparency counsels that we not accept seemingly neutral criteria of decision at face value. Most whites live and work in settings that are wholly or predominantly white. Thus whites rely on primarily white referents in formulating the norms and expectations that become criteria of decision for white decisionmakers. Given whites' tendency not to be aware of whiteness, it's unlikely that white decisionmakers do not similarly misidentify as race-neutral personal characteristics, traits, and behaviors that are in fact closely associated with whiteness. . . .

* * *

I recommend instead that whites adopt a deliberate and thorough-going skepticism regarding the race neutrality of facially neutral criteria of decision. This stance has the potential to improve the distribution across races of goods and power that whites currently control. In addition, skepticism may help to foster the development of a positive white racial identity that does not posit whites as superior to blacks.

* * *

Even when he looks for it, however, the white decisionmaker may not always be able to uncover the hidden racial content of the criteria he employs. In those instances, the skeptical stance may function to promote distributive justice in two different ways. First, the skeptical decisionmaker may opt to temper his judgment with a simultaneous acknowledgment of his uncertainty concerning nonobvious racial specificity. . . .

Second, white decisionmakers might choose to develop pluralistic criteria of decision as a prophylactic against covert white specificity. . . .

The skeptical stance may contribute to the development of a positive white racial identity by relativizing white norms. Even whites who do not harbor any conscious or unconscious belief in the superiority of white people participate in the maintenance of white supremacy whenever we impose white norms without acknowledging their whiteness. Any serious effort to dismantle white supremacy must include measures to dilute the effect of whites' dominant status, which carries with it the power to define as well as to decide. Because the skeptical stance prevents the unthinking imposition of white norms, it encourages white decisionmakers to consider adopting nonwhite ways of doing business, so that the formerly unquestioned white-specific criterion of decision becomes just one option among many. The skeptical stance thus can be instrumental in the development of a relativized white race consciousness, in which the white decisionmaker is conscious of the whiteness and contingency of white norms.

Most white people have no experience of a genuine cultural pluralism, one in which whites' perspectives, behavioral expectations, and values are not taken to be the standard from which all other cultural norms deviate. Whites therefore have no experiential basis for assessing the benefits of participating in a pluralist society so defined. On the assumption that prevailing egalitarian mores preclude white supremacy as a justification for the maintenance of the status quo, adopting the skeptical stance in the interest of exploring cultural pluralism seems the most appropriate course of action for any white person who acknowledges the transparency phenomenon.

III. A TRANSPARENCY-CONSCIOUS LOOK AT THE DISCRIMINATORY
       INTENT RULE

The threshold requirement that the constitutional plaintiff prove discriminatory intent operates to draw a sharp distinction between facially neutral but unconsciously race-specific instances of white decisionmaking, on the one hand, and the deliberate use of race, whether overt or covert, on the other; only the latter is constitutionally impermissible. Relying on a distinction among discriminators' states of mind seems a curious strategy for implementing the principle that the use of race as a criterion of decision is what constitutes the constitutional harm, because the racial criterion is equally present in either case. Indeed, the chosen rule appears more suited to drive the race specificity of white decisionmaking underground—out of whites' awareness—than to eradicate it altogether. However, the intent requirement might rest on either of two assumptions that, coupled with the perceived institutional costs of heightened scrutiny, provide ostensible justification for the decision to disapprove only the purposeful use of race in government decisionmaking. These foundational assumptions are, first, that unconsciously race-specific decisionmaking is relatively rare, or, second, that the conscious use of race as a factor in decisionmaking is more blameworthy than its unconscious use.

A. *The Belief in the Rarity of Unconscious Race Discrimination*

The Court's decision to adopt a discriminatory intent rule that does not reach unconscious race-specific decisionmaking might rest on a belief that such discrimination does not commonly occur. Such a belief is, perhaps, the natural corollary of whites' widespread faith in the pervasiveness of race-neutrality. This faith, for example, views Klan and other overtly white supremacist attitudes as extreme, perhaps pathological, deviations from the norm of white racial thinking, as if those attitudes can be comprehended in complete isolation from the culture in which they are embedded. Similarly, whites tend to adopt the "things are getting better" story of race relations, which allows us to suppose that our unfortunate history of socially approved race discrimination is largely behind us. This nexus of white confidence in race neutrality might dictate that the law should treat the unconscious use of nonobviously race-specific criteria of decision as nothing more than the occasional deviation from the prevailing practice of race-neutral government decisionmaking. From this perspective, given that significant institutional costs are associated with judicial intervention, unconscious race specificity seems too rare to justify heightened review.

The transparency phenomenon provides two arguments against the view that unconscious race specificity is uncommon. At minimum, it counsels that we hesitate to acquiesce in any view that accepts race neutrality at face value, whether as a matter of fact or of frequency of occurrence. Second, transparency supports the stronger, affirmative argument that unconscious race-specific decisionmaking is so common that it is in fact the norm for white decisionmakers.

The belief that race-neutral decisionmaking is relatively common and unconsciously race-specific decisionmaking relatively uncommon stands analytically distinct from the belief that any particular instance of facially neutral decisionmaking is in fact what it seems. Even if the unconscious use of race were extremely rare, whites could still misperceive the true character of every one of the few instances in which race in fact was a factor in the decision. Conversely, the fact that whites frequently are unaware of the white-specific factors that may be used in white decisionmaking does not dictate one conclusion or another regarding the frequency with which such factors actually are employed. This analytic distinction notwithstanding, transparency counsels skepticism with respect to the frequency of race-neutral decisionmaking as well.

Because the transparency phenomenon creates a risk that whites will misapprehend the race-specific nature of apparently race-neutral decisionmaking, it simultaneously creates a risk that we will systematically underestimate the incidence of such decisionmaking. Each circumstance in which we fail to perceive accurately the racial content of our decisions contributes to the overall perception that race neutrality is the more common way of doing business. Thus, even though the conclusion that race specificity is the norm does not necessarily follow from transparency alone, we ought to adopt a healthy skepticism toward, rather than a blind faith in the pervasiveness of, race neutrality if we wish to be able more accurately to assess the role of race in white decisionmaking.

Transparency also lends support to the stronger position that unconscious race-specific decisionmaking is so common that it is in fact the normal mode of white decisionmaking. This argument rests in part on an analysis of the outcomes of discretionary white decisionmaking. Numerous studies indicate that whites receive more favorable treatment than blacks in virtually every area of social interaction. The weight of the evidence supports the conclusion that race affects whites' discretionary decisionmaking in areas as diverse as hiring and performance evaluations in employment settings; mortgage lending, insurance redlining, and retail bargaining; psychiatric diagnoses; responses to patient violence in mental institutions; and virtually every stage in the criminal law process: arrest, the decision to charge, imprisonment, and capital sentencing.

* * *

B. *The Belief that Conscious Discrimination Is More Blameworthy than Unconscious Discrimination*

A second foundational belief that might be proffered to justify the line drawn by the discriminatory intent rule is that the conscious use of race-specific criteria of decision is more blameworthy than the unconscious use of race. That view is consistent with the familiar legal principle that conduct intended to cause a specified harmful result is more blameworthy than conduct that causes the same harm inadvertently. In other words, the law commonly recognizes degrees of culpability associated with different states of mind. . . .

In eschewing heightened scrutiny for racially disparate effects absent proof of discriminatory intent, the Court sends two messages that operate to legitimate unconscious race discrimination. First, the discriminatory intent rule recreates transparency at the level of constitutional doctrine, for it affords a presumption of race neutrality to facially neutral criteria of decision without regard to the possibility that those criteria in fact reflect white-specific characteristics, attitudes, or experiences. The rule tends to reassure whites that all is well so long as we avoid the conscious use of race-specific bases for decision.

The requirement of discriminatory intent also legitimates unconscious race discrimination by reinforcing a popular white story about progress in race relations. The central theme of this story is that our society has an unfortunate history of race discrimination that is largely behind us. In the past, the story goes, some unenlightened individuals practiced slavery and other forms of overt oppression of black people, but the belief in the inferiority of blacks upon which these practices were premised has almost entirely disappeared today. We, aside from the exceptional few who remain out of step with the times, think of blacks as the equals of whites and thus no longer accept race as a permissible basis for different treatment. The Court's discriminatory intent rule contributes to this dominant story insofar as it treats as blameworthy the form of race discrimination most common in the past but refuses to regard with suspicion the unconscious discrimination that is at least as significant a cause of the oppression of black people today.

The undesirable normative consequences of a rule that treats conscious race discrimination as more blameworthy than unconscious discrimination should not, however, raise the inference that the better approach would be to treat unconscious racism as equally blameworthy as conscious discrimination. The more fruitful response, I suggest, is to question the practice of blaming itself. Blaming is not an effective, empirically well-founded, or prudent way of addressing the complete range of contemporary manifestations of race discrimination.

The position implied by the discriminatory intent rule, that conscious discrimination is blameworthy but unconscious discrimination is not, is counterproductive of the ultimate goal of racial justice. Invalidating only conscious racism provides an incentive for whites to repress and deny whatever racist attitudes they in fact harbor. . . .

To hold both unconscious and conscious race discrimination equally blameworthy is also unlikely to produce desirable consequences. First, blaming individuals for unconsciously held attitudes may produce paralyzing guilt when the racist character of those attitudes comes to light. Furthermore, condemning the individual for matters not within his conscious control seems inconsistent with the very concept of blameworthiness. Finally, assessing blame for what, in effect, nearly every white person does seems equally incongruous.

The final option is to regard both conscious and unconscious race discrimination as morally acceptable. There is merit in the proposition that race neutrality is at least an overblown norm; that race consciousness may not be the overarching evil it often seems to be. But there should be no doubt about the moral status of the end to which race consciousness historically has been directed: white supremacy. To dismiss too easily the immorality of race-conscious decisionmaking, in a framework in which concepts of blame and innocence remain operative, would be to allow the inference that white domination of blacks is an acceptable social outcome.

* * *

Finally, the Court's use of the notions of blame, violation, and remedy is imprudent because the aura of criminality surrounding these concepts undoubtedly increases the Court's resistance to finding constitutional violations that it might otherwise recognize. The Court understandably hesitates to suggest that another branch of government has engaged in criminal conduct. In a nonblaming framework, however, courts might become more effective participants in the effort to address and eradicate all forms of race discrimination from government decisionmaking.

In this model, one takes responsibility for correcting undesirable states of affairs without thereby accepting either blame for, or even a causal connection with, the circumstance that requires correction.

* * *

Any white decisionmaker can choose to take responsibility for the form of unconscious race discrimination transparency describes by adopting the skeptical stance with respect to facially race-neutral criteria of decision she employs. Deliberate skepticism regarding race neutrality permits the decisionmaker to step outside the framework of blame and guilt that rarely offers more than a choice between legitimation of the status quo and paralysis. For government decisionmakers and the courts, deliberate skepticism provides an avenue for addressing unconscious discrimination while circumventing the problems of blaming described above. . . .

IV. A REFORMIST PROPOSAL

* * *

This Part sets forth a constitutional disparate impact rule designed to address the consequences of the transparency phenomenon as it affects government decisionmaking. I recognize that not all government actions that arguably violate the Equal Protection Clause are products of transparency, and I emphasize that this proposal does not foreclose finding some government decisions unconstitutional because motivated by racial animus. Other conduct might properly be invalidated because animated by racial stereotyping. Accordingly, the disparate impact rule I propose would be only one piece in a complete equal protection jurisprudence. Borrowing the familiar doctrinal concepts of heightened judicial scrutiny (from existing equal protection jurisprudence) and burdens of production and persuasion (from judicial interpretations of Title VII), the rule aims to reach government decisions that carry racially disparate consequences and would likely not have been adopted but for the transparency phenomenon.

In outline, the proposed rule calls for heightened scrutiny of governmental criteria of decision that have racially disparate effects. The constitutional challenger bears the burden of persuasion on the question of the existence of racially disparate effects. Once disparate impact is proven, the burden of production shifts to government to articulate the purposes behind the challenged rule of decision. The reviewing court ought to interpret government's purpose(s) in as pluralist a manner as possible, but government has the option of resisting that interpretation in favor of an assimilationist construction of its goals. In that event, government will bear a burden of justification similar to that imposed under traditional intermediate scrutiny. Finally, whether governmental purposes are construed pluralistically or in an assimilationist manner, the constitutional challenger has the obligation to produce alternative means of achieving government's goals. Government must implement the challenger's proposals unless it can demonstrate that those alternatives provide less effective means of implementing its goals than the criteria of decision originally employed.

A. A Reformist Disparate Impact Rule

The thoroughly skeptical white decisionmaker regards all facially neutral criteria of decision as presumptively white-specific; the existence of racially disparate effects only confirms what his skepticism already counsels. Thus, the individual decisionmaker who takes transparency seriously has no need for a rule that treats facially neutral criteria of decision with racially disparate effects differently from facially neutral criteria in general. However, that stance is unworkable as a constitutional rule because it would require heightened judicial scrutiny of virtually every governmental decision. A rule that requires a showing of disparate effects as a predicate for heightened scrutiny is a satisfactory alternative because it provides for judicial intervention whenever the presumed transparency phenomenon has produced concrete racial consequences.

Accordingly, the proposed rule anticipates the need for evidentiary guidelines concerning proof of adverse effects, and it permits the constitutional challenger to make such a demonstration by relying on a statistical disparity between the racial composition of the group selected by the challenged criteria of decision and that of the general population. . . .

Once a challenger has proved the existence of racially disparate effects, government should have to articulate the purpose or goal the challenged criteria are designed to accomplish. Initially this is simply a burden of production, so that challenger need not guess at government's policies or purposes. However, transparency can infect government's purposes as readily as it can affect chosen means, so the interpretation of government's articulated purpose is critical.

Heightened, transparency-conscious scrutiny of governmental purposes requires the reviewing court to construe those purposes in a manner that does not perpetuate the covert imposition of white norms. One way to avoid the reintroduction of transparency is for courts to interpret government's goals in as culturally pluralist a manner as possible. That is, the reviewing court should inquire whether and to what extent government's articulated goal, viewed at an appropriate level of generality, may be construed to encompass objectives that need not be understood as white-specific. For example, in *Fragante v. City & County of Honolulu* a Filipino job applicant who achieved the highest score on the applicable civil service examination was rejected for a position as a clerk at the Department of Motor Vehicles because the spoke English with a heavy Filipino accent. Had the case been litigated as a constitutional challenge to a facially neutral rule requiring clerks to speak "unaccented" English, the government most likely would have identified effective communication with the public as the purpose behind the rule.

The transparency of the norm of "unaccented" speech should be obvious. Fragante's speech was perceived as "difficult" by individuals who, consciously or unconsciously, preferred the speech of people with accents more nearly like that of white Americans. This case also illustrates the temptation for government to attempt to justify a transparently white criterion of decision with an equally white-specific purpose. From that perspective, the central problem of the case is the suppressed whiteness of the notion of "effective communication" with the public, government's proffered "legitimate, nondiscriminatory reason."

Under the disparate impact analysis proposed here, a reviewing court ought to construe government's purpose, if possible, in a manner that would not advantage whites. That is, the court would have to presume the "public" to be a diverse community and give "effective communication" the broadest possible reading. If the court unconsciously interpreted "effective communication" to mean "effective communication with whites," it would have reintroduced transparency in a manner that would defeat the underlying goals of heightened scrutiny.

On the other hand, government ought to have the option of insisting on a construction of its purpose that is white-specific, when it has good reasons for doing so. On occasion, context may provide a good reason: if, for example, all or nearly all of the persons with whom Mr. Fragante would come into contact were in fact white, government should be permitted to seek "effective communication" with that group, even if its purpose is thus effectively white-specific. However, a rule of general applicability would require a more thorough evaluation of government's goals. Suppose government argued that "effective communication" should be construed in a white-specific manner for the sake of uniformity and that a white norm had been adopted because whites are the dominant group in this society. At this stage the reviewing court would revert to a more traditional from of scrutiny, balancing government's interest in uniformity and whiteness against the burden the adoption of a white-specific rule would place on nonwhites. To prevail under this "mid-level" scrutiny, government's chosen purpose must be "important." At minimum, an asserted interest in administrative convenience would not be sufficient.

Once the question of purpose has been settled, whether in an assimilationist or a pluralist manner, the burden of production shifts to the challenger to introduce means of achieving that purpose that do not disproportionately disadvantage nonwhites. In the *Fragante* situation the challenger might propose one or more functional tests for "effective communication with the public" that would measure, for example, the actual ability of the relevant set of listeners to comprehend Mr. Fragante's speech. The challenger should be allowed at this stage to propose measures that would operate to the advantage of nonwhite applicants, as well as criteria of selection that would be racially neutral in effect.

Finally, government has the burden of persuasion on the question of means. Government must show that challenger's proposed alternative(s) will be less effective in achieving its purpose, as interpreted by the court, than the criteria of decision employed by the government. If government fails to carry its burden here, it will be required to employ challenger's criteria of decision either as a substitute for, or in parallel with, the criteria previously in use. In the abstract, parallel use of alternative criteria of decision would be preferable in cases in which challenger's proposed criteria of selection operate to advantage nonwhites, and substitution would be appropriate if the proffered alternative had racially neutral effects. For example, in the *Fragante* scenario, a functional, actual-ability-to-be-understood test would not systematically advantage nonwhites over whites, and so substitution of that test for the hypothesized requirement of "unaccented" speech would be preferable.

Like the traditional forms of heightened scrutiny employed in equal protection analysis, the disparate impact rule proposed here places increased burdens of justification on government with respect both to its purposes and its means, but the rule does so with special attention to the transparency phenomenon. Thus, where traditional heightened review requires that government's purpose be unusually weighty (and, arguably, that it be contemporaneous with the challenged rule or decision and adequately supported in fact), transparency-conscious scrutiny requires government to articulate purposes that are neither overtly nor transparently white-specific. Government may impose norms that are effectively white, but it must announce its choice candidly, and it must bear a substantial burden of justification when it wishes to do so. Traditional heightened scrutiny then demands a sufficiently tight "fit" between government's goal and its chosen means; the proposed rule requires the use of alternative criteria of decision that have no racially disparate impact whenever doing so will not negatively affect government's permissible purposes.

* * *

The deeper design of the proposed rule is to foster constructive dialogue concerning the necessity and appropriateness of assimilationist governmental purposes and means. The transparency phenomenon means that blacks evaluated under "facially neutral" norms in fact often face a choice between assimilation and exclusion. The proposed rule is intended to counteract the assimilationist force of transparency and to require government to confront the possibility of greater openness to cultural diversity in the formulation of public policy and the exercise of governmental power. At the same time, the constitutional challenger becomes responsible for proposing alternative means of achieving government's articulated goals. This requirement operates to relieve a white-controlled government of some of the burden of diversification; it does not require whites suddenly to be able to envision remedies for a phenomenon that has too often escaped our awareness altogether. Nonwhites who challenge transparently white-specific governmental criteria of decision must take an active role in reformulating them.

B. *The Colorblindness Objection*

The proposed rule clearly abandons the colorblindness principle, which disapproves any use of any race-specific criterion of decision, no matter what the race of the decisionmaker or of the persons respectively advantaged or burdened by that criterion. First, the proposed rule is founded on the presumption that facially neutral criteria of decision employed by white decisionmakers are in fact race-specific; the rule at least challenges the assumption of the colorblindness perspective that such a thing as a racially neutral criterion of decision is possible. Second, the rule permits government to take responsibility for disparate racial effects by adopting parallel race-conscious criteria of decision in appropriate instances. Finally, though the proposed rule does resemble colorblindness insofar as it mandates heightened scrutiny in the interest of mitigating the race-based effects of some covertly race-specific criteria of decision, it does so only when those effects flow from transparently white-specific bases of decision. That is, the rule contemplates heightened judicial scrutiny only when facially neutral criteria formulated or deployed by white governmental decisionmakers operate to disadvantage nonwhites. It is not symmetrical; heightened scrutiny is not appropriate when black governmental decisionmakers formulate and apply facially neutral criteria that negatively impact whites.

A transparency-conscious disparate impact rule should not be symmetrical because transparency itself is a white-specific phenomenon. In our society only whites have the social power that renders our point of view perspectiveless, that elevates our expectations to the status of "neutral" norms, and that permits us to see ourselves and our race-specific characteristics as raceless. Assuming there are, or can be, meaningful instances in which nonwhites gain the power to formulate as well as to apply governmental rules of decision, the existence of any disparate negative effect on whites would trigger at minimum an immediate inquiry, by whites, into the possible racial components of such facially neutral rules. Nonwhite decisionmaking never benefits from transparency.

* * *

Turning from the legal to the moral realm, the principal foundation of colorblindness seems to be its enormous intuitive appeal. To "judge a person by the color of his skin" just seems wrong. This moral insight may be the visceral rejection of its equally visceral opposite, the tendency of human beings to react negatively to persons of a different color than themselves. However, moral insights are at best problematic sources of constitutional doctrine and must in any event be subject to revision in the light of experience.

The colorblindness principle may also appear morally desirable by virtue of its relation to the liberal value of individual autonomy. Colorblindness often is seen as an expression of individual autonomy, which requires in part that persons not be held responsible or judged for personal characteristics not within their own control. Individuals ought to reap the fruits of their own industry, but they ought neither to benefit nor to be disadvantaged because of characteristics like race or gender that are a matter of birth.

However, colorblindness is at best a paradoxical means of implementing autonomy values. On the one hand, autonomy is not served when the individual is pigeonholed by race; certainly the whole person is much more than the color of her skin. On the other hand, individual autonomy ought to include the power of self-definition, the ability to make fundamental value choices and to select life strategies to implement them. . . .

The final category of arguments purporting to support the colorblindness principle may be characterized, loosely, as exemplifying antisubordinationist concerns. Race consciousness - the explicit use of racial classifications as a means of disadvantaging nonwhites - has been the primary vehicle of racial subordination until quite recently. The ideology of opposition to racial hierarchy evolved in reaction to the specific forms in which racial oppression had manifested itself. Rejecting racial distinctions seemed the natural avenue to reversing that history of oppression and achieving racial justice, especially during the "Second Reconstruction" of the 1950s and 1960s; colorblindness appeared to be the exact antithesis of the form of race consciousness that had been the root cause of racial subordination. If "color" had marked an individual as inferior, then the refusal to recognize "color" would be the way to elevate him to equal status with whites. In effect, colorblindness became the rule-like proxy for an underlying, historically based antisubordination principle.

The problem with the colorblindness principle as a strategy for achieving racial justice is that it has not been effective outside the social context in which it arose. Like all rules, colorblindness is both over- and underinclusive with respect to the underlying policy—antisubordination—it is intended to implement. It is underinclusive because the explicit use of racial classifications is no longer the principal vehicle of racial oppression; structural and institutional racism, of the sort illustrated by the transparency phenomenon, now are the predominant causes of blacks' continued inability to thrive in this society. Colorblindness is overinclusive insofar as it regards the explicit use of racial classifications to advantage blacks as equally blameworthy as the historical use of such classifications to blacks' disadvantage. In each respect colorblindness fails to implement racial justice; that it is a failed social policy is evident from the statistics revealing that blacks are scarcely better off today than they were before this ideology took hold in the 1950s and 1960s.

Liberals who wish to implement the goal of racial justice should give up the colorblindness principle in favor of a functional analysis of proposed means of achieving those ends. The proposed rule offers a better prospect for achieving racial equity because it permits nonwhites to engage white-controlled government in a dialogue concerning the scope of government's goals and the range of means that might be effective in attaining them. It requires government to define its goals in ways that do not systematically favor whites, and it also requires government to utilize diverse means of achieving its goals whenever possible. Unlike the inflexible, acontextual, and ahistorical colorblindness principle, the proposed rule offers the opportunity for government to take responsibility for racial justice.

C. An Institutional Objection

The institutional objection to the proposed rule mirrors the final, and for many, most persuasive argument articulated in *Washington v. Davis*.

* * *

In short, the proposed rule might require the courts to engage in a form of economic redistribution.

* * *

. . . [T]he proposed rule does have, and is intended to have, some racially redistributive effects. The *Davis* argument points out a core dilemma in liberal egalitarian rhetoric: while we approve and are willing in some respects to foster racial equality, we endorse no similar economic egalitarianism. Thus, because our history of the overt and covert, intentional and thoughtless oppression of blacks by whites has placed the former in a relatively disadvantaged economic position, any attempt at racial reform runs afoul of our at least equally strong resistance to intervention in the existing distribution of economic goods, a resistance that is especially acute when the federal judiciary assumes responsibility to alter the status quo.

The solution to the dilemma, I think, is for white people to acknowledge that taking responsibility for race discrimination does and should cost something. Implementing "Test 22" will indeed mean that fewer white officers will be hired onto the D.C. police force; employing criteria of selection that place more blacks in policymaking positions may well mean that government expends funds differently than before and expends relatively less to benefit whites. If the status quo results from a long history of the systematic privileging of whites, as it surely does, then one can only expect that a more racially just society would see a different, and more equal, distribution of societal goods.

The proposed rule in fact has relatively modest redistributive effects. It does no more than require government not to pursue thoughtlessly goals that advantage whites, and it permits nonwhites to propose inclusive means of accomplishing permissible goals; it does not mandate absolute distributional equality. It lays some of the burden of formulating more inclusive strategies at the feet of nonwhites, but it requires government to adopt those strategies whenever possible. To that extent, the proposed rule mandates a modest transfer of power as well as a somewhat more racially just distribution of benefits and burdens. We whites should expect no less from any rule that attempts seriously to address the structural racism of which transparency is one manifestation.

CONCLUSION

White people can do better than to continue to impose our beliefs, values, norms, and expectations on black people under the rubric of race neutrality. Recognizing transparency for the defining characteristic of whiteness that it is ought to impel us to a radical skepticism concerning the possibility of race-neutral decisionmaking. Operating from the presumption that facially neutral criteria of decision are in reality race-specific can prompt whites committed to the realization of racial justice to search for and adopt more racially inclusive ways of doing business. In this way, the skeptical stance can be instrumental in the development of a positive white racial identity, one that comprehends whiteness not as the (unspoken) racial norm, but as just one racial identity among many.

Whites who wish to see the destruction of racial hierarchy can hold government to the same standards of transparency consciousness. We can and ought to expect the institution designed to be representative of all the people not to contribute to the maintenance of white supremacy. The demand that government decisionmakers take responsibility for race discrimination by adopting the skeptical stance can be embodied in the rejection of the discriminatory intent requirement. A reformed disparate impact rule would prefer pluralist interpretations of government purposes, and it would require implementation through pluralist means whenever possible. Uncovering, naming, and counteracting the unrecognized whiteness of a white-dominated government and of the criteria of decision it employs is a first, crucial step in the realignment of social power that dismantling white supremacy entails.

Preferential and Diversification Policies

The concept of a color blind constitution was asserted a century ago by Justice Harlan. As he noted in dissenting from the Court's endorsement of official segregation, "there is in this country no superior, dominant, ruling class of citizens . . . [and] no caste . . . our Constitution is color-blind."[22] Although Harlan's sense of constitutional color blindness responded to methodology that subordinated a historically disadvantaged group, the rhetoric has been central to analysis of methods that purport to account for the nation's legacy of discrimination.[23] Richard A. Posner maintains that purportedly benign racial classifications are a source of harm to their intended beneficiaries. Thomas Sowell argues that the basic premises of race-conscious remediation are misplaced. Randall Kennedy contends that racially preferential policies have been effective and that opposition to them is exaggerated. Patricia J. Williams touts the potential of policies calculated to diversify and factor multicultural realities. David A. Straus suggests that the referencing of law to color blindness is delusionary.

Richard A. Posner, *The* DeFunis *Case and the Constitutionality of Preferential Treatment of Racial Minorities,* 1974 Sup. Ct. Rev. 1 (1974)*

* * *

II. THE REASONABLENESS OF REVERSE DISCRIMINATION

* * *

B. RACE AS A SURROGATE FOR OTHER, NONRACIAL CHARACTERISTICS

* * *

For a diversity argument to be convincing, it must identify a differentiating factor that is relevant to the educational experience. It would make no sense to argue that in selecting the entering first-year class a law school should strive for diversity in the height of the students, or in their weight, pulchritude, posture, depth of voice, or blood pressure, or that it should give a preference to (or disfavor) albinos, or people with freckles or double chins. Diversity in these superficial physical respects contributes nothing of value to the legal education of the students. Race *per se*—that is, race completely divorced from certain characteristics that may be strongly correlated with, but do not inevitably accompany, it—is also, and in a similar sense, irrelevant to diversity. There are black people (and Chicanos, Filipinos, etc.) who differ only in

---

22   Plessy v. Ferguson, 163 U.S. 537, 559 (1896)(Harlan, J., dissenting).

23   E.g., Fullilove v. Klutznick, 448 U.S. 448, 522 (1980)(Stewart and Rehnquist, JJ., dissenting). See generally City of Richmond v. J.A. Croson Co., 488 U.S. 469, 493-94 (1989).

*   Copyright © 1974 by the University of Chicago. Reprinted from 1974 Supreme Court Review 1 by permission.

the most superficial physical characteristics from whites—who have the same tastes, manners, experiences, aptitudes, and aspirations as the whites with whom one might compare them (here, white law school applicants). To give such people preferential treatment to the end of increasing the diversity of the student body would be equivalent to giving preferential treatment to albinos—were it not that race is frequently correlated with other attributes that are arguably relevant to meaningful diversity, and albinism is not. The average black applicant for admission is more likely than the average white to have known poverty and prejudice first hand, and his experience, communicated to his fellow students (and teachers) both inside and outside of the classroom, might enrich the educational process.

Race in this analysis is simply a proxy for a set of other attributes—relevant to the educational process—with which race, itself irrelevant to the process, happens to be correlated. The use of a racial proxy in making admissions decisions will produce some inaccuracy—blacks will be admitted who lack the attributes that contribute to genuine diversity—but this cost of using a racial proxy may be less than the cost, which is saved, of having to investigate the actual characteristics of each applicant.

The difficulty with this approach is that it closely resembles and could be viewed as imparting legitimacy to the case for regarding discrimination against racial minorities as proper, because (generally) efficient, from of conduct. There are several possible explanations for the presence of racial and ethnic discrimination. One is sheer irrationality; another is exploitation, another the desire to limit competition. But it may be that most discrimination in today's America can be explained simply by the cost of information. Suppose that a particular racial or ethnic identity is correlated with characteristics that are widely disliked for reasons not patently exploitive, anticompetitive, or irrational. A substantial proportion of the members of the group in question may be loud, or poor, or hostile, or irresponsible, or poorly educated, or dangerously irascible, or ill-mannered, or have different tastes, values, work habits from our own, or speak an unintelligible patois. To be averse to association (in housing, recreation, schooling, or employment) with an individual because he possessed such a characteristic would not ordinarily be regarded as a sign of prejudice. To be "prejudiced" means, rather, to ascribe to the members of a group defined by a racial or similarly arbitrary characteristic attributes typically or frequently possessed by members of the group without pausing to consider whether the individual member in question has that characteristic—sometimes without being willing even to consider evidence that he does not. The extreme bigot applies an irrebuttable presumption that every member of the group has the characteristic that he dislikes. The moderate bigot applies a rebuttable presumption to the same effect—and all of us are at least moderate bigots in some areas of life.

The history of this country contains examples of the unreasoning type of racial and ethnic prejudice, of exploitive discrimination illustrated by the treatment of the American Indian in the nineteenth century and by the enslavement of the black—and of the anticompetitive sort as well (e.g., exclusion of women from various occupations). But, today at least, it may be that most prejudice and discrimination are a product of the cost of making individual distinction with racial and ethnic groups. This is a type of economically efficient conduct similar to a consumer's reluctance to try a new brand, or more generally, to carry the process of searching for products beyond the point where the cost of searching is equal to its benefit in enabling a better purchase to be made. It is perfectly rational for an individual to support the exclusion of Armenians, or Jews, or blacks from his club if his experience, whether first or second hand, is that most or very many members of these groups do not have the characteristics that he likes in a social (or business) acquaintance and there is no scarcity of eligible applicants from other groups.

To say that discrimination is often a rational and efficient from of behavior is not to say that it is socially or ethically desirable. "Efficient" must never be confused with "good" or "right." Moreover, there is an important distinction to be drawn between private discrimination and discrimination that is compelled, practiced, or encouraged by the government, or that is practiced by a monopolist. But I am not interested in the normative basis of antidiscrimination policy. My purpose in noting that much discrimination may be applicable in terms of the costs of information is, rather, to suggest a doubt about the merits of the diversity justification for treating racial minorities preferentially. That justification, it will be recalled, rests on the correlation between racial identity and the possession of characteristics that promote meaningful diversity, and implicitly, therefore, on the cost of ascertaining whether a particular member of the racial group actually possesses the desired characteristic. Could not a policy against hostile discrimination be undermined by a program of benevolent discrimination rooted in the same habit of mind—that of using race or ethnic origin to establish a presumption, in the case of a racially preferential admissions program a conclusive one, that the individual possesses some other attribute as well, that is, some educationally relevant characteristic such as a background of deprivation or a cultural difference? The danger is underscored by the fact that the hostile and the well-disposed discriminators seem to be treating race as a proxy for the same set of characteristics. The characteristics that university admissions officers associate with "black" are the distinctive cultural attributes of many black people who have grown up in an urban slum or in the rural South, and these are the same characteristics that the white bigot ascribes to every black, although he uses a different terminology(e.g., "lazy" rather than "unmotivated").

I am not making the familiar argument that the member of the favored minority is humiliated by being singled out for preferential treatment. He may or may not be. My point is rather that the use of a racial characteristic to establish a presumption that the individual also possesses other, and socially relevant, characteristics exemplifies, encourages, and legitimizes the mode of thought and behavior that underlies most prejudice and bigotry in modern America.

This point is reinforced by considering some features of the actual implementation of a policy of racial preference. Here I shall supplement the meager record of the *DeFunis* case with information obtained from discussions with people involved in the law school admissions process. (This will also serve to illustrate why it is incorrect to assume that the next case to reach the Court on the question of racial preference in university admissions will add nothing to what the record of *DeFunis* contains on the question.) To administer a racial-preference program one needs an operational definition of membership in the favored group. The applicant cannot be relied upon to classify himself correctly. The correct racial classification is not always obvious; and since a benefit attaches to membership in particular racial groups, applicants have an incentive to misrepresent their race. Thus admissions officials confront the problem both of determining what constitutes membership in a racial group and of requiring appropriate evidence that an applicant belongs to it. In the case of blacks, it is necessary to determine what percentage of Negro ancestry should be required of an applicant claiming preferential treatment as a black. Additional problems of definition, and also of proof, arise with respect to Chicanos. If the president of Mexico marries an American woman and they have a child who is brought up in the United States, is the child a Chicano? Or is the term meant to imply some connection with life in a barrio? With regard to the problem of proof, Chicanos are less distinctive in physical appearance than most blacks; and the possession (or lack) of a Spanish surname is not decisive evidence since Puerto Ricans, Spaniards, and Latin Americans other than Mexicans also have Spanish surnames, and since a Chicano might be the product of the union of a Chicano woman and a nonChicano man. Similar problems exist with respect to American Indians. Many people have some Indian blood without being recognizable as Indian or having a characteristically Indian name. This problem could be avoided by limiting preferential treatment to Indians on reservations, but such a limitation would be difficult to justify to Indians who have recently (or not so recently) left the reservation and may have encountered substantial difficulties in adjusting to life on the outside. A simple solution to all such problems is to delegate the determination of whether an applicant is entitled to preferential treatment to the student association for the group in which he claims membership (the Black Students' Union, etc.), but the dangers of serious abuse in such a course are too great.

My point is not that the administrative problems, and therefore costs, of implementing a program of racial preferences in admissions should be decisive against adoption of such a program. The problems of definition and proof are relevant to the present discussion because they illustrate the distinction between racial or ethnic identity *per se* and the relevant characteristics for which that identity is a proxy. Suppose a family has so little Negro blood that it has been able to pass as white and has done so, suppressing all cultural traits that might betray its "true" identity. The family has a child, who has been brought up as a white but knows that he has some Negro ancestors and who, in applying for admission to law school, claims entitlement to preferential treatment as a black. Should his claim be honored? If it is, is not the law school's action fundamentally similar to the decision of a country club to deny this individual membership on the sole ground that it does not admit blacks? If the admissions committee takes the position that a single black great-great grandparent "makes a difference," if only as a matter of administrative convenience, on what basis could one criticize the country club (or employer, or school board) that reached the same conclusion on the same ground?

Another point that must be considered is that when race is used as a proxy for characteristics thought to be relevant to the educational experience, discrimination against people who have the characteristics, but not the racial identity, results. . . .

I have dwelled so long on the diversity argument for preferential treatment because it is the one argument that seems at first glance not racialistic at all. The argument is not that one race should be preferred over another but that a racial preference will benefit all members of the student body, regardless of race, by enriching the educational experience. Yet if one looks a little more closely at the argument it turns out to rest on a premise fundamentally inconsistent with that of a policy against hostile discrimination, for such a policy, if it is to be effective, requires rejection of administrative convenience as a justification for using racial criteria to allocate benefits or impose burdens.

C. RACIAL PROPORTIONAL REPRESENTATION

Where . . . a racial preference is based squarely, on a desire to increase the proportion of lawyers of a particular race, it is no longer possible to argue about whether the preference is a form of racial discrimination and it is more difficult to find a justification based on educational purposes, or for that matter on anything else. Four principal reasons are offered for attempting to achieve at least approximately proportional racial representation in the legal profession: (1) making amends for past discrimination against the minority group; (2) putting the group where it would have been but for the handicaps imposed on its members by past discrimination; (3)

improving the level of professional service received by the group; and (4) encouraging the aspirations of its members by the provision of suitable "role models." None of these four reasons would be any more persuasive to an objective observer than the sorts of arguments that could be offered for discriminating against racial minorities.

1. The members of the minority group who receive preferential treatment will often be those who have not been the victims of discrimination while the nonminority people excluded because of the preferences are unlikely to have perpetrated, or to have in any demonstrable sense benefited from, the discrimination. Indian reparations may be a distinct case, based on treaty (equivalent to contractual) obligations enforceable by the heirs of the original beneficiaries against the government; also distinguishable, though in my opinion only tenuously, is the use of racial quotas as part of a decree to remedy unlawful discrimination.

2. Many groups are under represented in various occupations for reasons of taste, opportunity, or aptitude unrelated to discrimination. . . .

3. There is no evidence of which I am aware that a substantial number or proportion of minority-group law school graduates will seek in their professional careers to serve the special needs of their minority group rather than follow the normal patterns of professional advancement.

4. The "role model" argument is similarly *ad hoc* and conjectural. So long as a significant number of members of a minority group enter the legal profession and succeed in it (one of the justices of the Supreme Court is black, after all), others will know that it is not closed to them. There is no basis for requiring proportional representation.

The reasons advanced for proportional representation are unimpressive. But more disturbing than the lack of solid intellectual foundations are the implications of the under representation approach for the overall structure of society. The ultimate logic of under representation is that the percentage of members of each minority racial and ethnic group in each desirable occupation, and in each level of achievement within the occupation, should be raised to equality with its percentage of the total population (either of the entire nation, or in some versions, of some region or local area). The proponents of proportional representation do not as yet urge adoption of the standard of perfect equality, but there seems to be no logical point short of it within the structure of their argument. This is true despite their soothing assurance that affirmative action is required only in a period of transition to a society in which, all vestiges of discrimination having been eliminated by affirmative action, society can resume a policy of color-blindness. If, as seems more likely than not, occupational preferences and abilities are not randomly distributed across all racial and ethnic groups, then governmental intervention in the labor markets (and in the educational process insofar as it affects occupational choice and success) will have to continue forever if proportional equality in the desirable occupations is to be secured. Consistently implemented, this sort of intervention would, by profoundly distorting the allocation of labor and by driving a wedge between individual merit and economic and professional success, greatly undermine the system of incentives on which a free society depends.

A superficially attractive variant of the under representation argument is that the demand for minority lawyers is greater at the present time than that for white lawyers, because of the special needs of minority-group members for legal representation and their preference for being represented by members of their own group. But to accept this argument would be once again to embrace the intellectual basis for the kinds of racial and ethnic discrimination that we do not like, for this argument would justify excluding an individual black, who had greater academic promise than some white applicant, on the ground that prejudice, or other factors, would limit the contribution that the black could make to the profession.

III. THE CONSTITUTIONAL ISSUE

A. PREVIOUS APPROACHES

* * *

A distinct argument for the constitutionality of discrimination in favor of minority groups has been made in a recent article by Professor Ely. He argues, along lines similar to those suggested earlier, that a policy of discrimination, favorable or unfavorable, might be adopted simply because the costs of individualized treatment were thought to exceed its benefits, but that when members of one racial group—such as the white majority of a state legislature—are appraising the costs and benefits of a proposed discrimination against another racial group the comparison is apt to be distorted by conscious or unconscious racial hostility. Hence, he argues, discrimination against a racial minority should be suspect under the Fourteenth Amendment, but discrimination in favor of a minority should not be since it does not involve any danger of majority exploitation of a minority.

There are two fundamental objections to this argument. One—that it misconceives the nature of the political process—I defer for the moment. The other is that it provides a mode of justifying discrimination against racial minorities. Professor Ely accepts the legitimacy of comparing the costs of discriminating against the members of a racial or ethnic minority with the benefits from thereby avoiding the need to make individual distinctions. He only wants assurance that the balance will be accurately struck. He is suspicious that the majority will fail to take adequate account of the costs, or will exaggerate the benefits, of the discriminatory measure, but this suspicion only warrants that the reviewing court satisfy itself that the legislature has in fact assessed the costs and benefits of the discrimination accurately. Suppose the Post Office were able to demonstrate convincingly that blacks had, on average, inferior aptitudes to whites for supervisory positions, that the costs to the postal system of inadequate supervisors were very great, and that the costs of conducting the inquiries necessary to ascertain whether an individual black had the requisite aptitudes were also great in relation to the probability of discovering qualified blacks. It would seem to follow from Ely's analysis that the Post Office could adopt a rule barring blacks from supervisory positions. By condemning only inefficient discriminations, Ely reduces the scope of the Equal Protection Clause to triviality, if I am correct in arguing that most discrimination in contemporary society is caused by the costs of information rather than by irrationality, exploitation, or the suppression of competition.

B. TOWARD AN OBJECTIVE CONSTITUTIONAL PRINCIPLE

In order to determine the constitutionality of racially preferential admissions policies, it is first necessary to derive from the Equal Protection Clause some rule, or principle, or standard for applying the constitutional formula (that no state may "deny to any person within its jurisdiction the equal protection of the laws") to racial discrimination. There are two extreme approaches to the task of constructing a constitutional rule to decide discrimination cases. One is to be guided completely by the specific expressions of intent on the part of the framers of the Fourteenth Amendment. If the scope of the Equal Protection Clause were so determined, *DeFunis* would have no leg to stand on. So bizarre would discrimination against whites in admission to institutions of higher learning have seemed to the framers of the Fourteenth Amendment that we can be confident that they did not consciously seek to erect a constitutional barrier against such discrimination. But it is equally clear that the framers did not contemplate that the Amendment would compel equal treatment of blacks in public education. The suggested approach to the interpretation of a constitutional provision is, in any event, unsound. The great costs of amending the Constitution counsel for a liberal interpretation of its provisions. A new constitutional amendment should not be needed to prevent states from imposing on blacks forms of discrimination unknown to the framers of the Fourteenth Amendment.

The opposite extreme would be to view the Equal Protection Clause as authorizing the Justices of the Supreme Court to enact into constitutional doctrine their personal values with respect to the society's social questions, such as poverty, racial discrimination, and equality between the sexes. The arguments against the Court's assuming the role of superlegislature have been made so compellingly by others that I shall not discuss this approach to constitutional interpretation.

There remains a middle course, which is to derive from the specific purposes of the constitutional framers a rule that, while sufficiently general to avoid constant recourse to the amendment process, is sufficiently precise and objective to limit a judge's exercise of personal whim and preference. The rule I derive on this basis is that the distribution of benefits and costs by government on racial or ethnic grounds is impermissible. Even though it is frequently efficient to sort people by race or ethnic origin, because racial or ethnic identity may be a good proxy for functional classifications, efficiency is rejected as a basis for governmental action in this context. The government is required to incur the additional costs of determining the individual applicant's fitness to hold a particular job, or patronize a particular facility, or be admitted to one of its educational institutions. To permit discrimination to be justified on efficiency grounds, as would Professor Ely, would not only thwart the purpose of the Equal Protection Clause by allowing much, perhaps most, discrimination to continue, but it would give the judges the power to pick and choose among discriminatory measures on the basis of personal values, for the weighing of the relevant costs and benefits would of necessity be largely subjective.

It is possible to object that the principle which I propose is itself subjective and arbitrary, because it does not explain why only race and ethnic origin, and not all immutable or involuntary characteristics, are subject to the principle. What is the difference between a rule forbidding women to be fighter pilots, premised on a belief that most women are unfit for such an occupation, and a rule forbidding Jews to be fighter pilots, premised on a similar belief? Alienage, nonresidence, height, homosexuality, youth, poverty, and low IQ are some other examples of immutable or involuntary characteristics used as criteria for governmental regulations. On what objective basis can these characteristics be distinguished from genealogy? There are two grounds for distinction. The first is one of necessity: if the constitutional principle were defined in terms of all involuntary characteristics, it would violate the requirement that a constitutional principle bind the judges. Since no one could argue that no involuntary characteristic should ever be used as a criterion of public regulation, the principle would give the judges interpreting it carte blanche to pick and choose among groups defined in accordance with one of the involuntary characteristics. Second, the grouping of people by an ancestral characteristic is surely not the same phenomenon as, say, grouping by sex or age. A rule forbidding blacks to work in mines, and one forbidding women to work in mines, and one forbidding children to work in mines may all be discriminatory, but one must strain to regard them as identical, in the sense that if one is invalid, so, obviously are the others. In contrast, it would be very difficult to distinguish a rule forbidding Chicanos, or Jews, or American Indians, or Italian-Americans to work in mines from a rule forbidding blacks to work in mines. If the last is invalid, so, clearly, are the others.

It remains to consider whether an exception to the rule forbidding discrimination on racial or ethnic grounds can be recognized where the discrimination can be said to be in favor of a racial or ethnic minority, and the race discriminated against is the white race. The exception is inadmissible, because it requires the court not only to consider whether there is discrimination but to decide whether the discrimination harms or hurts a particular racial group, and to weigh the competing claims of different racial groups, and the additional inquiries rob the principle of its precision and objectivity. The Court had no good evidence before it in the *Brown* case that segregated education in fact harmed blacks. The questions critical to the point were not even asked: Would blacks have fared better under a system of no public education (assuming that whites would prefer such a system to integrated public education)? Under a system where students were sorted by IQ? By family income? In later cases the Court stopped asking whether segregation actually hurt the blacks. (Today, of course, some blacks favor segregation.) The antidiscrimination principle is not only more objective, but more compelling, when it is divorced from empirical inquiries into the effects of particular forms of discrimination on the affected groups. The necessary inquiries are intractable and would leave the field open to slippery conjecture. As suggested earlier, a plausible argument could be made that various forms of discrimination nominally against Jews might actually advance the interests of the Jews as a whole, for example by reducing their prominence and visibility in certain areas where the conspicuousness of the Jews may stimulate anti-Semitism. Similar arguments could be made for various forms of conceivably well-intentioned discrimination against blacks (such as "benign housing quotas," or limitations on the migration of blacks from southern to northern states). The Supreme Court would reject such arguments, but not because they are substantially less compelling than the arguments it accepts when it upholds the constitutionality of governmental action. The arguments about the proper characterization of discrimination nominally in favor of racial minorities have a similar elusiveness. Is the position of the whites in this country so unassailable that they cannot be harmed by racial quotas? Or is the impact of such quotas likely to be concentrated on particular, and perhaps vulnerable, subgroups within the white majority? Do racial quotas actually help the minorities intended to be benefited, or harm them by impairing their self-esteem or legitimating stereotypical thinking about race? Are whites entitled to claim minority status when they are a minority within the political subdivision that enacted the measure discriminating against whites? If so, then by parity of reasoning would blacks lack standing to complain about an ordinance discriminating against them enacted by Newark, New Jersey, or Washington, D.C., or other cities in which blacks are a majority of the population eligible to vote? If these are litigable issues, we do not have a constitutional principle but merely a directive that the judges uphold those forms of racial and ethnic discrimination which accord with their personal values.

I contend, in short, that the proper constitutional principle is not, no "invidious" racial or ethnic discrimination, but no use of racial or ethnic criteria to determine the distribution of government benefits and burdens. . . .

* * *

D. THE ARGUMENT OF EXPEDIENCY

One last "argument" for countenancing preferential treatment is simply its prevalence. It is well known, for example, that law schools offer larger scholarships to outstanding black applicants than to equally qualified, and no more affluent, whites, in order to attract as many black students as possible who are not significantly less well qualified than their white students. This is an example of racial discrimination within the meaning of the concept proposed here. Preferential treatment for American Indians is a deeply embedded feature of our public policy and is contrary to the principle proposed here though perhaps justifiable in light of other principles—such as that of honoring treaty (i.e., contractual) obligations. Racially preferential treatment is becoming widespread in many employment contexts. But all that this amounts to saying is that the form of racial discrimination discussed in this article, only one aspect of which was involved in the *DeFunis* case itself, has become quite prevalent in the few years in which it has been practiced (I again except the Indian situation as a special case). That is not a good reason for affirming its constitutionality, once it is agreed that the *Realpolitik* arguments for legislation, while in general admissible and appropriate, are impermissible to justify infringement of a well defined and specific constitutional principle such as that forbidding racial discrimination.

Furthermore, the impact of eliminating racial preference is easily exaggerated. The preferred groups could be redefined as the underprivileged, the deprived, etc.— classifications not based on race or ethnic origin. The constitutional objection to preferential treatment would thereby be removed, without substantial impairment of the purposes of such treatment. The principal reason for using racial or ethnic criteria is, after all, convenience, and this implies that vindication of *DeFunis*'s claim would have created, at worst, some inconvenience for those who seek to use reverse racial and ethnic discrimination to increase the welfare of disadvantaged individuals in our society.

Thomas Sowell, Weber *and* Bakke, *and the Presuppositions of "Affirmative Action,"* 26 WAYNE L. REV. 1309 (1980)*

I. EVOLUTION

The central idea behind "affirmative action" is that it is often not enough to "cease and desist" from some harmful or proscribed activity. Sometimes the future consequences of the past activity must also be proscribed or mitigated. This idea was not new or peculiar to the civil rights issues of the 1960's.

In 1935, the Wagner Act used the identical phrase, "affirmative action," to describe an employer's duty to undo his past intimidation or harassment of union organizers and members, by posting notices of a new policy and by reinstating (with back pay) workers fired for union activity. Otherwise the future effect of past intimidation (physical and financial) would inhibit the "free choice" elections guaranteed by the Act. For the employer merely to cease and desist would not end the future detrimental effects of his past conduct.

---

*   Reprinted with permission.

Similar principles apply in the racial or ethnic area. The common employer practice of hiring new workers by word-of-mouth referrals from existing employees meant that a formerly discriminating employer with an all-white work force would probably continue to have an all-white work force, even after discrimination among applicants had ceased, because his applicants would be the relatives and friends of his existing employees. The effects of the past racially discriminatory choices of employees would be perpetuated after the policy of racially discriminatory choices among applicants had ended. In a similar vein, general channels of information and recruiting would tend to reflect past practices in the selection of students, executives, craftsmen, and in a wide variety of other selection situations and procedures. For this reason, to eliminate discrimination only at the decisionmaking point (employment, college admission, etc.) would not eliminate *de facto* discrimination—intentional or non-intentional—in the process as a whole, including information channels and recruiting networks established in an earlier era to reach some desired segments of the population, but not others. Therefore, "affirmative action" of *some kind* was considered necessary to make non-discrimination a reality throughout a whole information-recruiting-choosing process, at least until new informal information networks could form and special recruiting activities by employers, universities, and others could overcome fears among previously excluded groups that they would not be considered eligible or would not be judged fairly.

A. *The Distinction Between Information Networks and Decision Points*

"Affirmative action," as it was first applied in a racial or ethnic context in the 1960's, meant various activities aimed at spreading information about newly opened employment or other opportunities, so as to increase the number of minority individuals in the pool of applicants—from which the actual selection would then be made *without regard* to race, color, creed, or nationality. In such a context, it was meaningful to speak of "affirmative action" to promote "equal opportunity," as expressed in President Kennedy's Executive Order No. 10,925. The special targeting of designated groups for informational or recruiting activity was perfectly compatible, in principle, with disregarding all group designations when the time came to choosing among competing individuals. None of this implied goals, preferences, or quotas as regards the final choices. Nor was there any implication of "compensation" to individuals or groups for past societal or institutional wrongs. All these things require additional assumptions and presuppositions.

"Affirmative action" as a general term therefore includes specific policies which may or may not center on numerical results. Even as a very general concept, however, it is a transitional policy. This presents no special problems for administrative or even legislative policy. For judicial and especially constitutional decisionmaking, however, there are serious difficulties. Are courts the appropriate institutions to determine how long social transitions should last, or the principles or indicia of its duration? Can a program be *transitionally* constitutional?

* * *

B. *The Distinction Between Prospective Opportunity and Retrospective Results*

The shift from the prospective concept of "equal opportunity" to the retrospective concept of parity of "representation" (or "correction" of "imbalance") occurred in stages. The first use of the term "affirmative action" in an Executive Order (No. 10,925) was by John F. Kennedy in 1961, and the policy announced for federal contractors was hiring and treatment "without regard" to various ethnic considerations. Later Executive orders added age and sex to ethnicity as proscribed categories. The key Executive Order (No. 11,246) by President Johnson in 1965 created the Office of Federal Contract Compliance in the U.S. Department of Labor, and authorized it to issue guidelines to federal contractors. In May 1968, this Office issued guidelines containing the phrase "goals and timetables" and "representation," but in a context which did not yet make it clear that employers were to have specific numbers and percentages set forth as measures of their hiring practices. The next set of guidelines, in 1970, spoke of "results-oriented procedures," suggesting a shift from the still prospective 1968 language of "goals and timetables for the prompt achievement of full and equal employment opportunity" to a retrospective "results" criterion. The guidelines issued in December 1971 made it clear that "goals and timetables" were meant to "increase materially the utilization of minorities and women," with "under-utilization" being spelled out as "having fewer minorities or women in a particular job classification than would reasonably be expected by their availability." Employers were required to confess to "deficiencies" in the "utilization" of minorities and women whenever this statistical parity could not be found in all job classifications, as a first step toward correcting this situation. The burden of proof— and remedy—was on the employer. "Affirmative action" was now decisively transformed into a numerical concept, whether called "goals" or "quotas."

II. PRESUPPOSITIONS

To equate the retrospective fact of statistical under representation with the prospective act of discrimination requires additional presuppositions about the nature of social processes. So too does the belief that the extent of discrimination can be measured or monitored through numerical representation.

Group discrimination—differential treatment of similar individuals who belong to different groups—can be inferred from differences in group "representation" only insofar as the relevant characteristics by which individuals are chosen do not differ substantially from one group to another. *This is not even approximately true.*

Median age differences of a decade or more are common among American ethnic groups. Blacks, Hispanics, and American Indians are at least a decade younger than Americans of Irish, Polish, or Japanese ancestry—and more than twenty years younger than Americans of Jewish ancestry.

* * *

These huge age differences reflect, in part, differences in the number of children per family, which is twice as large in some groups as in others. Half of all Mexican Americans or Puerto Ricans in the United States are either infants, children or teenagers. To compare any group's representation in adult jobs with their representation in a *population* that includes five-year-olds is to compare apples and oranges. The comparison is especially inappropriate in the high-level occupations on which special attention is focused. These jobs typically require years of experience and/or education, and are consequently filled by individuals in their forties or fifties. In these age brackets, the *demographic* "representation" is so different from one group to another as to make an even occupational representation virtually impossible. . . .

Age differences of the magnitudes found among American ethnic groups play havoc with all the gross statistical comparisons that are commonly used, for age has a major impact, throughout all groups, on such variables as income, occupation, unemployment, fertility, and crime rates. Income differences between age brackets in the U.S. population are greater than income differences between blacks and whites.

* * *

In a country of the size and regional diversity of the United States, geographical distribution affects incomes as dramatically as demographic distribution does. Income differences between California and Arkansas, or between Alaska and Mississippi, are greater than income differences between blacks and whites. No ethnic group in the United States has an income that is as low as one-half the national average, but members of a given ethnic group in one location often earn less than half the income of members of the same ethnic group located elsewhere. Blacks in Mississippi earn less than half the income of blacks in New York state. Mexican Americans in the Laredo or Brownsville metropolitan areas in Texas earn less than half the income of Mexican Americans in the Detroit metropolitan area. Indians on reservations earn less than half the income of Indians located in Chicago, Detroit or New York City. In short, the effects of geographical distribution are profound, and are confounded with ethnic differences, as such, in gross statistical comparisons among groups. Virtually no two American ethnic groups have the same geographical distribution pattern. . . .

Age and location are variables with little moral or ideological significance, and are not very amenable to governmental policy control. This may explain, but in no way justifies, their being almost totally disregarded in analyses of causes of intergroup differences in income or occupations. Moreover, age and location are among various neglected factors which invalidate the presumption that all intergroup differences are due either to current discrimination or to some behavior in the past or present by a personified "society." In some cases, we feel certain *from other evidence* that discrimination has existed or does exist. But both intellectually and legally, a serious problem arises when the real basis for belief is replaced by pseudoscientific numerical indices—i.e., when issues are decided by gut feelings garnished with numbers. Many social processes and variables can and do generate the same numbers attributed to discrimination.

Many substantial economic and social differences among ethnic groups in the United States reflect historic differences that existed before they ever set foot on American soil—for example, the over representation of Jews in the clothing industry, Germans in the beer industry, or the Irish in politics and the priesthood, not to mention such general cultural differences as varying receptivity to formal education. In the New York City schools of 1911, German and Jewish children finished high school at a rate more than a hundred times greater than Irish or Italian children. Since the Irish were the dominant group in both municipal politics and among school teachers, these results could hardly have been due to discrimination against the Irish by either Germans or Jews. Similarly, in turn-of-the-century Boston, the Irish not only had more political power than the Jews but higher incomes and more education among the adults—and still the Jewish children went on to college at a higher rate than the Irish children.

The history of the Irish and the Jews in this era undermines the explanatory value of the usual socioeconomic indices, as well as those two favorite "causes" of social phenomena—"ability" and "discrimination." In addition to being better off than the Jews politically, economically, and educationally, the Irish also scored higher on mental tests administered to masses of soldiers in World War I. Because the Irish had immigrated to the United States in large numbers before the Jews, American "society" had given them more material and educational advantages over the years. What American society could not give them were the Jewish attitudes and values—and these proved decisive, as the Jews rose past the Irish by all the usual economic, educational, and other indices. In short, the actions of "society" are often far from decisive in the outcome, much less all-determining.

The case of blacks is obviously quite different from the case of Jews, for all sorts of historical and other reasons that remain largely implicit. But in terms of the explicit argument and the explicit evidence cited in "affirmative action" cases—and applied to all sorts of ethnic, sex, and other groups—the history of the Jews, Orientals, and other ethnic groups is relevant and fatally undermines their presuppositions. To the extent that the explicit evidence is merely *pro forma* recitation, the implicit argument is not tested for either its general validity or its applicability to each of the diverse groups covered by "affirmative action."

A. *The Ethnic Vision and the "National Average"*

A common theme in "affirmative action" arguments is comparison of one group's statistics with "the national average" or with local or regional data. This approach makes all deviations from the average look unusual or even suspicious. The implicit suggestion is that all groups would be "average" in the relevant respects, but for intervening discrimination or other societal action. But comparing each group with the national average seriatim is a very different process from looking at all the groups simultaneously—which may reveal that the national average is itself just one point on a wide-ranging continuum, and that "deviations" on either side are quite common. In other words, the national average is nothing more than a statistical amalgamation of highly diverse group characteristics, and not a norm measuring what most people actually do or should do.

The median family incomes of various American ethnic groups illustrates the point:

Ethnic Group	Income as Percent of National Average
Jewish	172 percent
Japanese	132 percent
Polish	115 percent
Chinese	112 percent
Italian	112 percent
German	107 percent
Anglo-Saxon	105 percent
Irish	102 percent
NATIONAL AVERAGE	100 percent
Filipino	99 percent
West Indian	94 percent
Mexican	76 percent
Puerto Rican	63 percent
Black	62 percent
Indian	60 percent

Source: U.S. Bureau of the Census and National Jewish Population Survey.

The notion of a national average unreachable by ethnic minority—or by non-white minorities—will not stand up, in the face of these data. Two of the top five incomes are by non-white groups. In addition, black West Indians have incomes not far from the national average, and considerably higher than the incomes of Puerto Ricans, most of whom are white.

The supposedly dominant Anglo-Saxons have incomes below various groups who arrived in American after them, and who faced varying degrees of discrimination on their way up. Anglo-Saxons may be envisioned as wealthy old families, but in fact they include poverty-stricken people scattered along hundreds of miles of the Appalachians, and numerous other places in American society. Even the supposed numerical dominance of the Anglo-Saxons is largely mythical. They are indeed the largest of the ethnically identifiable groups, but (1) half of all Americans cannot identify their ethnicity to Census surveyors, presumably because of intermixtures, and (2) Anglo-Saxons are only about 14 percent of the population. Despite widespread use of the majority-minority dichotomy, it is intellectually questionable to refer to 14 percent of the population as if they were a majority and to 13 percent (Germans) or 11 percent (blacks) as "minorities." Moreover, the inclusion of women as a disadvantaged group brings the total proportion of persons in the minority category up to about two-thirds of the total population.

Both the demographic and the economic data reveal the wholly arbitrary nature of the government's designations of various groups as "minorities" or "disadvantaged" groups—for the official list includes groups both above and below the national average, e.g., Japanese and Chinese as well as Indians or Mexicans. The only consistency in the list is with an implicit vision of racist and sexist discrimination as the reason for group deviations from the national average. Where those deviations include incomes nearly a third larger than the national average (Japanese), the data must at least suggest other very powerful influences at work—factors which cannot then be arbitrarily excluded from explanations of why other groups fall below the mythical national norm.

Many cultural differences do not lend themselves to quantification, but some have numerical effects. For example, half of all Mexican American women are married in their teens, while only 10 percent of Japanese American women marry that young. It requires little imagination to see how that must affect opportunities for college attendance and/or lucrative careers, quite aside from employer discrimination or the sins of "society."

B. *The Special Case of Blacks*

The unique history of blacks—both slavery and pervasive Jim Crow laws and practices—has been used as a justification for affirmative action programs, though as noted above, such programs are then applied to groups (including women) who add up to several times the size of the black population. But, putting aside this "entering wedge" approach to policymaking, how well do the presuppositions of affirmative action apply to the group which provides its strongest arguments? That is, how much of the still substantial black-white difference in incomes and occupations can be attributed to employer discrimination?

Despite a voluminous literature on discrimination, this is a question seldom addressed and often settled by assumption. . . .

One of the most obvious ways to test the effect of color against the effect of culture would be to compare the economic conditions of groups with the same color but with different cultures. Alternatively, the comparison could be made between groups with the same culture but of different colors. Seldom has either of these things been done.

Black West Indians living in the United States are a group physically indistinguishable from black Americans, but with a cultural background that is quite different. If current employer racial discrimination is the primary determinant of below average black income, West Indians' incomes would be similarly affected. Yet, as seen . . . West Indian incomes are 94 percent of the U.S. national average, while the incomes of blacks as a group are only 62 percent of the national average. That is, West Indians' incomes are 44 percent higher than the incomes of other blacks. Their "representation" in professional occupations is double that of blacks, and slightly higher than that of the U.S. population as a whole.

The argument has sometimes been made that white employers distinguish West Indians from other blacks by accent, birthplace or place of schooling and that this differentiation in their treatment explains the substantial intergroup economic differences between these two sets of blacks in the same economy. Again, the test is not plausibility but evidence. If accent, birthplace or place of schooling are responsible for West Indians' advantages in the market place, then those West Indians lacking such obvious clues for American employers would not be expected to have comparable advantages over other blacks. *Second-generation* West Indians—born in the United States of West Indian parents—are less likely to have an accent and would have no distinguishing place of birth or schooling. If employer discrimination explains the economic condition of blacks, and the different conditions of West Indians, then second-generation West Indians should not be expected to have as large an advantage over other blacks. If, on the other hand, West Indian advantages are cultural, then second-generation West Indians might be expected to continue to benefit from the values and behavior patterns of their parents, plus whatever additional benefits derive from their parents' socioeconomic success and their own greater familiarity with American society. In short, diametrically opposite predictions regarding second-generation West Indians derive from the theory of cultural differences and the theory of employer discrimination as explanations of black incomes below the national average.

The facts about the economic conditions of second-generation West Indians are rather dramatic in themselves, and decisive in their implications. Second-generation West Indians have even higher incomes than first generation West Indians, and higher incomes than the national average—or the incomes of Anglo-Saxons. Second-generation West Indians also have higher proportions in the professions than other blacks, first generation West Indians, the national average, or Anglo-Saxons. These data are from the 1970 Census, which is to say they are 1969 incomes—two years before the 1971 federal guidelines mandating quota hiring, and so cannot be explained as effects of affirmative action.

* * *

Looked at another way, the still large racial income difference was cultural rather than racial, as such. Data for earlier periods did not show such a similar pattern. Blacks made less than whites in earlier years, even when cultural indicators were the same. This is consistent with historical evidence of racial discrimination, while undermining the conclusion that all current differences can be automatically attributed to the same source.

There are many possible reasons for West Indians' advantages over other blacks. The purpose here is not to praise, blame, grade, or otherwise morally rank groups. In some ultimate sense, we are all born into a world we never made, including the values around us. The more important point, from a causal standpoint or policy relevance, is the source of the racial statistical discrepancies so often cited. West Indian data are simply a means to the end of testing alternative theories of racial discrepancies. Like the comparison between the Irish and the Jews, this comparison among different black groups suggests that cultural traits reaching far back in history have continuing contemporary impact, invalidating any presumption of equal "representation," income, etc., in the absence of current discriminatory institutional policies.

* * *

E. *The "Results" of Affirmative Action*

Despite the shift in the meaning of affirmative action, from prospective opportunity to retrospective results, the affirmative action program itself has little in the way of results to show for its own wide ranging, costly, activity. . . .

The automatic attribution that has occurred to affirmative action has been promoted by before-and-after comparisons in which "before" was long before the 1971 guidelines on goals and timetables, and before the whole equal opportunity phase that preceded affirmative action. This confounds the effects of two very different policies—equal opportunity with regard to race or ethnicity, and affirmative action with regard to those very same factors. There were dramatic improvements in the relative positions of low-income ethnic groups during the 1960's or equal opportunity era—more so than during the 1970's affirmative action policies. To attribute the total advancement of both phases to the latter is clearly invalid.

However little empirical support there is for the effectiveness of affirmative action, it would seem—theoretically—that quotas are a stronger measure that should have more effect than equal opportunity. In fact, however, there are theoretical as well as empirical reasons for doubting this.

The incentives provided by equal opportunity laws and policies are rather unequivocal. Discrimination against comparable individuals from different groups incurs liability under the law. Non-discrimination reduces or eliminates that liability, given that the burden of proof is on the employee to demonstrate employer policies that cannot be demonstrated, by hypothesis. In short, equal opportunity policies make the non-discriminatory alternative cheaper to the employer. Affirmative action, on the other hand, provides two opposing sets of incentives. An employer's immediate liabilities are lowered by hiring from the government-designated groups, but his longer run liabilities are raised insofar as employees from the government-designated groups can subject him to additional process costs whenever their pay, promotion, or discharge patterns do not coincide with those of others or with the preconceptions of government agencies. With the burden of proof on the employer—and often, either impossible or prohibitively expensive—it is by no means clear whether he is better off in the long run to have acquired such potentially expensive employees as a means of reducing government hiring pressures. Depending on the specifics of his circumstances, those offsetting incentives may make hiring members of government designated groups either advisable or inadvisable. The net effect is not nearly as clear-cut as under equal opportunity policies.

* * *

The uniqueness of the historic disabilities of blacks is often invoked by supporters of affirmative action. But that very uniqueness undermines both their causal and legal arguments. However much various data (income, education, etc.) for blacks differ from the national average, such data are not unique. Neither the median family income, occupation level, years of schooling, I.Q., or unemployment rate of blacks is the worst among American ethnic groups. There are non-enslaved, non-Jim Crowed, non-black groups worse off in each of these respects. This is hardly a reason for complacency, but the point is that the moral uniqueness of black history does not imply a causal uniqueness. Moreover, the economic performance of West Indian blacks in the United States suggests that color discrimination as an explanatory variable will not in fact bear the weight that is placed on it. But even if the factual evidence for the current uniqueness of blacks were far stronger than it is, that would hardly be an argument for a legal principle invoked on their behalf and then extended successively to other groups lacking that uniqueness and constituting—all together—a substantial majority of the American population.

* * *

Randall Kennedy, *Persuasion and Distrust: A Comment on the Affirmative Action Debate,* 99 HARV. L. REV. 1327 (1986)*

The controversy over affirmative action constitutes the more salient current battlefront in the ongoing conflict over the status of the Negro in American life. No domestic struggle has been more protracted or more riddled with ironic complication. One frequently noted irony is that the affirmative action controversy has contributed significantly to splintering the coalition principally responsible for the Civil Rights Revolution. That coalition was comprised of a broad array of groups—liberal Democrats, moderate Republicans, the national organizations of the black and Jewish communities, organized labor and others—that succeeded in invalidating de jure segregation and passing far-reaching legislation in support of the rights of blacks, including the Civil Rights Act of 1964 and the Voting Rights Act of 1965.

For over a decade this coalition has been riven by bitter disagreement over the means by which American society should attempt to overcome its racist past. Opponents of affirmative action maintain that commitment to a nonracist social environment requires strict color-blindness in decisionmaking as both a strategy and a goal. In their view, "one gets beyond racism by getting beyond it now: by a complete, resolute, and credible commitment *never* to tolerate in one's own life—or in the life or practices of one's government, the differential treatment of other human beings by race." Proponents of affirmative action insist that only *malign* racial distinctions should be prohibited—they favor benign distinctions that favor blacks. Their view is that "[i]n order to get beyond racism, we must first take race into account" and that "in order to treat some persons equally, we must treat them differently."

* * *

I. THE EFFICACY AND LAWFULNESS OF AFFIRMATIVE ACTION

A. The Case for Affirmative Action

Affirmative action has strikingly benefited blacks as a group and the nation as a whole. It has enabled blacks to attain occupational and educational advancement in numbers and at a pace that would otherwise have been impossible. These breakthroughs engender self-perpetuating benefits: the accumulation of valuable experience, the expansion of a professional class able to pass its material advantages and elevated aspirations to subsequent generations, the eradication of debilitating stereotypes, and the inclusion of black participants in the making of consequential decisions affecting black interests. Without affirmative action, continued access for black

---

applicants to college and professional education would be drastically narrowed. To insist, for example, upon the total exclusion of racial factors in admission decisions, especially at elite institutions, would mean classes of college, professional and graduate students that are virtually devoid of Negro representation.

Furthermore, the benefits of affirmative action redound not only to blacks but to the nation as a whole. For example, the virtual absence of black police even in overwhelmingly black areas helped spark the ghetto rebellions of the 1960s. The integration of police forces through strong affirmative action measures has often led to better relations between minority communities and the police, a result that improves public safety for all. Positive externalities have accompanied affirmative action programs in other contexts as well, most importantly by teaching whites that blacks, too, are capable of handling responsibility, dispensing knowledge, and applying valued skills.

B. The Claim That Affirmative Action Harms Blacks

In the face of arguments in favor of affirmative action, opponents of the policy frequently reply that it actually harms its ostensible beneficiaries. Various interrelated claims undergird the argument that affirmative action is detrimental to the Negro. The most weighty claim is that preferential treatment exacerbates racial resentment, entrenches racial divisiveness, and thereby undermines the consensus necessary for effective reform. The problem with this view is that intense white resentment has accompanied every effort to undo racial subordination no matter how careful the attempt to anticipate and mollify the reaction. The Supreme Court, for example, tried mightily to preempt white resistance to school desegregation by directing that it be implemented with "all deliberate speed." This attempt, however, to defuse white resistance may well have caused the opposite effect and, in any event, doomed from the outset the constitutional rights of a generation of black school children. Given the apparent inevitability of white resistance and the uncertain efficacy of containment, proponents of racial justice should be wary of allowing fear of white backlash to limit the range of reforms pursued. This admonition is particularly appropriate with respect to affirmative action insofar as it creates vital opportunities the value of which likely outweigh their cost in social friction. A second part of the argument that affirmative action hurts blacks is the claim that it stigmatizes them by implying that they simply cannot compete on an equal basis with whites. Moreover, the pall cast by preferential treatment is feared to be pervasive, hovering over blacks who have attained positions without the aid of affirmative action as well as over those who have been accorded preferential treatment. I do not doubt that affirmative action causes some stigmatizing effect. It is unrealistic to think, however, that affirmative action causes most white disparagement of the abilities of blacks. Such disparagement, buttressed for decades by the rigid exclusion of blacks from educational and employment opportunities, is precisely what engendered the explosive crisis to which affirmative action is a response. Although it is widely assumed that "qualified" blacks are now in great demand, with virtually unlimited possibilities for recognition, blacks continue to encounter prejudice that ignores or minimizes their talent. In the end, the uncertain extent to which affirmative action diminishes the accomplishments of blacks must be balanced against the stigmatization that occurs when blacks are virtually absent from important institutions in the society. The presence of blacks across the broad spectrum of institutional settings upsets conventional stereotypes about the place of the Negro and acculturates the public to the idea that blacks can and must participate in all areas of our national life. This positive result of affirmative action outweighs any stigma that the policy causes.

A third part of the argument against affirmative action is the claim that it saps the internal morale of blacks. It renders them vulnerable to a dispiriting anxiety that they have not truly earned whatever positions or honors they have attained. Moreover, it causes some blacks to lower their own expectations of themselves. Having grown accustomed to the extra boost provided by preferential treatment, some blacks simply do not try as hard as they otherwise would. There is considerable power to this claim, unaided accomplishment does give rise to a special pride felt by both the individual achiever and her community. But the suggestion that affirmative action plays a major role in undermining the internal morale of the black community is erroneous.

Although I am unaware of any systematic evidence on the self-image of beneficiaries of affirmative action, my own strong impression is that black beneficiaries do not see their attainments as tainted or undeserved—and for good reason. First, they correctly view affirmative action as rather modest compensation for the long period of racial subordination suffered by blacks as a group. Thus they do not feel that they have been merely *given* a preference; rather, they see affirmative discrimination as a form of social justice. Second, and more importantly, many black beneficiaries of affirmative action view claims of meritocracy with skepticism. They recognize that in many instances the objection that affirmative action represents a deviation from meritocratic standards is little more than disappointed nostalgia for a golden age that never really existed. Overt exclusion of blacks from public and private institutions of education and employment was one massive affront to meritocratic pretensions. Moreover, a longstanding and pervasive feature of our society is the importance of a wide range of nonobjective, nonmeritocratic factors influencing the distribution of opportunity. The significance of personal associations and informal networks is what gives durability and resonance to the adage, "It's not *what* you know, it's *who* you know." As Professor Wasserstrom wryly observes, "Would anyone claim that Henry Ford II [was] head of the Ford Company because he [was] the most qualified person for the job?"

Finally, and most importantly, many beneficiaries of affirmative action recognize the thoroughly political—which is to say contestable—nature of "merit"—they realize that it is a malleable concept, determined not by immanent, preexisting standards but rather by the perceived needs of society. Inasmuch as the elevation of blacks addresses pressing social needs, they rightly insist that considering a black's race as part of the bundle of traits that constitute "merit" is entirely appropriate.

A final and related objection to affirmative action is that it frequently aids those blacks who need it least and who can least plausibly claim to suffer the vestiges of past discriminational—the offspring of black middle-class parents seeking preferential treatment in admission to elite universities and black entrepreneurs seeking guaranteed set-asides for minority contractors on projects supported by the federal government. This objection too is unpersuasive. First, it ignores the large extent to which affirmative action has pried open opportunities for blue-collar black workers. Second, it assumes that affirmative action should be provided only to the most deprived strata of the black community or to those who can best document their victimization. In many circumstances, however, affirmative action has developed from the premise that special aid should be given to strategically important sectors of the black community—for example, those with the threshold ability to integrate the professions. Third, although affirmative action has primarily benefitted the black middle class, that is no reason to condemn preferential treatment. All that fact indicates is the necessity for additional social intervention to address unmet needs in those sectors of the black community left untouched by affirmative action. One thing that proponents of affirmative action have neglected to emphasize strongly enough is that affirmative discrimination is but part—indeed a rather small part—of the needed response to the appalling crisis besetting black communities. What is so remarkable—and ominous—about the affirmative action debate is that so modest a reform calls forth such powerful resistance.

C. Does Affirmative Action Violate the Constitution?

The constitutional argument against affirmative action proceeds as follows: *All* governmental distinctions based on race are presumed to be illegal and can only escape that presumption by meeting the exacting requirements of "strict scrutiny." Because the typical affirmative action program cannot meet these requirements, most such programs are unconstitutional. Behind this theory lies a conviction that has attained its most passionate and oft-quoted articulation in Alexander Bickel's statement:

> The lesson of the great decisions of the Supreme Court and the lesson of contemporary history have been the same for at least a generation: discrimination on the basis of race is illegal, immoral, unconstitutional, inherently wrong, and destructive of democratic society. Now this is to be unlearned and we are told that this is not a matter of fundamental principle but only a matter of whose ox is gored.

Among the attractions of this theory are its symmetry and simplicity. It commands that the government be color-blind in its treatment of persons, that it accord benefits and burdens to black and white individuals according to precisely the same criteria—no matter whose ox is gored. According to its proponents, this theory dispenses with manipulable sociological investigations and provides a clear *rule* that compels consistent judicial application.

In response, I would first note that the color-blind theory of the Constitution is precisely that—a "theory," one of any number of competing theories that seek to interpret the fourteenth amendment's delphic proscription of state action that denies any person "the equal protection of the laws." Implicitly recognizing that neither a theory or original intent nor a theory of textual construction provides suitable guidance, Professor Bickel suggests that a proper resolution of the affirmative action dispute can be derived from "the great decisions of the Supreme Court." Certainly what Bickel had in mind were *Brown v. Board of Education* and its immediate progeny, the cases that established the foundation of our post-segregation Constitution. To opponents of affirmative action, the lesson of these cases is that, except in the narrowest, most exigent circumstances, race can play no legitimate role in governmental decisionmaking.

This view, however, is too abstract and ahistorical. In the forties, fifties and early sixties, against the backdrop of laws that used racial distinctions to exclude Negroes from opportunities available to white citizens, it seemed that racial subjugation could be overcome by mandating the application of race-blind laws. In retrospect, however, it appears that the concept of race-blindness was simply a proxy for the fundamental demand that racial subjugation be eradicated. This demand, which matured over time in the face of myriad sorts of opposition, focused upon the *condition* of racial subjugation; its target was not only procedures that overtly excluded Negroes on the basis of race, but also the self-perpetuating dynamics of subordination that had survived the demise of American apartheid. The opponents of affirmative action have stripped the historical context from the demand for race-blind law. They have fashioned this demand into a new totem and insist on deference to it no matter what its effects upon the very group the fourteenth amendment was created to protect. *Brown* and its progeny do not stand for the abstract principle that governmental distinctions based on race are unconstitutional. Rather, those great cases, forged by the gritty particularities of the struggle against white racism, stand for the proposition that the Constitution prohibits any arrangements imposing racial subjugation—whether such arrangements are ostensibly race-neutral or even ostensibly race-blind.

This interpretation, which articulates a principle of antisubjugation rather than antidiscrimination, typically encounters two closely related objections. The first objection is the claim that the constitutional injury done to a white whose chances for obtaining some scarce opportunity are diminished because of race-based allocation schemes is legally indistinguishable from that suffered by a black victim of racial exclusion. Second, others argue that affirmative discrimination based on racial distinctions cannot be satisfactorily differentiated from racial subjugation absent controversial sociological judgments that are inappropriate to the judicial role.

As to the first objection, the injury suffered by white "victims" of affirmative action does not properly give rise to a constitutional claim, because the damage does not derive from a scheme animated by racial prejudice. Whites with certain credentials may be excluded from particular opportunities they would receive if they were black. But this diminished opportunity is simply an incidental consequence of addressing a compelling societal need: undoing the subjugation of the Negro. Whites who would be admitted to professional schools in the absence of affirmative action policies are not excluded merely because of prejudice, as were countless numbers of Negroes until fairly recently. Rather, whites are excluded "because of a rational calculation about the socially most beneficial use of limited resources for [professional] education."

As to the second objection, I concede that distinctions between affirmative and malign discrimination cannot be made in the absence of controversial sociological judgments. I reject the proposition, however, that drawing these distinctions is inappropriate to the judicial role. Such a proposition rests upon the assumption that there exists a judicial method wholly independent of sociological judgment. That assumption is false; to some extent, whether explicitly or implicitly, every judicial decision rests upon certain premises regarding the irreducibly controversial nature of social reality. The question, therefore, is not whether a court will make sociological judgments, but the content of the sociological judgments it must inevitably make.

Prior to *Brown*, the Supreme Court's validation of segregation statutes rested upon the premise that they did not unequally burden the Negro. A perceived difficulty in invalidating segregation statutes was that, as written, such laws were race-neutral; they excluded white children from Negro schools just as they excluded Negro children from white schools. The Court finally recognized in *Brown* that racial subjugation constituted the social meaning of segregation laws. To determine that social meaning, the Court had to look past form into substance and judge the legitimacy of segregation laws given their intended and actual effects. Just as the "neutrality" of the segregation laws obfuscated racial subjugation, so too may the formal neutrality of race-blind policies also obfuscate the perpetuation of racial subjugation. That issue can only be explored by an inquiry into the context of the race-blind policy at issue, an inquiry that necessarily entails judicial sociology.

* * *

Patricia J. Williams, Metro Broadcasting, Inc. v. FCC: *Regrouping in Singular Times*, 104 HARV. L. REV. 525 (1990)*

* * *

I. THE REAL ISSUES AT STAKE

One of the major issues in *Metro Broadcasting* was whether and to what extent the FCC's desire to promote racial and ethnic pluralism in programming is served by its choice to diversify broadcast ownership. Applying a standard of review that required the FCC's diversity program to be substantially related to an important governmental interest, the majority held that broadcast diversity was such an interest. According to the majority, although no necessary connection exists between ownership and diverse programming, congressional and FCC findings strongly suggested that diversity would be promoted by increasing the representation of groups currently under represent among owners. The dissenters, adhering to a standard of strict scrutiny, attacked the majority's use of the substantial relation test as a dangerous validation of racial classifications and challenged the notion that broadcast diversity was a compelling governmental interest. Moreover, the dissenters argued that without some guarantee that any particular minority station owner would structure programming differently than a non-minority owner, the FCC's use of race and ethnicity as factors in its licensing decisions could not be considered "narrowly tailored" enough to meet the declared interest in diversity.

Although the majority and the dissenters framed the issue in terms of disagreement about the standard of review, their underlying characterizations of the facts and weighing of the evidence were so polarized that the split probably would have remained even had they agreed on this doctrinal issue. The conflict underlying the opinions is revealed by the subtly nuanced and infinitely slippery vocabulary employed by each side. There was a covert adjectival war taking place in *Metro Broadcasting*, in which words were inflated like balloons in order to make the issue of diversity large or trivial, compelling or merely important, natural or momentary, grandly futuristic or of the local past.

The intensity of these divisions is rooted in profound differences in political philosophy about the nature of group identity, individualism, and the role of the market. Justice Brennan's analysis placed issues on a historical continuum that looks backward to our divided and ruthlessly co-optive past and forward to our long-term interest in the cooperative diversification of our airwaves and our lives. The dissenters' insistence, on the other hand, on a "guaranteed" link between diversity in ownership and diversity in programming arises from a highly individualistic notion of discriminatory action in which a court can consider little history beyond the limited confines of an arm's length commercially motivated bargain between neutrally feathered equals.

Similarly, the majority and the dissenters differed in their understandings of the very meaning of "necessity" in their respective descriptions of racial categorization as a means to desired ends. For the dissenters, necessity referred to an abstracted and absolute requirement of racial neutrality in the word of law. For the majority, necessity referred to the historically contextualized objective of media diversity, the achievement of which was constrained by a relative lack of alternative. Beyond that,

---

the starting points of each differed: for the majority, its sense of "narrowly tailoring" race-conscious efforts to eradicate discrimination had as its referential backdrop a larger social context, while for the dissenters, the sense of the menacing, unbounded "enormity" of the very same measures arose out of their singular focus on a methodological individualism.

Finally, although the majority described its measures as "not 'remedial' in the sense of being designed to compensate victims of past governmental or societal discrimination," its reasoning is clearly framed as a corrective for historical conditions that are hardly long buried in the shroud of some long-forgotten past, but whose effects are specifically identifiable and endlessly enumerable. In the dissents, on the other hand, persistent protests about future-oriented remedies divert attention from the fact that the dissenters would not have supported the outcome even if it had involved a remedial scheme for the past. The insistence that the FCC program is "'generalized'" with "'no logical stopping point'"—and the concomitant refusal even to entertain any of a host of logical stopping points suggested by the majority—amounts to an insistence on not just a personal or "identifiable" injury, but one with a completely privatized locus.

In fact, the dissenters described nothing more than contract law's limited expectation interest. The remedial frame for the dissenters was that of bargain theory— neither actual past nor future, but the *hypothetical* future of privately risked rather than constitutionally expressed expectations, not developed over time, but determined once and for all at the moment of entering into a four-cornered transaction. In the dissenters' view, constitutional rights are thus limited, as to both access and ability to enforce, not by superseding social duty, but by individually assumed obligation. The dissenters' analysis amounts to an implied requirement of notice and fault, thus constructing a civic identity that is limited to one-on-one encounters at specific business or employment sites. Judicial action may then be based only on a showing of specifically engaged and then interfered with expectations, and not on consideration of multiple lost opportunities.

In the swirl of all this, I would like to reframe some of the issues from a perspective that does not assume that simply because a problem such as discrimination is "societal" it is irremediable, nor that because a problem is individualized or privatized it is therefore effectively bounded. Whether racial imbalances are called societal or found to be the result of individualized injury, in either case there are overlooked (or underestimated) ways of looking at the problem that could provide both more latitude for courts and a clearer appreciation of the nuanced gradations that characterize judicial responses such as those in *Metro Broadcasting*.

II. DIVERSITY AND THE RECOGNITION OF GROUPS

Broadcasting diversity is often portrayed as an attempt to propagate special interest markets or to ghettoize audiences into "mass appeal" on the one hand and minority markets on the other. Its implications, however, are more complex; a real notion of diversity includes a concept of multiculturalism. This entails a view of a market in which there are not merely isolated interest groups, of which "mass market" may be one, but in which "mass" accurately reflects the complicated variety of many peoples and connotes "interactive" and "accommodative" rather than "dominant" or even just "majoritarian."

This perspective embodies the historical connotations of the quest for diversity and the underlying intersection of race and culture. In particular, although it is true that there is no guaranteed relation between race and taste in television and radio fare, the seeming simplicity of this statement deserves some qualification. For example, the literal biological truth that blacks (or members of any other racial or ethnic groups) are not born with genetic inclination for "things black" is often used to obscure the fact that "black" (like most racial or ethnic classification) also defines a culture. Blackness as culture (perhaps more easily understood as such in the designation "African-American") usually evokes a shared heritage of language patterns, habits, history, and experience.

Although all the cultures named by the FCC are exceedingly diverse, the most generalizable experience is that of battling cultural suppression if not obliteration, as well as discrimination and exclusion from the larger society. If we cannot conclude absolutely that the victims of racial oppression are always the best architects of its cure, we must nevertheless assume that the best insight and inspiration for its amelioration will come from those most immediately and negatively affected. This allowance is not merely a concession in a random contest of cultures; it is a recognition central to the checking and balancing, the fine line of restraint, that distinguishes a fluidly majoritarian society from a singularly tyrannical one.

This notion of blackness, for example, as a culture and the recognition that this culture may be consistently suppressed or denigrated under the guise of neutral "mass" entertainment, may be difficult for people who identify themselves as part of the dominant culture to understand. The parallelism of "whiteness" as culture—or as any kind of unified experience—is not immediately apparent. Although remaining convinced that there is a culture of whiteness in the United States, I appreciate the extent to which its contours are vaguely or even negatively discerned, so that its assertion is most clearly delineated as "not other," and most specifically as "not black." For so many Americans for whom minority cultures are themselves peripheral, I suspect that a realization that a culture of whiteness exists is occasioned only rarely. Perhaps the argument is more easily understood as a matter of ethnic heritage; perhaps it is easier to look at immigrant communities of those whom we now call whites in order to recapture the extent to which acculturation in the United States is assimilationist in a deeply color-coded sense. It is easy to forget, for example, that the first waves of Italian, Portuguese, Greek, Jewish, and Middle-Eastern immigrants to this country were frequently considered non-whites and suffered widespread discrimination.

It is therefore telling to note the degree to which we as Americans celebrate simultaneously our unity as a nation and the Ellis Island tradition of our variety. In the drive to achieve the unity to which our national mythology aspires, we frequently suppress if not undo the richness of our diversity by reconceptualizing any manifestation of it as a kind of unAmerican *dis*unity. I think we do this by consistently, if unconsciously, underestimating ourselves as a distinct national culture and even denying outright the possibility of our power as a consuming, assimilationist force. We tend to universalize the characteristics commonly, if romantically, attributed to middle-class America—individualism, self-interest, self-assertion—so that the very force of our desire to embrace one another becomes an impediment to the necessary recognition that "we" are not the world.

What is also troubling about this tendency is precisely the tendency to universalize individualism. In eliding singular and plural to create an abstract *Über-market-mensch*, we diminish the notion of collectivity as a collection of various overlapping others in favor of a collective *self*—again, a plural singularity—that is both condensed yet general, multiple yet monolithic, self-contained yet presumed representative.

Because the pluralism in our life and laws is so frequently unacknowledged and sometimes even suppressed, it is sometimes hard to see the extent to which we are constantly engaged in not merely discussions among equal individuals, but also complex power struggles of group against group. Recently, for example, I saw a television program in which commentators with important regionless male voices talked about the lack of educational opportunity for black children in inner-city schools. They cited statistics about dropout rates, drugs, crime, teacher apathy, lack of funding, inadequate facilities (particularly for math and science study), low expectations of civic officials and school administrators, and general conditions of hopelessness. At the end of this very depressing summary, the anchor turned to four young teenagers in the studio, all black, all excellent students in a special program designed to encourage inner-city black students with an interest in science. He asked: "We've just heard that black kids aren't very good in math and science; are you here to show us that that's a lie?" The students then proceeded to try to redeem themselves from the great group of the "not very good" by setting themselves apart as ambitious, dedicated, "different" in one sense, yet "just the same as" the majority of all other kids at the same time.

It was unbearable listening to these young people try to answer this question. It put them in an impossible double bind. On the one hand, the invisible norm was the "average" (achieving) white middle-class ideal; although this was never articulated, this is what they had to prove themselves the same as. On the other hand, these were lower class kids who came from tough inner-city neighborhoods where very few of their friends could realistically entertain aspirations to become neurosurgeons or microbiologists. It was this community from which they were being cued to be different. Let me be clear: I am not faulting these young people's aspirations or goals. What concerns me is the way in which not just this commentator, but also society at large forces them and others like them to reconcile their successful status with a covert cultural standard. In a very insidious way, the commentator's question actually limited their alternatives, compromised their function as role models, and prompted explanations of their good fortune that tended to kill their sense of communal affiliation as the only way of permitting the truth of their individualism to remain intact. Although this sort of rhetoric is frequently wrapped in aspirations of racial neutrality, it in fact pits group against individual in a way that is not just racist but classist as well.

Moreover, a question that asks children whether they prove statistics to be "a lie" does not treat statistics as genuinely informative. If the actual conditions of large numbers of people can be proved a lie by the accomplishments of an exemplary few, then statistics only reinforce an exception that proves the rule. They do not represent the likely consequences of social impoverishment; they bear no lessons about the chaotic costs of the last several years of having eliminated from our social commitment the life nets of basic survival. Rather, statistics are reduced to evidence of deserved destitution and chosen despair, the numerical tracking of people who dissemble their purported deprivation.

In another program on the failures of education, the commentator asked, do the parents care enough? "The Parents," he asked. As in "The Blacks." The plural specific. The singular generality. The monolithic multiple. Again, this type of question makes it impossible to acknowledge the complexity of the reality with a simple single answer. Well, yes, some parents care. Well, no, not enough care. Neither of these answers addresses whether "the" parents care; neither of these is as insistently summarizing as the from of the question—do the parents care, yes or no.

I cite these examples because the ability to understand statistics and use them sensibly depends on the ability to understand the difference between information about group behaviors and information that explains individual actions. The Supreme Court in recent cases, perhaps most vividly in *City of Richmond v. J.A. Croson Co.*, has persistently done something with statistical evidence that is very like asking four schoolchildren if they can make into a lie the lost opportunities of countless thousands of others. Richmond had a black population of approximately 50%, yet only 0.67% of public construction expenditures went to minority contractors. The city set a 30% goal in the awarding of its construction contracts to minorities, based on its findings that local, state, and national patterns of discrimination had resulted in all but complete lack of access for minority-owned businesses. The *Croson* majority dismissed these gross underrepresentations of people of color, of blacks in particular, as potentially attributable to their lack of "desire" to be contractors. In other words, the nearly one hundred percent absence of a given population from an extremely lucrative profession was explained away as mere lack of initiative. As long as the glass is 0.67% full . . ..

The dismissiveness of the dissenters' analysis of statistical evidence in *Metro Broadcasting* parallels that of the majority's reasoning in *Croson*. In contrast, one of the remarkable and good things about the majority's decision in *Metro Broadcasting* is that it does not supplant history with individualized hypotheses about free choice, in which each self chooses her destiny even if it is destitution. Rather, the decision takes into account past and present social constraints as realistic infringements on the ability to exercise choice; it puts our destinies on a historical continuum that gives at least as much weight to the possibility that certain minority groups have not had many chances to be in charge of things as to the possibility that they just do not want to or that they just can't. As Congress and the FCC have indicated, we as a society must change if we are not to become permanently divided. Such social necessity not only may have, but must have at least some place in the Court's consideration.

III. DIVERSITY AND BROADCASTING

Given the existence of minority cultures, and not just minority individuals, the attempt by the *Metro Broadcasting* dissenters to disclaim any relation between programming and ownership becomes rooted in paradox. The dissenting opinions contest any relation between the multiculturalism of programming and the racial or ethnic background of station owners. And yet clearly there is *some* relation between programming and the beliefs of an owner. And clearly there is some relation between one's heritage and one's beliefs.

Underlying the dissenters' attempted disavowal of the connection between ownership and broadcasting content is a paradigm in which the class characteristics of good ownership are assumed to transcend racial, ethnic, or other forms of identity. As a friend of mine is fond of saying, middle-class status is nothing more than the inner conquest of any perceived racial or ethnic identity at all. The complete Young Urban Professional (or the accomplished businessperson) is one who has achieved a certain tweedy neutrality of dress, speech, mannerism, and desire. Although there is facetiousness in this depiction, there is certainly nothing too unfamiliar in it: it merely updates and caricatures the model of the rational man who dutifully delays gratification, acts in perfect self-interest, lives with one finger on the pulse of market appetite, patterns a lifestyle upon strong if shifting trends, and under no circumstances wears anything louder than oxblood, loden, or slate.

Ironically, such an identity is not an expression of individuality. It is fashion, a collective aesthetic, a species of mass behavior wrapped in the discourse of self-interest. This deeply embedded notion of the rational market actor is in fact a conformed identity, so normalized that we seem to have lost the ability to see it as such. Nor is this identity really racially or ethnically neutral. For all the brilliant cultural mixtures in art, music, and film that America has given the world, middle- and upper-classness remains deeply steeped in Western European traditions and dominated by strong Protestant values. Ninety-five percent of all corporate executives, including communications executives, are still white males, "a figure that hasn't changed since 1979." As the *Metro Broadcasting* majority observed, "in 1986, [minorities] owned just 2.1 percent of the more than 11,000 radio and television stations in the United States. Moreover, . . . as late entrants who often have been able to obtain only the less valuable stations, many minority broadcasters serve geographically limited markets with relatively small audiences."

Furthermore, in an era of "infomercials," the media is increasingly used simply to spread (rather than exchange) information about markets (rather than ideas). Television and radio undoubtedly enable people to shop faster and better; it is easier than ever before to stay informed about a wide range of consumer goods and services. Yet even as they replace libraries (the traditional bastions of our culture), they do not seem to be serving the same interests or function as libraries. These media are not being geared for the sort of browsing in which there is no commercial stake. Although electronically conveyed knowledge indeed may be cheaper and easier to obtain in one sense, I wonder about a larger question: the degree to which information itself needs a patron or sponsor to be conveyed in the first place. Our modern-day patrons are no longer popes and princes; they are corporations and philanthropies. The degree to which advertising alone purveys and censors information seriously threatens genuine freedom of information. The degree to which the major media, the culture-creators in our society, are owned by very few or are subsidiaries of each other's financial interests, must be confronted as a skewing of the way in which cultural information is collected and distributed.

Thus, executives in the communications industry exercise a power that is not merely concentrated but also propagandistic. They make far-reaching choices in a way that few others in our society can. They project their images of the world out into the world. They do not merely represent, but also recreate themselves and their vision of the world as desirable, salable. What they reproduce is not neutral, not without consequence. To pretend (as we all do from time to time) that film or television, for example, is a neutral vessel, or contentless, mindless, or unpersuasive, is sheer denial. It is, for better and frequently for worse, one of the major forces in the shaping of our national vision, a chief architect of the modern American sense of identity.

Even assuming that profit-seeking behavior explains all or that materialism is itself a kind of culture, if the United States is to be anything more than a loose society of mercenaries—of suppliers and demanders, of vendors and consumers—then it must recognize that other forms of group culture and identity exist. We must respect the dynamic power of these groups and cherish their contributions to our civic lives, rather than pretend they do not exist as a way of avoiding argument about their accommodation. And we must be on guard against either privileging in our law a supposedly neutral "mass" culture that is in fact highly specific and historically contingent or legitimating a supposedly neutral ethic of individualism that is really a corporate group identity, radically constraining any sense of individuality, and silently advancing the claims of that group identity.

This is not to say that all women or blacks or men see the world in the same way or only according to their cultures. I do not believe that a "pure" black or feminist or cultural identity of any sort exists, any more than I think culture is biological. I am arguing against a perceived monolithism of "universal" culture that disguises our overlapping variety and that locates non-whites as "separate," "other," even "separatist" cultures or, as in the context of *Metro Broadcasting*, that argues about whether such cultures even exist.

The point then is not that whites cannot program for blacks, or that blacks would not watch programming aimed at Hispanic audiences. And the point is not, for example, whether white actors can convincingly portray Asian characters, as was so reductively maintained by the producers in the recent debate over the ill-fated Broadway version of *Miss Saigon*, or whether a black actor should be able to play the lead in Shakespeare's *Richard III*. I do maintain that a certain institutional skewing has taken place if within a supposedly diverse society it is only whites who represent Asians, only men who play women, or only children who fill black roles. It would suggest a profound social imbalance if only North Americans compose the intellectual canon of South American history. And if rape occurs mostly to women, it seems peculiar to reserve control over the standards for its remediation exclusively to men. In fact, it is precisely these sorts of disrespectful exclusivities that signal the most visible sites of oppression in any society.

In our society, the most obvious means of tearing down such exclusivities is dispersion of ownership. Participation in ownership of anything, but most particularly of broadcast stations or other tools of mass communication, is the gateway to our greatest power as Americans. Ownership enables one not merely to sell to others or to offer oneself to the call of the market. It provides the opportunity to propagate oneself in the marketplace of cultural images. Participation in the privileges of ownership thus involves more than the power to manipulate property itself; it lends an ability to express oneself through property as an instrument of one's interests. We think of freedom of expression as something creative, innovative, each word like a birth of something new and different. But it is also the power to manipulate one's resources to sanction what is not pleasing. The property of the communications industry is all about the production of ideas, images, and cultural representations, but it also selectively silences even as it creates. Like all artistic expression, it is a crafting process of production and negation, in the same way that a painting may involve choices to include yellow and blue while leaving out red and green.

Translating this understanding of ownership into the context of broadcast diversification, the issue becomes not only what is sanctioned, but also who is sanctioning. It is not that minorities live in wholly separate worlds, enclaves walled in by barriers of language, flavors, and music; minorities are not languishing on electronically underserved islands, starving for the rap-marimba beat of a feminist Korean-speaking radio deejay whom only like others can understand. Nevertheless, a feminist Korean deejay is more likely to sanction insulting images of herself and more likely to choose to propagate images of herself that humanize her and her interests. Likewise, it is not that white owners cannot be persuaded not to rerun old *Amos 'n' Andy* shows, in which white actors in blackface portrayed blacks in derogatory if comic ways and which reiterated the exclusive (until recently) image of blacks in the media. Rather, it is that it is much easier—and very likely not even necessary—to persuade Bill Cosby, for example, to choose to run programming that challenges and variegates the perpetual image of blacks as foolish and deviant.

In fact, I think that Bill Cosby's very success—as owner, producer, writer, and actor—in delivering an image of at least a certain middle-class segment of imagistic blackness into the realm of the "normal," rather than the deviant, has run him up against yet an even more complex (if instructive) level of cultural co-optation. As *The Cosby Show*'s warm, even smarmy appeal has made it a staple in homes around the country, black cultural inflections that were initially quite conspicuous (speech patterns, the undercurrent of jazz music, the role of Hillman College as the fictional black alma mater of the Huxtables, hairstyles ranging from dreadlocks to "high top fades") have become normalized and invisible.

Moreover, the process of normalizing has exaggerated the extent to which the black middle class and white middle class are not merely derivative, but identical, so that *The Cosby Show* has been described as little more than a portrayal of blacks costumed in cultural whiteface. Although this "whitening" of its appeal is refined into the language of "sameness," the process devalues and even robs the program of its black content.

Thus, as black cultural contributions are absorbed into mainstream culture, they actually become seen as exclusively white cultural property, with no sense of the rich multiculturalism actually at work. Ultimately, the minority set-aside policies at issue in *Metro Broadcasting* must address this consuming, unconscious power as well. It is not enough to have one Bill Cosby or two Oprah Winfreys if overall power is so concentrated in one community that it remains inconceivable that power could have any other source.

* * *

V. CONCLUSION

The majority opinion in *Metro Broadcasting* marks an important step toward a recognition of multiculturalism and of the need to take active steps to nurture such diversity. If the holding in this case does not guarantee that minority owners will change programming in any constructive way, it does increase the likelihood. Although the dissenters implicitly insisted on a guarantee that there be some relation, a necessary connection, such a strict guarantee can never be gained without expense to the freedoms provided by the first amendment. Even diversity of employment at other levels than ownership is largely at the will and whimsy of those owners. If cultural diversity is, as even the dissenters acknowledge, an acceptable social goal, then alternative creative means for its encouragement must be employed. That relation is fostered by making more frequent and enhancing the opportunities for minority owners and producers, who are more likely to hire minority writers, sponsor programs designed to serve the needs and interests of minority communities, and, perhaps most importantly, bring multiculturalism to mainstream programming.

Beyond the limited context of broadcasting, what I hope will be enduring about this opinion is the respect it gives to these pronounced social recognitions of the desirability of diversity in all aspects of our economy and of multiculturalism in our lives. A (probably too) concrete illustration may indicate the reconceptualization of equality that is so urgently needed. Imagine a glass half full (or half empty) of blue marbles. Their very hard-edged, discrete, yet identical nature makes it possible for the community of blue marbles to say to one another with perfect consistency both "we are all the same" and, if a few roll away and are lost in a sidewalk grate, "that's just their experience, fate, choice, bad luck." If, on the other hand, one imagines a glass full of soap-bubbles, with shifting permeable boundaries, expanding and contracting in size like a living organism, then it is not possible for the collective bubbles to describe themselves as "all the same." Furthermore, if one of the bubbles bursts, it cannot be isolated as a singular phenomenon. It will be felt as a tremor, a realignment, a reclustering among all.

Marbles and soap-bubbles are my crude way of elucidating competing conceptions of how to guarantee what we call "equal opportunity." One conception envisions that all citizens are equal, with very little variation from life to life or from lifetime to lifetime; even when there is differentiation among some, the remainder are not implicated in any necessary way.

The other conception holds that no one of us is the same and that although we can be grouped according to our similarities, difference and similarity are not exclusive categories but are instead continually evolving. Equal opportunity is not only about assuming the circumstances of hypothetically indistinguishable individuals, but also about accommodating the living, shifting fortunes of those who are very differently situated. What happens to one may be the repercussive history that repeats itself in the futures of us all.

David A. Strauss, *The Myth of Colorblindness*, 1986 SUP. CT. REV. 99 (1986)*

Sometimes great slogans make bad law, or, more precisely, misunderstood law. For decades, colorblindness was the great slogan of the civil right movements. That made it natural to believe that the movement's victories, such as *Brown v. Board of Education*, established colorblindness as the central principle of the law governing racial discrimination. It was also natural for the notion of colorblindness to set the terms of the debate over affirmative action.

Opponents of affirmative action, unsurprisingly, assert that *Brown* mandates colorblindness and that affirmative action is inconsistent with that mandate. Proponents of affirmative action seem to be put on the defensive by the invocation of colorblindness. In general, they acknowledge that there is a tension between affirmative action and *Brown*'s prohibition against racial discrimination, but they insist that the tension can be adequately resolved, at least so that affirmative action is not always unconstitutional.

Both approaches mistake a slogan for an analytical insight. The prohibition against discrimination established *Brown* is not rooted in colorblindness at all. Instead, it is, like affirmative action, deeply race-conscious; like affirmative action, the prohibition against discrimination reflects a deliberate decision to treat blacks differently from other groups, even at the expense of innocent whites. It follows that affirmative action is not at odds with the principle of nondiscrimination established by *Brown* but is instead logically continuous with that principle. It also follows that the interesting question is not whether the Constitution permits affirmative action but why the Constitution does not require affirmative action.

Reduced to its simplest terms, my argument is as follows. The prohibition against racial discrimination prohibits—and must necessarily prohibit—the use of accurate racial generalizations that disadvantage blacks. But to prohibit accurate racial generalizations is to engage in something very much like affirmative action. Specifically, a principle prohibiting accurate racial generalizations has many of the same characteristics as affirmative action; and the various possible explanations of why accurate racial generalizations are unconstitutional lead to the conclusion that failure to engage in affirmative action may also sometimes be unconstitutional.

I

In *Palmore v. Sidoti*, decided three terms ago, the Supreme Court, unanimously and with no apparent difficulty, overturned a Florida state court decision that took custody of a white child away from the divorced mother when she remarried a black man. *Palmore* is a particularly good illustration of certain essential features of the prohibition against discrimination, features that are present in racial discrimination cases generally. But *Palmore* also shows that affirmative action and nondiscrimination are, in important ways, the same thing. On the one hand, what the Supreme Court did in *Palmore* was plainly demanded by *Brown*; on the other hand, what the Court did in *Palmore* is indistinguishable from affirmative action in certain important respects. I am not suggesting at this point that it is impossible to draw a common-sense distinction between affirmative action and nondiscrimination. But critics of affirmative action attack it on the ground that it causes innocent people to suffer, and that instead of enforcing colorblindness, it draws attention to race. *Palmore* shows that the prohibition against discrimination has precisely these characteristics as well.

A

Linda and Anthony Sidoti are both white. When they were divorced, Linda was awarded custody of their three-year-old daughter, Melanie. About eighteen months after the divorce, Linda married Clarence Palmore, who is black. Anthony sued for custody of Melanie in the Circuit Court of Hillsborough County, Florida.

Florida law required Judge Buck of the county court to apply the traditional standard: he was to act in the best interests of the child. After hearing testimony, Judge Buck ordered that Anthony be given custody of the child. Judge Buck apparently regarded Anthony and Linda as equally fit parents. But he explained that notwithstanding "the strides that have been made in bettering relations between the races in this country," racial prejudice was still so pervasive, at least in central Florida, that a child raised by an interracial couple was "sure" to "suffer from . . . social stigmatization." Because Melanie would be adversely affected if she were raised in an interracial household, Judge Buck concluded that his obligation to act in the best interests of the child required him to divest Linda of custody and to award custody to Anthony.

Although, as the Supreme Court noted, a child custody determination by an inferior state court is "not ordinarily a likely candidate for review by this Court," the Supreme Court granted certiorari, and, in a brief opinion delivered only two months after oral argument, unanimously reversed the Florida court. The Supreme Court did not question Judge Buck's factual conclusion that Melanie would suffer psychological harm if she were raised by an interracial couple. Nor could the Court reasonably have questioned that determination; after all, Judge Buck was far closer to the facts of life in central Florida, and his finding was entirely plausible. Indeed, the Court explicitly acknowledged that it was subjecting Melanie to potential psychological harm "It would ignore reality to suggest that racial and ethnic prejudices do not exist or that all manifestations of those prejudices have been eliminated. There is a risk that a child living with a step-parent of a different race may be subject to a variety of pressures and stresses not present if the child were living with parents of the same racial or ethnic origin."

The Court nonetheless thought it entirely clear that Judge Buck's decision had to be reversed.

* * *

The effects of racial prejudice, however real, cannot justify a racial classification removing an infant child from the custody of its natural mother
found to be an appropriate person to have such custody.

* * *

The principle of *Brown*, therefore, required the Supreme Court to reverse the
Florida courts' decision in *Palmore*. At the same time, the reversal of the Florida decision was indistinguishable from affirmative action in important respects.

1. The principal argument used in litigation against affirmative action measures is that they violate the rights of innocent white victims. The Court's decision in
Palmore also created an innocent victim. Both by hypothesis and in fact, Melanie, the
child, will suffer psychological harm because of the Supreme Court's decision that she
would not have suffered if Judge Buck's decision had been allowed to stand. It will not
do to brush this harm aside as speculative or insignificant: nothing in the Court's
opinion suggests that it is either.

2. The Supreme Court in *Palmore* rejected an action—Judge Buck's decision—
that was, in an important sense, colorblind and race neutral. To understand why this
is so, consider the matter from Judge Buck's point of view. It was no part of the
Supreme Court's reasoning that he was in any way prejudiced against blacks or interracial couples. The Court assumed that he had applied a raceneutral standard—the
best interests of the child criterion—as straightforwardly and as conscientiously as
he could. In a custody dispute, the fact that a child will suffer psychological damage
with one parent but not another is a highly material fact, and a judge would be
derelict in his duty if he did not take that fact into account. Judge Buck, acting in a
colorblind fashion, treated *Palmore* exactly like every other case: he took into account
the prospective psychological damage to the child.

That, the Supreme Court told him, violated the Equal Protection Clause. In *Palmore*, unlike every other case, the Constitution required him to ignore that material
fact. Why was he to ignore that fact? One can give a variety of refined and complex
answers, but they all derive from one pivotal circumstance—*Palmore* involved a
black person. Judge Buck could say, in his own defense, that the import of the
Supreme Court's ruling is that he violated the Constitution by treating a case involving a black person in the same way he would have treated every other case.

Obviously, that statement is imprecise. The fact that a black person was
involved is only part of the story. But one can make this argument—that Judge
Buck acted in a colorblind fashion, and the Supreme Court held that race-conscious
action was required—more rigorously and abstractly as well. Suppose we design a
thought experiment in which a judge is literally blind to the races of the parties before
him. In particular, suppose the only evidence to which a family court judge has
access is a crystal ball that reveals nothing whatever about race. It only tells the judge
what the future of every child will be under alternative arrangements. In a case like
Palmore, Judge Buck's crystal ball will tell him that Melanie will be happier with her
father than with her mother. The cause of her unhappiness will be related to race, but
we are supposing that judge Buck—being ignorant of everyone's race—does not
know that; all his crystal ball allows him to know is that Melanie will be happier with
her father.

Suppose further that on the same day that a case like *Palmore* comes before
him, Judge Buck must also decide a case in which a divorced father seeks to regain
custody of a child from a mother who remarried, say, a notoriously ruthless industrialist who had made many enemies among members of the local community. Judge

Buck's crystal ball will look exactly the same in this case as it would have in *Palmore*. In each instance, he will see that allowing the mother to retain custody will be likely to cause the child to be ostracized by her peers and, as a result, to suffer psychological damage. In each case, therefore, Judge Buck will give the father custody of the child. When the mothers seek review in the Supreme Court, the mother who remarried the industrialist has no claim at all. But in a case like *Palmore*, the exact opposite is true: the Court would quickly and unanimously reverse Judge Buck, holding that he misunderstood a fundamental principle of the law of the Equal Protection Clause.

Judge Buck will surely be bewildered by the difference in the treatment of the cases. After all, they appeared absolutely identical to him: the crystal balls looked exactly alike. There is only one way that the Supreme Court will be able to explain its varying results to Judge Buck: the Court will have to introduce race into the picture. It will have to tell him that *Palmore* is different for some reason having to do with race. It will have to tell him that his error was that he did not take race into account. He made the mistake of focusing exclusively on his crystal ball, which revealed nothing about race. In other words, he should have been race-conscious. Judge Buck was colorblind; it was the Supreme Court that was race-conscious, and it held, in an important sense, that race-conscious action was constitutionally required.

3. The Court's justifications for its decision in *Palmore* closely resemble some of the standard justifications of affirmative action. Specifically, the Court seems to have relied on both (1) the unfairness of causing blacks (or those who associate with blacks, such as Linda Sidoti) to suffer disadvantages solely because others in society are prejudiced against them, and (2) the need to strike a blow against racial prejudice. But one common argument for allowing blacks with lesser credentials into universities, for example, is that their deficiencies were caused by racial prejudice—either prejudice against them or prejudice against their ancestors that had an adverse effect on them.

* * *

In sum, the Supreme Court's decision in *Palmore* declared that the colorblind application of a race-neutral standard was unacceptable. The Court ruled that benefits had to be given to blacks that would not be given to similarly situated whites (such as the industrialist). Such action was needed in order to prevent people from suffering the consequences of societal racial prejudice and to help bring about better race relations. These objectives warranted inflicting real harm on an innocent victim. This sounds exactly like conventional affirmative action. And the Supreme Court said that the Constitution requires this result.

I am not suggesting that it is impossible to distinguish between affirmative action and what the Court did in *Palmore*. Nor am I claiming to have proved, at this point, that the Constitution requires affirmative action. But *Palmore* does show that affirmative action and nondiscrimination have much in common. Specifically, those aspects of affirmative action that its critics most frequently invoke are characteristics of the prohibition against discrimination as well.

* * *

III

A

What this discussion principally demonstrates is the error of thinking that the law governing racial discrimination can be captured in a simple, comforting, easy-to-use term such as "colorblindness." This should not be surprising. Professor Wechsler's famous article on neutral principles argued that no principled foundation for *Brown* could be identified. Others answered him, but the one point he established is that it is not easy to articulate the principle underlying *Brown*. One cannot say that the principle is simply colorblindness. If the answer were that easy, surely Professor Wechsler and those who debated with him would have discovered it.

There are fundamental similarities between nondiscrimination and affirmative action. Moreover, while we have no fully satisfactory theory of why the Constitution forbids racial discrimination, the theories we do have suggest that affirmative action may sometimes be constitutionally required. And despite the theoretical uncertainty, my analysis has several clear implications about the kinds of arguments that can be used in the debate over affirmative action.

1. It is superficial and essentially incorrect to attack affirmative action on the ground that it is a step away from the colorblind society, or that it forces race back before our eyes. . . .

The prohibition against discrimination forces us to recognize that race is different from other bases for classifying people and forces us to act differently toward other characteristics. There is accordingly no basis for saying that affirmative action increases the consciousness of race.

2. The intense concern with the rights of innocent white victims that often characterizes the affirmative action debate is misplaced. Obviously one should never ignore the burden that any measure places on any person. But there is unquestionably an undertone in the affirmative action debate that affirmative action is different from nondiscrimination because affirmative action causes innocent people to suffer. The assertion that there is a difference in incorrect. Prohibiting discrimination also causes, and has caused, innocent people to suffer. And so far as I am a aware, no one has justified the suffering of these victims of nondiscrimination in a way that would not also justify the suffering of victims of affirmative action.

3. There is no basis for asserting that affirmative action is the moral equivalent of discrimination against blacks. This assertion reflects the myth of colorblindness at its worst: it assumes that an ill-defined notion of colorblindness is the correct state of affairs from which any deviation is wrong. I know of no theoretical justification for that view. There is, to be sure, a coherent (if unpersuasive) argument that the only principle that can be judicially administered is a prohibition against all racial generalizations. But as I noted, this argument does not explain why affirmative action is morally equivalent to discrimination against blacks.

The supposed justifications for the view that they are equivalent generally seem to assert that racial generalizations are intrinsically evil. Intrinsically, however, race is just another characteristic. One must provide some explanation of why racial generalizations are so bad. The explanations that have been given all seem to suggest, if anything, not that racial classifications are always unacceptable but the opposite: that sometimes race-neutral measures are equally bad.

It follows from this that the proponents of affirmative action should not bear the burden of proof. While there is theoretical uncertainty in this area, there is more reason to believe that deviations from race-neutrality are required than that they are forbidden. The proponents of affirmative action should not have to explain why they are not betraying *Brown*'s supposed principle of colorblindness; there is more reason to place the burden on the opponents of affirmative action to explain why maintaining a system in which there are dramatic economic and social disparities between the races is not destructive of the principles underlying *Brown*.

B

The conclusion that affirmative action may sometimes be constitutionally required is less novel than it appears. At one point, the position that the Fourteenth Amendment requires states to eliminate the racially disproportionate effects of at least certain measures was accepted, in one from or another, by several courts of appeals. Indeed, in the late 1960s and early 1970s, the position that de facto school segregation was unconstitutional—or at least, that it was to be treated in the same fashion as de jure segregation—gained considerable support. De facto segregation is segregation—a racially disproportionate effect—that results from racially neutral measures. To say that a school board must eliminate de facto segregation is to say that it must engage in affirmative action. Racial neutrality is not enough. The school board must ensure that the results are at least somewhat proportional.

In this connection, it is a mistake to suppose that constitutionally required affirmative action would mean rigid proportionality in every area. Both the areas in which affirmative action would be required and the extent to which it would be required depend on the underlying theory—that is, the theory, of what it is that makes even explicit racial discrimination wrong. If, for example, the point of prohibiting discrimination is to prevent blacks from being branded as inferior, then race-neutral measures need only be abrogated to the extent necessary to prevent that kind of stigmatization. There is no reason to believe that any form of strict proportionality would be necessary.

Finally, the close relationship between affirmative action and nondiscrimination tends to reinforce an argument used by opponents of affirmative action: the familiar argument that race-conscious measures intended to aid blacks can stigmatize them as much as oldfashioned segregation did. Perhaps this argument should have little weight in litigation brought by a white person, or in debates over legislation supported by blacks. . . .

Obviously this uncertainty about the explanation of why discrimination is wrong is unsatisfactory. Perhaps its effects can be mitigated by recalling that not all constitutional obligations need be enforced by courts. In view of the difficulty of determining with any degree of certainty when the application of race-neutral criteria is as unacceptable as the use of racial generalizations, there may be something to be said for imposing this obligation on the legislature alone. Courts could continue to enforce the principle that racial generalizations that disadvantage blacks are unlawful. Courts would still face the task of determining which racial generalizations those were, but in view of the infrequency with which blacks have challenged measures that arguably aid them, this task does not seem intractable.

It is frequently said that affirmative action is a difficult issue. It is important to be clear about why that is true. By common agreement, few institutions in our history have been as clearly wrong as the regime of racial discrimination against blacks. But it remains annoyingly difficult to articulate why it was wrong. As a result, it is sometimes difficult to identify with precision the objectives that the law in this area should pursue. And when we attempt to pursue those objectives, we inevitably impose burdens on innocent people.

These difficulties were, however, inherent in the prohibition against discrimination from the start. They did not begin with affirmative action. Only the myth of colorblindness says that they did.

Bibliography

EQUALITY CONCEPTS

Race

Slavery

Bell, Jr., Derrick A., AND WE ARE NOT SAVED (1987)

Bell, Jr., Derrick A., RACE, RACISM AND AMERICAN LAW (1980)

Fehrenbacher, Don E., THE DRED SCOTT CASE (1978)

Jordan, Winthrop D., WHITE OVER BLACK: AMERICAN ATTITUDES TOWARD THE NEGRO (1968)

Litwack, Leon F., NORTH OF SLAVERY (1961)

Lively, Donald E., THE CONSTITUTION AND RACE (1992)

Tushnet, Mark V., THE AMERICAN LAW OF SLAVERY (1981)

Wiecek, William M., THE SOURCES OF ANTISLAVERY CONSTITUTIONALISM IN AMERICA 1760-1848 (1977)

History and Understanding of the Fourteenth Amendment

ten Broek, Jacobus, ANTISLAVERY ORIGINS OF THE FOURTEENTH AMENDMENT (1951)

Cover, Robert, JUSTICE ACCUSED (1978)

Fairman, Charles, VII, HISTORY OF THE SUPREME COURT OF THE UNITED STATES, RECONSTRUCTION AND REUNION (1971)

Finkelman, Paul, AN IMPERFECT UNION (1981)

Graham, Howard J., The "Conspiracy Theory" of the Fourteenth Amendment, 47 YALE L.J. 371 (1938)

Hyman, Harold M., A MORE PERFECT UNION (1973)

Hyman, Harold M. & Wiecek, William M., EQUAL JUSTICE UNDER THE LAW (1982)

Kaczorowski, Robert J., THE POLITICS OF JUDICIAL INTERPRETATION: THE FEDERAL COURTS, DEPARTMENT OF JUSTICE AND CIVIL RIGHTS 1866-1876 (1985)

Kettner, James H., THE DEVELOPMENT OF AMERICAN CITIZENSHIP 1608-1870 (1978)

McGovney, D.O., Privileges or Immunities Clause, Fourteenth Amendment, 4 IOWA L. BULL. 219 (1918)

Woodward, C. Vann, THE BURDEN OF SOUTHERN HISTORY (1960)

Separate but Equal

Bickel, Alexander, *The Original Understanding and the Segregation Decision,* 69 HARV. L. REV. 1 (1955)

Glennon, Robert J., *Justice Henry Billings Brown: Values in Tension*, 44 U. COLO. L. REV. 553 (1973)

Kluger, Richard, SIMPLE JUSTICE (1976)

Myrdal, Gunnar, AN AMERICAN DILEMMA: THE NEGRO PROBLEM AND MODERN DEMOCRACY (1962)

Ripple, Kenneth, CONSTITUTIONAL LITIGATION (1984)

Schmidt, Benno C., Jr., *Principle and Prejudice: The Supreme Court and Race in the Progressive Era, Part 1: The Heyday of Jim Crow,* 82 COLUM. L. REV. 444 (1982).

Woodward, C. Vann, THE STRANGE CAREER OF JIM CROW (1974)

Brown and Beyond

Bell, Derrick A., Jr., *Serving Two Masters: Integration Ideals and Client Interests in School Desegregation Litigation*, 85 YALE L.J. 470 (1976)

Bickel, Alexander, *The Decade of School Segregation: Progress and Prospects*, 64 COLUM. L. REV. 193 (1964)

Gewirtz, Paul, *Remedies and Resistance*, 92 YALE L.J. 585 (1983)

Goodman, Frank I., *De Facto Segregation: A Constitutional and Empirical Analysis*, 60 CAL. L. REV. 275 (1972)

Graglia, Lino A., DISASTER BY DECREE: THE SUPREME COURT DECISIONS ON RACE AND THE SCHOOLS (1976)

Karst, Kenneth L., *Not One Law at Rome and Another at Athens: The Fourteenth Amendment in Nationwide Application*, 1972 WASH. U. L.Q. 383 (1972)

Lawrence , Charles R., III, *Segregation "Misunderstood: The Milliken Decision Revisited,* 12 U.S.F. L. REV. 15 (1977)

Lewis, Anthony, PORTRAIT OF A DECADE: THE SECOND AMERICAN REVOLUTION (1964)

Liebman, James S., *Implementing Brown in the Nineties: Political Reconstruction, Liberal Recollection, and Litigatively Enforced Legislative Reform*, 76 VA. L. REV. 349 (1990)

Steele, Roberta L., *All Things Not Being Equal: The Case for Race Separate Schools*, 43 CASE W. RES. L. REV. 591 (1973)

Yuof, Mark D., *Equal Educational Opportunity and the Courts*, 51 TEX. L. REV. 411 (1973)

Motive-Based Inquiry

Binion, Gayle, *Intent and Equal Protection: A Reconsideration*, 1983 SUP. CT. REV. 397 (1983)

Eisenberg, Theodore & Johnson, Sheri Lynn, *The Effects of Intent: Do We Know How Legal Standards Work?*, 76 CORNELL L. REV. 1151 (1991)

Eisenberg, Theodore J., *Disproportionate Impact and Illicit Motive: Theories of Constitutional Adjudication*, 52 N.Y.U. L. REV. 36 (1977)

Ely, John Hart, *Legislative and Administrative Motivation in Constitutional Law*, 79 YALE L.J. 1205 (1970)

Fiss, Owen, *Groups and the Equal Protection Clause*, 5 PHIL. & PUB. AFFS. 107 (1976)

Karst, Kenneth L., *The Costs of Motive-Centered Inquiry*, 15 SAN DIEGO L. REV. 1163 (1978)

Lively, Donald E. & Plass, Stephen, *Equal Protection: The Jurisprudence of Denial and Evasion*, 40 AM. U. L. REV. 1307 (1991)

Perry, Michael J., *The Disproportionate Impact Theory of Racial Discrimination*, 125 U. PA. L. REV. 540 (1977)

Preferential and Diversification Policies

Abram, Morris B., *Affirmative Action: Fair Shakers and Social Engineers*, 99 HARV. L. REV. 1312 (1986)

Carter, Stephen L., REFLECTIONS OF AN AFFIRMATIVE ACTION BABY (1991)

Fried, Charles, *Affirmative Action after City of Richmond v. J.A. Croson: A Response to the Scholars' Statement*, 99 YALE L.J. 155 (1989)

Fried, Charles, *Metro Broadcasting, Inc. v. FCC: Two Concepts of Equality*, 104 HARV. L. REV. 107 (1990)

Greenawalt, Kent, *The Unresolved Problems of Reverse Discrimination*, 67 CAL. L. REV. (1979)

Joint Statement, *Constitutional Scholars' Statement on Affirmative Action after* City of Richmond v. J.A. Croson Co., 98 YALE L.J. 1711 (1989)

Mishkin, Paul J., *The Uses of Ambivalence: Reflections on the Supreme Court and the Constitutionality of Affirmative Action*, 131 U. PA. L. REV. 907 (1983)

Nagel, Thomas, *Equal Treatment and Compensatory Discrimination*, 2 PHIL. & PUB. AFFS. 348 (1973)

Power, Robert C., *Affirmative Action and Judicial Incoherence*, 55 OHIO ST. L.J. (1994)

Rosenfeld, Michel, *Decoding* Richmond: *Affirmative Action and the Elusive Meaning of Constitutional Equality*, 87 MICH. L. REV. 1729 (1989)

Scholars Reply to Professor Fried, 99 YALE L.J. 163 (1989)

Steele, Shelby, THE CONTENT OF OUR CHARACTER (1990)

Sullivan, Kathleen M., *Sins of Discrimination: Last Term's Affirmative Action Cases*, 100 HARV. L. REV. 78 (1986)

Women and Other Marginalized Groups

The articles in this section primarily focus on the Constitution and gender equality, particularly the controversy concerning the treatment of gender- and sex-based classification schemes. The section also presents articles that consider the analytical alternatives available to resolve issues of inequality concerning other marginalized groups. In *The Supreme Court 1971 Term—Foreword: In Search of Evolving Doctrine on a Changing Court: A Model for a Newer Equal Protection,* Gerald Gunther suggests that the Burger Court paved the way for a more responsible judicial approach to equal protection than had been presented during the Warren era. He lauds the Court's engaging in "modest interventionism" in assuring rationality of means while being less willing to impinge on legislative prerogatives regarding ends because fundamental interests or suspect classes were affected.

In *The Politics of Women's Wrongs and the Bill of "Rights": A Bicentennial Perspective,* Mary E. Becker demonstrates how the Bill of Rights, though written in language which is gender neutral, not only better serves the interests of men than the interests of women or other groups outside the propertied white male class and may impede political participation of women and the opportunity for legislative reform in their interests and in the interests of other outsiders. Sylvia Law, in *Rethinking Sex and the Constitution,* challenges equality doctrine which denies the reality of biological difference in relation to reproduction, arguing that it is contrary to constituional ideals of individaul worth and perpetuates gender inequality. In *Deconstructing Gender,* Joan C. Williams confronts the "sameness" and "difference" split among feminists and proposes an alternative vision of gender which she claims avoids gender stereotypes and the oppressive gender system which affect men and women in family arrangements and in work.

In *Anti-Subordination Above All: Sex, Race, and Equal Protection,* Ruth Colker criticizes courts' application of the anti-discrimination principle in race and gender cases, arguing that the priciple of anti-subordination more fully addresses equality concerns than the anti-differentiation approach the Court has embraced. Judy Scales-Trent, in *Black Women and the Constitution: Finding Our Place; Asserting our Rights,* describes the dual disability experienced by Black women and considers whether Black women should be categorized as a distinct group entitled to enhanced protection under the Constitution in light of their "multiple statuses."

Janet Halley, in *The Politics of the Closet: Towards Equal Protection for Gay, Lesbian, and Bisexual Identity,* responds to the Suprme Court's holding in *Bowers v. Hardwick* by claiming that gay men, lesbians and bisexuals are entitled to protection from interference with political discourse about homosexual identity. She argues that they are entitled to heightened scrutiny of official acts punishing and deterring the public acknowledgement of gay, lesbian and bisexual identity. Finally, Martha Minow in *When Difference Has Its Home: Group Homes for the Mentally Retarded, Equal Protection and Legal Treatment of Difference* examines the concept of difference as she considers three approaches to the question of governmental treatment of people labeled as mentally incompetent: the "abnormal persons" approach, focusing on difference, a rights-analysis approach, emphasizing equal rights, and a relational approach which probes the social setting and power of the decision maker in resolving the controversy.

Gerald Gunther, *The Supreme Court 1971 Term— Foreword: In Search of Evolving Doctrine on a Changing Court: A Model for a Newer Equal Protection*, 86 HARV. L. REV. 1 (1972)*

* * *

I. The Warren Court Legacy

At the beginning of the 1960's, judicial intervention under the banner of equal protection was virtually unknown outside racial discrimination cases. The emergence of the "new" equal protection during the Warren Court's last decade brought a dramatic change. Strict scrutiny of selected types of legislation proliferated. The familiar signals of "suspect classification" and "fundamental interest" came to trigger the occasion for the new interventionist stance. The Warren Court embraced a rigid two-tier attitude. Some situations evoked the aggressive "new" equal protection with scrutiny that was "strict" in theory and fatal in fact; in other contexts, the deferential "old" equal protection reigned, with minimal scrutiny in theory and virtually none in fact.

The Warren Court left a legacy of anticipation as well as accomplishments. Its new equal protection was a dynamic concept, and the radiations encouraged hopes of further steps toward egalitarianism. "Once loosed, the idea of Equality is not easily cabined," Archibald Cox noted in the mid-sixties. The commentators' speculations, even more than the Court's results, confirmed the validity of that observation. The fundamental interests ingredient of the new equal protection was particularly open-ended. It was the element which bore the closest resemblance to freewheeling substantive due process, for it circumscribed legislative choices in the name of newly articulated values that lacked clear support in constitutional text and history. The list of interests identified as fundamental by the Warren Court was in fact quite modest: voting, criminal appeals and right of interstate travel were the primary examples. But in the extraordinary amount of commentary that followed, analysts searching for justifications for those enshrinements were understandably tempted to ponder analogous spheres that might similarly qualify. Welfare benefits, exclusionary zoning, municipal service, and school financing came to be the most inviting frontiers. The expansiveness of the speculations derived special impetus from the fact that, to an usual degree, litigation plans and doctrinal analyses came from the same hands.

Even with regard to suspect classifications, tantalizing statements from the Warren Court beckoned the searchers into the inner circle of strict scrutiny. For example, dicta suggested that wealth classifications were suspect—even though no case had actually invalidated a law solely because of differential impact on the poor, and even though it was difficult to believe that the Court seriously intended to impose broad affirmative equalizing obligations on government. But it was the fundamental interest analysis that especially invited the spinning of analogies to justify strict scrutiny of one area after another. Some strategists recognized that the open-endedness of fundamental interests might prove a fatal flaw: if the claims extended beyond schools and housing to golf courses and sewers, the sheer magnitude of the enterprise might stifle the Court's egalitarian zeal. Yet even while some proponents of the new equal protection sought to reassure critics that inclusion of education among the preferred fundamental interests would not compel extension of that cherished status to municipal services generally, others engaged in ever more far-reaching exercises in advocacy and analysis.

II. The Burger Court's Response

How has the Burger Court responded to the amalgamation of deeds and spurred hopes that constitutes the Warren Court's equal protection legacy? Those given to the assumption that substantial changes in personnel produce cataclysmic doctrinal shifts expected a root-and-branch abandonment of the interventionist new equal protection and a retreat to an extreme Holmesian deference in response to all equal protection claims, with the exception of race-related ones. But only Justice Rehnquist has urged so drastic a shift. The dominant response of the Burger Court has been less dramatic and more complex.

* * *

III. New Bite for the Old Equal Protection: A Sketch of a Model

The model suggested by recent developments would view equal protection as a means-focused, relatively narrow, preferred ground of decision in a broad range of cases. Stated most simply, it would have the Court take seriously a constitutional requirement that has never been formally abandoned: that legislative means must substantially further legislative ends. The equal protection requirement that legislative classifications must have a substantial relationship to legislative purposes is, after all, essentially a more specific formulation of that general principle. The core of that principle survived the constitutional revolution of 1937. In reality, however, it has received little more than lip service: extreme deference to imaginable supporting facts and conceivable legislative purposes was characteristic of the "hands off" attitude of the old equal protection. Putting consistent new bite into the old equal protection would mean that the Court would be less willing to supply justifying rationales by exercising its imagination. It would have the Court assess the means in terms of legislative proposes that have substantial basis in actuality, not merely in conjecture. Moreover, it would have the Justices gauge the reasonableness of questionable means on the basis of materials that are offered to the Court rather than resorting to rationalizations created by perfunctory judicial hypothesizing.

This relatively vigorous scrutiny would be more interventionist than the Warren Court's applications of old equal protection formulas. But it would be considerably less strict than the new equal protection. First, it would concern itself solely with means, not with ends. The "substantive equal protection" of the Warren era repeatedly asked whether legislative ends were "compelling" and repeatedly found legislative purposes inadequate to justify impingements on fundamental interests. An invigorated old equal protection scrutiny would not involve adjudication on the basis of fundamental interests with shaky constitutional roots. Nor would it require a critical evaluation of the relative weights of asserted state purposes. Rather, it would permit the state to achieve a wide range of objectives. The yardstick for the acceptability of the means would be the purposes chosen by the legislatures, not "constitutional" interests drawn from the value perceptions of the Justices.

Moreover, the strengthened "rationality" scrutiny would curtail the state's choice of means far less severely than the new equal protection approach. The Warren Court's strict scrutiny repeatedly asked whether the means were "necessary" and whether "less drastic means" were available to achieve the statutory purpose. That analysis sought to protect fundamental interests in part through value-laden restrictions on the legislative choice among effective means. The more modest interventionism, by contrast, would permit the state to select any means that substantially furthered the legislative purpose.

The avoidance of ultimate value judgments about the legitimacy and importance of legislative purposes would make the means-focused technique a preferred constitutional ground for a less interventionist Court. . . .

The . . . avoidance technique would build on insights offered by Justice Jackson's inadequately heeded concurrence in *Railway Express v. New York* in 1949. Justice Jackson stated:

> The burden should rest heavily upon one who would persuade us to use the due process clause to strike down a substantive law or ordinance. . . . Invalidation of a statute or an ordinance on due process grounds leaves ungoverned and ungovernable conduct which many people find objectionable.

* * *

Invocation of the equal protection clause, on the other hand, does not disable any governmental body from dealing with the subject at hand. It merely means that the prohibition or regulation must have a broader impact. I regard it as a salutary doctrine that cities, states and the Federal Government must exercise their powers so as not to discriminate between their inhabitants except upon some reasonable differentiation fairly related to the object of regulation.

The underinclusive classifications that were his special concern are an important part of equal protection analysis. But the distinction is not so much between equal protection and due process as between judicial scrutiny with regards to means and that directed at ends. The due process invalidations he shrank from were substantive due process adjudications, which, like substantive equal protection, foreclosed legislative purposes and left conduct "ungoverned and ungovernable." But due process, like equal protection, also purports to impose a requirement of a minimally rational means-end relationship. The emerging model of modest interventionism would have the courts do more than they have done for the last generation to assure rationality of means, without unduly impinging on legislative prerogatives regarding ends. The intensified means scrutiny would, in short, close the wide gap between strict scrutiny of the new equal protection and the minimal scrutiny of the old not by abandoning the strict but by raising the level of the minimal from virtual abdication to genuine judicial inquiry.

Mary E. Becker, *The Politics of Women's Wrongs and the Bill of "Rights": A Bicentennial Perspective,* 59 U. CHI. L. REV. 453 (1992)*

The language of the Bill of Rights is almost entirely gender neutral and its provisions have always applied to some women. But free white men of property designed the Bill of Rights in a political process from which they excluded most Americans and all women. Not surprisingly, the Bill of Rights served and serves the interests of such men better than the interests of others.

... In this Article, I assess the Bill of Rights from the perspective of women and other outsiders, with special emphasis on its continuing impact on women's political participation. I offer three kinds of criticisms in discussing specific clauses.

First, and most important, I make a point that is not normative or prescriptive but merely critical: the Bill of Rights does less to solve the problems of women and nonpropertied men than to solve the problems of men of property, especially white men of property. ... Some provisions overlook much more serious problems for women than the problems they address. ...

Some provisions operate differently for women and men in the sense that they perpetuate women's subordinate status. Although many historical inequities would have persisted without the Bill of Rights, the Bill magnifies these inequities. ...

Second, although the Bill of Rights may not cause a given problem, it sometimes impedes legislative reform. ...

My third point concerns politics. Several provisions of the Bill of Rights have continuing political effects, impeding women's effective political participation today. ...

More fundamentally, the Bill of Rights is inadequate in guaranteeing women the exercise of governmental power. Given that women were excluded from the process that produced the Bill of Rights and that few women occupy high government positions today, we should question the legitimacy of our purported democracy. Surely we would question whether another government was truly democratic if a majority group, other than women, had never held the top executive position and comprised only six percent of the national legislature. Only six percent of governors are women. Women hold only eighteen percent of state-wide elective offices. Women occupy only 18.1 percent of state legislative seats.

Women are similarly under-represented in judicial positions at the state and federal levels. At the state level, only 2.8 percent of the law-trained trial court judges are women; 5.5 percent of intermediate appellate state judges are women. On state supreme courts, 5.89 percent of justices are women; 0.56 percent are minority women. At the federal level, women comprise only 4.07 percent of administrative law judges; seven percent of district court judges; eight percent of appellate judges; and 11.11 percent of the Supreme Court. No women serve as senior appellate judges and less than two percent of the senior trial judges are women.

Two points recur in my criticisms of various clauses. The Bill of Rights incorporates a private-public split with only negative rights under a limited government. As a result, women's activities and concerns—from economic rights to religion— seem beyond the proper scope of government. That women are poorer than, and subordinate to, men appears "natural" and pre-political. Because the Bill of Rights incorporates only "negative" rights, it includes no provision guaranteeing, or even defining as an important concern of national government, the economic and educa-

---

* Reprinted with permission.

tional rights so important to women as caretakers. Indeed, women in the United States have fewer economic and educational supports than in any other North Atlantic nation.

To a large extent, my criticisms could apply to any written set of cryptic, abstract, and negative rights enforced by judges. Any such scheme will better protect the powerful against government action harmful to their interests than the less powerful, who need protection against the powerful as well as against the government. In part, this is because abstract rights enforced by judges, regardless of their wording, are unlikely to make radical changes in the distribution of power and resources. The less powerful need many concrete, positive rights. These rights require detailed implementation schemes and the expenditure of funds. Judges are not likely to order either when enforcing abstract clauses. For example, no matter how a constitution states its equality provision, it is unlikely that the provision would lead judges to restructure the social security system so as to provide equivalent old-age security to bread-winners and homemakers.

* * *

Some of my points focus on the underclass, rather than women as such. It is impossible to separate the interests of women from those of their class and race. When, for example, justice is denied the urban underclass in the criminal "justice" system, women inevitably suffer even though most of those caught directly in the system are men. Women suffer the destruction of their communities as well as the destruction of the men and boys who are, or might have been, in their lives.

. . . An ideal Constitution or Bill of Rights would contain a substantive sex equality provision. At a minimum, such a provision could require judges to take into account detrimental impact on women when approaching other constitutional provisions as well as legislation and other governmental action.

In the Conclusion, . . . I note that our constitutional structure, with its emphasis on individual rights conceived in absolutist and negative terms, particularly property rights, contributes to a culture in which the kinds of economic rights women need are difficult to achieve. Mary Ann Glendon makes this point in her most recent book. Absolutist individual rights are almost inevitably negative limits on government. Giving constitutional sanctity to negative rights only, with a central role for property rights, reinforces American faith in rugged individualism which is so incompatible with the needs of children and their caretakers.

I also discuss some of the ways in which our constitutional structure is countermajoritarian. The Framers deliberately devised a government that would protect the propertied minority from oppression by the propertyless majority. We should see it as a problem of democracy that, to date, women have not exercised their share of governmental power. I suggest that other governmental structures and electoral systems might be more democratic.

* * *

IV. CRIMINAL JUSTICE SYSTEM PROTECTIONS

The Bill of Rights contains a number of provisions designed to guard against governmental misuse of the criminal justice system. The Fourth Amendment proscribes unreasonable searches and seizures. The Fifth Amendment provides for indictment by a grand jury for serious crimes and for due process in criminal trials. The Sixth Amendment guarantees the accused a right to a trial by jury in criminal cases, and the assistance of counsel for his defense. The drafters intended these provisions to guard against misuse of the criminal justice system by government, particularly criminal prosecution of government critics.

Nothing in the Bill of Rights or the Fourteenth Amendment guards against systemic racism in the operation of the criminal justice system, or against its systematic misuse to "solve" problems associated with racism and poverty. In making these points, the emphasis in this section differs somewhat from the emphasis in other sections. Here, I stress that the Bill of Rights does less for poor minorities than it does for propertied white men. In other sections, I stress that the Bill of Rights does less for women than for men. This shift is appropriate even though my major concern is the latter. Although most of those caught in the criminal "justice" system are men, the problems with the way the system operates in poor minority communities pose major problems for women in those communities. One cannot separate the interests of poor minority women and men; their fates are intertwined in ways without precise parallel to white women and men, particularly propertied white women and men. Women who live in communities destroyed by drugs and by the "war" on drugs are devastated by the destruction around them even though they themselves are less likely to go to prison than are their sons, lovers, and husbands.

At the time the Bill of Rights was enacted, whites were free to enter the home and batter, rape, or kill African Americans with impunity. This was particularly true for African Americans who were slaves, but even free or freed African Americans were often subject to white violence without the criminal law protection afforded white men (and white women in some contexts). At the same time, black people, particularly slaves, were often punished for alleged crimes without any evidence of guilt. For African Americans in 1791, the criminal "justice" system was part of the problem, and the Bill of Rights did nothing to end these systemic abuses.

Racism persists within the criminal justice system. African American women receive less protection from the criminal justice system than white women. When African American women are raped, their rapists are less likely to serve time than the rapists of white women. Defendants in rape prosecutions often succeed by suggesting that the woman was a prostitute, and this may be especially effective when women live, as poor and African American women often must, in neighborhoods where prostitutes are on the streets. African Americans, women as well as men, more often fall into the police net because they fit the drug courier image, are more likely to be treated roughly or beaten severely by the police, and are more likely to be arrested. States are most likely to impose the death penalty on African American defendants whose victims were white.

Moreover, the criminal justice system is used today to "solve" problems caused by poverty—drugs and drug-related crime. As Randolph Stone has noted, "[t]he war on drugs has devastated the criminal justice system" as well as "some segments of the African-American community." Today, "the judicial system has become an assembly line." Most defendants do not receive trial by jury or the opportunity to confront witnesses against them. Because judges are pressured to treat cases summarily, counsel is more important than ever. But effective assistance of counsel is often denied, particularly to the poor or those accused of drug-related crimes. Public defenders handle unmanageable caseloads. In places without public defenders, poor defendants must rely on court-appointed counsel, who are often required to work pro bono or for token fees.

Once dragged into the criminal "justice" net, the consequences can be devastating, even if police and prosecutors lack sufficient evidence to proceed to trial. Under federal law and many states' laws, if the police suspect that property is related to drugs, they can seize it on grounds as slight as those required for a search warrant: probable cause to believe that the property was involved in illegal activities. Seizure of property makes it more difficult to hire counsel either to recover the property or for criminal defense. Given the fiscal crunch facing most law enforcement systems, these statutes create powerful incentives for misuse of seizure without trial.

Using the criminal justice system to battle problems caused by poverty and racism results in a prison population that is half African American men. There are more African American men in prison than in college. The incarceration rate in the United States is now the highest known in the world: 426 prisoners per 100,000 population. South Africa is second with a rate of 333 per 100,000 and the Soviet Union third with a rate of 268 per 100,000. Most of the world has much lower rates. For example, Western European rates are 35-120 per 100,000.

Although poor pregnant addicts cannot find the in-patient medicaid-funded rehabilitation treatment they need, they are increasingly subject to criminal prosecution for delivering drugs to minors.

The misuse of the criminal justice system to address problems of poverty and racism has political effects. People wrongly convicted of many crimes cannot vote in state elections while serving time and in most states even thereafter. More importantly, keeping the poor impoverished—rather than dealing with poverty effectively—means keeping them politically ineffective. The poor, disproportionately, do not vote and do not participate in political life.

The protections in the Bill of Rights against misuse of the criminal justice system do not "cause" these problems. But the Bill of Rights does less to guard against misuse of the criminal justice system to combat problems of poverty and racism than it does to guard against misuse of the criminal justice system to silence political dissidents. . . .

An interpretation of or amendment to the Bill of Rights might lessen these problems by directly addressing the economic and educational needs of the poor and by providing provisions more effective at ensuring justice for all within the criminal justice system. After discussing the "property" right enshrined in the Fifth Amendment, I suggest a number of positive economic and educational rights that we could incorporate in the Bill of Rights. In addition, the Bill of Rights could include provisions guaranteeing effective assistance of counsel and fair trials. For example, we could interpret effective assistance of counsel as proscribing the seizure of assets used to pay counsel and as requiring reasonable caseloads for public defenders and reasonable fees for court-appointed counsel. At a minimum, government should be prevented from seizing assets without a trial, and money paid to a lawyer prior to execution of a judgment should be no more recoverable than money paid to any other creditor. We could obtain this result by reasonable interpretation of the Fifth Amendment's Takings Clause.

V. SECURITY AT HOME

The Fourth Amendment provides that "[t]he right of the people to be secure in their persons, houses, papers, and effects, against unreasonable searches and seizures, shall not be violated." White male heads of family during the revolution and today face threats to physical security at home from two kinds of intruders: government actors and criminals. The criminal law has been used to protect against the latter, if not always effectively; the Fourth Amendment guards against the former.

Women, by contrast, face a third major source of physical insecurity within the home: battery and rape by someone who lives in the home—their sexual partners. Yet we have never accorded protection against domestic violence at the level accorded other crimes of violence. The Fourth Amendment does not address domestic violence. The Fourth Amendment protects women against governmental assault, but leaves governments free to treat "domestic" assaults differently from other crimes. Indeed, the criminal codes of many states still deny equal criminal protection to wives who are raped by their husbands. Although some states have eliminated this distinction, others have extended it to nonmarried cohabitants.

These inequities have political consequences. Women who fear violence redefine themselves as wanting to give what might otherwise be taken away, instead of asserting their own interests, particularly in a politically effective way. Women who are abused within their most intimate relationships are less able to assert their interests within those relationships. Abused women are unlikely to press strongly for change in the political arena, especially when their interests conflict with the interests of the abuser.

* * *

One can easily imagine improvements in the Bill of Rights from the perspective of violence against women. The Bill of Rights could include an equality standard for sex that would require the state to respond to domestic violence in the same way it responds to other crimes, and to proscribe marital rape. Such constitutional provisions would not by themselves revolutionize how police, prosecutors and jurors treat intersexual domestic violence, but they might contribute to changed attitudes. They would, moreover, ensure some of the prerequisites for effective control of domestic violence.

VI. PROPERTY

The Fifth Amendment provides that "[n]o person shall . . . be deprived of life, liberty, or property, without due process of law; nor shall private property be taken for public use without just compensation." There are a number of problems with this provision from the perspective of minorities and women. First, and most dramatically, at the time the Bill of Rights was adopted in 1789, slaves were property. They were protected as property of others; they could have no property themselves. This provision of the Fifth Amendment was an instrument of oppression for African American women and men.

Second, at the time of the passage of the Bill of Rights, married women could not own or control property. Thus, the Fifth Amendment protected only the property of men and single women.

Third, the protection of "property" meant and means the privileging of existing distributions, no matter how dubious. Consider, for example, the property rights of the newly-freed people vis-a-vis the property rights of their former owners. The fields cleared and cultivated by the freed people belonged to the owners. The buildings and plantations built by the freed people belonged to the owners.

Fourth, while "property" has always included realty and the goods produced by the kinds of labor in which most men spend their working lives, we have never recognized women's reproductive and domestic labor as property. Women's caretaking impedes women's ability to accumulate property in three distinct ways: (1) caretaking itself does not tend to produce property; (2) caretaking tends to limit one's ability to earn property; and (3) caretaking tends to require consumption of property. As a result, women have fewer resources than men and are far more likely to be poor.

Lack of property precludes effective political participation. The poor vote less often, are less politically active, and have fewer resources with which they can influence elections. It is more difficult for the poor to make contributions to candidates likely to represent their interests or to spend money themselves to advance candidates or political positions. . . .

Provisions in a Bill of Rights could lessen these problems. A Bill of Rights could provide for positive economic rights, ensuring women economic supports and safety nets as effective as those available to men. Such a Bill of Rights would be more detailed and specific, less elegant, brief, and abstract, than the Bill of Rights we have today. Against this aesthetic loss must be balanced the benefit to women and children, who form the majority of Americans. In addition, a society in which women have more power would be more democratic. Its government would have greater legitimacy.

Affirmative economic rights could include a right to health care under a national and universal health care system (the details of which would be specified by legislation); a requirement of a family allowance (tied to some independent economic indicator, such as a fractional percentage of gross national product); caretaking leave with wage support as part of the unemployment insurance system (with support required at the level generally provided for unemployment compensation); government-financed child care; a requirement that social security benefits be, on average, the same for women and men (within a limited level of tolerance); a right to a decent education (with a ban on financing schools through property taxes and a requirement that per pupil expenditures be uniform throughout the United States); and a requirement that breadwinners and homemakers be treated the same with respect to all substantive standards for disability. A ban on abortion should be seen as a taking (of women's reproductive labor) for government purposes without compensation. The Bill of Rights should also include a right to abortion, fully paid by the state, in light of (inter alia) the economic consequences of childbearing for women.

Further, the Bill of Rights should make family law a matter within the control of the national government and not the states. Gender relations in the family are of primary importance for a just society. Setting a framework for just relationships should be a priority for national government; living within such a framework should be a prerogative of national citizenship.

. . . The Due Process Clause of the Fifth Amendment also favors men's experiences, by enshrining as the "rule of law" a legal system developed by and for elite white men. . . .

VII. DUE PROCESS AND THE JURY PROVISIONS

The Fifth Amendment provides for "due process" before any person is deprived of "life, liberty, or property." The "due process" guaranteed by the Fifth Amendment thus entitled its framers, mostly elite white men, to the procedures and substantive rules of a legal system developed by and for people like themselves. At that time, women and African Americans could not participate as either lawyers or judges.

Today, the legal system remains one developed by and for propertied white men, with strong, built-in, conservative tendencies, in the form of well-developed substantive rules combined with rules favoring precedent. As I have described, the overwhelming majority of legislators and judges continue to be men. "Due process" continues to mean something quite different for propertied white men and other groups.

* * *

[J]udges and legislators, as well as jurors, should represent the population. We require that juries be representative with respect to race and somewhat representative with respect to sex, but have no constitutional provisions regarding judges or legislators. This is so even though the law developed and applied by judges and legislators is all the process that is "due" in any dispute before a jury or a judge. For any group other than white men, who is on the bench or in the legislature is more important than who is on the jury.

The Bill of Rights could require that judges represent the population with respect to sex and race. The African National Congress (ANC) Draft Bill of Rights includes a provision that "the judiciary shall be transformed in such a way as to consist of men and women drawn from all sectors of . . . society." The Bill of Rights could provide that women's representation in legislatures at appropriate levels is of prime importance in a democracy, and authorize Congress to enact a Voting Rights Act for Women. Such an act could offset the political problems women face as a result of freedoms we all value, such as freedom of religion and speech. If we had separate voting districts for women and men, women would be represented in legislatures in rough proportion to their presence in the population. Women tend to hold elective office in higher numbers in multi-member districts, under proportional representation, and with internal party quotas for women candidates. Our parties already have internal sex-based quotas for their national committees, and the Democrats have experimented with quotas for convention delegates. Our parties could be encouraged to experiment with such quotas by government funding tied to the number of women running in open elections.

CONCLUSION

The Bill of Rights serves the interests of those most like its drafters: relatively elite white men who tend to own more than their share of "property." Other groups—particularly women, the poor, and people of color—have fewer of their needs addressed by this revered document. I have shown three kinds of problems with the provisions of the Bill of Rights.

My major point has been critical: the Bill of Rights does less for other groups than it does for those in the class of propertied white men; often it perpetuates or even magnifies social inequities rather than eliminating them. When this happens, the Bill of Rights becomes part of the problem, rather than the solution. Second, the Bill of Rights is often an impediment to reform. Third, the problems ignored or even perpetuated by the Bill of Rights have political consequences for women and other outsider groups. More fundamentally, the Bill of Rights has done too little to ensure that women, a majority group, can exert their interests effectively in the political system.

* * *

In this Conclusion, I add three more general criticisms. First, part of the problem is that the Constitution contains no strong provision on sex discrimination. If such a provision were in the Bill of Rights, it might help judges balance other rights against the right of women to social equality. Such a provision should be a right to substantive, not formal, equality. In addition, as in the ANC Draft Bill of Rights, the Bill of Rights should ban discrimination on the basis of sexual orientation, both because lesbian and gay people are a vulnerable group needing protection, and because compulsory heterosexuality is a form of discrimination against women.

Second, the Bill of Rights and other provisions of the Constitution have created a structure posing obstacles to the implementation of the sorts of economic support systems and safety nets present in every other North Atlantic nation. Mary Ann Glendon makes this point powerfully and persuasively in her most recent book. Several features of our Constitution have reinforced the individualism so dominant in our culture: the absolutist wording of individual rights in the Bill of Rights; the failure of the Bill of Rights to include any positive economic rights; and the focus of both the Constitution and the Bill of Rights on limited government as the guarantor of liberty. Given these elements in our constitutional structure, it is not surprising that initial attempts at social legislation in this country were declared unconstitutional as violations of the Contracts Clause, a variation on the property right protected in the

Fifth Amendment. We abandoned this approach during the New Deal, but by then the United States was far behind the Continent in providing economic support systems. The gap persists today. Had we no written constitution so that a *Lochner* era never happened we might live today in a more just society.

My third and last general criticism has been made before by Jennifer Nedelsky, among others. Because the Framers focused on protection of private property as the key to liberty, they devised a "democratic" anti-majoritarian governmental structure. They saw the major problem of democracy as the "problem of majority oppression." The solution was to create barriers to ordinary people's participation, including multiple levels of government and rule by a distant elite. In addition, the Constitution limited directly the ability of less-distant state governments to experiment with the basic structure of the economy.

Seeing the problem of democracy as the problem of majority oppression of the propertied minority is particularly inappropriate from the perspective of women. Women are a majority of the population, who have never controlled or even exercised their proportionate share of influence. Surely we should regard men's domination of positions of power within government as at least a problem of democracy in light of women's ability to vote during the last seventy-one years.

We should consider whether other governmental structures and electoral systems would be more democratic. Three independent branches of government minimize governmental action, preserving the status quo. A requirement of coordination among three independent branches is countermajoritarian and conservative. Action is easier in parliamentary systems which integrate the legislative and executive power. We also should consider other electoral systems, such as the ones suggested above.

These are not all pragmatic proposals for change. Members of our legislative bodies are not likely to change the way the game is played when they have won under existing rules. My point is that our governmental structure is not ideal from the perspective of women, other outsider groups, or, indeed, democracy. We could imagine better structures, and many are in place in some parts of the world. We should not be exporting ours, as is, to Eastern Europe.

How should we assess a constitutional structure or a Bill of Rights? I suggest that we should consider, along with other factors, how well the system facilitates women's political participation, poverty rates (especially for women and children), physical safety, and incarceration rates. Measured by these standards, our constitutional system must be found wanting.

Sylvia A. Law, *Rethinking Sex and the Constitution,* 132 U. Pa. L. Rev. 955 (1984)*

INTRODUCTION

This Article attempts to articulate a stronger constitutional concept of sex-based equality than that which currently exists. The central thesis is that the development of modern constitutional sex equality doctrine has suffered from a lack of focus on biological reproductive differences between men and women. The reality of sex-based physical differences poses a significant problem for a society committed to ideals of individual human freedom and equality of opportunity. To the extent that constitutional doctrine shapes culture and individual identity, an equality doctrine that denies the reality of biological difference in relation to reproduction reflects an idea about personhood that is inconsistent with people's actual experience of themselves and the world. The constitutional ideal alienates people from their own experience. Given our history in which the idea of "man" is the linguistic and legal equivalent of "person," a concept of equality that denies biological difference has particularly adverse effects upon women.

The central biological difference between men and women is that only women have the capacity to create a human being. For many people, the decision to bear a child is jointly made by a man and a woman and is the occasion for joyous commitment to one another, to the child, and to the future. But it is not always so. Only women can grow a human being, and, although sperm is also needed, it is easily obtainable. The power to create people is awesome. Men are profoundly disadvantaged by the reality that only women can produce a human being and experience the growth of a child in pregnancy. Pregnancy and childbirth are also burdensome to health, mobility, independence, and sometimes to life itself, and women are profoundly disadvantaged in that they alone bear these burdens. And although men may be disadvantaged by their relatively minor role in reproduction, we have constructed a society in which men are advantaged, relative to women, in important material and spiritual ways.

* * *

The relationship between constitutional concepts and culture is reciprocal. The rise of the women's movement in the early 1970's provided impetus for Supreme Court revision of constitutional standards applicable to laws controlling reproduction and incorporating sex-based classifications. Contemporary ideas of equality are also reciprocal in relation to our past in two significant ways. First, historically, biology provided a central justification for the subjugation of women. That history partially explains the lack of focus on reproductive difference in contemporary equality doctrine and also suggests the need for close attention to such differences in developing new ideas of equality. Second, "protection" of women—construction of the pedestal/cage—was a core mechanism for oppression of women. Contemporary feminists are hence rightly skeptical of measures that protect women by providing them with special treatment.

* * *

A. Understanding Biological Differences According to Current Notions of Sex-Based Equality

It is possible to construct a constitutional sex equality concept in which laws governing sex-specific physical characteristics will have one of the following three implications: (1) the laws raise no concerns about sex equality; (2) the laws are considered in the same way as laws that classify explicitly on the basis of sex; and (3) the laws are considered under a reconceptualized idea of equality that applies a new, integrated test to any sex-related classification.

The first approach is essentially the Supreme Court's notion of sex equality—one in which laws governing reproductive biology raise no sex equality concerns. As the Court stated in *Geduldig v. Aiello,* for example, "[W]hile it is true that only women can become pregnant it does not follow that every legislative classification concerning pregnancy is a sex-based classification." This approach clearly denies the core reality that sex-based biological differences are related to sex. It is not easy to reconcile the ideal of sex-based equality with the reality of categorical biological difference, but the difficulty is not overcome by denying that laws governing reproductive biology are sex based. Further, because, as we have seen, it is easy for the Court to confuse real categorical biological differences with sex-based differences that are culturally imposed, an equality doctrine that exempts laws based on real physical differences from its concern is likely to be a weak one. Finally, and most importantly, in a society constitutionally committed to equality, the reality of biological difference in relation to reproduction should not be permitted to justify state action exaggerating the consequences of those differences. This is what happens when those actions escape scrutiny by courts.

The second approach to reconciling the ideal of equality with the reality of biological difference scrutinizes laws regulating reproductive differences in the same manner as laws that include explicit sex-based classifications using the Court's current gender-discrimination standard. This approach has the virtue of simplicity. It recognizes that laws based on sex-specific physical characteristics are related to sex and avoids the need to distinguish between these two types of sex-based laws.

The difficulty with this approach is that a central justification for limiting the use of explicit sex-based classifications is that they are not related to real differences between men and women. By contrast, laws governing reproductive characteristics, such as those prohibiting abortion or providing nutritional supplements for pregnant women, may be precisely related to the individual characteristics of the people they identify. The prevailing sex equality standard determines whether the sex-based classification at issue actually is responsive to real differences between men and women and rejects classifications when there are no such differences. This standard usually works in relation to explicit sex-based classifications because individual men and women escape stereotypical sex roles. The escapees disprove the judgment about men and women that motivated the explicit sex-based classification. However, because there are no escapees from biology, no pregnant men, or women sperm donors, a standard focusing solely on comparative equality does not provide a helpful tool for evaluating laws governing ways in which men and women categorically, biologically differ. This second approach is also troubling because of a related concern. As a practical matter, it is difficult to maintain an appropriately rigorous standard for evaluating the cultural restraints of explicit sex-based classifications if the same standard is also used to judge laws governing sex-specific physical characteristics. Similarly, the Supreme Court's current intermediate scrutiny may become much more deferential when the Court perceives that a rule is based on "real" differences between the sexes. A better approach would consider laws based on biological differences independently of laws employing categorical sex-based classifications, thereby reducing the Court's ability to distort its intermediate scrutiny in this way.

The final approach, as advocated by Professor Catherine MacKinnon, attempts to grapple with the pervasive totality of sex-based oppression. She describes sex discrimination as a systematic construct that defines women as inferior to men and "that cumulatively disadvantages women for their differences from men, as well as ignores their similarities." She urges a constitutional equality standard that would ask simply "whether the policy or practice in question integrally contributes to the maintenance of an underclass or a deprived position because of gender status."

Professor MacKinnon's approach is ambitious, but it adds unnecessary complexity to the application of sex equality doctrine in a large number of cases. The determination of what reinforces or undermines a sex-based underclass is exceedingly difficult. Professor MacKinnon may overestimate judges' capacities to identify and avoid socially imposed constraints on equality. She disregards our history in which laws justified as protecting women have been a central means of oppressing them. Most fundamentally, her proposed standard may incorporate and perpetuate a false belief that a judicially enforced constitutional standard can, by itself, dismantle the deep structures that "integrally contribute" to sex-based deprivation.

MacKinnon discusses how sex equality doctrine can focus on an analysis of either "differences" between sexes (current doctrine) or "inequality" (her proposed doctrine). MacKinnon correctly contends that under current gender doctrine, "[i]f the sexes can be considered relevantly the same, 'similarly situated,' or comparable on the dimension in question, differential treatment may be discriminatory; if not, differential treatment merely treats differences differently and is not discriminatory." We have seen, and MacKinnon herself argues, that this comparative analysis leads to the conclusion that there is no sex discrimination when a law is based on real biological differences between men and women. Notwithstanding this important limitation of current equality doctrine, broad use of

> an inequality approach poses tremendous risks. The very invisibility of discrimination against women makes it unlikely that the inequality approach can in fact be utilized successfully by litigators before the present judiciary. When, as in *Califano v. Goldfarb*, . . . a majority of the Court cannot agree that women are discriminated against by a system of social security benefits that provides greater coverage for the dependents of male workers than it does for the dependents of female workers, there are great dangers in pressing a view that subjects discrimination against women to more exacting scrutiny than it does discrimination against men. It is all too likely that the courts will simply uphold the discrimination because they fail to see that women have been disadvantaged. Moreover, as MacKinnon herself acknowledges, "woman's 'specialness' (is) the cornerstone of that separate-but-equal logic of complementarity that has assigned her those pursuits and those qualities that are glorified as female but denigrated as human. . . .

MacKinnon's proposal is mistaken, therefore, because it would require a search for hierarchy when only a search for difference may be necessary. Her approach is helpful, however, because it provides a framework for determining when a rule classifying on the basis of biological differences is actually discriminating on the basis of sex. Such a rule is discriminatory when it "integrally contributes to the maintenance of an underclass or a deprived position because of gender status."

The three approaches discussed above unsuccessfully confront the unique problem of evaluating laws based on biological differences. In articulating a new standard for evaluating such laws, I hope to incorporate the strengths while avoiding the weaknesses of these approaches.

B. A New Approach to Laws Based on Biological Differences

Professor Wendy Williams observes, "The instinct to treat pregnancy as a special case is deeply imbedded in our culture, indeed in every culture. It seems natural, and right, to treat it that way." Yet, this wise feminist and constitutional scholar urges that we resist the temptation to see pregnancy as unique. She argues that

> [c]onceptualizing pregnancy as a special case permits unfavorable as well as favorable treatment of pregnancy. . . . [T]he same doctrinal approach that permits pregnancy to be treated worse than other disabilities is the

same one that will allow the state constitutional freedom to create special benefits for pregnant women. . . . If we can't have it both ways, we need to think carefully about which way we want to have it.

But pregnancy, abortion, reproduction, and creation of another human being are special—very special. Women have these experiences. Men do not. An equality doctrine that ignores the unique quality of these experiences implicitly says that women can claim equality only insofar as they are like men. Such a doctrine demands that women deny an important aspect of who they are. Such a doctrine is, to say the least, reified. Further, deny as we might, the reality remains that only women experience pregnancy. If women are to achieve fully equal status in American society, including a sharing of power traditionally held by men, and retain control of their bodies, our understanding of sex equality must encompass a strong constitutional equality guarantee that requires "radically increasing the options available to each individual, and more importantly, allowing the human personality to break out of the present dichotomized system."

Because of the unique equality concerns raised by biological differences, sex equality doctrine must distinguish between laws drawing explicit sex-based lines and laws governing reproductive biology. Although both types of laws raise sex equality issues, the grounds for concern are different. The problem posed by laws that classify explicitly on the basis of sex is that sex, as a proxy for some functional characteristic, is often inaccurate in relation to particular individuals. More important, even when the sex generalization is accurate in the aggregate, these generalizations tend to be self-fulfilling and oppressive to the individual who fails to fit the mold. In using explicit sex classifications the state may perpetuate arbitrary limits on human freedom and equality. Based on these concerns, scrutiny of sex-based classifications is intended to ensure that there are important governmental reasons for treating men and women differently when they are in all relevant respects the same.

Also, the equality issues raised by laws affecting reproductive biology are related, in part, to accuracy, as when the state uses the fact that women may become pregnant to justify barring all women, pregnant or not, from public life and responsible work. In addition, the laws may generate a self-fulfilling expectation, as when the fact that women bear children is used to justify an assumption that women have greater responsibility to nurture them after birth. Because these concerns are raised in a context in which men and women seem to have real differences, the inaccuracy of the stereotype may not be apparent.

Because this context may present differences between the sexes that are relevant to lawmakers, a proper concern for equality requires scrutiny that is directly focused on the impact of the rule rather than its purpose or structure. For example, programs providing material support to pregnant women are not necessarily premised on inaccurate assumptions about their need. Laws restricting or facilitating access to abortion do not inaccurately assume that only women need abortions. Neither type of law crates a culturally imposed constraint on the ability to sustain or to avoid pregnancy. Still, these laws raise equality concerns because state control of a woman's reproductive capacity and exaggeration of the significance of biological difference has historically been central to the oppression of women. When the state bars pregnant women from doing work they are able to do or denies women access to reproductive health services, the state, as well as nature, denies women equality.

If we are persuaded that the fourteenth amendment's equality guarantee constrains legislative authority to regulate reproductive biology and that such laws raise issues different from those raised by laws that classify explicitly on the basis of sex, we must then consider what standard is appropriate for evaluating such laws. I propose that laws governing reproductive biology should be scrutinized by courts to ensure that (1) the law has no significant impact in perpetuating either the oppression of women or culturally imposed sex-role constraints on individual freedom or (2) if the law has this impact, it is justified as the best means of serving a compelling state purpose. Given how central state regulation of biology has been to the subjugation of women, the normal presumption of constitutionality is inappropriate and the state should bear the burden of justifying its rule in relation to either proposition.

This proposed test is a substantial improvement over current sex equality doctrine and the alternate approaches discussed above. Most fundamentally, the test recognizes that laws classifying according to biological differences raise equality concerns and must therefore be tested under equality norms. The test would also be consistent with a constitutional doctrine of sex equality grounded in the ERA—the test recognizes that the legislature may sometimes have legitimate reason to take account of biological reproductive difference, even if, as under an ERA standard, explicit sex-based classifications are prohibited.

The test departs from contemporary equal protection analysis in that it does not require any comparison between allegedly similarly situated classes of people. This departure is appropriate because laws governing reproductive biology, by definition, govern ways in which men and women are not similarly situated. The requirement that similarly situated individuals be treated the same does not exhaust the idea of equality. Equality is a substantive goal, not simply at neat classification or a rational relationship between means and ends. Instead of evaluating the extent to which men and women differ in relation to a particular classification, the proposed test requires that a court consider the impact of the classification. This approach is similar to Professor MacKinnon's but it limits the direct inquiry into a law's effect upon perpetuating inequality to those cases in which that difficult inquiry is necessary to ensure that the law is consistent with the constitutional requirement of sex equality.

The second part of the test is the compelling interest analysis. This strict scrutiny of the law is undertaken only after a court has determined that the law has a significant impact on perpetuating the inequality of women. Sometimes a law governing reproductive biology could be approved without a demonstration that it was the best means of serving a compelling state purpose, either because it had no discernable effect in oppressing women (for example, recordkeeping requirements) or because all of the effects we can discern are beneficial to women (for example, nutritional programs for pregnant women). But once we were convinced that a law governing reproductive biology oppressed women or perpetuated sex-role constraints, the state should bear the burden of justifying the law as the best means of serving a compelling state purposes. In race discrimination cases the requirement of compelling justification has been "strict" in theory and "fatal" in fact. This is not surprising given our broad cultural commitment to the assimilationist vision that explicit race classifications never accurately describe categorical differences. Since laws governing reproductive biology do accurately describe sex based differences, we should not expect that a standard that demands a high level of justification will always be fatal in fact. Given the core importance of reproduction, laws recognizing reproductive biology might well be the best means of serving a compelling state purpose. But, once we have determined that a law governing reproductive biology oppresses women and perpetuates sex-role constraints on human liberty, it is essential to require that the state demonstrate very strong justification to support its action. The demand for compelling justification for such laws is supported by our history in which biology has been so central to the subjugation of women.

The proposed two-level analysis also parallels the Supreme Court's contemporary reproductive freedom doctrine, which asks whether laws governing abortion restrict access to service and, if so, whether the legislation is supported by compelling state interests. This doctrine allows the states to adopt regulations—such as record-keeping requirements—that do not impinge on access to services, without demanding that the state show compelling justification in support of such regulations. Similarly, the proposed test would subject regulations to strict scrutiny only when they restrict access to services because only those regulations have a significant impact in perpetuating oppression of women and sex role constraints. The proposed standard departs from the contemporary constitutional standard governing abortion laws in one important respect. In the abortion cases only protection of maternal health is recognized as a compelling state interest prior to fetal viability. The more general equality standard proposed here allows a compelling state interest to be established in relation to the broader substantive concerns of sex equality, including the oppression of women and the constraints of traditional sex roles.

Two criticisms of the approach advocated here deserve brief examination. First, in relation to laws governing reproductive biology, it suffers from the same inadequacies I have observed in Professor MacKinnon's suggestion that constitutional equality doctrine should ask simply whether a challenged policy or practice contributes to the oppression of women; that is, it is exceedingly difficult to determine what perpetuates sex-based deprivation, and standards that rely on judicial discretion are likely to provide weak protection. However, under the approach advocated here, the area of discretion is limited to laws governing reproductive biology; explicit sex-based classifications would continue to be evaluated under an arguably more reliable comparative standard. A second possible criticism of my suggested approach is that, while it requires that equality concerns be brought to bear on laws governing biological difference, it does not allow a legislature to use explicit sex-based classifications to recognize or reward traditional women's work or supposed female virtues that are not based in biological difference. Achieving increased social valuation of women and their traditional work is a critically important enterprise. But judicial enforcement of constitutional norms seems better suited to the more modest objective of formal comparative equality, with its relatively more reliable standards.

Finally, it is important to understand that my argument that the constitutional guarantee of equality requires that courts carefully scrutinize whether laws governing reproductive biology perpetuate state-imposed restraints on sex equality is not a claim that the state has an affirmative obligation to mitigate the effects of biological difference. Analysis of the question when the state may take affirmative action to remedy race- or sex-based disadvantage is beyond the scope of this Article. However, a clear distinction between laws using explicit sex-based classifications and those governing reproductive biology may be helpful in thinking about this issue. Affirmative action programs using explicit sex- or race-based classifications are justifiable in relation to the reality of historic oppression and the need for transitional measures to make equality of opportunity possible. But compensatory laws based explicitly on sex or race may perpetuate stereotypes of inferiority. . . .

V. SEX-BASED EQUALITY AND LAWS GOVERNING REPRODUCTIVE BIOLOGY

Applying the test developed to laws classifying on the basis of biological differences entails several inquiries. The threshold inquiry is whether the law makes a classification that is based on biological differences. This inquiry is not trivial—a law that implicates biological differences may actually be a categorical sex-based classification. If the law is found to be based on biological differences, the court must then consider whether the law has a substantial impact on perpetuating the inequality of women. If so, the court must engage in traditional strict scrutiny analysis to see whether the law is justified by a compelling state interest.

This part first applies the proposed test to laws restricting access to abortion. Such laws classify according to a sex-specific physical characteristic and have been central to enforcing the inferior status of women. The second section applies the proposed standard to a variety of other laws that regulate according to biological differences.

* * *

The standard proposed here asks that we first distinguish between laws governing reproductive biology and laws that classify explicitly on the basis of sex and then recognize that laws governing reproductive biology raise serious concerns about sex equality and therefore must be justified by compelling state interests if they perpetuate the inequality of women. State policies that raise concerns about sex-based equality but would probably be subject only to minimum scrutiny under the current, flawed equality doctrine. Consider the following:

1. To protect the health of pregnant women, state policy requires that they quit public employment in the sixth month of pregnancy.

2. To protect the health of future children, state policy prohibits the employment of women of childbearing age in positions in which they may be exposed to substances that may be damaging to fetuses or future reproductive capacity.

3. To limit the cost of employee disability insurance, benefits for disabilities arising from normal pregnancy are excluded.

4. a) Recognizing the physical burdens that pregnancy imposes upon women, a state requires that employers allow pregnant workers reasonable absences from work for medical disabilities associated with pregnancy.

   b) Recognizing the special nutritional needs of pregnant women, the government provides supplemental food benefits for them.

5. a) The state allows up to six months of maternity leave at half pay to women employees who are nursing infants.

   b) The state allows all mothers, but not fathers, six months of child care leave at half pay, whether or not they are nursing.

6. In an effort to provide a social counterbalance to men's relatively minor role in reproduction and to encourage male involvement with young children, the state requires that a pregnant woman inform the man who impregnated her of the fact of pregnancy, unless she has reasonable grounds to believe that he would physically abuse her if he were informed.

The first three examples describe laws that govern reproductive biology and therefore are subject to strict scrutiny under the proposed standard. A requirement that women quit work once they reach the sixth month of pregnancy reflects a stereotype of incompetence that is most often inaccurate. This policy is similar to the rule that the Supreme Court struck down in *Cleveland Board of Education v. LaFleur* as an "irrebuttable presumption." The sex-equality analysis at the core of my proposed standard is, however, a stronger way of assessing the policy than the analysis that has grown out of the Court's limited understanding of sex equality. The law barring women from jobs that involve exposure to teratagenic chemicals stereotypes women as childbearers, a stereotype that is inaccurate in relation to the many women who cannot or intentionally do not bear children. The third example, which excludes payments for pregnancy-related disabilities from insurance plans, reflects a stereotype of women as temporary visitors to wage labor whose contributions are insignificant and for whom job continuity is unimportant.

Having determined that each of the three policies has a substantial impact upon perpetuating sex-role stereotypes, each policy must be strictly scrutinized. It is clear that alternative, sex-neutral means are available to promote any of the legitimate goals that the state might hope to serve by enforcing these rules. For example, a concern that workers be physically fit can be served by a more individualized approach that encompasses non-pregnancy-related disabilities and that recognizes that many pregnant women are not disabled. Professor Wendy Williams has outlined in comprehensive detail some of the ways in which a state might limit the destructive effects of teratagenic chemicals while minimizing the damage to women's equality as wage workers. There are many ways to limit the costs of employee disability programs without imposing the burdens exclusively on pregnant women.

The fourth example postulates a pair of laws, one requiring employers to allow pregnant workers reasonable absences from work without losing their jobs and the other providing special nutritional benefits to pregnant women. This type of law presents a closer case. When Montana adopted a law requiring that leave from work be allowed for pregnant women, feminists were divided in their views about whether it should be regarded as sex discriminatory. For more than a decade, the federal government has administered the Supplemental Food Program for Women, Infants, and Children (WIC), a program that provides nutritional benefits to pregnant women.

These two laws plainly govern reproductive biology. Whether they have a substantial impact upon perpetuating inequality is less clear. Such laws do not perpetuate cultural sex role stereotypes because they are tied precisely to the biological fact of pregnancy. A law providing help to pregnant women does not oppress women in an obvious way. The law requiring reasonable leave for pregnant women is dangerous, however, because the employer may decide to avoid the burden of providing the required protection by simply not hiring women who might become pregnant. Whether that danger is sufficiently real to enable one to conclude that the protective law oppresses women should, I believe, be treated as a question of fact and judgment, not as a matter of ideological preconception. It is possible that evidence would substantiate the fear that a mandatory leave rule would limit women's job opportunities.

Many issues are relevant to the assessment whether such a law oppresses women or whether it is supported by compelling state purposes. For example, can we foresee concrete ways in which the measure providing help to pregnant women can be used to hurt them? This inquiry distinguishes the WIC program from laws providing mandatory leaves for pregnant women, for it is difficult to see how the WIC program hurts women. Is the benefit provided so trivial that its primary function is to reinforce stereotypical ideas about men and women? At the other extreme, is the protection mandated for pregnant women so substantial that it is likely that those required to provide it would avoid dealing with women in order to escape it? For example, a law demanding that employers provide pregnant workers four months leave with pay would very likely have an adverse effect on women's employment opportunities. It is, however, difficult to imagine facts that would support a conclusion that the law providing nutritional benefits to pregnant women enforces cultural stereotypes or is oppressive. In either case, if a court concluded that the law in fact had a substantial impact in perpetuating inequality, the law would have to be struck down. The state could employ alternative, sex-neutral means of achieving its objective of protecting against dismissal for health-related absences or of ensuring a nutritionally adequate diet.

To understand fully the difficult issue posed by these two laws, it is useful to examine the feminist opposition to them. One objection to such laws, with which I fully agree, is that they are politically divisive. "Creating special privileges of the Montana type [example 4(a)] has, as one consequence, the effect of shifting attention away from the . . . state's failure to provide important protections to all workers and focusing it upon the unfairness of protecting one class of worker and not others." In developing a political strategy for the less affluent majority, it is vitally important to frame issues in ways that unite rather than divide people. But the political reality is that it is often easier to persuade a legislature to help or protect a particular group that is smaller than all who might need the help or protection.

A second feminist objection to laws providing special protections and benefits to pregnant women rests on a view of equality that says that "[c]onceptualizing pregnancy as a special case permits unfavorable as well as favorable treatment of pregnancy." This argument has tremendous power, given our present constitutional equality doctrine that persistently confuses reproductive biology with cultural patterns and that wholly denies the applicability of equality norms to laws governing reproductive biology. But this is not necessary as a matter of nature or logic. Rather we could, as I have urged here, develop a concept of equality that distinguishes between reproductive biological difference and cultural generalizations and that prohibits regulation of reproductive biology whenever it oppresses women or reinforces cultural sex-role stereotypes.

A final feminists' objection to such laws rests on an understanding of our history in which biological difference has been used to justify a separate role and world for women. Less than a century ago "doctors and scientists were generally of the view that a women's intellect, her capacity for education, for reasoning, for public undertakings, was biologically limited." This history demands profound skepticism of rules based on the fact that men and women are biologically different, but does it require that we reject any recognition of sex-based biological difference? Acknowledging the reality and importance of the reproductive biological difference does not necessarily set us on a slippery slope on which the state is allowed to exaggerate the costs of difference. Recognizing that men and women are different in relation to reproductive biology does not necessarily mean that the law can assume that we are different in relation to capacity to think, to lead, or to nurture. It is likely that courts would be less inclined to confuse biology with the social consequences of biology if a finding that a law was premised on biological differences between men and women were only the beginning and not the end of the equality inquiry. Confronting the myth and reality of biological differences may enable us to create a stronger equality concept in relation both to laws premised on cultural stereotypes and to laws that regulate reproductive biology.

The fifth example given above presents problems in relation to maternity and paternity leaves to care for young children. The policy providing child care leave to nursing mothers is one governing reproductive biology. Does the policy have a substantial impact in perpetuating inequality? It seems that it does. Either parent, or a stranger, is biologically capable of caring for a child. Limiting the childrearing to nursing women reinforces the cultural expectation that "the paramount destiny and mission of woman are to fulfill the noble and benign offices of wife and mother." Such a policy would have to be struck down because it could not withstand strict scrutiny; the state's interest in promoting the physical or psychic benefits of nursing is not sufficiently substantial to justify the burden upon men and women who would choose to take child care leave but who cannot nurse. Also, the oppressive effect upon women who would prefer not to nurse but are compelled to do so in order to qualify for the leave is not justified by the state's interest.

The second law presented in example 5 allows child care leave for mothers but not for fathers. This is not a law that governs reproductive biology but is instead a simple sex-based classification. A law based on what the government perceives to be the ability and willingness of certain citizens to care for children is not a law governing reproductive biology. A general maternal child care leave policy would be prohibited under the ERA and would need to be justified under the *Craig* standard as having a close relation to important government interests. The general maternal preference law would not be justifiable even under the more relaxed requirements of the *Craig* standard if challenged by a father who was able and eager to care for his child.

The final case, a statute requiring that a pregnant woman notify the man who impregnated her of the fact of the pregnancy, can be seen as a law governing reproductive biology. It addresses a problem of vital social importance—the law lends practical and symbolic force to the idea that men, as well as women, are responsible for the children they create and attempts to mitigate the effects of men's relatively minor role in relation to reproduction.

The hypothetical policy is far more sensitive to equality concerns than consent and notification requirements that are triggered by a woman's decision to have an abortion—requirements that have in the past been held unconstitutional. The hypothetical law directs the woman to provide the information, rather than imposing the requirement on a physician.

But even this more sensitive notification requirement is oppressive to women. The biological reality that "it is the woman who physically bears the child and who is the more directly and immediately affected by the pregnancy" must preclude the state from giving the man power over her decision whether to abort or to carry the pregnancy to term. A requirement of notification, as opposed to a formal veto, has effect only in those situations where the woman determines that communication with the man is unwise. It excuses notification when she has reason to fear violence. It gives the man only information, not a formal right of veto. Most significantly, it is not directed solely to women who seek abortions. A requirement that men be notified only when the pregnant woman seeks an abortion powerfully reinforces the cultural stereotype that motherhood is women's destiny. A man's concrete emotional, moral, and financial interest is vastly greater when a pregnancy he has helped to create is carried to term than when it ends in abortion. Abortion-only consent and notification policies express disapprobation for abortion, regard the woman as a "mother-machine," and are indefensible as a neutral means of increasing male involvement with reproductive decision-making.

A man's interest in a pregnancy he has helped to create is undeniably great. But a man's interest in having children does not justify imposing the burden of pregnancy and motherhood on a particular woman. Even if that woman is his wife, the burdens of pregnancy, which the woman inescapably bears, are too great to allow the man to impose them upon her. A man's interest in terminating a pregnancy he has helped to create may also be very great. He may be emotionally and financially incapable of assuming responsibility for a child. Perhaps society should allow biological parents greater freedom to reject the rights and responsibilities of parenthood. There is a strong public interest in encouraging fathers to be more involved in the nurturing and care of their children. The notification requirement may promote this interest. While this case is, for me, a difficult one, I do not believe that even this sensitive notification policy could survive the strict scrutiny that is appropriate to an analysis of laws that oppress women through the regulation of reproductive biology. We do not now require that mothers notify fathers at the point of birth and a multitude of public policies limit, rather than enhance, the father's participation in the nurturing of children. But parents' responsibilities to their children are not a function of reproductive biology. Such responsibilities can and should be defined in sex-neutral terms.

VI. THE FUTURE OF SEX-BASED EQUALITY UNDER THE FOURTEENTH AMENDMENT AND THE ERA

The Supreme Court's doctrine of sex-based equality under the fourteenth amendment is exceedingly unstable. This instability is manifest in the sharp divisions in analysis and result in cases such as *Parham v. Hughes, Caban v. Mohammed, Lehr v. Robertson,* and *Michael M. v. Superior Court.* The core principles of the Court's equality doctrine—the requirement that men and women be treated as individuals rather than stereotypes and the recognition that laws based on stereotypical assumptions are self-fulfilling as well as inaccurate in particular cases—are inconsistent with the approach that various members of the Court have taken in these cases. An unstable present necessarily implies an uncertain future.

The fourteenth amendment guarantees equal treatment under the law, and recognition of the injustice of denying men and women opportunities solely on the basis of sex is broad and deep. It would be possible to achieve greater strength and stability in sexual equality doctrine through the approach advocated here, which focuses directly on the reality and myth of biological differences. The Court could draw a sharp distinction between laws creating sex-based classifications and laws regulating sex-specific physical characteristics and still recognize that laws regulating sex-specific physical characteristics implicate the core concerns of sex-based equality.

For the most part the argument advanced here builds upon equality and privacy doctrine. Courts are skilled at the manipulation of doctrine. When doctrine develops quickly, in response to large changes in consciousness, modification in the light of experience and insight seems particularly appropriate. The analysis in cases such as *Michael M., Parham,* and *Caban* is not so compelling, nor the results so clear, that their approach need determine the way in which the Court analyzes future cases raising issues different than those resolved there. Other cases, notably *Geduldig,* are not so easily confined through the manipulation of doctrine. The Court should simply overrule *Geduldig,* recognizing it as the false step that Congress, nearly every commentator, and the Court itself have regarded it.

The Equal Rights Amendment has been defeated, but it is certain to rise again. What is not so certain is whether we will continue to regard laws regulating reproductive biology as tangential to the constitutional guarantee of sex-based equality. The direction in which the Court will move under the fourteenth amendment and the vision of sex-based equality reflected in the next ERA depend in large part upon the vision of equality adopted by those who shape claims of sex-based equality and reproductive freedom under existing constitutional guarantees and those who fight for the new ERA.

The ideas developed here are simply one woman's thoughts about the meaning of sex equality, under either the fourteenth amendment or the ERA. Although I support the Equal Rights Amendment, its major congressional proponents and the leaders of the struggle to enact it have expressed a different vision of sex-based equality. Strong reasons, both political and conceptual, support separation of doctrines of sex equality and reproductive freedom. The political reality is that extreme conservative religious and political groups have made opposition to abortion an organizing issue— a sine qua non political test. Although there is wide political support for equal pay for equal work and the claims of individual aspirational women seeking access to traditional male power, women's claims for control of their bodies present a more profound challenge to prevailing structures of male dominance, and are less widely accepted. Conceptual support for the separation of sex-based equality and reproductive freedom rests on skepticism whether courts are able to implement, with good faith and good sense, a concept of sex equality that recognizes the reality of biological difference. Further, privacy doctrine is richly developed in relation to reproductive freedom, and a shift to sex equality analysis in these cases seems, to many, unlikely. Nonetheless, as this Article has attempted to demonstrate, a strong concept of sex-based equality will require that we come to grips with the reality of sex-based biological differences, either through the approach proposed here or in some other way. A political struggle that embraces recognition that men and women are both limited by biology and able to transcend it may be stronger than one that ignores the core reality of sex difference in relation to reproductive biology.

Are we locked into the road we have taken? Are the two lines of constitutional doctrine—reproductive freedom and sex-based equality—which began as a unified whole to preserve male dominance and diverged in the early 1970's, now on fixed projections that move ineluctably further apart? I think not. The law is a social creation that produced the legal structure that made biology destiny and enforced the subjugation of women. In the 1970's we began the divergent movements to create a different social construct of sex equality and reproductive freedom. We can, if we choose, move toward a more unified understanding of the ways in which the law perpetuates sex-based restraints on human equality and liberty.

Joan C. Williams, *Deconstructing Gender,* 87 MICH. L. REV. 797 (1989)*

Mid-century feminism, now often referred to somewhat derisively as assimilationism, focused on providing opportunities to women in realms traditionally preserved for men. In the 1980s two phenomena have shifted feminists' attention from assimilationists' focus on how individual women are like men to a focus on gender differences, on how women as a group differ from men as a group. The first is the feminization of poverty, which dramatizes the chronic and increasing economic vulnerability of women. Feminists now realize that the assimilationists' traditional focus on gender-neutrality may have rendered women more vulnerable to certain gender-related disabilities that have important economic consequences. The second phenomenon that plays a central role in the current feminist imagination is that of career women "choosing" to abandon or subordinate their careers so they can spend time with their small children. These phenomena highlight the fact that deep-seated social differences continue to encourage men and women to make quite different choices with respect to work and family. Thus, "sameness" scholars are increasingly confronted by the existence of gender differences.

---

*   Originally published in 87 Mich. L. Rev. 797 (1989). Reprinted with permission of the Michigan Law Review Association.

Do these challenges to assimilationism prove that we should stop trying to kid ourselves and admit the "real" differences between men and women, as the popular press drums into us day after day, and as the "feminism of difference" appears to confirm? Do such phenomena mean that feminists' traditional focus on gender-neutrality is a bankrupt ideal? I will argue no on both counts, taking an approach quite different from that ordinarily taken by feminists on the sameness side of the spectrum. "Sameness" feminists usually have responded to the feminists of difference by reiterating their basic insight that individual men and women can be very similar. This is not an adequate response to the basic insight of "difference" feminists: that gender exists, that men and women differ as groups. While I take gender seriously, I disagree with the description of gender provided by difference feminists.

* * *

II. CHALLENGING THE GENDERED STRUCTURE OF WAGE LABOR

The challenge to "male norms" offered by the feminism of difference is comprised of two quite different elements. The first is the critique of "male" behavior and values, which in essence is the critique of possessive individualism. A second element is the critique of men's traditional life patterns. Like the first, this second critique has traditionally been linked with domesticity, but it need not be.

A rejection of men's traditional life patterns entails a fundamental challenge to the structure of wage labor. In articulating such a challenge, I begin from Catharine MacKinnon's analysis of gender as a system of power relations. While I disagree with many of MacKinnon's conclusions, her initial premise is a powerful one: that inequalities of power are the core feature of the gender system as we know it. MacKinnon and her followers have explored the implications of this insight primarily in the context of sexuality. Here I turn to a more conventional topic, and analyze the Western wage labor system as a system of power relations that leaves women economically and socially vulnerable.

Western wage labor is premised on an ideal worker with no child care responsibilities. In this system men and women workers are allocated very different roles. Men are raised to believe they have the right and the responsibility to perform as ideal workers. Husbands as a group therefore do far less child care, and earn far more, than their wives. Women are raised with complementary assumptions. They generally feel that they are entitled to the pleasure of spending time with their children while they are small. Moreover, even upon their return to work, the near-universal tendency is to assume that women's work commitment must be defined to accommodate continuing child-care responsibilities.

This gender system results in the impoverishment of women, since it leads mothers systematically to "choose" against performing as ideal workers in order to ensure that their children receive high-quality care. The phenomena that comprise the gender system today are often noted, but the way the system functions as a coherent whole remains largely hidden.

Before the industrial revolution, both men and women engaged in economic production, and though women were viewed as inferior, a certain fluidity existed between men's and women's roles. This situation changed with the shift from task-oriented to time-disciplined labor in the late eighteenth century. By the nineteenth century, men's and women's roles were sharply differentiated. Under the new gender system, married women ordinarily experienced utter financial dependence on their husbands, though a divorceless society protected wives from destitution so long as they stayed with their husbands and—perhaps more to the point—their husbands stayed with them.

This gendered division of labor had a certain logic during the colonial era, when the average white woman got pregnant once every 24 months, and had an average of more than seven live births. In addition, childbirth was hazardous and frequently incapacitated women for substantial periods. Marriage made biological reproduction a full-time job for most married women, even assuming that the household did not produce what it consumed, which many households did. Under these conditions the blanket assumption that married women were not suitable for life-long careers of time-disciplined labor may not have been far from the truth.

Since colonial times, childbirth has become safer and birth rates have fallen precipitously, yet the structure of wage labor remains unchanged. While women are keeping their side of the gender bargain, by "choosing" to marginalize themselves economically in order to allow their husbands to perform as ideal workers, many men no longer are honoring their commitment to support their mates and children. Divorced men in massive numbers pay little or no alimony or child support. Under these conditions, women's choice to eschew "ideal worker" status for the sake of their children often leads to impoverishment of their children as well as themselves.

The impoverishment of previously married women parallels the pattern among single mothers. With the breakdown of sexual taboos, increasing numbers of mothers are never married to the fathers of their children. These unwed fathers tend to play even less of a role in financial support of their children than do divorced fathers.

The wage gap, a third crucial element in the feminization of poverty, also appears to stem in part from the gendered distribution of wage labor and child-care responsibility. Economists employing "human capital" theory have argued that the wage gap is attributable not to discrimination but to women's choices. One study has estimated that roughly half of the wage gap between men and women is attributable to factors that, upon inspection, relate to women's childcare responsibilities. These factors include differences in work experience, work continuity, and ability to work full time and during illnesses of the worker or other family members. (Note that even were we to agree that women "choose" disproportionate child-care responsibilities, human capital theorists themselves implicitly acknowledge that such choices cannot account for all of the wage gap. Their own estimates leave 55 percent of the wage gap unexplained. This percentage may reflect discrimination.)

In fact, both discrimination against women and women's 'choices' must be seen as elements of an integrated system of power relations that systematically disadvantages women. Women's choices show the system's success in persuading women to buy into their own economic marginalization. Openly discriminatory treatment based on the notion that "women should stay at home" shows how gender ideology serves to police the gender system by eliminating options that would loosen the grip of gender roles. In sum, women's choices show how women perpetuate the gender system themselves; discrimination shows how others join them in policing the gender system.

* * *

The feminization of poverty reflects the way the gendered labor system invented at the time of the Industrial Revolution has adapted to modern conditions. In a world where many more women than ever before are raising children without significant financial assistance from men, the gender system has taken on a more repressive dynamic than at any time since its invention.

Why is this so difficult to see? In large part because of the ideology that women's disadvantaged position results from choices made by women themselves. . . .

The modern form of this argument is the contemporary celebration of women who either subordinate their careers or abandon them altogether because they "know their own priorities." "[A] woman shouldn't have to apologize for her priorities," said Betty Friedan in a recent interview on "sequencing," i.e., women dropping out of professional life for the period when their children are young. News articles on "sequencing" seem invariably to point to women such as Jeane J. Kirkpatrick, Sandra Day O'Connor, and D.C. Circuit Chief Judge Patricia Wald, each of whom took from five to fifteen years off to stay home with young children. Only occasionally do these articles note that such women are the exception. I suspect most women would take years off their careers if they could be guaranteed that upon their return they could become an ambassador to the United Nations, a Supreme Court Justice, or a D.C. Circuit Court judge—just as many men (and women) would take time off for a stint as an artist, a carpenter, or a ski bum if they could be offered the same assurance. But most "sequencers" are not so lucky. In the words of one company executive, "From a total career standpoint, anyone has to realize the realities of a big hiatus in their career—that it is certainly going to slow it down." (And this executive worked for a company that is actively seeking to hire reentering women—what do the executives of companies say who refuse to hire such women?)

There is growing evidence that a career hiatus, at least in some professions, does not merely slow women down, but places them permanently in a second-class, relatively low-paid "mommy track." This development has received particular attention in the law. One recent article notes the "frightening possibility" that law firms will evolve into institutions "top-heavy with men and childless women, supported by a pink-collar ghetto of mommy-lawyers," often with permanent associate status.

The professional who removes herself from the fast track is only part of the syndrome by which women systematically "choose" economic marginalization. Probably the more important aspect of the phenomenon is the tendency among women to select jobs that will allow them to fulfill their "family responsibilities," even if such jobs pay less and offer less opportunity for advancement.

These two phenomena are an integral part of the economic marginalization of women. Decoded, the current talk about women's priorities is a translation into new language of domesticity's old argument that women's values lead them to make different choices. The persistence of this classic argument makes it imperative for feminists to analyze why the argument has abiding persuasiveness. . . .

*   *   *

Feminists need to arm women to resist the argument that women's economic marginalization is the product of their own choice. Challenging this argument should be easy, since, in fact, in our deeply gendered system men and women face very different choices indeed. Whereas women, in order to be ideal workers, have to choose not to fulfill their "family responsibilities," men do not. The question women ask themselves is this: Should I make professional sacrifices for the good of my children? In order for the wife's "choice" to be equivalent to her husband's, she would first have to be in a position to ask herself whether or not she would choose to be an ideal worker if her husband would choose to stay home with the children. Second, she would have to pose the question in a context where powerful social norms told her he was peculiarly suited to raising children. When we speak of women's "choices" to subordinate their careers, we are so blinded by gender prescriptions that we can forget that the husband's decision to be an ideal worker rests upon the assumption that his wife will choose not to be in order to allow him that privilege. This is true whether the wife eschews a career altogether or whether (in the modern pattern) she merely subordinates her career to child-care responsibilities. The point is that the husband is doing neither. Women know that if they do not sacrifice no one will, whereas men assume that if they do not, women will.

Thus women do not enjoy the same choices as men. But the underlying point is a deeper one: that society is strucutred so that everyone, regardless of sex, is limited to two unacceptable choices—men's traditional life patterns or economic marginality. Under the current structure of wage labor, people are limited to being ideal workers, which leaves them with inadequate time to devote to parenting, and being primary parents condemned to relative poverty (if they are single parents) or economic vulnerability (if they are currently married to an ideal worker). Wage labor does not have to be structured in this way.

The increasing onerousness of the gender system makes a challenge to the structure of wage labor a priority of the highest order. Moreover, a historic opportunity exists for a challenge: the current revolution in wage labor itself.

This revolution is not that women work; women have always worked. The change is that the majority of mothers now engage in wage labor. . . .

This massive shift in the gendered distribution of wage labor has produced intense pressures to challenge the assumption that the ideal worker has no child care responsibilities. But this pressure is being evaded by a cultural decision to resolve the conflicts between home and work where they have always been resolved: on the backs of women. In the nineteenth century, married women "chose" total economic dependence in order to fulfill family responsibilities. Today, many women with children continue to make choices that marginalize them economically in order to fullfill those same responsibilities, through part-time work, "sequencing," the "mommy track" or "women's work." . . .

* * *

Feminists' goal must be to redesign wage labor to take account of reproduction. Such a goal today seems utopian—but then the eight-hour work day seemed utopian in the mid-nineteenth century. The notion that the wage-labor system should take account of the human life cycle has always faced the argument that such "private costs" as aging or raising children are of no concern to employers. Even in the United States, this view has been successfully challenged: old age is now acknowledged as a reality, and wage-labor expectations have been modified accordingly. That, too, once seemed a utopian goal. But expectations change: hegemony is never complete. Feminists should begin to work both towards cultural change and towards the kind of small, incremental steps that will gradually modify the wage-labor system to acknowledge the reality of society's reproductive needs.

III. REFOCUSING THE DEBATE

This section pursues two themes that will be crucial in refocusing the debate within feminism away from the destructive battle between "sameness" and "difference" towards a deeper understanding of gender as a system of power relations. I first argue that despite the force of Catharine MacKinnon's insight that gender involves disparities of power, her rejection of the traditional feminist ideal of gender-neutrality rests on misconceptions about this traditional goal, whose core aim is to oppose rules that institutionalize a correlation between gender and sex. Thus the traditional goal is not one of gender blindness; the goal instead is to deinstitutionalize gender, a long and arduous process that first requires us to see through the seductive descriptions of men and women offered by domesticity. I conclude the article by arguing that to the extent these descriptions offer an accurate description of gender differences, they merely reflect the realities of the oppressive gender system. Beyond that, the description is unconvincing.

A. From Gender-Neutrality to Deinstitutionalizing Gender

"Sameness" feminists' focus on the similarities between individual men and individual women led them to advocate "gender-neutral" categories that do not rely on gender stereotypes to differentiate between men and women. Recent feminists have challenged the traditional goal of gender neutrality on the grounds that it mandates a blindness to gender that has left women in a worse position than they were before the mid-twentieth-century challenge to gender roles.

This argument has been made in two different ways. Scholars such as Martha Fineman have argued that liberal feminists' insistence on gender-neutrality in the formulation of "no-fault" divorce laws has led to courts' willful blindness to the ways in which marriage systematically helps men's, and hurts women's, careers. Catharine MacKinnon has generalized this argument. She argues that because women are systematically disadvantaged by their sex, properly designed remedial measures can legitimately be framed by reference to sex.

MacKinnon's "inequality approach" would allow for separate standards for men and women so long as "the policy or practice in question [does not] integrally contribute[ ] to the maintenance of an underclass or a deprived position because of gender status." The strongest form her argument takes is that adherence to gender roles disadvantages women: Why let liberal feminists' taboo against differential treatment of women eliminate the most effective solution to inequality?

This debate is graced by a core truth and massive confusion. The core truth is that an insistence on gender neutrality by definition precludes protection for women victimized by gender.

The confusion stems from the use of the term gender neutrality. One could argue that problems created by the gendered structure of wage labor, or other aspects of the gender system, should not be remedied through the use of categories that identify the protected group by reference to the gender roles that have disadvantaged them. For example, one could argue that workers whose careers were disadvantaged by choices in favor of child care should not be given the additional support they need to "catch up" with their former spouses, on the grounds that the group protected inevitably would be mostly female, and this could reinforce the stereotype that women need special protections. Yet I know of no feminist of any stripe who makes this argument, which would be the position of someone committed to gender neutrality.

Traditionally, feminists have insisted not upon a blindness to gender, but on opposition to the traditional correlation between sex and gender. MacKinnon's crucial divergence is that she accepts the use of sex as a proxy for gender. Thus MacKinnon sees nothing inherently objectionable about protecting workers who have given up ideal worker status due to child-care responsibilities by offering protections to women. Her inequality approach allows disadvantages produced by gender to be remedied by reference to sex. This is in effect an acceptance and a reinforcement of the societal presumption that the social role of primary caretaker is necessarily correlated with possession of a vagina.

MacKinnon's approach without a doubt would serve to reinforce and to legitimize gender stereotypes that are an integral part of the increasingly oppressive gender system. Let's focus on a specific example. Scholars have found that the abolition of the maternal presumption in child-custody decisions has had two deleterious impacts on women. First, in the 90 percent of the cases where mothers received custody, mothers often find themselves bargaining away financial claims in exchange for custody of the children. Even if the father does not want custody, his lawyer often will advise him to claim it in order to have a bargaining chip with which to bargain down his wife's financial claims. Second, the abolition of the maternal preference has created situations where a father who wants custody often wins even if he was not the primary caretaker prior to the divorce—on the grounds that he can offer the children a better life because he is richer than his former wife. In these circumstances, the ironic result of a mother's sacrifice of ideal worker status for the sake of her children is that she ultimately loses the children.

While these results are no doubt infuriating, do they merit a return to a maternal presumption, as MacKinnon's approach seems to imply? No: the deconstruction of gender, by highlighting the chronic and increasing oppressiveness of the gender system, demonstrates the undesirability of the inequality approach, which would reinforce the gender system in both a symbolic way and a practical one. On a symbolic level, the inequality approach would reinforce and legitimize the traditional assumption that childrearing is "naturally" the province of women. MacKinnon's rule also would reinforce gender mandates in a very concrete way. Say a father chose to give up ideal worker status in order to undertake primary child care responsibility. MacKinnon's rule fails to help him, because the rule is framed in terms of biology, not gender. The result: a strong message to fathers that they should not deviate from established gender roles. MacKinnon's rule operates to reinforce the gender system.

What we need, then, is a rule that avoids the traditional correlation between gender and sex, a rule that is sex- but not gender-neutral. The traditional goal, properly understood, is really one of sex-neutrality, or, more descriptively, one of deinstitutionalizing gender. It entails a systematic refusal to institutionalize gender in any form. This approach mandates not an enforced blindness to gender, but rather a refusal to reinforce the traditional assumption that adherence to gender roles flows "naturally" from biological sex. Reinforcing that assumption reinforces the grip of the gender system as a whole.

* * *

This analysis shows that the traditional commitment, which is really one to deinstitutionalizing gender rather than to gender neutrality, need not preclude rules that protect people victimized by gender. People disadvantaged by gender can be protected by properly naming the group: in this case, not mothers, but anyone who has eschewed ideal worker status to fulfill child-care responsibilities. One court, motivated to clear thinking by a legislature opposed to rules that addressed gender disabilities by reference to sex, has actually framed child-custody rules in this way.

The traditional goal is misstated by the term "gender neutrality." The core feminist goal is not one of pretending gender does not exist. Instead, it is to deinstitutionalize the gendered structure of our society. There is no reason why people disadvantaged by gender need to be suddenly disowned. The deconstruction of gender allows us to protect them by reference to their social roles instead of their genitals.

B. Deconstructing Difference

How can this be done? Certainly the hardest task in the process of deconstructing gender is to begin the long and arduous process of seeing through the descriptions of men and women offered by domesticity. Feminists need to explain exactly how the traditional descriptions of men and women are false. To break free of traditional gender ideology, we need at the simplest level to see how men nurture people and relationships and how women are competitive and powerful. This is a task in which we as feminists will meet considerable resistance, both from inside and outside the feminist movement.

* * *

Our difficulty in seeing men's nurturing side stems in part from the word "nurture." Although its broadest definition is "the act of promoting development or growth," the word derives from nursing a baby, and still has overtones of "something only a mother can do." Yet men are involved in all kinds of relationships in which they promote another's development in a caring way: as fathers, as mentors, as camp counselors, as boy scout leaders. These relationships may have a somewhat different emotional style and tone than do those of women and often occur in somewhat different contexts: that is the gender difference. But a blanket assertion that women are nurturing while men are not reflects more ideology than reality.

* * *

Ideology not only veils men's needy side, it also veils the competitive nature of many women who want power as avidly as men. "Feminists have long been fiercely critical of male power games, yet we have often ignored or concealed our own conflicts over money, control, position, and recognition. . . . It is time to end the silence." The first step, as these authors note, is to acknowledge the existence of competition in women's lives. Women's desire for control may be exercised in running "a tight ship" on a small income, in tying children to apron strings, or in nagging husbands—the classic powerplay of the powerless. Note how these examples tend to deprecate women's desire for power. These are the stereotypes that come to mind because they confirm the ideology that "real" women don't need power. These are ways women's yearning for power has been used as evidence against them, as evidence they are not worthy as wives, as mothers, or as women. Feminists' taboo against competition has only reinforced the traditional view that real women don't need power. Yet women's traditional roles have always required them to be able to wield power with self-confidence and subtlety. Other cultures recognize that dealing with a two-year-old is one of the great recurring power struggles in the cycle of human life. But not ours. We are too wrapped up in viewing childrearing as nurturing, as something opposed by its nature to authoritative wielding of power, to see that nurturing involves a sophisticated use of power in a hierarchical relationship. The differences between being a boss and a mother in this regard are differences in degree as well as in kind.

* * *

CONCLUSION

. . . The traditional focus on how individuals diverge from gender stereotypes fails to come to terms with gender similarities of women as a group. I have tried to present an alternative response. By taking gender seriously, I have reached conclusions very different from those of the relational feminists. I have not argued that gender differences do not exist; only that relational feminists have misdescribed them.

* * *

The approach of deconstructing gender requires women to give up their claims to special virtue. But it offers ample compensation. It highlights the fact that women will be vulnerable until we redesign the social ecology, starting with a challenge to the current structure of wage labor. The current structure may not have been irrational in the eighteenth century, but it is irrational today. Challenging it today should be at the core of a feminist program.

The message that women's position will remain fundamentally unchanged until labor is restructured is both a hopeful and a depressing one. It is depressing because it shows that women will remain economically vulnerable in the absence of fundamental societal change. Yet it is hopeful because, if we heed it, we may be able to unite as feminists to seize the opportunity offered by mothers' entry into the work force, instead of frittering it away rediscovering traditional (and inaccurate) descriptions of gender differences.

Ruth Colker, *Anti-Subordination Above All: Sex, Race, and Equal Protection*, 61 N.Y.U. L. REV. 1003 (1986)*

* * *

INTRODUCTION

Feminists often criticize equal protection doctrine for not taking discrimination against women seriously enough. They consider the courts' use of intermediate rather than strict scrutiny in assessing sex-based equal protection claims a symptom of this problem. Civil rights advocates also criticize the race cases for not taking seriously enough the vision of equality for blacks. Although they generally applaud the use of strict scrutiny in race discrimination cases, they disagree with the courts' handling of some affirmative action cases.

I enter this discussion by starting from the premise that equal protection doctrine needs to do a better job understanding blacks' and womens' visions of equality and needs to have a framework that more effectively deals with the affirmative action cases. I posit a new model that can gain from the benefits of both the race and sex models of equal protection.

In order to facilitate an exploration of the strengths and weaknesses of the race and sex discrimination models, I analyze two principles that underlie these models: the principles of "anti-subordination" and "anti-differentiation." Under the anti-differentiation perspective, it is inappropriate to treat individuals differently on the basis of a particular normative view about race or sex. It is an individual rights perspective in two respects. First, it focuses on the motivation of the individual institution that has allegedly discriminated, without attention to the larger societal context in which the institution operates. Second, the anti-differentiation perspective focuses on the specific effect of the alleged discrimination on discrete individuals, rather than on groups. Race- and sex-specific policies or actions are invalid under this perspective because they reflect invidious motivation and result in dissimilar treatment for similarly situated individuals. It is equally individious for white men to be treated differently from black women as for black women to be treated differently from white men under this perspective, because both situations violate the preeminent norm of equal treatment. Anti-differentiation advocates therefore argue for "color-blindness" or "sex-blindness" in the development and analysis of legislative and institutional policies, and frequently criticize affirmative action as violating that principle.

In this Article, I argue that courts should analyze equal protection cases from an anti-subordination perspective. Under the anti-subordination perspective, it is inappropriate for certain groups in society to have subordinated status because of their lack of power in society as a whole. This approach seeks to eliminate the power disparities between men and women, and between whites and non-whites, through the development of laws and policies that directly redress those disparities. From an anti-subordination perspective, both facially differentiating and facially neutral policies are invidious only if they perpetuate racial or sexual hierarchy.

In contrast to the anti-differentiation approach, the anti-subordination perspective is a group-based perspective, in two ways. First, it focuses on society's role in creating subordination. Second, it focuses on the way in which this subordination affects, or has affected, groups of people. It is more invidious for women or blacks to be treated worse than white men than for men or whites to be treated worse than black women under this perspective, because of the differing histories and contexts of subordination faced by these groups. Anti-subordination proponents therefore advocate the use of race- or sex-specific policies, such as affirmative action, when those policies redress the subordination of racial minorities or women.

The courts have struggled with the choice between the anti-differentiation and anti-subordination perspectives. The most obvious sources of this tension have been the affirmative action cases, where the courts have grappled with the issue of whether the principle of anti-differentiation should be compromised by accommodation of race- or sex-specific policies that are instituted to overcome a prior history of subordination of racial minorities or women. This tension is also overt in the difference between the courts' treatment of race and sex discrimination cases, and the difference between strict scrutiny and intermediate scrutiny under constitutional equal protection doctrine.

Although much of the scholarship on equal protection doctrine assumes that the anti-differentiation principle is justifiably the dominant perspective, a comparison of race and sex cases, as well as of constitutional and statutory cases, reveals that the anti-subordination principle better explains both much of the law and the aversion we feel to race and sex discrimination.

. . . [T]he anti-subordination perspective is consistent with the history of the equal protection clause and reflects a living aspiration that will help us move towards a world of equality. Historically, the equal protection principle developed to remedy a history of subordination against a particular group in society, blacks. Aspirationally, it reminds us that no group should remain subordinated in our society and that we should therefore take seriously the claims of women and of other discrete minorities that they have been subjected to pervasive discrimination in our society.

The anti-differentiation principle, in contrast, does a disservice to this history and fundamental aspiration by asserting that discrimination against whites is as problematic as discrimination against blacks. We have not decided, as a nation, that all distinctions are invidious. We permit distinctions on the basis of intelligence or ability. We only prohibit distinctions that we have good reason to believe are biased or irrational, and it is group-based experiences that primarily inform us as to which kinds of distinctions are biased or irrational. Thus, the anti-subordination principle, by recognizing and drawing on the historical subordination of blacks and women, offers a substantive explanation for why certain distinctions are subjected to closer scrutiny.

* * *

In this Article, I argue that the courts have made their choices between the anti-differentiation and anti-subordination perspectives without a sound theoretical basis.

Historically, differentiation has been a powerful tool in perpetuating the subordination of minorities and women through segregation and exclusion. In the early equal protection cases, the principle of anti-differentiation was useful to abolish racial segregation and other practices that excluded blacks. Accordingly, the courts may not have seen the need to choose between the anti-differentiation and anti-subordination perspectives; they could describe the discrimination under either framework. The courts may therefore have uttered global assertions of anti-differentiation such as "separate can never be equal" when what they meant was "enforced segregation of blacks prevents their attainment of equality." . . .

* * *

[T]he framework I propose brings the principle of anti-subordination to the forefront of equal protection doctrine. The framework retains the bilevel inquiry that occurs in each equal protection lawsuit: the examination of the plaintiff's prima facie case, and the analysis of the defendant's proffered justification for the challenged policy or action. Yet the proposed framework reformulates the substance of each stage of the inquiry. First, the plaintiff would no longer be required to show the discriminatory intent behind a neutral policy or be able to establish a prima facie case of discrimination simply by asserting that a policy or action facially differentiates. Instead, every plaintiff would have to establish that the policy or action had a disparate impact on members of plaintiff's race or sex. This reformulation elevates anti-subordination over anti-differentiation in two ways: first, by emphasizing the effect of policies or actions on groups rather than individuals, and second, by eliminating the need to prove discriminatory motivation. Under this proposed approach, if the plaintiff could not show disparate impact a court would uphold a race- or sex-specific policy or action without ever getting to the stage of justification. By valuing impact over differentiation at the prima facie case stage, the framework ensures that only policies or actions that might be subordinating would reach the stage of justification.

In its second phase, the proposed approach would focus the justification inquiry on the principle of anti-subordination rather than on nebulous constructs of strict or intermediate scrutiny, which leave courts uncertain about what normative principles underlie the level of scrutiny. Only a goal of anti-subordination would justify a race- or sex-specific policy or action; no other justification would be permitted under the new framework. Courts would be unable to weaken the level of scrutiny to permit other kinds of justifications.

Thus, under the equal protection framework proposed in this Article, it would be permissible for a state actor to use facially differentiating policies to redress subordination; it would not be permissible for a state actor to use facially differentiating policies that perpetuate subordination. Indeed, the essential inquiry in any equal protection case would be how differentiating policies or actions connect to subordination, not whether policies are phrased in race- or sex-specific terms. The courts and private parties should be able to implement race- and sex-specific policies where they are best suited to the task of remedying subordination.

* * *

I

THE EVOLUTION OF EQUAL PROTECTION PRINCIPLES
IN THE RACE AND SEX CASES

Since the beginning of the 1950s, many black plaintiffs have brought cases alleging violations of the right to equal protection on either statutory or constitutional grounds, in which they challenged race-specific policies or actions that excluded them from important educational, employment, and general societal opportunities. These policies and actions were invalid from both anti-differentiation and anti-subordination perspectives because they explicitly differentiated on the basis of race and subordinated blacks. Congress responded with major civil rights legislation that made such race-specific policies or actions unlawful in the areas of public accommodations, federally financed programs or activities, voting, housing, and employment.

As the case law developed, courts had to confront two crucial issues. First, they had to determine whether evidence of a race-specific policy, action, or motivation—explicit "different treatment"—is always required to establish a prima facie case of discrimination, or whether evidence of "disparate impact," alone, is sufficient. The second issue confronting the Court was the level of scrutiny to apply to the justifications proffered for the discrimination once a prima facie case had been proved. Each issue will be treated in turn.

* * *

Faced with the prospect of arguing cases of unequal educational facilities one by one for the next half century, the LDF pushed for a stronger statement from the Court about the harm to blacks caused by segregation. Finally, in 1954, the Supreme Court held in *Brown v. Board of Education* that racially separate education cannot be equal education.

A superficial examination of *Brown* suggests that the Court was emphasizing the principle of anti-differentiation over the principle of anti-subordination in its ruling. However, closer examination shows that the anti-subordination principle dominated the Court's analysis. Post-*Brown* courts have focused on the strong anti-differentiation statement from the *Brown* Court, namely, that separate can never be equal, and overlooked that Court's central concern for remedying the subordination of blacks. Applying a 'strict scrutiny' standard, post-*Brown* courts have permitted virtually no justifications for racially-differentiating laws or policies, prompting Professor Gunther to describe strict scrutiny as "fatal in fact."

Yet, the strict standard of scrutiny did not survive importation to other, non-race-based claims of equal protection violation, such as claims of sex discrimination. In the early sex discrimination cases, male plaintiffs brought constitutional challenges to preferential policies for women, and women challenged subordinating sex-specific policies. After exploring various levels of scrutiny, the Court settled on approaching these cases with an "intermediate" level of scrutiny, under which some sex-specific policies or actions were invalidated, while others survived.

Intermediate scrutiny, or "intensified rational basis scrutiny" has developed gradually in the sex discrimination context. Before the advent of modern equal protection doctrine on sex-based classifications, courts were relatively unconcerned about the subordination of women. The courts easily accepted justifications for sex-specific policies or actions that served to perpetuate, rather than eliminate, the subordination of women to men. For example, in 1873, in *Bradwell v. Illinois*, the Court upheld a rule against women practicing law. Justice Bradley, in his famous concurrence, justified this rule on the basis that "civil law, as well as nature herself, has always recognized a wide difference in the respective spheres and destinies of man and woman. Man is, or should be, woman's protector and defender." Indeed, until the 1940s, virtually all of the cases challenging sex-specific classifications involved such subordinating views of women.

In these early cases, the Court did not even apply an equal protection framework. Hence, it upheld sex-based distinctions without inquiry into the problems of differentiation or subordination. It was not until the 1970s that the Court began to move toward intermediate scrutiny as a means to redress the subordination of women. In *Reed v. Reed*, the Court purported to use rational basis scrutiny in striking down an Idaho statute that provided a mandatory preference for males over females in the selection of the administrators of estates, but the Court actually applied a heightened level of scrutiny. Two years later, in *Frontiero v. Richardson*, a plurality of the Court used heightened scrutiny to invalidate a statute that presumed that servicemen but not servicewomen were the major providers in households. . . .

The *Frontiero* Court used history to justify the application of what it termed "strict judicial scrutiny." Despite this label, the scrutiny employed by the *Frontiero* Court, like the scrutiny used in later sex discrimination cases, was not as probing as the scrutiny used in race discrimination cases. The Court's decision in *Frontiero* exemplifies the development of this less probing model within modern sex-based equal protection doctrine. After justifying the use of heightened scrutiny, the Court considered justifications for the sex-specific policy, noting that the statutes in question were "not in any sense designed to rectify the effects of past discrimination against women." The Court thus suggested that it was appropriate to consider the principle of anti-subordination in ruling on the constitutionality of a sex-specific rule.

Unfortunately, it soon became clear that anti-subordination was not the only justification for sex-specific policies that the Court was willing to accept. Later cases revealed that other justifications were also to be considered, justifications that reflected a weak anti-differentiation model without an anti-subordination foundation.

A year after *Frontiero*, in *Kahn v. Shevin*, the Court used an explicitly lower level of scrutiny than that which it had purported to employ in *Frontiero*. In *Kahn*, a widower challenged a state property tax exemption that was available only to widows, blind persons, or totally and permanently disabled persons. The Supreme Court upheld the statute using the *Reed* heightened rational basis test, and its analysis provided the state with wide discretion in justifying sex-specific policies.

Two years later, the Court's decision in *Craig v. Boren* made clear that intermediate scrutiny was to be the standard of review in sex-discrimination cases. Invalidating an Oklahoma statute prohibiting the sale of 3.2% beer to males under 21 and to females under 18, the Court linked the use of intermediate scrutiny to its ability to consider sex-specific justifications, but bypassed an anti-subordination analysis because Oklahoma did not suggest that "the age-sex differential was enacted to . . . compensat[e] for previous deprivations."

These cases illustrate the general inconsistency on the Court's part in applying the principles of anti-differentiation and anti-subordination. In constructing the stage of justification, the Court developed a stronger anti-differentiation perspective in race cases than in sex cases by exhibiting less toleration of race-specific policies or actions than of sex-specific policies or actions.

* * *

II

THE DEVELOPMENT AND APPLICATION OF THE ANTI-DIFFERENTIATION AND ANTI-SUBORDINATION PRINCIPLES IN THE PRIMA FACIE CASE STAGE

* * *

. . . Under existing unconstitutional equal protection doctrine, a plaintiff may not establish a prima facie case of discrimination solely with evidence that a race- or sex-neutral policy or action had a disparate impact on a protected class of persons, but must instead offer proof of different treatment or invidious motivation. . . .

I question the construction of the prima facie case under the constitutional model. Like other commentators, I criticize the courts for choosing the principle of anti-differentiation over the principle of anti-subordination in the constitutional cases. . . .

Consideration of the following hypothetical situation will facilitate an understanding of my argument:

> A city agency has had a policy for the last five years that all professional employees may have a month of paid sick leave each year and the nonprofessional staff may have two weeks of paid sick leave. An employee is not required to justify the use of this sick leave. However, an employee who is absent more than the allotted sick leave may be terminated.
>
> The composition of this agency is: professional employees: 5% black, 10% female; nonprofessional employees: 60% black, 90% female. Black women comprise 90% of the individuals who earn income at the bottom two pay scales of this employer.
>
> Over the last five years, the only employees to be terminated for violating this policy were black women. These women missed work for a variety of reasons, such as transportation, health, crime, housing and child care problems.
>
> Would (or should) black women be able to bring a successful claim for violation of equal protection? If the employer or a court recognized a problem at the workplace, would (or should) it be able to order a race- and sex-specific leave policy to overcome this problem?

* * *

A. The Different Treatment Method of Proof

The different treatment approach requires black female plaintiffs to show that the defendant is treating them differently than it is treating similarly situated white or male workers. However, the black women in the hypothetical could not use this approach to challenge the policy because there are no similarly situated white or male workers who are being treated differently. This understanding of inequality is deficient because it permits the perpetuation of a system in which white men can generally take more sick leave than black women because of their differing status within the workplace. Hence, this understanding of inequality permits the perpetuation of the "horizontal" and "vertical" segregation of the workplace. Yet, a pure anti-differentiation analysis would not even perceive that a violation of equal protection exists here.

If anti-differentiation proponents did perceive that a problem exists here, they would insist that the employer respond only with race- and sex-neutral policies. They argue that the different treatment approach is important in defining discrimination and the scope of appropriate remedies because it reduces the risk of perpetuating racial or sex-role stereotypes. They believe that facially differentiating policies perpetuate racial and sex-role stereotypes by using race or sex as an inaccurate proxy for sociological conditions that could be defined in race- and sex-neutral terms. They therefore would not allow the employer to "correct" the disparate impact on black women through the use of a race- or sex-specific policy. Assuming that their argument is correct, can we be sure that their approach will avoid perpetuating stereotypes? Moreover, at what cost do we avoid perpetuating these stereotypes?

The cost of avoiding race- and sex-specific remedies is too high. A race- and sex-specific remedy may be the most effective because it makes it difficult for an uncooperative defendant to circumvent the court's order. The history of court-ordered desegregation illustrates this point strongly. After the *Brown* decision, many courts ordered desegregation of public facilities, but many did not prescribe the way in which the defendants should achieve desegregation. Some defendants responded by closing the segregated public facility to avoid having to desegregate it. Rather than recognize that race-specific remedies were necessary to insure that these facilities would be open to blacks, the Supreme Court avoided taking a strong position on this issue. The Court failed to recognize that closing these facilities would have a disparate impact on blacks who would not have access to the newly opened private facilities.

Similarly, in the hypothetical, if the court ordered the defendant to provide the same leave to all workers to eliminate the impact of the two-tier leave policy on black women, the employer could respond with a no-leave policy for all workers. Although this race- and sex-neutral policy would meet the court's requirements, it would have an even greater disparate impact on the black female workers, who would remain unable to afford good health care, child care, or transportation. Thus, race- and sex-neutral remedies may leave the underlying problem unresolved.

In addition, the anti-differentiation strategy may not always achieve its intended results. The fact that a plaintiff has argued from an anti-differentiation perspective does not mean that the courts will refrain from imposing a race- or sex-specific remedy. In the hypothetical, even if it were possible for a plaintiff to win a different treatment case and seek a prospective race- and sex-neutral prospective remedy, the court would be faced with many difficult choices. It could choose the plaintiff's preferred remedy of providing everyone with four weeks of leave time. This remedy would be race- and sex-neutral. Or it could search for a middle ground that would be reasonable in cost and tailored to remedy the underlying problem. The court might search for a remedy that would define all the factors that are causing black women to miss work disproportionately—housing, transportation, health care, child care, and the like. However, it might decide that it is not feasible to define all these factors in a way that would not lead to abuse of a new leave policy by other workers. Hence, it might opt for a race- and sex-specific remedy for black women. What will anti-differentiation proponents do at that point? Might they argue for no remedy at all rather than a race- or sex-specific remedy? No remedy at all would be an unfortunate development after a court has found that discrimination exists. Thus, employment of the different treatment approach does not necessarily avoid the possibility of race- or sex-specific policies or actions because the court may conclude that those are the best practical remedies.

The problem underlying these deficiencies in the different treatment approach is the law's definition of "discrimination." A prima facie case of discrimination can stand or fall solely on the basis of the language used in expressing a rule. By creating a distinction between "women" and "men," an employer is presumed to have discriminated on the basis of sex. Conversely, by creating facially neutral classes such as "veterans" and "nonveterans" rather than sex-specific distinctions like "men" and "women," governmental entities are able to avoid a finding of discrimination.

Prima facie discrimination need not be defined so superficially. Under the present framework, the law allows rulemakers to hide an invidious purpose behind facial neutrality. It would be more intellectually honest, and useful, for rules to say what they mean, rather than be drafted to meet the test of anti-differentiation. The real issue should be a policy's contribution to, or redress of, subordination, not the way in which it is phrased.

I therefore suggest that courts require some evidence of subordination in the presentation of the prima facie case. Evidence of differentiation should not be sufficient. One kind of evidence that could sufficiently establish subordination for the purpose of the prima facie case is evidence of disparate impact. Such evidence would indicate that the plaintiff is being treated differently because of her membership in a group, suggesting that group-based inequality is present within that institution. By arguing that the courts require some evidence of subordination at the prima facie case stage, I am not suggesting that evidence of differentiation is irrelevant to a showing of subordination or that courts ignore the implications of remedial differentiation. Rather, I argue that courts must specifically ask how differentiation influences subordination. Differentiation may contribute to subordination, or it may redress it as in the affirmative action setting. Courts should stop assuming, as anti-differentiation proponents would have them assume, that differentiation can only contribute to subordination and can never redress it.

In general, these criticisms reflect the failure of anti-differentiation advocates to grasp fully both the practical and theoretical limitations of the different treatment method of proof. This method of proof can neither challenge structural barriers to equality adequately nor facilitate the redress of group-based subordination. While the disparate impact theory may be more successful, much of its success depends, as the discussion that follows will show, on the ability of its proponents to formulate and advance race- and sex-specific policies that truly redress subordination.

* * *

B. Disparate Impact Method of Proof

The disparate impact approach would be more successful in combating the structural barriers to equality illustrated by the hypothetical. It does not require proof of individualized discriminatory motivation and would therefore permit consideration of a group-based claim by the black female plaintiffs in the hypothetical. These plaintiffs could aggregate evidence to show that the leave policy has a disparate impact on their employment opportunities within the workplace. Accordingly, they could challenge some of the structural inequalities of the workplace exemplified by the sick-leave policy. Finally, they could argue for race- or sex-specific prospective relief.

* * *

III

THE DEVELOPMENT OF THE ANTI-DIFFERENTIATION PRINCIPLE AT THE STAGE OF JUSTIFICATION

Once a plaintiff establishes a prima facie case of discrimination, the defendant has the burden of justifying the discrimination. The sex discrimination model of intermediate scrutiny permits courts to consider a much wider range of justifications for differentiations than does the race discrimination model of strict scrutiny. Sometimes, courts use the flexibility of intermediate scrutiny to permit sex-based policies to pass muster when they redress subordination; other times, they use this flexibility to accept less laudatory justifications. Thus, sex-based intermediate scrutiny does not reflect a rigid anti-differentiation perspective and can accommodate an anti-subordination perspective.

* * *

A. The Price of the Differing Levels of Scrutiny

Although *Brown v. Board of Education* could be said to stand for the proposition that it is equally invidious to exclude whites from predominantly black educational institutions as to exclude blacks from predominantly white educational institutions, the Court in *Brown* was not faced with that issue. Instead, the Court was faced with the historical reality that blacks were receiving an inferior education, as well as the ineffectiveness of remedying segregation on a case-by-case basis. . . .

It was the history of subordination of blacks that moved the Supreme Court to respond with its strict ruling that racially separate education cannot be equal education. Yet, the history in which *Brown* is rooted further suggests that race-specific policies or actions should be permitted to redress subordination. However, to uphold a justification of anti-subordination for a race-specific policy or action against constitutional challenge, some members of the Court have seen a need to lower the level of scrutiny.

Justice Brennan developed an intermediate level of scrutiny to be used in the affirmative action area that, in large part, encompasses the anti-subordination approach suggested in this Article. For example, in *Regents of the University of California v. Bakke*, Justice Brennan, joined by three other justices, stated that in race discrimination cases brought by whites that challenged race-specific policies and that did not involve fundamental rights, he would use an intermediate level of scrutiny that posed the following two questions: (1) Did the race-specific policy reflect an "important and articulated purpose," and (2) Did it "stigmatize[ ] any group or single[ ] out those least well represented in the political process to bear the brunt of a benign program"? The first question is the traditional question in intermediate scrutiny cases; the second question is not. This second question squarely places the focus on an anti-subordination justification by considering the impact on subordinated groups.

* * *

Thus, in *Bakke,* the difference in the levels of scrutiny employed by Justices Powell and Brennan determined the outcome of the case. Justice Powell's strict scrutiny was less tolerant of race-specific policies than Justice Brennan's intermediate scrutiny. Because only five of the members of the Court reached the constitutional issue in *Bakke*, and only four were in agreement, the case does not provide insight into what level of scrutiny a majority of the Court would favor in the affirmative action context.

* * *

On balance, it seems Justice Brennan headed toward a coherent articulation of the anti-subordination principle. But his framework leaves at least two problems unsettled. First, how does he know whether to apply strict scrutiny or intermediate scrutiny? Would he rely simply on whether the plaintiff is white in a race discrimination case or whether the plaintiff is male in a sex discrimination case? Chief Justice Rehnquist has suggested that such a simplistic approach would be appropriate in the sex discrimination context.

But differentiation based on the plaintiff's race or sex is not determinative of whether a policy or action is subordinating to blacks or women. For example, if a bar offers half-price drinks to women in order to attract more male and female customers, men might challenge the policy as discriminatory on the basis of sex, since they cannot take advantage of the offer. Under Rehnquist's approach, the case would be subjected to lowered scrutiny because the plaintiffs are men. However, such a practice directly reinforces sex-role stereotypes about women and perpetuates women's subordination. While the Brennan model tries to engage in a more probing analysis than simply asking the identity of the plaintiff, the model has dangerous implications in Chief Justice Rehnquist's hands.

Second, lowering the level of scrutiny in any subcategory of cases involving race discrimination might permit justifications other than redressing subordination, as has occurred in the cases treating sex-discrimination. Like race-based equal protection doctrine, sex-based equal protection doctrine has developed through the efforts of plaintiffs challenging subordination. For women, unlike blacks, this task was complicated by the need to attack "special protection" legislation that created sex-specific rules purportedly to assist women but that, in fact, helped to perpetuate paternalistic stereotypes about them. Thus, opponents of sex discrimination have often attacked the propriety of sex-specific rules in an attempt to eradicate the subordination that stems from paternalistic "special" protection.

The Supreme Court has not responded to these sex discrimination arguments consistently. Because it sometimes permits sex-specific policies or actions to withstand scrutiny, the Court does not appear to have a pure anti-differentiation perspective in this area. While modern sex-based equal protection cases emerged from the belief that women have faced a history of subordination that must be redressed, the decisions in *Reed v. Reed* and its progeny have made it clear that the subordination of women is not the only justification that can survive intermediate scrutiny.

The genesis of this problem can be found in *Kahn v. Shevin*. In its final footnote, the *Kahn* majority provided the first direct link between the level of scrutiny and the consideration of justifications for sex-specific policies or actions. Justifying its acceptance of the state's purported argument for passing a tax statute favoring women, the Court rejected the necessity of determining the state's real motivation for passing the statute because: "[g]ender has never been rejected as an impermissible classification in all instances. Congress has not so far drafted women in the Armed Services. The famous Brandeis Brief in *Muller v. Oregon*, on which the Court specifically relied, emphasized that the special physical structure of women has a bearing on the 'conditions under which she should be permitted to toil.'" Hence, *Kahn v. Shevin* shows that the development of intermediate scrutiny, which served to accommodate the principle of anti-subordination at the stage of justification, ironically also opened the door to affirmance of subordinating rationales for sex-specific policies. The Court in *Kahn* cited *Muller v. Oregon* with approval to justify upholding a sex-specific rule under a lowered level of scrutiny, even though the ruling in *Muller* had contributed to the subordination of women by upholding extremely paternalistic limitations on the hours women could work. . . .

. . . Since *Kahn*, the Court has repeatedly used intermediate scrutiny to consider justifications other than the eradication of subordination.

* * *

The fruits . . . can be seen in the most troubling recent sex discrimination case decided under intermediate scrutiny, *Michael M. v. Superior Court*. The petitioner in *Michael M.* challenged the constitutionality of California's statutory rape law, under which it was illegal to have sexual intercourse with a female under the age of eighteen but not illegal to have sexual intercourse with a male under the age of eighteen.

Justice Rehnquist, writing for a plurality, assumed that the state statute discriminated against men because it made "men alone criminally liable for the act of sexual intercourse." Relying on *Reed* and *Craig*, Justice Rehnquist applied intermediate scrutiny to the case, asking whether the gender-based classification had a fair and substantial relationship to legitimate state ends or important goverment objectives. He concluded that the statute served the strong state interest in preventing illegitimate pregnancy. In addition, he concluded that because all of the significant harmful and inescapable identifiable consequences of teenage pregnancy fall on the young female, the legislature had acted within its authority in electing only to punish the participant who, by nature, suffers few of the consequences of his conduct.

Although the Court purported to ask how this legislation affected women, it did not do so from an anti-subordination perspective. . . .

. . . The paucity of evidence before the Court strongly suggested that the desire to control pregnancy was, at best, a post hoc rationalization. Moreover, that rationalization did not even fit with the provisions of the statute because the statute also made sexual intercourse with prepubescent females unlawful. The interest in limiting teenage pregnancy seemed to be as much a reflection of the state's interests in protecting its financial resources as in protecting the interests of women.

The use of intermediate scrutiny enabled Justice Rehnquist to bring in considerations unrelated to elimination of women's subordination in order to uphold a sex-based statute. Under the sloppy framework of intermediate scrutiny, he was able to allow such a statute to pass muster, although it is doubtful that an analogous race-based statute could have passed muster under strict scrutiny.

* * *

In sum, then, the Court's experimentation with varying levels of scrutiny of race- and sex-specific policies has had positive and negative implications for the effort to bring forth an anti-subordination approach to equal protection. The greater tolerance of sex-specific policies has led to the positive result that policies and laws that differentiate for the purpose of eliminating subordination pass muster, but also to the negative result that sex-specific policies or actions serving less important, often invidious, purposes also survive. By contrast, the lesser tolerance of race-specific policies under strict scrutiny has led to the positive result that virtually no race-specific policy can pass muster, but has also led to a rather awkward attempt to accommodate race-specific remedies ordered for the purpose of redressing a particularly egregious case of subordination.

* * *

IV

BRINGING THE PRINCIPLE OF ANTI-SUBORDINATION TO THE FOREFRONT

Race- and sex-based equal protection doctrine emerged from a concern for the subordination of blacks and women. Nevertheless, the equal protection framework that has evolved does not allow that concern to have its fullest expression. At the stage of the prima facie case, the anti-differentiation principle currently dominates the constitutional analysis. That principle creates the presumption that all race- and sex-specific policies are discriminatory, and that no race- and sex-neutral policies are discriminatory unless accompanied by race- or sex-specific motivation. At the stage of justification, the anti-differentiation principle has dominated review of the discrimination claims that the courts have taken most seriously—race cases. In sex discrimination cases, courts have been more willing to deviate from the principle of anti-differentiation, sometimes to consider arguments less laudatory than anti-subordination.

These theoretical inconsistencies have created numerous practical difficulties. Race- or sex-specific policies are often necessary to overcome structural inequalities within an institution, yet such policies are rendered presumptively invalid at the prima facie case stage. Only sex-specific policies survive an equal protection challenge through an awkward and dangerous use of intermediate scrutiny at the justification stage; race-specific policies have almost no chance of survival under strict scrutiny. Given these difficulties with the existing framework, I propose modification of the existing approach in two respects.

The first modification eliminates the presumptive invalidity of race- or sex-specific policies at the prima facie case stage. Under the proposed framework, such a policy would not be presumed invalid unless it produces a negative disparate impact on a particular racial or ethnic group, or on a single sex. Under this framework, a race- or sex-specific rule could be viewed as a positive step towards eliminating race- or sex-based inequalities, as redressing subordination rather than creating differentiation.

The second modification more directly incorporates the anti-subordination approach into the stage of justification. The limited successes of anti-subordination advocates have come at the expense of the overall level of scrutiny. Rather than criticize the lowered level of scrutiny, anti-subordination advocates have tried to tailor their arguments to nebulous standards, like "compelling interests," that courts have used in effectuating the intermediate level of scrutiny. But the adverse effects that accompany lowered scrutiny need not be tolerated. A strict level of scrutiny can be preserved if it is recognized that the only justification for race- or sex-specific policies is the redress of a prior experience or history of subordination. This anti-subordination version of the equal protection model can bring the discussion of subordination to the forefront of the equal protection analysis.

The proposed framework has two key advantages. First, it would allow institutions to implement and defend remedial race- and sex-specific policies and actions without having to rely on stereotypes about minorities or women. A defendant would be able, at the justification stage, to show that its policy would help eliminate subordination. Second, the framework would ensconce the normative values of anti-subordination within the entire equal protection analysis and thereby make that analysis more meaningful. Under the existing equal protection model, the courts have yet to resolve fully whether they prefer the principle of anti-differentiation to that of anti-subordination. This framework would provide the analytic process of equal protection with a consistent theoretical base.

A. Making the Most of the Disparate Impact Method of Proof

The disparate impact model has been a powerful tool in the hands of plaintiffs challenging facially neutral rules that have discriminatory effects, although its use has thus far been too limited. To make it more effective, the concept of disparate impact should be expanded to include socially created impact. In addition, this model should be available to defendants to justify facially differentiating rules that help eradicate subordination. Instead of creating a presumption that a rule is invidious when it is phrased in race- or sex-specific terms, courts should consider the impact of the rule. Thus, both facially differentiating and facially neutral rules, when they cause disparate impact on the basis of race or sex, would have to be justified with heightened scrutiny.

This modification does not require that facial differentiation be wholly irrelevant. We have seen historically that facial differentiation can be extremely powerful in perpetuating subordination. However, it can also have a very powerful impact on redressing subordination. It is, difficult to imagine racial or sexual differentiation in rulemaking not having any impact one way or another on subordination. The important point is that we should not assume that differentiation always abets subordination. We should allow the courts to consider more fully the possibility that differentiation, on the contrary, often redresses subordination.

Accordingly, under the proposed framework, plaintiffs would continue to present evidence of differentiation at the prima facie case stage. However, they would be required to supplement that evidence with an explanation of how that differentiation contributes to their subordination. The trial court would make a specific finding as to whether the differentiation contributed to, or redressed, subordination. It would rarely have the option of finding that the differentiation had no effect on subordination, because differentiation is too powerful a tool not to have any effect in the vast majority of situations.

The implications of this proposed framework can be seen in its application to the earlier hypothetical about a leave policy that has a disparate impact on black women. Let us assume that the employer decides to implement a new four-week leave policy for nonprofessional black female workers who have primary childcare responsibilities that are exacerbated by extenuating circumstances, such as difficult schedules or unavailability of day care resources. The employer wishes to redress the disparate impact of the previous leave policy, and chooses this leave policy rather than a race- or sex-neutral leave policy because it does not feel a responsibility to subsidize the child care needs of all of its employees. Rather, it only wants to subsidize those needs when they have a negative impact on employment opportunities. In the employer's experience, that problem only exists for black nonprofessional female workers.

Under the current equal protection model, white male, black male, and white female nonprofessionals would be able to establish a prima facie case of discrimination because of the explicit differentiation embodied in the policy. By contrast, under the proposed framework, these plaintiffs would have an additional hurdle—they would also have to allege disparate impact. The issue then would become how to measure disparate impact. Are the white men, who receive only two weeks of leave time, suffering from a loss of employment opportunities by virtue of this new policy? Is the difference in leave time, alone, sufficient to establish disparate impact or should a more tangible loss of employment opportunities be required? This Article argues that these questions must be answered from an anti-subordination perspective. Thus, although white male employees might be able to show "disparate impact" from a literal point of view, in that they receive less leave time, they would probably be unable to show on these facts that it rose to the level of a subordinating disparate impact. By contrast, it is conceivable that nonprofessional white women might be able to make out a colorable claim of disparate impact with evidence of a more substantial loss of employment opportunities. The purpose of the proposed framework is to make a discussion of anti-subordination occur, not to provide an easy answer as to how it should be resolved.

B. Restricting the Means of Justification

If the plaintiffs challenging the new leave policy establish a prima facie case of discrimination, through disparate impact, then the case would proceed to the stage of justification. Under the existing equal protection framework, such a policy could not be justified without lowering the level of scrutiny to an intermediate level of scrutiny. Under the proposed framework, a strict level of scrutiny is maintained, and this policy could be justified only if it was established to overcome subordination. Was the employer acting on the basis of traditional stereotypes? Or was the employer acting consciously to eliminate subordination? How do the black women within the workplace view the policy? Do they believe that it is helping to establish equality within the workplace? Again, this is a factual inquiry. Even if the court found the policy unjustified, the proposed framework would have the crucial effect of basing the discussion on a normative principle of anti-subordination.

* * *

CONCLUSION: THE REMAINING DIFFICULTIES

One might argue that this Article's proposed framework raises more difficulties than it resolves. How does one define disparate impact? Can the analysis be applied to classifications other than race or sex? How subordinated must one's group be to trigger this analysis? At what point is the subordination of a group sufficiently redressed, so that it can no longer claim entitlement to differentiating policies designed to redress its prior history of subordination? What policies redress subordination? Are there truly no principles other than anti-subordination that should justify race- or sex-specific policies or actions?

These are hard questions that cannot be addressed theoretically. If we are committed to the principle of anti-subordination, then we should be equally committed to finding the answers to these questions in specific factual settings. . . .

* * *

Judy Scales-Trent, *Black Women and the Constitution: Finding Our Place; Asserting Our Rights,* 24 HARV. C.R.-C.L. L. REV. 9 (1989)*

Introduction

The economic, political, and social situation of black women in America is bad, and has been bad for a long time. Historically, they have borne both the disabilities of blacks and the disabilities which inhere in their status as women. These two statuses have often combined in ways which are not only additive, but synergistic—that is, they create a condition for black women which is more terrible than the sum of their two constituent parts. The result is that black women are the lowest paid group in America today when compared to white women, black men or white men. They also face significantly higher unemployment rates than any of those groups. Not surprisingly, studies have shown that when compared to whites and black men, black women lack an overall sense of well-being and satisfaction, while posessing a strong sense of powerlessness and lack of control over their lives.

Despite, or perhaps because of, this dual disability and its negative effects on life opportunities for black women, the problems of black women often go unrecognized. Black women have not been seen as a discrete group with a unique history, unique strengths and unique disabilities. By creating two separate categories for its major social problems—"the race problem," and "the women's issue"—society has ignored the group which stands at the interstices of these two groups, black women in America. For example, social reformist discussion tends to focus on the need to protect "minorities and women" from the hardships of discrimination. Although this term is intended to be inclusive, in fact, it misleads by overlooking those Americans who are both "minorities" and "women."

The legal system has incorporated the same dichotomous system—"minorities" and "women"—into its way of analyzing problems. Thus, the legal system, which is trying to protect the rights of "blacks" and "women," when faced with the existence of "black women," sometimes has difficulty categorizing this group. . . .

This Article discusses how the Constitution defines and protects black women. It then explores how black women should be defined by the Constitution—as women, as blacks, or as a distinct group with a legal identity of its own. The first section of this Article discusses how a new group, with new status—black women—is formed by the combination of multiple statuses in society. This section also addresses how the definitions of a group, within the legal system and within the larger society, interact and reinforce each other.

The second section of this Article explores the question of how the group "black women" should be defined under the Equal Protection Clause of the Constitution. It argues that, whether defined as a subset of women, as a subset of blacks or as a discrete group, black women should be granted the highest level of protection available under the Constitution: the "strict scrutiny" review used for race-based classifications. This section will also consider whether or not the Court should grant black women a higher level of protection than the "strict scrutiny" review it grants to the black group because of the long-standing and egregious nature of the harm inflicted on black women and because of the dual stigma of being black and female.

* * *

I. Black Women as a Discrete Group

"Status" is a term which sociologically identifies one's position in society. Each status carries a set of norms, defined as a pattern of behavior expected of persons of that particular status. Status is frequently used as a means of ranking one's social position or role.

Black women posess two statuses which derive from attributes over which they have no control: membership in the black race and membership in the female sex. The combination of these two statuses creates a new status, and because it is a combination of two degraded statuses, black and female, the new status is a particularly low-ranking one. In order to support this degraded status, society has created a system of mythology and misinterpretations about black women which further limits the life opportunities of black women.

In a society which sees as powerful both whiteness and maleness, black women possess no characteristic which is associated with power. They are therefore treated by society in a manner which reflects a status different from, and lower than, both black men (who have the status ascribed to maleness) and white women (who enjoy the status ascribed to whiteness). This is in no way inconsistent with the fact that black women are often treated badly along with black men solely because of their race; or because of their sex along with white women. A study on wages in New York State, conducted for the National Committee on Pay Equity in 1986, confirms this disparity in the treatment of black women. The researchers found that the wages of white women, minority men and minority women in job categories which were comprised largely of members of those groups, were systematically depressed. The studies further showed that the wages for women of color were depressed further than those of both men of color and white women. Two of the myths supporting the degraded status of black women are that they do not need money and are not worth money. Thus both of these myths are perpetuated by the economic structure of American society.

Since black women share a negative group label imposed from the outside, they feel a need to come together for mutual protection. This "perceived need to band together in defense against domination or hostility" is one major source of cultural identity. Although at one level it seems bizarre to request that "black women" be identified as a group with degraded social status, only through acceptance and utilization of this status will the group be able to work to defeat limitations imposed on its members from the outside. The Constitution protects both the choice to turn inward to the cultural group, and the choice to use that group identity to participate fully in the institutions of the wider society.

* * *

II. The Equal Protection Clause

The way in which a group is defined for purposes of the Equal Protection Clause both describes how that group is viewed by the larger society, and defines how that group should be viewed. The Court must see how the group has been treated historically by the larger society before it decides what level of protection it will provide the group. . . .

A. The Framework for Group Protection Under the Equal Protection Clause

The groups possessing the clearest definition, and therefore the highest level of protection under the Constitution, are racial and ethnic minorities. As the Court noted in *Korematsu v. U.S.*, "legal restrictions which curtail the civil rights of a single racial group are immediately suspect." Such laws are subject to strict scrutiny and will be sustained only if they serve a compelling state interest. Thus, black Americans, both male and female, are entitled to the highest level of protection under the Constitution when confronted with state action which restricts them due to their race.

Women, along with several other groups, come after racial and ethnic minorities in this hierarchy of protection. The Court has determined that a classification which has a negative effect on women is not "immediately suspect," although it is subject to a heightened standard of review. The government need only show that the classification is substantially related to an important government objective for it to be held constitutionally permissible under the Equal Protection Clause.

The third category of groups are those which have been defined by the Court as not needing and therefore not entitled to any heightened level of scrutiny. The Court will defer to the legislative body in cases of classifications based on age, out of state persons, new residents in the state or the mentally retarded, as long as the classification is "rationally related" to a legitimate state interest.

Given this scheme, black women can find specific protection under the Equal Protection Clause as either blacks or as women and, in fact, have already done so. Surely black women were protected as blacks in, for example, *Gomillion v. Lightfoot*, which involved racial gerrymandering for voting purposes. Black women were granted protection as women, along with white women, in *Califano v. Westcott*, which involved the use of a gender-based classification to allocate benefits to families with dependent children. If, however, a group of black women makes the claim that it is being denied the equal protection of the laws because its members are both black and women, it is not clear what kind of constitutional protection this group will be provided. Should the scrutiny level be "strict" because the women are black or should it be the lesser, heightened level of scrutiny because these blacks are women, or is the answer to acknowledge that black women constitute a discrete group in American culture whose position in society should be analyzed separately to determine what level of scrutiny should attach to state action which adversely affects them?

* * *

The Court has held that facially neutral laws, which impose heavier burdens on a suspect class, do not alone violate the Equal Protection Clause. That type of discriminatory impact is insufficient; plaintiffs must be able to show discriminatory intent. Although such discriminatory intent may be inferred from the totality of the relevant facts, a statistical showing of adverse impact on the protected group, standing alone, is not equivalent to proof of a constitutional violation. The question then becomes whether black women can prove an intent to discriminate against them, specifically, as a class. [S]tatistical proof of harm plus historical testimony tending to show an intent to discriminate would be sufficient to make out a constitutional violation.

* * *

B. The Protection of Black Women as a Class Within the Framework of the Equal Protection Clause

There are three possible ways to protect black women within the equal protection framework. The first is to treat black women as a subset of blacks or of women, and to grant their claims the level of protection accorded that group under the current tripartite analysis of the Court. The second is to treat black women as a discrete group seeking protection under the Constitution, and to assess that group on its own merits to determine the level of protection it should be afforded. One might analyze the situation of black women in this society as that of a "discrete and insular" minority which is unable to enjoy the benefits of full citizenship, and thus entitled to strict scrutiny protection under the Equal Protection Clause. Third, one might argue that since black women carry the burden of membership in the black group, which is already entitled to strict scrutiny protection, and in the disfavored female group, they should be entitled to more than strict scrutiny protection by the courts.

1. The Subset Theory

How are black women to be sub-classified: in the black group, or in the female group? This question is important because the level of protection granted black women will differ depending upon whether they are placed in the black group or the female group. Yet the notion that the level of protection would change depending upon which way they are classified is bizarre since black women are always both black and women. To the extent that they are always burdened by both classifications, the level of protection should be constant. Moreover, since black women are always sigmatized by the race classification, they should always be provided the highest level of protection available under the Constitution. If we accept the Court's formulation that race classifications are inherently more suspect than sex classifications, we must therefore conclude that the Court considers the status of racial minorities to be "lower" than the status of women. Thus if black women are provided only intermediate scrutiny, as women, a portion of the burden they carry will have gone completely unaddressed by the legal system. As long as race is part of the group identity, any classification which limits their opportunities should be reviewed under the highest level of scrutiny.

2. The "Discrete and Insular Minority" Theory

The second possibility is to treat black women as a discrete group seeking protection under the Constitution, and to assess the group on its own merits to determine the level of protection it should be afforded. Black women are entitled to the greatest constitutional protection under the Equal Protection Clause because they can be viewed just as the Court has viewed other groups which have sought the same level of protection. In making this determination, the Court has traditionally looked at several criteria to determine if a group is a "discrete and insular" minority, and thus unable to enjoy the benefits of full citizenship. The basic criteria are: whether or not the group is defined by immutable characteristics, whether or not there has been historical prejudice against the group, and the extent to which the group is politically powerless. A classification which reflects deep-seated prejudice against a particular group would be equally suspect.

a. Immutable Characteristics

Race, gender, national origin, mental retardation and (il)legitimacy are all immutable characteristics which often adversely affect the way certain people are treated in our society. Hence, the Court is more likely to see a group as one needing protection if one of these characteristics is part of its social group identity. . . . [C]learly race and sex are immutable characteristics, and black women thus satisfy this prong of the test.

b. Historical Prejudice

The role of history is critical in the determination of what level of protection a group receives. Justice Marshall has . . . stated on this point that:

> The lessons of history and experience are surely the best guide as to when, and with respect to what interests, society is likely to stigmatize individuals as members of an inferior caste or view them as not belonging to the community. Because prejudice spawns prejudice, and stereotypes produce limitations that confirm the stereotype on which they are based, a history of unequal treatment requires sensitivity to the prospect that its vestiges endure.

History proves that black women suffered a dual degradation, both as black slaves and as women. Although black women did not suffer any more than black men as a result of slavery, it is fair to say that they suffered differently, because they were women. As blacks they were exploited for their physical strength in the production of crops; as women, they performed a reproductive function which was crucial to the economic interests of the slaveholders. As one historian notes, "Blacks constituted a permanent labor force and metaphor that were perpetuated through the Black woman's womb." The reproductive function became especially important after 1801, when it became illegal to import slaves from Africa into the United States.

Black slave women were sexually exploited for other than reproductive reasons. Their objectification as sexual beings also served the function of demonstrating power, and of terrorizing the entire slave community. Rape and the constant threat of rape was not only a means of crushing attempts at resistance by black women, but was also a means of humiliating and symbolically attacking black men.

Statutes enacted during the pre-Civil War period legitimated this power relationship. . . .

* * *

. . . After the Civil War, both the states and the federal government acted in ways inimical to the interests of black women, treating them, again, differently from white women and black men. . . .

The subsequent history of black women as workers followed slave history by reinforcing the view of black women as either domestic servants or manual laborers.

After the Civil War, black women worked largely in rural areas in the South as sharecroppers or in urban areas as domestics in white households. Since the image of black women was limited to that of a domestic, and not, for example, worker in the cotton mills, domestic jobs were "reserved" for black women. . . .

During the Depression, southern black women returned to farm work and migratory labor camps; in the North, domestic servants were forced to look for jobs through "slave markets." . . .

These inequities were maintained throughout World War II, as black women moved into jobs in industry. There they were assigned to the most dangerous, backbreaking tasks in segregated job categories.

Within the past 20 years, the relative economic status of those black women with jobs has improved, in large part due to the increased convergence of their job structures with those of white women. This convergence only underscores the fact that black women are moving into essentially low-status, dead-end jobs. Despite this convergence, black women are still the lowest-paid group when compared to white women, black men, or white men. Even with the improvements, black women still face significantly higher unemployment rates than any other group. For example, black female unemployment rates have been twice those of white women throughout the past decade.

The history of dual oppression which has operated and continues to operate in the marketplace thus continues to limit the life opportunities of black women. The effects on the black community are devastating. In 1970, fifty-six percent of all poor black families were maintained by women; by 1981, that figure had jumped to seventy percent. In 1981, there were 22.1 maternal deaths per 100,000 live births to black women, compared to 6.5 maternal deaths per 100,000 births for white women.

c. Political Powerlessness

The political powerlessness of black women is best illustrated by their struggle for the right to vote. As members of two disenfranchised groups, they were forced to struggle twice, both as blacks and as women, to gain a meaningful franchise. Moreover, as the least powerful members within both the black and the female groups, black women have had to fight to make their voices heard at all. Thus the heaviest burden in terms of improving their social condition has fallen on, and continues to fall on, the group occupying the weakest political position.

* * *

The history of political powerlessness of black women becomes even more apparent when examining the number of group members who are elected officials on the local, state and federal government levels. If one's power be determined by the ability to elect representatives who are members of one's group and who are therefore more likely to represent that group's interests, the statistics for black women tell a tale of little power. In 1985, there were 392 black elected officials in the legislative bodies of forty-two states and the Virgin Islands. Of that number, only seventy-four were black women. Of the twenty black congressmen at the federal level, only one was a black woman. Of the twenty-six black mayors of cities with a population over 50,000, only one was a black woman.

If political power be determined by wealth, all indicators again point to black women as a group without power. Black women are over-represented among the poor. For example, although the incidence of poverty among all women with children under age eighteen is high, the poverty rate for black mothers is approximately three times that of white mothers. Even controlling for age and education, the poverty rates for black women are generally two to four times higher than the rates for white women. Their poverty rate is also higher than that of black men. For example, twenty-eight percent of all black women who have finished high school are poor, compared to sixteen percent of black male graduates.

Analyses of social indicators for political alienation also demonstrate that black women feel politically powerless. A 1972 study by the Center for Political Studies showed that black women are "polarized in a set of attitudes different from those of black men and whites": a set of attitudes exemplified by a sense of powerlessness and lack of control over their lives; a sense of being forced to live "unsatisfying and inse-cure lives." Black women, compared to white women and black and white men, were shown to have the lowest levels of trust in the political process and the lowest feel-ings of political efficacy. A 1976 study of the quality of American life reinforced this finding. The analysts discovered that black women were more negative in their over-all sense of well-being and satisfaction than black men or whites and concluded that "[t]he quality of life of the black female appears less positive than that of any of the other segments of the population. . . ." . . . [B]lack women clearly belong to a group which is entitled to be classified as "discrete and insular" for purposes of determin-ing the level of scrutiny applicable to equal protection claims.

3. The "More than Strict Scrutiny" Theory

The final possibility is that black women—who are burdened by the double stigma of race and sex—are entitled to more than even the "strict scrutiny" level of review accorded when there is a state action which harms based on race. If the race stigma alone is sufficient to trigger strict scrutiny review, the race stigma plus an additional stigma (sex) should entitle the group to an even higher level of scrutiny and protection by the Court. As noted above, these double burdens are at least additive. In some instances, the dual burdens create a level of harm even greater than the sum of the parts.

How could a court provide more than a "strict scrutiny" level of review? It could ease the burden of proof in equal protection cases brought by black women by lessening the requirement for a showing of intent, for example. . . . There are many ways a court could recognize that "race plus another burden" should be protected at the level of "strict scrutiny plus more." In analytical terms, such a step is a logical extension of the equal protection framework created by the Court. Realistically, however, it seems unlikely that the Court will break ground for a group that it barely acknowledges as a separate class. . . .

* * *

A Personal Postscript on Rights

This paper is situated squarely in a "rights" theory, that is, it seeks to protect a specific group from the ravages of racism and sexism by developing a new way of protecting their rights in the courts. As such, it flies in the face of the new criticism of rights consciousness and rights claims, which views such discourse as an obstacle to political development. Rights discourse is considered an impediment because of the indeterminate nature of rights claims and because of the way in which it emphasizes individual rather than group rights. In addition, the focus on rights can keep people passive, acquiescing in what the state determines to grant them as "rights." While there is much of value in these analyses of rights, we, the dispossessed, cling to the assertion of rights as our only source of protection in an overwhelmingly racist and sexist society. It is not that we believe that the law is good and just and will save us. Far from it. Rather, we believe that the law, and claims to rights under the law, are all that we have, all that stand between us and even greater oppression. As Pat Williams so eloquently stated: "To say that blacks never fully believed in rights is true; yet it is also true that blacks believed in them so much and so hard that we gave them life where there was none before." Not only have we held on to rights claims as our only hope in a hostile and legalistic world, but we have won some of these claims. These victories give us a sense of empowerment and the energy to face yet another day of onslaught, struggle, victory and defeat. Every successful step makes the thought of the next step possible.

Elizabeth Schneider explores this theme in her dialectic analysis of rights and politics in the development of social movements. In her view, rights discourse and political experience interact in a manner which shapes the development of the political process. Schneider further explores the positive aspects of rights discourse in political movements, including the development of a sense of group identity and pride, and the development of a means whereby the individual can become part of the group, and then link the group to the broader society. As she states, linking one's own experience with the "universal claim of rights" can be a "'radical and transforming notion."

Williams also articulates a positive aspect of rights discourse by pointing out how empowering it can be to claim one's rights, to claim, that is, the place one is entitled to in the society. "'Rights' feels so new in the mouths of most black people. It is still so deliciously empowering to say. It is a sign for and a gift of selfhood . . .. It is the magic wand of visibility and invisibility, of inclusion and exclusion, of power and no-power."

It is within this framework of rights discourse—one of self-definition and empowerment—that I wish to situate this work. And I want to discuss how the assertion of my rights claims—as a black woman with a keen interest in her rights under the Constitution—has been personally "radical and transforming."

I, like many other black women, have often felt torn between two distinct and often warring social movements: the black movement and the women's movement. In each of them, I could reflect and act upon one aspect of myself, and in each of them, I was one of a member of the (relatively) powerless outsider group. I had the sense of being fragmented, of being split into two entities with often competing goals. Certainly during the civil rights movement of the 1960s and 1970s, black women who expressed a concern about women's rights were considered traitors to the race.

Thinking about and writing about the constitutional rights of black women has allowed me to pull those fragments of self back into a whole, focused and centered. And one works more strongly and clearly from a centered self. Another empowering act has been to take charge of defining my group, of naming myself. Naming oneself, defining oneself and thereby taking the power to define out of the hands of those who wield that power over you, is an important act of empowerment. The "first power of the weak" is the "refusal to accept the definition of oneself that is put forth by the powerful." Defining a group of black women who see themselves with group rights under the Constitution is staking a claim to whatever those with privilege are entitled. The act of self-definition thus makes clear our worth and entitlement, and sets forth our view of ourselves as one which will have to be reckoned with.

. . . [B]y connecting rights discourse back to empowerment and community, I was able to find a community which empowered me to write and to assert my rights . . . a community of historians, poets, essayists, scholars. Audre Lorde, for one, yielded no ground. She said: "I am myself—a Black woman warrior poet doing my work—come to ask you, are you doing yours?" She sympathized: "Of course I am afraid, because the transformation of silence into language and action is an act of self-revelation, and that always seems fraught with danger. [But] . . . the machine will try to grind you into dust anyway, whether or not we speak." And finally, she urged:

> We can learn to work and speak when we are afraid in the same way we have learned to work and speak when we are tired. For we have been socialized to respect fear more than our own needs for language and defi-nition, and while we wait in silence for that final luxury of fearlessness, the weight of that silence will choke us.

Writing about rights for black women has put me in touch again with issues of self-definition, empowerment, staking my claim in the larger community, and creat-ing and working within a community of support. Like Alice Walker, I too "write all the things I should have been able to read."

Janet E. Halley, *The Politics of the Closet: Towards Equal Protection for Gay, Lesbian, and Bisexual Identity*, 36 UCLA L. REV. 915 (1989)*

In the summer of 1986, the U.S. Supreme Court made it resoundingly clear that no fundamental privacy right attaches to consensual homosexual sodomy. *Bowers v. Hardwick* forged an equally indubitable link between the question of homosexual rights under the Constitution and the proper scope of judicial review of legislative decisions. Invoking the specter of *Lochner v. New York* and "the face-off between the Executive and the Court in the 1930's," Justice White's majority opinion argued that "[t]he Court is most vulnerable and comes nearest to illegitimacy when it deals with judge-made constitutional law having little or no cognizable roots [sic] in the lan-guage or design of the Constitution." Chief Justice Burger concluded in his concurring opinion, "[t]his is essentially not a question of personal 'preferences' but rather of [sic] the legislative authority of the State." By refusing to extend its substantive due process jurisprudence, the Court remanded gay men and lesbians to the political arena to combat sodomy laws and their discriminatory enforcement through the majoritarian political process.

The history of the United States testifies eloquently to the fact that, when a despised minority must fend for itself in the tumult of electoral and legislative poli-tics, the majority may deny it a fair chance. Ever since *United States v. Carolene Prod-ucts*, the Supreme Court has acknowledged the constitutional dimension of this fact by committing itself to ensuring that the political process is not unfairly rigged. In the "most celebrated footnote in constitutional law," Justice Stone warned that the

Court, though forswearing the power to make substantive law under the rubric of due process, did not intend to abrogate its duty to enforce constitutional guarantees that the majoritarian process would not be poisoned.

* * *

Though Footnote Four is discreetly phrased as dictum and purports to canvass questions irrelevant to the present controversy, it remains the touchstone of process-based judicial review. The Footnote foresees that judicial interference with legislative decisions may be justified in three situations: (1) violations of terms of the Constitution; (2) direct interferences with the political process; and (3) indirect interferences with the political process, in the form of laws disadvantaging minorities. Placed back into its context, as a footnote to one of the line of cases jettisoning the jurisprudence of substantive due process, Footnote Four implicitly sets forth a vision of a renovated judiciary. No longer the intestine enemy of republican government, the judiciary is to be its champion; federal courts, while strictly restrained from frustrating the will of the people as expressed through the legislative process, are charged with a responsibility to interfere whenever that process has broken down. Judges must not usurp a power, under the due process clause, to void substantive legislative decisions made by political majorities; but neither may they abdicate a duty to guarantee that majorities will be formed and will exercise their powers in consonance with the Constitution.

The Court in *Bowers v. Hardwick*, far from rejecting the Footnote Four tradition, drew on its characterization of the judicial role. It made a constitutional promise to the very gay men and lesbians it spurned—a promise to guarantee us a full and unimpeded opportunity to advocate repeal of the sodomy statutes.

This Article attempts to clear the ground for such protection by demonstrating that sexual identity is produced by social interaction, and that that activity of production is so fundamental to the development of a genuine and fair public debate about the wisdom of the sodomy statutes that, under the mandate of the equal protection clause, courts are obliged to protect it. Advocates of gay and lesbian rights can look to the bill of rights for protection of rights expressly granted there; they can look to a rich constitutional tradition prohibiting direct interferences with the political process for protection of political speech about homosexuality; but when they voluntarily adopt or involuntarily bear the public identity "homosexual" and for that reason lose their employment and other public benefits, housing, custody of children, resident alien status, medical insurance, and even physical safety, they are hindered and deterred from entering the public debate surrounding the sodomy laws. The harms they suffer interfere sharply, albeit indirectly, with the political process. The *Carolene* formulation has determined that, when confronted with this third form of process failure, would-be advocates of legislative change can call on the equal protection clause.

To recognize the direct implication of both the majority and concurring opinions in *Bowers v. Hardwick* is to acknowledge that *Hardwick* is not an equal protection case. This point requires emphasis, because several courts have held that *Hardwick* is binding precedent in the equal protection context. As a panel of the Ninth Circuit observed in rejecting the argument that *Hardwick* is binding in the equal protection context, these cases vastly oversimplify the structure of the fourteenth amendment, which not only provides a guarantee of due process but also poses "an independent obligation on government not to draw invidious distinctions among its citizens."

Even if the two clauses are accorded the distinct analysis which clearly established precedent demands, however, one can interpret *Hardwick* to dictate the denial of heightened scrutiny under the equal protection clause by making a certain definition of the class of homosexuals. The argument turns on the relationship between homosexual identity and homosexual acts—specifically, the acts prohibited by statute in seven states. . . .

The reading of *Hardwick* as binding precedent in equal protection cases has brought new urgency to a project that has, until now, seemed rather academic: the project of ascertaining how the class of homosexuals is constituted. This Article argues that homosexual identity is the product not of sodomitic acts simpliciter, but of a complex political discourse that is threatened, in ways that the *Carolene Products* formulation prohibits, by antihomosexual discrimination. . . .

The full implications of this post-*Hardwick* equal protection jurisprudence cannot be understood without a recognition that recent, expansive readings of *Hardwick,* with their crudely essentialist notion of how the class of homosexuals is established, sound a weird echo of an argument repeatedly adopted by advocates of gay and lesbian rights. For until recently, gay rights advocates have fairly consistently argued that homosexual orientation is so unitary, fundamental, irresistable, and inalterable that homosexuals meet a supposed requirement of suspect classifications, that of immutability. After *Hardwick,* the argument for heightened scrutiny under the equal protection clause is now undermined, not bolstered, by claims that homosexuality is a fixed and immutable attribute of a rigidly demarcated class.

* * *

Confronted with the supposed requirement for heightened scrutiny that the proposed classification be based on an immutable trait, advocates of gay, lesbian, and bisexual rights have almost uniformly—though often with visible qualms—embraced the argument that homosexuality is immutable. . . .

Expansive readings of *Hardwick* should draw new, skeptical attention to the immutability argument. Clearly, it is time for gay advocates to rethink that argument—but even if it were not, the sheer facts demand that the argument be abandoned. In fact, the problem of the mutability of homosexual inclination is far more complex than the legal discourse has yet acknowledged. The patterns that emerge from recent empirical and theoretical work on the subject compel the conclusion that homosexual identity, far from being the equivalent of sodomy, is constituted in precisely the political process which, under the equal protection clause, the courts are pledged to protect. Far from closing constitutional debate on this issue, *Hardwick* opened it.

. . . Part I demonstrates that, in fact, immutability is not required by the Court's equal protection precedents, which focus instead on process implications often associated with apparently immutable traits. A proper reading of these precedents demonstrates that the equal protection clause vigilantly protects not monolithic groups but rather the dialogue that generates group identity and suggests that gay rights advocates and courts attend not to product but to process, not to the class but to the classification of homosexuals. Part II surveys the empirical literature on sexual orientation and the constitutive behavior of individuals in the legal process, to demonstrate that gay, lesbian, and bisexual identity are produced by a discourse so intrinsically political that it merits the most careful judicial scrutiny. Part III invokes the sociology of the political process developed under the first amendment in order to demonstrate that equal protection review committed to preserving that process will not only protect the public disclosure or assignment of gay or homosexual identity but also delimit the courts' role in protecting minorities from the will of the majority.

I. IMMUTABILITY DOCTRINE AND THE POLITICAL PROCESS

Legal lore has it that a group must be defined by an immutable characteristic before the Supreme Court will even consider whether it should be regarded as a suspect class. The contradiction implicit in this claim is perhaps most concisely expressed in the oxymoron "suspect class"—for it is surely not the class, but the classification, that is suspect. And classifications are highly contingent products of social relations, subject to change not only in their definitions but also in the roster of persons they can marshall at any given moment. I argue in this Section that the Supreme Court has, quite properly, repudiated the supposed requirement of immutability and focused its attention instead on the social process in which classifications are produced and policed.

A. Race and Immutability

If immuntability were a requirement for strict scrutiny under equal protection clause, race could not be a suspect classification. As the Supreme Court has shown in two recent cases recognizing that Arabs and Jews have a cause of action under 42 U.S.C. sections 1981 and 1982, the very conception of race, and the taxonomy of "races," are products of culture rather than nature. It conceded that it could not look to any "distinctive physiognomy" or to any sound modern scientific conception of race: instead, it had to turn to later nineteenth century dictionaries and floor debates before the passage of sections 1981 and 1982. The mere evidence relied on by the Court revals that race is historically contingent, that its contours have changed radically. If the boundaries between races can shift, the racial categorization of individuals can shift—a profound source of mutability.

* * *

B. The Displacement of Immutability by Process Analysis

The paradigm of race is so fundamental to equal protection doctrine that we should be disposed rather to discard a requirement of immutability for suspect classification, than to insist on it at the cost of the entire doctrinal tradition. But no such choice is even posed by the precedents set out by the Supreme Court: immutability is neither a necessary nor a sufficient precondition for the recognition of a suspect classification, and where it has appeared as a factor in the Court's analysis, it has always been shorthand for inquiry into the fairness of the political process burdening the group. . . .

* * *

In determining how stringent its review must be, the Court looks for acute vulnerability in the political process, not the immutability of any trait uniting or defiing the group. This vulnerability—not immutability—is what makes other suspect classifications "like race."

Where immutability does feature in the Court's analysis, it is merely a factor in the Court's review of two different sorts of process failure: mere irrationality and a pervasive prejudice that distorts the relationship of majority to minority. The Court has acknowledged further that the former inquiry is more properly invoked under the rational basis test, while the process failure implicated in the latter is just as likely to be signalled by mutability as by immutability of a target group's distinctive characteristics.

* * *

II. MUTABILITY IN THE SOCIAL CONTEXT OF SEXUAL IDENTITY

To display, or not to display; to tell or not to tell; to let on or not to let on; to lie or not to lie; and in each case, to whom, how, when and where.

Bowers v. Hardwick having indelibly drawn the link between judicial restraint and the question of homosexual rights, homosexual advocates must reconsider their litigation strategy. Heretofore homosexual-rights advocates have argued almost uniformly for suspect classification status on the grounds that homosexuality is immutable. Certainly they have been right when they have argued that homosexual orientation is not amenable to any recognized therapeutic "cure" and that the halting attempts at conversion sometimes undertaken are not only profoundly traumatic and expensive but are totally futile for all but a small population of "highly motivated" individuals of quavering sexual identity. This argument misses the point of the Supreme Court's actual jurisprudence of immutability and process failure. Moreover, it is factually inaccurate for the vast range of sexual identity—from personal self-description to the public disclosure of or subjection to homosexual or heterosexual identity—that is the proper object of constitutional process analysis.

Strict scrutiny must be triggered by the dynamics of mutability and immutability implicit in that empirical and analytical peculiarity of antihomosexual discrimination, the Closet. Antihomosexual discrimination encourages people to manipulate the identity they attach to themselves, both in the secrecy of their own minds and on the public stage. It ensures that personal desires, sexual behavior, subjective identity and public identity will frequently get out of sync with each other. However carefully an individual disposes these elements, they are all subject to sudden, either joyous or catastrophic, rearrangement. That is to say, they are mutable.

* * *

III. EQUAL PROTECTION, EQUAL PROCESS AND THE SPECTER OF SUBSTANTIVE REVIEW: PLACING LIMITS ON THE PROCESS-BASED EQUAL PROTECTION OF HOMOSEXUAL IDENTITY

* * *

The critics of process-based equal-protection review have argued that all judicial efforts to preserve the fairness of the legislative process are founded on substantive commitments, and charge that the *Carolene Products* tradition disingenuously denies those substantive implications. The arguments they advance acknowledge, moreover, that the conflict between the rights of homosexuals and the power of legislatures to deter homosexuality continually exemplifies these underlying substantive problems. These critiques challenge the Court and its advisory board of academics to abandon their pretense that process theories avoid substantive review, and to take up the job of crafting a theory of substantive judicial review that leaves some substantive legislative decisions—let's say a statute prohibiting burglary—beyond its scope. *Bowers v. Hardwick* makes it virtually impossible to imagine the Court taking up this challenge in the context of gay rights, sending those who would obtain some measure of constitutional justice back to the process theory assumed by the Court in that case. But the critiques of process theories require that any argument based on them carefully limit its invitation to the Court to reject substantive decisions of the political branches.

* * *

In the concluding Section of this Article, I propose that an intelligible line can be drawn between antihomosexual discrimination that blocks the political process and is properly subject to heightened judicial scrutiny and legislative decisions to deter homosexuality that remain unreviewable because they do not interfere with the public debate. That line has already been drawn, in the first amendment precedents distinguishing conduct from speech.

A. Conduct and Speech

. . . [G]ay rights advocates have argued that homosexuality is a status, legally similar to drug addiction and, under *Robinson v. California*, immune from criminal sanction. The act/status argument offers some strategic advantages. It directly parries the logic that would make *Hardwick* binding in an equal protection context: sodomy, like buying and selling drugs, may be criminalized without constitutional violation, but the status of homosexual, like the status of drug addict, is so inextricably intertwined with "the very fiber of an individual's personality," so "central" or "essential to personhood," that it cannot be the object of the legal sanction. In another sense, however, this view is extremely vulnerable after *Hardwick*: if a majority can criminalize what this essentializing viewpoint describes as "intimacies inherent in a homosexual orientation" and "the behavior that forms part of the very definition of homosexuality," what constitutional duty can that majority owe to restrain its moral indignation when confronted not with the act but with the personhood that inevitably produces it?

* * *

The first amendment thesis that we are safe from tyranny only so long as we engage (as speakers or listeners) in open social dialogue implicates a recognition that the protection of minority voices will be a most crucial function of the courts. . . . [W]hen the first amendment precedents providing positive law drawing the distinction between conduct and speech articulate a process rationale for protection of the latter, we are justified in expecting that light will be shed on the process protected by the equal protection clause as well. . . .

First amendment cases involving the political speech of gay activists, and indeed of anyone resisting homophobia, have acknowledged the fundamental process dangers imposed by the legal coercion of expression about sexual identity. As Judge Williams of the Northern District of California has recognized, the first amendment association rights of an acutely controversial gay-rights organization implicate precisely the process concerns that Justice Stone had in mind when he penned Footnote Four. Refusing to grant discovery of the membership list of Solidarity (a gay rights group sued by Adolph Coors Company), Judge Williams recognized the danger that "civil lawsuits could be misused as coercive devices to cripple, or subdue, vocal opponents," and took particular note that forcing the gay men and lesbians of Solidarity out of the closet would violate the first amendment because it constituted a "threat [ ] aimed at suppressing an attempted exercise of political rights" precisely of the kind foreseen by Justice Stone in *Carolene Products*.

* * *

. . . In the vision of political discourse attributed to the Constitution under the first amendment, the potential mutability of heterosexual behavior and identity—if it is an evil at all—is one that must be cured not by silence, but by more speech.

B. Sexual Identity as Political Discourse

. . . Public homosexual identity is so volatile, so problematically referential to a history of genital homosexual conduct, and so relentlessly controversial that it has become an element of political discourse distinguishable from the conduct that, *Hardwick* informs us, states may constitutionally criminalize.

When courts have denied to gay rights advocates protection for gay identity, they have made painfully clear the costs that discrimination exacts from the political process. These courts . . . conflate the opinions and the sexual identities of gay rights advocates and require that homosexual advocates keep both secret. . . .

* * *

. . . The mere disclosure of one's gay, lesbian, or bisexual identity ineluctably accumulates political significance, while one's mere participation in political action to alter laws affecting gays and lesbians can precipitously earn one a public homosexual identity. These legal and social prohibitions hobble everyone's discourse about gay rights, producing a process failure of constitutional magnitude. It is not the class of gays, lesbians, and bisexuals, but the classification of homosexuals—a group that could include anyone participating in the antihomophobic argument—that requires heightened scrutiny under the equal protection clause.

C. Equal Protection of Gay Identity

* * *

The distinction between speech and conduct not only grounds in the Constitution an understanding of the political process that requires heightened scrutiny of antihomosexual discrimination; it also limits judicial review. It stipulates that conduct is not speech, and is not part of the political process—at least, not a part that courts may protect under the theory of Footnote Four.

* * *

Hardwick may well be reversible on an equal protection analysis alert to these discursive implications, without creating any necessary implication that criminal prohibitions in constitutionally less sensitive areas are barred. But even if we assume that *Hardwick* was decided correctly, the "homosexual acts" encompassed by that case's holding are almost never at issue when government imposes burdens on homosexual identity. Here, the proportion of political speech to conduct—and of procedural to substantive review—is so high that heightened judicial scrutiny is not only proper but necessary.

Martha Minow, *When Difference Has its Home: Group Homes for the Mentally Retarded, Equal Protection and Legal Treatment of Difference*, 22 HARV. C.R.-C.L. L. REV. 111 (1987)*

Introduction

How should the law treat people whom the law labels as incompetent? This question seems to invite an inquiry into the ways in which our society should deal with an identifiable group of people, whose differences are understood as natural, immutable and given. That inquiry implicitly assumes that there exist "normal people" who govern society, and that their governance covers not only themselves, but also a separate and distinct group of "abnormal people."

A better approach begins with a more complex understanding of differences within society, and addresses the legal frameworks we devise as we construct our relationships with each other. The locus of choice in the naming of difference should be a central concern. Some differences are chosen and embraced by the "different" individual or group. Yet unavoidably implicated in the legal problems of difference are the relationships between people and between groups. Asking who is the same, who is different, and who defines those differences raises further questions about who has power over social life and resources and who is excluded from social life and denied access to resources. Differences, in this view, are neither "real" and absolute nor merely a function of words and names. Instead, differences are to be understood relationally.

Discussions of such matters can become abstract very quickly. To ground this discussion, I will focus on mental competence as an instance of the problem of difference, and examine a 1985 Supreme Court case considering the rights of the mentally retarded. I will suggest that behind the debate over the contents of equal protection analysis lie three different approaches for analyzing assertions of difference. I will explore the historical roots as well as the strengths and weaknesses of each approach, and will develop the third and most novel approach, while exploring its possible significance.

The chief purpose in this article is to demonstrate how categorical approaches— attributing difference to "different people"—undermine commitments to equality. Commitments to an egalitarian ideal would be better served by an approach that emphasizes the relationships between people, both in the construction of difference and in the creation of communities where "difference" can have a home.

* * *

In *City of Cleburne v. Cleburne Living Center*, the Supreme Court considered the constitutionality of a city's refusal to grant a group of mentally retarded people a permit to build a residential group home. The plaintiffs, applicants for the group home, challenged the city's action on the grounds that it discriminated against the mentally retarded, and argued that mental retardation should be treated as a "quasi-suspect" classification for the purpose of equal protection analysis.

* * *

Justice White, writing for the Supreme Court's majority, declined to treat the mentally retarded as a quasi-suspect class. Instead, the majority opinion concluded that under equal protection analysis, legislative categories based on mental retardation need only be rationally related to a legitimate end, since the mentally retarded are "different, immutably so, in relevant respects, and the states' interest in dealing with and providing for them is plainly a legitimate one." The effort by federal, state, and local governments to respond to the needs of the mentally retarded "belies a continuing antipathy or prejudice and a corresponding need for more intrusive oversight by the judiciary." To support this argument, the Court cited such reforms as section 504 of the Federal Rehabilitation Act of 1973, and the Bill of Rights portion of the Developmental Disabilities Assistance and Bill of Rights Act.

The Court expressed the view that when legislatures act to remedy historic exclusion and maltreatment of a minority, the minority does not deserve additional protection from the judiciary. The Court noted that elected officials require freedom from judicial scrutiny in developing such remedial efforts and the burden of satisfying heightened judicial scrutiny could inhibit the government from acting on behalf of the mentally retarded. Finally, the Court justified its refusal to accord heightened review to a classification based on mental retardation by noting the difficulty of distinguishing groups who, like the mentally retarded, also suffer from immutable disabilities, a lack of political power, and vulnerability to public prejudice. Apparently, granting heightened scrutiny to these other groups would produce judicial activity which the Court wished to restrain.

Nonetheless, even under its minimal "rational relationship" review, the majority actually offered a beefed up version of this usually minimal scrutiny. Legislative distinctions "between the mentally retarded and others must be rationally related to a legitimate governmental purpose," which can consist neither of a bare desire to harm a politically unpopular group, nor of negative attitudes and vague undifferentiated fears about the mentally retarded. The majority reasoned that it would not be rational to treat group homes for the mentally retarded differently from homes for other groups, in pursuing governmental purposes like controlling floods, limiting legal liability for the activities of residents, regulating residential density, and promoting the serenity of the neighborhood.

Applying this version of the rational relationship test, the majority rejected the facial challenge to the zoning ordinance insofar as it required special use permits for homes for the mentally retarded, but accepted the challenge to the ordinance as applied to the particular applicants in this case. The Court reasoned that the city had no rational basis to believe that the proposed home posed a special threat to the city's legitimate interests in protecting safety, restricting density, and the like, when the city did not require a special permit for apartments, dormitories, private clubs, fraternity and sorority houses, nursing homes for convalescents or the aged (who are not "insane, feeble-minded or alcoholics or drug addicts"), or other multiple dwellings. The Court thus invalidated the ordinance permit requirement as applied to the CLC applicants. But the Court left in place the regulatory scheme that could require other groups of mentally retarded people to apply for a special permit to maintain a home in the specified residential zones, and the Court did not specify what characteristics of the CLC applicants invalidated the applicability of the ordinance.

A partial dissent, authored by Justice Marshall and joined by Justices Brennan and Blackmun, disagreed with the majority's refusal to accept the facial challenge to the ordinance. Marshall speculated that the majority "appears to act out of a belief that the ordinance might be 'rational' as applied to some subgroup of the retarded under some circumstances" unspecified by the majority, even though some nine-tenths of the group covered by the term "mentally retarded" would fall into the category of "mildly retarded," which actually was the assigned label for the intended residents of the CLC home. While Marshall's opinion argued that heightened scrutiny should have been applied, it suggested that the majority had in essence accorded heightened scrutiny by forbidding the city to use imprecise categories. The opinion noted that in earlier decisions utilizing the rational relationship test, the Court had sustained legislative reforms taking "one step at at time"—reforms which address only one component of a more general problem. Here, however, the majority faulted the ordinance for singling out the mentally retarded in order to take a step towards achieving the city's safety and land-use goals.

Justice Stevens' concurrence, joined by Chief Justice Burger, rejected the three-tiered equal protection analysis which was advanced by the court of appeals and which implicitly informed the majority's analysis. In Justice Stevens' view, constitutional inquiry under equal protection analysis looks to whether the class harmed by the legislation has been subjected to a tradition of disfavor by the law, whether the public purpose is justifiable, and whether characteristics of the class are relevant to that purpose. In this case, he reasoned, "[t]he record convinces me that this permit was required because of the irrational fears of neighboring property owners, rather than for the protection of the mentally retarded persons" who could live in the group home.

How should we evaluate the strength of these three opinions? . . . One is a historical dispute: has the Court in the past articulated one, two, or three standards for equal protection analysis? The same dispute can be put in normative terms: should the Court have available more than one standard for equal protection analysis, and if so, how should such standards be articulated? And finally, what kind of equal protection analysis should apply to a classification based on mental competence, or, as in this case, mental retardation? Should such classifications be viewed with skepticism or disapproval, or should they be defensible on the basis of valid governmental purposes?

There are many competing views about all these issues in current constitutional adjudication. . . . Behind the argument lies a clash of world-views. First, there is the traditional view that classifications on the basis of mental incompetence are natural and immutable. A second view is concerned about errors in classifications and invokes what may be called rights analysis to unearth such errors. Third, there is an emerging view which focuses on the way in which classifications both reflect the power of those who classify and reveal relationships between those who label and those who are labeled—relationships that the label seeks to conceal. I will call these the "abnormal persons" approach, the "rights analysis" approach, and the "social relations" approach. . . .

A. The "Abnormal Persons" Approach

One version of the debate in *Cleburne* looks backward to a legal theory that society is composed of two classes of persons, normal and abnormal, and that different legal treatments follow from the assignment of individuals to one or the other class. Under this approach, which owes its origins in part to feudal notions of fixed status relations, that assignment rests on asserted facts about the person's basic or immutable nature, and most importantly, on those facts concerning the person's mental competence and capacity. Those with normal competence and capacity can enjoy rights and can be held responsible for their acts; those with abnormal competence and capacity can be subjected to legal restraints on their autonomy and rights, and can be submitted to legal protections to guard themselves and others from the effects of their incapacities. The mentally incompetent, in this view, are typically called disabled both because they have "natural" disabilities that affect their mental competence, and because they have legal disabilities that remove them from common legal, economic and political practices.

A further feature of this approach is that although abnormal persons themselves have many variations among them, these variations dim in contrast to their similarities when compared with normal persons. Thus, different legal treatment based on mental competence and incompetence is not only legally permitted; it advances the view that "all persons similarly situated should be treated alike" by implementing mental competence as a dividing line between two differently situated groups. . . .

In *Cleburne*, all the opinions manifest some aspects of this view. Mainly, the opinions treat the mentally retarded as one class of people who share more with each other than with the rest of the community. This, of course, presumes that the characteristic of mental retardation is a more important measure of similarity than, say, eye color, or age. The majority opinion, in particular, emphasizes this approach. It assumes that there is one easily discernible line that divides persons with sufficient mental capacity to be treated as normal from persons who lack such capacity. . . . The majority treats mental deficiency as a real and immutable difference, and the majority's mental universe is inhabited by various groups, some with immutable differences that set them apart from the rest of society and thus warrant different legal treatment. The majority expressly embraces the conception that because differences based on mental competence are real, natural and immutable, governmental action based on this difference is not suspicious but instead legitimate.

B. The Rights Analysis Approach

A contrasting approach applies to the mentally incompetent the rights apparatus utilized during eras of legal reform. Drawing primarily from the desegregation and civil liberties litigation strategies of the 1950's to the 1970's, groups of mentally handicapped individuals and their professional advocates have developed a rights analysis to challenge mental competence classifications.

Rights analysis begins with the view that legal rights apply to everyone: the facts of personhood and membership in the polity entitle each individual to rights against the state and rights to be treated by the state in the same way as others are treated. Rights historically have been denied to certain groups for reasons that can no longer be defended. Political and scientific innovations have rejected many old ideas about differences that used to justify denials of rights. Even though there persists an idea that some differences are true and natural, that notion is coupled here with a skepticism about the accuracy of particular assumptions and classifications, especially where there has been a history of prejudice and cruel treatment. This view animates the thought of those who seek the same legal rights enjoyed by "normal" people for those historically labeled abnormal and mentally incompetent.

At the same time, these advocates also champion new rights, programs and protections designed to benefit those labeled mentally incompetent, either as a quid pro quo for continued deprivation of such persons' basic rights, or as an entitlement founded on their special needs. In these respects, rights analysis contains a central instability. It starts with the idea that everyone enjoys the same rights, but proceeds with the possibility that some special rights may be necessary either to remove the effects of past exclusion or deprivation of rights, or to address some special characteristics of certain groups. This approach, then, uses differences to justify special rights—in contrast to a rights theory that emphasizes "sameness."

Like the "abnormal persons" approach, rights analysis asserts that "all persons similarly situated should be treated alike," and that those differently situated may be treated differently. In a real sense, rights analysis has its roots in the focus on abnormal persons insofar as that approach abides by the principle of equal treatment for similar groups. Yet unlike the "abnormal persons" approach, rights analysis acknowledges that historical attributions of difference have been in error at times, and to guard against error in the future it prescribes a constitutional rights analysis for those labeled mentally incompetent.

Rights analysis itself offers no answer to the question it poses: when are historic attributions of difference acceptable, and when are they false? Nor does it specify when a violation of rights is remedied by treating the retarded like non-retarded persons, and when such a violation justifies a new kind of special treatment. Instead, rights analysis calls for a careful judicial inquiry into these issues, and thus reposes confidence in the perceptions of the judiciary about similarities that transcend as well as differences that endure.

In many ways, all three opinions in *Cleburne* subscribe to this form of rights analysis, even though elements of the other two views can also be discerned. Yet the opinions in the case also demonstrate divergent views about when rights analysis should reject differential treatment and when it should approve it . . ..

* * *

. . . At its best, rights analysis adopts a skeptical perspective towards classifications historically used for discriminatory purposes, and seeks to expose hostility and thoughtlessness. In this sense, rights analysis simply calls for intensive examination by judges concerned with equality and liberty. Some governmental actions imposing differential treatment on the basis of group differences will survive the searching inquiry of rights analysis; yet, rights analysis itself does not explain why.

C. The Social Relations Approach

1. A Definition

Undoubtedly the least familiar and most difficult to define of the three approaches to difference, the social relations approach, is the youngest and the least embedded in language and practice. Nonetheless, the following elements can be identified. Unlike rights analysis, but bearing some resemblance to the "abnormal persons" approach, the social relations approach assumes that there is a basic connectedness between people, instead of assuming that autonomy is the prior and essential dimension of personhood. Yet like rights analysis, and unlike the view of abnormal persons, the social relations approach is dubious of the method of social organization that constructs human relationships in terms of immutable categories, fixed statuses and inherited or ascribed traits.

Indeed, even more fundamentally than rights analysis, the social relations approach challenges the categories and differences used to define and describe people on a group basis. Such suspicion stems not only from an awareness of historical errors in the attribution of difference, but also from a view that attribution itself hides the power of those who classify as well as those defined as different. . . . Relationships of power are often so unequal as to allow the namers to altogether ignore the perspective of the less powerful. The social relations approach embraces the belief that knowledge is rooted in specific perspectives, and that "prevailing views" or "consensus approaches" express the perspectives of those in positions to enforce their points of view in the structure and governance of society.

If one assumes that people are related to each other, then assertions of differences are actually statements of relationships, since they express a comparison between the one doing the asserting and the one about whom the assertion is made. Acts of comparison, then, express and distribute power. Differences do not reside in any one person. Instead, differences are comparisons drawn by some to locate themselves in relation to others.

. . . Attributions of difference should be sustained only if they do not express or confirm the distribution of power in ways that harm the less powerful and benefit the more powerful.

Undertaking such an analysis is a deeply problematic task for a court, which itself is in a position of power. The social relations approach exposes the court's own social relation of power vis-a-vis the litigants and other institutions. . . . Rights analysis treats as unproblematic the perspective of those looking into the bases for a challenged difference, even though the perspective of those doing the looking may itself construct the relationships behind the attributed difference. The social relations approach, in contrast, calls for the development of new strategies to expose the very problematic nature of a court's relationship to the question of difference.

One judicial strategy for analysis under this approach tries to take the perspective of the group which those in power have defined as different. There are two ways in which this strategy is problematic. First, no one can ever really take the perspective of another; at best, one can only try to imagine that perspective. Yet this very impossibility carries with it some benefits for judicial inquiry. It invites a certain amount of humility and self doubt in the enterprise of trying to know. These very qualities may allow the court to glimpse a point of view other than its own or at least develop a basis for knowing that its own point of view is not the only truth. The strategy of taking the perspective of another is problematic, though, for a second reason. This strategy attributes a unitary kind of difference to the "different" group, at the risk of obscuring the range of differences within that very group. A focus by male judges on the perspective of women, for example, could obscure the variety of perspectives among women, and could thereby reinforce, rather than challenge, the attribution by men of a particular conception of difference to women. Still, the very effort to imagine another perspective could sensitize the court to the possibility of a variety of perspectives. Once a judge recognizes that he does not possess the only truth, he may be more ready to acknowledge that there are even more than two truths, or two points of view.

A second judicial strategy taking the social relations approach explores the social meanings that exclusion and isolation carry in a community. The strategy builds on a premise of ongoing relationships, and considers the relationship between the namer and the named that is manifested in categories and labels and that is lived in daily experiences. Does the act of naming cut off or deny relationships? Affirmative answers to questions of this sort would support a conclusion that the attribution of difference violates the foundational premise of ongoing relationships. Such a violation should trigger protection for the constitutionally protected values of equality and freedom of association.

2. Social Relations in *Cleburne*

Although the majority's opinion in *Cleburne* barely hints of either of the judicial social relations strategies, Justice Stevens' opinion at a few points tries to take the perspective of mentally retarded persons burdened by the zoning ordinance requirement of a special permit for their group home. Justice Marshall's opinion adopts both this strategy and the focus on ongoing relationships, including relationships between the namer and the named. An exploration of the social relations ideas in these opinions suggests the relative merits of this approach.

In a remarkable flourish, Justice Stevens concluded his opinion by stating, "I cannot believe that a rational member of this disadvantaged class could ever approve of the discriminatory application of the city's ordinance in this case." The phrase is remarkable because it deems significant how the class burdened by the governmental classification views the treatment. . . . Imagining the perspective of the mentally retarded matters here is especially noteworthy, given the usual assessment of such persons as incapable of forming judgments about their own interests. Indeed, it is such attitudes that undergird the discussion in the majority opinion about why governments may continue to treat the mentally retarded differently from others.

Yet, in the very sentence making this remarkable call to consider the perspective of the mentally retarded, Justice Stevens also precludes much of the proximity, empathy and imagination necessary for such consideration. Perhaps instinctively, perhaps deliberately, Justice Stevens tempers his attention to the perspective of the mentally retarded person by the lawyerly "reasonable person" gloss: what would a rational mentally retarded person think about the special permit requirement for group homes for mentally retarded people? Justice Stevens attends to . . . the perspective of the mentally retarded filtered through the judicial lens of what would be reasonable to see or to want.

Perhaps even more revealing, Justice Stevens omits in the sentence an actual reference to "mental retardation," instead referring to "a rational member of this disadvantaged class." . . . Perhaps the author of the sentence could not bring himself to state next to each other the idea of "the rational"—with which he himself could identify—with the image of "the mentally retarded"—with which he has trouble identifying. . . .

There are implications in Justice Stevens' sentence that flesh out a social relations approach. Considering the perspective of the burdened class exposes the problematic relationship between those enacting the classification and those burdened by it, and between those reviewing constitutional challenges to the classification and those in the class itself. . . . [I]t also suggests that the judiciary may need to examine critically whether the political process for classification excluded or overshadowed the perspective of the burdened group.

Justice Stevens' approach sharply contrasts with the tack taken by the majority, which almost entirely ignores the possibility that the power the government and the courts have over the mentally retarded might allow them to ignore or even fail to see a contrasting perspective held by the mentally retarded. Power and knowledge are related, suggests Justice Stevens. The majority, in contrast, reasons that the remedial legislation singling out the retarded for special treatment reflects a civilized and decent society, and fails to acknowledge either that its own perspective may differ from the view of the mentally retarded, or that its power allows it to believe its perspective is the true perspective.

* * *

In the opinion by Justice Marshall, a focus on the relationships between the powerful and the less-powerful shapes an assessment of the meanings that exclusion and isolation carry. Thus, his opinion analyzes the historical experience of the mentally retarded by focusing on the meaning of segregating and excluding mentally retarded people from the rest of the community. . . . Continuing attribution of difference by the majority to the mentally retarded, and continuing fears and misunderstandings about the minority group, stem, in Justice Marshall's analysis, from the "prolonged social and cultural isolation of the retarded" and "continue to stymie recognition of the dignity and individuality of retarded people." Given a premise of relationships between people, isolation can be seen as a failure of connection and of relationship between the majority and the mentally retarded. To Justice Marshall, the history of isolation is "most important": "lengthy and continuing isolation of the retarded has perpetuated the ignorance, irrational fears, and stereotyping that long have plagued them." Here the opinion identifies a chief root of prejudice: separation among groups exaggerates difference.

Under this analysis, the zoning ordinance special permit requirement must be seen as excluding mentally retarded people from residential communities and preventing their integration into the community. This is how Justice Marshall describes the city's rule and the practices under it. In the course of explaining the significance of the home sought by the mentally retarded, here Justice Marshall combines his focus on the meanings of connectedness and separation in the context of relationships of unequal power, with an attempt to imagine the perspective of the less-powerful group. For retarded adults, the right to establish a home "means living together in group homes, for as deinstitutionalization has progressed, group homes have become the primary means by which retarded adults can enter life in the community." . . . Finally, reasoned Justice Marshall, "[e]xcluding group homes deprives the retarded of much of what makes for human freedom and fulfillment—the ability to form bonds and take part in the life of a community."

* * *

Attention to relationships between groups, and the power constructed in those relationships, also helps explain the importance that the opinion places on the contexts in which a given characteristic of difference is made to matter. This emphasis on context is in keeping with Justice Marshall's longstanding effort to establish a sliding scale of equal protection scrutiny based on the nature of the threatened interest as well as on the nature of the classification. In responding to the majority's claim that the standard of review varies depending on the number of classifications to which a given characteristic would be validly relevant, the partial dissent states: "that a characteristic may be relevant under some or even many circumstances does not suggest any reason to presume it relevant under other circumstances." And, "[a] sign that says 'men only' looks very different on a bathroom door than a courthouse door."

It is valuable to probe the layers of analysis implied by the last sentence. On one level, the point is simply that context can make something that seems the same quite different: the "men only" sign means something different in the context of the two settings. On another level, the sentence suggests that context can make differences become irrelevant and thus make different people the same: for the purpose of entrance to the courthouse, under current views, whatever differences there may be between men and women are irrelevant, and the two groups should be treated the same. On yet another level, the unstated distinction between the two contexts is the contrasting power represented by what lies beyond the two doorways: the bathroom versus the courthouse. It is not just difference in context that matters here; it is the relative power represented by the two contexts, and the meaning of inclusion and exclusion within the society that establishes those contexts. Finally, the sentence suggests but does not probe the question of who is doing the looking that makes the two contexts appear different. Perhaps implicit here is that the excluded group may see the two contexts for exclusion differently.

The opinions by both Justices Stevens and Marshall manifest strategies that advance the social relations approach. Neither opinion, however, fully embraces this view. . . . An opinion fully embracing the social relations approach would adopt new locutions. For example, it would not assign difference to a group and its members but instead locate it as a comparison drawn between groups. It would pay close attention to who exactly names the difference, and it would consider whether a more powerful group uses the assignment of meaning to difference in order to express and consolidate power. Similarly, the relationships between people, including the Court and those affected by the Court's decision, would be discussed overtly; the opinion would avoid the passive voice and its authors would thus have an obligation to disclose their own involvement and responsibility in the assertions they made.

The three approaches to legal treatment of difference help to identify the lines of disagreement among the Supreme Court Justices in contemporary cases. Yet, beneath the debates over the proper fit between ends and means of legislative action and the proper level of scrutiny for reviewing legislative classifications lies a sharp division about the meaning of difference. On one side is the perhaps contentiously labeled "abnormal persons" view, a conception of real differences used to treat certain people as legally different. On the other side is the perhaps ambiguously designated "social relations" view, which emphasizes how differences acquire significance through social attributions, rather than the other way around; how we each have relationships even with those we think are different; and how "we" are as different from those we call different as they are different from us. The "abnormal persons" view makes differential treatment seem natural, unavoidable, and unproblematic; the "social relations" view makes differential treatment a problem of social choice and meaning, a problem for which all onlookers are responsible. The "rights analysis" approach, perhaps the dominant framework of contemporary analysis, shares some elements with the other approaches, and yet cannot itself resolve the tension between them. What can? Which approach is better, and why?

* * *

Conclusion: A Case for Social Relations—and Its Ongoing Relations to Other Views

It is obvious by now that I am sympathetic towards the social relations view. Thinking about social relations offers:

(1)   Ways to challenge the complacency about fixed and assigned hierarchical statuses associated with a view that some people are simply abnormal—a view that has justified exclusion and denigration of racial minorities, women and mentally disabled people.

(2)   Ways to challenge the pretense of identity and sameness that animates rights analysis, a pretense that can undermine special programs aiming to assist mentally disabled people to function and flourish in a world not designed with them in mind.

(3)   Ways to integrate into law notions about the social dimensions of knowledge and the interpersonal dimensions of individual identity that have replaced earlier ideas about objectivity and autonomy in science, psychology and other fields.

(4)   Ways to highlight as human choices, rather than as acts of discovery, how we treat people, including those who seem or who are labeled "different."

(5)   Ways to direct legal inquiry into the social and historical patterns of power and exclusion in which a given problem arises, and thus, ways to direct legal decision-makers to address the practical meanings of their decisions for the people affected.

(6)   Ways to make the perspective of "different people" critical to decisions concerning difference; this could help erase the labels that separate, isolate and hide "different people" and bring them closer to the experience and imagination of those who judge them.

(7)   Ways to emphasize the responsibility of those in power for the decisions they make, especially in terms of the relationships they have with those affected by those decisions.

Working toward these directions through the social relations approach means embracing beliefs that society is a human invention and that those entrusted with societal power can and should exercise that power to recognize and deepen the shared humanity of others.

* * *

Perhaps most disturbing about the social relations approach, from my vantage point, is the loss of certainty it implies. Especially in an era when law reform on behalf of minority groups and social welfare programs in general suffer major political assaults, it seems foolhardy to abandon, much less undermine, the sharpness of rights claims. Perhaps due to its origins, rights analysis enables a devastating, if rhetorical, exposure of and challenge to hierarchies of power. As social policies turn to the politics of selfishness, exclusion and denial of public responsibility for social problems, those who have the weakest toeholds in the dominant social structure become most vulnerable to poverty and degradation. For people who still are members of groups traditionally labeled as "different," these risks are compounded by new forms of parentalism announced on their behalf. Claims to act on behalf of another have been used so often to justify exclusions, deprivations and attributions of difference that stigmatize rather than valorize or accept. Here the power of rights analysis seems especially appealing. It affords a purchase on the slippery matters of human relationships by commanding a searching inquiry from an allegedly certain point of view. And its equation of sameness with equality offers a spiritual commitment with a kind of positivist certainty: because we can measure characteristics of similarity and difference, we can tailor legal treatment to match.

Yet the internal instabilities of rights analysis, the mounting political reaction to its past successes, and the theoretical assault posed by newer theories of knowledge and meaning, make rights analysis vulnerable to critics on the right and the left, and to critics concerned with both practice and theory. There may be ways at once to strengthen and to embolden rights analysis with the kinds of probing inquiries offered by the social relations approach. . . . Rights analysis could come to emphasize as the prerequisite "sameness" the shared "right" to be included and to participate in society—on terms that may vary for each individual, but that may also entail special rights to make inclusion and participation possible.

* * *

Bibliography

Crenshaw, Kimberlé, *De-Marginalizing the Intersection of Race & Sex: A Black Feminist Critique of Antidiscrimination Doctrine, Feminist Theory and Antiracist Politics*, 1989 U. Chi. Legal F. 139

Harris, Angela, *Race and Essentialism in Feminist Legal Theory*, 42 Stan. L. Rev. 581 (1990)

Karst, Kenneth, *Paths to Belonging, The Constitution and Cultural Identity*, 64 N.C. L. Rev. 304 (1986)

Kay, Herma Hill, *Models of Equality*, 1985 U. Ill. L. Rev. 39

Law, Sylvia A., *Homosexuality and the Social Meaning of Gender*, 1988 Wisc. L. Rev. 187

Littleton, Christine A., *Equality and Feminist Legal Theory*, 48 U. Pitt. L. Rev. 1043 (1987)

MacKinnon, Catharine, *Reflections on Sex Equality Under Law*, 100 Yale L.J. 1281 (1991)

Olsen, Frances E., *Statutory Rape: A Feminist Critique of Rights Analysis*, 63 Tex. L. Rev. 387 (1984)

Roberts, Dorothy E., *Punishing Drug Addicts Who Have Babies: Women of Color, Equality and the Right of Privacy*, 104 Harv. L. Rev. 1419 (1991)

Symposium on Sexual Orientation and the Law, 79 Va. L. Rev. 1419 (1993)

Wildman, Stephanie, *The Legitimation of Sex Discrimination: A Critical Response to Supreme Court Jurisprudence*, 63 Or. L. Rev. 265 (1984)

Williams, Wendy Webster, *Equality's Riddle: Pregnancy and the Equal Treatment/Special Treatment Debate*, 13 N.Y.U. Rev. L. & Soc. Change 325 (1984)

Williams, Wendy Webster, *The Equality Crisis: Some Reflections on Culture, Courts and Feminism*, 7 Women's Rts. L. Rep. 175 (1982)

Williams, Patricia, *The Obliging Shell: An Informal Essay on Formal Equal Opportunity*, 87 Mich. L. Rev. 2128 (1989)

Part V
Litigative Prerequisites

This section is composed of articles discussing the doctrines of standing and political questions. In *The Doctrine of Standing as an Essential Element of the Separation of Powers,* Justice Antonin Scalia contends that the courts should insist more rigorously that a plaintiff's alleged injury be a particularized one that sets him apart from the citizenry at large. In *The Structure of Standing,* William A. Fletcher argues that federal "taxpayer" status cannot be considered in isolation for determining a plaintiff's standing. In *The New Law of Standing: A Plea for Abandonment,* Mark V. Tushnet suggests that the Court's professed law of standing, articulated in *Flast v. Cohen* (1968), makes possible concealed decisionmaking on the merits of each case. He advocates denying standing only if there is some doubt concerning the plaintiff's ability to present the case with adequate adverseness, or if another plaintiff more directly affected by the controversy is likely to bring the case. In *Should Trees Have Standing?—Toward Legal Rights for Natural Objects*, Christopher D. Stone argues that "natural objects"—trees, forests, oceans, rivers, animals—should be given legal rights, and that the "thing" should be able to institute legal action through a guardian. In *Is There a "Political Question" Doctrine?,* Louis Henkin questions whether use of the doctrine is ever necessary, suggesting that cases in which it has been invoked would come out the same had they been decided on the merits. Finally, in *Foreign Affairs and the Political Question Doctrine,* Michael J. Glennon suggests that the courts should not decline to decide foreign affairs cases just because they necessarily present political questions.

Antonin Scalia, *The Doctrine of Standing as an Essential Element of the Separation of Powers,* 17 SUFFOLK U. L. REV. 881, 894-99 (1983)*

* * *

Is standing functionally related to the distinctive role that we expect the courts to perform? The question is not of purely academic interest, because if there is a functional relationship it may have some bearing upon how issues of standing are decided in particular cases.

There is, I think, a functional relationship, which can best be described by saying that the law of standing roughly restricts courts to their traditional undemocratic role of protecting individuals and minorities against impositions of the majority, and excludes them from the even more undemocratic role of prescribing how the other two branches should function in order to serve the interest *of the majority itself.* Thus, when an individual who is the very *object* of a law's requirement or prohibition seeks to challenge it, he always has standing. That is the classic case of the law bearing down upon the individual himself, and the court will not pause to inquire whether the grievance is a "generalized" one.

Contrast that classic form of court challenge with the increasingly frequent administrative law cases in which the plaintiff is complaining of an agency's unlawful *failure* to impose a requirement or prohibition upon *someone else.* Such a failure harms the plaintiff, by depriving him, as a citizen, of governmental acts which the Constitution and laws require. But that harm alone is, so to speak, a *majoritarian* one. The plaintiff may *care* more about it; he may be a more ardent proponent of constitutional regularity or of the necessity of the governmental act that has been wrongfully omitted. But that does not establish that he has been harmed distinctively—only that he assesses the harm as more grave, which is a fair subject for democratic debate in which he may persuade the rest of us. Since our readiness to be persuaded is no less than his own (we are harmed just as much) there is no reason to remove the matter from the political process and place it in the courts. Unless the plaintiff can show some respect in which he is harmed *more* than the rest of us (for example, he is a worker in the particular plant where the Occupational Safety and Health Administration has wrongfully waived legal safety requirements) he has not established any basis for concern that the majority is suppressing or ignoring the rights of a minority that wants protection, and thus has not established the prerequisite for judicial intervention.

That explains, I think, why "concrete injury"—an injury apart from the mere breach of the social contract, so to speak, effected by the very fact of unlawful government action—is the indispensable prerequisite of standing. Only that can separate the plaintiff from all the rest of us who also claim benefit of the social contract, and can thus entitle him to some special protection from the democratic manner in which we ordinarily run our social-contractual affairs. Of course concrete injury is a necessary but not necessarily sufficient condition. The plaintiff must establish not merely minority status, but minority status relevant to the particular governmental transgression that he seeks to correct. If the concrete harm that he will suffer as a

---

*   Reprinted with permission.

consequence of the government's failure to observe the law is purely fortuitous—in the sense that the law was not specifically designed to avoid that harm, but rather for some other (usually more general) purpose—then the majority's failure to require observance of the law cannot be said to be directed *against him*, and his entitlement to the special protection of the courts disappears. That is the essential inquiry conducted under the heading of whether the plaintiff who claims standing has suffered any "legal wrong"; or whether he comes within the definition of "adversely affected" or "aggrieved" party under the various substantive statutes that employ such terms; or whether he is within a substantive statute's protected "zone of interests" under the post-*Data Processing* distortion of the APA.

If I am correct that the doctrine of standing, as applied to challenges to governmental action, is an essential means of restricting the courts to their assigned role of protecting minority rather than majority interests, several consequences follow. First of all, a consequence of some theoretical interest but relatively small practical effect: it would follow that not *all* "concrete injury" indirectly following from governmental action or inaction would be capable of supporting a congressional conferral of standing. One can conceive of such a concrete injury so widely shared that a congressional specification that the statute at issue was meant to preclude precisely that injury would nevertheless not suffice to mark out a subgroup of the body politic requiring judicial protection. For example, allegedly wrongful governmental action that affects "all who breathe." There is surely no reason to believe that an alleged governmental default of such general impact would not receive fair consideration in the normal political process.

A more practical consequence pertains not to congressional power to confer standing, but to judicial interpretation of congressional intent in that regard. If the doctrine does serve the separation-of-powers function I have suggested, then in the process of answering the abstruse question whether a "legal wrong" has been committed, or whether a person is "adversely affected or aggrieved," so that standing does exist, the courts should bear in mind the *object* of the exercise, and should not be inclined to assume congressional designation of a "minority group" so broad that it embraces virtually the entire population. I have in mind a recent case which found a congressional intent to confer standing upon a group no less expansive than all consumers of milk. It is hard to believe that the democratic process, if it works at all, could not and should not have been relied upon to protect the interests of that almost all-inclusive group.

But that is the ultimate question: Even if the doctrine of standing was once meant to restrict judges "solely, to decide on the rights of individuals," what is wrong with having them protect the rights of the majority as well? They've done so well at the one, why not promote them to the other? The answer is that there is no reason to believe they will be any good at it. In fact, they have in a way been specifically *designed* to be bad at it—selected from the aristocracy of the highly educated, instructed to be governed by a body of knowledge that values abstract principle above concrete result, and (just in case any connection with the man in the street might subsist) removed from all accountability to the electorate. That is just perfect for a body that is supposed to protect the individual against the people; it is just terrible (unless you are a monarchist) for a group that is supposed to decide what is good for the people. Where the courts, in the supposed interest of all the people, do enforce upon the executive branch adherence to legislative policies that the political process itself would not enforce, they are likely (despite the best of intentions) to be enforcing the political prejudices of their own class. Their greatest success in such an enterprise—ensuring strict enforcement of the environmental laws, not to protect particular minorities but for the benefit of all the people—met with approval in the classrooms of Cambridge and New Haven, but not in the factories of Detroit and the mines of West Virginia. It may well be, of course, that the judges know what is good for the people better than the people themselves; or that democracy simply does not permit the *genuine* desires of the people to be given effect; but those are not the premises under which our system operates.

Does what I have said mean that, so long as no minority interests are affected, "important legislative purposes, heralded in the halls of Congress, [can be] lost or misdirected in the vast hallways of the federal bureaucracy?" Of *course* it does—and a good thing, too. Where no peculiar harm to particular individuals or minorities is in question, lots of once-heralded programs ought to get lost or misdirected, in vast hallways or elsewhere. Yesterday's herald is today's bore—although we judges, in the seclusion of our chambers, may not be *au courant* enough to realize it. The ability to lose or misdirect laws can be said to be one of the prime engines of social change, and the prohibition against such carelessness is (believe it or not) profoundly conservative. Sunday blue laws, for example, were widely unenforced long before they were widely repealed—and had the first not been possible the second might never have occurred.

[In] the early 1970's—after *Flast* had pronounced that the doctrine of standing "does not, by its own force, raise separation of powers problems related to judicial interference in areas committed to other branches of the Federal Government," and after *Data Processing, Barlow v. Collins*, and *SCRAP* had demonstrated the Supreme Court's apparent intent to operate on that assumption—the subject addressed by the present paper would have been of merely historical interest. It might have been retitled "Former Relevance of Standing to the Separation of Powers." Since that time, however, the Supreme Court's theory has returned to earlier traditions, and there may be reason to believe that its practice will as well. The dictum of *Flast* has been disavowed by opinions that explicitly acknowledge that standing and separation of powers are intimately related. And the essential element that links the two—the requirement of *distinctive* injury not shared by the entire body politic—has been resurrected. *Flast* was essentially a repudiation of *Frothingham v. Mellon*, where the Court had disallowed a taxpayer suit to prevent expenditures in violation of the commerce clause, because it was not enough to allege an injury suffered in "some indefinite way in common with people generally." More recent cases, however, such as *United States v. Richardson* and *Schlesinger v. Reservists Committee to Stop the War*, not only restore *Frothingham* to a place of honor, but quote the following passage from the venerable case of *Ex parte Lévitt*:

> It is an established principle that to entitle a private individual to invoke the judicial power to determine the validity of executive or legislative action he must show that he has sustained or is immediately in danger of sustaining a direct injury as the result of that action and it is not sufficient that he has merely a general interest common to all members of the public.

It is unlikely that this reversion to former theory will not ultimately entail some degree of reversion to former practice. Apparently, *Flast* has already been limited strictly to its facts, and I anticipate that the Court's *SCRAP*-era willingness to discern breathlessly broad congressional grants of standing will not endure. There is already indication of this in opinions demonstrating a reluctance to "imply" in federal statutes rights of action against private parties, which opinions have been cited in the context of suits against executive officials as well. Though the APA's phrase "adversely affected or aggrieved within the meaning of a relevant statute" will not likely be restored to its original meaning, the effectively substituted phrase "adversely affected or aggrieved under a relevant statute" (involving application of the so-called "zone of interests" test) leaves plenty of room for maneuvering. I expect the direction of that maneuvering to be in the direction of separation of powers.

William A. Fletcher, *The Structure of Standing*, 98 YALE L.J. 221, 267-72 (1988)*

* * *

a. Federal Taxpayer Standing

Four cases are typically grouped under the heading of "federal taxpayer standing." In *Flast v. Cohen*, the Supreme Court granted standing to a federal taxpayer to seek an injunction against spending federal funds allegedly in violation of the establishment clause of the First Amendment. In *Valley Forge Christian College v. Americans United for Separation of Church and State, Inc.*, the Court denied standing to federal taxpayers to challenge a grant of federally owned real property to a religious college, also allegedly in violation of the establishment clause. In *United States v. Richardson*, the Court denied standing to a federal taxpayer to require the Central Intelligence Agency to provide an account of its expenditures under the "statement and account clause" of the Constitution. Finally, in *Schlesinger v. Reservists Committee to Stop the War*, the Court denied standing to federal taxpayers to enjoin members of congress from simultaneously sitting in Congress and holding positions in the military reserve allegedly in violation of the "incompatibility clause" of the Constitution.

In *Flast*, the majority formulated a two-part test designed to separate those cases in which federal taxpayer standing should be granted from those in which it should not. Under *Flast*, a federal taxpayer has standing to challenge a federal expenditure if (1) the challenged expenditure is an exercise of the federal government's taxing and spending power under Article I, section 8, of the Constitution, and (2) the challenged expenditure exceeds specific constitutional limitations on the taxing and spending power. Justices Stewart and Fortas each concurred separately, arguing that standing should be granted because of the special nature of the establishment clause and its relationship to the use of federal tax moneys. I suspect that Stewart's and Fortas' position (which I will here treat as one) was not adopted by the majority of the Court because it was seen as unseemly and "result oriented." Yet Stewart and Fortas asked precisely the question that was before the Court: Is the nature of the establishment clause guarantee such that a federal taxpayer should be permitted to sue to enforce it?

The Court's more recent decision in *Valley Forge* denied standing to federal taxpayers to challenge a grant of federally owned real property to a sectarian school as a violation of the establishment clause. It would be somewhat naive to argue that the result in *Valley Forge* would have been different if only *Flast* had been written differently. But it is at least apparent that the doctrinal formulation in *Flast* facilitated

---

* Reprinted by permission of The Yale Law Journal Company and Fred B. Rothman & Company from The Yale Law Journal, Vol. 98, pp. 221-291.

a thoroughgoing wrongheadedness in the Court's explanation of why it denied standing in *Valley Forge*.

In both *Flast* and *Valley Forge*, federal taxpayers asserted that federal actions violated the establishment clause. The difference between the two cases is that in *Flast* federal funds were spent, whereas in *Valley Forge* federally owned real property was granted. Although Justice Brennan argued in dissent in *Valley Forge* that the critical issue was the meaning of the establishment clause, the majority took the *Flast* test at face value. In an opinion by Justice Rehnquist, the Court held that the first part of the test was not satisfied because plaintiffs were challenging an action by the Department of Health, Education, and Welfare rather than a "congressional action," and because the grant of real property was an exercise of power under the property clause rather than an exercise of the taxing and spending power. The Court denied that plaintiffs' establishment clause claim was any more "fundamental" than the statement of account clause and incompatibility clause claims in *Richardson* and *Schlesinger*, and it repeated the statement in *Flast* that "the requirement of standing 'focuses on the party seeking to get his complaint before a federal court and not on the issues he wishes to have adjudicated.'"

Perhaps I should not dignify *Valley Forge* by pretending that it is anything more than an intellectually disingenuous way to undercut *Flast* and to return to the status quo ante. But it should be clear that either *Flast* or *Valley Forge* is wrongly decided. In each case, federal taxpayers alleged that something of economic value had been transferred by the United States to a religious institution in violation of the establishment clause. It is possible to argue, of course, that federal taxpayers should not be allowed to bring establishment clause challenges to federal expenditures; indeed, this was the state of the law before *Flast*. Whether a federal taxpayer should be permitted to bring such a challenge depends, and must depend, as Justices Stewart and Fortas said in their separate concurrences in *Flast*, and as Justice Brennan said in dissent in *Valley Forge*, on how one reads the establishment clause. The meaning of the clause, both as to what it prohibits and as to whom it permits to bring suit, is not irrelevant, as the *Flast* and *Valley Forge* Courts both suggested. It is, rather, the crux of the argument.

I believe that standing should have been allowed in both cases. My reasoning is much like that of Justices Stewart, Fortas, and Brennan—that the protection provided by the establishment clause cannot be fully realized unless there is easy and unrestricted access to the courts to challenge federal expenditures or grants that might violate the clause. Justice Brennan, like Justice Rutledge forty years earlier, has concluded that federal taxpayers should be given special status to challenge expenditures as violative of the establishment clause, based on the historical argument that the clause was enacted to prevent the forced exaction of moneys for the support of state-sponsored religion. There is much to be said for this argument, but I would prefer to read the establishment clause as protecting all members of our society, not merely taxpayers, from excessive entanglement of church and state. Federal taxpayer standing is, therefore, in my view, at once too narrow and too broad. It is too narrow in that a member of the society should not have to show that he pays federal taxes to invoke judicial enforcement of the clause. It is too broad in that a foreigner should not have standing to bring a challenge under the clause merely on the happenstance that he paid a federal tax.

I nevertheless would be willing to employ taxpayer status as the criterion to separate those who can bring establishment clause challenges from those who cannot, for as a practical matter the lack of fit between federal taxpayer standing and the intended protection of the clause is not serious. The narrowness of the taxpayer category is not a significant problem since virtually all adults in the country are federal taxpayers. Nor, in the absence of a showing that foreigners are flooding our courts with establishment clause litigation, am I greatly concerned about the overbreadth of the taxpayer category. Moreover, other general categories designed to encompass those who have sufficient stake in our society to warrant judicial protection by the clause may also turn out to have problems of fit. For example, one could argue that even general citizen standing is insufficiently broad for establishment clause purposes, given the stake that resident aliens and other non-citizens might be thought to have in our society.

In the end, however, I am less concerned with the proper reading of the establishment clause and the definition of the class of people entitled to its judicial enforcement, than with making the point that whether taxpayer standing should be permitted is not a question that can be answered in the abstract. It can be answered only by reference to the meaning and purposes of the particular clause at issue. A reader should not think that she should reject my general thesis because she disagrees with my reading of the establishment clause. Indeed, if she disagrees with my conclusion about standing because she argues that the establishment clause should be construed differently, she is agreeing with my thesis, for such an argument is precisely what I say should take place.

The Court's other two decisions in the taxpayer standing cases, *Richardson* and *Schlesinger*, further illustrate that the question of taxpayer standing cannot be considered in the abstract. In *Richardson*, plaintiff sought to compel the production of detailed information by the Central Intelligence Agency about its expenditures. Plaintiff contended that the Central Intelligence Agency Act, which allowed the CIA to account for its expenditures "solely on the certificate of the Director," violated the statement and account clause of the Constitution, which requires that "a regular Statement and Account of the Receipts and Expenditures of all public Money shall be published from time to time." The Supreme Court applied the *Flast* test and held that the plaintiff lacked standing as a federal taxpayer because there was "no 'logical nexus' between the asserted status of taxpayer" and the claimed constitutional violation.

The Court's decision in *Richardson* makes sense only if the statement and account clause should be read not to permit a member of the body politic—whether a federal taxpayer, a voter, or a citizen—to require, through judicial process, the production of the CIA's secret accounts. The Court seems to have sensed this, but its statement that there is "no logical nexus" between plaintiff's taxpayer status and the constitutional claim under the clause only hints at the reasoning that should support its decision. An explanation of the decision must be based, as the Court's opinion is not, on an explicit analysis of the purposes of the clause, and on whether those purposes would be served by granting standing to a member of the general public.

In *Schlesinger*, plaintiffs sought to prevent members of Congress from simultaneously serving as members of the United States military reserves on the ground that such simultaneous membership violated the incompatibility clause of the Constitution, which provides that "no Person holding any Office under the United States, shall be a Member of either House during his Continuance in Office." The Supreme Court denied standing to plaintiffs, both as citizens and as taxpayers. As in *Richardson*, the Court's decision in *Schlesinger* can be justified based on an analysis of the constitutional provision whose protection is invoked by the plaintiffs, but the Court failed to provide that analysis. In eleven pages devoted to the question of citizen standing, the Court mentioned the purpose of the incompatibility clause briefly, in only two places, and in both instances the Court appears to have considered such discussion irrelevant to the standing issue before it. The Court's denial of taxpayer standing was brief and similarly divorced from any consideration of the purpose of the incompatibility clause. Finally, at one point, the Court hinted that the clause was meant to be binding but not judicially enforceable, suggesting that plaintiffs had sought to adjudicate a political question. If this is so, the Court's decision means that no person has standing to enforce the clause, but argument about this issue is conspicuously absent.

In sum, *Flast*, *Valley Forge*, *Richardson*, and *Schlesinger* should not be seen as a group of "federal taxpayer cases." Rather, they should be seen as cases involving three different provisions of the Constitution. We may have a presumption that federal taxpayers ordinarily should not have standing to challenge activities of the federal government on constitutional grounds. But we should not make the mistake of thinking that there is something about federal taxpayer status, considered in isolation, that will allow us to arrive at the correct standing decision in particular cases. Nor, when federal taxpayers are granted standing, as in *Flast*, should we make the related mistake of thinking that the decision has changed the essence of federal taxpayer standing. Rather, we are dealing only with a presumption, which may be overcome when the purposes of the particular clause at issue will be best served by permitting federal taxpayers to sue to enforce its obligations.

* * *

Mark V. Tushnet, *The New Law of Standing: A Plea for Abandonment,* 62 CORNELL L. REV. 663, 688-97 (1977)*

* * *

Flast established a relatively coherent framework for analyzing constitutional questions of standing to sue. Unfortunately, Chief Justice Warren's opinion for the Court, after clearly setting out the proper framework, introduced unnecessary embellishments that have weakened the opinion's force and have confused the Court.

In *Flast*, the Chief Justice drew a distinction within the general doctrine of justiciability—between those policies served by the law of standing and those policies served by the law of political questions.

> Justiciability encompasses two complementary but somewhat different limitations. In part [it] limit[s] the business of the federal courts to questions presented [(1)] in an adversary context and in a form historically viewed as capable of resolution through the judicial process. And in part [it] define[s] the role assigned to the judiciary in a tripartite allocation of power [(2)] to assure that the federal courts will not intrude into areas committed to the other branches of government.

According to *Flast*, the constitutional doctrine of standing guarantees adverseness; the doctrine of political questions assures the proper judicial respect for the coordinate branches of government. This distinction represents Chief Justice Warren's major accomplishment in the opinion.

---

*   Copyright © 1977 by Cornell University. All rights reserved.

A. *Concrete Adverseness and its Surrogates*

The distinction drawn by the Chief Justice should have simplified the process of determining whether a plaintiff has standing; inquiry should focus on the "concrete adverseness" of the plaintiff's case. Unfortunately, the *Flast* Court's formulation of the test for standing added the more complicated requirement that there be a "logical nexus between the status asserted and the claim sought to be adjudicated" and that, in a taxpayer suit, the plaintiff "show that the challenged enactment exceeds specific constitutional limitations imposed upon the exercise of the congressional taxing and spending power." The point of the first part of this requirement is clear. When a nexus between status and claim exists, we can be relatively "confident that the questions will be framed with the necessary specificity, that the issues will be contested with the necessary adverseness and that the litigation will be pursued with the necessary vigor." The nexus serves as a substitute for the direct personal injury called for by the "private rights" model of constitutional adjudication.

This analysis, however, leaves open two related questions. First, it is not clear that the required nexus will guarantee concrete adverseness. Thus, the Court's attempt to substitute a more particularized test for concrete adverseness might permit a lawsuit where the policies underlying the case or controversy requirement would suggest that the suit should not be entertained. Second, the *Flast* Court never explained the necessity for an indirect test for concrete adverseness.

The *Flast* Court, by establishing a rule to limit standing, may have erroneously tried to generalize from the taxpayer cases to other, as yet unimagined cases of ideological plaintiffs. The Court's failure to justify its generalized rule sowed the seeds for subsequent decisions repudiating the fundamentally correct analysis of *Flast*. *Flast* itself thus illustrates the dangers of deciding cases not concretely before the Court.

1. *The Implicit Limitations in* Flast

Chief Justice Warren twice hinted in *Flast* that the absence of other plausible plaintiffs to challenge the government action at issue justified granting standing to taxpayers. He noted that free-exercise claims were distinguishable from establishment clause claims, since the former necessarily involved a specially burdened class of people, and "the proper party emphasis in the federal standing doctrine would require that standing be limited to the taxpayers within the affected class." In formulating the nexus requirement, the Chief Justice stated that taxpayers could not challenge expenditures incidental to "the administration of an essentially regulatory statute." In such a case, persons directly affected by the regulation could ordinarily be expected to challenge its constitutionality. If necessary, they could also assert claims affecting the general public interest in addition to claims based upon the direct burdens imposed on them by the regulation.

If these hints are taken seriously, taxpayers had standing in *Flast* because no one else was likely to present the claim for adjudication. A preference for "better" plaintiffs is justified by the self-evident truth that the more directly a person is affected by a governmental regulation, the harder he or she will fight to remove the restrictions it imposes; *i.e.*, adverseness is likely to be great. In addition, better plaintiffs allow the court to gauge the actual operation of the statute in question and ensure a fuller factual setting for deciding constitutional questions.

Conversely, the Court has repeatedly bestowed standing by default in the absence of better plaintiffs. Moot cases, for example, are ordinarily nonjusticiable, but the Court has often decided the merits of otherwise moot cases that are "capable of repetition, yet evad[e] review." These cases involve applications of a statute in concrete situations; therefore, only adverseness need be established.

In contrast, cases raising questions of first amendment overbreadth involve litigants with strong incentives to pursue the challenge but whose cases do little to illustrate the evil effects of unconstitutionally overbroad statutes. A defendant may challenge a statute as overbroad—prohibiting activity protected by the first amendment—even though his or her activity was plainly not constitutionally protected. The justification for the exception lies in the deterrent effect of an overbroad statute. Such a statute prohibits constitutionally protected activity. Conscientious citizens, knowing that the protected activity has been prohibited, will refrain from engaging in it. Thus, cases will seldom arise in which the state acts to penalize a person whose activity is indeed protected; the only prosecutions will involve those perfectly willing to break even a clearly constitutional law. However, in vagueness cases law-abiding citizens may misjudge the scope of a statute, engage in protected activity, and find themselves prosecuted. Thus, those who engage in constitutionally unprotected activity should be able to raise overbreadth claims, since plaintiffs engaging in protected activity are likely to feel the force of the law's operation, and state deterrence of constitutionally protected activity ought to be challenged. But those same individuals should not be permitted to raise vagueness claims, because of the probable availability of better plaintiffs. In fact, this is the state of the law.

The "no better plaintiff" concept stands as an implicit limitation of *Flast*. Two concluding observations are in order. First, if *Flast* suggests that standing should be granted to taxpayers or citizens when no other plaintiffs are available, the opinion does not assume that all constitutional questions are justiciable. The Court does not sanction the result feared by Professor Brown—that enactment of a statute would be a mere prelude to challenge of the statute in the courts. *Flast* clearly preserved other doctrines of justiciability, notably the political question limitation. Relaxed standing need not, as Professor Brown feared, turn the Supreme Court into a Council of Revision.

Second, Chief Justice Burger's opinion for the Court in *United States v. Richardson* argued that the absence of a plaintiff other than a citizen or taxpayer to challenge the failure of the Central Intelligence Agency (CIA) to make its budget public, indicated that the issue involved a political question. But the Chief Justice's argument departs from traditional political question analysis. The absence of better plaintiffs may suggest that there is a "textually demonstrable constitutional commitment" of the issue to Congress, the current test for determining whether a question is political in the constitutional sense. But the absence of a better plaintiff does not conclusively determine whether a question is political, as the Solicitor General recognized in *Richardson* when he conceded that even if standing were found, the suit might be barred by the political question doctrine. Perhaps the political question doctrine ought to be revitalized, but it confuses analysis to use dissatisfaction with the state of the law in one area to justify irrational decisions in another.

2. *The Repudiation of* Flast

Because *Flast* substituted an arbitrary nexus requirement for an inquiry into concrete adverseness, the Court could easily limit the implications of its holding. For example, when the plaintiff in *Richardson* attacked the nondisclosure of the CIA budget rather than a particular expenditure made by the agency, the Court simply held that the plaintiff had failed to satisfy the *Flast* nexus between his status as a taxpayer and the expenditure challenged. In a formal sense this was correct, but it is inconceivable that the result would have been different had the plaintiff alleged that CIA funds had been used to support right-wing Christian fundamentalist publications in violation of the establishment clause, and that disclosure of the CIA budget was necessary to prove that claim at trial.

The *Richardson* Court rejected the plaintiff's claim to standing as a citizen. The plaintiff had argued that he could not fulfill his obligation as a citizen to vote in an informed manner without knowing what expenditures Congress had approved for CIA activities. The Court held that citizen standing was unavailable because the plaintiff's grievances were "shared with 'all members of the public.'" This simply restates the problem; a party claiming standing as a citizen presents a claim shared by all members of the public. According to *Flast*, courts must inquire into the logical nexus between citizenship and the claim; the Court in *Richardson* simply refused to make the inquiry.

In a companion case to *Richardson*, the Court directly addressed the question of the concreteness necessary to permit informed adjudication. *Schlesinger v. Reservists Committee to Stop the War* was a suit by persons, claiming standing as citizens, challenging the enrollment of members of Congress in the Reserves. Plaintiffs claimed that this practice violated the constitutional prohibition of dual office holding. The Court held that the claimed injury, denial of the exercise of independent judgment by the dual office holders, was insufficiently concrete to permit informed adjudication. Unfortunately, the Court followed a standard that disregarded the inherently relative nature of concreteness. If the factual setting of a plaintiff's claim provides the best possible illumination of the operation of the challenged practice, then the Court ought to be able to consider the merits of the case. Of course, finding standing does not mean that the Court must decide the case in favor of the plaintiffs, or even that it must decide the merits at all. An amorphous injury may be evidence that the issue is not a proper one for judicial resolution, but that is a separate inquiry.

The Court's decisions in *Richardson* and *Reservists* rested on two unarticulated assumptions. First, the Court assumed that judicial inquiry into the constitutionality of a practice may offend coordinate branches of government. Although this assumption might be defensible if fully articulated, on its face it is odd. It is difficult to see why Congress and the President should be offended by being required to defend a lawsuit, particularly when the political question doctrine provides an adequate defense for their actions. The second assumption is simpler: the Court was convinced that the practices challenged in *Richardson* and *Reservists* were constitutional, and it made no sense to let those lawsuits go to trial when they were doomed to failure. But it made little sense to twist the law of standing to terminate the lawsuits. The Court's duty is to articulate principles of continuing applicability; hostility to the merits of particular lawsuits is not such a principle.

B. "Exceeds Specific Limitations"

The second part of the *Flast* test is pure fiat: no member of the Court has explained why a taxpayer has standing only to challenge expenditures that exceed specific limitations on the spending power. Perhaps the only explanation lies in a felt necessity to preserve the result in *Frothingham v. Mellon*. There the Court denied standing to a taxpayer who claimed that a federal expenditure violated the due process clause and invaded a sphere reserved to the states by the tenth amendment.

Another possible source of the second *Flast* requirement is more interesting. The concurring opinions of Justices Stewart and Fortas in *Flast* suggested rather strongly that *Flast* should be understood as an establishment clause case. They argued, in effect, that because of its particular history, the establishment clause conferred standing on taxpayers, just as in *Bivens v. Six Unknown Named Agents*, the fourth amendment conferred standing on persons whose homes had been searched. The second *Flast* requirement, then, is no more than a misguided attempt to articulate a general standard for determining which constitutional provisions confer standing on taxpayers. The attempt is misguided because under this analysis standing can be found only after interpretation of each particular constitutional provision. A constitutional provision on its face may not limit the spending power, but if examined in light of its history, the same provision might have been designed to limit impliedly Congress' power to spend. By attempting to generalize about the types of provisions that would confer standing, the Court in *Flast* weakened the force of its analysis.

Justice Stewart's recent foray into the field, in his dissenting opinion in *Richardson*, demonstrates the same eagerness to substitute a test which purportedly turns on concreteness, without direct inquiry into the facts of the case. He too sought to return to the "private rights" model by distinguishing between affirmative duties imposed on federal officials by the Constitution and specific prohibitions against federal action. Justice Stewart argued that when the Constitution imposes a duty, the plaintiff complaining of an official failure to perform the duty has alleged an infringement of a private right to benefit from the performance of the affirmative duty. For example, a plaintiff may claim that Congress has a duty to disclose the CIA budget and that it has not done so. He or she then assumes the same legal position as a person claiming that the Director of the CIA entered into a contract to provide the budget, but refused to perform; the constitutional duty is the analogue to the contract. The analysis of *Flast* comes into play only when a prohibition is involved.

Justice Stewart's distinction makes little sense when closely examined. Difficulties arise as soon as we try to decide which constitutional provisions impose affirmative duties and which contain only prohibitions. For example, Justice Stewart treats the establishment clause as a prohibition, and yet it could easily be characterized as a duty not to use taxpayers' money to support churches. The negative phrasing of this duty is linguistically and logically irrelevant. The clause at issue in *Richardson* provided that "a regular Statement and Account [shall] be published from time to time." A duty to publish is equally a duty not to withhold from publication. One is hard pressed to imagine why the happenstance that the Constitution puts it one way rather than the other should make any legal difference. Logically, too, the duty-prohibition distinction serves none of the underlying policies of the standing doctrine.

* * *

Christopher D. Stone, *Should Trees Have Standing?— Toward Legal Rights for Natural Objects*, 45 S. CAL. L. REV. 450, 464-73 (1972)*

* * *

It is not inevitable, nor is it wise, that natural objects should have no rights to seek redress in their own behalf. It is no answer to say that streams and forests cannot have standing because streams and forests cannot speak. Corporations cannot speak either; nor can states, estates, infants, incompetents, municipalities or uni-

---

*   Reprinted with permission of the Southern California Law Review.

versities. Lawyers speak for them, as they customarily do for the ordinary citizen with legal problems. One ought, I think, to handle the legal problems of natural objects as one does the problems of legal incompetents—human beings who have become vegetables. If a human being shows signs of becoming senile and has affairs that he is de jure incompetent to manage, those concerned with his well being make such a showing to the court, and someone is designated by the court with the authority to manage the incompetent's affairs. The guardian (or "conservator" or "committee"—the terminology varies) then represents the incompetent in his legal affairs. Courts make similar appointments when a corporation has become "incompetent"—they appoint a trustee in bankruptcy or reorganization to oversee its affairs and speak for it in court when that becomes necessary.

On a parity of reasoning, we should have a system in which, when a friend of a natural object perceives it to be endangered, he can apply to a court for the creation of a guardianship. Perhaps we already have the machinery to do so. California law, for example, defines an incompetent as "any person, whether insane or not, who by reason of old age, disease, weakness of mind, or other cause, is unable, unassisted, properly to manage and take care of himself or his property, and by reason thereof is likely to be deceived or imposed upon by artful or designing persons." Of course, to urge a court that an endangered river is "a person" under this provision will call for lawyers as bold and imaginative as those who convinced the Supreme Court that a railroad corporation was a "person" under the fourteenth amendment, a constitutional provision theretofore generally thought of as designed to secure the rights of freedmen. (As this article was going to press, Professor Byrn of Fordham petitioned the New York Supreme Court to appoint him legal guardian for an unrelated foetus scheduled for abortion so as to enable him to bring a class action on behalf of all foetuses similarly situated in New York City's 18 municipal hospitals. Judge Holtzman granted the petition of guardianship.) If such an argument based on present statutes should fail, special environmental legislation could be enacted along traditional guardianship lines. Such provisions could provide for guardianship both in the instance of public natural objects and also, perhaps with slightly different standards, in the instance of natural objects on "private" land.

The potential "friends" that such a statutory scheme would require will hardly be lacking. The Sierra Club, Environmental Defense Fund, Friends of the Earth, Natural Resources Defense Counsel, and the Izaak Walton League are just some of the many groups which have manifested unflagging dedication to the environment and which are becoming increasingly capable of marshalling the requisite technical experts and lawyers. If, for example, the Environmental Defense Fund should have reason to believe that some company's strip mining operations might be irreparably destroying the ecological balance of large tracts of land, it could, under this procedure, apply to the court in which the lands were situated to be appointed guardian. As guardian, it might be given rights of inspection (or visitation) to determine and bring to the court's attention a fuller finding on the land's condition. If there were indications that under the substantive law some redress might be available on the land's behalf, then the guardian would be entitled to raise the land's rights in the land's name, *i.e.*, without having to make the roundabout and often unavailing demonstration, discussed below, that the "rights" of the club's members were being invaded. Guardians would also be looked to for a host of other protective tasks, *e.g.*, monitoring effluents (and/or monitoring the monitors), and representing their "wards" at legislative and administrative hearings on such matters as the setting of state water quality standards. Procedures exist, and can be strengthened, to move a court for the removal and substitution of guardians, for conflicts of interest or for other reasons, as well as for the termination of the guardianship.

In point of fact, there is a movement in the law toward giving the environment the benefits of standing, although not in a manner as satisfactory as the guardianship approach. What I am referring to is the marked liberalization of traditional standing requirements in recent cases in which environmental action groups have challenged federal government action. *Scenic Hudson Preservation Conference v. FPC* is a good example of this development. There, the Federal Power Commission had granted New York's Consolidated Edison a license to construct a hydroelectric project on the Hudson River at Storm King Mountain. The grant of license had been opposed by conservation interests on the grounds that the transmission lines would be unsightly, fish would be destroyed, and nature trails would be inundated. Two of these conservation groups, united under the name Scenic Hudson Preservation Conference, petitioned the Second Circuit to set aside the grant. Despite the claim that Scenic Hudson had no standing because it had not made the traditional claim "of any personal economic injury resulting from the Commission's actions," the petitions were heard, and the case sent back to the Commission. On the standing point, the court noted that Section 313(b) of the Federal Power Act gave a right of instituting review to any party "aggrieved by an order issued by the Commission"; it thereupon read "aggrieved by" as not limited to those alleging the traditional personal economic injury, but as broad enough to include "those who by their activities and conduct have exhibited a special interest" in "the aesthetic, conservational, and recreational aspects of power development. . . ." A similar reasoning has swayed other circuits to allow proposed actions by the Federal Power Commission, the Department of Interior, and the Department of Health, Education and Welfare to be challenged by environmental action groups on the basis of, *e.g.*, recreational and esthetic interests of members, in lieu of direct economic injury. Only the Ninth Circuit has balked, and one of these cases, involving the Sierra Club's attempt to challenge a Walt Disney development in the Sequoia National Forest, is at the time of this writing awaiting decision by the United States Supreme Court.

Even if the Supreme Court should reverse the Ninth Circuit in the Walt Disney-Sequoia National Forest matter, thereby encouraging the circuits to continue their trend toward liberalized standing in this area, there are significant reasons to press for the guardianship approach notwithstanding. For one thing, the cases of this sort have extended standing on the basis of interpretations of specific federal statutes—the Federal Power Commission Act, the Administrative Procedure Act, the Federal Insecticide, Fungicide and Rodenticide Act, and others. Such a basis supports environmental suits only where acts of federal agencies are involved; and even there, perhaps, only when there is some special statutory language, such as "aggrieved by" in the Federal Power Act, on which the action groups can rely. Witness, for example, *Bass Angler Sportsman Society v. United States Steel Corp.* There, plaintiffs sued 175 corporate defendants located throughout Alabama, relying on 33 U.S.C. § 407 (1970), which provides:

> It shall not be lawful to throw, discharge, or deposit [any] refuse matter [into] any navigable water of the United States, or into any tributary of any navigable water from which the same shall float or be washed into such navigable water. . . .

Another section of the Act provides that one-half the fines shall be paid to the person or persons giving information which shall lead to a conviction. Relying on this latter provision, the plaintiff designated his action a *qui tam* action and sought to enforce the Act by injunction and fine. The District Court ruled that, in the absence of express language to the contrary, no one outside the Department of Justice had standing to sue under a criminal act and refused to reach the question of whether violations were occurring.

Unlike the liberalized standing approach, the guardianship approach would secure an effective voice for the environment even where federal administrative action and public lands and waters were not involved. It would also allay one of the fears courts—such as the Ninth Circuit—have about the extended standing concept: if any ad hoc group can spring up overnight, invoke some "right" as universally claimable as the esthetic and recreational interests of its members and thereby get into court, how can a flood of litigation be prevented? If an ad hoc committee loses a suit brought *sub nom.* Committee to Preserve our Trees, what happens when its very same members reorganize two years later and sue *sub nom.* the Massapequa Sylvan Protection League? Is the new group bound by res judicata? Class action law may be capable of ameliorating some of the more obvious problems. But even so, court economy might be better served by simply designating the guardian de jure representative of the natural object, with rights of discretionary intervention by others, but with the understanding that the natural object is "bound" by an adverse judgment. The guardian concept, too, would provide the endangered natural object with what the trustee in bankruptcy provides the endangered corporation: a continuous supervision over a period of time, with a consequent deeper understanding of a broad range of the ward's problems, not just the problems present in one particular piece of litigation. It would thus assure the courts that the plaintiff has the expertise and genuine adversity in pressing a claim which are the prerequisites of a true "case or controversy."

The guardianship approach, however, is apt to raise two objections, neither of which seems to me to have much force. The first is that a committee or guardian could not judge the needs of the river or forest in its charge; indeed, the very concept of "needs," it might be said, could be used here only in the most metaphorical way. The second objection is that such a system would not be much different from what we now have: is not the Department of Interior already such a guardian for public lands, and do not most states have legislation empowering their attorneys general to seek relief—in a sort of *parens patriae* way—for such injuries as a guardian might concern himself with?

As for the first objection, natural objects *can* communicate their wants (needs) to us, and in ways that are not terribly ambiguous. I am sure I can judge with more certainty and meaningfulness whether and when my lawn wants (needs) water, than the Attorney General can judge whether and when the United States wants (needs) to take an appeal from an adverse judgment by a lower court. The lawn tells me that it wants water by a certain dryness of the blades and soil—immediately obvious to the touch—the appearance of bald spots, yellowing, and a lack of springiness after being walked on; how does "the United States" communicate to the Attorney General? For similar reasons, the guardian-attorney for a smog-endangered stand of pines could venture with more confidence that his client wants the smog stopped, than the directors of a corporation can assert that "the corporation" wants dividends declared. We make decisions on behalf of, and in the purported interests of, others every day; these "others" are often creatures whose wants are far less verifiable, and even far more metaphysical in conception, than the wants of rivers, trees, and land.

As for the second objection, one can indeed find evidence that the Department of Interior was conceived as a sort of guardian of the public lands. But there are two points to keep in mind. First, insofar as the Department already is an adequate guardian it is only with respect to the federal public lands as per Article IV, section 3 of the Constitution. Its guardianship includes neither local public lands nor private lands. Second, to judge from the environmentalist literature and from the cases environmental action groups have been bringing, the Department is itself one of the bogeys of the environmental movement. (One thinks of the uneasy peace between the Indians and the Bureau of Indian Affairs.) Whether the various charges be right or wrong, one cannot help but observe that the Department has been charged with several institutional goals (never an easy burden), and is currently looked to for action by quite a variety of interest groups, only one of which is the environmentalists. In this context, a guardian outside the institution becomes especially valuable. Besides, what a person wants, fully to secure his rights, is the ability to retain independent counsel even when, and perhaps especially when, the government is acting "for him" in a beneficent way. I have no reason to doubt, for example, that the Social Security System is being managed "for me"; but I would not want to abdicate my right to challenge its actions as they affect me, should the need arise. I would not ask more trust of national forests, vis-à-vis the Department of Interior. The same considerations apply in the instance of local agencies, such as regional water pollution boards, whose members' expertise in pollution matters is often all too credible.

The objection regarding the availability of attorneys general as protectors of the environment within the existing structure is somewhat the same. Their statutory powers are limited and sometimes unclear. As political creatures, they must exercise the discretion they have with an eye toward advancing and reconciling a broad variety of important social goals, from preserving morality to increasing their jurisdiction's tax base. The present state of our environment, and the history of cautious application and development of environmental protection laws long on the books, testifies that the burdens of an attorney general's broad responsibility have apparently not left much manpower for the protection of nature. (*Cf. Bass Anglers*, above.) No doubt, strengthening interest in the environment will increase the zest of public attorneys even where, as will often be the case, well-represented corporate pollutors are the quarry. Indeed, the United States Attorney General has stepped up anti-pollution activity, and ought to be further encouraged in this direction. The statutory powers of the attorneys general should be enlarged, and they should be armed with criminal penalties made at least commensurate with the likely economic benefits of violating the law. On the other hand, one cannot ignore the fact that there is increased pressure on public law-enforcement offices to give more attention to a host of other problems, from crime "on the streets" (why don't we say "in the rivers"?) to consumerism and school bussing. If the environment is not to get lost in the shuffle, we would do well, I think, to adopt the guardianship approach as an additional safeguard, conceptualizing major natural objects as holders of their own rights, raisable by the court-appointed guardian.

* * *

Louis Henkin, *Is There a "Political Question" Doctrine?*, 85 YALE L.J. 597, 604-06 (1976)*

* * *

The Supreme Court has not recently held any issue to be textually committed by the Constitution to the other branches and therefore not justiciable—a "political question." And the Court's failure to require judicial abstention in those instances where scripture can most plausibly be read to require it leaves a strong sense that the present Justices are not disposed to find many—or any—issues in fact so textually committed. Justice Brennan, however, found textual commitment to another branch "prominent" in the doctrine as established by the older cases, and both he and Professor Bickel, trying to make sense of the constitutional jurisprudence they had inherited, apparently found instances of judicial abstention on grounds other than "textual commitment."

If any clauses in the Constitution are properly interpreted as conferring power not subject to judicial review, so be it (though there might be too few of such bricks, and it might be otherwise misleading to build a "political question doctrine"). If the cases have established that courts must, or should, or may, abstain from judicial review of constitutionality because of one or more of the considerations distilled by Justice Brennan or from Bickel's undifferentiated "prudence," so be that too (although Professor Wechsler is surely entitled to ask where the Court found authority for such abstention). I am not satisfied, however, that the older cases called for extraordinary judicial abstention in the sense of the pure "political question doctrine"; the considerations distilled from them by Justice Brennan seem rather to be elements of the ordinary respect which the courts show to the substantive decisions of the political branches. Different (perhaps only clearer) opinions might have been written in the leading cases that would justify and explain their result without even using the words "political question," and without suggesting a doctrine that would also be deemed to support an exception to our commitment to judicial review.

The Court, I suggest, was following (or might have followed) one of several established jurisprudential lines which are sometimes confused with the "political question doctrine" but which essentially have nothing to do with it:

1. The act complained of was within the power conferred upon the political branches of the federal government by the Constitution, and their action was law binding on the courts.

2. Contrary to petitioner's assertion, the act complained of fell within the enumerated powers conferred upon the political branches by the Constitution (or within the inherent powers of the state) and was not prohibited to them explicitly or by any warranted inference from the Constitution; nor did it violate any right reserved to the petitioner by the Constitution.

3. Although a legal claim existed, indeed although a constitutional violation may have been committed, the remedy sought was an equitable remedy and would not be granted in the circumstances by a court of equity in the exercise of sound discretion.

* Reprinted by permission of The Yale Law Journal Company and Fred B. Rothman & Company from The Yale Law Journal, Vol. 85, pages 597-625.

The first two are commonplace: courts have held one or the other of these in innumerable cases. In such cases, I stress, the court does not refuse judicial review; it exercises it. It is not dismissing the case or the issue as nonjusticiable; it adjudicates it. It is not refusing to pass on the power of the political branches; it passes upon it, only to affirm that they had the power which had been challenged and that nothing in the Constitution prohibited the particular exercise of it.

Denial of a particular, or any, equitable remedy is also not an exception to judicial review. The court may indeed review, find a violation, and still deny the remedy; or it may deny some remedy, say, an injunction, but grant other relief, *e.g.*, a declaratory judgment.

* * *

Michael J. Glennon, *Foreign Affairs and the Political Question Doctrine*, 83 AM. J. INT'L L. 814, 814-21 (1989)*

The unevenness of congressional oversight, the proclivity of executive foreign affairs agencies for violating the law and the traditional responsibility of the courts as the last guardians of the Constitution—all point to the propriety of an active role for the judiciary in ensuring governmental compliance with the law. Specifically, courts should not decline to resolve foreign affairs disputes between Congress and the President because they present "political questions." The recent case of *Lowry v. Reagan* illustrates the serious systemic damage wrought by judicial abstention in such disputes.

In *Lowry* a federal district court dismissed a challenge by 110 members of Congress to President Reagan's violation of the War Powers Resolution in the Persian Gulf, and a panel of the U.S. Court of Appeals for the District of Columbia Circuit dismissed their appeal. The district court grounded the dismissal on two doctrines: political question and remedial discretion.

The "now-classic catalogue of conditions to which the political question doctrine applies," as the *Lowry* court put it, was set forth by the United States Supreme Court in *Baker v. Carr*:

> Prominent on the surface of any case held to involve a political question is found a textually demonstrable constitutional commitment of the issue to a coordinate political department; or a lack of judicially discoverable and manageable standards for resolving it; or the impossibility of deciding without an initial policy determination of a kind clearly for nonjudicial discretion; or the impossibility of a court's undertaking independent resolution without expressing lack of respect due coordinate branches of government; or an unusual need for unquestioning adherence to a political decision already made; or the potentiality of embarrassment from multifarious pronouncements by various departments on one question.

A dispute falling within one or more of these categories is regarded as "nonjusticiable," or inappropriate for resolution by the courts. Such a controversy will thus be left for the political branches to resolve. The district court in *Lowry* found that judicial

---

decision of the dispute would have risked the last of the conditions enumerated in *Baker v. Carr*, "the potentiality of embarrassment [that would result] from multifarious pronouncements by various departments on one question."

A variety of rationales have been advanced in support of the political question doctrine. First, aside from constitutional requirements, the courts must be accorded prudential discretion to decline to hear cases that might undermine their legitimacy. The courts simply lack the institutional capacity to handle certain matters. This argument is made with particular force in the realm of foreign affairs. Professor Franck has contended, for example, that "[t]he courts should not [be] put in the position of actually stopping a war, a politically loaded task." Second, certain decisions are indeed committed by the Constitution to the political branches, rather than to the courts. Third, decision by the courts blocks the majoritarian resolution of a dispute; the answer arrived at by democratically constituted branches normally should be respected. Fourth, there are uncharted reaches of legal terrain where no rules can yet be said to exist. Here, especially, majoritarian processes should be left to work their will, even if that will is that there be *no* law. Fifth, judicial resolution of hot controversies merely encourages legislative buck-passing; the judiciary should encourage congressional responsibility by declining to "bite the bullet" for Congress. Finally, in separation of powers disputes particularly, there is little room for the Supreme Court to intervene because "each department possesses an impressive arsenal of weapons to demand observance of constitutional dictates by the other." Dean Choper thus concludes that "the federal judiciary should not decide constitutional questions concerning whether executive action (or inaction) violates the respective powers of Congress or whether legislative action (or inaction) transgresses the realm of the President." His theory seems to suggest that the courts should not have decided cases such as *Youngstown Sheet & Tube Co. v. Sawyer* and *United States v. Nixon*. And he, too, believes that "the federal courts should hold that the ultimate issue of the President's inherent constitutional power to lead the nation into a war is nonjusticiable."

In modern American society, these justifications for judicial abstention seem increasingly to be calls for judicial abdication. The courts have a core responsibility under the Constitution to resolve disputes. "It is emphatically the province and duty of the judicial department," Chief Justice Marshall wrote in *Marbury v. Madison*, "to say what the law is." The political question doctrine does not square with this fundamental tenet of our form of government: it is "at odds with our commitment to constitutionalism and limited government, to the rule of law monitored and enforced by judicial review." On close inspection, many of the arguments in favor of the political question doctrine are thus revealed to be bare attacks upon the idea of judicial review.

Few today could seriously believe, for example, that the Court places itself at risk by deciding a controversial case. It may have been true, before widespread public acceptance of judicial review, that an overzealous judiciary might have gotten "too far out in front" to continue to act as final legal arbiter. But that day has long passed. When President Nixon's Secretary of the Treasury, John Connally, implied that the President might disregard an illicit decision of the Supreme Court, the public outcry only hastened Nixon's downfall. There is no modern justification for use of the doctrine "as a means of escape for fearful judges unwilling to address challenges to governmental usurpation of authority in foreign affairs."

Choper places heavy reliance upon the argument that disputes between Congress and the President involve no genuine claims of abridgment of personal liberty. Should the courts decline to find that one branch has encroached upon the power of the other because "the 'liberty' claims are merely derivative"? I think not. The Constitution protects individual liberty not merely through the direct safeguards found in the Bill of Rights, but also through indirect protections inherent in the separation of powers. As the Supreme Court affirmed recently, "The Framers recognized that, in the long term, structural protections against abuse of power were critical to preserving liberty." Even assuming that the substance of individual and separation claims can be neatly distinguished—a proposition that the *Steel Seizure* case must surely call into question—there seems little ground for believing that the two should be subject to different rules of judicial review. It is worth remembering that *Marbury v. Madison* was at its most enduring level a dispute about the locus of governmental decision-making authority. At this point in our history, it seems bizarre to think that Chief Justice Marshall was precluded from striking down the statute that unconstitutionally conferred original jurisdiction on the Supreme Court if no claim of individual liberty had been directly implicated.

Concern about the courts' "lack of capacity" also seems misplaced. This concern animated the district court's dismissal of *Crockett v. Reagan*, which challenged noncompliance with the War Powers Resolution with respect to activities in El Salvador. The district court in *Crockett* reasoned that "[t]he question here belongs to the category characterized by a lack of judicially discoverable and manageable standards for resolution." Similarly, the court of appeals in *Lowry* wrote that a decision on the merits would have required an assessment of the stability of the cease-fire in the Persian Gulf; "an inquiry of this sort is beyond the judicial competence."

Apprehensions about judicial fact-finding incapacities are doctrinally misdirected. Its discussion in *Baker* makes clear that the Supreme Court meant to foreclose the judicial resolution of disputes characterized by indeterminate legal standards, not fact-finding difficulties. The "lack of criteria by which a court could determine which form of government was republican" was the reason that a political question was presented in *Luther v. Borden*. The Court did not suggest that judicial abstention was required by any proof problem presented by the facts of the case. Yet it is for the latter reason—the proof problem—that the *Crockett* court dismissed the plaintiff's complaint: "the Court no doubt would be presented conflicting evidence. . . . The Court lacks the resources and expertise (which are accessible to the Congress) to resolve disputed questions of fact concerning the military situation in El Salvador." Such questions of fact can be addressed as they always are, namely, through the use of interrogatories, depositions, testimony and all the other means of gathering evidence. It may or may not be correct that the plaintiffs would succeed in establishing their claim by a preponderance of the evidence; the opportunity to meet that burden, in any event, is one that the law accords them. The problem is addressed not by the political question doctrine but by the law of evidence.

As to claims that the courts' legitimacy is undermined by ventures into the political thicket, say, to stop a war, it must be remembered that *not* to stop an illegal war can also be a "politically loaded task." It is not self-evident that public respect for the courts would be enhanced if the courts sat idly by in the face of a manifest constitutional violation—for example, if a President ordered an invasion of Mexico to rectify Mexican election irregularities. Why is judicial *in*action in the face of controversy necessarily more prudent than judicial *action*? Professor Martin Redish put it well: "the moral cost of [permitting a manifest constitutional violation to continue], both to society in general and to the Supreme Court in particular, far outweighs whatever benefits are thought to derive from the judicial abdication of the review function."

It does not do to say that such decisions are allocated constitutionally to Congress or the President. The political question doctrine, the Supreme Court has reminded us, is "one of 'political questions,' not one of 'political cases.' The courts cannot reject as 'no law suit' a bona fide controversy as to whether some action denominated 'political' exceeds constitutional authority." In disputes between Congress and the President, the question is not whether one of the political branches had the authority in question, but *which* branch has that authority. In *Goldwater v. Carter*, for example, Justice Brennan correctly pointed out in dissent that, while the courts would have been precluded from reviewing the President's decision *if* the Constitution had committed that decision to the President, the nub of the case was *whether* the President had that authority.

Admittedly, judicial resolution of certain disputes may encourage legislative forbearance. Those who argue against such forbearance point out that courts inevitably make political decisions; why should a member of Congress cast a controversial vote if a judge will likely decide the issue anyway? In some cases, however, the likely intervention of the courts may actually *induce* Congress to act, on the notion that a clear statement of legislative intent could narrow the courts' latitude in subsequent litigation or even forestall judicial intervention. In other cases, the likelihood of judicial abstention may encourage Congress to poach on judicial terrain, as it did in the Good Friday agreements on aid for the Nicaraguan contras, by providing "informally" for congressional review of the implementation of the aid and its possible termination by congressional committees. In any event, the argument equates legislative forbearance with legislative irresponsibility, presupposing the preferability of legislation to adjudication. Why the courts should abstain from deciding disputes constitutionally within their jurisdiction is not explained.

Finally, the argument that Congress has enough arrows in its legislative quiver to respond successfully to executive illegality is unpersuasive as a justification for judicial abstention. For five decades, the Executive responded successfully to the putative illegality of the legislative veto simply by disregarding those it constitutionally contested—but that success did not discourage the Supreme Court from reaching the merits in *INS v. Chadha*. Further, the argument underestimates practical problems that frequently render Congress's textbook tools too unwieldly to use. Dean Choper himself acknowledges that the tactics to control executive usurpation of power—refusal to appropriate funds, enact laws and confirm appointments, and impeachment—"may reasonably be viewed as both unseemly and unreasonable." Moreover, if this argument were correct, there would seemingly be no case law on separation of powers controversies: in disputes from *Little v. Barreme* through *Steel Seizure*, Congress would have been left to fend for itself.

In rare circumstances, it may turn out that the question is one on which there is no law. If no primary source of constitutional power is available to resolve the dispute, the courts are justified in resorting to other sources of constitutional power. In *Goldwater v. Carter*, for example, the Court could have reached the merits and found that, while constitutional text and constitutional custom were not dispositive, functional and institutional considerations indicated that the matter fell within the President's concurrent, initiating power—as well as the concurrent power of Congress to act (or react) if it chose to do so.

The purported merits of judicial abstention in foreign affairs decision-making disputes thus shrink under scrutiny, while the drawbacks, frequently brushed aside by those who inveigh against "judicial activism," are substantial. Arguments against judicial resolution of such disputes are often, in reality, thinly disguised pleas for executive hegemony, for the Executive almost always wins if the courts sit on the sidelines. The reason is manifest: the Executive can move quickly—by introducing troops, making an international agreement, mining harbors, transferring arms—leaving Congress, if and when it finds out, faced with a fait accompli. During the Vietnam War, the state of Massachusetts put the argument cogently (if unsuccessfully) to the United States Supreme Court:

> [I]f the President takes the nation into war without Congressional authorization, the practical situation will [lead] [m]any legislators, for a variety of reasons [not to] vote for legislation which would cut off the use in the war of defense appropriations. Even if a majority of legislators could be amassed, the President could veto the bill and thus raise the burden much higher to the 2/3 majority level.

To permit the Executive to proceed unencumbered by judicial review would work a radical reallocation of constitutional power. If the Court declines to intervene when the Executive poses a fundamental threat to the separation of powers, the Executive, not the judiciary, becomes the ultimate arbiter of the meaning of the Constitution. Judicial abstention in such circumstances is unjustified for the same reason that it was unjustified in the face of electoral paralysis in *Baker*: operating alone, the political system is incapable of reestablishing an equilibrium of power, and the courts must step in to restore it.

Second, in time of crisis, exclusive reliance upon political processes can result in governmental gridlock. Cutting off all funds for the Department of Defense or the Department of State, or declining to confirm a Supreme Court nominee because a President has engaged in a foolish or unconstitutional foreign policy initiative, or commencing impeachment proceedings can hardly be seen as the constitutionally mandated way that the United States Government must resolve internal power disputes. Thus, even Dean Choper finds judicial intervention attractive where it is necessary to "preserve our constitutional equilibrium and to avoid the unseemly conversion of a grave constitutional crisis into a street corner brawl of naked self-help that would heap scorn on both departments."

Finally, an inevitable problem with the political question doctrine is hinted at in a passage that Choper quotes from *Baker v. Carr*: "The political question doctrine, a tool for maintenance of governmental order, will not be so applied as to promote only disorder." What are the preconditions of governmental order? Political regularity surely derives, at least at the outset, from legal predictability; and predictability of procedure presupposes *knowledge* of that procedure. However, the application of the doctrine ineluctably promotes disorder, for judicial failure to decide a bona fide case or controversy deprives litigants, as well as future actors, of that knowledge: the courts decline to say *what* legal procedure requires. The political question doctrine, by denying law-respecting governmental actors knowledge of the rules they must live by, undermines predictability in public affairs and maximizes chaos.

Not only is the doctrine incompatible with a public policy that favors predictability, but its practical application has actually undercut that objective. A case in point, again, is *Lowry v. Reagan*. As mentioned above, in dismissing the action on political question grounds, the district court worried that it would risk embarrassing U.S. foreign policy through "multifarious pronouncements" by different departments on the same issue. The "volatile situation in the Persian Gulf demands, in the words of *Baker v. Carr*, a 'single-voiced statement of the Government's views.'"

In fact, the dispute came before the courts precisely because the Government had *failed* to speak with one voice. Congress said in the War Powers Resolution that, under certain circumstances, the President must submit a certain report, and the

President declined to do so. "Multifarious pronouncements" therefore had already been made. Judicial intervention was needed to say which branch spoke for the Government—to cause the Government to speak with one voice. The court's refusal to step in merely prolonged the cacophony. *Lowry* thus indicates how, in practice, the political question doctrine can serve to perpetuate, rather than alleviate, conflicts between the political branches and to impede the ability of the United States to speak with a unified voice.

Bibliography

Broderick, Albert, *The Warth Optional Standing Doctrine: A Return to Judicial Supremacy?*, 25 Cath. U. L. Rev. 467 (1976)

Dodd, Walter F., *Judicially Non-Enforceable Provisions of Constitutions*, 80 U. Pa. L. Rev. 54 (1931)

Finkelstein, Maurice, *Further Notes on Judicial Self-Limitation*, 39 Harv. L. Rev. 221 (1925)

Finkelstein, Maurice, *Judicial Self-Limitation*, 37 Harv. L. Rev. 338 (1924)

Hart, Henry Melvin & Wechsler, Herbert, The Federal Courts and the Federal System (2nd ed. 1973)

Jackson, R., The Supreme Court in the American System (1955)

Rohr, Marc, *Fighting for the Rights of Others: The Troubled Law of Third Party Standing and Mootness in the Federal Courts*, 35 U. Miami L. Rev. 393 (1981)

Scharpf, Fritz W., *Judicial Review and the Political Question A Functional Analysis*, 75 Yale L.J. 517 (1966)

Thayer, James B., *The Origin and Scope of the American Doctrine of Constitutional Law*, 7 Harv. L. Rev. 129 (1893)

Wechsler, Herbert, *Toward Neutral Principles of Constitutional Law*, 73 Harv. L. Rev. 1 (1959)

Weston, Melville Fuller, *Political Questions*, 38 Harv. L. Rev. 296 (1925)